BaseBall america®
2013 PROSPECT
HANDBOOK

BASEBALL AMERICA INC. · DURHAM, N.C.

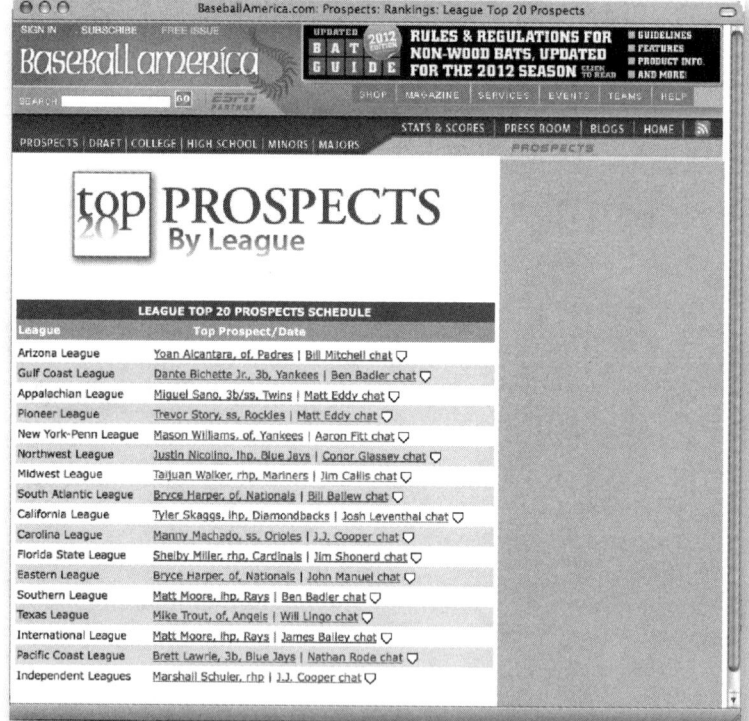
EDITOR'S NOTE: Transactions for this book go through Dec. 9, so the last significant player transactions included here came out of the Rule 5 draft and the Wil Myers/James Shields trade between the Royals and Rays. As always, you can find players even if they have changed organizations by using the handy index in the back. >>
For the purposes of this book, a prospect is any player who has no more than 50 innings pitched, 30 relief appearances or 130 at-bats in the major leagues, regardless of service time. Finally, the grades you'll find for each team's drafts are based solely on the quality of the players signed, with no consideration for whom players were traded for or how many picks a team might have lost.

BaseBall america
2013 PROSPECT
HANDBOOK

Editors
JIM CALLIS, WILL LINGO, JOHN MANUEL

Assistant Editors
BEN BADLER, J.J. COOPER, MATT EDDY, AARON FITT,

CONOR GLASSEY, JOSH LEVENTHAL, NATHAN RODE,

JIM SHONERD

Database and Application Development
TIM COLLINS, BRENT LEWIS

Contributing Writers
ANDY BAGGARLY, JAMES BAILEY, BILL BALLEW,

JACK ETKIN, MATTHEW FORMAN, DERRICK GOOLD,

TOM HAUDRICOURT, BILL MITCHELL, JOHN PERROTTO,

PHIL ROGERS

Photo Editor
NATHAN RODE

Design & Production
SARA HIATT MCDANIEL, LINWOOD WEBB

Cover Photo
JURICKSON PROFAR BY JOHN WILLIAMSON

NO PORTION OF THIS BOOK MAY BE REPRINTED OR REPRODUCED WITHOUT THE WRITTEN CONSENT OF THE PUBLISHER. FOR ADDITIONAL COPIES, VISIT OUR WEBSITE AT BASEBALLAMERICA.COM OR CALL 1-800-845-2726 TO ORDER. US $32.95, PLUS SHIPPING AND HANDLING PER ORDER. EXPEDITED SHIPPING AVAILABLE.

DISTRIBUTED BY SIMON & SCHUSTER   ISBN: 978-1-932391-44-2

STATISTICS PROVIDED BY MAJOR LEAGUE BASEBALL ADVANCED MEDIA AND COMPILED BY BASEBALL AMERICA

BaseBall america

PRESIDENT/PUBLISHER Lee Folger

EDITORIAL
EDITORS IN CHIEF Will Lingo, John Manuel
EXECUTIVE EDITOR Jim Callis
MANAGING EDITOR J.J. Cooper
NEWS EDITOR Josh Leventhal
NATIONAL WRITER Aaron Fitt
ASSOCIATE EDITOR Matt Eddy
ASSISTANT EDITORS Ben Badler, Conor Glassey, Nathan Rode, Jim Shonerd

PRODUCTION
DESIGN & PRODUCTION DIRECTOR Sara Hiatt McDaniel
MULTIMEDIA MANAGER Linwood Webb
PRODUCTION MANAGER Inna Cazares

ADVERTISING
DIRECTOR OF ADVERTISING Ryan Johnson
DIRECT MARKETING MANAGER Ximena Caceres
MARKETPLACE MANAGER Kristopher M. Lull
ADVERTISING SALES EXECUTIVE Edward Richards

BUSINESS
CUSTOMER SERVICE Ronnie McCabe, Jocelyn Dantini
MANAGER, FINANCE Susan Callahan
FINANCIAL ADMINISTRATOR Hailey Carpenter
TECHNOLOGY MANAGER Brent Lewis
TECHNOLOGY ASSISTANT Tim Collins

WHERE TO DIRECT QUESTIONS
ADVERTISING: advertising@baseballamerica.com
BUSINESS BEAT: joshleventhal@baseballamerica.com
COLLEGES: aaronfitt@baseballamerica.com
DESIGN/PRODUCTION: production@baseballamerica.com
DRAFT: johnmanuel@baseballamerica.com
HIGH SCHOOLS: nathanrode@baseballamerica.com
INDEPENDENT LEAGUES: jjcooper@baseballamerica.com
MAJOR LEAGUES: jimcallis@baseballamerica.com
MINOR LEAGUES: willlingo@baseballamerica.com
PHOTOS: photos@baseballamerica.com
PROSPECTS: benbadler@baseballamerica.com
REPRINTS: production@baseballamerica.com
SUBSCRIPTIONS/CUSTOMER SERVICE:
customerservice@baseballamerica.com
WEBSITE: customerservice@baseballamerica.com

GrindMedia

GRINDMEDIA MANAGEMENT
SVP, GROUP PUBLISHER Norb Garrett
norb.garrett@grindmedia.com
VP, DIGITAL Greg Morrow
greg.morrow@grindmedia.com
PRODUCTION DIRECTOR Kasey Kelley
kasey.kelley@grindmedia.com
EDITORIAL DIRECTOR–DIGITAL Chris Mauro
chris.mauro@grindmedia.com
FINANCE DIRECTOR Adam Miner
adam.miner@grindmedia.com

ADVERTISING SALES
SALES STRATEGY MGR/PRINT & EVENTS
Chris Engelsman chris.engelsman@grindmedia.com
SALES STRATEGY MGR/DIGITAL Elisabeth Murray
elisabeth.murray@grindmedia.com

DIGITAL
DIRECTOR OF ENGINEERING Jeff Kimmel
jeff.kimmel@grindmedia.com
SENIOR PRODUCT MANAGER Rishi Kumar
rishi.kumar@grindmedia.com
SENIOR PRODUCT MANAGER Marc Bartell
marc.bartell@grindmedia.com
CREATIVE DIRECTOR Peter Tracy
peter.tracy@grindmedia.com

MARKETING AND EVENTS
MARKETING DIRECTOR Jamey Stone
jameystone@grindmedia.com
DIRECTOR OF EVENT OPERATIONS Sean Nielsen
sean.nielsen@grindmedia.com

FACILITIES
MANAGER Randy Ward randy.ward@grindmedia.com
OFFICE COORDINATOR Ruth Hosea
ruth.hosea@grindmedia.com
ARCHIVIST Thomas Voehringer
thomas.voehringer@sorc.com

SOURCE INTERLINK MEDIA

OFFICERS OF SOURCE INTERLINK COMPANIES, INC.
PRESIDENT AND CHIEF EXECUTIVE OFFICER
Michael Sullivan
EVP, CHIEF FINANCIAL OFFICER John Bode
EVP, CHIEF ADMINISTRATIVE OFFICER
Stephanie Justice

SOURCE INTERLINK MEDIA, LLC
PRESIDENT Chris Argentieri
CHIEF CREATIVE OFFICER Alan Alpanian
SVP, FINANCE Dan Bednar
VP, SINGLE COPY SALES AND MARKETING Chris Butler
EVP, ENTHUSIAST AUTOMOTIVE Doug Evans
SVP, NEW PRODUCT DEVELOPMENT Howard Lim
CHIEF CONTENT OFFICER Angus MacKenzie
SVP, MANUFACTURING AND PRODUCTION
Kevin Mullan
SVP, CONSUMER MEDIA AND INTEGRATED SALES
Eric Schwab

DIGITAL MEDIA
CHIEF TECHNOLOGY OFFICER, DIGITAL MEDIA
Raghu Bala
SVP, DIGITAL MARKETING Craig Buccola
SVP, DIGITAL PRODUCT DEVELOPMENT Todd Busby
SVP, DIGITAL PRODUCT DEVELOPMENT Tom Furukawa
VP, DIGITAL PRODUCT DEVELOPMENT Dan Hong
VP, DIGITAL ADVERTISING PRODUCTS AND OPERATIONS Jung Park

CONSUMER MARKETING, ENTHUSIAST MEDIA SUBSCRIPTION COMPANY, INC.
VP, CONSUMER MARKETING Tom Slater
VP, RETENTION AND OPERATIONS FULFILLMENT
Donald T. Robinson III

446

JOHN WILLIAMSON

Jurickson Profar lit up the Futures Game with a home run, then became the big leagues' youngest player and homered off Cleveland's Zach McAllister in his first major league at-bat

FOREWORD

As I go through each major league season, I have the chance to cross paths with many of my former college teammates: Pedro Alvarez with the Pirates, Mike Baxter with the Mets, Ryan Flaherty with the Orioles, Mike Minor with the Braves. Seeing them always brings back great memories from my time at Vanderbilt. I remember going to the locker room early each day, because I loved being with those guys and all of our other great teammates. Coach Tim Corbin built a special program for us to be a part of.

Regularly while I was hanging out in the locker room, I would grab one of the copies of Baseball America that Coach Corbin would have in there for us. I was anxious to check the rankings and see where Vanderbilt stood against the rest of the country. I would read almost every word of the college coverage. I always enjoyed when Vandy was written about, but also liked to read up on guys I had played with on U.S. national teams or against in the Southeastern Conference. The college section helped me keep up with teams in other parts of the country, too.

I also would take a look at the team prospect lists when they came out. It was fun to see guys who we had played against in the SEC like Luke Hochevar, who played at Tennessee. It was also fun to think about the current guys I was playing with and against who might someday be a part of those lists, such as Alex Avila and Tommy Hunter from Alabama, Matt LaPorta from Florida, Gordon Beckham from Georgia, Zack Cozart at Mississippi, and J.P. Arencibia and Julio Borbon at Tennessee. There are a lot of great players from the SEC, but I'm proud to say I think Vanderbilt has produced the best group. I'm proud of our guys.

Today, my view of the BA prospect lists is totally different. I read to learn who is going to help us win the World Series. As I write this, my team, the Rays, has just traded for Wil Myers from the Royals. I don't know Wil, but I do know he ranks among the best prospects in baseball. Our 2013 team is going to be built with many former prospects and probably will have several current prospects helping out. Jeremy Hellickson, Desmond Jennings, Evan Longoria and Matt Moore all ranked high on our team's list previously. Now guys like Chris Archer are stepping up to play important roles and soon guys like Myers will, too. I'm disappointed when my teammates are traded away, but it makes me appreciate our team's drafting and developing of players each time my former teammates are replaced by these great young guys.

I hope you enjoy reading this year's Prospect Handbook. I'm sure you'll be seeing many of these guys at a major league stadium soon.

DAVID PRICE
TAMPA BAY RAYS
2012 AMERICAN LEAGUE CY YOUNG AWARD WINNER

INTRODUCTION

We had no idea what we were getting ourselves into.

Jim Callis told me that late one night at dinner as we brought this year's Prospect Handbook toward the finish line. He was talking about working on the 2001 Prospect Handbook, as we remembered sending that first edition of the book to press sometime in February 2001—or maybe even March—after slogging through 900 scouting reports for the first time and realizing just how much work it was.

But he could have been talking about the overall entity that is the Prospect Handbook. It has grown and evolved since that first edition, and we have added to the original formula, most significantly with the Organization Depth Charts for every team, and last year with the BA Grade for every player in the book.

We also quickly realized that, hey, this book would be a lot more useful if people could read it before the actual season started, so it now goes to press right before Christmas every year. We have established a pretty regular routine where the information starts flowing in soon after the season ends, building through the fall and then culminating in a crush in December. For the last week or so of book production, Jim uproots himself from his home and family in Chicago and comes down to North Carolina to get the book done.

A lot of people give a lot of time for the Prospect Handbook to be the outstanding book that it is—and make no mistake, there is no reference on prospects that even comes close to it—but Jim is the heart and soul of the book. There is no detail that is not considered, no tool that's overlooked, no ranking that isn't agonized over. It is maddening on those late nights when I'm waiting on a team to be edited so I can move it through the production process, but I've learned over the years that the book will always get done, and the result will always be worth it. So I don't get quite as anxious about it as I used to.

Jim is far from the only person who makes the book happen, of course. Pretty much everyone on the BA staff contributes to the Prospect Handbook effort, as well as some of our longtime correspondents. And design and production director Sara Hiatt McDaniel gets tired of my acknowledgement of her contributions, but I just don't know many people who would take the time to tweak the spacing on 900 numbers, along with countless other tweaks that we don't even notice because everything just looks *right*.

Each individual's focus on making his or her part of the book as good as it can be is what ultimately makes the final product so good, and makes working on it so rewarding. The Prospect Handbook is our signature publication, and in many ways it is both the culmination of all the work we have done in the last year, and the foundation for what we'll do in the year to come. It is the industry standard, and we're both proud of that and humble enough to know we can make it even better next year. For now, though, enjoy our latest effort.

WILL LINGO
EDITOR IN CHIEF
BASEBALL AMERICA

BA GRADES

For the second year in a row, Baseball America has assigned Grades and Risk Factors for each and every one of the 900 prospects in the Prospect Handbook. For the BA Grade, we used a 20-to-80 scale, similar to the scale scouts use, to keep it familiar. However, most major league clubs put an overall numerical grade on players, called the Overall Future Potential or OFP. Often the OFP is merely an average of the player's tools.

The BA Grade is *not* an OFP. It's a measure of a prospect's value and attempts to gauge the player's realistic ceiling. This year, we've adjusted our grades to try to be more realistic, and less optimistic, than they were last year.

Because we're writing about prospects, the lowest grade given for a realistic ceiling is a 40. Bryce Harper got a top-of-the-scale 80 last year, with a Risk Factor of Low, while Mike Trout and Matt Moore earned 75/Safe grades. No players in this year's book earned an 80 grade.

Also, the realistic ceiling grade doesn't tell a prospect's entire story. How close that player is to reaching his ceiling matters just as much. The less we believe scouts have to project on the prospect, the less risky he is. That's why we also have assigned every player a Risk Factor to go with their BA Grade. That scale is fairly self-explanatory, ranging from Safe (least risk) to Extreme (riskiest). The closer a player is to reaching his realistic ceiling, the safer he rates.

Only players who have appeared in the major leagues can earn a Safe, while Low risk players have performed well in Double-A or Triple-A or need little projection. Most players are labeled High or Medium risk, and High risk can incorporate a player's low level of experience, injury history or poor statistical profile, such as a lopsided strikeout-to-walk ratio for a hitter. The players with the largest gap between what they are and what they could be are labeled Extreme. The ideal combination is for prospects to have high ceilings thanks to prodigious, top-of-the-scale tools, success in the minor leagues, and a small gap between their potential and the "now" skills.

The goal of the Grade/Risk system is to allow readers to take a quick look at how strong their team's farm system is, and also how much immediate help the big league club can expect from its prospects. It should also help with our Organization Rankings, but those will not simply flow, in formulaic fashion, from the Grades/Risk Factor results. Some staff members favor star power in a farm system while others favor depth; that cannot be easily summed up in a spreadsheet.

The BA Grade has evolved in this second incarna-

BA Grade Scale

75-80: Franchise players and No. 1 starters, such as Mike Trout, Miguel Cabrera, Clayton Kershaw and Justin Verlander.

65-70: No. 2 starters and perennial all-stars in the mold of Matt Cain, Matt Kemp and Adrian Beltre.

55-60: First-division regulars and No. 3 starters and elite closers, such as Craig Kimbrel, James Shields and Austin Jackson would earn these grades.

45-50: Most players reside here. The 50s are second-division regulars with higher peaks, hard-throwing  eighth-inning relievers and fourth starters on playoff teams such as Joe Saunders, Cody Ross and Danny Espinosa. The 45s are platoon/utility players, back-end starters and middle relievers. Think of veterans such as Brandon Inge and Jake Westbrook.

35-40: Players with swingman or utility/backup catcher upside, or same-side relief specialists. This category includes the likes of Pete Orr, Cole De Vries and Clay Rapada.

Risk Factors

SAFE: Has shown realistic ceiling in big leagues; ready to contribute in 2013.

LOW: Likely to reach realistic ceiling, certain big league career barring injury.

MEDIUM: Still some work to do to turn tools into major league-caliber skills.

HIGH: Most draft picks in their first seasons, players with plenty of projection left.

EXTREME: Teenagers in Rookie ball or players with significant injury histories.

tion, just as the Prospect Handbook has evolved over the years. We keep trying to make the book better and believe the addition of the BA Grade system is the next step in making the Prospect Handbook more indispensable than ever to the game's fans and fantasy players.

AN OVERVIEW

Another feature of the Prospect Handbook is a depth chart of every organization's minor league talent. This shows you at a glance what kind of talent a system has and provides even more prospects beyond the Top 30.

Players are usually listed on the depth charts where we think they'll ultimately end up. To help you better understand why players are slotted at particular positions, we show you here what scouts look for in the ideal candidate at each spot, with individual tools ranked in descending order.

LF	CF	RF
Power	Fielding	Power
Hitting	Hitting	Hitting
Fielding	Speed	Arm Strength
Arm Strength	Power	Fielding
Speed	Arm Strength	Speed

3B	SS	2B	1B
Power	Fielding	Hitting	Power
Hitting	Arm Strength	Fielding	Hitting
Fielding	Hitting	Power	Fielding
Arm Strength	Speed	Speed	Arm Strength
Speed	Power	Arm Strength	Speed

C
Fielding
Hitting
Arm Strength
Power
Speed

STARTING PITCHERS

No. 1 starter	No. 2 starter	No. 3 starter	No. 4-5 starters
• Two plus pitches	• Two plus pitches	• One plus pitch	• Command of two major league pitches
• Average third pitch	• Average third pitch	• Two average pitches	• Average velocity
• Plus-plus command	• Average command	• Average command	• Consistent breaking ball
• Plus makeup	• Average makeup	• Average makeup	• Decent changeup

CLOSER
- One dominant pitch
- Second plus pitch
- Plus command
- Plus-plus makeup

When Baseball America ranks prospects, there's almost always a byline attributing the ranking to the person who finally put the players in order, who decided, "OK, this guy's No. 6 and this guy's No. 7." But in truth, all of our rankings are more than one person's opinion. They are most often a reflection of the consensus of sources on the subject—managers, coaches, scouts, front-office personnel, the whole spectrum—filtered through the expertise of our writers and editors.

Except here, really. In this section of the Handbook, we get personal. Sifting through all of the information we've gathered to this point, four of our editors give their own personal takes on the game's top 50 prospects. This helps form the basis of the arguments that shape Baseball America's official Top 100 Prospects list, which is released each February. We consider it the definitive guide to the best talent in the minor leagues, and you can find it in our print edition or online at BaseballAmerica.com.

The rules for these lists are the same for any prospect who appears in the Handbook: no more than 130 at-bats, 50 innings or 30 relief appearances in the major leagues. We do not consider service time in our eligibility requirements.

As with any prospect list, these rankings represent how each person regarded the top minor league talent in the game at a moment in time. Ask us again in a few months—or even tomorrow—how these prospects stack up, and you'll get a different answer.

JIM CALLIS

1. Jurickson Profar, ss, Rangers
2. Dylan Bundy, rhp, Orioles
3. Oscar Taveras, of, Cardinals
4. Wil Myers, of/3b, Rays
5. Shelby Miller, rhp, Cardinals
6. Jose Fernandez, rhp, Marlins
7. Gerrit Cole, rhp, Pirates
8. Byron Buxton, of, Twins
9. Zack Wheeler, rhp, Mets
10. Xander Bogaerts, ss, Red Sox
11. Javier Baez, ss, Cubs
12. Carlos Correa, ss, Astros
13. Miguel Sano, 3b, Twins
14. Trevor Bauer, rhp, Diamondbacks
15. Mike Zunino, c, Mariners
16. Taijuan Walker, rhp, Mariners
17. Travis d'Arnaud, c, Blue Jays
18. Christian Yelich, of, Marlins
19. Mike Olt, 3b/1b, Rangers
20. Tyler Skaggs, lhp, Diamondbacks
21. Billy Hamilton, of/ss, Reds
22. Danny Hultzen, lhp, Mariners
23. Kevin Gausman, rhp, Orioles
24. Kyle Zimmer, rhp, Royals
25. Francisco Lindor, ss, Indians
26. Anthony Rendon, 3b, Nationals
27. Archie Bradley, rhp, Diamondbacks
28. Jameson Taillon, rhp, Pirates
29. Nick Castellanos, 3b/of, Tigers
30. Jonathan Singleton, 1b, Astros
31. Max Fried, lhp, Padres
32. Jackie Bradley, of, Red Sox
33. Julio Teheran, rhp, Braves
34. Carlos Martinez, rhp, Cardinals
35. Mason Williams, of, Yankees
36. Albert Almora, of, Cubs
37. Bubba Starling, of, Royals
38. Lucas Giolito, rhp, Nationals
39. Jorge Soler, of, Cubs
40. Andrew Heaney, lhp, Marlins
41. Chris Archer, rhp, Rays
42. Nolan Arenado, 3b, Rockies
43. Matt Barnes, rhp, Red Sox
44. Oswaldo Arcia, of, Twins
45. Yasiel Puig, of, Dodgers
46. Gregory Polanco, of, Pirates
47. David Dahl, of, Rockies
48. Noah Syndergaard, rhp, Blue Jays
49. Aaron Sanchez, rhp, Blue Jays
50. Austin Hedges, c, Padres

J. J. COOPER

1. Jurickson Profar, ss, Rangers
2. Dylan Bundy, rhp, Orioles
3. Oscar Taveras, of, Cardinals
4. Wil Myers, of/3b, Rays
5. Jose Fernandez, rhp, Marlins
6. Xander Bogaerts, ss, Red Sox
7. Gerrit Cole, rhp, Pirates
8. Tyler Skaggs, lhp, Diamondbacks
9. Shelby Miller, rhp, Cardinals
10. Archie Bradley, rhp, Diamondbacks
11. Christian Yelich, of, Marlins
12. Zack Wheeler, rhp, Mets
13. Trevor Bauer, rhp, Diamondbacks
14. Kyle Zimmer, rhp, Royals
15. Kevin Gausman, rhp, Orioles
16. Javier Baez, ss, Cubs
17. Miguel Sano, 3b, Twins
18. Jonathan Singleton, 1b, Astros
19. Nick Castellanos, 3b/of, Tigers
20. Billy Hamilton, of/ss, Reds
21. Byron Buxton, of, Twins
22. Travis D'Arnaud, c, Blue Jays
23. Mike Zunino, c, Mariners
24. Mike Olt, 1b/3b, Rangers
25. Taijuan Walker, rhp, Mariners
26. Francisco Lindor, ss, Indians
27. Carlos Correa, ss, Astros
28. Jameson Taillon, rhp, Pirates
29. Danny Hultzen, lhp, Mariners
30. Adam Eaton, of, Diamondbacks
31. Jackie Bradley, of, Red Sox
32. Jorge Soler, of, Cubs
33. Robert Stephenson, rhp, Reds
34. Oswaldo Arcia, of, Twins
35. Mason Williams, of, Yankees
36. Addison Russell, ss, Athletics
37. Carlos Martinez, rhp, Cardinals
38. Chris Archer, rhp, Rays
39. Gregory Polanco, of, Pirates
40. Slade Heathcott, of, Yankees
41. Tony Cingrani, lhp, Reds
42. David Dahl, of, Rockies
43. Matt Barnes, rhp, Red Sox
44. Andrew Heaney, lhp, Marlins
45. Yasiel Puig, of, Dodgers
46. Trevor Rosenthal, rhp, Cardinals
47. Hyun-Jin Ryu, lhp, Dodgers
48. Bubba Starling, of, Royals
49. George Springer of, Astros
50. Anthony Rendon, 3b, Nationals

WILL LINGO

1. Dylan Bundy, rhp, Orioles
2. Jurickson Profar, ss, Rangers
3. Oscar Taveras, of, Cardinals
4. Wil Myers, of/3b, Rays
5. Xander Bogaerts, ss, Red Sox
6. Jose Fernandez, rhp, Marlins
7. Shelby Miller, rhp, Cardinals
8. Miguel Sano, 3b, Twins
9. Byron Buxton, of, Twins
10. Mike Olt, 3b/1b, Rangers
11. Carlos Correa, ss, Astros
12. Tyler Skaggs, lhp, Diamondbacks
13. Trevor Bauer, rhp, Diamondbacks
14. Gerrit Cole, rhp, Pirates
15. Billy Hamilton, of/ss, Reds
16. Jonathan Singleton, 1b, Astros
17. Nick Castellanos, 3b/of, Tigers
18. Mike Zunino, c, Mariners
19. Archie Bradley, rhp, Diamondbacks
20. Zack Wheeler, rhp, Mets
21. Taijuan Walker, rhp, Mariners
22. Christian Yelich, of, Marlins
23. Jameson Taillon, rhp, Pirates
24. Danny Hultzen, lhp, Mariners
25. Javier Baez, ss, Cubs
26. Francisco Lindor, ss, Indians
27. Carlos Martinez, rhp, Cardinals
28. George Springer, of, Astros
29. Travis d'Arnaud, c, Blue Jays
30. Kevin Gausman, rhp, Orioles
31. Kyle Zimmer, rhp, Royals
32. Jorge Soler, of, Cubs
33. Bubba Starling, of, Royals
34. Hyun-Jin Ryu, lhp, Dodgers
35. Trevor Rosenthal, rhp, Cardinals
36. Lucas Giolito, rhp, Nationals
37. Yasiel Puig, of, Dodgers
38. David Dahl, of, Rockies
39. Mason Williams, of, Yankees
40. Anthony Rendon, 3b, Nationals
41. Casey Kelly, rhp, Padres
42. Julio Teheran, rhp, Braves
43. Jackie Bradley, of, Red Sox
44. Oswaldo Arcia, of, Twins
45. Wily Peralta, rhp, Brewers
46. Matt Barnes, rhp, Red Sox
47. Kaleb Cowart, 3b, Angels
48. Jake Marisnick, of, Marlins
49. Albert Almora, of, Cubs
50. Chris Archer, rhp, Rays

Minor League Player of the Year Wil Myers was traded to the Rays in the offseason

2011 prep draftee Dylan Bundy made it to the major leagues by the end of 2012

JOHN MANUEL

1. Jurickson Profar, ss, Rangers
2. Dylan Bundy, rhp, Orioles
3. Oscar Taveras, of, Cardinals
4. Wil Myers, of/3b, Rays
5. Jose Fernandez, rhp, Marlins
6. Gerrit Cole, rhp, Pirates
7. Miguel Sano, 3b, Twins
8. Xander Bogaerts, ss, Red Sox
9. Carlos Correa, ss, Astros
10. Byron Buxton, of, Twins
11. Shelby Miller, rhp, Cardinals
12. Tyler Skaggs, lhp, Diamondbacks
13. Billy Hamilton, of/ss, Reds
14. Christian Yelich, of, Marlins
15. Jonathan Singleton, 1b, Astros
16. Trevor Bauer, rhp, Diamondbacks
17. Taijuan Walker, rhp, Mariners
18. Zack Wheeler, rhp, Mets
19. Jameson Taillon, rhp, Pirates
20. Danny Hultzen, lhp, Mariners
21. Javier Baez, ss, Cubs
22. Mike Zunino, c, Mariners
23. Archie Bradley, rhp, Diamondbacks
24. Travis d'Arnaud, c, Blue Jays
25. Mike Olt, 3b/1b, Rangers
26. Nick Castellanos, 3b/of, Tigers
27. Kyle Zimmer, rhp, Royals
28. Kevin Gausman, rhp, Orioles
29. Anthony Rendon, 3b, Nationals
30. George Springer, of, Astros
31. Bubba Starling, of, Royals
32. Francisco Lindor, ss, Indians
33. Mason Williams, of, Yankees
34. Carlos Martinez, rhp, Cardinals
35. Lucas, Giolito, rhp, Nationals
36. Chris Archer, rhp, Rays
37. Jackie Bradley, of, Red Sox
38. Andrew Heaney, lhp, Marlins
39. David Dahl, of, Rockies
40. Lance McCullers Jr., rhp, Astros
41. Hyun-Jin Ryu, lhp, Dodgers
42. Oswaldo Arcia, of, Twins
43. Matt Barnes, rhp, Red Sox
44. Yasiel Puig, of, Dodgers
45. Julio Teheran, rhp, Braves
46. Nolan Arenado, 3b, Rockies
47. Slade Heathcott, of, Yankees
48. Albert Almora, of, Cubs
49. Casey Kelly, rhp, Padres
50. Gary Sanchez, c, Yankees

01 ST. LOUIS CARDINALS: They used homegrown talent to win the 2011 World Series and make a run at repeating in 2012. They have a lot more that's nearly big league ready, led by Oscar Taveras, Shelby Miller and Trevor Rosenthal.

02 SEATTLE MARINERS: Their best prospects, including 2012 first-rounder Mike Zunino, already have had success in Double-A or higher. That bodes well for a big league turnaround in the near future.

03 TEXAS RANGERS: No team mines the international market as aggressively as the Rangers, and their next gem is the game's best prospect, Jurickson Profar. Texas' big league talent allows it to gamble on high-risk, high-reward players.

04 TAMPA BAY RAYS: After years of banner drafts, they haven't fared as well in recent years. But their system remains strong thanks to trades for Wil Myers, Chris Archer, Hak-Ju Lee and Jake Odorizzi.

05 MIAMI MARLINS: This system wasn't notable beyond the Marlins' last three first-rounders (Christian Yelich, Jose Fernandez, Andrew Heaney)—until Miami started dismantling and dealt veterans for prospects.

06 BOSTON RED SOX: September 2011 and most of the 2012 season weren't much fun for the Red Sox, but at least their system is in good shape thanks to Xander Bogaerts and their 2011 draft (Jackie Bradley, Matt Barnes and Co.).

07 ARIZONA DIAMONDBACKS: No system can match the Diamondbacks' trio of pitching prospects in Tyler Skaggs, Trevor Bauer and Archie Bradley. Arizona has some underrated hitters too, starting with Adam Eaton and Matt Davidson.

08 PITTSBURGH PIRATES: They still haven't figured out how to finish .500, but the Pirates do have plenty of blue-chip prospects in Gerrit Cole, Jameson Taillon, Luis Heredia, Gregory Polanco, Alen Hanson and Josh Bell.

09 HOUSTON ASTROS: Though the Astros have bottomed out in the last two years, GM Jeff Luhnow rebuilt the Cardinals system and is doing the same with Houston. A masterful 2012 draft and several trades have restocked the organization.

10 MINNESOTA TWINS: They've had little luck developing arms, which explains off-season deals for Alex Meyer and Trevor May. They do just fine with hitters and have a pair of potential superstars in Miguel Sano and Byron Buxton.

11 NEW YORK YANKEES: They're getting ancient in the big leagues and don't have replacements ready yet. Their best prospects (Mason Williams, Slade Heathcott, Gary Sanchez, Tyler Austin) are promising but a few years away.

12 TORONTO BLUE JAYS: After loading up on young talent in his first two years on the job, GM Alex Anthopoulos has shifted gears and started using his prospect depth to acquire veterans. The Jays did replenish with the 2012 draft, though.

13 CHICAGO CUBS: In their first season running the Cubs, president of baseball operations Theo Epstein and GM Jed Hoyer focused on the future. They added potential building blocks in Albert Almora, Jorge Soler and Arodys Vizcaino.

14 CINCINNATI REDS: They've done a fine job of building from within, though the system has thinned out thanks to graduations and trades that fueled two playoff berths in the last three years.

15 SAN DIEGO PADRES: They have more minor league depth than most teams but don't stand out as much in terms of star power. Ascending talents such as Max Fried and Austin Hedges could change that perception, however.

16 **WASHINGTON NATIONALS:** They ranked No. 1 in last year's Handbook, then traded for Gio Gonzalez and graduated Bryce Harper. This system can rebound quickly if Anthony Rendon and Lucas Giolito can stay healthy.

17 **BALTIMORE ORIOLES:** The good news is that they have the game's best pitching prospect in Dylan Bundy and another quality arm in Kevin Gausman. The bad news is that they don't have much else.

18 **KANSAS CITY ROYALS:** They placed a record nine players on our Top 100 Prospects list in 2011 and ranked second in our talent rankings last spring. Promotions, trades and downturns in performance have taken a toll since then.

19 **LOS ANGELES DODGERS:** Though they attracted more attention for their big-ticket trades and free agents, the Dodgers also bolstered their system by spending heavily on Hyun-Jin Ryu, Yasiel Puig and Corey Seager in 2012.

20 **COLORADO ROCKIES:** Bearing the brunt of weak drafts from 2006-08, the major league team posted its worst record ever last season. The Rockies have fared better recently with picks such as Nolan Arenado, David Dahl and Trevor Story.

21 **ATLANTA BRAVES:** They've built a playoff team around homegrown youngsters such as Jason Heyward and Craig Kimbrel. But the system is in a state of flux, and top prospect Julio Teheran endured a rough 2012 season.

22 **MILWAUKEE BREWERS:** They had extra draft picks to play with the last two years. The pitchers the Brewers loaded up on in 2011 (Taylor Jungmann, Jed Bradley and Co.) are off to slow starts, and they went mainly for bats in 2012.

23 **PHILADELPHIA PHILLIES:** It's hard to argue with their constant trading of products when it resulted in five straight division titles and a World Series championship. But the system has little left in the upper levels.

24 **CLEVELAND INDIANS:** For years, most of Cleveland's best big leaguers have been acquired via trade. The Tribe has struggled to develop its own talent, and has little to bank on beyond shortstops Francisco Lindor and Dorssys Paulino.

25 **OAKLAND ATHLETICS:** Over the course of a year, they traded their best veterans for prospects, graduated a ton of players to the big leagues and made a stunning playoff run. The A's need to reload again, and their 2012 draft may help.

26 **NEW YORK METS:** Beyond Zack Wheeler, who was stolen in a 2011 trade for Carlos Beltran, most of their best prospects are years from the majors. That doesn't spark hope for a Mets turnaround in the near future.

27 **DETROIT TIGERS:** They're building around Miguel Cabrera, Prince Fielder and Justin Verlander, and any assistance the system provides will be gravy. The Tigers have few obvious future starters after Nick Castellanos and Avisail Garcia.

28 **SAN FRANCISCO GIANTS:** Their system is at its lowest point in more than a decade, but no one is complaining. The Giants have won two of the last three World Series and have yet another power arm coming in Kyle Crick.

29 **CHICAGO WHITE SOX:** They'll need some time to build up a perennially weak system, but at least the White Sox are spending on the draft and making an effort internationally. Not doing so for years landed them here.

30 **LOS ANGELES ANGELS:** Well, at least they produced Mike Trout in 2012. But after Kaleb Cowart, the Angels' minor league talent falls off a cliff. And spending big on free agents makes it impossible to do so in the draft.

Arizona Diamondbacks

BY BILL MITCHELL

Diamondbacks general manager Kevin Towers hasn't been shy about overhauling his roster.

He made changes after taking the job at the end of the 2010 season, most notably to the bullpen, and Arizona improved by 29 victories and won the National League West in 2011.

The Diamondbacks geared up for another run at the postseason in 2012 by signing free agent Jason  Kubel and trading prospects Jarrod Parker, Ryan Cook and Collin Cowgill to the Athletics for Trevor Cahill and Craig Breslow. But injuries and the inability to duplicate the 48 come-from-behind victories of 2011 contributed to 13 fewer wins, a .500 record and a third-place finish.

Towers started remaking the 2013 roster before last season ended. When former franchise cornerstone Stephen Drew never got his bat going after he came back from ankle surgery, Towers shipped him to the Athletics for fringe shortstop prospect Sean Jamieson.

He swung another deal with the A's in October, a three-team transaction with the Marlins that brought Heath Bell and Cliff Pennington to Arizona in exchange for Chris Young, who wasn't the same after injuring his shoulder crashing into an outfield wall in April. Towers added more bullpen help by swapping third-base prospect Ryan Wheeler to the Rockies for Matt Reynolds, and boosted the rotation by signing free agent Brandon McCarthy.

And Towers might not be done. Rumors continued to swirl that the Diamondbacks' best player (Justin Upton) and the third overall pick in the 2011 draft (Trevor Bauer) were on the block as the GM searched for a frontline shortstop.

While the team's 2012 performance was a disappointment, a steady stream of rookies provided some hope for the future and more fodder with which Towers could remake his club. Wade Miley won 16 games, made the All-Star Game and finished second in NL rookie of the year voting.

Top prospects Tyler Skaggs and Bauer also joined the rotation, though neither was particularly effective. Bauer was demoted after posting a 6.06 ERA in four midseason starts, while Skaggs was shut down after six starts with a tired arm in mid-September. They were outperformed by lefthander Patrick Corbin, who came to Arizona from the Angels as part of the 2010 Dan Haren trade, and went 6-8, 4.54 in 107 innings with the big league club.

Adam Eaton, a 19th-round pick as a senior from

Wade Miley anchored the Diamondbacks rotation in his first full season in the majors

Miami (Ohio) in 2010, made Young expendable as he continued his meteoric rise through the farm system. Arizona's minor league player of the year, Eaton led the minors in batting (.375), hits (198) and doubles (47) and won the Triple-A Pacific Coast League MVP award. He drilled his first two major league homers in September and will start in center field in 2013.

Eaton was just part of the good news down on the farm. Reno won both the PCL playoffs and the Triple-A National Championship with a team that featured three of the league's top-four hitters (Eaton, Ryan Wheeler and Jake Elmore). Mobile grabbed its second straight Double-A Southern League title despite graduating the bulk of its rotation, including Bauer, Corbin and Skaggs. And Missoula earned the Rookie-level Pioneer League crown.

After Towers arrived in 2010 and senior vice president of scouting and player development Jerry Dipoto left to become the Angels general manager following the 2011 season, the front office was relatively stable in 2012. The only significant change came in November, when international scouting director Carlos Gomez followed Dipoto to the Angels in the same role. Arizona hired former Red Sox international director Craig Shipley as an assistant to Towers a week later.

THIS YEAR'S TOP 30

Player, Pos.		Grade
1.	Tyler Skaggs, lhp	65/Low
2.	Trevor Bauer, rhp	65/Medium
3.	Archie Bradley, rhp	70/High
4.	Adam Eaton, of	55/Low
5.	Matt Davidson, 3b	55/Medium
6.	David Holmberg, lhp	50/Medium
7.	Chris Owings, ss	50/High
8.	Stryker Trahan, c	50/High
9.	Andrew Chafin, lhp	50/High
10.	A.J. Pollock, of	45/Low
11.	Chase Anderson, rhp	45/Medium
12.	Michael Perez, c	50/High
13.	Anthony Meo, rhp	50/High
14.	Evan Marshall, rhp	45/Medium
15.	Keon Broxton, of	50/High
16.	Jake Lamb, 3b	50/High
17.	Jon Griffin, 1b	50/High
18.	Alfredo Marte, of	50/High
19.	Jake Barrett, rhp	50/High
20.	Felipe Perez, rhp	50/High
21.	Joe Munoz, ss	50/High
22.	Ben Eckels, rhp	45/High
23.	Kyle Winkler, rhp	45/High
24.	Andrew Velazquez, 2b/ss	45/High
25.	Jose Martinez, rhp	50/Extreme
26.	Starling Peralta, rhp	50/Extreme
27.	Tyler Green, rhp	45/High
28.	Kevin Munson, rhp	45/High
29.	Socrates Brito, of	50/Extreme
30.	Evan Marzilli, of	45/High

LAST YEAR'S TOP 30

Player, Pos.		Status
1.	Trevor Bauer, rhp	No. 2
2.	Archie Bradley, rhp	No. 3
3.	Tyler Skaggs, lhp	No. 1
4.	Matt Davidson, 3b/1b	No. 5
5.	A.J. Pollock, of	No. 10
6.	David Holmberg, lhp	No. 6
7.	Chris Owings, ss	No. 7
8.	Wade Miley, lhp	Majors
9.	Patrick Corbin, lhp	Majors
10.	Bobby Borchering, of/3b/1b	(Astros)
11.	Anthony Meo, rhp	No. 13
12.	Adam Eaton, of	No. 4
13.	Andrew Chafin, lhp	No. 9
14.	Keon Broxton, of	No. 15
15.	Evan Marshall, rhp	No. 14
16.	Marc Krauss, of	(Astros)
17.	Kyle Winkler, rhp	No. 23
18.	Ryan Wheeler, 3b/1b	(Rockies)
19.	Kevin Munson, rhp	No. 28
20.	Yonata Ortega, rhp	(Rangers)
21.	Charles Brewer, rhp	Dropped out
22.	Ty Linton, of	Dropped out
23.	David Nick, 2b	Dropped out
24.	Michael Perez, c	No. 12
25.	Tyler Green, rhp	No. 27
26.	Jesse Darrah, rhp	Dropped out
27.	J.R. Bradley, rhp	Dropped out
28.	Brett Lorin, rhp	Dropped out
29.	John Pedrotty, lhp	Dropped out
30.	Socrates Brito, of	No. 29

BEST TOOLS

Best Hitter for Average	Adam Eaton
Best Power Hitter	Matt Davidson
Best Strike-Zone Discipline	Mike Freeman
Fastest Baserunner	Adam Eaton
Best Athlete	Keon Broxton
Best Fastball	Archie Bradley
Best Curveball	Trevor Bauer
Best Slider	Andrew Chafin
Best Changeup	Chase Anderson
Best Control	David Holmberg
Best Defensive Catcher	Michael Perez
Best Defensive Infielder	Chris Owings
Best Infield Arm	Jake Lamb
Best Defensive Outfielder	A.J. Pollock
Best Outfield Arm	Adam Eaton

PROJECTED 2016 LINEUP

Catcher	Miguel Montero
First Base	Paul Goldschmidt
Second Base	Aaron Hill
Third Base	Matt Davidson
Shortstop	Chris Owings
Left Field	Gerardo Parra
Center Field	Adam Eaton
Right Field	Justin Upton
No. 1 Starter	Tyler Skaggs
No. 2 Starter	Trevor Bauer
No. 3 Starter	Archie Bradley
No. 4 Starter	Ian Kennedy
No. 5 Starter	Wade Miley
Closer	David Hernandez

TOP PROSPECTS OF THE DECADE

Year	Player, Pos.	2012 Org.
2003	Scott Hairston, 2b	Mets
2004	Scott Hairston, 2b	Mets
2005	Carlos Quentin, of	Padres
2006	Stephen Drew, ss	Athletics
2007	Justin Upton, of	Diamondbacks
2008	Carlos Gonzalez, of	Rockies
2009	Jarrod Parker, rhp	Athletics
2010	Jarrod Parker, rhp	Athletics
2011	Jarrod Parker, rhp	Athletics
2012	Trevor Bauer, rhp	Diamondbacks

TOP DRAFT PICKS OF THE DECADE

Year	Player, Pos.	2012 Org.
2003	Conor Jackson, 3b	White Sox
2004	Stephen Drew, ss	Athletics
2005	Justin Upton, of	Diamondbacks
2006	Max Scherzer, rhp	Tigers
2007	Jarrod Parker, rhp	Athletics
2008	Daniel Schlereth, lhp	Tigers
2009	Bobby Borchering, 3b	Astros
2010	*Barret Loux, rhp	Rangers
2011	Trevor Bauer, rhp	Diamondbacks
2012	Stryker Trahan, c	Diamondbacks

*Did not sign.

LARGEST BONUSES IN CLUB HISTORY

Travis Lee, 1996	$10,000,000
Justin Upton, 2005	$6,100,000
John Patterson, 1996	$6,075,000
Archie Bradley, 2011	$5,000,000
Stephen Drew, 2004	$4,000,000

ARIZONA DIAMONDBACKS

TOP 2013 ROOKIE: Tyler Skaggs, lhp. He made three strong starts for Arizona before tiring in September and has a good chance to win a rotation job in spring training.

BREAKOUT PROSPECT: Chase Anderson, rhp. After a forearm injury wiped out most of his 2011 season, he made a fine comeback last year, standing out for his changeup and command.

SLEEPER: Alex Glenn, of. A 12th-round pick last June, he has plus speed and raw power.

SOURCE OF TOP 30 TALENT			
Homegrown	27	Acquired	3
College	13	Trades	2
Junior college	1	Rule 5 draft	1
High school	9	Independent leagues	0
Nondrafted free agents	1	Free agents/waivers	0
International	3		

LF
Breland Almadova
Ty Linton
Yoguey Perez-Ramos
Ismael Pena

CF
Adam Eaton (4)
A.J. Pollock (10)
Keon Broxton (15)
Socrates Brito (29)
Evan Marzilli (30)
Chuck Taylor
Justin Bianco
Danny Poma

RF
Alfredo Marte (18)
Alex Glenn
Jose Ordaz
Yorman Garcia

3B
Matt Davidson (5)
Jake Lamb (16)
Cesar Carrasco
Tyler Bream
Matt Helm
Ryan Court

SS
Chris Owings (7)
Joe Munoz (21)
Sergio Alcantara
Pedro Ruiz
Gustavo Nunez
Kevin Medrano
Sean Jamieson

2B
Andrew Velazquez (24)
Tyler Bortnick
David Nick
Michael Freeman
Gerson Montilla

1B
Jon Griffin (17)
Yazy Arbelo
Wagner Mateo
Rudy Flores
Jacob House

C
Stryker Trahan (8)
Michael Perez (12)
Fidel Pena
Ronnie Freeman
Oswaldo Garcia
Raywilly Gomez
Phildrick Llewellyn

LHP

LHSP	LHRP
Tyler Skaggs (1)	Eury de la Rosa
David Holmberg (6)	Will Locante
Andrew Chafin (9)	Michael Blake
Anfernee Benitez	Keith Hessler
Alex Carreras	Patrick Schuster
Cody Wheeler	Jose Jose
John Pedrotty	

RHP

RHSP	RHRP
Trevor Bauer (2)	Evan Marshall (14)
Archie Bradley (3)	Jake Barrett (19)
Chase Anderson (11)	Kyle Winkler (23)
Anthony Meo (13)	Starling Peralta (26)
Felipe Perez (20)	Kevin Munson (28)
Ben Eckels (22)	D.J. Johnson
Jose Martinez (25)	Enrique Burgos
Tyler Green (27)	Willy Paredes
Charles Brewer	Eric Smith
Jeff Gibbs	Chris Cox
Erick Leal	
Blake Perry	
Jesus Castillo	

2012   BONUSES: $4.6 MILLION

BEST PURE HITTER: C Stryker Trahan's (1) power got him drafted in the first round, and the Diamondbacks believe he has the approach and swing to hit for average as well. SS/2B Kevin Medrano (18) batted .342 in four years at Missouri State, then hit .341 in his pro debut.

BEST POWER HITTER: Trahan lets his power come naturally, focusing more on hitting liners from gap to gap. 3B Jake Lamb (6) has nearly as much raw pop as Trahan and slugged .539 at Rookie-level Missoula.

FASTEST RUNNER: OFs Chuck Taylor (4), Evan Marzilli (8), Alex Glenn (12) and Breland Almadova (37) and 2B/SS Andrew Velazquez (7) all have plus speed. Velazquez is the youngest of that group but has the best basestealing instincts, swiping 22 bases in 43 pro games.

BEST DEFENSIVE PLAYER: Similar to his predecessor as South Carolina's center fielder, Jackie Bradley (now starring in the Red Sox system), Marzilli plays shallow and has uncanny instincts. Lamb has a strong arm and made just seven errors in 64 pro games.

BEST FASTBALL: RHP Jake Barrett (3) works at 93-96 mph and tops out at 98. RHP Robbie Buller (35) threw 93-95 before having Tommy John surgery, which cost him his senior season at Houston Baptist.

BEST SECONDARY PITCH: Arizona spent $400,000 to sign nondrafted free agent RHP Felipe Perez, in part because he has a true curveball with sharp break. From its draft class, Barrett's slider stands out the most.

BEST PRO DEBUT: Trahan made the Arizona League all-star team after batting .281/.422/.473 and topping the Rookie circuit with 40 walks. RHP Chase Stevens (30) struck out 59 in 34 innings at Missoula, thanks to his low-90s fastball and hard curveball.

BEST ATHLETE: Taylor quarterbacked Mansfield Timberview High to the Texas 5-A state semifinals last fall, rushing for 1,972 yards and 23 touchdowns while passing for 16 more TDs.

MOST INTRIGUING BACKGROUND: OF Cam Gibson's (38) father Kirk manages the Diamondbacks and is a former National League MVP and World Series hero. RHP Zane Hemond's (40) grandfather Roland is a special assistant to Arizona president Derrick Hall and has worked in baseball for 61 years. Neither player signed, with Gibson following in his father's footsteps by attending Michigan State.

CLOSEST TO THE MAJORS: Barrett, who debuted in low Class A and will move fast as a reliever.

BEST LATE-ROUND PICK: RHP Ben Eckels (11) slid because he's just 6 feet tall, but he has a low-90s fastball and a promising curve. He struck out 56 in 52 AZL innings.

THE ONE WHO GOT AWAY: RHP Holden Helmink (22) took his projectable 6-foot-4 frame and potential plus fastball and curve to Texas. South Carolina-bound 2B Max Schrock (28) is undersized at 5-foot-8 but has tremendous feel for hitting.

ASSESSMENT: After grabbing four pitchers in the first two rounds in 2011, the Diamondbacks took hitters with seven of their top eight picks in 2012. They believe Trahan can stay behind the plate, enhancing his value.

2011   BONUSES: $11.9 MILLION

The first team ever to have two of the top seven picks, the Diamondbacks drew a pair of aces in RHPs Trevor Bauer (1) and Archie Bradley (1). They added more intriguing arms in LHP Andrew Chafin (1s) and RHPs Anthony Meo (2) and Evan Marshall (4).

GRADE: A

2010   BONUSES: $4.4 MILLION

Arizona didn't sign RHP Barret Loux (1), the No. 6 overall pick, though it did turn the compensation choice for him into Bradley. OF Adam Eaton (19) has blown past all expectations. SS Zach Walters (9) also has overachieved, though he was traded to the Nationals for Jason Marquis.

GRADE: C+

2009   BONUSES: $9.3 MILLION

Arizona had seven picks in the top two rounds, but its best selection so far has been 1B Paul Goldschmidt (8). OF A.J. Pollock (1), 3B Matt Davidson (1s) and SS Chris Owings (1s) are three more potential big league regulars. Pollock and since-traded 3B/1B/OF Ryan Wheeler (5) have played in the majors.

GRADE: B+

2008   BONUSES: $4.5 MILLION

LHP Wade Miley (1s) won 16 games in his first full big league season in 2012, while RHPs Bryan Shaw (2) and Ryan Cook (27) are quality relievers. Cook and OF Collin Cowgill (5) were used to acquire Trevor Cahill from the Athletics. Cowgill, since-traded LHP Daniel Schlereth (1) and since-waived SS/2B Jake Elmore (34) all have played in the big leagues.

GRADE: B+

Draft analysis by Jim Callis. Numbers in parentheses indicate draft rounds.

1 TYLER SKAGGS, LHP

Born: July 13, 1991. **B-T:** L-L. **Ht.:** 6-4. **Wt.:** 195.
Drafted: HS—Santa Monica, Calif., 2009 (1st round supplemental). **Signed by:** Bobby DeJardin (Angels).

BA GRADE
65
LOW

BILL MITCHELL

Skaggs was a three-sport star at Santa Monica (Calif.) High, where his mother Debbie was the longtime softball coach. He eventually gave up basketball and football to focus on baseball and pitched his way into the supplemental first round of the 2009 draft. The Diamondbacks hoped to take him with the 41st overall selection, but the Angels beat them to the punch at No. 40. He was part of a strong Angels draft class that already has sent Mike Trout, Skaggs, Garrett Richards, Patrick Corbin and Drew Carpenter to the majors. Skaggs signed for $1 million just before the Aug. 17 deadline, giving up a Cal State Fullerton commitment. Arizona finally got him a year later, acquiring him as the centerpiece of a July 2010 trade for Dan Haren. The Diamondbacks also received Corbin, Rafael Rodriguez and Joe Saunders. Skaggs' fastball velocity and prospect stock have risen in each of his two full seasons with Arizona, and he represented the organization in the last two Futures Games. He ranked as the No. 3 prospect in the Double-A Southern League and No. 4 in the Triple-A Pacific Coast League in 2012, going a combined 9-6, 2.87 with 116 strikeouts in 123 innings before making his major league debut on Aug. 22. He beat the Marlins in his big league start and pitched well in his next two before he tired and his velocity dropped in his next three. Arizona shut him down for the season after the Padres beat him on Sept. 20.

The jewel of Skaggs' repertoire is a sharp 12-to-6 curveball that he throws in the mid-70s. It features late, sharp break and is regarded as one of the best in the minors. He set it up with a fastball that ranges from 89-94 mph and features some armside run. He delivers his heater with good downhill plane and spots it to both sides of the plate. He throws in the low 90s more consistently than he ever has, and he also has improved his fastball command. Skaggs' changeup gives him a potential third plus pitch, but he needs to trust it more. It arrives at 78-80 mph, has some fade and plays well off his fastball. He can dominate hitters when all three pitches are working for him. Skaggs has smooth, easy mechanics and uses a high three-quarters arm slot. His athleticism allows him to repeat his delivery and consistently command his pitches. He also stands out for his composure on the mound and his idea of what he needs to do with each hitter. He holds runners well with a strong pickoff move, permitting just five steals in eight attempts last year. He didn't give up a single swipe in his six major league starts. He fields his position well.

Skaggs will be just 21 when spring training rolls around, but he has an excellent chance of earning a spot in the Arizona rotation when camp breaks. There's still projection remaining in his lanky frame, so there's a chance he could continue to get stronger and add velocity to his fastball. One of the top lefthanded pitching prospects in the game, he projects as a No. 2 starter.

SCOUTING GRADES

Fastball: 60.   **Control:** 60.
Curveball: 65.   **Command:** 55.
Changeup: 55.

Based on 20-80 scouting scale, where 50 represents major league average, and future projection rather than present tools.

Year	Club (League)	Class	W	L	ERA	G	GS	CG	SV	IP	H	HR	BB	SO	K/9	WHIP	AVG
2009	Angels (AZL)	R	0	0	0.00	3	2	0	0	6	4	0	1	7	10.5	0.83	.182
	Orem (PIO)	R	0	0	4.50	2	0	0	0	4	5	0	1	6	13.5	1.50	.278
2010	Cedar Rapids (MWL)	LoA	8	4	3.61	19	14	0	0	82	78	6	21	82	9.0	1.20	.252
	South Bend (MWL)	LoA	1	1	1.69	4	4	0	0	16	13	1	4	20	11.3	1.06	.224
2011	Visalia (CAL)	HiA	5	5	3.22	17	17	0	0	101	81	6	34	125	11.2	1.14	.219
	Mobile (SL)	AA	4	1	2.50	10	10	0	0	58	45	4	15	73	11.4	1.04	.216
2012	Mobile (SL)	AA	5	4	2.84	13	13	0	0	70	63	8	21	71	9.2	1.21	.241
	Reno (PCL)	AAA	4	2	2.91	9	9	0	0	53	49	4	16	45	7.7	1.23	.253
	Arizona (NL)	MAJ	1	3	5.83	6	6	0	0	29	30	6	13	21	6.4	1.47	.256
Major League Totals			1	3	5.83	6	6	0	0	29	30	6	13	21	6.4	1.47	.256
Minor League Totals			27	17	2.98	77	69	0	0	389	338	29	113	429	9.9	1.16	.235

2 TREVOR BAUER, RHP

Born: Jan. 17, 1991. **B-T:** R-R. **Ht.:** 6-1. **Wt.:** 185. **Drafted:** UCLA, 2011 (1st round). **Signed by:** Hal Kurtzman.

Bauer had a storied career at UCLA, setting Bruins career records for wins (34) and whiffs (460) while topping NCAA Division I in strikeouts in consecutive seasons. He won the Baseball America College Player of the Year and Golden Spikes awards in 2011, when the Diamondbacks made him the No. 3 overall pick in the draft and signed him to a big league contract with a $3.4 million bonus and $4.45 million in guarantees. In his first full pro season, Bauer ranked as the Southern League's top prospect, made his big league debut in June and helped Reno win the Pacific Coast League playoffs and the Triple-A National Championship. But his unconventional approach, which includes extreme long-tossing and the desire to call his own pitches, drew criticism from teammates and even owner Ken Kendrick. Bauer lasted just four starts in his first shot at the major leagues, but he still has outstanding stuff. His mid-90s four-seam fastball touches 96 mph and bores in on right-handers. Both it and his hard curveball grade as plus-plus pitches. He also uses a splitter, slider and changeup, all of which are at least average pitches. Bauer needs to refine his plan on the mound. He gets caught up trying to strike out every hitter, which leads to control issues and high pitch counts. Rather than trying to make each pitch perfect, he just needs to trust his stuff. He puts considerable effort into each pitch, but his delivery works for him and adds deception. Bauer will get a fresh start in spring training and a chance to break camp in Arizona rotation. He needs to make some adjustments but has all the ingredients to be a No. 1 starter.

BA GRADE
65
MEDIUM

Year	Club (League)	Class	W	L	ERA	G	GS	CG	SV	IP	H	HR	BB	SO	K/9	WHIP	AVG
2011	Visalia (CAL)	HiA	0	1	3.00	3	3	0	0	9	7	1	4	17	17.0	1.22	.200
	Mobile (SL)	AA	1	1	7.56	4	4	0	0	17	20	2	8	26	14.0	1.68	.286
2012	Mobile (SL)	AA	7	1	1.68	8	8	0	0	48	33	1	26	60	11.2	1.22	.192
	Arizona (NL)	MAJ	1	2	6.06	4	4	0	0	16	14	2	13	17	9.4	1.65	.230
	Reno (PCL)	AAA	5	1	2.85	14	14	1	0	82	74	8	35	97	10.6	1.33	.241
Major League Totals			1	2	6.06	4	4	0	0	16	14	2	13	17	9.4	1.65	.230
Minor League Totals			13	4	3.00	29	29	1	0	156	134	12	73	200	11.5	1.33	.229

3 ARCHIE BRADLEY, RHP

Born: Aug. 10, 1992. **B-T:** R-R. **Ht.:** 6-4. **Wt.:** 225. **Drafted:** HS—Broken Arrow, Okla., 2011 (1st round). **Signed by:** Kyle Denney.

When the Diamondbacks failed to sign No. 6 overall selection Barrett Loux in 2010, they got the seventh choice in 2011 as compensation. That pick became Bradley, who turned down the chance to play quarterback at Oklahoma for a $5 million bonus. After pitching two innings in his first pro summer, he jumped to low Class A South Bend in 2012, ranking as the Midwest League's top pitching prospect while leading the circuit in opponent batting average (.181) but also in walks (84). Arizona has three potential No. 1 starters in the system, and Bradley has the most electric arm. His fastball ranges from 93-98 mph, though he doesn't always command it well because a high leg kick can throw off his mechanics. At least when he misses, he misses down in the strike zone. Bradley's above-average 12-to-6 curveball gives him a second swing-and-miss pitch, and he's developing feel for an average changeup with nice sink. He has the athleticism and easy delivery to develop solid control, as well as a strong build for durability. He made significant strides with his command during instructional league, so he could really take off in 2013. With a deep pool of pitching prospects ahead of him, the Diamondbacks won't have to rush Bradley, who will spend all or most of the year at high Class A Visalia.

BA GRADE
70
HIGH

Year	Club (League)	Class	W	L	ERA	G	GS	CG	SV	IP	H	HR	BB	SO	K/9	WHIP	AVG
2011	Missoula (PIO)	R	0	0	0.00	2	1	0	0	2	1	0	0	4	18.0	0.50	.143
2012	South Bend (MWL)	LoA	12	6	3.84	27	27	0	0	136	87	6	84	152	10.1	1.26	.181
Minor League Totals			12	6	3.78	29	28	0	0	138	88	6	84	156	10.2	1.25	.181

4 ADAM EATON, OF

Born: Dec. 6, 1988. **B-T:** L-L. **Ht.:** 5-9. **Wt.:** 185. **Drafted:** Miami (Ohio), 2010 (19th round). **Signed by:** Frankie Thon Jr.

Eaton won the Rookie-level Pioneer League batting title (.385) after signing for $35,000 as a 19th-round college senior in 2010, and he continues to prove that performance was no fluke. He reached the big leagues in 2012, when he also led the minors in batting (.375), hits (198) and doubles (47) and was named Pacific Coast League MVP. He played regularly for Arizona in September before an errant pitch broke his right hand. Though Eaton is undersized at 5-foot-9, he has plenty of tools. His plus-plus speed stands out the most, and he does an excellent job of putting the ball in play so he can use it. He gets to top speed quickly, making him a basestealing threat. He led the PCL with 38 stolen bases in 48 tries last year. A prototypical leadoff hitter, Eaton consistently puts together good at-bats and gets on base. He added more pop to his package in 2012 and now projects as a double-digit home run threat. He also made big strides defensively, convincing scouts that he can be a big league center fielder. He has a strong, accurate arm. Eaton has gone from draft afterthought to potential fourth outfielder to big league regular in two short years. Arizona cleared the way for him to be its everyday center fielder and leadoff hitter by trading Chris Young this offseason.

BA GRADE
55 LOW

Year	Club (League)	Class	AVG	G	AB	R	H	2B	3B	HR	RBI	BB	SO	SB	CS	OBP	SLG
2010	Missoula (PIO)	R	.385	68	226	48	87	14	4	7	37	35	44	20	8	.500	.575
2011	Visalia (CAL)	HiA	.332	65	244	54	81	15	3	6	39	42	41	24	8	.455	.492
	Mobile (SL)	AA	.302	56	212	31	64	7	4	4	28	30	35	10	6	.409	.429
2012	Mobile (SL)	AA	.300	11	40	11	12	1	0	0	3	6	8	6	1	.451	.325
	Reno (PCL)	AAA	.381	119	488	119	186	46	5	7	45	53	68	38	10	.456	.539
	Arizona (NL)	MAJ	.259	22	85	19	22	3	2	2	5	14	15	2	3	.382	.412
Major League Totals			.259	22	85	19	22	3	2	2	5	14	15	2	3	.382	.412
Minor League Totals			.355	319	1210	263	430	83	16	24	152	166	196	98	33	.456	.510

5 MATT DAVIDSON, 3B

Born: March 26, 1991. **B-T:** R-R. **Ht.:** 6-3 **Wt.:** 225. **Drafted:** HS—Yucaipa, Calif., 2009 (1st round supplemental). **Signed by:** Jeff Mousser.

The 35th overall pick in the 2009 draft, Davidson signed for $900,000. After sharing third base with 2009 first-rounder Bobby Borchering in their first two full pro seasons, Davidson had the hot corner to himself at Double-A Mobile last year. He improved his defense and slammed a career-high 23 homers. Davidson brings a professional approach and plenty of power to the plate. When he doesn't try to do too much, he can drive the ball to all fields. While he continued to improve his plate discipline in 2012, he'll always accumulate strikeouts and probably won't hit for a high average. The chance to play regularly at third base helped Davidson enhance his range and actions. His 28 errors led SL third basemen by a wide margin, so he needs more consistency, but he has the soft hands and average arm to play there. Better positioning would help him. He's a below-average runner. Arizona needs a starting third baseman and more power bats in its lineup. Davidson still needs some time in Triple-A but should make his major league debut at some point in 2013. He'll push incumbent Chris Johnson aside when he's ready.

BA GRADE
55 MEDIUM

Year	Club (League)	Class	AVG	G	AB	R	H	2B	3B	HR	RBI	BB	SO	SB	CS	OBP	SLG
2009	Yakima (NWL)	SS	.241	72	270	29	65	15	0	2	28	21	75	0	2	.312	.319
2010	South Bend (MWL)	LoA	.289	113	415	58	120	35	3	16	79	43	109	0	2	.371	.504
	Visalia (CAL)	HiA	.169	21	71	6	12	1	0	2	11	12	25	0	0	.298	.268
2011	Visalia (CAL)	HiA	.277	135	535	93	148	39	1	20	106	52	147	0	1	.348	.465
2012	Mobile (SL)	AA	.261	135	486	81	127	28	2	23	76	69	126	3	4	.367	.469
Minor League Totals			.266	476	1777	267	472	118	6	63	300	197	482	3	9	.351	.445

6 DAVID HOLMBERG, LHP

KEN WEISENBERGER

Born: July 19, 1991. **B-T:** R-L. **Ht.:** 6-4. **Wt.:** 219. **Drafted:** HS—Port Charlotte, Fla., 2009 (2nd round). **Signed by:** Joe Siers (White Sox).

Getting Daniel Hudson from the White Sox for Edwin Jackson was a nice return for the Diamondbacks in their 2010 deadline deal. As an added bonus, they also received Holmberg, a polished lefthander who has breezed through three levels in the last two seasons. One of the most polished pitchers in the system, Holmberg has the best command among Arizona farmhands. He knows how to pitch and can locate four offerings where he wants. His best pitch is a low-80s changeup with sink that he'll use in any situation. He spots his 88-91 mph fastball well, reaching as high as 93. He also has a good feel for a curveball and slider that can become average pitches. Holmberg is extremely poised on the mound and very sound mechanically. He has firmed up what used to be a doughy body and is now stronger and more athletic. Holmberg held his own but didn't dominate in Double-A, so he could open 2013 back in Mobile. He's on track to reach Triple-A before he turns 22 and could make his big league debut in 2014. While he may not match the upside of other pitching prospects in the system, the odds are pretty good that he'll reach his ceiling of a No. 3 or 4 starter.

BA GRADE

50

MEDIUM

Year	Club (League)	Class	W	L	ERA	G	GS	CG	SV	IP	H	HR	BB	SO	K/9	WHIP	AVG
2009	Bristol (APP)	R	2	2	4.73	14	7	0	0	40	40	5	18	37	8.3	1.45	.256
2010	Great Falls (PIO)	R	1	1	4.46	8	8	0	0	40	52	2	9	29	6.5	1.51	.315
	Missoula (PIO)	R	1	4	3.86	7	7	0	0	37	47	2	7	47	11.3	1.45	.294
2011	South Bend (MWL)	LoA	8	3	2.39	14	14	1	0	83	65	3	13	81	8.8	0.94	.212
	Visalia (CAL)	HiA	4	6	4.67	13	13	0	0	71	73	5	35	76	9.6	1.51	.263
2012	Visalia (CAL)	HiA	6	3	2.99	12	12	0	0	78	62	6	14	86	9.9	0.97	.214
	Mobile (SL)	AA	5	5	3.60	15	15	0	0	95	104	8	23	67	6.3	1.34	.281
Minor League Totals			27	24	3.64	83	76	1	0	445	443	31	119	423	8.5	1.26	.257

7 CHRIS OWINGS, SS

KEN WEISENBERGER

Born: Aug. 12, 1991. **B-T:** R-R. **Ht.:** 5-10. **Wt.:** 180. **Drafted:** HS—Gilbert, S.C., 2009 (1st round supplemental). **Signed by:** George Swain.

When the Angels took Tyler Skaggs with the 40th overall pick in the 2009 draft, the Diamondbacks used the next choice on Owings, who signed for $950,000. Plantar fasciitis in both feet abbreviated his first full pro season, and he struggled with pitch-recognition issues in 2011. He put up the best offensive numbers of his career when he repeated high Class A last year, though he leveled off after a midseason promotion. Owings uses his strong hands to generate above-average bat speed. He has more power potential than most middle infielders and could match the 17 homers he hit in 2012 at higher levels. He used a more compact swing and stayed on pitches better last year, improving his ability to handle curveballs. He still needs to draw more walks, however. Owings should be at least an average big league shortstop, with solid range and a strong arm. He runs well and could steal 20 or more bases on an annual basis once he refines his technique. He'll return to Mobile until he shows he can handle Double-A pitching. If he makes strides similar to 2012, he could reach Triple-A at midseason. Arizona's shortstop position has been wide open since the Stephen Drew trade in August, and Owings could challenge for the job by mid-2014.

BA GRADE

50

HIGH

Year	Club (League)	Class	AVG	G	AB	R	H	2B	3B	HR	RBI	BB	SO	SB	CS	OBP	SLG
2009	Missoula (PIO)	R	.306	24	108	20	33	5	1	2	10	3	25	3	0	.324	.426
2010	South Bend (MWL)	LoA	.298	62	255	39	76	19	2	5	28	9	50	1	3	.323	.447
2011	Visalia (CAL)	HiA	.246	121	521	67	128	29	6	11	50	15	130	10	4	.274	.388
2012	Visalia (CAL)	HiA	.324	59	241	51	78	16	2	11	24	13	63	8	3	.362	.544
	Mobile (SL)	AA	.263	69	297	35	78	10	3	6	28	11	69	4	3	.291	.377
Minor League Totals			.276	335	1422	212	393	79	14	35	140	51	337	26	13	.305	.425

8 STRYKER TRAHAN, C

Born: April 25, 1994. **B-T:** L-R. **Ht.:** 6-1. **Wt.:** 215. **Drafted:** HS—Lafayette, La., 2012 (1st round). **Signed by:** Rusty Pendergrass.

A tough but friendly Cajun kid named after a character in a Burt Reynolds movie, Trahan was the first high school catcher drafted in 2012. The 26th overall pick, he signed for $1.7 million before slugging .473 and leading the Rookie-level Arizona League with 40 walks in his pro debut. Because he's unrefined defensively, he spent the entire summer in the AZL so he could work with hitting coach Robby Hammock and catching coordinator Bill Plummer, both former big league catchers. Trahan's hitting is far ahead of his defense. He has advanced plate discipline, above-average bat speed and the strength to drive the ball out of the park. His plus power is his calling card, but he also has the potential to hit for solid average. Opinions are mixed as to whether Trahan can stay behind the plate despite a strong arm and good athleticism. He threw out just 24 percent of AZL basestealers and his blocking and receiving skills are below-average. He did show improvement during the summer. He runs well enough to play on an outfield corner if he has to move. Trahan has the hitting chops to warrant a move to a full-season team, but he'll likely stay behind in extended spring training to work on his defense at the start of 2013. His next stop likely will be short-season Hillsboro.

BA GRADE: 50 HIGH

Year	Club (League)	Class	AVG	G	AB	R	H	2B	3B	HR	RBI	BB	SO	SB	CS	OBP	SLG
2012	Diamondbacks (AZL)	R	.281	49	167	29	47	11	3	5	25	40	48	8	1	.422	.473
Minor League Totals			.281	49	167	29	47	11	3	5	25	40	48	8	1	.422	.473

9 ANDREW CHAFIN, LHP

Born: June 17, 1990. **B-T:** R-L. **Ht.:** 6-2. **Wt.:** 205. **Drafted:** Kent State, 2011 (1st round supplemental). **Signed by:** Nate Birtwell.

After signing Chafin for $875,000 as the 43rd overall pick in 2011, the Diamondbacks challenged him with a jump to high Class A in his first full pro season. He dominated in his first 10 starts, recording a 2.91 ERA and 77 strikeouts in 59 innings, before tiring and pulling bullpen duty for a month. The fatigue wasn't unexpected, considering it was just his second year back from Tommy John surgery, and he recovered to lead the California League in strikeouts per nine innings (11.0) and opponent average (.241). Chafin has the best slider in the system and it can be unhittable for both lefties and righties. He throws his 90-94 mph four-seam fastball to both sides of the plate, and he also uses a two-seamer with sink. He focused more on his average changeup when pitching in relief and began to use it more in the second half. Chafin's delivery lacks fluidity and features some upper-body tilt, leading some scouts to believe he might be better suite for the bullpen. He has the repertoire to remain in the rotation, though he'll need to stop nibbling so much and trust his stuff more. Scouts noted a more aggressive approach during instructional league. Chafin is ready to move to Double-A. He has a realistic ceiling of a mid-rotation starter or set-up man.

BA GRADE: 50 HIGH

KEN WEISENBERGER

Year	Club (League)	Class	W	L	ERA	G	GS	CG	SV	IP	H	HR	BB	SO	K/9	WHIP	AVG
2011	Diamondbacks (AZL)	R	0	0	0.00	1	1	0	0	1	1	0	0	2	18.0	1.00	.250
2012	Visalia (CAL)	HiA	6	6	4.93	30	22	0	0	122	112	12	69	150	11.0	1.48	.241
Minor League Totals			6	6	4.89	31	23	0	0	123	113	12	69	152	11.1	1.48	.241

10 A.J. POLLOCK, OF

Born: Dec. 5, 1987. **B-T:** R-R. **Ht.:** 6-1. **Wt.:** 205. **Drafted:** Notre Dame, 2009 (1st round). **Signed by:** Mike Daughtry.

The Diamondbacks expected Pollock to move quickly after signing him for $1.4 million as the 17th overall pick in 2009, but he missed the following season when he fractured a growth plate in his right elbow during spring training. He has made up for lost time by batting .312 in the upper minors during the last two seasons and getting three separate big league callups in 2012. Pollock's total package is more than the sum of its parts, with only his bat and makeup grading better than average. He's a gap-to-gap hitter who makes reliable contact but has yet to develop much over-the-fence power. The ball does come off his bat well, so Arizona believes he will eventually produce 10-15 homers per year. Pollock makes the most of his average speed, running the bases well and showing annual 20-steal potential. He's capable of playing all three outfield positions, getting good reads and displaying an average arm that's enough to handle right field. Scouts are split on Pollock, with some seeing him as a solid regular in center field and others thinking he profiles best as a fourth outfielder. The Diamondbacks have no shortage of starting outfield candidates in Adam Eaton, Jason Kubel,

BA GRADE: 45 LOW

Gerardo Parra and Justin Upton, so Pollock will have to settle for a reserve role in 2013.

Year	Club (League)	Class	AVG	G	AB	R	H	2B	3B	HR	RBI	BB	SO	SB	CS	OBP	SLG
2009	South Bend (MWL)	LoA	.271	63	255	36	69	12	3	3	22	16	36	10	4	.319	.376
2010	Did not play--Injured																
2011	Mobile (SL)	AA	.307	133	550	103	169	41	5	8	73	44	86	36	7	.357	.444
2012	Reno (PCL)	AAA	.318	106	428	65	136	25	3	3	52	32	52	21	8	.369	.411
	Arizona (NL)	MAJ	.247	31	81	8	20	4	1	2	8	9	11	1	2	.315	.395
Major League Totals			.247	31	81	8	20	4	1	2	8	9	11	1	2	.315	.395
Minor League Totals			.303	302	1233	204	374	78	11	14	147	92	174	67	19	.354	.418

11 CHASE ANDERSON, RHP

BA GRADE
45
MEDIUM

Born: Nov. 30, 1987. **B-T:** R-R. **Ht.:** 6-1. **Wt.:** 175. **Drafted:** Oklahoma, 2009 (9th round). **Signed by:** Jason Karegeannes.

Anderson was a reliever at Oklahoma prior to signing for $85,000 as a ninth-round pick in the 2009 draft, but the Diamondbacks have developed him as a starter. He missed nearly all of the 2011 season with a strained flexor tendon in his forearm that didn't require surgery, and Arizona was cautious with him last year by limiting most of his Double-A starts to five innings. He was the Game One starter for Mobile in both of its playoff series, helping the BayBears win their second straight Southern League championship. Anderson possesses the best changeup in the system. It's at least a plus pitch with excellent fade, and he doesn't hesitate to use it when behind in the count. While his fastball sat in the high 80s early in the season, he worked at 90-94 mph in the Arizona Fall League while maintaining good command. He delivers his curveball in the mid-70s with good depth, giving him an effective third pitch. He's also working on a slider and eventually could have four average or better offerings. Anderson throws with a high three-quarters arm slot and repeats his delivery. A strong AFL performance earned him a spot on the 40-man roster and enhanced his credentials as a potential No. 4 starter. He'll move up to Triple-A in 2013.

Year	Club (League)	Class	W	L	ERA	G	GS	CG	SV	IP	H	HR	BB	SO	K/9	WHIP	AVG
2009	Missoula (PIO)	R	3	1	2.38	18	4	0	0	45	35	1	13	48	9.5	1.06	.206
2010	South Bend (MWL)	LoA	2	4	2.82	7	7	1	0	38	36	1	9	31	7.3	1.17	.238
	Visalia (CAL)	HiA	5	3	3.60	19	4	0	3	70	58	7	16	83	10.7	1.06	.227
2011	Visalia (CAL)	HiA	1	1	5.40	3	3	0	0	13	14	1	1	20	13.5	1.13	.259
2012	Mobile (SL)	AA	5	4	2.86	21	21	0	0	104	91	9	25	97	8.4	1.12	.238
Minor League Totals			16	13	3.09	68	39	1	3	271	234	19	64	279	9.3	1.10	.231

12 MICHAEL PEREZ, C

BA GRADE
50
HIGH

Born: Aug. 7, 1992. **B-T:** L-R. **Ht.:** 5-11. **Wt.:** 180. **Drafted:** HS--San Juan, P.R., 2011 (5th round). **Signed by:** Frankie Thon Jr.

Perez, who signed for $235,000 out of the 2011 draft, took a big step forward in his first full pro season, showing the skills on offense and defense to be a potential starting major league catcher. Perez is a free swinger at the plate, striking out 72 times in 225 at-bats last season, but he squares up the ball well, makes solid contact and uses the whole field. He shows enough power that he might one day hit 20 homers a season. He had limited catching experience as an amateur, so he has made significant strides defensively. He's calm behind the plate, his footwork and exchange are good, and he blocks well. He has an above-average arm that could get stronger as he matures, and he threw out 52 percent of basestealers last year, the best figure in the Rookie-level Pioneer League. While some had concerns about whether he was big enough to handle the everyday rigors of catching, Perez got bigger and stronger in 2012 and now has a solid catcher's build. Scouts note that he resembles Miguel Montero in how he goes about his business on the field. With a surplus of catching prospects in the low minors, the Diamondbacks could choose to give Perez more time in short-season ball, but he is probably ready for a full-season assignment to South Bend.

Year	Club (League)	Class	AVG	G	AB	R	H	2B	3B	HR	RBI	BB	SO	SB	CS	OBP	SLG
2011	Diamondbacks (AZL)	R	.217	7	23	5	5	2	0	2	3	2	10	1	0	.280	.565
2012	Missoula (PIO)	R	.293	58	225	43	66	16	5	10	60	20	72	0	1	.358	.542
Minor League Totals			.286	65	248	48	71	18	5	12	63	22	82	1	1	.351	.544

13 ANTHONY MEO, RHP

BA GRADE
50
HIGH

Born: Feb. 19, 1990. **B-T:** R-R. **Ht.:** 6-2. **Wt.:** 185. **Drafted:** Coastal Carolina, 2011 (2nd round). **Signed by:** George Swain.

Meo was one of many college power arms that the Diamondbacks picked early in the 2011 draft, going in the second round after a strong junior season at Coastal Carolina. Like supplemental first-rounder Andrew Chafin, Meo was challenged with an assignment to high Class A in his first full pro season, and he responded well, tying for the California League lead with 153 strikeouts. Meo's best pitch is a 90-94 mph fastball and he shows the ability to maintain his velocity deep into his starts. His slider can be nasty at times, and he's developing a feel for a changeup. Meo pitches with a lot of effort, with a wrap in his arm action, and struggles repeating his delivery, so he probably profiles better in the bullpen, where his fastball and slider would play up. He could potentially be a late-inning reliever because of the good movement on his two-seam fastball. Meo will stay in the rotation for now, likely moving up to Double-A in 2013.

Year	Club (League)	Class	W	L	ERA	G	GS	CG	SV	IP	H	HR	BB	SO	K/9	WHIP	AVG
2011	Diamondbacks (AZL)	R	0	0	0.00	1	1	0	0	1	0	0	0	2	18.0	0.00	.000
	Missoula (PIO)	R	0	0	0.00	1	0	0	0	2	0	0	0	1	4.5	0.00	.000
2012	Visalia (CAL)	HiA	9	8	4.11	26	25	0	0	140	134	15	71	153	9.8	1.46	.251
Minor League Totals			9	8	4.03	28	26	0	0	143	134	15	71	156	9.8	1.43	.247

14 EVAN MARSHALL, RHP

BA GRADE
45
MEDIUM

Born: April 18, 1990. **B-T:** R-R. **Ht.:** 6-2. **Wt.:** 220. **Drafted:** Kansas State, 2011 (4th round). **Signed by:** Joe Robinson.

Marshall began his Kansas State career as a starter before moving to the bullpen and finding it suited him well. He was part of the Diamondbacks' infusion of pitching from the 2011 draft, signing for $232,500, and they have kept him in a relief role. He pitched at three levels in his pro debut, finishing the year in Double-A, then returned to that level for the entire 2012 season, closing games for Mobile as the team won a second consecutive Southern League championship. Marshall primarily uses a fastball/slider combination, with his biggest strength being average to plus command and the ability to keep the ball on the ground. His 91-93 mph fastball has good armside run and sink, and he has a decent feel for a slider. He worked on his changeup in the Arizona Fall League, so he now has a legitimate three-pitch mix. A lack of swings and misses may prevent Marshall from being an elite reliever. His maximum-effort delivery has him flying open quickly, which provides deception. Marshall will move to Triple-A in 2013 and could be one of the first relievers called to the big leagues when a need arises.

Year	Club (League)	Class	W	L	ERA	G	GS	CG	SV	IP	H	HR	BB	SO	K/9	WHIP	AVG
2011	Yakima (NWL)	SS	0	0	0.75	11	0	0	2	12	10	0	2	13	9.8	1.00	.213
	Visalia (CAL)	HiA	0	1	1.59	15	0	0	4	17	14	2	5	18	9.5	1.12	.212
	Mobile (SL)	AA	0	0	0.00	1	0	0	0	2	2	0	0	0	0.0	1.00	.286
2012	Mobile (SL)	AA	6	3	3.51	42	0	0	16	49	55	2	16	27	5.0	1.46	.284
Minor League Totals			6	4	2.60	69	0	0	22	80	81	4	23	58	6.6	1.31	.258

15 KEON BROXTON, OF

BA GRADE
50
HIGH

Born: May 7, 1990. **B-T:** R-R. **Ht.:** 6-3. **Wt.:** 195. **Drafted:** Santa Fe (Fla.) CC, 2009 (3rd round). **Signed by:** Luke Wrenn.

Broxton is another product of the rich 2009 draft, signed by the Diamondbacks away from a Florida Atlantic football commitment so he could try to translate his athleticism on the baseball diamond. A slow start in high Class A last season had some scouts jumping off the bandwagon, but something clicked in the second half and he finished strong, batting .333/.361/544 with 11 homers. That surge landed him on Arizona's 40-man roster in November. The key for Broxton was playing off his strengths and becoming more aggressive in hitting the fastball, allowing his power to emerge. He already plays major league-quality defense in center field. His plus speed and good routes and jumps in the outfield make him a plus defender, and his arm is also a plus tool. Below-average pitch recognition and difficulties with the curveball continue to be his biggest weaknesses and will determine if he reaches the big leagues. He is a hard worker with good makeup and has consistently ranked as the most athletic player in the system, but he's still a long way from proving he can be a big league regular.

Year	Club (League)	Class	AVG	G	AB	R	H	2B	3B	HR	RBI	BB	SO	SB	CS	OBP	SLG
2009	Missoula (PIO)	R	.246	72	272	38	67	11	9	11	37	19	93	6	1	.302	.474
2010	South Bend (MWL)	LoA	.228	133	531	74	121	17	19	5	32	65	172	21	13	.316	.360
2011	South Bend (MWL)	LoA	.231	20	78	8	18	0	2	0	1	7	30	6	4	.294	.282
	Visalia (CAL)	HiA	.251	110	406	69	102	14	5	7	44	62	142	27	8	.349	.362
2012	Visalia (CAL)	HiA	.267	130	490	84	131	24	1	19	62	40	136	21	8	.326	.437
Minor League Totals			.247	465	1777	273	439	66	36	42	176	193	573	81	34	.324	.396

16 JAKE LAMB, 3B

BA GRADE
50
HIGH

Born: Oct. 9, 1990. **B-T:** L-R. **Ht.:** 6-3. **Wt.:** 195. **Drafted:** Washington, 2012 (6th round). **Signed by:** Donnie Reynolds.

Lamb earned honorable mention all-Pacific-12 Conference recognition to wrap up his career at Washington, before the Diamondbacks picked him in the sixth round last June and signed him for $161,000. He began his pro career at Rookie-level Missoula, leading the team with a .929 OPS. Lamb stands out for his athleticism and his defense at third base, with his plus arm ranking as the best infield arm in the system. He has plus raw power that is starting to translate to game power and could grow as he matures physically, learns to hit off the fastball and adjusts better to offspeed pitches. His swing still gets a little too long. He's an adequate baserunner, stealing eight bases in 10 attempts at Missoula. Lamb plays the game the right way and is a hard worker. Scouts give him a legitimate chance to be a big league regular. After showing good progress in instructional league, he may be advanced enough to open 2013 in low Class A.

Year	Club (League)	Class	AVG	G	AB	R	H	2B	3B	HR	RBI	BB	SO	SB	CS	OBP	SLG
2012	Missoula (PIO)	R	.329	67	280	47	92	22	5	9	57	24	51	8	2	.390	.539
Minor League Totals			.329	67	280	47	92	22	5	9	57	24	51	8	2	.390	.539

17 JON GRIFFIN, 1B

BA GRADE
50
HIGH

Born: April 29, 1989. **B-T:** R-R. **Ht.:** 6-7. **Wt.:** 250. **Drafted:** Central Florida, 2011 (21st round). **Signed by:** Luke Wrenn.

The Diamondbacks took Griffin as a low-cost senior sign in 2011 out of Central Florida, where he earned all-Conference USA honors in his final year after batting .343/.394/.661 with 19 homers. He then hit 18 homers to lead the Pioneer League after signing, prompting Arizona to jump him to high Class A in his first full pro season. He continued to show his power potential, belting 28 homers and 102 RBIs as he moved up to Double-A for the end of the regular season and Southern League playoffs. Griffin has exceptional raw pop and it should translate into at least average game power at the big league level. He improved his approach at the plate, cutting his strikeout rate from 28 percent to 21 percent despite the two-level jump, and showed the ability to turn on balls in or adjust on balls away. He has good bat speed but a long swing path, and a tendency to cheat on the fastball. He's athletic for his size and has been a better defender than Arizona expected, with soft hands. Griffin has been compared to Paul Goldschmidt for his work ethic and preparation, and like Goldschmidt before him, Griffin will have to prove he can hit quality pitching as he moves up.

Year	Club (League)	Class	AVG	G	AB	R	H	2B	3B	HR	RBI	BB	SO	SB	CS	OBP	SLG
2011	Missoula (PIO)	R	.295	71	278	47	82	12	0	18	59	29	77	4	0	.355	.532
2012	Visalia (CAL)	HiA	.300	128	487	87	146	19	3	26	98	49	107	0	0	.363	.511
	Mobile (SL)	AA	.438	5	16	2	7	1	0	2	4	1	1	0	0	.471	.875
Minor League Totals			.301	204	781	136	235	32	3	46	161	79	185	4	0	.362	.526

18 ALFREDO MARTE, OF

BA GRADE
50
HIGH

Born: March 31, 1989. **B-T:** R-R. **Ht.:** 6-0. **Wt.:** 190. **Drafted:** Dominican Republic, 2005. **Signed by:** Junior Noboa.

Marte spent six years in the system without getting much recognition as a prospect until he broke out with a strong 2012 season in Double-A, earning him a spot on the World team in the Futures Game. After never hitting more than nine homers in any previous season, he went deep 20 times for Mobile in only 398 at-bats. Marte became more confident at the plate and carried over improvements he made in high Class A in 2011. He's aggressive at the plate and takes a big swing, but he has developed a better feel for hitting and made more solid contact in Double-A. He projects to be more of a gap-to-gap, doubles hitter but should be able to consistently hit 15-20 homers a year. He draws comparisons to Chris Young for his athleticism, and while speed is not expected to be a factor in his game, he's an average runner with average range in the outfield. Marte is better suited to a corner, and his average arm should be enough to handle right field. He missed time in 2012 with a hamstring injury, but he finished strong to earn a spot on Arizona's 40-man roster and should be ready for a move to Triple-A.

Year	Club (League)	Class	AVG	G	AB	R	H	2B	3B	HR	RBI	BB	SO	SB	CS	OBP	SLG
2006	Diamondbacks (DSL)	R	.250	19	68	9	17	4	0	1	10	5	10	0	1	.316	.353
2007	Diamondbacks (DSL)	R	.328	67	265	30	87	19	4	4	45	17	37	3	1	.377	.475
2008	Yakima (NWL)	SS	.251	70	267	37	67	18	0	1	27	24	44	19	5	.324	.330
2009	South Bend (MWL)	LoA	.251	120	475	49	119	27	3	7	71	25	78	5	2	.294	.364
2010	Visalia (CAL)	HiA	.260	130	516	76	134	26	3	9	61	34	107	9	5	.314	.374
2011	Visalia (CAL)	HiA	.299	59	234	35	70	15	3	7	33	14	43	5	0	.344	.479
	Mobile (SL)	AA	.233	17	43	4	10	1	0	1	6	4	10	1	0	.306	.326
2012	Mobile (SL)	AA	.294	113	398	68	117	25	3	20	75	34	72	6	6	.363	.523
Minor League Totals			.274	595	2266	308	621	135	16	50	328	157	401	48	20	.330	.414

19 JAKE BARRETT, RHP

BA GRADE
50
HIGH

Born: July 22, 1991. **B-T:** R-R. **Ht.:** 6-3. **Wt.:** 230. **Drafted:** Arizona State, 2012 (3rd round). **Signed by:** Matt Smith.

Barrett played his high school ball in the Phoenix area, leading Desert Ridge High to a 2009 state championship. The Blue Jays took him in the third round that June but he chose to go to Arizona

State instead. He moved from the rotation to a closer role in 2012 with the Sun Devils and was again a third-round pick, this time signing with the hometown Diamondbacks for $392,900. He jumped to full-season ball with South Bend and got knocked around a bit. Barrett has two plus pitches in his power arsenal, combining a 93-96 mph fastball that hits 98 with a hard slider. He worked on a changeup after signing, but it still lacks consistency. He has the big frame, demeanor and pitches to be a late-inning reliever. Fatigue and the adjustment to the grind of professional baseball caused Barrett's velocity and command to drop last season, but he should be ready for an assignment to high Class A in 2013. He has the repertoire to move quickly in an organization that values power bullpen arms.

Year	Club (League)	Class	W	L	ERA	G	GS	CG	SV	IP	H	HR	BB	SO	K/9	WHIP	AVG
2012	South Bend (MWL)	LoA	0	3	5.84	25	0	0	6	25	28	2	13	25	9.1	1.66	.283
Minor League Totals			0	3	5.84	25	0	0	6	25	28	2	13	25	9.1	1.66	.283

20 FELIPE PEREZ, RHP

BA GRADE 50 HIGH

Born: Jan. 22, 1994. **B-T:** R-R. **Ht.:** 6-3. **Wt.:** 200. **Drafted:** HS—Anaheim, NDFA 2012. **Signed by:** Jeff Mousser.

Perez had the talent to go in the third to fifth round of the 2012 draft, but a strong UCLA commitment caused him to go unselected. His stuff took a step forward when he pitched in a summer collegiate West Coast League, and with money left in their draft budget the Diamondbacks signed Perez as a non-drafted free agent for $400,000 just before he was to head to campus. He reported to the Arizona minor league complex but did not pitch in games until instructional league. Right now, Perez is more about arm strength and he shows limited feel for pitching. His fastball sits at 91-93 mph with average movement, sink and tail. His curveball has late break and his changeup has good tumble and works well off the fastball. His high three-quarters delivery is clean with good arm action. Perez can throw all three of his pitches for strikes, and they all project to be average or better pitches in time. He's very coachable and mature for his age. Perez will start the 2013 season in extended spring training before reporting to a short-season club.

Year	Club (League)	Class	W	L	ERA	G	GS	CG	SV	IP	H	HR	BB	SO	K/9	WHIP	AVG
2012	Did Not Play																

21 JOE MUNOZ, SS

BA GRADE 50 HIGH

Born: Dec. 28, 1993. **B-T:** R-R. **Ht.:** 6-3. **Wt.:** 195. **Drafted:** HS—Hacienda Heights, Calif., 2012 (2nd round). **Signed by:** Jeff Mousser.

Munoz didn't play in as many showcases as higher-profile Southern California high school prospects, so his draft stock was harder to judge. The Diamondbacks liked his natural shortstop frame, instincts on the field and power potential, so they made him a second-round pick and signed him away from San Diego State for $520,500. The comment most often made about Munoz is that he just looks like a shortstop, and one of his Arizona League coaches said: "You can't draw a better shortstop body than what he's got." Munoz's inexperience in the field showed in his first season, as he made 25 errors in 45 games, most from troubles with his footwork. He has the potential to be an above-average defender with enough arm for shortstop, and should be able to stay at the position unless he eventually grows too big. His defense is ahead of his offense right now, although he hit better in the latter half of the AZL season after making adjustments to his approach, and he put together nice at-bats in instructional league. Munoz shows good power in batting practice and projects to be an average hitter. He's a tick below-average runner. Scouts in the AZL thought that Munoz could be a late bloomer, and he'll certainly need another year of short-season ball.

Year	Club (League)	Class	AVG	G	AB	R	H	2B	3B	HR	RBI	BB	SO	SB	CS	OBP	SLG
2012	Diamondbacks (AZL)	R	.260	47	173	25	45	4	2	2	20	16	53	4	4	.326	.341
Minor League Totals			.260	47	173	25	45	4	2	2	20	16	53	4	4	.326	.341

22 BEN ECKELS, RHP

BA GRADE 45 HIGH

Born: Jan. 27, 1994. **B-T:** R-R. **Ht.:** 6-0. **Wt.:** 175. **Drafted:** HS—Davis, Calif., 2012 (11th round). **Signed by:** John Bartsch.

Eckels is an undersized righthander whose repertoire and bulldog mentality would have put him in the early rounds of the 2012 draft if he were two or three inches taller. The Diamondbacks grabbed him in the 11th round and signed him for a $125,000 bonus, steering him away from a commitment to Howard (Texas) JC. He quickly became a favorite of scouts covering the Arizona League, where he struck out 56 batters in 52 innings, and he may turn out to be one of the better sleepers of the draft. Eckels stands out for his composure and aggressiveness on the mound. His low-90s fastball has heavy sink, and he also has a promising curveball and changeup. He pitches aggressively in the zone and has the ability to throw all of his pitches for strikes. Eckels will likely head to a more advanced short-season stop in 2013, but with his advanced feel for pitching and command of three pitches, he might be able to earn an assignment to low Class A.

Year	Club (League)	Class	W	L	ERA	G	GS	CG	SV	IP	H	HR	BB	SO	K/9	WHIP	AVG
2012	Diamondbacks (AZL)	R	4	3	4.13	11	9	0	0	52	50	1	23	56	9.6	1.39	.248
Minor League Totals			4	3	4.13	11	9	0	0	52	50	1	23	56	9.6	1.39	.248

23 KYLE WINKLER, RHP

BA GRADE
45
HIGH

Born: June 18, 1990. **B-T:** R-R. **Ht.:** 5-11. **Wt.:** 205. **Drafted:** Texas Christian, 2011 (10th round). **Signed by:** Kyle Denney.

Winkler was the ace of the Texas Christian staff as a junior, going 8-2, 1.39 and looking like a likely first-round pick before coming down with an arm injury just before the 2011 draft. Arizona still took him in the 10th round, signing him for $240,000 just after he had surgery for a stress fracture in his elbow. He rehabbed at the Diamondbacks' complex for the rest of 2011, making his pro debut in 2012 in the Visalia bullpen. Winkler gets hitters out with a 93-95 mph fastball and a hard slider. His changeup looked much better in instructional league, when he was throwing it with nice fade and sink. He has a funky delivery in which his arm comes through late, putting some stress on his elbow, but it provides deception as he steps toward the plate. Winkler profiles as a reliever but may start some in the minors in order to get more innings under his belt and build up arm strength.

Year	Club (League)	Class	W	L	ERA	G	GS	CG	SV	IP	H	HR	BB	SO	K/9	WHIP	AVG
2012	Visalia (CAL)	HiA	3	1	5.44	31	0	0	0	43	51	2	24	38	8.0	1.74	.293
Minor League Totals			3	1	5.44	31	0	0	0	43	51	2	24	38	8.0	1.74	.293

24 ANDREW VELAZQUEZ, 2B/SS

BA GRADE
45
HIGH

Born: July 14, 1994. **B-T:** B-R. **Ht.:** 5-8. **Wt.:** 175. **Drafted:** HS—Bronx, N.Y., 2012 (7th round). **Signed by:** Todd Donovan.

Arizona scouted Velazquez in the summer before his senior year of high school and kept tabs on his progress before drafting him last June and signing him quickly for $200,000. After playing shortstop in high school, Velazquez spent most of his first pro season at second base, and that's where he looks best suited. The undersized infielder quickly became a favorite both of the Diamondbacks' Arizona League coaching staff and scouts covering the league for his athleticism, speed and gamer mentality on the field. Velazquez has good hands that help him generate above-average bat speed. His raw speed is above-average, and it plays up because he's a smart baserunner, stealing 22 bases in 25 attempts in his first season. He doesn't yet have much power (his only homer was inside the park), but started to show a little more pop during instructional league and could eventually hit 10-15 homers a year. While he's still relatively new to the infield, having been an outfielder earlier in his high school career, he should be a solid defender. He's capable of playing either middle-infield position, with enough arm for shortstop. Velazquez will need lots of development time, so he'll probably return to a short-season team in 2013.

Year	Club (League)	Class	AVG	G	AB	R	H	2B	3B	HR	RBI	BB	SO	SB	CS	OBP	SLG
2012	Diamondbacks (AZL)	R	.319	29	116	33	37	8	5	1	20	18	35	20	3	.406	.500
	Missoula (PIO)	R	.220	14	50	9	11	0	2	0	4	5	12	2	0	.286	.300
Minor League Totals			.289	43	166	42	48	8	7	1	24	23	47	22	3	.371	.440

25 JOSE MARTINEZ, RHP

BA GRADE
50
EXTREME

Born: April 14, 1994. **B-T:** R-R. **Ht.:** 6-1. **Wt.:** 160. **Drafted:** Dominican Republic, 2011. **Signed by:** Junior Noboa.

Martinez signed in 2011 for $55,000 under the name Jose Fermin. His fastball sat at 85-88 mph at the time, but shortly thereafter his velocity increased to 90-91 and he developed a harder-breaking curveball. Martinez made a strong pro debut at age 18 in the Rookie-level Dominican Summer League last season and was named the Diamondbacks' minor league pitcher of the month for July. He came to the United States for two late-season starts with short-season Yakima before reporting to Arizona for instructional league. Martinez commands his lively 91-96 mph fastball, and he could add more velocity as he gets bigger and stronger. He's got a tight power curveball that is tough to hit when he commands it, and a changeup that is still a work in progress. Martinez has an ideal, athletic pitcher's frame, fluid arm action and an over-the-top delivery that he repeats well, though with some effort. He keeps the same arm speed with all of his pitches. Martinez handled his late stint in Yakima well considering it was his first time in the United States. He's probably not yet ready for a full-season assignment and could return to the short-season Northwest League.

Year	Club (League)	Class	W	L	ERA	G	GS	CG	SV	IP	H	HR	BB	SO	K/9	WHIP	AVG
2012	Diamondbacks (DSL)	R	5	2	1.72	14	14	0	0	73	57	0	22	71	8.7	1.08	.218
	Yakima (NWL)	SS	0	1	4.22	2	2	0	0	11	8	1	6	8	6.8	1.31	.205
Minor League Totals			5	3	2.04	16	16	0	0	84	65	1	28	79	8.5	1.11	.216

26 STARLING PERALTA, RHP

BA GRADE
50
EXTREME

Born: Nov. 11, 1990. **B-T:** R-R. **Ht.:** 6-4. **Wt.:** 180. **Drafted:** Dominican Republic, 2008. **Signed by:** Jose Serra (Cubs).

Peralta spent three years in the Cubs' Dominican Summer League program before making his U.S. debut in 2011, starting with three games in Rookie ball before jumping to low Class A Peoria. He returned to Peoria in 2012 with better results after an early season hand injury, holding hitters to a .199 average in the second half. The Diamondbacks selected Peralta in the Rule 5 draft during the 2012 Winter Meetings when Chicago left the lanky righthander off the 40-man roster in his first year of eligibility. His fastball averages 94 mph and gets as high as 97. He pitches with a short-arm, upright delivery that is not loose and leads to command issues. Peralta tends to get slider happy at times instead of trusting the fastball, but the slider has the potential to be an average pitch. His third pitch is a below-average changeup that he seldom uses. With a two-pitch mix and effectiveness against righthanders, Peralta profiles better as a bullpen arm, and he'll attempt to make the Arizona roster in that role. The Diamondbacks have a history of making trades to retain Rule 5 picks they like and may do so again if he impresses during spring training. They can't send him to the minors in 2013 without exposing him to waivers and offering him back to the Cubs for half of his $50,000 draft price.

Year	Club (League)	Class	W	L	ERA	G	GS	CG	SV	IP	H	HR	BB	SO	K/9	WHIP	AVG
2008	Cubs 2 (DSL)	R	4	4	6.92	15	8	0	0	40	50	1	24	33	7.4	1.83	.314
2009	Cubs 1 (DSL)	R	1	3	4.10	7	3	0	0	26	32	2	4	22	7.5	1.37	.299
2010	Cubs 2 (DSL)	R	0	2	3.00	8	8	0	0	39	34	1	12	37	8.5	1.18	.239
	Cubs 1 (DSL)	R	1	2	4.82	7	7	1	0	28	26	1	7	30	9.6	1.18	.234
2011	Cubs (AZL)	R	2	1	3.46	3	2	0	0	13	14	0	2	18	12.5	1.23	.275
	Peoria (MWL)	LoA	3	5	5.68	12	12	0	0	57	67	9	26	40	6.3	1.63	.290
2012	Peoria (MWL)	LoA	5	8	3.44	20	17	0	0	99	80	11	42	86	7.8	1.23	.217
Minor League Totals			16	25	4.46	72	57	1	0	303	303	25	117	266	7.9	1.39	.259

27 TYLER GREEN, RHP

BA GRADE
45
HIGH

Born: Nov. 24, 1991. **B-T:** R-R. **Ht.:** 6-1. **Wt.:** 185. **Drafted:** HS—Clute, Texas, 2010 (8th round). **Signed by:** Trip Couch.

Green was on his way to Texas Christian as a two-way player before the Diamondbacks signed him at the 2010 deadline for an above-slot $750,000 bonus. He spent both of his first two professional seasons at South Bend, pitching mostly in the rotation, although his violent delivery and control issues indicate that he will likely wind up in the bullpen before long. Green's best pitch is an 88-92 mph fastball that gets up to 95 mph with good sink and angle. He also uses a power curveball and is starting to develop a better feel for a below-average changeup. Green's over-the-top delivery provides deception but also leads to command issues. He started to find himself late in the season when his work ethic and pitchability improved. Green will move up to high Class A, and he may wind up in a relief role where his bulldog mentality and power arsenal will play up well.

Year	Club (League)	Class	W	L	ERA	G	GS	CG	SV	IP	H	HR	BB	SO	K/9	WHIP	AVG
2011	South Bend (MWL)	LoA	6	8	4.97	25	22	0	1	114	118	10	49	79	6.2	1.46	.270
2012	South Bend (MWL)	LoA	4	9	3.78	26	20	0	1	126	132	8	60	75	5.3	1.52	.273
Minor League Totals			10	17	4.34	51	42	0	2	240	250	18	109	154	5.8	1.49	.271

28 KEVIN MUNSON, RHP

BA GRADE
45
HIGH

Born: Jan. 13, 1989. **B-T:** R-R. **Ht.:** 6-2. **Wt.:** 200. **Drafted:** James Madison, 2010 (4th round). **Signed by:** Shawn Barton.

Munson was a catcher at the beginning of his college career at James Madison but was quickly moved to the mound to take advantage of his arm strength. The Diamondbacks took Munson in the fourth round in 2010 and started him in full-season ball, assuming that he could move quickly and help the big league club sooner rather than later. Instead, command issues have plagued him throughout his career, caused in part by a delivery in which he opens up early, causing the stuff to flatten out and come up. He's no longer considered to have closer potential, but still possesses a 91-95 mph fastball that touches 97, as well as a hard slider. He fields his position well and displays good mound presence. Munson improved his command after the season's first two months and was dominating hitters by the end of the year, posting a 0.84 ERA with 16 strikeouts in 11 innings in August. His 2013 Opening Day assignment will depend on which Munson shows up in spring training.

Year	Club (League)	Class	W	L	ERA	G	GS	CG	SV	IP	H	HR	BB	SO	K/9	WHIP	AVG
2010	South Bend (MWL)	LoA	2	0	1.10	12	0	0	3	16	8	1	5	17	9.4	0.80	.143
	Visalia (CAL)	HiA	0	0	13.50	1	0	0	0	1	1	0	2	0	0.0	4.50	.333
2011	Visalia (CAL)	HiA	0	3	4.02	40	0	0	0	54	44	4	41	76	12.7	1.58	.221
	Mobile (SL)	AA	0	0	0.00	2	0	0	0	3	3	0	1	2	6.0	1.33	.273
2012	Mobile (SL)	AA	3	5	6.28	44	0	0	3	53	55	3	27	64	10.9	1.55	.266
Minor League Totals			9	8	4.55	101	0	0	6	127	111	8	76	159	11.3	1.48	.233

29 SOCRATES BRITO, OF

BA GRADE
50
EXTREME

Born: Sept. 6, 1992. **B-T:** L-L. **Ht.:** 6-2. **Wt.:** 197. **Drafted:** Dominican Republic, 2010. **Signed by:** Junior Noboa.

The Diamondbacks signed Brito out of the Dominican Republic for $190,000, then voided the deal when he failed a steroid test and re-signed him for $90,000 two months later. That small investment may pay off, though Brito is still a long way from the big leagues. One scout said that Brito has the biggest gap between his present and future grades, but that he's still someone to dream on. Brito spent his second year in the United States at Missoula, showing speed but no power. While his in-game power has not yet emerged, he shows enough pop in batting practice to prove that he will hit with power when he fills out his wiry strong frame and improves his pitch selection. Brito is one of the fastest players in the system once under way, and his speed gives him good range in the outfield, although his routes are sometimes poor. He has plus arm strength and is improving his accuracy. He is still years away but has the tools to profile as a big league regular if he figures everything out. He'll advance to low Class A in 2013.

Year	Club (League)	Class	AVG	G	AB	R	H	2B	3B	HR	RBI	BB	SO	SB	CS	OBP	SLG
2010	Diamondbacks (DSL)	R	.293	22	82	11	24	4	1	0	8	9	15	0	4	.363	.366
2011	Diamondbacks (AZL)	R	.275	55	236	29	65	3	7	1	29	13	50	18	10	.315	.360
2012	Missoula (PIO)	R	.312	69	279	47	87	15	5	4	39	21	73	15	9	.357	.444
Minor League Totals			.295	146	597	87	176	22	13	5	76	43	138	33	23	.342	.400

30 EVAN MARZILLI, OF

BA GRADE
45
HIGH

Born: March 13, 1991. **B-T:** L-L. **Ht.:** 5-11. **Wt.:** 175. **Drafted:** South Carolina, 2012 (8th round). **Signed by:** George Swain.

Marzilli was a key part of three straight College World Series runs at South Carolina, including national titles in 2010 and 2011. After the Gamecocks finished runner-up in 2012, he signed for $132,900 as an eighth-round pick. His knack for playing on winning teams continued, as he helped Missoula reach the Pioneer League playoffs, but a broken arm put him out of action for the playoffs. Marzilli is athletic with a deceptively strong body. Center-field defense is his strongest skill, and he's a plus defender with plus speed and excellent instincts. He worked hard on his throwing in school so that he now has an average arm. At the plate, Marzilli has a short, quick stroke and uses the whole field. He doesn't hit with much power, so he's best suited as a top of the order hitter, but he needs to work on plate discipline and understand how to work counts. His speed hasn't yet translated to stolen bases, something that the Diamondbacks will emphasize in his development plan. Marzilli is a grinder with an outstanding work ethic, and he brings a winning attitude to the game thanks to his three years in the South Carolina program. Because of his major college experience, Marzilli may be ready for full-season ball in 2013.

Year	Club (League)	Class	AVG	G	AB	R	H	2B	3B	HR	RBI	BB	SO	SB	CS	OBP	SLG
2012	Missoula (PIO)	R	.332	51	211	40	70	10	1	0	15	21	35	6	3	.403	.389
Minor League Totals			.332	51	211	40	70	10	1	0	15	21	35	6	3	.403	.389

Atlanta Braves

BY BILL BALLEW

In many ways, the 2012 season was one of redemption for the Braves, who were able to erase the memory of 2011's collapse by rebounding with a 94-68 record—their best mark since winning 96 games in 2004—and earning a spot in the first-ever National League Wild Card Game. They dropped that contest 6-3 to the Cardinals in an action-packed affair that featured a controversial infield-fly call.

Atlanta's front office didn't make any major changes after the disappointment of 2011, and that proved to be the right move. Manager Fredi Gonzalez, whom many fans blamed for the team's slide the year before, did a masterful job of handling an injury-ravaged pitching rotation and got more mileage out of his bullpen. He deployed third baseman Chipper Jones effectively as the Braves icon rode off into the sunset of his Hall of Fame career, and enjoyed a bounce-back year from outfielder Jason Heyward.

Jones' retirement severs the last tie to the team's run of 14 consecutive division titles from 1991-2005. Frank Wren took over as general manager after the 2007 season, replacing current team president John Schuerholz. Atlanta also has changed managers (Gonzalez replaced Bobby Cox, who retired after 2010), scouting directors (Tony DeMacio for Roy Clark, who joined the Nationals after the 2009 season) and farm directors (Ronnie Richardson for Kurt Kemp, who resigned in September 2011).

The roster continues to evolve, with Heyward and first baseman Freddie Freeman now relied upon as cornerstones and shortstop Andrelton Simmons stepping in as the next potential homegrown star. He nearly made the jump from high Class A to win the Braves' shortstop job in spring training, then claimed it in June. He batted .289 and played strong defense as a rookie.

Freeman, Heyward and Simmons are each 23, and there's plenty of youth on the pitching staff as well. Closer Craig Kimbrel, who set a major league record for relievers by averaging 16.7 strikeouts per nine innings in 2012, is 24. Atlanta's best starter last season was Kris Medlen (27), and Brandon Beachy (26), Mike Minor (25) and Randall Delgado (22) could join him in the 2013 rotation—though Beachy is returning from Tommy John surgery.

All of those players are products of the Braves farm system, and only Heyward and Minor were first-round draft picks. Building from within has become crucial as the big league payroll has moved to the

Andrelton Simmons filled a void at shortstop after his midseason promotion to Atlanta

middle of baseball's pack under Liberty Media, which has owned the team since a stock swap with Time Warner in May 2007.

Wren has operated under more financial constraints than Schuerholz ever did, both in acquiring major league talent and in bringing in players through the draft and international markets. And when Wren has made big investments, in players such as pitchers Kenshin Kawakami and Derek Lowe and infielder Dan Uggla, they haven't worked out that well.

In the minors, high Class A Lynchburg won its second Carolina League title in four years while low Class A Rome rebounded from an 18-52 start to reach the South Atlantic League playoffs.

While the Braves continue to do a fine job of developing their own talent, they've now gone seven straight seasons without finishing in first place. They haven't won a postseason series since sweeping the Astros in a NL Division Series in 2001.

Perhaps in reaction to those droughts, Atlanta made a big splash on the free agent market in November, signing outfielder B.J. Upton to a five-year, $75 million deal that represents the largest contract in franchise history. The Braves also picked up a $12 million option on Brian McCann for 2013, even though he had labrum surgery in the fall.

THIS YEAR'S TOP 30

Player, Pos.		Grade
1.	Julio Teheran, rhp	60/Medium
2.	J.R. Graham, rhp	50/Medium
3.	Christian Bethancourt, c	55/High
4.	Sean Gilmartin, lhp	50/Medium
5.	Lucas Sims, rhp	55/High
6.	Mauricio Cabrera, rhp	55/Extreme
7.	Alex Wood, lhp	50/High
8.	Evan Gattis, of/c	50/High
9.	Zeke Spruill, rhp	45/Medium
10.	Jose Peraza, ss	55/Extreme
11.	Nick Ahmed, ss	50/High
12.	Todd Cunningham, of	45/Medium
13.	Cody Martin, rhp	50/High
14.	Matt Lipka, of	50/High
15.	Navery Moore, rhp	50/High
16.	David Hale, rhp	45/Medium
17.	Edward Salcedo, 3b	50/High
18.	Joey Terdoslavich, 1b/3b	50/High
19.	Josh Elander, c	50/High
20.	Juan Jaime, rhp	50/Extreme
21.	Carlos Franco, 3b	50/Extreme
22.	Luis Merejo, rhp	50/Extreme
23.	Bryan de la Rosa, c	50/Extreme
24.	Billy Bullock, rhp	45/High
25.	Kyle Kubitza, 3b	45/High
26.	Nathan Hyatt, rhp	45/High
27.	Brandon Drury, 1b/3b	45/High
28.	Carlos Perez, lhp	45/High
29.	Robby Hefflinger, of	45/High
30.	Aaron Northcraft, rhp	45/High

LAST YEAR'S TOP 30

Player, Pos.		Status
1.	Julio Teheran, rhp	No. 1
2.	Arodys Vizcaino, rhp	(Cubs)
3.	Randall Delgado, rhp	Majors
4.	Andrelton Simmons, ss	Majors
5.	Sean Gilmartin, lhp	No. 4
6.	Edward Salcedo, 3b/ss	No. 17
7.	Tyler Pastornicky, ss	Majors
8.	Christian Bethancourt, c	No. 3
9.	Zeke Spruill, rhp	No. 9
10.	Brandon Drury, 3b	No. 27
11.	Joey Terdoslavich, 1b	No. 18
12.	J.J. Hoover, rhp	(Reds)
13.	J.R. Graham, rhp	No. 2
14.	Matt Lipka, ss/2b/of	No. 14
15.	Nick Ahmed, ss	No. 11
16.	Todd Cunningham, of	No. 12
17.	Kyle Kubitza, 3b	No. 25
18.	Dimasther Delgado, lhp	Dropped out
19.	Cody Martin, rhp	No. 13
20.	Navery Moore, rhp	No. 15
21.	David Hale, rhp	No. 16
22.	Adam Milligan, of	Dropped out
23.	Mycal Jones, of	Dropped out
24.	Billy Bullock, rhp	No. 24
25.	Carlos Perez, lhp	No. 28
26.	Erik Cordier, rhp	(Pirates)
27.	Evan Gattis, c	No. 8
28.	Tommy LaStella, 2b	Dropped out
29.	Cory Gearrin, rhp	Majors
30.	Phil Gosselin, 2b	Dropped out

BEST TOOLS

Best Hitter for Average	Todd Cunningham
Best Power Hitter	Evan Gattis
Best Strike-Zone Discipline	Chris Garcia
Fastest Baserunner	Jose Peraza
Best Athlete	Matt Lipka
Best Fastball	Juan Jaime
Best Curveball	Lucas Sims
Best Slider	Cody Martin
Best Changeup	Julio Teheran
Best Control	Gary Moran
Best Defensive Catcher	Christian Bethancourt
Best Defensive Infielder	Nick Ahmed
Best Infield Arm	Carlos Franco
Best Defensive Outfielder	Todd Cunningham
Best Outfield Arm	Robby Hefflinger

PROJECTED 2016 LINEUP

Catcher	Brian McCann
First Base	Freddie Freeman
Second Base	Jose Peraza
Third Base	Martin Prado
Shortstop	Andrelton Simmons
Left Field	Evan Gattis
Center Field	B.J. Upton
Right Field	Jason Heyward
No. 1 Starter	Kris Medlen
No. 2 Starter	Julio Teheran
No. 3 Starter	Mike Minor
No. 4 Starter	Brandon Beachy
No. 5 Starter	Randall Delgado
Closer	Craig Kimbrel

TOP PROSPECTS OF THE DECADE

Year	Player, Pos.	2012 Org.
2003	Adam Wainwright, rhp	Cardinals
2004	Andy Marte, 3b	Out of baseball
2005	Jeff Francoeur, of	Royals
2006	Jarrod Saltalamacchia, c	Red Sox
2007	Jarrod Saltalamacchia, c	Red Sox
2008	Jordan Schafer, of	Astros
2009	Tommy Hanson, rhp	Braves
2010	Jason Heyward, of	Braves
2011	Julio Teheran, rhp	Braves
2012	Julio Teheran, rhp	Braves

TOP DRAFT PICKS OF THE DECADE

Year	Player, Pos.	2012 Org.
2003	Luis Atiliano, rhp (1st round supp.)	Reds
2004	Eric Campbell, 3b (2nd rd)	Fargo (Amer. Assoc.)
2005	Joey Devine, rhp	Athletics
2006	Cody Johnson, of	Yankees
2007	Jason Heyward, of	Braves
2008	Brett DeVall (1st round supp.)	Out of baseball
2009	Mike Minor, lhp	Braves
2010	Matt Lipka, ss (1st round supp.)	Braves
2011	Sean Gilmartin, lhp	Braves
2012	Lucas Sims, rhp	Braves

LARGEST BONUSES IN CLUB HISTORY

Mike Minor, 2009	$2,420,000
Jeff Francoeur, 2002	$2,200,000
Matt Belisle, 1998	$1,750,000
Jason Heyward, 2007	$1,700,000
Lucas Sims, 2012	$1,650,000

ATLANTA BRAVES

TOP 2013 ROOKIE: Julio Teheran, rhp. After a difficult encore in Triple-A, he worked through some mechanical issues and should be back in contention for a starting job with Atlanta.

BREAKOUT PROSPECT: Juan Jaime, rhp. He lost two years to Tommy John surgery but came back last year with his trademark upper-90s fastball.

SLEEPER: Felix Marte, of. He has tremendous raw ability and is ready for his first extended shot at full-season ball.

SOURCE OF TOP 30 TALENT			
Homegrown	28	Acquired	2
College	13	Trades	1
Junior college	1	Rule 5 draft	0
High school	6	Independent leagues	0
Nondrafted free agents	0	Free agents/waivers	1
International	8		

LF	CF	RF
Evan Gattis (8)	Todd Cunningham (12)	Felix Marte
Josh Elander (19)	Matt Lipka (14)	
Robby Hefflinger (29)	Fernelys Sanchez	
Adam Milligan	Justin Black	
	Blake Brown	
	Connor Lien	
	Mycal Jones	
	Tony Mueller	

3B	SS	2B	1B
Edward Salcedo (17)	Jose Peraza (10)	Ross Heffley	Joey Terdoslavich (18)
Carlos Franco (21)	Nick Ahmed (11)	Tommy LaStella	Brandon Drury (27)
Kyle Kubitza (25)	Elmer Reyes	Phil Gosselin	Ernesto Mejia
Joe Leonard	Robert Luna		Chris Garcia
			William Beckwith
			Jackson Laumann

C
Christian Bethancourt (3)
Bryan de la Rosa (23)
Braeden Schlehuber
Tyler Tewell
Troy Snitker

LHP		RHP	
LHSP	**LHRP**	**RHSP**	**RHRP**
Sean Gilmartin (4)	Carlos Perez (28)	Julio Teheran (1)	David Hale (16)
Alex Wood (7)	Ryan Buchter	J.R. Graham (2)	Juan Jaime (20)
Dimasther Delgado	Chasen Shreve	Lucas Sims (5)	Billy Bullock (24)
Yohan Flande	Matt Chaffee	Mauricio Cabrera (6)	Nathan Hyatt (26)
David Starn	Ian Thomas	Zeke Spruill (9)	John Cornely
		Cody Martin (13)	Cory Rasmus
		Navery Moore (15)	Caleb Brewer
		Luis Merejo (22)	Shae Simmons
		Aaron Northcraft (30)	Wilson Rivera
		Gary Moran	Ryne Harper
		Gus Schlosser	Mark Lamm
		Ryan Weber	Jarrett Miller
		Wes Parsons	Jorge Montenegro
			Dave Peterson

2012

BEST PURE HITTER: Western Carolina's all-time leader in hits, 2B Ross Heffley (18) has a compact swing and a good two-strike approach, and he uses the whole field. He batted .296/.345/.412 in low Class A.

BEST POWER HITTER: There are questions about whether C Josh Elander (6) will remain behind the plate, but no one doubts his above-average right-handed pull power.

FASTEST RUNNER: OF Connor Lien (12) is a plus runner who covers a lot of ground in center field. OF Fernelys Sanchez (16) has shown well above-average speed in the past, but he broke his leg during the spring and was slower than Lien after signing. OFs Justin Black (4) and Blake Brown (5) are two more plus runners.

BEST DEFENSIVE PLAYER: C Bryan de la Rosa (3) was one of the best defensive catchers available in the draft. The Puerto Rico native possesses agile feet and soft hands behind the plate and can really throw, posting a 1.71-second pop time at a showcase last fall. He did commit 13 passed balls in 28 pro games, however.

BEST FASTBALL: RHP Nathan Hyatt (13) has a slight build at 6 feet and 180 pounds, but he has a live fastball that sits at 92-95 mph and touches 97. RHP Luke Sims' (1) and LHP Alex Wood's (2) heaters are just a tick slower.

BEST SECONDARY PITCH: A good athlete with a fast arm, Sims throws a tight downer curveball at 73-78 mph.

BEST PRO DEBUT: Though he never posted an ERA under 4.26 during three years at Appalachian State, Hyatt posted a 1.46 ERA while reaching low Class A. He also recorded six saves and a 37-8 K-BB ratio in 25 innings. Wood started 13 games in low Class A and pitched well, going 4-3, 2.22 with 52 strikeouts and 14 walks over 53 innings.

BEST ATHLETE: Lien has size (6-foot-3, 205 pounds) and tools. In addition to his speed, he has a plus arm and some strength. But questions about his bat persist after he hit .228/.352/.282 in the Rookie-level Gulf Coast League.

MOST INTRIGUING BACKGROUND: RHP Matt Kimbrel's (31) brother Craig is an all-star closer for the Braves. Unsigned C Levi Borders' (11) father Pat was MVP of the 1992 World Series and a 2000 Olympic gold medallist. Black (4) is the highest-drafted player out of Montana since 1984.

CLOSEST TO THE MAJORS: Wood is the highest-drafted college player in this Braves class. His funky delivery could cause him to wind up in the bullpen,
but he has the stuff to succeed in any role, with a fastball that touches 96 mph and an above-average changeup.

BEST LATE-ROUND PICK: Hyatt and Heffley, who were signed by the same area scout, Billy Best.

THE ONE WHO GOT AWAY: Borders was the highest-drafted player Atlanta didn't sign. He can catch and play shortstop, and he could hit in the middle of the order for South Florida as a freshman.

ASSESSMENT: The Braves had gotten away from mining their home state in recent years before using their first two 2012 picks on Peach State pitchers Sims and Wood. They headline a draft class that's short on polished hitters.

2011

Atlanta may not have loaded up on star power, but it found a number of potential contributors in RHPs Sean Gilmartin (1), J.R. Graham (4), Cody Martin (7) and Navery Moore (14), as well as SS Nick Ahmed (2).

GRADE: C+

2010

The Braves knew SS Andrelton Simmons (2) was a defensive whiz, but his bat and the speed with which he zoomed through the minors have been surprising. They didn't have a first-round pick, yet found three other interesting position players in OFs Matt Lipka (1s) and Todd Cunningham (2) and OF/C Evan Gattis (23).

GRADE: B+

2009

LHP Mike Minor (1) should be a solid mid-rotation starter in Atlanta for years to come. Unsigned LHP Josh Edgin (50) also has pitched in the big leagues.

GRADE: B

2008

Atlanta didn't have a first-rounder and blew its top choice on LHP Brett DeVall (1s), but it stole a difference-maker in RHP Craig Kimbrel (3). RHP Paul Clemens (7) and LHP Brett Oberholtzer (8) helped land Michael Bourn in a 2011 trade, while RHP J.J. Hoover (10) reached the majors after getting dealt for Juan Francisco.

GRADE: A

Draft analysis by Conor Glassey (2012) and Jim Callis (2008-11). Numbers in parentheses indicate draft rounds.

1 JULIO TEHERAN, RHP

Born: Jan. 27, 1991. **B-T:** R-R. **Ht.:** 6-2. **Wt.:** 170.
Signed: Colombia, 2007. **Signed by:** Miguel Teheran/
Carlos Garcia.

BA GRADE
60
MEDIUM

Expectations never have been a problem for Teheran. Signed as a 16-year-old out of Colombia in 2007 for $850,000, the largest bonus given to any international pitcher that year, he overcame a bout of shoulder tendinitis in the Rookie-level Appalachian League in 2008 to rank as that circuit's top prospect a year later. He then garnered the same recognition in the high Class A Carolina League in 2010 before earning pitcher and rookie of the year honors in the Triple-A International League in 2011. He also made his major league debut that year and entered last spring as a leading candidate to break camp in the Atlanta rotation. Instead, Teheran struggled with leaving pitches up in the strike zone and allowed nine homers while in big league camp. He performed well in the first two months at Triple-A Gwinnett and tossed the first nine-inning complete game of his career on June 3 before making an emergency start for the Braves. He wasn't the same pitcher after returning to the IL, going 2-7, 6.46 in his final 15 starts. Though Teheran was just 21 and trying to incorporate some mechanical adjustments, his downturn still was stunning.

Teheran has an electric arm, but his delivery had some violence that the Braves wanted to iron out in order to reduce his risk of injury. In 2012, they decided to reduce the bend on his back leg during his windup. He had been turning and coiling his body to generate more momentum toward the plate, placing additional strain on his right knee and elbow. Atlanta worked with Teheran on keeping his back leg straighter in order to create a better center of balance, particularly in his core. The alterations not only led to less initial success, but also to a reduction in fastball velocity. After sitting at 93-95 mph and reaching

97 in 2011, Teheran operated mostly at 90-93 last season. To his credit, he stuck with the changes and showed signs of regaining his previous velocity during the latter weeks of the campaign. He still has above-average fastball command and the ability to work both sides of the plate. His changeup remains the best in the system, a 79-81 mph offering with outstanding depth and fade. Teheran continues to search for a consistently reliable breaking ball. His curveball has good rotation but he hangs it too often, and he trusts his slider even less than his curve. After struggling with his confidence for most of 2012, he regained his swagger as he became more comfortable with the way he was throwing the ball. He has an impressive knowledge of how to set up hitters, along with impeccable work ethic and determination.

Though Teheran couldn't crack the Braves rotation in 2012, he remains firmly in their long-term plans and has as much upside as any starter in the organization—including the big league club. He won't be a No. 1 starter without a better breaking ball, but he definitely has the package to become a No. 2 or 3. He'll compete for a starting job again this spring, and Atlanta won't be concerned if he winds up back at Gwinnett to open the season. Either way, he should see a decent amount of time in the big leagues in 2013.

SCOUTING GRADES

Fastball: 65.   **Control:** 60.
Changeup: 65.   **Command:** 55.
Curveball: 45.

Based on 20-80 scouting scale, where 50 represents major league average, and future projection rather than present tools.

Year	Club (League)	Class	W	L	ERA	G	GS	CG	SV	IP	H	HR	BB	SO	K/9	WHIP	AVG
2008	Danville (APP)	R	1	2	6.60	6	6	0	0	15	18	2	4	17	10.2	1.47	.305
2009	Danville (APP)	R	2	1	2.68	7	7	0	0	44	36	2	7	39	8.0	0.98	.229
	Rome (SAL)	LoA	1	3	4.78	7	7	0	0	38	42	4	11	28	6.7	1.41	.288
2010	Rome (SAL)	LoA	2	2	1.14	7	7	0	0	39	23	1	10	45	10.3	0.84	.168
	Myrtle Beach (CAR)	HiA	4	4	2.98	10	10	0	0	63	56	6	13	76	10.8	1.09	.233
	Mississippi (SL)	AA	3	2	3.38	7	7	0	0	40	29	2	17	38	8.6	1.15	.204
2011	Gwinnett (IL)	AAA	15	3	2.55	25	24	0	0	145	123	5	48	122	7.6	1.18	.232
	Atlanta (NL)	MAJ	1	1	5.03	5	3	0	0	20	21	4	8	10	4.6	1.47	.276
2012	Gwinnett (IL)	AAA	7	9	5.08	26	26	1	0	131	146	18	43	97	6.7	1.44	.289
	Atlanta (NL)	MAJ	0	0	5.68	2	1	0	0	6	5	0	1	5	7.1	0.95	.217
Major League Totals			1	1	5.19	7	4	0	0	26	26	4	9	15	5.2	1.35	.263
Minor League Totals			35	26	3.50	95	94	1	0	515	473	38	153	462	8.1	1.22	.247

2 J.R. GRAHAM, RHP

Born: Jan. 14, 1990. **B-T:** R-R. **Ht.:** 6-0. **Wt.:** 185. **Drafted:** Santa Clara, 2011 (4th round). **Signed by:** Tom Davis.

A two-way player early in his career at Santa Clara, Graham didn't make his first college start until his draft year in 2011. He has thrived as a full-time starter in pro ball, leading the Appalachian League with a 1.72 ERA in his debut, then going 12-2, 2.80 while reaching Double-A Mississippi in his first full season. A fierce competitor who attacks hitters, Graham succeeds by generating a plethora of groundouts. His four-seam fastball has good movement while residing at 93-97 mph, but his best offering is a low-90s two-seamer with heavy sink. He does an impressive job of keeping hitters off balance with his sharp 82-85 mph slider and a changeup that has made steady progress. Graham is a quick-twitch athlete who repeats his delivery well, giving him the best command in the system. He's not big for a starter, yet he made 26 starts and worked 148 innings without missing a turn in 2012. The Braves believe Graham could fill one of several roles in the major leagues, depending on the team's needs. He'll continue to start in 2013 and has a ceiling of a No. 3 starter. He could open the year in Triple-A, and making his major league debut later in the season isn't out of the question.

BA GRADE
50
MEDIUM

Year	Club (League)	Class	W	L	ERA	G	GS	CG	SV	IP	H	HR	BB	SO	K/9	WHIP	AVG
2011	Danville (APP)	R	5	2	1.72	13	8	0	0	58	52	0	13	52	8.1	1.13	.245
2012	Lynchburg (CAR)	HiA	9	1	2.63	17	17	1	0	103	88	6	17	68	6.0	1.02	.236
	Mississippi (SL)	AA	3	1	3.18	9	9	0	0	45	35	2	17	42	8.3	1.15	.210
Minor League Totals			17	4	2.49	39	34	1	0	206	175	8	47	162	7.1	1.08	.233

3 CHRISTIAN BETHANCOURT, C

Born: Sept. 2, 1991. **B-T:** R-R. **Ht.:** 6-2. **Wt.:** 195. **Signed:** Panama, 2008. **Signed by:** Luis Ortiz.

Highly touted since starring for Panama in the 2004 Little League World Series, Bethancourt signed for $600,000 four years later. He rode his defense to a berth in the Futures Game in 2012, but he had his worst offensive performance as a pro and played in just 71 games because of a strained hamstring and broken hand. Bethancourt is a premier athlete behind the plate, with soft hands and one of the strongest arms among minor league catchers. He threw out 39 percent of basestealers last season. He moves well and does a good job of blocking pitches in the dirt, though he tends to get lazy and backhand balls on occasion. He has improved his game-calling ability and the way he works with pitchers. Bethancourt's bat lags considerably behind his defense, and he has hit just .253/.276/.304 above low Class A. His approach needs a lot of work, as he chases too many pitches far outside the strike zone and can't handle sharp breaking balls. He has raw power but doesn't tap into it because he has a flat swing. He runs well for a catcher. With Brian McCann recovering from offseason shoulder surgery, Bethancourt could make his major league debut in April. He'll likely spend most of 2013 in Triple-A after joining the 40-man roster in November.

BA GRADE
55
HIGH

Year	Club (League)	Class	AVG	G	AB	R	H	2B	3B	HR	RBI	BB	SO	SB	CS	OBP	SLG
2008	Braves (DSL)	R	.267	34	116	12	31	6	3	0	17	11	25	1	0	.328	.371
2009	Braves (GCL)	R	.284	32	116	22	33	9	1	2	19	11	22	7	0	.344	.431
	Danville (APP)	R	.260	14	50	10	13	5	0	2	8	6	16	1	1	.339	.480
2010	Rome (SAL)	LoA	.251	108	399	31	100	19	2	3	34	14	62	11	3	.276	.331
2011	Rome (SAL)	LoA	.303	54	221	25	67	10	3	4	33	8	27	6	3	.323	.430
	Lynchburg (CAR)	HiA	.271	45	166	11	45	6	0	1	20	3	35	3	2	.277	.325
2012	Mississippi (SL)	AA	.243	71	268	30	65	5	1	2	26	11	45	8	6	.275	.291
Minor League Totals			.265	358	1336	141	354	60	10	14	157	64	232	37	15	.297	.356

4 SEAN GILMARTIN, LHP

Born: May 8, 1990. **B-T:** L-L. **Ht.:** 6-2. **Wt.:** 195. **Drafted:** Florida State, 2011 (1st round). **Signed by:** Hugh Buchanan.

The No. 1 starter for three years at Florida State, Gilmartin went 28th overall in the 2011 draft and signed for $1,134,000. He lived up to his billing as an advanced college pitcher in his first full pro season, leading the Double-A Southern League in WHIP (1.15) and earning all-star honors before a July promotion to Triple-A. Considered by some scouts to be a poor man's Mike Minor, Gilmartin is a finesse lefthander who knows how to set up hitters and pitch to his strengths. His best pitch is a plus changeup with depth and fade. His 89-91 mph fastball has good movement, and he creates deception with a low-80s slider that has late break. He throws all three pitches for strikes and with the same arm speed. Gilmartin will need to get stronger after his fastball dipped to 86-88 mph late in the season. He remained effective even with diminished velocity because he continued to work the corners and pitch down in the strike zone. He's a good athlete who repeats his smooth delivery and fields his position well. Gilmartin is moving just as fast as the Braves expected, and he could see his first big league action in 2013. He'll open the season back in Gwinnett, however. His ultimate ceiling is as a No. 3 or 4 starter.

BA GRADE
50
MEDIUM

Year	Club (League)	Class	W	L	ERA	G	GS	CG	SV	IP	H	HR	BB	SO	K/9	WHIP	AVG
2011	Braves (GCL)	R	0	1	9.00	1	1	0	0	2	3	0	0	1	4.5	1.50	.333
	Rome (SAL)	LoA	2	1	2.53	5	5	0	0	21	18	3	2	30	12.7	0.94	.217
2012	Mississippi (SL)	AA	5	8	3.54	20	20	3	0	119	111	9	26	86	6.5	1.15	.248
	Gwinnett (IL)	AAA	1	2	4.78	7	7	0	0	38	41	6	13	25	6.0	1.43	.273
Minor League Totals			8	12	3.74	33	33	3	0	180	173	18	41	142	7.1	1.19	.251

5 LUCAS SIMS, RHP

Born: May 10, 1994. **B-T:** R-R. **Ht.:** 6-2. **Wt.:** 195. **Drafted:** HS—Snellville, Ga., 2012 (1st round). **Signed by:** Brian Bridges.

The 21st overall pick in the 2012 draft, Sims represents a return to the Braves' tradition of selecting local high school products and high-ceiling pitchers. Atlanta kept him on a tight pitch count after he turned down a Clemson commitment to sign for $1.65 million, yet he still struck out 39 in 34 pro innings. Though Sims struggled at times with his mechanics and release point during his pro debut, his arm works well and generates above-average velocity. His fastball sits in the low 90s and touches 95 mph with good running action. His velocity could continue to increase as he gains strength and becomes more efficient in his delivery. His 73-78 mph curveball has tight spin and is a plus pitch. Sims' changeup wasn't effective last summer, but he has shown solid feel for it in the past. He'll need to learn to do a better job of repeating his delivery so he can throw more strikes. He's an excellent athlete for a pitcher—he also played shortstop in high school—which should help him accomplish that goal. A potential contributor in the front half of a major league rotation, Sims should spend his first full pro season at low Class A Rome. The Braves' pitching depth in the upper levels means they can give him as much time as he needs to develop.

BA GRADE
55
HIGH

Year	Club (League)	Class	W	L	ERA	G	GS	CG	SV	IP	H	HR	BB	SO	K/9	WHIP	AVG
2012	Braves (GCL)	R	0	0	1.29	3	3	0	0	7	2	1	1	10	12.9	0.43	.091
	Danville (APP)	R	2	4	4.33	8	8	0	0	27	26	2	12	29	9.7	1.41	.243
Minor League Totals			2	4	3.71	11	11	0	0	34	28	3	13	39	10.3	1.21	.217

6 MAURICIO CABRERA, RHP

Born: Sept. 22, 1993. **B-T:** R-R. **Ht.:** 6-2. **Wt.:** 180. **Signed:** Dominican Republic, 2010. **Signed by:** Roberto Aquino.

After a lull, the Braves have pursued Latin American talent more aggressively in the last few years. Their latest top prospect from the region is Cabrera, who signed for $400,000 in 2010. He bypassed the Gulf Coast League and went to the system's more advanced Rookie affiliate in Danville for his U.S. debut in 2012, leading the Appalachian League in opponent average (.213). His older brother Alberto, also a righthanded pitcher, reached the majors with the Cubs last season. Cabrera has above-average arm strength and a strong frame for a 19-year-old. His 94-96 mph fastball has impressive cutting action and shows good sink when he stays on top of the pitch. He has the makings of a second plus offering in a low-80s slider that breaks down and in on lefthanders. He also has advanced feel for a changeup that could give him a third plus pitch. Cabrera is still learning to command

BA GRADE
55
EXTREME

all of his pitches, his slider in particular. He has a wrist wrap that makes that task more difficult. He has a solid mound presence and isn't afraid to challenge hitters. How well Cabrera can refine his secondary pitches and command will determine if he winds up in the rotation or bullpen. He has the upside of a No. 2 starter and will pitch alongside Lucas Sims in the Rome rotation in 2013.

Year	Club (League)	Class	W	L	ERA	G	GS	CG	SV	IP	H	HR	BB	SO	K/9	WHIP	AVG
2011	Braves (DSL)	R	1	5	4.30	19	9	0	0	52	51	3	24	36	6.2	1.43	.251
2012	Danville (APP)	R	2	2	2.97	12	12	0	0	58	45	2	23	48	7.5	1.18	.213
Minor League Totals			3	7	3.60	31	21	0	0	110	96	5	47	84	6.9	1.30	.232

7 ALEX WOOD, LHP

Born: Jan. 12, 1991. **B-T:** L-L. **Ht.:** 6-4. **Wt.:** 215. **Drafted:** Georgia, 2012 (2nd round). **Signed by:** Brian Bridges.

BA GRADE

50

HIGH

Wood posted the best ERA by a Georgia starter since ex-big leaguer Dave Fleming in 1989. The Braves liked Wood so much that they were leaning toward drafting him in the first round last June if Lucas Sims hadn't been on the board. A redshirt sophomore who had Tommy John surgery before his college career started, Wood went 88th overall and signed for $700,000. He made a seamless transition to low Class A, helping guide Rome to the playoffs before he was sidelined with a pulled back muscle. Wood pounds the strike zone on both sides of the plate with a low-90s fastball that touches 96 mph. He does a good job of working off his heater, then destroys hitters' timing with his above-average changeup. He can fall in love too much with his changeup at times. Scouts have two concerns with Wood: his breaking ball and mechanics. He struggles to throw his below-average slider for strikes and may need a better third pitch in order to remain a starter. He also employs a high-effort delivery in which he hops backward on his right leg after landing on it, though he does throw strikes. Wood's strong debut showed why Atlanta was so high on him. He should move quickly through the system and likely will finish his first full pro season in Double-A. With a better breaking ball, he could become a solid No. 3 starter.

Year	Club (League)	Class	W	L	ERA	G	GS	CG	SV	IP	H	HR	BB	SO	K/9	WHIP	AVG
2012	Rome (SAL)	LoA	4	3	2.22	13	13	0	0	53	39	1	14	52	8.9	1.01	.206
Minor League Totals			4	3	2.22	13	13	0	0	53	39	1	14	52	8.9	1.01	.206

8 EVAN GATTIS, OF/C

Born: Aug. 18, 1986. **B-T:** R-R. **Ht.:** 6-4. **Wt.:** 230. **Drafted:** Texas-Permian Basin, 2010 (23rd round). **Signed by:** Gerald Turner.

BA GRADE

50

HIGH

Gattis took a four-year hiatus from baseball before surfacing at NCAA Division II Texas-Permian Basin in 2010 and signing for $1,000 as a 23rd-rounder that June. He won the low Class A South Atlantic League batting title (.322) in his first full pro season, then slugged 18 homers in 74 games while battling tendinitis in his right wrist in 2012. Gattis possesses more raw power than any hitter in the system. He generates impressive bat speed with lightning-quick wrists and tremendous strength, producing power from foul pole to foul pole. He controls the strike zone and barrels the ball with consistency. Gattis' layoff shows how raw he is as a catcher. He has solid arm strength and threw out 39 percent of basestealers in 2012, but he's rough as a receiver and awkward behind the plate. He has enough athleticism to play left field adequately, where he saw most of his action in Double-A and in winter ball. He has below-average speed but moves well for his size and runs the bases aggressively. Gattis could follow the path of Josh Willingham, a catcher-turned-outfielder who didn't establish himself in the big leagues until age 27. A strong winter in Venezuela should prepare Gattis for Triple-A and possible big league shot in 2013.

Year	Club (League)	Class	AVG	G	AB	R	H	2B	3B	HR	RBI	BB	SO	SB	CS	OBP	SLG
2010	Danville (APP)	R	.288	60	222	33	64	10	0	4	29	6	44	0	0	.339	.387
2011	Rome (SAL)	LoA	.322	88	338	58	109	24	2	22	71	25	53	2	4	.386	.601
2012	Lynchburg (CAR)	HiA	.385	21	78	14	30	7	0	9	29	10	12	1	1	.468	.821
	Braves (GCL)	R	.500	4	12	2	6	0	0	0	1	1	2	0	0	.538	.500
	Mississippi (SL)	AA	.258	49	182	24	47	13	4	9	37	20	29	1	1	.343	.522
Minor League Totals			.308	222	832	131	256	54	6	44	167	62	140	4	6	.374	.546

9 ZEKE SPRUILL, RHP

Born: Sept. 11, 1989. **B-T:** B-R. **Ht.:** 6-4. **Wt.:** 185. **Drafted:** HS—Marietta, Ga., 2008 (2nd round). **Signed by:** Brian Bridges.

Spruill has overcome off-field issues and a broken right hand (from punching a dugout wall) early in his career to become a reliable, durable starter the last two seasons. He led the Southern League in starts (27) and innings (162) in 2012. He cemented a spot on the Atlanta's 40-man roster by performing well in the Arizona Fall League. Spruill uses his tall frame to pitch on a downhill plane, pounding the lower half of the strike zone while pitching to contact. His 91-94 mph fastball has good sink, and he uses it to get ahead in the count. His changeup also features nice sink and fades away from righthanders. He sells it well by throwing it with the same arm speed he uses with his fastball. His changeup helps him handle lefthanded hitters (.696 OPS in Double-A) almost as well as he handles righthanded hitters (.674). The key to Spruill's future is the consistency of his slider, which isn't particularly tight. He can get strikeouts with his slider when it's working, but

BA GRADE

45

MEDIUM

it also flattens out and hangs up in the strike zone at times. He doesn't miss a lot of bats, but he also doesn't beat himself by giving up walks or home runs. Counting the AFL, Spruill has made 61 starts and worked 359 innings in the last two years. He profiles as an innings-eater who can fill the No. 4 or 5 spot in a contender's rotation. He'll get his first Triple-A opportunity in 2013.

Year	Club (League)	Class	W	L	ERA	G	GS	CG	SV	IP	H	HR	BB	SO	K/9	WHIP	AVG
2008	Braves (GCL)	R	7	0	2.93	10	3	0	0	40	42	1	8	32	7.2	1.25	.268
2009	Braves (GCL)	R	1	0	4.58	4	4	0	0	20	24	2	5	23	10.5	1.47	.289
	Rome (SAL)	LoA	8	6	3.03	20	19	0	1	116	120	9	24	95	7.4	1.24	.261
2010	Braves (GCL)	R	0	0	3.00	2	2	0	0	3	4	0	1	1	3.0	1.67	.333
	Myrtle Beach (CAR)	HiA	3	5	5.54	14	13	1	0	65	83	4	13	41	5.7	1.48	.310
2011	Lynchburg (CAR)	HiA	7	9	3.19	20	20	5	0	130	108	7	23	92	6.4	1.01	.227
	Mississippi (SL)	AA	3	2	3.20	7	7	1	0	45	45	3	17	16	3.2	1.38	.266
2012	Mississippi (SL)	AA	9	11	3.67	27	27	1	0	162	158	8	46	106	5.9	1.26	.260
Minor League Totals			38	33	3.58	104	95	8	1	580	584	34	137	406	6.3	1.24	.262

10 JOSE PERAZA, SS

Born: April 30, 1994. **B-T:** R-R. **Ht.:** 5-11. **Wt.:** 170. **Signed:** Venezuela, 2010. **Signed by:** Rolando Petit.

The Braves signed both Peraza (for $350,000) and Mauricio Cabrera at the start of the international signing period in 2010. The organization's Rookie-level Dominican Summer League player of the year in his 2011 pro debut, Peraza played well at two more Rookie stops in the United States last summer. Peraza's strengths are his plus-plus speed and outstanding hand-eye coordination. He relishes the role of leadoff hitter, looking to get on base by any means necessary. He can beat out bunts and barrels the ball consistently when he swings away. He could use more patience to draw more walks, however. Peraza has surprising pop and may reach double-digits in home runs, but he stands out most with his quickness and basestealing instincts, which could result in 50 steals on an annual basis. He also has excellent first-step quickness at shortstop, where he has plus range and soft, sure hands. He has solid arm strength, but his throwing mechanics need work in order

BA GRADE

55

EXTREME

to improve his accuracy. Though he's nestled in an organization with plenty of depth at shortstop, Peraza has a higher ceiling than anyone the Braves have at the position—including Andrelton Simmons. Atlanta believes Peraza has the makeup to handle a jump to low Class A at age 19.

Year	Club (League)	Class	AVG	G	AB	R	H	2B	3B	HR	RBI	BB	SO	SB	CS	OBP	SLG
2011	Braves (DSL)	R	.281	66	235	29	66	5	3	1	22	15	27	28	7	.346	.340
2012	Braves (GCL)	R	.318	21	85	17	27	3	3	0	10	4	6	10	3	.348	.424
	Danville (APP)	R	.281	32	121	21	34	4	0	1	18	9	18	15	2	.351	.339
Minor League Totals			.288	119	441	67	127	12	6	2	50	28	51	53	12	.348	.356

11 NICK AHMED, SS

BA GRADE

50

HIGH

Born: March 15, 1990. **B-T:** R-R. **Ht.:** 6-3. **Wt.:** 205. **Drafted:** Connecticut, 2011 (2nd round). **Signed by:** Kevin Barry.

Ahmed had an outstanding first full pro season in 2012 at high Class A Lynchburg. He led the Carolina League in runs (84), doubles (36), steals (40) and fielding percentage at shortstop (.963). Managers rated him the fastest baserunner and best defensive shortstop in the CL, and he capped the year by leading Lynchburg to the league title by going 4-for-5 with three doubles in the deciding contest against Winston-Salem. Ahmed has great first-step quickness and above-average speed that give him outstanding lateral range at shortstop. He has soft hands and enhances his solid arm strength with a quick release and good accuracy. Ahmed is adept at working the count and can drive the ball but strikes out too much because he chases pitches up in the strike zone. He needs to use the opposite field more often and improve upon his bunting ability to increase his on-base percentage. Ahmed is a gritty player who proved his toughness by coming back quickly from a collapsed lung during his draft year at Connecticut. He continued to excel in the Arizona Fall League and will make the jump to Double-A in 2013. Andrelton Simmons looms as a significant obstacle ahead of him in Atlanta.

Year	Club (League)	Class	AVG	G	AB	R	H	2B	3B	HR	RBI	BB	SO	SB	CS	OBP	SLG
2011	Danville (APP)	R	.262	59	248	46	65	13	2	4	24	30	46	18	6	.346	.379
2012	Lynchburg (CAR)	HiA	.269	130	506	84	136	36	4	6	49	49	102	40	10	.337	.391
Minor League Totals			.267	189	754	130	201	49	6	10	73	79	148	58	16	.340	.387

12 TODD CUNNINGHAM, OF

Born: March 20, 1989. **B-T:** B-R. **Ht.:** 6-0. **Wt.:** 200. **Drafted:** Jacksonville State, 2010 (2nd round). **Signed by:** Brian Bridges.

BA GRADE
45
MEDIUM

Cunningham had a breakout Double-A season in 2012 after battling a strained right elbow the year before, ranking third in the Southern League in batting (.309) and runs (77) while serving as one of the few consistent offensive contributors at Mississippi. He has a smooth swing from both sides of the plate and drives the ball from gap to gap despite having limited power. He has strong hands and makes good contact but doesn't accumulate many walks, a trend that needs to change if he's to remain at the top of the batting order. He has made progress in getting better reads and jumps on stolen-base attempts, and he's an intelligent and productive runner with plus speed. Cunningham has good first-step quickness and moves well on balls hit in all directions in center field. His arm strength is fringy, but he makes accurate throws, hits the cutoff man and makes the right decisions. Cunningham will move up to Triple-A in 2013 and should be ready for a major league opportunity soon. It may not come with the Braves after they committed to B.J. Upton in center field for the next five years.

Year	Club (League)	Class	AVG	G	AB	R	H	2B	3B	HR	RBI	BB	SO	SB	CS	OBP	SLG
2010	Rome (SAL)	LoA	.260	65	231	32	60	9	3	1	20	14	30	7	4	.341	.338
2011	Braves (GCL)	R	.182	4	11	2	2	0	1	0	4	1	5	1	0	.286	.364
	Lynchburg (CAR)	HiA	.257	87	334	59	86	12	4	4	20	33	47	14	6	.348	.353
2012	Mississippi (SL)	AA	.309	120	466	77	144	23	6	3	51	38	51	24	8	.364	.403
Minor League Totals			.280	276	1042	170	292	44	14	8	95	86	133	46	18	.353	.372

13 CODY MARTIN, RHP

Born: Sept. 4, 1989. **B-T:** R-R. **Ht.:** 6-2. **Wt.:** 210. **Drafted:** Gonzaga, 2011 (7th round). **Signed by:** Brett Evert.

BA GRADE
50
HIGH

Martin was a reliever for three of his four seasons at Gonzaga, leading NCAA Division I with a 0.86 ERA in 2011 while filling that role, and had a strong pro debut out of the bullpen in 2011. The Braves were intrigued with his command of four pitches and decided to look at him as a starter in his first full pro season. He responded by ranking second in the Carolina League with 12 wins and tying for third with 123 strikeouts despite getting shut down in early August once he reached his innings limit. Martin has a lethal one-two punch in a 91-94 mph fastball with late movement and a mid-80s slider that's his out pitch. He also commands a solid curveball and a changeup with decent depth and fade, and he mixes all of his offerings with aplomb to keep hitters off balance. The Braves remain open-minded about Martin's future and believe he has the makeup and ability to succeed in virtually any role. The current plan calls for him to remain in the rotation in 2013 while moving up to Double-A.

Year	Club (League)	Class	W	L	ERA	G	GS	CG	SV	IP	H	HR	BB	SO	K/9	WHIP	AVG
2011	Danville (APP)	R	0	0	0.00	8	0	0	3	9	2	0	1	14	14.0	0.33	.069
	Rome (SAL)	LoA	1	0	1.48	14	0	0	6	24	18	2	4	35	12.9	0.90	.212
2012	Lynchburg (CAR)	HiA	12	7	2.93	22	19	1	0	107	93	7	34	123	10.3	1.18	.235
Minor League Totals			13	7	2.50	44	19	1	9	141	113	9	39	172	11.0	1.08	.222

14 MATT LIPKA, OF

Born: April 15, 1992. **B-T:** R-R. **Ht.:** 6-1. **Wt.:** 200. **Drafted:** HS—McKinney, Texas, 2010 (1st round supplemental). **Signed by:** Gerald Turner.

BA GRADE
50
HIGH

Signed for $800,000 as a 2010 sandwich pick, Lipka played center field for the first time last year after two seasons at shortstop and showed good instincts. He was limited to 51 games and didn't play again following a hamstring injury on June 23, but the standout high school wide receiver continued to bring an all-out, football mentality to the diamond. The Braves believe that once he gets comfortable and improves his routes, he'll make highlight-reel catches look routine. He had an awkward arm stroke at shortstop and has no better than average arm strength in the outfield but gets good accuracy on his throws. Lipka showed better plate discipline last season prior to getting hurt. With little power (46 extra-base hits in 937 career at-bats), he has to hone his small-ball approach, particularly with bunting, in order to utilize his plus speed. He also needs to get better reads while stealing bases in order to improve his success rate, which was 68 percent last year and 73 percent for his pro career. Because he missed the second half of last season, Lipka is likely to return to high Class A to open 2013.

Year	Club (League)	Class	AVG	G	AB	R	H	2B	3B	HR	RBI	BB	SO	SB	CS	OBP	SLG
2010	Braves (GCL)	R	.302	48	192	33	58	8	4	1	24	14	22	20	3	.357	.401
	Danville (APP)	R	.125	4	16	1	2	0	0	0	1	1	2	1	0	.176	.125
2011	Rome (SAL)	LoA	.247	127	530	78	131	21	3	1	37	42	83	28	14	.305	.304
2012	Lynchburg (CAR)	HiA	.271	51	199	32	54	5	1	2	13	20	32	12	6	.335	.337
Minor League Totals			.261	230	937	144	245	34	8	4	75	77	139	61	23	.320	.328

15 NAVERY MOORE, RHP

BA GRADE
50
HIGH

Born: Aug. 10, 1990. **B-T:** R-R. **Ht.:** 6-2. **Wt.:** 210. **Drafted:** Vanderbilt, 2011 (14th round). **Signed by:** Hugh Buchanan.

Moore had Tommy John surgery during high school and was used sparingly during his first two years at Vanderbilt before emerging as the Commodores' closer as a junior in 2011. The Braves' lone over-slot signing that summer—he got $400,000 in the 14th round—he made his pro debut in 2012 and spent the first half of the campaign in the Rome rotation before moving to the bullpen in order to limit his workload. The velocity of Moore's fastball improved as the season went on, sitting at 93-95 mph at its best while maintaining above-average movement. He worked hard on improving the consistency of his curveball and can generate good spin with sweeping action. His curve is more effective than his slider, which lacks a sharp, cutting action. His changeup also has made strides and shows flashes of being a solid pitch. The 103 innings he pitched in 2012 were by far the most action Moore has seen on the mound, and he will need more innings to refine his command and overall feel for pitching. The development of his breaking ball will determine whether he starts or relieves at higher levels, with most scouts seeing him as a potential force in the back of a bullpen. High Class A is next on his agenda.

Year	Club (League)	Class	W	L	ERA	G	GS	CG	SV	IP	H	HR	BB	SO	K/9	WHIP	AVG
2012	Rome (SAL)	LoA	8	3	3.86	26	13	0	0	103	83	3	45	84	7.4	1.25	.221
Minor League Totals			8	3	3.86	26	13	0	0	103	83	3	45	84	7.4	1.25	.221

16 DAVID HALE, RHP

BA GRADE
45
MEDIUM

Born: Sept. 27, 1987. **B-T:** R-R. **Ht.:** 6-2. **Wt.:** 205. **Drafted:** Princeton, 2009 (3rd round). **Signed by:** Kevin Barry.

After shifting Hale between starting and relieving during his first three minor league seasons, the Braves decided to stick him in their Double-A rotation in 2012 to help him develop all of his pitches. He responded by tying for the Southern League lead with 27 starts and ranking fourth with 124 strikeouts. He also ranked fourth with 67 walks, however, showing that he's still developing control. A two-way player at Princeton who saw more time in center field than on the mound, Hale continues to play catch-up in his development as a pitcher. He has a quick arm with a fluid delivery that produces a heavy 92-94 mph fastball that touches 96 mph. His slider can be a solid offering at times, while his feel for his changeup comes and goes. Hale needs to do a better job of getting ahead in the count, and of working off his fastball. Though he has proven to be durable as a starter, he could end up back in the bullpen at higher levels. He embraces relieving because his workload resembles that of an everyday player. Regardless of which role he fills this season, he'll make the jump to Triple-A after the Braves added him to their 40-man roster in November.

Year	Club (League)	Class	W	L	ERA	G	GS	CG	SV	IP	H	HR	BB	SO	K/9	WHIP	AVG
2009	Danville (APP)	R	2	1	1.13	7	1	0	1	16	7	0	5	12	6.8	0.75	.130
2010	Rome (SAL)	LoA	5	8	4.13	28	7	0	5	94	97	1	44	69	6.6	1.51	.268
2011	Lynchburg (CAR)	HiA	4	6	4.10	28	13	1	0	101	106	9	30	86	7.7	1.35	.275
2012	Mississippi (SL)	AA	8	4	3.77	27	27	0	0	146	121	11	67	124	7.7	1.29	.228
Minor League Totals			19	19	3.84	90	48	1	6	356	331	21	146	291	7.3	1.34	.248

17 EDWARD SALCEDO, 3B

Born: July 30, 1991. **B-T:** R-R. **Ht.:** 6-3. **Wt.:** 205. **Signed:** Dominican Republic, 2010. **Signed by:** Roberto Aquino.

The Braves knew Salcedo was raw when they signed him for $1.6 million in 2010, their largest bonus ever for an international amateur, yet they still have moved him aggressively through the system. In part that's because he lost more than two years of playing time while Major League Baseball investigated his age and identity after he first surfaced as a prospect on the international market in 2007. He didn't post great numbers in a season and a half in low Class A, but he got promoted anyway in 2012 and struggled both offensively and defensively. Salcedo generates impressive raw power with his quick swing, but his approach needs work after showing signs of improvement in 2011. He gets anxious and his lack of patience results in high-strikeout totals. Salcedo moved to third base from shortstop in 2011 and continued to struggle there last year with 42 errors, the third-highest total in the minor leagues. He has hard hands and makes bad throws while forcing too many plays. He has above-average arm strength that would play well on an outfield corner, where many scouts believe he would fit best. He has below-average speed and is too aggressive on the bases. Atlanta would like to push him to Double-A in 2013, but he may be better served by repeating high Class A.

Year	Club (League)	Class	AVG	G	AB	R	H	2B	3B	HR	RBI	BB	SO	SB	CS	OBP	SLG
2010	Braves (DSL)	R	.297	23	74	16	22	5	1	1	11	18	19	8	1	.453	.432
	Rome (SAL)	LoA	.197	54	193	23	38	5	4	2	16	11	56	6	5	.239	.295
2011	Rome (SAL)	LoA	.248	132	508	83	126	27	6	12	68	41	105	23	10	.315	.396
2012	Lynchburg (CAR)	HiA	.240	130	471	65	113	26	2	17	61	33	130	23	14	.295	.412
Minor League Totals			.240	339	1246	187	299	63	13	32	156	103	310	60	30	.306	.388

18 JOEY TERDOSLAVICH, 1B/3B

Born: Sept. 9, 1988. **B-T:** B-R. **Ht.:** 6-1. **Wt.:** 200. **Drafted:** Long Beach State, 2010 (6th round). **Signed by:** Steve Leavitt.

After setting a Carolina League record with 52 doubles, earning Braves minor league player of the year honors and performing well in the Arizona Fall League in 2011, Terdoslavich was heralded as the heir apparent to Chipper Jones. Two months into the 2012 season, however, the nephew of former all-star Mike Greenwell was demoted from Triple-A to Double-A and shifted from third base to first following a dismal showing in all phases of the game. To his credit, he bounced back at Mississippi and put together a solid performance. Terdoslavich is a switch-hitter with an uppercut swing that generates good backspin and is capable of spraying line drives to all fields, though he doesn't produce big home run totals. He generally does a good job of barreling the ball even with his aggressive approach, but Triple-A pitchers exposed holes in his swing. Terdoslavich is a below-average runner with an average arm, so finding a defensive home has been problematic. He made 25 errors in 56 games at third base last year and hasn't looked fluid in limited action in the outfield, so first base is his most likely long-term destination. He'll get another shot at Gwinnett in 2013.

Year	Club (League)	Class	AVG	G	AB	R	H	2B	3B	HR	RBI	BB	SO	SB	CS	OBP	SLG
2010	Danville (APP)	R	.296	49	189	27	56	10	2	2	24	15	27	3	3	.351	.402
	Rome (SAL)	LoA	.316	21	79	7	25	9	0	0	10	5	18	0	0	.365	.430
2011	Lynchburg (CAR)	HiA	.286	131	483	72	138	52	2	20	82	41	107	2	0	.341	.526
2012	Gwinnett (IL)	AAA	.180	53	194	19	35	4	0	4	20	19	50	3	0	.252	.263
	Mississippi (SL)	AA	.315	78	298	43	94	24	5	5	51	27	62	4	0	.372	.480
Minor League Totals			.280	332	1243	168	348	99	9	31	187	107	264	12	3	.338	.449

19 JOSH ELANDER, C

Born: March 19, 1991. **B-T:** R-R. **Ht.:** 6-1. **Wt.:** 215. **Signed:** Texas Christian, 2012 (6th round). **Signed by:** Gerald Turner.

A strong summer behind the plate with the U.S. national college team put Elander in position to go in the first round of the 2012 draft, but he wasn't as strong defensively last spring and lasted until the sixth round. The Braves were pleased to land a hitter of his caliber for $166,700. Elander has a compact swing and a lot of bat speed, which combine to produce above-average pull power. He does a good job of keeping his hands back and controlling the strike zone. More athletic than most catchers, he's close to an average runner and has heady instincts on the bases. Elander moves well behind the plate and enhances a fringy arm with a quick release, throwing out 29 percent of basestealers in his pro debut. His hands are hard, however, and he doesn't project to receive well enough at the major league level. He played some right field in college and figures to wind up on an infield or outfield corner, perhaps as early as 2013. His bat is advanced enough to get him to high Class A in his first full pro season.

Year	Club (League)	Class	AVG	G	AB	R	H	2B	3B	HR	RBI	BB	SO	SB	CS	OBP	SLG
2012	Danville (APP)	R	.260	36	123	19	32	6	2	4	19	16	19	3	1	.366	.439
Minor League Totals			.260	36	123	19	32	6	2	4	19	16	19	3	1	.366	.439

20 JUAN JAIME, RHP

BA GRADE
50
EXTREME

Born: Aug. 2, 1987. **B-T:** R-R. **Ht.:** 6-1. **Wt.:** 180. **Signed:** Dominican Republic, 2004. **Signed by:** Ismael Cruz (Nationals).

Jaime spent five seasons in the lower levels of the Nationals system before missing the entire 2010 and 2011 campaigns after Tommy John surgery in April 2010. Washington tried to slip him through waivers in late 2010 but the Diamondbacks claimed him, only to lose him in similar fashion to the Braves in August 2011. He finally returned to action last season and emerged as the closer at Lynchburg, ranking first in the system and second in the Carolina League with 18 saves. Though raw in many respects, Jaime has a classic power arm and a closer's mentality. He's not afraid to challenge hitters with his fastball, which flirts with 100 mph and sits in the upper 90s. He can be overpowering at times, though throwing strikes always has been an issue for him. His secondary pitches need work, with his slurvy curveball showing more promise than his below-average changeup. Atlanta placed Jaime on the 40-man roster in November, and he could be a factor in the majors by the end of 2013. He'll open the slate in Double-A.

Year	Club (League)	Class	W	L	ERA	G	GS	CG	SV	IP	H	HR	BB	SO	K/9	WHIP	AVG
2005	Nationals (DSL)	R	1	0	2.51	9	0	0	0	14	9	1	11	14	8.8	1.40	.176
2006	Nationals2 (DSL)	R	0	0	2.61	6	0	0	1	10	5	0	8	13	11.3	1.26	.135
2007	Nationals1 (DSL)	R	3	0	1.35	14	0	0	0	27	11	0	14	34	11.5	0.94	.121
2008	Nationals (GCL)	R	2	1	4.74	8	2	1	0	19	16	1	18	23	10.9	1.79	.232
2009	Vermont (NYP)	SS	2	1	1.88	6	5	0	0	24	15	0	15	36	13.5	1.25	.183
	Hagerstown (SAL)	LoA	3	1	2.27	8	7	0	0	32	22	2	16	40	11.4	1.20	.193
2010	Did Not Play—Injured																
2011	Did Not Play—Injured																
2012	Lynchburg (CAR)	HiA	1	3	3.16	42	0	0	18	51	31	4	33	73	12.8	1.25	.173
Minor League Totals			12	6	2.64	93	14	1	19	177	109	8	115	233	11.8	1.26	.175

21 CARLOS FRANCO, 3B

BA GRADE
50
EXTREME

Born: Dec. 20, 1991. **B-T:** B-R. **Ht.:** 6-2. **Wt.:** 170. **Signed:** Dominican Republic, 2009. **Signed by:** Roberto Aquino.

Franco entered 2012 as a career .205 hitter in three years of Rookie ball, but took a big step forward and earned team MVP honors at Danville. He displayed a variety of above-average tools and overall ability that make him one of the more intriguing position players in the system. Franco has solid pop from both sides of the plate. He has good plate discipline for a young player and makes consistent contact with solid hand-eye coordination. His frame is strong and sturdy, and he projects to generate above-average power as his body matures and he gains more experience. He runs well but won't be a big basestealing threat. Franco has good hands and well above-average arm strength at third base. He finally should be ready to make the jump to full-season ball in 2013.

Year	Club (League)	Class	AVG	G	AB	R	H	2B	3B	HR	RBI	BB	SO	SB	CS	OBP	SLG
2009	Braves (DSL)	R	.181	31	83	15	15	4	1	1	5	10	30	0	3	.274	.289
2010	Braves (DSL)	R	.218	37	142	8	31	4	1	2	19	18	31	3	0	.309	.303
	Braves (GCL)	R	.123	23	65	9	8	1	0	2	5	8	24	1	0	.256	.231
2011	Braves (GCL)	R	.239	44	155	22	37	9	1	1	21	15	38	10	0	.306	.329
2012	Danville (APP)	R	.271	50	166	35	45	6	3	2	20	37	36	6	5	.408	.380
Minor League Totals			.223	185	611	89	136	24	6	8	70	88	159	20	8	.326	.321

22 LUIS MEREJO, RHP

BA GRADE
50
EXTREME

Born: Oct. 8, 1994. **B-T:** L-L. **Ht.:** 6-0. **Wt.:** 170. **Signed:** Dominican Republic, 2011. **Signed by:** Matias Laureano Fortunato.

Signed out of the Dominican Republic a month into the 2011 international signing period for a modest $65,000, Merejo skipped the Dominican Summer League and made his pro debut in the Gulf Coast League last season. He finished third in the league with 53 strikeouts (against just nine walks) while mixing three pitches and repeating his delivery with consistency. He makes up for a lack of size with solid stuff and advanced feel for pitching. He works off his 89-93 mph fastball with good movement, and does an excellent job of getting ahead in the count by being aggressive in the strike zone. He struggled to throw strikes with his curveball, but it shows swing-and-miss potential when he has it dialed in. He also has some aptitude for throwing a changeup. The Braves were rewarded for being aggressive with the underrated Merejo and believe he has the makeup and ability to handle further challenges. His spring training performance will determine whether he spends 2013 at Danville or Rome.

Year	Club (League)	Class	W	L	ERA	G	GS	CG	SV	IP	H	HR	BB	SO	K/9	WHIP	AVG
2012	Braves (GCL)	R	0	5	4.61	10	8	0	0	41	38	1	9	53	11.6	1.15	.245
Minor League Totals			0	5	4.61	10	8	0	0	41	38	1	9	53	11.6	1.15	.245

23 BRYAN DE LA ROSA, C

BA GRADE
50
EXTREME

Born: March 3, 1994. **B-T:** R-R. **Ht.:** 5-8. **Wt.:** 193. **Drafted:** HS—Delray Beach, Fla., 2012 (3rd round). **Signed by:** Buddy Hernandez.

A native of Toa Alta, Puerto Rico, de la Rosa attended the Bucky Dent Baseball Academy (Delray Beach, Fla.), one of the growing number of baseball-oriented private schools that have popped up in Florida. That experience gave de la Rosa extra exposure, and he opened eyes at showcases with 1.71-second pop times and base and throws clocked at 85 mph. The Braves drafted him in the third round last June and signed him for $408,300. Short and stocky, de la Rosa has quick, agile feet behind the plate and soft hands. He still has some rough edges to smooth out after committing 13 passed balls in 28 pro games, though he did throw out 30 percent of basestealers. De la Rosa doesn't have as much upside with the bat, though he has decent power to his pull side and a relatively smooth swing. He has considerable work to do with his plate discipline after striking out 30 times and walking just twice in his pro debut. He's a below-average runner but is a good athlete for a catcher. He's not ready for a full-season assignment after his rough introduction to pro ball, so he'll likely play at Danville in 2013.

Year	Club (League)	Class	AVG	G	AB	R	H	2B	3B	HR	RBI	BB	SO	SB	CS	OBP	SLG
2012	Braves (GCL)	R	.162	29	68	5	11	1	0	1	3	2	30	0	1	.194	.221
Minor League Totals			.162	29	68	5	11	1	0	1	3	2	30	0	1	.194	.221

24 BILLY BULLOCK, RHP

BA GRADE
45
HIGH

Born: Feb. 27, 1988. **B-T:** R-R. **Ht.:** 6-6. **Wt.:** 225. **Drafted:** Florida, 2009 (2nd round). **Signed by:** Billy Corrigan (Twins).

Acquired from the Twins before the 2011 season as compensation for Rule 5 pickup Scott Diamond, Bullock has stalled in Double-A with the Braves. They thought he might be on the verge of the big leagues heading into 2012, but he struggled for most of the season and got knocked around when he got to Triple-A in mid-June. He had trouble finding a consistent feel for his release point, which hurt the effectiveness of his secondary pitches. In one four-game stretch in July, he allowed 16 earned runs in six innings. A closer at Florida, Bullock has a fearless approach on the mound and will challenge hitters and work inside with his 92-94 mph fastball. He uses his height to throw on a downhill plane. He tends to lose the feel for his slider and below-average changeup, however. Scouts say Bullock has the potential to be a set-up man in the majors if he gets more consistent. Atlanta was encouraged with the way he finished the season after going back down to Mississippi, and hopes he can maintain that momentum when he opens this year at Gwinnett. The Braves declined to protect him on their 40-man roster, however.

Year	Club (League)	Class	W	L	ERA	G	GS	CG	SV	IP	H	HR	BB	SO	K/9	WHIP	AVG
2009	Elizabethton (APP)	R	1	0	1.23	7	0	0	3	7	3	0	1	10	12.3	0.55	.125
	Beloit (MWL)	LoA	3	0	2.73	26	0	0	8	26	25	0	12	35	12.0	1.41	.253
2010	Fort Myers (FSL)	HiA	0	4	3.62	28	0	0	14	37	39	2	19	45	10.8	1.55	.281
	New Britain (EL)	AA	2	4	3.44	30	0	0	13	37	34	3	24	60	14.7	1.58	.239
2011	Mississippi (SL)	AA	3	1	4.53	50	0	0	11	50	35	2	34	65	11.8	1.39	.193
	Gwinnett (IL)	AAA	1	0	0.00	1	0	0	0	1	2	0	0	1	9.0	2.00	.400
2012	Mississippi (SL)	AA	1	2	3.89	26	0	0	1	39	30	3	33	41	9.4	1.60	.216
	Gwinnett (IL)	AAA	0	0	11.07	14	0	0	0	20	33	4	23	26	11.5	2.75	.355
Minor League Totals			11	11	4.33	182	0	0	50	218	201	14	146	283	11.7	1.59	.245

25 KYLE KUBITZA, 3B

BA GRADE
45
HIGH

Born: July 15, 1990. **B-T:** L-R. **Ht.:** 6-3. **Wt.:** 190. **Drafted:** Texas State, 2011 (3rd round). **Signed by:** John Barron.

Kubitza got off to a strong start last year, his first full pro season after becoming the highest-drafted (third round) position player in Texas State history in 2011, but he tailed off and batted just .229/.327/.335 in the second half. He has patience and manages the strike zone well, though he pressed at times last season and struck out 127 times. He has a smooth swing, his hands work well and he sees the ball well against southpaws, against whom he batted .302 in 2012. He's prone to tinker with his stance, but the Braves believe he'll settle down as he gains experience. Though primarily a line-drive hitter, Kubitza has solid raw power and could hit 20 homers if he adds some loft to his stroke and pulls more pitches. He's a good defender at the hot corner, with decent quickness and soft hands along with above-average arm strength. He also runs well for his size. He'll strive for more consistency when he advances to high Class A this year.

Year	Club (League)	Class	AVG	G	AB	R	H	2B	3B	HR	RBI	BB	SO	SB	CS	OBP	SLG
2011	Danville (APP)	R	.321	44	162	36	52	16	3	1	34	24	38	9	3	.407	.475
2012	Rome (SAL)	LoA	.239	128	448	68	107	24	9	9	59	73	127	18	11	.349	.393
Minor League Totals			.261	172	610	104	159	40	12	10	93	97	165	27	14	.364	.415

26 NATHAN HYATT, RHP

BA GRADE
45
HIGH

Born: Sept. **26, 1990. B-T:** R-R. **Ht.:** 6-0. **Wt.:** 180. **Drafted:** Appalachian State, 2012 (13th round). **Signed by:** Billy Best.

Hyatt jumped onto the radar of scouts last spring while helping Appalachian State win a school-record 41 games and reach the NCAA postseason for the first time since 1986. In his only season as a closer, he established the single-season school record with 16 saves, a total that led the Southern Conference and ranked sixth in NCAA Division I. That performance and an increase in velocity led the Braves to draft him in the 13th round and sign him for $100,000, and he continued to dominate in his pro debut. Hyatt doesn't have a classic closer's build, but the ball appears to jump out of his hand. His fastball sits at 92-95 mph and touches 97 while showing late life. He made improvements with the command and cutting action on his hard slider over the course of the year. His slider registers in the mid-80s and is difficult to hit, even when batters know its coming. More than one club official has said Hyatt resembles Craig Kimbrel as a minor leaguer. Hyatt has the stuff and makeup to work the late innings in the major leagues, and he might not need much time to get there. He'll open his first full pro season in high Class A.

Year	Club (League)	Class	W	L	ERA	G	GS	CG	SV	IP	H	HR	BB	SO	K/9	WHIP	AVG
2012	Danville (APP)	R	2	0	1.80	7	0	0	3	10	3	0	3	14	12.6	0.60	.100
	Rome (SAL)	LoA	0	0	1.23	11	0	0	3	15	10	0	5	23	14.1	1.02	.196
Minor League Totals			2	0	1.46	18	0	0	6	25	13	0	8	37	13.5	0.85	.160

27 BRANDON DRURY, 1B/3B

BA GRADE
45
HIGH

Born: March 11, 1991. **B-T:** R-R. **Ht.:** 6-0. **Wt.:** 190. **Drafted:** HS—Grants Pass, Ore., 2010 (13th round). **Signed by:** Brett Evert.

Drury blossomed at the plate in 2011, when he led the Appalachian League with 92 hits and narrowly missed winning the batting title with a .347 average. His quick, short stroke generated good backspin and he made consistent contact despite lacking patience at the plate. More advanced pitchers exploited his aggressiveness in 2012, particularly during the first half of the season. He started to figure things out after the all-star break, when he batted .279/.323/.407, but he's still going to have to tone down his approach. Drury gives away too many at-bats by chasing pitches, and he needs to wait for offerings he can drive if he's going to develop more than gap power. There's more pressure on his bat now that he's spending more time at first base. A shortstop in high school, Drury initially moved to third base as a pro. But his speed, range, arm strength and throwing accuracy are all below-average, and he saw more action at first base last year due to the presence of Kyle Kubitza at Rome. Drury will repeat low Class A to start the 2013 season, in hopes he can refine his approach at the plate.

Year	Club (League)	Class	AVG	G	AB	R	H	2B	3B	HR	RBI	BB	SO	SB	CS	OBP	SLG
2010	Braves (GCL)	R	.198	52	192	20	38	7	1	3	17	9	50	2	2	.248	.292
2011	Danville (APP)	R	.347	63	265	40	92	23	0	8	54	6	35	3	0	.367	.525
2012	Rome (SAL)	LoA	.229	123	445	47	102	22	3	6	51	20	73	3	4	.270	.333
Minor League Totals			.257	238	902	107	232	52	4	17	122	35	158	8	6	.293	.380

28 CARLOS PEREZ, LHP

BA GRADE
45
HIGH

Born: Nov. **20, 1991. B-T:** L-L. **Ht.:** 6-2. **Wt.:** 205. **Signed:** Dominican Republic, 2008. **Signed by:** Roberto Aquino.

Since he rated as the Appalachian League's top prospect in 2010, Perez's development has gone much more slowly than the Braves anticipated. He has bounced between Rome and Danville, battling his control and confidence while displaying an inability to repeat his delivery. His fastball dipped to the upper 80s in 2011 before returning to 91-95 mph last year. His curveball also showed tighter spin, though his changeup remains a distant third pitch. Perez's confidence is shaky, but he responded well after moving to the bullpen following a demotion to the Appy League last summer. He's still just 21, so time is on his side, but he needs to show he can clear the hurdle of low Class A this year in his new role. His inability to do so to this point led to Atlanta's decision to leave him off its 40-man roster this offseason.

Year	Club (League)	Class	W	L	ERA	G	GS	CG	SV	IP	H	HR	BB	SO	K/9	WHIP	AVG
2009	Braves (GCL)	R	1	2	5.28	10	5	0	0	31	35	2	13	23	6.8	1.57	.292
2010	Danville (APP)	R	2	0	1.13	6	6	0	0	32	20	0	14	27	7.6	1.06	.185
	Rome (SAL)	LoA	0	1	3.86	2	2	0	0	7	8	1	3	4	5.1	1.57	.267
2011	Rome (SAL)	LoA	4	10	4.82	28	23	0	1	125	138	7	66	109	7.8	1.63	.278
2012	Rome (SAL)	LoA	0	3	12.79	7	4	0	0	19	33	3	19	12	5.7	2.74	.379
	Danville (APP)	R	3	2	2.05	16	0	0	0	31	20	0	15	50	14.7	1.14	.182
Minor League Totals			10	18	4.64	69	40	0	1	244	254	13	130	225	8.3	1.57	.267

29 ROBBY HEFFLINGER, OF

BA GRADE
45
HIGH

Born: Jan. 3, 1990. **B-T:** R-R. **Ht.:** 6-4. **Wt.:** 220. **Drafted:** Georgia Perimeter CC, 2009 (7th round). **Signed by:** Brian Bridges.

After a dismal start in high Class A last year, the light came on for Hefflinger in the second half after he returned to Rome, where he had spent most of the previous two seasons. Instead of sulking, he worked hard in extensive sessions with hitting coordinator Don Long, and put together his best performance since turning pro in 2009. Much of the change centered on Hefflinger's approach at the plate. He had been taking too many pitches early in counts and then chasing breaking balls with two strikes. By hitting better pitches earlier in the count, he dialed into his easy plus power and used his smooth swing to hit the ball with authority to all fields. A good all-around athlete, Hefflinger runs the bases smartly with speed that's a tick above-average. He covers the outfield corners well and has above-average arm strength with good accuracy. He also generates raves for his leadership, getting a large share of the credit for Rome's worst-to-first turnaround in the second half of 2012. Hefflinger has the raw strength and overall tools to succeed at higher levels, but because he hasn't thus far, the Braves didn't bother protecting him on their 40-man roster this offseason. He'll have to show he can solve high Class A pitching in his third attempt this year.

Year	Club (League)	Class	AVG	G	AB	R	H	2B	3B	HR	RBI	BB	SO	SB	CS	OBP	SLG
2009	Danville (APP)	R	.242	61	240	23	58	11	1	7	37	16	76	1	0	.288	.383
2010	Rome (SAL)	LoA	.245	77	282	28	69	19	0	6	53	25	85	2	5	.302	.376
2011	Lynchburg (CAR)	HiA	.114	12	44	2	5	2	0	0	2	3	19	0	0	.170	.159
	Rome (SAL)	LoA	.256	112	425	55	109	34	3	8	56	24	123	1	1	.296	.407
2012	Lynchburg (CAR)	HiA	.228	37	123	14	28	8	0	4	11	18	47	1	1	.336	.390
	Rome (SAL)	LoA	.284	84	296	44	84	21	1	12	58	38	81	7	1	.362	.483
Minor League Totals			.250	383	1410	166	353	95	5	37	217	124	431	12	8	.310	.404

30 AARON NORTHCRAFT, RHP

BA GRADE
45
HIGH

Born: May 28, 1990. **B-T:** R-R. **Ht.:** 6-4. **Wt.:** 225. **Drafted:** HS—Newport Beach, Calif., 2009 (10th round). **Signed by:** Tom Battista.

Northcraft has made a slow but steady climb through the system and earned a spot on the Braves' 40-man roster after putting together his best season as a pro in 2012. He led the Carolina League with 27 starts and 160 strikeouts and pitched well in the playoffs as Lynchburg won the championship. Northcraft has good size and excellent mound presence. Throwing from a low three-quarters arm slot, he works fast and gets quick outs by coaxing groundballs. His main pitch is an 87-91 mph sinker, which he backs up with a solid changeup and fringy curveball. His breaking ball has continually improved since he signed, so there's hope that he could eventually have three average pitches. Scouts aren't crazy about his delivery, which includes a long arm action and a stiff front leg, so they're not convinced that he'll make it as a starter at the upper level. However, Northcraft is an intelligent pitcher who gets the most out of his ability. Atlanta is interested to see how he fares in his first taste of Double-A in 2013.

Year	Club (League)	Class	W	L	ERA	G	GS	CG	SV	IP	H	HR	BB	SO	K/9	WHIP	AVG
2009	Braves (GCL)	R	1	2	4.50	11	10	0	0	40	33	2	21	31	7.0	1.35	.229
2010	Danville (APP)	R	6	1	2.73	10	9	0	0	53	44	1	9	38	6.5	1.01	.228
	Rome (SAL)	LoA	1	3	8.16	4	3	0	0	14	21	1	15	8	5.0	2.51	.328
2011	Rome (SAL)	LoA	7	8	3.34	23	19	0	0	113	108	8	41	88	7.0	1.31	.254
2012	Lynchburg (CAR)	HiA	10	11	3.98	27	27	2	0	152	143	4	53	160	9.5	1.29	.247
Minor League Totals			25	25	3.82	75	68	2	0	372	349	16	139	325	7.9	1.31	.248

Baltimore Orioles

BY MATT FORMAN

Buckle up, Baltimore. The Orioles have reawakened baseball at Camden Yards.

After 14 straight losing seasons, the Orioles treated their fans to a magical, unexpected 2012 campaign that brought the franchise its first postseason berth and first home playoff victory since 1997.

Manager Buck Showalter flipped the script on a team that went 69-93 in his first full season, as the

Orioles went 93-69 and battled the Yankees for the American League East title down to the final day of the season. Baltimore dethroned the two-time defending AL champion Rangers in a one-game wild-card playoff, then pushed New York to the brink in the division series before losing in five games.

"We took a giant step forward this year and we re-energized the fan base," first-year general manager Dan Duquette said. "We're a first-division outfit. To win 96 games is really a significant accomplishment, and I'm proud of the work and effort that everyone did."

As Showalter said the day after the Orioles were eliminated in the Bronx: "Now the challenge is to hold on to it and continue to get better."

Baltimore knows nothing is guaranteed, and its accomplishments in 2012 were startling, given that it outscored its opponents by just seven runs during the regular season. The Orioles went 29-9 in one-run games and 16-2 in extra-inning affairs, as Showalter brilliantly navigated the season while relying on 52 different players to squeak out every victory. He did it without an ace pitcher, with a patchwork bullpen that developed into one of baseball's best (Jim Johnson led the majors with 51 saves) and with contributions from such unlikely sources as Miguel Gonzalez and Nate McLouth.

Duquette, who had been out of baseball since the Red Sox fired him as GM before the 2002 season, made many subtle but masterful moves. Taiwanese lefty Wei-Yin Chen, the only Baltimore pitcher to make more than 20 starts, was signed out of Japan's major league. Gonzalez, a hero in the second half and postseason, signed a minor league deal in March.

Other contributors such as Ryan Flaherty (major league Rule 5 draft), Jason Hammel (February trade for Jeremy Guthrie) and McLouth (minor league deal on June 5) also came aboard at little cost. Perhaps Duquette's best decision came in early August, when

Matt Wieters and the Orioles had plenty to celebrate in an unlikely run to the playoffs

he promoted 20-year-old Manny Machado to the big leagues in hopes of shoring up a huge defensive weakness at third base.

Machado did that despite having played just two games at the hot corner in the minors. He also exceeded offensive expectations by batting .262/.294/.445 in the regular season and became the third-youngest player ever to hit a postseason home run.

Along with Adam Jones, Nick Markakis and Matt Wieters, Machado is a lineup cornerstone for the Orioles. They also have the game's best pitching prospect in righthander Dylan Bundy, who made his major league debut in September at age 19. In scouting director Gary Rajisch's first draft with Baltimore, the club landed another potential frontline starter in Kevin Gausman, the No. 4 overall pick.

Baltimore was not nearly as successful in the minor leagues, and beyond Bundy and Gausman, the Orioles farm system lacks depth. Double-A Bowie was the only Baltimore affiliate to reach the postseason, and Baltimore's clubs finished dead last in the Carolina, South Atlantic and New York-Penn leagues.

But if the Orioles can continue to win at the major league level and Duquette can keep plugging holes, Baltimore won't have to rush prospects and will have time to build up its system.

THIS YEAR'S TOP 30

Player, Pos.		Grade
1.	Dylan Bundy, rhp	75/Medium
2.	Kevin Gausman, rhp	65/Medium
3.	Jonathan Schoop, 2b/ss	55/High
4.	Nick Delmonico, 1b/2b	50/High
5.	Eduardo Rodriguez, rhp	50/High
6.	L.J. Hoes, of	45/Low
7.	Xavier Avery, of	45/Medium
8.	Mike Wright, rhp	50/High
9.	Branden Kline, rhp	50/High
10.	Adrian Marin, ss	50/High
11.	Tim Berry, lhp	50/High
12.	Christian Walker, 1b	50/High
13.	Henry Urrutia, of	45/Medium
14.	Glynn Davis, of	50/High
15.	Torsten Boss, 3b	50/High
16.	Steve Johnson, rhp	40/Low
17.	Clay Schrader, rhp	45/Medium
18.	Devin Jones, rhp	50/High
19.	Josh Hader, lhp	45/High
20.	Zach Davies, rhp	45/High
21.	Tsuyoshi Wada, lhp	45/High
22.	T.J. McFarland, lhp	40/Medium
23.	Parker Bridwell, rhp	50/Extreme
24.	Mike Belfiore, lhp	45/High
25.	Lex Rutledge, lhp	45/High
26.	Tyler Wilson, rhp	40/Medium
27.	Brenden Webb, of	50/Extreme
28.	Oliver Drake, rhp	45/High
29.	Greg Lorenzo, of	45/High
30.	Ty Kelly, 2b/3b/of	40/Medium

LAST YEAR'S TOP 30

Player, Pos.		Status
1.	Dylan Bundy, rhp	No. 1
2.	Manny Machado, ss	Majors
3.	Jonathan Schoop, inf	No. 3
4.	Parker Bridwell, rhp	No. 23
5.	L.J. Hoes, of/2b	No. 6
6.	Nick Delmonico, 3b/1b	No. 4
7.	Ryan Flaherty, inf/of	Majors
8.	Jason Esposito, 3b	Dropped out
9.	Xavier Avery, of	No. 7
10.	Dan Klein, rhp	Dropped out
11.	Mike Wright, rhp	No. 8
12.	Clay Schrader, rhp	No. 17
13.	Joe Mahoney, 1b/of	(Marlins)
14.	Aaron Baker, 1b	Dropped out
15.	Ryan Berry, of	Dropped out
16.	Matt Angle, of	(Dodgers)
17.	Bobby Bundy, rhp	Dropped out
18.	Kyle Simon, rhp	(Phillies)
19.	Glynn Davis, of	No. 14
20.	Tim Berry, lhp	No. 11
21.	Gabriel Lino, c	(Phillies)
22.	Roderick Bernadina, of	Dropped out
23.	Ryan Adams, 2b	Dropped out
24.	Tyler Townsend, 1b	Dropped out
25.	Brandon Waring, 3b/1b	Dropped out
26.	Oliver Drake, rhp	No. 28
27.	Trent Mummey, of	Dropped out
28.	Wynn Pelzer, rhp	(Bridgeport/Atlantic League)
29.	Kyle Hudson, of	(Phillies)
30.	Eduardo Rodriguez, lhp	No. 5

BEST TOOLS

Best Hitter for Average	L.J. Hoes
Best Power Hitter	Jonathan Schoop
Best Strike-Zone Discipline	L.J. Hoes
Fastest Baserunner	Glynn Davis
Best Athlete	Xavier Avery
Best Fastball	Dylan Bundy
Best Curveball	Dylan Bundy
Best Slider	Clay Schrader
Best Changeup	Kevin Gausman
Best Control	Tyler Wilson
Best Defensive Catcher	Brian Ward
Best Defensive Infielder	Adrian Marin
Best Infield Arm	Jonathan Schoop
Best Defensive Outfielder	Glynn Davis
Best Outfield Arm	L.J. Hoes

PROJECTED 2016 LINEUP

Catcher	Matt Wieters
First Base	Nick Delmonico
Second Base	Jonathan Schoop
Third Base	J.J. Hardy
Shortstop	Manny Machado
Left Field	L.J. Hoes
Center Field	Adam Jones
Right Field	Nick Markakis
Designated Hitter	Chris Davis
No. 1 Starter	Dylan Bundy
No. 2 Starter	Kevin Gausman
No. 3 Starter	Jason Hammel
No. 4 Starter	Wei-Yin Chen
No. 5 Starter	Chris Tillman
Closer	Jim Johnson

TOP PROSPECTS OF THE DECADE

Year	Player, Pos.	2012 Org.
2003	Erik Bedard, lhp	Pirates
2004	Adam Loewen, lhp	Mets
2005	Nick Markakis, of	Orioles
2006	Nick Markakis, of	Orioles
2007	Billy Rowell, 3b	Orioles
2008	Matt Wieters, c	Orioles
2009	Matt Wieters, c	Orioles
2010	Brian Matusz, lhp	Orioles
2011	Manny Machado, ss	Orioles
2012	Dylan Bundy, rhp	Orioles

TOP DRAFT PICKS OF THE DECADE

Year	Player, Pos.	2012 Org.
2003	Nick Markakis, of	Orioles
2004	*Wade Townsend, rhp	Out of baseball
2005	Brandon Snyder, c	Rangers
2006	Billy Rowell, 3b	Orioles
2007	Matt Wieters, c	Orioles
2008	Brian Matusz, lhp	Orioles
2009	Matt Hobgood, rhp	Orioles
2010	Manny Machado, ss	Orioles
2011	Dylan Bundy, rhp	Orioles
2012	Kevin Gausman, rhp	Orioles

*Did not sign.

LARGEST BONUSES IN CLUB HISTORY

Matt Wieters, 2007	$6,000,000
Manny Machado, 2010	$5,250,000
Kevin Gausman, 2012	$4,320,000
Dylan Bundy, 2011	$4,000,000
Adam Loewen, 2002	$3,200,000
Brian Matusz, 2008	$3,200,000

BALTIMORE ORIOLES

TOP 2013 ROOKIE: Steve Johnson, rhp. He laid claim to a big league job for 2013 by going 4-0, 2.11 in 12 appearances with Baltimore last year.

BREAKOUT PROSPECT: Josh Hader, lhp. Lightly scouted in high school, Hader added velocity and took off last summer after signing as a 19th-round pick.

SLEEPER: Sander Beck, rhp. Signed as a non-drafted free agent after pitching four years at Maryland, he has good size and a low-90s fastball.

SOURCE OF TOP 30 TALENT			
Homegrown	27	Acquired	3
College	10	Trades	2
Junior college	2	Rule 5 draft	1
High school	9	Independent leagues	0
Nondrafted free agents	1	Free agents/waivers	0
International	5		

LF
L.J. Hoes (6)
Trent Mummey
Ronnie Welty

CF
Xavier Avery (7)
Glynn Davis (14)
Brenden Webb (27)
Greg Lorenzo (29)
Ray Hunnicutt

RF
Henry Urrutia (13)
Roderick Bernadina
John Ruettiger
Lucas Herbst

3B
Nick Delmonico (4)
Torsten Boss (15)
Ty Kelly (30)
Brandon Waring
Jason Esposito
Joel Hutter

SS
Adrian Marin (10)

2B
Jonathan Schoop (3)
Connor Narron

1B
Christian Walker (12)
Aaron Baker
Tyler Townsend

C
Brian Ward
Caleb Joseph
Luis Exposito

LHP

LHSP	LHRP
Eduardo Rodriguez (5)	Mike Belfiore (24)
Tim Berry (11)	Chris Petrini
Josh Hader (19)	Jason Gurka
Tsuyoshi Wada (21)	
T.J. McFarland (22)	
Lex Rutledge (25)	
Trent Howard	
Richard Zagone	
Elias Pinales	
Kevin Grendell	

RHP

RHSP	RHRP
Dylan Bundy (1)	Clay Schrader (17)
Kevin Gausman (2)	Dan Klein
Mike Wright (8)	Matt Price
Branden Kline (9)	Sander Beck
Steve Johnson (16)	Tom Boleska
Devin Jones (18)	Jose Nivar
Zach Davies (19)	Dioni Dominguez
Parker Bridwell (23)	Gene Escat
Tyler Wilson (26)	Nick Grim
Oliver Drake (28)	Janser Severino
Zach Clark	Tom Winegardner
Bobby Bundy	
Miguel Chalas	
Brady Wager	
Sean McAdams	
Luc Rennie	

2012   BONUSES: $7.4 MILLION

BEST PURE HITTER: 1B Christian Walker (3) controls the strike zone well and makes consistent line-drive contact. A member of the last three all-College World Series teams while winning two national championships at South Carolina, he tied Dustin Ackley's CWS career hits record with 28.

BEST POWER HITTER: Walker hit 30 homers in three years with the Gamecocks, and the Orioles think he has plus raw power and the hitting savvy to get to it.

FASTEST RUNNER: OF Ray Hunnicutt (40) can run the 60-yard dash in 6.5 seconds. SS Adrian Marin (3) is a step behind Hunnicutt but still has at least plus speed.

BEST DEFENSIVE PLAYER: For the second time in three years, Baltimore grabbed a South Florida prep shortstop. Marin doesn't have Manny Machado's offensive upside, but he's a solid defender who may have a better chance to remain at shortstop.

BEST FASTBALL: RHP Kevin Gausman (1) operates at 94-96 mph and routinely peaks at 98, and he continued to do so during instructional league. LHP Lex Rutledge (6) has hit 98 in the past but topped out at 94 after signing. RHPs Branden Kline (2) and Brady Wager (9) can reach 95.

BEST SECONDARY PITCH: Gausman's splitter/changeup devastates hitters who are geared up for his fastball. Kline's slider is the best breaking ball in this crop, while Rutledge flashes a plus curveball.

BEST PRO DEBUT: RHP Josh Hader (19) had a 1.88 ERA, 48-9 K-BB ratio and a .146 opponent average in 29 innings between two Rookie-ball stops.

BEST ATHLETE: If his power develops as the Orioles hope, Marin could have five average or better tools. Hunnicutt drew interest from college basketball programs as a guard, while RHP Sean McAdams (14) had football offers as a quarterback.

MOST INTRIGUING BACKGROUND: Unsigned 1B Ryan Ripken (20) is the son of Orioles legend Cal Jr.. His uncle Billy also played for the club and his grandfather Cal Sr. managed the team. C Steel Russell's (32) father John played in the majors and is Baltimore's bench coach.

CLOSEST TO THE MAJORS: Gausman threw three scoreless innings in the Double-A Eastern League playoffs. Once he masters a consistent slider, he'll be big league-ready.

BEST LATE-ROUND PICK: Hader, who commands three pitches and saw his fastball velocity shoot into the low 90s after he signed. McAdams has a big, athletic frame and throws in the low 90s as well.

THE ONE WHO GOT AWAY: LHP Colin Poche (5) was the highest Orioles pick not to sign and is now at Arkansas, but RHP Derick Velasquez (15) has a higher ceiling. Velasquez is projectable and athletic with the chance to have three plus pitches. He transferred from Merced (Calif.) JC to Fresno State.

ASSESSMENT: Despite picking fourth overall both years, the Orioles may have grabbed the best pitcher in each of the last two drafts. Gausman could move just as quickly to the majors as Dylan Bundy.

2011   BONUSES: $8.4 MILLION

RHP Dylan Bundy (1) is the best pitching prospect in baseball and made his big league debut at age 19. RHP Mike Wright (3) and 1B/2B Nick Delmonico (6) show promise as well.

GRADE: A

2010   BONUSES: $9.2 MILLION

The good news: SS/3B Manny Machado (1) looks like a star and arrived in Baltimore ahead of schedule. The bad news: No one else the Orioles drafted looks like he'll make much of an impact.

GRADE: A

2009   BONUSES: $8.7 MILLION

The Orioles overdrafted RHP Matt Hobgood (1) at No. 5 to save money, and he has been ineffective or injured ever since, missing all of 2012 following Tommy John surgery. Large investments in SS Mychal Givens (2), C Michael Ohlman (11) and LHP Cameron Coffey (22) also haven't panned out.

GRADE: F

2008   BONUSES: $6.9 MILLION

LHP Brian Matusz (1) got back on track in 2012 and may yet be a solid starter. OFs Xavier Avery (2), L.J. Hoes (3) and Kyle Hudson (4) also have played in the majors, though Baltimore released Hudson last offseason.

GRADE: C

Draft analysis by Jim Callis. Numbers in parentheses indicate draft rounds.

1 DYLAN BUNDY, RHP

Born: Nov. 15, 1992. **B-T:** R-R. **Ht.:** 6-1. **Wt.:** 195.
Drafted: HS—Owasso, Okla., 2011 (1st round).
Signed by: Ernie Jacobs.

BA GRADE
75
MEDIUM

CLIFF WELCH

Considered the most advanced prep pitcher in years, Bundy went fourth overall in a deep 2011 draft and signed a $6.225 million major league contract that included a $4 million bonus. Even the most ambitious predraft expectations sold him short, however. He threw his first professional pitch in April and five months later became the fourth player from his draft class to reach the big leagues, as well as the fourth 19-year-old to pitch in the majors in the last decade. After opening the season with 13 consecutive no-hit innings at low Class A Delmarva, he was promoted to high Class A Frederick, where he ranked as the Carolina League's top prospect. He earned a victory in the Futures Game and then made three starts for Double-A Bowie, including the Baysox's playoff opener. The Orioles kept him on a strict pitch count throughout the season and didn't let him venture into the sixth inning until August, a plan that left him with usable innings later in the year. Bundy went to instructional league, but the Orioles called him up in mid-September when they needed bullpen reinforcements. He made two scoreless appearances and was the obvious choice as the organization's minor league pitcher of the year.

Bundy offers a rare combination of polish and power at a young age, as well as four potential plus pitches, giving him true No. 1 starter upside. In shorter stints, Bundy attacks with a 95-98 mph fastball that touches triple digits, and in longer outings he settles in at 92-96 mph. Because his four-seam fastball has just average life, he added a two-seamer with more sink in the second half of the season. His best pitch as an amateur was an upper-80s cutter, but the Orioles asked him to scrap it in favor of developing his other secondary pitches. Bundy's downer curveball flashes well above-average potential, though it's inconsistent. His plus changeup has progressed more than any of his offerings since he signed. It's deceptive because of his consistent arm speed and

SCOUTING GRADES

Fastball: 70. **Control:** 65.
Curveball: 65. **Command:** 60.
Changeup: 60.

Based on 20-80 scouting scale, where 50 represents major league average, and future projection rather than present tools.

features slight sink. Reintroducing the cutter would give him a fourth plus offering and another weapon against lefthanders. Bundy's command and consistency need to improve, though he has a tremendous feel for pitching. He's a great athlete with good body control and balance, broad shoulders and a muscular lower half. His arm action is clean and he has worked to improve the tempo in his delivery. Despite his size, Bundy creates good plane on his pitches, though he runs into trouble when he leaves the ball up in the strike zone. Bundy draws praise for his work ethic, makeup and competitiveness.

Bundy already has passed his older brother Bobby, an Orioles 2008 eighth-round pick who spent time in Double-A before succumbing to an elbow injury in July. Regardless of whether Dylan gets a chance to make the big league club out of spring training, it won't be long before he's Baltimore's ace. He should be the Orioles' best homegrown pitcher since Mike Mussina.

Year	Club (League)	Class	W	L	ERA	G	GS	CG	SV	IP	H	HR	BB	SO	K/9	WHIP	AVG
2012	Delmarva (SAL)	LoA	1	0	0.00	8	8	0	0	30	5	0	2	40	12.0	0.23	.053
	Frederick (CAR)	HiA	6	3	2.84	12	12	0	0	57	48	5	18	66	10.4	1.16	.233
	Bowie (EL)	AA	2	0	3.24	3	3	0	0	17	14	1	8	13	7.0	1.32	.230
	Baltimore (AL)	MAJ	0	0	0.00	2	0	0	0	2	1	0	1	0	0.0	1.20	.200
Major League Totals			0	0	0.00	2	0	0	0	2	1	0	1	0	0.0	1.20	.200
Minor League Totals			9	3	2.08	23	23	0	0	104	67	6	28	119	10.3	0.92	.186

2 KEVIN GAUSMAN, RHP

Born: Jan. 6, 1991. **B-T:** R-R. **Ht.:** 6-4. **Wt.:** 185. **Drafted:** Louisiana State, 2012 (1st round). **Signed by:** Dave Jennings.

Considered a first-round talent out of high school, Gausman declined seven-figure overtures from clubs before the draft and turned down the Dodgers as a sixth-round pick to attend Louisiana State. A draft-eligible sophomore in 2012, he went fourth overall and signed for $4.32 million. Gausman's two premium pitches and developing third option give him No. 2 starter upside. His plus-plus fastball sits at 94-96 mph and touches 98, and he mixes in a sinking low-90s two-seamer to induce groundouts. His 84-86 mph changeup is an easy plus pitch, and some scouts ranked it among the best they've seen at the amateur level. Gausman threw both a 76-79 mph curveball and an 82-86 mph slider that blended together in college. His diving slider flashes more swing-and-miss potential and showed significant improvement during instructional league. A premium athlete with a live body, he has a smooth, high leg-kick delivery that helps him stay over the rubber.

BA GRADE

65

MEDIUM

His aptitude and intelligence help set him apart. Bundy and Gausman give the Orioles one of the minors' best 1-2 pitching punches. After making a playoff appearance for Bowie, Gausman might return to Double-A to open his first full pro season. He could reach Baltimore before the end of the season.

Year	Club (League)	Class	W	L	ERA	G	GS	CG	SV	IP	H	HR	BB	SO	K/9	WHIP	AVG
2012	Aberdeen (NYP)	SS	0	0	0.00	2	2	0	0	6	1	0	0	5	7.5	0.17	.053
	Frederick (CAR)	HiA	0	1	6.00	3	3	0	0	9	10	3	1	8	8.0	1.22	.278
Minor League Totals			0	1	3.60	5	5	0	0	15	11	3	1	13	7.8	0.80	.200

3 JONATHAN SCHOOP, 2B/SS

Born: Oct. 16, 1991. **B-T:** R-R. **Ht.:** 6-1. **Wt.:** 187. **Signed:** Curacao, 2008. **Signed by:** Ernst Meyer.

Throughout most of his minor league career, Schoop has been a double-play partner with Manny Machado. He played primarily second base before Machado's promotion to the big leagues, then saw time at shortstop afterward. In an organization not known for its international efforts, Schoop ranks as the system's headliner. Schoop showed flashes of brilliance in 2012 despite playing in Double-A at age 20 and battling tendinitis in both knees. He's an aggressive hitter who produces loud contact, but he has a bat wrap that causes timing issues and leaves him vulnerable to premium fastballs on the inner half. He needs to improve his pitch recognition to make the most of his above-average raw power. Though Schoop is a below-average runner, he has soft hands and works well around the bag. His plus arm will play anywhere in the infield. Depending on how his body fills out, he might be best suited for third base or an outfield corner, though he hasn't left the

BA GRADE

55

HIGH

infield yet. The Orioles will continue developing Schoop at shortstop until he plays his way off the position. After making a trip to the Arizona Fall League, he figures to return to Double-A to open 2013, which will be an important developmental year. He was added to the 40-man roster in the offseason and has the potential to be an above-average everyday player.

Year	Club (League)	Class	AVG	G	AB	R	H	2B	3B	HR	RBI	BB	SO	SB	CS	OBP	SLG
2009	Orioles (DSL)	R	.239	68	247	28	59	7	3	0	35	24	39	11	3	.320	.291
2010	Orioles (GCL)	R	.250	17	60	11	15	4	0	3	16	7	7	0	0	.329	.467
	Bluefield (APP)	R	.316	39	133	16	42	11	1	2	16	12	14	1	1	.372	.459
	Frederick (CAR)	HiA	.238	6	21	5	5	3	0	0	3	1	4	0	0	.273	.381
2011	Delmarva (SAL)	LoA	.316	51	212	45	67	12	3	8	34	20	32	6	4	.376	.514
	Frederick (CAR)	HiA	.271	77	299	37	81	12	2	5	37	22	44	6	3	.329	.375
2012	Bowie (EL)	AA	.245	124	485	68	119	24	1	14	56	50	103	5	3	.324	.386
Minor League Totals			.266	382	1457	210	388	73	10	32	197	136	243	29	14	.336	.396

4 NICK DELMONICO, 1B/2B

Born: July 12, 1992. **B-T:** L-R. **Ht.:** 6-2. **Wt.:** 196. **Drafted:** HS—Knoxville, Tenn., 2011 (6th round). **Signed by:** Adrian Dorsey.

As the son of former college coach Rod and brother of former Dodgers farmhand Tony, Nick grew up around the game. A disappointing high school senior season (caused in part by back problems) dropped him to the sixth round of the 2011 draft, though he signed for $1.525 million. Named MVP of the low Class A South Atlantic League all-star game in June, he suffered a slight tear in his left knee a week later that sidelined him for the balance of the 2012 season. Delmonico looks the part with a big, strong frame. His baseball IQ is evident with his advanced approach and feel for hitting. He recognizes breaking pitches and works counts. He gets good loft and projects to have average power, though there's some length to his swing. Delmonico's bat will be his carrying tool, as his future position is in question. He played 57 games at first base and 31 at second in his pro debut, though he might fit best at third. He doesn't have the hands and feet to turn the double play, but he should have enough first-step quickness for the hot corner. He's a below-average runner with a solid arm. Though his development has been slowed by injuries, Delmonico is advanced enough to handle a high Class A assignment in 2013. His ceiling is a first-division corner infielder.

BA GRADE
50
HIGH

Year	Club (League)	Class	AVG	G	AB	R	H	2B	3B	HR	RBI	BB	SO	SB	CS	OBP	SLG
2012	Delmarva (SAL)	LoA	.249	95	338	49	84	22	0	11	54	47	73	8	1	.351	.411
Minor League Totals			.249	95	338	49	84	22	0	11	54	47	73	8	1	.351	.411

5 EDUARDO RODRIGUEZ, LHP

Born: April 7, 1993. **B-T:** L-L. **Ht.:** 6-2. **Wt.:** 175. **Signed:** Venezuela, 2010. **Signed by:** Calvin Maduro.

Signed for $175,000 out of Venezuela, Rodriguez was one of few international splashes made by the Andy MacPhail regime. After making his U.S. debut in 2011, Rodriguez was Baltimore's most improved prospect in 2012. He more than held his own as a 19-year-old in low Class A while doubling his innings total. Previously known as a command-and-feel lefty with a funky delivery, Rodriguez has developed into a different animal as he continues growing into his lanky frame. His tailing fastball now sits at 90-94 mph, and the ball comes out of his hand well. His secondary pitches are inconsistent but have shown improvement. Both his 80-84 mph slider and 82-84 mph changeup flash plus potential, with the slider more advanced at this stage. He'll have at least average command. The Orioles have helped Rodriguez overhaul his delivery and get more on line toward the plate without robbing him of deception. He has benefited from committing to a consistent between-starts routine. With Bundy and Gausman possibly graduating to the big leagues in 2013, Rodriguez could rank as the organization's top pitching prospect a year from now. He likely will open the season in high Class A. He profiles as a mid-rotation starter, though some suggest he has an even higher ceiling.

BA GRADE
50
HIGH

Year	Club (League)	Class	W	L	ERA	G	GS	CG	SV	IP	H	HR	BB	SO	K/9	WHIP	AVG
2010	Orioles1 (DSL)	R	3	4	2.33	12	12	1	0	66	49	0	28	62	8.5	1.17	.213
2011	Orioles (GCL)	R	1	1	1.81	11	10	0	1	45	28	0	17	46	9.3	1.01	.177
	Aberdeen (NYP)	SS	0	0	6.75	1	1	0	0	4	6	1	1	4	9.0	1.75	.333
2012	Delmarva (SAL)	LoA	5	7	3.70	22	22	1	0	107	103	4	30	73	6.1	1.24	.251
Minor League Totals			9	12	2.97	46	45	2	1	221	186	5	76	185	7.5	1.18	.228

6 L.J. HOES, OF

Born: March 5, 1990. **B-T:** R-R. **Ht.:** 6-0. **Wt.:** 190. **Drafted:** HS—Washington D.C., 2008 (3rd round). **Signed by:** Dean Albany.

Hoes has been on Baltimore's radar since 2007, when he played on the organization's Youse's Orioles scout team in the Cal Ripken Collegiate League as a rising high school senior. Signed the next year as a third-round pick, he tried to make it as an infielder but didn't get his bat going until becoming a full-time outfielder in early 2011. He was the organization's minor league hitter of the year in 2012, when he became the first native Maryland position player to play for the big league club since Cal Ripken Jr. The organization's best pure hitter, Hoes batted .300 in Triple-A as one of the International League's youngest regulars. He has tremendous bat-to-ball skills and laces line drives to all fields. His plate discipline results in high on-base percentages, though the Orioles still are waiting for his power. Hoes is an above-average runner under way, though he doesn't get out of the box well and is working to improve his reads as a basestealer. He's a gliding

BA GRADE
45
LOW

outfielder who can play center field but fits best on a corner. He has a solid arm. If Hoes develops solid power, he could be an everyday left fielder. After a trip to the Arizona Fall League, he'll get a chance to win a big league job out of spring training.

Year	Club (League)	Class	AVG	G	AB	R	H	2B	3B	HR	RBI	BB	SO	SB	CS	OBP	SLG
2008	Orioles (GCL)	R	.308	48	159	36	49	4	3	1	18	30	22	10	0	.416	.390
2009	Delmarva (SAL)	LoA	.260	119	431	42	112	19	0	2	47	23	80	20	5	.299	.318
2010	Aberdeen (NYP)	SS	.464	8	28	8	13	5	1	1	5	2	1	1	1	.531	.821
	Bowie (EL)	AA	.222	3	9	1	2	0	0	0	1	0	1	0	0	.222	.222
	Frederick (CAR)	HiA	.278	97	353	52	98	19	2	3	44	53	70	10	8	.375	.368
2011	Frederick (CAR)	HiA	.241	41	158	23	38	7	0	3	17	10	25	4	2	.297	.342
	Bowie (EL)	AA	.305	95	344	47	105	17	1	6	54	43	56	16	7	.379	.413
2012	Bowie (EL)	AA	.265	51	196	25	52	9	3	2	16	31	33	12	5	.368	.372
	Norfolk (IL)	AAA	.300	82	317	54	95	14	4	3	38	34	43	8	7	.374	.397
	Baltimore (AL)	MAJ	.000	2	1	0	0	0	0	0	0	0	0	0	0	.000	.000
Major League Totals			.000	2	1	0	0	0	0	0	0	0	0	0	0	.000	.000
Minor League Totals			.283	544	1995	288	564	94	14	21	240	226	331	81	35	.358	.375

7 XAVIER AVERY, OF

Born: Jan 1, 1990. **B-T:** L-L. **Ht.:** 6-0. **Wt.:** 190. **Drafted:** HS—Ellenwood, Ga., 2008 (2nd round). **Signed by:** Dave Jennings.

Avery was slated to play running back at Georgia until the Orioles signed him for $900,000 as a second-round pick in 2008. Though raw, he reached the majors in his fourth full pro season, with three stints with Baltimore after first getting the call in early May. Consistently rated as the system's top athlete, Avery is still figuring things out at the plate. He has strong hands and good bat speed, though his power is below-average. He doesn't recognize pitches well, gets overly aggressive and chases pitches out of the strike zone. Some scouts wonder if he understands the type of hitter he should be, which is a top-of-the-order catalyst who gets on base. Avery is a plus-plus runner who's still learning the nuances of basestealing after getting caught 10 times in 38 tries in 2012. His speed translates to the outfield, where he's a solid defender in center with a fringy arm. Depending on Avery's ability to make adjustments, he could be an everyday center fielder, though Adam Jones is signed through 2018. He may work better as a quality fourth outfielder, though his bat must improve for him to serve in that role. Though he'll be in big league camp, Avery would benefit from additional development time at Triple-A Norfolk.

BA GRADE
45
MEDIUM

Year	Club (League)	Class	AVG	G	AB	R	H	2B	3B	HR	RBI	BB	SO	SB	CS	OBP	SLG
2008	Orioles (GCL)	R	.280	47	175	27	49	8	1	0	7	10	51	13	3	.333	.337
2009	Delmarva (SAL)	LoA	.262	129	473	55	124	15	8	2	36	27	111	30	10	.306	.340
2010	Frederick (CAR)	HiA	.280	109	447	73	125	25	6	4	48	42	96	28	14	.349	.389
	Bowie (EL)	AA	.234	27	107	10	25	6	0	3	18	7	34	10	0	.288	.374
2011	Bowie (EL)	AA	.259	138	557	72	144	31	2	4	26	49	156	36	14	.324	.343
2012	Norfolk (IL)	AAA	.236	102	390	57	92	13	5	8	34	51	106	22	7	.330	.356
	Baltimore (AL)	MAJ	.223	32	94	14	21	6	1	1	6	11	23	6	3	.305	.340
Major League Totals			.223	32	94	14	21	6	1	1	6	11	23	6	3	.305	.340
Minor League Totals			.260	552	2149	294	559	98	22	21	169	186	554	139	48	.325	.356

8 MIKE WRIGHT, RHP

Born: Jan. 3, 1990. **B-T:** R-R. **Ht.:** 6-5. **Wt.:** 195. **Drafted:** East Carolina, 2011 (3rd round). **Signed by:** Chris Gale.

Liking Wright more than the industry consensus in 2011, the Orioles drafted him in the third round. He impressed in his first spring training, striking out Mark Teixeira and two other Yankees in two innings to get on the fast track, and he reached Double-A in his first full season. He missed six weeks with a hamstring injury but made up for lost time in the Arizona Fall League. Wright doesn't have a true out pitch, but he gets good leverage out of his durable pitcher's frame, keeping the ball down and generating groundouts. His fastball operates from 89-95 mph and mostly sits at 92-93 with hard sink. His slider is inconsistent but flashes plus potential, and his changeup continues progressing. Wright threw a curveball in college, and Baltimore reintroduced it last year to give him a fourth pitch. Like most pitchers, he runs into trouble when he leaves the ball up and out over the plate. He's highly competitive. Given Wright's combination of size and stuff, Baltimore will leave him in the rotation and see if he can reach his No. 3 starter upside. Scouts outside the organization suggest he might fit best as a late-inning reliever, perhaps in a set-up role. He'll open 2013 in Triple-A.

BA GRADE
50
HIGH

Year	Club (League)	Class	W	L	ERA	G	GS	CG	SV	IP	H	HR	BB	SO	K/9	WHIP	AVG
2011	Orioles (GCL)	R	0	0	0.00	1	0	0	0	1	0	0	0	1	9.0	0.00	.000

Club (League)	Class	W	L	ERA	G	GS	CG	SV	IP	H	HR	BB	SO	K/9	WHIP	AVG
Aberdeen (NYP)	SS	2	1	3.77	7	7	0	0	31	29	3	6	29	8.4	1.13	.248
Delmarva (SAL)	LoA	1	1	10.54	4	1	0	0	14	21	3	4	12	7.9	1.83	.356
2012 Frederick (CAR)	HiA	5	2	2.91	8	8	0	0	46	47	3	5	35	6.8	1.12	.266
Bowie (EL)	AA	5	3	4.91	12	12	0	0	62	71	7	17	45	6.5	1.41	.289
Minor League Totals		13	7	4.55	32	28	0	0	154	168	16	32	122	7.1	1.30	.279

9 BRANDEN KLINE, RHP

Born: Sept. 29, 1991. **B-T:** R-R. **Ht.:** 6-3. **Wt.:** 195. **Drafted:** Virginia, 2012 (2nd round). **Signed by:** Chris Gale.

The Orioles have plenty of history with Kline, who grew up in Frederick, Md., the site of their high Class A affiliate. They liked him out of high school in 2009 but knew he was strongly committed to Virginia, as the Red Sox learned when they took him in the sixth round. Despite his inconsistent college career, they took him in the second round last June and signed him for $793,700. Kline's fastball sits at 92-95 mph, though it's a little straight. He threw a downer curveball in high school, but he ditched it in college in favor of an 81-84 mph slider that flashes plus potential. Baltimore likely will stick with the slider, but could bring back the curve as well. His low-80s changeup is a work in progress. Kline has a live, explosive body with long limbs. The Orioles have worked to add athleticism back into his delivery, which was removed in favor of Virginia's formulaic motion, in which pitchers start from a squat and stay low throughout. There never has been any question about his clean, quick arm action. Baltimore lauds his aptitude and intelligence. Some scouts see Kline as a mid-rotation starter, while others think he's destined for the bullpen. The Orioles like his chances of staying in the rotation and will send him to one of their Class A affiliates.

BA GRADE

50 HIGH

Year	Club (League)	Class	W	L	ERA	G	GS	CG	SV	IP	H	HR	BB	SO	K/9	WHIP	AVG
2012	Aberdeen (NYP)	SS	0	0	4.50	4	4	0	0	12	12	1	4	12	9.0	1.33	.273
	Minor League Totals		0	0	4.50	4	4	0	0	12	12	1	4	12	9.0	1.33	.273

10 ADRIAN MARIN, SS

Born: March 8, 1994. **B-T:** R-R. **Ht.:** 6-0. **Wt.:** 165. **Drafted:** HS—Miami, 2012 (3rd round). **Signed by:** Juan Alvarez.

The Orioles went to the South Florida well again to find a middle infielder, taking Marin in the third round of the 2012 draft and signing him for $481,100 just two years after selecting Manny Machado. Marin doesn't have Machado's upside, but scouts are impressed with his maturity and instincts. He was far and away the best player on Baltimore's Rookie-level Gulf Coast League club and spent the last week of the season in low Class A. A quick-twitch athlete, Marin has good actions, hands and feet, which should allow him to remain at shortstop. He has a solid arm and plus speed. Amateur scouts wondered about the impact of his bat because he doesn't have ideal hitting mechanics, starting in an upright stance and not utilizing his lower half. While he has below-average power, he smoked a triple against Rangers supplemental first-rounder Joey Gallo, who can throw in the mid-90s, in a spring showdown. Marin does handle the bat well, with quick hands and good bat speed. Like many young hitters, he's still learning to recognize pitches. He'll return to Delmarva for his first full pro season. With J.J Hardy and Machado in Baltimore and Jonathan Schoop in Double-A, the Orioles have no need to rush Marin.

BA GRADE

50 HIGH

Year	Club (League)	Class	AVG	G	AB	R	H	2B	3B	HR	RBI	BB	SO	SB	CS	OBP	SLG
2012	Orioles (GCL)	R	.287	47	178	24	51	7	3	0	13	11	34	6	1	.339	.360
	Delmarva (SAL)	LoA	.286	6	21	5	6	0	0	0	2	1	2	2	0	.348	.286
	Minor League Totals		.286	53	199	29	57	7	3	0	15	12	36	8	1	.340	.352

11 TIM BERRY, LHP

BA GRADE

50 HIGH

Born: March 18, 1991. **B-T:** L-L. **Ht.:** 6-3. **Wt.:** 180. **Drafted:** HS—San Marcos, Calif., 2009 (50th round). **Signed by:** Mark Ralston.

Berry put himself on the draft radar after he threw a 17-strikeout no-hitter as a prep senior in 2009, but he injured his elbow later that spring and required Tommy John surgery. The Orioles took a flier on Berry in the 50th round anyway and signed him away from an Oregon commitment for $125,000, and he hasn't had any setbacks since the surgery. He spent the early portion of last year repeating low Class A but earned two promotions and finished the season with a start in Double-A. Berry has a live, loose arm that delivers 90-94 mph fastballs, and some scouts think there could be more velocity to come as he continues adding strength to his skinny frame. He can spin the ball well and flashes plus curveballs in warmups but struggles with consistency during games. He has feel for a solid changeup that he throws with good arm speed. Berry needs to work on keeping the ball down in the strike zone. His command and control waver, and they ultimately will determine his future role. As his coordination has improved, so too has his delivery. Berry's three-pitch mix gives him a ceiling of a No. 3 starter, though he could end up in the bullpen. He'll return to Bowie in 2013.

Year	Club (League)	Class	W	L	ERA	G	GS	CG	SV	IP	H	HR	BB	SO	K/9	WHIP	AVG
2010	Orioles (GCL)	R	0	1	1.35	14	0	0	0	20	13	0	14	23	10.4	1.35	.181
2011	Delmarva (SAL)	LoA	3	7	5.17	26	26	0	0	117	107	11	61	96	7.4	1.44	.251
2012	Delmarva (SAL)	LoA	2	7	5.02	10	10	0	0	52	60	3	17	44	7.6	1.48	.282
	Frederick (CAR)	HiA	5	5	4.32	15	13	0	0	75	83	6	20	61	7.3	1.37	.285
	Bowie (EL)	AA	0	1	37.80	1	1	0	0	2	7	0	2	4	21.6	5.40	.583
Minor League Totals			10	21	4.82	66	50	0	0	265	270	20	114	228	7.7	1.45	.266

12 CHRISTIAN WALKER, 1B

Born: March 28, 1991. **B-T:** R-R. **Ht.:** 6-0. **Wt.:** 220. **Drafted:** South Carolina, 2012 (4th round). **Signed by:** Chris Gale.

Walker blasted 19 home runs to win the 2009 high school home run derby that is better known for sparking the Bryce Harper hoopla. Walker generated draft buzz that spring but turned down the Dodgers as a 49th-rounder to attend South Carolina. A key offensive contributor on Gamecocks teams that won national titles in 2010 and 2011 and finished runner-up in 2012, he tied Dustin Ackley's College World Series career hits record with 28 before signing with the Orioles for $349,900. He understands his fundamentally strong swing that features good hip rotation. He has uncanny bat-to-ball skills and a patient approach, which make him a tough out. Most scouts believe he has average game power, though Baltimore believes he has plus raw pop and the savvy to tap into it. Walker is limited to first base defensively and his bat will carry him as far as he goes. He moves well enough around the bag and has a below-average arm. Because of the offensive demands on first basemen, Walker is tough to profile, though several scouts say they won't be surprised if he outperforms expectations. He had drawn comparisons to Kevin Millar and Steve Pearce. Walker performed well in his pro debut at short-season Aberdeen, but he was limited with a lower-back injury during instructional league. He should open his first full pro season in low Class A, with the chance to earn a quick promotion.

Year	Club (League)	Class	AVG	G	AB	R	H	2B	3B	HR	RBI	BB	SO	SB	CS	OBP	SLG
2012	Aberdeen (NYP)	SS	.284	22	81	12	23	5	0	2	9	10	14	2	1	.376	.420
Minor League Totals			.284	22	81	12	23	5	0	2	9	10	14	2	1	.376	.420

13 HENRY URRUTIA, OF

Born: Feb. 13, 1987. **B-T:** B-R. **Ht.:** 6-3. **Wt.:** 180. **Signed:** Cuba, 2012. **Signed by:** Fred Ferreira.

The son of former Cuban national team outfielder Ermidelio Urrutia, Henry signed with the Orioles in July for a bonus of $778,500. He played for Cuba in the 2009 World Baseball Classic, then hit .397/.461/.597 during Cuba's Serie Nacional 2009-10 season. He was suspended for the 2010-11 season after an unsuccessful defection attempt, and he didn't play in any minor league or instructional league games in 2012 because he was dealing with visa issues. Urrutia is physically mature and doesn't offer much projection. He's a switch-hitting outfielder who should hit for a solid average with average power. He makes consistent line-drive contact from both sides but has a better swing plane from the left. An average runner with a strong arm, Urrutia fits best defensively in right field but may not have the prototypical pop for the position. Assuming he gets his visa, he'll open the 2013 season in Double-A. Baltimore believes he won't need much time in the minors.

Year	Club (League)	Class	AVG	G	AB	R	H	2B	3B	HR	RBI	BB	SO	SB	CS	OBP	SLG
Did Not Play																	

14 GLYNN DAVIS, OF

Born: Dec. 7, 1991. **B-T:** R-R. **Ht.:** 6-3. **Wt.:** 170. **Signed:** CC of Baltimore County-Catonsville (Md.), NDFA 2010. **Signed by:** Dean Albany/Chris Gale.

Though Davis went undrafted as a junior college sophomore in 2010, the Orioles had followed him throughout the spring. They continued watching him closely in the summer collegiate Cal Ripken League, where he was the circuit's No. 1 prospect playing for Youse's Orioles, which serves as a scout team for Baltimore. Since signing for $120,000 as a nondrafted free agent, Davis has been the system's fastest runner. His speed rates at the top of the scouting scale, and he led Baltimore farmhands with 37 steals in 47 tries last season. His quickness also helps him patrol center field, where he rates as an above-average defender despite spending his amateur career at shortstop. He has an average arm. Davis has a long, lanky body and the Orioles are waiting for his strength to develop, though they're wary of him bulking up and slowing down. He has a compact swing and good bat speed, though he is a singles hitter and power never will be part of his game. Baltimore has worked with him to use the whole field and keep the ball out of the air. He does have the patience to draw walks, and if his bat improves, he could be a tablesetter at the top of a lineup rather than a fourth outfielder. Davis receives Peter Bourjos comparisons for his overall package. He'll head back to high Class A to begin 2013.

Year	Club (League)	Class	AVG	G	AB	R	H	2B	3B	HR	RBI	BB	SO	SB	CS	OBP	SLG
2011	Orioles (GCL)	R	.435	6	23	4	10	2	0	1	2	4	3	1	1	.519	.652
	Aberdeen (NYP)	SS	.271	62	255	34	69	14	0	1	14	25	53	23	9	.337	.337
	Frederick (CAR)	HiA	.250	1	4	0	1	0	0	0	0	0	1	0	0	.250	.250
2012	Delmarva (SAL)	LoA	.252	101	397	53	100	16	2	0	25	51	91	29	9	.342	.302
	Frederick (CAR)	HiA	.256	22	82	11	21	1	1	0	4	12	25	8	1	.358	.293
Minor League Totals			.264	192	761	102	201	33	3	2	45	92	173	61	20	.347	.323

15 TORSTEN BOSS, 3B

BA GRADE
50
HIGH

Born: Dec. 27, 1990. **B-T:** L-R. **Ht.:** 6-0. **Wt.:** 190. **Drafted:** Michigan State, 2012 (8th round). **Signed by:** Bob Szymkowski.

When the Orioles took Boss in the eighth round in June, he became the highest-drafted player from Michigan State since 2002. Widely considered one of the best college hitters in the Midwest, he quickly signed for $139,500. Boss has a sweet lefthanded swing with solid bat speed, though it can get long on occasion. He has a good approach and works counts. He impressed scouts by homering off Texas A&M ace Michael Wacha (who would become a Cardinals first-round pick) early in the spring, but Boss may not have more than fringy to average power. He has solid speed and a strong arm, but scouts question whether he has a true defensive home. He spent most of his time at Michigan State and much of his pro debut at third base, though his pop doesn't profile well there. He also played second base as a collegian and pro and got some outfield time with the Spartans, but he doesn't have soft hands or smooth actions. Boss doesn't have any standout tools, but he also doesn't have any glaring weaknesses. Baltimore will continue to develop him as a third baseman, though he could wind up as a utilityman. He'll likely begin his first full pro season in low Class A.

Year	Club (League)	Class	AVG	G	AB	R	H	2B	3B	HR	RBI	BB	SO	SB	CS	OBP	SLG
2012	Frederick (CAR)	HiA	.143	2	7	1	1	0	0	0	0	0	2	0	0	.250	.143
	Aberdeen (NYP)	SS	.257	65	237	33	61	14	4	5	27	30	53	9	3	.360	.414
Minor League Totals			.254	67	244	34	62	14	4	5	27	30	55	9	3	.357	.406

16 STEVE JOHNSON, RHP

BA GRADE
40
LOW

Born: Aug. 31, 1987. **B-T:** R-R. **Ht.:** 6-1. **Wt.:** 220. **Drafted:** HS—Brooklandville, Md., 2005 (13th round). **Signed by:** Clair Rierson (Dodgers).

The son of former Orioles pitcher and current Baltimore broadcaster Dave Johnson, Steve made a long journey to realize his childhood dream of pitching in the big leagues for his hometown team. A Dodgers 13th-round pick out of a Baltimore-area high school in 2005, he first came to the Orioles with Josh Bell in a July 2009 trade for George Sherrill. That offseason, Johnson was left off Baltimore's 40-man roster and went to the Giants in the 2010 major league Rule 5 draft. San Francisco elected not to keep him and returned him to the Orioles for the 2011 season, after which he re-signed with Baltimore as a minor league free agent. He finally got summoned to Camden Yards last July, and he pitched well enough to earn a spot on the roster for the Orioles' American League Wild-Card Game. Johnson doesn't have loud stuff, instead thriving on feel and competitiveness. He has four fringy to average pitches in his 87-90 mph fastball, a 77-78 mph slider with bite, a get-me-over curveball and a changeup. He fits at the back of a rotation or in middle relief, and the Orioles like his versatility. He'll help the big league club in some capacity this season.

Year	Club (League)	Class	W	L	ERA	G	GS	CG	SV	IP	H	HR	BB	SO	K/9	WHIP	AVG
2005	Dodgers (GCL)	R	0	2	9.53	6	3	0	0	11	18	1	4	14	11.1	1.94	.360
2006	Jacksonville (SL)	AA	0	0	0.00	2	0	0	0	5	2	0	2	3	5.8	0.86	.133
	Ogden (PIO)	R	5	5	3.89	14	14	0	0	79	79	4	25	86	9.8	1.32	.267
2007	Great Lakes (MWL)	LoA	3	6	4.85	18	16	0	0	82	90	2	40	65	7.2	1.59	.280
2008	Great Lakes (MWL)	LoA	9	2	2.34	13	13	0	0	73	59	4	25	57	7.0	1.15	.223
	Inland Empire (CAL)	HiA	3	6	7.10	11	11	0	0	52	68	9	21	55	9.5	1.71	.318
2009	Inland Empire (CAL)	HiA	4	4	3.82	18	16	0	1	97	94	14	42	102	9.5	1.41	.260
	Chattanooga (SL)	AA	1	1	1.69	2	2	0	0	11	8	1	3	15	12.7	1.03	.205
	Bowie (EL)	AA	3	2	2.84	7	7	0	0	38	24	3	17	37	8.8	1.08	.179
2010	Bowie (EL)	AA	7	8	5.09	28	28	0	0	145	144	24	78	128	7.9	1.53	.259
2011	Bowie (EL)	AA	5	1	2.16	10	10	0	0	58	40	7	15	59	9.1	0.94	.194
	Norfolk (IL)	AAA	2	7	5.56	17	17	0	0	87	101	7	47	63	6.5	1.69	.294
2012	Norfolk (IL)	AAA	4	8	2.86	19	14	1	0	91	66	7	31	86	8.5	1.06	.202
	Baltimore (AL)	MAJ	4	0	2.11	12	4	0	0	38	23	4	18	46	10.8	1.07	.174
Major League Totals			4	0	2.11	12	4	0	0	38	23	4	18	46	10.8	1.07	.174
Minor League Totals			50	52	4.17	165	151	1	1	829	793	83	350	770	8.4	1.38	.253

17 CLAY SCHRADER, RHP

BA GRADE
45
MEDIUM

Born: April 28, 1990. **B-T:** L-R. **Ht.:** 5-11. **Wt.:** 200. **Drafted:** San Jacinto (Texas) JC, 2010, (10th round). **Signed by:** Rich Morales.

After transferring from Texas-San Antonio, where he had middling success as a two-way player, Schrader helped San Jacinto (Texas) to the Junior College World Series in 2010. The Orioles drafted him and signed him away from an Oklahoma commitment for $300,000. Schrader attracts attention for two plus pitches and turns heads for his aggressively violent delivery. He's strictly a bullpen arm, but he gets outs and has averaged 12.2 strikeouts per nine innings as a pro. His lively fastball sits at 91-95 mph and his 79-82 mph slider has hard bite. Schrader throws across his body, lands with a stiff front leg and has a recoiling arm action, which provide deception but raise red flags. He missed time at the end of 2011 with elbow tendinitis and tenderness. He struggles to throw consistent strikes, which will be a greater concern as he moves up the ladder. If he can develop better control and command, Schrader will profile as a set-up man and could move quickly. Otherwise he'll be a middle reliever. After a stint in the Arizona Fall League, he'll likely return to Double-A to open 2013.

Year	Club (League)	Class	W	L	ERA	G	GS	CG	SV	IP	H	HR	BB	SO	K/9	WHIP	AVG
2010	Aberdeen (NYP)	SS	1	0	0.00	7	0	0	1	8	4	0	4	10	11.3	1.00	.148
	Delmarva (SAL)	LoA	0	1	6.75	3	0	0	0	4	4	0	2	6	13.5	1.50	.250
2011	Delmarva (SAL)	LoA	1	1	2.05	12	0	0	2	22	11	1	13	38	15.5	1.09	.145
	Frederick (CAR)	HiA	1	1	1.13	15	0	0	3	24	8	1	19	35	13.1	1.13	.101
2012	Frederick (CAR)	HiA	1	1	1.29	23	0	0	4	35	20	0	27	51	13.1	1.34	.165
	Bowie (EL)	AA	1	0	2.74	19	0	0	1	23	15	1	24	17	6.7	1.70	.192
Minor League Totals			5	4	1.78	79	0	0	11	116	62	3	89	157	12.2	1.30	.156

18 DEVIN JONES, RHP

BA GRADE
50
HIGH

Born: July 4, 1990. **B-T:** R-R. **Ht.:** 6-2. **Wt.:** 170. **Drafted:** Mississippi State, 2011 (9th round). **Signed by:** Dave Jennings.

Used mostly as a reliever at Mississippi State, Jones stayed in the bullpen at the outset of his pro career after signing for $97,500 as a ninth-rounder in 2011. Shifted into the rotation following a promotion to high Class A last July, he responded by going 7-1, 2.80, albeit with a greatly reduced strikeout rate (4.8 per nine innings). When he starts, Jones' fastball sits at 90-94 mph with sinking action that generates a lot of groundouts. As a reliever, he can reach 96 mph. His second pitch is an 82-84 mph slider that's a solid offering at times, though he doesn't always command it well. He has worked with the Orioles' player-development staff to add a changeup, which will go a long way toward determining his future role. Jones' sound delivery allows him to work downhill and live in the bottom of the strike zone. His competitiveness and aptitude also draw praise. He reminds some scouts of former Baltimore reliever Rick Bauer, though the club hopes Jones can become a No. 3 or 4 starter. He'll open 2013 in Double-A.

Year	Club (League)	Class	W	L	ERA	G	GS	CG	SV	IP	H	HR	BB	SO	K/9	WHIP	AVG
2011	Aberdeen (NYP)	SS	2	4	6.08	14	0	0	2	24	29	2	13	21	8.0	1.77	.290
2012	Delmarva (SAL)	LoA	1	6	2.65	19	0	0	3	54	49	1	11	51	8.4	1.10	.241
	Frederick (CAR)	HiA	7	1	2.80	9	9	2	0	55	53	5	12	29	4.8	1.19	.255
Minor League Totals			10	11	3.32	42	9	2	5	133	131	8	36	101	6.9	1.26	.256

19 JOSH HADER, LHP

BA GRADE
45
HIGH

Born: April 7, 1994. **B-T:** L-L. **Ht.:** 6-3. **Wt.:** 160. **Drafted:** HS—Millersville, Md., 2012 (19th round). **Signed by:** Dean Albany.

Hader didn't generate much draft hype in the spring of 2012 as a lanky lefthander who threw 84-87 mph. But Orioles scout Dean Albany kept close tabs on him and saw him pitch a 13-strikeout complete game in May, prompting the team to select him in the 19th round. Shortly after the draft, Hader struck out three in two innings of the Brooks Robinson all-star game—a Maryland high school showcase at Camden Yards—in front of general manager Dan Duquette and manager Buck Showalter. The next day, Baltimore signed Hader away from an Anne Arundel (Md.) CC commitment for $40,000. His velocity soared as Baltimore's development staff helped him gain weight, straighten out his delivery and get on a long-toss program. Hader's fastball now ranges from 89-94 mph, and he starred in his pro debut and during instructional league. Long and loose, he creates deception from a low three-quarters delivery. His secondary stuff is a work in progress, but he has the makings of a plus changeup and an average slider. He also has a slurvy curveball and throws strikes with all his pitches. For his body type and delivery, he draws comparisons to Chris Sale. Hader's first full pro season should start in low Class A Delmarva. If he lives up to his potential, he could blossom into a No. 3 starter.

Year	Club (League)	Class	W	L	ERA	G	GS	CG	SV	IP	H	HR	BB	SO	K/9	WHIP	AVG
2012	Orioles (GCL)	R	2	0	2.66	12	0	0	2	20	12	2	7	35	15.5	0.93	.174
	Aberdeen (NYP)	SS	0	0	0.00	5	0	0	0	8	2	0	2	13	14.0	0.48	.074
Minor League Totals			2	0	1.88	17	0	0	2	29	14	2	9	48	15.1	0.80	.146

20 ZACH DAVIES, RHP

BA GRADE

45

HIGH

Born: Feb. **7, 1993. B-T:** R-R. **Ht.:** 6-0. **Wt.:** 150. **Drafted:** HS—Chandler, Ariz., 2011 (26th round). **Signed by:** John Gillette.

As an undersized righty with a strong commitment to Arizona State, Davies was overlooked coming out of high school in suburban Phoenix. The Orioles took a chance on him in the 26th round of the 2011 draft and signed him for $575,000. Aggressively assigned to low Class A for his 2012 pro debut, he more than held his own as one of the South Atlantic League's youngest pitchers. Davies doesn't overwhelm with his stuff, but he does just enough for scouts to buy into his package. Some see him as another Mike Leake because he's athletic with a four-pitch mix and has feel for his craft and a competitive edge. Only 6 feet tall, Davies has a slight frame with room to fill out, though he needs to work to create plane for his pitches. He has a simple, repeatable delivery and a quick arm action that allows his fastball to operate at 88-91 mph. Davies' secondary stuff is improving. He has a 73-75 mph curveball with good 12-to-6 shape and depth, but he struggles to throw it for strikes. His fading changeup could be an average offering, and he also has a slider that he rarely uses. Davies has No. 4 starter upside, but he's a long way from reaching it. He'll make the jump to high Class A at age 20.

Year	Club (League)	Class	W	L	ERA	G	GS	CG	SV	IP	H	HR	BB	SO	K/9	WHIP	AVG
2012	Delmarva (SAL)	LoA	5	7	3.86	25	17	0	1	114	109	11	46	91	7.2	1.36	.255
Minor League Totals			5	7	3.86	25	17	0	1	114	109	11	46	91	7.2	1.36	.255

21 TSUYOSHI WADA, LHP

BA GRADE

45

HIGH

Born: Feb. 21, 1981. **B-T:** L-L. **Ht.:** 5-11. **Wt.:** 180. **Signed:** Japan, 2011. **Signed by:** Brett Ward.

Baltimore landed a pair of lefty pitchers from the Japanese majors last winter in Wada and Wei-Yin Chen, who had very different 2012 seasons. Chen was the only Oriole to make 30 starts, while Wada hurt his elbow in spring training after signing a two-year, $8.14 million contract. He made a single rehab appearance in Triple-A before ligament damage requiring Tommy John surgery was discovered. In nine seasons in Japan, Wada went 107-61, 3.41 in 207 starts with the Fukuoka SoftBank Hawks. He also pitched in the 2004 and 2008 Olympics. When he's healthy, his fastball sits at 84-87 mph with sink. His changeup is his best secondary offering, and he also throws a below-average slider. With fringy stuff, Wada survives on feel and deception provided by a quirky drop-and-drive delivery. Because he'll be 32 when the 2013 season starts, it's hard to predict how Wada will bounce back from the surgery, specifically in terms of regaining the pitchability he thrived on. He could fit as a back-of-the-rotation starter, or as a multi-inning reliever in a Troy Patton-like role.

Year	Club (League)	Class	W	L	ERA	G	GS	CG	SV	IP	H	HR	BB	SO	K/9	WHIP	AVG
2003	Daiei (PL)	JPN	14	5	3.38	26	18	8	0	189	165	26	61	195	9.3	1.20	—
2004	Daiei (PL)	JPN	10	6	4.35	19	11	7	0	128	110	23	38	115	8.1	1.15	—
2005	SoftBank (PL)	JPN	12	8	3.27	25	0	4	0	182	154	17	57	167	8.3	1.16	—
2006	SoftBank (PL)	JPN	14	6	2.98	24	18	6	0	163	137	18	42	136	7.5	1.10	—
2007	SoftBank (PL)	JPN	12	10	2.82	26	0	2	0	182	168	15	42	169	8.4	1.15	—
2008	SoftBank (PL)	JPN	8	8	3.61	23	23	3	0	162	167	12	36	123	6.8	1.25	—
2009	SoftBank (PL)	JPN	4	5	4.06	15	0	1	0	84	72	13	24	87	9.3	1.14	—
2010	SoftBank (PL)	JPN	17	8	3.14	26	0	1	0	169	145	11	55	169	9.0	1.18	—
2011	SoftBank (PL)	JPN	16	5	1.51	26	—	4	0	185	145	7	40	168	8.2	1.00	—
2012	Norfolk (IL)	AAA	0	1	20.25	1	1	0	0	3	6	1	4	1	3.4	3.75	.429
Minor League Totals			0	1	20.25	1	1	0	0	3	6	1	4	1	3.4	3.75	.429
Japanese League Totals			107	61	3.13	210	70	36	0	1445	1263	142	395	1329	8.3	1.15	—

22 T.J. MCFARLAND, LHP

BA GRADE

40

MEDIUM

Born: June 8, 1989. **B-T:** L-L. **Ht.:** 6-3. **Wt.:** 220. **Drafted:** HS—Palos Heights, Ill., 2007 (4th round). **Signed by:** Mike Soper (Indians).

McFarland made steady progress in five years in the Indians system, reaching Triple-A and tying for the minor league lead with 16 wins in 2012. When Cleveland declined to protect him on its 40-man roster, the Orioles took him in the major league Rule 5 draft in December. He can't be sent to the minors in 2013 without being exposed to waivers and offered back to the Indians for half his $50,000 draft price, but he has a decent chance of winning a job on Baltimore's staff, perhaps even in the back of the rotation. McFarland relies on command and deception more that stuff. His best pitch is his average 77-81 mph slider, which he sets up by spotting his 87-90 mph fastball all over the strike zone. He also has a fringy changeup. The Orioles made their surprising 2012 playoff run in part because they found unlikely pitching help from a variety of sources, and McFarland could be another useful pickup. If he can't cut it as a starter, his slider could help him make it as a situational reliever.

Year	Club (League)	Class	W	L	ERA	G	GS	CG	SV	IP	H	HR	BB	SO	K/9	WHIP	AVG
2008	Indians (GCL)	R	3	4	5.07	12	10	0	0	55	70	3	15	38	6.2	1.55	.314
2009	Lake County (SAL)	LoA	9	4	3.58	25	23	0	1	121	128	6	42	85	6.3	1.41	.275

Year	Club (League)	Class	W	L	ERA	G	GS	CG	SV	IP	H	HR	BB	SO	K/9	WHIP	AVG
2010	Akron (EL)	AA	0	0	11.25	1	1	0	0	4	9	1	2	5	11.3	2.75	.429
	Kinston (CAR)	HiA	11	5	3.13	24	19	1	0	127	121	9	40	92	6.5	1.27	.246
2011	Kinston (CAR)	HiA	0	1	2.25	2	2	0	0	12	9	2	1	12	9.0	0.83	.191
	Akron (EL)	AA	9	9	3.87	25	25	2	0	137	140	9	50	103	6.8	1.38	.265
2012	Akron (EL)	AA	8	2	2.69	10	10	1	0	60	61	1	12	41	6.1	1.21	.272
	Columbus (IL)	AAA	8	6	4.82	17	17	1	0	103	112	9	33	55	4.8	1.41	.279
Minor League Totals			48	31	3.83	116	107	5	1	619	650	40	195	431	6.3	1.37	.271

23 PARKER BRIDWELL, RHP

BA GRADE
50
EXTREME

Born: Aug. 2, 1991. **B-T:** R-R. **Ht.:** 6-4. **Wt.:** 190. **Drafted:** HS—Hereford, Texas, 2010 (9th round). **Signed by:** Ernest Jacobs.

A three-sport high school star who drew interest from college football programs as a quarterback, Bridwell passed up a baseball commitment to Texas Tech for a chance to pursue his lifelong dream of playing professional baseball. The Orioles selected him in the ninth round in 2010 and signed him for an over-slot $625,000 bonus. He ranked No. 4 on this list a year ago before getting hit hard in low Class A for the second straight season. Despite his struggles, scouts still like Bridwell's long, loose frame and live arm. His fastball works anywhere from 87-94 mph with good sink, though his velocity dipped late in 2012 as his innings accumulated. His overhand curveball shows the most potential among his secondary pitches. He also throws a slider and changeup. Baltimore has worked with Bridwell to smooth out his delivery, though he has trouble repeating it, which leads to varying arm angles and wavering command. Given his lack of experience, the Orioles think Bridwell just needs time to develop. The raw material is there for a mid-rotation starter, but he's a long way from reaching his ceiling. He may see more time in Delmarva to open the 2013 season.

Year	Club (League)	Class	W	L	ERA	G	GS	CG	SV	IP	H	HR	BB	SO	K/9	WHIP	AVG
2010	Orioles (GCL)	R	0	0	5.40	2	2	0	0	2	1	0	3	4	21.6	2.40	.167
	Aberdeen (NYP)	SS	0	0	0.00	2	0	0	0	4	3	0	1	2	4.5	1.00	.214
2011	Aberdeen (NYP)	SS	2	5	4.53	12	11	0	0	54	56	2	22	57	9.6	1.45	.271
	Delmarva (SAL)	LoA	0	3	7.06	5	5	0	0	22	23	0	13	13	5.4	1.66	.271
2012	Delmarva (SAL)	LoA	5	9	5.98	23	22	1	0	114	122	15	63	71	5.6	1.62	.281
Minor League Totals			7	17	5.58	44	40	1	0	195	205	17	102	147	6.8	1.57	.275

24 MIKE BELFIORE, LHP

BA GRADE
45
HIGH

Born: Oct. 3, 1988. **B-T:** R-L. **Ht.:** 6-2. **Wt.:** 220. **Drafted:** Boston College, 2009 (1st round supplemental). **Signed by:** Matt Merullo (Diamondbacks).

Acquired as the player to be named in a trade that sent Josh Bell to the Diamondbacks, Belfiore joined the Orioles in May and immediately jumped to Double-A, where he turned in the best performance of his pro career. Arizona took him with the 45th overall pick in 2009, after the Boston College two-way star pitched 9 ⅔ innings of scoreless relief in an epic 25-inning NCAA regional game against Texas. The Diamondbacks signed him for $725,000 with the intention of developing him as a starter, but he never was effective or comfortable in that role. Belfiore has solid stuff across the board, and it plays up because he's deceptive and competitive. He dials up his fastball to 89-92 mph with running life, backing it up with a sweeping slider and changeup. His command comes and goes because he has a slight stab in the back of his arm action. Belfiore throws from a high three-quarters slot and gets in trouble when he doesn't keep the ball down. He's especially tough on lefthanders, who hit .160/.218/.200 in 50 at-bats against him in Double-A. At the very least, he should be a serviceable left-on-left specialist. If his command improves, Belfiore could help in Baltimore sooner rather than later. He figures to spend 2013 in Triple-A after getting added to the 40-man roster in November.

Year	Club (League)	Class	W	L	ERA	G	GS	CG	SV	IP	H	HR	BB	SO	K/9	WHIP	AVG
2009	Missoula (PIO)	R	2	2	2.17	14	11	0	0	58	59	2	13	55	8.5	1.24	.259
2010	South Bend (MWL)	LoA	3	10	3.99	25	25	0	0	126	139	6	42	105	7.5	1.43	.277
2011	Visalia (CAL)	HiA	4	4	5.92	35	8	0	0	79	86	17	57	79	9.0	1.81	.278
2012	Visalia (CAL)	HiA	0	0	2.37	12	0	0	1	19	13	2	5	28	13.3	0.95	.197
	Bowie (EL)	AA	5	1	2.85	28	0	0	2	47	43	2	21	50	9.5	1.35	.239
Minor League Totals			14	17	3.88	114	44	0	3	330	340	29	138	317	8.7	1.45	.265

25 LEX RUTLEDGE, LHP

BA GRADE
45
HIGH

Born: June 28, 1991. **B-T:** L-L. **Ht.:** 6-1. **Wt.:** 195. **Drafted:** Samford, 2012 (6th round). **Signed by:** Dave Jennings.

Rutledge spurned the Brewers to attend Samford when he was a 26th-round selection as a Mississippi prep product. He struggled with his command as a college starter, but thrived in the closer role as a freshman and junior, and he showed upper-90s velocity in two summers in the Cape Cod League. Impressed by his lefty arm strength, the Orioles snagged him in the sixth round in June and signed him for $196,200. Rutledge's velocity wavers, though he sat at 90-93 mph with cutting action as a starter in his pro debut. He has a straight overhand curveball that can be a plus pitch at times, and he's working to develop a changeup. Rutledge throws from an extreme overhand arm slot, which leads to command and control difficulties, and he might attain better feel by lowering it. He has an unorthodox delivery that Baltimore has worked to refine. If he can improve his changeup, delivery and overall feel for pitching, Rutledge could reach his ceiling as a mid-rotation starter. The Orioles will develop him in that role, though he might be best suited for the back of a bullpen. He'll make the jump to low Class A for his first full pro season.

Year	Club (League)	Class	W	L	ERA	G	GS	CG	SV	IP	H	HR	BB	SO	K/9	WHIP	AVG
2012	Orioles (GCL)	R	0	1	1.64	6	0	0	0	11	9	0	3	13	10.6	1.09	.220
	Aberdeen (NYP)	SS	0	3	9.49	6	6	0	0	12	16	1	13	12	8.8	2.35	.291
Minor League Totals			0	4	5.79	12	6	0	0	23	25	1	16	25	9.6	1.76	.260

26 TYLER WILSON, RHP

BA GRADE
40
MEDIUM

Born: Sept. 25, 1989. **B-T:** R-R. **Ht.:** 6-2. **Wt.:** 185. **Drafted:** Virginia, 2011 (10th round). **Signed by:** Chris Gale.

The Robin to 2011 No. 2 overall pick Danny Hultzen's Batman in Virginia's weekend rotation, Wilson went in the 10th round that June and received $20,000 as a senior sign. He won an award recognizing him as the outstanding senior student-athlete in NCAA Division I baseball. Wilson reached high Class A in his first full pro season while demonstrating the system's best command. With fringy stuff across the board, he doesn't have a high ceiling but succeeds with competitiveness and moxie. Wilson knows how to get outs by keeping the ball down. He works off a sinking, grounder-inducing 87-91 mph fastball that he maintains deep into games. He also throws an average slider and an inconsistent changeup. Baltimore overhauled Wilson's delivery throughout last season, and it's now clean and repeatable. He has earned an assignment to Double-A, where more advanced hitters will test him. Though he doesn't project as more than a No. 5 starter or middle reliever, his resolve may get him to the big leagues.

Year	Club (League)	Class	W	L	ERA	G	GS	CG	SV	IP	H	HR	BB	SO	K/9	WHIP	AVG
2011	Orioles (GCL)	R	0	0	0.00	2	2	0	0	3	0	0	1	3	9.0	0.33	.000
	Aberdeen (NYP)	SS	0	0	2.10	6	6	0	0	30	19	4	4	24	7.2	0.77	.176
2012	Delmarva (SAL)	LoA	3	3	5.06	6	6	0	0	32	30	4	11	29	8.2	1.28	.252
	Frederick (CAR)	HiA	7	7	3.49	19	19	0	0	111	95	12	19	114	9.2	1.03	.228
Minor League Totals			10	10	3.48	33	33	0	0	176	144	20	35	170	8.7	1.02	.221

27 BRENDEN WEBB, OF

BA GRADE
50
EXTREME

Born: Feb. 20, 1990. **B-T:** L-L. **Ht.:** 6-3. **Wt.:** 190. **Drafted:** Palomar (Calif.) JC, 2009 (30th round). **Signed by:** Mark Ralston.

Webb was committed to attend Southern California after spending the 2009 season at Palomar (Calif.) JC. The Orioles liked what they saw of him in the Northwoods League that summer, however, so they signed him for $250,000 after having taken a flier on him in the 30th round. He's a good athlete who flashes five-tool potential, which makes him one of the more exciting prospects in the system, though he's still raw. Scouts who get short looks at him come away comparing him to David Justice in face and frame. Webb is strong and has above-average raw power, but he doesn't reach it during games because he doesn't have much of an approach. He has a long, uppercut swing with a lot of pre-pitch movement that leaves him with a hole on the inner half. He struck out 138 times in 124 games across two levels last year, though he also walked 98 times. Webb is a stylish, gliding outfielder who can handle center field but might fit better on a corner with his solid speed and average arm. For all his upside, he won't be more than a fourth outfielder if he can't make more consistent contact. He'll return to high Class A to start the season after finishing 2012 there.

Year	Club (League)	Class	AVG	G	AB	R	H	2B	3B	HR	RBI	BB	SO	SB	CS	OBP	SLG
2009	Orioles (GCL)	R	.186	13	43	7	8	2	0	0	1	10	14	2	0	.352	.233
2010	Bluefield (APP)	R	.227	61	194	25	44	5	8	5	25	32	58	5	2	.348	.412
2011	Delmarva (SAL)	LoA	.218	121	400	42	87	14	1	4	29	75	152	14	8	.344	.288
2012	Delmarva (SAL)	LoA	.251	101	311	51	78	23	4	11	48	87	108	18	3	.422	.457
	Frederick (CAR)	HiA	.270	23	74	14	20	6	1	3	13	11	30	1	3	.382	.500
Minor League Totals			.232	319	1022	139	237	50	14	23	116	215	362	40	16	.373	.376

28 OLIVER DRAKE, RHP

BA GRADE
45
HIGH

Born: Jan. 13, 1987. **B-T:** R-R. **Ht.:** 6-4. **Wt.:** 215. **Drafted:** Navy, 2008 (43rd round). **Signed by:** Dean Albany.

Most teams didn't realize Drake had attended a year of prep school before he attended the Naval Academy, making him draft-eligible as a sophomore in 2008, or that he wouldn't have to fulfill his military commitment if he didn't return for his junior year. Baltimore had background with Drake because he had played for the Youse's Orioles club that serves as their scout team, knew his situation and signed him for

$100,000 as a 43rd-rounder. He worked his way to Double-A and onto the Orioles' 40-man roster in 2011. He began last year on the disabled list with shoulder inflammation, made three starts for Bowie in May, then felt discomfort in the shoulder again. He was shut down for the season and had surgery. Drake's last start, a six-inning no-hitter, was arguably the best of his career. That day, his fastball sat at 92-95 mph with sink, and he showed an 82-83 mph splitter/changeup with late tumble and downer curveball. His secondary pitches lack consistency, but he does a good job of throwing strikes. Big and strong, Drake works quickly and mixes his offerings well. If he fully recovers, he could fit at the back of a big league rotation but might be best suited for bullpen work. He'll make a third trip to Double-A this year after getting outrighted off the 40-man roster in November.

Year	Club (League)	Class	W	L	ERA	G	GS	CG	SV	IP	H	HR	BB	SO	K/9	WHIP	AVG
2008	Bluefield (APP)	R	1	0	0.77	7	0	0	0	12	7	1	2	11	8.5	0.77	.167
	Aberdeen (NYP)	SS	0	0	0.87	5	0	0	1	10	9	0	1	13	11.3	0.97	.214
2009	Delmarva (SAL)	LoA	8	9	4.34	25	24	0	0	131	138	6	42	104	7.2	1.38	.277
2010	Frederick (CAR)	HiA	6	6	4.36	24	21	0	0	128	135	19	37	100	7.0	1.34	.272
2011	Norfolk (IL)	AAA	0	0	0.00	1	0	0	0	2	1	0	1	2	9.0	1.00	.143
	Frederick (CAR)	HiA	8	3	2.14	14	13	2	0	97	78	1	18	80	7.4	0.99	.224
	Bowie (EL)	AA	3	5	5.20	12	12	2	0	64	77	8	24	47	6.6	1.58	.292
2012	Bowie (EL)	AA	1	1	1.50	3	3	0	0	18	8	1	4	15	7.5	0.67	.125
Minor League Totals			27	24	3.71	91	73	4	1	461	453	36	129	372	7.3	1.26	.257

29 GREG LORENZO, OF

BA GRADE 45 HIGH

Born: May 31, 1991. **B-T:** R-R. **Ht.:** 6-0. **Wt.:** 160. **Signed:** Dominican Republic, 2009. **Signed by:** David Stockstill/Carlos Bernhardt.

A small, athletic outfielder from the Dominican Republic, Lorenzo stands out for his ability to run and throw. He has top-of-the-scale speed, getting down the first-base line in less than 4.0 seconds from the right side, and he stole 16 bases in 53 games last year. His quickness helps him cover ground in center field, and his arm grades out as plus. The rest of Lorenzo's game is still in progress. He has some bat speed, slaps at the ball to put it in play and is willing to bunt to get on base. He's still learning the strike zone, and like many young hitters has difficulty recognizing breaking pitches. His approach won't yield much power, and he doesn't get caught up trying to drive the ball. Lorenzo will need a lot of time to develop but will get his first extended shot at full-season ball in 2013.

Year	Club (League)	Class	AVG	G	AB	R	H	2B	3B	HR	RBI	BB	SO	SB	CS	OBP	SLG
2009	Orioles/Brewers (DSL)	R	.174	26	69	9	12	0	2	0	6	11	17	5	3	.289	.232
2010	Orioles1 (DSL)	R	.252	69	226	41	57	4	5	0	15	34	49	27	6	.360	.314
2011	Orioles (GCL)	R	.232	48	164	25	38	8	6	0	8	14	46	8	5	.298	.354
2012	Orioles (GCL)	R	.316	25	76	9	24	4	3	2	7	3	15	4	3	.381	.526
	Aberdeen (NYP)	SS	.317	9	41	8	13	1	0	0	6	1	5	6	1	.364	.341
	Delmarva (SAL)	LoA	.333	19	72	13	24	2	2	1	3	1	22	6	2	.368	.458
Minor League Totals			.259	196	648	105	168	19	18	3	45	64	154	56	20	.340	.358

30 TY KELLY, 2B/3B/OF

BA GRADE 40 MEDIUM

Born: July 20, 1988. **B-T:** B-R. **Ht.:** 6-0. **Wt.:** 185. **Drafted:** UC Davis, 2009 (13th round). **Signed by:** James Keller.

Kelly wasn't on the prospect radar entering 2012, but he hit his way onto it, batting .327/.425/.413 while walking more than he struck out and rising three levels to Triple-A. Kelly can hit from both sides of the plate, and his future is tied entirely to his bat. He doesn't have much power, but he flares line drives from foul line to foul line, keeping his bat on a level plane through the hitting zone. Kelly still is looking for a position, however. He has below-average speed, range and arm strength, though his defensive instincts are sound. He has played every position but catcher, pitcher and center field during his minor league career, with more than half of his time coming at third base. He doesn't have the power to profile on an infield or outfield corner, nor the defensive chops to play up the middle. That leaves Kelly looking for a role as an offensive utilityman. He'll return to Norfolk to open 2013.

Year	Club (League)	Class	AVG	G	AB	R	H	2B	3B	HR	RBI	BB	SO	SB	CS	OBP	SLG
2009	Aberdeen (NYP)	SS	.265	61	226	31	60	5	1	1	18	33	29	3	3	.357	.310
2010	Delmarva (SAL)	LoA	.259	129	487	68	126	30	6	4	58	68	81	5	4	.352	.370
2011	Delmarva (SAL)	LoA	.274	120	457	63	125	13	0	4	46	67	63	11	4	.369	.328
2012	Norfolk (IL)	AAA	.278	11	36	3	10	1	0	1	2	4	3	1	0	.350	.389
	Frederick (CAR)	HiA	.346	76	263	47	91	17	0	9	41	54	41	2	3	.460	.513
	Bowie (EL)	AA	.308	46	172	24	53	11	2	1	27	21	28	1	0	.384	.413
Minor League Totals			.283	443	1641	236	465	77	9	20	192	247	245	23	14	.379	.378

Boston Red Sox

BY JIM CALLIS

For the Red Sox, 2012 was as embarrassing as 2011 was painful.

Boston lost 20 of its final 27 games in 2011, with the biggest September collapse in baseball history taking the team from the American League's best record to out of the playoffs. Two days after the season ended, the Red Sox declined the option on the contract of Terry Francona, their most successful manager ever. General manager Theo Epstein, the architect of the franchise's first World Series championship teams since 1918, left to become the Cubs' president of baseball operations in late October.

Senior vice president/assistant GM Ben Cherington was promoted to take over for his former boss in the GM's chair. His first major task was to hire Francona's replacement, with Dale Sveum as his top choice. But ownership declined to make an offer to Sveum, who ended up joining Epstein in Chicago as Cubs manager, and pushed for Bobby Valentine, who hadn't managed in the major leagues since 2002 with the Mets.

Concerns that Valentine's outspoken personality wouldn't mesh well with a veteran club quickly came true. He alienated many of his players by calling out Mike Aviles during spring training and Kevin Youkilis in April. Four days after Valentine left Jon Lester in to give up 11 runs to the Blue Jays on July 22, players met with owner John Henry and president Larry Lucchino to blast the manager.

At that point, the Red Sox were on the fringe of wild-card contention with a 49-50 record. When Boston dropped 16 of its next 27 games, ownership and Cherington decided to blow up the roster.

The Red Sox shipped Adrian Gonzalez and Carl Crawford, who had joined the club in blockbuster moves three days apart in December 2010, to the Dodgers. World Series hero-turned-malcontent Josh Beckett and Nick Punto also headed to Los Angeles. Boston not only shed $261 million in salary commitments, but also managed to acquire a pair of quality arms in Rubby de la Rosa and Allen Webster, along with James Loney (who departed to the Rays as a free agent after the season), Jerry Sands and Ivan DeJesus Jr.

While the trade gave the Red Sox much more flexibility for the future, it destroyed their present. They won just nine of their last 36 games, finishing at 69-93. Boston fired Valentine the day after the end of their worst season since 1965, and traded Aviles to get manager John Farrell from the Blue Jays. Farrell worked well with the Red Sox front office when he

The low Class A Greenville mascot wasn't the only one to mock Bobby Valentine in 2012

was the team's pitching coach from 2007-10.

Farrell takes over a team that hasn't won a playoff game since 2008, its longest drought in 15 years, and hasn't reached the postseason in the last three seasons despite baseball's second-largest payroll during that time. Both the rotation and the bullpen wilted in 2012, and the club's primary focus this offseason was on rebuilding the pitching staff.

Young players did provide positive developments in Boston in 2012, with third baseman Will Middlebrooks homering 15 times in 75 games and essentially making Youkilis expendable. Middlebrooks' season ended early when he broke his wrist in August, but he is expected to be healthy in spring training and is penciled in as the Opening Day starter at third. First-year starter Felix Doubront tied for the team lead with 11 victories, and he'll be expected to man a spot in the middle of the rotation again.

Down on the farm, shortstop Xander Bogaerts continued to develop rapidly, while several 2011 draft picks (outfielder Jackie Bradley, righthander Matt Barnes, lefthander Henry Owens, catcher Blake Swihart) provided intriguing early returns.

Even so, the Red Sox will need more than those youngsters to ease the pain and embarrassment of the last two seasons.

THIS YEAR'S TOP 30

Player, Pos.	Grade
1. Xander Bogaerts, ss	70/Medium
2. Jackie Bradley, of	60/Medium
3. Matt Barnes, rhp	60/Medium
4. Allen Webster, rhp	60/Medium
5. Henry Owens, lhp	60/High
6. Blake Swihart, c	60/Extreme
7. Garin Cecchini, 3b	55/High
8. Bryce Brentz, of	50/Medium
9. Jose Iglesias, ss	45/Low
10. Deven Marrero, ss	50/Medium
11. Drake Britton, lhp	55/High
12. Brandon Workman, rhp	50/Medium
13. Brandon Jacobs, of	50/High
14. Anthony Ranaudo, rhp	50/High
15. Brian Johnson, lhp	50/High
16. Tzu-Wei Lin, ss	55/Extreme
17. Jose Vinicio, ss	50/High
18. Alex Wilson, rhp	45/Medium
19. Christian Vazquez, c	50/High
20. Manuel Margot, of	55/Extreme
21. Pat Light, rhp	50/High
22. Frank Montas, rhp	55/Extreme
23. Travis Shaw, 1b/3b	50/High
24. Sean Coyle, 2b	50/High
25. Keury de la Cruz, of	50/High
26. Ty Buttrey, rhp	50/High
27. Cody Kukuk, lhp	50/High
28. Simon Mercedes, rhp	50/High
29. Stolmy Pimentel, rhp	50/High
30. Miguel Pena, lhp	50/High

LAST YEAR'S TOP 30

Player, Pos.	Status
1. Will Middlebrooks, 3b	Majors
2. Xander Bogaerts, ss	No. 1
3. Blake Swihart, c	No. 6
4. Anthony Ranaudo, rhp	No. 14
5. Bryce Brentz, of	No. 8
6. Brandon Jacobs, of	No. 13
7. Garin Cecchini, 3b	No. 7
8. Matt Barnes, rhp	No. 3
9. Ryan Lavarnway, c	Majors
10. Jackie Bradley, of	No. 2
11. Alex Wilson, rhp	No. 18
12. Jose Iglesias, ss	No. 9
13. Miles Head, 1b	(Athletics)
14. Sean Coyle, 2b	No. 24
15. Brandon Workman, rhp	No. 12
16. Drake Britton, lhp	No. 11
17. Felix Doubront, lhp	Majors
18. Henry Owens, lhp	No. 5
19. Kolbrin Vitek, 3b	Dropped out
20. Kyle Stroup, rhp	Dropped out
21. Jose Vinicio, ss	No. 17
22. Kyle Weiland, rhp	(Astros)
23. Stolmy Pimentel, rhp	No. 29
24. Oscar Tejeda, 2b	(Pirates)
25. Derrik Gibson, ss	Dropped out
26. Alex Hassan, of	Dropped out
27. Raul Alcantara, rhp	(Athletics)
28. Lars Anderson, 1b	(Indians)
29. Christian Vazquez, c	No. 19
30. Heiker Meneses, inf	Dropped out

BEST TOOLS

Best Hitter for Average	Jackie Bradley
Best Power Hitter	Xander Bogaerts
Best Strike-Zone Discipline	Jackie Bradley
Fastest Baserunner	Tzu-Wei Lin
Best Athlete	Xander Bogaerts
Best Fastball	Matt Barnes
Best Curveball	Brandon Workman
Best Slider	Alex Wilson
Best Changeup	Henry Owens
Best Control	Brandon Workman
Best Defensive Catcher	Christian Vazquez
Best Defensive Infielder	Jose Iglesias
Best Infield Arm	Garin Cecchini
Best Defensive Outfielder	Jackie Bradley
Best Outfield Arm	Jackie Bradley

PROJECTED 2016 LINEUP

Catcher	Blake Swihart
First Base	Mike Napoli
Second Base	Dustin Pedroia
Third Base	Will Middlebrooks
Shortstop	Xander Bogaerts
Left Field	Jacoby Ellsbury
Center Field	Jackie Bradley
Right Field	Bryce Brentz
Designated Hitter	Garin Cecchini
No. 1 Starter	Jon Lester
No. 2 Starter	Clay Buchholz
No. 3 Starter	Matt Barnes
No. 4 Starter	Allen Webster
No. 5 Starter	Henry Owens
Closer	Rubby de la Rosa

TOP PROSPECTS OF THE DECADE

Year	Player, Pos.	2012 Org.
2003	Hanley Ramirez, ss	Dodgers
2004	Hanley Ramirez, ss	Dodgers
2005	Hanley Ramirez, ss	Dodgers
2006	Andy Marte, 3b	Out of baseball
2007	Daisuke Matsuzaka, rhp	Red Sox
2008	Clay Buchholz, rhp	Red Sox
2009	Lars Anderson, 1b	Indians
2010	Ryan Westmoreland, of	Red Sox
2011	Jose Iglesias, ss	Red Sox
2012	Will Middlebrooks, 3b	Red Sox

TOP DRAFT PICKS OF THE DECADE

Year	Player, Pos.	2012 Org.
2003	David Murphy, of	Rangers
2004	Dustin Pedroia, ss (2nd round)	Red Sox
2005	Jacoby Ellsbury, of	Red Sox
2006	Jason Place, of	Out of baseball
2007	Nick Hagadone, lhp (1st round supp.)	Indians
2008	Casey Kelly, rhp/ss	Padres
2009	Reymond Fuentes, of	Padres
2010	Kolbrin Vitek, 3b	Red Sox
2011	Matt Barners, rhp	Red Sox
2012	Deven Marrero, ss	Red Sox

LARGEST BONUSES IN CLUB HISTORY

Jose Iglesias, 2009	$6,250,000
Casey Kelly, 2008	$3,000,000
Anthony Ranaudo, 2010	$2,550,000
Blake Swihart, 2011	$2,500,000
Tzu-Wei Lin, 2012	$2,050,000
Deven Marrero, 2012	$2,050,000

BOSTON RED SOX

TOP 2013 ROOKIE: Jose Iglesias, ss. The potential Gold Glover is the favorite to replace Mike Aviles at shortstop.

BREAKOUT PROSPECT: Tzu-Wei Lin, ss. His all-around ability stands out in a system deep in shortstops.

SLEEPER: Mookie Betts, 2b/ss. He has the speed, athleticism and approach to provide solid offense and defense at second base.

SOURCE OF TOP 30 TALENT

Homegrown	29	**Acquired**	1
College	10	Trades	1
Junior college	1	Rule 5 draft	0
High school	9	Independent leagues	0
Nondrafted free agents	0	Free agents/waivers	0
International	9		

LF
Brandon Jacobs (13)
Keury de la Cruz (25)
Jeremy Hazelbaker
Alex Hassan
Aneury Tavarez

CF
Jackie Bradley (2)
Manuel Margot (20)
Shannon Wilkerson
Cody Koback
Iseha Conklin
Shaq Thompson

RF
Bryce Brentz (8)
J.C. Linares
Henry Ramos
Jose Colorado

3B
Garin Cecchini (7)
Kolbrin Vitek
David Renfroe
Nick Moore

SS
Xander Bogaerts (1)
Jose Iglesias (9)
Deven Marrero (10)
Tzu-Wei Lin (16)
Jose Vinicio (17)
Cleuluis Rondon
Wendell Rijo

2B
Sean Coyle (24)
Mookie Betts
Heiker Meneses
Ivan DeJesus Jr.
Jose Garcia
Mike Meyers

1B
Travis Shaw (23)
Mauro Gomez
Michael Almanzar
Boss Moanaroa

C
Blake Swihart (6)
Christian Vazquez (19)
Dan Butler

LHP

LHSP	LHRP
Henry Owens (5)	Chris Hernandez
Drake Britton (11)	Dylan Chavez
Brian Johnson (15)	
Cody Kukuk (27)	
Miguel Pena (30)	
Francisco Taveras	
Daniel McGrath	

RHP

RHSP	RHRP
Matt Barnes (3)	Alex Wilson (18)
Allen Webster (4)	Frank Montas (22)
Brandon Workman (12)	Stolmy Pimentel (29)
Anthony Ranaudo (14)	Chris Carpenter
Pat Light (21)	Austin Maddox
Ty Buttrey (26)	Sandy Rosario
Simon Mercedes (28)	Madison Younginer
William Cuevas	Aaron Kurcz
Jamie Callahan	Kyle Kaminska
Kyle Stroup	Chris Martin
Miguel Celestino	Neifi Ogando
Graham Godfrey	Yunior Ortega
Justin Haley	Mike Augliera
Jose Almonte	Braden Kapteyn
Steven Wright	J.B. Wendelken
Noe Ramirez	Stephen Williams
Sergio Gomez	
Kevin Heras	
Willie Ethington	

2012   BONUSES: $7.9 MILLION

BEST PURE HITTER: SS Deven Marrero (1) hit just .284 in the spring at Arizona State, but Boston believes in his track record of producing with wood bats.

BEST POWER HITTER: The best raw power belongs to LHP Brian Johnson (1) and RHP Austin Maddox (3), who were two-way players at Florida but will focus on pitching as pros. Among the long-term hitters, 1B Nathan Minnich (8) has the most usable pop. The 2012 NCAA Division II player of the year, he led that level with a .980 slugging percentage while setting Shepherd (W.Va.) records for single-season (21) and career (58) homers.

FASTEST RUNNER: OF Khiry Cooper (25) also uses his plus-plus speed as a wide receiver at Tulsa. OF Iseha Conklin (19) has 65 speed on the 20-80 scouting scale.

BEST DEFENSIVE PLAYER: Marrero is a rare college shortstop who shouldn't have any problems staying at the position. He has smooth actions to go with plenty of range and arm strength.

BEST FASTBALL: The Red Sox rated RHP Pat Light's (1s) fastball as one of the best in the draft because of its combination of velocity and heavy life. He sits at 92-94 mph and has reached 97. Johnson stunned Boston by hitting 98 when facing a college rival in pro ball, but he usually pitches 88-91 mph. Maddox and RHP Ty Buttrey (4) can get to 96.

BEST SECONDARY PITCH: Buttrey, who signed for $1.3 million, has a knuckle-curve that needs more consistency but could develop into a true out pitch. Johnson has outstanding feel for both a curveball and slider that could be solid pitches.

BEST PRO DEBUT: RHP J.B. Wendelken (13) had a 1.27 ERA, 28-3 K-BB ratio and .147 opponent average in 21 innings in the Rookie-level Gulf Coast League.

BEST ATHLETE: OF Shaq Thompson (18), who went 0-for-39 with 37 strikeouts in the GCL, is starting at safety for Washington as a freshman. Cooper also plays college football, as does OF Brandon Magee (23), an Arizona State linebacker with NFL potential. Among the baseball-only group, Conklin has the most athleticism.

MOST INTRIGUING BACKGROUND: Johnson's mother is a former Doublemint twin. C J.T. Watkins' (10) father Danny scouts for Boston. J.T. signed but will fulfill his Army commitment first. Marrero's cousin Chris was a 2006 first-rounder and has played in the majors. 1B Jake Davies' (21) brother Kyle pitched in the big leagues, and Thompson's brother Syd'Quan played in the NFL.

CLOSEST TO THE MAJORS: Johnson, provided he doesn't have any setbacks after taking a liner to the face in mid-August. The sleeper candidate is RHP Mike Augliera (5), a reliever who lives off his command of his solid fastball.

BEST LATE-ROUND PICK: Wendelken, who posted a 0.20 ERA at Middle Georgia JC, commands his 91-92 mph fastball well. RHP Stephen Williams (16) touched 94 mph in instructional league.

THE ONE WHO GOT AWAY: RHP Carson Fulmer (15), who has a 92-95 mph fastball, headed to Vanderbilt, and 2B Alex Bregman (29), an undersized but gifted hitter, opted for Louisiana State.

ASSESSMENT: The Red Sox were thrilled to get Marrero at No. 24. He was the only position player they signed for more than $100,000, and after him they focused on restocking the system's pitching.

2011   BONUSES: $11.0 MILLION

RHP Matt Barnes (1) and OF Jackie Bradley (1s) could help the Red Sox before the end of 2013. C Blake Swihart (1) and LHP Henry Owens (1s) have equally high ceilings.

GRADE: B+

2010   BONUSES: $10.7 MILLION

Boston's top pick, 3B Kolbrin Vitek (1), has stalled and their $2.55 million investment in RHP Anthony Ranaudo (1s) has yet to bear fruit. But it still has several potential contributors, including OF Bryce Brentz (1s), RHP Brandon Workman (2) and 3B Garin Cecchini (4)

GRADE: C+

2009   BONUSES: $7.1 MILLION

RHP Alex Wilson (2) could join the Red Sox bullpen in 2013, and OF Brandon Jacobs (10) has some of the system's best offensive upside. OF Reymond Fuentes (1) was part of a trade for Adrian Gonzalez, while 3B/1B Miles Head (26) helped land Andrew Bailey.

GRADE: C

2008   BONUSES: $10.5 MILLION

Boston signed five big leaguers, though only C Ryan Lavarnway (6) remains in the organization. RHP Casey Kelly (1) was the headline in the Gonzalez deal, and RHPs Stephen Fife (3), Kyle Weiland (3) and C Tim Federowicz (7) also were traded.

GRADE: C+

Draft analysis by Jim Callis. Numbers in parentheses indicate draft rounds.

1 XANDER BOGAERTS, SS

Born: Oct. 1, 1992. **B-T:** R-R. **Ht.:** 6-3. **Wt.:** 175.
Signed: Aruba, 2009. **Signed by:** Mike Lord.

BA GRADE
70
MEDIUM

TOM PRIDDY

The Red Sox's best international prospect since Hanley Ramirez, Bogaerts keeps raising his performance and raising expectations. Boston signed him for $410,000 out of Aruba in 2009, promising his mother that he could finish high school before making his pro debut. He hit .314/.396/.423 in the Rookie-level Dominican Summer League in 2010, then came to United States. The Red Sox planned on sending him to the Rookie-level Gulf Coast League in 2011, but Bogaerts so dominated extended spring training that they sent him to low Class A Greenville at age 18, and he responded with 16 homers in 72 games. He was just warming up for 2012, when he was Boston's minor league offensive player of the year and appeared in the Futures Game. Bogaerts batted a combined .307/.373/.523 and reached Double-A Portland, where he was the youngest position player in the Eastern League. About the only negative in his year came when the Sox sent his twin brother Jair, a first baseman, to the Cubs in March when the teams exchanged players as compensation for former Boston GM Theo Epstein. Chicago released Jair in June.

Bogaerts has the offensive potential to be an all-star at any position, and that position just might be shortstop. He's a confident, strong hitter who doesn't muscle up to tap into his plus-plus raw power. He has an easy swing with plenty of bat speed, and he does a nice job of keeping his weight back and using the entire field. Despite his youth, he has a feel for making in-game adjustments. He improved his selectivity in 2012, though he still expands the strike zone at times. While that flaw doesn't hurt him much because he still makes hard contact on balls off the plate, the Red Sox want him to draw more walks. His walk rate was acceptable at high Class A Salem (43 in 104 games), but he drew just one free pass in 23 Double-A contests. Though scouts look at Bogaerts' 6-foot-3 frame and wonder if he'll outgrow shortstop, he has good actions at the position and could stay there longer than expected. His plus arm isn't a question and he played more under control on defense in 2012.

He made just 21 errors in 119 games, after making 26 in 72 games the year before, boosting his fielding percentage from .924 to .959. He's an average runner who's not quite as quick as a typical shortstop, but he still exhibits solid range. He's athletic and has good body control for his size. If Bogaerts has to move, he'd profile best at third base or right field. Along with his considerable tools, he draws praise for his intelligence and work ethic.

Bogaerts likely will open 2013 in Double-A to focus on his plate discipline, but Boston has had a hard time holding him back. He easily could hit his way to Triple-A Pawtucket before he turns 21. The Red Sox don't have a clear starter at shortstop, so it's not out of the question that he could put himself in the major league mix before the end of the season. More realistically, Bogaerts will make his Boston debut in 2014. Whether he does so at shortstop likely depends on how much slick-fielding Jose Iglesias shows at the plate between now and then.

SCOUTING GRADES

Batting: 60.   **Defense:** 55.
Power: 70.   **Arm:** 60.
Speed: 50.

Based on 20-80 scouting scale, where 50 represents major league average, and future projection rather than present tools.

Year	Club (League)	Class	AVG	G	AB	R	H	2B	3B	HR	RBI	BB	SO	SB	CS	OBP	SLG
2010	Red Sox (DSL)	R	.314	63	239	39	75	7	5	3	42	30	37	4	5	.396	.423
2011	Greenville (SAL)	LoA	.260	72	265	38	69	14	2	16	45	25	71	1	3	.324	.509
2012	Salem (CAR)	HiA	.302	104	384	59	116	27	3	15	64	43	85	4	4	.378	.505
	Portland (EL)	AA	.326	23	92	12	30	10	0	5	17	1	21	1	1	.351	.598
Minor League Totals			.296	262	980	148	290	58	10	39	168	99	214	10	13	.366	.495

2 JACKIE BRADLEY, OF

Born: April 19, 1990. **B-T:** L-R. **Ht.:** 5-10. **Wt.:** 180. **Drafted:** South Carolina, 2011 (1st round supplemental). **Signed by:** Quincy Boyd.

The Most Outstanding Player at the 2010 College World Series, Bradley slipped to No. 40 in 2011 after a wrist injury and lower production with toned-down NCAA bats. Signed for $1.1 million, he regained his form in 2012. The Red Sox named him their minor league defensive player of the year, while managers rated him as having the best bat, plate discipline, baserunning skills, outfield defense and outfield arm in the high Class A Carolina League before his promotion in June. Bradley is an outstanding center fielder who can run down almost any ball, thanks to his quickness and instincts, and he has a plus arm as a bonus. An on-base machine with quick hands, Bradley works deep counts and sprays line drives to all fields. He has enough power to hit 10-15 homers annually, though it can make him too pull-conscious at times. He's an average runner whose speed plays up on the basepaths. The Red Sox love his competitive makeup, which sparked consecutive national championships at South Carolina. Ticketed for Triple-A to start 2013, Bradley has no major adjustments to make. He's a better center fielder than Jacoby Ellsbury, who becomes a free agent after 2013.

BA GRADE

60

MEDIUM

Year	Club (League)	Class	AVG	G	AB	R	H	2B	3B	HR	RBI	BB	SO	SB	CS	OBP	SLG
2011	Lowell (NYP)	SS	.190	6	21	5	4	0	0	0	0	4	5	0	2	.320	.190
	Greenville (SAL)	LoA	.333	4	15	2	5	1	0	1	3	0	3	0	0	.333	.600
2012	Salem (CAR)	HiA	.359	67	234	53	84	26	2	3	34	52	40	16	6	.480	.526
	Portland (EL)	AA	.271	61	229	37	62	16	2	6	29	35	49	8	3	.373	.437
Minor League Totals			.311	138	499	97	155	43	4	10	66	91	97	24	11	.423	.473

3 MATT BARNES, RHP

Born: June 17, 1990. **B-T:** R-R. **Ht.:** 6-4. **Wt.:** 205. **Drafted:** Connecticut, 2011 (1st round). **Signed by:** Ray Fagnant.

Barnes set a Connecticut career record with 247 strikeouts and pitched the Huskies to their first-ever NCAA super-regional in 2011, before Boston drafted him 19th overall and signed him for $1.5 million. His 2012 pro debut was a tale of two halves, as he went 7-1, 0.99 before the all-star break before tiring and going 0-4, 5.74 afterward. He required just a pair of 95 mph fastballs to record two outs at the Futures Game. Barnes pitches aggressively with his swing-and-miss fastball. He effortlessly throws heaters with riding life, usually sitting at 93-95 mph and topping out at 98. The Red Sox had him scrap a slider he started to fiddle with in college and had him focus on throwing his hard curveball, a plus downer at times. Barnes is learning the need for a changeup, which he throws a bit too hard in the upper 80s but sells well with his arm speed. He's not afraid to throw strikes or pitch inside. If Barnes can refine his secondary pitches, he can become a No. 2 or 3 starter. After easing him into pro ball with 120 innings, Boston will turn him loose in 2013. He'll start in Double-A and could push for a spot in the big league rotation by the end of the season.

BA GRADE

60

MEDIUM

Year	Club (League)	Class	W	L	ERA	G	GS	CG	SV	IP	H	HR	BB	SO	K/9	WHIP	AVG
2012	Greenville (SAL)	LoA	2	0	0.34	5	5	0	0	27	12	0	4	42	14.2	0.60	.130
	Salem (CAR)	HiA	5	5	3.58	20	20	1	0	93	85	6	25	91	8.8	1.18	.250
Minor League Totals			7	5	2.86	25	25	1	0	120	97	6	29	133	10.0	1.05	.225

4 ALLEN WEBSTER, RHP

Born: Feb. 10, 1990. **B-T:** R-R. **Ht.:** 6-3. **Wt.:** 185. **Drafted:** HS—Madison, N.C., 2008 (18th round). **Signed by:** Lon Joyce (Dodgers).

Mainly a shortstop in high school, Webster threw 91-92 mph in a pitching appearance late in his senior year in front of a Dodgers scout who was evaluating another player. Signed for $20,000 as an 18th-rounder, he has blossomed into a top pitching prospect. Other teams marveled that Boston was able to acquire him while also dumping $261 million in salaries in the Adrian Gonzalez trade in August. Webster turns bats into kindling and generates groundballs with a 92-95 mph fastball that peaks at 97 but is most notable for its late sink and armside run. In 2012, he ranked fourth in the minors in home run rate (0.1 per nine innings). His changeup can be just as devastating with its fade and sink. His mid-80s slider lacks consistency but has the makings of a third plus offering. Webster's pitches move so much that he can struggle to command them, and he gets hit when he falls behind in the count. He also tends to revert to predictable pitch patterns. Some prefer him to Matt Barnes because he has a deeper repertoire, though Webster still must learn to harness his stuff. A potential No. 2 or 3 starter, he's ready to graduate to Triple-A after getting added to the 40-man roster and could

BA GRADE

60

MEDIUM

make his major league debut in 2013.

Year	Club (League)	Class	W	L	ERA	G	GS	CG	SV	IP	H	HR	BB	SO	K/9	WHIP	AVG
2008	Dodgers (GCL)	R	1	1	3.44	12	0	0	1	18	12	1	17	13	6.4	1.58	.197
2009	Dodgers (AZL)	R	2	1	2.08	12	8	0	0	48	35	0	14	56	10.6	1.03	.197
	Ogden (PIO)	R	2	0	3.00	4	3	0	0	21	23	1	4	21	9.0	1.29	.277
2010	Great Lakes (MWL)	LoA	12	9	2.88	26	23	0	0	131	119	6	53	114	7.8	1.31	.239
2011	R. Cucamonga (CAL)	HiA	5	2	2.33	9	9	0	0	54	46	2	21	62	10.3	1.24	.228
	Chattanooga (SL)	AA	6	3	5.04	18	17	1	0	91	101	7	36	73	7.2	1.51	.286
2012	Chattanooga (SL)	AA	6	8	3.55	27	22	0	0	122	120	1	57	117	8.7	1.45	.260
	Portland (EL)	AA	0	1	8.00	2	2	0	0	9	13	1	4	12	12.0	1.89	.325
Minor League Totals			34	25	3.43	110	84	1	1	494	469	19	206	468	8.5	1.37	.250

5 HENRY OWENS, LHP

Born: July 21, 1992. **B-T:** L-L. **Ht.:** 6-6. **Wt.:** 190. **Drafted:** HS—Huntington Beach, Calif., 2011 (1st round supplemental). **Signed by:** Tom Battista.

Yet another member of what is shaping up as a strong 2011 draft class for the Red Sox, Owens went 36th overall and signed for $1.55 million. Though kept on a short leash in his 2012 pro debut, Owens led the system with 12 wins and ranked second with 130 strikeouts. Owens is a rare lefthander who can get swings and misses with three different pitches. His fastball has mostly average velocity and life, ranging from 88-94 mph, but plays up because his tall body and long limbs give him deceptive angle and plane. He has advanced feel for his plus changeup and an average breaking ball. He varies his breaker, using a loopy 67-72 mph curveball early in counts for strikes and a 78-81 mph slurve to put hitters away. While Owens' lanky frame gives him plenty of room to add strength, he won't require more power to succeed. His control is better than his average of 4.2 walks per nine innings would indicate, but his command needs refinement. He's athletic and repeats his delivery well. Owens is further away than Matt Barnes or Allen Webster but may have more upside. He'll head to high Class A in 2013 and should advance quickly as soon as he starts to locate his pitches with more precision.

BA GRADE

60 HIGH

Year	Club (League)	Class	W	L	ERA	G	GS	CG	SV	IP	H	HR	BB	SO	K/9	WHIP	AVG
2012	Greenville (SAL)	LoA	12	5	4.87	23	22	0	0	102	100	10	47	130	11.5	1.45	.256
Minor League Totals			12	5	4.87	23	22	0	0	102	100	10	47	130	11.5	1.45	.256

6 BLAKE SWIHART, C

Born: April 3, 1992. **B-T:** B-R. **Ht.:** 6-1. **Wt.:** 175. **Drafted:** HS—Rio Rancho, N.M., 2011 (1st round). **Signed by:** Matt Mahoney.

The 26th overall pick in 2011, Swihart was the highest-drafted player out of New Mexico since Shane Andrews in 1990, and it was the earliest Boston has taken a catcher since John Marzano in 1984. Adjusting to tougher competition while becoming a full-time backstop, Swihart hit just .198 through mid-May but rallied to bat .289/.329/.439 afterward. As an athletic catcher who projects as an above-average hitter, Swihart's overall tool package is similar to a young Buster Posey. Swihart has a good swing from both sides of the plate, with bat speed and the ability to keep the bat in the hitting zone for a long time. He's still learning to recognize pitches and tone down his aggressiveness. He makes a lot of hard, line-drive contact that should produce average power once he adds strength and loft to his stroke. Swihart is still learning behind the plate but has made progress with shortening his release and cleaning up his footwork. He threw out 31 percent of basesteal-ers in 2012 while showing average arm strength. He has quick feet and soft hands but needs to quiet down his receiving. He's an average runner. Swihart is a long way from becoming the next Posey, and the Red Sox will develop him patiently. He'll likely spend all of 2013 in high Class A.

BA GRADE

60 EXTREME

Year	Club (League)	Class	AVG	G	AB	R	H	2B	3B	HR	RBI	BB	SO	SB	CS	OBP	SLG
2011	Red Sox (GCL)	R	.000	2	6	0	0	0	0	0	0	0	2	0	0	.000	.000
2012	Greenville (SAL)	LoA	.262	92	344	44	90	17	4	7	53	26	68	6	2	.307	.395
Minor League Totals			.257	94	350	44	90	17	4	7	53	26	70	6	2	.302	.389

7 GARIN CECCHINI, 3B

Born: April 20, 1991. **B-T:** L-R. **Ht.:** 6-2. **Wt.:** 200. **Drafted:** HS—Lake Charles, La., 2010 (4th round). **Signed by:** Matt Dorey.

After blowing out his right knee as a high school senior and having a pitch break his right wrist in his pro debut, Cecchini finally stayed healthy in 2012. The $1.31 million bonus signee ranked third in the low Class A South Atlantic League in doubles (38) and steals (51 in 57 attempts) and was named Red Sox minor league baserunner of the year. The Mets drafted his younger brother Gavin 12th overall in June. Garin is a pure hitter who excels at controlling the strike zone, managing at-bats and making adjustments. He has enough bat speed to develop average power once he learns to load his hands better in his swing. It's hard to believe considering his 51 swipes, but Cecchini is a below-average runner out of the box. Though he has a quick first step and tremendous instincts on the bases, he won't be a huge basestealing threat at higher levels. He's also savvy in the field, leading SAL third basemen in fielding percentage (.944). He moves well

BA GRADE
55
HIGH

laterally, and managers rated his infield arm as the best in the league. He has the tools to be a solid regular at third base, but Will Middlebrooks and possibly Xander Bogaerts may preclude Cecchini from playing there in Boston. If his power comes, he'd profile well on an outfield corner. He'll open 2013 in high Class A.

Year	Club (League)	Class	AVG	G	AB	R	H	2B	3B	HR	RBI	BB	SO	SB	CS	OBP	SLG
2011	Lowell (NYP)	SS	.298	32	114	21	34	12	1	3	23	17	19	12	2	.398	.500
2012	Greenville (SAL)	LoA	.305	118	455	84	139	38	4	4	62	61	90	51	6	.394	.433
Minor League Totals			.304	150	569	105	173	50	5	7	85	78	109	63	8	.395	.446

8 BRYCE BRENTZ, OF

Born: Dec. 30, 1988. **B-T:** R-R. **Ht.:** 6-0. **Wt.:** 190. **Drafted:** Middle Tennessee State, 2010 (1st round supplemental). **Signed by:** Danny Watkins.

Brentz topped NCAA Division I in batting (.465), home runs (28) and slugging (.930) in 2009, then went 36th overall in the next year's draft and signed for $889,200. He hit 30 homers in his first full pro season and reached Triple-A in his second. He batted .333/.385/.792 in the International League playoffs to lead Pawtucket to a championship. Brentz has the two most important tools for a right fielder, as both his power and arm grade as better than average. His bat speed and pure strength give him at least 65 raw pop on the 20-80 scouting scale. He'll always pile up strikeouts, but he has shortened his swing and used the whole field more often as he has risen through the minors. He can get out of control at times, trying to uppercut and pull pitches, and his biggest weakness is a propensity to chase breaking balls. Managers rated Brentz's outfield arm as the Eastern League's best in 2012, when he recorded 10 assists and cut down on needless throws that led to

BA GRADE
50
MEDIUM

errors in the past. He's a below-average runner with average range in right. The Red Sox view Brentz as a potential solid regular in right field. After more Triple-A seasoning, he could compete for a starting job in Boston in 2014.

Year	Club (League)	Class	AVG	G	AB	R	H	2B	3B	HR	RBI	BB	SO	SB	CS	OBP	SLG
2010	Lowell (NYP)	SS	.198	69	262	28	52	14	4	5	39	21	76	5	4	.259	.340
2011	Greenville (SAL)	LoA	.359	40	170	43	61	10	3	11	36	14	35	2	2	.414	.647
	Salem (CAR)	HiA	.274	75	288	48	79	15	1	19	58	26	80	1	1	.336	.531
2012	Portland (EL)	AA	.296	122	456	62	135	30	1	17	76	40	130	7	5	.355	.478
	Pawtucket (IL)	AAA	.118	5	17	0	2	0	0	0	0	1	6	0	0	.167	.118
Minor League Totals			.276	311	1193	181	329	69	9	52	209	102	327	15	12	.335	.479

9 JOSE IGLESIAS, SS

Born: Jan. 5, 1990. **B-T:** R-R. **Ht.:** 5-11. **Wt.:** 185. **Signed:** Cuba, 2009. **Signed by:** Craig Shipley/Johnny DiPuglia.

A Cuban defector, Iglesias signed in 2009 for an $8.25 million major league contract that included a Red Sox-record $6.25 million bonus. He made his major league debut in 2011 but spent the bulk of 2012 in Triple-A. Iglesias may be the best defensive shortstop prospect in the game. Rated as the International League's top defensive shortstop for two years running, he has exceptionally quick hands and feet. His arm is strong and former manager Bobby Valentine said Iglesias has more range than Rey Ordonez, the Gold Glover he had with the Mets. The problem is that Iglesias has hit .251/.302/.287 in Triple-A and looked helpless at the plate with Boston. While he has bat speed and makes contact, he draws few walks and offers no power. With average speed and good instincts, he can steal 10-15 bases a season. After trading Mike Aviles to the Blue Jays in order to get new manager John Farrell, the Red Sox will give Iglesias the opportunity to win the

BA GRADE
45
LOW

shortstop job in spring training. His defense can make him a valuable regular, even if his bat relegates him to the bottom of the lineup.

Year	Club (League)	Class	AVG	G	AB	R	H	2B	3B	HR	RBI	BB	SO	SB	CS	OBP	SLG
2010	Lowell (NYP)	SS	.350	13	40	8	14	2	2	0	7	7	8	2	1	.458	.500
	Portland (EL)	AA	.285	57	221	29	63	10	3	0	13	8	49	5	2	.315	.357
2011	Pawtucket (IL)	AAA	.235	101	357	35	84	9	0	1	31	21	58	12	4	.285	.269
	Boston (AL)	MAJ	.333	10	6	3	2	0	0	0	0	0	2	0	0	.333	.333
2012	Lowell (NYP)	SS	.375	2	8	1	3	1	0	0	0	1	1	1	0	.444	.500
	Pawtucket (IL)	AAA	.266	88	353	46	94	9	1	1	23	27	46	12	3	.318	.306
	Boston (AL)	MAJ	.118	25	68	5	8	2	0	1	2	4	16	1	0	.200	.191
Major League Totals			.135	35	74	8	10	2	0	1	2	4	18	1	0	.210	.203
Minor League Totals			.264	261	979	119	258	31	6	2	74	64	162	32	10	.313	.314

10 DEVEN MARRERO, SS

Born: Aug. 25, 1990. **B-T:** R-R. **Ht.:** 6-1. **Wt.:** 194. **Drafted:** Arizona State, 2012 (1st round). **Signed by:** Vaughn Williams.

Marrero entered 2012 as a potential No. 1 overall draft pick, but he lasted until No. 25 after hitting just .284 as a junior at Arizona State. A rare college shortstop who looks like a good bet to remain at the position, he signed with the Red Sox for $2.05 million. His cousin Chris was a Nationals first-rounder in 2006 and has appeared briefly in the majors. Marrero reads balls well and has fluid actions at shortstop, with the above-average range and arm strength to make all the plays. He can improve his focus and consistency on defense, though that can be said of most players entering pro ball. Marrero hit better with wood bats in summer play than he did with metal bats during the college season, and the Red Sox think he'll produce at the plate. He stays inside the ball well, controls the strike zone and may flash enough pull power to hit 10 homers a year. With solid speed, a quick first step and keen instincts, he could add 20 steals a year. He isn't in Iglesias' class defensively, but Marrero is a plus defender with much more offensive upside. Those two represent Boston's future at shortstop if Xander Bogaerts outgrows the position. Marrero figures to skip a level and start his first full pro season in high Class A.

BA GRADE
50
MEDIUM

Year	Club (League)	Class	AVG	G	AB	R	H	2B	3B	HR	RBI	BB	SO	SB	CS	OBP	SLG
2012	Lowell (NYP)	SS	.268	64	246	45	66	14	3	2	24	34	48	24	6	.358	.374
Minor League Totals			.268	64	246	45	66	14	3	2	24	34	48	24	6	.358	.374

11 DRAKE BRITTON, LHP

BA GRADE
55
HIGH

Born: May 22, 1989. **B-T:** L-L. **Ht.:** 6-2. **Wt.:** 200. **Drafted:** HS—Tomball, Texas, 2007 (23rd round). **Signed by:** Jim Robinson.

Since he signed for $700,000 as a 23rd-round pick in 2007, Britton's stock has been as volatile as anything offered on Wall Street. He blew out his elbow and needed Tommy John surgery in 2008, bounced back in 2010 to surge to No. 3 on this list, then posted a 6.91 ERA at Salem in a hugely disappointing 2011. He's on the upswing again, after he shook off more struggles in high Class A and closed the 2012 season with a 2.23 ERA and 45 strikeouts in 44 innings over his final eight Double-A starts. For Britton, his success comes down to confidence rather than stuff. Few lefthanders can match the velocity on his fastball, which averaged 94 mph in Double-A and peaks at 97. He maintains that velocity deep into games, and his heater plays up further because it features plenty of sink. He doesn't have a plus secondary pitch, but he has made strides with an 81-86 mph slider that has supplanted his curveball as his go-to breaking ball. His changeup has deception and sink. Britton hasn't always trusted his stuff, leading to deep counts and getting hit harder than he should, but he did a better job of attacking hitters and battling through jams down the stretch in 2012. His finish has the Red Sox encouraged again that he can make it as a starter, and if he doesn't, he could be a dynamic late-inning reliever. He should see Triple-A at some point in 2013, with a chance to make his big league debut late in the year.

Year	Club (League)	Class	W	L	ERA	G	GS	CG	SV	IP	H	HR	BB	SO	K/9	WHIP	AVG
2008	Lowell (NYP)	SS	1	2	4.28	8	7	0	0	34	30	3	16	26	7.0	1.37	.234
2009	Red Sox (GCL)	R	0	0	0.00	4	4	0	0	7	2	0	4	11	14.1	0.86	.080
	Lowell (NYP)	SS	0	0	1.93	3	3	0	0	5	4	0	3	8	15.4	1.50	.235
2010	Greenville (SAL)	LoA	2	3	2.97	21	21	0	0	76	69	5	23	78	9.3	1.22	.240
2011	Salem (CAR)	HiA	1	13	6.91	26	26	0	0	98	111	12	55	89	8.2	1.70	.285
2012	Salem (CAR)	HiA	3	5	5.80	10	8	0	0	45	42	5	19	42	8.4	1.36	.246
	Portland (EL)	AA	4	7	3.72	16	16	0	0	85	86	3	38	76	8.1	1.46	.266
Minor League Totals			11	30	4.68	88	85	0	0	348	344	28	158	330	8.5	1.44	.257

12 BRANDON WORKMAN, RHP

BA GRADE

50

MEDIUM

Born: Aug. 13, 1988. **B-T:** R-R. **Ht.:** 6-4. **Wt.:** 195. **Drafted:** Texas, 2010 (2nd round). **Signed by:** Jim Robinson.

Workman receives less hype than comparable Red Sox prospects, but he's accustomed to getting overshadowed. Though he was a second-round pick in 2010, he spent that spring as Texas' No. 3 starter. He signed for $800,000, but that was just the sixth-highest bonus in Boston's draft class. He generated little attention when the Red Sox eased him into pro ball in 2011, and not much more when he won their minor league pitcher of the year award in 2012. Workman doesn't have the sexiest stuff, but he does a good job of locating a vast array of pitches where he wants. His fastball sits at 92-94 mph into the late innings and reaches 96. His heater has nice life and he throws it on a steep downhill plane, and his command of the pitch improved after Boston made that a priority for his first pro season. His No. 2 option is a pitch that varies between a true slider and an 85-88 mph cutter, and both versions are effective. Workman also has an average curveball and changeup, not to mention the best mound presence in the system. There's some stiffness in his delivery, which leads some scouts to project him as a reliever, but he repeats it well and pounds the strike zone. The Red Sox see him as a workhorse No. 3 starter and expect him to reach Triple-A during 2013.

Year	Club (League)	Class	W	L	ERA	G	GS	CG	SV	IP	H	HR	BB	SO	K/9	WHIP	AVG
2011	Greenville (SAL)	LoA	6	7	3.71	26	26	0	0	131	128	10	33	115	7.9	1.23	.260
2012	Salem (CAR)	HiA	7	7	3.40	20	20	0	0	114	104	10	20	107	8.5	1.09	.244
	Portland (EL)	AA	3	1	3.96	5	5	0	0	25	23	2	5	23	8.3	1.12	.247
Minor League Totals			16	15	3.60	51	51	0	0	270	255	22	58	245	8.2	1.16	.252

13 BRANDON JACOBS, OF

BA GRADE

50

HIGH

Born: Dec. 8, 1990. **B-T:** R-R. **Ht.:** 6-1. **Wt.:** 225. **Drafted:** HS—Lilburn, Ga., 2009 (10th round). **Signed by:** Tim Hyers.

Jacobs has one of the more intriguing bats in the system, but aside from his 2011 breakout season in low Class A, he has hit a combined .248/.318/.407 in his other three years as a pro. To be fair, a hamate injury in his left hand hampered him throughout much of 2012. A talented running back who turned down an Auburn football scholarship to sign for $750,000 as a 10th-round pick in 2009, Jacobs remains an unfinished product on the diamond. His strength and bat speed give him impressive raw power, though he's still refining his swing and approach. He must adapt to quality breaking pitches and learn to make adjustments. Jacobs has remade his body since his football days, trimming from 240 to 225 pounds and reducing his body fat to under 10 percent. He has gotten quicker, exhibiting solid speed and a knack for stealing an occasional base. He has become an average left fielder as he has learned to take better routes on balls, and he even saw his first action (27 games) in center field in 2012. He has fringy arm strength, which rules out right field as a possibility. Jacobs still has youth on his side and will compete for a Double-A job in spring training.

Year	Club (League)	Class	AVG	G	AB	R	H	2B	3B	HR	RBI	BB	SO	SB	CS	OBP	SLG
2009	Red Sox (GCL)	R	.250	8	24	1	6	2	0	0	0	2	8	0	0	.333	.333
2010	Lowell (NYP)	SS	.242	64	236	30	57	18	2	6	31	21	59	4	1	.308	.411
2011	Greenville (SAL)	LoA	.303	115	442	75	134	32	3	17	80	43	123	30	7	.376	.505
2012	Salem (CAR)	HiA	.252	114	437	62	110	30	0	13	61	39	128	17	9	.322	.410
Minor League Totals			.270	301	1139	168	307	82	5	36	172	105	318	51	17	.341	.445

14 ANTHONY RANAUDO, RHP

BA GRADE

50

HIGH

Born: Sept. 9, 1989. **B-T:** R-R. **Ht.:** 6-7. **Wt.:** 231. **Drafted:** Louisiana State, 2010 (1st round supplemental). **Signed by:** Matt Dorey.

Ranaudo's pro career has been as much of a roller-coaster ride as his time at Louisiana State. He pitched just 12 innings as a college freshman because of elbow tendinitis, then rebounded in 2009 to win the College World Series clincher and establish himself as the top college prospect for the 2010 draft, only to come down with a stress reaction in his elbow and post a 7.32 ERA in 2010. The Red Sox still drafted him 39th overall in 2010, and when he threw 30 innings without an earned run in the Cape Cod League that summer, they rewarded him with a $2.55 million bonus. Ranaudo began his pro career with a strong stint in low Class A in 2011 but wasn't as impressive after a midseason promotion. He looked poised for a big 2012 when he popped 97 mph fastballs in spring training, only to come down with a strained groin that sidelined him until mid-May. He never got right during nine starts in Double-A, as his mechanics got out of whack before he was shut down in early July with shoulder inflammation. Some club officials thought his problems were as much mental as physical. Before Ranaudo got hurt, he was throwing 93-96 mph in short stints and showing a better curveball than he had previously as a pro. Both can be plus pitches, and he complements them with a solid changeup. When he's on, he repeats his delivery, uses his tall frame to leverage pitches down in the strike zone and works both sides of the plate. Ranaudo threw well in instructional league before heading to the Puerto Rican League, but he had to leave Puerto Rico after aggravating his groin injury. The Red Sox still can dream on him as a No. 2 or 3 starter, but it's hard to ignore the reality that he has dealt with injury problems in three of the previous five seasons.

Year	Club (League)	Class	W	L	ERA	G	GS	CG	SV	IP	H	HR	BB	SO	K/9	WHIP	AVG
2011	Greenville (SAL)	LoA	4	1	3.33	10	10	0	0	46	35	4	16	50	9.8	1.11	.211
	Salem (CAR)	HiA	5	5	4.33	16	16	0	0	81	80	6	30	67	7.4	1.36	.262
2012	Portland (EL)	AA	1	3	6.69	9	9	0	0	38	41	4	27	27	6.5	1.81	.283
Minor League Totals			10	9	4.59	35	35	0	0	165	156	14	73	144	7.9	1.39	.253

15 BRIAN JOHNSON, LHP

BA GRADE
50
HIGH

Born: Dec. 7, 1990. **B-T:** L-L. **Ht.:** 6-3. **Wt.:** 225. **Drafted:** Florida, 2012 (1st round). **Signed by:** Anthony Turco.

A two-way star at Florida, Johnson won 22 games and hit 15 homers while leading the Gators to three straight College World Series appearances from 2010-12. Though he offers potential as a lefthanded hitter, most teams preferred him on the mound. That includes the Red Sox, who drafted him 31st overall in June and signed him for $1.575 million. Johnson stands out more for his ability to command four pitches than his pure stuff, though he may add velocity now that he's concentrating on pitching full-time. He usually pitched at 88-91 mph with his fastball in college, but he worked at 92-93 mph during brief outings at short-season Lowell and touched 98 when he faced former Florida State rival Jayce Boyd. Johnson hides the ball well with his delivery, so his fastball gets more swings and misses than might be expected. He also has good feel for both a curveball and a slider, changing speeds easily with them. His changeup helps him keep righthanders at bay. While he doesn't have the most athletic body, he controls it well and repeats his delivery. Johnson earned a start in the annual Futures at Fenway event in Boston in mid-August, only to get struck in the face by a line drive off the bat of the leadoff hitter. The shot broke multiple bones in his face and ended his first pro summer. He returned to work out but didn't see any game action during instructional league. Assuming there are no lasting effects from the injury, he has the polish to move faster than most Red Sox pitching prospects. Johnson will open 2013 at one of the club's Class A affiliates. He has a ceiling as a durable No. 3 starter.

Year	Club (League)	Class	W	L	ERA	G	GS	CG	SV	IP	H	HR	BB	SO	K/9	WHIP	AVG
2012	Lowell (NYP)	SS	0	0	0.00	4	4	0	0	6	2	0	1	4	6.4	0.53	.111
Minor League Totals			0	0	0.00	4	4	0	0	6	2	0	1	4	6.4	0.53	.111

16 TZU-WEI LIN, SS

BA GRADE
55
EXTREME

Born: Feb. 15, 1994. **B-T:** L-R. **Ht.:** 5-9. **Wt.:** 155. **Signed:** Taiwan, 2012. **Signed by:** Louie Lin/Jon Deeble/Eddie Romero.

The Red Sox have several talented shortstop prospects, led by Xander Bogaerts and including Jose Iglesias, Deven Marrero, Jose Vinicio and Cleuluis Rondon. In the end, Lin could develop into a better all-around shortstop than any of them. After winning MVP honors at the 18-and-under World Championship in 2010, he nearly signed with the Yankees for $350,000 as a 16-year-old. That deal collapsed, however, when the Chinese Taipei Baseball Association threatened to block him from ever playing or coaching in Taiwan if he signed before graduating from high school. Lin waited to do so, then signed with Boston for $2.05 million in June, setting a bonus record for Taiwanese position players. The fastest runner in the system, he has plus-plus speed and perhaps more offensive upside than any of the Red Sox' shortstop hopefuls aside from Bogaerts. Though he's not big, Lin has a quick bat and an advanced approach for his age. He repeatedly squares balls up, though he sometimes drifts out in front on pitches. He won't have much power but has the ingredients to become a quality leadoff man. Reports on his overall defense and arm strength range from average to plus, though no one doubts Lin can stay at shortstop. He played in the world 18-and-under tournament again after the 2012 season, earning recognition as the event's top defensive player. If Marrero and Vinicio open 2013 as the everyday shortstops at Boston's two Class A affiliates, Lin could wind up at Lowell.

Year	Club (League)	Class	AVG	G	AB	R	H	2B	3B	HR	RBI	BB	SO	SB	CS	OBP	SLG
2012	Red Sox (GCL)	R	.255	29	110	21	28	5	1	0	16	16	28	4	2	.341	.318
Minor League Totals			.255	29	110	21	28	5	1	0	16	16	28	4	2	.341	.318

17 JOSE VINICIO, SS

BA GRADE
50
HIGH

Born: July 10, 1993. **B-T:** B-R. **Ht.:** 5-11. **Wt.:** 150. **Signed:** Dominican Republic, 2009. **Signed by:** Manny Nanita.

The Red Sox invested heavily in international shortstops in 2009, signing Vinicio for $1.95 million in July and Jose Iglesias for $8.25 million two months later. After Iglesias, Vinicio is the top defensive shortstop in the system and he shows more promise at the plate. He has the actions, quickness, range, hands and arm strength to make all the plays at shortstop, though at times he can get too flashy for his own good. He made 25 errors in 72 games last year, though his .925 fielding percentage represented a career high. Vinicio has quick hands and some life in his bat, though he's frail and won't ever hit for power. If he fills out and develops more patience, he could be a contact hitter who produces solid batting averages and decent on-base percentages. He has plus speed but still is learning the nuances of basestealing. Added strength also would help him cope with the grind of the long season, as assorted nicks and bruises limited him to 72 games last season. With 2012 first-rounder Deven Marrero ticketed for high Class A, Vinicio figures to return to Greenville to begin 2013.

Year	Club (League)	Class	AVG	G	AB	R	H	2B	3B	HR	RBI	BB	SO	SB	CS	OBP	SLG
2010	Red Sox (GCL)	R	.253	43	158	23	40	4	6	1	22	7	26	13	1	.290	.373
2011	Red Sox (GCL)	R	.291	50	179	22	52	7	5	2	18	7	33	19	10	.337	.419
2012	Lowell (NYP)	SS	.000	2	8	0	0	0	0	0	0	0	2	0	0	.000	.000
	Greenville (SAL)	LoA	.277	70	256	37	71	9	3	3	32	13	56	24	11	.320	.371
Minor League Totals			.271	165	601	82	163	20	14	6	72	27	117	56	22	.313	.381

18 ALEX WILSON, RHP

BA GRADE
45
MEDIUM

Born: Nov. 3, 1986. **B-T:** R-R. **Ht.:** 6-0. **Wt.:** 215. **Drafted:** Texas A&M, 2009 (2nd round). **Signed by:** Jim Robinson.

Though Wilson was Boston's minor league pitcher of the year in 2011 as a starter and didn't make a single relief appearance in his first three pro seasons, scouts long have projected him as a bullpen arm. He made three more starts to open 2012 before becoming a full-time reliever in mid-April. He had ups and downs in his new role but was lights-out in the International League playoffs, working five perfect innings as Pawtucket won the championship. Wilson mainly works with a 91-94 mph fastball and a 81-85 mph slider that devastates hitters at times. His stuff didn't kick up a notch as expected, however, when he made the move to the bullpen. Wilson's fastball lacks life, and his command, control and changeup are average at best, which is why he profiles better as a reliever. He has a maximum-effort delivery that contributed to Tommy John surgery while he was in college in 2007. Wilson has the mentality to work the late innings, and could wind up in that role with slightly better stuff and improved command. For now, he has a good shot to break into Boston's bullpen as a middle reliever in 2013.

Year	Club (League)	Class	W	L	ERA	G	GS	CG	SV	IP	H	HR	BB	SO	K/9	WHIP	AVG
2009	Lowell (NYP)	SS	0	1	0.50	13	13	0	0	36	10	0	7	33	8.3	0.47	.085
2010	Salem (CAR)	HiA	2	1	3.40	11	11	0	0	56	43	4	15	50	8.1	1.04	.212
	Portland (EL)	AA	4	5	6.66	16	16	0	0	78	95	15	34	56	6.4	1.65	.302
2011	Portland (EL)	AA	9	4	3.05	21	21	0	0	112	103	8	37	99	8.0	1.25	.246
	Pawtucket (IL)	AAA	1	0	3.43	4	4	0	0	21	19	2	7	24	10.3	1.24	.235
2012	Pawtucket (IL)	AAA	5	3	3.72	40	3	0	1	73	76	3	33	78	9.7	1.50	.270
Minor League Totals			21	14	3.76	105	68	0	1	376	346	32	133	340	8.1	1.28	.244

19 CHRISTIAN VAZQUEZ, C

BA GRADE
50
HIGH

Born: Aug. 21, 1990. **B-T:** R-R. **Ht.:** 5-9. **Wt.:** 195. **Drafted:** HS—Gurabo, P.R., 2008 (9th round). **Signed by:** Edgar Perez.

After smashing 18 homers in 2011, Vazquez got too power-conscious to open last season. He hit just .211 with one homer through the end of May before making adjustments. With a shorter swing and more of an up-the-middle approach, he batted .322/.434/.534 in the next two months to earn a promotion to Double-A. He swings and misses too much to hit for a high average, but he draws his share of walks and has solid power. He should provide more than enough offense to profile as a regular, because he stands out most with his work behind the plate. Managers rated him the Carolina League's best defensive catcher in 2012, and he led the circuit by throwing out 42 percent of basestealers. He enhances average arm strength with a fast release, regularly recording 1.9-second pop times. He has improved as a receiver and blocker. He speaks both English and Spanish well, allowing him to communicate effectively with his pitching staff. He's a well below-average runner but has instincts on the bases. Vazquez struggled offensively during his month in Portland, so he'll head back there at the outset of 2013.

Year	Club (League)	Class	AVG	G	AB	R	H	2B	3B	HR	RBI	BB	SO	SB	CS	OBP	SLG
2008	Red Sox (GCL)	R	.190	21	58	7	11	1	0	0	5	6	17	0	0	.266	.207
2009	Red Sox (GCL)	R	.278	10	36	5	10	5	0	0	7	4	7	0	0	.366	.417
	Lowell (NYP)	SS	.123	21	65	4	8	2	0	2	9	11	16	0	0	.250	.246
2010	Greenville (SAL)	LoA	.263	79	270	34	71	11	0	3	32	23	62	3	1	.328	.337
2011	Greenville (SAL)	LoA	.283	105	392	71	111	27	3	18	84	43	84	1	1	.358	.505
2012	Salem (CAR)	HiA	.266	81	293	43	78	17	0	7	41	40	70	2	2	.360	.396
	Portland (EL)	AA	.205	20	73	11	15	4	0	0	5	8	9	0	0	.280	.260
Minor League Totals			.256	337	1187	175	304	67	3	30	183	135	265	6	4	.337	.393

20 MANUEL MARGOT, OF

BA GRADE
55
EXTREME

Born: Sept. 28, 1994. **B-T:** R-R. **Ht.:** 5-11. **Wt.:** 170. **Signed:** Dominican Republic, 2011. **Signed by:** Manny Nanita/Craig Shipley.

Margot has done nothing but impress the Red Sox since signing for $800,000 in 2011. He tripled, homered and drove in six runs in his first pro game this June and went on to win the organization's Latin American program player of the year award. After that, he was one of the standouts in Boston's instructional league camp. Margot has an advanced approach for his age, works counts and recognizes pitches well. He has a fast bat and wiry strength, with the potential for average power as he gets stronger. He showed promising opposite-field power during instructional league. Margot is an above-average runner who's still raw on the bases, though he did rank third in the Rookie-level Dominican Summer League with 33 steals in 68 games. His speed also makes him an asset in center field, where he reads balls well, and he even has a solid arm. Margot will make his U.S. debut in the Gulf Coast League in June.

Year	Club (League)	Class	AVG	G	AB	R	H	2B	3B	HR	RBI	BB	SO	SB	CS	OBP	SLG
2012	Red Sox (DSL)	R	.285	68	260	49	74	10	7	4	45	36	25	33	9	.382	.423
Minor League Totals			.285	68	260	49	74	10	7	4	45	36	25	33	9	.382	.423

21 PAT LIGHT, RHP

BA GRADE
50
HIGH

Born: March 29, 1991. **B-T:** R-R. **Ht.:** 6-5. **Wt.:** 195. **Drafted:** Monmouth, 2012 (1st round supplemental). **Signed by:** Ray Fagnant.

A 28th-round pick by the Twins out of high school in 2009, Light opted to attend Monmouth, where he set a Hawks single-season strikeout record (102 in 101 innings) last spring and became the highest-drafted player in school history. Selected 39th overall in June, he signed for $1 million, well below the assigned pick value of $1,394,300. But he's far more than a bargain-bin draftee. The Red Sox took pitchers with eight of their top nine choices in 2012, and Light has a better fastball package than any of them. He operates at 92-94 mph and can reach 97, and his heater is just as impressive for its heavy sink. He commands it well, too. Plagued by blister issues on one of his pitching fingers during the spring, he added power and velocity to his slider once he put those behind him in pro ball. He threw a fringy splitter/changeup as an amateur, but Boston had him switch to a true changeup in instructional league. The Red Sox will develop Light as a potential No. 3 starter, and if that doesn't work out he could make a living as late-inning reliever who works off his sinker. He'll spend his first full pro season in Class A.

Year	Club (League)	Class	W	L	ERA	G	GS	CG	SV	IP	H	HR	BB	SO	K/9	WHIP	AVG
2012	Lowell (NYP)	SS	0	2	2.37	12	12	0	0	30	27	1	5	30	8.9	1.05	.243
Minor League Totals			0	2	2.37	12	12	0	0	30	27	1	5	30	8.9	1.05	.243

22 FRANK MONTAS, RHP

BA GRADE
55
EXTREME

Born: March 21, 1993. **B-T:** R-R. **Ht.:** 6-2. **Wt.:** 185. **Signed:** Dominican Republic, 2009. **Signed by:** Manny Nanita.

No one in the system can light up a radar gun like Montas. Signed for $75,000 in 2009, he hit 99-100 mph in the Dominican Summer League two years later. He regularly reached triple digits a few times a game in his 2012 U.S. debut, and did a better job of staying under control and not overthrowing. The angle and armside run on his fastball make it that much tougher to hit, and when he's on he can be untouchable. He blew away the Twins' Byron Buxton, the No. 2 overall pick in the 2012 draft, with three straight 97-100 mph heaters during instructional league. Montas still is far from a finished product, however. His fastball command needs significant improvement and his other pitches are works in progress. He'll flash impressive sliders but without much consistency, and he often throws his changeup too hard in the upper 80s. There's a good chance that Montas eventually will wind up in the bullpen, though he'll continue to get innings as a starter for now. If he throws enough strikes in spring training, he can earn an assignment to low Class A.

Year	Club (League)	Class	W	L	ERA	G	GS	CG	SV	IP	H	HR	BB	SO	K/9	WHIP	AVG
2010	Red Sox (DSL)	R	0	3	9.55	12	4	0	0	22	28	2	18	18	7.5	2.12	.322
2011	Red Sox (DSL)	R	0	1	4.26	5	5	0	0	13	7	0	12	12	8.5	1.50	.159
2012	Red Sox (GCL)	R	1	5	3.98	12	9	0	0	41	34	0	12	41	9.1	1.13	.228
	Lowell (NYP)	SS	0	0	0.00	1	1	0	0	4	5	0	1	4	9.8	1.64	.357
Minor League Totals			1	9	5.38	30	19	0	0	79	74	2	43	75	8.6	1.49	.252

23 TRAVIS SHAW, 1B/3B

BA GRADE
50
HIGH

Born: April 16, 1990. **B-T:** L-R. **Ht.:** 6-4. **Wt.:** 225. **Drafted:** Kent State, 2011 (9th round). **Signed by:** Jon Adkins.

The Red Sox originally drafted Shaw in the 32nd round out of an Ohio high school in

2008, but they had to wait until he played three years at Kent State to sign him for $110,000 as a ninth-rounder in 2011. The son of former all-star reliever Jeff Shaw, Travis was one of the most pleasant surprises in the system last year. He led the Carolina League in on-base percentage (.397) and slugging (.517) and continued to hit after a promotion to Double-A. He also earned MVP honors at the California/Carolina League all-star game after hitting a two-run homer, and recognition from managers as the CL's best defensive first baseman. Shaw has a fluid lefthanded stroke suited for Fenway Park, as he can pull pitches for home runs or take them the other way for potential doubles off the Green Monster. His disciplined approach never wavers, as he continued to work counts even when he went 27 games without a homer to open the 2012 season or when he tired at the end of his first full pro season. Boston thinks he can post high batting averages and on-base percentages while hitting for solid power. Shaw has below-average speed and athleticism, but he moves well for his size and has a strong arm. A third baseman in college, he has shown soft hands and good footwork since moving to first base in pro ball. Now that his stock has surpassed that of Michael Almanzar and Kolbrin Vitek, Shaw could get more of an opportunity at the hot corner in 2013. He'll likely return to Portland to open the season.

Year	Club (League)	Class	AVG	G	AB	R	H	2B	3B	HR	RBI	BB	SO	SB	CS	OBP	SLG
2011	Lowell (NYP)	SS	.262	57	202	33	53	13	0	8	36	34	47	3	0	.371	.446
	Greenville (SAL)	LoA	.333	2	9	1	3	1	0	0	1	1	0	0	0	.400	.444
2012	Salem (CAR)	HiA	.305	99	354	69	108	31	3	16	73	59	81	11	2	.405	.545
	Portland (EL)	AA	.227	31	110	13	25	13	0	3	12	21	34	1	1	.353	.427
Minor League Totals			.280	189	675	116	189	58	3	27	122	115	162	15	3	.390	.495

24 SEAN COYLE, 2B

BA GRADE
50
HIGH

Born: Jan. 17, 1992. **B-T:** R-R. **Ht.:** 5-8. **Wt.:** 175. **Drafted:** HS—Fort Washington, Pa., 2010 (3rd round). **Signed by:** Chris Calciano.

One of the Carolina League's youngest players last year at age 20, Coyle got off to a slow start and compounded his problems by overswinging and chasing pitches out of the strike zone. He hit just .211/.285/.343 in the first half before tightening his approach and batting .297/.355/.451 after the all-star break. That's the kind of offensive production that led the Red Sox to invest $1.3 million in him as a third-round pick in 2010. Because he's a 5-foot-8 second baseman in the Boston system, he inevitably draws Dustin Pedroia comparisons. Those are a stretch, though Coyle does have surprising pop for his size and plays an aggressive, instinctive game. His bat speed, strong lower half and hand-eye coordination give him average power. He's at his best when he works counts and uses the middle of the field. The Red Sox expected that he might have growing pains in high Class A, but they were surprised that his walk total dropped to 29 from 60 the year before. Coyle has plus speed and went a perfect 16-for-16 stealing bases last season, but scouts would like him to get more out of his quickness by bunting and attempting steals more often. He has solid range, hands and arm strength on defense, and he topped Carolina League second basemen with a .967 fielding percentage. Coyle will advance to Double-A in 2013 and should be close to big league-ready when Pedroia's contract expires after the 2014 season.

Year	Club (League)	Class	AVG	G	AB	R	H	2B	3B	HR	RBI	BB	SO	SB	CS	OBP	SLG
2010	Red Sox (GCL)	R	.200	3	10	5	2	1	0	0	0	1	1	0	0	.333	.300
2011	Greenville (SAL)	LoA	.247	106	384	77	95	27	7	14	64	60	110	20	6	.362	.464
2012	Salem (CAR)	HiA	.249	116	437	60	109	31	2	9	63	29	116	16	0	.316	.391
Minor League Totals			.248	225	831	142	206	59	9	23	127	90	227	36	6	.339	.424

25 KEURY DE LA CRUZ, OF

BA GRADE
50
HIGH

Born: Nov. 28, 1991. **B-T:** L-L. **Ht.:** 5-11. **Wt.:** 185. **Signed:** Dominican Republic, 2009. **Signed by:** Luciano del Rosario.

De la Cruz was Boston's Latin American program player of the year in his 2009 pro debut and encored by leading the Gulf Coast League with 94 total bases in 2010, but his lack of a consistent approach caught up to him at Lowell in 2011. He hit more under control in 2012, which combined with improved strength and bat speed resulted in the first 20-20 season by a Red Sox farmhand since George Lombard in 2005. De la Cruz's swing is more sound, his balance is improved and he's more willing to use the opposite field than he was in the past. He's still overly aggressive at the plate, which more experienced pitchers may be able to exploit. Signed as a center fielder, de la Cruz has taken on a different profile as he has filled out. He now has fringy speed, and basestealing won't be a big part of his game despite his 20 steals last season. His below-average arm will relegate him to left field, and he topped South Atlantic League outfielders with nine errors in 2012. Some scouts don't think he puts forth enough effort on defense. His bat will have to carry him, and it may because de la Cruz has the upside of an above-average hitter with solid power. He finished last season in high Class A and will return there to begin 2013.

Year	Club (League)	Class	AVG	G	AB	R	H	2B	3B	HR	RBI	BB	SO	SB	CS	OBP	SLG
2009	Red Sox (DSL)	R	.259	67	251	31	65	16	4	3	50	42	43	13	8	.368	.390
2010	Red Sox (GCL)	R	.263	51	198	35	52	10	7	6	31	17	50	8	6	.320	.475
2011	Lowell (NYP)	SS	.263	71	300	31	79	14	6	4	24	10	56	15	11	.292	.390

2012	Greenville (SAL)	LoA	.308	116	474	71	146	35	8	19	81	26	101	19	7	.352	.536
	Salem (CAR)	HiA	.280	6	25	1	7	2	0	1	6	1	2	1	1	.308	.480
Minor League Totals			.280	311	1248	169	349	77	25	33	192	96	252	56	33	.336	.461

26 TY BUTTREY, RHP

BA GRADE

50

HIGH

Born: March 31, 1993. **B-T:** L-R. **Ht.:** 6-5. **Wt.:** 210. **Drafted:** HS—Charlotte, 2012 (4th round). **Signed by:** Quincy Boyd.

Buttrey is the latest top prospect to come out of Charlotte's Providence High, following Richie Shaffer, who became a Rays 2012 first-round pick after three years at Clemson, and Brett Austin, a Padres 2012 supplemental first-rounder. Buttrey's price tag and commitment to Arkansas dropped him to the fourth round in June, with his $1.3 million bonus more indicative of his true value. While he's just getting going in pro ball, he has the potential to be a No. 2 or 3 starter. Buttrey's velocity fluctuated during the spring, but he's capable of sitting at 90-93 mph and reaching 96. He throws a 77-79 mph knuckle-curve that has downer action and a chance to become an out pitch. His changeup shows nice fade. Buttrey's large frame creates tough angles for hitters and should lend him the durability needed to start. He's advanced for a high schooler and will turn 20 before the start of the 2013 season, giving him a chance to open it in low Class A.

Year	Club (League)	Class	W	L	ERA	G	GS	CG	SV	IP	H	HR	BB	SO	K/9	WHIP	AVG
2012	Red Sox (GCL)	R	0	0	1.80	4	3	0	0	5	5	0	1	5	9.0	1.20	.278
Minor League Totals			0	0	1.80	4	3	0	0	5	5	0	1	5	9.0	1.20	.278

27 CODY KUKUK, LHP

BA GRADE

50

HIGH

Born: April 10, 1993. **B-T:** L-L. **Ht.:** 6-4. **Wt.:** 200. **Drafted:** HS—Lawrence, Kan., 2011 (7th round). **Signed by:** Chris Mears.

A potential third-round pick in the 2011 draft, Kukuk lasted until the eighth round because he had a reported seven-figure asking price. He signed for $800,000 that August but didn't make his pro debut for another 12 months. He was arrested and charged with drunken driving in May while in extended spring training, and the Red Sox held him out of game action until the charges were dropped for lack of probable cause. He overpowered Gulf Coast League hitters, who went just 3-for-35 (.083) with 16 strikeouts against him, and continued to impress during instructional league. After pitching at 88-91 mph as a high school starter, Kukuk sat at 92-93 mph and peaked at 95 in short pro stints. His fastball has life as well, and he's improving his feel for a hard slider that shows the potential to give him a second plus pitch. His changeup isn't as far along as his other two offerings. Like most young pitchers, Kukuk needs more consistency with his stuff, command and delivery. But there's no doubting that he has a quality left arm and plenty of upside. Because he has just 10 pro innings under his belt, it remains to be seen whether Boston will deem him ready for a full-season assignment to start 2013.

Year	Club (League)	Class	W	L	ERA	G	GS	CG	SV	IP	H	HR	BB	SO	K/9	WHIP	AVG
2012	Red Sox (GCL)	R	2	0	0.90	5	0	0	0	10	3	0	3	16	14.4	0.60	.086
Minor League Totals			2	0	0.90	5	0	0	0	10	3	0	3	16	14.4	0.60	.086

28 SIMON MERCEDES, RHP

BA GRADE

50

HIGH

Born: Feb. 17, 1992. **B-T:** R-R. **Ht.:** 6-4. **Wt.:** 220. **Signed:** Dominican Republic, 2012. **Signed by:** Manny Nanita/Eddie Romero.

In the murky world of Latin American signings, several players have had deals voided after Major League Baseball investigations into their identities and birthdays, only to land bigger bonuses from a second team. The Red Sox got burned when they landed Dominican righthander Carlos Matias for $160,000 in 2009, lost him when MLB didn't clear him, then saw him develop into a top prospect with the Cardinals after signing for $1.5 million as Carlos Martinez. In a reversal of that, Boston signed Mercedes for $800,000 in March 2012, after he had agreed to a $400,000 deal with the Giants in March 2011, only to have MLB kill it and declare him ineligible to sign for one year. He used the same name and birthdate on both contracts, and he finally received a U.S. visa and MLB approval last August. Mercedes has one of the heaviest fastballs in the system, sitting at 92-94 mph and topping out at 96. His hard curveball is a swing-and-miss pitch at times, but he sometimes gets under the pitch and doesn't command it well. He also throws a splitter to keep hitters off balance. Mercedes could become more efficient if he can smooth out his delivery. He draws physical comparisions to Guillermo Mota and could wind up in the bullpen if he can't refine his secondary pitches and command. He'll be 21 at the start of the 2013 season, so the Red Sox may send him to low Class A with just four innings of pro experience.

Year	Club (League)	Class	W	L	ERA	G	GS	CG	SV	IP	H	HR	BB	SO	K/9	WHIP	AVG
2012	Red Sox (DSL)	R	0	0	0.00	1	1	0	0	4	4	0	2	4	9.0	1.50	.250
Minor League Totals			0	0	0.00	1	1	0	0	4	4	0	2	4	9.0	1.50	.250

29 STOLMY PIMENTEL, RHP

BA GRADE
50
HIGH

Born: Feb. 1, 1990. **B-T:** R-R. **Ht.:** 6-4. **Wt.:** 230. **Signed:** Dominican Republic, 2006. **Signed by:** Luis Scheker.

The Red Sox read a lot of positives into Pimentel's 6-7, 4.59 performance in Double-A last year. Though his results were mediocre, they represented a marked improvement from his previous stint at Portland (0-9, 9.12), and he made strides with his stuff and command. A growth spurt resulted in extra fastball velocity in 2011 but threw his mechanics and the rest of his game out of sync. Pimentel worked to tighten his delivery and throw in a more direct line to the plate last season, which helped add life and deception to his pitches. While he's capable of reaching 98 mph with his four-seam fastball, he's learning that he's more effective when he works with 91-94 mph two-seamers. He generates weak contact with a cutter/slider hybrid, and he has regained the feel for a quality changeup that he lost in 2011. The next step is for Pimentel to miss more bats and achieve more consistent success. If he can't, he'll make the transition from possible No. 3 starter to potential set-up man. He should make his Triple-A debut at some point in 2013.

Year	Club (League)	Class	W	L	ERA	G	GS	CG	SV	IP	H	HR	BB	SO	K/9	WHIP	AVG
2007	Red Sox (DSL)	R	3	1	2.90	14	13	0	0	62	44	2	22	60	8.7	1.06	.202
2008	Lowell (NYP)	SS	5	2	3.14	13	11	0	0	63	51	7	17	61	8.7	1.08	.224
2009	Greenville (SAL)	LoA	10	7	3.82	24	23	1	0	118	135	12	29	103	7.9	1.39	.290
2010	Salem (CAR)	HiA	9	11	4.06	26	26	0	0	129	120	11	42	102	7.1	1.26	.248
2011	Portland (EL)	AA	0	9	9.12	15	15	0	0	50	75	8	23	30	5.4	1.95	.352
	Salem (CAR)	HiA	6	4	4.53	11	10	0	0	52	50	8	16	35	6.1	1.28	.259
2012	Portland (EL)	AA	6	7	4.59	22	22	1	0	116	115	9	42	86	6.7	1.36	.259
Minor League Totals			39	41	4.37	125	120	2	0	589	590	57	191	477	7.3	1.33	.263

30 MIGUEL PENA, LHP

BA GRADE
50
HIGH

Born: Oct. 24, 1990. **B-T:** L-L. **Ht.:** 6-2. **Wt.:** 175. **Drafted:** San Jacinto (Texas) JC, 2011 (6th round). **Signed by:** Matt Dorey.

The Nationals made Pena a fifth-round pick out of a Texas high school in 2008 because he was a projectable lefthander with three pitches. During two years at San Jacinto (Texas) JC and two in pro ball, he hasn't gotten much stronger and his stuff hasn't gotten much better. Yet he remains intriguing because he's a southpaw whose pitchability gives him a chance to develop into a No. 4 starter. Pena is athletic and has a clean delivery, which allows him to command all three of his pitches with ease. His best offering is a changeup that projects as a plus pitch. He also throws an 87-92 mph fastball that sits around 90, and a mid-70s curveball with some bite. He's fearless on the mound, attacking hitters while also keeping them off balance. Pena's first full pro season in 2012 went well, highlighted by six perfect innings May 8 as part of the first no-hitter in Greenville franchise history, though he missed most of July with a strained hamstring. The Red Sox will send him to high Class A this year and could move him quickly if he keeps getting results.

Year	Club (League)	Class	W	L	ERA	G	GS	CG	SV	IP	H	HR	BB	SO	K/9	WHIP	AVG
2011	Lowell (NYP)	SS	1	0	2.35	5	2	0	0	15	10	0	3	22	12.9	0.85	.185
2012	Red Sox (GCL)	R	0	1	4.50	1	0	0	0	4	3	0	1	4	9.0	1.00	.214
	Greenville (SAL)	LoA	8	7	2.95	20	19	0	0	101	95	7	21	91	8.1	1.15	.253
Minor League Totals			9	8	2.93	26	21	0	0	120	108	7	25	117	8.8	1.11	.244

Chicago Cubs

BY JIM CALLIS

Optimism reigned when the Cubs gave their a front office a full makeover last offseason. New president of baseball operations Theo Epstein, general manager Jed Hoyer and vice president of player development and scouting Jason McLeod had built two World Series champions with the Red Sox. Hoyer and McLeod also had revitalized the Padres farm system when they went to San Diego.

Because Chicago had focused on the short term in the last years of GM Jim Hendry's tenure and were left with an old and overpriced roster, fans understood that the club was going to have to get worse before it could get better.

That's exactly what happened in 2012. Winning at the major league level wasn't a priority—or a common occurrence. The Cubs' victory total dropped for the fourth straight season, culminating with a 61-101 record that was their worst in 46 seasons.

For all the losses, there was plenty of good news. Chicago's priority was to procure impact talent, and they found some.

The Cubs spent the No. 6 overall pick in the draft and $3.9 million in bonus money on center fielder Albert Almora, one of the most polished high school position players in recent memory. To restock an organization bereft of pitching, they spent their next seven choices on arms, starting with Missouri State righthander Pierce Johnson.

A week after the draft, Chicago landed Cuban slugger Jorge Soler with the biggest deal for an amateur in franchise history. Soler received a nine-year, $30 million big league contract that included a $6 million bonus, then teamed with Almora in the Rookie-level Arizona League.

At the trade deadline, the Cubs picked up righthander Arodys Vizcaino from the Braves in a deal for reliable veterans Reed Johnson and Paul Maholm. Vizcaino never would have been available if he hadn't had Tommy John surgery in March, but pitching-starved Chicago was thrilled to grab someone who ranked among the game's better pitching prospects before he got hurt.

Those were the headline moves, but there were several more. The Cubs spent heavily on three international pitchers, with $1.5 million Dominican righthander Juan Carlos Paniagua generating positive reviews and $6 million Cuban lefthander Gerardo Concepcion getting panned and shelled in low Class A. They imported Hanshin Tigers closer Kyuji

Albert Almora (left) and Jorge Soler hope to usher in a better future for the Cubs

Fujikawa from Japan in December for a two-year deal worth $9.5 million.

Of the many trades Epstein and Hoyer made in their first 14 months on the job, one of their best came three months before the season began. They shipped Andrew Cashner, Chicago's 2008 first-round pick, to the Padres for Anthony Rizzo, whom they had drafted in Boston. Rizzo was the biggest threat in the Cubs lineup after they called him up in late June, batting .285/.342/.463 at age 22.

There were more comings and goings in the front office, too. Vice president of player personnel Oneri Fleita, who had been with the organization since 1995, was fired as part of a mid-August shakeup. Minor league field coordinator Brandon Hyde was promoted to take over Fleita's farm director duties. Padres scouting director Jaron Madison took the same job with the Cubs. He replaced Tim Wilken, who took an expanded role as a special assistant to Epstein. And at the end of October, the Cubs hired Vanderbilt pitching coach Derek Johnson—who helped mentor current big leaguers such as David Price and Mike Minor while with the Commodores—as their new minor league pitching coordinator.

That's a lot of change in one year. But Chicago believes it was necessary and will be for the better.

THIS YEAR'S TOP 30

Player, Pos.		Grade
1.	Javier Baez, ss	65/High
2.	Albert Almora, of	60/Medium
3.	Jorge Soler, of	65/High
4.	Arodys Vizcaino, rhp	60/High
5.	Brett Jackson, of	55/High
6.	Pierce Johnson, rhp	50/High
7.	Dan Vogelbach, 1b	50/High
8.	Jeimer Candelario, 3b	50/High
9.	Kyuji Fujikawa, rhp	45/Low
10.	Arismendy Alcantara, ss	50/High
11.	Juan Carlos Paniagua, rhp	55/Extreme
12.	Christian Villanueva, 3b	50/High
13.	Alberto Cabrera, rhp	45/Medium
14.	Matt Szczur, of	50/High
15.	Junior Lake, ss/3b	50/High
16.	Paul Blackburn, rhp	50/High
17.	Duane Underwood, rhp	50/High
18.	Dillon Maples, rhp	50/High
19.	Logan Watkins, 2b/ss/of	45/Medium
20.	Marco Hernandez, ss	50/High
21.	Gioskar Amaya, 2b	50/High
22.	Tony Zych, rhp	45/High
23.	Robert Whitenack, rhp	50/High
24.	Trey McNutt, rhp	50/High
25.	Josh Vitters, 3b	45/Medium
26.	Barret Loux, rhp	45/Medium
27.	Matt Loosen, rhp	45/Medium
28.	Lendy Castillo, rhp	45/Medium
29.	Marcus Hatley, rhp	45/Medium
30.	Trey Martin, of	50/High

LAST YEAR'S TOP 30

Player, Pos.		Status
1.	Brett Jackson, of	No. 5
2.	Javier Baez, ss	No. 1
3.	Matt Szczur, of	No. 14
4.	Trey McNutt, rhp	No. 24
5.	Dillon Maples, rhp	No. 18
6.	Welington Castillo, c	Majors
7.	Rafael Dolis, rhp	Majors
8.	Junior Lake, ss	No. 15
9.	Josh Vitters, 3b/1b	No. 25
10.	Dan Vogelbach, 1b	No. 7
11.	Dae-Eun Rhee, rhp	Dropped out
12.	Dallas Beeler, rhp	Dropped out
13.	Chris Carpenter, rhp	(Red Sox)
14.	Zeke DeVoss, 2b	Dropped out
15.	Tony Zych, rhp	No. 22
16.	Marco Hernandez, ss/2b	No. 20
17.	Reggie Golden, of	Dropped out
18.	Jae-Hoon Ha, of	Dropped out
19.	Robert Whitenack, rhp	No. 23
20.	Jeimer Candelario, 3b	No. 8
21.	Steve Clevenger, c	Majors
22.	Jose Rosario, rhp	Dropped out
23.	Logan Watkins, 2b/ss/of	No. 19
24.	Jeff Beliveau, lhp	Majors
25.	Ben Wells, rhp	Dropped out
26.	Marcus Hatley, rhp	No. 29
27.	Casey Weathers, rhp	Dropped out
28.	Taiwan Easterling, of	Dropped out
29.	Hayden Simpson, rhp	Dropped out
30.	Shawon Dunston Jr., of	Dropped out

BEST TOOLS

Best Hitter for Average	Albert Almora
Best Power Hitter	Dan Vogelbach
Best Strike-Zone Discipline	Logan Watkins
Fastest Baserunner	Matt Szczur
Best Athlete	Matt Szczur
Best Fastball	Arodys Vizcaino
Best Curveball	Arodys Vizcaino
Best Slider	Alberto Cabrera
Best Changeup	Brooks Raley
Best Control	Kyle Hendricks
Best Defensive Catcher	Chadd Krist
Best Defensive Infielder	Javier Baez
Best Infield Arm	Junior Lake
Best Defensive Outfielder	Albert Almora
Best Outfield Arm	Jorge Soler

PROJECTED 2016 LINEUP

Catcher	Welington Castillo
First Base	Anthony Rizzo
Second Base	Starlin Castro
Third Base	Jeimer Candelario
Shortstop	Javier Baez
Left Field	Brett Jackson
Center Field	Albert Almora
Right Field	Jorge Soler
No. 1 Starter	Jeff Samardzija
No. 2 Starter	Matt Garza
No. 3 Starter	Arodys Vizcaino
No. 4 Starter	Pierce Johnson
No. 5 Starter	Paul Blackburn
Closer	Juan Carlos Paniagua

TOP PROSPECTS OF THE DECADE

Year	Player, Pos.	2012 Org.
2003	Hee Seop Choi, 1b	Kia (Korea)
2004	Angel Guzman, rhp	Dodgers
2005	Brian Dopirak, 1b	Out of baseball
2006	Felix Pie, of	Braves
2007	Felix Pie, of	Braves
2008	Josh Vitters, 3b	Cubs
2009	Josh Vitters, 3b	Cubs
2010	Starlin Castro, ss	Cubs
2011	Chris Archer, rhp	Rays
2012	Brett Jackson, of	Cubs

TOP DRAFT PICKS OF THE DECADE

Year	Player, Pos.	2012 Org.
2003	Ryan Harvey, of	Lancaster (Atlantic)
2005	Mark Pawelek, lhp	Out of baseball
2006	Tyler Colvin, of	Rockies
2007	Josh Vitters, 3b	Cubs
2008	Andrew Cashner, rhp	Padres
2009	Brett Jackson, of	Cubs
2010	Hayden Simpson, rhp	Cubs
2011	Javier Baez, ss	Cubs
2012	Albert Almora, of	Cubs

LARGEST BONUSES IN CLUB HISTORY

Jorge Soler, 2012	$6,000,000
Mark Prior, 2001	$4,000,000
Kosuke Fukudome, 2007	$4,000,000
Albert Almora, 2012	$3,900,000
Corey Patterson, 1998	$3,700,000

CHICAGO CUBS

TOP 2013 ROOKIE: Kyuji Fujikama, rhp. Japanese import could be the Opening Day closer if the Cubs jettison Carlos Marmol.

BREAKOUT PROSPECT: Paul Blackburn, rhp. Solid stuff and advanced pitchability could help this 2012 supplemental first-rounder move quickly for a prep product.

SLEEPER: Jose Arias, rhp. He already throws 91-94 mph and is starting to figure the rest of pitching out.

SOURCE OF TOP 30 TALENT

Homegrown	26	Acquired	4
College	6	Trades	3
Junior college	1	Rule 5 draft	1
High school	9	Independent leagues	0
Draft-and-follow	1	Free agents/waivers	0
Nondrafted free agents	0		
International	9		

LF
Ricardo Marcano

CF
Albert Almora (2)
Brett Jackson (5)
Matt Szczur (14)
Trey Martin (30)
Jae-Hoon Ha
Taiwan Easterling
Shawon Dunston Jr.
Pin-Chieh Chen
Rubi Silva
Rashad Crawford

RF
Jorge Soler (3)
Reggie Golden
Bijan Rademacher

3B
Jeimer Candelario (8)
Christian Villanueva (12)
Junior Lake (15)
Josh Vitters (25)
Dustin Geiger
Wes Darvill
Mark Malave

SS
Javier Baez (1)
Arismendy Alcantara (10)
Marco Hernandez (20)
Tim Saunders
Frandy de la Rosa

2B
Logan Watkins (19)
Gioskar Amaya (21)
Ronald Torreyes
Zeke DeVoss
Stephen Bruno
David Bote

1B
Dan Vogelbach (7)
Justin Bour
Rock Shoulders
Ben Carhart

C
Willson Contreras
Chadd Krist
Justin Marra
Carlos Escobar

LHP

LHSP	LHRP
Brooks Raley	Michael Heesch
Chris Rusin	Jeffry Antigua
Eric Jokisch	Jeffrey Lorick
Austin Kirk	Nathan Dorris
Anthony Prieto	
Frank del Valle	
Gerardo Concepcion	

RHP

RHSP	RHRP
Arodys Vizcaino (4)	Kyuji Fujikawa (9)
Pierce Johnson (6)	Alberto Cabrera (13)
Juan Carlos Paniagua (11)	Tony Zych (22)
Paul Blackburn (16)	Trey McNutt (24)
Duane Underwood (17)	Lendy Castillo (28)
Dillon Maples (18)	Marcus Hatley (29)
Robert Whitenack (23)	Austin Reed
Barret Loux (26)	Hector Rondon
Matt Loosen (27)	Kevin Rhoderick
Jose Arias	Casey Weathers
Dallas Beeler	Josh Conway
Kyle Hendricks	Trey Lang
Michael Jensen	Marcel Carreno
Nick Struck	P.J. Francescon
Zach Cates	Jose Rosario
Ben Wells	Justin Amlung
Ryan McNeil	Luis Liria
Tayler Scott	

2012   BONUSES: $9.2 MILLION

BEST PURE HITTER: OF Albert Almora (1) has a quick bat and repeatedly makes line-drive contact with ease. The Cubs had their eyes opened by the bats of three lower draft picks—INF Stephen Bruno (7), SS/3B Tim Saunders (32) and 3B Ben Carhart (35).

BEST POWER HITTER: Power might be the least obvious of Almora's tools, but he has the hitting prowess to produce 20 homers annually once he gets stronger. 1B Jacob Rogers (40) has the most strength in this draft crop.

FASTEST RUNNER: OF Rashad Crawford (11) has plus-plus speed that also served him well on the basketball court. An above-average runner, Saunders stole 17 bases in 49 pro games.

BEST DEFENSIVE PLAYER: Almora has impressive tools and even better instincts, and he has all the ingredients to be a Gold Glove center fielder. C Chadd Krist (9) is solid behind the plate and ranks as the system's best defensive catcher.

BEST FASTBALL: RHP Duane Underwood's (2) velocity fluctuates, but at his best he can get to 98 mph. RHP Pierce Johnson (1s) has more consistent velocity, sitting at 92-94 mph and peaking at 96. RHP Josh Conway (4) maxed out at 96 mph before having Tommy John surgery during the spring while still at Coastal Carolina.

BEST SECONDARY PITCH: Johnson's hard curveball gives him a second strikeout pitch. RHP Paul Blackburn (1s), who has the best overall feel for pitching among Cubs draftees, has the makings of a plus curve as well.

BEST PRO DEBUT: Bruno led the short-season Northwest League in batting (.361), hits (91) and on-base percentage (.442). Saunders outhit him while reaching high Class A, batting a combined .381/.431/.536 between three stops.

BEST ATHLETE: Crawford is the most explosive athlete, as YouTube clips of him dunking from the foul line will attest. Almora is the best baseball athlete, with the chance to have solid or better tools across the board.

MOST INTRIGUING BACKGROUND: Unsigned 3B Rustin Sveum's (39) father Dale manages the Cubs and played in the big leagues for 12 seasons.

CLOSEST TO THE MAJORS: Johnson, who could start his first full pro season in high Class A. Almora's instincts make him a good bet to be the first prep position player from the entire draft class to get to the big leagues.

BEST LATE-ROUND PICK: Saunders, the 2012 NCAA Division III College World Series MVP in June, has versatility to go with his plus bat and wheels. LHP Nathan Dorris (17) has the makings of a solid fastball and above-average curveball.

THE ONE WHO GOT AWAY: Chicago never got close to landing OF Rhett Wiseman (25), a quality athlete with a raw bat who could have gone in the top three rounds if he could have been signed away from Vanderbilt. The Cubs thought they had a deal with LHP Jake Drossner (23) but ultimately lost him to Maryland.

ASSESSMENT: The Cubs desperately need pitching in their system but couldn't pass up Almora with the No. 6 overall pick. After that, they focused on the mound and used their next seven picks on arms.

2011   BONUSES: $12.0 MILLION

SS Javier Baez (1), the system's top prospect, has hit as hoped and defended better than expected. 1B Dan Vogelbach (2) has massive power. RHP Tony Zych (4) could help Chicago's bullpen in the near future.

GRADE: A

2010   BONUSES: $4.7 MILLION

RHP Hayden Simpson (1), a surprise choice at No. 16 overall, hasn't worked out. OF Matt Szczur (5) is still turning his physical tools into baseball skills after giving up a potential NFL career.

GRADE: D

2009   BONUSES: $4.0 MILLION

Four players from this crop have reached the majors, but only OF Brett Jackson (1) has the potential to be more than a role player—and he struck out 217 times last year. 2B/3B D.J. LeMahieu (2) was traded to the Rockies in the Ian Stewart deal last offseason, while LHPs Chris Rusin (4) and Brooks Raley (6) got battered in Chicago's rotation.

GRADE: C+

2008   BONUSES: $5.5 MILLION

The Cubs got value out of RHP Andrew Cashner (1) by dealing him to the Padres for Anthony Rizzo last January. Seven additional draftees have played in the majors. Of those, only OF Tony Campana (13), RHP Casey Coleman (15) and LHP Jeff Beliveau (18) remain in the organization. OF/3B Ryan Flaherty (1s), RHPs Chris Carpenter (3) and Eric Hamren (37) and INF/OF Josh Harrison (6) have departed.

GRADE: C+

Draft analysis by Jim Callis. Numbers in parentheses indicate draft rounds.

1 JAVIER BAEZ, SS

Born: Dec. 1, 1992. **B-T:** R-R. **Ht.:** 6-1. **Wt.:** 205.
Drafted: HS—Jacksonville, Fla., 2011 (1st round).
Signed by: Tom Clark.

BA GRADE
65
HIGH

MIKE JANES

Born in Puerto Rico, Baez moved to Florida when he was 12. Going into his senior season at the Arlington Country Day School (Jacksonville, Fla.), he projected as a late first-round pick. He and Montverde (Fla.) Academy shortstop Francisco Lindor drew more than 100 scouts to a February showdown, and Baez kept impressing evaluators all spring. He batted .711 with 20 homers and went ninth overall to the Cubs—one pick after the Indians took Lindor—playing five pro games after signing for $2,625,000. Chicago kept him in extended spring training at the start of 2012 in order to tame his wild approach. That didn't really work, but his aggressiveness didn't stop him from posting a .979 OPS after he got to low Class A Peoria in late May. Managers named him the most exciting player in the Midwest League, where he also rated as the No. 1 prospect, and one scout said watching Baez take batting practice was the highlight of his summer. It took him just two months to hit his way to high Class A Daytona, where more advanced pitchers took advantage of his belief that he can hit any pitch in or out of the strike zone. The Cubs continued to challenge him after the season, taking the rare step of sending a teenager to the Arizona Fall League. He kept swinging from his heels, batting .211 but drilling four homers in 14 games, before breaking the tip of his left thumb in a pregame accident. He'll be fine by spring training.

Baez has electric bat speed that elicits comparisons to the gold standard (Gary Sheffield), and he turns it loose every time. At some point he's going to have to tone down his swing and take more pitches—probably once he understands that opponents won't challenge him if they don't have to—but he has an uncanny ability to impart a lot of topspin on balls even when he doesn't square them up. His offensive ceiling is ridiculous, as it's not out of the question that he could develop into a well above-average hitter for both average and power. His bat alone could make him a superstar, but Baez offers a lot more in his tool kit. He sur-

SCOUTING GRADES

Batting: 60.   **Defense:** 55.
Power: 65.   **Arm:** 65.
Speed: 50.

Based on 20-80 scouting scale, where 50 represents major league average, and future projection rather than present tools.

prised MWL observers and the Cubs with his smooth actions and range at shortstop. He eventually may outgrow the position, but scouts give him a chance to stay there for a while. His arm gives him a third well above-average tool, and he'd have no problem fulfilling the offensive and defensive requirements at third base. He has strong instincts and is much more under control as both a defender and baserunner. With average speed, he swiped 24 bases in 29 attempts last year. Baez plays with a cockiness that tends to infuriate opponents, which explains why he was hit by 10 pitches in 57 MWL games.

As an offensive-minded shortstop, he could be better than Starlin Castro. Baez has better defensive tools, more power and similar hitting ability. The Cubs probably won't displace Castro, but they'll keep Baez at shortstop until he shows he can't play there. He should see Double-A Tennessee at some point in 2013, perhaps even on Opening Day. Once he moderates his approach at the plate, he could get to Wrigley Field in a hurry.

Year	Club (League)	Class	AVG	G	AB	R	H	2B	3B	HR	RBI	BB	SO	SB	CS	OBP	SLG
2011	Cubs (AZL)	R	.333	3	12	2	4	2	0	0	0	0	2	2	0	.333	.500
	Boise (NWL)	SS	.167	2	6	0	1	0	0	0	1	0	2	0	0	.167	.167
2012	Peoria (MWL)	LoA	.333	57	213	41	71	10	5	12	33	9	48	20	3	.383	.596
	Daytona (FSL)	HiA	.188	23	80	9	15	3	1	4	13	5	21	4	2	.244	.400
Minor League Totals			.293	85	311	52	91	15	6	16	47	14	73	26	5	.342	.534

2 ALBERT ALMORA, OF

Born: April 16, 1994. **B-T:** R-R. **Ht.:** 6-1. **Wt.:** 170. **Drafted:** HS—Hialeah, Fla., 2012 (1st round). **Signed by:** John Koronka/Laz Llanos.

Scouts say Almora has more polish and better makeup than any high schooler in recent memory. His tools are solid or better across the board too, so the Cubs selected him sixth overall in June and signed him for $3.9 million. It was no surprise that he was able to make an easy transition to pro ball, hitting .321/.331/.464 at the two lowest levels of the system. Thanks to his bat speed, loose swing and hand-eye coordination, Almora makes line-drive contact with ease. He has natural hitting rhythm and pitch-recognition skills beyond his years. He will need to develop more patience, however, after walking just twice in 145 pro plate appearances. He's not the most physical player, but he has the hitting acumen and projection to grow into annual 20-homer power. As gifted as he is offensively, scouts rave even more about Almora's defense. He has incredible instincts, allowing his average speed to play up a grade on the bases and well above that in center field. He gets

BA GRADE

60

MEDIUM

outstanding jumps and takes precise routes. He also has a strong, accurate arm. A quality teammate, he has helped Cuban defector Jorge Soler with his English. Almora profiles as a Gold Glove center fielder who could hit third in the batting order. He'll be part of a very talented lineup at Chicago's new low Class A Kane County affiliate in 2013, and he might only need two years in the minors.

Year	Club (League)	Class	AVG	G	AB	R	H	2B	3B	HR	RBI	BB	SO	SB	CS	OBP	SLG
2012	Cubs (AZL)	R	.347	18	75	18	26	5	1	1	13	2	8	5	1	.363	.480
	Boise (NWL)	SS	.292	15	65	9	19	7	0	1	6	0	5	0	1	.292	.446
Minor League Totals			.321	33	140	27	45	12	1	2	19	2	13	5	2	.331	.464

3 JORGE SOLER, OF

Born: Feb. 25, 1992. **B-T:** R-R. **Ht.:** 6-3. **Wt.:** 205. **Signed:** Cuba, 2012. **Signed by:** Louie Eljaua/Jose Serra/Alex Suarez.

The best prospect on Cuba's bronze-medal team at the 2010 World Junior Championships, Soler was unsuccessful in his initial attempt to defect but escaped in 2011. The Cubs were linked to Soler months before he was cleared to sign by the U.S. government and MLB in June, and they quickly signed him to a nine-year, $30 million contract that includes a club-record $6 million bonus. Despite his long layoff, he easily handled low Class A pitching in his pro debut. The ball explodes off Soler's bat, and his well above-average power can make any ballpark look small. He hit two balls onto Waveland Avenue while taking batting practice at Wrigley Field in September. He has feel for hitting too, as he uses a game plan, recognizes pitches well and can make two-strike adjustments. Some scouts worry about an arm bar and some stiffness in his swing. Soler has solid speed once he gets going and good instincts on the bases. Once he improves his

BA GRADE

65

HIGH

routes to balls, he'll be an asset in right field. He has well above-average arm strength and makes accurate throws. A prototypical right fielder, Soler has a ceiling that rivals Javier Baez's as the highest among Chicago farmhands. The Cubs may be conservative to start 2013, letting Soler tear up the Midwest League while he continues to get acclimated to the United States. He and Albert Almora may race through the system together.

Year	Club (League)	Class	AVG	G	AB	R	H	2B	3B	HR	RBI	BB	SO	SB	CS	OBP	SLG
2012	Cubs (AZL)	R	.241	14	54	14	13	2	0	2	10	6	13	8	0	.328	.389
	Peoria (MWL)	LoA	.338	20	80	14	27	5	0	3	15	6	6	4	1	.398	.513
Minor League Totals			.299	34	134	28	40	7	0	5	25	12	19	12	1	.369	.463

4 ARODYS VIZCAINO, RHP

Born: Nov. 13, 1990. **B-T:** R-R. **Ht.:** 6-0. **Wt.:** 190. **Signed:** Dominican Republic, 2007. **Signed by:** Alfredo Dominguez (Yankees).

After the Braves acquired him in a four-player trade that sent Javier Vazquez to the Yankees in December 2009, Vizcaino missed time the following season with a partially torn elbow ligament. He rose from high Class A to the majors in 2011, but the ligament gave out last spring and required Tommy John surgery in March that cost him the 2012 season. Atlanta parted with him and righthander Jaye Chapman in July to get Reed Johnson and Paul Maholm from the Cubs. Before he got hurt, Vizcaino was one of baseball's top pitching prospects. He had a 93-95 mph fastball that topped out at 97, and it might be his second-best pitch. The only negative about his sharp curveball was that he threw it too much. Refining his changeup and improving his fastball command were on

BA GRADE

60

HIGH

his to-do list. Assuming Vizcaino regains full health, which is often the case with elbow reconstructions, the biggest question will be his future role. Chicago sees a potential No. 2 starter while detractors point to his injury track record, which indicates he won't hold up in a rotation even if his mechanics are fine. At worst, the Cubs think they have a closer. Chicago will handle Vizcaino, far and away their best upper-level pitching prospect, with great care. He should be able to return early in the 2013 season, but the goal is to have him ready to start for the big league club in 2014.

Year	Club (League)	Class	W	L	ERA	G	GS	CG	SV	IP	H	HR	BB	SO	K/9	WHIP	AVG
2008	Yankees (GCL)	R	3	2	3.68	12	6	0	0	44	38	5	13	48	9.8	1.16	.222
2009	Staten Island (NYP)	SS	2	4	2.13	10	10	0	0	42	34	2	15	52	11.1	1.16	.211
2010	Myrtle Beach (CAR)	HiA	0	0	4.61	3	3	0	0	14	16	1	3	11	7.2	1.39	.296
	Rome (SAL)	LoA	9	4	2.39	14	14	0	0	72	63	1	9	68	8.5	1.00	.229
2011	Lynchburg (CAR)	HiA	2	2	2.45	9	9	0	0	40	31	3	10	37	8.3	1.02	.207
	Mississippi (SL)	AA	2	3	3.81	11	8	0	0	50	44	3	18	55	10.0	1.25	.234
	Gwinnett (IL)	AAA	1	0	1.29	6	0	0	0	7	7	1	0	8	10.3	1.00	.259
	Atlanta (NL)	MAJ	1	1	4.67	17	0	0	0	17	16	1	9	17	8.8	1.44	.239
2012	Did Not Play—Injured																
Major League Totals			1	1	4.67	17	0	0	0	17	16	1	9	17	8.8	1.44	.239
Minor League Totals			19	15	2.91	65	50	0	0	269	233	16	68	279	9.3	1.12	.227

5 BRETT JACKSON, OF

Born: Aug. 2, 1988. **B-T:** L-R. **Ht.:** 6-2. **Wt.:** 210. **Drafted:** California, 2009 (1st round). **Signed by:** John Bartsch.

BA GRADE
55
HIGH

The Cubs thought Jackson had the draft's best bat speed in 2009, when they selected him 31st overall and signed him for $972,000. He had swing-and-miss issues as an amateur, but appeared to have them under control until he got to Triple-A. He has fanned 222 times in 592 at-bats at Iowa over the last two years, and whiffed 59 times in 120 at-bats after he joined the Cubs in August. Jackson's problems may be mechanical. He has developed a bad habit of drifting toward the plate, blocking off his hands and leaving him easy prey for inside fastballs. He also takes or swings through too many hittable pitches. As his problems got worse, he started chasing more offspeed pitches. Even if Jackson doesn't hit for a high average, he still can do a lot to help a club. He draws walks and has plus power and speed, still managing to produce 60 extra-base hits (including 19 homers) and 27 steals in 2012 despite his struggles. He can play a solid center field and provide above-average defense on the corners. His arm is average and accurate. Jackson may have gotten caught up trying to do too much as he got close to and then reached the majors. If he can relax and make some adjustments, he could be a 20-20 player. He should open 2013 as Chicago's center fielder unless he tanks in spring training.

Year	Club (League)	Class	AVG	G	AB	R	H	2B	3B	HR	RBI	BB	SO	SB	CS	OBP	SLG
2009	Cubs (AZL)	R	.455	3	11	6	5	0	1	0	4	3	4	0	0	.533	.636
	Boise (NWL)	SS	.330	24	88	14	29	1	1	1	15	17	20	2	1	.443	.398
	Peoria (MWL)	LoA	.295	26	112	30	33	5	1	7	17	11	32	11	1	.383	.545
2010	Daytona (FSL)	HiA	.316	67	263	56	83	19	8	6	38	43	63	12	7	.420	.517
	Tennessee (SL)	AA	.276	61	228	47	63	13	6	6	28	30	63	18	4	.366	.465
2011	Tennessee (SL)	AA	.256	67	246	45	63	10	3	10	32	45	74	15	6	.373	.443
	Iowa (PCL)	AAA	.297	48	185	39	55	13	2	10	26	28	64	6	1	.388	.551
2012	Iowa (PCL)	AAA	.256	106	407	66	104	22	12	15	47	47	158	27	5	.338	.479
	Chicago (NL)	MAJ	.175	44	120	14	21	6	1	4	9	22	59	0	3	.303	.342
Major League Totals			.175	44	120	14	21	6	1	4	9	22	59	0	3	.303	.342
Minor League Totals			.282	402	1540	303	435	83	34	55	207	224	478	91	25	.379	.488

6 PIERCE JOHNSON, RHP

Born: May 10, 1991. **B-T:** R-R. **Ht.:** 6-3. **Wt.:** 170. **Drafted:** Missouri State, 2012 (1st round supplemental). **Signed by:** Stan Zielinski.

BA GRADE
50
HIGH

Since 2001, Missouri State has had four pitchers selected in the first or sandwich round, and the Bears have sent seven arms to the big leagues. Their latest quality hurler is Johnson, who went 43rd overall last June and lasted that long only because he missed two starts with a forearm strain in the spring. His stuff looked as crisp as ever after he signed for $1,196,000. Johnson consistently works at 92-94 mph and reaches 96 with his lively fastball. His hammer curveball gives him two pitches that can get swings and misses. He also has a mid-80s cutter and a changeup that's coming along nicely. Johnson is more about power than finesse, and his control and command are no better than average at this point. He doesn't have a clean medical history, as he had forearm issues as a high school senior and college freshman and dislocated a kneecap while warming up in the summer Cape Cod League in 2011. The Cubs rave about his work ethic and character almost as much as they do about Albert Almora's. How thin is the system's pitching? Among Chicago prospects with a legitimate chance to pitch in the front half of a big league rotation, Johnson already is the second-most advanced despite having just 11 innings of pro experience. The Cubs will expedite his development, which could mean starting his first full pro season in high Class A.

Year	Club (League)	Class	W	L	ERA	G	GS	CG	SV	IP	H	HR	BB	SO	K/9	WHIP	AVG
2012	Cubs (AZL)	R	0	0	0.00	2	2	0	0	3	4	0	0	2	6.0	1.33	.364
	Boise (NWL)	SS	0	0	4.50	4	4	0	0	8	10	0	3	12	13.5	1.63	.323
Minor League Totals			0	0	3.27	6	6	0	0	11	14	0	3	14	11.5	1.55	.333

7 DAN VOGELBACH, 1B

Born: Dec. 17, 1992. **B-T:** L-R. **Ht.:** 6-0. **Wt.:** 260. **Drafted:** HS—Fort Myers, Fla., 2011 (2nd round). **Signed by:** Lukas McKnight.

The Cubs spent a franchise-record $12 million on the 2011 draft, highlighted by a pair of high schoolers with light-tower power in Javier Baez and Vogelbach. He barely played that summer after signing late for $1.6 million, but he made up for lost time by hitting .322/.410/.641 with 17 homers in 61 games last year. He has more usable power than Baez or Jorge Soler, which is saying a lot. He has plenty of bat speed and strength, but Vogelbach does more than just grip it and rip it. He earns high marks for his advanced approach and feel for hitting. He controls the strike zone, takes his walks and uses the entire field with an effortless swing. He can get pull-conscious at times but generally hits from gap to gap. He will need to keep producing at the plate because he can't do anything else. He has improved his conditioning since ballooning to 280 pounds in 2010, but he'll always carry a lot of weight. He's a liability on the basepaths and adequate at best as a first baseman. A lot of teams see him purely as a DH, which wouldn't do a National League club any good. Vogelbach's build and background as a Florida prep product are similar to Billy Butler and Prince Fielder, and he too has the offensive upside to become an all-star one day. Vogelbach and Soler should put on some unreal shows in batting practice at Kane County this year.

BA GRADE 50 HIGH

Year	Club (League)	Class	AVG	G	AB	R	H	2B	3B	HR	RBI	BB	SO	SB	CS	OBP	SLG
2011	Cubs (AZL)	R	.292	6	24	4	7	3	0	1	6	2	2	1	0	.370	.542
2012	Cubs (AZL)	R	.324	24	102	16	33	12	2	7	31	12	14	1	0	.391	.686
	Boise (NWL)	SS	.322	37	143	23	46	9	1	10	31	23	34	0	1	.423	.608
Minor League Totals			.320	67	269	43	86	24	3	18	68	37	50	2	1	.406	.632

8 JEIMER CANDELARIO, 3B

Born: Nov. 24, 1993. **B-T:** B-R. **Ht.:** 6-1. **Wt.:** 180. **Signed:** Dominican Republic, 2010. **Signed by:** Jose Serra/Marino Encarnacion.

Signed for $500,000 in 2010, Candelario tore up the Rookie-level Dominican Summer League in his pro debut the following year. The Cubs threw a two-level promotion at him for 2012, making him the youngest regular in the short-season Northwest League, and he was up to the challenge. Though he's just 19, Candelario already shows a fluid swing and feel for hitting from both sides of the plate. He's advanced for his age in terms of plate discipline, pitch recognition and willingness to use the entire field. He didn't drive the ball a lot last summer, but he has the bat speed and projectable frame to develop 20-homer power. He'll need to get stronger after hitting just .265 with two homers in the final two months of the NWL season. Candelario has the soft hands and strong arm for third base but it's questionable whether he can play there at the highest levels. He has below-average speed and fringy range, and his concentration wanders at times. He led

BA GRADE 50 HIGH

NWL third basemen with 20 errors in 59 games. Candelario will stay at third base for now as he advances to low Class A. Moving to first base wouldn't be an attractive option, because he'd have to battle Anthony Rizzo and Dan Vogelbach for future playing time.

Year	Club (League)	Class	AVG	G	AB	R	H	2B	3B	HR	RBI	BB	SO	SB	CS	OBP	SLG
2011	Cubs 2 (DSL)	R	.337	72	249	50	84	16	2	5	53	50	42	4	4	.443	.478
2012	Boise (NWL)	SS	.281	71	278	34	78	14	0	6	47	26	55	2	1	.345	.396
Minor League Totals			.307	143	527	84	162	30	2	11	100	76	97	6	5	.393	.435

9 KYUJI FUJIKAWA, RHP

Born: July 21, 1980. **B-T:** L-R. **Ht.:** 6-0. **Wt.:** 190. **Signed:** Japan, 2012. **Signed by:** Paul Weaver.

Fujikawa made his Nippon Professional Baseball debut at age 19 and has been once of Japan's top relievers since 2005. He led the Central League with 46 saves in 2007 and 41 in 2011, and he recorded 220 saves and a 1.77 ERA in 12 seasons with Hanshin. He also was a regular on national teams, pitching in the 2008 Olympics and the 2006 and 2009 World Baseball Classics. Fujikawa had asked the Hanshin Tigers to post him to a major league club for several years, but they declined and he had to wait to become a free agent this offseason. Chicago signed him in December to a two-year deal that's worth $9.5 million and includes a vesting option for 2015. Fujikawa throws harder than most Japanese pitchers, regularly operating with a 91-94 mph fastball. His out pitch is a mid-80s splitter, and he also uses an upper-70s slurve. He commands and controls his pitches well, with career averages of 11.9 strikeouts and 2.7 walks per nine innings in Japan. With his track record of pitching in the late innings and in international tournaments, he has no problems dealing with pressure. The Cubs are confident Fujikawa can handle the late innings but won't determine his specific role until spring training. Whether they ask him to close games probably depends on whether they trade Carlos Marmol.

BA GRADE
45
LOW

Year	Club (League)	Class	W	L	ERA	G	GS	CG	SV	IP	H	HR	BB	SO	K/9	WHIP	AVG
2007	Hanshin (NPB)	INTL	5	5	1.63	71	0	0	46	83	50	2	18	115	12.5	0.82	—
2008	Hanshin (NPB)	INTL	8	1	0.67	63	0	0	38	68	34	2	13	90	12.0	0.70	—
2009	Hanshin (NPB)	INTL	5	3	1.25	49	0	0	25	58	32	4	15	86	13.4	0.82	—
2010	Hanshin (NPB)	INTL	3	4	2.01	58	0	0	28	63	47	7	20	81	11.6	1.07	—
2011	Hanshin (NPB)	INTL	3	3	1.24	56	0	0	41	51	25	2	13	80	14.1	0.75	—
2012	Hanshin (NPB)	INTL	2	2	1.32	48	0	0	24	48	34	1	15	58	11.0	1.03	—
Japanese League Totals			42	25	1.77	562	14	0	220	692	460	40	207	914	11.9	0.96	—

10 ARISMENDY ALCANTARA, SS

Born: Oct. 29, 1991. **B-T:** B-R. **Ht.:** 5-10. **Wt.:** 170. **Signed:** Dominican Republic, 2008. **Signed by:** Jose Serra/Marino Encarnacion/Carlos Reyes.

Alcantara finally started to translate his intriguing tools into on-field performance in 2012, but his season came to a premature end when he broke a bone in his foot on July 11. Before he got hurt, he already had set career highs in most offensive categories and earned recognition from managers as the best infield arm in the high Class A Florida State League. He returned to play with Licey in the Dominican League. Alcantara is a live-bodied switch-hitter who can hit for average and provide solid power for a middle infielder from both sides of the plate. His further offensive development will be tied to improved selectivity at the plate, as he still gives away at-bats at times. He has plus speed and knows how to use it, stealing 25 bases in 29 tries in 2012. Alcantara has the quickness, range and arm strength to make all the plays at shortstop. But he loses focus at times and makes too many off-target throws, leading to 30 errors in 71 games at short last year. The game may just be too fast for him there, so he might be better off at second base. Scouts throw some Jimmy Rollins comparisons on Alcantara, though at the same point of his career, Rollins already had reached Triple-A. Alcantara will seek better health and consistency when he advances to Double-A in 2013.

BA GRADE
50
HIGH

Year	Club (League)	Class	AVG	G	AB	R	H	2B	3B	HR	RBI	BB	SO	SB	CS	OBP	SLG
2009	Cubs 1 (DSL)	R	.275	65	258	44	71	11	8	3	32	30	47	20	2	.349	.415
2010	Boise (NWL)	SS	.283	59	219	29	62	5	6	3	24	10	53	7	3	.315	.402
2011	Peoria (MWL)	LoA	.271	99	369	45	100	14	5	2	37	16	76	8	8	.303	.352
2012	Daytona (FSL)	HiA	.302	85	331	47	100	13	7	7	51	19	61	25	4	.339	.447
Minor League Totals			.283	308	1177	165	333	43	26	15	144	75	237	60	17	.326	.402

11 JUAN CARLOS PANIAGUA, RHP

BA GRADE
55
EXTREME

Born: April 4, 1990. **B-T:** R-R. **Ht.:** 6-1. **Wt.:** 175. **Signed:** Dominican Republic, 2012. **Signed by:** Louie Eljaua/Jose Serra/Alex Suarez.

It took three tries, but Paniagua finally found a home with a big league club when MLB approved his $1.5 million deal with the Cubs last August. He originally signed with the Diamondbacks for $17,000 in May 2009, using the name Juan Carlos Collado and an April 4, 1990 birthdate. He pitched parts of two seasons in the Dominican Summer League waiting for MLB approval that never came. MLB terminated that deal and declared him ineligible to sign for one year because of falsified paperwork. Afterward, he used the Paniagua surname and the same birthdate to sign with the Yankees for $1.1 million. Again, MLB rejected him and ruled him ineligible for year for using fraudulent documents. When he agreed to terms with the Cubs,

MLB decided it couldn't determine his birthdate and let the team proceed as it wished. Even if he's older than his listed age of 22, Paniagua has a valuable right arm. Club officials saw his fastball sit at 94-98 mph and touch 100 in multiple-inning stints. His second-best pitch is his changeup, with his 82-84 mph slider more notable for its velocity than its break. Paniagua has a long, slinging arm action, leading many scouts to believe he's better suited for the bullpen. Chicago will audition him first as a starter and probably will send him to low Class A to open 2013.

Year	Club (League)	Class	W	L	ERA	G	GS	CG	SV	IP	H	HR	BB	SO	K/9	WHIP	AVG
2009	Diamondbacks (DSL)	R	1	1	4.66	18	0	0	2	29	40	0	15	33	10.2	1.90	.323
2010	Diamondbacks (DSL)	R	0	0	5.40	3	0	0	0	7	11	1	1	8	10.8	1.80	.379
2011	Did Not Play—Ineligible																
2012	Cubs (AZL)	R	1	0	0.00	2	0	0	0	4	0	0	1	4	9.8	0.27	.000
Minor League Totals			2	1	4.35	23	0	0	2	39	51	1	17	45	10.3	1.73	.313

12 CHRISTIAN VILLANUEVA, 3B

BA GRADE
50
HIGH

Born: June 19, 1991. **B-T:** R-R. **Ht.:** 5-11. **Wt.:** 180. **Signed:** Mexico, 2008. **Signed by:** Bill McLaughlin/Mike Daly (Rangers).

Blocked by Adrian Beltre and Mike Olt in Texas, Villanueva's chances for future playing time improved dramatically when the Rangers dealt him and strike-throwing righthander Kyle Hendricks to the Cubs for Ryan Dempster. He still has to worry about Jeimer Candelario and perhaps Javier Baez (if he moves to third base), but Villanueva suddenly has a lot more upward mobility. On the 20-80 scouting scale, one Cubs official described him as having 80 makeup, 70 defense and questionable power. Villanueva's short stroke is conducive to line drives more than longballs, and he tends to inside-out quality fastballs and serve them to the opposite field. He has the potential for average power, but he'll have to get stronger and turn on more pitches to get there. He can hit for solid average and provide some doubles. He has fringy speed but has the instincts to steal bases if the defense doesn't pay attention to him. Defense is where Villanueva really shines. He has the first-step quickness, hands, arm strength and savvy to make tough plays look routine. Chicago added him to its 40-man roster and will send him to Double-A in 2013. He could get a big league audition sometime the following year.

Year	Club (League)	Class	AVG	G	AB	R	H	2B	3B	HR	RBI	BB	SO	SB	CS	OBP	SLG
2009	Rangers 2 (DSL)	R	.208	8	24	2	5	1	0	0	3	6	5	1	0	.375	.250
2010	Rangers (AZL)	R	.314	51	188	30	59	14	1	2	35	13	42	6	2	.365	.431
2011	Hickory (SAL)	LoA	.278	126	467	78	130	30	3	17	84	37	86	32	6	.338	.465
2012	Myrtle Beach (CAR)	HiA	.285	100	375	45	107	19	1	10	59	24	83	9	9	.356	.421
	Daytona (FSL)	HiA	.250	25	84	14	21	5	0	4	9	10	24	5	2	.337	.452
Minor League Totals			.283	310	1138	169	322	69	5	33	190	90	240	53	19	.349	.439

13 ALBERTO CABRERA, RHP

BA GRADE
45
MEDIUM

Born: Oct. 25, 1988. **B-T:** R-R. **Ht.:** 6-4. **Wt.:** 210. **Signed:** Dominican Republic, 2005. **Signed by:** Jose Serra/Sandy Nin.

Cabrera completed an arduous seven-year journey to the majors on Aug. 1, when he needed just 10 pitches to work a 1-2-3 inning against the Pirates. Along the way, he battled shoulder and elbow tenderness, not to mention control issues and inconsistency. He seemed to have turned a corner when he performed well in high Class A and earned a spot on the 40-man roster in 2010, but he recorded a 6.16 ERA as an encore the following season. That downturn convinced the new Cubs regime to make Cabrera a full-time reliever in 2012, a role change that allowed him to conquer the upper levels of the minors and get to Chicago. It's easy to dream on him as a starter because he'll show three plus pitches at times. His fastball ranges from 93-98 mph, his changeup features some sink and fade, and his power slider added some bite when he worked with big league pitching coach Chris Bosio. However, Cabrera's pitches tend to play down because he lacks control and command. His fastball is fairly straight and gets hit when he doesn't keep it down in the strike zone. He's better in shorter stints when he can go all out and not worry as much about trying to mix his pitches. Cabrera will compete for a big league bullpen job in spring training and has a ceiling as a set-up man.

Year	Club (League)	Class	W	L	ERA	G	GS	CG	SV	IP	H	HR	BB	SO	K/9	WHIP	AVG
2006	Cubs (DSL)	R	5	6	2.27	15	14	0	0	71	69	4	18	55	6.9	1.22	.257
2007	Boise (NWL)	SS	3	3	5.40	9	9	0	0	38	41	4	18	33	7.7	1.54	.287
2008	Peoria (MWL)	LoA	4	6	5.71	12	11	0	0	52	55	7	30	37	6.4	1.63	.281
2009	Peoria (MWL)	LoA	8	2	4.48	27	8	0	1	96	94	6	54	73	6.8	1.54	.256
2010	Daytona (FSL)	HiA	7	5	3.28	18	17	1	0	93	92	6	26	90	8.7	1.26	.253
	Tennessee (SL)	AA	0	4	6.33	10	9	0	0	43	57	1	24	35	7.4	1.90	.315
2011	Tennessee (SL)	AA	6	2	5.36	9	9	0	0	49	60	4	21	34	6.3	1.66	.308
	Iowa (PCL)	AAA	3	6	6.60	19	17	0	0	89	118	11	53	67	6.8	1.93	.330
2012	Tennessee (SL)	AA	2	1	2.52	23	0	0	5	36	30	2	10	45	11.4	1.12	.217
	Iowa (PCL)	AAA	2	0	4.19	13	0	0	0	19	29	4	4	29	13.5	1.71	.337
	Chicago (NL)	MAJ	1	1	5.40	25	0	0	0	22	16	1	18	27	11.2	1.57	.205
Major League Totals			1	1	5.40	25	0	0	0	22	16	1	18	27	11.2	1.57	.205
Minor League Totals			40	35	4.59	155	94	1	6	586	645	49	258	498	7.6	1.54	.281

14 MATT SZCZUR, OF

BA GRADE
50
HIGH

Born: July 20, 1989. **B-T:** R-R. **Ht.:** 6-1. **Wt.:** 195. **Drafted:** Villanova, 2010 (5th round). **Signed by:** Tim Adkins.

The Cubs bought Szczur out of a potential football career, signing him for a $100,000 bonus in 2010 with the provision he could play his final football season at Villanova. When that ended, Chicago paid him an additional $1.4 million to concentrate on baseball full-time. Szczur is the best athlete and fastest player in the system, but he has yet to maximize his physical gifts on the diamond. He's strong enough to hit for average power, but he cuts off his swing and rolls over on a lot of fastballs. He has become a more selective hitter and focuses on getting on base to take advantage of his plus-plus speed. He has improved his bunting and his basestealing instincts, becoming more aggressive about picking spots to run. He has made himself into a solid center fielder with an average, accurate arm. Some scouts think he still can blossom into a quality everyday player; others see him as a second-division regular. Both sides agree he has stellar makeup and brings energy to the park everyday. A knee injury sustained on a bad slide right before his Double-A promotion hindered him down the stretch, but he played in the Arizona Fall League and will take another shot at Double-A in 2013.

Year	Club (League)	Class	AVG	G	AB	R	H	2B	3B	HR	RBI	BB	SO	SB	CS	OBP	SLG
2010	Cubs (AZL)	R	.500	1	2	1	1	0	0	0	0	1	0	1	0	.750	.500
	Boise (NWL)	SS	.397	18	73	17	29	9	0	0	8	6	11	1	0	.439	.521
	Peoria (MWL)	LoA	.192	6	26	6	5	1	1	0	2	3	5	0	0	.300	.308
2011	Peoria (MWL)	LoA	.314	66	274	55	86	15	1	5	27	21	28	17	5	.366	.431
	Daytona (FSL)	HiA	.260	43	173	20	45	7	2	5	19	5	20	7	0	.283	.410
2012	Daytona (FSL)	HiA	.295	78	295	68	87	19	4	2	34	47	50	38	12	.394	.407
	Tennessee (SL)	AA	.210	35	143	24	30	7	4	2	6	14	29	4	2	.285	.357
Minor League Totals			.287	247	986	191	283	58	12	14	96	97	143	68	19	.355	.413

15 JUNIOR LAKE, SS/3B

BA GRADE
50
HIGH

Born: March 27, 1990. **B-T:** R-R. **Ht.:** 6-3. **Wt.:** 215. **Signed:** Dominican Republic, 2007. **Signed by:** Jose Serra.

While Lake's 2008 Rookie-level Arizona League teammate Starling Castro raced through the minors and reached the big leagues to stay in May 2010, Lake still hasn't gotten to Triple-A. A stellar AFL performance in 2011 gave him momentum going into last season, but he hurt his back in spring training and missed a month. When he returned, it was the same old Lake: tantalizing tools and inconsistent performance. He has a big league body, one of the strongest infield arms in the minor leagues, raw power and solid speed. He never has developed patience at the plate and gets himself out by chasing breaking pitches. Staying at shortstop past his expiration date hasn't helped Lake's cause. He's too big and not quite quick enough for the position, and he might get more out of his bat if he played a less challenging spot. Scouts on other clubs see him as a third baseman or right fielder, and some would like to see him try pitching. Lake had a fine winter in the Dominican League and will try to build off that in Double-A this year.

Year	Club (League)	Class	AVG	G	AB	R	H	2B	3B	HR	RBI	BB	SO	SB	CS	OBP	SLG
2007	Cubs (DSL)	R	.274	62	223	41	61	16	2	3	30	16	53	9	3	.341	.404
2008	Cubs (AZL)	R	.286	47	168	24	48	4	6	2	23	13	42	12	2	.335	.417
2009	Peoria (MWL)	LoA	.248	131	463	71	115	19	7	7	42	18	138	10	7	.277	.365
2010	Daytona (FSL)	HiA	.264	120	394	56	104	18	4	9	46	35	99	13	9	.333	.398
2011	Daytona (FSL)	HiA	.315	49	203	39	64	11	4	6	34	6	49	19	4	.336	.498
	Tennessee (SL)	AA	.248	67	242	41	60	10	2	6	17	13	60	19	2	.300	.380
2012	Tennessee (SL)	AA	.279	103	405	56	113	26	3	10	50	35	105	21	12	.341	.432
Minor League Totals			.269	579	2098	328	565	104	28	43	242	136	546	103	39	.320	.407

16 PAUL BLACKBURN, RHP

BA GRADE
50
HIGH

Born: Dec. 4, 1993. **B-T:** R-R. **Ht.:** 6-2. **Wt.:** 185. **Drafted:** HS—Brentwood, Calif., 2012 (1st round supplemental). **Signed by:** Scott Fairbanks.

The Cubs used seven of their first eight picks in the 2012 draft on arms, and Blackburn stands out as having the best feel for pitching among that group. The 56th overall pick, he turned down an Arizona State commitment to sign for $911,700. Blackburn works down in the strike zone and to both sides of the plate with a 90-92 mph fastball that peaks at 94. He hasn't filled out yet, so there could be more velocity in his future. He's athletic and repeats his smooth delivery well, which bodes well for the development of his secondary pitches and command. Chicago believes he'll eventually have a plus curveball, and his changeup has similar promise. He gets high marks for his mound presence. Blackburn has the ingredients necessary to become a No. 3 starter, and he's advanced enough to consider sending him to low Class A in his first full pro season.

Year	Club (League)	Class	W	L	ERA	G	GS	CG	SV	IP	H	HR	BB	SO	K/9	WHIP	AVG
2012	Cubs (AZL)	R	2	0	3.48	9	6	0	0	21	23	2	7	13	5.7	1.45	.284
Minor League Totals			2	0	3.48	9	6	0	0	21	23	2	7	13	5.7	1.45	.284

17 DUANE UNDERWOOD, RHP

BA GRADE

50

HIGH

Born: July 20, 1994. **B-T:** R-R. **Ht.:** 6-2. **Wt.:** 205. **Drafted:** HS—Marietta, Ga., 2012 (2nd round). **Signed by:** Keith Lockhart.

Underwood was one of the more enigmatic players in the 2012 draft. On some days, he'd hit 98 mph with his fastball and flash first-round talent. On others, he couldn't command his heater and would dip into the upper 80s quickly, looking more like a fourth-rounder. The Cubs split the difference, drafting him in the second round and signing him away from a Georgia commitment for $1.05 million. He's very athletic for a pitcher and would have been a two-way player for the Bulldogs. Underwood generally pitches at 91-94 mph with his fastball but it varies from 88-98 and he doesn't always know where it's going. His curveball is similarly inconsistent. He'll show some feel for spinning the ball, but he'll also overthrow the curve and wind up with a soft, loopy offering that's begging to be crushed. He controls his changeup better than his other pitches, but he throws it too hard and doesn't get enough separation from his fastball. The Cubs worked to get Underwood to stop rushing his delivery in instructional league, and they were pleased with the results. They'll probably keep him in extended spring to start 2013 before sending him to short-season Boise in June.

Year	Club (League)	Class	W	L	ERA	G	GS	CG	SV	IP	H	HR	BB	SO	K/9	WHIP	AVG
2012	Cubs (AZL)	R	0	1	5.19	5	5	0	0	9	7	1	6	7	7.3	1.50	.206
Minor League Totals			0	1	5.19	5	5	0	0	9	7	1	6	7	7.3	1.50	.206

18 DILLON MAPLES, RHP

BA GRADE

50

HIGH

Born: May 9, 1992. **B-T:** R-R. **Ht.:** 6-2. **Wt.:** 195. **Drafted:** HS—Southern Pines, N.C., 2011 (14th round). **Signed by:** Billy Swoope.

Teams considered Maples virtually unsignable in 2011 because he was strongly committed to North Carolina, where he would have played baseball and kicked for the football team. The Cubs fell in love with his stuff, took him in the 14th round and got him away from the Tar Heels for $2.5 million—a maneuver that would have cost them two future first-round picks under new draft rules that went into effect in 2012. They have yet to see what they got with that investment because he has pitched just 10 pro innings. He signed too late to debut in 2011, then tweaked his elbow in spring training and didn't get on the mound again until June. Maples' main weapons are a heavy 91-96 mph fastball and a hard curveball. His non-athletic delivery and short arm action turn off a lot of scouts and could lead to health and control problems. Chicago won't give him a complete makeover but wants to simplify his mechanics to make it easier for him to throw strikes. He'll need to add a changeup as well. Maples will turn 21 early in the 2013 season, so the Cubs would like to get him to low Class A and, they hope, on the road to becoming a No. 2 starter.

Year	Club (League)	Class	W	L	ERA	G	GS	CG	SV	IP	H	HR	BB	SO	K/9	WHIP	AVG
2012	Cubs (AZL)	R	0	1	4.35	6	4	0	0	10	6	0	10	12	10.5	1.55	.162
Minor League Totals			0	1	4.35	6	4	0	0	10	6	0	10	12	10.5	1.55	.162

19 LOGAN WATKINS, 2B/SS/OF

BA GRADE

45

MEDIUM

Born: Aug. 29, 1989. **B-T:** L-R. **Ht.:** 5-11. **Wt.:** 170. **Drafted:** HS—Goddard, Kan., 2008 (21st round). **Signed by:** Brandon Mozley.

The Cubs named Watkins their minor league player of the year and placed him on their 40-man roster after he led the Double-A Southern League with 93 runs and established career highs in most categories. Signed for $500,000 as a 21st-rounder in 2008, Watkins has an interesting package of tools and has the aptitude to get the most out of them. He has a contact approach at the plate, hitting the ball where it's pitched and spraying line drives all over the field. He draws walks and he's stronger than he looks, though his power goes mostly to the gaps. An all-star quarterback and defensive back in high school, he has above-average speed and exploits it by bunting for hits. His biggest needs offensively are to cut down a few more strikeouts and to attempt more steals. Watkins has spent most of his pro career at second base, where his average arm and solid range fit best. He also has seen extended time at shortstop and center field, and he's versatile enough to play almost anywhere on the diamond. Watkins' biggest backers project him as an everyday second baseman, and he may have a better collection of tools than Cubs incumbent Darwin Barney. Scouts outside the organization see him more as a utilityman. Watkins' bat ultimately will determine which group is correct. He'll move up to Triple-A in 2013.

Year	Club (League)	Class	AVG	G	AB	R	H	2B	3B	HR	RBI	BB	SO	SB	CS	OBP	SLG
2008	Cubs (AZL)	R	.325	27	80	15	26	3	0	0	14	20	19	2	0	.462	.363
2009	Boise (NWL)	SS	.326	72	279	48	91	14	2	0	29	27	31	14	7	.389	.391
2010	Peoria (MWL)	LoA	.261	118	440	69	115	15	8	1	30	58	97	19	10	.351	.339
2011	Daytona (FSL)	HiA	.281	125	441	70	124	15	12	5	45	44	97	21	5	.352	.404
2012	Tennessee (SL)	AA	.281	133	488	93	137	20	11	9	52	76	97	28	7	.383	.422
Minor League Totals			.285	475	1728	295	493	67	33	15	170	225	341	84	29	.372	.388

20 MARCO HERNANDEZ, SS

BA GRADE
50
HIGH

Born: Sept. 6, 1992. **B-T:** B-R. **Ht.:** 6-0. **Wt.:** 170. **Signed:** Dominican Republic, 2009. **Signed by:** Jose Serra/Jose Estevez.

It was Hernandez and not 2011 first-round pick Javier Baez who opened last season as Peoria's starting shortstop. Hernandez wasn't ready to make the jump from Rookie-ball to low Class A and didn't get his bat going until he went to Boise in June. While he can't match the tools of Baez or Arismendy Alcantara, Hernandez has no glaring weaknesses and a better chance to stay at shortstop in the long term. A switch-hitter, he has an easy swing from both sides of the plate and more pop as a lefty. His Midwest League performance aside, he makes reliable contact and should have solid gap power once he gets stronger. He'll have to improve his plate discipline and pitch recognition to handle better pitching. Hernandez has above-average speed but still is learning to make the most of it on the bases. He has the actions, quickness and solid arm required at shortstop, but he let the game speed up too much on him defensively in 2012, committing 32 errors in 105 games. He'll be better equipped to handle low Class A when he opens there in 2013.

Year	Club (League)	Class	AVG	G	AB	R	H	2B	3B	HR	RBI	BB	SO	SB	CS	OBP	SLG
2010	Cubs 2 (DSL)	R	.272	23	92	10	25	8	0	0	7	6	6	6	5	.316	.359
	Cubs 1 (DSL)	R	.294	46	163	21	48	13	1	1	14	15	21	16	7	.364	.405
2011	Cubs (AZL)	R	.333	51	210	39	70	16	5	2	42	16	29	9	7	.375	.486
2012	Peoria (MWL)	LoA	.210	43	157	18	33	2	3	2	12	9	40	2	1	.249	.299
	Boise (NWL)	SS	.286	67	269	39	77	12	4	5	38	10	36	8	3	.310	.416
Minor League Totals			.284	230	891	127	253	51	13	10	113	56	132	41	23	.326	.404

21 GIOSKAR AMAYA, 2B

BA GRADE
50
HIGH

Born: Dec. 13, 1992. **B-T:** R-R. **Ht.:** 5-11. **Wt.:** 175. **Signed:** Dominican Republic, 2009. **Signed by:** Hector Ortega/Julio Figueroa.

Amaya starred alongside Marco Hernandez in the Rookie-level Arizona League during their 2011 U.S. debuts, and again at Boise last summer. Amaya can do a little bit of everything, but he stands out most for how easy he makes it all look. When the Cubs needed an emergency infielder in Triple-A in mid-May, they sent him to Iowa and he delivered a double in his lone at-bat. Amaya uses a short, quick swing that has produced a .333 batting average in two years in the United States. He's growing into some sneaky power and has plus speed, and he hinted at both with his Northwest League-leading 12 triples last summer. After alternating between second base and shortstop with Hernandez in the AZL, Amaya played exclusively at the keystone in 2012 with Boise. His range and arm strength weren't quite good enough at shortstop but are solid at second. He topped NWL second basemen with a .968 fielding percentage. Club officials love his makeup and how he's locked in to play every day. If Amaya keeps producing at the plate when he gets to full-season ball in 2013, he'll start to move quickly.

Year	Club (League)	Class	AVG	G	AB	R	H	2B	3B	HR	RBI	BB	SO	SB	CS	OBP	SLG
2010	Cubs 1 (DSL)	R	.282	69	238	33	67	8	3	1	29	28	33	18	8	.375	.353
2011	Cubs (AZL)	R	.377	52	204	37	77	11	8	0	36	13	39	13	8	.417	.510
2012	Iowa (PCL)	AAA	1.000	1	1	1	1	1	0	0	0	0	0	0	0	1.000	2.000
	Boise (NWL)	SS	.298	69	272	61	81	6	12	8	33	33	65	15	5	.381	.496
Minor League Totals			.316	191	715	132	226	26	23	9	98	74	137	46	21	.389	.455

22 TONY ZYCH, RHP

BA GRADE
45
MEDIUM

Born: Aug. 7, 1990. **B-T:** R-R. **Ht.:** 6-3. **Wt.:** 190. **Drafted:** Louisville, 2011 (4th round). **Signed by:** Tim Adkins.

The Cubs drafted Zych out of a suburban Chicago high school in the 46th round of the 2008 draft, but he turned them down to attend Louisville. He emerged as one of the top college relief prospects for 2011 after starring in the Cape Cod League, yet the Cubs were able to get him in the fourth round thanks to mixed signals about his asking price. Signed for $400,000, he reached Double-A in his first full pro season. Zych has the same approach he had in high school. He rears back and throws as hard as he can from a funky, max-effort delivery. And he can throw plenty hard, working at 94-96 mph and reaching 99. The life on his fastball and the deception his mechanics provide make it seem even quicker. His delivery makes it difficult to maintain consistent break on his slider, which arrives in the mid-80s but can flatten out. His arm action and lack of a consistent second pitch leave most scouts hesitant to give him the closer stamp of approval, but he profiles as a seventh- or eighth-inning reliever in the big leagues. Zych could get there by the end of 2013.

Year	Club (League)	Class	W	L	ERA	G	GS	CG	SV	IP	H	HR	BB	SO	K/9	WHIP	AVG
2011	Cubs (AZL)	R	0	0	4.50	2	0	0	0	2	2	0	1	3	13.5	1.50	.250
	Boise (NWL)	SS	0	0	0.00	2	0	0	0	2	0	0	1	2	9.0	0.50	.000
2012	Daytona (FSL)	HiA	3	3	3.19	27	0	0	6	37	32	0	7	36	8.8	1.06	.239
	Tennessee (SL)	AA	2	1	4.38	20	0	0	0	25	26	1	12	28	10.2	1.54	.268
Minor League Totals			5	4	3.58	51	0	0	6	65	60	1	21	69	9.5	1.24	.245

23 ROBERT WHITENACK, RHP

BA GRADE
50
HIGH

Born: Nov. 20, 1988. **B-T:** R-R. **Ht.:** 6-5. **Wt.:** 185. **Drafted:** SUNY Old Westbury, 2009 (8th round). **Signed by:** Billy Blitzer.

The only player ever drafted out of SUNY Old Westbury, Whitenack was making a case for being the system's top pitching prospect during a breakout 2011 season—until he blew out his elbow in June. Instead of getting consideration for a late-season callup, he had Tommy John surgery instead. Before he got hurt, Whitenack's fastball had jumped from the high-80s to 89-96 mph while keeping its hard sink. He scrapped a knuckle-curve for a more effective slider in the low-80s and had some success with his changeup. Whitenack's stuff didn't come all the way back in 2012, as his fastball resided around 90 mph and his slider lacked bite. The Cubs weren't concerned about his radar-gun readings or statistics. They just wanted to build his arm back up so he'd be at full strength in 2013, and they added him to the 40-man roster in November. If he can recover his 2011 form, he could develop into a No. 3 starter.

Year	Club (League)	Class	W	L	ERA	G	GS	CG	SV	IP	H	HR	BB	SO	K/9	WHIP	AVG
2009	Boise (NWL)	SS	0	4	4.80	15	12	0	0	54	66	1	20	33	5.5	1.58	.296
2010	Peoria (MWL)	LoA	8	7	4.96	21	20	0	1	103	102	5	30	63	5.5	1.28	.262
	Daytona (FSL)	HiA	3	1	2.04	7	7	0	0	40	32	2	10	28	6.4	1.06	.218
2011	Daytona (FSL)	HiA	3	0	1.17	4	4	0	0	23	11	0	1	25	9.8	0.52	.141
	Tennessee (SL)	AA	4	0	2.39	7	7	0	0	38	32	1	13	22	5.3	1.19	.237
2012	Daytona (FSL)	HiA	1	6	5.96	15	15	0	0	51	70	4	27	31	5.4	1.89	.332
Minor League Totals			19	18	4.13	69	65	0	1	309	313	13	101	202	5.9	1.34	.265

24 TREY McNUTT, RHP

BA GRADE
50
HIGH

Born: Aug. 2, 1989. **B-T:** R-R. **Ht.:** 6-4. **Wt.:** 220. **Drafted:** Shelton State (Ala.) CC, 2009 (32nd round). **Signed by:** Jim Crawford/Al Geddes.

McNutt looked like a 32nd-round draft steal when he dealt two plus-plus pitches early in his first full year as a pro. But he hasn't shown the same stuff since and stalled since reaching Double-A at the end of 2010. The Cubs gave up on trying to make him a starter midway through 2012. Working in shorter stints gave a boost to McNutt's fastball, which now sits at 94-95 mph. He always has thrown both a curveball and a slider, each of which could be devastating at its best, but he focused more on the slider when coming out of the bullpen. He doesn't have to worry any longer about trying to develop his changeup. McNutt has had recurring blisters on the index finger of his pitching hand, which contribute to his subpar control and command. He has the mental toughness to work the late innings, but he'll be better suited for the sixth or seventh until he can throw more strikes. The Cubs saw enough in him to protect him on their 40-man roster after the season. McNutt's new role may be his ticket to Triple-A in 2013.

Year	Club (League)	Class	W	L	ERA	G	GS	CG	SV	IP	H	HR	BB	SO	K/9	WHIP	AVG
2009	Cubs (AZL)	R	0	1	0.00	6	4	0	0	7	5	0	3	7	8.6	1.09	.167
	Boise (NWL)	SS	3	0	1.33	7	2	0	0	20	9	1	12	21	9.3	1.03	.132
2010	Peoria (MWL)	LoA	6	0	1.51	13	13	0	0	60	43	0	24	70	10.6	1.12	.202
	Daytona (FSL)	HiA	4	0	2.63	9	9	0	0	41	29	3	9	49	10.8	0.93	.191
	Tennessee (SL)	AA	0	1	5.74	3	3	0	0	16	21	2	4	13	7.5	1.60	.333
2011	Tennessee (SL)	AA	5	6	4.55	23	22	0	0	95	120	5	39	65	6.2	1.67	.319
2012	Tennessee (SL)	AA	9	8	4.26	34	17	0	0	95	93	12	45	66	6.3	1.45	.251
Minor League Totals			27	16	3.45	95	70	0	0	334	320	23	136	291	7.8	1.37	.251

25 JOSH VITTERS, 3B

BA GRADE
45
MEDIUM

Born: Aug. 27, 1989. **B-T:** R-R. **Ht.:** 6-2. **Wt.:** 200. **Drafted:** HS--Cypress, Calif., 2007 (1st round). **Signed by:** Denny Henderson.

Vitters made his major league debut last August at age 22, but the Cubs expected more after drafting him third overall in 2007 and signing him for $3.2 million. He never has destroyed minor league pitching and was overmatched by big leaguers in a September callup. Chicago's third-base job was wide open but he failed to seize it, and the club re-signed veteran Ian Stewart in the offseason. Vitters still possesses the strength, bat speed, short stroke and feel for the barrel that made him an elite draft pick. There still are scouts inside and outside the organization who feel comfortable projecting him as a .275 hitter with 20 homers annually. Others think that he gets himself out too often because he's not selective enough—his 30 walks in 2012 represented a career high—and because he brings little intensity to the ballpark. He could be best suited for platoon duty because he destroys lefthanders, hitting .331/.377/.625 against them in Triple-A last year. Vitters doesn't help his cause with his defense at third base, which remains adequate at best. He has the arm strength for the hot corner but struggled with his throws in the majors, and his speed and range are below average. Vitters has a track record of performing much better in his second stint at a level, so maybe he'll handle big league pitching the next time he gets the chance. When the new Cubs regime will give him that opportunity remains to be seen.

CHICAGO CUBS

Year	Club (League)	Class	AVG	G	AB	R	H	2B	3B	HR	RBI	BB	SO	SB	CS	OBP	SLG
2007	Cubs (AZL)	R	.067	7	30	0	2	0	0	0	2	1	9	0	0	.094	.067
	Boise (NWL)	SS	.190	7	21	2	4	0	0	0	1	2	5	1	1	.261	.190
2008	Peoria (MWL)	LoA	.214	4	14	1	3	3	0	0	1	0	5	0	0	.214	.429
	Boise (NWL)	SS	.328	61	259	38	85	25	2	5	37	13	45	1	3	.365	.498
2009	Peoria (MWL)	LoA	.316	70	269	42	85	12	1	15	46	7	42	4	0	.351	.535
	Daytona (FSL)	HiA	.238	50	189	21	45	7	2	3	22	5	23	2	1	.260	.344
2010	Daytona (FSL)	HiA	.291	28	110	16	32	8	0	3	13	8	22	4	1	.350	.445
	Tennessee (SL)	AA	.223	63	206	28	46	12	0	7	26	13	41	2	0	.292	.383
2011	Tennessee (SL)	AA	.283	129	449	56	127	28	2	14	81	22	54	4	10	.322	.448
2012	Iowa (PCL)	AAA	.304	110	415	54	126	32	2	17	68	30	77	6	3	.356	.513
	Chicago (NL)	MAJ	.121	36	99	7	12	2	0	2	5	7	33	2	0	.193	.202
Major League Totals			.121	36	99	7	12	2	0	2	5	7	33	2	0	.193	.202
Minor League Totals			.283	529	1962	258	555	127	9	64	297	101	323	24	19	.327	.455

26 BARRET LOUX, RHP

BA GRADE **45** MEDIUM

Born: April 6, 1989. **B-T:** R-R. **Ht.:** 6-5. **Wt.:** 215. **Signed:** Texas A&M, 2010. **Signed by:** Randy Taylor (Rangers).

The Diamondbacks selected Loux sixth overall in 2010, in part because he agreed to a below-slot $2 million bonus before the draft. Arizona revoked its offer, however, when it didn't like the wear and tear revealed on his shoulder and elbow during a postdraft physical. MLB declared Loux a free agent and he signed with the Rangers for $312,000, roughly third-round money, that November. He came to the Cubs in a trade in November. Chicago had traded Geovany Soto to Texas in July for righthander Jake Brigham and a player to be named. When concerns arose about Brigham's elbow, the Cubs sent him back to the Rangers for Loux and a player to be named. Loux has a simple, repeatable delivery and an idea of how to pitch. He works downhill and commands his 90-92 mph fastball to both sides of the plate, though neither his velocity nor his secondary pitches separate him from the pack. His average slider and curveball blend together, but most scouts like his changeup best, and he knows how and when to use it. Loux requires a long time to warm up prior to appearances, so his future is in the rotation, where he profiles as an innings-eating back-of-the-rotation starter. Chicago will deploy him in Triple-A to begin 2013 and he could make his big league debut later in the year.

Year	Club (League)	Class	W	L	ERA	G	GS	CG	SV	IP	H	HR	BB	SO	K/9	WHIP	AVG
2011	Myrtle Beach (CAR)	HiA	8	5	3.80	21	21	0	0	109	106	6	34	127	10.5	1.28	.252
2012	Frisco (TL)	AA	14	1	3.47	25	25	0	0	127	120	10	41	100	7.1	1.27	.251
Minor League Totals			22	6	3.62	46	46	0	0	236	226	16	75	227	8.7	1.28	.251

27 MATT LOOSEN, RHP

BA GRADE **45** MEDIUM

Born: April 10, 1989. **B-T:** R-R. **Ht.:** 6-2. **Wt.:** 205. **Drafted:** Jacksonville, 2010 (23rd round). **Signed by:** Tom Clark.

Signed for $30,000 as a 23rd-round pick in 2010, Loosen broke out last year and made the Florida State League all-star team after pacing the circuit with 11 wins. Chicago has worked to smooth out Loosen's delivery, and he no longer throws across his body. His stuff has improved too, as he works his fastball from 89-95 mph and has a sharper curveball. His curve grades as a plus pitch at times, though he sometimes loses his feel for it. When that happens, he'll turn to his decent slider. Loosen's changeup has gotten better but still lacks consistency. While he's not excessively wild, his control and command could use some more fine-tuning. Headed to Double-A in 2013, Loosen has a No. 4 starter's ceiling.

Year	Club (League)	Class	W	L	ERA	G	GS	CG	SV	IP	H	HR	BB	SO	K/9	WHIP	AVG
2010	Cubs (AZL)	R	1	0	0.00	3	1	0	0	7	4	0	1	8	10.8	0.75	.174
	Boise (NWL)	SS	3	3	4.54	11	6	0	0	38	39	4	8	32	7.6	1.25	.267
2011	Tennessee (SL)	AA	0	2	5.73	2	2	0	0	11	6	2	8	7	5.7	1.27	.167
	Peoria (MWL)	LoA	2	1	1.74	6	5	0	0	31	21	2	6	28	8.1	0.87	.194
	Daytona (FSL)	HiA	2	3	4.42	9	6	0	0	37	40	4	13	39	9.6	1.45	.274
2012	Daytona (FSL)	HiA	11	5	4.07	23	23	0	0	113	83	8	46	110	8.8	1.14	.202
Minor League Totals			17	14	3.86	54	43	0	0	236	193	20	82	224	8.6	1.17	.222

28 LENDY CASTILLO, RHP

BA GRADE **45** MEDIUM

Born: April 8, 1989. **B-T:** R-R. **Ht.:** 6-1. **Wt.:** 170. **Signed:** Dominican Republic, 2006. **Signed by:** Sal Agostinelli/Wil Tejada (Phillies).

Originally signed as a shortstop, Castillo hit .239 in three seasons of Rookie ball before the Phillies decided to make him a pitcher in 2010. When the Phillies left him off their 40-man roster, the Cubs plucked Castillo in the Rule 5 draft, and they retained his rights by keeping him on their big league roster for most of 2012. He only pitched 36 innings, however, a significant setback because he needs more experience to improve. Castillo is all about arm strength. His fastball ranges from 93-97 mph in short stints, and sat at 90-93 when he started in previous years. He can run his hard slider up to 86 mph but it doesn't feature much break and finds the strike zone more than his fastball. If Chicago wants to develop him as a starter, he'll probably open 2013 in high Class A. If they keep him in the bullpen, he'll proceed to Double-A.

Year	Club (League)	Class	AVG	G	AB	R	H	2B	3B	HR	RBI	BB	SO	SB	CS	OBP	SLG
2007	Phillies (DSL)	R	.286	60	196	36	56	6	1	1	20	16	23	12	2	.343	.342
2008	Phillies (GCL)	R	.212	45	170	23	36	8	1	3	19	7	36	7	0	.243	.324
2009	Phillies (GCL)	R	.179	27	78	3	14	3	0	0	7	6	15	4	6	.235	.218
Minor League Totals			.239	133	444	62	106	17	2	4	46	29	74	23	8	.287	.313

Year	Club (League)	Class	W	L	ERA	G	GS	CG	SV	IP	H	HR	BB	SO	K/9	WHIP	AVG
2010	Phillies (DSL)	R	0	1	3.52	3	3	0	0	15	13	0	6	11	6.5	1.24	.224
	Phillies (GCL)	R	3	1	2.22	13	6	0	0	45	33	2	18	51	10.3	1.14	.212
	Williamsport (NYP)	SS	0	0	0.00	1	1	0	0	5	3	0	2	3	5.4	1.00	.167
2011	Lakewood (SAL)	LoA	4	2	2.54	21	2	0	0	46	37	1	16	46	9.0	1.15	.220
2012	Cubs (AZL)	R	0	0	0.69	4	4	0	0	13	7	0	3	16	11.1	0.77	.156
	Daytona (FSL)	HiA	0	0	0.00	1	1	0	0	4	3	0	1	4	9.0	1.00	.200
	Tennessee (SL)	AA	0	0	3.00	2	2	0	0	3	3	0	2	2	6.0	1.67	.273
	Chicago (NL)	MAJ	0	1	7.88	13	0	0	0	16	24	2	12	13	7.3	2.25	.343
Major League Totals			0	1	7.88	13	0	0	0	16	24	2	12	13	7.3	2.25	.343
Minor League Totals			7	4	2.20	45	19	0	0	131	99	3	48	133	9.1	1.12	.210

29 MARCUS HATLEY, RHP

BA GRADE 45 MEDIUM

Born: March 26, 1988. **B-T:** R-R. **Ht.:** 6-5. **Wt.:** 220. **Drafted:** Palomar (Calif.) JC, D/F 2006 (39th round). **Signed by:** Denny Henderson.

The Cubs selected Hatley as an outfielder in the 39th round in 2006, and he made just two relief appearances as a Palomar freshman, but Chicago saw enough to sign him as a pitcher for $40,000. He didn't reach full-season ball until 2009, when he blew out his elbow and required Tommy John surgery. On the right night, Hatley uses his size and good delivery to fire 93-96 mph fastballs on a steep downhill plane. His mid-80s slider and upper-80s splitter flash plus ability, though his slider lacks consistent break. Hatley's control and command are scattershot and he lacks deception, so he gets knocked around more than someone with his stuff should. He failed his first shot at Triple-A. Hatley has both a high ceiling and a low floor, and Chicago will try to polish him up some more in 2013.

Year	Club (League)	Class	W	L	ERA	G	GS	CG	SV	IP	H	HR	BB	SO	K/9	WHIP	AVG
2007	Cubs (AZL)	R	1	3	3.82	13	6	0	0	38	36	0	12	26	6.2	1.27	.254
	Boise (NWL)	SS	1	0	3.86	3	0	0	1	5	3	1	2	3	5.8	1.07	.167
2008	Boise (NWL)	SS	1	3	5.71	12	6	0	0	35	46	3	21	30	7.8	1.93	.317
2009	Peoria (MWL)	LoA	6	6	4.64	30	16	0	0	95	103	10	41	64	6.1	1.52	.278
2010	Boise (NWL)	SS	0	0	2.45	2	2	0	0	4	2	0	2	4	9.8	1.09	.154
	Cubs (AZL)	R	0	0	0.00	2	2	0	0	3	2	0	0	3	9.0	0.67	.182
	Peoria (MWL)	LoA	0	0	3.38	7	7	0	0	13	14	0	7	13	8.8	1.58	.318
2011	Peoria (MWL)	LoA	2	1	2.35	13	0	0	3	15	9	0	8	21	12.3	1.11	.170
	Daytona (FSL)	HiA	0	0	1.76	13	0	0	4	15	10	0	11	19	11.2	1.37	.192
	Tennessee (SL)	AA	3	0	4.66	22	0	0	4	29	30	2	11	20	6.2	1.41	.278
2012	Tennessee (SL)	AA	3	1	3.40	28	0	0	4	45	36	3	20	46	9.2	1.24	.232
	Iowa (PCL)	AAA	1	0	8.22	12	0	0	0	15	14	0	10	18	10.6	1.57	.237
Minor League Totals			18	14	4.27	157	39	0	16	312	305	19	145	267	7.7	1.44	.260

30 TREY MARTIN, OF

BA GRADE 50 HIGH

Born: Dec. 11, 1992. **B-T:** R-R. **Ht.:** 6-2. **Wt.:** 188. **Drafted:** HS--Snellville, Ga., 2011 (13th round). **Signed by:** Keith Lockhart.

Martin flew under the scouting radar in the 2011 draft, but former big leaguer and first-year area scout Keith Lockhart found him for the Cubs. They signed him for $250,000 and have raved about his center-field defense ever since. He draws Devon White comparisons for his long, gliding strides and effortless range. He still can improve his jumps and reads, but he's also good enough to play center in Wrigley Field right now. He even adds a solid arm to his defensive package. Martin has interesting offensive potential as well with a projectable frame, good hand-eye coordination and long arms to create leverage giving him some power potential down the line. The downside to those long arms is that they add length to his swing and he can get tied up inside. He has well above-average speed but is still learning how to parlay it into stolen bases. Martin got a scare during instructional league, when he was hit in the face by a pitch. He required surgery to repair a broken cheekbone, but unless there are any setbacks, he'll be able to report to low Class A in 2013.

Year	Club (League)	Class	AVG	G	AB	R	H	2B	3B	HR	RBI	BB	SO	SB	CS	OBP	SLG
2011	Cubs (AZL)	R	.243	18	70	10	17	0	4	0	8	4	17	3	2	.289	.357
2012	Cubs (AZL)	R	.448	7	29	5	13	5	1	0	6	2	3	2	0	.515	.690
	Boise (NWL)	SS	.270	57	204	26	55	5	4	3	23	13	48	6	5	.318	.377
Minor League Totals			.281	82	303	41	85	10	9	3	37	19	68	11	7	.331	.403

Chicago White Sox

BY PHIL ROGERS

Ken Williams got the keys to the White Sox when predecessor Ron Schueler walked away after a 95-win playoff season in 2000. After 12 seasons as general manager, Williams would have loved to go out in similar fashion. Instead, he stepped aside to make room for Rick Hahn, his longtime assistant, after a season that saw the White Sox lead the American League Central for four months before an 11-17 September dropped them behind the Tigers and out of the playoffs.

The 2012 White Sox were like all of Williams' teams: competitive mostly because of talent imported for the short haul rather than a homegrown core with staying power. Chicago made its run in part because Williams' deals for Adam Dunn, Jake Peavy and Alex Rios turned around, but in the end the team overachieved to win 85 games. The good news was that the organization showed signs of getting back to its roots in scouting and player development.

The last two No. 1 prospects on this list, Chris Sale and Addison Reed, emerged as building blocks for the pitching staff. Sale went 17-8, 3.05 in his first year as a starter, while Reed converted 29 of 33 save opportunities as a rookie. Hector Santiago, a 30th-round draft-and-follow in 2006, opened the season as the closer and ended it as a probable member of the 2013 rotation after posting a 2.70 second-half ERA. The White Sox added another quality young arm in Jose Quintana, a minor league free agent recommended by scouts Joe Siers and Daraka Shaheed. Quintana hadn't pitched above high Class A before 2012, but he proved to be a lifesaver when John Danks injured his shoulder by posting a 6-6, 3.76 record over 136 innings.

For once, Williams resisted the urge to trade top prospects. He bolstered the big league club by dealing for Francisco Liriano, Brett Myers and Kevin Youkilis without giving up any youngsters who will be missed.

One nagging issue for the franchise was a sixth consecutive season of decreased attendance at U.S. Cellular Field. Chicago drew 1,965,955 fans to rank 24th in the majors. That figure is down from 2,500,642 in 2008, when Chicago ranked 16th in the majors. Williams, whose new job title is executive vice president, will try to help owner Jerry Reinsdorf turn around that troubling trend.

The club did reverse another negative by investing more heavily in the draft. After spending less money on bonuses ($18.3 million) than any team during the

After 12 years of building contenders, Ken Williams is passing GM duties to Rick Hahn

2007-11 drafts, the White Sox paid $6.5 million for their 2012 draftees, spending every cent of their draft bonus pool allocated by Major League Baseball. That included $2.475 million—the third-highest draft bonus in franchise history—for 13th overall pick Courtney Hawkins.

After a decade of relative inactivity in Latin America, the White Sox also began rounding up talent more aggressively under Marco Paddy, who left the Blue Jays to take a job as special assistant to the general manager in charge of international operations. Paddy's most significant signing in 2012 was power-hitting Dominican third baseman Luis Castillo for $450,000.

Two of the White Sox's three highest affiliates finished as runners-up in their playoffs. Triple-A Charlotte went to the International League finals, featuring a lineup that included three of the system's best position players in outfielders Jared Mitchell and Trayce Thompson and shortstop Carlos Sanchez. Thompson and Sanchez each opened the season with high Class A Winston-Salem, which posted the Carolina League's best regular-season record at 87-51 and made its playoff run with Chicago's top picks in the last two drafts (Hawkins and outfielder Keenyn Walker) and two of its best pitching prospects (Erik Johnson and Scott Snodgress).

THIS YEAR'S TOP 30

Player, Pos.		Grade
1.	Courtney Hawkins, of	60/High
2.	Trayce Thompson, of	55/High
3.	Carlos Sanchez, 2b	50/Medium
4.	Erik Johnson, rhp	50/High
5.	Keenyn Walker, of	50/High
6.	Scott Snodgress, lhp	50/High
7.	Andre Rienzo, rhp	50/High
8.	Keon Barnum, 1b	55/Extreme
9.	Jared Mitchell, of	50/High
10.	Chris Beck, rhp	50/High
11.	Charlie Leesman, lhp	45/Medium
12.	Andy Wilkins, 1b	45/Medium
13.	Jhan Marinez, rhp	45/Medium
14.	Marcus Semien, ss/2b	45/Medium
15.	Blake Tekotte, of	45/Medium
16.	Jake Petricka, rhp	50/High
17.	Brian Omogrosso, rhp	45/Medium
18.	Josh Phegley, c	45/Medium
19.	Kevin Vance, rhp	45/Medium
20.	Simon Castro, rhp	45/Medium
21.	Santos Rodriguez, lhp	45/Medium
22.	Sammy Ayala, c	45/High
23.	Brandon Brennan, rhp	45/High
24.	Joey DeMichele, 2b	45/High
25.	Micah Johnson, 2b	45/High
26.	Tyler Saladino, ss/2b	45/High
27.	Kevan Smith, c	45/High
28.	Nestor Molina, rhp	45/High
29.	Jeff Soptic, rhp	50/Extreme
30.	Jefferson Olacio, lhp	50/Extreme

LAST YEAR'S TOP 30

Player, Pos.		Status
1.	Addison Reed, rhp	Majors
2.	Nestor Molina, rhp	No. 28
3.	Trayce Thompson, of	No. 2
4.	Jake Petricka, rhp	No. 16
5.	Keenyn Walker, of	No. 5
6.	Jhan Marinez, rhp	No. 13
7.	Tyler Saladino, ss	No. 26
8.	Juan Silverio, 3b	Dropped out
9.	Osvaldo Martinez, ss	(Dodgers)
10.	Eduardo Escobar, ss/2b	(Twins)
11.	Hector Santiago, lhp	Majors
12.	Andy Wilkins, 1b	No. 12
13.	Erik Johnson, rhp	No. 4
14.	Charlie Leesman, lhp	No. 11
15.	Jefferson Olacio, lhp	No. 30
16.	Jared Mitchell, of	No. 9
17.	Andre Rienzo, rhp	No. 7
18.	Brandon Short, of	Dropped out
19.	Josh Phegley, c	No. 18
20.	Mike Blanke, c	Dropped out
21.	Carlos Sanchez, 2b/ss	No. 3
22.	Nate Jones, rhp	Majors
23.	Gregori Infante, rhp	Dropped out
24.	Dylan Axelrod, rhp	Majors
25.	Jose Martinez, of	Dropped out
26.	Blair Walters, lhp	(Astros)
27.	Tyler Kuhn, inf/of	(Diamondbacks)
28.	Kevin Smith, c	No. 27
29.	Jordan Danks, of	Dropped out
30.	Deunte Heath, rhp	Dropped out

BEST TOOLS

Best Hitter for Average	Carlos Sanchez
Best Power Hitter	Courtney Hawkins
Best Strike-Zone Discipline	Tyler Saladino
Fastest Baserunner	Keenyn Walker
Best Athlete	Courtney Hawkins
Best Fastball	Jeff Soptic
Best Curveball	Kevin Vance
Best Slider	Erik Johnson
Best Changeup	Charlie Leesman
Best Control	Nestor Molina
Best Defensive Catcher	Miguel Gonzalez
Best Defensive Infielder	Carlos Sanchez
Best Infield Arm	Juan Silverio
Best Defensive Outfielder	John Danks
Best Outfield Arm	Courtney Hawkins

PROJECTED 2016 LINEUP

Catcher	Tyler Flowers
First Base	Andy Wilkins
Second Base	Gordon Beckham
Third Base	Carlos Sanchez
Shortstop	Alexei Ramirez
Left Field	Courtney Hawkins
Center Field	Trayce Thompson
Right Field	Alex Rios
Designated Hitter	Dayan Viciedo
No. 1 Starter	Chris Sale
No. 2 Starter	John Danks
No. 3 Starter	Jake Peavy
No. 4 Starter	Gavin Floyd
No. 5 Starter	Jose Quintana
Closer	Addison Reed

TOP PROSPECTS OF THE DECADE

Year	Player, Pos.	2012 Org.
2003	Joe Borchard, of	Out of baseball
2004	Joe Borchard, of	Out of baseball
2005	Brian Anderson, of	Somerset (Atlantic)
2006	Bobby Jenks, rhp	Red Sox
2007	Ryan Sweeney, of	Red Sox
2008	Aaron Poreda, lhp	Pirates
2009	Gordon Beckham, ss	White Sox
2010	Jared Mitchell, of	White Sox
2011	Chris Sale, lhp	White Sox
2012	Addison Reed, rhp	White Sox

TOP DRAFT PICKS OF THE DECADE

Year	Player, Pos.	2012 Org.
2003	Brian Anderson, of	Rockies
2004	Josh Fields, 3b	Dodgers
2005	Lance Broadway, rhp	Out of baseball
2006	Kyle McCulloch, rhp	Out of baseball
2007	Aaron Poreda, lhp	Pirates
2008	Gordon Beckham, ss	White Sox
2009	Jared Mitchell, of	White Sox
2010	Chris Sale, lhp	White Sox
2011	Keenyn Walker, of (1st round supp.)	White Sox
2012	Courtney Hawkins, of	White Sox

LARGEST BONUSES IN CLUB HISTORY

Joe Borchard, 2003	$5,300,000
Dayan Viciedo, 2008	$4,000,000
Gordon Beckham, 2008	$2,600,000
Courtney Hawkins, 2012	$2,475,000
Jason Stumm, 1999	$1,750,000

CHICAGO WHITE SOX

TOP 2013 ROOKIE: Jhan Marinez, rhp. Part of the Ozzie Guillen compensation package, he has the power fastball/slider combination to be a bullpen weapon.

BREAKOUT PROSPECT: Santos Rodriguez, lhp. He's starting to figure out his command and could help Chicago in a relief role in the near future.

SLEEPER: Euclides Leyer, rhp. A product of the organization's renewed efforts in Latin America, he can hit 94 mph and throw strikes.

SOURCE OF TOP 30 TALENT			
Homegrown	27	Acquired	5
College	15	Trades	5
Junior college	3	Rule 5 draft	0
High school	4	Independent leagues	0
Nondrafted free agents	0	Free agents/waivers	0
International	3		

LF	CF	RF
Brady Shoemaker	Trayce Thompson (2)	Courtney Hawkins (1)
Brandon Short	Keenyn Walker (5)	Mark Haddow
	Jared Mitchell (9)	
	Blake Tekotte (15)	
	Jordan Danks	

3B	SS	2B	1B
Juan Silverio	Carlos Sanchez (3)	Joey DeMichele (24)	Keon Barnum (8)
Rangel Ravelo	Marcus Semien (14)	Micah Johnson (25)	Andy Wilkins (12)
Eric Grabe	David Herbek	Tyler Saladino (26)	Dan Black
	Nick Basto	Drew Garcia	Seth Loman
		Daniel Wagner	

C
Josh Phegley (18)
Sammy Ayala (22)
Kevan Smith (27)
Mike Blanke
Hector Gimenez
Miguel Gonzalez
Zach Stoner
Jose Barraza

LHP		RHP	
LHSP	**LHRP**	**RHSP**	**RHRP**
Scott Snodgress (6)	Santos Rodriguez (21)	Erik Johnson (4)	Jhan Marinez (13)
Charlie Leesman (11)	Matt Lane	Andre Rienzo (7)	Brian Omogrosso (17)
Jefferson Olacio (30)		Chris Beck (10)	Kevin Vance (19)
Jordan Guerrero		Jake Petricka (16)	Jeff Soptic (29)
Spencer Arroyo		Simon Castro (20)	Duente Heath
		Brandon Brennan (23)	Leyson Septimo
		Nestor Molina (28)	Kyle Hansen
		Euclides Leyer	Zach Isler
		Charlie Shirek	Taylor Thompson
		Myles Jaye	Ryan Kussmaul
		Chris Bassitt	Steven Upchurch
		Bryan Blough	Sal Sanchez
			Nick McCully
			Ryan Buch
			Daniel Webb
			Eric Jaffe
			Mitch Mustain

2012 BONUSES: $6.5 MILLION

BEST PURE HITTER: 2B Joey DeMichele (3) was Arizona State's top hitter the last two seasons, and he avoids slumps because of his knack for finding the barrel. He earns Adam Kennedy comparisons for his swing and overall profile.

BEST POWER HITTER: 1B Keon Barnum (1s) missed time after signing with a shoulder injury and he's raw. But he blistered the ball in a personal workout with White Sox GM Ken Williams and has at least plus-plus raw power, drawing comparisons to Ryan Howard. OF Courtney Hawkins (1) doesn't quite have Barnum's light-tower power but may have more usable pop and hit a pair of homers in the high Class A Carolina League playoffs.

FASTEST RUNNER: 2B Micah Johnson (9) has plus speed, though he needs to polish his baserunning skills. His quickness could lead him to move to center field down the line.

BEST DEFENSIVE PLAYER: 3B/2B Eric Grabe (24) showed reliable hands and arm strength at both second and third base. He also can fill in at shortstop.

BEST FASTBALL: RHP Kyle Hansen (6) reaches 96-97 mph in shorter stints. RHP Chris Beck (2) hit 95-96 mph in the summer and fall of 2011 but topped out at 93 in 2012.

BEST SECONDARY PITCH: Beck still flashes a hard slider/cutter that touches 86-87 mph. He has battled his conditioning and lowered his release point since peaking in the summer and fall of 2011, but the White Sox believe they can address his issues. LHP Jordan Guerrero (15) has a solid curveball that flashes plus.

BEST PRO DEBUT: Hawkins hit .284/.317/.480 with eight homers and 11 steals while finishing the summer in high Class A. Grabe was old for Rookie ball at 22 but batted .357/.434/.521 at Bristol. DeMichele reached low Class A while hitting .275/.328/.479 with seven homers.

BEST ATHLETE: Hawkins has good strength and speed and has retained some of his cheerleading skills, as evidenced by the backflip he performed during the draft broadcast on MLB Network.

MOST INTRIGUING BACKGROUND: Hansen's brother Craig had a similar big fastball before injuries struck. He's still attempting a comeback in the Mets system but hasn't pitched in the majors since 2009. Unsigned RHP Ryan Castellanos' (34) brother Nick is the Tigers' top prospect.

CLOSEST TO THE MAJORS: DiMichele may start 2013 at Double-A Birmingham.

BEST LATE-ROUND PICK: The White Sox are high on the physicality of C Sammy Ayala (17), a three-sport prep athlete who's raw but has power potential and plus arm strength. Signed for $258,800, he's a beast at 6-foot-3 and 225 pounds.

THE ONE WHO GOT AWAY: Chicago expects to sign OF Jason Coats (29), a college senior rehabbing a knee injury, once he passes a physical prior to spring training. That would leave John A. Logan (Ill.) CC LHP Derek Thompson (13) as its only unsigned pick in the top 32 rounds.

ASSESSMENT: The White Sox spent less money than any team under the previous labor agreement but opened things up with the new draft rules. Hawkins is a high-ceiling athlete and Chicago added its usual array of strong arms.

2011 BONUSES: $2.8 MILLION

The White Sox didn't have a first-round pick and spent less than any other team. On the positive side, OF Keenyn Walker (1s), RHP Erik Johnson (2) and LHP Scott Snodgress (5) rank among their best prospects.

GRADE: C

2010 BONUSES: $3.9 MILLION

When LHP Chris Sale's (1) price tag scared off other teams, Chicago stole him at No. 13 and got him to the big leagues quickly. RHP Addison Reed (3) became the club's closer as a rookie in 2012.

GRADE: A

2009 BONUSES: $4.2 MILLION

Injuries derailed OF Jared Mitchell's (1) development, and OF Trayce Thompson (2) has been slow to progress. The White Sox have hopes for both, though neither is as attractive as OF Brian Goodwin (17), who signed for $3 million in 2011. LHP David Holmberg (2) took off after joining the Diamondbacks in a trade for Edwin Jackson.

GRADE: C

2008 BONUSES: $4.7 MILLION

Chicago also gave up RHP Daniel Hudson (5) for Jackson, and he won 16 games in 2011 before having Tommy John surgery in 2011. 2B Gordon Beckham (1) hasn't lived up to getting chosen eighth overall, and 3B Brent Morel (3) and OF Jordan Danks (7) haven't met expectations in the majors.

GRADE: B

Draft analysis by John Manuel (2012) and Jim Callis (2008-11). Numbers in parentheses indicate draft rounds.

1 COURTNEY HAWKINS, OF

Born: Nov. 12, 1993. **B-T:** R-R. **Ht.:** 6-3. **Wt.:** 220.
Drafted: HS—Corpus Christi, Texas, 2012 (1st round).
Signed by: Keith Staab.

BA GRADE
60
HIGH

BILL MITCHELL

The White Sox didn't need Hawkins to do a backflip to show off his athleticism, but he did one anyway for the MLB Network after the Sox took him with 13th overall pick in the 2012 draft. He's a Texan with the speed and strength to be a football star, but he chose baseball and quickly became a standout. He has been a favorite of scouts since helping Carroll High of Corpus Christi win the Texas 5-A title as a sophomore in 2010, when he earned MVP honors in the clincher as a starting pitcher. The White Sox got to know Hawkins in the summer of 2011 during the Double Duty Classic at U.S. Cellular Field, an event honoring the history of Negro League baseball in Chicago. Hawkins helped Carroll get back to the 5-A final as a senior before signing for $2.475 million, the third-highest draft bonus in franchise history. He played well at three levels of pro ball, finishing the season at high Class A Winston-Salem and homering twice in the Carolina League playoffs. Hawkins has the kind of talent Chicago's system has lacked over the last decade, and the club might not have risked drafting him if not for the new restrictions on bonus spending, which White Sox owner Jerry Reinsdorf helped push through. Chicago hadn't taken a high school player in the first round since Kris Honel in 2001.

Hawkins has tremendous bat speed, strength and leverage, which combine to give him well above-average power. As a 16-year-old, he launched a monster shot into the upper deck at Round Rock's Dell Diamond in the 2010 state playoffs. Though the White Sox pushed him aggressively in his pro debut, he homered 10 times in 66 games, counting the postseason. Hawkins' swing can get long, which contributes to his tendency to strike out a lot. He could improve as a hitter if he cut down on the effort in his swing, as his bat stays in the hitting zone for a long time. He needs to do a better job recognizing pitches, an area he focused on during instructional league. Chicago is confident that he'll be able to make those adjustments. Hawkins has solid speed and currently runs well enough to

SCOUTING GRADES

Batting: 55.	**Defense:** 55.
Power: 65.	**Arm:** 60.
Speed: 50.	

Based on 20-80 scouting scale, where 50 represents major league average, and future projection rather than present tools.

play center field, though he may lose a half-step as he continues to mature physically, which would push him to an outfield corner. He won't be a significant basestealer but runs the bases well. His fastball sat in the low 90s as a pitcher and that arm strength is a major asset in the outfield. He's a hard worker who made a quick transition to pro ball.

Hawkins has the potential to become the best all-around outfielder the White Sox have produced since they drafted Mike Cameron in the 18th round of the 1991 draft, in part because he has shown the ability to grasp the subtleties of the game. Hawkins has the makings of a middle-of-the-order hitter and solid right fielder, with an outside chance of staying in center. He'll probably return to Winston-Salem to begin his first full pro season. It will be interesting to see whether an organization starved for homegrown impact players will allow him a full season at each minor league level or shortcut his development to write him into the picture in 2015, an option year in Alex Rios' contract.

Year	Club (League)	Class	AVG	G	AB	R	H	2B	3B	HR	RBI	BB	SO	SB	CS	OBP	SLG
2012	Bristol (APP)	R	.272	38	147	25	40	8	1	3	16	7	37	8	2	.314	.401
	Kannapolis (SAL)	LoA	.308	16	65	11	20	5	2	4	15	4	17	3	2	.352	.631
	Winston-Salem (CAR)	HiA	.294	5	17	3	5	2	0	1	2	0	2	0	1	.294	.588
Minor League Totals			.284	59	229	39	65	15	3	8	33	11	56	11	5	.324	.480

2 TRAYCE THOMPSON, OF

Born: March 15, 1991. **B-T:** R-R. **Ht.:** 6-3. **Wt.:** 195. **Drafted:** HS—Santa Margarita, Calif., 2009 (2nd round). **Signed by:** George Kachigian.

A rare above-slot signing for the White Sox, Thompson got $625,000 as a second-round pick in 2009. After repeating low Class A in 2011, he took off in 2012, leading the Carolina League in homers (22), extra-base hits (55) and RBIs (90) and reaching Triple-A Charlotte. He's the son of former NBA No. 1 overall pick Mychal Thompson and the brother of NBA players Klay and Mychel Thompson. Thompson is making his family's athletic ability translate to baseball. He offers a combination of power and speed along with the ability to play center field at a high level. He has worked hard to shorten a long, uppercut swing and use the entire field. He still strikes out too much, in large part because he gets fooled on a lot of breaking pitches. He used his solid speed to steal a career-high 21 bases in 2012 and improved his reads and jumps in center field. He has solid arm strength. Farm director Nick Capra says Thompson has a chance to be a superstar, but he also has to continue to get better. The key will be making more consistent contact after fanning 338 times in the last two seasons. He'll be tested in Double-A Birmingham in 2013 and could receive big league consideration the following year.

BA GRADE

55

HIGH

Year	Club (League)	Class	AVG	G	AB	R	H	2B	3B	HR	RBI	BB	SO	SB	CS	OBP	SLG
2009	Bristol (APP)	R	.188	25	85	8	16	3	1	0	10	4	33	2	0	.247	.247
	Great Falls (PIO)	R	.238	7	21	2	5	0	0	0	0	3	8	1	0	.333	.238
2010	Kannapolis (SAL)	LoA	.229	58	210	28	48	13	3	8	31	21	69	6	4	.302	.433
2011	Kannapolis (SAL)	LoA	.241	136	519	95	125	36	2	24	87	60	172	8	4	.329	.457
2012	Winston-Salem (CAR)HiA	.254	116	449	77	114	28	5	22	90	45	144	18	3	.325	.486
	Birmingham (SL)	AA	.280	14	50	10	14	1	1	3	6	8	16	2	0	.379	.520
	Charlotte (IL)	AAA	.167	6	18	1	3	2	0	0	0	2	6	1	0	.250	.278
Minor League Totals			.240	362	1352	221	325	83	12	57	224	143	448	38	11	.319	.446

3 CARLOS SANCHEZ, SS/2B

Born: June 29, 1992. **B-T:** B-R. **Ht.:** 5-11. **Wt.:** 175. **Signed:** Venezuela, 2009. **Signed by:** Amador Arias.

While the White Sox were falling behind internationally, Venezuelan scout Amador Arias still found infielder Eduardo Escobar (since traded to the Twins for Francisco Liriano) and Sanchez. The latter won the Carolina League batting title (.315) in 2012, then hit .370 in Double-A. He has played all over the infield, including an appearance at third base in the 2012 Futures Game, and first stood out with his glove in pro ball. In 2011, Kannapolis manager Tommy Thompson said Sanchez was as good defensively as any second baseman he had ever seen. He has enough arm to play on the left side of the infield and the Sox haven't ruled him out as a shortstop. He has quick hands that are good on the double-play pivot and a quick first step. Offensively, Sanchez features a short swing and good bat speed, hitting line drives all over the park from both sides of the plate. Smaller than his listed size, he offers little power and needs to walk more often. He has average speed and runs the bases aggressively. While Alexei Ramirez (2015) and Gordon Beckham (2016) are under White Sox control for several years, Sanchez could make one of them trade bait. A potential Gold Glover, he could play as a 20-year-old shortstop in Triple-A in 2013 before making a push for the big leagues before season's end.

BA GRADE

50

MEDIUM

Year	Club (League)	Class	AVG	G	AB	R	H	2B	3B	HR	RBI	BB	SO	SB	CS	OBP	SLG
2009	White Sox (DSL)	R	.156	22	32	7	5	0	0	0	3	8	10	1	0	.341	.156
2010	White Sox (DSL)	R	.269	52	156	26	42	5	2	1	18	41	26	7	3	.431	.346
2011	Bristol (APP)	R	.250	5	16	4	4	1	0	0	3	5	2	1	2	.500	.313
	Kannapolis (SAL)	LoA	.288	63	264	44	76	10	1	1	27	15	49	7	8	.341	.345
2012	Winston-Salem (CAR)HiA	.315	92	365	58	115	14	6	1	42	31	64	19	10	.374	.395
	Birmingham (SL)	AA	.370	30	119	17	44	9	1	0	13	10	22	7	5	.424	.462
	Charlotte (IL)	AAA	.256	11	39	4	10	2	0	0	1	0	6	0	0	.256	.308
Minor League Totals			.299	275	991	160	296	41	10	3	107	110	179	42	28	.379	.369

4 ERIK JOHNSON, RHP

Born: Dec. 30, 1989. **B-T:** R-R. **Ht.:** 6-3. **Wt.:** 240. **Drafted:** California, 2011 (2nd round). **Signed by:** Adam Virchis.

White Sox coaches were thrilled when Johnson arrived at their Arizona complex in 2011, with one saying, "This is what we're looking for." After he recovered from shoulder fatigue in spring training that delayed his 2012 debut until June, Johnson posted a 2.53 ERA in 17 regular season starts and took a no-hitter into the sixth inning in the first round of the Carolina League playoffs. He uses his strong build to throw a low-90s fastball that peaks at 96. His slider is a potential plus pitch with depth and bite, and his curveball is nearly as good. He's still learning to add and subtract from his changeup, which lags behind his other pitches. He worked on his changeup during instructional league, with club officials encouraged by the results. Johnson has refined his mechanics since signing, which paid off with extra velocity and improved control late in the 2012 season. He still needs to prove he can hold up over the course of a full season. White Sox scouts compare him to Curt Schilling, though realistically Johnson's ceiling is more as a No. 3 starter. He could open 2013 in Double-A and compete for a big league rotation spot in 2014.

BA GRADE

50

HIGH

Year	Club (League)	Class	W	L	ERA	G	GS	CG	SV	IP	H	HR	BB	SO	K/9	WHIP	AVG
2011	Great Falls (PIO)	R	0	0	4.50	2	0	0	0	2	4	0	1	2	9.0	2.50	.444
2012	Kannapolis (SAL)	LoA	2	2	2.30	9	9	0	0	43	39	3	19	39	8.2	1.35	.235
	Winston-Salem (CAR)	HiA	4	3	2.74	8	8	0	0	49	43	0	10	48	8.8	1.07	.230
Minor League Totals			6	5	2.58	19	17	0	0	94	86	3	30	89	8.5	1.23	.238

5 KEENYN WALKER, OF

Born: Aug. 12, 1990. **B-T:** B-R. **Ht.:** 6-3. **Wt.:** 195. **Drafted:** Central Arizona JC, 2011 (1st round supplemental). **Signed by:** John Kazanas.

A star defensive back in high school, Walker drew football interest from Boise State and some Pacific-12 Conference programs. He chose to play baseball at Central Arizona JC, where he led national juco players with 70 steals and became Chicago's top pick (supplemental first round) in 2011. Signed for $795,000, he topped the system with 56 swipes in his first full pro season. He missed a month with two disabled-list stints in the second half after sustaining nagging knee and shoulder injuries during baserunning mishaps. Walker's plus-plus speed allows him to run wild on the bases and cover a lot of ground in center field. He likes to play shallow and has a solid arm. His quickness also allows him to collect infield hits, and his ability to draw walks gives him strong on-base skills. However, Walker strikes out too much from both sides of the plate. The White Sox have worked with him on widening his stance and improving his pitch recognition. He doesn't have much power from either side but is a little more dangerous as a lefty. Walker struggled when he got to high Class A in mid-July, so he'll probably return to Winston-Salem to begin 2013. He'll need time to develop and may not be ready for the majors until the end of 2015.

BA GRADE

50

HIGH

Year	Club (League)	Class	AVG	G	AB	R	H	2B	3B	HR	RBI	BB	SO	SB	CS	OBP	SLG
2011	Great Falls (PIO)	R	.333	15	60	16	20	7	1	0	9	7	17	11	5	.431	.483
	Kannapolis (SAL)	LoA	.228	39	162	25	37	1	2	0	15	14	64	10	4	.296	.259
2012	Kannapolis (SAL)	LoA	.282	74	266	53	75	15	5	1	39	50	93	39	11	.395	.387
	Winston-Salem (CAR)	HiA	.238	37	143	31	34	7	1	3	16	24	50	17	4	.345	.364
Minor League Totals			.263	165	631	125	166	30	9	4	79	95	224	77	24	.363	.358

6 SCOTT SNODGRESS, LHP

Born: Sept. 20, 1989. **B-T:** L-L. **Ht.:** 6-5. **Wt.:** 210. **Drafted:** Stanford, 2011 (5th round). **Signed by:** Adam Virchis.

Snodgress never put the pieces together at Stanford, going 4-7, 5.47 in three seasons. Nevertheless, the White Sox loved his size and arm strength enough to draft him in the fifth round in 2011, and he has had much more consistent success as a pro. He finished his first full pro season with eight strong starts in high Class A. Snodgress has improved his delivery and experienced a jump in velocity since signing, now operating at 91-93 mph and hitting 95 with his fastball. His curveball and his changeup also have gotten better, though the latter needs more work. He no longer telegraphs his changeup by slowing his arm speed, but he still doesn't throw it for strikes consistently. Snodgress' overall command and composure are two more areas where he has made strides as a pro. He has natural deception in his delivery, which allows him to be effective against righties as well as lefties. Snodgress should get to Double-A at some point in 2013. He still needs to throw more

BA GRADE

50

HIGH

strikes, but if he continues to make strides toward mastering a three-pitch mix, he could develop into a No. 3 starter. At worst, he should have late-inning value as a lefthanded reliever.

Year	Club (League)	Class	W	L	ERA	G	GS	CG	SV	IP	H	HR	BB	SO	K/9	WHIP	AVG
2011	Great Falls (PIO)	R	3	3	3.34	16	12	0	0	59	61	5	17	68	10.3	1.31	.262
2012	Kannapolis (SAL)	LoA	3	3	3.64	19	19	0	0	99	86	4	49	84	7.6	1.36	.233
	Winston-Salem (CAR)	HiA	4	0	1.50	8	8	0	0	42	26	2	15	44	9.4	0.98	.176
Minor League Totals			10	6	3.10	43	39	0	0	200	173	11	81	196	8.8	1.27	.231

7 ANDRE RIENZO, RHP

Born: July 5, 1988. **B-T:** R-R. **Ht.:** 6-3. **Wt.:** 160. **Signed:** Brazil, 2006. **Signed by:** Orlando Santana.

Left off Chicago's 40-man roster following a disappointing 2011 season, Rienzo didn't endear himself to the club when he got hit with a 50-game suspension in April for testing positive for performance-enhancing drugs. Once he returned, he pitched well in Double-A and the Arizona Fall League. Brazil tabbed him to pitch for its World Baseball Classic team, and he could be the first pitcher from his nation to reach the majors. Rienzo's fastball usually sits it the low 90s and touches 95 mph, running in on lefthanders. Improved secondary pitches helped him hold opponents to a .206 average in 2012. He throws his overhand curveball in the upper 70s, getting swings and misses. He has started to use his low-80s cutter more often, and it too has been effective. Rienzo hasn't added much size or strength since signing, and his ultra-thin build doesn't fit the profile of a big league starter. Neither does his lack of command or an effective changeup. Rienzo is knocking on the door of the big leagues. His work in Triple-A in 2013 will determine whether he arrives as a starter or reliever. His most realistic ceiling is as a set-up man, but he also could be a No. 4 starter.

BA GRADE 50 HIGH

Year	Club (League)	Class	W	L	ERA	G	GS	CG	SV	IP	H	HR	BB	SO	K/9	WHIP	AVG
2007	White Sox 2 (DSL)	R	1	1	7.63	7	3	0	0	15	16	1	11	22	12.9	1.76	.286
2008	White Sox 2 (DSL)	R	2	1	1.64	5	4	0	0	22	17	0	6	22	9.0	1.05	.218
	White Sox 1 (DSL)	R	3	0	0.96	3	3	0	0	19	15	0	3	22	10.6	0.96	.214
2009	Bristol (APP)	R	2	6	4.14	13	9	0	0	54	55	4	13	49	8.1	1.25	.263
2010	Kannapolis (SAL)	LoA	8	4	3.65	20	18	2	0	101	95	5	32	125	11.1	1.26	.242
2011	Winston-Salem (CAR)	HiA	6	5	3.41	25	22	1	0	116	108	4	66	118	9.2	1.50	.247
2012	Winston-Salem (CAR)	HiA	3	0	1.08	4	4	0	0	25	17	0	7	31	11.2	0.96	.193
	Birmingham (SL)	AA	4	3	3.27	13	13	1	0	72	56	2	33	72	9.0	1.24	.209
	Charlotte (IL)	AAA	0	0	0.00	1	1	0	0	7	5	0	2	10	13.5	1.05	.227
Minor League Totals			29	20	3.30	91	77	4	0	431	384	16	173	471	9.8	1.29	.237

8 KEON BARNUM, 1B

Born: Jan. 6, 1993. **B-T:** L-L. **Ht.:** 6-5. **Wt.:** 225. **Drafted:** HS—Tampa, 2012 (1st round supplemental). **Signed by:** Joe Siers.

The White Sox haven't developed many power hitters in recent years, so they looked to change that by taking Courtney Hawkins with their first pick and Barnum with their second in the 2012 draft. Signed for $950,000, he has drawn comparisons to Ryan Howard and Fred McGriff. Barnum homered three times in his first five professional games, but then missed six weeks with a shoulder injury and wasn't the same after he returned to the field. Barnum has more raw power than Hawkins, using his long arms to hit balls hard and with enviable loft. He can crush all but the best fastballs and has the strength to get hits even when he's jammed. But a lot of scouts consider him a one-trick pony. Barnum struggles to control his oversized strike zone, easily gets fooled by breaking balls and can look clueless by chasing bad pitches. Chicago wants to shorten his swing, which can get loopy at times. He has fringy speed and solid arm strength. His defense at first base needs work, and he may be able to give left field a try. Barnum likely will open his first full pro season at low Class A Kannapolis. His plus-plus raw power could play well at U.S. Cellular Field, but he could need 2,000 pro at-bats before he's polished enough to be ready to play there.

BA GRADE 55 EXTREME

Year	Club (League)	Class	AVG	G	AB	R	H	2B	3B	HR	RBI	BB	SO	SB	CS	OBP	SLG
2012	Bristol (APP)	R	.279	13	43	6	12	1	0	3	8	5	13	0	0	.347	.512
Minor League Totals			.279	13	43	6	12	1	0	3	8	5	13	0	0	.347	.512

9 JARED MITCHELL, OF

Born: Oct. 11, 1998. **B-T:** L-L. **Ht.:** 5-11. **Wt.:** 192. **Drafted:** Louisiana State, 2009 (1st round). **Signed by:** Warren Hughes.

Mitchell was an electrifying athlete who won national championships in baseball and football (as a wide receiver) at Louisiana State. The 23rd overall pick in the 2009 draft, he signed for $1.2 million and immediately ranked as the organization's top prospect. But he hasn't been quite the same player since he crashed into an outfield fence in spring training in 2010, tearing tendons in his left ankle that resulted in him missing the entire season. Mitchell has a quick bat, the willingness to work counts and solid speed, so he should be able to hit for average. But he's patient to a fault, often falling behind in the count and struggling when he does so. He has struck out 362 times in his two full pro seasons. He has a lot of holes in his long swing and is especially ineffective against lefthanders. He has average raw power. Mitchell is still aggressive on the bases, though he's no longer the plus-plus runner he was before his injury. He was less tentative in center field in 2012 than he was the year before. He's a solid defender with an average arm. Unless he can make some major adjustments at the plate, Mitchell may not be more than a platoon player in the big leagues. He's ticketed for a full year in Triple-A in 2013.

BA GRADE
50
HIGH

Year	Club (League)	Class	AVG	G	AB	R	H	2B	3B	HR	RBI	BB	SO	SB	CS	OBP	SLG
2009	Kannapolis (SAL)	LoA	.296	34	115	13	34	12	2	0	10	23	40	5	3	.417	.435
2010	Did Not Play—Injured																
2011	Winston-Salem (CAR)HiA		.222	129	477	74	106	31	8	9	58	52	183	14	6	.304	.377
2012	Birmingham (SL)	AA	.240	94	334	51	80	13	12	10	54	62	126	20	5	.368	.440
	Charlotte (IL)	AAA	.231	36	121	18	28	11	1	1	13	16	53	1	1	.329	.364
Minor League Totals			.237	293	1047	156	248	67	23	20	135	153	402	40	15	.341	.402

10 CHRIS BECK, RHP

Born: Sept. 4, 1990. **B-T:** R-R. **Ht.:** 6-3. **Wt.:** 210. **Drafted:** Georgia Southern, 2012 (2nd round). **Signed by:** Kevin Burrell.

After a strong summer in the Cape Cod League, Beck projected as a top 10 overall selection for the 2012 draft. But his stock dropped as he lost his arm slot and much of his command during the spring, and the White Sox signed him for $600,000 as the No. 76 choice. Their pick came down to him and Paco Rodriguez, who went at No. 82 and reached the big leagues in September with the Dodgers. When he's right, Beck has a classic pitcher's frame and the stuff to go with it. He worked at 91-94 mph and touched 96 in 2011, though he operated at 89-93 throughout 2012. His mid-80s slider/cutter is filthy at times albeit inconsistent, and his changeup shows flashes of becoming a plus pitch. Chicago believes Beck's problems stemmed from being overweight and lowering his release point. He has to work to keep his mechanics and command in order. He seemed to find a better arm slot working with White Sox coaches but needs innings to refine the changes. Beck will open his first full pro season in low Class A. He'll advance quickly if he stays in shape and develops more consistency, with the ceiling of a No. 2 or 3 starter if it all comes together.

BA GRADE
50
HIGH

Year	Club (League)	Class	W	L	ERA	G	GS	CG	SV	IP	H	HR	BB	SO	K/9	WHIP	AVG
2012	Great Falls (PIO)	R	4	3	4.69	15	6	0	0	40	51	3	12	36	8.0	1.56	.319
Minor League Totals			4	3	4.69	15	6	0	0	40	51	3	12	36	8.0	1.56	.319

11 CHARLIE LEESMAN, LHP

BA GRADE
45
MEDIUM

Born: March 10, 1987. **B-T:** L-L. **Ht.:** 6-4. **Wt.:** 210. **Drafted:** Xavier, 2008 (11th round). **Signed by:** Mike Shirley/Phil Gulley.

While the White Sox used 12 rookie pitchers in 2012, Leesman spent a full season in Triple-A as one of the International League's top starters. He might have been Chicago's 13th rookie pitcher if he hadn't torn up his left knee while covering first base during the IL playoffs, an injury that required surgery and will put him behind to start 2013. He finished second in the IL with a 2.47 ERA while improving his control and command from the previous season. Leesman has reached double digits in victories in each of his four full pro seasons since signing for $50,000. He has succeeded by mixing four pitches, including a changeup that's a plus offering at times, but his 86-89 mph fastball is a caution sign for scouts. His fastball has late life and sink, and hitters don't barrel it consistently despite its lack of velocity. He also throws a curveball and cutter, though neither is a swing-and-miss pitch. When Leesman misses with his pitches, he tends to miss down, as he has surrendered just 23 homers in 603 pro innings. He doesn't profile as more than a No. 4 or 5 starter, but he's ready for the opportunity to show whether he can hold down that role with the White Sox.

Year	Club (League)	Class	W	L	ERA	G	GS	CG	SV	IP	H	HR	BB	SO	K/9	WHIP	AVG
2008	Bristol (APP)	R	0	0	0.00	2	0	0	1	5	5	0	1	6	10.1	1.13	.263
	Kannapolis (SAL)	LoA	0	0	0.00	1	1	0	0	5	3	0	2	5	9.6	1.07	.188
2009	Kannapolis (SAL)	LoA	13	5	3.08	27	27	1	0	158	165	4	58	117	6.7	1.41	.275
2010	Winston-Salem (CAR)	HiA	9	4	5.10	17	17	0	0	85	98	6	44	39	4.1	1.68	.294
	Birmingham (SL)	AA	5	2	2.69	11	11	0	0	64	47	1	20	51	7.2	1.05	.210
2011	Birmingham (SL)	AA	10	7	4.03	27	27	0	0	152	150	4	83	113	6.7	1.53	.264
2012	Charlotte (IL)	AAA	12	10	2.47	26	26	0	0	135	129	8	52	103	6.9	1.34	.255
Minor League Totals			49	28	3.37	111	109	1	1	603	597	23	260	434	6.5	1.42	.264

12 ANDY WILKINS, 1B

BA GRADE
45
MEDIUM

Born: Sept. 13, 1988. **B-T:** L-R. **Ht.:** 6-2. **Wt.:** 225. **Drafted:** Arkansas, 2010 (5th round). **Signed by:** Clay Overcash.

Scouts have mixed opinions on Wilkins, as some see him as a rising prospect and others think he's just a good organization player. Big and strong, he has slugged 40 homers in his two full pro seasons, but his batting average plunged to .239 last season in Double-A. Birmingham is a tough place to hit for power, and at times he seemed to overswing and become pull-conscious. Wilkins has a bat wrap that alarms scouts, though he has the bat speed to still drive balls out of the park. He has been more productive against righthanders (.785 OPS in 2012) than against lefties (.687 OPS), so he might not be more than a platoon player. He has worked hard to do a better job of staying on the ball against southpaws, and he did hit them well in the Arizona Fall League. Wilkins is adequate at first base but looked awkward when the White Sox tried him at third in 2010. He had enough arm strength for the hot corner but not much range. He's a below-average runner who's aggressive on the bases. Wilkins moves to Triple-A and a hitter's park in 2013, with Paul Konerko in the last year of his contract. If Konerko retires, as he has hinted he might, Wilkins appears first in line to replace him.

Year	Club (League)	Class	AVG	G	AB	R	H	2B	3B	HR	RBI	BB	SO	SB	CS	OBP	SLG
2010	Great Falls (PIO)	R	.307	53	218	37	67	14	1	6	40	33	31	7	2	.396	.463
2011	Winston-Salem (CAR)	HiA	.278	134	493	72	137	33	0	23	89	56	91	2	2	.349	.485
2012	Birmingham (SL)	AA	.239	116	435	68	104	28	1	17	69	63	94	6	4	.335	.425
Minor League Totals			.269	303	1146	177	308	75	2	46	198	152	216	15	8	.353	.458

13 JHAN MARINEZ, RHP

BA GRADE
45
MEDIUM

Born: Aug. 12, 1988. **B-T:** R-R. **Ht.:** 6-1. **Wt.:** 200. **Signed:** Dominican Republic, 2006. **Signed by:** Sandy Nin (Marlins).

A year after the White Sox essentially traded former manager Ozzie Guillen to the Marlins for Marinez and Osvaldo Martinez, Miami had fired Guillen and Chicago had sold Martinez to the Dodgers. Marinez, however, is still in the system and on the verge of making big league contributions. He threw more strikes after working on his mechanics with Triple-A pitching coach Rich Dotson, finished the season as Charlotte's closer and demonstrated his improvement nicely in a perfect inning against the Rays on Sept. 9. Marinez's stuff got him to the big leagues as a 21-year-old with the Marlins, but he never has developed command to go along with his live arm. He may be on the verge of doing that after cutting his walk ratio from 6.5 per nine innings in 2011 to 4.3 last year. The White Sox believe his low three-quarters arm slot works for his two-pitch arsenal—a 93-98 mph fastball with late life and an 83-87 mph slider—but he battles a tendency to get under his pitches, leaving them up in the strike zone. He did a better job of staying on top of his offerings under Dotson's tutelage. Marinez will compete for a bullpen job in spring training and could make a veteran like Jesse Crain expendable, helping new GM Rick Hahn out of a payroll squeeze. Marinez profiles as a seventh- or eighth-inning arm in the big leagues but is still young enough that he could evolve into a closer down the road.

Year	Club (League)	Class	W	L	ERA	G	GS	CG	SV	IP	H	HR	BB	SO	K/9	WHIP	AVG
2006	Marlins (DSL)	R	2	1	7.00	20	2	0	1	36	44	0	26	22	5.5	1.94	.324
2007	Marlins (GCL)	R	0	0	10.80	3	0	0	0	3	5	0	4	4	10.8	2.70	.357
	Marlins (GCL)	R	2	3	4.70	5	1	0	0	23	14	1	19	25	9.8	1.43	.163
2008	Marlins (GCL)	R	1	1	6.11	12	1	0	1	18	21	0	14	18	9.2	1.98	.296
2009	Jupiter (FSL)	HiA	1	1	3.14	29	0	0	1	43	28	4	20	42	8.8	1.12	.185
2010	Florida (NL)	MAJ	0	0	6.75	4	0	0	0	3	3	1	3	3	10.1	2.25	.273
	Jupiter (FSL)	HiA	0	1	1.42	21	1	0	4	25	12	1	14	44	15.6	1.03	.148
	Jacksonville (SL)	AA	1	0	2.16	15	0	0	6	17	9	1	7	20	10.8	0.96	.164
2011	Jacksonville (SL)	AA	3	8	3.57	56	0	0	3	58	47	7	42	74	11.5	1.53	.223
2012	Charlotte (IL)	AAA	4	2	2.86	40	0	0	4	63	39	6	30	65	9.3	1.10	.177
	Chicago (AL)	MAJ	0	0	0.00	2	0	0	0	3	2	0	2	1	3.4	1.50	.250
Major League Totals			1	1	3.38	6	0	0	0	5	5	1	5	4	6.8	1.88	.263
Minor League Totals			14	17	3.84	201	9	0	20	286	219	19	176	314	9.9	1.38	.214

14 MARCUS SEMIEN, SS/2B

BA GRADE
45
MEDIUM

Born: Sept. 17, 1990. **B-T:** R-R. **Ht.:** 6-1. **Wt.:** 190. **Drafted:** California, 2011 (6th round). **Signed by:** Adam Virchis.

The son of former California wide receiver Eric Semien, Marcus was a three-sport standout in high school who followed his father's footsteps to Berkeley, where he focused on baseball. The White Sox drafted him in the 34th round out of high school but didn't land him until 2011, when they took him in the sixth round and gave him a $130,000 bonus. He was more highly regarded as a fielder than a hitter in college, but Chicago projected he would make major strides at the plate as a pro—and he did in his first full season. Semien shook off shoulder tendinitis in the first half to bat .290/.392/.514 after the all-star break. He opened his stance slightly last year, allowing him to barrel more pitches. Some scouts are still skeptical about his bat, questioning his strength and whether he'll get on base enough to bat anywhere but the bottom of a lineup. Semien has average speed but isn't a basestealing threat. He has solid arm strength and reliable hands, though his range is average and may push him to second base down the road. How Semien performs in Double-A in 2013 will shed light as to whether he eventually can become a big league regular or will top out as a utility type.

Year	Club (League)	Class	AVG	G	AB	R	H	2B	3B	HR	RBI	BB	SO	SB	CS	OBP	SLG
2011	Kannapolis (SAL)	LoA	.253	60	229	35	58	15	2	3	26	22	53	3	4	.320	.376
2012	Winston-Salem (CAR)	HiA	.273	107	418	80	114	31	5	14	59	55	97	11	5	.362	.471
Minor League Totals			.266	167	647	115	172	46	7	17	85	77	150	14	9	.347	.437

15 BLAKE TEKOTTE, OF

BA GRADE
45
MEDIUM

Born: May 24, 1987. **B-T:** L-R. **Ht.:** 5-11. **Wt.:** 175. **Drafted:** Miami, 2008 (3rd round). **Signed by:** Rob Sidwell (Padres).

The Padres have one of the deepest farm systems in baseball, and Tekotte found himself a victim of a numbers crunch after the worst season of his career. San Diego needed 40-man roster space and designated him for assignment in November, and the White Sox picked him up in a trade for journeyman righthander Brandon Kloess. Tekotte got knocked off course in 2012 by recurring hamstring problems and an unsuccessful attempt to change his swing to fare better against lefthanders. His plate discipline fell apart and he got away from his strength, which is to get on base and use his plus speed. He has a quick bat and close to average power, though he gets too pull-conscious at times. He's a legitimate basestealer who's aggressive on the basepaths. Tekotte is a good athlete and solid center-field defender, with his only real weakness a below-average arm. Tekotte probably will start 2013 in Triple-A, but he could win a reserve role on the big league club during spring training. He could benefit if the White Sox decide to move Dayan Viciedo to third base.

Year	Club (League)	Class	AVG	G	AB	R	H	2B	3B	HR	RBI	BB	SO	SB	CS	OBP	SLG
2008	Eugene (NWL)	SS	.285	47	193	43	55	15	0	6	29	27	45	7	4	.379	.456
2009	Fort Wayne (MWL)	LoA	.258	134	530	83	137	24	5	13	56	68	97	30	12	.345	.396
2010	Lake Elsinore (CAL)	HiA	.310	59	203	41	63	17	1	8	27	36	46	22	8	.419	.522
	San Antonio (TL)	AA	.250	67	268	44	67	8	7	10	37	26	63	6	9	.324	.444
2011	San Diego (NL)	MAJ	.176	19	34	1	6	1	1	0	1	4	21	2	1	.263	.265
	San Antonio (TL)	AA	.285	106	414	77	118	27	2	19	67	67	108	36	12	.393	.498
2012	San Diego (NL)	MAJ	.133	11	15	0	2	0	0	0	0	0	4	1	0	.133	.133
	Tucson (PCL)	AAA	.243	89	321	38	78	20	2	9	26	18	92	9	8	.284	.402
Major League Totals			.163	30	49	1	8	1	1	0	1	4	25	3	1	.226	.224
Minor League Totals			.269	502	1929	326	518	111	17	65	242	242	451	110	53	.355	.445

16 JAKE PETRICKA, RHP

BA GRADE
50
HIGH

Born: June 5, 1988. **B-T:** R-R. **Ht.:** 6-5. **Wt.:** 210. **Drafted:** Indiana State, 2010 (2nd round). **Signed by:** Mike Shirley.

One of the system's top pitching prospects entering last season, Petricka was his own worst enemy at times and got hammered at two levels. He still has a high ceiling, but he won't reach it or have success against more advanced hitters until he can develop a reliable breaking ball and command his pitches. Originally drafted by the White Sox as a 38th-rounder out of a Minnesota high school in 2006, Petricka played in college at Iowa Western CC and Indiana State. He also had Tommy John surgery before signing with Chicago as a second-rounder in 2010. Petricka has a big-boy fastball that can sit in the mid-90s and has reached 100 mph, though he also pitched in the low 90s at times in 2012. His changeup shows the making of becoming a solid pitch, but he's handicapped by an inconsistent curveball. Even when his stuff is on, he doesn't always locate it effectively, and he needs to learn to deal with failure better. If there was a positive to Petricka's 2012 season, it was that he held up for 29 starts after missing time the previous year with back issues. He'll return to Double-A to begin 2013, and he could be headed for the bullpen if he doesn't deliver better results.

Year	Club (League)	Class	W	L	ERA	G	GS	CG	SV	IP	H	HR	BB	SO	K/9	WHIP	AVG
2010	Bristol (APP)	R	2	4	2.86	8	8	0	0	35	25	1	7	38	9.9	0.92	.197

	Club (League)	Class	W	L	ERA	G	GS	CG	SV	IP	H	HR	BB	SO	K/9	WHIP	AVG
	Kannapolis (SAL)	LoA	0	1	3.72	9	0	0	0	10	13	0	8	10	9.3	2.17	.295
2011	Kannapolis (SAL)	LoA	3	1	2.81	8	8	0	0	42	39	0	13	48	10.4	1.25	.255
	Bristol (APP)	R	0	0	0.00	2	1	0	0	4	4	0	0	5	11.3	1.00	.286
	Winston-Salem (CAR)	HiA	4	7	4.39	13	13	0	0	68	71	3	26	46	6.1	1.43	.265
2012	Winston-Salem (CAR)	HiA	5	5	5.33	19	19	0	0	83	93	2	46	84	9.1	1.68	.284
	Birmingham (SL)	AA	3	3	5.46	10	10	0	0	58	63	7	35	27	4.2	1.70	.290
Minor League Totals			17	21	4.38	69	59	0	0	298	308	13	135	258	7.8	1.49	.268

17 BRIAN OMOGROSSO, RHP

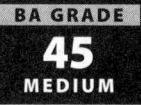

BA GRADE

45

MEDIUM

Born: April 26, 1984. **B-T:** R-R. **Ht.:** 6-4. **Wt.:** 230. **Drafted:** Indiana State, 2006 (6th round). **Signed by:** Nathan Durst/Keith Staab/Mike Shirley.

Give Omogrosso credit for never giving up on himself, and the White Sox kudos for not writing him off. He survived Tommy John surgery at Indiana State and a torn labrum in 2009 to reach the big leagues in his seventh pro season. He looked comfortable enough that manager Robin Ventura gave him big innings in a playoff race. Omogrosso has one of the highest leg kicks in baseball and comes at hitters like a modern-day Sam McDowell. His fastball sits at 93-95 mph and hits 97. He backs it up with a hard slider in the low 80s and an occasional curve. After showing better control and command than ever in Triple-A last year, Omogrosso wasn't as accurate in Chicago yet still was effective. His peak value is probably as a seventh- or eighth-inning reliever, and he could slot into Jesse Crain's role if the White Sox find a taker for Crain's salary.

Year	Club (League)	Class	W	L	ERA	G	GS	CG	SV	IP	H	HR	BB	SO	K/9	WHIP	AVG
2006	Kannapolis (SAL)	LoA	1	2	3.19	22	0	0	2	37	27	2	13	23	5.6	1.09	.209
2007	Winston-Salem (CAR)	HiA	8	8	3.74	40	14	1	5	120	94	7	57	108	8.1	1.25	.211
2008	Birmingham (SL)	AA	2	3	3.69	17	5	0	1	39	32	2	25	26	6.0	1.46	.230
2009	Birmingham (SL)	AA	7	2	4.19	13	13	0	0	73	67	4	40	64	7.9	1.47	.245
	Charlotte (IL)	AAA	0	0	15.88	4	0	0	0	6	12	2	3	6	9.5	2.65	.429
2010	Bristol (APP)	R	0	0	0.00	2	0	0	0	2	1	0	2	2	9.0	1.50	.167
	Birmingham (SL)	AA	0	1	3.00	3	0	0	0	3	2	0	1	3	9.0	1.00	.182
2011	Birmingham (SL)	AA	0	2	2.51	31	0	0	2	43	36	2	16	53	11.1	1.21	.225
	Charlotte (IL)	AAA	1	1	4.03	11	1	0	0	22	24	1	8	19	7.7	1.43	.282
2012	Charlotte (IL)	AAA	0	2	4.56	33	0	0	9	47	43	3	12	59	11.2	1.16	.240
	Chicago (AL)	MAJ	0	0	2.57	17	0	0	0	21	20	3	9	18	7.7	1.38	.247
Major League Totals			0	0	2.57	17	0	0	0	21	20	3	9	18	7.7	1.38	.247
Minor League Totals			19	21	3.90	176	33	1	19	392	338	23	177	363	8.3	1.31	.232

18 JOSH PHEGLEY, C

BA GRADE

45

MEDIUM

Born: Feb. 12, 1988. **B-T:** R-R. **Ht.:** 5-10. **Wt.:** 210. **Drafted:** Indiana, 2009 (1st round supplemental). **Signed by:** Mike Shirley.

Phegley won a Rawlings minor league Gold Glove in 2012 after leading International League catchers with a .996 fielding percentage and ranking second by throwing out 46 percent of basestealers. He has caught 48 percent of basestealers during his pro career, thanks to his solid arm strength. Despite his Gold Glove, he's not a particularly advanced receiver. He has committed 32 passed balls in 195 games during the last two seasons and is somewhat stiff behind the plate. Phegley is still raw at the plate as well. He makes contact but lacks patience, and he also doesn't have the bat speed to catch up to good fastballs. He can drive mistakes and has power, but his consistently low on-base percentages relegate him to the bottom of the order. He's a well below-average runner. Phegley's throwing ability earned him a spot on Chicago's 40-man roster in November and could put him into the mix for a big league job in 2013 if the White Sox don't re-sign A.J. Pierzynski. He isn't likely to be more than a backup in the long term unless he finds a way to become more productive at the plate.

Year	Club (League)	Class	AVG	G	AB	R	H	2B	3B	HR	RBI	BB	SO	SB	CS	OBP	SLG
2009	Kannapolis (SAL)	LoA	.224	52	196	27	44	9	0	9	33	11	40	1	1	.277	.408
2010	Bristol (APP)	R	.200	5	15	1	3	1	0	0	1	2	4	0	0	.333	.267
	Winston-Salem (CAR)	HiA	.292	25	89	16	26	3	0	3	12	7	22	0	0	.337	.427
	Birmingham (SL)	AA	.292	18	72	7	21	4	0	2	13	2	22	0	0	.316	.431
2011	Charlotte (IL)	AAA	.241	22	79	9	19	4	0	2	6	8	18	0	0	.326	.367
	Birmingham (SL)	AA	.242	94	364	43	88	21	2	7	50	23	61	1	2	.292	.368
2012	Charlotte (IL)	AAA	.266	102	394	40	105	22	1	6	48	20	60	3	0	.306	.373
Minor League Totals			.253	318	1209	143	306	64	3	29	163	73	227	5	3	.302	.383

19 KEVIN VANCE, RHP

BA GRADE

45

MEDIUM

Born: July 8, 1990. **B-T:** R-R. **Ht.:** 6-0. **Wt.:** 208. **Drafted:** Connecticut, 2011 (19th round). **Signed by:** Ryan Dorsey.

Part of loaded Connecticut teams that featured top prospects Matt Barnes (now with the Red Sox), Mike Olt (Rangers) and George Springer (Astros), Vance saved games as a closer and sometimes won them with his bat. He slid to the 19th round in 2011 after losing fastball velocity that spring, but his stock has surged since he signed for $40,000 and focused on pitching full-time. He had middling success as a starter in the first two months of last season before posting a 1.66 ERA with 67 strikeouts in 60 innings after moving to the bullpen. Vance's fastball continues to fluctuate. He'll work in the low 90s at times and the upper 80s at others, but he piles up outs because he generates weak contact thanks to his solid curveball. He also has a fringy changeup that he didn't use often as a reliever. Vance pitches with a lot of poise, digging in and throwing strikes when he's in trouble. If he can find more consistent fastball velocity and build on his success when he gets to Double-A in 2013, he could put himself in position for big league consideration before the season is over.

Year	Club (League)	Class	W	L	ERA	G	GS	CG	SV	IP	H	HR	BB	SO	K/9	WHIP	AVG
2011	Great Falls (PIO)	R	2	1	4.54	22	1	0	1	36	45	3	10	58	14.6	1.54	.294
2012	Kannapolis (SAL)	LoA	4	2	3.05	19	9	0	0	80	70	4	28	70	7.9	1.23	.236
	Winston-Salem (CAR)	HiA	1	0	1.66	11	0	0	0	22	19	3	5	29	12.0	1.11	.235
Minor League Totals			7	3	3.22	52	10	0	1	137	134	10	43	157	10.3	1.29	.252

20 SIMON CASTRO, RHP

Born: April 9, 1988. **B-T:** R-R. **Ht.:** 6-5. **Wt.:** 230. **Signed:** Dominican Republic, 2006. **Signed by:** Randy Smith/Felix Francisco (Padres).

BA GRADE 45 MEDIUM

Castro ranked as one of the top prospects in the Padres system, leading the low Class A Midwest League in strikeouts (157) in 2009 and skipping a level and ranking second in the Double-A Texas League in ERA (2.92) in 2010. But his career took a downturn after he gave up two runs in the first inning of the 2010 Futures Game, and San Diego packaged him with Pedro Hernandez in a trade for Carlos Quentin in December 2011. Castro still has a low-90s fastball that can touch 95, but he's having trouble rounding out his repertoire. His low-80s slider has regressed and lost bite, his changeup is average at times and he flashes a splitter that might play well in the bullpen. He has significant issues repeating his delivery, costing him velocity and command. He spent time on the disabled list in the second half of 2012 with what the White Sox called general soreness before finishing the season on a tight pitch count. Chicago is tempted to make him a reliever but probably will give him one more chance as a starter when he returns to Triple-A this year.

Year	Club (League)	Class	W	L	ERA	G	GS	CG	SV	IP	H	HR	BB	SO	K/9	WHIP	AVG
2006	Padres (DSL)	R	1	3	4.63	12	12	0	0	47	40	2	21	58	11.2	1.31	.219
2007	Padres (AZL)	R	2	6	6.22	14	12	0	0	51	61	4	30	55	9.8	1.80	.298
2008	Eugene (NWL)	SS	2	3	3.99	15	15	0	0	65	54	3	29	64	8.8	1.27	.223
2009	Fort Wayne (MWL)	LoA	10	6	3.33	28	27	1	0	140	118	9	37	157	10.1	1.10	.226
2010	San Antonio (TL)	AA	7	6	2.92	24	23	0	0	130	107	8	36	107	7.4	1.10	.223
	Portland (PCL)	AAA	0	1	7.84	2	2	0	0	10	16	1	6	6	5.2	2.13	.333
2011	Tucson (PCL)	AAA	2	2	10.17	6	6	0	0	26	37	5	18	21	7.4	2.14	.333
	San Antonio (TL)	AA	5	6	4.33	16	16	0	0	89	95	9	16	73	7.4	1.24	.271
2012	Charlotte (IL)	AAA	1	1	4.32	5	5	0	0	25	32	2	6	16	5.8	1.52	.317
	Bristol (APP)	R	0	0	4.50	1	1	0	0	2	3	0	0	0	0.0	1.50	.429
	Birmingham (SL)	AA	6	4	3.70	15	15	0	0	90	89	4	21	72	7.2	1.22	.254
Minor League Totals			36	38	4.17	138	134	1	0	675	652	47	220	629	8.4	1.29	.251

21 SANTOS RODRIGUEZ, LHP

Born: Jan 2, 1988. **B-T:** L-L. **Ht.:** 6-5. **Wt.:** 180. **Signed:** Dominican Republic, 2006. **Signed by:** Roberto Aquino (Braves).

BA GRADE 45 MEDIUM

A high-ceiling arm acquired from the Braves in a package that also included Tyler Flowers, Brent Lillibridge and third-base prospect Jon Gilmore for Javier Vazquez in December 2008, Rodriguez has progressed slowly. The White Sox have remained patient and protected him on their 40-man roster in November because he has a live arm and has made strides smoothing out a maximum-effort delivery and improving his command. Rodriguez throws harder than most lefthanders, working at 91-95 mph and peaking at 98. He did a better job of not overthrowing and not pitching to the radar gun in 2012, though he still doesn't locate his pitches with anything close to precision. His breaking ball has evolved from a slurve into more of a true slider with depth, and it's a swing-and-miss pitch when his delivery is working. He also can mix in a changeup. Confidence has been an issue in Rodriguez's development, and his improved when he fared well in his first exposure to Double-A. He could win a big league job in the spring, but he'd benefit from extended time in Triple-A.

Year	Club (League)	Class	W	L	ERA	G	GS	CG	SV	IP	H	HR	BB	SO	K/9	WHIP	AVG
2007	Braves (GCL)	R	0	1	6.67	12	2	0	2	28	29	3	21	35	11.1	1.76	.248
2008	Braves (GCL)	R	1	2	2.79	14	0	0	5	29	16	0	13	45	14.0	1.00	.155
2009	Bristol (APP)	R	2	0	1.33	19	0	0	4	27	18	0	17	42	14.0	1.30	.189
	Kannapolis (SAL)	LoA	0	0	0.00	3	0	0	0	4	3	0	1	8	18.0	1.00	.200
2010	Winston-Salem (CAR)	HiA	2	0	3.57	32	0	0	40	27	0	32	59	13.2	1.46	.193
2011	Winston-Salem (CAR)	HiA	2	3	3.77	40	5	0	2	62	70	4	33	49	7.1	1.66	.293
2012	Birmingham (SL)	AA	2	4	2.81	37	0	0	8	64	33	6	33	60	8.4	1.03	.153
	Charlotte (IL)	AAA	0	0	3.68	5	0	0	0	7	7	0	2	9	11.0	1.23	.250
Minor League Totals			9	10	3.40	162	7	0	21	262	203	13	152	307	10.5	1.35	.213

22 SAMMY AYALA, C

Born: July 12, 1984. **B-T:** L-R. **Ht.:** 6-3. **Wt.:** 225. **Drafted:** HS—La Jolla, Calif., 2012 (17th round). **Signed by:** George Kachigian.

BA GRADE
45
HIGH

A three-sport athlete in high school, Ayala put himself on the scouting radar by producing against advanced prospects Max Fried (the No. 7 overall pick in 2012) and Andrew Potter in a tournament at the MLB Urban Youth Academy before his senior year. Ayala lasted until the 531st pick in June because teams thought he would honor his commitment to UC Santa Barbara. The White Sox were able to sign him for $258,800, the equivalent of fifth-round money. He had a reputation for being pull-conscious in high school and often looked overmatched in his pro debut. Chicago believes he'll improve at the plate now that his focus is on baseball, and he has solid power potential. A defensive end in football, Ayala has a nice build for a catcher. He's athletic, with good speed for the position and a plus arm, though he has a long way to go behind the plate. He needs to improve his flexibility and quicken his transfer on throws after erasing just 15 percent of pro basestealers. Ayala isn't ready for a full-season assignment at age 18, so his next stop figures to be Rookie-level Great Falls.

Year	Club (League)	Class	AVG	G	AB	R	H	2B	3B	HR	RBI	BB	SO	SB	CS	OBP	SLG
2012	Bristol (APP)	R	.202	24	84	12	17	3	0	1	5	5	23	0	1	.261	.274
Minor League Totals			.202	24	84	12	17	3	0	1	5	5	23	0	1	.261	.274

23 BRANDON BRENNAN, RHP

Born: July 26, 1991. **B-T:** R-R. **Ht.:** 6-4. **Wt.:** 220. **Drafted:** Orange Coast (Calif.) CC, 2012 (4th round). **Signed by:** Mike Baker.

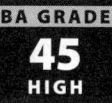

BA GRADE
45
HIGH

Like Chris Beck, who was selected two rounds ahead of him last June, Brennan passes the eye test for a big league starter. He has a power pitcher's build and a low-90s fastball that has the sink the White Sox look for at hitter-friendly U.S. Cellular Field. Brennan began his college career at Oregon but redshirted as a freshman, prompting his transfer to California juco power Orange Coast for 2012. Eager to get his pro career started, he gave up a Houston commitment to sign for $320,800. Brennan's fastball sits at 91-93 mph, and he uses his high three-quarters arm slot to generate armside run and heavy sink, producing plenty of groundouts. His slider and changeup are still works in progress, but he has made strides with them since turning pro. He also needs to improve his substandard command. The difference between him and Beck lies largely with Beck's changeup and ability to change speeds. Brennan looks like he could develop into a workhorse, though he could wind up as a reliever if his secondary pitches don't get better. He'll open next season in the Kannapolis rotation.

Year	Club (League)	Class	W	L	ERA	G	GS	CG	SV	IP	H	HR	BB	SO	K/9	WHIP	AVG
2012	Great Falls (PIO)	R	3	2	4.34	14	7	0	0	37	44	2	16	31	7.5	1.61	.297
Minor League Totals			3	2	4.34	14	7	0	0	37	44	2	16	31	7.5	1.61	.297

24 JOEY DeMICHELE, 2B

Born: Feb. 5, 1991. **B-T:** L-R. **Ht.:** 5-11. **Wt.:** 185. **Drafted:** Arizona State, 2012 (3rd round). **Signed by:** John Kazanas.

BA GRADE
45
HIGH

DeMichele isn't especially toolsy, but he definitely can hit. He won the Pacific-10 Conference batting title with a .368 average as a sophomore in 2011, then hit .336 last spring to become just the sixth Arizona State player ever to lead the team in consecutive seasons. His prowess at the plate got DeMichele drafted in the third round, where he signed for $400,000. With a compact swing and impressive bat control, he held his own in low Class A during his pro debut. He uses the whole field and should be able to stay out of slumps. Most of his power comes to the gaps, though the White Sox think he has the strength to post double-digit home run totals as he develops. DeMichele played mostly DH as a Sun Devils sophomore, and it remains to be seen whether he can remain at second base. He has limited range and average arm strength, and he has work to do improving his hands. He has fringy speed but runs the bases fairly well. DeMichele could start his first full pro season in Double-A. He could develop into an Adam Kennedy type if he can field his position adequately.

Year	Club (League)	Class	AVG	G	AB	R	H	2B	3B	HR	RBI	BB	SO	SB	CS	OBP	SLG
2012	Bristol (APP)	R	.348	12	46	7	16	4	3	2	9	3	8	3	0	.412	.696
	Kannapolis (SAL)	LoA	.261	58	234	30	61	12	7	5	29	19	54	5	4	.319	.436
Minor League Totals			.275	70	280	37	77	16	10	7	38	22	62	8	4	.334	.479

25 MICAH JOHNSON, 2B

Born: Dec. 18, 1990. **B-T:** B-R. **Ht.:** 5-11. **Wt.:** 190. **Drafted:** Indiana, 2012 (9th round). **Signed by:** Mike Shirley.

BA GRADE
45
HIGH

Johnson is more athletic than the typical second baseman. Legend has it that he once beat former NBA No. 1 overall draft pick Greg Oden in a one-on-one basketball game when both were in high school, and he was the fastest runner in Chicago's 2012 draft class, clocking a 6.6-second 60-yard dash for scouts.

Johnson hurt his elbow in the Cape Cod League in 2011 and tried to play through it last spring before succumbing to arthroscopic surgery and missing two months. His inactivity helped drop him to the ninth round, where he signed for $127,600. A switch-hitter, Johnson has surprising pop for his size but tries to do too much at the plate at times. He draws walks and has the speed to be a factor at the top of the order, but he doesn't focus on making contact and strikes out too often. Though he has raw speed, he needs to improve his baserunning. A below-average defender at second because he lacks soft hands, he made 10 errors in 43 pro games. He has the quickness and average arm strength to perhaps fit in center field, but he'd have a hard time profiling as a regular if he had to play on an outfield corner. He'll stay at second base as he opens his first full pro season in low Class A.

Year	Club (League)	Class	AVG	G	AB	R	H	2B	3B	HR	RBI	BB	SO	SB	CS	OBP	SLG
2012	Great Falls (PIO)	R	.273	69	271	49	74	10	5	4	25	43	74	19	6	.375	.391
Minor League Totals			.273	69	271	49	74	10	5	4	25	43	74	19	6	.375	.391

26 TYLER SALADINO, SS/2B

BA GRADE 45 HIGH

Born: July 20, 1989. **B-T:** R-R. **Ht.:** 5-11. **Wt.:** 180. **Drafted:** Oral Roberts, 2010 (7th round). **Signed by:** Clay Overcash.

A productive hitter in college at Palomar (Calif.) JC and Oral Roberts and in his first two pro seasons, Saladino faced adversity for the first time in 2012. The year started on a positive note, as he earned a mid-spring promotion from minor league camp and caught manager Robin Ventura's eye during Cactus League action. But Saladino hit just .236 during the regular season, 46 points below his previous career average, and his .315 slugging percentage represented a 164-point drop. Though he hit 16 homers in high Class A in 2011, he projects as a line-drive hitter with occasional pop. To his credit, Saladino maintained his plate discipline through his struggles, and his on-base ability may be the best part of his offensive game. He's just an average runner but managed to steal 39 bases in 47 attempts. A surehanded fielder with a strong arm and good instincts, Saladino doesn't have true shortstop range. He could wind up at second base and played 21 games there last year. He'll try to bounce back in 2013, likely beginning the season in Double-A.

Year	Club (League)	Class	AVG	G	AB	R	H	2B	3B	HR	RBI	BB	SO	SB	CS	OBP	SLG
2010	Bristol (APP)	R	.292	13	48	7	14	3	0	1	6	5	12	1	2	.364	.417
	Kannapolis (SAL)	LoA	.309	47	165	40	51	14	1	2	18	22	44	4	2	.397	.442
2011	Winston-Salem (CAR)HiA		.270	102	397	75	107	26	9	16	55	51	90	7	7	.363	.501
2012	Charlotte (IL)	AAA	.224	15	49	9	11	2	0	0	6	4	16	1	0	.296	.265
	Birmingham (SL)	AA	.237	112	418	71	99	15	4	4	39	75	91	38	8	.359	.321
Minor League Totals			.262	289	1077	202	282	60	14	23	124	157	253	51	19	.364	.408

27 KEVAN SMITH, C

BA GRADE 45 HIGH

Born: June 28, 1988. **B-T:** R-R. **Ht.:** 6-4. **Wt.:** 240. **Drafted:** Pittsburgh, 2011 (7th round). **Signed by:** Phil Gulley.

Because he spent the first half of his college career as a quarterback at Pittsburgh—even starting as a freshman and breaking Dan Marino's school record with 202 passing yards in his debut—Smith was old when he signed as a redshirt senior in 2011, turning 23 two weeks after signing for $50,000 as a seventh-round pick. He helped Great Falls win the Pioneer League title in his first pro summer and homered twice for Winston-Salem in the Carolina League playoffs last year. Smith has the strength to drive the ball to all fields. His plus raw power stands out more than his hitting ability, because he gets too aggressive and chases pitches. Smith has good athleticism for his size, though he's raw behind the plate. He's ironing out his throwing and receiving and is making progress learning to call a game. He has average arm strength and erased 33 percent of basestealers in 2012. A slow runner, he could become a serious baseclogger as he gets older. Smith will advance to Double-A in 2013. He may never become a big league regular but could have value as an offensive-minded backup.

Year	Club (League)	Class	AVG	G	AB	R	H	2B	3B	HR	RBI	BB	SO	SB	CS	OBP	SLG
2011	Bristol (APP)	R	.396	26	96	24	38	10	1	7	32	14	14	1	2	.482	.740
	Great Falls (PIO)	R	.318	30	107	22	34	12	2	2	16	14	16	1	0	.417	.523
2012	Kannapolis (SAL)	LoA	.282	86	340	48	96	26	0	7	60	25	62	0	1	.344	.421
	Winston-Salem (CAR)HiA		.273	22	77	8	21	4	2	3	23	5	17	0	0	.314	.494
Minor League Totals			.305	164	620	102	189	52	5	19	131	58	109	2	3	.376	.497

28 NESTOR MOLINA, RHP

BA GRADE 45 HIGH

Born: Jan. 9, 1989. **B-T:** R-R. **Ht.:** 6-1. **Wt.:** 180. **Signed:** Venezuela, 2006. **Signed by:** Rafael Mancada (Blue Jays).

When the White Sox were trying to pare payroll last offseason, they traded closer Sergio Santos to the Blue Jays in December 2011 for Molina. Santos barely pitched for Toronto before requiring shoulder surgery, and Molina was a huge disappointment as well. He was rocked early in spring training and didn't live up to his billing as the system's top starting pitching prospect. Molina threw a lot of strikes, but they were hit at an alarming rate. Command within the zone troubled him, as his 87-92 mph fastball doesn't afford him the luxury of bad location. Molina throws five pitches, but none qualify as better than average. His splitter features nice tumble at times and gets more swings and misses than his other offerings. He doesn't have much feel for a breaking ball and uses both a curveball and slider, and he also has an average changeup. Molina was briefly sidelined with elbow concerns in June, but MRIs didn't reveal any significant damage. Some scouts felt he profiled best as a reliever when Chicago acquired him, but former GM Ken Williams saw more upside in the converted third baseman. Molina still needs to prove he can get Double-A hitters out, so that's where he will start 2013.

Year	Club (League)	Class	AVG	G	AB	R	H	2B	3B	HR	RBI	BB	SO	SB	CS	OBP	SLG
2006	Twins/Blue Jays (VSL)	R	.252	38	107	19	27	1	1	0	9	20	24	3	2	.380	.280
2007	Blue Jays 2 (DSL)	R	.208	52	144	23	30	4	3	0	13	26	32	11	3	.354	.278
2008	Blue Jays 2 (DSL)	R	.000	4	5	0	0	0	0	0	1	5	1	0	0	.500	.000
Minor League Totals			.223	94	256	42	57	5	4	0	23	51	57	14	5	.369	.273

Year	Club (League)	Class	W	L	ERA	G	GS	CG	SV	IP	H	HR	BB	SO	K/9	WHIP	AVG
2007	Blue Jays 2 (DSL)	R	0	0	0.00	1	0	0	0	1	0	0	1	0	0.0	1.00	.000
2008	Blue Jays 2 (DSL)	R	4	1	0.96	20	0	0	4	37	30	1	5	27	6.5	0.94	.213
2009	Blue Jays (GCL)	R	3	0	1.69	15	2	0	1	37	31	0	4	32	7.7	0.94	.226
	Auburn (NYP)	SS	0	1	1.59	2	0	0	0	6	9	1	1	6	9.5	1.76	.346
2010	Lansing (MWL)	LoA	8	2	3.17	37	2	0	4	77	64	4	20	61	7.2	1.10	.224
	Dunedin (FSL)	HiA	0	0	2.08	2	0	0	0	4	7	0	0	3	6.2	1.62	.350
2011	Dunedin (FSL)	HiA	10	3	2.58	21	18	0	0	108	102	8	14	115	9.6	1.07	.248
	New Hampshire (EL)	AA	2	0	0.41	5	5	0	0	22	12	0	2	33	13.5	0.64	.156
2012	Charlotte (IL)	AAA	0	1	13.50	1	1	0	0	4	9	2	1	4	9.0	2.50	.450
	Birmingham (SL)	AA	6	10	4.26	22	21	0	0	123	156	7	26	84	6.2	1.48	.312
Minor League Totals			33	18	2.92	126	49	0	9	419	420	23	74	365	7.8	1.18	.259

29 JEFF SOPTIC, RHP

BA GRADE 50 EXTREME

Born: April 8, 1991. **B-T:** R-R. **Ht.:** 6-6. **Wt.:** 210. **Drafted:** Johnson County (Kan.) CC, 2011 (3rd round). **Signed by:** Clay Overcash.

With Nate Jones in the big leagues, Soptic becomes the system's high-risk, high-reward pitcher. He had one of the best arms in the 2011 draft, hitting 100 mph and showing easy mid-90s heat at Johnson County (Kan.) CC, but he slid to the third round because he was so raw. His inconsistent mechanics scared away a lot of teams and still cause opposing scouts to roll their eyes, but the White Sox are thrilled at the improvement he showed over the course of his first full pro season. Soptic has smoothed out his delivery a bit and was repeating it better during the fall. He still has plus-plus fastball velocity and will flash a plus slider at times, though he has trouble throwing it for strikes. He has become more willing to throw his changeup, but it remains a show-me pitch. Soptic has a ceiling as a closer, though Chicago wants to get him innings as a starter in 2013. Soptic's control, command and consistency would have to improve dramatically for him to stick in the rotation. He'll probably open the season in high Class A.

Year	Club (League)	Class	W	L	ERA	G	GS	CG	SV	IP	H	HR	BB	SO	K/9	WHIP	AVG
2011	Bristol (APP)	R	0	1	0.00	3	0	0	1	3	2	0	2	2	6.8	1.50	.182
2012	Kannapolis (SAL)	LoA	3	2	5.40	27	0	0	0	43	26	1	29	36	7.5	1.27	.176
Minor League Totals			3	3	5.09	30	0	0	1	46	28	1	31	38	7.4	1.28	.176

30 JEFFERSON OLACIO, LHP

BA GRADE 50 EXTREME

Born: Jan. 16, 1994. **B-T:** L-L. **Ht.:** 6-7. **Wt.:** 230. **Signed:** Dominican Republic, 2010. **Signed by:** Jerry Krause.

He looks like C.C. Sabathia and has similar fastball potential, so the White Sox signed Olacio for $125,000 in 2010. Two years before that, he stood 6-foot-3 and couldn't hit 80 mph with his fastball, so he has come a long way in a hurry. Chicago knows his development will take time and figured correctly that he would struggle in his U.S. debut last season. Olacio can throw 90-92 mph consistently, but he has to dial down his velocity to throw strikes, and hitters sit and wait for a diminished fastball. He has a below-average slider that he tips off by slowing down his arm speed, and he lacks feel for a changeup. He doesn't have a pitch to trust when he falls behind in the count, which happens regularly. Olacio is a true lottery ticket who will have to progress step by step through the system. The White Sox aggressively assigned him to low Class A to begin last season, but he still may not be advanced enough to succeed there at the start of 2013.

Year	Club (League)	Class	W	L	ERA	G	GS	CG	SV	IP	H	HR	BB	SO	K/9	WHIP	AVG
2011	White Sox (DSL)	R	3	5	5.50	11	11	0	0	38	30	0	38	42	10.0	1.81	.227
2012	Kannapolis (SAL)	LoA	1	5	5.35	15	5	0	0	37	43	3	26	34	8.3	1.86	.287
	Bristol (APP)	R	2	6	5.03	12	12	1	0	59	57	4	38	55	8.4	1.61	.254
Minor League Totals			6	16	5.25	38	28	1	0	134	130	7	102	131	8.8	1.74	.257

Cincinnati Reds

BY J.J. COOPER

For a team on a budget, this is how you're supposed to get things done.

With a largely homegrown lineup and pitching staff, the Reds rolled to 97 wins and a National League Central title in 2012, the second-best record in the majors and the club's most wins since the Big Red Machine won 102 games and a World Series in 1976.

Cincinnati didn't have the money to make a  big splash on the free-agent market, and it didn't need to. At $2 million, Ryan Ludwick was the most expensive free-agent acquisition to make the 25-man roster. The Reds did spend $8.5 million to sign reliever Ryan Madson, but he missed the entire season with an elbow injury that required Tommy John surgery.

After cultivating a talented farm system, the Reds are reaping the dividends, with homegrown players like Jay Bruce, Johnny Cueto and Joey Votto serving as franchise cornerstones. Before the season, they traded prospects Yonder Alonso, Yasmani Grandal and Brad Boxberger to the Padres to acquire Mat Latos, adding another frontline starter to pair with Cueto. They also traded prospects to acquire lefthanded reliever Sean Marshall. Rookies played key roles in Cincinnati as well, with Zack Cozart holding down the everyday shortstop job and Todd Frazier hitting 19 homers while playing first base, third base and left field.

It all culminated in the Reds' second division title in three years, after what had been a 15-year playoff drought. While the NL Division Series against the Giants ended in disappointment, as Cincinnati won the first two games in San Francisco before losing the last three, the team is positioned for long-term success and was recognized as Baseball America's Organization of the Year.

The revitalization has been slow and steady. The Reds had one of the least-talented systems in baseball for most of the late 1990s and much of the early 2000s. From 1992-2003, outfielder Austin Kearns was their only first-round pick who became a multi-year regular in Cincinnati.

Since then, the Reds have rarely missed on their top picks. In fact, every first-rounder from 2004-10 has become a big league regular, with the exception of Devin Mesoraco, who's still expected to after ranking No. 1 on this list a year ago. Former scouting director Terry Reynolds (2004-05) and successor Chris Buckley (2006-present) have produced a series of

Todd Frazier provided position versatility and power in a productive rookie season

productive drafts while rarely stretching the budget.

A franchise that had also been unable to develop starting pitchers for more than a decade had three homegrown arms who made 30 or more starts in 2012 in Cueto and former first-round picks Homer Bailey and Mike Leake. Cincinnati's $30.25 million investment in Aroldis Chapman has paid off, as he earned all-star recognition while saving 38 games. He'll get an opportunity to join the rotation in 2013.

Through trades and promotions, 11 members of last year's Reds Top 30 Prospects list no longer qualify, so the system's depth has understandably taken a hit. There's still elite talent at the top with outfielder/shortstop Billy Hamilton, who created perhaps the biggest story of the 2012 minor league season by stealing a professional-record 155 bases. The Reds also have enviable front-end pitching depth with Robert Stephenson, Tony Cingrani and Daniel Corcino.

The farm system beyond the top four is thinner than it has been in years, but Cincinnati won't be counting on many prospects to make the jump to the majors in the next couple of years. The club simply doesn't have many holes at the big league level. Among the Reds' projected regulars, all but Bronson Arroyo and Homer Bailey are under team control through the 2015 season.

THIS YEAR'S TOP 30

Player, Pos.		Grade
1.	Billy Hamilton, of/ss	65/Medium
2.	Robert Stephenson, rhp	60/High
3.	Tony Cingrani, lhp	55/Medium
4.	Daniel Corcino, rhp	55/Medium
5.	Didi Gregorius, ss	55/Medium
6.	Nick Travieso, rhp	50/High
7.	Jesse Winker, of	50/High
8.	J.J. Hoover, rhp	45/Safe
9.	Ismael Guillon, lhp	50/High
10.	Jonathan Reynoso, of	55/Extreme
11.	Dan Langfield, rhp	50/High
12.	Kyle Lotzkar, rhp	50/High
13.	Carlos Contreras, rhp	50/High
14.	Jeff Gelalich, of	50/High
15.	Amir Garrett, lhp	55/Extreme
16.	Yorman Rodriguez, of	55/Extreme
17.	Pedro Diaz, rhp	50/High
18.	Donald Lutz, of/1b	50/High
19.	Seth Mejias-Brean, 3b	50/High
20.	Tanner Rahier, 3b	50/High
21.	Ryan LaMarre, of	50/High
22.	Kyle Waldrop, of	50/High
23.	Tucker Barnhart, c	40/Low
24.	Henry Rodriguez, 3b/2b	45/Medium
25.	Devin Lohman, 2b/ss	45/Medium
26.	Neftali Soto, 1b	45/Medium
27.	Curtis Partch, rhp	45/Medium
28.	Chad Rogers, rhp	45/Medium
29.	Gabriel Rosa, 3b	50/Extreme
30.	Sal Romano, rhp	50/Extreme

LAST YEAR'S TOP 30

Player, Pos.		Status
1.	Devin Mesoraco, c	Majors
2.	Billy Hamilton, ss	No. 1
3.	Yonder Alonso, of/1b	(Padres)
4.	Yasmani Grandal, c	(Padres)
5.	Zack Cozart, ss	Majors
6.	Daniel Corcino, rhp	No. 4
7.	Robert Stephenson, rhp	No. 2
8.	Didi Gregorius, ss	No. 5
9.	Todd Frazier, 3b/1b/of	Majors
10.	Brad Boxberger, rhp	(Padres)
11.	Neftali Soto, 1b	No. 26
12.	J.C. Sulbaran, rhp	(Royals)
13.	Ronald Torreyes, 2b	(Cubs)
14.	Ryan LaMarre, of	No. 21
15.	Tony Cingrani, lhp	No. 3
16.	Dave Sappelt, of	(Cubs)
17.	Henry Rodriguez, 3b	No. 24
18.	Amir Garrett, lhp	No. 15
19.	Yorman Rodriguez, of	No. 16
20.	Gabriel Rosa, 3b	No. 29
21.	Chris Valaika, ss	(Marlins)
22.	Kyle Waldrop, of	No. 22
23.	Ryan Wright, 2b	Dropped out
24.	Sean Buckley, 3b/of	Dropped out
25.	Tucker Barnhart, c	No. 23
26.	David Vidal, 3b	Dropped out
27.	Donnie Joseph, lhp	(Royals)
28.	Juan Duran, of	Dropped out
29.	Jonathan Perez, rhp	Dropped out
30.	Kyle Lotzkar, rhp	No. 12

BEST TOOLS

Best Hitter for Average	Jesse Winker
Best Power Hitter	Donald Lutz
Best Strike-Zone Discipline	Josh Fellhauer
Fastest Baserunner	Billy Hamilton
Best Athlete	Billy Hamilton
Best Fastball	Robert Stephenson
Best Curveball	Robert Stephenson
Best Slider	Daniel Corcino
Best Changeup	Ismael Guillon
Best Control	Drew Cisco
Best Defensive Catcher	Tucker Barnhart
Best Defensive Infielder	Didi Gregorius
Best Infield Arm	Didi Gregorius
Best Defensive Outfielder	Ryan LaMarre
Best Outfield Arm	Yorman Rodriguez

PROJECTED 2016 LINEUP

Catcher	Devin Mesoraco
First Base	Joey Votto
Second Base	Brandon Phillips
Third Base	Todd Frazier
Shortstop	Zack Cozart
Left Field	Jesse Winker
Center Field	Billy Hamilton
Right Field	Jay Bruce
No. 1 Starter	Johnny Cueto
No. 2 Starter	Aroldis Chapman
No. 3 Starter	Mat Latos
No. 4 Starter	Robert Stephenson
No. 5 Starter	Homer Bailey
Closer	Daniel Corcino

TOP PROSPECTS OF THE DECADE

Year	Player, Pos.	2012 Org.
2003	Chris Gruler, rhp	Out of baseball
2004	Ryan Wagner, rhp	Out of baseball
2005	Homer Bailey, rhp	Reds
2006	Homer Bailey, rhp	Reds
2007	Homer Bailey, rhp	Reds
2008	Jay Bruce, of	Reds
2009	Yonder Alonso, 1b	Padres
2010	Todd Frazier, 3b/of	Reds
2011	Aroldis Chapman, lhp	Reds
2012	Devin Mesoraco, c	Reds

TOP DRAFT PICKS OF THE DECADE

Year	Player, Pos.	2012 Org.
2003	Ryan Wagner, rhp	Out of baseball
2004	Homer Bailey, rhp	Reds
2005	Jay Bruce, of	Reds
2006	Drew Stubbs, of	Reds
2007	Devin Mesoraco, c	Reds
2008	Yonder Alonso, 1b	Padres
2009	Mike Leake, rhp	Reds
2010	Yasmani Grandal, c	Padres
2011	Robert Stephenson, rhp	Reds
2012	Nick Travieso, rhp	Reds

LARGEST BONUSES IN CLUB HISTORY

Aroldis Chapman, 2010	$16,250,000
Chris Gruler, 2002	$2,500,000
Yorman Rodriguez, 2008	$2,500,000
Homer Bailey, 2004	$2,300,000
Mike Leake, 2009	$2,270,000

CINCINNATI REDS

TOP 2013 ROOKIE: Tony Cingrani, lhp. While he has upside as a starter, he could serve the Reds as a lefty reliever if needed this year.

BREAKOUT PROSPECT: Pedro Diaz, rhp. If Daniel Corcino could be the next Johnny Cueto, Diaz could be the next Corcino.

SLEEPER: Aristides Aquino, of. He has hit .193 in two years in the Rookie-level Dominican Summer League, but his tools rank among the best in the system.

SOURCE OF TOP 30 TALENT

Homegrown	29	Acquired	1
College	6	Trades	1
Junior college	2	Rule 5 draft	0
High school	12	Independent leagues	0
Nondrafted free agents	0	Free agents/waivers	0
International	9		

LF
Jesse Winker (7)
Jeff Gelalich (14)
Kyle Waldrop (22)
Sean Buckley
Steve Selsky
Juan Silva
Cody Puckett
Daniel Pigott

CF
Billy Hamilton (1)
Jonathan Reynoso (10)
Ryan LaMarre (21)
Theo Bowe
Felix Perez
Beau Amaral
Bryson Smith

RF
Yorman Rodriguez (16)
Aristides Aquino
Juan Duran
Josh Fellhauer

3B
Seth Mejias-Brean (19)
Tanner Rahier (20)
Henry Rodriguez (24)
Gabriel Rosa (29)
David Vidal
Travis Mattair

SS
Didi Gregorius (5)
Devin Lohman (25)
Brent Peterson
Zach Vincej

2B
Ryan Wright
Juan Perez
Brodie Greene
Avain Rachal

1B
Donald Lutz (18)
Neftali Soto (26)

C
Tucker Barnhart (23)
Brandon Dailey
Daniel Paula
Jose Ortiz
Joe Hudson

LHP
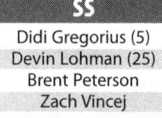

LHSP	LHRP
Tony Cingrani (3)	Chris Manno
Ismael Guillon (9)	Ryan Dennick
Amir Garrett (15)	Sean Lucas
Mason Felt	Nolan Becker

RHP
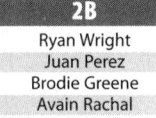

RHSP	RHRP
Robert Stephenson (2)	J.J. Hoover (8)
Daniel Corcino (4)	Kyle Lotzkar (12)
Nick Travieso (6)	Carlos Contreras (13)
Dan Langfield (11)	Curtis Partch (27)
Pedro Diaz (17)	Josh Ravin
Chad Rogers (28)	Nick Christani
Sal Romano (30)	Justin Freeman
Jeremy Kivel	James Allen
Jonathan Perez	Wes Mugarian
Jonathan Moscot	Alejandro Chacin
Drew Cisco	Michael Dennhardt
	Kyle McMyne
	Brooks Pinckard
	Abel de los Santos
	Luke Moran
	Jackson Stephens

2012   BONUSES: $7.5 MILLION

BEST PURE HITTER: OF Jesse Winker (1s) established a reputation for a balanced, strong swing as an amateur, when he worked out with ex-big leaguer David Eckstein and his brother Rick. Winker enhanced his reputation by hitting .338/.443/.500 in the Rookie-level Pioneer League.

BEST POWER HITTER: 3B Seth Mejias-Brean (8) hit only one homer in the spring for College World Series champion Arizona, then hit eight in the Pioneer League after adding loft to his swing. At 6-foot-2 and 210 pounds, he has the strength and size to maintain his power gain.

FASTEST RUNNER: OF Jeff Gelalich (1s) has plus speed, giving him a slight edge over fellow Pacific-12 Conference products OF Beau Amaral (7), his former teammate at UCLA, and Mejias-Brean.

BEST DEFENSIVE PLAYER: While he's no burner, Amaral has tremendous instincts and is a quality center fielder. Mejias-Brean moves well for his size and has the hands and arm strength for third.

BEST FASTBALL: The first two pitchers Cincinnati drafted have fastballs that sit in the mid-90s. RHP Nick Travieso (1) hit 98 in the spring and topped out at 96 this summer. RHP Dan Langfield (3) hits 97 mph regularly in shorter stints and may do so as a starter after smoothing out his delivery with professional coaching. RHP Jeremy Kivel (10) blew out his knee and missed most of the spring, but a fastball clocked up to 95 mph before he got hurt earned him a $500,000 bonus.

BEST SECONDARY PITCH: Langfield's downer curveball has power and depth. Travieso's slider lacks consistency but shows flashes of becoming a plus pitch with mid-80s power. He didn't start throwing it much until last spring.

BEST PRO DEBUT: Winker led the Pioneer League in on-base percentage and ranked third in batting. Mejias-Brean nearly matched him with a .925 OPS. Langfield shined with a 2.68 ERA, 54 strikeouts and one homer allowed in 37 Pioneer League innings.

BEST ATHLETE: Amaral, Mejias-Brean and SS Brent Peterson (12), a versatile middle infielder who runs well, all deserve mention.

MOST INTRIGUING BACKGROUND: Peterson has a brother in the Army and spurned the Reds as a 17th-round pick out of high school in 2010 to attend West Point. He hit .255 as a freshman before transferring back home to Bakersfield (Calif.) JC in 2012. Amaral's father Rich was a big league utilityman for parts of 10 seasons. Unsigned OF Kyle Wren (30) is the son of Braves GM Frank.

CLOSEST TO THE MAJORS: Langfield, particularly if it's as a reliever.

BEST LATE-ROUND PICK: Peterson. Also keep an eye on RHP Jackson Stephens (18), who touches 94 mph, and SS Zach Vincej (37), a grinder out of Pepperdine who batted .336 at Billings.

THE ONE WHO GOT AWAY: LHP Matt Boyd (13) improved significantly in the summer Cape Cod League, hitting 96 mph before returning to Oregon State, and will be one of the top seniors in the 2013 draft.

ASSESSMENT: The Reds put a premium on finding bats going into the draft but couldn't pass up Travieso. Then they landed potential impact position players in Winker, Gelalich, Mejias-Brean and Peterson.

2011   BONUSES: $6.4 MILLION

RHP Robert Stephenson (1) has frontline starter potential. LHP Tony Cingrani (3) isn't far behind, and he already has pitched in the majors. LHP Amir Garrett (22) has tantalizing talent but divides his attention as a starter on St. John's basketball team.

GRADE: B+

2010   BONUSES: $5.7 MILLION

C Yasmani Grandal (1), far and away the best talent in this crop, went to the Padres in the Mat Latos trade. OFs Ryan LaMarre (2) and Kyle Waldrop (2) are the top prospects still in the system.

GRADE: B

2009   BONUSES: $5.9 MILLION

RHP Mike Leake (1) went straight from Arizona State to Cincinnati's rotation. He figures to be eclipsed by OF/SS Billy Hamilton (2), who set a pro record with 155 steals last year. RHP Brad Boxberger (1s), who has reached the big leagues, and LHP Donnie Joseph (3) were parts of deals for Latos and Jonathan Broxton.

GRADE: B+

2008   BONUSES: $4.8 MILLION

The Reds traded three major leaguers: 1B Yonder Alonso (1) to get Latos, RHP Zach Stewart (3) to acquire Scott Rolen and OF Dave Sappelt (9) to land Sean Marshall. They've held onto a fourth, RHP Pedro Villareal (7).

GRADE: B+

*Draft analysis by John Manuel (2012) and Jim Callis (2008-11).
Numbers in parentheses indicate draft rounds.*

1 BILLY HAMILTON, OF/SS

Born: Sept. 9, 1990. **B-T:** B-R. **Ht.:** 6-1. **Wt.:** 159.
Drafted: HS—Taylorsville, Miss., **2009 (2nd round).**
Signed by: Tyler Jennings.

BA GRADE

65

MEDIUM

TONY FARLOW

A few years ago, the Internet spawned a meme called Matt Wieters facts, where impossible feats were attributed to baseball's top prospect. (One sample: Matt Wieters draws intentional walks in batting practice.) Billy Hamilton facts seem equally overblown—except they're true. When a left fielder lost sight of a fly ball, Hamilton ran out from his shortstop position to catch it near the warning track. He scored a game-winning run on a sacrifice fly that didn't leave the infield. He scored from second on an infield grounder. And along the way, he set the professional baseball single-season stolen base record last year with 155, eclipsing Vince Coleman's 30-year-old mark of 145. After Hamilton had played shortstop and second base throughout his pro career, the Reds moved him to center field in the Arizona Fall League. The position change should speed his arrival to the big leagues, as concerns about his arm and hands at shortstop were the biggest knocks on him. The 57th overall pick in the 2009 draft, he turned down the chance to play wide receiver at Mississippi State for a $623,600 bonus.

Every scouting report ever written about Hamilton has to start with his speed. There may be current players who can run a faster 60-yard dash, but no one is faster on a diamond. He turns in hard-to-comprehend 3.35-3.4 second times to first base on bunts from the left side. His aggressiveness makes his speed play up, if that's even possible. His ability to turn routine plays into nail-biters forces infielders to hurry, and he's a threat to take an extra base on any ball to the outfield. Hamilton has made more use of his speed as he has improved at the plate. A switch-hitter, he has smoothed out his less-natural lefthanded swing, which has left him less vulnerable to high fastballs that he used to chase and pop up. Pitchers with good fastballs can still bust him up and in at times. He's rail-thin and never will have home run power, but he does show some gap pop, especially from the right side.

SCOUTING GRADES

Batting: 60.	**Defense:** 65.
Power: 30.	**Arm:** 50.
Speed: 80.	

Based on 20-80 scouting scale, where 50 represents major league average, and future projection rather than present tools.

His speed also means that singles sometimes turn into doubles, while doubles can become triples or more. He has improved his pitch recognition and selectivity, with his 86 walks in 2012 nearly matching his previous career total from three pro seasons. The move to center field should fit Hamilton's aggressive approach. He still has some work to do on jumps and routes, but his quickness allows him to outrun mistakes and play shallower than most center fielders. He projects as a plus defender, perhaps even a Gold Glover, with an average arm. Hamilton is as durable as he is fast.

Despite taking the pounding of countless steal attempts and dives back to the base on pick-offs, he never has spent a day on the disabled list.

Hamilton's speed ensures him some sort of big league job, and his continued development at the plate will determine whether he ends up being an all-star or a bottom-of-the-order speedster. He might get a chance to unseat Drew Stubbs as Cincinnati's center fielder in spring training, but Hamilton could use some time at Triple-A Louisville to refine his game. When he arrives in the big leagues, he'll spur ticket sales with his style of play.

Year	Club (League)	Class	AVG	G	AB	R	H	2B	3B	HR	RBI	BB	SO	SB	CS	OBP	SLG
2009	Reds (GCL)	R	.205	43	166	19	34	6	3	0	11	11	47	14	3	.253	.277
2010	Billings (PIO)	R	.318	69	283	61	90	13	10	2	24	28	56	48	9	.383	.456
2011	Dayton (MWL)	LoA	.278	135	550	99	153	18	9	3	50	52	133	103	20	.340	.360
2012	Bakersfield (CAL)	HiA	.323	82	337	79	109	18	9	1	30	50	70	104	21	.413	.439
	Pensacola (SL)	AA	.286	50	175	33	50	4	5	1	15	36	43	51	16	.406	.383
Minor League Totals			.289	379	1511	291	436	59	36	7	130	177	349	320	69	.364	.389

2 ROBERT STEPHENSON, RHP

RODGER WOOD

Born: Feb. 24, 1993. **B-T:** R-R. **Ht.:** 6-2. **Wt.:** 185. **Drafted:** HS—Martinez, Calif., 2011 (1st round). **Signed by:** Rich Bordi.

He has pitched just 65 pro innings, but Stephenson already has shown the best pure stuff of any Reds draftee back to at least 2004 first-rounder Homer Bailey. Signed for $2 million as the 27th overall pick in 2011, he ranked as the Rookie-level Pioneer League's top pitching prospect in his pro debut last summer. Stephenson's fastball velocity has improved in pro ball, rising from 92-95 in his draft year to 93-97 in 2012, and he touched 100 mph at low Class A Dayton. His heater has excellent life as well. What makes him stand out from the average prep flamethrower is that he also has a good feel for his secondary pitches. His changeup also has gotten better since his high school days, and some scouts project it as a plus pitch. His curveball has similar potential. Stephenson can get too intense at times—he sometimes throws in the mid-90s warming up in the bullpen—and needs to avoid rushing his delivery, which detracts from his control. Cincinnati kept a tight leash on Stephenson and will turn him loose in 2013, when he'll open back in low Class A. He has all of the ingredients to become a frontline starter.

BA GRADE
60
HIGH

Year	Club (League)	Class	W	L	ERA	G	GS	CG	SV	IP	H	HR	BB	SO	K/9	WHIP	AVG
2012	Billings (PIO)	R	1	0	2.05	7	7	0	0	31	22	2	8	37	10.9	0.98	.195
	Dayton (MWL)	LoA	2	4	4.19	8	8	0	0	34	32	4	15	35	9.2	1.37	.246
Minor League Totals			3	4	3.18	15	15	0	0	65	54	6	23	72	10.0	1.18	.222

3 TONY CINGRANI, LHP

PAUL BRESKI

Born: July 5, 1989. **B-T:** L-L. **Ht.:** 6-5. **Wt.:** 205. **Drafted:** Rice, 2011 (3rd round). **Signed by:** Jerry Flowers.

Cingrani was so bad as a Rice junior that he asked his coaches if they wanted him to come back for his senior season. The Owls simplified his delivery and fixed a timing issue in which his arm lagged behind his lower half, and the results were immediate. He improved his fastball velocity and control, pitched his way into the third round of the 2011 draft and led the minors with a 1.73 ERA last year before joining the Reds in September. Cingrani's success begins with his fastball, which generates plenty of swings and misses thanks to excellent life and some deception in his delivery. He adds and subtracts from his fastball, varying it from 88-95 mph, and locates it to both sides of the plate. It looks even quicker because he pairs it with a plus change with good fade that gives him a weapon against righthanders. His slider is fringy, as it is too often flat and it lacks bite. He generally throws strikes, though his control slipped at Double-A Pensacola. Cingrani's slider will determine his future role. He can thrive in the bullpen with two pitches, but needs a better breaking ball to succeed as a starter. With a full starting rotation in Cincinnati, he'll head to Triple-A to begin 2013.

BA GRADE
55
HIGH

Year	Club (League)	Class	W	L	ERA	G	GS	CG	SV	IP	H	HR	BB	SO	K/9	WHIP	AVG
2011	Billings (PIO)	R	3	2	1.75	13	13	0	0	51	35	1	6	80	14.0	0.80	.190
2012	Bakersfield (CAL)	HiA	5	1	1.11	10	10	0	0	57	39	2	13	71	11.3	0.92	.189
	Pensacola (SL)	AA	5	3	2.12	16	15	1	0	89	59	7	39	101	10.2	1.10	.192
	Cincinnati (NL)	MAJ	0	0	1.80	3	0	0	0	5	4	1	2	9	16.2	1.20	.200
Major League Totals			0	0	1.80	3	0	0	0	5	4	1	2	9	16.2	1.20	.200
Minor League Totals			13	6	1.73	39	38	1	0	197	133	10	58	252	11.5	0.97	.191

4 DANIEL CORCINO, RHP

Born: Aug. 26, 1990. **B-T:** R-R. **Ht.:** 5-11. **Wt.:** 205. **Signed:** Dominican Republic, 2008. **Signed by:** Richard Jimenez.

Even before he arrived in the United States, Corcino has been known as the Reds' "next Cueto." He draws comparisons to Cincinnati's ace because he's a short but powerfully built Dominican righthander with a low three-quarters arm slot. And like Cueto, he has had success wherever he goes. In 2012, he pitched the first eight innings of the first no-hitter in Pensacola franchise history and ranked second in the Southern League with a 3.01 ERA. Because of his arm slot, cross-fire delivery and understanding of how to manipulate the baseball, Corcino throw 91-94 mph fastballs with either cutting action or armside run. His slider shows flashes of being a plus pitch, though it needs more consistency. His changeup has good sink at the plate, giving him the potential for three solid or better pitches. Corcino has some effort to his delivery. His control wasn't as sharp in Double-A, with his walk rate (4.1 per nine innings) nearly doubling from the year before (2.2). If the Reds needed a power arm out of the pen, Corcino is ready right now. Because he'll have more value

BA GRADE
55
MEDIUM

as a starter, he'll head to Triple-A to continue to refine his secondary stuff and control. Added to the 40-man roster in November, he projects as a middle-of-the-rotation starter, much like Cueto did as he climbed the minor league ladder.

Year	Club (League)	Class	W	L	ERA	G	GS	CG	SV	IP	H	HR	BB	SO	K/9	WHIP	AVG
2008	Reds (DSL)	R	6	2	5.29	23	0	0	0	34	37	2	14	26	6.9	1.50	.280
2009	Reds (GCL)	R	0	1	0.00	2	0	0	0	3	5	0	1	2	6.8	2.25	.455
	Billings (PIO)	R	1	4	4.91	20	0	0	3	26	23	2	15	30	10.5	1.48	.245
2010	Billings (PIO)	R	1	3	3.40	9	9	0	0	40	38	2	17	31	7.0	1.39	.255
	Dayton (MWL)	LoA	1	1	4.31	6	6	0	0	31	31	1	15	29	8.3	1.47	.254
2011	Dayton (MWL)	LoA	11	7	3.42	26	26	1	0	139	128	10	34	156	10.1	1.16	.238
2012	Pensacola (SL)	AA	8	8	3.01	26	26	0	0	143	111	9	65	126	7.9	1.23	.216
Minor League Totals			28	26	3.57	112	67	1	3	416	373	26	161	400	8.7	1.28	.239

5 DIDI GREGORIUS, SS

Born: Feb. 18, 1990. **B-T:** L-R. **Ht.:** 6-1. **Wt.:** 185. **Signed:** Curacao, 2007. **Signed by:** Jim Stoeckel.

Even when he hit .155 with zero extra base hits as an overmatched 18-year-old in his 2008 pro debut, the Reds felt that they might have something special in Gregorius. He held his own in an emergency stint at high Class A the next year and has made steady progress every since, debuting in the big leagues last September. Gregorius is the Reds' best defensive shortstop. He has smooth actions, plus range and a sniper rifle of an arm. His arm rates as a 70 on the 20-80 scouting scale, allowing him to make plays from deep in the hole that other shortstops can't. He showed improved consistency in 2012, making just 18 errors in 128 games after committing 21 in 80 contests the year before. Scouts are divided on Gregorius' bat. Some think he could end up as a No. 2 hitter, while others think he'll fit at the bottom of a lineup. He's too aggressive and needs to use the whole field more, and he does have gap power. He's an average runner. He doesn't have to worry about Billy Hamilton now that the speedster is moving to center field, but Gregorius still is blocked by Zack Cozart in Cincinnati. Gregorius could use more Triple-A time to work on his offense, and he ultimately may end up as a trade chip.

BA GRADE 55 MEDIUM

Year	Club (League)	Class	AVG	G	AB	R	H	2B	3B	HR	RBI	BB	SO	SB	CS	OBP	SLG
2008	Reds (GCL)	R	.155	31	97	6	15	0	0	0	9	10	10	2	1	.241	.155
2009	Sarasota (FSL)	HiA	.254	22	71	8	18	4	0	0	2	1	9	0	0	.274	.310
	Billings (PIO)	R	.314	50	204	28	64	10	1	1	16	12	27	8	6	.363	.387
2010	Dayton (MWL)	LoA	.273	120	501	65	137	16	11	5	41	33	62	16	7	.327	.379
	Lynchburg (CAR)	HiA	.240	7	25	4	6	0	0	0	0	2	6	0	0	.321	.240
2011	Bakersfield (CAL)	HiA	.303	46	188	30	57	12	1	5	28	10	25	8	8	.333	.457
	Carolina (SL)	AA	.270	38	148	18	40	6	3	2	16	9	25	3	2	.312	.392
2012	Pensacola (SL)	AA	.278	81	316	45	88	11	8	1	31	29	49	3	4	.344	.373
	Louisville (IL)	AAA	.243	48	185	25	45	10	3	6	23	12	31	0	2	.288	.427
	Cincinnati (NL)	MAJ	.300	8	20	1	6	0	0	0	2	0	5	0	0	.300	.300
Major League Totals			.300	8	20	1	6	0	0	0	2	0	5	0	0	.300	.300
Minor League Totals			.271	443	1735	229	470	69	27	20	166	118	244	40	30	.323	.376

6 NICK TRAVIESO, RHP

Born: Jan. 31, 1994. **B-T:** R-R. **Ht.:** 6-2. **Wt.:** 215. **Drafted:** HS—Southwest Ranches, Fla., 2012 (1st round). **Signed by:** Tony Arias/Miguel Machado.

In the final month before the 2012 draft, Travieso's velocity ticked up as he helped Archbishop McCarthy High (Southwest Ranches, Fla.) win its third straight 6-A state title. He pitched just 15 innings as a junior because the team was stacked and he was still raw on the mound. The Reds had plenty of history with him because international scouting director Tony Arias has a son on the team, and they selected Travieso 14th overall and signed him for $2 million—$375,000 less than the assigned pick value. While Travieso's fastball touched 98 mph in high school, he sat at 90-93 mph and peaked at 96 as pro as Cincinnati worked on getting him to repeat his delivery and avoid opening up too early. Some scouts think his fastball lacks life and deception. He shows the ability to spin a tight slider in the mid-80s, but he doesn't stay on top of it or command it consistently. His changeup is a long ways away, which isn't surprising considering his limited innings. The Reds will give Travieso plenty of chances to start, but many observers see him ending up as a power reliever. Cincinnati probably will put him on the same path as 2011 first-rounder Robert Stephenson, sending Travieso to extended spring training and then on to Rookie-level Billings or Dayton.

BA GRADE 50 HIGH

Year	Club (League)	Class	W	L	ERA	G	GS	CG	SV	IP	H	HR	BB	SO	K/9	WHIP	AVG
2012	Reds (AZL)	R	0	2	4.71	8	8	0	0	21	20	3	5	14	6.0	1.19	.250
Minor League Totals			0	2	4.71	8	8	0	0	21	20	3	5	14	6.0	1.19	.250

7 JESSE WINKER, OF

BA GRADE

50

HIGH

Born: Aug. 17, 1993. **B-T:** L-L. **Ht.:** 6-3. **Wt.:** 195. **Drafted:** HS—Orlando, 2012 (1st round supplemental). **Signed by:** Greg Zunino.

When he was a sophomore, Winker watched Olympia High (Orlando) teammate Mason Williams hit his way to a $1.45 million signing bonus as a fourth-round pick. Two years later, Winker and righthander Walker Weickel gave Olympia a pair of 2012 supplemental first-round picks. After signing for $1 million, Winker led the Pioneer League in on-base percentage (.443) and ranked third in hitting (.338) and OPS (.993). Winker has a sweet lefthanded swing and keeps his bat in the hitting zone for a long time. He's an extremely disciplined hitter who isn't afraid to work counts, though he'll have to cut down his strikeouts as he advances. His stroke generates natural loft that could produce 20 homers annually as he adds further muscle. He has strong legs that he uses well in his swing. Reds coaches compare his stroke to Jay Bruce's, though Winker isn't nearly as athletic. He's a below-average runner now and will get slower as he fills out. He's most likely a left fielder in the long term, though he has enough arm to handle right. Following a fabulous pro debut, Winker is more than ready to move up for low Class A. His big league future depends on his bat, but it looks like it will be up to the challenge. He's a potential No. 3 hitter in a contender's lineup.

Year	Club (League)	Class	AVG	G	AB	R	H	2B	3B	HR	RBI	BB	SO	SB	CS	OBP	SLG
2012	Billings (PIO)	R	.338	62	228	42	77	16	3	5	35	40	50	1	3	.443	.500
Minor League Totals			.338	62	228	42	77	16	3	5	35	40	50	1	3	.443	.500

8 J.J. HOOVER, RHP

BA GRADE

45

SAFE

Born: Aug. 13, 1987. **B-T:** R-R. **Ht.:** 6-3. **Wt.:** 230. **Drafted:** Calhoun (Ala.) CC, 2008 (10th round). **Signed by:** Brian Bridges (Braves).

The Braves drafted 11 pitchers in the first 12 rounds of the 2008 draft. They have already released three of their first six choices, but they did get Craig Kimbrel (third round) and Hoover. Traded to Cincinnati for Juan Francisco at the end of spring training in 2012, he impressed the Reds so much during a September callup that they added him to their playoff roster. He made two scoreless appearances in the National League Division Series. The thick-bodied Hoover has been dominant ever since he moved to the bullpen early in 2011. His fastball velocity increased with the move, now sitting at 92-93 mph with plenty of sink. Because of his background as a starter, he has a varied repertoire. Hoover junked his slider last year in favor of a slow curveball that he can command better. His curve can handcuff hitters who are gearing up to catch up to his fastball. He also throws a useable changeup and has average control. Hoover already has demonstrated that he can pitch in a big league bullpen. He'll serve as a set-up man for Jonathan Broxton in 2013, and he could grow into the closer role if needed down the road.

Year	Club (League)	Class	W	L	ERA	G	GS	CG	SV	IP	H	HR	BB	SO	K/9	WHIP	AVG
2008	Danville (APP)	R	1	0	0.00	2	0	0	0	5	4	0	1	6	11.6	1.07	.235
2009	Myrtle Beach (CAR)	HiA	0	0	9.00	1	1	0	0	3	3	1	5	2	6.0	2.67	.250
	Rome (SAL)	LoA	7	6	3.35	25	18	0	1	134	135	9	25	148	9.9	1.19	.259
2010	Myrtle Beach (CAR)	HiA	11	6	3.26	24	24	0	0	133	126	7	35	118	8.0	1.21	.245
	Mississippi (SL)	AA	3	1	3.48	4	4	0	0	21	15	1	15	34	14.8	1.45	.203
2011	Mississippi (SL)	AA	2	5	2.48	31	12	0	1	87	65	5	28	86	8.9	1.07	.206
	Gwinnett (IL)	AAA	1	1	3.38	12	2	0	1	19	12	0	12	31	14.9	1.29	.174
2012	Louisville (IL)	AAA	4	0	1.22	30	0	0	13	37	15	1	12	55	13.4	0.73	.121
	Cincinnati (NL)	MAJ	1	0	2.05	28	0	0	1	31	17	2	13	31	9.1	0.98	.160
Major League Totals			1	0	2.05	28	0	0	1	31	17	2	13	31	9.1	0.98	.160
Minor League Totals			29	19	2.98	129	61	0	16	438	375	24	133	480	9.9	1.16	.227

9 ISMAEL GUILLON, LHP

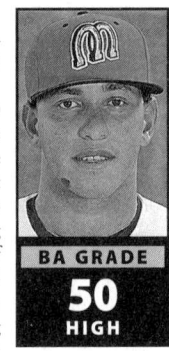

Born: Feb. 13, 1992. **B-T:** L-L. **Ht.:** 6-1. **Wt.:** 200. **Drafted:** Venezuela, 2009. **Signed by:** Tony Arias.

Other teams scouted Guillon more as a hitter, but the Reds signed him for $220,000 as a pitcher in 2008. When he was found to need Tommy John surgery, they voided his original deal and re-signed him at a significantly reduced rate. The renegotiation made him eligible for the Rule 5 draft if he wasn't on the 40-man roster, and while he went unpicked in 2010 and 2011, Cincinnati protected him this offseason. Guillon's changeup is a true plus pitch. He throws it with the same arm speed as his fastball and is willing to double up on it, baffling even hitters who are looking for the pitch. The quality of his changeup helps his fastball play up. He usually works at 89-92 mph, touching 94 on some nights but struggling to top 90 on others. His curveball is well below average, but Guillon's biggest weakness is his control. He has smoothed out his delivery, reducing a pronounced wrap in the back, but he still needs to repeat his mechanics better. His delivery does give him some deception. While Guillon's 40-man roster spot means he'll head to big league spring training, he has a lot of development ahead of him. He'll open 2013 in low Class A after making four strong starts there to conclude last season.

BA GRADE

50

HIGH

Year	Club (League)	Class	W	L	ERA	G	GS	CG	SV	IP	H	HR	BB	SO	K/9	WHIP	AVG
2009	Did Not Play—Injured																
2010	Reds (AZL)	R	3	3	3.32	12	10	0	0	57	39	1	23	73	11.5	1.09	.193
2011	Billings (PIO)	R	3	6	6.57	15	15	0	0	63	78	11	46	61	8.7	1.97	.305
2012	Billings (PIO)	R	4	1	2.29	11	10	0	0	51	39	1	24	63	11.1	1.24	.210
	Dayton (MWL)	LoA	2	0	2.55	4	4	0	0	25	22	2	7	27	9.9	1.18	.247
Minor League Totals			12	10	4.00	42	39	0	0	196	178	15	100	224	10.3	1.42	.243

10 JONATHAN REYNOSO, OF

Born: Jan. 7, 1993. **B-T:** R-R. **Ht.:** 6-3. **Wt.:** 177. **Signed:** Dominican Republic, 2010. **Signed by:** Richard Jimenez.

In a system thinned out by big league promotions and trades, Reynoso is one of the toolsiest players. Signed for only $45,000, he batted .223 in two seasons in the Rookie-level Dominican Summer League before taking a big step forward in his 2012 U.S. debut. He hit .311 and led the Rookie-level Arizona League with 30 steals. Only Yorman Rodriguez can match Reynoso's all-around physicality among Reds farmhands. His best present tool is his plus speed, though he's still learning to use it. He led the AZL by getting caught stealing nine times and doesn't take good routes in center field. His 6-foot-3 frame has plenty of room to add strength, which means he could end up as a power-hitting right fielder, though his high-waisted build leads observers to believe he'll retain most of his speed as he matures. Reynoso has solid hand-eye coordination and squares up pitches over the plate. He's comfortable lining pitches off the plate to the opposite field, but he does have trouble turning on inside offerings. He has well above-average arm strength, though he's not always accurate with his throws and he needs to speed up his release. The jump from the AZL to full-season ball is steep, but Reynoso might be ready for low Class A after some time in extended spring training. The Reds are anxious to see how he'll handle better competition.

BA GRADE

55

EXTREME

Year	Club (League)	Class	AVG	G	AB	R	H	2B	3B	HR	RBI	BB	SO	SB	CS	OBP	SLG
2010	Reds (DSL)	R	.202	35	104	16	21	3	2	0	7	9	20	9	0	.272	.269
2011	Reds (DSL)	R	.236	56	178	27	42	8	4	0	24	19	38	22	5	.340	.326
2012	Reds (AZL)	R	.311	50	190	37	59	7	3	2	16	6	23	30	9	.328	.411
Minor League Totals			.258	141	472	80	122	18	9	2	47	34	81	61	14	.321	.347

11 DAN LANGFIELD, RHP

BA GRADE

50

HIGH

Born: Jan. 21, 1991. **B-T:** R-R. **Ht.:** 6-2. **Wt.:** 196. **Drafted:** Memphis, 2012 (3rd round). **Signed by:** Joe Katuska.

In 2011, the Reds drafted Tony Cingrani, a pitcher projected by most scouts to end up in the bullpen, and let him start, and by the end of 2012 they were encouraged that Cingrani had a chance to stick there. They may have made a similar discovery in Langfield, whose father Paul was a 10th-round pick of the Blue Jays in 1980 and peaked in Class A ball. After signing him for $436,800 as a third-round pick last June, Cincinnati smoothed out a delivery that had a lot of effort in college, making his approach much cleaner, freer and easier without losing anything off his fastball. In college Langfield seemed to be pitching to the radar gun too often, as his 93-97 mph fastball was his calling card. The Reds slowed down his delivery, toned down the arm-jarring recoil and were rewarded with a strong pro debut. His fastball and hard slider both could be plus pitches and allowed him to lead Conference USA in strikeouts last year, and his changeup and curveball show flashes of being solid offerings as well. His control improved as his delivery cleaned up, but it still needs further refinement. He has been durable throughout his amateur career. Langfield's ability to tone down his delivery has shelved efforts to move him to the bullpen for now. He heads to full-season ball with a chance to anchor the Dayton rotation.

Year	Club (League)	Class	W	L	ERA	G	GS	CG	SV	IP	H	HR	BB	SO	K/9	WHIP	AVG
2012	Billings (PIO)	R	3	0	2.68	15	5	0	0	37	27	1	17	54	13.1	1.19	.197
Minor League Totals			3	0	2.68	15	5	0	0	37	27	1	17	54	13.1	1.19	.197

12 KYLE LOTZKAR, RHP

BA GRADE
50
HIGH

Born: Oct. 24, 1989. **B-T:** L-R **Ht.:** 6-4. **Wt.:** 205. **Drafted:** HS—Delta, B.C., 2007 (1st round supplemental). **Signed by:** Bill Bychowski.

Lotzkar's to-do list for 2012 had one big item at the top: Stay healthy. He has endured a stress fracture in his elbow followed by Tommy John surgery, as well as a strained hamstring, and never had topped 67 innings in a season. He finally reached that threshold last year, but even then the Reds were cautious with him. He was pulled at 80 pitches or less in seven of his last nine starts as his stuff backed up, and he went 1-4, 7.25 in the second half with 31 walks and 10 homers allowed in 45 innings. At his best, Lotzkar has some of the best stuff in the system and is one of the few pitchers who can generate swings and misses with his curveball. It's harder than the average curveball and can be almost described as a slurve. His 90-94 mph fastball is a tick above average as well. He also throws a fringy, firm changeup but locates it well; it just doesn't offer much deception. Health concerns still cloud Lotzkar's potential. Although many of the worst aspects of his delivery have been cleaned up, the team still hasn't felt comfortable letting him just go out and pitch. His stuff will work as a power reliever, which may save some wear and tear. For now, he'll stay a starter and return to Double-A.

Year	Club (League)	Class	W	L	ERA	G	GS	CG	SV	IP	H	HR	BB	SO	K/9	WHIP	AVG
2007	Reds (GCL)	R	0	2	3.86	7	7	0	0	21	21	2	7	24	10.3	1.33	.263
	Billings (PIO)	R	0	0	1.13	2	2	0	0	8	1	1	3	12	13.5	0.50	.040
2008	Dayton (MWL)	LoA	2	3	3.58	10	10	0	0	38	29	2	24	50	11.9	1.41	.215
2009	Did Not Play—Injured																
2010	Reds (AZL)	R	1	1	3.33	8	6	0	0	24	20	1	12	27	10.0	1.32	.230
	Billings (PIO)	R	2	0	0.45	4	4	0	0	20	8	1	2	33	14.9	0.50	.119
2011	Dayton (MWL)	LoA	3	2	4.32	14	14	0	0	67	51	8	25	72	9.7	1.14	.213
2012	Bakersfield (CAL)	HiA	3	0	2.39	5	5	0	0	26	22	2	10	27	9.2	1.22	.224
	Pensacola (SL)	AA	4	6	5.21	18	17	0	0	86	77	12	53	96	10.0	1.51	.238
Minor League Totals			15	14	3.84	68	65	0	0	290	229	29	136	341	10.6	1.26	.217

13 CARLOS CONTRERAS, RHP

BA GRADE
50
HIGH

Born: Jan. 8, 1991. **B-T:** R-R. **Ht.:** 6-0. **Wt.:** 165. **Signed:** Dominican Republic, 2008. **Signed by:** Richard Jimenez.

The Reds have had to be patient with Contreras, but after struggling for most of his career, his results started to catch up to his stuff. He needed two years in the Dominican Summer League before coming to the United States, and he spent two further years in Rookie ball before making his full-season debut in 2012. He earned a late-season promotion to high Class A Bakersfield and was added to Cincinnati's 40-man roster after the season. Contreras' stuff is among the best in the system, and his 20 saves last season led the system. His fastball sits at 93-95 mph and touches 98. His changeup shows good late fade. It is a plus pitch that he trusts to throw early and late in counts. His breaking ball is much less consistent, which helps explain why he consistently puts up reverse splits—.656 career OPS against lefthanders compared to a .750 career OPS against righthanders. Contreras delivery is long in the back, which has led to control issues and limits him to a bullpen role. He projects as a big league set-up man and will return to high Class A to open 2013.

Year	Club (League)	Class	W	L	ERA	G	GS	CG	SV	IP	H	HR	BB	SO	K/9	WHIP	AVG
2008	Reds (DSL)	R	0	1	8.64	17	0	0	0	17	14	0	30	17	9.2	2.64	.241
2009	Reds (DSL)	R	4	4	5.60	14	12	0	0	72	65	6	30	58	7.2	1.31	.242
2010	Reds (AZL)	R	2	4	6.45	10	6	0	2	38	44	8	16	30	7.2	1.59	.288
2011	Billings (PIO)	R	2	1	5.00	18	0	0	0	36	35	5	23	38	9.5	1.61	.259
2012	Dayton (MWL)	LoA	0	1	3.20	40	0	0	16	51	29	6	19	51	9.1	0.95	.158
	Bakersfield (CAL)	HiA	1	0	2.70	9	0	0	4	10	9	1	5	12	10.8	1.40	.225
Minor League Totals			9	11	5.20	108	18	0	22	223	196	26	123	206	8.3	1.43	.234

14 JEFF GELALICH, OF

Born: March 16, 1991. **B-T:** L-R. **Ht.:** 6-1. **Wt.:** 180. **Drafted:** UCLA, 2012 (1st round supplemental). **Signed by:** Rex de la Nuez.

A high school teammate of Astros 2009 first-rounder Jio Mier, Gelalich is part of a baseball family. His younger brother Matt is a starting outfielder for Pepperdine, while his younger brother Danny is a high school center fielder. Jeff had an All-America season at UCLA in 2012, helping the team to the College World Series for the second time in his career, playing his way into the supplemental first round and an $825,000 bonus. He didn't get to show much as a pro as a hand injury limited his effectiveness. When healthy, Gelalich is an above-average runner with a knack for getting good jumps on the basepaths. He's a tick above average defensively in right or left field, though his average arm makes him a better fit for left, and he can play center field for a game if needed. At the plate, Gelalich projects as an average to solid hitter with average power. He was a patient hitter in college, unafraid to go deep in counts, but that didn't show in his pro debut. Gelalich never really got a chance to get going as a pro in 2012, but now healthy, he'll get a shot at low Class A in 2013.

Year	Club (League)	Class	AVG	G	AB	R	H	2B	3B	HR	RBI	BB	SO	SB	CS	OBP	SLG
2012	Billings (PIO)	R	.244	35	127	27	31	7	2	2	9	14	42	4	1	.336	.378
Minor League Totals			.244	35	127	27	31	7	2	2	9	14	42	4	1	.336	.378

15 AMIR GARRETT, LHP

Born: May 3, 1992. **B-T:** L-L **Ht.:** 6-5. **Wt.:** 210. **Drafted:** HS—Henderson, Nev., 2011 (22nd round). **Signed by:** Clark Crist.

Cincinnati has been willing to get creative to bring in premium talent, from signing Cuban defector Aroldis Chapman to a $30 million contract to signing Garrett for $1 million even though Garrett hadn't played high school baseball as a senior, focusing instead on basketball. Teams including the Reds saw intriguing talent when Garrett lit up radar guns in predraft workouts in 2011, and they signed him while still allowing him to play basketball at St. John's, where he was starting as a sophomore. Understandably, Garrett showed how raw he was in his pro debut. But he also showed himself to be a quick learner, as his breaking ball and changeup improved dramatically. His fastball sits at 92-94 mph, touching 96, and it's easily his best pitch for now. He flashed a plus slider and average changeup by late in the season. Garrett showed significant improvement as the season went on and impressed in his brief stay during instructional league. The Reds hope that at some point he'll focus on baseball, but with the opportunity to develop a lefthander with plus stuff they're willing to share him for now. Garrett should be slated for a return to Billings in 2013 once he finishes his sophomore basketball season.

Year	Club (League)	Class	W	L	ERA	G	GS	CG	SV	IP	H	HR	BB	SO	K/9	WHIP	AVG
2012	Reds (AZL)	R	0	2	5.79	7	5	0	0	14	14	1	12	13	8.4	1.86	.255
	Billings (PIO)	R	0	0	0.00	2	2	0	0	6	4	0	1	5	7.5	0.83	.211
Minor League Totals			0	2	4.05	9	7	0	0	20	18	1	13	18	8.1	1.55	.243

16 YORMAN RODRIGUEZ, OF

Born: Aug. 15, 1992. **B-T:** R-R. **Ht.:** 6-2. **Wt.:** 185. **Signed:** Venezuela, 2008. **Signed by:** Tony Arias.

Signed for what was then a Venezuelan amateur record $2.5 million signing bonus, Rodriguez has had a rocky couple of seasons. He carried bad at-bats into the field and did not fit in well with his teammates in Dayton in 2011. He showed similar problems while struggling at the plate in high Class A early in 2012, but after a demotion back to low Class A, he was more receptive to coaching and gave more consistent effort. Rodriguez still has some of the best tools in the system. His throwing arm and speed both rate as plus, and his raw power earns plus-plus grades. Poor pitch recognition short-circuits his power, though he still led the Dragons in slugging last season. He chases too many fastballs up and out of the zone and tries to pull everything. He has to show a better feel for making adjustments at the plate. Defensively, Rodriguez is average in right field, and his tools should work in center, although he doesn't look as comfortable there. If the light bulb goes on, Rodriguez is a potential all-star outfielder, but he'll have to make a lot of progress with the bat. Added to the 40-man roster in November, he'll give Bakersfield a second chance in 2013.

Year	Club (League)	Class	AVG	G	AB	R	H	2B	3B	HR	RBI	BB	SO	SB	CS	OBP	SLG
2009	Reds (GCL)	R	.274	22	84	9	23	2	1	0	2	10	23	5	0	.347	.321
	Billings (PIO)	R	.219	46	183	21	40	10	2	3	17	9	61	5	2	.259	.344
2010	Billings (PIO)	R	.339	43	171	25	58	8	3	2	39	8	30	12	2	.361	.456
2011	Dayton (MWL)	LoA	.254	79	280	38	71	10	4	7	40	25	84	20	8	.318	.393
2012	Bakersfield (CAL)	HiA	.156	23	90	7	14	4	0	0	7	3	39	4	0	.181	.200
	Dayton (MWL)	LoA	.271	65	258	35	70	17	3	6	44	12	61	7	5	.307	.430
Minor League Totals			.259	278	1066	135	276	51	13	18	149	67	298	53	17	.303	.382

17 PEDRO DIAZ, RHP

BA GRADE
50
HIGH

Born: April 23, 1993. **B-T:** R-R. **Ht.:** 6-0. **Wt.:** 180. **Signed:** Dominican Republic, 2010. **Signed by:** Richard Diaz.

The Reds have ignored the adage that short righthanders can't succeed, signing Johnny Cueto and seeing him develop into an ace, and getting Daniel Corcino to the brink of the majors. They now have Diaz in the pipeline, drawing Cueto and Corcino comparisons last season as he made his U.S. debut. Like Cueto and Corcino before him, Diaz wasn't a big name on the international scouting circuit—he signed for $30,000. He throws a little harder than either Cueto or Corcino did at the same age, sitting around 92-94 mph and touching 98 in the Arizona League, with a promising changeup and a hard slider. His delivery has no obvious flaws and his control is advanced for his age. Cueto made the jump from complex ball to low Class A, but Diaz is more likely to head to Billings to start 2013. Long-term, he has given no indication he can't remain a starter, other than his size. He projects as a potential frontline starter if he can survive the long trip from Arizona's complexes to the big leagues.

Year	Club (League)	Class	W	L	ERA	G	GS	CG	SV	IP	H	HR	BB	SO	K/9	WHIP	AVG
2011	Reds (DSL)	R	0	3	2.36	15	0	0	3	34	25	0	18	29	7.6	1.25	.203
2012	Reds (AZL)	R	1	6	5.72	14	12	0	0	46	60	3	14	43	8.5	1.62	.303
Minor League Totals			1	9	4.28	29	12	0	3	80	85	3	32	72	8.1	1.46	.265

18 DONALD LUTZ, OF/1B

BA GRADE
50
HIGH

Born: Feb. 6, 1989. **B-T:** L-R. **Ht.:** 6-3. **Wt.:** 235. **Signed:** Germany, 2007. **Signed by:** Jim Stoeckel.

The best German hockey player in the minors, Lutz didn't pick up a baseball bat until he was a teenager. He ended up hitting lefthanded because of his hockey background—it felt more natural even though he's usually righthanded. Signed out of MLB's European academy, Lutz is a dual German/American citizen who was born in the United States but has lived most of his life in Germany. He is a better athlete than his 6-foot-3, 235-pound frame would suggest. He's an average runner who turns in 4.2-second times to first. Lutz is still raw defensively, especially at first base. His best hope to make the big leagues with the Reds is as an outfielder. He has enough athleticism to play in left field, but he's currently well below average there thanks to inexperience, modest instincts and below-average arm. At the plate, Lutz is more promising. He has well above-average power with the potential to be an average hitter, though he needs to improve his selectivity at the plate. His numbers dropped off significantly after a midseason promotion to Double-A, in part because he was recovering from an oblique injury. Lutz remains raw for his age thanks to his unusual background. He'll have to improve defensively and prove he can hit advanced pitching to make the big leagues. He'll return to Pensacola to try to do that.

Year	Club (League)	Class	AVG	G	AB	R	H	2B	3B	HR	RBI	BB	SO	SB	CS	OBP	SLG
2008	Reds (GCL)	R	.250	34	108	22	27	9	0	1	19	9	21	4	1	.317	.361
2009	Reds (GCL)	R	.169	16	59	9	10	1	2	1	10	5	14	2	1	.246	.305
2010	Billings (PIO)	R	.286	55	203	36	58	10	4	7	28	21	45	6	2	.356	.478
2011	Dayton (MWL)	LoA	.301	123	465	85	140	23	3	20	75	34	125	5	4	.358	.492
2012	Reds (AZL)	R	.643	4	14	3	9	2	2	0	5	3	4	0	0	.706	1.071
	Bakersfield (CAL)	HiA	.265	63	253	42	67	18	3	17	51	19	71	7	2	.325	.561
	Pensacola (SL)	AA	.242	40	149	17	36	5	1	5	15	13	32	1	3	.315	.389
Minor League Totals			.277	335	1251	214	347	68	15	51	203	104	312	25	13	.341	.478

19 SETH MEJIAS-BREAN, 3B

BA GRADE
50
HIGH

Born: April 5, 1991. **B-T:** R-R. **Ht.:** 6-2. **Wt.:** 210. **Drafted:** Arizona, 2012 (8th round). **Signed by:** Clark Crist.

Mejias-Brean finished his college career in style, helping Arizona win the 2012 College World Series title. Scouts loved his defense and his athleticism but were concerned that a hitter with two homers in three college seasons may not have enough pop to stick in pro ball. The Reds signed him for $125,000 in the eighth round, taking a chance that they could tweak his swing for more power while reaping the benefits of his glove. The early returns were promising, as he was a Pioneer League all-star in his pro debut. Mejias-Brean's calling card is polished defense that fits the third-base profile thanks to agility, plus range and plenty of arm strength. At the plate, he focused on being more pull-conscious, which paid off in significantly improved power numbers. He has always hit for average and has solid hand-eye coordination. He still projects to have no more than average power, but that's a big step up for him, and his glove is good enough that even average power to go with his feel for hitting gives him a prospective path to the big leagues. He's a solid runner. Mejias-Brean will head to low Class A in 2013.

Year	Club (League)	Class	AVG	G	AB	R	H	2B	3B	HR	RBI	BB	SO	SB	CS	OBP	SLG
2012	Billings (PIO)	R	.313	46	179	35	56	12	2	8	40	21	29	6	0	.389	.536
Minor League Totals			.313	46	179	35	56	12	2	8	40	21	29	6	0	.389	.536

20 TANNER RAHIER, 3B

BA GRADE
50
HIGH

Born: Oct. 12, 1993. **B-T:** R-R. **Ht.:** 6-2. **Wt.:** 205. **Drafted:** HS—Palm Desert, Calif., 2012 (2nd round). **Signed by:** Mike Misuraca.

Rahier has been focused on becoming a pro baseball player for years. His father owns a chain of workout facilities, and he built a facility at their house and designed a special workout regime for his son. Rahier also decided not to play his 2012 senior season at Palm Desert (Calif.) High, choosing instead to play for a spring showcase team. For a relatively polished Southern California hitter who had spent plenty of time on the showcase circuit, Rahier had a surprisingly difficult adjustment to pro ball after signing for $649,700 in the second round. He got caught up in overswinging and trying to pull everything, and the Arizona League's more advanced pitchers found they could get him to chase out of the zone. His swing also has a bit of funk to it that needs to be cleaned up. Long-term he projects to have average power, although he needs to fill out and get stronger. A high school shortstop, Rahier had limited range there but made a relatively easy transition to third base, where his good hands and plus arm are a good fit. He's a fringy runner and may slow down as he matures physically. If Rahier doesn't fit at third base, he also could be an intriguing prospect to convert to catching. He's likely to open in extended spring training before moving up to Billings for 2013.

Year	Club (League)	Class	AVG	G	AB	R	H	2B	3B	HR	RBI	BB	SO	SB	CS	OBP	SLG
2012	Reds (AZL)	R	.192	51	193	21	37	9	1	4	30	21	43	5	2	.266	.311
Minor League Totals			.192	51	193	21	37	9	1	4	30	21	43	5	2	.266	.311

21 RYAN LAMARRE, OF

BA GRADE
50
HIGH

Born: Nov. 21, 1988. **B-T:** R-L. **Ht.:** 6-1. **Wt.:** 209. **Drafted:** Michigan, 2010 (2nd round). **Signed by:** Brad Meador.

A four-year starter in hockey, football and baseball in high school in Jackson, Mich., LaMarre wasn't drafted out of high school and went to Michigan to play baseball. He didn't let a broken thumb ruin his draft status as a junior, hitting .419 upon his return and climbing into the second round. LaMarre is one of the safer bets to be a big leaguer in the system because he has a pair of big league skills. He's a 65 runner on the 20-80 scouting scale, and a 65 defender in center field, where his average arm is more than enough. On the basepaths, he reads pitchers well, though after stealing 52 bases in 2011 he slowed down last year thanks to plantar fasciitis in his right foot. Because he couldn't injure it further, he decided to play through the injury and had surgery after the season. LaMarre strikes out a lot, but he also shows the ability to draw walks, which is important considering he profiles as a top-of-the-order hitter. His power is limited to hitting doubles to the gaps. He's expected to be healthy for spring training, and if so LaMarre is nearly ready for a major league backup role. He'll probably open the season in Triple-A, just a phone call away.

Year	Club (League)	Class	AVG	G	AB	R	H	2B	3B	HR	RBI	BB	SO	SB	CS	OBP	SLG
2010	Dayton (MWL)	LoA	.282	60	227	44	64	11	0	5	29	21	53	18	7	.370	.396
	Lynchburg (CAR)	HiA	.222	8	27	2	6	2	0	1	3	2	4	1	1	.276	.407
2011	Bakersfield (CAL)	HiA	.279	117	445	78	124	17	3	6	47	42	97	52	14	.347	.371
	Carolina (SL)	AA	.267	5	15	3	4	1	0	0	0	3	3	3	0	.421	.333
2012	Pensacola (SL)	AA	.263	133	482	68	127	22	3	5	32	60	119	30	10	.356	.353
Minor League Totals			.272	323	1196	195	325	53	6	17	111	128	276	104	32	.355	.369

22 KYLE WALDROP, OF

BA GRADE
50
HIGH

Born: Nov. 26, 1991. **B-T:** L-L. **Ht.:** 6-3. **Wt.:** 190. **Drafted:** HS—Fort Myers, Fla., 2010 (12th round). **Signed by:** Greg Zunino.

When Joey Votto came to Dayton for an injury rehab assignment last August, he joined Waldrop's batting practice group. With a big crowd gathered to see Votto, Waldrop put on a show, hitting long homer after long homer. That power doesn't always show up in games much yet, but it's a reason the Reds have high hopes for the former South Florida football commitment. He hit eight homers in 2012 but projects to have above-average power once he figures out how to translate it into game production. He generally has a fluid swing, though he will get caught sometimes trying too hard to muscle the ball out of the park. He hit .301 the second half of the season and projects to be a solid hitter. His below-average arm will limit him to left field, but as with many former football players, it has improved as he has focused on baseball. He's a solid defender, though he's a below-average runner who likely will slow down. He needs to improve his baserunning. Waldrop will head to high Class A in 2013. As a bat-first left fielder, he knows he'll have to keep hitting to get to the big leagues.

Year	Club (League)	Class	AVG	G	AB	R	H	2B	3B	HR	RBI	BB	SO	SB	CS	OBP	SLG
2010	Reds (AZL)	R	.214	7	28	1	6	1	0	0	1	1	9	0	0	.241	.250
2011	Billings (PIO)	R	.273	68	278	38	76	22	9	5	29	10	65	4	4	.305	.471
2012	Dayton (MWL)	LoA	.284	117	416	59	118	21	6	8	50	38	77	10	6	.346	.421
Minor League Totals			.277	192	722	98	200	44	15	13	80	49	151	14	10	.327	.434

23 TUCKER BARNHART, C

Born: Jan. 7, 1991. **B-T:** B-R **Ht.:** **5-10. Wt.:** 185. **Drafted:** HS—Brownsburg, Ind., 2009 (10th round). **Signed by:** Rick Sellers.

Barnhart may never hit .250 in the big leagues, yet he could still have a major league career as a backup catcher because of his glove. The best defensive catcher in the system, he has a heady approach behind the plate. He calls a good game, blocks pitches well and does a good job of pitch framing. His arm isn't especially strong, but his good footwork and quick release generate 1.95-second pop times, allowing him to throw out 38 percent of basestealers in 2012. At the plate, the switch-hitting Barnhart has a better swing from the left side. All six of his homers and both of his triples last year came against righthanders, while lefties held him to a .168 average. He has a short stroke from the left side and tries to spray line drives. From the right side, the swing is a little sweepier with less power. His hitting ability is ahead of his power, but both tools grade below average if not worse, so his glove will have to get him to the big leagues. Barnhart struggled in his first exposure to Double-A pitchers, he'll continue grinding by returning there to start the 2013 season.

Year	Club (League)	Class	AVG	G	AB	R	H	2B	3B	HR	RBI	BB	SO	SB	CS	OBP	SLG
2009	Reds (GCL)	R	.208	14	48	5	10	2	0	0	6	6	9	0	0	.291	.250
2010	Billings (PIO)	R	.306	35	111	17	34	9	0	0	12	18	25	4	1	.412	.387
2011	Dayton (MWL)	LoA	.273	97	326	47	89	24	2	3	43	37	59	2	1	.344	.387
2012	Bakersfield (CAL)	HiA	.278	59	198	26	55	12	1	4	22	29	45	0	2	.371	.409
	Pensacola (SL)	AA	.200	41	130	10	26	4	1	2	12	11	22	1	1	.262	.292
Minor League Totals			.263	246	813	105	214	51	4	9	95	101	160	7	5	.345	.369

24 HENRY RODRIGUEZ, 3B/2B

Born: Feb. 9, 1990. **B-T:** B-R. **Ht.:** 5-10. **Wt.:** 150. **Signed:** Venezuela, 2007. **Signed by:** Tony Arias.

A thumb injury, a pair of promotions and a lack of plate discipline exploited by Triple-A pitchers helped end what had been an impressive streak for Rodriguez. For the first time in five years he failed to hit .300, putting up a combined line of .282/.310/.370 last season. He still carries a .303 career minor league average, and he made his big league debut as a September callup. In recent years Rodriguez has had a run of bad luck with injuries. He broke his ankle in late August 2011, then missed six weeks with a broken thumb last year. His biggest liability, however, is his defensive limitations. He's a tick below-average third baseman with an average arm for the position. He's well below average at second base because of his limited range and his difficulty with the pivot on double plays. He has played shortstop at times, but no scouts project him as anything more than an emergency fill-in there. Rodriguez has the look of a utilityman, but he'll have to polish his defense across the infield to do that. He's likely to spend some more time with Louisville in 2013.

Year	Club (League)	Class	AVG	G	AB	R	H	2B	3B	HR	RBI	BB	SO	SB	CS	OBP	SLG
2007	Devil Rays/Reds (VSL)	R	.267	54	206	30	55	14	5	3	25	28	29	4	2	.361	.427
	Reds (DSL)	R	.235	7	17	3	4	0	0	0	4	1	1	1	0	.263	.235
2008	Reds (DSL)	R	.240	13	50	5	12	1	0	0	3	7	9	5	1	.328	.260
	D'backs/Reds (DSL)	R	.337	46	181	25	61	8	3	1	18	20	14	16	6	.405	.431
2009	Reds (GCL)	R	.322	42	152	24	49	10	1	1	19	7	18	9	0	.354	.421
2010	Dayton (MWL)	LoA	.307	124	514	76	158	37	3	14	78	22	70	33	13	.337	.473
	Lynchburg (CAR)	HiA	.250	6	24	2	6	0	0	0	4	0	4	0	0	.250	.250
2011	Bakersfield (CAL)	HiA	.340	58	238	37	81	17	0	8	44	14	35	12	7	.378	.513
	Carolina (SL)	AA	.302	69	278	39	84	19	1	5	37	25	43	18	3	.367	.432
2012	Pensacola (SL)	AA	.348	33	132	19	46	6	0	2	15	9	18	3	0	.385	.439
	Reds (AZL)	R	.235	5	17	1	4	1	0	0	1	1	2	0	0	.278	.294
	Louisville (IL)	AAA	.244	51	213	23	52	10	0	3	20	6	35	5	4	.264	.333
	Cincinnati (NL)	MAJ	.214	12	14	0	3	1	0	0	2	2	2	0	0	.313	.286
Major League Totals			.214	12	14	0	3	1	0	0	2	2	2	0	0	.313	.286
Minor League Totals			.303	508	2022	284	612	123	13	37	268	140	278	106	36	.350	.431

25 DEVIN LOHMAN, 2B/SS

Born: April 14, 1989. **B-T:** R-R. **Ht.:** 6-1. **Wt.:** 185. **Drafted:** Long Beach State, 2010 (3rd round). **Signed by:** Mike Misuraca.

The best thing that ever happened to Lohman was to get away from Billy Hamilton. He's a better shortstop than second baseman, and as long as Hamilton was in Bakersfield, Lohman's games at shortstop were going to be few and far between. He returned to short after Hamilton moved up to Double-A last year, and re-energized his career. He struggled offensively in the first half of the season, then posted an OPS 70 points higher when playing shortstop rather than second base. Defensively, he showed similar improvement. His plus arm is his best tool, and it was somewhat wasted at second. He shows average range with good hands and easy infield actions. He's an average runner, and while he's no Hamilton, he ranked third in the system with 34 steals. At the plate, he handles the bat well enough to hit for average. Reds officials think he will one day hit for average power, though opposing scouts see that as a longshot. He projects as a useful backup middle infield, and the Cincinnati sees enough similarities to Zack Cozart to think he could be a little more than that.

Year	Club (League)	Class	AVG	G	AB	R	H	2B	3B	HR	RBI	BB	SO	SB	CS	OBP	SLG
2010	Billings (PIO)	R	.239	64	230	33	55	12	2	1	31	24	47	2	5	.324	.322
2011	Dayton (MWL)	LoA	.208	62	207	14	43	5	1	1	31	17	47	9	2	.269	.256
	Billings (PIO)	R	.322	29	115	23	37	4	0	4	21	16	22	6	2	.420	.461
	Bakersfield (CAL)	HiA	.331	39	130	25	43	10	2	5	17	13	23	4	2	.400	.554
2012	Bakersfield (CAL)	HiA	.257	130	494	80	127	23	3	14	70	60	108	34	9	.353	.401
Minor League Totals			.259	324	1176	175	305	54	8	25	170	130	247	55	20	.345	.383

26 NEFTALI SOTO, 1B

BA GRADE
45
MEDIUM

Born: Feb. 28, 1989. **B-T:** R-R. **Ht.:** 6-2. **Wt.:** 200. **Drafted:** HS—Manati, P.R., 2007 (3rd round). **Signed by:** Tony Arias.

Part of the 2007 Reds draft class that produced Devin Mesoraco, Todd Frazier and Zack Cozart, Soto has had a much slower climb to the big leagues, and he took a step back in 2012. Drafted as a shortstop, he has moved from third base to catcher to first base as a pro, slowing his progress. He's entrenched as a first baseman now, which is bad news when you play in an system where Joey Votto is signed through 2023. After hitting 31 homers in 2011, Soto regressed significantly, getting too pull-happy and dealing with a mid-season stint on the disabled list with a back injury, which hurt his chances to get out of his slump. Soto doesn't need to sell out to hit the ball over the fence, as his above-average raw power gives him the ability to hit the ball out to all fields. Power is his calling card, as he's a below-average hitter overall, a well below-average runner and an average defender at first base. Soto is unlikely to get a full-time big league shot until the Reds either trade him or drop him from their 40-man roster and someone else claims him, so he'll head back to Triple-A and try to improve his performance.

Year	Club (League)	Class	AVG	G	AB	R	H	2B	3B	HR	RBI	BB	SO	SB	CS	OBP	SLG
2007	Reds (GCL)	R	.303	40	152	18	46	7	5	2	28	11	31	2	0	.355	.454
2008	Billings (PIO)	R	.388	15	67	12	26	10	1	4	11	4	10	1	0	.423	.746
	Dayton (MWL)	LoA	.326	52	218	26	71	15	1	7	36	7	36	1	1	.343	.500
2009	Sarasota (FSL)	HiA	.248	131	505	53	125	21	2	11	57	23	95	1	3	.282	.362
2010	Lynchburg (CAR)	HiA	.268	134	522	73	140	33	2	21	73	32	105	0	0	.319	.460
2011	Carolina (SL)	AA	.272	102	379	70	103	19	3	30	76	25	96	0	1	.329	.575
	Louisville (IL)	AAA	.412	4	17	1	7	0	0	1	4	1	2	0	0	.444	.588
2012	Louisville (IL)	AAA	.245	122	465	55	114	30	0	14	59	41	116	2	1	.313	.400
Minor League Totals			.272	600	2325	308	632	135	14	90	344	144	491	7	6	.320	.458

27 CURTIS PARTCH, RHP

BA GRADE
45
MEDIUM

Born: Feb. 13, 1987. **B-T:** R-R. **Ht.:** 6-4. **Wt.:** 230. **Drafted:** Merced (Calif.) JC, 2007 (26th round). **Signed by:** Tom Wheeler.

Originally drafted by the Giants in 2005, Partch instead headed to Merced (Calif.) JC and signed with Cincinnati after two seasons there. One of two Reds relief prospects who pitched their way onto the 40-man roster in part because of their Arizona Fall League performance, Partch doesn't throw quite as hard as Josh Ravin, but he's a better prospect because he has better idea of what he's doing on the mound. Partch isn't one to paint the corners himself, but he does find the strike zone enough to make hitters respect his 94-97 mph fastball. His fastball has good armside run and is tough to lift. His slider and changeup are fringy, though at times the breaking ball flashes low-80s power and bite. The lack of a consistently effective second pitch helps explain why he struggled against lefties, who posted a .922 OPS against Partch in Double-A last year, while he held righties to a .692 OPS. Primarily a starter prior to 2012, Partch took to the bullpen and will head to Triple-A for 2013.

Year	Club (League)	Class	W	L	ERA	G	GS	CG	SV	IP	H	HR	BB	SO	K/9	WHIP	AVG
2007	Reds (GCL)	R	0	0	1.29	5	0	0	2	7	2	0	7	4	5.1	1.29	.083
	Billings (PIO)	R	1	0	3.29	12	1	0	1	27	21	3	21	22	7.2	1.54	.221
2008	Dayton (MWL)	LoA	5	11	5.00	33	17	0	1	112	118	6	42	74	6.0	1.43	.267
2009	Carolina (SL)	AA	1	0	1.80	1	1	0	0	5	5	0	2	2	3.6	1.40	.238
	Dayton (MWL)	LoA	8	7	4.67	19	19	0	0	104	107	11	39	77	6.7	1.40	.270
	Sarasota (FSL)	HiA	1	7	4.35	7	7	0	0	39	38	0	18	25	5.7	1.42	.257
2010	Carolina (SL)	AA	0	1	21.00	1	1	0	0	3	7	2	2	1	3.0	3.00	.467
	Lynchburg (CAR)	HiA	7	11	4.98	28	24	0	0	132	165	11	45	96	6.5	1.59	.308
2011	Bakersfield (CAL)	HiA	7	5	5.25	21	21	2	0	122	161	14	28	93	6.9	1.55	.317
	Carolina (SL)	AA	2	2	6.92	7	7	0	0	39	55	3	13	33	7.6	1.74	.337
2012	Bakersfield (CAL)	HiA	0	0	1.50	7	0	0	2	12	7	1	3	15	11.3	0.83	.167
	Pensacola (SL)	AA	7	4	4.73	45	4	0	6	70	75	7	33	64	8.2	1.54	.274
Minor League Totals			40	49	4.91	186	102	2	12	672	761	58	253	506	6.8	1.51	.286

28 CHAD ROGERS, RHP

Born: Aug. 3, 1989. **B-T:** R-R. **Ht.:** 5-11. **Wt.:** 175. **Drafted:** Galveston (Texas) CC, 2010 (28th round). **Signed by:** Jerry Flowers.

Unless he has a lengthy big league career or cures cancer, the first line of Rogers' bio will likely always include the words "bitten by a shark." Rogers was surfing in waters off Galveston, Texas, when a shark took a bite out of his foot. The injury occurred after Cincinnati drafted him but before he signed a contract, and he was happy the club still wanted to sign him after he demonstrated that despite 60 stitches, he had no permanent damage. To his credit, he has started to do enough as a prospect to prove he's more than just a human interest story. Another of the Reds' short righthanders, Rogers has thrived with average stuff. His fastball is effective despite its 88-92 mph velocity because it has plenty of sink. His slider is a hard pitch that can almost be confused for a cutter. If he's going to remain a starter, Rogers will need to improve his below-average changeup, which is too firm to get proper separation from his fastball. His assortment may work better out of the bullpen long-term, where his velocity could gain a tick—he has touched 94 mph in short stretches. Rogers has repaid Cincinnati's faith in him by showing more success than the average late-round pick. After an impressive finish in Double-A last year, he could make it to Triple-A at some point in 2013.

Year	Club (League)	Class	W	L	ERA	G	GS	CG	SV	IP	H	HR	BB	SO	K/9	WHIP	AVG
2011	Dayton (MWL)	LoA	6	4	2.99	37	1	0	1	69	57	3	24	72	9.3	1.17	.227
2012	Bakersfield (CAL)	HiA	6	4	3.15	21	21	0	0	111	113	11	29	88	7.1	1.28	.263
	Pensacola (SL)	AA	3	1	1.99	6	6	0	0	32	27	3	6	23	6.5	1.04	.241
Minor League Totals			15	9	2.92	64	28	0	1	212	197	17	59	183	7.8	1.21	.249

29 GABRIEL ROSA, 3B

Born: July 2, 1993. **B-T:** R-R. **Ht.:** 6-4. **Wt.:** 185. **Drafted:** HS—Rio Grande, P.R., 2011 (2nd round). **Signed by:** Tony Arias.

After a promising pro debut, Rosa endured a lost year in 2012. A torn labrum in his hip forced him to shut it down after just 21 games, and he wasn't healthy in time for instructional league and may not be ready for spring training. When healthy, Rosa has shown promising tools, but his approach at the plate needs work. His leg kick is too pronounced to survive against pro pitchers, as it forces him to commit too early. It makes him vulnerable to offspeed pitches and makes it hard to lay off pitches out of the zone. With his 6-foot-4 frame, he has plenty of power potential if he can make enough contact. Rosa could be average defensively at third base, and he played shortstop well enough that the Reds may let him stay there in the short-term. With above-average speed, he could play outfield as well. He played one game in left field last year and could even be a center fielder if he doesn't fill out too much. His plus arm would also work in right field. Rosa has to show he's healthy before Cincinnati can assess where he'll play in 2013, but Billings seems a likely spot for a return trip.

Year	Club (League)	Class	AVG	G	AB	R	H	2B	3B	HR	RBI	BB	SO	SB	CS	OBP	SLG
2011	Reds (AZL)	R	.245	28	106	17	26	5	3	2	10	8	28	4	3	.314	.406
2012	Billings (PIO)	R	.179	21	78	8	14	6	0	0	5	1	25	2	0	.188	.256
Minor League Totals			.217	49	184	25	40	11	3	2	15	9	53	6	3	.263	.342

30 SAL ROMANO, RHP

Born: Oct. 12, 1993. **B-T:** L-R. **Ht.:** 6-5. **Wt.:** 220. **Drafted:** HS—Southington, Conn., 2011 (23rd round). **Signed by:** Lee Seras.

In most years, scouts don't have a lot of reasons to scour Connecticut high schools for talent. Romano, a Tennessee signee who was flashing a low-90s fastball as a 17-year-old senior, brought them to Southington in 2011, however. He had missed much of the high school showcase circuit after his jaw was broken on a comebacker to the mound, but Cincinnati saw enough during his senior year to sign him for $450,000. As would be expected with a 6-foot-5 Northeast pitcher, Romano is quite raw. Like many tall pitchers, his coordination hasn't caught up to his height yet. He doesn't always repeat his delivery, and he has to work on getting his upper half and lower half to work together, but he fires 92-94 mph fastballs with sink that are hard to get into the air. He gave up one homer in 286 plate appearances last season. His curveball and changeup both project to be average pitches or better. Despite his delivery issues, Romano throws enough strikes; he just needs to continue to improve his command. Depending on how he pitches in spring training he could make his full-season debut in low Class A in 2013.

Year	Club (League)	Class	W	L	ERA	G	GS	CG	SV	IP	H	HR	BB	SO	K/9	WHIP	AVG
2012	Billings (PIO)	R	5	6	5.32	15	15	0	0	64	74	1	23	52	7.3	1.51	.288
Minor League Totals			5	6	5.32	15	15	0	0	64	74	1	23	52	7.3	1.51	.288

Cleveland Indians

BY BEN BADLER

A s their 68-94 season drew to a close, the Indians fired manager Manny Acta, then quickly replaced him with former Red Sox skipper Terry Francona.

While Francona puts a fresh face in the dugout, there's little Acta could have done given the players at his disposal. Cleveland ranked 22nd in baseball in runs scored, but the pitching was worse as only the Rockies allowed more runs.

The Indians have struggled to add talent in recent years, most notably through the market for amateur players. While Jason Kipnis has proven to be an excellent use of a second-round pick in 2009, the draft continues to be an area that has provided little help.

Vinnie Pestano (20th round, 2006) and Tony Sipp (45th round, 2004) have been useful relievers and Cody Allen (23rd round, 2011) made a rapid rise to join them in the big league bullpen, but years of missing on first-round picks and getting little from the later rounds have hampered Cleveland.

Further development from 2008 first-rounder Lonnie Chisenhall would represent a major draft breakthrough, but he has hit .260/.295/.421 and played substandard defense in the majors the last two years.

The international market also has been a dry spot. The Indians signed Victor Martinez out of Venezuela in 1996, then former Latin American director Rene Gayo (now with the Pirates) helped the team add Roberto Hernandez and Jhonny Peralta, among others. The Indians' more recent forays into international waters have yet to deliver any impact players.

Other than Hernandez and Rafael Perez, the only other international free agent Cleveland signed and had on its 2012 team was nondescript Jeanmar Gomez. The Indians hope that Chen Lee perhaps can offer some relief help in 2013 after losing 2012 to Tommy John surgery.

Former GM and current club president Mark Shapiro helped build his reputation on trades that landed such players as Asdrubal Cabrera, Shin-Soo Choo, Travis Hafner, Cliff Lee, Brandon Phillips, Carlos Santana and Grady Sizemore.

But Shapiro received little in return when he traded C.C. Sabathia in 2008 and Lee in 2009, a major reason why the team hasn't had a winning season since blowing a 3-1 lead in the 2007 American League Championship Series. Matt LaPorta, the centerpiece

Zach McAllister was one of the few bright spots on a staff that ranked 29th in ERA

of the Sabathia trade, has been a bust, though Michael Brantley did emerge as a solid regular in 2012. Carlos Carrasco, who missed 2012 after Tommy John surgery. is the last hope to salvage much value from the Lee deal.

Making the opposite move, trading prospects in exchange for a supposed ace, also has turned sour. With the Indians contending in mid-2011, GM Chris Antonetti traded his two best young arms to the Rockies as part of a four-player package for Ubaldo Jimenez.

Neither Drew Pomeranz and Alex White has done much in the major leagues yet, but Jimenez has posted a 5.32 ERA in 42 starts for Cleveland.

The Indians did get value when they traded Austin Kearns in 2010, getting Zach McAllister from the Yankees. He had a 4.24 ERA in 22 major league starts in 2012.

If the Indians are counting on help from the minors, impact talent is still at least a couple of years away. Francisco Lindor is a potential all-star and fellow shortstop Dorssys Paulino may be the best international player they've signed since Peralta in 1999. But neither has played above low Class A, nor has 2012 first-rounder Tyler Naquin, and beyond them the system is thin.

THIS YEAR'S TOP 30

Player, Pos.		Grade
1.	Francisco Lindor, ss	65/High
2.	Dorssys Paulino, ss	60/Extreme
3.	Tyler Naquin, of	55/High
4.	Cody Allen, rhp	50/Low
5.	Mitch Brown, rhp	50/High
6.	Danny Salazar, rhp	50/High
7.	Luigi Rodriguez, of	50/High
8.	Ronny Rodriguez, ss/2b	50/High
9.	Jesus Aguilar, 1b	50/High
10.	Chen Lee, rhp	45/Medium
11.	Scott Barnes, lhp	45/Medium
12.	Luis Lugo, lhp	50/High
13.	Anthony Santander, of	50/High
14.	Trey Haley, rhp	45/Medium
15.	D'Vone McClure, of	50/High
16.	Dylan Baker, rhp	50/High
17.	Tony Wolters, 2b/ss	50/High
18.	Chris McGuiness, 1b	45/Medium
19.	Tim Fedroff, of	45/Medium
20.	Shawn Armstrong, rhp	45/Medium
21.	Kieran Lovegrove, rhp	50/High
22.	Giovanny Urshela, 3b	50/High
23.	Jose Ramirez, 2b	50/High
24.	Austin Adams, rhp	50/Extreme
25.	Dillon Howard, rhp	50/Extreme
26.	Elvis Araujo, lhp	50/Extreme
27.	Yan Gomes, c/1b/3b	45/Medium
28.	Thomas Neal, of	45/Medium
29.	Cody Anderson, rhp	45/High
30.	Jordan Smith, of	45/High

LAST YEAR'S TOP 30

Player, Pos.		Status
1.	Francisco Lindor, ss	No. 1
2.	Dillon Howard, rhp	No. 25
3.	Nick Hagadone, lhp	Majors
4.	Chen Lee, rhp	No. 10
5.	Luigi Rodriguez, of	No. 7
6.	Zach McAllister, rhp	Majors
7.	Tony Wolters, ss	No. 17
8.	Austin Adams, rhp	No. 24
9.	Scott Barnes, lhp	No. 11
10.	Zach Putnam, rhp	(Free agent)
11.	Elvis Araujo, lhp	No. 26
12.	Tyler Sturdevant, lhp	Dropped out
13.	Ronny Rodriguez, ss	No. 8
14.	Jake Sisco, rhp	Dropped out
15.	Cord Phelps, 2b/ss	Dropped out
16.	Trey Haley, rhp	No. 14
17.	Mike Rayl, lhp	Dropped out
18.	Nick Weglarz, of	Dropped out
19.	LeVon Washington, of	Dropped out
20.	Felix Sterling, rhp	Dropped out
21.	T.J. McFarland, lhp	Dropped out
22.	Hector Rondon, rhp	Dropped out
23.	Josh Judy, rhp	(Free agent)
24.	Bryce Stowell, rhp	Dropped out
25.	Jesus Aguilar, 1b	No. 9
26.	Chun Chen, c	Dropped out
27.	Jake Lowery, c/1b	Dropped out
28.	Bryson Myles, of	Dropped out
29.	Matt Packer, lhp	Dropped out
30.	Jordan Smith, 3b/of	No. 30

BEST TOOLS

Best Hitter for Average	Dorssys Paulino
Best Power Hitter	Jesus Aguilar
Best Strike-Zone Discipline	Francisco Lindor
Fastest Baserunner	Luigi Rodriguez
Best Athlete	D'Vone McClure
Best Fastball	Trey Haley
Best Curveball	Cody Allen
Best Slider	Shawn Armstrong
Best Changeup	Danny Salazar
Best Control	T.J. McFarland
Best Defensive Catcher	Roberto Perez
Best Defensive Infielder	Francisco Lindor
Best Infield Arm	Giovanny Urshela
Best Defensive Outfielder	Tyler Holt
Best Outfield Arm	Tyler Naquin

PROJECTED 2016 LINEUP

Catcher	Carlos Santana
First Base	Lonnie Chisenhall
Second Base	Asdrubal Cabrera
Third Base	Dorssys Paulino
Shortstop	Francisco Lindor
Left Field	Jason Kipnis
Center Field	Michael Brantley
Right Field	Tyler Naquin
Designated Hitter	Shin-Soo Choo
No. 1 Starter	Justin Masterson
No. 2 Starter	Carlos Carrasco
No. 3 Starter	Ubaldo Jimenez
No. 4 Starter	Zach McAllister
No. 5 Starter	Mitch Brown
Closer	Cody Allen

TOP PROSPECTS OF THE DECADE

Year	Player, Pos.	2012 Org.
2003	Brandon Phillips, ss/2b	Reds
2004	Grady Sizemore, of	Indians
2005	Adam Miller, rhp	Yankees
2006	Adam Miller, rhp	Yankees
2007	Adam Miller, rhp	Yankees
2008	Adam Miller, rhp	Yankees
2009	Carlos Santana, c	Indians
2010	Carlos Santana, c	Indians
2011	Lonnie Chisenhall, 3b	Indians
2012	Francisco Lindor, ss	Indians

TOP DRAFT PICKS OF THE DECADE

Year	Player, Pos.	2012 Org.
2003	Michael Aubrey, 1b	Out of baseball
2004	Jeremy Sowers, lhp	Out of baseball
2005	Trevor Crowe, of	Angels
2006	David Huff, lhp (1st round supplemental)	Indians
2007	Beau Mills, 3b/1b	Reds
2008	Lonnie Chisenhall, 3b	Indians
2009	Alex White, rhp	Rockies
2010	Drew Pomeranz, lhp	Rockies
2011	Francisco Lindor, ss	Indians
2012	Tyler Naquin, of	Indians

LARGEST BONUSES IN CLUB HISTORY

Danys Baez, 1999	$4,500,000
Jeremy Guthrie, 2002	$3,000,000
Francisco Lindor, 2011	$2,900,000
Drew Pomeranz, 2010	$2,650,000
Jeremy Sowers, 2004	$2,475,000

CLEVELAND INDIANS

TOP 2013 ROOKIE: Cody Allen, rhp. With his stuff, don't be surprised if he finishes the year as Cleveland's closer.

BREAKOUT PROSPECT: Luis Lugo, lhp. With his projectable frame, he could add velocity and take off.

SLEEPER: Josh Schubert, of. The 2012 seventh-rounder is raw, but he has plus power potential, solid speed and a strong arm.

SOURCE OF TOP 30 TALENT			
Homegrown	26	Acquired	4
College	6	Trades	3
Junior college	2	Rule 5 draft	1
High school	7	Independent leagues	0
Nondrafted free agents	0	Free agents/waivers	0
International	11		

LF
Anthony Santander (13)
Tim Fedroff (19)
Thomas Neal (28)
Russ Canzler
Bryson Myles
Hector Caro

CF
Tyler Naquin (3)
Luigi Rodriguez (7)
LeVon Washington
Tyler Holt
Jordan Henry
Delvi Cid
Tyler Booth

RF
D'Vone McClure (15)
Jordan Smith (30)
Josh Schubert
Logan Vick
Carlos Moncrief
Bo Greenwell

3B
Dorssys Paulino (2)
Giovanny Urshela (22)
Jorge Martinez
Grofi Cruz

SS
Francisco Lindor (1)
Ronny Rodriguez (8)
Juan Diaz

2B
Tony Wolters (17)
Jose Ramirez (23)
Cord Phelps
Robel Garcia
Joe Wendle

1B
Jesus Aguilar (9)
Chris McGuiness (18)
Mike McDade
Lars Anderson
Chun Chen
Nelson Rodriguez

C
Yan Gomes (27)
Alex Monsalve
Jake Lowery
Roberto Perez
Alex Lavisky
Jeremy Lucas
Eric Haase
Yoiber Marquina
Richard Stock

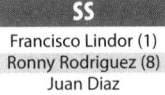

LHP

LHSP	LHRP
Luis Lugo (12)	Scott Barnes (11)
T.J. House	Elvis Araujo (26)
Matt Packer	Tyler Sturdevant
Giovanni Soto	Mike Rayl
Shawn Morimando	Kyle Petter

RHP

RHSP	RHRP
Mitch Brown (5)	Cody Allen (4)
Danny Salazar (6)	Chen Lee (10)
Dylan Baker (16)	Trey Haley (14)
Kieran Lovegrove (21)	Shawn Armstrong (20)
Dillon Howard (25)	Austin Adams (24)
Cody Anderson (29)	Bryce Stowell
Clayton Cook	Rob Bryson
Jake Sisco	Fabio Martinez
Kyle Blair	Felix Sterling
Caleb Hamrick	Kota Kobayashi
Jacob Lee	Jeff Johnson
Luis DeJesus	Cole Cook
Nick Pasquale	Preston Guilmet
	Jose Flores
	Francisco Valera
	Jim Stokes

2012

BEST PURE HITTER: The Indians weren't the only club that considered OF Tyler Naquin (1) the draft's best pure hitter. He has good swings whether he's ahead or behind in the count and has a knack for centering the baseball.

BEST POWER HITTER: 1B Nelson Rodriguez (15) packs present strength into his 6-foot-2, 205-pound frame. He has a track record of hitting for power, including with USA Baseball's 18-and-under squad.

FASTEST RUNNER: OF Tyler Booth (13) is a 6-foot, 155-pounder with plus-plus speed and wiry athleticism. Naquin's above-average speed has allowed him to move to center field after playing right in college.

BEST DEFENSIVE PLAYER: Cleveland is confident Naquin will be an above-average center fielder. He had one of the best outfield arms in the draft as well.

BEST FASTBALL: RHP Jacob Lee (9) pitched at 89-92 mph at Arkansas State, then bumped his fastball to 92-94 and touched 96 after signing. He throws plenty of strikes with his heater as well and could provide excellent value for his $2,500 bonus. RHP Dylan Baker (5) sits at 94-95 mph at times and touches 97 but doesn't command his fastball as well as Lee.

BEST SECONDARY PITCH: RHP Mitch Brown (2) has two potentially excellent breaking balls in a true curveball at 76-78 mph and a hard cutter/slider that ranges from 83-87.

BEST PRO DEBUT: 2B/3B Joe Wendle (6) ranked third in the short-season New York-Penn League in batting and on-base percentage, hitting .327/.375/.469. Lee went 4-2, 3.12 with 47 strikeouts in 43 innings in the NY-P, including a five-inning no-hit start.

BEST ATHLETE: OF D'Vone McClure (4) offers the best combination of power and speed in this class. He has enticing bat speed to go with a developing 6-foot-3, 190-pound frame. He drew interest from college football programs as a wide receiver.

MOST INTRIGUING BACKGROUND: RHP Kieran Lovegrove (3) was born in South Africa and pitched for his homeland in a World Baseball Classic qualifier. 3B Nick Hamilton's (35) father Tom has been an Indians radio broadcaster for 23 seasons. 3B Joe Sever (21) is the nephew of NFL Hall of Fame quarterback John Elway. Brown's father is a Korean-born powerlifter who was adopted and brought to Minnesota as a child. C Richard Stock's (23) brother Robert is a Cardinals farmhand who was Baseball America's 2005 Youth Player of the Year.

CLOSEST TO THE MAJORS: Naquin should be one of the first college position players from the entire draft to get to the big leagues.

BEST LATE-ROUND PICK: Rodriguez or RHP Nick Pasquale (20). A sinkerballer with command, Pasquale walked just five in 50 innings as a pro.

THE ONE WHO GOT AWAY: The Indians hoped to sign OF Andrew Calica (17), an athletic switch-hitter. He headlined a strong UC Santa Barbara recruiting class instead.

ASSESSMENT: As a polished college performer, Naquin was a classic Tribe first-rounder. After him, Cleveland's draft class had a heavier high school tilt than usual with Brown, Lovegrove and McClure.

2011

SS Francisco Lindor (1) looks like a future all-star and Gold Glover for years to come. RHP Cody Allen (23) raced to the majors and could take over as the Indians' closer in short order.

GRADE: A

2010

LHP Drew Pomeranz (1) also got to the big leagues quickly, but did so with the Rockies after becoming part of the ill-fated Ubaldo Jimenez trade. Seven-figure investments in OF LeVon Washington (2) and C Alex Lavisky (8) aren't looking so hot, but a third in 2B/SS Tony Wolters (3) may pay off.

GRADE: B

2009

2B Jason Kipnis (2) already looks like the best position player drafted and developed by Cleveland since it signed Luke Scott in 2001. RHP Alex White (1) was another piece of the Jimenez package, and RHP Cory Burns (8) got to the majors with the Padres after getting dealt for Aaron Cunningham.

GRADE: B

2008

3B Lonnie Chisenhall (1) still may be the Indians' third baseman for the long term, but it has taken longer than expected for him to seize that role. 2B Cord Phelps (3), since-traded RHP Zach Putnam (5) and unsigned RHP Adam Warren (36) also have played in the big leagues but lack high ceilings.

GRADE: C+

Draft analysis by John Manuel (2012) and Jim Callis (2008-11).
Numbers in parentheses indicate draft rounds.

1 FRANCISCO LINDOR, SS

Born: Nov. 14, 1993. **B-T:** B-R. **Ht.:** 5-11. **Wt.:** 175.
Drafted: HS—Montverde, Fla., 2011 (1st round).
Signed by: Mike Soper.

BA GRADE
65
HIGH

PAUL GIERHART

Lindor moved to the United States from Puerto Rico at age 12. He rose to prominence in 2009 as the captain of a Team USA squad that captured the gold medal at the 16-and-under World Championship in Taiwan, batting .500 in 11 games. He continued to boost his stock with a strong summer showcase tour in 2010, including a shocking win in the Aflac All-American Game's home run derby at Petco Park. Known for typically college-heavy drafts, the Indians drafted Lindor with the eighth overall pick in 2011, making him their first prep first-rounder since Dan Denham and Alan Horne in 2001. Lindor signed for $2.9 million, the biggest bonus Cleveland ever has given a position player or high school draftee. The youngest everyday player in the low Class A Midwest League in his first pro season in 2012, he stood out not only for his tools but also for his remarkable maturity as an 18-year-old. He batted .333 in the playoffs as Lake County reached the semifinals.

An excellent athlete, Lindor is one of the best defensive shortstops in the minors. In addition to above-average defensive tools, he has phenomenal instincts. He knows how to position himself and always seems to be in the right spot at the right time. He gets great reads off the bat and has terrific fundamentals. His range and arm are both better than average, and his feet and hands work well together. Lindor has a quiet, simple approach in the batter's box. He has a compact swing with good bat speed from both sides of the plate and hits line drives to all fields. His pitch-recognition skills are above average, as he shows the ability to handle offspeed pitches and lays off pitches outside the strike zone to take his walks. With his bat control, he doesn't swing and miss much.

Lindor could be a plus hitter who gets on base at a high clip, though his power is more to the gaps than over the fence. He has some surprising strength in his lower half and can occasionally pull a ball over the fence, but he'll likely top out around 10-15 homers per year. He's a slightly above-average runner whose 27 steals in 2012 were somewhat of a surprise, though he needs to become more efficient after getting thrown out 12 times. The game never seems to speed up on Lindor, and seemingly everyone who comes in contact with him raves about his makeup. Indians officials marvel at the way he approaches his routine every day and never wavers from his preparation. After hitting .285/.369/.410 in the first half, he batted .228/.355/.299 in 62 games after the all-star break, so he'll need to get stronger to hold up over a full season.

Lindor has the look of a future all-star shortstop. His defense is already major league caliber, while additional strength and refinement should help bring his offensive game to the next level. Ticketed for high Class A Carolina in 2013, he's the best infield prospect the franchise has had since Brandon Phillips (who was originally drafted by the Expos and obtained in the 2002 Bartolo Colon trade) and the best position prospect who was originally signed by the Indians since Victor Martinez. Lindor has a chance to get to Cleveland before he turns 21.

SCOUTING GRADES

Batting: 60. **Defense:** 70.
Power: 40. **Arm:** 60.
Speed: 55.

Based on 20-80 scouting scale, where 50 represents major league average, and future projection rather than present tools.

Year	Club (League)	Class	AVG	G	AB	R	H	2B	3B	HR	RBI	BB	SO	SB	CS	OBP	SLG
2011	Mahoning Valley (NYP)	SS	.316	5	19	4	6	0	0	0	2	1	5	1	0	.350	.316
2012	Lake County (MWL)	LoA	.257	122	490	83	126	24	3	6	42	61	78	27	12	.352	.355
Minor League Totals			.259	127	509	87	132	24	3	6	44	62	83	28	12	.352	.354

2 DORSSYS PAULINO, SS

Born: Nov. 21, 1994. **B-T:** R-R. **Ht.:** 6-0. **Wt.:** 175. **Signed:** Dominican Republic, 2011. **Signed by:** Ramon Pena/Claudio Brito/Felix Nivar.

The son of former big league lefthander Jesus Sanchez, Paulino drew plenty of attention as an amateur in the Dominican Republic for his bat. Signed for $1.1 million, he starred in his 2012 pro debut, ranking second in the Rookie-level Arizona League in batting (.355) and third in OPS (1.014) despite being one of the league's youngest players at 17. Paulino has quick hands and a short, simple swing that stays in the hitting zone a long time, giving him excellent plate coverage. His approach is mature for his age. He can get the barrel out front against good fastballs and recognizes spin, doesn't chase much out of the strike zone and uses the whole field. While international scouts pegged Paulino with average power, he showed surprising pop in his debut, so he might end up with more. He's an above-average runner and the Indians would like him to stay at shortstop, though scouts outside the organization think he's a better fit at second or third base. He has a strong arm but made 25 errors in 46 games at short. One of the most exciting hitters to sign with the Indians in years, Paulino should move quickly and will open 2013 in low Class A.

BA GRADE
60
EXTREME

Year	Club (League)	Class	AVG	G	AB	R	H	2B	3B	HR	RBI	BB	SO	SB	CS	OBP	SLG
2012	Indians (AZL)	R	.355	41	172	42	61	14	6	6	30	15	31	9	1	.404	.610
	Mahoning Valley (NYP)	SS	.271	15	59	5	16	5	0	1	8	3	14	2	1	.306	.407
Minor League Totals			.333	56	231	47	77	19	6	7	38	18	45	11	2	.380	.558

3 TYLER NAQUIN, OF

Born: April 24, 1991. **B-T:** L-R. **Ht.:** 6-2. **Wt.:** 175. **Drafted:** Texas A&M, 2012 (1st round). **Signed by:** Kyle Van Hook.

Naquin led NCAA Division I with 104 hits for Texas A&M in 2011, and he won consecutive Big 12 Conference batting titles the last two seasons with .381 and .380 averages. He parlayed his status as one of the best pure hitters in college baseball into a $1.75 million bonus as the 15th overall pick in the 2012 draft. A back injury kept him out for most of August. Naquin's quick, handsy swing helps him stay inside the ball, use the opposite field and generate line drives. He has nice balance and a mature approach. He has good hand-eye coordination and has no issues handling breaking pitches. Naquin could benefit from incorporating his lower half more in his swing and turning on pitches with greater authority. He has below-average power and his narrow shoulders raise questions about his ability to add more pop. A right fielder for the Aggies, Naquin played center field in pro ball. He's a solid runner with a well above-average arm, though he needs to improve his routes. Whether Naquin will have the defensive chops to handle center field or the power to profile on a corner is still a question, as some scouts consider him a tweener. His bat is advanced enough for him to make the jump to high Class A.

BA GRADE
55
HIGH

Year	Club (League)	Class	AVG	G	AB	R	H	2B	3B	HR	RBI	BB	SO	SB	CS	OBP	SLG
2012	Mahoning Valley (NYP)	SS	.270	36	137	22	37	11	2	0	13	17	26	4	3	.379	.380
Minor League Totals			.270	36	137	22	37	11	2	0	13	17	26	4	3	.379	.380

4 CODY ALLEN, RHP

Born: Nov. 20, 1988. **B-T:** R-R. **Ht.:** 6-1. **Wt.:** 210. **Drafted:** High Point, 2011 (23rd round). **Signed by:** Bob Mayer.

There was little hype when the Indians signed Allen out of mid-major High Point for $40,000 as a 23rd-round pick in 2011. His stuff kicked into a higher gear in 2012, when he made his major league debut in July to become the second-fastest 2011 draftee to reach the majors, behind only No. 3 overall pick Trevor Bauer. Allen had Tommy John surgery and was a starter in college, but his fastball velocity spiked when he became a reliever in pro ball. An 88-92 mph guy who touched 94 in college, he now sits at 94-96 mph and hits 97 with late life. His mid-80s breaking ball is a plus pitch with plenty of depth, resembling a curveball more than a slider. He's still learning how to command his breaking ball in the strike zone, but it can miss bats against both lefties and righties. Allen's increased velocity has dramatically changed his outlook, improving his profile to that of a late-inning reliever. His stuff is on par with current Cleveland closer Chris Perez, and Allen could take his job in the near future.

BA GRADE
50
LOW

Year	Club (League)	Class	W	L	ERA	G	GS	CG	SV	IP	H	HR	BB	SO	K/9	WHIP	AVG
2011	Mahoning Valley (NYP)	SS	3	1	2.14	14	0	0	0	34	21	1	9	42	11.2	0.89	.183

Year	Club (League)	Class	W	L	ERA	G	GS	CG	SV	IP	H	HR	BB	SO	K/9	WHIP	AVG
	Lake County (MWL)	LoA	2	0	0.00	7	0	0	0	17	10	0	5	28	14.8	0.88	.164
	Akron (EL)	AA	0	0	18.00	1	0	0	0	1	3	0	0	2	18.0	3.00	.500
	Kinston (CAR)	HiA	0	0	0.00	1	0	0	0	3	1	0	0	3	9.0	0.33	.100
2012	Carolina (CAR)	HiA	0	0	0.00	2	0	0	0	4	1	0	0	8	18.0	0.25	.077
	Akron (EL)	AA	0	0	1.17	5	0	0	1	8	2	1	0	10	11.7	0.26	.080
	Columbus (IL)	AAA	3	2	2.27	24	0	0	2	32	22	3	9	35	9.9	0.98	.195
	Cleveland (AL)	MAJ	0	1	3.72	27	0	0	0	29	29	2	15	27	8.4	1.52	.266
Major League Totals			0	1	3.72	27	0	0	0	29	29	2	15	27	8.4	1.52	.266
Minor League Totals			8	3	1.74	54	0	0	3	98	60	5	23	128	11.8	0.85	.175

5 MITCH BROWN, RHP

BA GRADE

50

HIGH

Born: April 13, 1994. **B-T:** R-R. **Ht.:** 6-1. **Wt.:** 195. **Drafted:** HS—Rochester, Minn., 2012 (2nd round). **Signed by:** Les Pajari.

Brown became just the fourth Minnesota prep pitcher ever to go as high as the second round, giving up a San Diego scholarship to sign for $800,000. The son of a Korean powerlifter, Brown has a sturdy build and pitches with poise. His fastball velocity is inconsistent, but he can sit around 90-93 mph and reached as high as 96 after signing. The Indians love the upside of both of his breaking pitches, a true curveball in the upper 70s and a cutter/slider in the mid-80s. In his debut, he focused mainly on the cutter/slider and worked with Rookie-level Arizona League pitching coach Steve Karsay in the bullpen to improve his curve. Brown also has an average changeup that could get better. He has a relatively low-maintenance delivery, and while he does throw across his body, it doesn't impede his command and helps him hide the ball. Brown has the stuff and polish to make the jump from Rookie ball low Class A at age 19. If he can refine his secondary pitches, he'll combine solid stuff across the board with good feel for pitching and project as a possible No. 3 starter.

Year	Club (League)	Class	W	L	ERA	G	GS	CG	SV	IP	H	HR	BB	SO	K/9	WHIP	AVG
2012	Indians (AZL)	R	2	0	3.58	8	8	0	0	28	20	3	10	26	8.5	1.08	.204
Minor League Totals			2	0	3.58	8	8	0	0	28	20	3	10	26	8.5	1.08	.204

6 DANNY SALAZAR, RHP

BA GRADE

50

HIGH

Born: Jan. 11, 1990. **B-T:** R-R. **Ht.:** 6-0. **Wt.:** 190. **Signed:** Dominican Republic, 2006. **Signed by:** Lino Diaz.

Salazar did little in his first five years as a pro to garner much attention as a prospect. Elbow problems limited him to seven starts in 2010, and he eventually succumbed to Tommy John surgery in August that year. Though he hadn't pitched above low Class A, the Indians protected him on the 40-man roster after the 2011 season, then saw his stuff pick up significantly in 2012 amidst the best year of his career. As the season wore on and Salazar grew further removed from his surgery, his velocity took off. His fastball now sits at 94-97 mph at times and reaches 100. He's still learning how to use his secondary pitches to miss bats, but his breaking ball has power and depth to it and his changeup stands out in a system that doesn't feature many good ones. He still has to prove his durability because his career high in innings remains the 107 he threw in 2009. If he can't hold up as a starter, his power fastball could be electric in the bullpen. He'll either return to Double-A Akron or make the jump to Triple-A Columbus in 2013, when he could see big league time by the end of the season.

Year	Club (League)	Class	W	L	ERA	G	GS	CG	SV	IP	H	HR	BB	SO	K/9	WHIP	AVG
2007	Indians (DSL)	R	5	3	1.96	14	14	0	0	64	52	1	12	49	6.9	0.99	.221
2008	Indians (GCL)	R	4	2	2.87	11	11	0	0	53	46	5	13	43	7.3	1.11	.231
2009	Lake County (SAL)	LoA	5	7	4.44	21	20	0	0	107	114	10	40	65	5.5	1.43	.271
2010	Lake County (MWL)	LoA	1	1	4.45	7	7	0	0	32	34	7	13	23	6.4	1.45	—
2011	Indians (AZL)	R	0	0	2.70	5	5	0	0	7	6	1	2	11	14.9	1.20	.231
	Lake County (MWL)	LoA	0	2	3.38	3	3	0	0	8	8	0	2	7	7.9	1.25	.258
2012	Carolina (CAR)	HiA	3	2	2.68	16	16	0	0	54	46	3	19	53	8.9	1.21	.237
	Akron (EL)	AA	4	0	1.85	6	6	0	0	34	25	1	8	23	6.1	0.97	.203
Minor League Totals			20	17	3.20	83	82	0	0	360	331	28	109	274	6.9	1.22	.244

7 LUIGI RODRIGUEZ, OF

Born: Nov. 13, 1992. **B-T:** B-R. **Ht.:** 5-11. **Wt.:** 160. **Signed:** Dominican Republic, 2009. **Signed by:** Lino Diaz.

Rodriguez began his pro career as a second baseman. The infield never came naturally to him, however, so he moved to center field a month into his first season. He has held his own as a teenager in low Class A. Rodriguez is a plus-plus runner with good bat speed from both sides of the plate. Strikeouts weren't an issue early in his career, though his swing can get big and leads to too many strikeouts. He has surprising strength, though he'll probably never have more than average power. He does have a decent idea of the strike zone and is patient enough to take his walks. While his speed and athleticism give him the chance to make plays in center field, he's still learning how to take the right routes. His average arm is fine for center. Some scouts see Rodriguez as an everyday player in the big leagues, while others see him as more of a good fourth outfielder. After reaching low Class A at the end of the 2011 season as an 18-year-old, he was still one of the youngest players in the Midwest League last season, and he's ready to advance to high Class A at age 20.

BA GRADE: 50 HIGH

Year	Club (League)	Class	AVG	G	AB	R	H	2B	3B	HR	RBI	BB	SO	SB	CS	OBP	SLG
2010	Indians (DSL)	R	.301	63	206	43	62	7	10	2	27	36	35	31	9	.403	.461
2011	Indians (AZL)	R	.379	25	95	18	36	6	2	3	14	5	19	12	5	.408	.579
	Lake County (MWL)	LoA	.250	34	132	10	33	4	2	0	5	14	36	6	5	.320	.311
2012	Lake County (MWL)	LoA	.268	117	463	75	124	21	5	11	48	50	133	24	9	.338	.406
Minor League Totals			.285	239	896	146	255	38	19	16	94	105	223	73	28	.358	.423

8 RONNY RODRIGUEZ, SS/2B

Born: April 17, 1992. **B-T:** R-R. **Ht.:** 6-0. **Wt.:** 170. **Signed:** Dominican Republic, 2010. **Signed by:** Ramon Pena/Miguel Valdez.

Born in the Dominican Republic, Rodriguez moved to Lawrence, Mass., when he was 12 and attended high school in the United States before moving back to the island. He signed for $375,000 in 2010, making him the Indians' top international signing that year. His odd path is evident in his game, as Rodriguez stands out more for his tools than his refinement. He has plus raw power that has led to 30 homers in two years in Class A, but his free-swinging approach restricts his on-base ability. He has a tendency to step in the bucket and doesn't recognize breaking pitches well. Rodriguez also has plus speed, though his baserunning still needs work. He's a good athlete with a well above-average arm and the range to play shortstop, but he still makes way too many mistakes at the position, including 28 errors in 80 games in 2012. His footwork reduces the accuracy of his throws. Rodriguez will stay on the fast track, jumping to Double-A at age 21 in 2013. He has much to clean up, but he ultimately could profile along the lines of Clint Barmes or Khalil Greene as a shortstop with defensive promise who won't get on base much but flashes impressive power for the position.

BA GRADE: 50 HIGH

Year	Club (League)	Class	AVG	G	AB	R	H	2B	3B	HR	RBI	BB	SO	SB	CS	OBP	SLG
2011	Lake County (MWL)	LoA	.246	98	370	41	91	28	7	11	42	13	83	10	7	.274	.449
2012	Carolina (CAR)	HiA	.264	126	454	67	120	20	4	19	66	19	88	7	7	.300	.452
Minor League Totals			.256	224	824	108	211	48	11	30	108	32	171	17	14	.289	.450

9 JESUS AGUILAR, 1B

Born: June 30, 1990. **B-T:** R-R. **Ht.:** 6-3. **Wt.:** 257. **Signed:** Venezuela, 2007. **Signed by:** Jesus Mendoza.

Aguilar broke out in his fourth pro season, slamming 23 homers in Class A and performing well in the Arizona Fall League in 2011. He built upon that with a solid 2012 season that included a strong August showing in Double-A. The Indians left him off their 40-man roster, but teams passed on him in the Rule 5 draft. Aguilar's game is based around strength and power. He has plus raw pop and can drive the ball out of the park to all fields. He's not a rhythmic hitter, as he has an upper-body dominant swing and still needs work on his approach. He can get beat with good fastballs in on him, but if he learns to free up his hands, his power will show up more frequently in games. Some scouts think he needs to become better at recognizing breaking pitches, but he doesn't strike out excessively. Aguilar is a bottom-of-the-scale runner who lacks range and athleticism but has sure hands at first base. He did improve markedly at first base in 2012. Aguilar will head back to Akron to open the 2013 season. If he shows that his hitting approach will work at the upper levels, he could be in line for a shot at Cleveland's first-base job in 2014.

BA GRADE: 50 HIGH

Year	Club (League)	Class	AVG	G	AB	R	H	2B	3B	HR	RBI	BB	SO	SB	CS	OBP	SLG
2008	Indians (DSL)	R	.209	68	235	23	49	12	0	4	45	23	29	4	3	.286	.311
2009	Indians (DSL)	R	.305	55	200	33	61	16	0	5	46	31	24	5	1	.412	.460
2010	Indians (AZL)	R	.259	29	112	15	29	2	1	7	22	5	33	1	1	.293	.482
	Mahoning Valley (NYP)	SS	.244	32	123	8	30	9	0	2	17	11	28	2	0	.301	.366
2011	Lake County (MWL)	LoA	.292	95	349	58	102	27	2	19	69	35	98	1	0	.370	.544
	Kinston (CAR)	HiA	.257	31	113	12	29	3	0	4	13	11	28	1	0	.323	.389
2012	Carolina (CAR)	HiA	.277	107	368	63	102	25	2	12	58	45	91	0	1	.365	.454
	Akron (EL)	AA	.292	20	72	12	21	6	0	3	13	13	24	0	0	.402	.500
Minor League Totals			.269	437	1572	224	423	100	5	56	283	174	355	14	6	.350	.446

10 CHEN LEE, RHP

Born: Oct. 21, 1986. **B-T:** R-R. **Ht.:** 5-11. **Wt.:** 190. **Signed:** Taiwan, 2008. **Signed by:** Jason Lee.

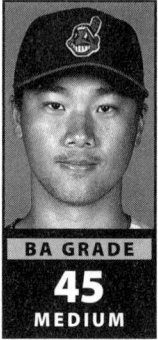

BA GRADE

45

MEDIUM

The Indians tried to sign Lee out of high school, but they had to wait until he attended college and pitched for Taiwan in the 2008 Olympics before landing him for $400,000. He pitched for Taiwan again in the 2009 World Baseball Classic as he steadily made his way up the ladder in the Indians minor league system. After a strong 2011 season, he was poised to make his major league debut in 2012. Instead, he blew out his elbow in Triple-A in April and had Tommy John surgery in June. When healthy, Lee has shown the ability to miss bats. He has averaged 11.0 strikeouts per nine innings in the minors, thanks to a lively fastball that sits at 92-93 mph and reaches 95. His velocity is unusually high for a pitcher with a low three-quarters arm slot, and his delivery adds to his deception. He keeps the ball down in the strike zone and gets groundballs. Lee's slider is inconsistent, getting him swings and misses at times but also flattening out when his low slot makes it difficult to stay on top of the pitch. He doesn't have a reliable weapon to combat lefthanders. His command is average, as he doesn't always locate his pitches as well as he'd like. Lee should return to game action by May or June. A potential big league set-up man, Lee was added to the 40-man roster and could get to Cleveland before the end of 2013 if he regains his previous form.

Year	Club (League)	Class	W	L	ERA	G	GS	CG	SV	IP	H	HR	BB	SO	K/9	WHIP	AVG
2009	Kinston (CAR)	HiA	4	6	3.35	45	0	0	2	83	67	5	28	97	10.5	1.14	.220
2010	Akron (EL)	AA	5	4	3.22	44	0	0	6	73	59	6	22	82	10.2	1.11	.219
2011	Akron (EL)	AA	2	1	2.50	23	0	0	0	40	27	1	11	56	12.7	0.96	.196
	Columbus (IL)	AAA	4	0	2.27	21	0	0	1	32	26	2	12	43	12.2	1.20	.228
2012	Columbus (IL)	AAA	2	0	2.57	5	0	0	0	7	5	1	1	8	10.3	0.86	.208
Minor League Totals			17	11	3.00	138	0	0	3	234	184	15	74	286	11.0	1.10	.216

11 SCOTT BARNES, LHP

BA GRADE

45

MEDIUM

Born: Sept. 5, 1987. **B-T:** L-L. **Ht.:** 6-4. **Wt.:** 200. **Drafted:** St. John's, 2008 (8th round). **Signed by:** John DiCarlo (Giants).

Barnes pitched well in the Giants system for two seasons before San Francisco shipped him to the Indians in exchange for Ryan Garko at the 2009 trade deadline. Barnes struggled in his first full season in the Cleveland system in 2010 but rebounded in 2011 before tearing the anterior cruciate ligament in his left knee while fielding a bunt. Moved to the bullpen full-time last season, he made his major league debut in May and bounced up and down between Cleveland and Columbus afterward. Barnes' fastball velocity plays up when he comes out of the bullpen, sitting in the low 90s and reaching 96 mph. He worked more at 88-92 as a starter. He leans heavily on his slider, which ranges from an average to plus pitch. He also mixes in a useable changeup, though he uses the pitch less as a reliever. He has some effort in his delivery, but he has gotten better at repeating it to be able to throw more strikes. During a September callup, Barnes didn't allow a run in his final nine innings with the Indians. He profiles as a middle reliever and should fill that role in Cleveland this year.

Year	Club (League)	Class	W	L	ERA	G	GS	CG	SV	IP	H	HR	BB	SO	K/9	WHIP	AVG
2008	Giants (AZL)	R	0	1	3.38	3	0	0	0	5	3	0	4	11	18.6	1.31	.167
	Salem-Keizer (NWL)	SS	0	0	4.76	2	1	0	0	6	6	0	1	11	17.5	1.24	.250
	Augusta (SAL)	LoA	3	2	1.38	6	6	0	0	33	15	0	7	41	11.3	0.67	.133
2009	San Jose (CAL)	HiA	12	3	2.85	18	18	0	0	98	82	7	29	99	9.1	1.13	.227
	Kinston (CAR)	HiA	0	0	2.13	3	3	0	0	13	14	1	6	10	7.1	1.58	.280
	Akron (EL)	AA	2	2	5.68	6	6	0	0	32	35	7	14	29	8.2	1.55	.292
2010	Akron (EL)	AA	6	11	5.22	26	26	0	0	138	126	15	58	127	8.3	1.33	.241
2011	Akron (EL)	AA	1	0	1.64	2	2	0	0	11	5	0	2	17	13.9	0.64	.139
	Columbus (IL)	AAA	7	4	3.68	16	15	0	0	88	80	12	34	90	9.2	1.30	.240
2012	Columbus (IL)	AAA	2	3	3.98	31	3	0	2	52	37	1	23	67	11.6	1.15	.196
	Cleveland (AL)	MAJ	0	0	4.26	16	0	0	0	19	17	1	7	16	7.6	1.26	.236
Major League Totals			0	0	4.26	16	0	0	0	19	17	1	7	16	7.6	1.26	.236
Minor League Totals			33	26	3.88	113	80	0	2	475	403	43	178	502	9.5	1.22	.228

12 LUIS LUGO, LHP

BA GRADE
50
HIGH

Born: March 5, 1994. **B-T:** L-L. **Ht.:** 6-5. **Wt.:** 200. **Signed:** Venezuela, 2011. **Signed by:** Ramon Pena/Antonio Caballero.

Lugo became eligible to sign on July 2, 2010, but he developed late and didn't sign until the following year. One of the top pitchers on the 2011 international market, he landed a $415,000 bonus. Lugo has an extra-large, projectable body that should help him add to his present 88-92 mph fastball. His arm works well and he could eventually throw in the mid-90s. Lugo has the stuff to miss bats, though his curveball and changeup are still inconsistent. He's a good athlete for his size and scouts like his competitiveness, but his control needs to improve. At this point, Lugo is more about projection than polish, but there are a lot of ingredients to like if added velocity comes with increased physical maturity. Given his age and lack of experience, the Indians may want to keep his workload down, so he may end up in short-season Mahoning Valley in 2013. That would still put him in line to make his full-season debut at age 20.

Year	Club (League)	Class	W	L	ERA	G	GS	CG	SV	IP	H	HR	BB	SO	K/9	WHIP	AVG
2011	Indians (DSL)	R	0	3	3.38	9	7	0	0	29	21	3	16	36	11.0	1.26	.194
	Indians (AZL)	R	0	2	6.14	3	2	0	0	7	10	1	8	8	9.8	2.45	.303
2012	Indians (AZL)	R	2	4	4.50	11	10	0	0	42	38	4	21	51	10.9	1.40	.242
Minor League Totals			2	9	4.23	23	19	0	0	79	69	8	45	95	10.9	1.45	.232

13 ANTHONY SANTANDER, OF

BA GRADE
50
HIGH

Born: Oct. 19, 1994. **B-T:** B-R. **Ht.:** 6-2. **Wt.:** 187. **Signed:** Venezuela, 2011. **Signed by:** Ramon Pena/Antonio Caballero.

After signing Santander for $385,000 out of Venezuela, the Indians pushed him to the Arizona League for his 2012 pro debut and he didn't disappoint with his performance. He began switch-hitting just about a year before he signed, so his strong showing was even more surprising given that the natural right-hander faced predominantly righty pitching in the AZL. He doesn't have a pure stroke from either side, but it works for him and he has curbed his tendency to overswing and try to do too much. With broad shoulders and a strong lower half, Santander has average raw power that could become plus as he matures physically. His speed and arm are average, so he's best suited for an outfield corner. He spent most of his debut playing left field, where he still needs to improve his reads and routes. He has a chance to start 2013 in low Class A as an 18-year-old.

Year	Club (League)	Class	AVG	G	AB	R	H	2B	3B	HR	RBI	BB	SO	SB	CS	OBP	SLG
2012	Indians (AZL)	R	.305	43	154	27	47	15	1	4	32	13	37	6	3	.381	.494
Minor League Totals			.305	43	154	27	47	15	1	4	32	13	37	6	3	.381	.494

14 TREY HALEY, RHP

BA GRADE
45
MEDIUM

Born: June 21, 1990. **B-T:** R-R. **Ht.:** 6-3. **Wt.:** 180. **Drafted:** HS—Nacogdoches, Texas (2nd round). **Signed by:** Kevin Cullen.

The Indians paid Haley $1.25 million as a second-round pick out of high school in 2008, an investment that quickly looked like it might not yield any return. After struggling as a starter, he moved to the bullpen in 2011, a transition that helped restore his prospect status. Despite missing two months in the middle of 2012 because he had surgery to repair a sports hernia in June, he had the best year of his career. After sitting at 88-92 mph and touching 95 when he started, Haley's fastball now operates at 93-98 mph, has touched 100 and features late, heavy life. His curveball had good depth to begin with, and he has added more power to it coming out of the bullpen. It shows flashes of becoming a plus offering. Haley's biggest obstacle is his lack of control, which stems from his delivery. He throws with effort and finishes with a head whack, so repeating his mechanics isn't easy for him. If he can develop even fringe-average control, he has the power stuff to eventually earn a major league bullpen role. Added to Cleveland's 40-man roster in November, he could open 2013 in Triple-A and make his big league debut later in the season.

Year	Club (League)	Class	W	L	ERA	G	GS	CG	SV	IP	H	HR	BB	SO	K/9	WHIP	AVG
2008	Indians (GCL)	R	0	0	0.00	1	1	0	0	1	0	0	1	1	9.0	1.00	.000
	Mahoning Valley (NYP)	SS	0	1	54.00	2	1	0	0	1	4	0	6	1	6.8	7.50	.571
2009	Lake County (SAL)	LoA	4	8	5.56	19	16	0	0	78	70	6	65	57	6.6	1.74	.241
2010	Lake County (MWL)	LoA	5	11	5.97	27	26	0	0	116	122	13	86	97	7.5	1.79	—
2011	Lake County (MWL)	LoA	0	0	2.84	8	2	0	1	13	5	0	8	17	12.1	1.03	.125
	Indians (AZL)	R	0	0	0.00	2	1	0	0	3	0	0	0	4	12.0	0.00	.000
	Kinston (CAR)	HiA	1	1	3.77	19	0	0	1	29	25	1	17	27	8.5	1.47	.240
2012	Indians (AZL)	R	1	0	7.50	4	0	0	0	6	8	0	2	10	15.0	1.67	.320
	Carolina (CAR)	HiA	0	0	1.04	12	0	0	2	17	8	0	6	16	8.3	0.81	.133
	Akron (EL)	AA	3	1	1.76	9	0	0	0	15	10	0	11	23	13.5	1.37	.189
Minor League Totals			14	22	5.13	103	47	0	4	279	252	20	202	253	8.2	1.63	.244

15 D'VONE McCLURE, OF

BA GRADE
50
HIGH

Born: Jan. 22, 1994. **B-T:** R-R. **Ht.:** 6-3. **Wt.:** 190. **Drafted:** HS—Jacksonville, Ark., 2012 (4th round). **Signed by:** Steve Abney.

McClure gained attention in 2011 when he got the better end of several Arkansas high school showdowns with righthander Dillon Howard, who would go on to sign for $1.85 million as the Indians' second-round pick that year. McClure went two rounds later last June, signed for $765,000 and became Howard's teammate in the Arizona League. An outstanding athlete, McClure attracted the interest of college football programs as a wide receiver. He has excellent bat speed and above-average raw power, though he's going to have to make adjustments to hit for average. He has a loose, handsy swing, but it gets long and leads to swings and misses. He's an average runner who sometimes turns in subpar times going from home to first. A center fielder for now, McClure has an average arm and will have to improve his instincts to stick there because he doesn't have prototypical speed for the position. He'll head to low Class A for his first full pro season.

Year	Club (League)	Class	AVG	G	AB	R	H	2B	3B	HR	RBI	BB	SO	SB	CS	OBP	SLG
2012	Indians (AZL)	R	.211	24	90	15	19	4	0	1	12	11	19	2	1	.305	.289
Minor League Totals			.211	24	90	15	19	4	0	1	12	11	19	2	1	.305	.289

16 DYLAN BAKER, RHP

BA GRADE
50
HIGH

Born: April 6, 1992. **B-T:** R-R. **Ht.:** 6-2. **Wt.:** 215. **Drafted:** Western Nevada JC, 2012 (5th round). **Signed by:** Don Lyle.

A graduate of Douglas High in Juneau, Alaska, Baker pitched at Tacoma (Wash.) CC in 2011 before transferring to Western Nevada JC. Baker pitched the Wildcats to the Junior College World Series, topping national juco players in strikeouts per nine innings (13.4). He became the highest-drafted player in school history and the second highest-drafted Alaska native ever (behind Braves 2000 fourth-rounder Brian Montalbo), signing with the Indians for $200,000 as a fifth-rounder. Baker has a strong, physical frame and a fastball that usually ranges from 90-95 mph and gets up to 97. He throws a hard slider that has a shorter, cutter-type break rather than true two-plane depth. He'll mix in a true curveball that peaks in the low 80s and an occasional changeup, but he's mainly a fastball/slider guy. He doesn't always stay on line to the plate and has some effort in his delivery, contributing factors in his struggles to throw strikes at times. Some scouts think he's best suited for a late-inning relief role, but the Indians want to see how he develops as a starter. He'll open his first full pro season in low Class A.

Year	Club (League)	Class	W	L	ERA	G	GS	CG	SV	IP	H	HR	BB	SO	K/9	WHIP	AVG
2012	Indians (AZL)	R	0	1	4.13	8	8	0	0	24	24	1	15	30	11.3	1.63	.255
Minor League Totals			0	1	4.13	8	8	0	0	24	24	1	15	30	11.3	1.63	.255

17 TONY WOLTERS, 2B/SS

BA GRADE
50
HIGH

Born: June 9, 1992. **B-T:** L-R. **Ht.:** 5-10. **Wt.:** 165. **Drafted:** HS—Vista, Calif., 2010, (3rd round). **Signed by:** Jason Smith.

Cleveland handed out four seven-figure bonuses in the 2010 draft, and only one of those recipients appears on this Top 30. First-rounder Drew Pomeranz went to the Rockies in the Ubaldo Jimenez trade, while second-rounder LeVon Washington and eighth-rounder Alex Lavisky haven't hit. That leaves Wolters, who signed for $1.35 million in the third round. Wolters didn't get his batting average get past .200 until May 22, but he rebounded to hit .291/.344/.474 in 64 games in the second half. He's a solid hitter who's at his best when he works the middle of the field and drives the ball into the gaps. He struggles when his front side flies open and can get into free-swinging mode, but he learned to manage his plate appearances better as the season progressed. Wolters broke his hamate bone in spring training in 2011, an injury that required surgery and sapped his power. He showed more pop in 2012 and has the potential to hit 10-15 homers annually in his prime. His above-average arm and clean hands fit at shortstop, but his fringy speed limits his range. Wolters could be an offensive-oriented second baseman, though he may be better suited as a backup. He'll advance to Double-A in 2013.

Year	Club (League)	Class	AVG	G	AB	R	H	2B	3B	HR	RBI	BB	SO	SB	CS	OBP	SLG
2010	Indians (AZL)	R	.211	5	19	2	4	0	0	0	3	2	5	2	0	.286	.211
2011	Mahoning Valley (NYP)	SS	.292	69	267	50	78	10	3	1	20	30	49	19	4	.385	.363
2012	Carolina (CAR)	HiA	.260	125	485	66	126	30	8	8	58	36	104	5	9	.320	.404
Minor League Totals			.270	199	771	118	208	40	11	9	81	68	158	26	13	.342	.385

18 CHRIS McGUINESS, 1B

BA GRADE
45
MEDIUM

Born: April 11, 1988. **B-T:** L-L. **Ht.:** 6-1. **Wt.:** 210. **Drafted:** The Citadel, 2009 (13th round). **Signed by:** Quincy Boyd (Red Sox).

When the Rangers shipped Jarrod Saltalamacchia to the Red Sox in July 2010, they received McGuiness and righthander Roman Mendez in return. An oblique strain, back strain and bruised knee limited him to just 55 games in 2011, but McGuinness got healthy and hit 23 homers to rank fourth in the Texas League, and he also finished fourth with 69 walks. The Rangers opted not to protect him on their 40-man roster after the season, and the Indians grabbed him in the major league Rule 5 draft. If he doesn't stick on the major league roster, he has to clear waivers and get offered back to Texas for half his $50,000 draft price. McGuiness stays inside the ball, hits with power to all fields and shows a disciplined approach. He gets through a hitch in his swing that doesn't seem to affect his timing. McGuiness will have to prove he can go deep outside of Frisco's Dr. Pepper Ballpark, where 18 of 23 homers came last year. Though he's not very athletic, he's a fine defensive first baseman with agility, good hands and an average arm. He's a well below-average runner.

Year	Club (League)	Class	AVG	G	AB	R	H	2B	3B	HR	RBI	BB	SO	SB	CS	OBP	SLG
2009	Greenville (SAL)	LoA	.150	6	20	2	3	1	0	0	1	3	5	0	0	.320	.200
2009	Lowell (NYP)	SS	.255	54	196	26	50	17	0	6	38	36	40	0	1	.374	.434
2010	Greenville (SAL)	LoA	.298	78	282	41	84	20	1	12	46	53	59	2	3	.416	.504
2010	Bakersfield (CAL)	HiA	.250	34	120	19	30	3	0	7	22	24	32	1	1	.381	.450
2011	Rangers (AZL)	Rk	.200	2	5	3	1	0	0	1	2	1	1	0	0	.429	.800
2011	Myrtle Beach (CAR)	HiA	.214	53	196	19	42	10	0	2	26	30	51	1	0	.320	.296
2012	Frisco (TL)	AA	.268	123	456	65	122	25	0	23	77	69	107	0	1	.366	.474
Minor League Totals			.260	350	1275	175	332	76	1	51	212	216	295	4	6	.373	.442

19 TIM FEDROFF, OF

BA GRADE
45
MEDIUM

Born: Feb. 4, 1987. **B-T:** R-L. **Ht.:** 5-11. **Wt.:** 220. **Drafted:** North Carolina, 2008 (7th round). **Signed by:** Bob Mayer.

The Indians spent $725,000 to sign Fedroff in 2008, but he has moved slower than expected. He has split the last two seasons between Double-A and Triple-A and was one of the International League's top hitters in the second half last year, which helped him claim a spot on the Indians' 40-man roster in November. Fedroff always has stood out for his compact swing, selective approach and ability to hit to all fields. He doesn't expand his strike zone but his lack of power has been an issue since he signed. He adjusted his set-up to be able to get to inside pitches more easily and pull them with more authority, and his 12 homers in 2012 exceeded his total for his four previous pro seasons. His pop still projects as fringy at best, however. Despite his stocky build, Fedroff is athletic and possesses average speed, showing even a little more quickness under way. He has split time between left field and center, but he struggles getting good reads off the bat, so he's better suited for left—where his lack of power limits his value. He'll be 26 this season and still has time to carve out a big league role as an extra outfielder.

Year	Club (League)	Class	AVG	G	AB	R	H	2B	3B	HR	RBI	BB	SO	SB	CS	OBP	SLG
2008	Mahoning Valley (NYP)	SS	.319	23	91	12	29	6	1	0	12	10	20	1	1	.382	.407
2009	Kinston (CAR)	HiA	.278	99	378	70	105	23	2	4	39	64	95	13	3	.383	.381
2010	Akron (EL)	AA	.274	118	445	65	122	19	5	4	36	48	90	7	5	.349	.366
2011	Akron (EL)	AA	.338	70	266	42	90	13	5	2	35	27	39	7	5	.399	.447
	Columbus (IL)	AAA	.272	62	224	29	61	15	1	1	28	35	35	3	2	.370	.362
2012	Akron (EL)	AA	.305	54	203	27	62	9	5	3	22	30	33	5	6	.396	.443
	Columbus (IL)	AAA	.325	69	265	52	86	14	5	9	32	31	45	9	0	.393	.517
Minor League Totals			.296	495	1872	297	555	99	24	23	204	245	357	45	22	.378	.412

20 SHAWN ARMSTRONG, RHP

BA GRADE
45
MEDIUM

Born: Sept. 11, 1990. **B-T:** R-R. **Ht.:** 6-2. **Wt.:** 210. **Drafted:** East Carolina, 2011 (18th round). **Signed by:** Bob Mayer.

Armstrong was North Carolina's top high school pitcher going into 2008, but a sore arm dropped his fastball from the low 90s to the high 80s. He chose to go to East Carolina rather than sign with the Astros as a 33rd-round pick, signing with the Indians three years later for $325,000 as an 18th-rounder. He has a 1.55 ERA as a pro and finished his first full season in Double-A, thanks to sneaky stuff that misses bats. Armstrong's fastball now parks in the low 90s and touches 95. He gets great extension, providing deception and generating swings and misses with his fastball. He throws a tight mid-80s slider that's inconsistent but can be an out pitch when he gets ahead in the count. He uses an occasional changeup that's just a show-me pitch. The key for Armstrong will be throwing more strikes, as he's averaged 4.8 walks per nine innings as a pro. If he improves his control, he could fit as a middle reliever and get a shot at a major league job in 2014.

Year	Club (League)	Class	W	L	ERA	G	GS	CG	SV	IP	H	HR	BB	SO	K/9	WHIP	AVG
2011	Mahoning Valley (NYP)	SS	0	0	0.00	1	0	0	0	2	1	0	0	2	9.0	0.50	.167
2012	Lake County (MWL)	LoA	0	0	0.00	2	0	0	0	4	1	0	2	4	9.8	0.82	.091
	Carolina (CAR)	HiA	1	3	2.06	26	0	0	1	44	31	0	23	52	10.7	1.24	.205
	Akron (EL)	AA	1	0	0.89	17	0	0	3	20	12	0	12	22	9.7	1.18	.176
Minor League Totals			2	3	1.55	46	0	0	4	70	45	0	37	80	10.3	1.18	.191

21 KIERAN LOVEGROVE, RHP

BA GRADE
50
HIGH

Born: July 28, 1994. **B-T:** R-R. **Ht.:** 6-4. **Wt.:** 185. **Drafted:** HS—Mission Viejo, Calif., 2012 (3rd round). **Signed by:** Jason Smith.

Scouts had a hard time getting a read on Lovegrove out of high school, as he flashed plus stuff at times but not on a consistent basis. The Indians drafted him in the third round in June and paid him a $400,000 bonus. At his best, Lovegrove will operate in the low 90s with his fastball, but it ranges anywhere from 86-94 mph. With his big, projectable frame, more velocity may come. He showed a wicked mid-80s slider as the draft approached, but it usually has slurvier break. The slider has two-plane break, so if he can tighten it up, it can be a putaway pitch. He also shows the beginnings of a changeup. There are questions about Lovegrove's durability, as he needs to show that he can maintain his velocity from inning to inning as well as throughout a full season. His inconsistency might stem from his unorthodox delivery, which is complicated and includes a short stride. He may not be ready for an assignment to low Class A, so Mahoning Valley could be his next destination.

Year	Club (League)	Class	W	L	ERA	G	GS	CG	SV	IP	H	HR	BB	SO	K/9	WHIP	AVG
2012	Indians (AZL)	R	0	2	6.00	8	7	0	0	21	28	1	9	18	7.7	1.76	.318
Minor League Totals			0	2	6.00	8	7	0	0	21	28	1	9	18	7.7	1.76	.318

22 GIOVANNY URSHELA, 3B

BA GRADE
50
HIGH

Born: Oct. 11, 1991. **B-T:** R-R. **Ht.:** 6-0. **Wt.:** 197. **Signed:** Colombia, 2008. **Signed by:** Jose Quintero.

When Urshela signed with the Indians for $300,000 in 2008, he was one of the top prospects out of Colombia. His biggest strength so far has been his defense, which has the potential to be well above-average. He's a smooth defender with range to his left and down the line, clean hands, good instincts and a plus-plus arm. His hand-eye coordination is evident in the field, though in some ways it hampers him at the plate. Urshela doesn't swing and miss much, but because his he puts the bat on the ball so easily, he gets himself in trouble by expanding the strike zone rather than waiting for a good pitch to hit. He has raw power that could develop into average or slightly better pop, which he hinted at with a career-high 14 homers in 2012, but he must become less of a free swinger. He's a below-average runner. Still young, Urshela should make the jump to Double-A at age 21 this year.

Year	Club (League)	Class	AVG	G	AB	R	H	2B	3B	HR	RBI	BB	SO	SB	CS	OBP	SLG
2009	Indians (DSL)	R	.269	27	108	10	29	8	1	1	24	7	14	2	2	.316	.389
	Indians (AZL)	R	.257	32	105	10	27	2	0	0	11	10	12	3	0	.322	.276
2010	Mahoning Valley (NYP)	SS	.290	58	221	22	64	8	0	3	35	12	32	5	3	.326	.367
2011	Lake County (MWL)	LoA	.238	126	505	57	120	24	2	9	46	14	69	3	0	.262	.347
2012	Carolina (CAR)	HiA	.278	114	439	50	122	30	1	14	59	16	60	1	1	.309	.446
Minor League Totals			.263	357	1378	149	362	72	4	27	175	59	187	14	6	.296	.380

23 JOSE RAMIREZ, 2B

BA GRADE
45
HIGH

Born: Sept. 17, 1992. **B-T:** B-R. **Ht.:** 5-9. **Wt.:** 165. **Signed:** Dominican Republic, 2009. **Signed by:** Lino Diaz/Omar Rogers.

Only 5-foot-9, Ramirez is undersized but has managed to garner attention by hitting .342/.383/.459 through two minor league seasons. With his size, he doesn't have much of a strike zone, but what's there he covers well. He's difficult to strike out, showing natural hand-eye coordination along with good bat speed from both sides of the plate and the ability to hit line drives to all fields. He also has plus-plus speed. Ramirez has little power and minimal physical projection, so some scouts worry that more advanced pitchers will eat him up. He's a solid defender at second base who makes the routine plays and turns the double play well. He endears himself to managers with how hard he plays. Ramirez lacks a high ceiling, but he's a well-rounded player who may continue to surprise as he moves through the system. He's ready for high Class A at age 20.

Year	Club (League)	Class	AVG	G	AB	R	H	2B	3B	HR	RBI	BB	SO	SB	CS	OBP	SLG
2010	Did Not Play																
2011	Indians (AZL)	R	.325	48	194	30	63	13	4	1	20	7	17	12	6	.351	.448
2012	Mahoning Valley (NYP)	SS	.364	3	11	2	4	2	0	0	0	1	0	2	1	.417	.545
	Lake County (MWL)	LoA	.354	67	277	54	98	13	4	3	27	24	26	15	6	.403	.462
Minor League Totals			.342	118	482	86	165	28	8	4	47	32	43	29	13	.383	.459

24 AUSTIN ADAMS, RHP

BA GRADE
50
EXTREME

Born: Aug. 19, 1986. **B-T:** R-R. **Ht.:** 5-11. **Wt.:** 190. **Drafted:** Faulkner (Ala.), 2009 (5th round). **Signed by:** Chuck Bartlett.

Adams rode his fastball to the No. 8 spot on this list a year ago, but he ended up losing the entire 2012 season. He experienced a shoulder impingement in spring training, and when he tried to start throwing again in May his shoulder still bothered him, and by the end of the month he had surgery. A two-way player as a shortstop and pitcher at NAIA Faulkner (Ala.), Adams became a full-time pitcher as a senior before signing for $70,000 in 2009. Before his injury, he delivered fastballs that sat in the mid-90s and reached 100 mph. Both his curveball and a slider show signs of becoming average pitches, with the slider the better of his two breaking balls. He also throws a below-average changeup. The lost development time is especially damaging for Adams, who is still raw as a pitcher. He has shown the athleticism to make mechanical adjustments. He does throw across his body, which may have contributed to his shoulder woes and hampers his control. Shoulder injuries are more worrisome than elbow maladies, so Adams will have to show his fastball is still there when he returns. Already 26 and having never topped 136 innings in a season, his future may be in the bullpen.

Year	Club (League)	Class	W	L	ERA	G	GS	CG	SV	IP	H	HR	BB	SO	K/9	WHIP	AVG
2009	Mahoning Valley (NYP)	SS	3	1	4.86	17	0	0	1	37	39	4	15	29	7.1	1.46	.269
2010	Lake County (MWL)	LoA	2	4	3.54	13	8	0	1	53	40	7	21	61	10.3	1.14	—
	Kinston (CAR)	HiA	6	1	1.53	13	12	0	0	59	50	5	15	51	7.8	1.11	.228
2011	Akron (EL)	AA	11	10	3.77	26	26	0	0	136	147	6	63	131	8.7	1.54	.280
2012	Did Not Play—Injured																
Minor League Totals			22	16	3.41	69	46	0	2	285	276	22	114	272	8.6	1.37	.255

25 DILLON HOWARD, RHP

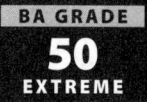

BA GRADE
50
EXTREME

Born: July 1, 1992. **B-T:** R-R. **Ht.:** 6-4. **Wt.:** 210. **Drafted:** HS—Searcy, Ark., 2011, (2nd round). **Signed by:** Steve Abney.

A projected first-rounder in the 2011 draft, Howard had a so-so high school senior season and scared some teams off with his bonus expectations. After the Indians signed him for a $1.85 million bonus in the second round, his 2012 pro debut was the biggest disappointment in the system. He arrived at spring training out of shape and didn't make a full-season club. Nearly 20 when he arrived in the Arizona League, he got hammered for a 7.90 ERA. While that was a disaster, Cleveland also hopes it was a wakeup call for Howard. He dealt with elbow and knee issues, as well as an illness early in the year that cut into his weight and strength. As a result, his fastball often sat at 85-88 mph, though he did get back to touching 92 mph by the end of the year. In high school, he regularly threw in the low 90s. Howard induced a lot of grounders in the AZL, but his typically lively two-seamer flattened out and became hittable. Scouts from other organizations had concerns about his fastball command as an amateur that were borne out in his debut. Howard flashes an average changeup, but he wasn't ahead in enough counts to use the pitch. His curveball is slurvy because he has trouble staying on top of it. If Howard can return to his 2011 form, he'll still have the potential to be a solid starter, but his regression in 2012 was troubling.

Year	Club (League)	Class	W	L	ERA	G	GS	CG	SV	IP	H	HR	BB	SO	K/9	WHIP	AVG
2012	Indians (AZL)	R	1	7	7.90	12	10	0	0	41	65	3	18	35	7.7	2.02	.348
Minor League Totals			1	7	7.90	12	10	0	0	41	65	3	18	35	7.7	2.02	.348

26 ELVIS ARAUJO, LHP

BA GRADE
50
EXTREME

Born: July 15, 1991. **B-T:** L-L. **Ht.:** 6-6. **Wt.:** 215. **Signed:** Venezuela, 2007. **Signed by:** Otilio Chourio.

When the Indians signed Araujo for $125,000 on his 16th birthday in 2007, their scouts saw a long-limbed lefthander oozing projection. Yet after a promising 2008 pro debut in the Dominican Summer League, he didn't pitch in a game for another two years. He had Tommy John surgery that cost him the 2009 season, followed by a setback in his recovery that prevented him from taking the mound in 2010. When he returned in 2011, his fastball jumped to as high as 98 mph. Araujo's heater still sits around 90-94 mph with heavy life. The rest of his game is still raw, however. He throws a slider that's average at times and sweepy at others. He doesn't have much of a changeup yet. Araujo's arm action is long and he has trouble repeating an unorthodox delivery, which is why he doesn't throw enough strikes. The Indians didn't protect Araujo on the 40-man roster, but he didn't get picked in the Rule 5 draft. Throwing a career-high 135 innings in 2012 was a big step for Araujo, but he is likely to end up a reliever. For now, Araujo will remain in the rotation and advance to high Class A.

Year	Club (League)	Class	W	L	ERA	G	GS	CG	SV	IP	H	HR	BB	SO	K/9	WHIP	AVG
2008	Indians (DSL)	R	4	2	1.89	14	14	0	0	57	46	0	23	37	5.8	1.21	.230
2009	Did Not Play—Injured																
2010	Did Not Play—Injured																

2011	Indians (AZL)	R	9	1	2.86	13	11	0	0	63	54	2	18	58	8.3	1.14	.228
	Mahoning Valley (NYP)	SS	0	0	8.10	2	2	0	0	7	11	0	7	5	6.8	2.70	.393
2012	Lake County (MWL)	LoA	7	10	5.00	28	28	1	0	135	141	7	61	111	7.4	1.50	.270
Minor League Totals			20	13	3.89	57	55	1	0	262	252	9	109	211	7.3	1.38	.255

27 YAN GOMES, C/1B/3B

BA GRADE
45
MEDIUM

Born: July 19, 1987. **B-T:** R-R. **Ht.:** 6-2. **Wt.:** 215. **Drafted:** Barry (Fla.), 2009 (10th round). **Signed by:** Carlos Rodriguez (Blue Jays).

Gomes was a highly regarded recruit for Tennessee, but transferred to NCAA Division II Barry (Fla.) for his junior season. He hit .405 with 21 homers and a school-record 92 RBIs before signing with the Blue Jays for $85,000 in the 2009 draft. He became the first Brazilian ever to play in the major leagues when he reached Toronto last May. In November, he joined the Indians along with Mike Aviles in a trade for Esmil Rogers before playing for Brazil in a World Baseball Classic qualifier. Gomes generates good bat speed that produces solid power. His hands are high in his load, which can create a little length to his swing, but he's pretty direct to the ball and has shown the ability to make adjustments. Gomes' primary position is catcher, and he has seen action on both infield corners and brief time in left field. He has good hands and feet that allow him to provide solid defense behind the plate. He also has an average arm and threw out 23 percent of Triple-A basestealers in 2012. He's a below-average runner but moves decently for his size. Gomes may not quite profile as a regular, but he could be useful as a backup catcher who can play multiple positions and provide power.

Year	Club (League)	Class	AVG	G	AB	R	H	2B	3B	HR	RBI	BB	SO	SB	CS	OBP	SLG
2009	Blue Jays (GCL)	R	.357	4	14	1	5	0	0	0	2	3	2	0	0	.471	.357
	Auburn (NYP)	SS	.296	60	223	22	66	23	2	2	44	22	37	0	2	.363	.444
2010	Lansing (MWL)	LoA	.231	7	26	2	6	2	0	0	8	3	11	0	0	.290	.308
	Dunedin (FSL)	HiA	.275	68	233	37	64	21	1	9	40	9	64	0	0	.312	.489
2011	Las Vegas (PCL)	AAA	.214	4	14	1	3	1	0	0	1	1	4	0	0	.267	.286
	New Hampshire (EL)	AA	.250	79	276	34	69	18	1	13	51	25	75	0	0	.317	.464
2012	Las Vegas (PCL)	AAA	.328	79	305	44	100	29	1	13	59	25	72	4	0	.380	.557
	Toronto (AL)	MAJ	.204	43	98	9	20	4	0	4	13	6	32	0	0	.264	.367
Major League Totals			.204	43	98	9	20	4	0	4	13	6	32	0	0	.264	.367
Minor League Totals			.287	301	1091	141	313	94	5	37	205	88	265	4	2	.344	.484

28 THOMAS NEAL, OF

BA GRADE
45
MEDIUM

Born: Aug. 17, 1987. **B-T:** R-R. **Ht.:** 6-2. **Wt.:** 220. **Drafted:** Riverside (Calif.) CC, D/F 2005 (36th round). **Signed by:** Lee Carballo (Giants).

Signing with the Giants through the now defunct draft-and-follow process, Neal earned a $220,000 bonus in 2006 after getting selected in the 36th round the year before. He had his breakout year in 2009, when he led the high Class A California League with a .431 on-base percentage, but his stock had dropped by the time San Francisco traded him to Cleveland for Orlando Cabrera in July 2011. After spending most of 2011 in Triple-A, Neal went back down to Double-A last year, had a nice season and made his major league debut as a September callup. He has a quick bat and takes an aggressive swing, though he does show enough selectivity not to chase too many pitches out of the strike zone. He can handle balls in on his hands and his plate coverage is solid, though his average power isn't prototypical for a corner outfielder. Neal is athletic for a man his size, but with his below-average speed and arm strength, he's limited to left field. Most scouts don't think he has enough offensive potential to hold down an everyday job, but a big year in Triple-A in 2013 could help him get back to the big leagues.

Year	Club (League)	Class	AVG	G	AB	R	H	2B	3B	HR	RBI	BB	SO	SB	CS	OBP	SLG
2006	Salem-Keizer (NWL)	SS	.250	50	176	26	44	6	2	4	20	7	44	1	3	.289	.375
2007	Giants (AZL)	R	.308	10	39	7	12	3	0	1	4	5	7	0	0	.413	.462
2008	Augusta (SAL)	LoA	.276	117	428	69	118	25	1	15	81	48	103	3	4	.359	.444
2009	San Jose (CAL)	HiA	.337	129	475	102	160	41	4	22	90	65	98	3	0	.431	.579
2010	Richmond (EL)	AA	.291	136	525	69	153	40	1	12	69	46	94	11	5	.359	.440
2011	Fresno (PCL)	AAA	.295	60	220	35	65	13	3	2	25	13	50	7	6	.351	.409
	Columbus (IL)	AAA	.250	10	36	5	9	1	0	0	1	1	7	1	0	.289	.278
2012	Akron (EL)	AA	.314	117	405	77	127	24	1	12	51	46	71	11	8	.400	.467
	Cleveland (AL)	MAJ	.217	9	23	2	5	1	0	0	2	0	6	0	0	.250	.261
Major League Totals			.217	9	23	2	5	1	0	0	2	0	6	0	0	.250	.261
Minor League Totals			.299	629	2304	390	688	153	12	68	341	231	474	37	26	.376	.464

29 CODY ANDERSON, RHP

BA GRADE
45
HIGH

Born: Sept. 14, 1990. **B-T:** R-R. **Ht.:** 6-4. **Wt.:** 220. **Drafted:** Feather River (Calif.) JC, 2011 (14th round). **Signed by:** Don Lyle.

Anderson expressed interest in going on a Mormon mission while at Feather River (Calif.) JC, and he turned down the Rays as a 17th-round pick in 2010. The Indians drafted him three rounds earlier in 2011, signing him away from a Texas Christian commitment for $250,000. Because Anderson threw just 40 innings in two years as a juco reliever, Cleveland limited him to just 98 innings. Anderson's best pitch is a lively 89-94 mph fastball that touches 96, leveraging the ball downhill from a high three-quarters slot. He doesn't have the secondary stuff to rack up big strikeout numbers. His curveball shows occasional downward action but falls into more of a three-quarters break at times. He'll mix in a cutter to try to offset lefties. Despite his relative inexperience, his arm works well and he's able to repeat his delivery to spot his fastball throughout the zone. The Indians envision him as a potential back-of-the-rotation starter, and he'll move up to high Class A in 2013.

Year	Club (League)	Class	W	L	ERA	G	GS	CG	SV	IP	H	HR	BB	SO	K/9	WHIP	AVG
2011	Mahoning Valley (NYP)	SS	0	0	1.80	3	1	0	0	5	4	0	4	3	5.4	1.60	.235
2012	Lake County (MWL)	LoA	4	7	3.20	24	23	0	0	98	92	8	29	72	6.6	1.23	.249
Minor League Totals			4	7	3.14	27	24	0	0	103	96	8	33	75	6.5	1.25	.248

30 JORDAN SMITH, OF

BA GRADE
45
HIGH

Born: July 5, 1990. **B-T:** L-R. **Ht.:** 6-4. **Wt.:** 205. **Drafted:** St. Cloud State (Minn.), 2011 (9th round). **Signed by:** Les Pajari.

Wherever Smith goes, he has shown the ability to hit, be it at NCAA Division II St. Cloud State (Minn.), the collegiate Northwoods League in the summer of 2010 or with the Indians. Smith is quiet in the box with good rhythm and balance at the plate. He manages his plate appearances well and uses the whole field. He has an easy, natural swing and uses his hands well, but with his size there's a natural tendency for his stroke to get long. Smith has a hit-first, power-second profile with average raw pop. He could become a more complete offensive player once he learns to pull with more authority. Smith spent time at third base in college and during his pro debut before becoming a right fielder in 2012. He's a below-average runner but has a solid arm. If his power comes around, Smith has the potential to be a late-round gem. He's ready for high Class A in 2013.

Year	Club (League)	Class	AVG	G	AB	R	H	2B	3B	HR	RBI	BB	SO	SB	CS	OBP	SLG
2011	Mahoning Valley (NYP)	SS	.300	65	243	36	73	20	1	0	47	35	30	3	1	.403	.391
2012	Lake County (MWL)	LoA	.316	116	468	70	148	23	7	9	74	35	52	9	3	.367	.453
Minor League Totals			.311	181	711	106	221	43	8	9	121	70	82	12	4	.380	.432

Colorado Rockies

BY JACK ETKIN

The Rockies plumbed new depths in 2012, compiling the worst record in franchise history at 64-98, so significant changes were probably to be expected.

After reaching the playoffs in 2009 when Jim Tracy took over as manager in May, Colorado has been in steady decline, going from 92 wins to 83 to 73 to 64. The organization has tried various fixes without success, so it got radical in 2012.

In mid-June, the Rockies implemented a four-man rotation and allotted each starter about 80 pitches. That plan reduced the opportunity for valuable side  work between starts, among other problems, and was scrapped after two months.

The pitching staff ended the season with a 5.22 ERA, the highest in the majors and the team's worst since 2004, as the organization continues to struggle with the vagaries of playing at altitude. Colorado's 35-46 record at Coors Field last season was its worst ever, and its starters' ERA at home was 6.70.

In August, general manager Dan O'Dowd and assistant GM Bill Geivett essentially switched responsibilities, with O'Dowd shifting his focus to player development and scouting while keeping the GM title. Geivett became senior director of major league operations and established an office in the clubhouse conference room, where he exerted significant influence over just about everything associated with the team except game management.

Uncomfortable with his reduced authority under the new front-office arrangement, Tracy resigned after the season, walking away from the $1.4 million salary he had coming in 2013. To replace him, the Rockies hired Walt Weiss, the shortstop on their first-ever playoff club in 1995 and a former special assistant to O'Dowd for seven years, most recently in 2008. Weiss hasn't managed or coached professionally, and he had coached a Denver-area high school team for one successful season when hired.

Colorado has a long history of loyalty to its employees, so the one-year deal Weiss received is less significant than it seems. He has the pedigree of playing most of his career for Tony La Russa and Bobby Cox, and he's familiar with the organization.

Amid the rubble, there was some good news. Injuries created big league opportunities for a host of relatively inexperienced position players. Charlie Blackmon, Tyler Colvin, D.J. LeMahieu, Chris

Shortstop Josh Rutledge hit well for the Rockies in the second half of the season

MIKE JANES

Nelson, Jordan Pacheco, Wilin Rosario, Josh Rutledge and Eric Young Jr.—none older than 27—got the at-bats to show that they have major league value.

However, the big leagues were a struggle for young starters Tyler Chatwood, Christian Friedrich, Drew Pomeranz and Alex White. In another effort to solve their pitching conundrum, the Rockies hired Mark Wiley to the newly created position of director of pitching operations in October. He's another former special assistant to O'Dowd and will work closely with him to find a way to develop effective pitchers in Colorado.

Four of the Rockies' six U.S.-based minor league affiliates made the playoffs in 2012 as the organization puts three highly unproductive drafts from 2006-08 further in its rear-view mirror. Recent efforts have infused more talent into the system.

Closer-in-waiting Rex Brothers and third baseman Nolan Arenado (the system's top prospect) were drafted in 2009, followed by outfielder Kyle Parker, righthander Chad Bettis (its best pitching prospect) and Rutledge in 2010. Lefthander Tyler Anderson and shortstop/third baseman Trevor Story were the top selections in 2011, while 2012 first-rounder David Dahl won Rookie-level Pioneer League MVP honors in his pro debut.

THIS YEAR'S TOP 30

	Player, Pos.	Grade
1.	Nolan Arenado, 3b	55/Medium
2.	David Dahl, of	60/High
3.	Trevor Story, ss/3b	55/High
4.	Kyle Parker, of	50/High
5.	Chad Bettis, rhp	50/High
6.	Eddie Butler, rhp	50/High
7.	Tyler Anderson, lhp	50/High
8.	Tyler Matzek, lhp	55/Extreme
9.	Jayson Aquino, lhp	50/High
10.	Ryan Wheeler, 3b/1b/of	45/Low
11.	Tim Wheeler, of	45/Medium
12.	Rob Scahill, rhp	45/Medium
13.	Corey Dickerson, of	50/High
14.	Tom Murphy, c	50/High
15.	Rafael Ortega, of	50/High
16.	Kent Matthes, of	50/High
17.	Edwar Cabrera, lhp	45/Medium
18.	Josh Sullivan, rhp	45/Medium
19.	Cristhian Adames, ss	50/High
20.	Julian Yan, of	50/High
21.	Will Swanner, c	50/High
22.	Danny Rosenbaum, lhp	45/Medium
23.	Harold Riggins, 1b	50/High
24.	Seth Willoughby, rhp	50/High
25.	Max White, of	50/High
26.	Ryan Warner, rhp	50/Extreme
27.	Wilfredo Rodriguez, c	50/Extreme
28.	Christian Bergman, rhp	45/Medium
29.	Peter Tago, rhp	50/Extreme
30.	Parker Frazier, rhp	40/Medium

LAST YEAR'S TOP 30

	Player, Pos.	Status
1.	Drew Pomeranz, lhp	Majors
2.	Nolan Arenado, 3b	No. 1
3.	Chad Bettis, rhp	No. 5
4.	Wilin Rosario, c	Majors
5.	Tim Wheeler, of	No. 11
6.	Trevor Story, ss/3b	No. 3
7.	Tyler Anderson, lhp	No. 7
8.	Kent Matthes, of	No. 16
9.	Kyle Parker, of	No. 4
10.	Josh Rutledge, ss	Majors
11.	Charlie Blackmon, of	Majors
12.	Tyler Matzek, lhp	No. 8
13.	D.J. LeMahieu, 3b/2b	Majors
14.	Christian Friedrich, lhp	Majors
15.	Peter Tago, rhp	No. 29
16.	Rosell Herrera, ss/3b	Dropped out
17.	Jordan Pacheco, c/1b/3b	Majors
18.	Edwar Cabrera, lhp	No. 17
19.	Hector Gomez, ss	(Brewers)
20.	Cristhian Adames, ss	No. 19
21.	Will Swanner, c	No. 21
22.	Rafael Ortega, of	No. 15
23.	Ben Paulsen, 1b	Dropped out
24.	Rob Scahill, rhp	No. 12
25.	Joe Gardner, rhp	Dropped out
26.	Jayson Aquino, lhp	No. 9
27.	Tommy Field, 2b/ss	(Angels)
28.	Parker Frazier, rhp	No. 30
29.	Coty Woods, rhp	(Rangers)
30.	Michael Marbry, rhp	Dropped out

BEST TOOLS

Best Hitter for Average	Nolan Arenado
Best Power Hitter	Kyle Parker
Best Strike-Zone Discipline	Kyle Parker
Fastest Baserunner	Max White
Best Athlete	David Dahl
Best Fastball	Eddie Butler
Best Curveball	Tyler Matzek
Best Slider	Chad Bettis
Best Changeup	Edwar Cabrera
Best Control	Tyler Anderson
Best Defensive Catcher	Lars Davis
Best Defensive Infielder	Nolan Arenado
Best Infield Arm	Nolan Arenado
Best Defensive Outfielder	Rafael Ortega
Best Outfield Arm	Julian Yan

PROJECTED 2016 LINEUP

Catcher	Wilin Rosario
First Base	Nolan Arenado
Second Base	Josh Rutledge
Third Base	Troy Tulowitzki
Shortstop	Trevor Story
Left Field	Dexter Fowler
Center Field	David Dahl
Right Field	Carlos Gonzalez
No. 1 Starter	Drew Pomeranz
No. 2 Starter	Jhoulys Chacin
No. 3 Starter	Chad Bettis
No. 4 Starter	Eddie Butler
No. 5 Starter	Tyler Anderson
Closer	Rex Brothers

TOP PROSPECTS OF THE DECADE

Year	Player, Pos.	2012 Org.
2003	Aaron Cook, rhp	Red Sox
2004	Chin-Hui Tsao, rhp	Out of baseball
2005	Ian Stewart, 3b	Cubs
2006	Ian Stewart, 3b	Cubs
2007	Troy Tulowitzki, ss	Rockies
2008	Franklin Morales, lhp	Red Sox
2009	Dexter Fowler, of	Rockies
2010	Tyler Matzek, lhp	Rockies
2011	Drew Pomeranz, lhp	Rockies
2012	Drew Pomeranz, lhp	Rockies

TOP DRAFT PICKS OF THE DECADE

Year	Player, Pos.	2012 Org.
2003	Ian Stewart, 3b	Cubs
2004	Chris Nelson, ss	Rockies
2005	Troy Tulowitzki, ss	Rockies
2006	Greg Reynolds, rhp	Rangers
2007	Casey Weathers, rhp	Cubs
2008	Christian Friedrich, lhp	Rockies
2009	Tyler Matzek, lhp	Rockies
2010	Kyle Parker, of	Rockies
2011	Tyler Anderson, lhp	Rockies
2012	David Dahl, of	Rockies

LARGEST BONUSES IN CLUB HISTORY

Tyler Matzek, 2009	$3,900,000
Greg Reynolds, 2006	$3,250,000
Jason Young, 2000	$2,750,000
David Dahl, 2012	$2,600,000
Troy Tulowitzki, 2005	$2,300,000

COLORADO ROCKIES

TOP 2013 ROOKIE: Rob Scahill, rhp. He has the stuff and versatility to help the Rockies as a starter or reliever.

BREAKOUT PROSPECT: Tom Murphy, c. A third-round pick in June, he has intriguing power plus the raw tools to be a solid defender behind the plate.

SLEEPER: Mike Mason, lhp. The 24th-round pick from 2012 hit 95 mph when he moved to the bullpen in his pro debut.

SOURCE OF TOP 30 TALENT

Homegrown	28	Acquired	2
College	12	Trades	1
Junior college	1	Rule 5 draft	1
High school	10	Independent leagues	0
Nondrafted free agents	0	Free agents/waivers	0
International	5		

LF
Corey Dickerson (13)
Carl Thomore
Dillon Thomas
Derek Jones

CF
David Dahl (2)
Rafael Ortega (15)
Max White (25)
Michael Mitchell
Kyle Von Tungeln

RF
Kyle Parker (4)
Tim Wheeler (11)
Kent Matthes (16)
Julian Yan (20)
Matt McBride

3B
Nolan Arenado (1)
Ryan Wheeler (10)
Sam Mende
Brett Tanos
Joey Wong
Matt Wessinger

SS
Trevor Story (3)
Cristhian Adames (19)
Rosell Herrera
Matt Wessinger

2B
Angelys Nina
Taylor Featherston
Juan Ciriaco
Tim Smalling

1B
Harold Riggins (23)
Ben Paulsen
Corelle Prime
Jordan Ribera
Jared Clark

C
Tom Murphy (14)
Will Swanner (21)
Wilfredo Rodriguez (27)
Lars Davis
Jose Gonzalez
Ryan Casteel
Dustin Garneau

LHP

LHSP	LHRP
Tyler Anderson (7)	Mike Mason
Tyler Matzek (8)	Isaiah Froneberger
Jayson Aquino (9)	Ken Roberts
Edwar Cabrera (17)	Kraig Sitton
Danny Rosenbaum (22)	Craig Bennigson
Roberto Padilla	

RHP

RHSP	RHRP
Chad Bettis (5)	Josh Sullivan (18)
Eddie Butler (6)	Seth Willoughby (24)
Rob Scahill (12)	Joe Gardner
Ryan Warner (26)	Scott Oberg
Christian Bergman (28)	Mike Marbry
Peter Tago (29)	Raul Fernandez
Parker Frazier (30)	Adam Jorgenson
Ben Hughes	Stephen Dodson
Chris Jensen	Tyler Gagnon
Ben Alsup	Nelson Gonzalez
Dan Houston	Jefri Hernandez
Dan Winkler	Jesse Meaux
Matt Carasiti	Rayan Gonzalez
Zach Jemiola	Chad Rose
T.J. Oakes	Nick Schnaitmann
Shane Broyles	

2012   BONUSES: $7.0 MILLION

BEST PURE HITTER: OF David Dahl (1) showed a natural feel for hitting against older college competition by leading the Rookie-level Pioneer League in batting at .379.

BEST POWER HITTER: C Tom Murphy (3) set a Buffalo record with 13 homers in the spring and went deep six times at short-season Tri-City. Dahl may catch up to Murphy once he matures physically, and 1B Ben Waldrip (10) also is packed with raw power.

FASTEST RUNNER: OF Max White (2) runs the 60-yard dash in 6.5 seconds and has Steve Finley upside. Dahl is nearly as fast.

BEST DEFENSIVE PLAYER: INF Matt Wessinger (5) has the range and arm strength to be a solid defender anywhere in the infield. Dahl has good range and uncommon arm strength for a center fielder.

BEST FASTBALL: RHP Eddie Butler (1s) threw 94-95 and topped out at 97 all summer, with sinking life that was just as impressive as his velocity. He reached 99 during instructional league. RHPs Seth Willoughby (4) and Matt Carasiti (6) hit the mid-90s during the college season but were worn down a bit in their pro debuts.

BEST SECONDARY PITCH: Willoughby wasn't on many follow lists and was slated to double as a shortstop and reliever at Xavier entering the year. He focused on pitching after he broke his left hamate bone in the third game of the season, and his stuff took off, with his 88-90 mph cutter becoming unhittable.

BEST PRO DEBUT: Dahl was the MVP and top prospect in the Pioneer League, which he also led in hits (106), extra-base hits (41), total bases (175) and slugging (.625). Butler led the circuit in ERA (2.13), WHIP (1.06) and opponent average (.230). RHP Scott Oberg (15) joined them on the Pioneer all-star team and paced the league with 13 saves.

BEST ATHLETE: White, who drew interest as a pitcher who threw in the low 90s before he hurt his shoulder. Dahl is nearly as athletic and more polished. RHP Ryan Warner (3s) has exceptional body control for a 6-foot-7 teenager and quarterbacked Pine Creek High to the Colorado 4-A championship game last fall.

MOST INTRIGUING BACKGROUND: OF Ryan Garvey's (33) father Steve won a National League MVP award and made 10 all-star teams. Unsigned SS Kevin Bradley's (36) dad Scott played in the majors and is now Princeton's head coach. C Aaron Jones (18) gave up baseball to become a fireman.

CLOSEST TO THE MAJORS: As a reliever, Willoughby has a quicker path to Colorado than Butler, who will be developed as a starter.

BEST LATE-ROUND PICK: Oberg missed all of 2011 following Tommy John surgery but bounced back with a solid fastball and curveball. 1B Correlle Prime (12) is raw but is a 6-foot-5, 200-pounder with intriguing offensive upside. LHP Mike Mason's (24) fastball topped out at 95 mph once he moved to the bullpen in pro ball.

THE ONE WHO GOT AWAY: SS A.J. Simcox (32, Tennessee) and Dansby Swanson (38, Vanderbilt) are projectable middle infielders who could be early-round picks in 2015.

ASSESSMENT: The Rockies benefited from the Pirates' decision to scrap a deal with Dahl and take Mark Appel instead at No. 8. Colorado pounced on Dahl at No. 10, and he set the tone for a draft class that had several strong debuts.

2011   BONUSES: $4.0 MILLION

Polished LHP Tyler Anderson (1) could start to rise quickly. So could multitooled SS/3B Trevor Story (1s), who shouldn't have lasted until the 45th overall pick.

GRADE: B

2010   BONUSES: $4.8 MILLION

SS/2B Josh Rutledge (3) took the majors by storm when he was promoted last July, though he cooled off in September. He'll eventually be eclipsed by OF Kyle Parker (1) and RHP Chad Bettis (2). The best pro in this crop is 2B Russell Wilson (4), who played two summers in the system and now is starring as a rookie quarterback in the NFL.

GRADE: B

2009   BONUSES: $7.9 MILLION

3B Nolan Arenado (2) is the system's best prospect. LHP Rex Brothers (1s) looks like Colorado's closer of the future, and RHP Rob Scahill (8) joined him in the big league bullpen last September. LHP Tyler Matzek (1) and OF Tim Wheeler (1) have had up-and-down careers, to say the least.

GRADE: B+

2008   BONUSES: $4.2 MILLION

LHP Christian Friedrich (1) and OF Charlie Blackmon (2) have made it to the majors and could wind up as regulars or role players. SS Tommy Field (24) got big league cameos the last two years before the Rockies lost him on waivers in November.

GRADE: C

Draft analysis by Jim Callis. Numbers in parentheses indicate draft rounds.

1 NOLAN ARENADO, 3B

Born: April 16, 1991. **B-T:** R-R. **Ht.:** 6-1. **Wt.:** 205.
Drafted: HS—El Toro, Calif., 2009 (2nd round).
Signed by: Jon Lukens.

BA GRADE
55
MEDIUM

JOHN WILLIAMSON

Arenado earned an invitation to his first big league spring training last year after leading the minors with 122 RBIs in 2011 at high Class A Modesto and then winning MVP honors in the Arizona Fall League. He went 5-for-26 in 12 Cactus League games, including just three hits in his final 19 at-bats as he tried too hard to make a good impression. It turned out to be a prelude to Arenado's most challenging season since he turned down an Arizona State commitment to sign for $625,000 as the 59th overall pick in the 2009 draft. Having gotten a whiff of the major leagues last spring and hearing from people outside the organization that he might be in the big leagues as early as June, he spent too much time wondering when he might get called up. He watched other players in the Double-A Texas League get promoted, including Tulsa teammate Josh Rutledge in mid-July. During a midseason conference call with Rockies' season-ticket holders, GM Dan O'Dowd said that Arenado's "maturity level still hasn't caught up with his ability level," which sent the player into another funk. He went .165/.252/.272 in July, but snapped out of it and hit .358/.375/.569 in August.

A high school teammate of Yankees catcher Austin Romine, Arenado has a knack for making steady contact and getting the barrel of his bat to the ball. His swing gets long through the ball, so his finish looks unorthodox, but he has great hand speed. He has been difficult to strike out throughout his career, with just 181 whiffs in 414 pro games. He derives his power more from bat speed than muscle at this point, and as he gets stronger he should be capable of hitting 20 homers annually. Arenado entered pro ball with an opposite-field stroke but has learned to turn on inside pitches, sometimes to a fault because he strays from hitting to the center of the field. Nevertheless, he should always be able to hit for high averages. After the 2010 season, the Rockies expected Arenado to move to first base because he was such a defensive liability at

SCOUTING GRADES

Batting: 65.   **Defense:** 60.
Power: 55.   **Arm:** 60.
Speed: 30.

Based on 20-80 scouting scale, where 50 represents major league average, and future projection rather than present tools.

the hot corner, with minimal range and no feel for the position. But he got in better shape, worked hard on his first-step quickness and has blossomed into a quality third baseman. He lacks speed but compensates by reading and reacting to balls instinctively. He has a strong arm, throws accurately from various angles and has become adept at charging balls and fielding them barehanded. He can get caught flat-footed at times but still gets to balls that a lot of other third basemen don't. Arenado has terrific feel for the game in all phases, even on the bases despite his below-average speed. Maximizing his agility, an area of emphasis this offseason, may make him a half-step quicker. He's generally a hard worker but the Rockies want to see him improve his focus with more consistent effort.

Arenado will start 2013 at Triple-A Colorado Springs and should reach Colorado during the season. Former first-round pick Chris Nelson played well at the hot corner for the Rockies last year, but Arrenado has a much higher ceiling offensively and defensively. The final step of his development will be to take a more mature approach when dealing with failure.

Year	Club (League)	Class	AVG	G	AB	R	H	2B	3B	HR	RBI	BB	SO	SB	CS	OBP	SLG
2009	Casper (PIO)	R	.300	54	203	28	61	15	0	2	22	16	18	5	2	.351	.404
2010	Asheville (SAL)	LoA	.308	92	373	45	115	41	1	12	65	19	52	1	3	.338	.520
2011	Modesto (CAL)	HiA	.298	134	517	82	154	32	3	20	122	41	53	2	1	.349	.487
2012	Tulsa (TL)	AA	.285	134	516	55	147	36	1	12	56	39	58	0	2	.337	.428
Minor League Totals			.296	414	1609	210	477	124	5	46	265	121	181	8	8	.343	.466

2 DAVID DAHL, OF

Born: April 1, 1994. **B-T:** L-R. **Ht.:** 6-2. **Wt.:** 185. **Drafted:** HS—Birmingham, 2012 (1st round). **Signed by:** Damon Iannelli.

The Pirates agreed to a predraft deal to take Dahl with the No. 8 pick in the 2012 draft, then switched gears and opted for Mark Appel, who didn't sign. The Rockies grabbed Dahl at No. 10, making him the first high school outfielder they've ever taken with their first pick and their first prep position player in the first round since Chris Nelson in 2004. After signing for $2.6 million, Dahl won MVP honors in the Rookie-level Pioneer League after topping the circuit in batting (.379), hits (106), extra-base hits (41), total bases (175) and slugging (.625). Dahl is a pure hitter with exceptional hand-eye coordination and the rare ability for a young player to make adjustments from at-bat to at-bat and even pitch to pitch. He also offers power that will include a lot of doubles and triples and 15-20 homers per year in the big leagues. He hits lefthanders well, and his above-average speed will lead to leg hits that will further boost his average. He needs to get better reads to steal bases.

BA GRADE
60
HIGH

Dahl has a plus arm and covers a lot of ground in center field. His routes and reads need work, but he has the potential to be a Gold Glove outfielder. Dahl profiles as a No. 3 hitter with five-tool ability. He should be able to handle the jump to low Class A Asheville at age 19.

Year	Club (League)	Class	AVG	G	AB	R	H	2B	3B	HR	RBI	BB	SO	SB	CS	OBP	SLG
2012	Grand Junction (PIO)	R	.379	67	280	62	106	22	10	9	57	21	42	12	7	.423	.625
Minor League Totals			.379	67	280	62	106	22	10	9	57	21	42	12	7	.423	.625

3 TREVOR STORY, SS/3B

Born: Nov. 15, 1992. **B-T:** R-R. **Ht.:** 6-1. **Wt.:** 175. **Drafted:** HS—Irving, Texas, 2011 (1st round supplemental). **Signed by:** Dar Cox.

After Story went 45th overall in the 2011 draft and signed for $915,000, he ranked as the Pioneer League's top prospect in his pro debut. He moved up to low Class A in 2012 and rated as the South Atlantic League's best position prospect. He shared time with Rosell Herrera at shortstop and third base early in the year, then became the full-time shortstop when Herrera was demoted in early July. Story has more all-around ability than most shortstops. He recognizes breaking pitches well for his age, is adept at staying inside the ball and has impressive bat speed. He led the SAL with 43 doubles and 67 extra-base hits as a 19-year-old. He has a knack for driving the ball the other way, though he can become too pull-conscious. Better pitchers took advantage of his aggressiveness last year, and he ran up high strikeout totals, though the Rockies expect he'll make more contact as he learns his swing. Managers rated Story as the SAL's best defensive shortstop, though

BA GRADE
55
HIGH

some scouts questioned his actions and arm strength. He's a calm, instinctive defender who covers ground and rarely makes ill-advised throws. He does lay back somewhat on balls hit right at him. He's a solid runner. He might outgrow shortstop and Troy Tulowitzki is blocking him there anyway, but Story has the tools to develop into an all-star at third base or second. He'll play in high Class A at age 20.

Year	Club (League)	Class	AVG	G	AB	R	H	2B	3B	HR	RBI	BB	SO	SB	CS	OBP	SLG
2011	Casper (PIO)	R	.268	47	179	37	48	8	2	6	28	26	41	13	1	.364	.436
2012	Asheville (SAL)	LoA	.277	122	477	96	132	43	6	18	63	60	121	15	3	.367	.505
Minor League Totals			.274	169	656	133	180	51	8	24	91	86	162	28	4	.366	.486

4 KYLE PARKER, OF

Born: Sept. 30, 1989. **B-T:** R-R. **Ht.:** 6-0. **Wt.:** 200. **Drafted:** Clemson, 2010 (1st round). **Signed by:** Jay Matthews.

A former Clemson quarterback, Parker is the only player in NCAA Division I history to throw 20 touchdown passes and hit 20 homers in the same school year. The son of former NFL wide receiver Carl Parker went 26th overall in the 2010 draft. He turned down a $2.2 million offer that would have forced him to give up football, signing instead for $1.4 million and playing one more fall at Clemson. Though wrist and thumb injuries limited him to 102 games last year, he bashed 23 homers and topped the high Class A California League with a .415 on-base percentage. Parker's standout tool is his tremendous raw power, especially to right center, and he has become a much better overall hitter in his two pro seasons. His strike-zone awareness improved last year, as he let the ball travel deeper and took it to the opposite field more often. He can wait before deciding to swing because of his quick wrists and quiet approach. Parker has a solid, accurate arm but he

BA GRADE
50
HIGH

fits in left field because he's a below-average runner. He's a subpar defender right now, but the Rockies think he'll improve with time and practice. If he doesn't, first base is a possibility. Parker showed more intensity last season and seemed more committed to baseball than in 2011. He will move up to Double-A Tulsa to open the season, and if can stay healthy he could reach the majors in 2014.

Year	Club (League)	Class	AVG	G	AB	R	H	2B	3B	HR	RBI	BB	SO	SB	CS	OBP	SLG
2011	Asheville (SAL)	LoA	.285	117	445	75	127	23	1	21	95	48	133	2	0	.367	.483
2012	Modesto (CAL)	HiA	.308	102	390	86	120	18	6	23	73	66	88	1	2	.415	.562
Minor League Totals			.296	219	835	161	247	41	7	44	168	114	221	3	2	.390	.520

5 CHAD BETTIS, RHP

Born: April 26, 1989. **B-T:** R-R. **Ht.:** 6-1. **Wt.:** 210. **Drafted:** Texas Tech, 2010 (2nd round). **Signed by:** Dar Cox.

Bettis was the 2011 California League pitcher of the year after going 12-5, 3.34 and leading the league in innings (170), strikeouts (184), WHIP (1.10) and opponent average (.225). But he hasn't pitched in an official game since. He strained a muscle behind his shoulder in his second Cactus League outing last spring, sidelining him until instructional league. Bettis is tenacious and attacks hitters with everything he throws. His fastball ranges from 91-96 mph and sits at 93, and he got back up to 96 in instructional league. He throws a tight, two-plane slider that gives him a second plus pitch. His changeup is average and has the potential to get better. Bettis has good command works the bottom of the zone consistently. His height creates concerns about a lack of a downhill plane for his pitches that might make it more difficult to get through a lineup three times, but his ability to hold his velocity means he'll continue to start for now. Bettis will open 2013 in Double-A and could be a solid No. 3 starter or more in the majors. If he moves to the bullpen, he could get to Colorado faster and wind up as a closer.

Year	Club (League)	Class	W	L	ERA	G	GS	CG	SV	IP	H	HR	BB	SO	K/9	WHIP	AVG
2010	Tri-City (NWL)	SS	4	1	1.12	10	9	0	0	48	44	0	10	39	7.3	1.12	.227
	Asheville (SAL)	LoA	2	0	0.96	3	3	0	0	19	14	1	3	17	8.2	0.91	.209
2011	Modesto (CAL)	HiA	12	5	3.34	27	27	0	0	170	142	10	45	184	9.8	1.10	.225
2012	Did Not Play—Injured																
Minor League Totals			18	6	2.70	40	39	0	0	237	200	11	58	240	9.1	1.09	.224

6 EDDIE BUTLER, RHP

Born: March 13, 1991. **B-T:** R-R. **Ht.:** 6-2 **Wt.:** 165. **Drafted:** Radford, 2012 (1st round supplemental). **Signed by:** Jay Matthews.

As compensation for the loss of Mark Ellis to the Dodgers as a free agent, the Rockies got the 46th overall pick in the 2012 draft. They used it on Butler, who signed for $1 million before leading the Pioneer League in ERA (2.13), WHIP (1.06) and opponent average (.230). He allowed just one homer in 68 innings. Butler's stuff is electric. He touched 99 mph in instructional league with his fastball after hitting 97 several times during the season. He usually pitches at 94-96 mph with his fastball, and its sinking action makes it even more effective. Butler throws two breaking balls, a solid slider and an average curveball. He overmatched Pioneer League hitters who geared up for his fastball by getting them to chase sliders off the plate. His changeup is improving but is behind his other pitches. He commands his arsenal well. It didn't happen too often during his banner debut, but he shows too much emotion when things don't go his way. Despite his velocity, Butler will need to tighten his secondary stuff get more strikeouts against more advanced hitters. Butler proved even better than advertised, showing a ceiling of a No. 2 starter. He'll advance to low Class A for his first full pro season.

Year	Club (League)	Class	W	L	ERA	G	GS	CG	SV	IP	H	HR	BB	SO	K/9	WHIP	AVG
2012	Grand Junction (PIO)	R	7	1	2.13	13	12	0	0	68	59	1	13	55	7.3	1.06	.230
Minor League Totals			7	1	2.13	13	12	0	0	68	59	1	13	55	7.3	1.06	.230

7 TYLER ANDERSON, LHP

Born: Dec 30, 1989. **B-T:** L-L. **Ht.:** 6-4. **Wt.:** 215. **Drafted:** Oregon, 2011 (1st round). **Signed by:** Jesse Retzlaff.

The 20th overall pick in the 2011 draft, Anderson signed for $1.4 million at the deadline and made his pro debut in 2012. Despite pitching with a sports hernia, he led the South Atlantic League in ERA (2.13) and WHIP (1.06). He had surgery in September and will be ready for spring training. Anderson has no single pitch that stands out, but his command makes his whole repertoire better. He's smart and analytical, traits that will help him as he faces more advanced hitters. Anderson sits at 89-90 mph with a fastball that has good tilt to the plate. His best pitch is a plus changeup with good deception and fade, and he also throws a solid cutter and an average curveball that has more sweeping than downward action. He hides the ball well and is quick to the plate. Anderson profiles as a No. 4 starter, though as a lefty with fine pitchability, he might exceed that expectation. Now that he's fully healthy, he could move fast and possibly skip a level to open 2013 in Double-A.

BA GRADE

50

HIGH

Year	Club (League)	Class	W	L	ERA	G	GS	CG	SV	IP	H	HR	BB	SO	K/9	WHIP	AVG
2012	Asheville (SAL)	LoA	12	3	2.47	20	20	2	0	120	102	5	28	81	6.1	1.08	.232
Minor League Totals			12	3	2.47	20	20	2	0	120	102	5	28	81	6.1	1.08	.232

8 TYLER MATZEK, LHP

Born: Oct. 19, 1990. **B-T:** L-L. **Ht.:** 6-3. **Wt.:** 210. **Drafted:** HS—Capistrano Valley, Calif., 2009 (1st round). **Signed by:** Jon Lukens.

Matzek received a franchise-record $3.9 million bonus as the 11th overall pick in the 2009 draft and has struggled to live up to it. He took time off during the 2011 season to go home and work with his youth pitching coach. He finally showed signs of coming around late last season after he stopped being overly analytical, recording a 1.14 ERA and 31 strikeouts in 32 inning in his final five starts (including two playoff elimination games). He led the California League in both strikeouts (153) and walks (95). Matzek still has better stuff than most lefthanders. He averages 91-92 mph and reaches 95 with his fastball. He has raised his lead arm in his delivery, giving him more leverage and downhill plane. That has helped his curveball immensely, and it's now a plus pitch. Matzek worked on softening his changeup in instructional league and threw some at 85 mph, notable improvement from his usual 89 mph. His control and command have improved but still need to get a lot better. He has become more receptive to coaching, which the Rockies see as a sign of maturity. Advancing to Double-A will provide Matzek a stiff test to see how consistently he can throw strikes and handle adversity. With better command, he could become a No. 2 or 3 starter.

BA GRADE

55

EXTREME

Year	Club (League)	Class	W	L	ERA	G	GS	CG	SV	IP	H	HR	BB	SO	K/9	WHIP	AVG
2010	Asheville (SAL)	LoA	5	1	2.92	18	18	0	0	89	62	6	62	88	8.9	1.39	.204
2011	Modesto (CAL)	HiA	0	3	9.82	10	10	0	0	33	34	5	46	37	10.1	2.42	.266
	Asheville (SAL)	LoA	5	4	4.36	12	12	0	0	64	45	3	50	74	10.4	1.48	.202
2012	Modesto (CAL)	HiA	6	8	4.62	28	28	0	0	142	134	7	95	153	9.7	1.61	.246
Minor League Totals			16	16	4.63	68	68	0	0	329	275	21	253	352	9.6	1.61	.229

9 JAYSON AQUINO, LHP

Born: Nov. 22, 1992. **B-T:** L-L. **Ht.:** 6-1. **Wt.:** 170. **Signed:** Dominican Republic, 2009. **Signed by:** Rolando Fernandez/Jhonathan Leyba/Frank Roa.

After two years in the Rookie-level Dominican Summer League, Aquino came to his first minor league spring training in 2012. He looked too heavy, his work ethic and intensity were lacking and he didn't pitch well, so the Rockies sent him back to the DSL. He got the message, dominated the DSL and pitched well when he came to Rookie-level Grand Junction in August. Aquino used to show fear on the mound, but he was a different pitcher in the Pioneer League. His 88-89 mph fastball is a good pitch that he can locate well to his glove side, but he needs to throw it more. He tops out at 91 mph and could gain velocity because he's young and getting stronger. His curveball and changeup both show the potential to become plus pitches. Because he's so adept at throwing his curve and changeup for strikes, Aquino uses them too often. As he gains experience, he should have above-average command of all three pitches. Aquino profiles as a No. 4 starter, and he could be more if his velocity improves. He'll get his first full-season assignment to low Class A in 2013.

BA GRADE

50

HIGH

Year	Club (League)	Class	W	L	ERA	G	GS	CG	SV	IP	H	HR	BB	SO	K/9	WHIP	AVG
2010	Rockies (DSL)	R	4	3	1.02	12	12	2	0	62	35	0	9	59	8.6	0.71	.161
2011	Rockies (DSL)	R	8	2	1.30	14	14	3	0	90	55	1	22	80	8.0	0.86	.175
2012	Rockies (DSL)	R	6	1	1.52	9	9	2	0	65	45	1	9	74	10.2	0.83	.191
	Grand Junction (PIO)	R	4	0	1.87	7	7	0	0	43	32	2	11	36	7.5	0.99	.203
Minor League Totals			22	6	1.39	42	42	7	0	260	167	4	51	249	8.6	0.84	.180

10 RYAN WHEELER, 3B/1B/OF

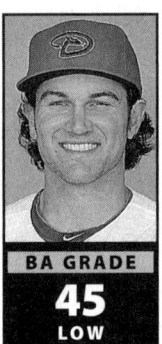

Born: July 10, 1988. **B-T:** L-R. **Ht.:** 6-4. **Wt.:** 220. **Drafted:** Loyola Marymount, 2009 (5th round). **Signed by:** Hal Kurtzman (Diamondbacks).

Wheeler, who spent most of his college career as a first baseman, made the shift to third base in 2010 and has improved his offensive profile each year. He was one of the top hitters on a Reno squad that won the Triple-A National Championship in 2012, batting .351/.388/.572 before getting called up in mid-July. The Diamondbacks traded him to the Rockies for Matt Reynolds in November. Wheeler has strong wrists and gets good leverage with his swing. While he has the ability to drive the ball to the opposite field, he's working on developing more pull power. He makes consistent contact, though somewhat at the expense of drawing walks. Wheeler made strides defensively in 2012, showing a strong arm and working on his agility and mobility in order to increase his range. He won't ever be an asset at the hot corner, but he can make the routine play and has cut down on his errors. He also has seen time in the outfield, but his well below-average speed doesn't provide him with much range. It's not certain that Wheeler will have enough glove to profile as an everyday third baseman or enough power to be a regular at first base. He'll get a chance to make the big league club in spring training as an extra bat off the bench, but more Triple-A time may be in his future.

BA GRADE 45 LOW

Year	Club (League)	Class	AVG	G	AB	R	H	2B	3B	HR	RBI	BB	SO	SB	CS	OBP	SLG
2009	Yakima (NWL)	SS	.363	64	234	44	85	20	3	5	36	37	28	7	4	.461	.538
	South Bend (MWL)	LoA	.345	8	29	4	10	1	1	1	5	5	4	0	1	.472	.552
2010	Visalia (CAL)	HiA	.284	113	465	62	132	25	2	9	57	35	98	3	1	.340	.404
	Mobile (SL)	AA	.254	19	67	8	17	3	0	3	10	5	16	0	0	.315	.433
2011	Mobile (SL)	AA	.294	131	480	69	141	30	2	16	89	45	102	3	4	.358	.465
2012	Reno (PCL)	AAA	.351	93	362	56	127	27	4	15	90	26	67	3	1	.388	.572
	Arizona (NL)	MAJ	.239	50	109	11	26	6	1	1	10	9	22	1	0	.294	.339
Major League Totals			.239	50	109	11	26	6	1	1	10	9	22	1	0	.294	.339
Minor League Totals			.313	428	1637	243	512	106	12	49	287	153	315	16	11	.376	.482

11 TIM WHEELER, OF

BA GRADE 45 MEDIUM

Born: Jan. 21, 1988. **B-T:** L-R. **Ht.:** 6-4. **Wt.:** 215. **Drafted:** Sacramento State, 2009 (1st round). **Signed by:** Gary Wilson.

Wheeler's power fell off drastically last season, from 33 home in Double-A in 2011 to two last season in Triple-A. He broke his right hamate bone eight games into the season and was understandably rusty when he returned in June, but he also hadn't hit for power in spring training when he was healthy. Wheeler went into last season wanting to hit lefthanders better and cut his strikeouts and succeeded on both counts. While it made him a better overall hitter, though, it short-circuited the power that is his only standout tool. He has a tendency to get bent over in his stance, which causes him to break down on his back side and get under the ball, rather than staying firm and tall and getting full extension in his swing to create backspin. He hits to all fields, especially up the middle. Wheeler projects as a corner outfielder, with average speed, but his arm limits him to left field. Wheeler is an intense player and a dedicated worker, so the Rockies expect him to make the adjustments to tap into his power again. They added him to the 40-man roster in November and will send him back to Triple-A, where he'll need to show more power to put himself in position for a promotion to the majors.

Year	Club (League)	Class	AVG	G	AB	R	H	2B	3B	HR	RBI	BB	SO	SB	CS	OBP	SLG
2009	Tri-City (NWL)	SS	.256	68	273	44	70	13	3	5	35	29	60	10	4	.332	.381
2010	Modesto (CAL)	HiA	.249	129	510	88	127	21	6	12	63	60	114	22	8	.341	.384
2011	Tulsa (TL)	AA	.287	138	561	105	161	28	6	33	86	59	142	21	12	.365	.535
2012	Colo. Springs (PCL)	AAA	.303	92	379	67	115	27	4	2	37	29	69	7	7	.357	.412
Minor League Totals			.275	427	1723	304	473	89	19	52	221	177	385	60	31	.351	.439

12 ROB SCAHILL, RHP

BA GRADE 45 MEDIUM

Born: Feb. 15, 1987. **B-T:** L-R. **Ht.:** 6-2. **Wt.:** 220. **Drafted:** Bradley, 2009 (8th round). **Signed by:** Mark Germann.

Scahill has quality stuff, and toward the end of last season began seeing better results thanks to mechanical adjustments. In his final four starts at Colorado Springs, he had a 3.42 ERA with seven walks and 32 strikeouts in 24 innings, earning a September callup to Colorado, where he had a 1.04 ERA in six relief appearances. Scahill touches 96 mph and sits at 93-94 with his fastball. His upper-70s curveball is ahead of his 84-88 mph slider, but both are good pitches. He rarely throws his changeup, which is below average. Scahill raised his arm slot and became more consistent staying on top of the ball and driving it downward, which helped him become less rotational in his delivery and not have his body get ahead of his arm. He's aggressive on the mound and has a sturdy frame. His control is solid but his command is below average on all of his pitches and must improve. If it does, he could still be a starter, but with his stuff he could be a valuable member of the Rockies bullpen, particularly if they continue using piggyback relievers.

Year	Club (League)	Class	W	L	ERA	G	GS	CG	SV	IP	H	HR	BB	SO	K/9	WHIP	AVG
2009	Tri-City (NWL)	SS	1	4	3.14	15	15	0	0	63	58	2	20	58	8.3	1.24	.245
2010	Modesto (CAL)	HiA	10	7	4.73	27	27	1	0	156	173	9	59	140	8.1	1.49	.284
2011	Tulsa (TL)	AA	12	11	3.92	27	26	1	0	161	164	12	60	104	5.8	1.39	.266
2012	Colorado Springs (PCL)	AAA	9	11	5.68	29	29	1	0	152	168	11	74	159	9.4	1.59	.280
	Colorado (NL)	MAJ	0	0	1.04	6	0	0	0	9	7	0	3	4	4.2	1.15	.233
Major League Totals			0	0	1.04	6	0	0	0	9	7	0	3	4	4.2	1.15	.233
Minor League Totals			32	33	4.57	98	97	3	0	532	563	34	213	461	7.8	1.46	.273

13 COREY DICKERSON, OF

BA GRADE
50
HIGH

Born: May 22, 1989. **B-T:** L-R. **Ht.:** 6-2. **Wt.:** 210. **Drafted:** Meridian (Miss.) CC, 2010 (8th round). **Signed by:** Damon Iannelli.

Though he hit 32 homers at Asheville in 2011, taking advantage of a short right-field porch, Dickerson worked exceptionally hard after the season to become a more complete player. He reported to spring training in the best shape since joining the organization and played as if on a mission. After dominating the California League, he earned a promotion to Double-A in mid-June. He broke his nose when hit with a pitch July 23 but was back in the lineup five days later, albeit hitting with a mask attached to his helmet that complicated matters for a couple of weeks. Dickerson has become a much better overall hitter. He has learned to use the entire field and drives the ball well to left-center. His quick hands enable him to consistently move the barrel of his bat to the ball. He has good pitch recognition and is adept at fighting off a good pitch to keep an at-bat alive. Dickerson worked on his agility and has become a slightly better than average runner. His defense in left field had been a huge liability and remains a work in progress, but is notably better, though he still has a below-average arm. He likely will open 2013 in Triple-A.

Year	Club (League)	Class	AVG	G	AB	R	H	2B	3B	HR	RBI	BB	SO	SB	CS	OBP	SLG
2010	Casper (PIO)	R	.348	69	276	54	96	22	9	13	61	28	51	12	6	.412	.634
2011	Asheville (SAL)	LoA	.282	106	383	78	108	27	5	32	87	39	99	9	6	.356	.629
2012	Modesto (CAL)	HiA	.338	60	240	43	81	24	4	9	43	25	42	9	5	.396	.583
	Tulsa (TL)	AA	.274	67	266	40	73	16	3	13	38	18	51	7	3	.322	.504
Minor League Totals			.307	302	1165	215	358	89	21	67	229	110	243	37	20	.370	.592

14 TOM MURPHY, C

BA GRADE
50
HIGH

Born: Jan. 3, 1991. **B-T:** R-R. **Ht.:** 6-1. **Wt.:** 220. **Drafted:** Buffalo, 2012 (3rd round). **Signed by:** Ed Santa.

Signed for $454,000 as a third-round pick in 2012, Murphy is just the fifth catcher the Rockies have selected that high since they began drafting in 1992. They took Ben Petrick in the second round in 1995, Jeff Winchester as a supplemental first-round pick in 1998, and in the third round have taken Josh Bard (1999), Lars Davis (2007) and Pete O'Brien (2011), who didn't sign. Murphy's best tool is his power, which isn't evident from his six homers because Gesa Stadium, where short-season Tri-City plays, is a pronounced pitcher's park. He has the upside to hit 25 homers annually in the big leagues and won't be an all-or-nothing type. Murphy has a short, compact swing and because of his good strike-zone awareness, he doesn't strike out excessively for a young power hitter. He needs to get better at recognizing and hitting breaking pitches, but he's not overmatched by them. Murphy is a physical presence behind the plate and has an above-average arm but needs work on all nuances of his defense. He threw out just 21 percent of basestealers in his pro debut. In instructional league, he did a much better job taking charge behind the plate. He could bypass Asheville and begin his first full pro season in high Class A.

Year	Club (League)	Class	AVG	G	AB	R	H	2B	3B	HR	RBI	BB	SO	SB	CS	OBP	SLG
2012	Tri-City (NWL)	SS	.288	55	212	26	61	13	3	6	38	14	52	1	1	.349	.462
Minor League Totals			.288	55	212	26	61	13	3	6	38	14	52	1	1	.349	.462

15 RAFAEL ORTEGA, OF

BA GRADE
50
HIGH

Born: May 15, 1991. **B-T:** L-R. **Ht.:** 5-11. **Wt.:** 160. **Drafted:** Venezuela, 2008. **Signed by:** Rolando Fernandez/Francisco Cartaya/Carlos Gomez.

After completing the 2012 season at Modesto, Ortega was in instructional league when the Rockies, their outfield corps depleted by injuries, called him to Colorado. He had two hits and reached base three times in his major league debut Sept. 30 and made one other pinch-hitting appearance. He returned to instructional league to work on bunting, reading pitchers and getting better leads, and he showed improvement. Those will be big factors in Ortega's success because he's an energetic leadoff hitter with good speed. He has a short swing and stays inside the ball well, and he'll maximize his value with better strike-zone awareness and plate discipline—he has a combined 187 strikeouts and 76 walks the past two seasons. Despite his size, he has surprising power but needs to guard against falling in love with his power stroke after he hits a homer, and then hitting the ball in the air for a series of at-bats. His speed plays on the bases, as he stole 36 bases for Modesto, but he was caught 18 times. Ortega is a true center fielder, and fearless when it comes to outfield walls. His reads on flyballs and routes are good, and his plus arm is very accurate. He should move up to Double-A in 2013.

Year	Club (League)	Class	AVG	G	AB	R	H	2B	3B	HR	RBI	BB	SO	SB	CS	OBP	SLG
2008	Rockies (DSL)	R	.277	52	188	38	52	4	2	1	11	20	20	17	3	.349	.335
2009	Rockies (DSL)	R	.324	70	256	45	83	7	8	0	39	32	23	39	12	.395	.414
2010	Casper (PIO)	R	.358	71	288	69	103	17	3	7	45	28	42	23	9	.416	.510
2011	Asheville (SAL)	LoA	.294	113	479	77	141	26	8	9	66	28	90	32	19	.335	.438
2012	Modesto (CAL)	HiA	.283	114	495	81	140	23	8	8	60	46	93	36	18	.344	.410
	Colorado (NL)	MAJ	.500	2	4	0	2	0	0	0	0	1	2	1	0	.667	.500
Major League Totals			.500	2	4	0	2	0	0	0	0	1	2	1	0	.667	.500
Minor League Totals			.304	420	1706	310	519	77	29	25	221	154	268	147	61	.362	.427

16 KENT MATTHES, OF

BA GRADE
50
HIGH

Born: Jan. 8, 1987. **B-T:** R-R. **Ht.:** 6-2. **Wt.:** 215. **Drafted:** Alabama, 2009 (4th round). **Signed by:** Damon Iannelli.

Three different injuries have slowed Matthes in each of the past three seasons. A torn patellar tendon in his left knee limited him to 21 games at Asheville in 2010, and his 2011 season at Modesto ended after 93 games when a pitch hit him and broke his left hand—though he still won the California League MVP award. A right oblique strain cut short his 2012 season at Tulsa after 94 games. Matthes' power and arm give him two plus tools. The lingering effects of his hand injury and a right groin strain he sustained just prior to spring training last year led to a slow start at Tulsa. Trying to repeat the strong season he had in Modesto, he admitted that he pressed badly. His intensity level can be a problem, as he tries too hard to hit the ball with maximum effort, which can prevent him from keeping the bat in the zone for a long time. Before his oblique injury, he was slowing down somewhat and staying back rather than charging for the ball. In spite of his injuries he's an average runner, and with one of the strongest arms in the system he fits well in right field, where he's a solid defender. Matthes benefited from making up some at-bats in the Arizona Fall League, though the Rockies declined to protect him on their 40-man roster and he went unpicked in the Rule 5 draft. He'll have a chance to move up to Triple-A in 2013.

Year	Club (League)	Class	AVG	G	AB	R	H	2B	3B	HR	RBI	BB	SO	SB	CS	OBP	SLG
2009	Tri-City (NWL)	SS	.289	63	239	39	69	23	1	5	35	21	77	6	4	.364	.456
2010	Asheville (SAL)	LoA	.185	21	81	9	15	7	1	1	11	5	32	0	0	.261	.333
2011	Modesto (CAL)	HiA	.334	93	371	70	124	39	3	23	95	22	80	7	4	.378	.642
2012	Tulsa (TL)	AA	.214	94	336	44	72	18	2	17	40	22	80	6	2	.273	.432
Minor League Totals			.273	271	1027	162	280	87	7	46	181	70	269	19	10	.331	.505

17 EDWAR CABRERA, LHP

BA GRADE
45
MEDIUM

Born: Oct. 20, 1987. **B-T:** L-L. **Ht.:** 6-0. **Wt.:** 175. **Signed:** Dominican Republic, 2008. **Signed by:** Rolando Fernandez/Jhonathan Leyba/Martin Cabrera.

The Rockies needed a starter on June 27 and promoted Cabrera from Tulsa, where he had pitched well, to face the Nationals at Coors Field. He was knocked out in the third inning and was quickly optioned to Triple-A. He got another chance on July 24 at Arizona and didn't make it through the fourth. He went back down to Colorado Springs, where his season ended Aug. 3 due to an oblique strain, compounded by elbow soreness. As his big league time showed, Cabrera badly needs to develop a third pitch. His best attributes are an outstanding changeup and a fearless mindset. His 87-91 mph fastball is nothing special—though that didn't prevent him from leading the minors with 217 strikeouts in 2011—and he must command it better. His curveball has improved marginally but remains below average. He either needs to develop that pitch or a cutter and learn to work both sides of the plate. He's very good pitching to his arm side but needs to get better to his glove side, which will make his already formidable changeup that much better. With improved fastball command

and an average third pitch, Cabrera profiles as a No. 4 or 5 starter. He'll get an opportunity to make the big league staff in spring training but more likely will get more time in Triple-A.

Year	Club (League)	Class	W	L	ERA	G	GS	CG	SV	IP	H	HR	BB	SO	K/9	WHIP	AVG
2008	Rockies (DSL)	R	5	1	0.92	8	8	0	0	49	26	1	18	75	13.9	0.90	.158
	Casper (PIO)	R	0	4	7.80	9	5	0	0	30	38	7	15	38	11.4	1.77	.304
2009	Rockies (DSL)	R	1	0	1.16	7	3	0	0	31	16	0	10	50	14.5	0.84	.145
	Casper (PIO)	R	0	0	3.38	9	1	0	0	21	19	2	12	28	11.8	1.45	.235
2010	Tri-City (NWL)	SS	1	8	3.07	14	14	0	0	73	71	2	24	87	10.7	1.30	.251
2011	Asheville (SAL)	LoA	4	2	3.14	13	13	0	0	86	77	10	18	110	11.5	1.10	.237
	Modesto (CAL)	HiA	4	1	3.56	13	13	0	0	81	78	8	23	107	11.9	1.25	.252
2012	Tulsa (TL)	AA	8	4	2.94	15	15	0	0	98	65	15	23	82	7.5	0.90	.186
	Colorado (NL)	MAJ	0	2	11.12	2	2	0	0	6	9	3	7	5	7.9	2.82	.346
	Colorado Springs (PCL)	AAA	3	1	3.41	6	6	1	0	32	26	6	12	39	11.1	1.20	.224
Major League Totals			0	2	11.12	2	2	0	0	6	9	3	7	5	7.9	2.82	.346
Minor League Totals			26	21	3.13	94	78	1	0	501	416	51	155	616	11.1	1.14	.223

18 JOSH SULLIVAN, RHP

BA GRADE

45

MEDIUM

Born: July 5, 1984. **B-T:** R-R. **Ht.:** 6-4. **Wt.:** 215. **Drafted:** Auburn, 2005 (5th round). **Signed by:** Damon Iannelli.

Sullivan never topped 70 innings in any of his first six pro seasons and didn't even make it to 30 in five of them due to three arm operations: shoulder surgery in October 2005, a nerve transposed in his elbow in April 2008 and Tommy John surgery in March 2009. He finally reached Double-A in 2011 and returned there in 2012, when he moved to the bullpen and did well enough in the closer role to earn a spot on Colorado's 40-man roster in November. Given his medical history, the Rockies carefully monitored Sullivan's workload early in the season, and he adjusted well to relieving. He touches 96 mph with a fastball that sits at 92-93 and has heavy sinking action, a reason he allowed just three homers in 62 innings last year. He throws an 86-88 mph slider that's above average at times, and a developing changeup. Sullivan has a long stride and a long arm action in back that can make it hard for him to repeat his delivery and causes his command to be inconsistent. He'll need to improve that as he moves up to Triple-A and the big leagues. With his power arm, Sullivan has the potential to be a late-inning reliever, but because of his age he can't afford many developmental missteps.

Year	Club (League)	Class	W	L	ERA	G	GS	CG	SV	IP	H	HR	BB	SO	K/9	WHIP	AVG
2005	Tri-City (NWL)	SS	0	1	27.00	1	0	0	0	1	3	0	1	1	9.0	4.00	.500
2006	Tri-City (NWL)	SS	3	4	2.71	13	13	0	0	70	49	2	21	74	9.6	1.00	.188
2007	Asheville (SAL)	LoA	3	2	3.26	13	9	0	0	50	42	3	25	45	8.2	1.35	.223
2008	Tri-City (NWL)	SS	0	1	3.38	3	3	0	0	11	12	0	5	8	6.8	1.59	.286
2009	Did Not Play—Injured																
2010	Tri-City (NWL)	SS	1	2	6.23	5	5	0	0	22	25	2	9	15	6.2	1.57	.275
	Modesto (CAL)	HiA	3	3	5.86	9	8	0	0	28	29	2	18	23	7.5	1.70	.274
2011	Tulsa (TL)	AA	5	9	5.51	25	20	1	0	118	122	19	54	87	6.7	1.50	.272
2012	Tulsa (TL)	AA	1	2	2.76	60	0	0	17	62	56	3	24	63	9.1	1.29	.241
Minor League Totals			16	24	4.25	129	58	1	17	360	338	31	157	316	7.9	1.38	.246

19 CRISTHIAN ADAMES, SS

BA GRADE

50

HIGH

Born: July 26, 1991. **B-T:** B-R. **Ht.:** 6-0. **Wt.:** 160. **Signed:** Dominican Republic, 2007. **Signed by:** Rolando Fernandez/Felix Feliz.

Since signing out of the Dominican Republic, Adames has moved up steadily through the system and played well at Modesto in 2012, overcoming a .191 April to hit .297 the rest of the season. He was the best player in Colorado's instructional league program, where he pushed himself, played harder and ran better. Adames is the best defensive shortstop in the system, but he is getting bigger, which may mean a move to second base or even third eventually, particularly if his power improves as expected. He has very good hands, a quick release and throws easy, with plenty of arm strength. His range is solid, as is his speed, and he is a heady, instinctive player. A switch-hitter, he stays inside the ball well, does a good job of using the opposite-field gap from both sides and is able to recognize pitches to pull. On offense and defense, Adames has done a better job of using his lower half. That will help him get more stability at the plate and perhaps have his power not just show up as doubles and triples but in double-digit home run totals. Added to the 40-man roster in November, Adames will move up to Double-A in 2013.

Year	Club (League)	Class	AVG	G	AB	R	H	2B	3B	HR	RBI	BB	SO	SB	CS	OBP	SLG
2008	Rockies (DSL)	R	.262	51	168	22	44	5	0	6	8	18	26	7	8	.339	.292
2009	Rockies (DSL)	R	.231	36	121	17	28	6	0	1	19	18	24	8	3	.340	.306
2010	Casper (PIO)	R	.290	37	145	30	42	9	0	1	15	14	24	4	5	.356	.372
2011	Asheville (SAL)	LoA	.273	108	399	63	109	17	2	8	44	42	74	2	0	.350	.386
2012	Modesto (CAL)	HiA	.280	115	418	59	117	21	7	2	54	47	82	4	2	.352	.378
Minor League Totals			.272	347	1251	191	340	58	9	12	140	139	230	25	18	.349	.361

20 JULIAN YAN, OF

BA GRADE

50

HIGH

Born: Nov. 27, 1991. **B-T:** R-R. **Ht.:** 6-2. **Wt.:** 180. **Signed:** Dominican Republic, 2008. **Signed by:** Rolando Fernandez/Jhonathan Leyba/Frank Roa.

Yan spent two lackluster seasons in the Dominican Summer League before making his domestic debut in 2011. He showed glimpses of his talent then but was inconsistent, not unusual for a 19-year-old playing in the United States for the first time. He returned to the Pioneer League in 2012 and led the league in homers (16), though he also struck out in nearly one-third of his at-bats. Yan has easy power but often tries to force it by swinging hard, and worse, doing it with complex mechanics. He waggled his bat up and down and employed a toe tap with a leg kick, conflicting movements that meant he had to make decisions very early and resulted in fishing for balls and striking out often. He simplified his swing, making changes that got his hands ready sooner, and in the second half batted .313/.383/.664 with 12 homers. He has plus bat speed, and as long as he doesn't try too hard to hit the ball far, he has enough power to develop into a big-time home run hitter with piles of doubles, particularly at Coors Field. Yan has a tremendous arm and runs well enough to develop into a very good outfielder, though he can improve his routes in right field. He will play at Asheville in 2013.

Year	Club (League)	Class	AVG	G	AB	R	H	2B	3B	HR	RBI	BB	SO	SB	CS	OBP	SLG
2009	Rockies (DSL)	R	.197	47	152	17	30	7	1	2	14	22	45	1	7	.307	.296
2010	Rockies (DSL)	R	.201	64	209	26	42	3	1	6	25	16	59	15	11	.285	.311
2011	Casper (PIO)	R	.249	53	201	22	50	8	2	3	26	11	60	6	1	.285	.353
2012	Grand Junction (PIO)	R	.282	66	255	50	72	13	1	16	57	21	82	9	4	.357	.529
Minor League Totals			.237	230	817	115	194	31	5	27	122	70	246	31	23	.312	.387

21 WILL SWANNER, C

BA GRADE

50

HIGH

Born: Sept. 10, 1991. **B-T:** R-R. **Ht.:** 6-2. **Wt.:** 185. **Drafted:** HS—Carlsbad, Calif., 2010 (15th round). **Signed by:** Jon Lukens.

Swanner looked to be headed to Pepperdine heading into the 2010 draft, but the Rockies were able to sign him away with a $495,000 bonus in the 15th round. He got his feet wet in the Pioneer League, returned there in 2011 and moved up to Asheville last season. He had 41 extra-base hits, including 16 homers, and finished with a .302 average despite batting .182 after July. Swanner's best tool is his power, which played particularly well at Asheville's McCormick Field because he hits a lot of balls to right-center. He has a deep wrap in his swing that causes his bat head to get flat in his load, raising questions about whether he'll be able to adjust to better pitching and loft the ball. He can have balance issues at the plate because he taps back and over-strides, and he tends to be too aggressive and strikes out a lot. On defense, Swanner shows average arm strength at times, but in games he has been unable to break the habit of pausing at the top of his throwing motion. He surrendered an astonishing 120 steals in 75 games last year, throwing out just 13 runners (10 percent). His height makes getting low to block balls a challenge, leading to 14 passed balls in 2012. Swanner is fine catching organizational pitchers but isn't as adept handling those with better stuff. He's a below-average runner. He might end up at first base, which would put more pressure on his bat. He likely will begin 2013 at Modesto and will need to take a step forward with his bat or his defense behind the plate to have an everyday major league role.

Year	Club (League)	Class	AVG	G	AB	R	H	2B	3B	HR	RBI	BB	SO	SB	CS	OBP	SLG
2010	Casper (PIO)	R	.303	18	76	14	23	4	0	7	13	0	33	0	1	.321	.632
2011	Casper (PIO)	R	.264	43	159	33	42	14	1	10	24	20	60	1	2	.357	.553
2012	Asheville (SAL)	LoA	.302	88	325	60	98	24	1	16	61	38	101	3	2	.385	.529
Minor League Totals			.291	149	560	107	163	42	2	33	98	58	194	4	5	.369	.550

22 DANNY ROSENBAUM, LHP

BA GRADE

45

MEDIUM

Born: Oct. 10, 1987. **B-T:** R-L. **Ht.:** 6-1. **Wt.:** 210. **Drafted:** Xavier, 2009 (22nd round). **Signed by:** Alex Smith (Nationals).

After helping Xavier reach its first NCAA regional in 2009, Rosenbaum signed with the Nationals for $20,000 and went about carving up hitters at every level for the next three years. He carried a 2.35 career ERA into 2012, when he got off to a sterling start at Double-A Harrisburg, going 6-1, 1.69 through the end of May. But he went 2-9, 5.76 over the final three months of the season, as his stuff flattened out and he struggled to locate to his arm side. The Nationals left him off their 40-man roster, and the Rockies grabbed him in the major league Rule 5 draft. Rosenbaum relies more on his craftiness and feel for pitching than his stuff, so his command must be precise. His below-average fastball ranges from 84-90 mph, and he can cut it and spot it when he's going right. His best secondary pitch is a solid changeup that he throws with good arm speed. His curveball is fringy but serviceable. Rosenbaum lacks upside, but he has a decent chance to be a touch-and-feel lefty at the back of a big league rotation. He will get the opportunity to join a Colorado staff desperately in need of help, and if he doesn't stick on the big league roster he'll have to clear waivers and be offered back to the Nationals for half his $50,000 draft price.

Year	Club (League)	Class	W	L	ERA	G	GS	CG	SV	IP	H	HR	BB	SO	K/9	WHIP	AVG
2009	Nationals (GCL)	R	4	1	1.95	11	8	0	0	37	29	1	9	38	9.2	1.03	.215
2010	Hagerstown (SAL)	LoA	2	5	2.32	18	18	0	0	101	95	5	28	84	7.5	1.22	.253
	Potomac (CAR)	HiA	3	2	2.09	8	7	0	0	43	35	2	13	31	6.5	1.12	.230
2011	Potomac (CAR)	HiA	6	5	2.59	20	19	2	0	132	113	4	41	108	7.4	1.17	.234
	Harrisburg (EL)	AA	3	1	2.29	6	6	0	0	39	27	0	11	27	6.2	0.97	.190
2012	Harrisburg (EL)	AA	8	10	3.94	26	26	2	0	155	164	8	39	99	5.7	1.31	.278
Minor League Totals			26	24	2.84	89	84	4	0	508	463	20	141	387	6.9	1.19	.247

23 HAROLD RIGGINS, 1B

BA GRADE
50
HIGH

Born: March 6, 1990. **B-T:** R-R. **Ht.:** 6-2. **Wt.:** 240. **Drafted:** North Carolina State, 2011 (7th round). **Signed by:** Jay Matthews.

Riggins was drafted by the White Sox in the 35th round out of high school in 2008 but chose to attend North Carolina State. The Rockies took him in the seventh round in 2011 and signed him for $125,000. Back stiffness limited him in 2012 at Asheville and in instructional league, where he was finally able to play late in the program. Riggins has size, strength and good bat speed, but with a big leg kick his swing can get long. In instructional league, his hands had gotten buried, almost behind his body, and he needs to free them up so he can catch up to balls out front. Riggins uses the opposite field well, to the point that Colorado tried to get him to pull the ball more last season, but that's easier said than done at Asheville, where right field is cozy. Riggins moves well in the field, and his first-step quickness, hands and arm strength are pluses, though he's an average runner at best. Some have wondered if Riggins shouldn't shift to third base or catcher to maximize his value, figuring he can always return to first base if need be. For now he will move up to Modesto and continue proving the value of his bat.

Year	Club (League)	Class	AVG	G	AB	R	H	2B	3B	HR	RBI	BB	SO	SB	CS	OBP	SLG
2011	Casper (PIO)	R	.279	67	215	42	60	13	1	8	35	46	85	1	3	.416	.460
2012	Asheville (SAL)	LoA	.302	87	328	63	99	23	0	19	76	37	104	8	5	.388	.546
Minor League Totals			.293	154	543	105	159	36	1	27	111	83	189	9	8	.400	.512

24 SETH WILLOUGHBY, RHP

BA GRADE
50
HIGH

Born: June 28, 1990. **B-T:** R-R. **Ht.:** 6-2. **Wt.:** 195. **Drafted:** Xavier, 2012 (4th round). **Signed by:** Ed Santa.

Willoughby was a two-way player for Xavier until he broke the hamate bone in his left hand in the sixth game of his junior season. That meant he had to concentrate on pitching and could no longer hit cleanup, which turned out to be a boon for his professional prospects. Previously a draft afterthought, Willoughby's stuff improved markedly, and the Rockies took him in the fourth round in June and signed him for $330,300. As the 138th player taken overall, he became Xavier's highest-ever draft pick, besting Rich Donnelly, who was taken 158th overall by the Yankees in 1967. Willoughby is a strike-thrower who attacks hitters and doesn't get rattled by any situation. His out pitch is an 88-90 mph cutter that sets him apart, though he sometimes relies on it too much. Colorado took it away from him in instructional league so he could concentrate on his fastball and changeup, which he rarely threw while closing games at Tri-City. His fastball ranges from 92-95 mph, and he needs to hone his command of it. Willoughby pitched in three games for Asheville in the final week of the season and will begin 2013 there if he doesn't jump to Modesto in spring training. Strictly a reliever, he could move through the system quickly.

Year	Club (League)	Class	W	L	ERA	G	GS	CG	SV	IP	H	HR	BB	SO	K/9	WHIP	AVG
2012	Tri-City (NWL)	SS	2	1	1.44	21	0	0	8	25	18	1	4	27	9.7	0.88	.200
	Asheville (SAL)	LoA	0	0	3.00	3	0	0	0	3	4	0	0	3	9.0	1.33	.333
Minor League Totals			2	1	1.61	24	0	0	8	28	22	1	4	30	9.6	0.93	.216

25 MAX WHITE, OF

BA GRADE
50
HIGH

Born: Oct. 10, 1993. **B-T:** L-L. **Ht.:** 6-2. **Wt.:** 175. **Drafted:** HS—Williston, Fla., 2012 (2nd round). **Signed by:** Alan Matthews.

White was a two-way prospect early in his high school career, but shoulder surgery dented his professional prospects as a pitcher. He still had plenty of appeal as an athletic, speedy center fielder, however, and the Rockies took him 73rd overall in June and signed him away from a Florida commitment for $1 million. He had a humbling pro debut at Grand Junction, though he did show improvement as the season went on, batting .151/.295/.233 in the first half and .237/.342/.412 in the second. White is wiry and athletic, with a smooth lefthanded swing. His two best attributes are his hand speed and ability to run. His hand speed helped White fare better against the hardest throwers because he just reacted and got his barrel on the ball and didn't try to hit homers. He attempted the latter too often, which caused his swing to become long and his strikeouts to mount. As he grows into his body, White could develop enough power to hit 15 homers a year, but he'll need to improve his approach at the plate to tap into it. He has the potential to hit a lot of doubles and triples, steal bases and cover ground in center field. His arm strength isn't what it was before surgery, but it's plenty strong enough for center field, where he should be a good defender, though he needs work on his routes. White has not faced a lot of quality pitching, so he'll probably return to a short-season stop to get up to speed in pro ball.

Year	Club (League)	Class	AVG	G	AB	R	H	2B	3B	HR	RBI	BB	SO	SB	CS	OBP	SLG
2012	Grand Junction (PIO)	R	.200	50	170	30	34	5	3	4	18	29	72	6	5	.322	.335
Minor League Totals			.200	50	170	30	34	5	3	4	18	29	72	6	5	.322	.335

26 RYAN WARNER, RHP

BA GRADE
50
EXTREME

Born: Jan. 21, 1994. **B-T:** L-R. **Ht.:** 6-7. **Wt.:** 195. **Drafted:** HS—Colorado Springs, 2012 (3rd round supplemental). **Signed by:** Marc Gustafson.

Warner committed to North Carolina State and would have gone there had any team but the Rockies drafted him. Growing up in nearby Colorado Springs, he seized the opportunity to play for the team he followed growing up and signed for $363,700 as a supplemental third-round pick last summer. He made his pro debut in the Pioneer League, where he was on a 60-pitch limit and got knocked around a bit. For his size, Warner is a very good athlete, and he played at quarterback and wide receiver on his high school football team. His 6-foot-7 frame is the kind scouts can dream on, and his size gives him the natural ability to create a downward angle with his fastball that causes a lot of ground balls and swings and misses over the top of the ball. He has a quick arm and usually ranged from 89-90 mph with his fastball, topping out at 93, so his velocity is likely to rise as he fills out. He has a true, firm curveball that he'll be able to command well and could turn into a strikeout pitch, and he shows good deception with his changeup, though it needs development. He shows maturity and competitiveness on the mound, complemented by intelligence and an ability to make adjustments. Warner will likely move up to Tri-City in 2013. He's a project but offers intriguing upside.

Year	Club (League)	Class	W	L	ERA	G	GS	CG	SV	IP	H	HR	BB	SO	K/9	WHIP	AVG
2012	Grand Junction (PIO)	R	3	0	7.00	14	10	0	0	45	63	9	13	36	7.2	1.69	.333
Minor League Totals			3	0	7.00	14	10	0	0	45	63	9	13	36	7.2	1.69	.333

27 WILFREDO RODRIGUEZ, C

BA GRADE
50
EXTREME

Born: Jan. 25, 1994. **B-T:** R-R. **Ht.:** 5-10. **Wt.:** 200. **Drafted:** HS—Gurabo, P.R., 2012 (7th round). **Signed by:** Rafael Reyes.

Rodriguez was a teammate at the Puerto Rico Baseball Academy of shortstop Carlos Correa, who was the No. 1 overall pick in the 2012 draft by the Astros. The Rockies took Rodriguez six rounds later and signed him for $185,000, sending him to the Pioneer League, where he was the youngest catcher in the league but more than held his own. Club officials said he was easily the hardest worker on the Grand Junction team and extremely coachable. Rodriguez has a compact stroke but swings at just about anything. He makes steady, solid contact, however, which is rare for an 18-year-old who will often venture outside the strike zone. Against better pitching, he will need to refine his plate discipline. He has learned to hit against, rather than over his front foot and should develop enough power to hit 10-15 homers annually with a lot of doubles. Rodriguez overcame the habit of dropping his target and then raising it and has already become a much calmer receiver. His blocking needs work simply because as an amateur he caught few pitchers with decent velocity. He showed an above-average arm early in the season before starting to wear down, and he threw out 21 percent of basestealers in his pro debut. He's a bottom-of-the-scale runner. Rodriguez should develop into an average catcher whose strength will be his bat. He could begin 2013 in low Class A.

Year	Club (League)	Class	AVG	G	AB	R	H	2B	3B	HR	RBI	BB	SO	SB	CS	OBP	SLG
2012	Grand Junction (PIO)	R	.319	43	166	26	53	14	1	2	27	13	23	1	1	.370	.452
Minor League Totals			.319	43	166	26	53	14	1	2	27	13	23	1	1	.370	.452

28 CHRISTIAN BERGMAN, RHP

BA GRADE
45
MEDIUM

Born: May 4, 1988. **B-T:** R-R. **Ht.:** 6-1. **Wt.:** 180. **Drafted:** UC Irvine, 2010 (24th round). **Signed by:** Jon Lukens.

Bergman was pitcher of the year in the short-season Northwest League in 2011, and he came to spring training last year ticketed to move up one level to Asheville. But instead he pitched his way to Modesto and ended up as the pitcher of the year in the California League after tying for the minor league lead with 16 wins. After he lost June 16 in the final game of the first half, Bergman won eight straight in the second half and went 1-1, 1.50 in two playoff games. Bergman succeeds with standout command. All of his pitches are average, but they play better than that because of his feel for locating them. He pitches at 89-92 mph with his fastball, also throws a curveball and changeup, and has started to mix in a cutter/slider. He has also proven to be durable. After succeeding at the lower levels, where he was always on the old side, Bergman will move up to Double-A in 2013 and face the challenge of getting out better hitters. He profiles as a fifth starter and has a strong track record of success.

Year	Club (League)	Class	W	L	ERA	G	GS	CG	SV	IP	H	HR	BB	SO	K/9	WHIP	AVG
2010	Casper (PIO)	R	1	4	5.96	14	5	0	0	48	62	5	11	37	6.9	1.51	.304
2011	Tri-City (NWL)	SS	7	5	2.59	15	15	2	0	97	83	4	11	68	6.3	0.97	.226
2012	Modesto (CAL)	HiA	16	5	3.65	27	27	0	0	163	161	16	37	121	6.7	1.22	.259
Minor League Totals			24	14	3.68	56	47	2	0	308	306	25	59	226	6.6	1.18	.257

29 PETER TAGO, RHP

BA GRADE
50
EXTREME

Born: July 5, 1992. **B-T:** R-R. **Ht.:** 6-2. **Wt.:** 170. **Drafted:** HS—Dana Point, Calif., 2010 (1st round supplemental). **Signed by:** Jon Lukens.

When the Rockies took Tago 47th overall in the 2010 draft, with a compensation pick for the loss of free agent pitcher Jason Marquis, scouting director Bill Schmidt compared his loose, easy arm action to that of Pedro Astacio and Esmil Rogers. Tago signed late for $982,500 and didn't begin his career until 2011, and he hasn't shown much progress in his first two seasons. He regressed from Asheville in 2011 to Tri-City in 2012 and now has a career 6.36 ERA, and compounding matters has been his lack of maturity off the field. But Colorado saw a change in instructional league, as Tago made great progress with his delivery and had better focus. He had been using a robotic delivery, with a stabbing arm action when he separated. But now he is separating with a short little arc and taking his hand more straight back, which enables him to throw his fastball down in the zone more consistently. Tago's fastball reaches 95 mph at its best, and he'll usually pitch at 91. His curveball is average at times, though it has been more often below average in pro ball. Rockies officials report the bite returned in instructional league. His changeup remains a work in progress. Tago's fall progress was encouraging, but he needs to finally move his career forward in 2013, which he's likely to begin back at Asheville.

Year	Club (League)	Class	W	L	ERA	G	GS	CG	SV	IP	H	HR	BB	SO	K/9	WHIP	AVG
2011	Asheville (SAL)	LoA	3	5	7.07	19	19	0	0	90	88	10	72	58	5.8	1.77	.267
2012	Tri-City (NWL)	SS	2	7	5.47	14	14	0	0	72	68	4	39	37	4.6	1.48	.249
Minor League Totals			5	12	6.36	33	33	0	0	163	156	14	111	95	5.3	1.64	.259

30 PARKER FRAZIER, RHP

BA GRADE
40
MEDIUM

Born: Nov. 11, 1988. **B-T:** R-R. **Ht.:** 6-5. **Wt.:** 185. **Drafted:** HS—Tulsa, 2007 (8th round). **Signed by:** Dar Cox.

Frazier pitched at Tulsa, his hometown, in 2012 and led the Texas League with 167 innings, which tied for fifth in the minors. He also led the TL in losses and home runs allowed. He has a very good idea of what he's doing with each hitter, a cerebral approach to pitching that isn't surprising because his father George is a former reliever in the majors and a current Rockies television analyst. Parker's fastball, slider and changeup all improved in 2012. He's a strike-thrower who doesn't have fine command but controls the zone with a sinker that sits at 90-91 mph, gets up to 93 and induces a lot of grounders. He's tough, competitive and aggressive, sometimes to the point where he overthrows and leaves his fastball up in the zone. His arm speed on his changeup has gotten better, along with his ability to stay on top of the pitch and keep it down, and his slider gotten a little tighter. Frazier profiles as a middle reliever or swingman. Though he wasn't added to the 40-man roster in the offseason, he has a chance to get his first major league callup this year after getting some time in Triple-A.

Year	Club (League)	Class	W	L	ERA	G	GS	CG	SV	IP	H	HR	BB	SO	K/9	WHIP	AVG
2007	Casper (PIO)	R	3	5	10.07	16	10	0	0	45	78	8	18	22	4.4	2.15	.386
2008	Tri-City (NWL)	SS	5	5	3.83	15	15	0	0	87	94	3	20	47	4.9	1.31	.281
2009	Asheville (SAL)	LoA	10	7	4.48	23	23	1	0	131	158	7	33	98	6.8	1.46	.303
2010	Tri-City (NWL)	SS	1	3	7.52	5	5	0	0	20	28	1	8	15	6.6	1.77	.318
	Modesto (CAL)	HiA	2	2	4.70	9	9	0	0	46	49	1	11	38	7.4	1.30	.269
2011	Modesto (CAL)	HiA	11	11	4.50	27	27	0	0	154	171	15	46	105	6.1	1.41	.281
2012	Tulsa (TL)	AA	5	14	3.88	27	27	0	0	167	182	19	40	93	5.0	1.33	.285
Minor League Totals			37	47	4.74	122	116	1	0	650	760	54	176	418	5.8	1.44	.295

Detroit Tigers

BY CONOR GLASSEY

Despite being in first place in the American League Central for just 34 days during the season and finishing with the seventh-best record (88-74) in the league, the Tigers returned to the playoffs in 2012, making back-to-back trips to the postseason for the first time since 1934-35.

Tied with the White Sox for the division lead with eight games left, the Tigers finished with a 6-2 kick. Detroit needed all five games to beat the Athletics in an AL Division Series, then swept the Yankees in the American League Championship Series before suffering the same fate at the hands of the Giants in the World Series.

Though Detroit is the poorest of America's 25 largest cities, fans supported the club by making it one of just nine teams to draw three million fans in 2012. They repaid 83-year-old Tigers owner Mike Ilitch, who authorized the game's fifth-highest Opening Day payroll ($132 million) in an attempt to win his first World Series and the franchise's first since 1984.

Three players accounted for nearly half of that payroll total. Prince Fielder ($23 million), signed as a free agent in the offseason, delivered as expected by hitting .313 with 30 homers. Miguel Cabrera ($21 million) was even better, winning baseball's first triple crown since 1967 by batting .330 with 44 homers and 139 RBIs. Justin Verlander ($20 million) followed his MVP/Cy Young season of 2011 by going 17-8, 2.68 and leading the majors in strikeouts and innings.

That may be the best nucleus in the game, and the Tigers will continue fielding it. Verlander is signed through 2014, Cabrera is locked up through 2015 and Fielder is extended through 2020, with a total of $296 million remaining on their contracts. The Tigers continued to spend on the free agent market this winter, adding Torii Hunter for two years and $26 million.

Cabrera, Fielder and Verlander will have to keep producing, because the farm system has little to offer in the way of solid regulars and starting pitchers beyond third baseman Nick Castellanos and outfielder Avisail Garcia.

The soft spot of the 2012 club was the bullpen. Tigers relievers ranked 10th in the American League in ERA and closer Jose Valverde melted down in the playoffs. But the Tigers' Top 30 is loaded with hard throwers who are already relievers or profile best in that role, and team officials sounded comfortable in the winter going into 2013 with No. 3 prospect Bruce Rondon penciled in as the team's closer.

Miguel Cabrera moved to third base in 2012 and won the first Triple Crown since 1967

The Tigers used to be one of the most aggressive teams in the draft, but they have forfeited their last three first-round picks as free-agent compensation for Jose Valverde, Victor Martinez and Fielder. Detroit spent $6 million on the 2011-12 drafts, the second-lowest total in baseball.

While the Tigers haven't finished in the top half of Baseball America's annual organization talent rankings since 2007, they have gotten production out of their system. They're tied with the Cubs with 12 players who have reached the majors from the 2008-12 drafts, most notably Alex Avila and Andy Dirks.

Detroit also has been able to trade minor leaguers for key additions to the major league roster during the last three seasons. The Tigers astutely picked up Jhonny Peralta (from the Indians for lefthander Giovanni Soto) in 2010, and Doug Fister (from the Mariners for big leaguers Charlie Furbush and Casper Wells, third baseman Francisco Martinez and righty Chance Ruffin) and Delmon Young (from the Twins for lefty Cole Nelson and righty Lester Oliveros) in 2011. Last season, they grabbed Anibal Sanchez and Omar Infante from the Marlins for former No. 1 overall prospect Jacob Turner, catcher Rob Brantly, lefty Brian Flynn and a swap of competitive-balance lottery picks.

ORGANIZATION OVERVIEW

THIS YEAR'S TOP 30

Player, Pos.		Grade
1.	Nick Castellanos, 3b/of	65/Medium
2.	Avisail Garcia, of	55/Medium
3.	Bruce Rondon, rhp	55/Medium
4.	Jake Thompson, rhp	50/High
5.	Austin Schotts, of	50/High
6.	Danry Vasquez, of	50/High
7.	Tyler Collins, of	50/High
8.	Casey Crosby, lhp	50/High
9.	Eugenio Suarez, ss/2b	50/High
10.	Adam Wilk, lhp	45/Low
11.	James McCann, c	45/Medium
12.	Tyler Clark, rhp	45/Medium
13.	Melvin Mercedes, rhp	50/High
14.	Drew VerHagen, rhp	45/High
15.	Steven Moya, of	50/Extreme
16.	Jose Ortega, rhp	45/High
17.	Harold Castro, 2b	45/High
18.	Montreal Robertson, rhp	50/Extreme
19.	Kyle Lobstein, lhp	45/High
20.	Jeff Kobernus, 2b	45/High
21.	Brenny Paulino, rhp	50/Extreme
22.	Endrys Briceno, rhp	50/Extreme
23.	Curt Casali, c	45/High
24.	Bryan Holaday, c	40/Medium
25.	Luke Putkonen, rhp	40/Medium
26.	Ramon Cabrera, c	45/High
27.	Dixon Machado, ss	45/High
28.	Hernan Perez, 2b/ss	45/High
29.	Edgar de la Rosa, rhp	50/Extreme
30.	Daniel Fields, of	50/Extreme

LAST YEAR'S TOP 30

Player, Pos.		Status
1.	Jacob Turner, rhp	(Marlins)
2.	Nick Castellanos, 3b	No. 1
3.	Drew Smyly, lhp	Majors
4.	Casey Crosby, lhp	No. 8
5.	Andy Oliver, lhp	(Pirates)
6.	Brenny Paulino, rhp	No. 21
7.	Rob Brantly, c	(Marlins)
8.	Alex Burgos, lhp	Dropped out
9.	James McCann, c	No. 11
10.	Avisail Garcia, of	No. 2
11.	Ramon Lebron, rhp	Dropped out
12.	Bruce Rondon, rhp	No. 3
13.	Tyler Collins, of	No. 7
14.	Aaron Westlake, 1b	Dropped out
15.	Brayan Villarreal, rhp	Majors
16.	Matt Hoffman, lhp	Dropped out
17.	Tyler Stohr, rhp	Dropped out
18.	Danry Vasquez, of	No. 6
19.	Brandon Loy, ss	Dropped out
20.	Tyler Gibson, of	Dropped out
21.	Duane Below, lhp	Majors
22.	Adam Wilk, lhp	No. 10
23.	Luis Marte, rhp	Dropped out
24.	Brian Flynn, lhp	(Marlins)
25.	Dixon Machado, ss	No. 27
26.	Kevin Eichhorn, rhp	Dropped out
27.	Daniel Fields, of	No. 30
28.	Eugenio Suarez, ss	No. 9
29.	Jose Ortega, rhp	No. 16
30.	Hernan Perez, 2b/ss	No. 28

BEST TOOLS

Best Hitter for Average	Nick Castellanos
Best Power Hitter	Avisail Garcia
Best Strike-Zone Discipline	Nick Castellanos
Fastest Baserunner	Austin Schotts
Best Athlete	Austin Schotts
Best Fastball	Bruce Rondon
Best Curveball	Casey Crosby
Best Slider	Bruce Rondon
Best Changeup	Adam Wilk
Best Control	Adam Wilk
Best Defensive Catcher	James McCann
Best Defensive Infielder	Dixon Machado
Best Infield Arm	Dixon Machado
Best Defensive Outfielder	Daniel Fields
Best Outfield Arm	Avisail Garcia

PROJECTED 2016 LINEUP

Catcher	Alex Avila
First Base	Prince Fielder
Second Base	Jhonny Peralta
Third Base	Nick Castellanos
Shortstop	Eugenio Suarez
Left Field	Austin Jackson
Center Field	Austin Schotts
Right Field	Avisail Garcia
Designated Hitter	Miguel Cabrera
No. 1 Starter	Justin Verlander
No. 2 Starter	Max Scherzer
No. 3 Starter	Doug Fister
No. 4 Starter	Drew Smyly
No. 5 Starter	Rick Porcello
Closer	Bruce Rondon

TOP PROSPECTS OF THE DECADE

Year	Player, Pos.	2012 Org.
2003	Jeremy Bonderman, rhp	Out of baseball
2004	Kyle Sleeth, rhp	Out of baseball
2005	Curtis Granderson, of	Yankees
2006	Justin Verlander, rhp	Tigers
2007	Cameron Maybin, of	Padres
2008	Rick Porcello, rhp	Tigers
2009	Rick Porcello, rhp	Tigers
2010	Jacob Turner, rhp	Marlins
2011	Jacob Turner, rhp	Marlins
2012	Jacob Turner, rhp	Marlins

TOP DRAFT PICKS OF THE DECADE

Year	Player, Pos.	2012 Org.
2003	Kyle Sleeth, rhp	Out of baseball
2004	Justin Verlander, rhp	Tigers
2005	Cameron Maybin, of	Padres
2006	Andrew Miller, lhp	Red Sox
2007	Rick Porcello, rhp	Tigers
2008	Ryan Perry, rhp	Nationals
2009	Jacob Turner, rhp	Marlins
2010	Nick Castellanos, 3b (1st round supp.)	Tigers
2011	James McCann, c (2nd round)	Tigers
2012	Jake Thompson, rhp (2nd round)	Tigers

LARGEST BONUSES IN CLUB HISTORY

Jacob Turner, 2009	$4,700,000
Rick Porcello, 2007	$3,580,000
Andrew Miller, 2006	$3,550,000
Eric Munson, 1999	$3,500,000
Nick Castellanos, 2010	$3,450,000

DETROIT TIGERS

TOP 2013 ROOKIE: Avisail Garcia, of. Expectations are high for the toolsy outfielder after he hit .455 in the American League Championship Series.

BREAKOUT PROSPECT: Montreal Robertson, rhp. The 29th-round pick from 2011 is a big, smooth athlete with a fastball that touches 98 mph.

SLEEPER: Jose Valdez, rhp. He used a mid-90s fastball and nasty slider to lead the Rookie-level Gulf Coast League with 15 saves last summer.

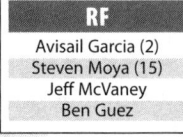

SOURCE OF TOP 30 TALENT			
Homegrown	27	Acquired	3
College	7	Trades	3
Junior college	2	Rule 5 draft	0
High school	5	Independent leagues	0
Nondrafted free agents	0	Free agents/waivers	0
International	13		

LF
Danry Vasquez (6)
Tyler Collins (7)

CF
Austin Schotts (5)
Daniel Fields (30)
Jake Stewart
Tyler Gibson
Rashad Brown

RF
Avisail Garcia (2)
Steven Moya (15)
Jeff McVaney
Ben Guez

3B
Nick Castellanos (1)
Wade Gaynor
Jason King

SS
Eugenio Suarez (9)
Dixon Machado (27)
Brandon Loy

2B
Harold Castro (17)
Jeff Kobernus (20)
Hernan Perez (28)
Devon Travis

1B
Dean Green
Jordan Lennerton
Aaron Westlake

C
James McCann (11)
Curt Casali (23)
Bryan Holaday (24)
Ramon Cabrera (26)
Adolfo Reina
Bennett Pickar
Franklin Navarro

LHP

LHSP	LHRP
Casey Crosby (8)	Darin Downs
Adam Wilk (10)	Matt Hoffman
Kyle Lobstein (19)	Joe Rogers
Alex Burgos	Ryan Robowski
Logan Ehlers	
Jay Voss	
Kyle Ryan	
Josh Turley	
Jordan John	
Preston Jamison	

RHP

RHSP	RHRP
Jake Thompson (4)	Bruce Rondon (3)
Drew VerHagen (14)	Tyler Clark (12)
Montreal Robertson (18)	Melvin Mercedes (13)
Brenny Paulino (21)	Jose Ortega (16)
Endrys Briceno (22)	Luke Putkonen (25)
Edgar de la Rosa (29)	Luis Marte
Hudson Randall	Jose Valdez
Tommy Collier	Will Clinard
Kevin Eichhorn	Mike Morrison
	Tyler White
	Tyler Stohr
	Robbie Weinhardt
	Ramon Lebron
	Slade Smith
	Yorfrank Lopez
	Dan Bennett
	Hunter Scantling
	Juan Falcon
	Julio Felix
	Matt Davenport

2012   BONUSES: $3.2 MILLION

BEST PURE HITTER: OF Austin Schotts (3) displayed his natural feel for hitting in his pro debut, batting .310/.360/.449 in the Rookie-level Gulf Coast League.

BEST POWER HITTER: OF Jake Stewart's (9) power goes more to the gaps than over the fence, but the Tigers didn't sign any true mashers. Stewart was an enigma at Stanford, batting just .265 with nine homers in three seasons as his athleticism never quite translated to college baseball.

FASTEST RUNNER: Schotts is a plus-plus runner who stole 16 bases in 42 pro games. He was a short-stop in high school but has fringy arm strength, so Detroit moved him to center field. OF Rashad Brown (26) is also a well above-average runner.

BEST DEFENSIVE PLAYER: With his tools, Schotts should develop into an asset in center field. He naturally takes good routes on flyballs and impressed Tigers officials with his ability to retain instruction and make quick adjustments. Stewart has plus speed and is a quality defender in center field as well.

BEST FASTBALL: RHP Drew VerHagen (4) has a big frame at 6-foot-6 and 230 pounds and a fastball that is just as intimidating, topping out at 97 mph. His lack of an average secondary pitch limits his ability to miss bats, however.

BEST SECONDARY PITCH: RHP Jake Thompson (2) shows the makings of two plus pitches, pairing a hard slider with a fastball that peaks at 95 mph.

BEST PRO DEBUT: Detroit's top two picks both performed well in the GCL. Thompson went 1-2, 1.91 with 31 strikeouts in 28 innings, while Schotts led the GCL Tigers with an .812 OPS and stole 15 bases.

BEST ATHLETE: Stewart was a three-sport stand-out in high school. Schotts played safety for his high school football team.

MOST INTRIGUING BACKGROUND: OF Jeff McVaney's (8) father John is a minority owner of the Astros.

CLOSEST TO THE MAJORS: Detroit didn't draft any players who will shoot through the system. If VerHagen develops a better breaking ball, he could be the first to arrive in Comerica Park. LHP Joe Rogers (5) also has a shot because he has two solid pitches and had a nice debut.

BEST LATE-ROUND PICK: 2B Devon Travis (13) shows a good feel for hitting to go with solid range and smooth actions at second base. RHP Will Clinard (19) has a big frame and touches 94 mph with his fastball.

THE ONE WHO GOT AWAY: 3B Dylan LaVelle (18) fell in the draft after missing most of his senior year with a dislocated left shoulder. He spurned his commitment to Oregon State and headed to Everett (Wash.) CC so he'll be draft-eligible again in 2013. RHP Clate Schmidt (36) was a potential fourth- to sixth-round talent even after a down spring, but he slid in the draft because of his strong commitment to Clemson.

ASSESSMENT: With their first pick coming at No. 91, the Tigers had baseball's second-smallest bonus pool for the first 10 rounds at $2.1 million. They started their draft with two high school players for the first time since 2007.

2011   BONUSES: $2.9 MILLION

Detroit didn't have a first-round pick and spent conservatively, taking C James McCann (2) with its top choice. OF Tyler Collins (6) is the best prospect from this group, while LHP Brian Flynn (7) was part of the Anibal Sanchez/Omar Infante trade with the Marlins in July.

GRADE: C

2010   BONUSES: $7.3 MILLION

In another year without a first-rounder, the Tigers shelled out $3.45 million for 3B/OF Nick Castellanos (1s), now their best prospect. They also landed LHP Drew Smyly (2) and three other players who already have reached the majors in RHP Chance Ruffin (1s) and Cs Rob Brantly (3) and Bryan Holaday (6). Ruffin helped bring back Doug Fister in a 2011 trade and Brantly was part of the Sanchez/Infante package.

GRADE: B+

2009   BONUSES: $9.4 MILLION

Detroit invested $8.9 million in RHP Jacob Turner (1), LHP Andy Oliver (2) and OF Daniel Fields (6), and none of them has developed as hoped. Turner (part of the Sanchez/Infante deal) and Oliver (traded to the Pirates) have pitched in the big leagues, as has LHP Adam Wilk (11).

GRADE: C+

2008   BONUSES: $3.7 MILLION

C Alex Avila (5) and OF Andy Dirks (8) have exceeded expectations and become quality big league regulars. Since-traded RHPs Ryan Perry (1), Robbie Weinhardt (10) and Thad Weber (16) also have gotten to the majors.

GRADE: B+

Draft analysis by Conor Glassey (2012) and Jim Callis (2008-11). Numbers in parentheses indicate draft rounds.

1 NICK CASTELLANOS, 3B/OF

Born: March 4, 1992. **B-T:** R-R. **Ht.:** 6-4. **Wt.:** 210.
Drafted: HS—Southwest Ranches, Fla., 2010 (1st round supplemental). **Signed by:** Rolando Casanova.

BA GRADE
65
MEDIUM

MIKE JANES

A South Florida native, Castellanos spent his first two years of high school at American Heritage High, where he played with 2008 Royals first-round pick Eric Hosmer and 2012 Red Sox first-rounder Deven Marrero on a team that won the 2008 national title, then played his final two seasons at Archbishop McCarthy High, which won the 2011 national championship the year after he left. The Tigers had Castellanos ranked near the top of their 2010 draft board but didn't expect to get the opportunity to draft him after losing their first-round pick for signing free agent Jose Valverde. But Castellanos slid amid reports that he wanted $6 million to sign, allowing Detroit to grab him with the 44th overall selection. He signed at the deadline for a supplemental first round-record $3.45 million. After leading the low Class A Midwest League with 158 hits in his first full season, Castellanos started 2012 as the third-youngest player in the high Class A Florida State League. He hit .405 in 55 games to earn selection to the FSL all-star game, but he already had moved up to Double-A Erie by the time the contest took place. He did get to play in the Futures Game, however, going 3-for-4 with a home run and a walk to win the game's MVP award. The bat he used in the game was taken to the Hall of Fame.

One of the best pure hitters in the minor leagues, Castellanos has batted .316 while advancing quickly. With natural, loose, wristy actions, he's a rare righthander whose swing is described as pretty. He recognizes pitches well, lets balls travel deep and has no problems catching up to premium velocity. He makes loud contact and can hit all types of pitching. Castellanos has a tall, well-proportioned frame with wiry strength. His natural power is to right-center field, but he truly uses the entire ballpark. Of his 42 doubles and homers in 2012, 15 went to left field, 10 to center and 17 to right. Though more advanced pitchers got him to chase sliders away in Double-A, he has shown the ability to make adjustments. Overall, he has the upside of a .300 hitter who could hit 40 doubles and 20-25 homers annually. Defensively, Castellanos is still looking for a permanent home. He came up as a third baseman, and still might end up there eventually, but the Tigers moved him to right field at midseason. He has earned mixed reviews at third base. Some scouts think he has stiff actions and can be too timid on balls, often getting caught in between hops. Others felt he was solid at the hot corner with quick reactions and above-average arm strength. In mid-July, the Tigers shifted him to right field. He's still learning to read balls off the bat and to take clean routes on flyballs. With more experience, he could be an average outfielder. He has below-average speed but moves well for his size and runs the bases well.

Moving Castellanos to the outfield makes sense in the short term. The Tigers have $116 million committed to Miguel Cabrera, Prince Fielder and Victor Martinez for 2013-14, tying up their infield corners and DH spot. Castellanos likely will start 2013 back in Double-A but it won't be long before he adds another impact bat to the middle of an already fearsome Detroit lineup.

SCOUTING GRADES

Batting: 70. **Defense:** 50.
Power: 55. **Arm:** 55.
Speed: 40.

Based on 20-80 scouting scale, where 50 represents major league average, and future projection rather than present tools.

Year	Club (League)	Class	AVG	G	AB	R	H	2B	3B	HR	RBI	BB	SO	SB	CS	OBP	SLG
2010	Tigers (GCL)	R	.333	7	24	5	8	2	0	0	3	4	5	0	1	.414	.417
2011	West Michigan (MWL)	LoA	.312	135	507	65	158	36	3	7	76	45	130	3	2	.367	.436
2012	Lakeland (FSL)	HiA	.405	55	215	37	87	17	3	3	32	22	42	3	2	.461	.553
	Erie (EL)	AA	.264	79	322	35	85	15	1	7	25	14	76	5	4	.296	.382
Minor League Totals			.316	276	1068	142	338	70	7	17	136	85	253	11	9	.367	.443

2 AVISAIL GARCIA, OF

BA GRADE

55

MEDIUM

Born: June 12, 1991. **B-T:** R-R. **Ht.:** 6-4. **Wt.:** 240. **Signed:** Venezuela, 2007. **Signed by:** Alejandro Rodriguez/Pedro Chavez.

Signed for $200,000 out of Venezuela, Garcia developed slowly in his first four pro seasons before taking off in 2012, when he moved from high Class A Lakeland to the majors. He made the Tigers' postseason roster, starting against lefthanded pitchers. Dubbed "Little Miggy" by his teammates for his physical resemblance to Miguel Cabrera, Garcia has a similar stance, set-up and swing to his fellow countryman. He doesn't have Cabrera's upside, but Garcia is loaded with tools and could become an average hitter with above-average power. He cut down on his strikeouts in 2012, but he's overly aggressive at the plate and rarely walks. He has the brute strength to get away with hitting pitchers' pitches and Garcia has a surprising athleticism considering his size. He's an average runner with good instincts who could be a 20-20 threat in the majors. At least an average defender in right field, he played 44 games in center in Double-A and has a strong arm. He'll need to improve his plate discipline, and he has the tools to be a solid regular with all-star potential.

Year	Club (League)	Class	AVG	G	AB	R	H	2B	3B	HR	RBI	BB	SO	SB	CS	OBP	SLG
2008	Tigers (VSL)	R	.298	63	245	33	73	12	2	7	34	15	39	7	5	.342	.449
2009	Lakeland (FSL)	HiA	.250	3	8	1	2	0	0	0	0	0	2	0	0	.250	.250
	West Michigan (MWL)	LoA	.264	81	299	36	79	11	2	1	31	8	70	8	7	.289	.324
2010	West Michigan (MWL)	LoA	.281	125	494	58	139	17	4	4	63	20	113	20	4	.313	.356
2011	Lakeland (FSL)	HiA	.264	129	488	53	129	16	6	11	56	18	132	14	5	.297	.389
2012	Lakeland (FSL)	HiA	.289	67	266	47	77	8	5	8	36	11	57	14	4	.324	.447
	Erie (EL)	AA	.312	55	215	31	67	9	3	6	22	7	38	9	4	.345	.465
	Detroit (AL)	MAJ	.319	23	47	7	15	0	0	0	3	3	10	0	2	.373	.319
Major League Totals			.319	23	47	7	15	0	0	0	3	3	10	0	2	.373	.319
Minor League Totals			.281	523	2015	259	566	73	22	37	242	79	451	72	29	.314	.394

3 BRUCE RONDON, RHP

BA GRADE

55

MEDIUM

Born: Dec. 9, 1990. **B-T:** R-R. **Ht.:** 6-3. **Wt.:** 271. **Signed:** Venezuela, 2007. **Signed by:** German Robles/Pedro Chavez/Miguel Garcia.

Rondon's prospect status has risen nearly as fast as his weight. The organization's 2012 minor league pitcher of the year after finishing third in the minors with 29 saves, he weighed 190 pounds when he signed out of Venezuela in 2007 (where he initially tried out for teams as a catcher) but now tips the scales at nearly 300. Rondon hit 102 mph with his first pitch at the Futures Game in July, touched 103 during the season and normally works at 97-100 mph. Along with its top-of-the-charts velocity, his fastball has boring action and breaks its fair share of bats. Rondon worked in spring training to get more comfortable with his slider grip. He has tightened and improved his slider, but it still gets slurvy at times. His slider shows signs of becoming an average offering, as does his high-80s changeup with late sink. He made significant strides with his control and command in 2012, but both still have a long way to go and likely will always be an issue because of his lack of athleticism. He's fearless on the mound and will get a chance to close in Detroit in 2013.

Year	Club (League)	Class	W	L	ERA	G	GS	CG	SV	IP	H	HR	BB	SO	K/9	WHIP	AVG
2008	Tigers (VSL)	R	2	6	3.58	13	13	1	0	55	48	0	20	34	5.5	1.23	.225
2009	Tigers (GCL)	R	0	1	4.76	3	3	0	0	11	12	0	8	15	11.9	1.76	.267
	Tigers (VSL)	R	0	0	13.50	3	0	0	0	4	5	0	7	4	9.0	3.00	.313
2010	Tigers (GCL)	R	0	0	0.70	24	0	0	15	26	11	1	14	26	9.1	0.97	.133
	Lakeland (FSL)	HiA	0	0	1.35	4	0	0	2	7	2	1	2	7	9.5	0.60	.095
2011	West Michigan (MWL)	LoA	2	2	2.03	41	0	0	19	40	22	0	34	61	13.7	1.40	.164
2012	Lakeland (FSL)	HiA	1	0	1.93	22	0	0	15	23	12	1	10	34	13.1	0.94	.152
	Erie (EL)	AA	0	1	0.83	21	0	0	12	22	15	1	9	23	9.6	1.11	.195
	Toledo (IL)	AAA	1	0	2.25	9	0	0	2	8	5	1	7	9	10.1	1.50	.167
Minor League Totals			6	10	2.53	140	16	1	65	196	132	5	111	213	9.8	1.24	.189

4 JAKE THOMPSON, RHP

Born: Jan. 31, 1994. **B-T:** R-R. **Ht.:** 6-4. **Wt.:** 235. **Drafted:** HS—Heath, Texas, 2012 (2nd round). **Signed by:** Tim Grieve.

The Tigers didn't have a first-round pick in 2012 after signing Prince Fielder, so their top choice didn't come until 91st overall. Detroit went with Thompson, who turned down a commitment to Texas Christian to sign for $531,800. He pitched Rockwall-Heath High to the Texas 4-A championship, going 12-1, 0.73 on the mound and hitting .448 with nine homers as a first baseman. Thompson looks like a future rotation workhorse with his physical, proportioned frame. He throws fastballs that sit at 88-92 mph and top out at 95. His fastball has heavy life and he works on a steep downhill plane to the plate. His slider shows occasional tight bite and the flashes of being a plus pitch down the road, though it flattens out at times. He also shows feel for a changeup. Thompson held his velocity deep into games during his high school season, but he pitched 90 innings as a senior and started to wear down in pro ball. The Tigers shut him down in early August and kept him out of instructional league. His stuff and consistency should improve now that he's focusing on pitching. Thompson has the stuff, athleticism and work ethic to profile as a mid-rotation starter. After his abbreviated pro debut, he'll likely start 2013 in extended spring training before heading to short-season Connecticut in June.

BA GRADE
50
HIGH

Year	Club (League)	Class	W	L	ERA	G	GS	CG	SV	IP	H	HR	BB	SO	K/9	WHIP	AVG
2012	Tigers (GCL)	R	1	2	1.91	7	7	0	0	28	14	1	10	31	9.8	0.85	.149
Minor League Totals			1	2	1.91	7	7	0	0	28	14	1	10	31	9.8	0.85	.149

5 AUSTIN SCHOTTS, OF

Born: Sept. 16, 1993. **B-T:** R-R. **Ht.:** 5-10. **Wt.:** 163. **Drafted:** HS—Frisco, Texas, 2012 (3rd round). **Signed by:** Tim Grieve.

Schotts wasn't a big name on the high school showcase circuit, but he shot up draft boards last spring thanks to his natural athleticism. He also starred as a safety and kick returner in football. A third-round pick in June who signed for $389,100, he hit .388 in his first month in pro ball before dislocating a finger and then cooling off. Schotts has excellent bat speed with a short, balanced swing. Thanks to his quick wrists and strong forearms, he has surprising pop for a smaller player. He has the potential to be a solid hitter with fringy home run power and plenty of doubles and stolen bases. He used his plus-plus speed to steal 16 bases in 42 pro games. A shortstop in high school, Schotts moved to center field after signing. The change better utilizes his speed and mitigates his below-average arm strength. He's a high-energy player who made a seamless transition to pro ball and a new position because of his work ethic and ability to retain information. Schotts has the tools and makeup to handle a full-season assignment to low Class A West Michigan as a 19-year-old. He needs to continue to get stronger and make adjustments to pro pitching but profiles as a first-division center fielder.

BA GRADE
50
HIGH

Year	Club (League)	Class	AVG	G	AB	R	H	2B	3B	HR	RBI	BB	SO	SB	CS	OBP	SLG
2012	Tigers (GCL)	R	.310	40	155	31	48	11	1	3	21	12	41	15	4	.360	.452
	Lakeland (FSL)	HiA	.333	2	3	1	1	0	0	0	0	0	1	1	0	.333	.333
Minor League Totals			.310	42	158	32	49	11	1	3	21	12	42	16	4	.360	.449

6 DANRY VASQUEZ, OF

Born: Jan. 8, 1994. **B-T:** L-R. **Ht.:** 6-3. **Wt.:** 177. **Signed:** Venezuela, 2010. **Signed by:** Oscar Garcia/Pedro Chavez.

The Tigers scouted Vasquez for two years before signing him for $1.2 million, their largest bonus ever for a Venezuelan amateur. The youngest player in the Midwest League at the start of the 2012 season, he was overmatched by low Class A pitching as an 18-year-old. Following a demotion, he rebounded to lead the short-season New York-Penn League with 90 hits. Vasquez has an advanced approach at the plate and good pitch recognition for his age. He has explosive bat speed and a compact, balanced swing. He has a quiet load, creates natural leverage and has a knack for centering the ball. He shows advanced feel for driving pitches the other way and has power to all parts of the park. Most of Vasquez's value comes from his offense. He's a below-average runner who's still learning how to read the ball off the bat and take proper routes in the outfield. He's likely limited to left field—so the bat will really have to play—and he has a solid arm. Vasquez will get another crack at the Midwest League in 2013, when he'll still be one of the circuit's youngest players at age 19. As he adds strength, he projects as a solid hitter with plus power potential.

BA GRADE
50
HIGH

Year	Club (League)	Class	AVG	G	AB	R	H	2B	3B	HR	RBI	BB	SO	SB	CS	OBP	SLG
2011	Tigers (GCL)	R	.272	54	206	25	56	8	1	2	30	7	34	3	2	.306	.350
2012	West Michigan (MWL)	LoA	.162	29	99	5	16	3	0	1	7	7	20	0	0	.218	.222
	Connecticut (NYP)	SS	.311	72	289	36	90	16	2	2	35	13	45	6	4	.341	.401
Minor League Totals			.273	155	594	66	162	27	3	5	72	27	99	9	6	.308	.354

7 TYLER COLLINS, OF

Born: June 6, 1990. **B-T:** L-L. **Ht.:** 5-11. **Wt.:** 205. **Drafted:** Howard (Texas) JC, 2011 (6th round). **Signed by:** Tim Grieve.

After batting .404 as a Baylor freshman in 2010, Collins became academically ineligible, so he transferred to Howard (Texas) JC. He became the 2011 national junior college player of the year after topping NJCAA Division I in hits (105), doubles (34) and home runs (19) while ranking second in batting (.488) and RBIs (82). He has continued to hit in pro ball, jumping to high Class A for his first full pro season and ranking among the Florida State League leaders in several categories. Collins has a thick, muscular build and a compact stroke. He has a patient, polished approach at the plate. He knows how to work the count well and uses the entire field, making consistent hard contact. While his power is geared more toward doubles than homers, he has strength in his swing with solid average bat speed. Collins has average foot speed and good instincts on the bases, as evidenced by his 20 steals in 23 attempts in 2012. He's an average defender with solid arm strength on the outfield corners. He's a hard-nosed player. Collins may not have profile power for a corner outfielder, which could make him more of a fourth outfielder than a regular. His pure hitting ability, on-base skills, gap power and grinder mentality could make him a poor man's Jason Kubel. Collins will begin 2013 in Double-A.

BA GRADE: 50 HIGH

2012 Club (Class)	AVG	OBP	SLG	AB	R	H	2B	3B	HR	RBI	BB	SO	SB
Lakeland (HiA)	.290	.371	.429	473	68	137	35	5	7	66	58	64	20

8 CASEY CROSBY, LHP

Born: Sept. 17, 1988. **B-T:** R-L. **Ht.:** 6-5. **Wt.:** 200. **Drafted:** HS—Maple Park, Ill., 2007 (5th round). **Signed by:** Marty Miller.

Crosby has had one of the best arms in the system since signing for $748,500 in 2007. He hurt his elbow in instructional league right after he was drafted and missed most of 2008 after Tommy John surgery. Then he missed most of 2010 with swelling in the joint. Healthy for the last two seasons, he made his big league debut in June when Doug Fister went on the disabled list with a ribcage strain. Crosby has better stuff than most lefthanders. When he's on, he has a 91-94 mph fastball that tops out at 96 and a power curveball in the low 80s. He has learned to back off his fastball a bit and save a little extra for when he really needs it. He also has shown the ability to add and subtract from his curveball. Crosby has tinkered with his grip—now using a three-finger grip—and made improvements with his changeup. He backspins the pitch well, which creates deception, but it's still fringy. He has reduced the effort in his delivery and taken a more direct line to the plate, though his control still needs work. If Crosby can throw enough quality strikes, he has the stuff to be a solid No. 3 starter. The Tigers currently have a crowded rotation, so he figures to start 2013 in Triple-A or in the big league bullpen.

BA GRADE: 50 HIGH

Year	Club (League)	Class	W	L	ERA	G	GS	CG	SV	IP	H	HR	BB	SO	K/9	WHIP	AVG
2008	Tigers (GCL)	R	0	0	0.00	3	3	0	0	5	4	0	3	2	3.9	1.50	.211
2009	West Michigan (MWL)	LoA	10	4	2.41	24	24	0	0	105	70	3	48	117	10.1	1.13	.195
2010	Tigers (GCL)	R	0	1	8.76	3	3	0	0	12	21	1	4	10	7.3	2.03	.382
2011	Erie (EL)	AA	9	7	4.10	25	25	0	0	132	122	11	77	121	8.3	1.51	.253
2012	Detroit (AL)	MAJ	1	1	9.49	3	3	0	0	12	15	2	11	9	6.6	2.11	.313
	Toledo (IL)	AAA	7	9	4.01	22	22	2	0	126	112	12	65	112	8.0	1.41	.238
Major League Totals			1	1	9.49	3	3	0	0	12	15	2	11	9	6.6	2.11	.313
Minor League Totals			26	21	3.70	77	77	2	0	379	329	27	197	362	8.6	1.39	.237

9 EUGENIO SUAREZ, SS/2B

Born: July 18, 1991. **B-T:** B-R. **Ht.:** 6-0. **Wt.:** 178. **Signed:** Venezuela, 2008. **Signed by:** Alejandro Rodriguez.

Suarez made the leap to full-season ball in 2012, his fourth professional season. He was one of the best all-around infielders in the Midwest League, ranking second in the league in hits (147) and fielding percentage at shortstop (.971) and playing in the circuit's all-star game. Suarez has a short, quick stroke and works himself into hitter's counts. He barrels balls consistently and can drive them to the gaps, but he sometimes gets too pull-conscious and needs to work on using the middle of the field more often. His on-base skills stand out more than his below-average power. Suarez has smooth defensive actions, soft hands and a plus arm, but his range at shortstop is limited by his fringe-average speed. He's able to compensate in the field because of his above-average instincts for the game. He's steady and makes plays on all the balls he gets to, though he can get a little too comfortable at times in the field. He played errorless ball in 15 games at second base for West Michigan. Suarez's instincs also show on the bases, where he's a good baserunner and can read pitchers. He wore down toward the end of the year, so he'll need to do a better job preparing for the grind of a full season schedule. While he might be a little stretched at shortstop, Suarez still is Detroit's top prospect at the position. He'll spend 2013 in high Class A.

BA GRADE

50

HIGH

Year	Club (League)	Class	AVG	G	AB	R	H	2B	3B	HR	RBI	BB	SO	SB	CS	OBP	SLG
2009	Tigers (VSL)	R	.262	57	206	29	54	9	3	1	15	17	32	8	4	.360	.350
2010	Tigers (VSL)	R	.311	61	225	32	70	12	2	1	18	23	44	8	6	.389	.396
2011	Tigers (GCL)	R	.341	12	44	11	15	7	0	2	9	3	4	2	0	.408	.636
	Connecticut (NYP)	SS	.250	58	204	37	51	11	5	5	24	18	43	9	5	.323	.426
2012	West Michigan (MWL)	LoA	.288	135	511	82	147	34	5	6	67	65	116	21	9	.380	.409
Minor League Totals			.283	323	1190	191	337	73	15	15	133	126	239	48	24	.370	.408

10 ADAM WILK, LHP

Born: Dec. 8, 1987. **B-T:** L-L. **Ht.:** 6-2. **Wt.:** 180. **Drafted:** Long Beach State, 2009 (11th round). **Signed by:** Phil Huttmann.

At Cypress (Calif.) High, Wilk played with Josh Vitters and Tigers minor leaguer Mike Morrison while setting school records for career wins (23) and ERA (1.50). He went undrafted, however, and spent three years at Long Beach State before signing for $68,000 as an 11th-rounder in 2009. He's the 11th 49ers pitcher selected in the last 11 drafts to make the big leagues, joining the likes of Jered Weaver and Jason Vargas. A classic pitch-ability lefthander, Wilk doesn't blow hitters away with his 86-89 mph fastball but can run it up to 91 when needed. He has an average slider and the ability to change its shape and speed, throwing it anywhere from 79-85 mph. He has an average changeup with a 10 mph differential from his fastball and occasionally uses a curveball as a show-me pitch. Wilk's biggest asset is his excellent command and feel for pitching, which allowed him to lead Detroit farmhands with 128 strikeouts in 2012. He's a student of the game and shows excellent poise on the mound. While he's been roughed up in his brief big league stints, Wilk has the command and moxie to pitch at the back of a big league rotation. He compares favorably with Tommy Milone.

BA GRADE

45

LOW

Year	Club (League)	Class	W	L	ERA	G	GS	CG	SV	IP	H	HR	BB	SO	K/9	WHIP	AVG
2009	Oneonta (NYP)	SS	2	0	1.45	7	7	1	0	37	23	0	5	34	8.2	0.75	.173
	West Michigan (MWL)	LoA	2	1	1.49	7	7	0	0	36	30	2	2	33	8.2	0.88	.222
2010	Lakeland (FSL)	HiA	9	5	3.01	24	24	1	0	144	139	8	19	100	6.3	1.10	.250
	Erie (EL)	AA	2	0	1.14	3	3	0	0	24	10	1	5	14	5.3	0.63	.128
2011	Detroit (AL)	MAJ	0	0	5.40	5	0	0	0	13	14	3	3	10	6.8	1.28	.259
	Toledo (IL)	AAA	8	6	3.24	18	18	0	0	103	105	15	14	76	6.7	1.16	.262
2012	Detroit (AL)	MAJ	0	3	8.18	3	3	0	0	11	21	4	3	7	5.7	2.18	.412
	Toledo (IL)	AAA	7	11	2.77	24	24	3	0	150	123	13	28	128	7.7	1.01	.221
Major League Totals			0	3	6.66	8	3	0	0	24	35	7	6	17	6.3	1.68	.333
Minor League Totals			30	23	2.66	83	83	5	0	493	430	39	73	385	7.0	1.02	.231

11 JAMES McCANN, C

BA GRADE

45

MEDIUM

Born: June 13, 1990. **B-T:** R-R. **Ht.:** 6-2. **Wt.:** 210. **Drafted:** Arkansas, 2011 (2nd round). **Signed by:** Chris Wimmer.

The Tigers gave up their 2011 first-round pick as compensation for free agent Victor Martinez, so their first choice didn't come until No. 76 overall. They took McCann, who signed for $577,900, continuing their affinity for players from the Southeastern Conference. Of the 224 SEC players drafted from 2010-12, the Tigers picked 23 of them, by far the most of any team. Some scouts viewed McCann as a fringy receiver coming out of Arkansas, but he has improved in that regard and is now the system's best defensive catcher. He has worked hard to improve his blocking, framing and footwork. He has solid arm strength and threw out 43 percent of basestealers last year. He's a leader on the field with a take-charge attitude, and pitchers love throwing to him. McCann's defensive skills are good enough to get him to the big leagues, but his bat is a question. Using a long, flat swing path with an opposite-field approach, he has hit an anemic .227/.272/.304 in pro ball. He's a well below-average hitter with gap power at best and he's a 20 runner on the 20-80 scouting scale. With his defensive skills and makeup, McCann should at least be a useful big league backup. He'll probably return to Double-A to open 2013.

Year	Club (League)	Class	AVG	G	AB	R	H	2B	3B	HR	RBI	BB	SO	SB	CS	OBP	SLG
2011	Tigers (GCL)	R	.357	5	14	1	5	1	0	1	6	1	1	0	0	.438	.643
	West Michigan (MWL)	LoA	.059	9	34	0	2	1	0	0	1	2	12	0	0	.132	.088
2012	Lakeland (FSL)	HiA	.288	45	160	24	46	10	0	0	20	10	29	3	0	.345	.350
	Erie (EL)	AA	.200	64	220	15	44	12	0	2	19	8	44	2	2	.227	.282
Minor League Totals			.227	123	428	40	97	24	0	3	46	21	86	5	2	.272	.304

12 TYLER CLARK, RHP

BA GRADE 45 MEDIUM

Born: Jan. 4, 1989. **B-T:** R-R. **Ht.:** 6-2. **Wt.:** 185. **Drafted:** Missouri, 2010 (24th round). **Signed by:** Marty Miller.

Clark was Detroit's biggest breakout prospect in 2012. A 24th-round pick who signed for $20,000 in 2010, he held Florida State League hitters to a .137 average and two homers while recording a 0.63 ERA and 59 strikeouts in 43 innings. Clark pitches with a funky delivery with a little pause at his balance point and a quick leg kick as he comes to the plate. That adds deception to a fastball that can sit at 92-94 mph and get as high as 98. Even better than the velocity on his fastball is its natural cutting movement. Clark's best secondary pitch is an 87-89 mph cutter with tight break and three-quarter tilt. He also has a solid changeup and a decent curveball that he's working to feel more comfortable with. Clark is a hard worker and spent the fall in the Arizona Fall League. If he continues to perform in 2013, he could see the big leagues by the end of the season.

Year	Club (League)	Class	W	L	ERA	G	GS	CG	SV	IP	H	HR	BB	SO	K/9	WHIP	AVG
2010	Connecticut (NYP)	SS	3	1	2.05	21	0	0	3	44	39	1	20	43	8.8	1.34	.234
2011	Tigers (GCL)	R	0	0	3.71	13	0	0	0	17	15	1	13	25	13.2	1.65	.238
	West Michigan (MWL)	LoA	0	0	2.89	6	0	0	0	9	9	1	4	6	5.8	1.39	.250
2012	Lakeland (FSL)	HiA	6	1	0.63	31	0	0	9	43	19	1	17	59	12.4	0.84	.137
	Erie (EL)	AA	0	0	7.36	7	0	0	0	7	8	1	6	7	8.6	1.91	.276
Minor League Totals			9	2	2.17	78	0	0	12	120	90	5	60	140	10.5	1.25	.207

13 MELVIN MERCEDES, RHP

BA GRADE 50 HIGH

Born: Nov. 2, 1990. **B-T:** R-R. **Ht.:** 6-1. **Wt.:** 269. **Signed:** Dominican Republic, 2008. **Signed by:** Miguel Rodriguez/Ramon Perez.

Mercedes reminds the Tigers of Bruce Rondon because of his size, stuff and fearlessness. Another pitcher approaching 300 pounds, Mercedes intimidates hitters with his 93-98 mph fastball. His heater shows sink when he throws down in the zone, and he can elevate it and blow it by hitters too. Mercedes throws his short slider in the upper 80s. It's a fringy pitch that occasionally shows the potential to be an above-average offering, but it hasn't progressed much over the past few years. Mercedes had Tommy John surgery in 2010 and pitches with well below-average command. He has an aggressive delivery with a fast arm. He has the stuff to be a dominant set-up man if he can improve his control and develop a complement to his fastall. Added to Detroit's 40-man roster in November, he'll spend 2013 in high Class A.

Year	Club (League)	Class	W	L	ERA	G	GS	CG	SV	IP	H	HR	BB	SO	K/9	WHIP	AVG
2008	Tigers (DSL)	R	2	2	3.19	24	0	0	6	37	28	1	24	33	8.1	1.42	.207
2009	Tigers (GCL)	R	1	1	1.82	26	0	0	16	25	19	0	14	20	7.3	1.34	.221
	West Michigan (MWL)	LoA	0	1	11.57	3	0	0	0	2	1	0	3	1	3.9	1.71	.125
2010	West Michigan (MWL)	LoA	1	2	5.03	15	0	0	3	20	16	0	19	12	5.5	1.78	.225
2011	West Michigan (MWL)	LoA	0	0	10.80	2	0	0	0	2	3	0	1	1	5.4	2.40	.375
	Connecticut (NYP)	SS	3	1	2.67	21	0	0	3	34	32	0	16	21	5.6	1.43	.246
2012	West Michigan (MWL)	LoA	0	3	2.80	37	0	0	9	64	54	3	23	43	6.0	1.20	.230
	Lakeland (FSL)	HiA	0	0	0.00	1	0	0	0	1	1	0	0	0	0.0	2.00	.250
Minor League Totals			7	10	3.13	129	0	0	37	184	154	4	101	131	6.4	1.39	.227

14 DREW VERHAGEN, RHP

BA GRADE 45 HIGH

Born: Oct. 22, 1990. **B-T:** R-R. **Ht.:** 6-6. **Wt.:** 230. **Drafted:** Vanderbilt, 2012 (4th round). **Signed by:** Harold Zonder.

VerHagen played with Jake Thompson, Detroit's top 2012 draft pick, at Rockwall-Heath HS (Heath, Texas) for one season before pitching for three different colleges in three years. He went to

Oklahoma as a freshman, helped Navarro (Texas) JC win the Junior College World Series as a sophomore and attended Vanderbilt as a junior. He pitched well down the stretch for the Commodores, earning a fourth-round selection and $392,500 bonus. VerHagen throws a fastball that operates at 92-94 mph and tops out at 97. He has a big, strong frame, but some scouts don't like his arm action because of a wrist wrap and stiffness. He had Tommy John surgery as a senior in high school. Because of his arm action, VerHagen has a tendency to get under his curveball at times. The pitch shows hard 12-to-6 break when he gets on top of it. His changeup is a work in progress. VerHagen never has shown a reliable secondary pitch or consistent command, so his ability to remain a starter is questionable. He has pitched as both a starter and a reliever in college and pro ball, and the Tigers will keep him in the rotation for now. He finished his pro debut in high Class A and likely will return there to begin 2013.

Year	Club (League)	Class	W	L	ERA	G	GS	CG	SV	IP	H	HR	BB	SO	K/9	WHIP	AVG
2012	Tigers (GCL)	R	0	0	2.25	2	0	0	0	4	5	0	0	2	4.5	1.25	.313
	Lakeland (FSL)	HiA	0	3	3.67	8	6	0	0	27	20	0	14	17	5.7	1.26	.206
Minor League Totals			0	3	3.48	10	6	0	0	31	25	0	14	19	5.5	1.26	.221

15 STEVEN MOYA, OF

BA GRADE
50
EXTREME

Born: Sept. 8, 1991. **B-T:** L-R. **Ht.:** 6-7. **Wt.:** 229. **Signed:** Dominican Republic, 2008. **Signed by:** Miguel Rodriguez/Ramon Perez/Miguel Garcia.

Moya was born in Puerto Rico but signed out of the Dominican Republic in 2008. He's a physical monster who draws body comparisons to Dave Winfield. With his 6-foot-7 frame, Moya obviously has long limbs—which come with pros and cons. They add length to his swing, which leads to problems making contact, though he was able to shorten his stroke last year and cut his strikeout rate to 24 percent of his at-bats, down from 39 percent in his previous tour of the Midwest League. He also learned to use the opposite field, leading to the belief that he could be an average hitter. On the positive side, his size gives him excellent leverage and above-average power potential. Moya has surprisingly good athleticism and is an average runner. He has the plus arm strength necessary for right field, but his season ended in June when he needed Tommy John surgery. The recovery time isn't as long for position players as it is for pitchers, and he was ahead of schedule in the fall. Moya should be ready for spring training and could remain in Lakeland with the high Class A team.

Year	Club (League)	Class	AVG	G	AB	R	H	2B	3B	HR	RBI	BB	SO	SB	CS	OBP	SLG
2009	Tigers (DSL)	R	.252	60	218	36	55	8	0	6	33	33	58	4	2	.361	.372
2010	Tigers (GCL)	R	.190	40	137	12	26	5	2	6	11	6	64	0	0	.229	.299
2011	West Michigan (MWL)	LoA	.204	86	323	38	66	10	1	13	39	12	127	1	1	.234	.362
2012	West Michigan (MWL)	LoA	.288	59	243	28	70	14	3	9	47	11	59	5	3	.319	.481
Minor League Totals			.236	245	921	114	217	37	6	30	130	62	308	10	6	.288	.387

16 JOSE ORTEGA, RHP

BA GRADE
45
HIGH

Born: Oct. 12, 1988. **B-T:** R-R. **Ht.:** 5-11. **Wt.:** 185. **Signed:** Venezuela, 2006. **Signed by:** German Robles.

Ortega didn't reach full-season ball until 2010, his fourth year as a pro, and he has recorded a 5.99 ERA in Triple-A during the last two seasons. Nevertheless, he always has had a big arm and made his major league debut last year. Managers rated his fastball the International League's best in 2012. It sits at 95-98 mph with tremendous movement and grades out as at least a 70 pitch on the 20-80 scouting scale. His mid-80s slider has explosive life too and gives him a second plus pitch. Ortega hasn't had much success because his control and command are poor. He has a thin, wiry frame with some effort in his delivery. If he can learn to slow things down and realizes he can take a little off his fastball without losing effectiveness, he should be able to throw strikes more consistently. Ortega has the upside of a set-up man, and his consistency will determine how much big league managers will trust him in key situations.

Year	Club (League)	Class	W	L	ERA	G	GS	CG	SV	IP	H	HR	BB	SO	K/9	WHIP	AVG
2007	Tigers (VSL)	R	0	0	2.45	10	0	0	0	11	9	1	3	11	9.0	1.09	.209
2008	Tigers (VSL)	R	1	1	2.20	23	0	0	5	45	43	5	15	27	5.4	1.29	.256
2009	Oneonta (NYP)	SS	2	2	3.97	25	0	0	1	34	28	2	23	32	8.5	1.50	.220
2010	West Michigan (MWL)	LoA	0	3	4.56	18	0	0	1	26	28	1	17	22	7.7	1.75	.275
	Lakeland (FSL)	HiA	2	1	0.95	10	0	0	4	19	14	0	7	20	9.5	1.11	.212
	Erie (EL)	AA	1	0	3.04	15	1	0	0	24	22	2	7	19	7.2	1.23	.242
2011	Toledo (IL)	AAA	1	3	6.30	33	0	0	0	50	61	7	27	44	7.9	1.76	.310
2012	Detroit (AL)	MAJ	0	0	3.38	2	0	0	0	3	3	1	1	4	13.5	1.50	.250
	Toledo (IL)	AAA	5	8	5.74	45	0	0	1	63	76	4	51	68	9.8	2.03	.311
Major League Totals			0	0	3.38	2	0	0	0	3	3	1	1	4	13.5	1.50	.250
Minor League Totals			12	18	4.22	179	1	0	8	271	281	22	150	243	8.1	1.59	.271

17 HAROLD CASTRO, 2B

BA GRADE

45

HIGH

Born: Nov. 30, 1993. **B-T:** L-R. **Ht.:** 6-0. **Wt.:** 145. **Signed:** Venezuela, 2011. **Signed by:** Pedro Chavez.

When the Tigers signed Castro for $29,000 in March 2011, he weighed only 140 pounds but showed plus speed and the ability to consistently put the barrel on the ball. He continued to display those tools during a strong debut in the Rookie-level Venezuelan Summer League in 2011, which persuaded Detroit to have him make the jump to the United States in 2012. He didn't disappoint, ranking third in the Rookie-level Gulf Coast League with 14 doubles and fifth with a .311 batting average. Even with his slender frame, Castro generates good bat speed and is more than just a slap hitter. He's aggressive at the plate yet has a sound approach. He can turn on inside pitches or flick his wrists at pitches on the outer half to drive the ball to left field. He needs to get stronger and still doesn't project to have much more than gap power. Castro's speed makes him a stolen-base threat and his athleticism helps him in the field, but defense doesn't come as naturally to him as hitting. He's still raw at second base and has fringy arm strength. Castro is advanced enough to handle the jump to Class A this year at age 19.

Year	Club (League)	Class	AVG	G	AB	R	H	2B	3B	HR	RBI	BB	SO	SB	CS	OBP	SLG
2011	Tigers (VSL)	R	.313	63	252	44	79	10	0	1	32	11	21	24	7	.352	.365
2012	Tigers (GCL)	R	.311	51	193	24	60	14	2	1	21	10	25	15	3	.343	.420
Minor League Totals			.312	114	445	68	139	24	2	2	53	21	46	39	10	.348	.389

18 MONTREAL ROBERTSON, RHP

BA GRADE

50

EXTREME

Born: June 19, 1990. **B-T:** R-R. **Ht.:** 6-4. **Wt.:** 220. **Drafted:** Coahoma (Miss.) CC, 2011 (29th round). **Signed by:** Bryson Barber.

Robertson may wind up being one of the bigger steals in the 2011 draft. The first player ever selected from Coahoma (Miss.) CC, he went in the 29th round and signed for $15,000. He has a physical frame with long arms and legs plus tremendous athleticism for his size. That athleticism allows him to throw with a smooth, effortless delivery and the ball jumps out of his hand. His fastball took a step forward this year in 2012 as he used his legs more in his delivery, and it now sits at 94-96 mph and tops out at 98. His fastball shows heavy sink and armside run at times, and he shows the potential to have future average fastball command. Robertson relies heavily on his heater because his secondary stuff is still a work in progress. He throws a short slider in the mid-80s that breaks more like a cutter than a true slider, and he's still trying to develop feel for his changeup. The Tigers love Robertson's toughness and throwback demeanor on the mound and are excited about his upside. If Robertson can make strides with his secondary pitches like he has with his fastball, he has the potential to be a mid-rotation starter. If not, he'll have value as a power reliever. After two summers in pro ball, he's ready for a full-season assignment in 2013.

Year	Club (League)	Class	W	L	ERA	G	GS	CG	SV	IP	H	HR	BB	SO	K/9	WHIP	AVG
2011	Tigers (GCL)	R	3	2	2.73	24	0	0	9	26	29	0	14	22	7.5	1.63	.290
	Connecticut (NYP)	SS	0	0	0.00	2	0	0	1	4	3	0	2	0	1.36	.214
2012	Connecticut (NYP)	SS	0	4	4.69	11	9	0	0	48	42	2	20	33	6.2	1.29	.239
Minor League Totals			3	6	3.81	37	9	0	10	78	74	2	36	55	6.3	1.41	.255

19 KYLE LOBSTEIN, LHP

BA GRADE

45

HIGH

Born: Aug. 12, 1989. **B-T:** L-L. **Ht.:** 6-3. **Wt.:** 200. **Drafted:** HS—Flagstaff, Ariz., 2008 (2nd round). **Signed by:** Jayson Durocher (Rays).

Expectations have been high for Lobstein ever since the Rays made him the 47th overall pick in the 2008 draft and gave him an over-slot $1.5 million baseball. After touching the low 90s on the showcase circuit prior to his senior year of high school, he hasn't displayed that type of velocity since. He has reached Double-A and developed into a consistent innings-eater, but that wasn't enough for Tampa Bay to protect him on its 40-man roster before the 2012 season. The Mets took him in the major league Rule 5 draft and sold him to the Tigers in a prearranged deal. Per Rule 5 guidelines, Detroit must keep him on its major league roster throughout 2013, or else put him on waivers and offer him back to the Rays for half his $50,000 draft price. Lobstein has learned how to pitch with a below-average fastball. He throws with flawless mechanics and has good feel for pitching. His fastball resides in the upper 80s and is more notable for its movement and deception. His upper-70s curveball has sharp downward break, and he uses a solid changeup to keep hitters off balance. He doesn't project as more than a back-of-the-rotation starter unless more velocity kicks in, but Lobstein does have the craftiness to pitch in the majors.

Year	Club (League)	Class	W	L	ERA	G	GS	CG	SV	IP	H	HR	BB	SO	K/9	WHIP	AVG
2009	Hudson Valley (NYP)	SS	3	5	2.58	14	14	0	0	73	55	4	23	74	9.1	1.06	.204
2010	Bowling Green (MWL)	LoA	9	8	4.14	27	27	1	0	148	140	14	54	128	7.8	1.31	—
2011	Charlotte (FSL)	HiA	9	9	3.71	22	21	1	0	121	120	11	30	85	6.3	1.24	.257
	Montgomery (SL)	AA	1	1	7.36	2	2	0	0	11	14	4	6	11	9.0	1.82	.318

2012	Montgomery (SL)	AA	8	7	4.06	27	27	0	0	144	140	12	69	129	8.1	1.45	.260
Minor League Totals			30	30	3.85	92	91	2	0	498	469	45	182	427	7.7	1.31	.250

20 JEFF KOBERNUS, 2B

BA GRADE
45
HIGH

Born: June 30, 1988. **B-T:** R-R. **Ht.:** 6-2. **Wt.:** 210. **Drafted:** California, 2009 (2nd round). **Signed by:** Ryan Fox (Nationals).

The son of a former minor leaguer of the same name, Kobernus is a baseball rat who plays the game hard. His career has been marked by a succession of nagging injuries, and 2012 was more of the same. He came out of the chute healthy, but a thumb injury sidelined him for some of May and June, and when he returned to action his timing was off, causing him to press. Then he was hit by a pitch on July 26, resulting in a cracked rib that ended his season. The Nationals left him off their 40-man roster and saw him taken in the major league Rule 5 draft by the Red Sox, who immediately shipped him to the Tigers in a prearranged trade for infielder/outfielder Justin Henry. Kobernus' best tool is his speed, which easily rates as a 70 and sometimes flashes 80 on the 20-80 scouting scale. He's a smart, aggressive baserunner who puts pressure on defenses by stealing and taking extra bases. When he's in a groove at the plate, Kobernus swings at strikes and hits hard line drives all over the field. He got into hack mode during the second half of 2012, getting out in front on pitches and struggling to control the strike zone. He projects as an average hitter with well below-average power, though he should drive his share of extra-base hits into the gaps. Kobernus' hands are a bit stiff at second base, but he has an average arm and makes most of the routine plays. Detroit acquired him with the idea that he can help the major league club as a speed-oriented utilityman. He has to stick on the major league roster for the entire season, unless the Tigers are willing to place him on waivers and offer him back to Washington for half of his $50,000 draft price.

Year	Club (League)	Class	AVG	G	AB	R	H	2B	3B	HR	RBI	BB	SO	SB	CS	OBP	SLG
2009	Vermont (NYP)	SS	.220	10	41	8	9	1	0	0	2	2	5	4	0	.273	.244
2010	Hagerstown (SAL)	LoA	.279	74	312	40	87	18	0	1	42	17	58	21	10	.316	.346
2011	Potomac (CAR)	HiA	.282	124	489	67	138	22	4	7	52	21	87	53	8	.313	.387
2012	Harrisburg (EL)	AA	.282	82	330	41	93	10	2	1	19	19	57	42	11	.325	.333
Minor League Totals			.279	290	1172	156	327	51	6	9	115	59	207	120	29	.316	.356

21 BRENNY PAULINO, RHP

BA GRADE
50
EXTREME

Born: Feb. 21, 1993. **B-T:** R-R. **Ht.:** 6-4. **Wt.:** 170. **Signed:** Dominican Republic, 2009. **Signed by:** Carlos Santana/Ramon Perez/Miguel Garcia.

Signed for $100,000 in 2009, Paulino pitched well in his U.S. debut in 2011 and claimed the No. 6 spot on this list a year ago. But he missed the entire 2012 season with arm problems and had minor shoulder surgery in June. When he's healthy, Paulino flashes tantalizing upside with his tall, projectable frame and quick, loose arm. His fastball operated at 92-95 mph in 2011, peaked at 97 and held its velocity deep into outings. His fastball showed good life and he could throw it by hitters up in the zone. His other pitches weren't nearly as impressive, as his curveball was inconsistent and his changeup was below-average. Paulino's long arms allow him to pitch with a steep downhill plane. He showed better body control in 2011, but his command still needed work. The Tigers are going to take it slow with Paulino and ease him back in 2013, so he may begin in extended spring training before heading to Connecticut in June. If he regains the stuff he had before he got hurt, he has the potential to be a mid-rotation starter.

Year	Club (League)	Class	W	L	ERA	G	GS	CG	SV	IP	H	HR	BB	SO	K/9	WHIP	AVG
2010	Tigers (DSL)	R	1	6	3.88	16	15	0	0	46	34	0	45	55	10.7	1.71	.205
2011	Tigers (GCL)	R	4	3	2.36	11	8	2	0	46	34	1	18	45	8.9	1.14	.202
	Lakeland (FSL)	HiA	0	2	21.94	2	2	0	0	5	9	0	9	7	11.8	3.38	.346
2012	Did Not Play—Injured																
Minor League Totals			5	11	4.16	29	25	2	0	97	77	1	72	107	9.9	1.53	.214

22 ENDRYS BRICENO, RHP

BA GRADE
50
EXTREME

Born: Feb. 7, 1992. **B-T:** R-R. **Ht.:** 6-5. **Wt.:** 171. **Signed:** Venezuela, 2009. **Signed by:** German Robles.

The Tigers are one of just four teams with a Venezuelan academy, and consequently they are one of the more active teams in the nation. They signed Briceno there in March 2009 and kept him in the Venezuelan Summer League for two years before bringing him to the United States in 2011. He has pitched exclusively as a starter the past two years and has the stuff to remain in that role. He works with a 92-93 mph fastball that features above-average sink, touches 95 regularly and sometimes reaches 97. He also has an average changeup and shows flashes of an average slider. He has below-average command right now, but it has the potential to be average. If Briceno's slender build can't handle a rotation workload, he also would be an asset in a big league bullpen. His frame and stuff remind some club officials of Ramiro Mendoza. Briceno hasn't posted a sub-5.00 ERA since his 2009 pro debut but he'll probably get his first full-season assignment this year.

Year	Club (League)	Class	W	L	ERA	G	GS	CG	SV	IP	H	HR	BB	SO	K/9	WHIP	AVG
2009	Tigers (VSL)	R	0	0	3.41	16	0	0	2	32	36	4	12	16	4.5	1.52	.295
2010	Tigers (VSL)	R	2	5	5.63	14	9	0	0	46	56	2	16	33	6.4	1.55	.303
2011	Tigers (GCL)	R	2	5	5.34	12	12	0	0	59	72	2	19	49	7.5	1.54	.310
2012	Connecticut (NYP)	SS	4	3	5.15	12	12	0	0	58	60	3	22	30	4.7	1.42	.269
Minor League Totals			8	13	5.04	54	33	0	2	195	224	11	69	128	5.9	1.51	.294

23 CURT CASALI, C

BA GRADE
45
HIGH

Born: Nov. 9, 1988. **B-T:** R-R. **Ht.:** 6-2. **Wt.:** 220. **Drafted:** Vanderbilt, 2011 (10th round). **Signed by:** Harold Zonder.

The Tigers were able to deal Rob Brantly to the Marlins in July as part of a package for Anibal Sanchez and Omar Infante because they had catching depth. Like Alex Avila, Brantly, James McCann and Bryan Holaday, Casali was a catcher drafted in the top 10 rounds out of a major college program. He signed for $40,000 as a Vanderbilt senior taken in the 10th round in 2011. While with the Commodores, he proved he could handle quality arms, as nine pitchers he worked with eventually were drafted in the first five rounds. Casali has solid defensive tools across the board, and they play up because of his natural leadership and work ethic. He threw out 33 percent of basestealers in 2012 and committed just four passed balls in 87 games. At the plate, he puts together quality at-bats, works the count and uses a short, simple swing. With his bat control, he'll hit for a decent average, and he has enough pop to make things interesting. Like most catchers, he has well below-average speed. Casali profiles as a solid backup catcher at the major league level.

Year	Club (League)	Class	AVG	G	AB	R	H	2B	3B	HR	RBI	BB	SO	SB	CS	OBP	SLG
2011	Connecticut (NYP)	SS	.278	10	36	7	10	2	0	1	2	6	5	0	0	.409	.417
	West Michigan (MWL)	LoA	.227	25	75	10	17	7	0	2	14	13	9	0	0	.344	.400
2012	West Michigan (MWL)	LoA	.288	48	170	25	49	12	0	8	25	27	18	2	1	.402	.500
	Lakeland (FSL)	HiA	.250	46	160	18	40	13	0	1	18	11	28	0	0	.322	.350
Minor League Totals			.263	129	441	60	116	34	0	12	59	57	60	2	1	.365	.422

24 BRYAN HOLADAY, C

BA GRADE
40
MEDIUM

Born: Nov. 19, 1987. **B-T:** R-R. **Ht.:** 6-0. **Wt.:** 205. **Drafted:** Texas Christian, 2010 (6th round). **Signed by:** Tim Grieve.

Holaday made a name for himself at Texas Christian by being one of the few collegians to homer off Stephen Strasburg, and by leading the Horned Frogs to their first-ever College World Series appearance in 2010. Holaday started his pro career in high Class A and hasn't posted an OPS higher than .665 at any of his stops, but he spent most of 2012 in Triple-A and made his big league debut in June when Alex Avila strained a hamstring. Holaday has a thick, sturdy build and solid catch-and-throw skills. He isn't flashy behind the plate, but he gets the job done. His arm is average and he threw out 34 percent of International League basestealers last year. He has decent footwork and handles pitchers well. Holaday's bat will determine his ultimate role. He has strength and average raw power, but his pure hitting ability is well below-average, just like his speed. His upside is similar to that of Gerald Laird, whose free-agent departure from Detroit this offseason could create a big league opening for Holaday.

Year	Club (League)	Class	AVG	G	AB	R	H	2B	3B	HR	RBI	BB	SO	SB	CS	OBP	SLG
2010	Lakeland (FSL)	HiA	.220	44	159	14	35	8	0	3	12	21	43	0	0	.335	.327
2011	Erie (EL)	AA	.242	95	330	35	80	18	0	7	42	27	76	6	1	.304	.361
2012	Toledo (IL)	AAA	.240	75	250	18	60	12	1	2	25	22	43	2	0	.312	.320
	Detroit (AL)	MAJ	.250	6	12	3	3	1	0	0	0	0	2	0	0	.250	.333
Major League Totals			.250	6	12	3	3	1	0	0	0	0	2	0	0	.250	.333
Minor League Totals			.237	214	739	67	175	38	1	12	79	70	162	8	1	.314	.340

25 LUKE PUTKONEN, RHP

BA GRADE
40
MEDIUM

Born: May 10, 1986. **B-T:** R-R. **Ht.:** 6-6. **Wt.:** 210. **Drafted:** North Carolina, 2007 (3rd round). **Signed by:** Grant Brittain.

After he spent four and a half years as a starter, the Tigers moved Putkonen to the bullpen midway through the 2011 season. He arrived in Detroit less than a year later, arriving last April and becoming one of eight former Tar Heels to debut in the majors in the last two seasons. Becoming a reliever gave a boost to Putkonen's fastball. He worked from 89-94 mph as a starter, but he's now throwing 93-95 mph and topping out at 97. His heater has heavy life that makes it even more effective. Putkonen also mixes in a hard 79-81 mph curveball and uses a splitter as a changeup. He has a smooth, easy delivery but just fringy control, mainly because of the long levers in his tall frame. He could work on showing a more aggressive demeanor on the mound. Putkonen profiles as a solid seventh- or eighth-inning guy in a big league bullpen and could fill that role in Detroit this year.

Year	Club (League)	Class	W	L	ERA	G	GS	CG	SV	IP	H	HR	BB	SO	K/9	WHIP	AVG
2007	Tigers (GCL)	R	0	1	4.15	3	3	0	0	9	8	0	0	9	9.3	0.92	.229
2008	Oneonta (NYP)	SS	2	1	3.65	6	6	0	0	25	24	1	8	17	6.2	1.30	.270
2009	West Michigan (MWL)	LoA	7	8	3.13	28	28	1	0	149	148	3	47	115	6.9	1.31	.260
2010	Lakeland (FSL)	HiA	9	7	3.18	27	26	1	0	153	144	8	44	87	5.1	1.23	.257
2011	Erie (EL)	AA	1	7	7.57	11	11	0	0	52	68	8	22	23	4.0	1.72	.315
	Lakeland (FSL)	HiA	2	6	5.54	18	8	1	0	65	77	10	18	52	7.2	1.46	.297
2012	Toledo (IL)	AAA	3	3	4.92	24	2	0	0	57	68	3	20	46	7.3	1.55	.304
	Detroit (AL)	MAJ	0	2	3.94	12	0	0	1	16	19	0	8	10	5.6	1.69	.302
Major League Totals			0	2	3.94	12	0	0	1	16	19	0	8	10	5.6	1.69	.302
Minor League Totals			24	33	4.15	117	84	3	0	509	537	33	159	349	6.2	1.37	.275

26 RAMON CABRERA, C

BA GRADE **45** **HIGH**

Born: Nov. 5, 1989. **B-T:** B-R. **Ht.:** 5-8. **Wt.:** 195. **Drafted:** Venezuela, 2008. **Signed by:** Rene Gayo/Rodolfo Petit (Pirates).

Cabrera's father Alex Cabrera played for the Diamondbacks in 2000 before becoming a prolific power hitter in Japan. Signed by the Pirates for $100,000, Ramon won the Florida State League batting title with a .343 average in 2011. After he turned in a lackluster encore in Double-A last year, Pittsburgh traded him to the Tigers for Andy Oliver. Cabrera can put the bat on the ball consistently and hit for a solid average, but he doesn't contribute much offensively beyond that. While he doesn't strike out much, he also doesn't walk a lot. He didn't receive his father's power genes and hasn't hit more than three homers in any of his five pro seasons. Cabrera made strides defensively in 2012, especially from a receiving standpoint. However, his throwing is still erratic and he has difficulty controlling the running game. He threw out just 20 percent of basestealers last season. As expected with a catcher, he's a well below-average runner. Cabrera profiles as a backup catcher in the major leagues, and he'll have to battle Curt Casali and Bryan Holaday to eventually win that job in Detroit.

Year	Club (League)	Class	AVG	G	AB	R	H	2B	3B	HR	RBI	BB	SO	SB	CS	OBP	SLG
2008	Pirates (VSL)	R	.264	56	178	24	47	16	0	3	22	28	27	5	0	.367	.404
2009	Pirates (VSL)	R	.312	20	77	10	24	6	0	2	19	12	11	1	2	.400	.468
	Pirates (GCL)	R	.291	37	127	15	37	11	1	1	16	16	16	2	1	.372	.417
2010	West Virginia (SAL)	LoA	.269	90	342	49	92	14	4	1	40	22	42	3	4	.312	.342
2011	Bradenton (FSL)	HiA	.343	92	327	46	112	25	4	3	53	38	29	5	1	.410	.471
2012	Altoona (EL)	AA	.276	112	384	47	106	22	2	3	50	39	44	0	3	.342	.367
	Indianapolis (IL)	AAA	.400	1	5	1	2	1	0	0	0	0	0	0	0	.400	.600
Minor League Totals			.292	408	1440	192	420	95	11	13	200	155	169	16	11	.360	.400

27 DIXON MACHADO, SS

BA GRADE **45** **HIGH**

Born: Feb. 22, 1992. **B-T:** R-R. **Ht.:** 6-0. **Wt.:** 160. **Signed:** Venezuela, 2008. **Signed by:** German Robles.

The report hasn't changed on Machado, whom the Tigers signed as soon as he became eligible on July 2, 2008. He was 16 at the time and looked much younger because of his 130-pound build. He has added about 30 pounds since then, but his frame is still slight. He remained at the team's training base in Lakeland, Fla., in the offseason to work with strength coaches and try to add a little more punch to his all-Judy approach. Machado had the lowest OPS (.534) of any Florida State League regular last year, and his .252 slugging percentage actually represented a five-point increase from 2011. He makes contact and draws walks, but that's the extent of his offensive contributions. Defense is Machado's calling card. He has graceful agility and excellent athleticism in the field. He's a treat to watch with his soft hands, above-average arm strength and acrobatic play. He has three plus tools in his fielding, arm and speed, but his bat will have to evolve for him to have any chance at being an everyday player in the big leagues. He has 20 power on the 20-80 scouting scale, so a utility player in the mold of Wilson Valdez is Machado's most likely ceiling. Detroit added him to the 40-man roster in November even though he may need to repeat high Class A.

Year	Club (League)	Class	AVG	G	AB	R	H	2B	3B	HR	RBI	BB	SO	SB	CS	OBP	SLG
2009	Tigers (VSL)	R	.205	63	234	41	48	6	1	3	26	32	32	27	6	.310	.278
2010	Tigers (GCL)	R	.261	43	165	22	43	4	3	0	11	14	27	12	3	.315	.321
	Connecticut (NYP)	SS	.292	7	24	4	7	1	0	0	1	3	5	1	2	.393	.333
2011	West Michigan (MWL)	LoA	.235	124	429	47	101	1	2	0	28	46	77	25	5	.314	.247
2012	Lakeland (FSL)	HiA	.195	119	421	59	82	16	1	2	37	51	61	23	5	.283	.252
Minor League Totals			.221	356	1273	173	281	28	7	5	103	146	202	88	21	.305	.266

28 HERNAN PEREZ, 2B/SS

BA GRADE **45** **HIGH**

Born: March 26, 1991. **B-T:** R-R. **Ht.:** 6-1. **Wt.:** 185. **Signed:** Venezuela, 2007. **Signed by:** Jesus Garces/Pedro Chavez.

The Tigers immediately signed Perez for $237,000 when the 2007 international sign-

ing period opened. After showing little offensively in his first four pro seasons, he batted .302/.318/.397 in the Arizona Fall League in 2011 to earn a spot on 40-man roster. His addition came in handy when Detroit needed him for an emergency callup when Jhonny Peralta went on paternity leave in early June. He's more physical than Eugenio Suarez or Dixon Machado, with a chance to hit for average and the strength for gap power. He doesn't walk much, however, and Perez's other tools will always be ahead of his offense. He can fill in at shortstop but is a better second baseman. His arm strength is also a plus, but he still needs more consistency to be considered an above-average defender. He has quick-twitch athleticism in his tightly wound frame, along with excellent instincts. He has above-average speed and led all Tigers farmhands with 27 steals in 2012. If his bat comes around, Perez could be a nice utility player similar to current Tiger Ramon Santiago.

Year	Club (League)	Class	AVG	G	AB	R	H	2B	3B	HR	RBI	BB	SO	SB	CS	OBP	SLG
2008	Tigers (VSL)	R	.226	68	265	38	60	8	4	1	22	16	35	4	4	.278	.298
2009	West Michigan (MWL)	LoA	.227	12	44	0	10	0	1	0	5	0	8	2	1	.227	.273
	Tigers (GCL)	R	.222	21	81	9	18	9	1	1	9	3	14	2	0	.259	.395
	Lakeland (FSL)	HiA	.264	21	72	7	19	4	1	0	10	3	21	0	0	.289	.347
2010	West Michigan (MWL)	LoA	.235	124	473	45	111	15	0	5	50	25	98	5	1	.273	.298
2011	West Michigan (MWL)	LoA	.258	129	503	69	130	23	3	8	42	38	87	23	6	.314	.364
2012	Detroit (AL)	MAJ	.500	2	2	1	1	0	0	0	0	0	0	0	0	.500	.500
	Lakeland (FSL)	HiA	.261	124	441	50	115	11	4	5	44	24	70	27	4	.298	.338
Major League Totals			.500	2	2	1	1	0	0	0	0	0	0	0	0	.500	.500
Minor League Totals			.246	499	1879	218	463	70	14	20	182	109	333	63	16	.290	.330

29 EDGAR DE LA ROSA, RHP

BA GRADE
50
EXTREME

Born: Nov. 20, 1990. **B-T:** R-R. **Ht.:** 6-6. **Wt.:** 215. **Signed:** Dominican Republic, 2009. **Signed by:** Miguel Rodriguez/Ramon Perez/Miguel Garcia.

De La Rosa is yet another big-bodied Tigers righthander who's years away from the big leagues. He made his U.S. debut in 2011 as part of a Gulf Coast League club that would place 11 players on this list. De La Rosa has a heavy 92-93 mph fastball and can run it up to 96 on occasion. His fastball has late boring life and he loves to challenge righthanders inside, running his heater in on their hands. His slider and changeup are below average right now. His slider has plenty of velocity at 81-85 mph and shows flashes of being an average pitch in the future. He slows his delivery and his arm down on his 78-81 mph changeup, but he does have some feel for commanding the pitch. De La Rosa has loose, easy mechanics but will need to sharpen up below-average control and work on controlling his emotions on the mound. He doesn't strike out as many hitters as one might expect from a pitcher with his arsenal. He could develop into a No. 4 starter, though some scouts believe he'll ultimately wind up in the bullpen. He'll pitch in West Michigan's rotation this year.

Year	Club (League)	Class	W	L	ERA	G	GS	CG	SV	IP	H	HR	BB	SO	K/9	WHIP	AVG
2009	Tigers (DSL)	R	3	3	5.70	17	11	0	1	54	64	1	28	40	6.7	1.71	.299
2010	Tigers (DSL)	R	2	9	4.43	20	11	0	2	65	76	2	25	64	8.9	1.55	.295
2011	Tigers (GCL)	R	2	4	3.19	12	12	0	0	68	70	5	18	50	6.7	1.30	.277
2012	Connecticut (NYP)	SS	4	4	3.10	15	15	0	0	73	66	3	35	54	6.7	1.39	.242
Minor League Totals			11	20	4.00	64	49	0	3	259	276	11	106	208	7.2	1.47	.277

30 DANIEL FIELDS, OF

BA GRADE
50
EXTREME

Born: Jan. 23, 1991. **B-T:** L-R. **Ht.:** 6-2. **Wt.:** 215. **Drafted:** HS—Detroit, 2009 (6th round). **Signed by:** Tom Osowski.

It's impossible to know what Fields' career might look like now if he hadn't been pushed to high Class A after signing for $1,625,000 out of high school in 2009. It makes for interesting game of "what if" because his production never has matched his intriguing tools. While he hit just .266/.318/.357 in his third stint at Lakeland last year, he was still relatively young for his level and played well when he advanced to Double-A in August. Expectations for Fields' bat have diminished. He's a below-average hitter but has a pro-fessional approach and knows how to use the whole field, lessons imparted by his father Bruce, a former Tigers outfielder and hitting coach. Daniel has strength and above-average raw power, but it doesn't translate into games because he doesn't make enough contact. He's a good athlete who played shortstop in high school. He has solid speed and is learning to read pitchers, resulting in a career-high 23 steals in 2012. He takes good routes and has average arm strength in center field. Fields still is young enough to develop into a regular, but a more realistic projection is that he could become a useful fourth outfielder. He'll open this season back in Erie.

Year	Club (League)	Class	AVG	G	AB	R	H	2B	3B	HR	RBI	BB	SO	SB	CS	OBP	SLG
2010	Lakeland (FSL)	HiA	.240	109	375	33	90	13	6	8	47	55	119	8	9	.343	.371
2011	Lakeland (FSL)	HiA	.220	124	432	57	95	14	4	8	46	49	133	4	4	.308	.326
2012	Lakeland (FSL)	HiA	.266	62	244	31	65	11	4	1	26	19	55	14	7	.318	.357
	Erie (EL)	AA	.264	29	106	13	28	4	0	2	7	13	21	9	1	.352	.358
Minor League Totals			.240	324	1157	134	278	42	14	19	126	136	328	35	21	.326	.350

Houston Astros

BY JOHN MANUEL

No organization needed a fresh start more than the Astros.

And no team has made more alterations since November 2011, when Major League Baseball approved Jim Crane's purchase of the team from Drayton McLane.

The changes have come in rapid-fire fashion. For a $70 million discount on the $680 million purchase price (which included a 60 percent share in the Houston Regional Sports Network), Crane agreed to move the Astros to the American League West, effective in 2013. Then he fired general manager Ed Wade and hired Jeff Luhnow, formerly vice president of scouting and player development for the Cardinals, to succeed him.

Luhnow immediately started a makeover of Houston's front office. Assistant GM Bobby Heck, who ran the club's drafts from 2008-12, didn't have his contract renewed, and several amateur and pro scouts also were fired. Farm director Fred Nelson, a member of the organization since 1985, was offered a different position after getting replaced by former big league outfielder Quinton McCracken.

Luhnow also completed the dismantling of the big league roster that Wade started in 2010-11, when he traded veterans such as Lance Berkman, Michael Bourn, Roy Oswalt and Hunter Pence. The 2012 Astros weren't competitive to begin with, and fell to absurd levels after Luhnow dealt Chris Johnson, Carlos Lee, Brett Myers and Wandy Rodriguez through the season, slashing an Opening Day payroll of $61 million to barely more than $10 million.

The Astros suffered through a 4-33 stretch after the deals, costing manager Brad Mills his job, and went 55-107 overall. Triple-A manager Tony DeFrancesco took over for Mills on an interim basis, until Luhnow hired Nationals third-base coach Bo Porter as the permanent replacement. DeFrancesco will return to manage Triple-A Oklahoma City.

While five of the 2011 trade acquisitions made the Astros Top 10 Prospects list a year ago, none of this year's additions cracked this Top 10. Houston did add potential impact players in the draft, however, while picking No. 1 overall for the first time since 1992.

Twenty years earlier, the Astros passed on Derek Jeter to take the more signable Phil Nevin. This time around, Luhnow, Heck and special assistant Mike Elias (now scouting director) devised and executed a plan to stretch Houston's $11.2 million bonus pool

Four of the Astros' top 12 prospects, like Jonathan Singleton, arrived via trade

with impressive results.

Though the consensus had the Astros taking Stanford righthander Mark Appel at No. 1, they opted instead for Puerto Rican prep shortstop Carlos Correa. Houston signed him quickly for $4.8 million, $2.4 million less than the assigned value for his pick, and used the savings to sign supplemental first-round righthander Lance McCullers Jr. ($2.5 million) and fourth-round third baseman Rio Ruiz ($1.85 million) to above-value bonuses. The rest of the draft followed Luhnow's playbook from his days with the Cardinals, with promising college draft picks.

The trades and recent drafts have brought depth the system lacked for years. That allowed the Astros to let former first-rounders Delino DeShields Jr. and Mike Foltynewicz to repeat low Class A at age 20, and they both responded with strong seasons.

After finishing with the worst cumulative minor league record in 2008, 2009 and 2011 (and 29th in 2010), Houston affiliates had the best winning percentage (.546) in the game in 2012.

In November, the Astros unveiled a new uniform and logo, harkening back to their 1980s caps and color scheme. Coming off back-to-back seasons that were the worst in franchise history, it's a good time to make a clean break with their recent past.

THIS YEAR'S TOP 30

Player, Pos.	Grade
1. Carlos Correa, ss	70/High
2. Jonathan Singleton, 1b/of	65/Medium
3. George Springer, of	65/High
4. Lance McCullers Jr., rhp	65/Extreme
5. Mike Foltynewicz, rhp	55/High
6. Delino DeShields Jr., 2b	55/High
7. Jarred Cosart, rhp	55/High
8. Rio Ruiz, 3b	55/Extreme
9. Nick Tropeano, rhp	50/Medium
10. Nolan Fontana, ss	50/High
11. Domingo Santana, of	50/High
12. Jonathan Villar, ss	50/High
13. Vincent Velasquez, rhp	50/High
14. Asher Wojciechowski, rhp	50/High
15. Jose Cisnero, rhp	45/Medium
16. Adrian Houser, rhp	50/High
17. Robbie Grossman, of	45/Medium
18. Brett Phillips, of	50/High
19. Rob Rasmussen, lhp	45/Medium
20. Brett Oberholtzer, lhp	45/Medium
21. Ross Seaton, rhp	45/Medium
22. Chia-Jen Lo, rhp	50/High
23. Brady Rodgers, rhp	45/Medium
24. Andrew Aplin, of	45/Medium
25. Josh Fields, rhp	45/Medium
26. Austin Wates, of	45/Medium
27. Paul Clemens, rhp	45/High
28. Carlos Perez, c	45/Medium
29. Aaron West, rhp	50/High
30. Tyler Heineman, c	45/High

LAST YEAR'S TOP 30

Player, Pos.	Status
1. Jonathan Singleton, 1b/of	No. 2
2. Jarred Cosart, rhp	No. 7
3. George Springer, of	No. 3
4. Jonathan Villar, ss	No. 12
5. Paul Clemens, rhp	No. 27
6. Domingo Santana, of	No. 11
7. Brett Oberholtzer, lhp	No. 20
8. Delino DeShields Jr., 2b	No. 6
9. Mike Foltynewicz, rhp	No. 5
10. Telvin Nash, 1b/of	Dropped out
11. Adrian Houser, rhp	No. 16
12. Nick Tropeano, rhp	No. 9
13. Jake Buchanan, rhp	Dropped out
14. Ariel Ovando, of	Dropped out
15. R.J. Alaniz, rhp	Dropped out
16. Ross Seaton, rhp	No. 21
17. J.B. Shuck, of	(Angels)
18. Austin Wates, of	No. 26
19. Juan Abreu, rhp	(Dodgers)
20. Marwin Gonzalez, ss/2b	Majors
21. Dallas Keuchel, lhp	Majors
22. Jorge DeLeon, rhp	Dropped out
23. Jio Mier, ss	Dropped out
24. Tanner Bushue, rhp	Dropped out
25. Mike Kvasnicka, 3b	Dropped out
26. Jose Cisnero, rhp	No. 15
27. Vincent Velasquez, rhp	No. 13
28. Rhiner Cruz, rhp	Majors
29. Jack Armstrong Jr., rhp	Dropped out
30. Chris Wallace, c	Dropped out

BEST TOOLS

Best Hitter for Average	Jonathan Singleton
Best Power Hitter	Carlos Correa
Best Strike-Zone Discipline	Nolan Fontana
Fastest Baserunner	Delino DeShields Jr.
Best Athlete	George Springer
Best Fastball	Lance McCullers Jr.
Best Curveball	Jarred Cosart
Best Slider	Lance McCullers Jr.
Best Changeup	Nick Tropeano
Best Control	Brady Rodgers
Best Defensive Catcher	Roberto Pena
Best Defensive Infielder	Carlos Correa
Best Infield Arm	Carlos Correa
Best Defensive Outfielder	George Springer
Best Outfield Arm	George Springer

PROJECTED 2016 LINEUP

Catcher	Jason Castro
First Base	Jonathan Singleton
Second Base	Jose Altuve
Third Base	Jed Lowrie
Shortstop	Carlos Correa
Left Field	Domingo Santana
Center Field	Delino DeShields Jr.
Right Field	George Springer
Designated Hitter	Rio Ruiz
No. 1 Starter	Lance McCullers Jr.
No. 2 Starter	Mike Foltynewicz
No. 3 Starter	Bud Norris
No. 4 Starter	Jordan Lyles
No. 5 Starter	Nick Tropeano
Closer	Jarred Cosart

TOP PROSPECTS OF THE DECADE

Year	Player, Pos.	2012 Org.
2003	John Buck, c	Marlins
2004	Taylor Buchholz, rhp	Out of baseball
2005	Chris Burke, 2b	Out of baseball
2006	Jason Hirsh, rhp	Out of baseball
2007	Hunter Pence, of	Giants
2008	J.R. Towles, c	Twins
2009	Jason Castro, c	Astros
2010	Jason Castro, c	Astros
2011	Jordan Lyles, rhp	Astros
2012	Jonathan Singleton, 1b	Astros

TOP DRAFT PICKS OF THE DECADE

Year	Player, Pos.	2012 Org.
2003	Jason Hirsh, rhp (2nd round)	Out of baseball
2004	Hunter Pence, of (2nd round)	Giants
2005	Brian Bogusevic, lhp	Astros
2006	Max Sapp, c	Out of baseball
2007	*Derek Dietrich, 3b (3rd round)	Rays
2008	Jason Castro, c	Astros
2009	Jio Mier, ss	Astros
2010	Delino DeShields Jr., 2b	Astros
2011	George Springer, of	Astros
2012	Carlos Correa, ss	Astros

*Did not sign.

LARGEST BONUSES IN CLUB HISTORY

Carlos Correa, 2012	$4.800,000
Ariel Ovando, 2010	$2,600,000
George Springer, 2011	$2,525,000
Lance McCullers Jr., 2012	$2,500,000
Delino DeShields Jr., 2010	$2,150,000

HOUSTON ASTROS

TOP 2013 ROOKIE: Jonathan Singleton, 1b/DH. He has the polished bat to wrest Houston's first-base job from Brett Wallace.

BREAKOUT PROSPECT: Vincent Velasquez, rhp. Now that he's fully recovered from Tommy John surgery, he should be ready for his full-season closeup.

SLEEPER: Michael Feliz. rhp. Signed for $400,000 out of the Dominican Republic, he touches 97 mph with his fastball.

SOURCE OF TOP 30 TALENT			
Homegrown	19	Acquired	11
College	8	Trades	10
Junior college	0	Rule 5 draft	1
High school	9	Independent leagues	0
Nondrafted free agents	0	Free agents/waivers	0
International	2		

LF
Austin Wates (26)
Marc Krauss
Jake Goebbert
Brandon Meredith
Adam Bailey
Terrell Joyce

CF
George Springer (3)
Robbie Grossman (17)
Brett Phillips (18)
Andrew Aplin (24)
Brandon Barnes
Che-Hsuan Lin
D'Andre Toney

RF
Domingo Santana (11)
Preston Tucker
Michael Burgess
Teoscar Hernandez
Drew Muren

3B
Rio Ruiz (8)
Brandon Laird
Jonathan Meyer
Matt Duffy

SS
Carlos Correa (1)
Nolan Fontana (10)
Jonathan Villar (12)
Jio Mier

2B
Delino DeShields Jr. (6)
Jake Elmore
Jose Martinez
Austin Elkins
Joe Sclafani

1B
Jonathan Singleton (2)
Nate Freiman
Bobby Borchering
Ariel Ovando
Telvin Nash

C
Carlos Perez (28)
Tyler Heineman (30)
Roberto Pena
Chris Wallace
Ben Heath

LHP

LHSP	LHRP
Rob Rasmussen (19)	Kevin Chapman
Brett Oberholtzer (20)	Alex Sogard
Rudy Owens	Kenny Long
Wes Musick	Pat Urckfitz
David Rollins	Reymin Guduan
Colton Cain	Mitchell Lambson
Luis Cruz	
Brian Holmes	
Blair Walters	
Joe Bircher	

RHP

RHSP	RHRP
Lance McCullers Jr. (4)	Chia-Jen Lo (22)
Mike Foltynewicz (5)	Josh Fields (25)
Jarred Cosart (7)	Mickey Storey
Nick Tropeano (9)	Drew Robinson
Vincent Velasquez (13)	Arcenio Leon
Asher Wojciechowski (14)	Jason Stoffel
Jose Cisnero (15)	Josh Zeid
Adrian Houser (16)	David Martinez
Ross Seaton (21)	Jorge DeLeon
Brady Rodgers (23)	Jandel Gustave
Paul Clemens (27)	Joe Musgrove
Aaron West (29)	Kevin Comer
Bobby Doran	Jordan Jankowski
Jake Buchanan	Dayan Diaz
Michael Feliz	Carlos Quevedo
R.J. Alaniz	Travis Ballew
Chris Devenski	Juri Perez
Matt Heidenreich	Tanner Bushue
Alex Gillingham	
Jack Armstrong Jr.	

2012
BONUSES: $12.1 MILLION

BEST PURE HITTER: The Astros had plenty of history with 3B Rio Ruiz (4) and believed his swing was as sweet as any in the draft. That's why they were willing to give him $1.8 million even though he missed most of the spring with a blood clot in his neck that required surgery. He has balance, bat speed and bat-to-ball skills to spare.

BEST POWER HITTER: SS Carlos Correa (1), the draft's No. 1 overall pick, hit what Houston called "freak show" homers in instructional league. At 6-foot-4 he has plenty of leverage in his swing, and his natural opposite-field power bodes well for his future home run totals.

FASTEST RUNNER: OF Brett Phillips (6) has consistent plus speed and will turn in some well above-average times.

BEST DEFENSIVE PLAYER: Correa has tremendous footwork, balance, hands and arm strength. If he outgrows shortstop, he'll be a Gold Glove-caliber third baseman. OF Andrew Aplin (5) is just a fringy runner but smoothly patrols center field thanks to his instincts and excellent reads off the bat. He also has a solid arm.

BEST FASTBALL: RHP Lance McCullers Jr. (1s) hit 100 mph in the spring and sits at 93-97 mph as a starter. By saving bonus-pool money when they landed Correa for $4.8 million, the Astros were able to meet McCullers' $2.5 million asking price. RHP Aaron West (17) had a velocity jump after signing, working from 90-96 mph after rarely touching 95 in the spring.

BEST SECONDARY PITCH: McCullers has a terrific power slurve with mid-80s velocity and tilt. When he's locating it, hitters have no hope.

BEST PRO DEBUT: OF Preston Tucker (7) helped push short-season Tri-City into the New York-Penn League playoffs by hitting .321/.390/.509 with eight homers. C Tyler Heineman (8) won the NY-P batting title (.358) and ranked second in the league in on-base percentage (.452) and plate appearances per strikeout (19.4). Alpin started in Tri-City and jumped to high Class A Lancaster, batting .313/.378/.493 overall with 24 stolen bases. LHP Kenny Long (22) joined him at Lancaster and struck out 38 in 22 innings overall while posting a 1.61 ERA.

BEST ATHLETE: Phillips has quick-twitch explosiveness that Correa lacks, but Correa's combination of graceful actions and body control speak to his overall athleticism.

MOST INTRIGUING BACKGROUND: McCullers and his father, who pitched seven seasons in the majors, were the 41st overall picks in the draft 30 years apart. SS Nolan Fontana (2) is the grandson of 203-game winner Lew Burdette. Unsigned C Jimmy Sinatro's (35) father Matt caught in the big leagues and coaches with the Cardinals.

CLOSEST TO THE MAJORS: Fontana and Alpin, two polished college hitters and defenders.

BEST LATE-ROUND PICK: West, who throws three pitches for strikes and should remain a starter.

THE ONE WHO GOT AWAY: The Astros took LHP Hunter Virant (11) and SS C.J. Hinojosa (26) as insurance in case higher picks didn't sign. Virant wound up at UCLA and Hinojosa went to Texas.

ASSESSMENT: The Astros used the second-largest bonus pool ($11.2 million) to stage baseball's best draft, with obvious impact at the top complemented by college draftees like Fontana, Alpin and Heineman.

2011
BONUSES: $5.5 MILLION

Five-tool college players don't usually last 11 picks in the draft, but OF George Springer (1) did, to the Astros' good fortune. They also added promising RHPs Adrian Houser (2) and Nick Tropeano (5).

GRADE: B

2010
BONUSES: $7.3 MILLION

2B Delino DeShields Jr. (1) and RHP Mike Foltynewicz (1) finally started coming into their own when they repeated low Class A in 2012. RHP Vincent Velasquez (2) is making an encouraging comeback in his return from Tommy John surgery.

GRADE: C+

2009
BONUSES: $4.2 MILLION

Houston found three big leaguers in the late rounds, but neither LHP Dallas Keuchel (7) nor OF J.D. Martinez (20) looks like a regular and LHP Paco Rodriguez (48) didn't sign. SS Jio Mier (1) isn't a major part of the club's future.

GRADE: C

2008
BONUSES: $6.5 MILLION

Similar to 2009, the Astros drafted three major leaguers but may not have a regular in the bunch. C Jason Castro (1) and RHP Jordan Lyles (1s) have scuffled in Houston, while OF J.B. Shuck (6) departed as a free agent

GRADE: C

Draft analysis by John Manuel (2012) and Jim Callis (2008-11). Numbers in parentheses indicate draft rounds.

1 CARLOS
CORREA, SS

Born: Sept. 22, 1994. **B-T:** R-R. **Ht.:** 6-4. **Wt.:** 190.
Drafted: HS—Gurabo, P.R., 2012 (1st round). **Signed by:** Larry Pardo/Joey Sola.

BA GRADE
70
HIGH

TONY FARLOW

Correa is a product of the Puerto Rico Baseball Academy, the top finishing school on the island for prospective draft picks. The academy has produced 56 draft picks since 2004, though none has reached the major leagues yet. With a strong tour of high school showcase events in 2011, Correa vaulted himself into first-round consideration for 2012. The Miami recruit starred at Puerto Rico's Excellence Games in May and wowed clubs in workouts shortly before the draft. The Astros considered him a legitimate top-of-the-draft talent but took him No. 1 overall in part because he signed quickly for $4.8 million. His bonus set a club record though it was well below the $7.2 million assigned value for his pick, which allowed Houston to use the savings elsewhere in the draft. Correa became the highest selection ever from Puerto Rico, surpassing Ramon Castro, whom Houston took 17th overall in 1994. The Astros challenged Correa late in the summer, sending him to advanced Rookie-level Greeneville as a 17-year-old in August, and he responded well.

Correa has tools worthy of a No. 1 overall pick, earning comparisons to players such as Troy Tulowitzki and Ryan Zimmerman. Tall and athletic, Correa has the potential to hit for power while playing the left side of the infield. His best attributes are his well above-average pop to all fields, which Houston scouting director Mike Elias describes as "freak-show power," and his cannon arm. Correa has an easy swing with plenty of bat speed and leverage. He's balanced at the plate, uses his hands well and has natural hitting rhythm, and the Astros expect him to hit for average as well as power. He impressed club officials by laying off breaking balls out of the zone after signing. At his size, he has holes in his swing that he'll have to tighten. Correa is the best present defender the organization has at shortstop. His arm strength earns 70 grades, and he has excellent footwork and body control. There's some concern he'll outgrow shortstop as he matures physically. If so, scouts expect him to be a premium defender if he

has to slide to third base. He has excellent defensive instincts and work ethic, and he did nothing after signing to convince scouts he'll have to move. He lost weight this summer while playing every day for the first time, so his lanky frame should keep him at shortstop for at least the short term. Correa plays with energy, consistently producing above-average running times to first base. He's likely to slow down as he grows, and stealing bases isn't expected to be a significant part of his game. Correa got straight "A's" in high school and speaks English well.

Houston has tried to temper expectations for Correa, but with his talent, work ethic and personality, it's hard not to see him becoming a star. He's advanced enough to earn a spot at the organization's new low Class A Quad Cities affiliate to start his first full pro season, and a strong performance could put him on the fast track. If all goes well, he could reach Houston as early as 2015.

SCOUTING GRADES

Batting: 55. **Defense:** 60.
Power: 65. **Arm:** 70.
Speed: 55.

Based on 20-80 scouting scale, where 50 represents major league average, and future projection rather than present tools.

Year	Club (League)	Class	AVG	G	AB	R	H	2B	3B	HR	RBI	BB	SO	SB	CS	OBP	SLG
2012	Astros (GCL)	R	.232	39	155	23	36	11	1	2	9	7	36	5	1	.270	.355
	Greeneville (APP)	R	.371	11	35	5	13	3	1	1	3	5	8	1	0	.450	.600
Minor League Totals			.258	50	190	28	49	14	2	3	12	12	44	6	1	.305	.400

2 JONATHAN SINGLETON, 1B/OF

BA GRADE

65

MEDIUM

Born: Sept. 18, 1991. **B-T:** L-L. **Ht.:** 6-2. **Wt.:** 235. **Drafted:** HS—Long Beach, 2009 (8th round). **Signed by:** Demetrius Pittman (Phillies).

The son of a former Oregon quarterback, Singleton signed with the Phillies for $200,000 in 2009, then was traded to Houston with righthanders Jarred Cosart and Josh Zeid and outfielder Domingo Santana in the 2011 Hunter Pence deal. He set career highs with 27 doubles, 21 homers and 88 walks in his first full season as an Astro. Singleton has a smooth swing with strength, and he knows his strike zone well. He uses his advanced plate discipline to focus on a particular hitting zone, takes aim and unleashes his well above-average raw power. He has a knack for hitting, showing enough bat speed to turn on fastballs while also using the whole field. Advanced lefthanders with good breaking balls still can handle him. Singleton has the tools to be an average first baseman but made too many careless errors in 2012. He's a well below-average defender in left field, where his lack of speed and arm strength hinder him. Scouts would like to see him play with more energy. Singleton remains the best first-base prospect in baseball. Brett Wallace hasn't sewn up the big league job, leaving the door open for Singleton as soon as he proves he's ready. His next stop is Triple-A Oklahoma City.

Year	Club (League)	Class	AVG	G	AB	R	H	2B	3B	HR	RBI	BB	SO	SB	CS	OBP	SLG
2009	Phillies (GCL)	R	.290	31	100	12	29	9	0	2	12	18	13	1	0	.395	.440
2010	Lakewood (SAL)	LoA	.290	104	376	64	109	25	2	14	77	62	74	9	7	.393	.479
2011	Clearwater (FSL)	HiA	.284	93	320	48	91	14	0	9	47	56	83	3	3	.387	.413
	Lancaster (CAL)	HiA	.333	35	129	20	43	9	1	4	16	14	40	0	0	.405	.512
2012	Corpus Christi (TL)	AA	.284	131	461	94	131	27	4	21	79	88	131	7	2	.396	.497
Minor League Totals			.291	394	1386	238	403	84	7	50	231	238	341	20	12	.394	.470

3 GEORGE SPRINGER, OF

BA GRADE

65

HIGH

Born: Sept. 19, 1989. **B-T:** R-R. **Ht.:** 6-3. **Wt.:** 200. **Drafted:** Connecticut, 2011 (1st round). **Signed by:** John Kosciak/Bobby Heck.

The highest-drafted player in Connecticut history, Springer went 11th overall and signed for $2.525 million in 2011. In his first full pro season, he ranked in the top six in the high Class A California League in all three slash stats at .316/.398/.557 before finishing at Double-A Corpus Christi. Springer is a true power/speed threat. His strong, quick hands generate tremendous whip and bat speed, giving him power to all fields. He doesn't have to cheat to drive the ball, but he does leak out with his front side at times, leading to strikeouts. He tends to play too fast, though scouts think he'll adjust with experience. Springer's above-average speed plays well on the bases and in center field, and managers rated him the Cal League's top defensive outfielder. His arm is above-average as well. His energy is infectious, and the Astros credit him with helping Delino DeShields Jr. play harder after rooming with him in instructional league and spring training. If Springer can make more consistent contact, he'll be a five-tool player. Whether he sticks in center field or shifts to right will depend in part on how other players fall into place. He'll return to Double-A to start 2013.

Year	Club (League)	Class	AVG	G	AB	R	H	2B	3B	HR	RBI	BB	SO	SB	CS	OBP	SLG
2011	Tri-City (NYP)	SS	.179	8	28	8	5	3	0	1	3	2	2	4	0	.303	.393
2012	Lancaster (CAL)	HiA	.316	106	433	101	137	18	10	22	82	56	131	28	6	.398	.557
	Corpus Christi (TL)	AA	.219	22	73	8	16	3	0	2	5	6	25	4	2	.288	.342
Minor League Totals			.296	136	534	117	158	24	10	25	90	64	158	36	8	.378	.519

4 LANCE McCULLERS JR., RHP

BA GRADE

65

EXTREME

Born: Oct. 2, 1993. **B-T:** L-R. **Ht.:** 6-1. **Wt.:** 190. **Drafted:** HS—Tampa, 2012 (1st round supplemental). **Signed by:** John Martin.

McCullers' father Lance Sr. was drafted 41st overall in 1982 and pitched seven seasons in the majors. Lance Jr. went in the same spot 30 years later, with his high price tag helping him fall that far. He signed for $2.5 million, the biggest bonus in franchise history for a pitcher. Powerful and athletic, McCullers flashed two of the best pitches in the 2012 draft class: a fastball that reaches 100 mph and sits at 93-97 late into games, and a slider with depth and late bite that hits the mid-80s. His changeup shows signs of becoming an average pitch. McCullers pitched sparingly early in his prep career and didn't become a full-time starter until 2012, when he showed a better feel for pitching to go with his electric stuff. He's still new to a starter's routine and will have to improve his control and command to stay in that role. He has effort in his delivery, but scouts credit his Jesuit High

(Tampa) pitching coach, 1997 first-round pick Geoff Goetz, with improving it. Some scouts believe McCullers will wind up in the bullpen like his father. The Astros will give him every chance to remain in the rotation, and he could be a frontline starter if he does. He'll begin his first full pro season in low Class A.

Year	Club (League)	Class	W	L	ERA	G	GS	CG	SV	IP	H	HR	BB	SO	K/9	WHIP	AVG
2012	Astros (GCL)	R	0	1	1.64	4	4	0	0	11	10	0	2	12	9.8	1.09	.227
	Greeneville (APP)	R	0	3	4.80	4	4	0	0	15	10	2	10	17	10.2	1.33	.182
Minor League Totals			0	4	3.46	8	8	0	0	26	20	2	12	29	10.0	1.23	.202

5 MIKE FOLTYNEWICZ, RHP

Born: Oct. 7, 1991. **B-T:** R-R. **Ht.:** 6-4. **Wt.:** 200. **Drafted:** HS—Minooka, Ill., 2010 (1st round). **Signed by:** Troy Hoerner.

Foltynewicz signed for $1,305,000 as the 19th overall pick in 2010. After a rough introduction to full-season ball in 2011, he benefited as much as any Astros farmhand from increased depth in the organization. He repeated low Class A in 2012 and was named the South Atlantic League's pitcher of the year, tying for the league lead in wins (14) while ranking fourth in ERA (3.14). More mature physically and in terms of his preparation, Foltynewicz learned to pitch off his fastball in 2012. He now relies more on a four-seamer that ranges from 93-99 mph, a pitch he pairs with his curveball to work up and down in the strike zone. His curve shows signs of becoming a plus pitch with good shape and bite, though it gets slow and loopy at times. Scouts see the ability to spin a breaking ball, however. Foltynewicz's changeup remains ahead of his curve, earning average to plus grades from scouts. He has an ideal frame with athleticism, and the Astros believe he should develop into an innings-eater. He's still a bit raw when it comes to defense and holding runners. Improving his fastball command and the consistency of his secondary pitches are Foltynewicz's goals for 2013, when he'll either have to survive high Class A Lancaster or skip a level to Double-A. He has the upside of a No. 2 starter.

BA GRADE 55 HIGH

Year	Club (League)	Class	W	L	ERA	G	GS	CG	SV	IP	H	HR	BB	SO	K/9	WHIP	AVG
2010	Greeneville (APP)	R	0	3	4.03	12	12	0	0	45	46	3	15	39	7.9	1.37	.272
2011	Lexington (SAL)	LoA	5	11	4.97	26	26	0	0	134	149	10	51	88	5.9	1.49	.289
2012	Lexington (SAL)	LoA	14	4	3.14	27	27	0	0	152	145	11	62	125	7.4	1.36	.250
Minor League Totals			19	18	4.00	65	65	0	0	331	340	24	128	252	6.9	1.42	.269

6 DELINO DeSHIELDS JR., 2B

Born: Aug. 16, 1992. **B-T:** R-R. **Ht.:** 5-9. **Wt.:** 190. **Drafted:** HS—College Park, Ga., 2010 (1st round). **Signed by:** Lincoln Martin.

Delino DeShields Sr. stole 463 bases in a 13-year big league career and now manages in the Reds system. He helped mentor Billy Hamilton, whose pro-record 155 stolen bases in 2012 obscured the fact that DeShields Jr.—who signed for $2.125 million as the eighth overall pick in 2010—stole 101 himself in a breakout year. Humbled after hitting .220/.305/.322 at low Class A in 2011, DeShields got in better shape and regained his speed, which grades as a 75 on the 20-80 scouting scale. He also played harder and smarter, and his bat heated up when he stopped trying to pull everything and used the whole field. He's surprisingly strong for his size and could develop average power. He draws walks, so he'll profile as an elite leadoff hitter if he can maintain his improvements. DeShields is an aggressive basestealer who reads pitchers well and has a quick first step. He also has worked to grow as a defender, improving his footwork around the bag at second, though his arm strength and accuracy remain erratic. DeShields batted .318 in the California League playoffs and may advance to Double-A to start 2013. If he can't stay at second base, center field is always an option for a player with his explosive speed.

BA GRADE 55 HIGH

Year	Club (League)	Class	AVG	G	AB	R	H	2B	3B	HR	RBI	BB	SO	SB	CS	OBP	SLG
2010	Astros (GCL)	R	.111	2	9	3	1	0	0	0	0	1	2	0	0	.200	.111
	Greeneville (APP)	R	.313	16	67	11	21	6	1	0	8	5	18	5	1	.356	.433
2011	Lexington (SAL)	LoA	.220	119	469	73	103	17	2	9	48	52	118	30	11	.305	.322
2012	Lexington (SAL)	LoA	.298	111	440	96	131	22	5	10	52	70	108	83	14	.401	.439
	Lancaster (CAL)	HiA	.237	24	97	17	23	2	3	2	9	13	23	18	5	.336	.381
Minor League Totals			.258	272	1082	200	279	47	11	21	117	141	269	136	31	.350	.380

7 JARRED COSART, RHP

Born: May 25, 1990. **B-T:** R-R. **Ht.:** 6-3. **Wt.:** 180. **Drafted:** HS—League City, Texas, 2008 (38th round). **Signed by:** Steve Cohen (Phillies).

Signed by the Phillies for $550,000 in 2008, Cosart quickly emerged as one of their more electric arms. Houston targeted him and Singleton in the 2011 Hunter Pence trade, but blisters interrupted his first full season with the Astros in 2012. He rallied late, allowing no earned runs in five of his last 10 starts, then threw well in the Arizona Fall League despite poor numbers. Cosart has a live, quick arm that produces a hard sinker that sits at 94-97 mph and touched 99 in the AFL. His fastball has excellent life down in the zone, which produces plenty of ground balls but makes the pitch tough to control. He excels at keeping the ball in the park, and he nearly got as many double plays (18) as he allowed extra-base hits (26) in 2012. Cosart throws his curveball with power, reaching 81-82 mph with good shape, and his solid straight changeup plays off his fastball well. Better command of his curveball would produce the strikeouts expected of a pitcher with such electric stuff. Cosart has shown flashes of brilliance but not consistency. While Houston intends to keep developing him as a starter, many scouts believe he'll wind up as a closer. He's slated for the Triple-A rotation to start 2013.

BA GRADE

55

HIGH

Year	Club (League)	Class	W	L	ERA	G	GS	CG	SV	IP	H	HR	BB	SO	K/9	WHIP	AVG
2009	Phillies (GCL)	R	2	2	2.22	7	5	0	0	24	12	0	7	25	9.2	0.78	.143
2010	Lakewood (SAL)	LoA	7	3	3.79	14	14	1	0	71	60	3	16	77	9.7	1.07	.224
2011	Clearwater (FSL)	HiA	9	8	3.92	20	19	0	0	108	98	7	43	79	6.6	1.31	.243
	Corpus Christi (TL)	AA	1	2	4.71	7	7	0	0	36	33	4	13	22	5.4	1.27	.234
2012	Corpus Christi (TL)	AA	5	5	3.52	15	15	0	0	87	83	3	38	68	7.0	1.39	.250
	Oklahoma City (PCL)	AAA	1	2	2.60	6	5	0	0	28	26	0	13	24	7.8	1.41	.250
Minor League Totals			25	22	3.65	69	65	1	0	355	312	17	130	295	7.5	1.25	.234

8 RIO RUIZ, 3B

Born: May 22, 1994. **B-T:** L-R. **Ht.:** 6-1. **Wt.:** 180. **Drafted:** HS—La Puente, Calif., Year (4th round). **Signed by:** Tim Costic.

Ruiz was a high-profile prep athlete as a star quarterback and baseball player at Bishop Amat High (La Puente, Calif.), the alma mater of Michael Young and several NFL players. A sprained left knee sidelined Ruiz as a senior in football, and a blood clot in his neck that required surgery ended his baseball season in March. The Astros had scouted him extensively and believed he had the sweetest swing in the 2012 draft, so they invested a fourth-round pick and $1.85 million in him. Houston loves Ruiz's pretty swing path, track record of hitting and balance at the plate. He has powerful hands and forearms, producing homers with strength and bat speed. Some club officials project him as a plus-plus hitter with above-average power, though area scouts saw Ruiz as merely solid in both regards. He has plenty of arm strength for third base, having hit 95 mph off the mound as a junior. He's athletic with good body control and soft hands, so he should just need repetitions to become a dependable defender. He has below-average speed. As a lefthanded-hitting, Southern California third baseman with power and an easygoing demeanor, he draws comparisons to Eric Chavez. Ruiz will play alongside No. 1 overall pick Carlos Correa in low Class A in 2013.

BA GRADE

55

EXTREME

Year	Club (League)	Class	AVG	G	AB	R	H	2B	3B	HR	RBI	BB	SO	SB	CS	OBP	SLG
2012	Astros (GCL)	R	.271	23	85	13	23	8	2	0	11	12	22	2	0	.361	.412
	Greeneville (APP)	R	.220	15	50	8	11	3	1	1	7	4	10	0	0	.291	.380
Minor League Totals			.252	38	135	21	34	11	3	1	18	16	32	2	0	.336	.400

9 NICK TROPEANO, RHP

Born: Aug. 27, 1990. **B-T:** R-R. **Ht.:** 6-4. **Wt.:** 205. **Drafted:** Stony Brook, 2011 (6th round). **Signed by:** John Kosciak.

Before the whole world found out about Stony Brook with its trip to the 2012 College World Series, Tropeano served as the team's ace the previous two seasons. The first two-time America East Conference pitcher of the year, he has gone 15-9, 2.85 since signing for $155,700 as a 2011 sixth-round pick. Tropeano's plus changeup has been his out pitch since his amateur days. He throws it with good arm speed, and it features fade and sink. It's even more effective now that he pitches off his fastball more and has added velocity. He worked at 86-90 mph in college but now sits at 90-95 mph, thanks to using his fastball more often and incorporating his lower half better in his delivery. Tropeano also throws a solid split-finger fastball that gets swings and misses when it's on. His slurvy slider remains below-average and he gets on the side of it too often, though he keeps it down in the strike zone. He needs to focus on making it shorter and deeper instead of forcing the spin and getting on the side of the ball. He throws strikes and commands his fastball well. Following a strong stint in the Arizona Fall League, Tropeano is headed for a faster track in 2013. He'll open the season in Double-A and may not be much more than a year away from the majors. He has a ceiling of a No. 3 starter.

BA GRADE

50

MEDIUM

Year	Club (League)	Class	W	L	ERA	G	GS	CG	SV	IP	H	HR	BB	SO	K/9	WHIP	AVG
2011	Tri-City (NYP)	SS	3	2	2.36	12	12	0	0	53	42	1	21	63	10.6	1.18	.212
2012	Lexington (SAL)	LoA	6	4	2.78	15	14	0	0	87	77	3	26	97	10.0	1.18	.238
	Lancaster (CAL)	HiA	6	3	3.31	12	12	0	0	71	72	8	21	69	8.8	1.32	.265
Minor League Totals			15	9	2.85	39	38	0	0	211	191	12	68	229	9.8	1.23	.241

10 NOLAN FONTANA, SS

Born: June 6, 1991. **B-T:** L-R. **Ht.:** 5-11. **Wt.:** 190. **Drafted:** Florida, 2012 (2nd round). **Signed by:** John Martin.

Fontana's grandfather Lew Burdette won 203 games in the majors and beat the Yankees three times in the Braves' 1957 World Series triumph. Fontana made three College World Series trips as Florida's starting shortstop, making just 23 errors in three seasons. The 61st pick in the 2012 draft, he signed for $844,100 and went straight to low Class A. Fontana evokes compliments such as "ballplayer" and "grinder." He has excellent defensive instincts, soft hands and solid arm strength. He doesn't have ideal range for a shortstop, but it would shock few scouts if he willed himself to be an average big league defender there. He would thrive at second base and provides enough offense to profile there. Fontana knows the strike zone, works counts and handles the bat well. He walked 65 times in 49 pro games, though he struck out 44 times and may need to get a little more aggressive. He has doubles power to the gaps, above-average speed and good baserunning instincts. He wore down at the end of the season and will have to get stronger to hold up over a 162-game schedule. While Fontana may not be a star, scouts are certain he'll be a big leaguer, likely in the mold of another former Gator, David Eckstein. Fontana will push toolsier shortstops Jonathan Villar and Jio Mier in 2013 and could start his first full pro season in Double-A.

BA GRADE

50

HIGH

Year	Club (League)	Class	AVG	G	AB	R	H	2B	3B	HR	RBI	BB	SO	SB	CS	OBP	SLG
2012	Lexington (SAL)	LoA	.225	49	151	37	34	9	1	2	25	65	44	12	2	.464	.338
Minor League Totals			.225	49	151	37	34	9	1	2	25	65	44	12	2	.464	.338

11 DOMINGO SANTANA, OF

BA GRADE

50

HIGH

Born: Aug. 5, 1992. **B-T:** R-R. **Ht.:** 6-5. **Wt.:** 228. **Signed:** Dominican Republic, 2009. **Signed by:** Sal Agostinelli (Phillies).

The Phillies originally signed Santana for $330,000 out of the Dominican Republic in 2009, and he was advanced enough to make his pro debut in the United States that year as a 16-year-old. The Astros acquired him along with first baseman/outfielder Jonathan Singleton and righthanders Jarred Cosart and Josh Zeid in the 2011 Hunter Pence trade. Some scouts see significant first-division right-field regular tools with Santana, who has size, long levers and significant raw power. He's an average runner with above-average speed underway, and he has a plus throwing arm. The biggest question with Santana is how athletic he is and how much he'll adjust against better pitching. He hits to the opposite field well for his age and experience level, and scouts are split on whether he has the aptitude to learn to pull the ball with authority. He has holes in his swing thanks to his long arms, and some scouts wonder about his hands and timing, grading him as a fringy hitter. Others think he's athletic enough to make the adjustments to fully tap into his power. Santana figures to play alongside George Springer in the outfield again in 2013, this time in Double-A.

Year	Club (League)	Class	AVG	G	AB	R	H	2B	3B	HR	RBI	BB	SO	SB	CS	OBP	SLG
2009	Phillies (GCL)	R	.288	37	118	17	34	6	1	6	28	15	44	3	1	.388	.508
2010	Lakewood (SAL)	LoA	.182	49	165	27	30	10	0	3	16	29	76	5	6	.322	.297
	Williamsport (NYP)	SS	.237	54	186	28	44	9	0	5	20	23	73	4	4	.336	.366
2011	Lakewood (SAL)	LoA	.269	96	350	45	94	29	4	7	32	26	120	4	1	.345	.434
	Lexington (SAL)	LoA	.382	17	68	13	26	4	0	5	21	6	15	1	0	.447	.662
2012	Lancaster (CAL)	HiA	.302	119	457	87	138	26	6	23	97	55	148	7	1	.385	.536
Minor League Totals			.272	372	1344	217	366	84	11	49	214	154	476	24	13	.363	.461

12 JONATHAN VILLAR, SS

Born: May 2, 1991. **B-T:** B-R. **Ht.:** 6-1. **Wt.:** 195. **Signed:** Dominican Republic, 2008. **Signed by:** Sal Agostinelli (Phillies).

The fourth ex-Phillies farmhand among the Astros' top dozen prospects, Villar arrived in the 2010 Roy Oswalt trade along with Anthony Gose (who was traded immediately for Brett Wallace) and J.A. Happ. Villar was in the midst of a breakthrough 2012 season when he punched a door between innings of a July game and broke his right hand, ending his season. If he'd stayed healthy, he likely would have made his big league debut filling in for an injured Jed Lowrie. Villar was healthy enough to return to the field in the Dominican Winter League, though he served mostly as a pinch-runner. Villar is well-suited for that role because he's a plus runner and aggressive player with plenty of tools. His arm also rates as above-average, and he has plenty of range at shortstop. He continues to make errors in bunches, with 24 in 85 Double-A games, and scouts believe he hasn't slowed the game down yet. He plays frenetically on defense and doesn't trust his tools. The switch-hitting Villar hit 11 homers in his interrupted season, with most of his power improvement coming from the left side. Aggressive to a fault, he strikes out too often because he chases breaking balls and expands his zone. That unpolished approach and recklessness on both sides of the ball limits his ceiling, though he still has the tools to be a quality regular. Added to the 40-man roster, Villar figures to advance to Triple-A and see some big league time in 2013.

Year	Club (League)	Class	AVG	G	AB	R	H	2B	3B	HR	RBI	BB	SO	SB	CS	OBP	SLG
2008	Phillies (DSL)	R	.271	62	214	37	58	6	3	1	21	30	56	27	8	.367	.341
2009	Phillies (GCL)	R	.277	31	94	14	26	7	1	0	14	13	24	11	2	.364	.372
	Williamsport (NYP)	SS	.231	11	39	6	9	1	1	0	5	4	14	6	0	.302	.308
2010	Lakewood (SAL)	LoA	.272	100	371	61	101	18	4	2	36	26	103	38	13	.332	.358
	Lancaster (CAL)	HiA	.225	32	129	18	29	6	2	3	19	12	50	7	2	.294	.372
2011	Lancaster (CAL)	HiA	.259	47	174	26	45	7	4	4	26	25	56	20	6	.353	.414
	Corpus Christi (TL)	AA	.231	83	324	52	75	16	2	10	26	29	100	14	6	.301	.386
2012	Corpus Christi (TL)	AA	.261	86	326	54	85	7	2	11	50	35	87	39	8	.336	.396
Minor League Totals			.256	452	1671	268	428	68	19	31	197	174	490	162	45	.332	.375

13 VINCENT VELASQUEZ, RHP

Born: June 7, 1992. **B-T:** B-R. **Ht.:** 6-3. **Wt.:** 185. **Drafted:** HS—Garey, Calif., 2010 (2nd round). **Signed by:** Tim Costic/Bobby Heck.

The Astros haven't had much success developing high school arms, with Jordan Lyles by far their best success story in the last decade. Velasquez is a ways away, but he has the best stuff of any recent Houston prep draft pick other than Mike Foltynewicz. Velasquez has rebounded from Tommy John surgery in the fall after his 2010 pro debut, returning in instructional league a year later. He pitched well at short-season Tri-City last summer, though he was shut down for a month after getting hammered in his ninth start. Velasquez remains loose and athletic. At his best, he sits at 91-93 mph with his fastball and throws strikes with it, though not yet with the same frequency he did in his debut. He touches some 96s and tends to pitch downhill. His changeup still shows flashes of becoming a plus pitch, as he continues to show good arm speed and feel with it. His curveball has some sharpness and grades as average, though he gets on the side of it at times. Velasquez had a stress fracture and ligament strain in his elbow as a high schooler, and he has obvious durability questions. Houston hopes he'll make it through a full season in low Class A in 2013.

Year	Club (League)	Class	W	L	ERA	G	GS	CG	SV	IP	H	HR	BB	SO	K/9	WHIP	AVG
2010	Greeneville (APP)	R	2	2	3.07	8	6	0	0	29	24	4	5	25	7.7	0.99	.216
2011	Did Not Play—Injured																
2012	Tri-City (NYP)	SS	4	1	3.35	9	9	0	0	46	37	2	17	51	10.1	1.18	.223
Minor League Totals			6	3	3.24	17	15	0	0	75	61	6	22	76	9.1	1.11	.220

14 ASHER WOJCIECHOWSKI, RHP

Born: Dec. 21, 1988. **B-T:** R-R. **Ht.:** 6-4. **Wt.:** 235. **Drafted:** The Citadel, 2010 (1st round supplemental). **Signed by:** John Hendricks (Blue Jays).

The Blue Jays drafted righthanders with each of their first four picks before the second round of the 2010 draft. Two years later, they have cast their lot with the high schoolers (Aaron Sanchez, Noah Syndergaard) while souring on college picks Deck McGuire and Wojciechowski. They included the latter along with big leaguers Francisco Cordero and Ben Francisco and prospects Kevin Comer, Joe Musgrove, Carlos Perez and David Rollins to get David Carpenter, J.A. Happ and Brandon Lyon from the Astros in July. Wojciechowski had struggled through 43 outings and two seasons in high Class A, then threw well after the trade in his first action at Double-A. Corpus Christi was making a playoff run, and the Astros believe the winning atmosphere brought out the best in him. Wojciechowski throws a 90-94 mph fastball that touches 96. He has worked hard to command his fastball as a pro but has lost a bit of feel for his slider. He leaned heavily on a plus slider in college, but it's now more of a cutter in shape. He throws the cutter at 87-88 mph. He now uses a solid curveball as his breaking ball and can get swings and misses with it. His changeup can be too firm but has some run and can be effective. Wojciechowski has a durable starter's body and throws strikes but lacks pitch efficiency, working more than six innings just twice all season. He's likely to start 2013 back in Double-A.

Year	Club (League)	Class	W	L	ERA	G	GS	CG	SV	IP	H	HR	BB	SO	K/9	WHIP	AVG
2010	Auburn (NYP)	SS	0	0	0.75	3	3	0	0	12	6	0	4	11	8.3	0.83	.146
2011	Dunedin (FSL)	HiA	11	9	4.70	25	22	0	0	130	156	15	31	96	6.6	1.43	.292
2012	Dunedin (FSL)	HiA	7	3	3.57	18	18	0	0	93	91	3	22	76	7.3	1.21	.261
	Corpus Christi (TL)	AA	2	2	2.06	8	8	0	0	44	30	0	14	34	7.0	1.01	.190
Minor League Totals			20	14	3.74	54	51	0	0	279	283	18	71	217	7.0	1.27	.261

15 JOSE CISNERO, RHP

BA GRADE
45
MEDIUM

Born: April 11, 1989. **B-T:** R-R. **Ht.:** 6-3. **Wt.:** 185. **Signed:** Dominican Republic, 2007. **Signed by:** Felix Francisco/Andre Lopez.

Cisnero survived Lancaster, where he posted a 6.06 ERA in 2011 due mostly to too many walks and poor luck with his strand rate. He also averaged more than 11.1 strikeouts per nine innings, and the Astros promoted him to Double-A for 2012. He responded by making every start for the third straight season and finishing in Triple-A. Cisnero generates good velocity and sink on his fastball. He pitches at 90-92 mph with his sinker, at times working at 94-95. His slider is his main secondary pitch, an average if unspectacular breaking ball that he keeps down in the zone when he's going well. His changeup is fringy but has some sink and helped hold lefthanders homerless in 316 plate appearances against him last year. Cisnero threw more strikes in 2012 but his long arm action makes it tough for him to repeat his release point, so he'll never have precise command. Some scouts think he'll wind up in the bullpen. His durability and sturdy pitcher's frame gives him value as a sinker-slider innings-eater. Added to the 40-man roster this offseason, Cisnero will compete for a rotation spot in Houston but likely will start the year in Triple-A.

Year	Club (League)	Class	W	L	ERA	G	GS	CG	SV	IP	H	HR	BB	SO	K/9	WHIP	AVG
2008	Astros (DSL)	R	0	3	3.10	10	6	0	2	29	18	0	11	34	10.6	1.00	.180
2009	Greeneville (APP)	R	4	2	3.56	13	13	0	0	56	32	5	30	64	10.3	1.11	.165
2010	Lexington (SAL)	LoA	8	6	3.65	26	26	0	0	133	106	11	65	106	8.5	1.29	.221
2011	Lancaster (CAL)	HiA	8	11	6.06	27	27	0	0	123	115	13	75	152	11.1	1.54	.246
2012	Corpus Christi (TL)	AA	9	6	3.40	20	20	2	0	109	93	7	46	116	9.6	1.28	.227
	Oklahoma City (PCL)	AAA	4	1	4.54	8	8	0	0	40	52	1	18	32	7.3	1.76	.329
Minor League Totals			33	29	4.23	104	100	2	2	489	416	37	245	524	9.6	1.35	.230

16 ADRIAN HOUSER, RHP

BA GRADE
50
HIGH

Born: Feb. 2, 1993. **B-T:** R-R. **Ht.:** 6-4. **Wt.:** 205. **Drafted:** HS—Locust Grove, Okla., 2011 (2nd round). **Signed by:** Jim Stevenson.

The Astros decided to take it slow with Houser, who signed for a $530,100 bonus in 2011 as a second-round pick. He repeated Greeneville last summer and was fairly consistent, giving up two or fewer runs in eight of his 11 starts. Houser has a good frame and a promising repertoire. He stays tall and delivers an 88-92 mph fastball that regularly touches 95 and features cutting, sinking action at times. His downhill plane with his fastball keeps hitters from elevating the ball against him, and he has allowed just two homers in 106 pro innings. Houser can get swings and misses with his 12-to-6 curveball. He doesn't throw much of a changeup yet and uses the curve as his change of pace, sometimes slowing his arm on both pitches. Houser still is growing into his lanky body and could stand to add strength to better maintain his velocity. Innings and throwing his changeup more are other obvious needs as he advances to low Class A this year.

Year	Club (League)	Class	W	L	ERA	G	GS	CG	SV	IP	H	HR	BB	SO	K/9	WHIP	AVG
2011	Astros (GCL)	R	1	2	4.03	6	5	0	0	22	24	0	10	25	10.1	1.52	.273
	Greeneville (APP)	R	1	2	4.56	6	6	0	0	26	25	1	15	19	6.7	1.56	.258
2012	Greeneville (APP)	R	3	4	4.19	11	11	0	0	58	53	1	23	54	8.4	1.31	.245
Minor League Totals			5	8	4.25	23	22	0	0	106	102	2	48	98	8.3	1.42	.254

17 ROBBIE GROSSMAN, OF

BA GRADE
45
MEDIUM

Born: Sept. 16, 1989. **B-T:** B-L. **Ht.:** 6-0. **Wt.:** 205. **Drafted:** HS—Cypress, Texas, 2008 (6th round). **Signed by:** Mike Leuzinger (Pirates).

Signed for $1 million by the Pirates in 2008, Grossman led the minors with 127 runs and 104 walks three years later. He became the first minor leaguer to reach triple digits in both categories in the same season since Nick Swisher in 2004, and finally established himself as one of Pittsburgh's top prospects. With the Pirates chasing a playoff spot last July, they packaged him and minor league lefties Colton Cain and Rudy Owens to acquire Wandy Rodriguez. Grossman took a step back in his 2012 performance, with his power numbers, walk rate and stolen-base efficiency all dipping, but did claim a spot on the Astros' 40-man roster in November. Grossman never has had a standout tool, with his on-base ability his strongest attribute. From either side of the plate, his power comes mostly to the gaps, and profiles better if he can handle center field. He takes good routes and is a solid defender in center, but he lacks the prototypical plus speed for the spot. He's more of an average runner who lacks the first-step burst to be a big stolen-base threat. His arm is average. Grossman's profile screams fourth outfielder, but center field is wide open in Houston. He could win the job with a strong spring.

Year	Club (League)	Class	AVG	G	AB	R	H	2B	3B	HR	RBI	BB	SO	SB	CS	OBP	SLG
2008	Pirates (GCL)	R	.188	5	16	3	3	1	0	0	1	4	7	1	0	.381	.250
2009	West Virginia (SAL)	LoA	.266	116	451	83	120	21	2	5	42	75	164	35	12	.373	.355
2010	Bradenton (FSL)	HiA	.245	125	470	84	115	29	3	4	50	66	118	15	8	.344	.345
2011	Bradenton (FSL)	HiA	.294	134	490	127	144	34	2	13	56	104	111	24	10	.418	.451
2012	Altoona (EL)	AA	.266	95	350	59	93	20	4	7	36	59	78	9	10	.378	.406
	Corpus Christi (TL)	AA	.267	36	135	22	36	8	2	3	11	18	43	4	1	.371	.422
Minor League Totals			.267	511	1912	378	511	113	13	32	196	326	521	88	41	.379	.390

18 BRETT PHILLIPS, OF

BA GRADE
50
HIGH

Born: May 30, 1994. **B-T:** L-R. **Ht.:** 6-0. **Wt.:** 175. **Drafted:** HS—Seminole, Fla., 2012 (6th round). **Signed by:** John Martin.

Phillips was known among area scouts in Florida, but some thought they'd lost him to football when he earned all-county honors as a wide receiver as a senior in the fall of 2011, his only season as a varsity player. A North Carolina State recruit, he had late helium, and his package of twitchy athleticism, size and speed prompted the Astros to draft him 189th overall and sign him for $300,000 last June. Some scouts graded Phillips with two plus-plus tools as an amateur: his speed and arm. His throws have carry and are a tick better than his speed, which was somewhat muted after he signed when he tweaked his knee. Phillips doesn't have a lot of advanced baseball experience and has a somewhat raw approach at the plate. Scouts like his strength but want to see a more consistent, repeatable swing before they project him to hit for power. He has bat speed, though, and can drive the ball from gap to gap. His speed allows him to cover center field well. It may take him some time to develop, but Phillips profiles as an everyday center fielder. He'll start 2013 in extended spring training, then head either to Greenville or Tri-City in 2013.

Year	Club (League)	Class	AVG	G	AB	R	H	2B	3B	HR	RBI	BB	SO	SB	CS	OBP	SLG
2012	Astros (GCL)	R	.251	54	175	26	44	7	6	0	13	28	48	7	5	.360	.360
Minor League Totals			.251	54	175	26	44	7	6	0	13	28	48	7	5	.360	.360

19 ROB RASMUSSEN, LHP

BA GRADE
45
MEDIUM

Born: April 2, 1989. **B-T:** R-L. **Ht.:** 5-10. **Wt.:** 160. **Drafted:** UCLA, 2010 (2nd round). **Signed by:** Tim McDonnell (Marlins).

The third starter behind Trevor Bauer and Gerrit Cole on UCLA's 2010 College World Series runners-up, Rasmussen won 11 games that spring, including the clinchers in the NCAA regionals and super-regionals. Signed by the Marlins for $499,500 as a second-rounder, he advanced quickly and spent his full pro season in high Class A. In the midst of his second, Miami shipped him and Matt Dominguez to the Astros for Carlos Lee. Houston pushed Rasmussen to Double-A, where he scuffled a bit but finished with seven shutout innings in a playoff start. The small-bodied Rasmussen has topped 140 innings in each of his two full seasons and gets swings and misses with two breaking balls. He throws both a curveball and slider, and his feel for spin has been his calling card since high school. Rasmussen has added polish as a pro, pitching on the corners with his fastball and changeup. He throws his fastball at 89-92 mph, though it tends to come in flat. His pitchability allows him to pitch backwards, but Rasmussen tends to nibble and get in trouble with walks. Scouts are split on whether he should remain a surprisingly durable, back-of-the-rotation starter or slide to the bullpen, where being lefthanded and throwing two breaking balls would make him an asset. He could see his first big league action in 2013.

Year	Club (League)	Class	W	L	ERA	G	GS	CG	SV	IP	H	HR	BB	SO	K/9	WHIP	AVG
2010	Greensboro (SAL)	LoA	0	0	1.35	5	0	0	0	7	6	0	2	4	5.4	1.20	.240
2011	Jupiter (FSL)	HiA	12	10	3.64	28	27	1	0	148	140	10	71	118	7.2	1.42	.254

2012	Jupiter (FSL)	HiA	4	7	3.90	16	16	0	0	88	83	6	36	75	7.7	1.36	.250
	Corpus Christi (TL)	AA	4	4	4.80	11	10	0	0	54	58	6	18	44	7.3	1.40	.276
Minor League Totals			20	21	3.88	60	53	1	0	297	287	22	127	241	7.3	1.39	.257

20 BRETT OBERHOLTZER, LHP

BA GRADE

45

MEDIUM

Born: July 1, 1989. **B-T:** L-L. **Ht.:** 6-2. **Wt.:** 230. **Drafted:** Seminole (Fla.) JC, 2008 (8th round). **Signed by:** Gregg Kilby (Braves).

Acquired from the Braves in the 2011 Michael Bourn trade along with Juan Abreu, Jordan Schafer and righthander Paul Clemens, Oberholtzer gives the Astros yet another durable innings-eater. He made every start in 2012, earning a midseason promotion to Triple-A. He has little flash about him, but he's big and strong and has a 90-92 mph fastball that gets on hitters quick thanks to an easy arm action and clean delivery. His fastball has a bit of sink, as does his solid changeup, which may be his best pitch. His slider is more of a cutter, but he does spin a reliable curveball. Oberholtzer's issue is his propensity for pitching up in the strike zone. He doesn't have the velocity to get away with elevating his pitches and gave up 24 homers last season. He has control but not the command to keep the ball out of hitters' hot zones, making him more of a fourth or fifth starter down the line. Protected on the 40-man roster in November, he figures to open 2013 as part of an intriguing Oklahoma City rotation with Jarred Cosart, Jose Cisnero, Ross Seaton and Clemens.

Year	Club (League)	Class	W	L	ERA	G	GS	CG	SV	IP	H	HR	BB	SO	K/9	WHIP	AVG
2008	Braves (GCL)	R	4	1	2.89	10	0	0	0	37	34	1	10	32	7.7	1.18	.241
2009	Danville (APP)	R	6	2	2.01	12	12	1	0	67	46	1	6	56	7.5	0.78	.191
2010	Rome (SAL)	LoA	0	2	1.96	4	4	0	0	23	22	1	5	19	7.4	1.17	.262
	Myrtle Beach (CAR)	HiA	6	6	4.15	22	18	0	2	113	123	7	18	107	8.5	1.25	.279
2011	Mississippi (SL)	AA	9	9	3.74	21	21	1	0	128	119	6	42	93	6.6	1.26	.249
	Corpus Christi (TL)	AA	2	3	5.27	6	6	0	0	27	28	3	10	28	9.2	1.39	.267
2012	Corpus Christi (TL)	AA	5	3	4.21	13	13	0	0	77	81	11	21	68	7.9	1.32	.267
	Oklahoma City (PCL)	AAA	5	7	4.52	15	15	0	0	90	105	13	19	69	6.9	1.38	.292
Minor League Totals			37	33	3.75	103	89	2	2	562	558	43	131	472	7.6	1.23	.259

21 ROSS SEATON, RHP

BA GRADE

45

MEDIUM

Born: Sept. 18, 1989. **B-T:** L-R. **Ht.:** 6-4. **Wt.:** 225. **Drafted:** HS—Houston, 2008 (3rd round supplemental). **Signed by:** Rusty Pendergrass/Mike Burns.

Few Astros farmhands embody the Bobby Heck era more than Seaton. The club's first draft under its former scouting director/assistant GM was in 2008, and four of the top five picks were high schoolers, including Seaton. He signed for $700,000, well above-slot money for the supplemental third round. Those prospects entered a system with zero depth, so they all were thrown into full-season competition in their first full pro seasons—and all of them except for Jordan Lyles struggled with the assignment. First-rounder Jason Castro (a college product) and Lyles are big leaguers but don't appear to be future stars, and Seaton is the only player with big league potential left in the system from that draft. He set career bests for innings (169), strikeout rate (6.2 per nine innings) and walk rate (2.0 per nine) in 2012, earning a pair of promotions to Triple-A. Seaton threw 91-94 mph earlier in his career, but now he's a sinker-slider pitcher with average velocity on both offerings. He'll pitch at 87-92 mph with his sinking two-seamer, commanding it well down and away to both sides of the plate. He keeps his hard slider down in the zone, and he has the pitchability to throw both his curveball and changeup—fringy pitches at best—for strikes in fastball counts. He doesn't have enough stuff to miss up in the strike zone and remains fairly homer prone. Seaton hasn't missed a start in three seasons and profiles as a back-of-the-rotation innings-eater. Added to the 40-man roster in November, he'll head to Triple-A for the full 2013 season.

Year	Club (League)	Class	W	L	ERA	G	GS	CG	SV	IP	H	HR	BB	SO	K/9	WHIP	AVG
2008	Greeneville (APP)	R	0	0	13.50	3	3	0	0	4	8	1	2	4	9.0	2.50	.381
2009	Lexington (SAL)	LoA	8	10	3.29	24	24	1	0	137	137	11	39	88	5.8	1.29	.261
2010	Lancaster (CAL)	HiA	6	13	6.64	28	28	0	0	146	198	22	45	85	5.2	1.66	.327
2011	Corpus Christi (TL)	AA	4	9	5.23	28	28	0	0	155	168	19	47	97	5.6	1.39	.279
2012	Oklahoma City (PCL)	AAA	0	1	3.09	4	4	0	0	23	24	2	7	11	4.2	1.33	.258
	Corpus Christi (TL)	AA	8	8	4.07	25	25	1	0	146	155	17	31	106	6.5	1.27	.271
Minor League Totals			26	41	4.83	112	112	2	0	611	690	72	171	391	5.8	1.41	.285

22 CHIA-JEN LO, RHP

BA GRADE

50

HIGH

Born: April 7, 1986. **B-T:** R-R. **Ht.:** 5-11. **Wt.:** 185. **Signed:** Taiwan, 2008. **Signed by:** Glen Barker.

The Astros signed Lo to a $250,000 bonus three months after he'd pitched for Taiwan in the Beijing Olympics. He reached Double-A in his first season in the United States, though elbow pain caused him to miss most of 2010. Diagnosed with a partially torn ligament, he tried to rehab the injury but eventually had Tommy John surgery. After working just 17 innings in 2010-11, he finally returned healthy last season and pitched well enough to earn a spot on the 40-man roster. Lo has regained his velocity, pumping a heavy 94-96 mph fastball to go with a solid curveball. Lo gets most of his strikeouts with his fastball, and when his curve is on he can pitch up and down in the strike zone. His changeup is just for show. Lo led the Arizona Fall League with 14 appearances after the season and should be ready for a full load in 2013. He could factor into Houston's bullpen in the near future. He has the upside of a closer if the stays healthy and maintains his improved control.

Year	Club (League)	Class	W	L	ERA	G	GS	CG	SV	IP	H	HR	BB	SO	K/9	WHIP	AVG
2009	Lancaster (CAL)	HiA	1	0	1.78	12	0	0	1	25	10	1	13	36	12.8	0.91	.120
	Corpus Christi (TL)	AA	0	2	2.31	30	0	0	2	39	30	1	20	39	9.0	1.28	.213
2010	Corpus Christi (TL)	AA	0	1	1.80	7	0	0	0	15	9	0	10	13	7.8	1.27	.176
2011	Lexington (SAL)	LoA	0	0	13.50	2	0	0	0	2	2	1	2	3	13.5	2.00	.250
2012	Astros (GCL)	R	0	1	0.00	8	5	0	0	11	5	0	2	11	9.0	0.64	.128
	Lancaster (CAL)	HiA	0	0	1.42	11	0	0	0	19	14	1	4	20	9.5	0.95	.222
Minor League Totals			1	4	1.94	70	5	0	3	111	70	4	51	122	9.9	1.09	.182

23 BRADY RODGERS, RHP

BA GRADE
45
MEDIUM

Born: Sept. 17, 1990. **B-T:** R-R. **Ht.:** 6-2. **Wt.:** 187. **Drafted:** Arizona State, 2012 (3rd round). **Signed by:** Mike Brown.

Rodgers posted the second-best career ERA (2.39) in Arizona State history while going 23-10 with just 36 walks in 286 innings over the last three years. He had similar success in his pro debut after signing for a $495,200 bonus as the 96th overall selection, helping Tri-City to a 51-25 record with the same mix of efficiency and stinginess with walks. Rodgers' wiry build gives scouts some pause, but he maintained his stuff through the college and pro seasons, working 184 innings (counting the New York-Penn League playoffs). At his best, Rodgers pitches with an 88-92 mph fastball and puts it where he wants to, exhibiting solid average command already. His slider gives him an above-average pitch, coming in at 82-85 mph at times. His feel for spin also helps him throw a solid curveball that can have sharp downer action in the mid-70s. His changeup gives him a reliable fourth pitch. Rodgers' competitiveness serves him well. He'll join Lance McCullers Jr., Vincent Velasquez and Adrian Houser in a talented Cedar Rapids rotation in 2013.

Year	Club (League)	Class	W	L	ERA	G	GS	CG	SV	IP	H	HR	BB	SO	K/9	WHIP	AVG
2012	Tri-City (NYP)	SS	7	2	2.89	12	12	0	0	62	60	5	11	49	7.1	1.14	.251
Minor League Totals			7	2	2.89	12	12	0	0	62	60	5	11	49	7.1	1.14	.251

24 ANDREW APLIN, OF

BA GRADE
45
MEDIUM

Born: March 21, 1991. **B-T:** L-L. **Ht.:** 6-0. **Wt.:** 190. **Drafted:** Arizona State, 2012 (5th round). **Signed by:** Mike Brown.

When he was Cardinals scouting director, Astros GM Jeff Luhnow and his staff excelled at finding college players whom other clubs regarded as organization players or fringe big leaguers but wound up as prospects or big league regulars. Allen Craig, Daniel Descalso and Jon Jay are just a few examples. Houston has several college players from the 2012 draft whom they believe can follow the same successful path. A fifth-rounder signed for $220,000 in June, Aplin draws comparisons to Jay. As one club official put it, Aplin has average tools and well above-average feel for the game. That makes for a good quote, but his tools actually are a bit better than that. He's no burner, yet Aplin impresses scouts with great reads and smooth, easy routes in center field that make him a plus defender. Aside from his glove, his arm strength might be his best pure tool, earning some 55 grades on the 20-80 scouting scale. Aplin controls the strike zone well and makes consistent line-drive contact. He has below-average power, though he slugged .493 in his pro debut compared to .454 in three years at Arizona State. He's a smart baserunner who's a threat to steal despite fringy speed. A strong start with Tri-City prompted an August promotion to Lancaster, where he replaced George Springer in center field, hit third and the JetHawks to the California League championship. Aplin has a fourth outfielder's toolset and already has hopped on the fast track. He's likely to return to high Class A to start his first full pro season.

Year	Club (League)	Class	AVG	G	AB	R	H	2B	3B	HR	RBI	BB	SO	SB	CS	OBP	SLG
2012	Tri-City (NYP)	SS	.348	44	164	38	57	9	5	4	25	24	22	20	7	.441	.537
	Lancaster (CAL)	HiA	.260	24	104	19	27	4	2	3	13	4	16	4	3	.287	.423
Minor League Totals			.313	68	268	57	84	13	7	7	38	28	38	24	10	.386	.493

25 JOSH FIELDS, RHP

BA GRADE
45
MEDIUM

Born: Aug. 19, 1985. **B-T:** R-R. **Ht.:** 6-0. **Wt.:** 185. **Drafted:** Georgia, 2008 (1st round). **Signed by:** Chuck Carlson (Mariners).

A rare college senior first-rounder when the Mariners took him 20th overall in 2008, Fields took until February 2009 to sign for $1.75 million. He never got untracked in the Seattle system, battling a dead arm along with oblique and forearm strains, and went to Boston as a throw-in in a three-team Erik Bedard trade in July 2011. Fields turned a corner last year after working with Double-A Portland pitching coach

Bob Kipper and Red Sox minor league pitching coordinator Ralph Treuel. Fields did a better job of repeating his maximum-effort delivery, his stuff improved and he performed consistently. His fastball averaged 95 mph (up from 92 the year before) and peaked at 97 with improved gloveside run. He also added power to his curveball, which became the downer that was his bread and butter in college. He gained the confidence to challenge hitters more aggressively and did a better job of working down in the strike zone. Left off Boston's 40-man roster, the Astros made him the No. 1 pick in the major league Rule 5 draft in December. If Fields can maintain the gains he made in 2012, he should stick in the Houston bullpen. If he doesn't, he'll have to clear waivers and get offered back to the Red Sox for half his $50,000 draft price before he can be sent to the minors.

Year	Club (League)	Class	W	L	ERA	G	GS	CG	SV	IP	H	HR	BB	SO	K/9	WHIP	AVG
2009	West Tenn (SL)	AA	2	2	6.48	31	0	0	1	33	33	2	22	36	9.7	1.65	.254
2010	West Tenn (SL)	AA	1	1	3.14	21	0	0	6	29	19	0	18	28	8.8	1.29	.190
2011	Jackson (SL)	AA	1	2	2.77	20	0	0	3	26	17	0	19	26	9.0	1.38	.185
	Tacoma (PCL)	AAA	0	0	6.23	9	0	0	0	13	11	2	13	13	9.0	1.85	.229
	Portland (EL)	AA	3	0	3.12	9	0	0	1	17	10	2	10	25	13.0	1.15	.179
2012	Portland (EL)	AA	3	3	2.62	32	0	0	8	45	30	4	16	59	11.9	1.03	.185
	Pawtucket (IL)	AAA	1	0	0.00	10	0	0	4	14	8	0	2	19	12.5	0.73	.174
Minor League Totals			11	8	3.57	132	0	0	23	177	128	10	100	206	10.5	1.29	.202

26 AUSTIN WATES, OF

BA GRADE 45 MEDIUM

Born: Sept. 2, 1988. **B-T:** R-R. **Ht.:** 6-2. **Wt.:** 179. **Drafted:** Virginia Tech, 2010 (3rd round). **Signed by:** Everett Stull.

Since signing for $550,000 as a 2010 third-round pick, Wates has been one of the best hitters in the system. With an unconventional swing and an inside-out approach, he's content to shoot balls the other way rather than turn on them and pull them with authority. He displays natural hitting rhythm and timing. He batted a career-high .310 in 2012 despite landing on the disabled list twice with a quadriceps problem in June and a hamstring pull in July. However, Wates won't profile as more than a fourth outfielder unless he starts to draw more walks. While he's an above-average runner, his leg injuries set him back a bit and he's not an efficient basestealer. His swing keeps him from hitting for power in games despite surprising raw juice in batting practice. His arm and instincts are better suited for left field than center. Wates is headed to Triple-A for 2013.

Year	Club (League)	Class	AVG	G	AB	R	H	2B	3B	HR	RBI	BB	SO	SB	CS	OBP	SLG
2010	Astros (GCL)	R	.000	1	3	1	0	0	0	0	0	0	2	0	0	.250	.000
	Tri-City (NYP)	SS	.316	12	38	11	12	2	1	1	6	8	6	9	0	.447	.500
2011	Lancaster (CAL)	HiA	.300	132	526	85	158	23	9	6	75	47	86	26	7	.366	.413
2012	Astros (GCL)	R	.556	3	9	2	5	0	0	1	2	0	2	0	0	.556	.889
	Corpus Christi (TL)	AA	.304	95	359	58	109	16	4	7	48	31	71	17	11	.375	.429
Minor League Totals			.304	243	935	157	284	41	14	15	131	86	167	52	18	.374	.426

27 PAUL CLEMENS, RHP

BA GRADE 45 HIGH

Born: Feb. 14, 1988. **B-T:** R-R. **Ht.:** 6-4. **Wt.:** 180. **Drafted:** Louisburg (N.C.) JC, 2008 (7th round). **Signed by:** Billy Best (Braves).

Another piece in the 2011 Michael Bourn trade, Clemens arrived with a reputation as a hard thrower with a bit of a wild streak. He pitched well in big league camp last spring but never got going in Triple-A. He won six of his first 10 decisions but, but his season fell off a cliff as his control failed him. Clemens has a live fastball that ranges from 90-96 mph with good sink. His curveball shows flashes of being a plus pitch, and his sinking changeup gives him a solid third offering when it's on. As with most pitchers, Clemens' success is predicated on fastball command, which comes down to consistency on and off the field. Those issues have dogged him since his amateur days. He lacks the durable frame typical of a starting pitcher, though he has topped 140 innings in each of the last two seasons. The issues with his command, frame and preparation point toward Clemens being a reliever long-term. He'll get another chance as a starter in Triple-A this year.

Year	Club (League)	Class	W	L	ERA	G	GS	CG	SV	IP	H	HR	BB	SO	K/9	WHIP	AVG
2008	Braves (GCL)	R	1	0	0.00	1	0	0	0	3	1	0	0	2	6.0	0.33	.111
	Danville (APP)	R	3	3	3.39	12	8	0	1	58	57	6	18	57	8.8	1.29	.252
	Rome (SAL)	LoA	0	1	9.00	1	1	0	0	4	7	0	2	0	0.00	2.25	.412
2009	Rome (SAL)	LoA	6	5	5.91	26	11	0	3	85	105	7	49	64	6.8	1.80	.296
2010	Rome (SAL)	LoA	2	0	1.42	8	0	0	1	19	11	1	8	16	7.6	1.00	.164
	Myrtle Beach (CAR)	HiA	0	4	3.69	27	8	0	2	76	83	5	28	65	7.7	1.47	.275
2011	Mississippi (SL)	AA	6	5	3.73	20	20	0	0	109	103	8	44	93	7.7	1.35	.249
	Corpus Christi (TL)	AA	2	1	2.35	5	5	0	0	31	23	3	12	26	7.6	1.14	.200
	Oklahoma City (PCL)	AAA	0	1	15.43	1	1	0	0	5	4	1	6	6	11.6	2.14	.250
2012	Oklahoma City (PCL)	AAA	8	8	6.73	20	20	0	0	102	145	16	32	68	6.0	1.74	.341
	Corpus Christi (TL)	AA	3	2	3.46	7	7	0	0	42	41	7	11	37	8.0	1.25	.255
Minor League Totals			31	30	4.55	128	81	0	7	533	580	54	210	434	7.3	1.48	.275

28 CARLOS PEREZ, C

BA GRADE
45
MEDIUM

Born: Oct. 27, 1990. **B-T:** R-R. **Ht.:** 5-11. **Wt.:** 200. **Signed:** Venezuela, 2008.
Signed by: Rafael Moncada (Blue Jays).

Signed by the Blue Jays, Perez was selected MVP of his teams in the Dominican Summer, Gulf Coast and New York-Penn leagues in his first three pro seasons. His career appeared to plateau when he hit full-season ball, however, and he got buried in a logjam of catchers in the Toronto organization. The Jays included him as one of five prospects in the 10-player July trade that sent David Carpenter, J.A. Happ and Brandon Lyon to Toronto. Perez immediately became the top catcher in the Houston system, though Roberto Pena has a bit better defensive ability. Scouts like Perez's defensive tools, as he's fluid behind the plate, handles velocity well and has a solid arm. He posts consistent pop times of 1.95-2.0 seconds and threw out 34 percent of basestealers last year. After slumping in his first exposure to low Class A in 2011, Perez rebounded last year but scouts still aren't sure how much offense he'll provide. He has adopted a contact approach that sacrifices power. His swing gets long when he tries to drive the ball, and his hands don't work as well at the plate as they do behind it. He draws some walks and has some strength to the gaps, so he's not an offensive zero. The Astros declined to protect him on their 40-man roster after the season and will send him back to high Class A to start 2013.

Year	Club (League)	Class	AVG	G	AB	R	H	2B	3B	HR	RBI	BB	SO	SB	CS	OBP	SLG
2008	Blue Jays 1 (DSL)	R	.306	58	196	27	60	10	2	0	29	52	28	7	5	.459	.378
2009	Blue Jays (GCL)	R	.291	43	141	17	41	11	3	1	21	16	23	2	5	.364	.433
2010	Auburn (NYP)	SS	.298	66	235	44	70	11	8	2	41	34	41	7	3	.396	.438
2011	Lansing (MWL)	LoA	.256	95	383	58	98	17	6	3	41	37	74	6	2	.320	.355
2012	Lansing (MWL)	LoA	.275	71	273	48	75	22	5	5	40	35	38	3	2	.358	.447
	Lancaster (CAL)	HiA	.318	26	88	11	28	6	1	0	10	6	17	0	1	.368	.409
Minor League Totals			.283	359	1316	205	372	77	25	11	182	180	221	25	18	.372	.404

29 AARON WEST, RHP

BA GRADE
50
HIGH

Born: June 1, 1990. **B-T:** R-R. **Ht.:** 6-1. **Wt.:** 195. **Drafted:** Washington, 2012 (17th round). **Signed by:** Paul Gale.

The Astros scouted Stanford righthander Mark Appel hard while considering him for the No. 1 overall pick in 2012. While doing so, they spotted West, who emerged as one of the Pacific-12 Conference's better starters as a redshirt junior two years removed from surgery to repair frayed cartilage in his elbow. He took a loss against Appel, but West also sat at 89-93 mph and touched 95 with his fastball. Houston signed him for $50,000 in the 17th round and was rewarded with a promising debut. West worked more off his fastball more after turning and his velocity increased to a consistent 90-96 mph. He has average command of his fastball. While neither his cutter/slider nor changeup projects as a plus pitch, they both find the strike zone and help him keep hitters off balance. West has a body built for durability and his delivery has no major red flags. He could jump on the fast track and will spend some if not all of 2013 in high Class A.

Year	Club (League)	Class	W	L	ERA	G	GS	CG	SV	IP	H	HR	BB	SO	K/9	WHIP	AVG
2012	Tri-City (NYP)	SS	6	2	2.04	12	12	0	0	62	50	3	9	59	8.6	0.96	.218
Minor League Totals			6	2	2.04	12	12	0	0	62	50	3	9	59	8.6	0.96	.218

30 TYLER HEINEMAN, C

BA GRADE
45
HIGH

Born: June 19, 1991. **B-T:** B-R. **Ht.:** 5-11. **Wt.:** 205. **Drafted:** UCLA, 2012 (8th round). **Signed by:** Tim Costic.

A baseball rat, Heineman has an uncle who played at Arizona State, while his brother Scott is a sophomore infielder for Oregon. Heineman's UCLA career included two trips to the College World Series but he was a little-used backup in his first two seasons, when he caught Rob Rasmussen and two of the top three picks in the 2011 draft, Gerrit Cole and Trevor Bauer. In his lone season as a regular, Heineman's grit, solid tools and surprising skills shined through, earning him a $125,000 bonus in the eighth round last June. Scouts laud him for his toughness as he shakes off home-plate collisions, coaxes his pitchers to compete and handles his staff in a professional manner. He has solid catch-and-throw skills and threw out 41 percent of basestealers while helping Tri-City to the New York-Penn League finals. Heineman led the NY-P in batting (.358) while ranking second in on-base percentage (.452) and plate appearances per strikeout (19.4). He's a switch-hitter with a contact approach and an excellent notion of the strike zone. He's willing to take one for the team, getting hit by 27 pitches between college and pro ball last year, and he handles the bat well in hit-and-run and bunt situations. His power potential is limited and he'll have to prove he can hit quality fastballs as he moves up the later. He runs well for a catcher and is a smart baserunner. Even with modest offensive upside, Heineman fits as a fast-moving future backup, and added power could make him an eventual regular. He'll open his first full pro season in low Class A.

Year	Club (League)	Class	AVG	G	AB	R	H	2B	3B	HR	RBI	BB	SO	SB	CS	OBP	SLG
2012	Tri-City (NYP)	SS	.358	55	193	33	69	14	0	0	26	26	12	6	2	.452	.430
Minor League Totals			.358	55	193	33	69	14	0	0	26	26	12	6	2	.452	.430

Kansas City Royals

BY J.J. COOPER

The Royals' 2012 marketing slogan was Our Time. It should have been Déjà Vu All Over Again.

Kansas City again found itself unable to contend in one of the weakest divisions in baseball, the American League Central. The Royals finished below .500 for the 18th time in 19 seasons and have gone 27 years since their last playoff appearance. Many players on the current major league roster weren't alive the last time the club made the postseason.

A playoff run in 2012 would have been a serendipitous early arrival for a team fielding rookies or second-year players at catcher, first base, second base, shortstop, third base and center field. But those hopes took a hit early with the loss of closer Joakim Soria and starters Danny Duffy and Felipe Paulino to Tommy John surgeries, gutting an already thin pitching staff.

There will be no such excuses in 2013. Now two seasons removed from being the first club ever to place nine players on Baseball America's Top 100 Prospects list, Kansas City will field largely the same lineup as the one it rolled out for most of the second half of 2012.

GM Dayton Moore and his staff have developed a group of position players who should be an asset if they continue to mature. Likewise, the bullpen is equally young, homegrown and talented. If the Royals fall flat in 2013, it likely will be for the same reason they've struggled throughout Moore's 6½ years as GM: an inability to produce starting pitching.

The six drafts Moore has overseen in Kansas City have produced a total of just 26 big league starts, 18 by Duffy and eight by Everett Teaford, the 10th-worst total in baseball. High-dollar draft picks Chris Dwyer, Tim Melville and Mike Montgomery haven't developed as hoped, nor has $6.9 million Cuban defector Noel Arguelles. Right before Moore took over in 2006, the Royals spent the No. 1 overall pick on Luke Hochevar, who has gone 38-59, 5.39 in parts of six seasons and posted the second-worst ERA (5.73) among major league qualifiers last year.

As a result, Moore aggressively rebuilt his rotation this offseason. He acquired Ervin Santana from the Angels in exchange for minor league reliever Brandon Sisk in October, then gave free agent Jeremy Guthrie a three-year, $25 million deal in November. Moore's boldest move came two weeks before Christmas, when he packaged four prospects—outfielder Wil

The Royals had to turn to other teams to get established pitchers like Ervin Santana

Myers, Baseball America's 2012 Minor League Player of the Year, plus righthander Jake Odorizzi, lefty Mike Montgomery and third baseman Patrick Leonard—to get James Shields and Wade Davis from the Rays.

Trading away the club's top position prospect has left the Royals thin in position prospects at the upper levels of the system. Christian Colon could help at second base or shortstop in 2013, but the rest of the Royals' premium position players are a year or two away. But that was a tradeoff Kansas City felt was worth taking—as the offseason moves have brought much-needed depth and talent to the starting rotation.

Moore and his front office have plenty of incentive to solve their pitching problems. Just eight clubs have failed to make the playoffs since he was hired in May 2006, and the Royals are the lone team in the group that hasn't made a GM change.

If Kansas City fails to advance to the postseason in 2013, Moore will have one of the five longest GM tenures without a playoff appearance in the last two decades. Former Royals GM Herk Robinson leads that list with nine playoff-less seasons.

The Royals sacked the ad agency that came up with the Our Time slogan. If their time doesn't come in 2013, more firings may ensue.

THIS YEAR'S TOP 30

Player, Pos.		Grade
1.	Kyle Zimmer, rhp	65/Medium
2.	Bubba Starling, of	70/Extreme
3.	Yordano Ventura, rhp	60/High
4.	Jorge Bonifacio, of	55/High
5.	Adalberto Mondesi, ss	60/Extreme
6.	Sam Selman, lhp	50/High
7.	Orlando Calixte, ss	50/High
8.	Jason Adam, rhp	50/High
9.	Cheslor Cuthbert, 3b	50/High
10.	Miguel Almonte, rhp	55/Extreme
11.	John Lamb, lhp	55/Extreme
12.	Kyle Smith, rhp	50/High
13.	Christian Colon, ss/2b	45/Medium
14.	Donnie Joseph, lhp	45/Medium
15.	Cameron Gallagher, c	50/High
16.	Elier Hernandez, of	55/Extreme
17.	Bryan Brickhouse, rhp	55/Extreme
18.	Angel Baez, rhp	50/High
19.	Jack Lopez, ss	50/High
20.	Humberto Arteaga, ss	50/High
21.	Chris Dwyer, lhp	50/High
22.	Ramon Torres, ss	50/High
23.	Fred Ford, of	50/High
24.	David Lough, of	40/Low
25.	Colin Rodgers, lhp	50/High
26.	Christian Binford, rhp	50/High
27.	Jake Junis, rhp	50/High
28.	Robinson Yambati, rhp	45/High
29.	Brett Eibner, of	50/Extreme
30.	Brian Fletcher, of/1b	45/High

LAST YEAR'S TOP 30

Player, Pos.		Status
1.	Mike Montgomery, lhp	(Rays)
2.	Bubba Starling, of	No. 2
3.	Wil Myers, of	(Rays)
4.	Jake Odorizzi, rhp	(Rays)
5.	Cheslor Cuthbert, 3b	No. 9
6.	John Lamb, lhp	No. 11
7.	Kelvin Herrera, rhp	Majors
8.	Jason Adam, rhp	No. 8
9.	Chris Dwyer, lhp	No. 21
10.	Yordano Ventura, rhp	No. 3
11.	Christian Colon, ss/2b	No. 13
12.	Brett Eibner, of	No. 29
13.	Jeremy Jeffress, rhp	(Blue Jays)
14.	Elier Hernandez, of	No. 16
15.	Jorge Bonifacio, of	No. 4
16.	Bryan Brickhouse, rhp	No. 17
17.	Noel Arguelles, lhp	Dropped out
18.	Kevin Chapman, lhp	(Astros)
19.	Tim Melville, rhp	Dropped out
20.	Orlando Calixte, ss	No. 7
21.	Clint Robinson, 1b	(Pirates)
22.	Will Smith, lhp	Majors
23.	Cameron Gallagher, c	No. 15
24.	Mike Antonio, ss	Dropped out
25.	Jack Lopez, ss	No. 19
26.	Everett Teaford, lhp	Majors
27.	Brian Fletcher, of	No. 30
28.	Danny Mateo, 2b/3b	Dropped out
29.	Humberto Arteaga, ss	No. 20
30.	David Lough, of	No. 24

BEST TOOLS

Best Hitter for Average	Jorge Bonifacio
Best Power Hitter	Bubba Starling
Best Strike-Zone Discipline	Christian Colon
Fastest Baserunner	Terrance Gore
Best Athlete	Bubba Starling
Best Fastball	Yordano Ventura
Best Curveball	Kyle Zimmer
Best Slider	Donnie Joseph
Best Changeup	John Lamb
Best Control	Kyle Zimmer
Best Defensive Catcher	Manny Pina
Best Defensive Infielder	Humberto Arteaga
Best Infield Arm	Cheslor Cuthbert
Best Defensive Outfielder	Bubba Starling
Best Outfield Arm	Brett Eibner

PROJECTED 2016 LINEUP

Catcher	Salvador Perez
First Base	Eric Hosmer
Second Base	Johnny Giavotella
Third Base	Mike Moustakas
Shortstop	Alcides Escobar
Left Field	Alex Gordon
Center Field	Bubba Starling
Right Field	Jorge Bonifacio
Designated Hitter	Billly Butler
No. 1 Starter	Kyle Zimmer
No. 2 Starter	James Shields
No. 3 Starter	Ervin Santana
No. 4 Starter	Yordano Ventura
No. 5 Starter	Wade Davis
Closer	Kelvin Herrera

TOP PROSPECTS OF THE DECADE

Year	Player, Pos.	2012 Org.
2003	Zack Greinke, rhp	Angels
2004	Zack Greinke, rhp	Angels
2005	Billy Butler, 1b	Royals
2006	Alex Gordon, 3b	Royals
2007	Alex Gordon, 3b	Royals
2008	Mike Moustakas, ss	Royals
2009	Mike Moustakas, 3b	Royals
2010	Mike Montgomery, lhp	Royals
2011	Eric Hosmer, 1b	Royals
2012	Mike Montgomery, lhp	Royals

TOP DRAFT PICKS OF THE DECADE

Year	Player, Pos.	2012 Org.
2003	Chris Lubanski, of	Out of baseball
2004	Billy Butler, 1b	Royals
2005	Alex Gordon, 3b	Royals
2006	Luke Hochevar, rhp	Royals
2007	Mike Moustakas, ss	Royals
2008	Eric Hosmer, 1b	Royals
2009	Aaron Crow, rhp	Royals
2010	Christian Colon, ss	Royals
2011	Bubba Starling, of	Royals
2012	Kyle Zimmer, rhp	Royals

LARGEST BONUSES IN CLUB HISTORY

Bubba Starling, 2011	$7,500,000
Eric Hosmer, 2008	$6,000,000
Alex Gordon, 2005	$4,000,000
Mike Moustakas, 2007	$4,000,000
Luke Hochevar, 2006	$3,500,000

KANSAS CITY ROYALS

TOP 2013 ROOKIE: Donnie Joseph, lhp. Picked up in the Jonathan Broxton deal with the Reds last summer, he has a tough fastball-slider combination.

BREAKOUT PROSPECT: Cameron Gallagher, c. Minor injuries slowed down Gallagher in 2012. If he stays healthy, he should show he'a solid defensive catcher with power.

SLEEPER: Justin Marks, lhp. Part of the David DeJesus trade with the Athletics in 2010, he has four average pitches and threw well in the Arizona Fall League.

SOURCE OF TOP 30 TALENT

Homegrown	29	Acquired	1
College	7	Trades	1
Junior college	1	Rule 5 draft	0
High school	10	Independent leagues	0
Nondrafted free agents	0	Free agents/waivers	0
International	11		

LF
Fred Ford (23)
David Lough (24)
Whit Merrifield

CF
Bubba Starling (2)
Brett Eibner (29)
Lane Adams
Terrance Gore
Alfredo Escalera-Maldonado
Ethan Chapman

RF
Jorge Bonifacio (4)
Elier Hernandez (16)
Alexis Rivera

3B
Cheslor Cuthbert (9)
Mauricio Ramos
Mike Antonio
Anthony Seratelli
Nick Cuckovich

SS
Adalberto Mondesi (5)
Orlando Calixte (7)
Jack Lopez (19)
Humberto Arteaga (20)
Ramon Torres (22)
Alex McClure

2B
Christian Colon (13)
Irving Falu
Danny Mateo
Kenny Diekroeger
Rey Navarro
Justin Trapp

1B
Brian Fletcher (30)
Mark Threlkeld
Matt Fields

C
Cameron Gallagher (15)
Manny Pina
Chad Johnson
Julio Rodriguez
Jose Bonilla
Beau Maggi

LHP

LHSP	LHRP
Sam Selman (6)	Donnie Joseph (14)
John Lamb (11)	Francisley Bueno
Chris Dwyer (21)	Buddy Baumann
Colin Rodgers (25)	Jon Keck
Justin Marks	Blaine Hardy
Daniel Stumpf	
Ryan Verdugo	
Matt Strahm	
Austin Fairchild	
Noel Arguelles	
Crawford Simmons	
Hunter Haynes	
Dylan Sons	
Matt Tenuta	

RHP

RHSP	RHRP
Kyle Zimmer (1)	Robinson Yambati (28)
Yordano Ventura (3)	Patrick Keating
Jason Adam (8)	Tyler Sample
Miguel Almonte (10)	Matt Ridings
Kyle Smith (12)	Edwin Carl
Bryan Brickhouse (17)	Andrew Triggs
Angel Baez (18)	Michael Mariot
Christian Binford (26)	Zeb Sneed
Jake Junis (27)	Andrew Triggs
Tim Melville	John Walter
J.C. Sulbaran	
Brooks Pounders	
Sugar Ray Marimon	
Zach Lovvorn	
Greg Billo	
Aroni Nina	

2012
BONUSES: $7.6 MILLION

BEST PURE HITTER: The Royals drafted OF Alexis Rivera (10) primarily for his power, then were floored when he hit over .400 for much of his debut before slumping in August. He has a short swing, uses the whole field and controls the strike zone well.

BEST POWER HITTER: OF Fred Ford (7) hit four home runs for Jefferson (Mo.) CC at the Junior College World Series, then 13 more at Rookie-level Burlington. He has well above-average raw power, though he also has holes in his swing.

FASTEST RUNNER: OF Marsalis Holloway (34) is the Royals' annual raw draftee with well above-average speed. OF Ethan Chapman (30) is a plus runner who knows how to use his speed better than Holloway.

BEST DEFENSIVE PLAYER: C Chad Johnson (5) has steady receiving tools and savvy to go with an average arm. He has added strength since signing, and his overall package resembles that of Brian Schneider.

BEST FASTBALL: RHP Kyle Zimmer (1) was the top pitcher on Kansas City's draft board thanks to a four-seam fastball that ranges from 92-99 mph. He threw 22 straight fastballs for strikes in his second start of the spring for San Francisco. He had surgery after the season to remove bone chips from his elbow, but the Royals don't think it's a long-term concern. LHP Sam Selman (2) topped out at 98 this summer and sat at 90-95.

BEST SECONDARY PITCH: Zimmer throws a hammer curveball with power and downer action. LHP Colin Rodgers (3) has the makings of a plus curveball and changeup.

BEST PRO DEBUT: Selman was the Rookie-level Pioneer League pitcher of the year, going 5-4, 2.09 with 89 strikeouts in 60 innings. Idaho Falls teammate Chapman was a leadoff force, batting .313/.383/.420 with 25 steals. Rivera finished at .341/.417/.477 in the Rookie-level Arizona League season.

BEST ATHLETE: In a pitching-focused draft, Zimmer stands out. He played basketball and water polo as well as baseball in high school. OF Alfredo Escalera-Maldonado (8) is the best athlete among Kansas City's position players.

MOST INTRIGUING BACKGROUND: Escalera-Maldonado was the youngest player in the entire 2012 draft class, having turned 17 in February. Unsigned OF Raphael Andrades (36) is a freshman wide receiver at Florida. C Beau Maggi's (24) brother Drew is a Pirates farmhand.

CLOSEST TO THE MAJORS: Despite his surgery, Zimmer still should move quickly. RHP Andrew Triggs (19) could do the same as a reliever

BEST LATE-ROUND PICK: RHP John Walter (29) quickly adapted to a relief role as Burlington's closer. Chapman's polish and speed fit the fourth-outfielder profile.

THE ONE WHO GOT AWAY: The Royals thought they could sign 2B Jackson Willeford (12), but he'll help defending national champion Arizona reload.

ASSESSMENT: The Royals' plan to focus on pitching paid off when Zimmer, Selman and Rodgers were all available. Considering Kansas City's crying need for arms, Zimmer becomes the system's most important prospect.

2011
BONUSES: $14.1 MILLION

The Royals have high hopes for their first five picks, even if OF Bubba Starling (1) will need time for his skills to catch up to his athleticism. They're also pleased with C Cameron Gallagher (2), RHPs Bryan Brickhouse (3) and Kyle Smith (4), and 3B Patrick Leonard (5).

GRADE: B

2010
BONUSES: $6.7 MILLION

Passing on pitchers like Chris Sale and Matt Harvey to take SS/2B Christian Colon (1) fourth overall was a mistake, even if Colon could be in the majors this year. RHP Jason Adam (5) may be the best player from this crop, which lacks an impact player—a situation not helped by OF Brett Eibner's (2) struggles with the bat.

GRADE: C+

2009
BONUSES: $6.7 MILLION

OF/3B Wil Myers (3) has legitimized his $2 million bonus, and Baseball America's 2012 Minor League Player of the Year is ready to step into the middle of Kansas City's order. The club also found a pair of nice bullpen pieces in RHPs Aaron Crow (1) and Louis Coleman (5).

GRADE: A

2008
BONUSES: $11.1 MILLION

This group still has promise but took a step backward last year. 1B Eric Hosmer (1) and 2B Johnny Giavotella (2) slumped terribly in the majors, LHP Mike Montgomery (1s) couldn't get anyone out and LHP John Lamb's (5) recovery from Tommy John surgery has taken longer than expected.

GRADE: B

Draft analysis by John Manuel (2012) and Jim Callis (2008-11). Numbers in parentheses indicate draft rounds.

1 KYLE ZIMMER, RHP

Born: Sept. 13, 1991. **B-T:** R-R. **Ht.:** 6-3. **Wt.:** 215.
Drafted: San Francisco, 2012 (1st round). **Signed by:**
Max Valencia.

BA GRADE
70
LOW

MIKE JANES

A high school basketball, water polo and baseball player who originally went to San Francisco as a third baseman, Zimmer pitched only sparingly in high school and just five innings as a freshman. As a sophomore in 2011, he beat UCLA and No. 1 overall pick Gerrit Cole with a shutout in the NCAA regional playoffs, then had a strong summer in the Cape Cod League. Zimmer further established himself as one of the top prospects for the 2012 draft with his first outing as a junior, during which he hit 99 mph and started with 22 consecutive strikes. He overwhelmed scouts with his stuff and his athleticism, which runs in the family. His father Eric pitched at UC San Diego, his mother Cathy ran the hurdles at San Diego State and his younger brother Bradley is a Dons outfielder and a prospect for the 2014 draft. The pressure of the spotlight didn't affect Zimmer, as he posted a 3.90 grade-point average while working toward a degree in business administration. Hamstring woes caused his velocity to fluctuate as the draft approached and a predraft physical detected bone chips in his elbow, but that couldn't stop him from becoming the highest draft pick in San Francisco history. Signed for $3 million, he made nine pro starts before having surgery to remove the bone chips. Post-surgical exams showed a healthy elbow ligament, and Zimmer is expected to be at full speed by spring training.

Zimmer is a power pitcher with a nasty mound demeanor to match. He consistently sits at 93-95 mph with his four-seam fastball, reaching the upper 90s on his best nights. His heater also has late life and excellent armside run, generating swings and misses. Hitters have trouble making contact with his hammer curveball as well, and it grades as a 70 pitch on the 20-80 scouting scale at times. He actually has more confidence in his slider, though it's more of an average offering. Zimmer junked a splitter he threw as a freshman and has developed an erratic but promising changeup with late tumble. It needs work because he didn't need to use it much in college, but it shows

SCOUTING GRADES

Fastball: 70.   **Control:** 65.
Curveball: 65.   **Command:** 55.
Changeup: 55.

Based on 20-80 scouting scale, where 50 represents major league average, and future projection rather than present tools.

flashes of becoming a plus pitch. His natural athleticism and strong lower body bode well for his ability to maintain his delivery and his stuff late into games. Because of his athleticism, his command and his feel for his delivery are much more advanced than would be expected for a pitcher with just two years of experience. He pounds the strike zone with all four of his pitches. The former infielder also fields his position with aplomb. Zimmer fits perfectly with the Royals' organizational philosophies on pitching. They favor four-seam fastballs and curveballs, and he doesn't even throw a two-seamer.

Kansas City desperately wanted a frontline starter with top-five picks in 2010 and 2011, and it finally got one in Zimmer. He's likely to start his first full pro season at high Class A Wilmington and should pitch his way to Double-A Northwest Arkansas at some point during 2013. The Royals' offseason makeover of their rotation eases some of the pressure to hurry Zimmer to the big leagues, but his potential as a true No. 1 could force the issue before too long. He could arrive at Kauffman Stadium in 2014.

Year	Club (League)	Class	W	L	ERA	G	GS	CG	SV	IP	H	HR	BB	SO	K/9	WHIP	AVG
2012	Royals (AZL)	R	1	0	0.90	3	3	1	0	10	5	0	0	13	11.7	0.50	.152
	Kane County (MWL)	LoA	2	3	2.43	6	6	0	0	30	34	1	8	29	8.8	1.42	.301
Minor League Totals			3	3	2.04	9	9	1	0	40	39	1	8	42	9.5	1.18	.267

2 BUBBA STARLING, OF

Born: Aug. 3, 1992. **B-T:** R-R. **Ht.:** 6-4. **Wt.:** 205. **Drafted:** HS—Gardner, Kan., 2011 (1st round). **Signed by:** Blake Davis.

A three-sport star in high school, Starling turned down a scholarship to play quarterback at Nebraska when the Royals selected him fifth overall and paid him $7.5 million in 2011. He remained in extended spring training at the start of 2012 to retool his set-up and swing, then headed to Rookie-level Burlington. Of the 13 high school first-rounders from 2011, he was one of three who didn't play full-season ball during the year. Starling has well above-average raw power and his speed, center-field defense and arm strength all project as at least plus tools. His ultimate impact will be determined by his bat, however. He's still raw at the plate and swings and misses a lot—he struck out in 35 percent of his at-bats, fifth-worst in the system. He too often drops his bat head during his load, which leads to a long, flat swing. Kansas City is working on having him pull his bat back with his top hand instead of pushing it back with his bottom hand to help him control the bat head better. He also has to improve in recognizing breaking balls. Defensively, he's more advanced than expected and projects as a plus center fielder. Starling's power and speed will allow the Royals to live with some strikeouts, but he still has a long way to go at the plate. He'll advance to Kansas City's new low Class A Lexington affiliate in 2013.

BA GRADE
70
EXTREME

Year	Club (League)	Class	AVG	G	AB	R	H	2B	3B	HR	RBI	BB	SO	SB	CS	OBP	SLG
2012	Burlington (APP)	R	.275	53	200	35	55	8	2	10	33	28	70	10	1	.371	.485
Minor League Totals			.275	53	200	35	55	8	2	10	33	28	70	10	1	.371	.485

3 YORDANO VENTURA, RHP

Born: June 3, 1991. **B-T:** R-R. **Ht.:** 5-11. **Wt.:** 167. **Signed:** Dominican Republic, 2008. **Signed by:** Pedro Silverio.

Signed for $28,000 as a 17-year-old with a mid-80s fastball, Ventura quickly blossomed into one of the hardest throwers in the organization. Slated to return to low Class A in 2012, he earned a spot at high Class A during spring training, then merited a Double-A promotion and Futures Game appearance at midseason. Nicknamed "Lil' Pedro" because of his combination of size and velocity, Ventura has a fastball that sits at 94-97 mph and reaches 102. He can throw his curveball for strikes by taking a little off it, or use it as a chase pitch by breaking it off harder. It's a true downer curve that should end up as a plus pitch if he continues to refine it. His changeup has more deception than movement, and he needs to show more trust in it. Ventura still is working to improve his command and control. Some scouts worry that his fastball will lack effectiveness at higher levels because his size doesn't give him much angle or downward plane. Despite Ventura's small stature, Kansas City hopes he can fill one of the holes in their big league rotation, perhaps as soon as mid-2013. His stuff makes him a safe bet to at least be a power reliever.

BA GRADE
60
HIGH

Year	Club (League)	Class	W	L	ERA	G	GS	CG	SV	IP	H	HR	BB	SO	K/9	WHIP	AVG
2009	Royals (DSL)	R	0	1	2.78	10	5	0	3	23	28	0	5	11	4.4	1.46	.304
2010	Royals (DSL)	R	0	1	2.31	3	3	0	0	12	9	0	1	13	10.0	0.86	.209
	Royals (AZL)	R	4	2	3.25	14	6	0	0	53	49	3	17	58	9.9	1.25	.236
2011	Kane County (MWL)	LoA	4	6	4.27	19	19	0	0	84	82	8	24	88	9.4	1.26	.258
2012	Wilmington (CAR)	HiA	3	5	3.30	16	16	0	0	76	66	7	28	98	11.6	1.23	.229
	Royals (AZL)	R	0	0	2.45	1	1	0	0	4	3	0	1	7	17.2	1.09	.214
	NW Arkansas (TL)	AA	1	2	4.60	6	6	0	0	29	23	1	13	25	7.7	1.23	.221
Minor League Totals			12	17	3.62	69	56	0	3	281	260	19	89	300	9.6	1.24	.244

4 JORGE BONIFACIO, OF

Born: June 4, 1993. **B-T:** R-R. **Ht.:** 6-1. **Wt.:** 216. **Signed:** Dominican Republic, 2009. **Signed by:** Edis Perez.

The brother of big leaguer Emilio Bonifacio, Jorge couldn't be more different from his older sibling. Where Emilio is a light-hitting infielder who stands out for his speed, Jorge is a barrel-chested, power-hitting right fielder. In his first taste of full season ball, he hit .314/.369/.469 in the first half of 2012 as a teenager in low Class A, before slumping and missing much of August with an injured right wrist. Now that Wil Myers is gone, Bonifacio is the best pure hitter in the system. He produces line drive after line drive with quick wrists and plenty of strength in his hands. His swing can get long at times and it isn't picture perfect, but he hasn't had problems catching up to good velocity and he consistently barrels the ball. Unlike many young hitters, Bonifacio already knows that the opposite-field gap is his friend. He also has the strength to produce plus power as he matures, but he'll have to learn to pull inside pitches more frequently. He's an adequate right fielder with plenty of arm for the position, though he figures to slow from his current average speed as he matures and his stocky frame continues to fill out. If he continues to develop, Bonifacio has the tools to become an impact right fielder. He'll head to a more difficult hitting environment in Wilmington in 2013.

BA GRADE
55
HIGH

Year	Club (League)	Class	AVG	G	AB	R	H	2B	3B	HR	RBI	BB	SO	SB	CS	OBP	SLG
2010	Royals (DSL)	R	.335	48	164	22	55	16	2	1	28	26	27	13	5	.429	.476
	Royals (AZL)	R	.211	21	76	9	16	0	5	0	6	6	31	1	2	.271	.342
2011	Burlington (APP)	R	.284	62	236	26	67	20	4	7	30	16	58	5	6	.333	.492
2012	Kane County (MWL)	LoA	.282	105	412	54	116	20	6	10	61	30	84	6	3	.336	.432
Minor League Totals			.286	236	888	111	254	56	17	18	125	78	200	25	16	.348	.448

5 ADALBERTO MONDESI, SS

Born: July 27, 1995. **B-T:** B-R. **Ht.:** 6-1. **Wt.:** 162. **Drafted:** Signed: Dominican Republic, 2011. **Signed by:** Edis Perez/Alvin Cuevas.

The son of 1994 National League rookie of the year Raul Mondesi and the brother of Rays' minor leaguer Raul Mondesi Jr., Adalberto signed with the Royals for a $2 million bonus. Some international scouts didn't think his bat was worth such a hefty price tag, but he has been working to convert the critics. He was the youngest player in the Rookie-level Pioneer League in 2012 and didn't turn 17 until midseason, yet he more than held his own against players three to five years his senior. A switch-hitter, Mondesi has an advanced approach and present gap power. Some scouts project him to have average home run power as he gets older and matures physically. He already has started to fill out and has gotten quicker since signing, becoming an above-average runner. He'll need to improve his plate discipline, but time is on his side. At shortstop, he has excellent instincts, hands so quick that his transfers seem like a blur, and a strong arm. He made 23 errors in 47 games in 2012, the result of his youth and ability to get to balls that other shortstops can't reach. Mondesi should be the youngest player in full-season ball in 2013, when he'll play in Lexington. If he advances one level a year, he could still get to Kansas City at the age of 21.

BA GRADE
60
EXTREME

Year	Club (League)	Class	AVG	G	AB	R	H	2B	3B	HR	RBI	BB	SO	SB	CS	OBP	SLG
2012	Idaho Falls (PIO)	R	.290	50	207	35	60	7	2	3	30	19	65	11	2	.346	.386
Minor League Totals			.290	50	207	35	60	7	2	3	30	19	65	11	2	.346	.386

6 SAM SELMAN, LHP

Born: Nov. 14, 1990. **B-T:** R-L. **Ht.:** 6-3. **Wt.:** 195. **Drafted:** Vanderbilt, 2012 (2nd round). **Signed by:** Sean Gibbs.

Selman totaled just 12 innings as a freshman and sophomore at Vanderbilt because of control problems, and he was demoted to a midweek starter as a junior when they persisted. He recovered, returned to the weekend rotation in May and pitched his way into the second round of the 2012 draft. The Royals signed him for $750,000 and then watched him lead the Pioneer League with 89 strikeouts despite falling one inning short of qualifying for the ERA title. Even as a 160-pound high school senior, Selman could touch 94 mph. Now that he's a much more robust 195-pounder, he sits at 90-95 mph and peaks at 98. He also snaps off a nasty slider at times, giving him the potential for two plus pitches. His changeup is fringy at best. He showed improvement with his control as a pro, but it's still a concern. He has a wrap in his arm action that inhibits his ability to repeat his release point and secondary pitches. Once projected as a power lefty out of the

BA GRADE
50
HIGH

bullpen, Selman now has a realistic chance at becoming a mid-rotation starter. He'll open his first full season at one of Kansas City's Class A affiliates, with his ability to find the strike zone dictating how quickly he advances.

Year	Club (League)	Class	W	L	ERA	G	GS	CG	SV	IP	H	HR	BB	SO	K/9	WHIP	AVG
2012	Idaho Falls (PIO)	R	5	4	2.09	13	12	0	0	60	45	1	22	89	13.3	1.11	.204
Minor League Totals			5	4	2.09	13	12	0	0	60	45	1	22	89	13.3	1.11	.204

7 ORLANDO CALIXTE, SS

BA GRADE
50
HIGH

Born: Feb. 3, 1992. **B-T:** R-R. **Ht.:** 6-0. **Wt.:** 174. **Signed:** Dominican Republic, 2010. **Signed by:** Alvin Cuevas/Hector Pineda.

Known as Paul Carlixte before teams discovered that he and his brother had swapped identities, Calixte signed with the Royals in 2010 after they had scouted him for more than three years. The questions about his identity didn't cost him much, as he still signed for $1 million. After he struggled in an aggressive assignment to low Class A in 2011, he showed better feel at the plate and thrived after a midseason promotion to high Class A in 2012. Calixte has more power and hitting ability than the average shortstop prospect. Wilmington's tough hitting environment kept his home run numbers down after his promotion, but Calixte has average power to go with a solid bat. He has yet to show the patience to draw walks, as he's aggressive early and late in the count. With good range, excellent hands and a strong arm, he is a solid to plus defender at shortstop. He played some third base in the Arizona Fall League, but shortstop is his long-term home. Calixte's impressive second half in Wilmington gives him a chance to play in Double-A at age 21. Kansas City has several legitimate shortstop prospects, and he's the closest to the big leagues.

Year	Club (League)	Class	AVG	G	AB	R	H	2B	3B	HR	RBI	BB	SO	SB	CS	OBP	SLG
2010	Royals (DSL)	R	.227	20	66	10	15	6	0	0	12	13	13	3	1	.350	.318
2011	Kane County (MWL)	LoA	.208	81	289	19	60	5	1	3	31	20	70	11	4	.256	.263
2012	Kane County (MWL)	LoA	.241	62	228	31	55	13	4	10	34	21	44	2	5	.303	.465
	Wilmington (CAR)	HiA	.281	63	256	38	72	17	4	4	28	15	65	8	3	.326	.426
Minor League Totals			.241	226	839	98	202	41	9	17	105	69	192	24	13	.298	.372

8 JASON ADAM, RHP

BA GRADE
50
HIGH

Born: Aug. 4, 1991. **B-T:** R-R. **Ht.:** 6-4. **Wt.:** 225. **Drafted:** HS—Overland Park., Kan., 2010 (5th round). **Signed by:** Steve Gossett.

A native of suburban Kansas City who had played at Kauffman Stadium while in high school, Adam lasted five rounds in the 2010 draft because of his up-and-down senior season and commitment to Missouri. Signed for a well above-slot $800,000, he opened eyes by touching 98 mph in instructional league shortly after signing. He hasn't shown the same velocity during his two pro seasons. Adam usually works at 90-92 mph and occasionally hits 94 with his fastball. While he has had some success, the Royals aren't ready to give up on finding that lost velocity. They believe he needs to return to the bigger hip turn and higher leg kick he showed in high school, instead of the more tall-and-fall delivery he has used as a pro. He had trouble repeating his high school mechanics, so returning to them could detract from his command, which has been better than expected. Adam's below-average curveball needs more bite, though he controls it well. His changeup is also below-average because he struggles to maintain his usual arm speed. Adam will make the jump to Double-A at age 21. How he performs in 2013 will shed light on whether he can be a No. 2 or 3 starter, or more of a back-of-rotation option.

Year	Club (League)	Class	W	L	ERA	G	GS	CG	SV	IP	H	HR	BB	SO	K/9	WHIP	AVG
2011	Kane County (MWL)	LoA	6	9	4.23	21	21	0	0	104	94	9	25	76	6.6	1.14	.235
2012	Wilmington (CAR)	HiA	7	12	3.53	27	27	0	0	158	148	18	36	123	7.0	1.16	.251
Minor League Totals			13	21	3.81	48	48	0	0	262	242	27	61	199	6.8	1.16	.245

9 CHESLOR CUTHBERT, 3B

Born: Nov. **16, 1992. B-T:** R-R. **Ht.:** 6-0. **Wt.:** 193. **Signed:** Nicaragua, 2009. **Signed by:** Orlando Esteves/Juan Lopez.

The pride of Big Corn Island, a four-square-mile island 40 miles off the coast of Nicaragua, Cuthbert has played in front of minor league crowds larger than the 6,000 people who inhabit his homeland. After a great start in 2011, his production has fallen through the floor. He posted an OPS of .800 or better in his first three months as an 18-year-old in low Class A, but he hasn't topped .710 since. Once a patient hitter, Cuthbert now chases too many pitches out of the zone. His plus power potential stopped showing up in games, as he couldn't get into counts to consistently get pitches to drive. While he has good hand-eye coordination, his bat control needs improvement as he sometimes overswings. At third base, Cuthbert continues to make all the routine plays and occasionally a Web Gem despite below-average speed and quickness. His arm is above-average and the strongest among the system's infielders. Cuthbert does not appear to have any significant mechanical problem with his swing, so the Royals are optimistic that his recent struggles are more a case of being young for his levels. They haven't ruled out promoting him to Double-A to start 2013.

BA GRADE

50

HIGH

Year	Club (League)	Class	AVG	G	AB	R	H	2B	3B	HR	RBI	BB	SO	SB	CS	OBP	SLG
2010	Royals (AZL)	R	.265	18	68	14	18	3	2	1	5	6	19	1	1	.342	.412
	Idaho Falls (PIO)	R	.233	14	60	10	14	4	1	2	10	3	16	1	0	.281	.433
2011	Kane County (MWL)	LoA	.267	81	300	33	80	13	1	8	51	36	65	2	0	.345	.397
2012	Wilmington (CAR)	HiA	.240	124	475	47	114	18	0	7	59	37	80	6	3	.296	.322
Minor League Totals			.250	237	903	104	226	38	4	18	125	82	180	10	4	.315	.361

10 MIGUEL ALMONTE, RHP

Born: April 4, 1993. **B-T:** R-R. **Ht.:** 6-2. **Wt.:** 160. **Signed:** Dominican Republic, 2010. **Signed by:** Fausto Morel/Alvin Cuevas.

Several prospects will rise two levels in a year, but few covered the amount of distance that Almonte did to pull off his jump in 2012. Signed for $25,000 in 2010, he started last season in the Rookie-level Dominican Summer League, earned a promotion to the Rookie-level Arizona League, then flew cross-country to Burlington, N.C., for the Appalachian League playoffs. He's still flying under the radar because he has moved so quickly. He's just 19 and has thrown only 27 regular season innings in the United States. Almonte has a good three-pitch mix with a heavy 91-93 mph fastball that touches 96, an average changeup and an inconsistent curveball. He does show feel for spinning the ball, so he could have three solid offerings in time. Almonte repeats his delivery well and has shown the ability to diagnose his own mechanical flaws and fix them when they crop up, giving him advanced command for his age. Despite Almonte's inexperience, the Royals think the potential No. 3 starter is ready to handle the jump to low Class A.

BA GRADE

50

HIGH

Year	Club (League)	Class	W	L	ERA	G	GS	CG	SV	IP	H	HR	BB	SO	K/9	WHIP	AVG
2011	Royals (DSL)	R	0	0	5.40	5	1	0	0	12	11	0	7	9	6.9	1.54	.256
2012	Royals (DSL)	R	6	1	1.44	10	10	0	0	50	34	2	8	46	8.3	0.84	.194
	Royals (AZL)	R	2	1	2.33	6	2	0	0	27	22	0	5	28	9.3	1.00	.212
Minor League Totals			8	2	2.23	21	13	0	0	89	67	2	20	83	8.4	0.98	.208

11 JOHN LAMB, LHP

BA GRADE

55

EXTREME

Born: July 10, 1990. **B-T:** L-L. **Ht.:** 6-3. **Wt.:** 195. **Drafted:** HS—Laguna Hills, Calif., 2008 (5th round). **Signed by:** Gary Johnson/John Ramey.

Before he blew out his elbow in 2011, Lamb was the Royals' best pitching prospect and a half-season or so away from a big league callup. He strained a lat muscle during spring training that year, and his torn ligament was discovered after he struggled to regain his velocity. He was slated to return to the mound last June, but that was delayed by a bout of tendinitis in his left foot resulting from his running work at the Royals' Arizona training complex. He threw 13 innings over six abbreviated starts before being shut down for the four months of offseason rest that is part of Kansas City's rehab protocol for Tommy John surgery. Lamb has shown signs that he was getting back to full strength, but in those starts a fastball that sat at 90-95 mph before his injury operated at just 85-91. The Royals expect he'll pick up velocity once he gets fully stretched out in 2013. He still possesses the organization's best changeup, and before he got hurt he also had an average curveball to go with excellent command. He was still shaking the rust off his curve when his season ended. Added to the 40-man roster in November, Lamb will return to Double-A to start 2013 and try to get back on the path of becoming a No. 2 starter. If he shows he's fully recovered, he could make his major league debut before the season ends.

Year	Club (League)	Class	W	L	ERA	G	GS	CG	SV	IP	H	HR	BB	SO	K/9	WHIP	AVG
2009	Burlington (APP)	R	2	2	3.95	6	6	0	0	27	24	4	9	25	8.2	1.21	.238
	Idaho Falls (PIO)	R	3	1	3.70	8	8	0	0	41	33	4	11	46	10.0	1.06	.217
2010	Burlington (MWL)	LoA	2	3	1.58	8	8	0	0	40	26	2	17	43	9.7	1.08	.188
	Wilmington (CAR)	HiA	6	3	1.45	13	13	0	0	75	59	1	15	90	10.8	0.99	.219
	NW Arkansas (TL)	AA	2	1	5.45	7	7	0	0	33	37	2	13	26	7.1	1.52	.280
2011	NW Arkansas (TL)	AA	1	2	3.09	8	8	0	0	35	33	3	13	22	5.7	1.31	.246
2012	Royals (AZL)	R	0	0	6.35	4	4	0	0	6	6	0	2	6	9.5	1.41	.250
	Idaho Falls (PIO)	R	0	1	7.36	2	2	0	0	7	9	2	2	8	9.8	1.50	.300
Minor League Totals			16	13	3.06	56	56	0	0	264	227	18	82	266	9.1	1.17	.231

12 KYLE SMITH, RHP

BA GRADE
50
HIGH

Born: Sept. 10, 1992. **B-T:** R-R. **Ht.:** 5-11. **Wt.:** 175. **Drafted:** HS—Lantana, Fla., 2011 (4th round). **Signed by:** Alex Mesa.

The Royals nabbed a pair of high school righthanders with consecutive picks and over-slot bonuses in 2011, but Bryan Brickhouse (third round, $1.5 million) and Smith (fourth, $695,000) couldn't be more different. Where Brickhouse is a big, raw hard thrower, Smith is 5-foot-11, as polished as they come and generally works at 88-91 mph with his fastball. What he lacks in stature and velocity, Smith makes up for with advanced feel for pitching, solid secondary stuff and an athletic, compact delivery that he repeats well. He can handcuff hitters with his plus curveball and average changeup, but he still pitches off his fastball. He changes hitters' eye levels by working up and down, and he is comfortable locating to both sides of the plate. Smith touches 93-94 mph pretty regularly, and some scouts think he could gain a tick more velocity as he matures. Even if his stuff doesn't get firmer, his savvy should help him move quickly. He needed just one start to earn a promotion from Rookie-level Idaho Falls last June, and he's ready for high Class A as a 20-year-old with just 14 pro starts of experience. He has a ceiling of a No. 3 starter.

Year	Club (League)	Class	W	L	ERA	G	GS	CG	SV	IP	H	HR	BB	SO	K/9	WHIP	AVG
2012	Idaho Falls (PIO)	R	1	0	1.80	1	1	0	0	5	3	0	1	11	19.8	0.80	.167
	Kane County (MWL)	LoA	4	3	2.94	13	13	0	0	67	62	3	20	87	11.6	1.22	.241
Minor League Totals			5	3	2.86	14	14	0	0	72	65	3	21	98	12.2	1.19	.236

13 CHRISTIAN COLON, SS/2B

BA GRADE
45
MEDIUM

Born: May 14, 1989. **B-T:** R-R. **Ht.:** 6-1. **Wt.:** 180. **Drafted:** Cal State Fullerton, 2010 (1st round). **Signed by:** Scott Groot.

If Colon had been drafted 20th overall in 2010 he would likely be seen as a safe produc-tive pick. But because he went fourth overall, ahead of pitchers the Royals desperately need such as Chris Sale and Matt Harvey, Colon's steady climb toward the majors has seemed less impressive. Signed for $2.75 million, he was slowed in 2012 by a pair of freak injuries. He missed the Double-A Texas League all-star game and lost six weeks after hurting his foot when he stepped on a bat, then saw his season end three weeks early in mid-August when he fouled off a ball that hit him in the face. The latter injury didn't affect his vision. Colon's eventual move to second base became more obvious once the Royals signed shortstop Alcides Escobar to a long-term deal last March. Colon's tools fit better at second, as his average range is less of an issue there than it is at shortstop. He's average across the board in terms of his bat, speed and arm, with his power projecting as slightly below-average. He controls the strike zone well, and his exceptional instincts help him maximize his physical ability. Scouts from outside the organization expect Colon will end up as a solid utility infielder, but Kansas City still views him as an everyday second baseman and hopes he'll push for the job in late 2013 after more time in Triple-A Omaha.

Year	Club (League)	Class	AVG	G	AB	R	H	2B	3B	HR	RBI	BB	SO	SB	CS	OBP	SLG
2010	Wilmington (CAR)	HiA	.278	60	245	38	68	12	2	3	30	13	33	2	4	.326	.380
2011	NW Arkansas (TL)	AA	.257	127	491	69	126	14	2	8	61	46	51	17	7	.325	.342
2012	NW Arkansas (TL)	AA	.289	73	273	33	79	9	2	5	27	31	27	12	6	.364	.392
	Royals (AZL)	R	.364	7	22	6	8	3	0	0	4	4	0	1	1	.481	.500
	Omaha (PCL)	AAA	.412	5	17	4	7	1	0	1	5	2	1	0	0	.429	.647
Minor League Totals			.275	272	1048	150	288	39	6	17	127	96	112	32	18	.341	.372

14 DONNIE JOSEPH, LHP

BA GRADE
45
MEDIUM

Born: Nov. 1, 1987. **B-T:** L-L. **Ht.:** 6-3. **Wt.:** 190. **Drafted:** Houston, 2009 (3rd round). **Signed by:** Jerry Flowers (Reds).

After bombing with a 6.94 ERA in Double-A in 2011, Joseph just as quickly reversed course last season. Acquired along with righthander J.C. Sulbaran from the Reds in July for Jonathan Broxton, Joseph immediately became the Royals' best lefthanded relief prospect. He filled a void created when Kansas City traded Kevin Chapman to the Astros in March. His stuff rates a tick better than Chapman's, as he pairs a 92-95 mph fastball with a slider that's devastating at times. Joseph's success depends on his delivery. When he overthrows, he opens up too soon, taking away the bite from his slider. But when he stays under control, he's nearly unhittable for lefthanders and is capable of getting righties out as well. Command isn't his strong suit, but he generally throws enough strikes to succeed. Joseph likely will return to Triple-A after joining the Royals' 40-man roster in November. When they need another lefty in their bullpen, his will be the first number they call.

Year	Club (League)	Class	W	L	ERA	G	GS	CG	SV	IP	H	HR	BB	SO	K/9	WHIP	AVG
2009	Billings (PIO)	R	2	1	0.77	8	0	0	0	12	6	0	4	11	8.5	0.86	.146
	Dayton (MWL)	LoA	2	2	4.35	16	0	0	4	21	13	0	10	31	13.5	1.11	.176
2010	Dayton (MWL)	LoA	2	1	0.78	19	0	0	6	23	13	0	7	40	15.7	0.87	.160
	Lynchburg (CAR)	HiA	0	4	2.31	31	0	0	17	35	23	2	16	56	14.4	1.11	.181
	Carolina (SL)	AA	1	0	5.14	7	0	0	1	7	7	0	2	7	9.0	1.29	.250
2011	Carolina (SL)	AA	1	3	6.94	57	0	0	8	58	67	8	30	66	10.2	1.66	.286
2012	Pensacola (SL)	AA	4	2	0.89	26	0	0	13	30	13	1	8	46	13.6	0.69	.129
	Louisville (IL)	AAA	4	1	2.86	18	0	0	5	22	22	0	9	22	9.0	1.41	.259
	Omaha (PCL)	AAA	1	0	4.15	11	0	0	2	17	21	1	13	19	9.9	1.96	.296
Minor League Totals			17	14	3.55	193	0	0	56	225	185	12	99	298	11.9	1.26	.220

15 CAMERON GALLAGHER, C

BA GRADE 50 HIGH

Born: Dec. 6, 1992. **B-T:** R-R. **Ht.:** 6-3. **Wt.:** 216. **Drafted:** HS—Lancaster, Pa., 2011 (2nd round). **Signed by:** Jim Farr.

Gallagher's big frame led some scouts to wonder whether he would be able to stick behind the plate as a pro, but the Royals liked his work as a backstop enough to sign him away from East Carolina for an over-slot $750,000 in the second round of the 2011 draft. He went one round earlier than his father Glenn (who reached Double-A) and brother Austin (currently in the Dodgers system). Gallagher missed time last summer with minor hand and shoulder injuries, but otherwise had a solid year at Burlington. He has proven to be a more polished receiver than expected and already shows aptitude for calling a game. He has a strong arm and threw out 26 percent of basestealers in 2012. Though Gallagher has shortened his somewhat lengthy swing, his calling card continues to be above-average power for a catcher. As might be expected, he shows a good understanding of how pitchers are trying to get him out, helping him make consistent contact. He's a well below-average runner. In a system thin on catching prospects, Gallagher stands out as the only one whom scouts project as a big league regular. He'll advance to low Class A this year.

Year	Club (League)	Class	AVG	G	AB	R	H	2B	3B	HR	RBI	BB	SO	SB	CS	OBP	SLG
2011	Royals (AZL)	R	.141	20	78	6	11	0	0	1	7	7	15	0	0	.209	.179
	Idaho Falls (PIO)	R	.200	8	30	2	6	0	0	1	2	3	4	0	0	.273	.300
2012	Burlington (APP)	R	.276	36	127	13	35	10	0	3	15	10	16	1	3	.331	.425
Minor League Totals			.221	64	235	21	52	10	0	5	24	20	35	1	3	.283	.328

16 ELIER HERNANDEZ, OF

BA GRADE 55 EXTREME

Born: Nov. 21, 1994. **B-T:** R-R. **Ht.:** 6-3. **Wt.:** 200. **Signed:** Dominican Republic, 2011. **Signed by:** Rene Francisco.

Rated by many clubs as the top international amateur prospect for the 2011 signing period, Hernandez signed for $3.05 million, earning kudos for his impressive bat speed and solid feel for the game. The Royals thought he and fellow 2011 signee Adalberto Mondesi were advanced enough to make their professional debuts at Idaho Falls. Mondesi, the son of a longtime big leaguer, flourished in the challenging environment, but Hernandez struggled to keep his head above water. He struggled to recognize breaking balls and developed bad habits. Where he impressed scouts with his quick wrists as an amateur, he started trying to push balls to the opposite field too often instead of using his bat speed to turn on pitches he could drive. Hernandez is a solid athlete who profiles as a right fielder with the ability to hit for average and power, though his power potential requires a lot of projection for now. He's an average runner with a strong arm. Hernandez is young enough that a return to Rookie ball in 2013 still would get him to full-season ball as a 19-year-old.

Year	Club (League)	Class	AVG	G	AB	R	H	2B	3B	HR	RBI	BB	SO	SB	CS	OBP	SLG
2012	Idaho Falls (PIO)	R	.208	60	250	30	52	10	4	0	34	14	66	2	0	.256	.280
Minor League Totals			.208	60	250	30	52	10	4	0	34	14	66	2	0	.256	.280

17 BRYAN BRICKHOUSE, RHP

BA GRADE 55 EXTREME

Born: June 6, 1992. **B-T:** R-R. **Ht.:** 6-0. **Wt.:** 209. **Drafted:** HS—The Woodlands, Texas, 2011 (3rd round). **Signed by:** Brian Rhees.

The Royals knew the 2011 draft would be the last chance to spend money under less restrictive bonus rules, with a new labor agreement bringing spending restrictions in 2012, so they spent $14.1 million in bonuses. Brickhouse was one of the beneficiaries, getting $1.5 million in the third round to give up his commitment to North Carolina. He throws nearly as hard as former high school teammate Jameson Taillon, the No. 2 overall pick in the 2010 draft by the Pirates, though Taillon has better feel and secondary stuff. At his best, Brickhouse has a fastball that touches 95-96 mph with excellent late movement that leads more to weak contact than strikeouts. His breaking ball and changeup are inconsistent, but both show flashes of being plus offerings. His biggest problem is that his command often disappears for batters or innings at a time because he struggles to repeat his delivery. As with many young fireballers, his control will determine his fate. If Brickhouse solves his mechanics, he could be a No. 2 or 3 starter. If not, he'll likely end up as a power reliever. It's possible that he could repeat low Class A at the beginning of 2013 to help build his confidence.

Year	Club (League)	Class	W	L	ERA	G	GS	CG	SV	IP	H	HR	BB	SO	K/9	WHIP	AVG
2012	Idaho Falls (PIO)	R	0	0	37.80	1	1	0	0	2	5	1	3	1	5.4	4.80	.500
	Kane County (MWL)	LoA	3	3	5.61	10	10	0	0	51	50	3	23	40	7.0	1.42	.249
Minor League Totals			3	3	6.62	11	11	0	0	53	55	4	26	41	7.0	1.53	.261

18 ANGEL BAEZ, RHP

BA GRADE
50
HIGH

Born: Feb. 14, 1991. **B-T:** R-R. **Ht.:** 6-3. **Wt.:** 226. **Signed:** Dominican Republic, 2008. **Signed by:** Edis Perez.

When Baez won his Kane County debut on May 26, it ended quite a drought. He had gone 0-15, 4.90 in 43 previous pro appearances. Obviously a win-loss record doesn't tell much about a young pitcher, but his stuff is much better than his 6-20 career mark would indicate. Baez throws a heavy fastball that sits at 92-96 mph and peaks at 98. His changeup shows the potential to become an average pitch, though his curveball isn't as impressive. It's more of a slurve, and his low arm slot may work better for a slider in the long term. He did a better job of throwing strikes in 2012 but still has room for improvement, especially with his command. Scouts from other teams envision Baez becoming a late-inning reliever, but the Royals see no reason to close the door on starting yet. He'll pitch in their high Class A rotation this year.

Year	Club (League)	Class	W	L	ERA	G	GS	CG	SV	IP	H	HR	BB	SO	K/9	WHIP	AVG
2009	Royals (DSL)	R	0	6	3.88	14	11	0	0	49	54	0	19	45	8.3	1.50	.280
2010	Royals (DSL)	R	0	1	2.93	8	7	0	0	31	29	1	14	25	7.3	1.40	.257
	Royals (AZL)	R	0	2	5.40	7	4	0	0	15	9	1	10	14	8.4	1.27	.167
2011	Burlington (APP)	R	0	6	7.09	14	14	0	0	47	67	3	30	41	7.9	2.06	.321
2012	Kane County (MWL)	LoA	6	5	3.17	16	15	1	0	77	65	5	31	83	9.7	1.25	.220
Minor League Totals			6	20	4.29	59	51	1	0	218	224	10	104	208	8.6	1.50	.259

19 JACK LOPEZ, SS

BA GRADE
50
HIGH

Born: Dec. 16, 1992. **B-T:** R-R. **Ht.:** 5-8. **Wt.:** 170. **Drafted:** HS—Deltona, Fla., 2011 (16th round). **Signed by:** Colin Gonzales.

Many scouts who saw Lopez in high school liked his glove and feel for the game, but they also saw him as a player who would do well to fulfill his commitment to Miami so he could develop physically before entering pro ball. The Royals decided they were willing to let him mature on their dime, as they signed the 16th-rounder for $750,000 in 2011. The son of Reds bullpen coach Juan Lopez often looked overmatched at the plate during his pro debut last year, mainly because he just didn't have the strength to drive the ball consistently. Lopez has good pitch recognition and a solid approach at the plate, but at this point pitchers can knock the bat out of his hands. He's a solid runner with the instincts to steal a few bases. Lopez has above-average range, soft hands and an adequate arm. If he can get stronger, he could be an everyday shortstop and perhaps hit second in a big league batting order. If not, his feel for the game could make him a useful utilityman.

Year	Club (League)	Class	AVG	G	AB	R	H	2B	3B	HR	RBI	BB	SO	SB	CS	OBP	SLG
2012	Idaho Falls (PIO)	R	.385	3	13	6	5	0	1	0	3	2	1	1	0	.467	.538
	Kane County (MWL)	LoA	.222	64	261	30	58	9	2	0	16	14	43	14	4	.271	.272
Minor League Totals			.230	67	274	36	63	9	3	0	19	16	44	15	4	.281	.285

20 HUMBERTO ARTEAGA, SS

BA GRADE
50
HIGH

Born: Jan. 23, 1994. **B-T:** R-R. **Ht.:** 6-0. **Wt.:** 195. **Signed:** Venezuela, 2010. **Signed by:** Orlando Estevez/Richard Castro.

Signed for $1.1 million in 2010 as part of the Royals' push to fix a gaping hole at shortstop in the organization, Arteaga has impressed with a steady, heady approach since turning pro. Kansas City has other shortstop prospects who can provide more offense, as Arteaga lacks Adalberto Mondesi's pop, Orlando Calixte's strength in his swing, Jack Lopez's feel for the game and Ramon Torres' strike-zone judgment. But when he's standing in the dirt with a glove on his hand, Arteaga is better than any of them. He reads the ball off the bat well and has a decisive first step, which explains how he has plenty of range despite below-average speed. He also has soft hands and an average arm. At the plate, Arteaga is a line-drive hitter who tries to find the gaps. He won't ever offer much power of speed, so any offensive value he provides will come from getting on base. He'll play in low Class A at age 19 this year, likely splitting time at shortstop with Mondesi or Torres.

Year	Club (League)	Class	AVG	G	AB	R	H	2B	3B	HR	RBI	BB	SO	SB	CS	OBP	SLG
2011	Royals (AZL)	R	.254	47	213	30	54	11	2	0	28	9	39	8	2	.290	.324
2012	Burlington (APP)	R	.274	58	234	40	64	13	3	2	29	9	31	7	3	.313	.380
Minor League Totals			.264	105	447	70	118	24	5	2	57	18	70	15	5	.303	.353

21 CHRIS DWYER, LHP

BA GRADE

50

HIGH

Born: April 10, 1988. **B-T:** L-L. **Ht.:** 6-2. **Wt.:** 210. **Drafted:** Clemson, 2009 (4th round). **Signed by:** Steve Connelly.

The Royals believed Dwyer was one of the top lefties in the 2009 draft, paying him a well above-slot $1.45 million in the fourth round as a rare draft-eligible freshman. But after getting his career off to a strong start in 2010, he has gone backward in two seasons since. He had to be shut down in 2012 after a thyroid condition caused him to lose nearly 20 pounds. His normally 90-92 mph fastball dipped to 83-86 in his final start of the season. His condition has since been treated with medication and he's expected to be back to full strength by spring training. Fixing Dwyer's control problems will not be as straightforward. He has yet to repeat his delivery enough to consistently stay ahead of hitters, which means he can't use his 12-to-6 curveball as much as he would like. His breaking ball has been a plus pitch in the past but has regressed since he reached Double-A. He has improved his changeup to the point where it's average. Kansas City protected Dwyer on its 40-man roster in November and is set on giving him more time to develop as a starter. Some scouts believe his command trouble points to a future as a reliever.

Year	Club (League)	Class	W	L	ERA	G	GS	CG	SV	IP	H	HR	BB	SO	K/9	WHIP	AVG
2009	Idaho Falls (PIO)	R	0	0	4.15	4	4	0	0	9	12	1	8	15	15.6	2.31	.324
2010	Wilmington (CAR)	HiA	6	3	2.99	15	15	1	0	84	79	3	33	93	9.9	1.33	.246
	NW Arkansas (TL)	AA	2	1	3.06	4	4	0	0	18	11	2	10	20	10.2	1.19	.175
2011	NW Arkansas (TL)	AA	8	10	5.60	27	27	2	0	141	124	14	78	126	8.0	1.43	.238
2012	NW Arkansas (TL)	AA	5	8	5.25	17	16	0	0	86	79	13	44	71	7.5	1.44	.242
	Omaha (PCL)	AAA	3	4	6.97	9	9	1	0	50	73	10	24	33	5.9	1.93	.349
Minor League Totals			24	26	4.99	76	75	4	0	388	378	43	197	358	8.3	1.48	.256

22 RAMON TORRES, SS

BA GRADE

50

HIGH

Born: Jan. 22, 1993. **B-T:** B-R. **Ht.:** 5-10. **Wt.:** 161. **Signed:** Dominican Republic, 2009. **Signed by:** Fausto Morel.

If Kansas City didn't have so many interesting shortstop prospects, Torres would get significantly more attention. As it is, he's intriguing but ranks behind Adalberto Mondesi, Orlando Calixte, Jack Lopez and Humberto Arteaga. Torres wore down at the end of each of his first two pro seasons but has added strength and held up better in the Arizona League last year. The Royals have spread him out in his stance, giving him a more balanced swing. A switch-hitter, he has an excellent batting eye and a good two-strike approach. He's a tick above-average as a runner. At shortstop, Torres has average range, soft hands and a plus arm. His on-base skills give him a chance to be a top-of-the-order hitter, but he's a long way from Kansas City and may spend another year in Rookie ball. He may end up moving to second base because of the logjam of shortstops in the organization.

Year	Club (League)	Class	AVG	G	AB	R	H	2B	3B	HR	RBI	BB	SO	SB	CS	OBP	SLG
2010	Royals (DSL)	R	.229	56	179	30	41	6	1	1	20	22	26	15	7	.319	.291
2011	Royals (DSL)	R	.260	60	204	35	53	16	3	2	24	26	36	14	5	.351	.397
2012	Royals (AZL)	R	.316	49	193	47	61	5	4	3	27	23	25	17	8	.385	.430
Minor League Totals			.269	165	576	112	155	27	8	6	71	71	87	46	20	.352	.375

23 FRED FORD, OF

BA GRADE

50

HIGH

Born: April 10, 1992. **B-T:** R-R. **Ht.:** 6-5. **Wt.:** 200. **Drafted:** Jefferson (Mo.) CC, 2012 (7th round). **Signed by:** Scott Melvin / Keith Connolly.

After helping Jefferson (Mo.) CC to back-to-back Junior College World Series appearances. Ford proceeded to show the best raw power Royals scouts had seen in a Kauffman Stadium workout since Wil Myers came to town in 2009. Kansas City took Ford in the seventh round last June and signed him for $125,000, then converted the athletic first baseman to the outfield. He was able to translate his plus-plus raw power into home runs, as he went deep 13 times in 62 pro contests. But he'll struggle to maintain that production at higher levels if he can't close the holes in his long swing. He struck out in 39 percent of his at-bats, the second-worst rate among Royals farmhands. He sells out for power too much and needs to shorten his stride and stay back on pitches. An average runner, Ford played right field in his pro debut, but his below-average arm eventually will push him to left. Kansas City is eager to see how his power will play in low Class A this year.

Year	Club (League)	Class	AVG	G	AB	R	H	2B	3B	HR	RBI	BB	SO	SB	CS	OBP	SLG
2012	Burlington (APP)	R	.248	62	214	38	53	11	1	13	35	36	83	5	5	.362	.491
Minor League Totals			.248	62	214	38	53	11	1	13	35	36	83	5	5	.362	.491

24 DAVID LOUGH, OF

BA GRADE
40
LOW

Born: Jan. 20, 1986. **B-T:** L-L. **Ht.:** 6-0. **Wt.:** 180. **Drafted:** Mercyhurst (Pa.), 2007 (11th round). **Signed by:** Jason Bryan.

After six years and 640 games in the minors, Lough finally reached the majors last September. The highest-drafted Mercyhurst player ever, Lough began his college career as a football wide receiver and baseball walk-on before signing for $49,500 as an 11th-round pick in 2007. He became the program's third big leaguer, following John Costello and David Lee. Lough profiles as a tweener in the outfield but has enough tools to serve as a useful backup. He can hit for average and possesses above-average speed and the ability to play all three outfield positions. He makes consistent line-drive contact and employs an all-fields approach. Lough's 35 power on the 20-80 scouting scale isn't enough for him to be a regular on a corner, and he's not good enough defensively to play center field on an everyday basis. His below-average arm is overtaxed in right field. After hitting safely in his final six starts in September, Lough will compete for a reserve role in spring training.

Year	Club (League)	Class	AVG	G	AB	R	H	2B	3B	HR	RBI	BB	SO	SB	CS	OBP	SLG
2007	Burlington (APP)	R	.337	24	86	15	29	6	0	2	12	4	13	6	1	.380	.477
2008	Burlington (MWL)	LoA	.268	126	488	76	131	21	11	16	62	35	70	12	11	.329	.455
2009	Wilmington (CAR)	HiA	.320	65	222	28	71	15	2	5	30	12	34	6	4	.370	.473
	NW Arkansas (TL)	AA	.331	61	236	41	78	13	2	9	31	12	30	13	4	.371	.517
2010	Omaha (PCL)	AAA	.280	120	460	65	129	15	12	11	58	40	72	14	5	.346	.437
2011	Omaha (PCL)	AAA	.318	114	456	87	145	26	11	9	65	36	49	14	8	.367	.482
2012	Omaha (PCL)	AAA	.275	130	491	69	135	19	11	10	69	25	65	26	4	.317	.420
	Kansas City (AL)	MAJ	.237	20	59	9	14	2	1	0	2	4	9	1	0	.292	.305
Major League Totals			.237	20	59	9	14	2	1	0	2	4	9	1	0	.292	.305
Minor League Totals			.294	640	2439	381	718	115	49	62	327	164	333	91	37	.346	.458

25 COLIN RODGERS, LHP

BA GRADE
50
HIGH

Born: Dec. 2, 1993. **B-T:** L-L. **Ht.:** 6-0. **Wt.:** 180. **Drafted:** HS—Baton Rouge, 2012 (3rd round). **Signed by:** Travis Ezi.

Rodgers confounded scouts when his fastball velocity fluctuated last spring, but the Royals believed in him enough to go well over his assigned pick value in the third round and sign him for $700,000. Kansas City usually breaks draftees in with an Arizona League assignment, but made an exception with Rodgers because of his polish. He had no problem handling older hitters in the Appalachian League, and is 2.05 ERA would have led the circuit if the Royals' strict innings limits hadn't kept him from qualifying. Rodgers' calling cards are guile and deception. He rarely throws back-to-back fastballs at the same velocity. He'll toss his fastball over the plate at 84 mph against the bottom of the order, then run it up to 93 against the cleanup hitter. His delivery shows no more effort when he's pitching at 90-93 mph than it does when he's working at 84-86. It's not an inability to maintain velocity, as he purposely changes speeds with his fastball. He has the makings of a plus curveball and changeup, with the latter his best secondary pitch during his pro debut. Rodgers could be part of a very interesting Lexington rotation in 2013.

Year	Club (League)	Class	W	L	ERA	G	GS	CG	SV	IP	H	HR	BB	SO	K/9	WHIP	AVG
2012	Burlington (APP)	R	3	1	2.05	11	11	0	0	48	40	2	16	25	4.7	1.16	.226
Minor League Totals			3	1	2.05	11	11	0	0	48	40	2	16	25	4.7	1.16	.226

26 CHRISTIAN BINFORD, RHP

BA GRADE
50
HIGH

Born: Dec. 20, 1992. **B-T:** R-R. **Ht.:** 6-7. **Wt.:** 215. **Drafted:** HS—Mercersburg, Pa., 2011 (30th round). **Signed by:** Jim Farr.

If Binford were a year younger, he'd probably be in college rather than pro ball. He didn't pitch much as a high school junior as he recovered from Tommy John surgery, and he entered 2011 as a raw project at a small Pennsylvannia private school who was strongly committed to Virginia. In the final year before MLB installed stricter draft spending restrictions, the Royals took him in the 30th round and persuaded him to sign for $575,000—something not feasible under the current draff rules. In his 2012 pro debut, Kansas City discovered that Binford was more physical and tougher than they expected. He showed advanced feel for pitching and surprising control, at one point going five straight starts without allowing a walk. Binford gets ahead of hitters with an 89-93 mph fastball and good boring action. He can throw his curveball for strikes in any count, though it's a fringy pitch that's better when it catches hitters off guard. His changeup shows some potential but is further away. Binford lacks much more projection but profiles as a No. 4 starter who could soak up innings. He's ready to make the jump to low Class A

Year	Club (League)	Class	W	L	ERA	G	GS	CG	SV	IP	H	HR	BB	SO	K/9	WHIP	AVG
2012	Burlington (APP)	R	2	3	2.03	8	8	0	0	40	40	1	4	31	7.0	1.10	.252
Minor League Totals			2	3	2.03	8	8	0	0	40	40	1	4	31	7.0	1.10	.252

27 JAKE JUNIS, RHP

BA GRADE

50

HIGH

Born: Sept. 16, 1992. **B-T:** R-R. **Ht.:** 6-3. **Wt.:** 210. **Drafted:** HS—Rock Falls, Ill., 2011 (29th round). **Signed by:** Scott Melvin.

Another late-round bonus baby from the 2011 draft, Junis received $675,000 as a 29th-rounder to give up a North Carolina State scholarship. He had to be shut down halfway through his 2012 pro debut with an elbow strain, though he didn't require surgery and should be ready for spring training. Also a star basketball player and a power-hitting third baseman in high school, Junis is a quality athlete who has no problem throwing strikes. His long-term success depends in part on how much projection remains in his strong frame. He currently sits at 88-90 mph with his fastball, though some scouts believe he could work at 92-94 once he matures. He shows the ability to snap off a power breaking ball and has an advanced changeup for his age. If he's healthy, he could open 2013 in low Class A.

Year	Club (League)	Class	W	L	ERA	G	GS	CG	SV	IP	H	HR	BB	SO	K/9	WHIP	AVG
2012	Burlington (APP)	R	2	2	4.15	7	6	0	0	35	39	2	5	22	5.7	1.27	.283
Minor League Totals			2	2	4.15	7	6	0	0	35	39	2	5	22	5.7	1.27	.283

28 ROBINSON YAMBATI, RHP

BA GRADE

50

EXTREME

Born: Jan. 15, 1991. **B-T:** R-R. **Ht.:** 6-3. **Wt.:** 208. **Signed:** Dominican Republic, 2008. **Signed by:** Edis Perez.

Much like Royals great Bret Saberhagen did on a much bigger stage, Yambati seems to alternate between good and bad years. In the 1980s, Saberhagen was dominant during odd-numbered seasons and merely adequate in even-numbered years. Yambati has been awful in odd-numbered seasons and intriguing in even-numbered ones. After struggling with his mechanics in 2009, he nearly matched Yordano Ventura pitch for pitch in 2010. But while Ventura successfully made the leap to full-season ball in 2011, Yambati again lost the feel for his delivery, saw his stuff take a step back and posted horrific numbers. He managed to pull it back together in 2012, when he became a full-time reliever. He smoothed out his delivery and regained the velocity on his fastball, which once again sat at 93-95 mph and touched 97. Working out of the bullpen, Yambati has simplified his approach. He largely pitches off his fastball, mixing in an occasional slider that has the potential to be average. He generates strikeouts but must continue to refine his control and command. He could move quickly as a reliever and will battle for a job in Double-A during spring training.

Year	Club (League)	Class	W	L	ERA	G	GS	CG	SV	IP	H	HR	BB	SO	K/9	WHIP	AVG
2008	Royals (DSL)	R	4	1	3.09	14	8	0	0	55	49	0	16	40	6.5	1.17	.236
2009	Royals (DSL)	R	2	0	0.77	5	5	0	0	23	16	1	9	16	6.2	1.07	.198
	Royals (AZL)	R	2	3	8.89	12	1	0	1	27	41	3	14	18	5.9	2.01	.333
2010	Royals (AZL)	R	8	2	2.71	14	6	0	0	66	65	0	12	64	8.7	1.16	.252
2011	Burlington (APP)	R	0	5	18.85	8	8	0	0	18	44	6	11	9	4.6	3.11	.458
2012	Kane County (MWL)	LoA	2	1	3.22	16	4	0	2	45	40	1	17	33	6.6	1.28	.231
	Wilmington (CAR)	HiA	2	1	2.16	17	0	0	5	25	22	0	10	31	11.2	1.28	.234
Minor League Totals			20	13	4.40	86	32	0	8	260	277	11	89	211	7.3	1.41	.268

29 BRETT EIBNER, OF

BA GRADE

50

EXTREME

Born: Dec. 2, 1988. **B-T:** R-R. **Ht.:** 6-4. **Wt.:** 210. **Drafted:** Arkansas, 2010 (2nd round). **Signed by:** Lloyd Simmons.

When Eibner came out of Arkansas as a two-way player in 2010, many scouts thought he had more promise as pitcher than as a hitter. He wanted to hit and the Royals liked his potential at the plate, so they gave him $1.25 million in the second round and made him an everyday player. Two pro seasons later, it looks like the scouts who preferred him on the mound were correct. For a player with significant Southeastern Conference experience, he has found it surprisingly difficult to hit minor league pitching. Eibner has batted .203 and struck out 255 times in 196 pro games. His noisy set-up makes it tough for him to catch up to good velocity, and he sometimes swings through hittable pitches. He has some of the best raw power in the system but throws too many at-bats away. A solid runner and center-field defender, Eibner's most usable tool may be his arm. With the Razorbacks, he showed a 92-93 mph fastball that touched 97. He also showed flashes of a plus slider and a developing changeup. He'll continue to try to make it as a hitter in 2013 when he repeats high Class A, but the clamor to see him pitch will get louder and louder unless he starts to have some success.

Year	Club (League)	Class	AVG	G	AB	R	H	2B	3B	HR	RBI	BB	SO	SB	CS	OBP	SLG
2011	Kane County (MWL)	LoA	.213	76	272	46	58	13	2	12	31	48	90	2	3	.340	.408
2012	Wilmington (CAR)	HiA	.196	120	423	60	83	26	5	15	53	57	165	5	2	.299	.388
Minor League Totals			.203	196	695	106	141	39	7	27	84	105	255	7	5	.315	.396

30 BRIAN FLETCHER, 1B/OF

BA GRADE
45
MEDIUM

Born: Oct. 26, 1988. **B-T:** R-R. **Ht.:** 6-0. **Wt.:** 190. **Drafted:** Auburn, 2010 (18th round). **Signed by:** Sean Gibbs.

Now that Mike Moustakas and Eric Hosmer are in the big leagues and Wil Myers and Clint Robinson have been traded, the Royals don't have many possible big league bats in the upper levels of the system. Fletcher is one possibility, though he'll have to cut down on his strikeouts to allow his plus power potential to play in games. While he has succeeded throughout most of his career with an unconventional front-foot approach because his hands work well, he had problems against more advanced pitching, striking out in 38 percent of his Double-A at-bats last year. The son of former big leaguer Scott Fletcher, Brian will have to produce at the plate because the rest of his tools are lacking. He's a well below average runner with subpar arm strength. He projects as average at best at first base, and his lack of speed limits him in left field. Fletcher's status as a righthanded-hitting first baseman will make his road to the majors tougher, but his power gives him a chance.

Year	Club (League)	Class	AVG	G	AB	R	H	2B	3B	HR	RBI	BB	SO	SB	CS	OBP	SLG
2010	Burlington (APP)	R	.313	4	16	4	5	0	0	2	4	1	5	2	0	.353	.688
2011	Kane County (MWL)	LoA	.328	91	341	54	112	31	3	14	60	24	80	4	4	.386	.560
2012	Wilmington (CAR)	HiA	.289	67	246	27	71	15	0	5	25	19	51	5	2	.353	.411
	NW Arkansas (TL)	AA	.256	65	254	32	65	11	2	10	34	15	96	6	3	.318	.433
Minor League Totals			.295	227	857	117	253	57	5	31	123	59	232	17	9	.356	.482

Los Angeles Angels

BY BEN BADLER

After signing Albert Pujols and C.J. Wilson last December, the Angels introduced their expensive new free agents outside Angel Stadium at a press conference that more closely resembled a pep rally.

While the team stopped short of guaranteeing a multitude of championships a la the Miami Heat, its grandiose celebration for winning the offseason looked just as silly when the 2012 regular season ended without a trip to the playoffs.

The Angels won 89 games—one more than the American League pennant-win-  ning Tigers—and featured an offense that finished fourth in baseball in scoring despite play-ing in one of baseball's most pitcher-friendly home parks. Yet a 6-14 start sunk them to nine games behind the Rangers in the AL West early in the season, a hole that proved to be insurmountable.

The highlight of the season—and perhaps the big-gest story in all of baseball—was the emergence of Mike Trout. He became the first player to ever win Baseball America's Major League Player of the Year and Rookie of the Year honors in the same season, though he finished second in the AL MVP vote to Miguel Cabrera.

Trout, who spent the first month of the season in Triple-A Salt Lake, hit .326/.399/.564 in 639 plate appearances. He led the American League with 129 runs scored and 49 stolen bases and regularly made highlight plays in center field.

Trout's 10.7 Wins Above Replacement (as mea-sured by Baseball-Reference.com) was the highest single-season mark since Barry Bonds in 2002 (11.6) and the third-highest ever for a center fielder, trailing only Mickey Mantle (11.1 in 1957) and Willie Mays (10.9 in 1965).

There isn't another premium prospect in the farm system, which is now one of the worst in baseball. Third baseman Kaleb Cowart stands out as the orga-nization's best prospect, but behind him the system lacks both impact talent and depth—though there are reasons for that beyond talent evaluation.

A 2009 high school first-round pick, Trout zipped to the big leagues. The Angels used three players who would have ranked among their Top 10 Prospects (shortstop Jean Segura, righthanders Johnny Hellweg and Ariel Pena) in a July trade with the Brewers to acquire Zack Greinke, who became a free agent after the season.

LARRY GOREN

Mike Trout's dynamite rookie season earned him Major League Player of the Year honors

Righthander Donn Roach also would have been in the Top 10 had they not included him in a May deal with the Padres for Ernesto Frieri.

Additionally, signing Pujols and Wilson cost the club its first- and second-round picks in the 2012 draft as compensation. That left the team with base-ball's smallest bonus pool ($1.6 million) for the first 10 rounds, hampering its efforts to restock the farm system.

The Angels made a series of personnel changes in scouting and player development. The most notable departure was that of Tom Kotchman, who had man-aged in the system since 1984 and doubled as an area scout in Florida since 1990.

Kotchman, who signed more than a dozen big leaguers for the club, resigned after the Angels asked him to focus solely on scouting and took a job with the Red Sox.

International scouting director Marc Russo, who helped rebuild the Angels' Latin American program after they cleaned house in mid-2009, also wasn't retained.

General manager Jerry Dipoto brought in Carlos Gomez, who had worked with Dipoto in Arizona as the Diamondbacks' international scouting director, to replace Russo.

THIS YEAR'S TOP 30

Player, Pos.	Grade
1. Kaleb Cowart, 3b	60/High
2. Nick Maronde, lhp	50/Medium
3. C.J. Cron, 1b	50/High
4. Mike Clevinger, rhp	50/High
5. Austin Wood, rhp	50/High
6. Randal Grichuk, of	50/High
7. Taylor Lindsey, 2b	50/High
8. R.J. Alvarez, rhp	50/High
9. Mark Sappington, rhp	50/High
10. Alex Yarbrough, 2b	50/High
11. Kole Calhoun, of	40/Low
12. A.J. Schugel, rhp	45/Medium
13. Ryan Chaffee, rhp	45/Medium
14. Eric Stamets, ss	50/High
15. Reid Scoggins, rhp	50/Extreme
16. Yency Almonte, rhp	50/Extreme
17. Luis Jimenez, 3b	45/Medium
18. Victor Alcantara, rhp	50/Extreme
19. Jose Rondon, ss	45/High
20. Daniel Tillman, rhp	45/High
21. Andrew Romine, inf	40/Low
22. Arjenis Fernandez, rhp	50/Extreme
23. Eduar Lopez, rhp	50/Extreme
24. Travis Witherspoon, of	45/High
25. Ryan Brasier, rhp	40/Medium
26. Steven Geltz, rhp	40/Medium
27. Drew Taylor, lhp	40/Medium
28. Cam Bedrosian, rhp	45/High
29. Kevin Johnson, rhp	40/Medium
30. Michael Roth, lhp	45/High

LAST YEAR'S TOP 30

Player, Pos.	Status
1. Mike Trout, of	Majors
2. Jean Segura, ss	(Brewers)
3. Garrett Richards, rhp	Majors
4. Johnny Hellweg, rhp	(Brewers)
5. C.J. Cron, 1b	No. 3
6. Kaleb Cowart, 3b	No. 1
7. Taylor Lindsey, 2b	No. 7
8. Daniel Tillman, rhp	No. 20
9. Ariel Pena, rhp	(Brewers)
10. Nick Maronde, lhp	No. 2
11. Jeremy Moore, of	(Free Agent)
12. Luis Jimenez, 3b	No. 17
13. Fabio Martinez, rhp	(Indians)
14. Nick Mutz, rhp	Dropped out
15. Travis Witherspoon, of	No. 24
16. Mike Clevinger, rhp	No. 4
17. Randal Grichuk, of	No. 6
18. Cam Bedrosian, rhp	No. 28
19. Alexi Amarista, 2b/of	(Padres)
20. Kole Calhoun, of/1b	No. 11
21. Carlos Ramirez, c	Dropped out
22. Trevor Reckling, lhp	(White Sox)
23. Donn Roach, rhp	(Padres)
24. Austin Wood, rhp	No. 5
25. Andrew Romine, inf	No. 21
26. Orangel Arenas, rhp	Dropped out
27. Matt Shoemaker, rhp	Dropped out
28. A.J. Schugel, rhp	No. 12
29. Ryan Brasier, rhp	No. 25
30. Loek Van Mil, rhp	(Free Agent)

BEST TOOLS

Best Hitter for Average	Kaleb Cowart
Best Power Hitter	C.J. Cron
Best Strike-Zone Discipline	Drew Heid
Fastest Baserunner	Eric Stamets
Best Athlete	Travis Witherspoon
Best Fastball	R.J. Alvarez
Best Curveball	Ryan Chaffee
Best Slider	Austin Wood
Best Changeup	Mike Clevinger
Best Control	Nick Maronde
Best Defensive Catcher	Carlos Ramirez
Best Defensive Infielder	Eric Stamets
Best Infield Arm	Kaleb Cowart
Best Defensive Outfielder	Travis Witherspoon
Best Outfield Arm	Kole Calhoun

PROJECTED 2016 LINEUP

Catcher	Chris Iannetta
First Base	Albert Pujols
Second Base	Howie Kendrick
Third Base	Kaleb Cowart
Shortstop	Erick Aybar
Left Field	Mark Trumbo
Center Field	Mike Trout
Right Field	Randal Grichuk
Designated Hitter	Kendrys Morales
No. 1 Starter	Jered Weaver
No. 2 Starter	C.J. Wilson
No. 3 Starter	Tommy Hanson
No. 4 Starter	Garrett Richards
No. 5 Starter	Nick Maronde
Closer	Ernesto Frieri

TOP PROSPECTS OF THE DECADE

Year	Player, Pos.	2012 Org.
2003	Francisco Rodriguez, rhp	Brewers
2004	Casey Kotchman 1b	Indians
2005	Casey Kotchman, 1b	Indians
2006	Brandon Wood, ss	Rockies
2007	Brandon Wood, ss	Rockies
2008	Brandon Wood, ss	Rockies
2009	Nick Adenhart, rhp	Deceased
2010	Hank Conger, c	Angels
2011	Mike Trout, of	Angels
2012	Mike Trout, of	Angels

TOP DRAFT PICKS OF THE DECADE

Year	Player, Pos.	2012 Org.
2003	Brandon Wood, ss	Rockies
2004	Jered Weaver, rhp	Angels
2005	Trevor Bell, rhp (1st round supp.)	Angels
2006	Hank Conger, c	Angels
2007	Jon Bachanov, rhp (1st round supp.)	White Sox
2008	Tyler Chatwood, rhp (2nd round)	Indians
2009	Randal Grichuk, of	Angels
2010	Kaleb Cowart, 3b	Angels
2011	C.J. Cron, 1b	Angels
2012	R.J. Alvarez (3rd round)	Angels

LARGEST BONUSES IN CLUB HISTORY

Jered Weaver, 2004	$4,000,000
Kendrys Morales, 2004	$3,000,000
Kaleb Cowart, 2010	$2,300,000
Troy Glaus, 1997	$2,250,000
Joe Torres, 2000	$2,080,000

LOS ANGELES ANGELS

TOP 2013 ROOKIE: Nick Maronde, lhp. It's not clear yet whether the Angels will ask him to start or relieve, but he should make an impact in either role.

BREAKOUT PROSPECT: Victor Alcantara, rhp. He may end up ticketed for the bullpen, but his fastball hit 100 mph during his 2012 pro debut.

SLEEPER: Kody Eaves, 2b. A 16th-round pick last June, he's an aggressive lefthanded hitter with some pop in his bat.

SOURCE OF TOP 30 TALENT			
Homegrown	30	Acquired	0
College	13	Trades	0
Junior college	6	Rule 5 draft	0
High school	5	Independent leagues	0
Nondrafted free agents	1	Free agents/waivers	0
International	5		

LF
Robbie Widlansky
Zach Borenstein

CF
Travis Witherspoon (24)
Chevy Clarke

RF
Randal Grichuk (6)
Kole Calhoun (11)
Natanael Delgado
Andrew Ray

3B
Kaleb Cowart (1)
Luis Jimenez (17)

SS
Eric Stamets (14)
Jose Rondon (19)
Andrew Romine (21)
Tommy Field
Wendell Soto
Rolando Gomez

2B
Taylor Lindsey (7)
Alex Yarbrough (10)
Kody Eaves
Sherman Johnson
Matt Long

1B
C.J. Cron (3)
Mike Snyder

C
Sandy Martinez
Carlos Ramirez
Chase Patterson

LHP

LHSP	LHRP
Nick Maronde (2)	Drew Taylor (27)
Michael Roth (30)	Brandon Sisk
	Buddy Boshers

RHP

RHSP	RHRP
Mike Clevinger (4)	R.J. Alvarez (8)
Austin Wood (5)	Ryan Chaffee (13)
Mark Sappington (9)	Reid Scoggins (15)
A.J. Schugel (12)	Victor Alcantara (18)
Yency Almonte (16)	Daniel Tillman (20)
Arjenis Fernandez (22)	Ryan Brasier (25)
Eduar Lopez (23)	Steven Geltz (26)
Cam Bedrosian (28)	Kevin Johnson (29)
Jairo Diaz	Nick Mutz
Manny Correa	Austin Adams
Lay Batista	Mike Morin
Angel Guerra	
Gabriel Perez	

2012   BONUSES: $2.3 MILLION

BEST PURE HITTER: 2B Alex Yarbrough (4) has strong hands, a compact swing and very good bat control. He has natural pitch-recognition skills and manages his at-bats well. He went straight to low Class A and batted .287.

BEST POWER HITTER: 3B/1B Mike Snyder (23) is big and physical at 6-foot-4 and 230 pounds. He has strength and bat speed and shows 70 raw power on the 20-80 scouting scale.

FASTEST RUNNER: SS Eric Stamets (6) has well above-average speed, turning in home-to-first times in the 4.1-second range from the right side of the plate.

BEST DEFENSIVE PLAYER: Stamets' speed also helps him cover a lot of ground at shortstop, where he shows soft hands and solid arm strength.

BEST FASTBALL: Angels scouting director Ric Wilson saw both RHP R.J. Alvarez (3) and RHP Reid Scoggins (15) touch 100 mph this spring. Both sit at 95-97 mph, with Alvarez doing so it a little easier. RHP Mark Sappington (5) pitches at 94-95 mph and reaches 97.

BEST SECONDARY PITCH: While it needs to be a little more consistent, Alvarez throws a power slider in the mid-80s. RHP Mike Morin (14) has a quality changeup.

BEST PRO DEBUT: 1B Wade Hinkle (27) crushed in his debut for Rookie-level Orem, hitting .338/.430/.586 with 21 doubles and 15 homers in 266 at-bats. He made the Pioneer League all-star team, as did Snyder, who batted .332/.393/.531, and OF Joel Capote (28), who hit .335/.434/.504.

BEST ATHLETE: In addition to his speed and defense, Stamets has a live, loose body and very good athleticism.

MOST INTRIGUING BACKGROUND: RHP Kenny Hatcher's (36) uncle Mickey played in the majors and was the Angels' hitting coach before getting fired in May. Snyder's father Brian and brother Brandon also reached the big leagues, and the Yankees drafted his twin Matt in the 10th round. Unsigned C Justin Morhardt's (39) dad Greg is one of the team's national crosscheckers. LHP Michael Roth (9), whose mother is English, pitched for Great Britain in the World Baseball Classic qualifying round.

CLOSEST TO THE MAJORS: As a strong-armed college reliever, Alvarez could move through the minors quickly.

BEST LATE-ROUND PICK: Scoggins. The Angels also are excited about RHP Yency Almonte (17), who has a loose, athletic build at 6-foot-4 and 185 pounds. He has a 90-94 mph fastball and some feel for spin-ning a breaking ball.

THE ONE WHO GOT AWAY: "There were about 113 guys ahead of us that got away," Wilson joked, because the Angels didn't pick until No. 114 after giving up their top two choices as compensation for free agents Albert Pujols and C.J. Wilson. They signed 36 of their 38 selections, with the only exceptions SS Jeff Kemp (31), who returned to Radford, and Morhardt, who honored his commitment to Oral Roberts.

ASSESSMENT: Without a first- or second-round pick, the Angels had baseball's lowest bonus pool ($1.6 million). Still, they added a fast-moving reliever in Alvarez and some interesting sleepers.

2011   BONUSES: $3.3 MILLION

1B C.J. Cron (1) led the minors with 123 RBIs in his first full pro season. LHP Nick Maronde (3) surpassed that by jumping all the way to the majors and posting a 1.50 ERA in 12 relief appearances.

GRADE: B

2010   BONUSES: $8.1 MILLION

The Angels had five picks before the second round and found a potential all-star (3B Kaleb Cowart), a possible regular (2B Taylor Lindsey) and three guys who have struggled (RHP Cam Bedrosian, OF Chevy Clarke, OF Ryan Bolden). OF Kole Calhoun (8) already reached Anaheim but profiles as a reserve.

GRADE: C+

2009   BONUSES: $6.8 MILLION

OF Mike Trout (1) alone would make this an outstanding crop. The Angels didn't stop there, also signing four more big leaguers in LHPs Tyler Skaggs (1s) and Patrick Corbin (2) and RHPs Garrett Richards (1s) and Drew Carpenter (9). They gave up Skaggs and Corbin to get Dan Haren from the Diamondbacks, and lost Carpenter on waivers this offseason.

GRADE: A

2008   BONUSES: $2.7 MILLION

Without a first-round pick, the Angels still found marginal big leaguers in RHPs Tyler Chatwood (2) and Michael Kohn (13) and LHP Will Smith (7). Their best pick was RHP Johnny Hellweg (16), sent to the Brewers in the Zack Greinke deal last summer. They've traded Chatwood and Smith, too.

GRADE: C+

Draft analysis by Conor Glassey (2012) and Jim Callis (2008-11). Numbers in parentheses indicate draft rounds.

1 KALEB COWART, 3B

Born: June 2, 1992. **B-T:** B-R. **Ht.:** 6-3. **Wt.:** 190.
Drafted: HS—Adel, Ga., 2010 (1st round). **Signed by:**
Chris McAlpin.

BA GRADE
60
HIGH

LARRY GOREN

Cowart won Baseball America's 2010 High School Player of the Year award thanks to his dominance as a two-way player, hitting .654 with 11 home runs in 107 at-bats and going 10-1, 1.05 with 116 strikeouts in 73 innings. Most teams at the time preferred him on the mound, where he showed a plus fastball in the low 90s with sink along with a hard slider. He preferred to hit, however, and the Angels thought enough of his future as a third baseman to draft him 18th overall and pay him $2.3 million at the signing deadline. He didn't make much of a splash in his first two pro seasons, barely playing in 2010 and hitting .283/.345/.420 at Rookie-level Orem in 2011. He finally reached full-season ball in 2012 and had a breakthrough year in 135 games split between low Class A Cedar Rapids and high Class A Inland Empire.

Cowart has developed into a well-rounded prospect at third base. A switch-hitter with strong hands, he shows the ability to drive the ball to the opposite field when he's going well. The book on him coming out of high school and entering the 2012 season was that his swing was more natural from the right side. His lefthanded stroke does still tend to get loopy, which causes him to pop the ball up more than he should, but he became more comfortable as a lefty last season. He hit 14 of his 16 homers from the left side of the plate in 2012. He has plus bat speed from both sides of the plate and the potential to hit more than 20 home runs annually when he reaches the big leagues. His plate discipline also has improved markedly, helping him to get into better hitter's counts to drive the ball and to increase his on-base percentage with more walks. He didn't have as much success following his promotion to high Class A, yet he didn't stray from his patient approach. Cowart is athletic, has a quick first step and has become a solid defender at third base. He's a surehanded defender who makes all the routine plays, gets good jumps on balls and is adept at fielding bunts and slow choppers hit right at him, though he does

need to get better on balls to his left. His long, over-the-top throwing motion is a little unorthodox for a third baseman, but it works for him because he has above-average arm strength and consistent accuracy. He had just 16 errors in 125 games in 2012 after making the same number in 66 games the year before. Cowart has below-average speed but runs the bases well. He earns praise for his aptitude and ability to make adjustments, and for being a good teammate.

In a farm system that lacks impact talent and depth, Cowart stands out as the lone farmhand whom scouts feel comfortable about projecting as an everyday player in the big leagues. The Angels have produced just two homegrown all-star third basemen in their first 52 seasons—Dave Chalk and Troy Glaus—and Cowart has the potential to become their third. He should make the jump to Double-A Arkansas during the 2013 season, with a chance to compete for a starting job in the major leagues at some point in 2014.

Year	Club (League)	Class	AVG	G	AB	R	H	2B	3B	HR	RBI	BB	SO	SB	CS	OBP	SLG
2010	Angels (AZL)	R	.143	6	21	0	3	0	0	0	4	0	6	0	0	.136	.143
	Orem (PIO)	R	.400	1	5	1	2	0	0	1	3	1	2	0	0	.500	1.000
2011	Orem (PIO)	R	.283	72	283	49	80	12	3	7	40	25	81	11	4	.345	.420
2012	Cedar Rapids (MWL)	LoA	.293	66	263	42	77	16	3	9	54	22	44	9	4	.348	.479
	Inland Empire (CAL)	HiA	.259	69	263	48	68	15	4	7	49	45	67	5	3	.366	.426
Minor League Totals			.275	214	835	140	230	43	10	24	150	93	200	25	11	.349	.437

2 NICK MARONDE, LHP

Born: Sept. 5, 1989. **B-T:** R-R. **Ht.:** 6-3. **Wt.:** 205. **Drafted:** Florida, 2011 (3rd round).
Signed by: Tom Kotchman.

After ranking as the No. 1 prospect in the Rookie-level Pioneer League in his 2011 pro debut, Maronde rocketed to the big leagues in his first full pro season. Despite missing most of May and June with back and elbow injuries, he became the fourth player from the 2011 draft to reach the majors. Maronde has excellent command of a deceptive fastball that ranges from 89-95 mph. He keeps his fastball down and locates it on both sides of the plate. His 82-85 mph slider is a plus pitch that features good depth. It can flatten out when he doesn't stay on top of the ball, but when it's on he can throw it for strikes or as a chase pitch. The Angels want Maronde to improve his below-average changeup, though he rarely threw it as a big league reliever. Maronde's athleticism helps him repeat his delivery, while his arm action makes some scouts worry about his durability. Maronde has the stuff and command to be a No. 3 starter, but durability concerns and lack of a third pitch may keep him in the bullpen. He could open 2013 in the big leagues in the latter role.

BA GRADE
50
MEDIUM

Year	Club (League)	Class	W	L	ERA	G	GS	CG	SV	IP	H	HR	BB	SO	K/9	WHIP	AVG
2011	Orem (PIO)	R	5	0	2.14	11	11	0	0	46	36	5	15	50	9.7	1.10	.217
2012	Angels (AZL)	R	0	1	1.13	3	3	0	0	8	3	0	2	9	10.1	0.63	.107
	Inland Empire (CAL)	HiA	3	1	1.82	10	10	0	0	59	40	4	14	60	9.1	0.91	.187
	Arkansas (TL)	AA	3	2	3.34	7	5	0	0	32	39	1	3	21	5.8	1.30	.300
	Los Angeles (AL)	MAJ	0	0	1.50	12	0	0	0	6	6	0	3	7	10.5	1.50	.261
Major League Totals			0	0	1.50	12	0	0	0	6	6	0	3	7	10.5	1.50	.261
Minor League Totals			11	4	2.22	31	29	0	0	146	118	10	34	140	8.6	1.04	.219

3 C.J. CRON, 1B

Born: Jan. 5, 1990. **B-T:** R-R. **Ht.:** 6-4. **Wt.:** 235. **Drafted:** Utah, 2011 (1st round).
Signed by: John Gracio.

The 17th overall pick in the 2011 draft and recipient of a $1.467 million bonus, Cron came into spring training in 2012 out of shape. He looked lost early in his first full pro season before losing weight and rebounding to lead the minors with 123 RBIs. Following the season, he had surgery to repair a torn labrum in his right shoulder, which he had played with since his final season at Utah. Cron also had an operation on his right knee following his pro debut. His father Chris played briefly in the majors with the Angels and his brother was an unsigned third-rounder in 2011 that now attends Texas Christian. The ball makes a different sound coming off Cron's bat. He has plus-plus raw power, and thanks to his hand-eye coordination he doesn't strike out excessively. But he also doesn't walk much because he swings at borderline strikes and chases breaking balls. His ability to handle breaking pitches improved as the season went on, though some scouts have reservations about his ability to catch up to quality fastballs. All of his value lies in his bat, as he's slow-footed and a limited defender at first base. His hands and feet are adequate, but he needs to improve his flexibility and first-step quickness to avoid becoming a DH. Cron will have to show improved plate discipline to reach his ceiling as a middle-of-the-order bat. He should start 2013 in Double-A.

BA GRADE
50
HIGH

Year	Club (League)	Class	AVG	G	AB	R	H	2B	3B	HR	RBI	BB	SO	SB	CS	OBP	SLG
2011	Orem (PIO)	R	.308	34	143	30	44	5	1	13	41	10	34	0	0	.371	.629
2012	Inland Empire (CAL)	HiA	.293	129	525	73	154	32	2	27	123	17	72	3	4	.327	.516
Minor League Totals			.296	163	668	103	198	37	3	40	164	27	106	3	4	.337	.540

4 MIKE CLEVINGER, RHP

Born: Dec. 21, 1990. **B-T:** R-R. **Ht.:** 6-4. **Wt.:** 202. **Drafted:** Seminole State (Fla.) JC, 2011 (4th round). **Signed by:** Tom Kotchman.

Clevinger boosted his draft stock in the Cape Cod League in the summer of 2010 before signing for a slightly above-slot $250,000 in the 2011 draft. He made a strong impression in low Class A to start the 2012 season, but he made just eight starts before needing Tommy John surgery. Clevinger has four pitches that grade as average or better. He throws an 89-93 mph fastball from a three-quarters arm slot and has reached 96 as a reliever. He gets plenty of swings and misses with his secondary stuff, most notably an above-average 81-84 mph slider with wide break. His changeup is average and shows the potential to give him another plus pitch. His curveball is average as well, though he tips it off by throwing it from a slightly higher release point. Some scouts think Clevinger tries to get too many swings and misses on chase pitches early in the count rather than pitching off his quality fastball. His delivery creates deception, though it's an aggressive motion and he tends to overthrow when he gets jacked up. He has average control but could use better command. Clevinger has the repertoire to be a mid-rotation starter, but concerns about his durability may make a relief role more likely. He may not return to game action until late in the 2013 season.

BA GRADE

50

HIGH

Year	Club (League)	Class	W	L	ERA	G	GS	CG	SV	IP	H	HR	BB	SO	K/9	WHIP	AVG
2011	Orem (PIO)	R	0	0	2.25	3	0	0	0	4	3	0	2	5	11.3	1.25	.200
2012	Cedar Rapids (MWL)	LoA	1	1	3.73	8	8	0	0	41	37	3	13	34	7.5	1.22	.243
Minor League Totals			1	1	3.60	11	8	0	0	45	40	3	15	39	7.8	1.22	.240

5 AUSTIN WOOD, RHP

Born: July 11, 1990. **B-T:** R-R. **Ht.:** 6-4. **Wt.:** 225. **Drafted:** Southern California, 2011 (6th round). **Signed by:** Tim Corcoran.

After struggling at Florida State in 2009 and falling out of the St. Petersburg (Fla.) JC rotation in 2010, Wood still was a fourth-round pick of the Rays and dominated the Cape Cod League that summer. He did not sign and transferred to Southern California, but he fell to the sixth round after posting a 5.61 ERA as a junior. As a pro, he has continued to produce pedestrian results despite quality stuff. Wood's fastball ranges from 91-96 mph and he can hit 99. His plus slider has power and hard bite, but he doesn't miss as many bats as expected because he gets behind in the count too frequently. He left fastballs up in the zone early in 2012, though he did a better job of keeping them down as the year went along. Wood has shown feel for his changeup, but it regressed last season because he rarely used it. He prefers to pitch away from hitters, rather than attacking them inside. He's athletic but has trouble repeating his mechanics and rushes his delivery, which leads to poor control and command—as evidenced by his 72 walks in 128 innings this season. Wood has the arsenal to be a starter if he can improve his changeup, but his lack of success and control may lead him to the bullpen. He should advance to high Class A in 2013.

BA GRADE

50

HIGH

Year	Club (League)	Class	W	L	ERA	G	GS	CG	SV	IP	H	HR	BB	SO	K/9	WHIP	AVG
2011	Orem (PIO)	R	0	0	20.25	2	0	0	0	1	4	1	0	1	6.8	3.00	.500
2012	Cedar Rapids (MWL)	LoA	5	12	4.30	26	26	0	0	128	125	4	72	109	7.7	1.54	.264
Minor League Totals			5	12	4.47	28	26	0	0	129	129	5	72	110	7.7	1.56	.268

6 RANDAL GRICHUK, OF

Born: Aug. 13, 1991. **B-T:** R-R. **Ht.:** 6-1. **Wt.:** 195. **Drafted:** HS—Rosenberg, Texas, 2009 (1st round). **Signed by:** Kevin Ham.

Taken one pick ahead of Mike Trout in the 2009 draft, Grichuk signed for $1.242 million as the 24th overall selection. He battled thumb and wrist injuries in 2010, then hurt both of his knees in 2011. His ability to stay healthy for a full season in 2012 was a step in the right direction, and he nearly doubled his career at-bat total. Grichuk has strong wrists, a quick bat and above-average raw power. His swing can get complicated, but he has made adjustments with his set-up, widening his base and quieting his hands. He wraps his bat, which adds length to his stroke, but he has good hands and accelerates the barrel into contact well. He hits breaking balls when he maintains a gap-to-gap approach, but he's vulnerable to them when he flies open with his swing. He doesn't strike out excessively but needs more discipline at the plate after putting up just a .335 on-base percentage in 2012. Grichuk is coachable and has made huge strides with his defense and baserunning, both of which were poor when he entered pro ball. He's now a reliable right fielder with a solid, accurate arm.

BA GRADE

50

HIGH

Trout and Grichuck are friends, and their proximity in the 2009 draft drives Grichuk to join Trout in the majors. His free-swinging approach will be tested in Double-A in 2013.

Year	Club (League)	Class	AVG	G	AB	R	H	2B	3B	HR	RBI	BB	SO	SB	CS	OBP	SLG
2009	Angels (AZL)	R	.322	53	236	47	76	13	10	7	53	9	64	6	4	.352	.551
2010	Angels (AZL)	R	.327	12	49	7	16	3	2	4	10	3	9	0	0	.365	.714
	Cedar Rapids (MWL)	LoA	.292	52	202	41	59	19	4	7	36	9	50	4	0	.327	.530
2011	Angels (AZL)	R	.333	7	24	2	8	1	1	0	6	2	4	0	0	.357	.458
	Cedar Rapids (MWL)	LoA	.230	32	122	12	28	7	4	2	13	6	29	0	1	.267	.402
	Inland Empire (CAL)	HiA	.283	14	53	13	15	4	2	1	6	0	13	0	0	.316	.491
2012	Inland Empire (CAL)	HiA	.298	135	537	79	160	30	9	18	71	23	92	16	6	.335	.488
Minor League Totals			.296	305	1223	201	362	77	32	39	195	52	261	26	11	.331	.507

7 TAYLOR LINDSEY, 2B

Born: Dec. 2, 1991. **B-T:** L-R. **Ht.:** 6-0. **Wt.:** 195. **Drafted:** HS—Scottsdale, Ariz., 2010 (1st round supplemental). **Signed by:** John Gracio.

The Angels surprised several teams when they drafted Lindsey 37th overall and signed him for $873,000 in 2010, but he responded with a Rookie-level Pioneer League MVP season in 2011. The club's new front office chose to skip him a level in 2012 and jumped him to high Class A, where he held his own offensively at age 20. Lindsey is an unorthodox hitter who succeeds largely because of his impressive hand-eye coordination. He has a narrow stance and scouts would like to see him use his legs more in his swing, but he has strong forearms and wrists along with good hands, which gives him a knack for squaring up the baseball. He sets up with his hands unconventionally low, then raises them late to get to his trigger. The Angels tried raising his hand position to help his timing, but it's still something he's getting comfortable with. He's not a major power threat and works more line to line. A below-average runner, Lindsey has enhanced his footwork to avoid having to move to the outfield, but his lateral movement and range need to get better. While his arm strength has improved, it's still fringy. Lindsey will move to Double-A in 2013. He'll have to stay at second base to profile as a regular.

Year	Club (League)	Class	AVG	G	AB	R	H	2B	3B	HR	RBI	BB	SO	SB	CS	OBP	SLG
2010	Angels (AZL)	R	.284	45	194	26	55	12	6	0	18	12	33	8	3	.325	.407
2011	Orem (PIO)	R	.362	63	290	64	105	28	6	9	46	13	46	10	4	.394	.593
2012	Inland Empire (CAL)	HiA	.289	134	547	79	158	26	6	9	58	29	66	8	6	.328	.408
Minor League Totals			.308	242	1031	169	318	66	18	18	122	54	145	26	13	.346	.460

8 R.J. ALVAREZ, RHP

Born: June 8, 1991. **B-T:** R-R. **Ht.:** 6-1. **Wt.:** 180. **Drafted:** Florida Atlantic, 2012 (3rd round). **Signed by:** Ralph Reyes.

Alvarez went a combined 9-7, 5.17 as a starter in his first two seasons at Florida Atlantic, and excelled as a reliever in the Cape Cod League for two summers. The Owls moved him to the bullpen in 2012 and he responded by posting a 0.53 ERA and 45 strikeouts in 34 innings. The Angels, who lost their picks in the first two rounds as compensation for signing Albert Pujols and C.J. Wilson as free agents and had the lowest bonus pool allotment, used their top choice (114th overall) to draft Alvarez in the third round and signed him for $416,300. Alvarez has a quick arm that produces fastballs ranging from 95-97 mph in most outings and reaching as high as 100 mph. He can miss bats with his fastball and his mid-80s slider, which features late action. He does have a tendency to get around his slider, causing it to morph into more of a power slurve. He has a fringy changeup in his arsenal, though he doesn't need it as a reliever. He has a high-effort delivery and throws across his body, which adds deception but affects his command. The Angels would like to move Alvarez through the system quickly, though his command will dictate that more than his stuff. He has the repertoire to eventually pitch in the back of their bullpen if everything comes together.

Year	Club (League)	Class	W	L	ERA	G	GS	CG	SV	IP	H	HR	BB	SO	K/9	WHIP	AVG
2012	Cedar Rapids (MWL)	LoA	3	2	3.29	23	0	0	0	27	22	2	11	38	12.5	1.21	.216
Minor League Totals			3	2	3.29	23	0	0	0	27	22	2	11	38	12.5	1.21	.216

9 MARK SAPPINGTON, RHP

Born: Nov. 17, 1990. **B-T:** R-R. **Ht.:** 6-5. **Wt.:** 209. **Drafted:** Rockhurst (Mo.), 2012 (5th round). **Signed by:** Joel Murrie.

Sappington's fastball parked in the mid-80s when he was a high school senior, so he didn't get much attention from college recruiters. He spent three years at NCAA Division II Rockhurst (Mo.), where his velocity improved dramatically. He became the highest-drafted player in school history when the Angels took him in the fifth round in June and signed him for $218,000. Sappington now cruises at 94-95 mph and reaches 97. He has a big, physical frame and throws his fastball with downhill angle and late, heavy sink, which helps him generate plenty of groundballs. His secondary stuff lacks consistency, but his slider shows flashes of becoming a plus pitch and his changeup has the potential to develop into an average offering. Sappington has a unique delivery, with effort, twists and turns that result in a lot of knees and elbows flying at the batter. His mechanics create deception but lead scouts to wonder how good his command can be and if he might be better suited to the bullpen. Sappington got hit hard in Orem, though the Angels say he was just tired after pitching 96 innings in the spring. They'll keep deploying him as a starter in 2013, most likely at their new low Class A Burlington affiliate. Even if he winds up as a reliever, he needs innings for development.

**BA GRADE
50
HIGH**

Year	Club (League)	Class	W	L	ERA	G	GS	CG	SV	IP	H	HR	BB	SO	K/9	WHIP	AVG
2012	Orem (PIO)	R	1	1	5.15	15	12	0	0	37	31	3	16	34	8.3	1.28	.231
Minor League Totals			1	1	5.15	15	12	0	0	37	31	3	16	34	8.3	1.28	.231

10 ALEX YARBROUGH, 2B

Born: Aug. 3, 1991. **B-T:** B-R. **Ht.:** 5-11. **Wt.:** 180. **Drafted:** Mississippi, 2012 (4th round). **Signed by:** J.T. Zink.

The Angels system is littered with free swingers, so it was notable that the first position player drafted under GM Jerry Dipoto has the patient approach the organization is trying to emphasize. After hitting .380 as a Mississippi junior, Yarbrough went in the fourth round in June and signed for $302,800. Yarbrough's barrel stays in the hitting zone a long time and he has excellent hands at the plate, which results in a high contact rate. He showed modest pop in college and didn't homer in 63 pro games, so he'll have to get stronger. He likes to use the opposite field, even on inside pitches, and some scouts are concerned that his lack of bat speed could get exposed at upper levels against good fastballs on the inner half. Yarbrough is a modest athlete and there's nothing flashy about his defense. He's a fringy runner who doesn't have great range or arm strength, but his hands are clean and he's reliable on the balls he reaches. He needs to improve his double-play pivot but he shows aptitude for receiving instruction. Yarbrough reached Double-A at the end of 2012, but he might start his first full pro season in high Class A. He profiles as an offensive second baseman, albeit not as talented as Howie Kendrick, who's signed through 2015.

**BA GRADE
50
HIGH**

Year	Club (League)	Class	AVG	G	AB	R	H	2B	3B	HR	RBI	BB	SO	SB	CS	OBP	SLG
2012	Cedar Rapids (MWL)	LoA	.287	58	244	35	70	12	9	0	27	10	20	9	2	.320	.410
	Arkansas (TL)	AA	.111	5	18	1	2	1	0	0	0	0	3	0	0	.111	.167
Minor League Totals			.275	63	262	36	72	13	9	0	27	10	23	9	2	.307	.393

11 KOLE CALHOUN, OF

**BA GRADE
40
LOW**

Born: Oct. 14, 1987. **B-T:** L-L. **Ht.:** 5-10. **Wt.:** 190. **Drafted:** Arizona State, 2010 (8th round). **Signed by:** John Gracio.

After Calhoun spent his first full pro season in high Class A Inland Empire in 2011, the Angels pushed him to Triple-A Salt Lake to start 2012 and he didn't disappoint. He made his major league debut in May and stayed with the Angels for a couple of weeks before returning to Triple-A, then came back to Anaheim at the end of August. Calhoun's tools are uninspiring, but club officials gush about his makeup. He's a smart player with outstanding instincts and a leader who brings out the best in his teammates. He's an aggressive player in all aspects of the game. Calhoun compensates for modest bat speed by getting himself ready to hit with a compact swing and a keen idea of the strike zone. He keeps the barrel in the zone a long time and surprises with sneaky power that grades out as close to average. He's a below-average runner but a good defender in right field. His arm, above-average in terms of both strength and accuracy, is his best tool. Calhoun's ceiling is probably limited to that of an extra outfielder, but he's a lefty bat in a predominantly righthanded-hitting Angels outfield and he's the type of players managers love, so he should get plenty of opportunities to stick around. He'll try to crack the Opening Day roster, though the Angels' November waiver claim of Scott Cousins didn't help Calhoun's cause.

Year	Club (League)	Class	AVG	G	AB	R	H	2B	3B	HR	RBI	BB	SO	SB	CS	OBP	SLG
2010	Orem (PIO)	R	.292	56	202	43	59	14	4	7	42	39	45	3	1	.411	.505
2011	Inland Empire (CAL)	HiA	.324	133	512	94	166	36	6	22	99	73	96	20	10	.410	.547
2012	Salt Lake (PCL)	AAA	.298	105	410	79	122	30	7	14	73	44	88	12	3	.369	.507
	Los Angeles (AL)	MAJ	.174	21	23	2	4	1	0	0	1	2	6	1	0	.240	.217
Major League Totals			.174	21	23	2	4	1	0	0	1	2	6	1	0	.240	.217
Minor League Totals			.309	294	1124	216	347	80	17	43	214	156	229	35	14	.396	.525

12 A.J. SCHUGEL, RHP

BA GRADE
45
MEDIUM

Born: June 27, 1989. **B-T:** R-R. **Ht.:** 6-1. **Wt.:** 190. **Drafted:** Central Arizona JC, 2010 (25th round). **Signed by:** John Gracio.

Schugel didn't sign with the Padres drafted him as a high school third baseman in the 33rd round in 2007. He turned pro for $40,000 three years later as a 25th-round pick, and while he didn't pitch much at Central Arizona JC, he quickly found success on the mound with the Angels. His father Jeff is a big league scout for the team. From a three-quarters arm slot, Schugel throws strikes with an 89-93 mph fastball that has late sink and tail and can touch 95. His changeup has improved significantly to become an average pitch that can get swings and misses. Some scouts think his changeup can continue to develop into a plus offering. His breaking ball is more slider than curve, but it's a below-average pitch that's often soft and slurvy. Schugel has a fairly fluid delivery with a slight hook in the back of his arm action. He throws across his body but he repeats his delivery, creates deception and keeps the ball in the bottom of the zone. His athleticism helps him field his position extremely well. While his breaking ball is a concern, Schugel's fastball/changeup combination and ability to stay around the strike zone could be enough to fit into the back of a rotation. He'll advance to Triple-A in 2013.

Year	Club (League)	Class	W	L	ERA	G	GS	CG	SV	IP	H	HR	BB	SO	K/9	WHIP	AVG
2010	Angels (AZL)	R	0	0	1.72	11	0	0	2	16	15	0	5	12	6.9	1.28	.259
	Orem (PIO)	R	2	2	8.59	6	0	0	1	7	8	0	6	9	11.0	1.91	.267
2011	Cedar Rapids (MWL)	LoA	4	3	2.59	25	12	0	1	90	73	2	39	80	8.0	1.24	.220
	Inland Empire (CAL)	HiA	1	2	5.03	4	4	0	0	20	22	1	6	15	6.9	1.42	.278
2012	Arkansas (TL)	AA	6	8	2.89	27	27	0	0	140	117	9	55	109	7.0	1.23	.232
Minor League Totals			13	15	3.03	73	43	0	4	273	235	12	111	225	7.4	1.27	.234

13 RYAN CHAFFEE, RHP

BA GRADE
45
MEDIUM

Born: May 18, 1988. **B-T:** R-R. **Ht.:** 6-2. **Wt.:** 195. **Drafted:** Chipola (Fla.) JC, 2008 (3rd round). **Signed by:** Tom Kotchman.

The winning pitcher for Chipola (Fla.) JC in the 2007 Junior College World Series championship game as a freshman, Chaffee broke a bone in his foot the next March, requiring surgery to insert a screw. He returned to the mound and signed with the Angels for $338,000 as a third-round pick in 2008, but he reinjured the foot that summer and didn't make his pro debut until 2009. After three unsuccessful seasons as a starter, he moved to the bullpen late in 2011 and finally found success in the role last season. Working from a three-quarters arm slot, Chaffee has excellent arm speed that produces a lively 90-95 mph fastball with downhill plane. His curveball can be a power hook in the low 80s that comes out of the same line of his fastball and disappears to get swings and misses, though it gets slurvy and is still inconsistent. He has shown feel for a changeup with solid fade but doesn't use it frequently. Chaffee's command and control are still below-average, and he gets in trouble when he leaves the ball up. He works quickly with a high-effort delivery. Chaffee has the stuff to carve out a role in middle relief and could get his chance to make his big league debut in 2013. However, the Angels opted not to protect him on their 40-man roster during the offseason.

Year	Club (League)	Class	W	L	ERA	G	GS	CG	SV	IP	H	HR	BB	SO	K/9	WHIP	AVG
2008	Did Not Play—Injured																
2009	Cedar Rapids (MWL)	LoA	8	8	4.33	23	23	0	0	116	84	6	65	121	9.4	1.28	.206
2010	R. Cucamonga (CAL)	HiA	7	6	6.36	20	20	0	0	105	126	13	46	83	7.1	1.64	.301
2011	Inland Empire (CAL)	HiA	2	10	7.26	30	14	0	0	97	114	11	48	87	8.1	1.68	.284
	Salt Lake (PCL)	AAA	1	1	6.52	4	1	0	0	10	13	3	4	8	7.4	1.76	.317
2012	Inland Empire (CAL)	HiA	2	0	2.38	18	0	0	7	23	17	2	9	28	11.1	1.15	.218
	Arkansas (TL)	AA	5	1	2.72	37	0	0	0	43	24	3	27	56	11.7	1.19	.164
Minor League Totals			25	26	5.36	132	58	0	7	393	378	38	199	383	8.8	1.47	.253

14 ERIC STAMETS, SS

BA GRADE
50
HIGH

Born: Sept. 25, 1991. **B-T:** R-R. **Ht.:** 6-0. **Wt.:** 185. **Drafted:** Evansville, 2012 (6th round). **Signed by:** John Burden.

Stamets was one of the best defensive shortstops in college baseball in 2012, though concerns about his bat dropped him to the sixth round, where he signed for $169,000. He makes all the routine plays with excellent hands, clean footwork and a solid arm. He's also a plus-plus runner whose speed and first-step quickness give him the range to make spectacular plays. He's especially good on balls to his right, showing the ability to jump and make a throw from deep in the hole. He's more athletic and explosive than Andrew Romine, another plus defender at shortstop in the system. While Stamets' defense gets glowing reviews, his bat is a huge question mark. He has good hand-eye coordination and doesn't strike out excessively, but there's funkiness to his swing and he rolls over a lot of balls because he tries to hook them rather than use the whole field. He has limited power, and some scouts are concerned he won't be able to catch up to good fastballs as he moves up the system. He could hit for a decent average while providing little in the way of on-base or slugging percentage. Stamets held his own offensively against low Class A pitching in his pro debut, so he'll move up to high Class A this year.

Year	Club (League)	Class	AVG	G	AB	R	H	2B	3B	HR	RBI	BB	SO	SB	CS	OBP	SLG
2012	Cedar Rapids (MWL)	LoA	.274	62	248	34	68	13	1	1	20	15	35	7	2	.323	.347
Minor League Totals			.274	62	248	34	68	13	1	1	20	15	35	7	2	.323	.347

15 REID SCOGGINS, RHP

BA GRADE
50
EXTREME

Born: July 18, 1990. **B-T:** R-R. **Ht.:** 6-3. **Wt.:** 210. **Drafted:** Howard (Texas) JC, 2012 (15th round). **Signed by:** Rudy Vasquez.

After Scoggins missed the 2011 season because of Tommy John surgery, area scouts made their way to Howard (Texas) JC last spring when word spread that he was hitting triple digits with his fastball. He pitched just 20 innings out of the bullpen, so he fell to the Angels in the 15th round, where they signed him for $100,000. He struck out 34 of the 78 batters he faced in the Rookie-level Arizona League, though he also walked nearly a batter per inning in his pro debut. Scoggins' fastball will range from 91-100 mph, and he usually works at 95-97. His slider has the potential to become an average or better pitch, but it's slurvy and he needs to improve the timing of his delivery when he throws it. He also has a rudimentary changeup but rarely throws it. Scoggins has a huge amount of effort in his delivery, including a pronounced head whack when he finishes that impedes his control. Even coming out of the bullpen, he'll need to refine his mechanics so he can be around the strike zone more often. He'll open his first full pro season where he ended his debut, in low Class A.

Year	Club (League)	Class	W	L	ERA	G	GS	CG	SV	IP	H	HR	BB	SO	K/9	WHIP	AVG
2012	Angels (AZL)	R	1	0	4.24	15	0	0	0	17	13	0	14	34	18.0	1.59	.210
	Cedar Rapids (MWL)	LoA	0	0	5.40	3	0	0	0	3	3	0	4	7	18.9	2.10	.231
Minor League Totals			1	0	4.43	18	0	0	0	20	16	0	18	41	18.1	1.67	.213

16 YENCY ALMONTE, RHP

BA GRADE
50
EXTREME

Born: June 4, 1994. **B-T:** B-R. **Ht.:** 6-4. **Wt.:** 185. **Drafted:** HS—Miami, 2012 (17th round). **Signed by:** Ralph Reyes.

The younger brother of Mariners minor league outfielder Denny Almonte, Yency generated attention early in the 2012 high school season before a dead arm cost him several weeks. Hamstrung by the loss of their first two picks as free-agent compensation and a $1.6 million bonus pool for the first 10 rounds, the Angels looked for ways to add extra talent in the draft. They grabbed Almonte in the 17th round and signed him for $250,000, though he had a setback with his shoulder after turning pro and pitched just three innings. He has an athletic, projectable frame and fires low-90s fastballs that have reached as high as 94 mph. He has feel for spinning the ball and threw a three-quarters breaking ball for strikes during instructional league. He's working on a changeup but hasn't used it much yet. Almonte doesn't have much pitching experience and he comes with durability concerns, but he has become a favorite of some club officials among the newer players in the system.

Year	Club (League)	Class	W	L	ERA	G	GS	CG	SV	IP	H	HR	BB	SO	K/9	WHIP	AVG
2012	Angels (AZL)	R	0	0	6.00	3	0	0	0	3	5	0	1	0	0.0	2.00	.357
Minor League Totals			0	0	6.00	3	0	0	0	3	5	0	1	0	0.0	2.00	.357

17 LUIS JIMENEZ, 3B

BA GRADE
45
MEDIUM

Born: Jan. 18, 1988. **B-T:** R-R. **Ht.:** 6-1. **Wt.:** 205. **Signed:** Dominican Republic, 2005. **Signed by:** Leo Perez.

Jimenez may not always look pretty, but he has been a productive offensive player who has hit for average and power at every level of the minors. He has solid raw power, though there are questions about how much he'll be able to get to it at the big league level. He takes an uppercut swing and gets pull-conscious, which limits his coverage of the outer half of the plate. The biggest thing holding Jimenez back is his pitch selection. He's a free swinger who doesn't walk much and chases borderline pitches instead of waiting for something he can drive. Despite having below-average speed, he has stolen at least 15 bases in each of the last three seasons. He takes pride in being an aggressive baserunner with good instincts. Jimenez has an average arm, but his footwork costs him accuracy on his throws and his limited range makes him a below-average third baseman. He's a good teammate, though Angels personnel have met with him to improve his focus on the field. Jimenez may get a chance to make his big league debut in 2013, but he also has Kaleb Cowart breathing down his neck at third base.

Year	Club (League)	Class	AVG	G	AB	R	H	2B	3B	HR	RBI	BB	SO	SB	CS	OBP	SLG
2006	Angels (DSL)	R	.284	25	74	12	21	9	1	1	10	7	9	4	0	.341	.473
2007	Angels (DSL)	R	.313	67	256	49	80	19	2	11	55	10	27	16	4	.347	.531
2008	Orem (PIO)	R	.331	66	284	57	94	28	6	15	65	11	45	6	2	.361	.630
2009	Did Not Play—Injured																
2010	Cedar Rapids (MWL)	LoA	.292	43	168	32	49	15	5	2	38	11	27	6	2	.332	.476
	R. Cucamonga (CAL)	HiA	.286	81	318	52	91	31	4	12	43	13	43	15	8	.324	.522
2011	Arkansas (TL)	AA	.290	125	490	62	142	40	1	18	94	27	72	15	6	.335	.486
2012	Salt Lake (PCL)	AAA	.309	122	485	78	150	38	2	16	85	19	70	17	7	.334	.495
Minor League Totals			.302	529	2075	342	627	180	21	75	390	98	293	79	29	.338	.518

18 VICTOR ALCANTARA, RHP

BA GRADE
50
EXTREME

Born: April 3, 1993. **B-T:** R-R. **Ht.:** 6-2. **Wt.:** 190. **Signed:** Dominican Republic, 2011. **Signed by:** Roman Ocumarez.

Martin Alcantara signed with the Indians in February 2011, four months before his younger brother agreed to a $174,000 bonus with the Angels. Victor was attractive because he was an 18-year-old with a projectable, athletic frame and a fastball that touched 93 mph. He since has morphed into a power arm, hitting 96 the winter after he signed and reaching 100 during his 2012 pro debut. Alcantara has a quick arm and a durable body, which allows him to hold mid-90s velocity deep into outings. He features a pure power approach, backing up his heater with an 86-88 mph slider. He's still learning a changeup, which won't get better unless he uses it more frequently. His control still needs a lot of work, and it could improve if the Angels succeed in smoothing out his delivery. If he can't develop an offspeed pitch and throw more strikes, Alcantara might not be more than a late-inning reliever, but he's still young and the Angels will develop him as a slider. They may challenge him with an assignment beyond the Arizona League in 2013.

Year	Club (League)	Class	W	L	ERA	G	GS	CG	SV	IP	H	HR	BB	SO	K/9	WHIP	AVG
2012	Angels (DSL)	R	5	4	2.13	14	14	0	0	72	51	0	40	77	9.6	1.26	.199
Minor League Totals			5	4	2.13	14	14	0	0	72	51	0	40	77	9.6	1.26	.199

19 JOSE RONDON, SS

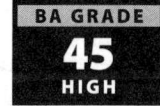

BA GRADE
45
HIGH

Born: March 3, 1994. **B-T:** R-R. **Ht.:** 6-1. **Wt.:** 180. **Signed:** Venezuela, 2011. **Signed by:** Lebi Ochoa.

After signing for $70,000 in January 2011, Rondon had a strong pro debut in the Rookie-level Dominican Summer League. When he arrived in spring training last year, the organization game him a mandate to get bigger. He responded by going from 160 to 180 pounds by the end of the year while holding his own at the plate. Rondon is young, raw and aggressive. He has good bat-to-ball ability and loves to hit the fastball, though he's too much of a free swinger right now and often goes after the first fastball he sees. Though he has gotten stronger, he still has minimal power. He's also a fringy runner, so his offensive contributions may be limited to his batting average. Rondon shows flashes of becoming a solid shortstop with a strong arm and reliable hands. He still gets caught on his heels and gets poor jumps on balls, and he tries to make too many routine plays look flashy. If he outgrows shortstop, he might have to slide over to third base, and his bat wouldn't profile well there. Rondon has a realistic ceiling of a utilityman, though he'll have to show more impact with the bat and slow the game down to get there. The Angels plan to push some of their players more aggressively than they have in the past, so Rondon could jump to low Class A in 2013.

Year	Club (League)	Class	AVG	G	AB	R	H	2B	3B	HR	RBI	BB	SO	SB	CS	OBP	SLG
2011	Angels (DSL)	R	.315	49	165	28	52	11	2	0	21	17	16	9	4	.378	.406
2012	Angels (AZL)	R	.260	48	192	26	50	13	2	1	20	14	24	5	5	.314	.365
	Orem (PIO)	R	.300	6	20	4	6	1	1	0	1	2	3	1	0	.348	.450
Minor League Totals			.286	103	377	58	108	25	5	1	42	33	43	15	9	.344	.387

20 DANIEL TILLMAN, RHP

Born: March 14, 1989. **B-T:** R-R. **Ht.:** 6-1. **Wt.:** 205. **Drafted:** Florida Southern, 2010 (2nd round). **Signed by:** Tom Kotchman.

BA GRADE
45
HIGH

After he cruised through the lower minors in his first two pro seasons, Tillman was a major disappointment in 2012. Pushed to Double-A after spending most of the previous year in low Class A, he showed a power arm but little feel for the strike zone. He recorded a 12.10 ERA and 19 walks in 19 innings, necessitating a demotion to high Class A, where he managed to have success in the second half. Tillman's fastball operates at 92-95 mph and gets as high as 98 mph. His heater has occasional sink, though some scouts think it's too flat. His No. 2 pitch is a below-average slider that lacks depth and can get slurvy. Tillman has high-effort mechanics and struggles to find his release point, which leads to erratic control. He's an emotional pitcher, and once he starts to struggle, he gets rattled and lets the game speed up on him. His velocity makes him an intriguing bullpen possibility, but he still has plenty of adjustments before he can help the Angels. He'll take another shot at Double-A in 2013.

Year	Club (League)	Class	W	L	ERA	G	GS	CG	SV	IP	H	HR	BB	SO	K/9	WHIP	AVG
2010	Orem (PIO)	R	2	2	1.95	22	0	0	10	32	23	0	10	50	13.9	1.02	.195
2011	Cedar Rapids (MWL)	LoA	5	3	2.04	36	5	0	12	66	53	1	32	70	9.5	1.28	.218
	Inland Empire (CAL)	HiA	1	0	4.50	7	0	0	2	8	7	1	2	8	9.0	1.13	.212
2012	Arkansas (TL)	AA	1	5	12.10	20	0	0	0	19	23	3	19	21	9.8	2.17	.303
	Inland Empire (CAL)	HiA	1	1	1.88	22	0	0	8	24	10	0	14	31	11.6	1.00	.127
Minor League Totals			10	11	3.42	107	5	0	32	150	116	5	77	180	10.8	1.29	.211

21 ANDREW ROMINE, INF

Born: Dec. 24, 1985. **B-T:** L-R. **Ht.:** 6-1. **Wt.:** 190. **Drafted:** Arizona State, 2007 (5th round). **Signed by:** John Gracio.

BA GRADE
40
LOW

Romine comes from a baseball family. His father Kevin played for the Red Sox for seven seasons, while his brother Austin is a Yankees catching prospect who has played briefly in the big leagues. Andrew has had short stints in the majors in each of the last three seasons, thanks to his defensive ability. He's a quality shortstop who can play anywhere in the infield with his solid range, clean hands and plus arm with tremendous accuracy from an over-the-top slot. He's an excellent decision-maker in the field and has a knack for taking advantage of baserunners' mistakes. Romine's athleticism works well in the field but doesn't carry over to the batter's box. He gave up switch-hitting last year to bat exclusively lefthanded, but the results weren't noticeably different. Romine has good hand-eye coordination and strong hands, but his bat speed is fringy, his power is limited and he doesn't hit the ball hard. He has a simple, no-stride approach yet deviates from his plan at the plate too often. He's an average runner and bunts well. With Maicer Izturis signing with the Blue Jays as a free agent in the offseason, the door is open for Romine to show he can fill a utility spot at the big league level.

Year	Club (League)	Class	AVG	G	AB	R	H	2B	3B	HR	RBI	BB	SO	SB	CS	OBP	SLG
2007	Orem (PIO)	R	.286	56	231	38	66	6	6	5	35	16	38	12	4	.337	.429
2008	Cedar Rapids (MWL)	LoA	.260	126	461	79	120	21	4	2	34	55	76	62	18	.347	.336
2009	R. Cucamonga (CAL)	HiA	.278	131	479	68	133	13	9	1	36	51	83	26	11	.351	.349
2010	Arkansas (TL)	AA	.282	106	383	55	108	15	4	3	34	50	66	21	9	.370	.366
	Los Angeles (AL)	MAJ	.091	5	11	0	1	0	0	0	0	0	4	0	0	.091	.091
2011	Salt Lake (PCL)	AAA	.281	105	381	67	107	9	2	4	35	45	87	23	6	.363	.346
	Los Angeles (AL)	MAJ	.125	10	16	2	2	0	0	0	0	1	6	1	0	.176	.125
2012	Salt Lake (PCL)	AAA	.285	87	351	57	100	11	7	4	39	24	46	23	10	.336	.390
	Los Angeles (AL)	MAJ	.412	12	17	2	7	0	0	0	1	3	3	1	0	.500	.412
Major League Totals			.227	27	44	4	10	0	0	0	1	4	13	2	0	.292	.227
Minor League Totals			.277	611	2286	364	634	75	32	19	213	241	396	167	58	.352	.363

22 ARJENIS FERNANDEZ, RHP

Born: July 29, 1993. **B-T:** R-R. **Ht.:** 6-4. **Wt.:** 195. **Signed:** Dominican Republic, 2011. **Signed by:** Roman Ocumarez.

BA GRADE
50
EXTREME

The Angels worked on a restricted budget during Marc Russo's brief tenure as international scouting director, but he and his staff managed to find a few intriguing arms. One of those is Fernandez, who signed for $150,000 out of the Dominican Republic in August 2011 at age 18. After he impressed the Angels during the club's Dominican winter program, they decided to start him in the Dominican Summer League and bring him to the United States as soon as the Arizona League season began. Fernandez has a big frame and comes straight over the top with a fastball that sits at 89-92 mph and touches 94. He flashes some feel for his 74-77 mph curveball and maintains his arm speed on his changeup, though he doesn't miss many bats yet. He has a sound delivery. While he doesn't project to match the velocity of fellow 2011 Dominican signee Victor Alcantara, Fernandez has a wider array of pitches and a better chance to remain a starter. The Angels gave him a start in low Class A at the end of last season and could push him there in 2013.

Year	Club (League)	Class	W	L	ERA	G	GS	CG	SV	IP	H	HR	BB	SO	K/9	WHIP	AVG
2012	Angels (DSL)	R	1	0	2.57	3	3	0	0	14	7	0	7	10	6.4	1.00	.156
	Angels (AZL)	R	3	2	4.68	13	12	0	0	60	56	5	22	33	5.0	1.31	.248
	Cedar Rapids (MWL)	LoA	0	1	16.20	1	1	0	0	3	5	1	3	3	8.1	2.40	.357
Minor League Totals			4	3	4.79	17	16	0	0	77	68	6	32	46	5.4	1.30	.239

23 EDUAR LOPEZ, RHP

BA GRADE

50

EXTREME

Born: Feb. 1, 1995. **B-T:** R-R. **Ht.:** 6-0. **Wt.:** 180. Signed: Dominican Republic, 2012. **Signed by:** Roman Ocumarez.

Lopez signed out of the Dominican Republic last year for just $45,000, but he made a strong impression during his pro debut. He ranked third in the Dominican Summer League with 83 strikeouts and would have ranked first with 14.0 whiffs per nine innings if he had enough innings to qualify. Lopez has a compact frame and an 89-91 mph fastball that he can get up to 93 mph and throw for strikes. He has a mid-70s curveball with quick break and solid depth, and DSL hitters often swung over it or froze up when he threw it. Like most pitchers with his experience level, he's still learning a changeup. A pleasant surprise in 2012, he'll head to the Arizona League this year.

Year	Club (League)	Class	W	L	ERA	G	GS	CG	SV	IP	H	HR	BB	SO	K/9	WHIP	AVG
2012	Angels (DSL)	R	2	1	3.54	12	11	0	0	53	42	5	23	83	14.0	1.22	.212
Minor League Totals			2	1	3.54	12	11	0	0	53	42	5	23	83	14.0	1.22	.212

24 TRAVIS WITHERSPOON, OF

BA GRADE

45

HIGH

Born: April 16, 1989. **B-T:** R-R. **Ht.:** 6-2. **Wt.:** 190. **Drafted:** Spartanburg Methodist (S.C.) JC, 2009 (12th round). **Signed by:** Chris McAlpin.

The Angels knew Witherspoon was a raw project who might not hit when they signed him for $100,000 as a 12th-rounder in 2009, but they were drawn to his speed and athleticism. Four years later, his profile is still much the same. He posted an .869 OPS in high Class A during the first two months of the 2012 season, but his offense cratered when he got to Double-A. Witherspoon has a quick bat and is at his best when he uses the whole field. He doesn't often stay with that approach, however. He has below-average power, yet he still takes a big swing and his barrel doesn't spend much time in the hitting zone. After he got to Arkansas, he chased too many pitches and had trouble recognizing breaking balls, an issue he's had since signing. Witherspoon's carrying tool is his above-average speed. He gets great jumps off the bat and takes good routes on flyballs, making him a plus defender in center field with an average arm. He also has stolen bases at an 83 percent success rate. Mike Trout is about as big a roadblock as there could be, though Witherspoon still needs to prove he can hit enough to get to the big leagues. The Angels still believe in his upside and protected him on their 40-man roster in November.

Year	Club (League)	Class	AVG	G	AB	R	H	2B	3B	HR	RBI	BB	SO	SB	CS	OBP	SLG
2009	Angels (AZL)	R	.231	5	13	2	3	1	0	0	1	3	0	0		.286	.308
	Orem (PIO)	R	.227	58	194	37	44	3	6	6	26	10	61	10	1	.281	.397
2010	Orem (PIO)	R	.309	71	288	57	89	11	3	10	45	24	73	20	0	.365	.472
2011	Cedar Rapids (MWL)	LoA	.245	102	404	60	99	16	4	12	42	36	103	44	9	.313	.394
	Inland Empire (CAL)	HiA	.279	16	68	15	19	4	0	1	10	5	14	2	2	.338	.382
2012	Inland Empire (CAL)	HiA	.319	67	270	52	86	10	5	7	27	33	52	25	7	.399	.470
	Arkansas (TL)	AA	.202	54	208	28	42	9	2	6	21	24	54	9	4	.286	.351
Minor League Totals			.264	373	1445	251	382	54	20	42	171	133	360	110	23	.332	.417

25 RYAN BRASIER, RHP

BA GRADE

40

MEDIUM

Born: Aug. 26, 1987. **B-T:** R-R. **Ht.:** 6-0. **Wt.:** 205. **Drafted:** Weatherford (Texas) JC, 2007 (6th round). **Signed by:** Arnold Brathwaite.

A high school catcher, Brasier moved to the mound when he got to Weatherford (Texas) JC. He pitched his way into the sixth round of the 2007 draft and began his pro career as a reliever. The Angels tried to make him a starter in 2009-10, but he was ill-suited for the role and moved back to the bullpen in 2011. While Brasier has yet to dominate as a pro, he does have a fastball that can range from 92-96 mph with late hop and run. His secondary pitches are what hold him back. He flashes an average slider, but it doesn't have a lot of depth so he doesn't miss many bats. His changeup is well below-average, and he throws it only occasionally against lefthanders. Brasier has a stocky build, stabs in the back of his arm action and has effort in his delivery, so his command never has been a strong suit. He'll need a more consistent slider and better location for his pitches before he's ready for a big league callup, which could come this season. The Angels added him to the 40-man roster in November.

Year	Club (League)	Class	W	L	ERA	G	GS	CG	SV	IP	H	HR	BB	SO	K/9	WHIP	AVG
2007	Orem (PIO)	R	1	2	2.08	26	0	0	9	30	22	2	7	26	7.7	0.96	.212

Year	Club (League)	Class	W	L	ERA	G	GS	CG	SV	IP	H	HR	BB	SO	K/9	WHIP	AVG
2008	Cedar Rapids (MWL)	LoA	1	3	1.59	23	0	0	9	28	22	0	14	24	7.6	1.27	.210
	Angels (AZL)	R	1	0	3.86	4	0	0	1	5	3	0	1	2	3.9	0.86	.188
	R. Cucamonga (CAL)	HiA	0	0	2.70	3	0	0	1	3	3	0	2	0	0.0	1.50	.300
2009	Arkansas (TL)	AA	2	1	5.56	8	0	0	2	11	13	1	7	6	4.8	1.76	.283
	R. Cucamonga (CAL)	HiA	5	4	5.23	27	14	0	0	98	103	17	32	93	8.5	1.38	.270
2010	Arkansas (TL)	AA	7	12	5.07	28	23	1	0	142	127	28	68	94	6.0	1.37	.242
2011	Arkansas (TL)	AA	0	1	0.71	25	0	0	16	25	18	1	14	26	9.2	1.26	.198
	Salt Lake (PCL)	AAA	2	1	5.00	25	0	0	3	27	26	2	9	26	8.7	1.30	.257
2012	Salt Lake (PCL)	AAA	7	3	4.37	55	0	0	13	60	66	1	24	54	8.1	1.51	.286
Minor League Totals			26	27	4.29	224	37	1	54	430	403	52	178	351	7.3	1.35	.250

26 STEVEN GELTZ, RHP

BA GRADE
40
MEDIUM

Born: Nov. 1, 1987. **B-T:** R-R. **Ht.:** 5-10. **Wt.:** 170. **Signed:** Buffalo, NDFA 2008.
Signed by: Greg Morhardt.

Signed as a nondrafted free agent in 2008, Geltz made his major league debut last season and became the first Buffalo player in the big leagues since Joe Hesketh wrapped up an 11-year career in 1994. There's not much that jumps out about Geltz, yet he has averaged 12.1 strikeouts per nine innings in the minors. He keeps hitters off balance with a lot of deception from a high three-quarters arm slot. Talent evaluators use words like "fearless," "moxie" and "bulldog" to describe Geltz, who attacks hitters mostly with a 91-94 mph fastball that features late hop. He locates his fastball well on the outside corner against lefthanders, but his control is no better than average. He's had a lot of success with mostly one pitch, though he does flash an average breaking ball and mixes in an occasional splitter. Geltz has a middle-relief ceiling, and there's still concern that his smoke-and-mirrors act might not work against big leaguers.

Year	Club (League)	Class	W	L	ERA	G	GS	CG	SV	IP	H	HR	BB	SO	K/9	WHIP	AVG
2008	Angels (AZL)	R	1	0	3.86	3	0	0	0	2	3	0	0	7	27.0	1.29	.300
	Orem (PIO)	R	1	0	6.15	16	0	0	0	26	31	4	9	36	12.3	1.52	.295
2009	R. Cucamonga (CAL)	HiA	7	1	3.76	34	0	0	0	65	52	7	32	73	10.2	1.30	.225
2010	R. Cucamonga (CAL)	HiA	3	1	3.44	22	0	0	2	34	20	4	10	51	13.5	0.88	.167
	Arkansas (TL)	AA	1	0	2.41	16	0	0	0	19	9	0	16	36	17.4	1.34	.145
2011	Salt Lake (PCL)	AAA	0	0	21.60	2	0	0	0	2	4	0	2	1	5.4	3.60	.444
	Arkansas (TL)	AA	3	3	3.09	32	0	0	0	47	31	5	14	67	12.9	0.96	.190
2012	Arkansas (TL)	AA	3	0	0.36	21	0	0	6	25	13	0	6	37	13.1	0.75	.148
	Salt Lake (PCL)	AAA	0	1	5.08	25	0	0	0	5	34	29	4	14	33	8.8	1.28	.236
	Los Angeles (AL)	MAJ	0	0	4.50	2	0	0	0	2	2	0	3	1	4.5	2.50	.286
Major League Totals			0	0	4.50	2	0	0	0	2	2	0	3	1	4.5	2.50	.286
Minor League Totals			19	6	3.69	171	0	0	13	253	192	24	103	341	12.1	1.16	.211

27 DREW TAYLOR, LHP

BA GRADE
40
MEDIUM

Born: Aug. 18, 1986. **B-T:** R-L. **Ht.:** 6-2. **Wt.:** 195. **Drafted:** North Carolina State, 2008 (34th round). **Signed by:** Chris McAlpin.

Taylor made only one start in three years at North Carolina State, but the Angels tinkered with him in that role here and there over parts of his first four pro seasons after signing him for $45,000 as a 34th-round pick. He got hammered as a starter in Double-A in 2011, so they moved him back to the bullpen full-time last season and he got to the majors for three appearances in September. Taylor has a high-effort delivery, but his game is more about keeping hitters off balance than power. His fastball sits around 88-89 mph and touches 91. He can get sink and tail on his fastball, but when he leaves it up it flattens out and gets pounded. Taylor likes to pitch backward by leaning on his slider, an average pitch with late break. He has a changeup but rarely uses it because it doesn't have enough separation from his fastball to be effective. Taylor struggled with his control both in Triple-A and the big leagues, and he'll have to throw more strikes to carve out a role as a situational lefty.

Year	Club (League)	Class	W	L	ERA	G	GS	CG	SV	IP	H	HR	BB	SO	K/9	WHIP	AVG
2008	Orem (PIO)	R	2	1	4.37	21	3	0	5	35	33	4	13	39	10.0	1.31	.248
2009	R. Cucamonga (CAL)	HiA	1	0	9.53	5	0	0	0	6	8	2	8	8	12.7	2.82	.320
	Cedar Rapids (MWL)	LoA	3	0	1.23	40	0	0	8	51	29	0	19	83	14.6	0.94	.166
2010	R. Cucamonga (CAL)	HiA	4	1	2.06	20	0	0	0	35	24	1	14	39	10.0	1.09	.186
	Arkansas (TL)	AA	1	3	4.70	15	4	0	0	38	38	2	18	21	4.9	1.46	.264
2011	Arkansas (TL)	AA	2	11	5.14	29	19	0	0	112	125	13	71	73	5.9	1.75	.287
2012	Arkansas (TL)	AA	2	4	4.61	37	0	0	2	41	44	4	14	39	8.6	1.41	.273
	Salt Lake (PCL)	AAA	1	0	3.50	16	0	0	0	18	16	3	11	17	8.5	1.50	.229
	Los Angeles (AL)	MAJ	0	0	11.57	3	0	0	0	2	3	0	4	0	0.0	3.00	.300
Major League Totals			0	0	11.57	3	0	0	0	2	3	0	4	0	0.0	3.00	.300
Minor League Totals			16	20	4.01	183	26	0	15	336	317	29	168	319	8.5	1.44	.249

28 CAM BEDROSIAN, RHP

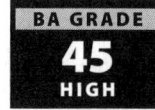

BA GRADE
45
HIGH

Born: Oct. 2, 1991. **B-T:** R-R. **Ht.:** 6-0. **Wt.:** 205. **Drafted:** HS—Sharpsburg, Ga., **2010 (1st round). Signed by:** Chris McAlpin.

Steve Bedrosian won the National League Cy Young Award in 1987. Twenty-three years later, the Angels drafted his son Cam 29th overall and signed him for $1,116,000. He came down with a sore elbow a month after turning pro and had Tommy John surgery in May 2011. He returned to the mound last May in low Class A, but he struggled with his stuff and control, failing to make it out of the third inning in several outings. Bedrosian's fastball touched 96 mph in high school, but his arm wasn't as quick last year and his fastball varied from 87-94 mph. His curveball was big and loopy and often missed the strike zone, so he tinkered with a slider at the end of the year. He didn't get much of a chance to work on his raw changeup because he fell behind in the count too often. If there was a positive to his trying 2012 season, it was that Bedrosian stayed healthy, though he understandably tired toward the end. He's at a crossroads as he enters the 2013 season, and he could wind up in the bullpen if he can't regain his high school form. He'll probably return to Cedar Rapids.

Year	Club (League)	Class	W	L	ERA	G	GS	CG	SV	IP	H	HR	BB	SO	K/9	WHIP	AVG
2010	Angels (AZL)	R	0	2	4.50	5	4	0	0	12	13	0	7	10	7.5	1.67	.283
2011	Did Not Play—Injured																
2012	Cedar Rapids (MWL)	LoA	3	11	6.31	21	21	0	0	83	91	5	52	48	5.2	1.73	.286
Minor League Totals			3	13	6.08	26	25	0	0	95	104	5	59	58	5.5	1.72	.286

29 KEVIN JOHNSON, RHP

BA GRADE
40
MEDIUM

Born: Aug. 19, 1988. **B-T:** L-R. **Ht.:** 6-4. **Wt.:** 240. **Drafted:** West Florida, 2010 (20th round). **Signed by:** Tom Kotchman.

Johnson went undrafted out of high school, two years at Alabama Southern CC and after his first year at NCAA Division II West Florida. After his senior season ended, he pitched two games with the independent Pensacola Pelicans (American Association) before the Angels took him in the 20th round of the 2010 draft and signed him for $2,000. He reached Triple-A two years later and is on track to possibly make his major league debut in 2013. Johnson succeeded in college with a high-80s sinker that touched 91 mph, but he has added velocity in pro ball. His fastball now ranges anywhere from 88-96 mph and still features the heavy sink that results in an abundance of groundballs. He mostly gets by on one pitch, as his slider is a fringy offering without much depth. He averaged just 4.4 strikeouts per nine innings last season, so the development of his slider will be key. He has a lot of effort in his delivery, but he still throws plenty of strikes. If he can find a way to miss a few more bats, he could earn a middle-relief job with the Angels.

Year	Club (League)	Class	W	L	ERA	G	GS	CG	SV	IP	H	HR	BB	SO	K/9	WHIP	AVG
2010	Pensacola (A-A)	IND	0	1	22.85	2	1	0	0	4	12	1	9	3	6.2	4.85	—
	Orem (PIO)	R	1	4	4.75	18	9	0	0	61	71	3	24	44	6.5	1.57	.293
2011	Cedar Rapids (MWL)	LoA	1	1	3.38	12	0	0	4	13	9	1	4	9	6.1	0.98	.200
	Inland Empire (CAL)	HiA	3	2	3.33	33	0	0	5	51	52	6	16	42	7.4	1.32	.260
2012	Arkansas (TL)	AA	1	4	2.37	36	0	0	16	38	35	3	11	18	4.3	1.21	.250
	Salt Lake (PCL)	AAA	1	2	5.68	20	0	0	2	25	37	4	5	13	4.6	1.66	.349
Minor League Totals			7	13	3.91	119	9	0	27	189	204	17	60	126	6.0	1.40	.278

30 MICHAEL ROTH, LHP

BA GRADE
45
HIGH

Born: Feb. 15, 1990. **B-T:** L-L. **Ht.:** 6-1. **Wt.:** 210. **Drafted:** South Carolina, 2012 (9th round). **Signed by:** Brandon McArthur.

On pure stuff, Roth would just be another arm in the organization, a senior sign who saved money in the ninth round with his $20,000 bonus. But his stellar college track record and performance on college baseball's biggest stage are hard to ignore. A reliever for most of his first two seasons at South Carolina, he made his first two starts (including a shutout of Clemson) at the 2010 College World Series as the Gamecocks won their first national championship. As a junior, he topped NCAA Division I in wins (14-3) and ERA (1.06) as South Carolina repeated as national champions. He led the Gamecocks to a national runner-up finish in 2012, setting career CWS records for starts (eight) and innings (60) while ranking second in wins (four) and fifth in ERA (1.49). While scouts respect what Roth did in college, there are obvious questions about how well his skill set will translate to pro ball. He has outstanding savvy, but his fastball parks around the mid-80s and peaks at 89 mph. He has a deceptive delivery, varies his arm angles and moves the ball around the strike zone. His best pitch is his changeup, which has deep action and late sink. He mixes in an upper-70s slider, can bust cutters in on the hands of righthanders and throws an occasional slow curve. His funkiness could work in relief, where he doesn't have to get through a lineup multiple times. He could begin his first full year in high Class A because he'll be 23.

Year	Club (League)	Class	W	L	ERA	G	GS	CG	SV	IP	H	HR	BB	SO	K/9	WHIP	AVG
2012	Orem (PIO)	R	0	2	4.91	11	9	0	0	22	23	2	11	21	8.6	1.55	.274
Minor League Totals			0	2	4.91	11	9	0	0	22	23	2	11	21	8.6	1.55	.274

Los Angeles Dodgers

BY JIM SHONERD

What a difference a year makes. The Dodgers have gone from the thriftiness and legal battles of the Frank McCourt era to buying the biggest houses in Beverly Hills, with no signs of slowing down.

After two years of watching McCourt's ownership spiral downward, the Dodgers finally began turning the page when he agreed to sell the team via bankruptcy auction in November 2011. In late March 2012, it was announced that Guggenheim Baseball Management won control of the team, beating out Dallas Mavericks owner Mark Cuban among others.

GBM bid $2.15 billion for the Dodgers, obliterating the U.S. sports record of $1.1 billion the Miami Dolphins went for in 2009. The group, which is led by Mark Walter and also includes Los Angeles Lakers icon Magic Johnson and former Braves and Nationals president Stan Kasten, figures to make back its money with a proposed deal to start a new regional sports network that will be worth an estimated $6 billion.

Money has been flowing freely since the sale. No longer shackled by McCourt's financial limitations, the Dodgers have most decidedly entered win-now mode.

General manager Ned Colletti went all-out to fortify the big league roster during the season, making a pair of blockbuster trades. He picked up Hanley Ramirez and the $36.5 million remaining on his contract from the Marlins in late July, then took on $261 million in salary commitments by acquiring Josh Beckett, Carl Crawford and Adrian Gonzalez from the Red Sox in August.

The moves didn't pan out, at least not in 2012. Los Angeles held first place in the National League West as late as Aug. 19, but went 19-21 the rest of the way to finish with 86 wins, eight fewer than the Giants. Undaunted, the Dodgers kept spending.

In early December, Los Angeles signed Korean lefthander Hyun-Jin Ryu for six years and $36 million and also paid his former team a $25,737,737.33 posting fee. On the same weekend, the Dodgers made Zack Greinke the second highest-paid pitcher ever with a six-year, $147 million deal. The club is poised to open 2013 with a big league payroll north of $210 million.

With Los Angeles locked into veterans up and down the roster, opportunities for young players look limited in the immediate future. In all, the Dodgers

The Dodgers' new financial might allowed them to add players like Adrian Gonzalez

LARRY GOREN

sent 12 prospects or young big leaguers away in various trades in 2012, with first baseman James Loney the only true veteran shipped out. The list of the departed included talented righthanders Rubby de la Rosa, Nate Eovaldi, Ethan Martin and Allen Webster. Martin was a first-round pick in 2008, while Eovaldi and Webster both ranked among Los Angeles' top 10 prospects a year ago.

Still, the franchise's new wealth should trickle down to benefit player development. Though new rules prevented Los Angeles from spending freely in the draft, their $6.3 million in bonus expenditures represented a sizeable increase over the $3.5 million McCourt authorized in 2011. The Dodgers made a much bigger splash internationally in June, landing Cuban outfielder Yasiel Puig with a $42 million big league deal that shocked many clubs who were more skeptical of his ability.

Puig and first-round shortstop Corey Seager now rank as the best hitters in the system. Despite the departure of several valuable young arms via trades, the strength of system remains pitching, with seven hurlers among the top 10 prospects on this list. Ryu headlines an impressive crop of lefthanders that also features Chris Reed, Onelki Garcia and Paco Rodriguez, all premium picks from the last two drafts.

THIS YEAR'S TOP 30

Player, Pos.	Grade
1. Hyun-Jin Ryu, lhp	55/Low
2. Yasiel Puig, of	65/Extreme
3. Corey Seager, ss	55/High
4. Joc Pederson, of	55/High
5. Zach Lee, rhp	55/High
6. Chris Reed, lhp	55/High
7. Onelki Garcia, lhp	55/Extreme
8. Paco Rodriguez, lhp	45/Safe
9. Matt Magill, rhp	50/Medium
10. Ross Stripling, rhp	50/High
11. Alex Castellanos, 2b/3b/of	45/Low
12. Chris Withrow, rhp	50/High
13. Tim Federowicz, c	45/Low
14. Jesmuel Valentin, ss	50/High
15. Bobby Coyle, of	45/Medium
16. Scott Van Slyke, of/1b	45/Medium
17. Garrett Gould, rhp	50/High
18. Scott Griggs, rhp	50/Extreme
19. Zach Bird, rhp	50/Extreme
20. Josh Wall, rhp	45/Medium
21. Steve Ames, rhp	45/Medium
22. James Baldwin III, of	50/Extreme
23. Alex Santana, 3b	50/Extreme
24. Scott Barlow, rhp	50/Extreme
25. Angel Sanchez, rhp	50/Extreme
26. Brian Cavazos-Galvez, of	45/Medium
27. Aaron Miller, lhp	45/Medium
28. Blake Smith, of	45/Medium
29. Jeremy Rathjen, of	45/High
30. Joey Curletta, of	50/Extreme

LAST YEAR'S TOP 30

Player, Pos.	Status
1. Zach Lee, rhp	No. 5
2. Allen Webster, rhp	(Red Sox)
3. Nate Eovaldi, rhp	(Marlins)
4. Alfredo Silverio, of	(Marlins)
5. Chris Reed, lhp	No. 6
6. Garrett Gould, rhp	No. 17
7. Chris Withrow, rhp	No. 12
8. Josh Lindblom, rhp	(Rangers)
9. Joc Pederson, of	No. 4
10. Tim Federowicz, c	No. 13
11. James Baldwin III, of	No. 22
12. Angel Sanchez, rhp	No. 25
13. Jonathan Garcia, of	Dropped out
14. Scott Barlow, rhp	No. 24
15. Shawn Tolleson, rhp	Majors
16. Aaron Miller, lhp	No. 27
17. Ethan Martin, rhp	(Phillies)
18. Alex Santana, 3b	No. 23
19. Alex Castellanos, of	No. 11
20. Kyle Russell, of	Dropped out
21. Scott Van Slyke, of/1b	No. 16
22. Angelo Songco, of/1b	Dropped out
23. Ryan O'Sullivan, rhp	(Phillies)
24. Josh Wall, rhp	No. 20
25. Pratt Maynard, c	Dropped out
26. Ivan De Jesus Jr., inf	(Red Sox)
27. Jake Lemmerman, ss	Dropped out
28. Gorman Erickson, c	Dropped out
29. O'Koyea Dickson, 1b	Dropped out
30. Blake Smith, of	No. 28

BEST TOOLS

Best Hitter for Average	Corey Seager
Best Power Hitter	Yasiel Puig
Best Strike-Zone Discipline	Joc Pederson
Fastest Baserunner	James Baldwin III
Best Athlete	Yasiel Puig
Best Fastball	Chris Withrow
Best Curveball	Onelki Garcia
Best Slider	Chris Reed
Best Changeup	Zach Lee
Best Control	Hyun-Jin Ryu
Best Defensive Catcher	Tim Federowicz
Best Defensive Infielder	Jesmuel Valentin
Best Infield Arm	Jesmuel Valentin
Best Defensive Outfielder	Joc Pederson
Best Outfield Arm	Yasiel Puig

PROJECTED 2016 LINEUP

Catcher	Tim Federowicz
First Base	Adrian Gonzalez
Second Base	Jesmuel Valentin
Third Base	Corey Seager
Shortstop	Hanley Ramirez
Left Field	Andre Ethier
Center Field	Matt Kemp
Right Field	Yasiel Puig
No. 1 Starter	Clayton Kershaw
No. 2 Starter	Zack Greinke
No. 3 Starter	Hyun-Jin Ryu
No. 4 Starter	Zach Lee
No. 5 Starter	Chris Reed
Closer	Kenley Jansen

TOP PROSPECTS OF THE DECADE

Year	Player, Pos.	2012 Org.
2003	James Loney, 1b	Red Sox
2004	Edwin Jackson, rhp	Nationals
2005	Joel Guzman, ss/of	Laguna (Mexican)
2006	Chad Billingsley, rhp	Dodgers
2007	Andy LaRoche, 3b	Red Sox
2008	Clayton Kershaw, lhp	Dodgers
2009	Andrew Lambo, of	Pirates
2010	Dee Gordon, ss	Dodgers
2011	Dee Gordon, ss	Dodgers
2012	Zach Lee, rhp	Dodgers

TOP DRAFT PICKS OF THE DECADE

Year	Player, Pos.	2012 Org.
2003	Chad Billingsley, rhp	Dodgers
2004	Scott Elbert, rhp	Dodgers
2005	*Luke Hochevar, rhp (1st round supp.)	Royals
2006	Clayton Kershaw, lhp	Dodgers
2007	Chris Withrow, rhp	Dodgers
2008	Ethan Martin, rhp	Phillies
2009	Aaron Miller, lhp (1st round supp.)	Dodgers
2010	Zach Lee, rhp	Dodgers
2011	Chris Reed, lhp	Dodgers
2012	Corey Seager, ss	Dodgers

*Did not sign.

LARGEST BONUSES IN CLUB HISTORY

Yasiel Puig, 2012	$12,000,000
Hiroki Kuroda, 2007	$7,300,000
Zach Lee, 2010	$5,250,000
Hyun-Jin Ryu, 2012	$5,000,000
Corey Seager, 2012	$2,350,000

LOS ANGELES DODGERS

TOP 2013 ROOKIE: Hyun-Jin Ryu, rhp. The Dodgers spent $61.7 million to import the big Korean into the middle of their rotation.

BREAKOUT PROSPECT: Jeremy Rathjen, of. An 11th-round pick last year, he has the approach and all-around tools to move up quickly.

SLEEPER: Justin Chigbogu, 1b. A 2012 fourth-rounder who was an all-state defensive end, he has exciting power potential.

SOURCE OF TOP 30 TALENT

Homegrown	28	Acquired	2
College	10	Trades	2
Junior college	0	Rule 5 draft	0
High school	14	Independent leagues	0
Cuban/drafted	1	Free agents/waivers	0
International	3		

LF
Alex Castellanos (11)
Bobby Coyle (15)
Scott Van Slyke (16)
Brian Cavazos-Galvez (26)
Theo Alexander
Josh Henderson
Pat Stover

CF
Joc Pederson (4)
James Baldwin III (22)
Jeremy Rathjen (29)
Matt Angle
Jacob Scavuzzo

RF
Yasiel Puig (2)
Blake Smith (28)
Joey Curletta (30)
Kyle Russell
Jonathan Garcia
Noel Cuevas

3B
Alex Santana (23)
C.J. Retherford

SS
Corey Seager (3)
Jesmuel Valentin (14)
Darnell Sweeney

2B
Jake Lemmerman
Scott Wingo
Zach Babitt

1B
Justin Chigbogu
O'Koyea Dickson
Austin Gallagher
Angelo Songco
Jesus Valdez

C
Tim Federowicz (13)
Gorman Erickson
Pratt Maynard
Eric Smith

LHP

LHSP	LHRP
Hyun-Jin Ryu (1)	Paco Rodriguez (8)
Chris Reed (6)	Eric Eadington
Onelki Garcia (7)	Alfredo Unzue
Aaron Miller (27)	
Miguel Sulbaran	

RHP

RHSP	RHRP
Zach Lee (5)	Chris Withrow (12)
Matt Magill (9)	Scott Griggs (18)
Ross Stripling (10)	Josh Wall (20)
Garrett Gould (17)	Steve Ames (21)
Zach Bird (19)	Jose Dominguez
Scott Barlow (24)	Yimi Garcia
Angel Sanchez (25)	Jharel Cotton
Andres Santiago	Red Patterson
Stephen Fife	Matthew Reckling
Ralston Cash	Javier Solano
Jonathan Martinez	
Duke von Schamann	

2012

BEST PURE HITTER: SS Corey Seager's (1) simple lefthanded swing and all-fields approach helped him bat .309 as one of the youngest regulars in the Rookie-level Pioneer League.

BEST POWER HITTER: Once he gets stronger, Seager could have power to match his hitting ability and the Dodgers think he'll produce 25 homers annually. 1B Justin Chigbogu (4) and OF Joey Curletta (6) have huge power potential but are very raw.

FASTEST RUNNER: SS Darnell Sweeney (13), the lone plus runner in this crop, stole 27 bases in 67 pro games.

BEST DEFENSIVE PLAYER: SS Jesmuel Valentin (1s) played second base alongside No. 1 overall pick Carlos Correa in Puerto Rico, but he has all the tools for shortstop, starting with outstanding hands and a strong arm. Sweeney and Seager are also good defenders, though Seager may eventually move to third base.

BEST FASTBALL: LHP Onelki Garcia (3) hit 97 mph in the Double-A Southern League playoffs and usually pitches at 91-94. Los Angeles has seen RHP Scott Griggs (8) up to 98, RHPs Zach Bird (9) and Jharel Cotton (20) up to 96 and RHP Matthew Reckling (14) up to 95.

BEST SECONDARY PITCH: Garcia's power curveball is even tougher to hit than his fastball. LHP Paco Rodriguez's (2) high-80s cutter is nearly as filthy.

BEST PRO DEBUT: Rodriguez posted a 0.92 ERA and struck out 32 in 20 minor league innings, then allowed just one run in 11 big league outings. 1B Paul Hoenecke (24) won the Arizona League batting title at .382, though he was old for Rookie ball at 21. Pioneer League all-star OF Jeremy Rathjen (11) hit .324/.443/.500 with a league-high 67 runs.

BEST ATHLETE: OF Jacob Scavuzzo (21) requires polish, but he has strength, solid speed and a quick bat. Chigbogu was an all-state defensive end at his Missouri high school.

MOST INTRIGUING BACKGROUND: RHP Jordan Hershiser's (34) father Orel won a Cy Young Award and made three all-star teams for the Dodgers. Four other draftees have big league connections: Seager (brother Kyle), Valentin (father Jose), 2B Zach Babitt (10, father Shooty) and unsigned 3B Jose Vizcaino (34, father Jose, who's a special adviser for the club). RHP Duke von Schamann's (15) dad Uwe was an NFL kicker. Reckling played at Rice, where the baseball stadium is named after his grandparents, its lead donors.

CLOSEST TO THE MAJORS: Rodriguez was the first 2012 draftee to reach the majors. Garcia could be the second. The Dodgers considered him with their 2011 first-round pick before MLB pulled him out of that draft at the last minute.

BEST LATE-ROUND PICK: Cotton, who dropped in the draft after a stress fracture in his elbow hampered him in the spring at East Carolina.

THE ONE WHO GOT AWAY: RHP David Graybill (31) is a two-way player with power potential and a 90-93 mph fastball. He opted to attend Arizona State.

ASSESSMENT: Freed from previous financial limitations, the Dodgers spent more up-front money than they ever had before. Seager was one of the best bats available, and Rodriguez and Garcia should help the big league pitching staff in a hurry.

2011

LHP Chris Reed (1) reached Double-A in his first full pro season, but no one else has emerged as a top prospect. RHP Ryan O'Sullivan (4) became trade bait for Joe Blanton last summer.

GRADE: C+

2010

The Dodgers found two of their better prospects by paying over-slot bonuses—a rarity under then-owner Frank McCourt—to RHP Zach Lee (1) and OF Joc Pederson (11). RHP Shawn Tolleson (30) joined the big league bullpen last year.

GRADE: B

2009

Los Angeles didn't have a first-round pick and failed to sign three future first-rounders in 3B Richie Shaffer (25), LHP Brian Johnson (27) and OF/3B Stephen Piscotty (45). Its top choice, LHP Aaron Miller (1s), couldn't crack the 40-man roster this offseason.

GRADE: D

2008

The Dodgers signed four big leaguers in RHPs Josh Lindblom (2) and Nathan Eovaldi (11), SS Dee Gordon (4) and OF/1B Jerry Sands (25). They traded Lindblom and RHP Ethan Martin (1) for Shane Victorino, included Eovaldi in the Hanley Ramirez deal and put Sands and RHP Allen Webster (18) in the Adrian Gonzalez/Josh Beckett/Carl Crawford blockbuster with the Red Sox. Keep an eye on RHP Matt Magill (31), who blossomed in 2012.

GRADE: B+

Draft analysis by Jim Callis. Numbers in parentheses indicate draft rounds.

1 HYUN-JIN RYU, LHP

Born: March 25, 1987. **B-T:** L-L. **Ht.:** 6-2. **Wt.:** 215.
Signed: Korea, 2012. **Signed by:** Byung-Hwan An.

BA GRADE
55
LOW

RICH PILLING-MLB PHOTOS

The Dodgers have known Ryu since he was in high school and followed him throughout his pro career in Korea. He had Tommy John surgery as an amateur yet took the Korean Baseball Organization by storm in 2006 when he went 18-6, 2.23 for Hanwha at age 19 and became the first player in league history to win rookie of the year and MVP awards in the same season. Ryu won two games for South Korea at the 2008 Olympics, including the gold-medal victory over Cuba. He worked in relief at the 2009 World Baseball Classic and kept putting up numbers in the KBO. He led the league in strikeouts five times in his seven seasons, including last year with 210 in 183 innings, and compiled a 98-52, 2.80 record. However, he went just 9-9 in 2012 for Hanwha and at times seemed bored pitching against inferior hitters for the KBO's worst team. Ryu repeatedly had expressed a desire to play in the United States, and Hanwha granted his wish by posting him after the season. Los Angeles, continuing its new willingness to spend to the max, submitted the winning bid of $25,737,737.33 in November. He was represented by Scott Boras and negotiations stretched to the limit of the 30-day window to come to terms, after which Ryu would have had to return to Hanwha. On the same December weekend that the Dodgers made Zack Greinke the second-highest paid pitcher in big league history, they got a deal done with Ryu. He signed a six-year, $36 million contract that included a $5 million bonus and an opt-out clause after five seasons if he reaches certain performance levels.

Ryu has the weapons to step into Los Angeles' rotation immediately. He runs his fastball up to 94 mph and sits at 92-93. His heater has some cutting action and he can locate it to both sides of the plate. Most scouts who watched him in Korea thought his changeup was his best secondary offering, though the Dodgers believe more in his slider. Both are quality options. His slider is crisp with sharp, late

break when he has it going. He does sometimes get around the ball, causing the slider to get slurvy. He gets good arm speed on his fading changeup, eliciting some swings and misses with it. He also has a fourth pitch in a slow curveball he can flip up to the plate. The curve has good depth but sits in the high 60s, and he uses it mainly as an early-count pitch. Ryu isn't a bad athlete, but he has a portly build and will have to keep his weight in check. He had gotten overweight at the end of 2012 but is back in shape. He does a fine job of repeating his delivery, throwing strikes and getting downhill plane on his pitches. Some major league teams were wary of his workload in Korea, where he worked 1,269 innings in seven years from ages 19-25.

Ryu's contract includes a clause that forbids him from being sent to the minor leagues without his consent. That shouldn't be an issue. The first player to go directly from the KBO to the major leagues, he'll become the Dodgers' No. 3 starter behind Clayton Kershaw and Greinke.

SCOUTING GRADES

Fastball: 60.   **Control:** 60.
Slider: 55.   **Command:** 55.
Changeup: 55.

Based on 20-80 scouting scale, where 50 represents major league average, and future projection rather than present tools.

Year	Team	Class	W	L	ERA	G	GS	CG	SV	IP	H	HR	BB	SO	K/9	WHIP	AVG
2006	Hanwha (KBO)	INTL	18	6	2.23	30	28	6	1	202	159	11	52	204	9.1	1.05	.221
2007	Hanwha (KBO)	INTL	17	7	2.94	30	30	6	0	211	195	15	68	178	7.6	1.25	.251
2008	Hanwha (KBO)	INTL	14	7	3.31	26	26	2	0	166	144	12	67	143	7.8	1.27	.240
2009	Hanwha (KBO)	INTL	13	12	3.57	28	27	4	0	189	180	19	67	188	9.0	1.30	.254
2010	Hanwha (KBO)	INTL	16	4	1.82	25	25	5	0	193	149	11	45	187	8.7	1.01	.220
2011	Hanwha (KBO)	INTL	11	7	3.36	24	18	3	0	126	101	12	38	128	9.1	1.10	.217
2012	Hanwha (KBO)	INTL	9	9	2.66	27	27	1	0	183	153	12	46	210	10.3	1.09	.232
Korean League Totals			98	52	2.80	190	181	27	1	1269	1081	92	383	1238	8.8	1.15	.234

2 YASIEL PUIG, OF

BILL MITCHELL

Born: Dec. 7, 1990. **B-T:** R-R. **Ht.:** 6-3. **Wt.:** 215. **Signed:** Cuba, 2012. **Signed by:** Mike Brito/Paul Fryer.

One of the Dodgers' first big outlays under new ownership was a seven-year, $42 million major league contract for Puig that included a club-record $12 million bonus. The deal was widely questioned around the game given his history. Before defecting to Mexico, he had been barred from playing in Cuba's professional league during the 2011-12 season for disciplinary reasons. He hadn't played in a live game in nearly a year when he signed, with teams only getting to see him in a few workouts. Puig has the tools to justify his contract. He's a physical specimen, generating explosive bat speed and plus-plus raw power. He could stand to incorporate his lower body a little better in his swing, but he shows a good load and an ability to get through the ball, so he should hit for solid averages. He does need to be more selective, however, and not get impatient when he sees fewer fastballs. Puig has the speed to be a center fielder but his above-average arm makes him a better fit in right. Some observers question his maturity, as he rubbed opponents and scouts the wrong way during his time with high Class A Rancho Cucamonga. Los Angeles sees Puig as the most talented position player to come through its system since Matt Kemp. He'll likely begin 2013 back in high Class A but will move quickly if he produces.

BA GRADE 65 EXTREME

Year	Club (League)	Class	AVG	G	AB	R	H	2B	3B	HR	RBI	BB	SO	SB	CS	OBP	SLG
2012	Dodgers (AZL)	R	.400	9	30	10	12	0	3	4	11	6	7	1	1	.500	1.000
	R. Cucamonga (CAL)	HiA	.327	14	52	10	17	2	0	1	4	6	8	7	4	.407	.423
Minor League Totals			.354	23	82	20	29	2	3	5	15	12	15	8	5	.442	.634

3 COREY SEAGER, SS

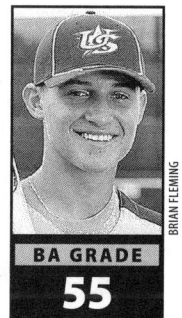

BRIAN FLEMING

Born: April 27, 1994. **B-T:** L-R. **Ht.:** 6-3. **Wt.:** 195. **Drafted:** HS—Concord, N.C., 2012 (1st round). **Signed by:** Lon Joyce.

The younger brother of Mariners third baseman Kyle Seager, Corey rose up draft boards last spring, eventually landing an above-slot $2.35 million bonus from the Dodgers as the 18th overall pick. Los Angeles hadn't used its top choice on a position player since taking James Loney 19th overall in 2002. Seager has an advanced bat and easily transitioned to pro ball in his debut. He has a clean swing, with good direction to the ball and the ability to keep the bat head in the hitting zone a long time. He ropes line drives to all fields, and he generates enough backspin and loft to hit for above-average power down the road. Seager exudes polish for his age and shows a natural ability to slow the game down, both at the plate and in the field. He already has a physical frame and should get stronger in time. He's an average runner who doesn't have great range at shortstop, though he makes up for it with first-step quickness and his feel for positioning. He has soft hands and the arm to stay on the left side of the infield. Seager likely will face a move to third base at some point, but the Dodgers will keep him at shortstop for now. He has all the makings of an impact bat and could move quickly for a high school player. He'll begin his first full pro season at low Class A Great Lakes.

BA GRADE 55 HIGH

Year	Club (League)	Class	AVG	G	AB	R	H	2B	3B	HR	RBI	BB	SO	SB	CS	OBP	SLG
2012	Ogden (PIO)	R	.309	46	175	34	54	9	2	8	33	21	33	8	2	.383	.520
Minor League Totals			.309	46	175	34	54	9	2	8	33	21	33	8	2	.383	.520

4 JOC PEDERSON, OF

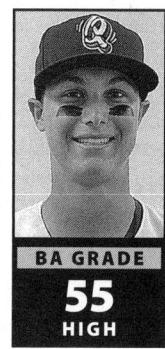

Born: April 21, 1992. **B-T:** L-L. **Ht.:** 6-1. **Wt.:** 185. **Drafted:** HS—Palo Alto, Calif., 2010 (11th round). **Signed by:** Orsino Hill.

Pederson could have played baseball at Southern California and walked on to the football team as a wide receiver, but he instead turned pro for $600,000 at the 2010 signing deadline. His father Stu played briefly for the Dodgers in 1985. Joc took off in the second half of 2012, batting .328/.410/.595 with 16 homers and 18 steals, and won the organization's minor league player of the year award. He played in the Arizona Fall League and for Israel in a World Baseball Classic qualifier after the season. Pederson swings with controlled aggression. He attacks balls yet does a good job of keeping his hands back, spraying line drives all over the field. Los Angeles wants him to improve his posture in his swing, as he tends to dip his head, but the ball jumps off his bat. He does a good job of imparting backspin, leading the Dodgers to believe his power has a chance to keep emerging as he gets older, as it did with Andre Ethier. Pederson isn't a blazer, but he has the athleticism and speed to play center field. His average arm gives him a chance to play in right field as well.

BA GRADE 55 HIGH

His tireless work ethic and grinder mentality draw praise. Pederson will see time at all three outfield positions moving forward, given that he's unlikely to unseat Matt Kemp in center field. Pederson still has the tools to be an above-average regular, and he'll move up to Double-A Chattanooga for 2013.

Year	Club (League)	Class	AVG	G	AB	R	H	2B	3B	HR	RBI	BB	SO	SB	CS	OBP	SLG
2010	Dodgers (AZL)	R	.000	3	7	1	0	0	0	0	0	4	5	0	0	.417	.000
2011	Great Lakes (MWL)	LoA	.160	16	50	4	8	0	0	0	1	7	9	2	0	.288	.160
	Ogden (PIO)	R	.353	68	266	54	94	20	2	11	64	36	54	24	5	.429	.568
2012	R. Cucamonga (CAL)	HiA	.313	110	434	96	136	26	4	18	70	51	81	26	14	.396	.516
Minor League Totals			.314	197	757	155	238	46	6	29	135	98	149	52	19	.401	.506

5 ZACH LEE, RHP

Born: Sept. 13, 1991. **B-T:** R-R. **Ht.:** 6-4. **Wt.:** 190. **Drafted:** HS—McKinney, Texas, 2010 (1st round). **Signed by:** Calvin Jones.

Considered one of the toughest players to sign out of the 2010 draft, Lee had committed to play quarterback and pitch at Louisiana State. But the Dodgers selected him 25th overall and signed him to a heavily backloaded two-sport deal worth $5.25 million, the largest draft bonus in franchise history. He has advanced rapidly, reaching Double-A at age 20 last year and going 3-1, 2.34 in August as the second-youngest player in the Southern League. Lee doesn't have a truly dominant pitch, but his ability to command four solid offerings sets him apart from his peers. He has a physical frame and throws his fastball from 90-95 mph, with the projection to add more velocity. He can give his heater sinking or cutting action. Lee's curveball and slider come in with similar 1-to-7 break. His slider has tighter rotation and rates slightly higher than his curve, which is softer and has more depth. He has feel for using his changeup, which could become a plus pitch. He

BA GRADE
55
HIGH

shored up his direction to home plate last season, helping him work both sides of the plate. He's ahead of his years in terms of pitchability and mound presence. Lee's lack of a knockout pitch keeps him from having true frontline potential, but he's a fairly safe bet to become a quality No. 3 starter. He could be ready to pitch in the majors in 2013, though Los Angeles won't rush him. He's ticketed for a return to Chattanooga.

Year	Club (League)	Class	W	L	ERA	G	GS	CG	SV	IP	H	HR	BB	SO	K/9	WHIP	AVG
2011	Great Lakes (MWL)	LoA	9	6	3.47	24	24	0	0	109	101	9	32	91	7.5	1.22	.242
2012	R. Cucamonga (CAL)	HiA	2	3	4.55	12	12	0	0	55	60	9	10	52	8.5	1.27	.270
	Chattanooga (SL)	AA	4	3	4.25	13	13	0	0	66	69	6	22	51	7.0	1.39	.272
Minor League Totals			15	12	3.95	49	49	0	0	230	230	24	64	194	7.6	1.28	.257

6 CHRIS REED, LHP

Born: May 20, 1990. **B-T:** L-L. **Ht.:** 6-4. **Wt.:** 195. **Drafted:** Stanford, 2011 (1st round). **Signed by:** Orsino Hill.

Though he grew up in California, Reed was born in London and represented Great Britain in the 2012 Futures Game and in a World Baseball Classic qualifier in September. A reliever throughout his career at Stanford, he converted to a starter after signing for $1,589,000 as the 16th overall pick in 2011. Blister problems plagued him in his first full pro season, but he did reach Double-A. Reed has better raw stuff than 2010 first-rounder Zach Lee, his teammate at two stops last year, but he lacks Lee's command. Reed's fastball operates at 92-96 mph with heavy sink, and he complements it with a devastating spike slider that's hard with late movement when he has it working. The slider was the culprit behind his blister problems, however, and they remain a concern going forward. Reed's changeup looks good in flashes but remains a work in progress. His command has to improve, and Los Angeles wants him to stay more upright in his delivery, which should

BA GRADE
55
HIGH

help him stay behind the ball better. The Dodgers will loosen the reins on Reed in 2013. He could reach the majors quickly if he went back to the bullpen, but Los Angeles will continue developing him as a potential No. 3 starter. He'll head back for more fine-tuning at Chattanooga to open the season.

Year	Club (League)	Class	W	L	ERA	G	GS	CG	SV	IP	H	HR	BB	SO	K/9	WHIP	AVG
2011	R. Cucamonga (CAL)	HiA	0	1	7.71	3	3	0	0	7	9	1	4	9	11.6	1.86	.321
2012	R. Cucamonga (CAL)	HiA	1	4	3.09	7	6	0	0	35	25	1	14	38	9.8	1.11	.203
	Chattanooga (SL)	AA	0	4	4.84	12	11	0	0	35	31	2	20	29	7.4	1.44	.242
Minor League Totals			1	9	4.31	22	20	0	0	77	65	4	38	76	8.8	1.33	.233

7 ONELKI GARCIA, LHP

BILL MITCHELL

BA GRADE

55

EXTREME

Born: Aug. 2, 1989. **B-T:** L-L. **Ht.:** 6-3. **Wt.:** 220. **Drafted:** Los Angeles (no school), 2012 (3rd round). **Signed by:** Dennis Moeller.

After Garcia defected from Cuba in January 2011, MLB originally decided he would have to enter the draft rather than making him a free agent. Los Angeles considered taking him with the first-round pick it eventually spent on Chris Reed, until MLB tabled Garcia's case and made him wait a year. The Dodgers stayed on him throughout, watching him pitch winter ball in Puerto Rico and in a local adult league, before taking him in the third round last June and signing him for $382,000. Garcia has two above-average pitches in his fastball and curveball. He sits in the low 90s with running action on his heater, and he touched 97 mph during his pro debut. His 12-to-6 curve is even tougher to square up, featuring good rotation and depth. He also throws a slider/cutter and a changeup, though these two pitches aren't as advanced. Garcia arrived with a good delivery and arm action to go with his strong, athletic build. The Dodgers like his makeup as much as his stuff. Garcia struck out seven over three no-hit innings in a Double-A playoff game in September. He's 23 and certainly could reach the majors quickly, though he's expected to begin his first full season back in Chattanooga.

Year	Club (League)	Class	W	L	ERA	G	GS	CG	SV	IP	H	HR	BB	SO	K/9	WHIP	AVG
2012	R. Cucamonga (CAL)	HiA	0	0	0.00	1	1	0	0	2	0	0	0	4	18.0	0.00	.000
Minor League Totals			0	0	0.00	1	1	0	0	2	0	0	0	4	18.0	0.00	.000

8 PACO RODRIGUEZ, LHP

BA GRADE

45

SAFE

Born: April 16, 1991. **B-T:** L-L. **Ht.:** 6-3. **Wt.:** 215. **Drafted:** Florida, 2012 (2nd round). **Signed by:** Scott Hennessey.

Rodriguez was a bullpen mainstay for Florida teams that reached three straight College World Series from 2010-12. Dodgers scouts who watched him saw a major league-ready reliever and he lived up to that billing after signing for $610,800 as a second-rounder. He became the first 2012 draftee to reach the majors, allowing one run in 11 September appearances. Rodriguez does have quality stuff, but his deception is what sets him apart. He hides the ball well and has funk to his arm action. Los Angeles had him tone down the high leg lift he used in college because an umpire they asked to review tape of Rodriguez said he'd likely be called for balks in the majors. His best pitch is a high-80s cutter that continually beats up the hands of righties. His fastball ranges from 88-93 mph with arm-side life, so he can run his pitches to either side of the plate. He also has a sweepy slider and occasionally will unveil a changeup. Rodriguez's control and mound poise are two more assets. He wasn't awed by his surroundings in the big leagues. While Rodriguez may not have the upside of a closer, the future is now for him as a set-up man. He should be back in Los Angeles to open 2013.

Year	Club (League)	Class	W	L	ERA	G	GS	CG	SV	IP	H	HR	BB	SO	K/9	WHIP	AVG
2012	Great Lakes (MWL)	LoA	0	0	0.00	6	0	0	2	6	4	0	0	10	15.0	0.67	.182
	Chattanooga (SL)	AA	1	0	1.32	15	0	0	3	14	7	0	6	22	14.5	0.95	.149
	Los Angeles (NL)	MAJ	0	1	1.35	11	0	0	0	7	3	0	4	6	8.1	1.05	.136
Major League Totals			0	1	1.35	11	0	0	0	7	3	0	4	6	8.1	1.05	.136
Minor League Totals			1	0	0.92	21	0	0	5	20	11	0	6	32	14.6	0.86	.159

9 MATT MAGILL, RHP

BA GRADE

50

MEDIUM

Born: Nov. 10, 1989. **B-T:** R-R. **Ht.:** 6-3. **Wt.:** 190. **Drafted:** HS—Simi Valley, Calif., 2008 (31st round). **Signed by:** Chuck Crim.

Magill had a below-average fastball and rough mechanics as a high school senior in 2008, but area scout Chuck Crim persuaded Los Angeles to invest a 31st-round pick and $75,000 in him. A former big league pitcher, Crim shifted to coaching in 2009, and the two have reunited at several stops, including last season in Double-A. Magill led the Southern League in strikeouts (168) and the Dodgers give Crim much of the credit for his development. Magill has added mass to his frame and smoothed out his delivery over the years, adding velocity to his fastball. He can reach 94-95 mph early in games and sits at 91-92. He pounds the strike zone with his fastball, which runs in on righthanders. Magill has a legitimate strikeout pitch in his sharp, late-breaking slider, which he can also throw for a strike in any count. His changeup is rudimentary but does have some fade. He draws raves for his blend of pitching smarts and aggressiveness. Los Angeles added Magill to its 40-man roster to protect him from the Rule 5 draft and will send him to Triple-A Albuquerque in 2013. He has the ceiling of a No. 3 starter and could be ready to pitch in the majors by the end of the season.

Year	Club (League)	Class	W	L	ERA	G	GS	CG	SV	IP	H	HR	BB	SO	K/9	WHIP	AVG
2008	Dodgers (GCL)	R	1	2	3.34	11	3	0	1	30	30	2	9	25	7.6	1.31	.265
2009	Ogden (PIO)	R	6	3	4.00	15	15	0	0	72	59	7	30	55	6.9	1.24	.224
2010	Great Lakes (MWL)	LoA	7	4	3.28	24	20	1	2	126	87	13	52	135	9.6	1.10	.194
2011	R. Cucamonga (CAL)	HiA	11	5	4.33	26	21	0	0	139	156	15	52	126	8.1	1.49	.280
2012	Chattanooga (SL)	AA	11	8	3.75	26	26	0	0	146	127	8	61	168	10.3	1.28	.232
Minor League Totals			36	22	3.80	102	85	1	3	514	459	45	204	509	8.9	1.29	.238

10 ROSS STRIPLING, RHP

Born: Nov. 23, 1989. **B-T:** R-R. **Ht.:** 6-3. **Wt.:** 190. **Drafted:** Texas A&M, 2012 (5th round). **Signed by:** Clint Bowers.

Stripling didn't take up pitching full-time until his senior year of high school and originally joined Texas A&M as a walk-on. He blossomed in 2011, tying for the NCAA Division I lead with 14 wins, then spurned the Rockies as a ninth-round pick that summer. He threw a no-hitter against San Diego State on the day he was scheduled to graduate last May before signing a month later for $130,000 as a fifth-rounder. In his pro debut, Stripling impressed the Dodgers both with his stuff and his feel for using it. His fastball sat at 92-93 mph with run and sink last summer at Rookie-level Ogden. His velocity picked up from the 88-91 mph he showed in college, and Los Angeles believes there's more in there if can incorporate his lower half better in his delivery. Stripling's best pitch is a 12-to-6 curveball with plus potential, and he also has a fading changeup. He's extremely athletic, has a clean arm action and commands the ball to both sides of the plate. The Dodgers felt fortunate to get Stripling in the fifth round. They see the makings of a No. 3 starter who can climb through the system quickly. He could skip a level and begin his first full pro season in high Class A.

BA GRADE 50 HIGH

Year	Club (League)	Class	W	L	ERA	G	GS	CG	SV	IP	H	HR	BB	SO	K/9	WHIP	AVG
2012	Ogden (PIO)	R	1	0	1.24	14	12	0	0	36	26	0	6	37	9.2	0.88	.197
Minor League Totals			1	0	1.24	14	12	0	0	36	26	0	6	37	9.2	0.88	.197

11 ALEX CASTELLANOS, 2B/3B/OF

BA GRADE 45 LOW

Born: Aug. 4, 1986. **B-T:** R-R. **Ht.:** 5-11. **Wt.:** 195. **Drafted:** Belmont Abbey (N.C.), 2008 (10th round). **Signed by:** Mike Juhl (Cardinals).

Castellanos can hit. He batted .408 in two seasons at NCAA Division II Belmont Abbey and became the tiny North Carolina Catholic school's first draft pick since 1972 when the Cardinals took him in 2008. He then became its first big leaguer since Hal Haid in 1933 when the Dodgers called him up last May. He came to Los Angeles in the Rafael Furcal deal at the 2011 trade deadline. Castellanos made the most of his first full season in his new organization, finishing in the top five in the Triple-A Pacific Coast League in both on-base (.420) and slugging percentage (.590). He lacks a standout tool but is solid across the board. His hands work well in his swing while providing enough bat speed to give him sneaky power. His swing can get long at times, making it hard for him to get around on elevated fastballs. Castellanos played second base in college and stayed in the dirt at Triple-A last year, playing second and third, but the Dodgers consider him better suited for the outfield, where they used him during his big league time. An average runner, he played center field in the Venezuelan League this winter. Castellanos should fit in Los Angeles as a utility option, capable of playing anywhere except catcher and shortstop, as soon as this season.

Year	Club (League)	Class	AVG	G	AB	R	H	2B	3B	HR	RBI	BB	SO	SB	CS	OBP	SLG
2008	Johnson City (APP)	R	.298	49	181	42	54	14	4	7	31	8	45	20	2	.354	.536
	Batavia (NYP)	SS	.269	10	26	6	7	2	2	0	4	2	7	0	1	.345	.500
2009	Quad Cities (MWL)	LoA	.270	82	311	51	84	21	4	5	34	20	89	21	4	.336	.412
	Palm Beach (FSL)	HiA	.189	21	53	5	10	1	1	1	2	2	19	0	2	.232	.302
2010	Palm Beach (FSL)	HiA	.270	129	459	62	124	35	7	13	58	38	112	19	9	.339	.462
2011	Springfield, MO (TL)	AA	.319	93	354	72	113	21	4	19	62	24	94	10	1	.379	.562
	Chattanooga (SL)	AA	.322	32	121	30	39	14	4	4	23	15	24	4	1	.406	.603
2012	Albuquerque (PCL)	AAA	.328	94	344	74	113	25	7	17	52	46	85	16	8	.420	.590
	Los Angeles (NL)	MAJ	.174	16	23	3	4	0	1	1	3	0	8	0	0	.200	.391
Major League Totals			.174	16	23	3	4	0	1	1	3	0	8	0	0	.200	.391
Minor League Totals			.294	510	1849	342	544	133	33	66	266	155	475	90	28	.365	.509

12 CHRIS WITHROW, RHP

BA GRADE 50 HIGH

Born: April 1, 1989. **B-T:** R-R. **Ht.:** 6-4. **Wt.:** 220. **Drafted:** HS—Midland, Texas, 2007 (1st round). **Signed by:** Calvin Jones.

Withrow learned the game from his father Mike, who pitched three seasons in the White Sox organization and was Chris' pitching coach at Midland (Texas) Christian High. The Dodgers gave

Withrow a $1.35 million bonus as the 20th overall pick in 2007, and he reached Double-A in 2009, but he has stalled there. He got off to another slow start last year, going 1-1, 5.71 through the end of May, when Los Angeles decided to shift him to the bullpen. He posted his best sustained performance in his three full years in the Southern League after the move, going 2-2, 2.37 the rest of the way. His season was delayed early and interrupted late by muscle strains in his back and oblique. Withrow has a major league arm, pitching in the mid-90s and reaching 98 mph. His curveball had been his best secondary pitch in past years, but it took a back seat to his slider last season. The slider comes in at 85-87 mph with tilt and sharp break, looking like a legitimate big league weapon. He still has the curveball, along with a solid changeup, but he'll focus on the fastball and slider as a reliever. He has a clean delivery and arm action but still lacks command. His walk rate has climbed in each of his years in Double-A, reaching 5.40 per nine innings last year, and it's his biggest obstacle to reaching the majors. Though Withrow could still have potential as a starter, the Dodgers will stick with him in the bullpen, where he has the pure stuff pitch in the late innings. He's on the 40-man roster and will try to take a step up to Triple-A.

Year	Club (League)	Class	W	L	ERA	G	GS	CG	SV	IP	H	HR	BB	SO	K/9	WHIP	AVG
2007	Dodgers (GCL)	R	0	0	5.00	6	4	0	0	9	5	0	4	13	13.0	1.00	.167
2008	Inland Empire (CAL)	HiA	0	0	4.50	4	0	0	0	4	2	0	6	1	2.3	2.00	.182
2009	Inland Empire (CAL)	HiA	6	6	4.69	19	16	0	0	86	80	3	45	105	10.9	1.45	.252
	Chattanooga (SL)	AA	2	2	3.95	6	6	0	0	27	24	2	12	26	8.6	1.32	.240
2010	Chattanooga (SL)	AA	4	9	5.97	27	27	1	0	130	146	13	69	120	8.3	1.66	.285
2011	Chattanooga (SL)	AA	6	6	4.20	25	25	1	0	129	111	8	75	130	9.1	1.45	.239
2012	Chattanooga (SL)	AA	3	3	4.65	22	7	0	2	60	52	3	36	64	9.6	1.47	.233
Minor League Totals			21	26	4.87	109	85	2	2	445	420	29	247	459	9.3	1.50	.253

13 TIM FEDEROWICZ, C

BA GRADE 45 LOW

Born: Aug. 5, 1987. **B-T:** R-R. **Ht.:** 5-10. **Wt.:** 215. **Drafted:** North Carolina, 2008 (7th round). **Signed by:** Quincy Boyd (Red Sox).

Federowicz arrived in a three-team deal with the Red Sox and Mariners at the 2011 trade deadline. The Dodgers sent Trayvon Robinson to Seattle and got Federowicz and righthanders Stephen Fife and Juan Rodriguez from Boston. The Red Sox also received Erik Bedard and righthander Josh Fields from the Mariners and sent outfielder Chin-Hsien Chiang to Seattle. Federowicz looks like he'll be the most significant player in the trade. Playing his first full season in the system last year, he posted career bests in both on-base percentage (.371) and OPS (.832), though he did much of his damage in hitter-friendly Albuquerque, batting just .245/.331/.370 on the road. Federowicz has been hailed for his standout defense throughout his pro career and came as advertised when the Dodgers got him. He's a fine receiver who gains the trust of his pitchers with his ability block balls and call games. He has a strong arm and led the Pacific Coast League by throwing out 39 percent of basestealers last year, and Los Angeles felt his catch-and-throw ability improved. He won BA's Captain's Catcher's Award as the minors' top defender at the spot. If Federowicz carves out a big league career, it will be on the strength of his defense. He has strength and could be a double-digit home run threat, but he can get too pull-conscious and struggles with breaking pitches. The Dodgers would like to see him stay more up the middle and drive balls into the right-center field gap. He has little speed. Federowicz has little left to prove in the minors and goes into 2013 well positioned to be Los Angeles' backup catcher behind A.J. Ellis. He has the defensive chops to be a starter down the road.

Year	Club (League)	Class	AVG	G	AB	R	H	2B	3B	HR	RBI	BB	SO	SB	CS	OBP	SLG
2008	Lowell (NYP)	SS	.244	36	127	14	31	6	0	1	15	19	24	10	3	.338	.315
2009	Greenville (SAL)	LoA	.345	55	226	34	78	19	0	10	34	15	42	1	0	.393	.562
	Salem (CAR)	HiA	.257	51	187	18	48	13	0	4	24	5	22	1	0	.276	.390
2010	Salem (CAR)	HiA	.253	109	407	47	103	34	1	4	61	43	86	1	1	.324	.371
2011	Portland (EL)	AA	.277	90	339	46	94	20	0	8	52	32	63	1	0	.338	.407
	Albuquerque (PCL)	AAA	.325	25	83	17	27	7	0	6	17	15	20	0	0	.431	.627
	Los Angeles (NL)	MAJ	.154	7	13	0	2	0	0	0	1	2	4	0	0	.313	.154
2012	Albuquerque (PCL)	AAA	.294	115	412	71	121	34	1	11	76	52	91	0	1	.371	.461
	Los Angeles (NL)	MAJ	.333	3	3	0	1	0	0	0	0	1	2	0	0	.500	.333
Major League Totals			.188	10	16	0	3	0	0	0	1	3	6	0	0	.350	.188
Minor League Totals			.282	481	1781	247	502	133	2	44	279	181	348	14	5	.348	.433

14 JESMUEL VALENTIN, SS

BA GRADE 50 HIGH

Born: May 12, 1994. **B-T:** B-R. **Ht.:** 5-10. **Wt.:** 174. **Drafted:** HS—Gurabo, P.R., 2012 (1st round supplemental). **Signed by:** Rob Sidwell.

Valentin has spent plenty of time in others' shadows. He's the son of longtime big leaguer Jose Valentin and played his high school baseball alongside 2012 No. 1 overall pick Carlos Correa. Valentin frequently played second base in deference to Correa, but Los Angeles will give him a chance to play shortstop after signing him for $984,700 as a sandwich pick last June. More of a prototypical, glove-first shortstop than Dodgers 2012 first-rounder Corey Seager, Valentin has a quick first step and above-average range. His hands work well and he has the arm strength to stay at short. He's capable of making flashy plays but is still learning to stay under control and not make reckless throws after committing 20 errors in 43 games in his pro debut. Naturally righthanded, Valentin didn't take up switch-hitting until late in his high school career. His lefty swing tends to get sweepy and causes him to get under the ball. He's more compact from the right side. He won't hit for a lot of power, but Los Angeles does believe he has the potential to sting the ball. On the bases, he has good speed that plays up because he's already a savvy baserunner. If Seager can stay at shortstop, Valentin could end up back at second base, but the team will develop him as a shortstop for now. He'll likely stay a level behind Seager in 2013, going to extended spring training to keep working on his swing before taking an assignment to Ogden.

Year	Club (League)	Class	AVG	G	AB	R	H	2B	3B	HR	RBI	BB	SO	SB	CS	OBP	SLG
2012	Dodgers (AZL)	R	.211	43	152	34	32	6	2	2	18	35	24	5	2	.352	.316
Minor League Totals			.211	43	152	34	32	6	2	2	18	35	24	5	2	.352	.316

15 BOBBY COYLE, OF

BA GRADE 45 MEDIUM

Born: March 6, 1989. **B-T:** L-L. **Ht.:** 6-1. **Wt.:** 215. **Drafted:** Fresno State, 2010 (10th round). **Signed by:** Dennis Moeller.

Coyle played in the shadows of 2007 first-round picks Matt Dominguez and Mike Moustakas at Chatsworth (Calif.) High. He was a 19th-round pick of the Indians out of high school but opted to go to Arizona, where he played two seasons before transferring to Fresno State. He hit .360 with 11 homers for the Bulldogs in 2010, garnering a $95,000 bonus from the Dodgers as a 10th-rounder. After battling oblique issues that kept him on the shelf early last year, he broke out in high Class A. Coyle has a physical build and quick-twitch athleticism. He maintains a short, compact swing that helps him spray line drives all over the park. He has the strength and bat speed to hit for solid home run power, though that shows up mainly to his pull side. Coyle has no standout tool defensively, where he's adequate but needs to get better reads and jumps on balls. His average arm allows him to scrape by in right field, though left suits him better. He's an average runner. Los Angels also wants him to improve his work habits, though they believe he's made progress. Coyle's bat is good enough to keep carrying him through the upper levels of the system, and he'll take on a full season of Double-A in 2013.

Year	Club (League)	Class	AVG	G	AB	R	H	2B	3B	HR	RBI	BB	SO	SB	CS	OBP	SLG
2010	Ogden (PIO)	R	.316	54	237	38	75	16	1	4	52	10	29	7	1	.345	.443
2011	Great Lakes (MWL)	LoA	.250	98	380	42	95	16	1	9	44	30	68	3	2	.303	.368
2012	R. Cucamonga (CAL)	HiA	.378	56	201	34	76	17	2	8	32	11	18	3	1	.408	.602
	Chattanooga (SL)	AA	.324	13	37	4	12	0	1	1	5	3	9	0	1	.375	.459
Minor League Totals			.302	221	855	118	258	49	5	22	133	54	124	13	5	.342	.448

16 SCOTT VAN SLYKE, OF/1B

BA GRADE 45 MEDIUM

Born: July 24, 1986. **B-T:** R-R. **Ht.:** 6-5. **Wt.:** 250. **Drafted:** HS—Ladue, Mo., 2005 (14th round). **Signed by:** Mitch Webster.

Van Slyke's father Andy played 13 seasons in the majors, and Scott made his big league debut when the Dodgers called him up in early May. He made a splash initially, slugging a game-winning pinch-hit homer against the Cardinals on May 20, but he struggled thereafter and returned to Triple-A in early July. He went back to mashing against Triple-A pitching, finishing fourth in the Pacific Coast League in slugging (.578). Van Slyke has a nice, wristy swing, with the strength to generate above-average raw power. He has a big leg kick, though, and his timing suffered last season when he wasn't getting consistent at-bats in the majors, so he may be ill suited for a bench role. His swing is long as well, given that he's a big guy with long arms. He saw action at both corner outfield spots and first base last season. He shows soft hands at first base and has a capable arm in the outfield. He runs well for his size, though just fringy overall. Van Slyke is blocked at all of his potential positions in Los Angeles, so he'll likely be back in Albuquerque to open 2013 to keep getting regular playing time.

Year	Club (League)	Class	AVG	G	AB	R	H	2B	3B	HR	RBI	BB	SO	SB	CS	OBP	SLG
2005	Dodgers (GCL)	R	.282	24	85	15	24	4	1	2	15	4	19	4	3	.330	.424
2006	Ogden (PIO)	R	.256	45	156	18	40	5	2	2	17	14	41	5	3	.320	.353
2007	Great Lakes (MWL)	LoA	.254	104	351	38	89	18	1	2	35	27	68	4	4	.310	.328
2008	Great Lakes (MWL)	LoA	.148	22	61	4	9	4	0	0	7	12	11	0	0	.280	.213
	Inland Empire (CAL)	HiA	.261	48	176	29	46	9	2	5	26	11	35	7	4	.309	.420
2009	Inland Empire (CAL)	HiA	.294	132	496	75	146	42	4	23	100	61	128	10	7	.373	.534
	Albuquerque (PCL)	AAA	.167	3	6	1	1	0	0	0	0	0	2	1	0	.375	.167
2010	Chattanooga (SL)	AA	.235	65	217	28	51	7	3	4	29	18	37	4	2	.300	.350
	Inland Empire (CAL)	HiA	.307	48	189	34	58	12	2	9	35	17	39	3	1	.368	.534
	Albuquerque (PCL)	AAA	.289	12	38	5	11	4	0	1	5	0	7	0	0	.289	.474
2011	Chattanooga (SL)	AA	.348	130	457	81	159	45	4	20	92	65	100	6	5	.427	.595
2012	Los Angeles (NL)	MAJ	.167	27	54	4	9	2	0	2	7	2	14	1	0	.196	.315
	Albuquerque (PCL)	AAA	.327	95	358	68	117	34	1	18	67	46	64	5	3	.404	.578
Major League Totals			.167	27	54	4	9	2	0	2	7	2	14	1	0	.196	.315
Minor League Totals			.290	728	2590	396	751	184	20	86	428	277	550	48	32	.360	.476

17 GARRETT GOULD, RHP

BA GRADE
50
HIGH

Born: July 19, 1991. **B-T:** R-R. **Ht.:** 6-4. **Wt.:** 190. **Drafted:** HS—Maize, Kan., 2009 (2nd round). **Signed by:** Scott Little.

Gould steadily built momentum leading up to the 2009 draft, first by winning MVP honors at the 2008 World Wood Bat Association Championships and then by breaking Nate Robertson's strikeout record at Maize (Kan.) High in the spring of 2009. He landed the largest signing bonus in the Dodgers' 2009 class, $900,000, and looked to be on the right track after a strong 2011 season in low Class A, but his stock took a hit last season with a disappointing showing in high Class A. Gould's fastball sat in the low 90s in 2011, but he mostly operated at 89-90 mph last season amid concerns he had gotten out of shape. His overhand curveball remained a plus pitch with tilt and depth, but he struggled to throw strikes and got in trouble whenever hitters were able to lay off the curve. His fastball lacks movement, and the results were predictable when he fell behind in the count and had to lay it in the zone. He has a decent changeup with sink and fade and needs to throw it more. While his velocity has dropped, his mechanics have actually gotten smoother since he signed, and he's softened how he lands on his front leg. Gould likely will graduate to Double-A for 2013, trying to re-establish himself as a future mid-rotation starter if his velocity bounces back and his command steps forward.

Year	Club (League)	Class	W	L	ERA	G	GS	CG	SV	IP	H	HR	BB	SO	K/9	WHIP	AVG
2009	Ogden (PIO)	R	0	1	10.13	3	3	0	0	3	4	1	2	4	13.5	2.25	.333
2010	Ogden (PIO)	R	1	4	4.06	13	13	0	0	58	68	4	20	52	8.1	1.53	.292
2011	Great Lakes (MWL)	LoA	11	6	2.40	27	24	0	0	124	102	8	37	104	7.6	1.12	.220
2012	R. Cucamonga (CAL)	HiA	5	10	5.75	27	23	0	0	130	140	19	54	123	8.5	1.49	.275
Minor League Totals			17	21	4.16	70	63	0	0	314	314	32	113	283	8.1	1.36	.258

18 SCOTT GRIGGS, RHP

BA GRADE
50
EXTREME

Born: May 13, 1991. **B-T:** R-R. **Ht.:** 6-3. **Wt.:** 185. **Drafted:** UCLA, 2012 (8th round). **Signed by:** Dennis Moeller.

Griggs long has frustrated scouts with electric stuff but poor command. He turned down the Mariners as a 34th-round pick in 2009 to go to UCLA, where he saw little action his first two years but broke through in 2012, taking over as the Bruins' closer and setting a school record with 15 saves to go with a 2.65 ERA. The Dodgers took him in the eighth round and signed him for a $135,100 bonus. Scouts who saw Griggs on the right night last spring envisioned a surefire future big leaguer. He has the power arm to ramp his fastball up to 98 mph and sit at 94-95. He backs it up with a hard, late-breaking curveball. He also has a changeup that he toys with but doesn't use much in games. He has a good frame and a clean delivery when everything's in sync, driving his fastball down through the zone with good downhill plane. Los Angeles doesn't believe Griggs' control problems come from mechanical flaws, but rather when he tries to do too much and overthrows. They aren't new, as he walked 60 in 63 college innings prior to issuing 21 free passes in 23 pro frames. He has the raw ability to move through the system quickly and be a major league closer, but he must throw strikes to reach that ceiling. He'll begin his first full pro season with one of the Dodgers' Class A affiliates.

Year	Club (League)	Class	W	L	ERA	G	GS	CG	SV	IP	H	HR	BB	SO	K/9	WHIP	AVG
2012	Ogden (PIO)	R	0	0	4.09	11	0	0	5	11	5	0	8	18	14.7	1.18	.135
	Great Lakes (MWL)	LoA	1	0	3.86	8	0	0	0	12	7	0	13	14	10.8	1.71	.175
Minor League Totals			1	0	3.97	19	0	0	5	23	12	0	21	32	12.7	1.46	.156

19 ZACH BIRD, RHP

BA GRADE
50
EXTREME

Born: July 14, 1994. **B-T:** R-R. **Ht.:** 6-3. **Wt.:** 177. **Drafted:** HS—Jackson, Miss., 2012 (9th round). **Signed by:** Matthew Paul.

Bird's father Eugene played defensive back at Southern Mississippi from 1971-73 and was an 11th-round pick of the New York Jets in the 1974 NFL draft, though he never played in the pros. Zach would've followed in his father's footsteps to Southern Miss, but the Dodgers steered him to pro ball with a $140,000 bonus as their ninth-round pick last June. Coaches and scouts who watched Bird in the Rookie-level Arizona League last summer were surprised his name wasn't called sooner. His fastball ranges from 90-96 mph, and he has plenty of projection in his tall, lean frame. His curveball shows plus potential with its sharp break and depth. He's still learning his changeup but does show feel for it. He needs to repeat his delivery better, which could come with added strength. He generates good downhill plane on his fastball and shows an ability to command his curveball. He has already impressed Los Angeles with his pitching IQ, along with how quickly he soaks up instruction. He garners comparisons to former Dodgers prospect James McDonald, though Bird should be able to throw harder. Bird will compete for a spot in the low Class A Great Lakes rotation in 2013, with a stay in extended spring training and assignment to Ogden as the fallback option.

Year	Club (League)	Class	W	L	ERA	G	GS	CG	SV	IP	H	HR	BB	SO	K/9	WHIP	AVG
2012	Dodgers (AZL)	R	1	2	4.54	10	10	0	0	40	36	2	17	46	10.4	1.34	.237
Minor League Totals			1	2	4.54	10	10	0	0	40	36	2	17	46	10.4	1.34	.237

20 JOSH WALL, RHP

BA GRADE
45
MEDIUM

Born: Jan. 21, 1987. **B-T:** R-R. **Ht.:** 6-6. **Wt.:** 220. **Drafted:** HS—Walker, La., 2005 (2nd round). **Signed by:** Dennis Moeller.

Wall needed time to mature, physically and mentally, after the Dodgers took him in the second round of the 2005 draft and signed him for $480,000. A rangy, long-limbed 6-foot-6, he struggled to maintain his stuff consistently as a starter, but he turned a corner after converting to relief in 2011. Braving the hitter's haven in Albuquerque last year, he led the Pacific Coast League and ranked fourth in the minors with 28 saves and made his big league debut in July. Wall has the weapons to pitch in the back of a big league bullpen, with a fastball that sits at 94-96 mph and a hard, late-breaking slider. The slider can get sweepy but has been a plus pitch for him. He also has a curveball and changeup left over from his days as a starter, but he is primarily a two-pitch reliever. He has a clean delivery but his size makes it difficult to repeat, and his command remains below average. That hinders him against lefthanders, who posted an .811 OPS against him in Triple-A. Los Angeles has been encouraged by Wall's maturation, as he has come to take his career more seriously. He'll have a chance to make the big league bullpen in spring training.

Year	Club (League)	Class	W	L	ERA	G	GS	CG	SV	IP	H	HR	BB	SO	K/9	WHIP	AVG
2005	Dodgers (GCL)	R	1	3	3.86	5	4	0	0	14	13	2	8	5	3.2	1.50	.245
2006	Ogden (PIO)	R	3	5	5.86	14	14	0	0	66	80	5	33	41	5.6	1.71	.305
2007	Great Lakes (MWL)	LoA	6	10	4.18	26	24	1	1	129	136	8	48	103	7.2	1.42	.269
2008	Inland Empire (CAL)	HiA	9	6	6.28	27	25	0	0	129	152	12	63	101	7.0	1.67	.297
2009	Inland Empire (CAL)	HiA	5	8	5.98	23	22	0	0	111	135	9	51	77	6.2	1.67	.310
2010	Great Lakes (MWL)	LoA	9	7	4.24	26	26	1	0	153	144	11	68	151	8.9	1.39	.248
2011	Chattanooga (SL)	AA	4	5	3.93	51	0	0	1	69	72	6	27	57	7.5	1.44	.271
2012	Albuquerque (PCL)	AAA	2	1	4.53	55	0	0	28	54	50	7	20	52	8.7	1.30	.242
	Los Angeles (NL)	MAJ	1	0	4.76	7	0	0	0	6	3	1	1	4	6.4	0.71	.158
Major League Totals			1	0	4.76	7	0	0	0	6	3	1	1	4	6.4	0.71	.158
Minor League Totals			39	45	4.99	227	115	2	30	725	782	60	318	587	7.3	1.52	.277

21 STEVE AMES, RHP

BA GRADE
45
MEDIUM

Born: March 15, 1988. **B-T:** R-R. **Ht.:** 6-1. **Wt.:** 205. **Drafted:** Gonzaga, 2009 (17th round). **Signed by:** Hank Jones.

Ames has performed at every stop along the way in his pro career. He went 8-2, 3.91 while working as a starter in his lone season at Gonzaga in 2009, but the Dodgers converted him to relief right away. He has put up a 1.93 career ERA in four seasons as a pro and earned a spot on Los Angeles' 40-man roster after last season. His brother Jeff pitches in the Rays system. Ames has the prototypical reliever's mentality, coming to the mound in attack mode. He works fast and pounds the bottom of the strike zone with 92-94 mph fastballs. He struggles to maintain a consistent release point for his slider at times, but it looks like a solid major league pitch when he has it going. He has an early-count curveball as well, and he sometimes gets caught between the two breaking pitches. He has some feel for a below-average changeup but uses it infrequently. Ames' delivery is a bit herky-jerky, but it's nothing major and his command is solid. He should make his big league debut at some point in 2013, fitting in as a useful seventh- or eighth-inning option down the road.

Year	Club (League)	Class	W	L	ERA	G	GS	CG	SV	IP	H	HR	BB	SO	K/9	WHIP	AVG
2009	Ogden (PIO)	R	1	1	2.10	17	0	0	7	30	20	2	6	47	14.1	0.87	.192
2010	Dodgers (AZL)	R	0	0	0.00	3	0	0	0	3	2	0	0	4	12.0	0.67	.182
	Great Lakes (MWL)	LoA	0	2	2.54	23	0	0	16	28	21	0	3	44	14.0	0.85	.196
2011	R. Cucamonga (CAL)	HiA	0	0	1.17	15	0	0	9	15	10	1	2	28	16.4	0.78	.182
	Chattanooga (SL)	AA	2	2	2.48	28	0	0	5	33	32	3	11	41	11.3	1.32	.260
2012	Chattanooga (SL)	AA	3	3	1.56	54	0	0	18	63	52	2	13	72	10.2	1.03	.222
Minor League Totals			6	8	1.93	140	0	0	55	173	137	8	35	236	12.3	1.00	.216

22 JAMES BALDWIN III, OF

BA GRADE
50
EXTREME

Born: Oct. 10, 1991. **B-T:** L-R. **Ht.:** 6-3. **Wt.:** 190. **Drafted:** HS—Southern Pines, N.C., 2010 (4th round). **Signed by:** Lon Joyce.

Baldwin played for his father, longtime big league pitcher James Jr., at Pinecrest High in Southern Pines, N.C. His father was Pinecrest's pitching coach and Baldwin played both ways in high school, but his father encouraged him to make the outfield his future, and he signed for $180,000 with the Dodgers out of the 2010 draft. Getting his first shot at a full-season league last year, he opened the season in a 1-for-30 rut, and his average hovered around the Mendoza Line most of the year. The tools are there, but Baldwin needs a lot of polish. He's an outstanding athlete and wiry strong, unleashing plenty of bat speed to generate power. His power potential has been a double-edged sword, however. He sells out far too much, not taking advantage of his speed, becoming too pull-conscious and giving away at-bats. Los Angeles wants him to bunt more and focus on hitting balls on the ground because he has well above-average speed. He ranges well in all directions to track balls down in center field and led the low Class A Midwest League with 53 steals last year despite his struggles to get on base. Baldwin's ceiling remains high as a center fielder and potential top-of-the-order hitter, but he has a long way to go, beginning with likely repeating low Class A in 2013.

Year	Club (League)	Class	AVG	G	AB	R	H	2B	3B	HR	RBI	BB	SO	SB	CS	OBP	SLG
2010	Dodgers (AZL)	R	.274	46	179	25	49	6	2	2	22	9	60	17	3	.313	.363
2011	Ogden (PIO)	R	.250	50	196	47	49	9	3	10	39	18	74	22	5	.348	.480
2012	Great Lakes (MWL)	LoA	.209	123	440	62	92	18	8	7	40	45	177	53	8	.293	.334
Minor League Totals			.233	219	815	134	190	33	13	19	101	72	311	92	16	.311	.375

23 ALEX SANTANA, 3B

BA GRADE
50
EXTREME

Born: Aug. 21, 1993. **B-T:** R-R. **Ht.:** 6-4. **Wt.:** 200. **Drafted:** HS—Cape Coral, Fla., 2011 (2nd round). **Signed by:** Rob Sidwell.

Santana played shortstop in high school like his father, Rafael, who was a big league shortstop for seven seasons. Alex will take a different road to the majors, though, as the Dodgers saw in his tall, lanky frame that he was already outgrowing shortstop and moved him to third base after signing him for $499,500 as the No. 73 overall pick in 2011. Santana was just 17 when he was drafted, making him one of the youngest players in the 2011 class, and Los Angeles knows his development will take time. He's a line-drive, gap-to-gap hitter, but he has the bat speed and leverage in his swing to produce 20-homer power once he fills out his frame. His swing gets out of sync, though. He gets too long to the ball and needs to maintain a good bat path more consistently, as he gets in trouble when he tries to hit for power. He needs to put bad at-bats behind him and tends to be too hard on himself when he gets in a hitting funk. His third base play is still raw as well. He shows good hands and an above-average arm, but his set-up and first-step movements need to get better, and he's just a fringy runner. He made 24 errors in 50 games last season. The tools are there for Santana to be a run producer at the hot corner, but he's several years away and will likely head back to Ogden in 2013.

Year	Club (League)	Class	AVG	G	AB	R	H	2B	3B	HR	RBI	BB	SO	SB	CS	OBP	SLG
2011	Dodgers (AZL)	R	.238	50	189	30	45	10	3	1	19	10	64	8	1	.298	.339
2012	Ogden (PIO)	R	.269	24	93	14	25	8	1	1	19	4	29	1	2	.297	.409
	Dodgers (AZL)	R	.240	26	96	12	23	3	1	1	12	11	41	4	1	.315	.323
Minor League Totals			.246	100	378	56	93	21	5	3	50	25	134	13	4	.302	.352

24 SCOTT BARLOW, RHP

BA GRADE
50
EXTREME

Born: Dec. 18, 1992. **B-T:** R-R. **Ht.:** 6-3. **Wt.:** 170. **Drafted:** HS—Santa Clarita, Calif., 2011 (6th round). **Signed by:** Fred Costello.

Barlow was one of the stars of Los Angeles' instructional league contingent in 2011 but never got to build on that momentum in 2012, missing the entire season following Tommy John surgery. A gangly righthander who had a fringy fastball in high school, he added strength to his frame following his selection in the sixth round of the 2011 draft, and Los Angeles spent $150,000 that August to sign him away from a Fresno State commitment. The Dodgers saw a lot of projection in his frame, and his velocity picked up into the low 90s, peaking at 95 mph, by the end of 2011. His curveball got the highest marks of his secondary offerings, but he has a four-pitch mix that also includes a slider and changeup that have a chance to play as quality weapons. He drew rave reviews for how well he competed and for his feel for pitching. He has a good delivery and arm action that shouldn't cause any future problems, and Los Angeles wonders if he was overworked before he signed. Barlow had his operation early enough that he should be able to have a productive 2013 season, and his rehab was proceeding on track. Once he gets a clean bill of health, he could head to low Class A or stay back in extended spring training before going to Ogden.

Year	Club (League)	Class	W	L	ERA	G	GS	CG	SV	IP	H	HR	BB	SO	K/9	WHIP	AVG
2011	Dodgers (AZL)	R	0	1	27.00	2	0	0	0	2	5	1	2	1	5.4	4.20	.500
2012	Did Not Play—Injured																
Minor League Totals			0	1	27.00	2	0	0	0	2	5	1	2	1	5.4	4.20	.500

25 ANGEL SANCHEZ, RHP

BA GRADE
50
EXTREME

Born: Nov. 28, 1989. **B-T:** R-R. **Ht.:** 6-3. **Wt.:** 177. **Signed:** Dominican Republic, 2010. **Signed by:** Ezequiel Sepulveda.

The Dodgers signed Sanchez out of an unusual source, Santo Domingo Autonomous University, a college in the Dominican Republic. He cost them a mere $7,500 bonus in July 2010 and had a breakout pro debut the next year, going 8-4, 2.82 in low Class A. His follow-up campaign was a disaster. After an up-and-down first half in high Class A, Sanchez lost nine straight decisions and had the worst ERA in the minors in the second half at 8.75. His stock understandably took a hit, but he does still have an exciting arm. His fastball ranges from 92-96 mph, and he backs it up with a tight, late-breaking slider. He can also turn to an underused changeup, which is inconsistent but shows flashes of becoming an average pitch, and a show-me curveball. He struggled with command last season, particularly with his slider. The team also worried that he didn't put in the same effort in his start-to-start preparation as he did in 2011, and hopes last season was a wakeup call. Sanchez will get another crack at Rancho Cucamonga in 2013. Continued struggles with his secondary stuff could force a move to the bullpen sooner than later.

Year	Club (League)	Class	W	L	ERA	G	GS	CG	SV	IP	H	HR	BB	SO	K/9	WHIP	AVG
2011	Great Lakes (MWL)	LoA	8	4	2.82	20	16	0	0	99	72	5	39	84	7.6	1.12	.198
2012	R. Cucamonga (CAL)	HiA	6	12	6.58	27	23	0	0	130	157	26	51	103	7.1	1.60	.300
Minor League Totals			14	16	4.95	47	39	0	0	229	229	31	90	187	7.3	1.39	.258

26 BRIAN CAVAZOS-GALVEZ, OF

BA GRADE

45

MEDIUM

Born: May 17, 1987. **B-T:** R-R. **Ht.:** 6-0. **Wt.:** 215. **Drafted:** New Mexico, 2009 (12th round). **Signed by:** Calvin Jones.

Cavazos-Galvez's father Balvino Galvez came up through the Dodgers organization in the 1980s and pitched briefly in the majors in 1986, but he has not been in contact with his son since leaving to play overseas in the 1990s. Cavazos-Galvez got off to a terrible start at Double-A last spring and was sent back to high Class A to refocus. He ironed out some issues in his swing as well and took off when an injury opened a spot for him in Albuquerque, where he was born and where he played his college ball. He had been too pull-conscious, trying to hook balls and getting himself out when he chased breaking pitches. Working with Triple-A hitting coach John Valentin, he got his bat on a better path and is now able to keep the barrel in the hitting zone longer. He does have the strength and quick hands to hit for solid power. He's still a free swinger, though he did a better job of laying off early count breaking pitches last year. He runs well enough to keep play either outfield corner and plays with energy. His arm is better suited for left field, though, and he needs to improve his routes and jumps. His 2012 season ended early when he went down with an ankle injury in July, but he should be ready to go back for a full season of Triple-A ball in 2013. The Dodgers didn't protect him on the 40-man roster but he went unpicked in the Rule 5 draft.

Year	Club (League)	Class	AVG	G	AB	R	H	2B	3B	HR	RBI	BB	SO	SB	CS	OBP	SLG
2009	Ogden (PIO)	R	.322	71	301	59	97	29	3	18	63	10	43	17	8	.353	.618
2010	Great Lakes (MWL)	LoA	.318	121	490	76	156	43	4	16	77	12	60	43	13	.343	.520
2011	Chattanooga (SL)	AA	.277	116	411	60	114	27	5	14	61	12	63	13	11	.311	.470
2012	Chattanooga (SL)	AA	.167	20	78	11	13	3	0	4	11	6	17	5	0	.233	.359
	R. Cucamonga (CAL)	HiA	.346	12	52	14	18	2	1	3	11	2	4	4	2	.370	.596
	Albuquerque (PCL)	AAA	.354	57	178	33	63	11	3	7	32	5	24	1	1	.376	.567
	Dodgers (AZL)	R	.389	6	18	4	7	4	0	1	4	0	3	2	0	.389	.778
Minor League Totals			.306	403	1528	257	468	119	16	63	259	47	214	85	35	.336	.529

27 AARON MILLER, LHP

BA GRADE

45

MEDIUM

Born: Sept. 18, 1987. **B-T:** L-L. **Ht.:** 6-3. **Wt.:** 200. **Drafted:** Baylor, 2009 (1st round supplemental). **Signed by:** Chris Smith.

The Rockies drafted Miller as an outfielder in the 11th round out of high school in 2006, but he didn't sign and headed to Baylor, where he continued to focus on hitting through his first two years. He got back on the mound as a junior and landed an $889,200 bonus as the Dodgers' top pick in the 2009 draft. He has battled injuries since signing, most notably a torn muscle in his abdomen that required surgery in 2011, but got through the full season healthy last year, encouraging club officials. The discouraging news is that the 91-94 mph velocity he featured in college hasn't come back. His velocity varied last season, as he could pitch at 90-92 mph with tailing action at times, while at others his fastball sat at 86-89. He has a pair of average secondary pitches in his slider and changeup. Los Angeles hopes he'll recover some of his velocity, but Miller has had to make do with becoming more reliant on command and pitchability. He has a good pitcher's frame, his arm works well and he does show a feel for pitching, but with his current stuff his command will have to become above average if he's going to pitch in the majors. His ceiling may not be more than a back-of-the-rotation starter at this point, and the Dodgers didn't bother to protect him on their 40-man roster this offseason. He's likely to return to the Chattanooga rotation to open 2013.

Year	Club (League)	Class	W	L	ERA	G	GS	CG	SV	IP	H	HR	BB	SO	K/9	WHIP	AVG
2009	Dodgers (AZL)	R	0	0	6.35	3	3	0	0	6	8	0	2	10	15.9	1.76	.320
	Great Lakes (MWL)	LoA	3	1	2.08	7	7	0	0	30	22	3	10	38	11.3	1.05	.208
2010	Chattanooga (SL)	AA	1	4	7.04	6	6	0	0	23	28	3	18	22	8.6	2.00	.304
	Inland Empire (CAL)	HiA	6	4	2.92	19	17	0	0	102	76	6	48	99	8.8	1.22	.207
2011	Dodgers (AZL)	R	1	0	0.00	1	0	0	0	2	1	0	1	3	13.5	1.00	.143
	R. Cucamonga (CAL)	HiA	3	2	3.97	10	6	0	0	34	37	2	18	30	7.9	1.62	.282
2012	Chattanooga (SL)	AA	6	6	4.45	25	25	0	0	121	117	10	71	110	8.2	1.55	.261
Minor League Totals			20	17	3.88	71	64	0	0	318	289	24	168	312	8.8	1.44	.246

28 BLAKE SMITH, OF

Born: Dec. 9, 1987. **B-T:** L-R. **Ht.:** 6-2. **Wt.:** 225. **Drafted:** California, 2009 (2nd round). **Signed by:** Fred Costello.

BA GRADE
45
MEDIUM

The Dodgers have toyed with the idea of putting Smith on the mound, but he has earned the right to keep hitting and playing the outfield. He was a two-way player at California, and his power potential prompted Los Angeles to sign him for $643,500 as the 56th overall pick in 2009. Reaching Double-A for the first time last season, he was hitting .298/.382/.480 at the all-star break but tailed off afterward. Smith did a better job of not leaking out on the front side in his swing last year, allowing him to stay through the ball and hit more to all fields. He whips his bat through the zone and should hit for at least average power, but he must make more consistent contact for his bat to play as an everyday regular. Smith was Chattanooga's primary right fielder last year and started a smattering of games in center. He has the tools for either spot. He's a solid runner whose speed plays up thanks to outstanding routes and jumps, and he has a strong arm. The Dodgers expect to get him some time in left field next season to increase his versatility. Smith wasn't added to the 40-man roster after the season despite his progress, but he should get a chance to move up to Triple-A in 2013.

Year	Club (League)	Class	AVG	G	AB	R	H	2B	3B	HR	RBI	BB	SO	SB	CS	OBP	SLG
2009	Dodgers (AZL)	R	.227	6	22	3	5	1	0	0	2	2	9	0	0	.346	.273
	Ogden (PIO)	R	.212	30	104	14	22	7	0	1	12	13	38	0	0	.311	.308
2010	Great Lakes (MWL)	LoA	.281	115	430	77	121	28	2	19	76	49	135	2	3	.363	.488
2011	Dodgers (AZL)	R	.450	6	20	7	9	2	0	4	10	3	1	0	0	.522	1.150
	R. Cucamonga (CAL)	HiA	.294	74	293	59	86	24	0	16	63	32	83	3	2	.359	.539
2012	Chattanooga (SL)	AA	.267	133	461	69	123	29	4	13	65	64	134	14	6	.358	.432
Minor League Totals			.275	364	1330	229	366	91	6	53	228	163	400	19	11	.359	.472

29 JEREMY RATHJEN, OF

Born: Jan. 28, 1990. **B-T:** R-R. **Ht.:** 6-6. **Wt.:** 190. **Drafted:** Rice, 2012 (11th round). **Signed by:** Clint Bowers.

BA GRADE
45
HIGH

Rathjen first got on the scouting radar when he was a high school teammate of Blue Jays 2007 first-rounder Kevin Ahrens. He passed on signing with the Diamondbacks as a 45th-rounder in 2008 to go to Rice, and he looked like a potential top-five-rounds pick going into 2011 before tearing his ACL 16 games into his junior season. The Yankees took a shot at him in the 41st round, but he went back for one more year at Rice, hitting .329 with nine homers last spring. The Dodgers were ecstatic to get him in the 11th round for $75,000, as his athleticism reminds them of Justin Ruggiano, who began his career as Los Angeles' 25th-round pick in 2004. Rathjen's speed hasn't come all the way back to where it was before his knee injury, but he's still a good runner and has a chance to stick as a center fielder. His arm would work in right field if he needs to move. He's an intelligent hitter with advanced pitch-recognition skills, and he posted the third-best on-base percentage (.443) in the Rookie-level Pioneer League in his pro debut. His swing gets long at times, but he shows the bat speed to drive balls, giving him at least average power. Rathjen has the tools and advanced approach to push through the lower levels of the system quickly. He'll begin his first full pro season at one of Los Angeles' Class A affiliates.

Year	Club (League)	Class	AVG	G	AB	R	H	2B	3B	HR	RBI	BB	SO	SB	CS	OBP	SLG
2012	Ogden (PIO)	R	.324	68	262	67	85	17	1	9	53	48	55	16	8	.443	.500
Minor League Totals			.324	68	262	67	85	17	1	9	53	48	55	16	8	.443	.500

30 JOEY CURLETTA, OF

Born: March 8, 1994. **B-T:** R-R. **Ht.:** 6-4. **Wt.:** 225. **Drafted:** HS—Phoenix, 2012 (6th round). **Signed by:** Dustin Yount.

BA GRADE
50
EXTREME

Curletta mashed 21 homers as a junior at Mountain Pointe High in Phoenix in 2011 before his production dropped off to just four homers in his draft year, but the Dodgers still believed enough in his tools to sign him away from an Arizona commitment for $171,600 in the sixth round. Despite his home run dropoff, Curletta has a chance for two well above-average tools in his raw power and throwing arm, which also made him a prospect on the mound. He garners physical comparisons to the Angels' Mark Trumbo and has similar raw power. He'll need to tweak his swing to show it in games, though. He needs a better bat path, as he tends to collapse and try too much to hook and lift balls. Scouts who watched Curletta in high school felt he would be limited to first base, but Los Angeles believes he runs well enough to try in the outfield and doesn't want to waste his arm at first base, either. He was capable of throwing 94 mph in high school but prefers hitting. The Dodgers will give him a chance to make it as a hitter but would put him on the mound if he doesn't make progress within a few years. He'll likely begin his career in extended spring training in 2013 before heading to Ogden.

Year	Club (League)	Class	AVG	G	AB	R	H	2B	3B	HR	RBI	BB	SO	SB	CS	OBP	SLG
2012	Dodgers (AZL)	R	.149	25	74	5	11	2	0	0	6	7	25	0	0	.235	.176
Minor League Totals			.149	25	74	5	11	2	0	0	6	7	25	0	0	.235	.176

Miami Marlins

BY JAMES BAILEY

After years of frugality, the Marlins stole the headlines at the 2011 Winter Meetings. They lavished $191 million worth of contracts on free agents Jose Reyes, Mark Buehrle and Heath Bell, and even made runs at Albert Pujols and C.J. Wilson.

Miami's plan was to make the first season in new Marlins Park one to remember. Owner Jeffrey Loria's sudden largesse seemed a fitting thank-you for a  stadium largely financed by the public.

The goodwill proved fleeting. Eleven months later, all three players had followed embattled manager Ozzie Guillen out the door.

The disappointing Bell was dumped on the Diamondbacks in a three-team trade in October, one month before Reyes and Buehrle went to the Blue Jays in a landscape-shifting, 12-player blockbuster. Combined with in-season deals that shipped former face of the franchise Hanley Ramirez to the Dodgers and Anibal Sanchez and Omar Infante to the Tigers, the moves left the big league roster in smoldering ruins, angering both fans and remaining players alike.

Ironically, the Marlins' first significant swap of 2012 added a veteran bat at the expense of prospects. With a 39-42 record on July 4, they picked up Carlos Lee from the Astros in exchange for third baseman Matt Dominguez and lefthander Rob Rasmussen. Just two weeks later, however, a five-game losing skid flipped the switch to rebuilding mode.

Sanchez and Infante brought pitchers Jacob Turner and Brian Flynn and catcher Rob Brantly from Detroit, along with the first-ever trade of draft picks. Two days after that, the underperforming Ramirez went to the Dodgers for righthanders Nate Eovaldi and Scott McGough. In other deadline deals for Edward Mujica and Gaby Sanchez, Miami scored third baseman Zack Cox, center fielder Gorkys Hernandez and a competitive-balance lottery pick.

By season's end, Brantly, Eovaldi, Hernandez and Turner were regulars in a Marlins lineup and rotation that barely resembled those the team opened the season with. Guillen, whose ill-advised profession of love of Cuban dictator Fidel Castro earned him a five-game suspension less than a week into the season, was fired in late October. A 69-93 last-place finish was hardly what Miami hoped for when it traded two prospects for Guillen and gave him a four-year, $10 million contract.

Jose Reyes (left) and Ozzie Guillen didn't last very long as part of the makeover in Miami

Then came the bombshell.

While the Reyes/Buehrle trade completed the decimation of the big league roster—Emilio Bonifacio, John Buck and Josh Johnson also went to Toronto—it did beef up a thin farm system. The Marlins added four prospects in outfielder Jake Marisnick, lefthander Justin Nicolino, shortstop Adeiny Hechavarria and righty Anthony DeSclafani. Miami also picked up three veterans in Henderson Alvarez, Yunel Escobar and Jeff Mathis, then spun Escobar to the Rays for middle infielder Derek Dietrich.

The cream of the system's existing talent mostly played together at high Class A Jupiter in 2012, finishing runner-up in the Florida State League playoffs. The Hammerheads' prospect-laden lineup included outfielders Christian Yelich and Marcell Ozuna and catcher J.T. Realmuto. They were joined at midseason by righthander Jose Fernandez and lefthander Adam Conley, who were promoted after dominating in low Class A.

Fernandez and Yelich give the Marlins two true impact talents. The club's last three first-rounders (Yelich, Fernandez, lefthander Andrew Heaney) rank as its best prospects, though the upper levels of the system are feeling the effects of disappointing drafts in 2008-09.

THIS YEAR'S TOP 30

	Player, Pos.	Grade
1.	Jose Fernandez, rhp	70/Medium
2.	Christian Yelich, of	65/Medium
3.	Andrew Heaney, lhp	60/Medium
4.	Jake Marisnick, of	60/High
5.	Marcell Ozuna, of	60/High
6.	Justin Nicolino, lhp	55/Medium
7.	Adeiny Hechavarria, inf	50/Medium
8.	Jose Urena, rhp	55/High
9.	J.T. Realmuto, c	50/High
10.	Adam Conley, lhp	50/High
11.	Rob Brantly, c	45/Medium
12.	Derek Dietrich, ss/2b	50/High
13.	Alfredo Silverio, of	55/Extreme
14.	A.J. Ramos, rhp	45/Low
15.	Zack Cox, 3b	50/High
16.	Austin Brice, rhp	50/High
17.	Avery Romero, 3b/2b	50/High
18.	Kolby Copeland, of	50/High
19.	Austin Dean, of	50/High
20.	Jesus Solorzano, of	50/Extreme
21.	Chris Hatcher, rhp	45/Medium
22.	Raudel Lazo, lhp	45/Medium
23.	Jake Esch, rhp	50/Extreme
24.	Brian Flynn, lhp	45/Medium
25.	Grant Dayton, lhp	45/Medium
26.	Chad James, lhp	50/Extreme
27.	Jose Ceda, rhp	45/High
28.	Danny Black, ss	45/High
29.	Austin Barnes, 2b/c	45/High
30.	Brent Keys, of	45/High

LAST YEAR'S TOP 30

	Player, Pos.	Status
1.	Christian Yelich, of	No. 2
2.	Marcell Ozuna, of	No. 5
3.	Jose Fernandez, rhp	No. 1
4.	Matt Dominguez, 3b	(Astros)
5.	J.T. Realmuto, c	No. 9
6.	Chad James, lhp	No. 26
7.	Rob Rasmussen, lhp	(Astros)
8.	Noah Perio, 2b	Dropped out
9.	Scott Cousins, of	(Angels)
10.	Adam Conley, lhp	No. 10
11.	Jose Urena, rhp	No. 8
12.	Austin Brice, rhp	No. 16
13.	Ryan Fisher, 3b	Dropped out
14.	Chris Hatcher, rhp	No. 21
15.	Jose Ceda, rhp	No. 27
16.	Jesus Solorzano, of	No. 20
17.	Grant Dayton, lhp	No. 25
18.	Michael Brady, rhp	Dropped out
19.	Kyle Jensen, of	Dropped out
20.	A.J. Ramos, rhp	No. 14
21.	Kyle Skipworth, c	Dropped out
22.	Mark Canha, 1b/of	Dropped out
23.	Mason Hope, rhp	Dropped out
24.	Evan Reed, rhp	Dropped out
25.	Joey O'Gara, rhp	Dropped out
26.	Tom Koehler, rhp	Dropped out
27.	Kevin Mattison, of	Dropped out
28.	Josh Hodges, rhp	Dropped out
29.	Sandy Rosario, rhp	(Red Sox)
30.	Daniel Jennings, lhp	Dropped out

BEST TOOLS

Best Hitter for Average	Christian Yelich
Best Power Hitter	Marcell Ozuna
Best Strike-Zone Discipline	Jake Smolinski
Fastest Baserunner	Kevin Mattison
Best Athlete	Jake Marisnick
Best Fastball	Jose Fernandez
Best Curveball	Jose Fernandez
Best Slider	Andrew Heaney
Best Changeup	Justin Nicolino
Best Control	Justin Nicolino
Best Defensive Catcher	J.T. Realmuto
Best Defensive Infielder	Adeiny Hechavarria
Best Infield Arm	Yordy Cabrera
Best Defensive Outfielder	Jake Marisnick
Best Outfield Arm	Marcell Ozuna

PROJECTED 2016 LINEUP

Catcher	J.T. Realmuto
First Base	Logan Morrison
Second Base	Avery Romero
Third Base	Derek Dietrich
Shortstop	Adeiny Hechavarria
Left Field	Christian Yelich
Center Field	Jake Marisnick
Right Field	Giancarlo Stanton
No. 1 Starter	Jose Fernandez
No. 2 Starter	Andrew Heaney
No. 3 Starter	Justin Nicolino
No. 4 Starter	Nathan Eovaldi
No. 5 Starter	Jacob Turner
Closer	A.J. Ramos

TOP PROSPECTS OF THE DECADE

Year	Player, Pos.	2012 Org.
2003	Miguel Cabrera, 3b	Tigers
2004	Jeremy Hermida, of	Padres
2005	Jeremy Hermida, of	Padres
2006	Jeremy Hermida, of	Padres
2007	Chris Volstad, rhp	Cubs
2008	Cameron Maybin, of	Padres
2009	Cameron Maybin, of	Padres
2010	Giancarlo Stanton, of	Marlins
2011	Matt Dominguez, 3b	Astros
2012	Christian Yelich, of	Marlins

TOP DRAFT PICKS OF THE DECADE

Year	Player, Pos.	2012 Org.
2003	Jeff Allison, rhp	Out of baseball
2004	Taylor Tankersley, lhp	Out of baseball
2005	Chris Volstad, rhp	Cubs
2006	Brett Sinkbeil, rhp	Out of baseball
2007	Matt Dominguez, 3b	Astros
2008	Kyle Skipworth, c	Marlins
2009	Chad James, lhp	Marlins
2010	Christian Yelich, of	Marlins
2011	Jose Fernandez, rhp	Marlins
2012	Andrew Heaney, lhp	Marlins

LARGEST BONUSES IN CLUB HISTORY

Josh Beckett, 1999	$3,625,000
Adrian Gonzalez, 2000	$3,000,000
Andrew Heaney, 2012	$2,600,000
Livan Hernandez, 1996	$2,500,000
Kyle Skipworth, 2008	$2,300,000

MIAMI MARLINS

TOP 2013 ROOKIE: Adeiny Hechavarria, inf. After coming over from the Blue Jays in the Jose Reyes blockbuster, he's the logical choice to replace Reyes.

BREAKOUT PROSPECT: Jake Esch, rhp. Despite his inexperience on the hill, the former college infielder has good stuff and knows what to do with it.

SLEEPER: Andy Beltre, rhp. He has a projectable 6-foot-4 frame and command of a lively mid-90s fastball.

SOURCE OF TOP 30 TALENT			
Homegrown	21	Acquired	9
College	8	Trades	8
Junior college	0	Rule 5 draft	1
High school	9	Independent leagues	0
Nondrafted free agents	0	Free agents/waivers	0
International	4		

LF
Austin Dean (19)
Jake Smolinski

CF
Christian Yelich (2)
Jake Marisnick (4)
Kolby Copeland (18)
Brent Keys (30)
Kevin Mattison
Isaac Galloway
Cody Keefer
Juancito Martinez

RF
Marcell Ozuna (5)
Alfredo Silverio (13)
Jesus Solorzano (20)
Kyle Jensen

3B
Zack Cox (15)
Avery Romero (17)
Yordy Cabrera
Ryan Fisher
Josh Adams
Ryan Goetz

SS
Adeiny Hechavarria (7)
Danny Black (28)
Javier Lopez
Austin Nola
Yeison Hernandez
Christian Rivera
Rehiner Cordova

2B
Derek Dietrich (12)
Noah Perio
Anthony Gomez
Alfredo Lopez
Yefri Perez

1B
Joe Mahoney
Mark Canha
Viosergy Rosa
Matt Smith
Aaron Senne
Ryan Rieger
Felix Munoz
Ron Miller

C
J.T. Realmuto (9)
Rob Brantly (11)
Austin Barnes (29)
Kyle Skipworth
Wilfredo Gimenez
Michael Vaughn

LHP

LHSP
Andrew Heaney (3)
Justin Nicolino (6)
Adam Conley (10)
Brian Flynn (24)
Chad James (26)
Braulio Lara
Charlie Lowell
Edgar Olmos

LHRP
Raudel Lazo (22)
Grant Dayton (25)
Dan Jennings
Greg Nappo
Tyler Kehrer

RHP

RHSP
Jose Fernandez (1)
Jose Urena (8)
Austin Brice (16)
Jake Esch (23)
Mason Hope
Josh Hodges
Robert Morey
Andy Beltre
Joey O'Gara
Elih Villanueva
Zach Neal
Helpi Reyes
Scott Lyman
Ramon del Orbe
Drew Steckenrider
Blake Logan
Ryan Newell

RHRP
A.J. Ramos (14)
Chris Hatcher (21)
Jose Ceda (27)
Evan Reed
Tom Koehler
Nick Wittgren
Tyler Higgins
Michael Brady
Arquimedes Caminero
Kevin Cravey
Scott McGough
Pete Andrelczyk
Matt Milroy
Dane Stone
Rett Varner
Jordan Conley
Chris Squires

2012
BONUSES: $5.8 MILLION

BEST PURE HITTER: All three of the Marlins' high school position players from the top four rounds—3B/2B Avery Romero (3), OFs Kolby Copeland (3s) and Austin Dean (4)—show some feel with the bat. Copeland has the best pure hitting ability. He has a compact lefthanded stroke and a flat swing path that keeps his bat in the zone for a long time.

BEST POWER HITTER: Romero (3) has a thicker build, similar to that of Dan Uggla. While it's not clear where he'll wind up defensively, Romero has a strong, short swing with above-average power potential.

FASTEST RUNNER: The Marlins didn't draft any burners. OF Cody Keefer (15) has above-average speed and plays a good center field.

BEST DEFENSIVE PLAYER: SS Austin Nola (5) lacks impact with the bat and hit just .211/.305/.268 in his debut, but he's a steady defender with soft hands, quick feet and good infield actions.

BEST FASTBALL: For pure velocity, RHP Ryan Newell (7) was up to 97 mph in the spring but topped out at 95 after signing. LHP Andrew Heaney (1) sits mostly in the 92-93 mph range, but did touch 97 in his final pro outing this year and his fastball plays up because of its action and his command.

BEST SECONDARY PITCH: Heaney's slider is a 65 offering on the 20-80 scouting scale, typically arriving at 83-85 mph. The pitch has late downer action, making it a weapon against lefties and righties alike. His fastball and slider helped him lead NCAA Division I pitchers with 140 strikeouts at Oklahoma State in the spring.

BEST PRO DEBUT: With his 91-93 mph fastball and hard curveball, RHP Nick Wittgren (9) posted a 1.17 ERA, 13 saves and a 47-5 K-BB ratio in 31 innings between short-season Jamestown and low Class A Greensboro.

BEST ATHLETE: Copeland was a high school quarterback and shows good instincts, body control and hand-eye coordination. Though he played mostly first base in high school, Dean has solid speed and athleticism.

MOST INTRIGUING BACKGROUND: C Michael Vaughn (14) is a quadruplet whose uncle, Shawn Gilbert, spent parts of three seasons in the big leagues. Unsigned SS Lucas Hunter's (31) father Brian L. and OF Eddie Sappelt's (37) brother Dave also played in the majors.

CLOSEST TO THE MAJORS: Heaney's stuff and advanced feel should allow him to start his first full pro season in high Class A. Wittgren could do the same. Best Late-Round Pick: In addition to his speed and defense, Keefer has a smooth lefthanded swing with some sneaky power.

THE ONE WHO GOT AWAY: The Marlins drew the line at paying any draft tax, letting 3B/RHP Cody Gunter go to Grayson County (Texas) CC rather than paying him $200,000. He offers lefthanded power and also throws 90-92 off the mound.

ASSESSMENT: The Marlins avoided disaster by signing Heaney after breaking off negotiations and by landing Romero at the deadline. Romero, Copeland and Dean add some much-needed offensive talent to the system.

2011
BONUSES: $4.1 MILLION

A steal with the 14th overall pick, RHP Jose Fernandez (1) quickly has become one of the game's top pitching prospects. LHP Adam Conley (2) could team with him in Miami's rotation in the near future.

GRADE: A

2010
BONUSES: $4.4 MILLION

Like Fernandez, OF Christian Yelich (1) is a first-rounder who has exceeded expectations. The Marlins also are bullish on C J.T. Realmuto (3) and RHP Austin Brice (9). LHP Rob Rasmussen (2) was lost in the ill-advised Carlos Lee trade with the Marlins last summer.

GRADE: B+

2009
BONUSES: $4.1 MILLION

LHP Chad James (1) is headed in the wrong direction, leaving RHP A.J. Ramos (21) as the brightest hope for this class.

GRADE: D

2008
BONUSES: $5.4 MILLION

The Marlins hoped for a catcher, and after missing on Buster Posey by one pick, they busted with C Kyle Skipworth (1). They did find five big leaguers in LHPs Brad Hand (2) and Dan Jennings (9), RHPs Tom Koehler (18) and Elih Villanueva (27) and OF Kevin Mattison (28), but none may be more than a role player. Unsigned OF Mikie Mahtook (39) developed into a 2011 first-rounder.

GRADE: D

Draft analysis by Conor Glassey (2012) and Jim Callis (2008-11). Numbers in parentheses indicate draft rounds.

1 JOSE FERNANDEZ, RHP

Born: July 31, 1992. **B-T:** R-R. **Ht.:** 6-3. **Wt.:** 215.
Drafted: HS—Tampa, 2011 (1st round). **Signed by:** Brian Kraft.

BA GRADE
70
MEDIUM

MIKE JANES

It took four tries before a 15-year-old Fernandez, his mother and his sister finally escaped Cuba via speedboat in 2008. As punishment for their failed attempts, he was expelled from school, kicked off the baseball team and briefly jailed. When waves swept his mother overboard, Fernandez dove in to rescue her, swimming back to the boat with her clinging to his neck. After a harrowing 36-hour journey to Mexico they reached the United States and reunited with his father, who had fled three years earlier. Fernandez learned English after settling in Tampa, where he led Alonso High to two Florida 6-A state titles in three years. The 14th overall pick in the 2011 draft, he signed for an above-slot $2 million bonus. That looks like a bargain after he ranked as the No. 1 prospect in the low Class A South Atlantic and high Class A Florida State leagues in his first full pro season, leading the minors with an overall 0.93 WHIP.

Fernandez's confidence—or cockiness—earns him comparisons to Roger Clemens. It's not arrogance if you can back it up, which Fernandez can. Numerous scouts cited his stuff as the best of any hurler in the 2012 Futures Game. His four-seam fastball sits at 94-95 mph and touches 99 with unbelievable explosion. Using an easy arm action, he'll dial his velocity up and down and climb the ladder on hitters. He also mixes in a 92-93 mph two-seamer to induce groundouts. Fernandez also can overmatch hitters with a hard three-quarters breaking ball that he can run up to 85 mph. He can command it for both called strikes and swinging misses, and he'll throw it any count. He also can use a true slider that's effective. He flashes a plus changeup with deception and nice fade, though he doesn't consistently command it down in the strike zone. With so many weapons to choose from, Fernandez doesn't always throw the right pitch in every situation, though he's getting better at letting a hitter's reaction to certain pitches determine which ones he sees the rest of the night. The Marlins rave about his work ethic, aptitude and drive to win.

SCOUTING GRADES

Fastball: 75.   **Control:** 65.
Curveball: 65.   **Command:** 60.
Changeup: 55.

Based on 20-80 scouting scale, where 50 represents major league average, and future projection rather than present tools.

In one May start, he struck out six hitters in the first two innings, then fanned just two more while working into the eighth. When asked about his change in approach, he told a coach he began pitching to contact to keep his pitch count low so he could stay in the game longer. That kind of maturity is uncommon for a player in his first full year as a pro. Strong and durable, Fernandez had plenty left in the tank when the season concluded. Much of his power comes from his strong lower half, which allows him to explode through his hips. He has good athleticism for his size, though he'll have to watch his conditioning as he ages. The only hiccup in his 2012 season came after his midseason promotion, when he tried to overpower FSL hitters at times instead of simply trusting his stuff.

Fernandez might tempt the big league staff to keep him during spring training, but he'll probably open 2013 in Double-A Jacksonville. He could reach Miami by midseason and has the stuff and mindset to become a true No. 1 starter.

Year	Club (League)	Class	W	L	ERA	G	GS	CG	SV	IP	H	HR	BB	SO	K/9	WHIP	AVG
2011	Marlins (GCL)	R	0	0	0.00	1	1	0	0	2	1	0	1	3	13.5	1.00	.125
	Jamestown (NYP)	SS	0	1	19.29	1	1	0	0	2	4	0	3	4	15.4	3.00	.400
2012	Greensboro (SAL)	LoA	7	0	1.59	14	14	0	0	79	51	2	18	99	11.3	0.87	.189
	Jupiter (FSL)	HiA	7	1	1.96	11	11	0	0	55	38	0	17	59	9.7	1.00	.193
Minor League Totals			14	2	2.02	27	27	0	0	138	94	2	39	165	10.7	0.96	.194

2 CHRISTIAN YELICH, OF

AMANDA WILLIAMS

Born: Dec. 5, 1991. **B-T:** L-R. **Ht.:** 6-4. **Wt.:** 190. **Drafted:** HS—Westlake Village, Calif., 2010 (1st round). **Signed by:** Tim McDonnell.

Since signing for a $1.7 million bonus as the 23rd overall pick in 2010, Yelich has been Marlins minor league player of the year in each of his two full seasons. He topped the Florida State League in slugging (.519) and OPS (.923) and finished second in hitting (.330) in 2012 despite missing time with an elbow injury and a concussion. Yelich has the pure swing of a future batting champion and an advanced approach. Quick, strong hands allow him to line balls to all fields, though he makes a particular effort to stay in the middle of the diamond. While he projects to hit more for average than power, some scouts envision 25-homer potential once he fills out. Yelich uses his plus speed well on the bases, where he has succeeded on 53 of 64 (83 percent) pro steal attempts. It also plays well in center field, where he gets good jumps and can run balls down in the gaps. A long arm stroke has hampered his throwing since high school, but extra repetitions and improved footwork mean his arm plays as average. The Marlins love his attitude and competitive nature. Yelich's defensive progress has silenced any talk of a move to left field. He should anchor the middle of Miami's outfield and batting order soon. His next stop is Double-A.

BA GRADE
65
MEDIUM

Year	Club (League)	Class	AVG	G	AB	R	H	2B	3B	HR	RBI	BB	SO	SB	CS	OBP	SLG
2010	Marlins (GCL)	R	.375	6	24	3	9	1	1	0	3	2	7	1	0	.423	.500
	Greensboro (SAL)	LoA	.348	6	23	2	8	2	0	0	2	1	6	0	0	.375	.435
2011	Greensboro (SAL)	LoA	.312	122	461	73	144	32	1	15	77	55	102	32	5	.388	.484
2012	Marlins (GCL)	R	.250	1	4	0	1	0	0	0	0	0	0	0	0	.250	.250
	Jupiter (FSL)	HiA	.330	106	397	76	131	29	5	12	48	49	85	20	6	.404	.519
Minor League Totals			.322	241	909	154	293	64	7	27	130	107	200	53	11	.395	.497

3 ANDREW HEANEY, LHP

Born: June 5, 1991. **B-T:** L-L. **Ht.:** 6-3. **Wt.:** 180. **Drafted:** Oklahoma State, 2012 (1st round). **Signed by:** Steve Taylor.

The top college lefthander in the 2012 draft, Heaney led NCAA Division I with 140 strikeouts in 118 innings last spring. Negotiations turned acrimonious after the Marlins selected him ninth overall, though they signed him near the deadline for $2.6 million. Heaney got better with each start, with his fastball climbing from 88-90 mph after the layoff to touching 97 in his final pro outing. It should settle at 90-94, and he commands it easily to both sides of the plate. His 83-85 mph slider is already at least a plus pitch, though he's working to give it more deception with late, hard break that will finish out of the hitting zone. His changeup improved in league after Miami got him to finish with his upper half coming more toward the plate. Heaney has a loose arm, effortless delivery and excellent control. While he worked to gain strength coming into his junior season at Oklahoma State, he could stand to add more muscle to his lean frame. Heaney will open his first full pro season at high Class A Jupiter and may not stay there long. He projects as a No. 2 or 3 starter who could join the Marlins at some point in 2014.

BA GRADE
60
MEDIUM

Year	Club (League)	Class	W	L	ERA	G	GS	CG	SV	IP	H	HR	BB	SO	K/9	WHIP	AVG
2012	Marlins (GCL)	R	0	0	2.57	2	2	0	0	7	7	0	2	9	11.6	1.29	.259
	Greensboro (SAL)	LoA	1	2	4.95	4	4	0	0	20	25	0	4	21	9.5	1.45	.287
Minor League Totals			1	2	4.33	6	6	0	0	27	32	0	6	30	10.0	1.41	.281

4 JAKE MARISNICK, OF

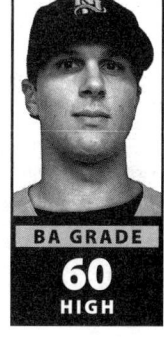

Born: March 30, 1991. **B-T:** R-R. **Ht.:** 6-4. **Wt.:** 200. **Drafted:** HS—Riverside, Calif., 2009 (3rd round). **Signed by:** Rick Ingalls (Blue Jays).

Signed for $1 million as a Blue Jays third-rounder in 2009, Marisnick had a breakout .320/.392/.496 season at low Class A Lansing two years later. He found the going rougher in 2012 while reaching Double-A, then became the top prospect included in the 12-player blockbuster that sent Jose Reyes and Mark Buehrle from Miami to Toronto. Marisnick has the potential to be a five-tool player, though questions linger about his bat. He has made adjustments to eliminate a hitch in his swing, but he still has a big frame that leads to a long stroke with a lot of moving parts. He needs to do a better job of staying short to the ball, letting pitches travel deep and avoiding chasing them out of the strike zone. It's hard to find fault with the rest of Marisnick's package. His strength and ability to backspin the ball give him plus power. His speed, center-field defense and arm strength all grade as

BA GRADE
60
HIGH

above average. He has a knack for stealing bases, succeeding on 84 of 100 pro attempts. Even if he loses a step, he'll easily fit the profile for right field. Marisnick will return to Double-A at age 22. If he can make the necessary offensive adjustments, he's on target to reach Miami during the 2014 season. He's talented enough defensively to push Christian Yelich to left field.

Year	Club (League)	Class	AVG	G	AB	R	H	2B	3B	HR	RBI	BB	SO	SB	CS	OBP	SLG
2010	Blue Jays (GCL)	R	.287	35	122	17	35	12	0	3	14	13	18	14	1	.373	.459
	Lansing (MWL)	LoA	.220	34	127	16	28	8	2	1	12	9	37	9	2	.298	.339
2011	Lansing (MWL)	LoA	.320	118	462	68	148	27	6	14	77	43	91	37	8	.392	.496
2012	Dunedin (FSL)	HiA	.263	65	266	41	70	18	7	6	35	26	55	10	5	.349	.451
	New Hampshire (EL)	AA	.233	55	223	25	52	11	3	2	15	11	45	14	4	.286	.336
Minor League Totals			.278	307	1200	167	333	76	18	26	153	102	246	84	20	.351	.436

5 MARCELL OZUNA, OF

Born: Nov. 12, 1990. **B-T:** R-R. **Ht.:** 6-2. **Wt.:** 190. Signed: Dominican Republic, 2008.
Signed by: Sandy Nin.

Despite not going deep in July, Ozuna led the Florida State League in homers (24)—as well as in runs (89), RBIs (95) and total bases (233)—in 2012. He has topped 20 homers in each of the least three seasons and nearly replicated his 2011 stat line despite moving from cozy low Class A Greensboro to cavernous Jupiter. Ozuna oozes tools, particularly with his plus-plus raw power and a cannon arm. He has the power to drive the ball well out of any part of the park, though he tends to get pull-happy at times, flying open with his front side instead of staying back and punishing the ball. Plate-discipline issues that plagued him early in his career have eased significantly as he has advanced, though at times he'll revert to guessing and chasing breaking balls down and out of the strike zone. When he swings at strikes, he rarely misses, thanks to excellent hand-eye coordination. With slightly above-average speed and average instincts, Ozuna should reach double figures in stolen bases. He has plus range and a well above-average arm in right field. He plays with an infectious passion at all times. After gaining a spot on Miami's 40-man roster, Ozuna will head to Double-A. If he can lay off bad breaking pitches and trust his swing, he can become an all-star capable of hitting 30 home runs.

BA GRADE
60
HIGH

Year	Club (League)	Class	AVG	G	AB	R	H	2B	3B	HR	RBI	BB	SO	SB	CS	OBP	SLG
2008	Marlins (DSL)	R	.279	63	233	33	65	14	0	6	43	23	61	8	1	.335	.416
2009	Marlins (GCL)	R	.313	55	214	32	67	22	0	5	39	22	52	4	2	.377	.486
2010	Greensboro (SAL)	LoA	.160	6	25	3	4	0	0	1	2	2	10	0	0	.222	.280
	Jamestown (NYP)	SS	.267	68	270	53	72	11	2	21	60	17	94	3	1	.314	.556
2011	Greensboro (SAL)	LoA	.266	131	496	87	132	28	5	23	71	46	121	17	2	.330	.482
2012	Jupiter (FSL)	HiA	.266	129	489	89	130	27	2	24	95	44	116	8	3	.328	.476
Minor League Totals			.272	452	1727	297	470	102	9	80	310	154	454	40	9	.332	.481

6 JUSTIN NICOLINO, LHP

Born: Nov. 22, 1991. **B-T:** L-L. **Ht.:** 6-3. **Wt.:** 195. **Drafted:** HS—Orlando, 2010 (2nd round). **Signed by:** Carlos Rodriguez (Blue Jays).

Armed with extra picks in 2010, the Blue Jays rolled the dice on Nicolino, considered a tough sign away from a Virginia commitment. Since signing for an above-slot $615,000 in the second round, he has dominated pro hitters. He ranked as the No.1 prospect in the short-season Northwest League in 2011, then led the low Class A Midwest League in ERA (2.46) and WHIP (1.07) as an encore. He came to the Marlins in the Jose Reyes/ Mark Buehrle trade. Nicolino's polish is more impressive than his stuff, but he's not a soft-tosser. He spots a fastball that sits at 88-92 mph and touches 94 to both sides of the plate, and he's not afraid to come inside on hitters. His best pitch is a plus changeup that he sells with deceptive arm speed. He gets under his changeup at times but has the aptitude to make corrections quickly. Nicolino needs to stay on top of his curveball too, but it's a solid third pitch with good shape. Though there's some crossfire to his delivery, that doesn't prevent him from throwing all three pitches for strikes. Nicolino profiles as a mid-rotation starter with an ultimate ceiling of a No. 2. He'll advance to high Class A at age 21. His savvy could put him on the fast track after Toronto handled him cautiously early in his career.

BA GRADE
55
MEDIUM

Year	Club (League)	Class	W	L	ERA	G	GS	CG	SV	IP	H	HR	BB	SO	K/9	WHIP	AVG
2011	Vancouver (NWL)	SS	5	1	1.03	12	9	1	0	52	28	0	11	64	11.0	0.75	.156
	Lansing (MWL)	LoA	1	1	3.12	3	3	0	0	9	11	0	2	9	9.3	1.50	.297
2012	Lansing (MWL)	LoA	10	4	2.46	28	22	0	0	124	112	6	21	119	8.6	1.07	.241
Minor League Totals			16	6	2.09	43	34	1	0	185	151	6	34	192	9.3	1.00	.222

7 ADEINY HECHAVARRIA, INF

Born: April 15, 1989. **B-T:** R-R. **Ht.:** 5-11. **Wt.:** 180. Signed: Cuba, 2010. **Signed by:** Marco Paddy (Blue Jays).

Hechavarria defected from the Cuban junior national team in July 2009. After signing nine months later for a $10 million big league contract that included a Blue Jays-record $4 million bonus, he didn't produce much at the plate until reaching hitter-friendly Triple-A Las Vegas in 2011. He continued to hit there in 2012, earning a big league callup in August. Three months later, he became a Marlin after the Jose Reyes/Mark Buehrle deal. Hechavarria has all the tools to contend for Gold Gloves at shortstop. He has plus range, hands and arm strength, though he's prone to throwing errors because he tends to flip the ball to first base. He's also an above-average runner though not a prolific basestealer. Scouts still aren't sold on Hechavarria's offensive ability, however. He has a simple swing and some bat speed but is still learning how to put together professional at-bats. While he's strong and has gap power, he doesn't project as a home run threat. His command of the strike zone regressed in his first taste of the majors. His defense alone will allow Hechavarria to carve out a big league career. If his offense is simply adequate, he'll secure an everyday job. He'll enter 2013 as the favorite to replace Reyes as Miami's shortstop.

BA GRADE
50
MEDIUM

Year	Club (League)	Class	AVG	G	AB	R	H	2B	3B	HR	RBI	BB	SO	SB	CS	OBP	SLG
2010	Dunedin (FSL)	HiA	.193	41	161	21	31	7	3	1	7	5	25	7	0	.217	.292
	New Hampshire (EL)	AA	.273	61	253	36	69	11	1	3	34	12	40	6	3	.305	.360
2011	New Hampshire (EL)	AA	.235	111	464	58	109	22	6	6	46	25	78	19	13	.275	.347
	Las Vegas (PCL)	AAA	.389	25	108	16	42	6	2	2	11	8	21	1	2	.431	.537
2012	Las Vegas (PCL)	AAA	.312	102	443	78	138	20	6	6	63	38	86	8	2	.363	.424
	Toronto (AL)	MAJ	.254	41	126	10	32	8	0	2	15	4	32	0	0	.280	.365
Major League Totals			.254	41	126	10	32	8	0	2	15	4	32	0	0	.280	.365
Minor League Totals			.272	340	1429	209	389	66	18	18	161	88	250	41	20	.314	.381

8 JOSE URENA, RHP

Born: Sept. 12, 1991. **B-T:** R-R. **Ht.:** 6-3. **Wt.:** 175. Signed: Dominican Republic, 2008. **Signed by:** Sandy Nin.

After signing for $52,000 in 2008, Urena spent two seasons in the Rookie-level Dominican Summer League before finally reaching the United States in 2011. The Marlins took a cautious approach in his first year in full-season ball, piggybacking him and Austin Brice in the Greensboro rotation in the first half of 2012. Urena has a loose, live arm and a lean, projectable frame. He fills the strike zone with fastballs that sit at 94-96 mph and touch 98. His heater is explosive at times but flat at others. His slider gives him a second potential plus pitch, though it too lacks consistency. It has good tilt and life when it's on, but his arm often comes through late, causing it to flatten. He mixes in an occasional curveball to keep hitters off balance. He sells his straight changeup with fastball arm speed, and it can become an average offering if he can soften it up. Urena's control is better than his command at this stage. He's not yet able to consistently hit his targets within the strike zone, particularly inside on hitters. He works with enthusiasm and a smile. If Urena's slider and command become more reliable, he could reach his ceiling of a No. 2 or 3 starter. He's still raw and will progress slowly for now, with high Class A his next stop.

BA GRADE
55
HIGH

Year	Club (League)	Class	W	L	ERA	G	GS	CG	SV	IP	H	HR	BB	SO	K/9	WHIP	AVG
2009	Marlins (DSL)	R	3	3	6.75	14	2	0	2	27	36	0	11	15	5.1	1.76	.313
2010	Marlins (DSL)	R	5	6	2.61	13	13	3	0	83	76	2	7	66	7.2	1.00	.241
2011	Jamestown (NYP)	SS	4	7	4.33	15	15	0	0	73	74	4	29	48	5.9	1.42	.264
2012	Greensboro (SAL)	LoA	9	6	3.38	27	22	1	2	138	143	13	29	101	6.6	1.24	.266
Minor League Totals			21	22	3.68	69	52	4	4	320	329	19	76	230	6.5	1.26	.264

9 J.T. REALMUTO, C

Born: March 18, 1991. **B-T:** R-R. **Ht.:** 6-1. **Wt.:** 190. **Drafted:** HS—Midwest City, Okla., 2010 (3rd round). **Signed by:** Steve Taylor.

A shortstop in high school, Realmuto set national records with 88 hits and 119 RBIs while hitting .595 with 28 homers as a senior in 2010. The Marlins saw one of his rare appearances behind the plate and converted him to catcher after signing him for $600,000 as a third-rounder that summer. Realmuto has the potential to become a solid hitter with average power. He uses the entire field and cut his strikeout rate from one per 4.5 at-bats in 2011 to one per 7.0 last season. The rigors of catching wore on him as the year progressed and he occasionally cheated on pitches, sometimes pulling off and opening up too soon. That should happen less frequently as he gets more accustomed to the grind. Managers rated Realmuto the Florida State League's best defensive catcher in in 2012. The former prep quarterback combines quality arm strength with quick footwork and a fast release, turning in sub-1.8-second pop times. He threw out 36 percent of FSL basestealers. His receiving and game-calling took big steps forward last season, though he still must improve at blocking balls and handling tough pitches. He's a tick above-average runner but figures to lose a step as he continues catching. Realmuto will spend 2013 in Double-A.

BA GRADE
50
HIGH

Year	Club (League)	Class	AVG	G	AB	R	H	2B	3B	HR	RBI	BB	SO	SB	CS	OBP	SLG
2010	Marlins (GCL)	R	.175	12	40	2	7	0	0	0	4	7	11	0	1	.298	.175
2011	Greensboro (SAL)	LoA	.287	96	348	46	100	16	3	12	49	26	78	13	6	.347	.454
2012	Jupiter (FSL)	HiA	.256	123	446	63	114	16	0	8	46	37	64	13	5	.319	.345
Minor League Totals			.265	231	834	111	221	32	3	20	99	70	153	26	12	.329	.382

10 ADAM CONLEY, LHP

Born: May 24, 1990. **B-T:** L-L. **Ht.:** 6-3. **Wt.:** 185. **Drafted:** Washington State, 2011 (2nd round). **Signed by:** Gabe Sandy.

A closer early in his college career, Conley moved into the Washington State rotation as a junior in 2011 and earned a second-round selection and $625,000 bonus. He formed a stellar 1-2 punch with Jose Fernandez at Greensboro last spring, but Conley couldn't maintain his success after they moved to high Class A. Conley's fastball sits at 92-95 mph and touches 97, and it features so much life that he occasionally has trouble keeping it over the plate. He throws his average changeup with fastball arm speed, and it can dive out of the strike zone. His slider is below average, however, as it's often too big and wide. Conley has a little funk to his delivery that adds deception, though the Marlins are working to simplify it. He appeared tired when he got to Jupiter and his command and control suffered. A perfectionist, he wore himself down further by throwing too much between starts. By September, he was overstriding toward third base and throwing across his body. He bounced back well from rough starts and showed advanced pitchability for someone in his first full pro season. How he holds up in 2013 could help determine whether Conley remains a starter, though he'd still need a better slider to fill a high-leverage relief role. He should see Double-A at some point during the season.

BA GRADE
50
HIGH

Year	Club (League)	Class	W	L	ERA	G	GS	CG	SV	IP	H	HR	BB	SO	K/9	WHIP	AVG
2011	Marlins (GCL)	R	0	0	0.00	2	0	0	0	2	1	0	0	2	9.0	0.50	.143
2012	Greensboro (SAL)	LoA	7	3	2.78	14	14	0	0	74	58	4	24	84	10.2	1.10	.213
	Jupiter (FSL)	HiA	4	2	4.44	12	12	0	0	53	59	0	19	51	8.7	1.48	.282
Minor League Totals			11	5	3.42	28	26	0	0	129	118	4	43	137	9.6	1.25	.242

11 ROB BRANTLY, C

BA GRADE
45
MEDIUM

Born: July 14, 1989. **B-T:** L-R. **Ht.:** 6-2. **Wt.:** 188. **Drafted:** UC Riverside, 2010 (3rd round). **Signed by:** Steve Pack (Tigers).

A third-round pick by the Tigers in 2010 as a draft-eligible sophomore, Brantly came to the Marlins along with Jacob Turner and Brian Flynn last July in a deal for Anibal Sanchez and Omar Infante. After a stint with Triple-A New Orleans, Brantly was called to the majors and pressed into regular duty. He profiles as an offensive-minded catcher with a solid bat. He makes consistent contact to all fields with a short stroke more suited to line drives into the gaps than clearing the fences, though he has the strength to reach double figures in homers. While he has lacked patience at times, he drew 13 walks in his big league apprenticeship, which may be a function of hitting lower in the order. His speed is solid for a catcher, though he runs more upright than most. Brantly's hands and feet are good behind the plate, and he gets rid of the ball quickly with average arm strength. He threw out 29 percent of basestealers in 2012. His receiving skills need further development, and he's prone to taking an occasional pitch off. Though stronger than he appears, he could benefit by filling out his lean frame. Having proven himself capable of hitting big league pitching, Brantly is in the mix for a significant big league role in 2013. He may be best suited as the lefthanded portion of a platoon with veteran Jeff Mathis, which would alleviate concerns about his durability.

Year	Club (League)	Class	AVG	G	AB	R	H	2B	3B	HR	RBI	BB	SO	SB	CS	OBP	SLG
2010	West Michigan (MWL)	LoA	.255	52	188	26	48	10	1	1	21	23	22	2	2	.352	.335
2011	West Michigan (MWL)	LoA	.303	75	284	42	86	16	1	7	44	24	39	2	2	.366	.440
	Lakeland (FSL)	HiA	.219	39	146	16	32	6	0	3	18	5	17	0	0	.239	.322
2012	Erie (EL)	AA	.311	46	180	16	56	16	1	3	24	12	17	0	3	.359	.461
	Toledo (IL)	AAA	.254	36	130	11	33	4	0	0	6	7	25	0	0	.295	.285
	New Orleans (PCL)	AAA	.365	14	52	7	19	4	0	2	11	1	9	0	0	.389	.558
	Miami (NL)	MAJ	.290	31	100	14	29	8	0	3	8	13	16	1	1	.372	.460
Major League Totals			.290	31	100	14	29	8	0	3	8	13	16	1	1	.372	.460
Minor League Totals			.280	262	980	118	274	56	3	16	124	72	129	4	7	.336	.392

12 DEREK DIETRICH, SS/2B

BA GRADE 50 HIGH

Born: July 18, 1989. **B-T:** L-R. **Ht.:** 6-1. **Wt.:** 200. **Drafted:** Georgia Tech, 2010 (2nd round). **Signed by:** Milt Hill (Rays).

A third-round pick of the Astros in 2007, Dietrich opted to attend Georgia Tech and went a round higher in the 2010 draft to the Rays. After he reached Double-A and moved from shortstop to second base, Tampa Bay traded him for Yunel Escobar after the Marlins added Escobar in their massive deal with the Blue Jays. Dietrich has good power for a middle infielder, as his quick hands and natural strength allow him to drive the ball. He has homered 36 times in his two full pro seasons. While his plate discipline has improved, he struggles at times trying to do too much at the plate, leading to an uppercut stroke. It was only a matter of time before he moved off shortstop, because Dietrich lacks the actions, first-step quickness and range for the position. His hands are soft and he has plenty of arm strength to turn double plays. He's a below-average runner. The trade opens possibilities for Dietrich, as neither second nor third base is settled in Miami. He's likely to start 2013 at second base in Double-A, but he also could supplant Zack Cox as the organization's best third-base option. If he's not a regular, Dietrich's lefthanded bat should help him earn a spot as a utility infielder.

Year	Club (League)	Class	AVG	G	AB	R	H	2B	3B	HR	RBI	BB	SO	SB	CS	OBP	SLG
2010	Hudson Valley (NYP)	SS	.279	45	179	33	50	12	2	3	20	11	42	2	2	.340	.419
2011	Bowling Green (MWL)	LoA	.277	127	480	73	133	34	4	22	81	38	128	5	7	.346	.502
2012	Charlotte (FSL)	HiA	.282	98	372	49	105	21	9	10	58	25	78	4	2	.343	.468
	Montgomery (SL)	AA	.271	34	133	22	36	7	1	4	17	7	36	0	1	.324	.429
Minor League Totals			.278	304	1164	177	324	74	16	39	176	81	284	11	12	.342	.470

13 ALFREDO SILVERIO, OF

BA GRADE 55 EXTREME

Born: May 6, 1987. **B-T:** R-R. **Ht.:** 6-0. **Wt.:** 205. **Signed:** Dominican Republic, 2003. **Signed by:** Angel Santana (Dodgers).

Signed for $50,000 as a raw 16-year-old, Silverio made a slow climb through the Dodgers chain. He exploded in Double-A in 2011, earning a spot in the Futures Game, then was seriously injured in a car accident in January 2012. He missed spring training with back, shoulder and elbow injuries from the accident, as well as concussion symptoms, then needed Tommy John surgery in May. The Marlins plucked him in the major league Rule 5 draft in December. When healthy, Silverio shows five average or better tools. He has a quick, powerful swing, generating line drives from gap to gap and average home run power, mostly to the pull side. His progress in 2011 was a result of improving his strike-zone discipline, which allowed him to put together quality at-bats and make pitchers work harder to get him out. He's an aggressive hitter and will never walk much. Silverio has played all three outfield positions, seeing significant time in center, and is a slightly above-average runner who profiles better on a corner. His solid arm strength and accuracy play well in right field. He DHed in the Dodgers' Dominican instructional league in the fall, where he ran fine and showed a crisp swing, but he hadn't been cleared to throw by December. Silverio must stick with the big league club or else clear waivers and be offered back to the Dodgers for half his $50,000 draft price.

Year	Club (League)	Class	AVG	G	AB	R	H	2B	3B	HR	RBI	BB	SO	SB	CS	OBP	SLG
2004	Dodgers2 (DSL)	R	.240	59	192	18	46	6	2	1	16	7	36	5	6	.273	.307
2005	Dodgers (DSL)	R	.244	25	82	11	20	2	0	1	14	10	15	2	2	.316	.305
2006	Dodgers (DSL)	R	.276	61	225	36	62	12	6	6	48	18	44	6	3	.335	.462
2007	Dodgers (GCL)	R	.373	51	193	38	72	9	3	6	46	11	32	5	3	.406	.544
2008	Great Lakes (MWL)	LoA	.263	95	376	37	99	15	4	10	45	7	83	6	3	.279	.404
2009	Great Lakes (MWL)	LoA	.284	132	490	75	139	34	6	13	61	26	104	2	5	.320	.457
2010	Inland Empire (CAL)	HiA	.292	95	387	66	113	27	6	12	43	18	63	17	7	.324	.486
	Chattanooga (SL)	AA	.063	4	16	1	1	0	0	0	0	0	3	0	0	.063	.063
2011	Chattanooga (SL)	AA	.306	132	533	90	163	42	18	16	85	30	91	11	12	.340	.542
2012	Did Not Play—Injured																
Minor League Totals			.287	654	2494	372	715	147	45	65	358	127	471	54	41	.322	.460

14 A.J. RAMOS, RHP

BA GRADE
45
MEDIUM

Born: Sept. 20, 1986. **B-T:** R-R. **Ht.:** 5-10. **Wt.:** 212. **Drafted:** Texas Tech, 2009 (21st round). **Signed by:** Dennis Cardoza.

Ramos signed for $1,500 as a senior in 2009, a year after tearing an elbow ligament at Texas Tech. A starter in college, he has averaged 12.3 strikeouts per nine innings as a pro reliever and fanned the side on 13 pitches in his big league debut in September. The 5-foot-10 mighty mite shows no fear on the hill. Ramos used to try to simply throw his fastball past hitters but has learned to hit his spots. He'll mix in a cutter against lefthanders to keep them off the plate, then go back outside with his fastball, which sits at 92-95 mph and touches 97. He'll back-door his hard-breaking slider or bounce it for a swing and miss. He also throws a solid changeup with deceptive arm speed. Ramos' command with all of his pitches has improved significantly since he signed, though occasionally he'll struggle with his location, particularly with his fastball. He's constantly in attack mode and can get too amped up at times. Humble and hardworking, he pitches like he has something to prove every night. Ramos' September audition puts him in the mix for a set-up role going into spring training. He has the stuff to handle an eighth-inning role and eventually may work his way into closing games.

Year	Club (League)	Class	W	L	ERA	G	GS	CG	SV	IP	H	HR	BB	SO	K/9	WHIP	AVG
2009	Jamestown (NYP)	SS	2	2	2.14	25	0	0	9	34	22	0	14	50	13.4	1.07	.182
2010	Greensboro (SAL)	LoA	3	7	3.70	49	0	0	28	58	40	3	32	78	12.0	1.23	.198
2011	Jupiter (FSL)	HiA	1	4	1.78	49	0	0	25	51	37	2	19	71	12.6	1.11	.200
2012	Jacksonville (SL)	AA	3	3	1.44	55	0	0	21	69	36	3	21	89	11.7	0.83	.151
	Miami (NL)	MAJ	0	0	3.86	11	0	0	0	9	8	2	4	13	12.5	1.29	.229
Major League Totals			0	0	3.86	11	0	0	0	9	8	2	4	13	12.5	1.29	.229
Minor League Totals			9	16	2.26	178	0	0	83	211	135	8	86	288	12.3	1.05	.181

15 ZACK COX, 3B

BA GRADE
50
HIGH

Born: May 9, 1989. **B-T:** L-R. **Ht.:** 6-0. **Wt.:** 215. **Drafted:** Arkansas, 2010 (1st round). **Signed by:** Jay Catalano (Cardinals).

Regarded as the best pure hitter in the 2010 draft, Cox went 25th overall and netted a $3.2 million big league contract from the Cardinals that included a $2 million bonus. He rocketed through the system, reaching Triple-A last spring, but fell out of favor and was dealt to the Marlins for Edward Mujica in July. Cox still has quick hands and shows gap power with a compact, line-drive swing. When he's on, he works up the middle. Attempts to get him to pull the ball threw off his timing and mechanics last year, when he hit just .254/.301/.409. He has the strength to hit 15-20 home runs a year, though without much lift in his swing he projects as more of a doubles hitter. Cox's body has gotten thick and a little stiff. He needs to get leaner to regain flexibility and fluidity, both at bat and in the field. He must improve his range and footwork at third base, where he's susceptible to bunts and rarely seems to find easy hops. While his arm is strong enough for the hot corner, some scouts foresee an eventual move to first base. He's a below-average runner. The Marlins felt Cox belonged in Double-A when they acquired him, and that may still be the best place for him to open the 2013 season. Third base is wide open in Miami, but someone else will have to keep it warm until Cox proves he's ready.

Year	Club (League)	Class	AVG	G	AB	R	H	2B	3B	HR	RBI	BB	SO	SB	CS	OBP	SLG
2010	Cardinals (GCL)	R	.400	4	15	0	6	1	0	0	1	1	3	0	0	.471	.467
2011	Palm Beach (FSL)	HiA	.335	42	164	22	55	8	0	3	20	11	29	2	2	.380	.439
	Springfield (TL)	AA	.293	93	352	54	103	19	0	10	48	29	69	0	1	.355	.432
2012	Memphis (PCL)	AAA	.254	84	299	27	76	23	0	9	30	12	63	1	0	.294	.421
	Jacksonville (SL)	AA	.253	24	95	14	24	6	1	1	13	10	27	0	0	.321	.368
Minor League Totals			.285	247	925	117	264	57	1	23	112	63	191	3	3	.339	.424

16 AUSTIN BRICE, RHP

BA GRADE
50
HIGH

Born: June 19, 1992. **B-T:** R-R. **Ht.:** 6-4. **Wt.:** 205. **Drafted:** HS—Pittsboro, N.C., 2010 (9th round). **Signed by:** Joel Matthews.

The top-rated North Carolina high school pitcher in the 2010 draft, Brice parlayed his raw arm strength into a $205,000 deal as a ninth-round pick. He led Greensboro with 122 strikeouts last year in his full-season debut. To protect his arm the Marlins alternated him with Jose Urena early in the season, with one starting and the other relieving. Brice already shows an ability to spot his fastball, which sits at 91-95 mph and could step up as he learns to pitch. He gets natural spin on a downer curveball that is also a plus pitch at times, though the break gets big and could be tightened up. His changeup needs work but has the potential to become an average third pitch. His command can be erratic, but his control is better than his high walk totals suggest. Brice needs to be more consistent with the release point on all of his pitches. His head also tends to drift left, causing his pitches to flatten out and allowing hitters to see them better. When he keeps his delivery together, he can be dominating. He maintains his poise well. Because he's still learning to pitch, Brice could return to low Class A to open the season. He projects as a No. 3 or 4 starter.

Year	Club (League)	Class	W	L	ERA	G	GS	CG	SV	IP	H	HR	BB	SO	K/9	WHIP	AVG
2010	Marlins (GCL)	R	0	1	4.32	6	0	0	0	8	7	0	7	8	8.6	1.68	.219
2011	Marlins (GCL)	R	6	0	2.96	11	9	0	0	49	32	2	33	55	10.2	1.34	.189
2012	Greensboro (SAL)	LoA	8	6	4.35	25	19	0	3	110	96	13	68	122	10.0	1.50	.237
Minor League Totals			14	7	3.94	42	28	0	3	167	135	15	108	185	10.0	1.46	.223

17 AVERY ROMERO, 3B/2B

BA GRADE

50

HIGH

Born: May 11, 1993. **B-T:** R-R. **Ht.:** 5-11. **Wt.:** 195. **Drafted:** HS—St. Augustine, Fla., 2012 (3rd round). **Signed by:** Brian Kraft.

Just before the signing deadline last summer, Romero inked a $700,000 deal as a third-round pick. His stocky frame reminds many in the organization of Dan Uggla, who hit 154 homers in five season with the Marlins. Romero has an advanced approach at the plate and uses quick hands, good hand-eye coordination and a short swing to rip line drives into the gaps. He hangs in well on breaking pitches and hits the ball where it's pitched. He projects as an above-average hitter and has the raw power to match. Though he's a below-average runner, he shows good instincts and a quick first step. A shortstop in high school, Romero split his time between third and second base in his pro debut. Despite his build, he's a quality athlete. He has soft hands and quick feet, though he has to work on turning the double play at second. His arm is strong enough for third base, where he looks more comfortable. The Marlins would like Romero to settle into a position, but they have yet to pick that spot. His bat may be polished enough for him to handle low Class A in his first full pro season.

Year	Club (League)	Class	AVG	G	AB	R	H	2B	3B	HR	RBI	BB	SO	SB	CS	OBP	SLG
2012	Marlins (GCL)	R	.223	33	121	8	27	6	0	3	15	10	21	0	1	.309	.347
	Jamestown (NYP)	SS	.381	7	21	3	8	0	0	0	4	3	0	1	0	.458	.381
Minor League Totals			.246	40	142	11	35	6	0	3	19	13	21	1	1	.331	.352

18 KOLBY COPELAND, OF

BA GRADE

50

HIGH

Born: Feb. 5, 1994. **B-T:** L-R. **Ht.:** 6-0. **Wt.:** 190. **Drafted:** HS—Bossier City, La., 2012 (3rd round supplemental). **Signed by:** Mark Willoughby.

A baseball and football star in high school, Copeland was suspended for part of his 2012 senior season due to a drunken-driving charge. He impressed enough upon his return to entice the Marlins to take him with a supplemental third-round pick and sign him for $367,200. He's physically mature, with a good approach and a compact, line-drive swing that should make him an above-average hitter. There's not a lot of loft in his stroke, but the barrel stays in the hitting zone a long time and he makes consistent hard contact. He showed plenty of extra-base pop in his debut, and despite not homering he projects to have at least average power when he learns how to turn on pitches. Copeland has average speed and runs the bases well, though he doesn't project as a big basestealing threat. He shows good instincts and a quick first step in center field, but he likely will wind up on a corner. His arm is average and more suited for left field than right. Copeland has been well coached and doesn't make the mistakes many young players do. He could jump to low Class A for his first full pro season.

Year	Club (League)	Class	AVG	G	AB	R	H	2B	3B	HR	RBI	BB	SO	SB	CS	OBP	SLG
2012	Marlins (GCL)	R	.286	56	217	34	62	14	6	0	34	16	27	2	6	.331	.406
	Jamestown (NYP)	SS	.227	6	22	5	5	0	1	0	0	3	2	2	0	.320	.318
Minor League Totals			.280	62	239	39	67	14	7	0	34	19	29	4	6	.330	.397

19 AUSTIN DEAN, OF

BA GRADE

50

HIGH

Born: Oct. 14, 1993. **B-T:** R-R. **Ht.:** 6-1. **Wt.:** 190. **Drafted:** HS—Spring, Texas, 2012 (4th round). **Signed by:** Ryan Wardinsky.

An infielder at perennial Houston-area power Klein Collins High, Dean moved to the outfield after signing as a fourth-round pick last June for $367,200. Though Dean hit just .223/.337/.338 in the Rookie-level Gulf Coast League, the Marlins raved about the adjustments he made both during the summer and in fall minicamp. His bat speed compares with anyone's in the system, and the ball makes a nice sound coming off his bat. He wants to pull the ball too much, even on outside pitches that he should take the other way, and needs to learn to let the ball travel a little deeper and trust his quick hands. He also needs to narrow his strike zone. He made mechanical adjustments to his lower half to improve his balance, which should allow him to tap into his above-average raw power. Dean is an average runner with enough athleticism to handle left or right field. He saw time in center but profiles better on a corner. His arm is average. Dean's spring showing will determine whether he jumps to low Class A or waits for a short-season assignment in June.

Year	Club (League)	Class	AVG	G	AB	R	H	2B	3B	HR	RBI	BB	SO	SB	CS	OBP	SLG
2012	Marlins (GCL)	R	.223	47	148	15	33	11	0	2	15	24	35	2	2	.337	.338
Minor League Totals			.223	47	148	15	33	11	0	2	15	24	35	2	2	.337	.338

20 JESUS SOLORZANO, OF

BA GRADE
50
EXTREME

Born: Aug. **8, 1990. B-T:** R-R. **Ht.:** 6-0. **Wt.:** 190. **Signed:** Venezuela, 2009. **Signed by:** Wilmer Castillo.

Solorzano spent two years in the Dominican Summer League before making his U.S. debut in 2011. He led the short-season New York-Penn League in slugging (.519) and OPS (.894) last year, though he was old for the league, having turned 22 in August. An aggressive hitter who can turn around a good fastball, Solarzano has the raw strength to develop plus power. He needs to rein in his all-out approach and recognize different game situations instead of always going with his free-swinging mentality. He makes strong contact when he stays in the strike zone but too often gets himself out by chasing pitches. His speed is a tick above average, and while he's a good baserunner he hasn't shown the instincts to steal bases. A solid defender, Solarzano has played all three outfield spots and profiles best on a corner. His arm strength is average and he needs to improve the accuracy of his throws. He's prone to mental lapses in the field and at the plate. He'll get his first crack at full-season ball this spring.

Year	Club (League)	Class	AVG	G	AB	R	H	2B	3B	HR	RBI	BB	SO	SB	CS	OBP	SLG
2009	Marlins (DSL)	R	.109	23	55	6	6	0	1	1	6	5	18	2	1	.219	.200
2010	Marlins (DSL)	R	.286	51	175	22	50	7	2	0	13	11	47	12	3	.365	.349
2011	Marlins (GCL)	R	.299	51	194	34	58	13	4	3	31	13	30	18	7	.355	.454
2012	Jamestown (NYP)	SS	.314	59	210	36	66	13	3	8	27	17	49	7	6	.374	.519
Minor League Totals			.284	184	634	98	180	33	10	12	77	46	144	39	17	.352	.424

21 CHRIS HATCHER, RHP

BA GRADE
45
MEDIUM

Born: Jan. 12, 1985. **B-T:** B-R. **Ht.:** 6-2. **Wt.:** 206. **Drafted:** UNC Wilmington, 2006 (5th round). **Signed by:** Joel Matthews.

The top defensive catcher in the system just three years ago, Hatcher shifted to the mound in 2011 and reached the big leagues within months. Though a poor camp cost him a shot at last year's Opening Day roster, he was called up several times during the season and excelled in Triple-A. Despite his relative inexperience, Hatcher is a natural strike-thrower. His fastball sits at 93-94 mph and touches 96 with a little armside run. His sharp, late-breaking slider gives him a second plus pitch. His changeup has nice fade and could be an average offering, but he uses it sparingly. Hatcher brings a bulldog mentality to the mound and isn't afraid to work inside. His delivery is compact and he has a quick arm. Hatcher's Miami appearances were limited to losses and blowout wins last year, so his next hurdle is convincing new manager Mike Redmond that he's ready for a more significant role. He has the stuff and makeup to be a set-up man.

Year	Club (League)	Class	AVG	G	AB	R	H	2B	3B	HR	RBI	BB	SO	SB	CS	OBP	SLG
2006	Jamestown (NYP)	SS	.181	36	127	19	23	4	2	2	17	11	40	3	1	.273	.291
2007	Greensboro (SAL)	LoA	.242	102	356	62	86	23	1	15	50	34	104	8	6	.312	.438
2008	Jupiter (FSL)	HiA	.178	63	202	22	36	12	0	6	28	23	78	3	1	.278	.327
2009	Jupiter (FSL)	HiA	.333	6	18	4	6	1	0	0	2	1	8	0	1	.400	.389
	Jacksonville (SL)	AA	.218	51	156	29	34	9	3	8	27	14	43	1	0	.294	.468
2010	Jacksonville (SL)	AA	.202	84	267	23	54	9	1	3	26	20	92	1	2	.261	.277
	New Orleans (PCL)	AAA	.167	17	48	10	8	1	0	2	10	9	19	0	0	.333	.313
	Florida (NL)	MAJ	.000	5	6	0	0	0	0	0	0	2	5	0	0	.250	.000
Major League Totals			.000	26	7	0	0	0	0	0	0	2	5	0	0	.222	.000
Minor League Totals			.210	411	1179	169	248	59	7	36	160	112	386	17	11	.290	.364

Year	Club (League)	Class	W	L	ERA	G	GS	CG	SV	IP	H	HR	BB	SO	K/9	WHIP	AVG
2009	Jacksonville (SL)	AA	0	0	0.00	1	0	0	0	0	0	0	0	0	0.0	0.00	.000
2010	Jacksonville (SL)	AA	1	0	0.00	1	0	0	0	1	0	0	0	1	9.0	0.00	.000
2011	Jacksonville (SL)	AA	2	1	1.90	42	0	0	6	47	32	2	19	57	10.8	1.08	.192
	Florida (NL)	MAJ	0	0	6.97	11	0	0	0	10	14	2	4	8	7.0	1.74	.341
2012	New Orleans (PCL)	AAA	1	0	0.77	37	0	0	11	47	33	1	15	45	8.6	1.02	.196
	Miami (NL)	MAJ	0	0	4.30	11	0	0	0	15	17	3	6	10	6.1	1.57	.288
Major League Totals			0	0	5.40	22	0	0	0	25	31	5	10	18	6.5	1.64	.310
Minor League Totals			4	1	1.32	81	0	0	17	96	65	3	34	103	9.7	1.03	.192

22 RAUDEL LAZO, LHP

BA GRADE
45
MEDIUM

Born: April 12, 1989. **B-T:** L-L. **Ht.:** 5-10. **Wt.:** 175. **Signed:** Cuba, 2011. **Signed by:** Albert Gonzalez.

Lazo's uncle is Pedro Luis Lazo, the all-time wins leader in Cuba's Serie Nacional and the closer on Cuba's national team for more than a decade. Raudel also pitched on the national team until he defected in early 2011. Though his fastball sat at 87-88 mph when he worked out for teams in Mexico, the Marlins liked his projectable, wiry frame and signed him for $60,000. He proved a pleasant surprise during his 2012 pro debut, showing a quick arm and good feel for three pitches. Lazo throws strikes and generally works ahead in the count. His fastball has jumped to 90-92 mph and runs up to 94 with good life. He commands it well most of the time, but occasionally it wanders on him. He varies the speed on a hammer curveball that's an out pitch. He can make it break straight down or give it more of an 11-to-4 bend with some sweep to it. At times he'll throw it harder for strikes, with velocity that gives it more of a slider look. Lazo's changeup has sinking action that generates a lot of swings and misses. He's lights out against lefties (.176 average last year) and effective enough against righties to project as a set-up man. Despite his small build, he proved durable and served as the go-to guy in Jupiter's bullpen. He should start 2013 in Double-A and could move quickly.

Year	Club (League)	Class	W	L	ERA	G	GS	CG	SV	IP	H	HR	BB	SO	K/9	WHIP	AVG
2012	Jupiter (FSL)	HiA	7	1	2.44	41	0	0	3	59	53	4	16	61	9.3	1.17	.243
	New Orleans (PCL)	AAA	0	0	0.00	1	0	0	0	0	0	0	0	0	0.0	0.00	.000
Minor League Totals			7	1	2.43	42	0	0	3	59	53	4	16	61	9.3	1.16	.242

23 JAKE ESCH, RHP

BA GRADE
50
EXTREME

Born: March 27, 1990. **B-T:** R-R. **Ht.:** 6-4. **Wt.:** 190. **Drafted:** Georgia Tech, 2011 (11th round). **Signed by:** Carmen Carcone.

Esch played baseball, basketball and football at Cretin-Derham Hall, the same St. Paul high school that produced Joe Mauer, before heading to Georgia Tech. A relief pitcher as a freshman, he played second base for a season alongside Derek Dietrich, then replaced Dietrich at shortstop in 2011. Though Esch worked just five innings in his draft year, the Marlins had seen him throw well during fall practice. They took him as a pitcher and paid him $200,000 in the 11th round. Despite his inexperience, he has a clean delivery and a feel for throwing strikes. His fastball sits at 92-94 mph and reaches 96 with good downhill plane. He throws both a slider and a curveball and separates them well, and both should become average offerings. He has the elements of a nice changeup, but it's lags behind his other pitches for now. He fields his position like an extra infielder, popping off the hill to snare anything in his vicinity. Esch has the stuff to be a solid mid-rotation starter and made as much progress as anyone in the system last year. He pitched for Great Britain in a World Baseball Classic qualifier in the fall and will likely return to low Class A to open 2013.

Year	Club (League)	Class	W	L	ERA	G	GS	CG	SV	IP	H	HR	BB	SO	K/9	WHIP	AVG
2011	Marlins (GCL)	R	2	0	1.29	4	0	0	0	7	4	0	2	6	7.7	0.86	.182
	Jamestown (NYP)	SS	1	1	4.63	8	0	0	0	12	13	0	6	11	8.5	1.63	.283
2012	Jamestown (NYP)	SS	3	0	3.16	10	2	0	1	37	31	3	13	27	6.6	1.19	.233
	Greensboro (SAL)	LoA	1	3	3.13	6	4	0	0	32	27	1	11	26	7.4	1.20	.231
Minor League Totals			7	4	3.19	28	6	0	1	87	75	4	32	70	7.2	1.23	.236

24 BRIAN FLYNN, LHP

BA GRADE
45
MEDIUM

Born: April 19, 1990. **B-T:** L-L. **Ht.:** 6-8. **Wt.:** 240. **Drafted:** Wichita State, 2011 (7th round). **Signed by:** Chris Wimmer (Tigers).

A year after the Tigers signed Flynn for $125,000 as a seventh-round pick, they packaged him with Jacob Turner and Rob Brantly to acquire Anibal Sanchez and Omar Infante from the Marlins. The big, physical lefty is raw but reached Double-A in his first full pro season. Flynn commands the bottom half of the strike zone with an 89-92 mph fastball that touches 94 and has decent movement. He throws two breaking balls, getting more swings and misses with his slider than with his curveball. He's not afraid to throw his changeup, which improved significantly by the end of last season. Flynn attacks the zone and has good angle on his pitches. Though he's a quick study who's willing and able to make adjustments, he has been susceptible to lapses in focus. His lack of athleticism shows at times, particularly on defense and with the running game. Flynn projects as a back-of-the-rotation starter and will challenge for a Triple-A job in spring training.

Year	Club (League)	Class	W	L	ERA	G	GS	CG	SV	IP	H	HR	BB	SO	K/9	WHIP	AVG
2011	West Michigan (MWL)	LoA	7	2	3.46	13	13	0	0	68	58	3	23	57	7.6	1.20	.235
2012	Lakeland (FSL)	HiA	8	4	3.71	18	18	0	0	102	113	5	32	84	7.4	1.42	.280
	Erie (EL)	AA	0	1	9.00	1	1	0	0	5	8	1	2	3	5.4	2.00	.381
	Jacksonville (SL)	AA	3	0	3.80	8	8	0	0	45	48	3	13	32	6.4	1.36	.273
Minor League Totals			18	7	3.77	40	40	0	0	220	227	12	70	176	7.2	1.35	.268

25 GRANT DAYTON, LHP

BA GRADE
45
MEDIUM

Born: Nov. 25, 1987. **B-T:** L-L. **Ht.:** 6-2. **Wt.:** 200. **Drafted:** Auburn, 2010 (11th round). **Signed by:** Mark Willoughby.

Dayton had relieved exclusively since turning pro in 2010, but the Marlins moved him into the Jupiter rotation for six starts last spring so he could work on his breaking pitches. His fastball, which sat at 94-97 mph in 2011, dipped to 89-91 but came back once he returned to the bullpen in May. Its late life makes it difficult for hitters to square up. His fastball command remains an issue, however, and he walked eight in 12 innings in the Arizona Fall League. Dayton mixed in a curveball while starting, but once back in the pen he used his 83-84 mph slider as his primary breaking pitch. He gets good depth and angle on his slider, and he can drop it on the back foot of righthanders. He shows good feel for his changeup, which can be a solid pitch. Dayton attacks with quality stuff and keeps the ball down, working both sides of the plate. He projects as a middle reliever who could face both lefties and righties. He'll head back to Double-A to start 2013.

Year	Club (League)	Class	W	L	ERA	G	GS	CG	SV	IP	H	HR	BB	SO	K/9	WHIP	AVG
2010	Marlins (GCL)	R	0	0	0.00	1	0	0	1	1	0	0	0	1	9.0	0.00	.000
	Jamestown (NYP)	SS	1	1	1.26	17	0	0	1	29	18	0	15	23	7.2	1.15	.186
2011	Greensboro (SAL)	LoA	7	1	2.89	49	0	0	5	72	59	5	24	99	12.4	1.16	.223
2012	Jupiter (FSL)	HiA	2	5	2.10	31	6	0	2	60	48	1	18	71	10.7	1.10	.214
	Jacksonville (SL)	AA	2	1	4.15	7	0	0	0	13	12	2	4	19	13.2	1.23	.245
Minor League Totals			12	8	2.43	105	6	0	9	174	137	8	61	213	11.0	1.14	.215

26 CHAD JAMES, LHP

BA GRADE
50
EXTREME

Born: Jan. 23, 1991. **B-T:** L-L. **Ht.:** 6-3. **Wt.:** 185. **Drafted:** HS—Yukon, Okla., 2009 (1st round). **Signed by:** Ryan Wardinsky.

The 18th overall pick in the 2009 draft, James has notched double-digit losses in each of his three seasons since signing for $1.7 million. His 2012 season ended in late August when he was suspended for a violation of team policies. His fastball, which once sat at 95 mph, now runs 90-93 mph. He gets nice downward action on his slurvy slider, which has the potential to be an average or better pitch. He'll also throw a big, loopy curve. His straight changeup is good at times but lacks consistency, which could be said for all of his pitches as well as his delivery. James fails to repeat his mechanics, and when he gets moving side to side he loses downhill tilt, his pitches flatten out and hitters have little difficulty seeing the ball. His command is poor and he has particular trouble throwing his secondary pitches for strikes. James needs to field his position better and make strides controlling the running game. When he reported last spring, it was clear he hadn't put much effort into his offseason conditioning, a mistake he vowed not to repeat this winter. James has flashed the stuff to be an effective mid-rotation starter, but his commitment to the game will determine whether he reaches that ceiling.

Year	Club (League)	Class	W	L	ERA	G	GS	CG	SV	IP	H	HR	BB	SO	K/9	WHIP	AVG
2010	Greensboro (SAL)	LoA	5	10	5.12	24	24	0	0	114	116	3	65	105	8.3	1.58	.269
2011	Jupiter (FSL)	HiA	5	15	3.80	27	27	0	0	149	173	12	51	124	7.5	1.50	.294
2012	Jupiter (FSL)	HiA	6	10	4.87	24	23	0	0	115	138	9	50	80	6.3	1.64	.299
Minor League Totals			16	35	4.52	75	74	0	0	378	427	24	166	309	7.4	1.57	.288

27 JOSE CEDA, RHP

BA GRADE
45
HIGH

Born: Jan. 28, 1987. **B-T:** R-R. **Ht.:** 6-4. **Wt.:** 275. **Signed:** Dominican Republic, 2004. **Signed by:** Felix Francisco/Randy Smith (Padres).

Originally signed by the Padres in 2004, Ceda went to the Cubs in a 2006 trade for Todd Walker and came to the Marlins in a 2008 deal for Kevin Gregg. Managers rated Ceda the best relief prospect in the Triple-A Pacific Coast League in 2011, and he was making a case for a big league job last spring when he tore a ligament in his elbow and required Tommy John surgery. Before he got hurt, Ceda's fastball was clocked at 95-96. He also had a solid slider and added a splitter as to combat lefthanders. A lack of command has troubled him, though he did a better job of locating his pitches in 2011. Last year marked the second time in four seasons he had missed an entire campaign, as he spent 2009 working his way back from shoulder surgery. Conditioning has been an issue for him in the past. Ceda is on schedule to return this spring, though he'll need to build his arm back up in the minors before he's ready to help in Miami.

Year	Club (League)	Class	W	L	ERA	G	GS	CG	SV	IP	H	HR	BB	SO	K/9	WHIP	AVG
2005	Padres (DSL)	R	4	2	1.50	13	9	2	2	60	38	2	29	83	12.5	1.12	.174
2006	Padres (AZL)	R	2	0	5.09	8	4	0	0	23	20	1	13	31	12.1	1.43	.235
	Cubs (AZL)	R	0	0	0.75	5	3	0	0	12	6	0	7	21	15.8	1.08	.154
	Boise (NWL)	SS	1	0	3.27	3	3	0	0	11	5	1	2	11	9.0	0.64	.139
2007	Cubs (AZL)	R	0	0	2.45	2	1	0	0	4	2	0	3	3	7.4	1.36	.182
	Peoria (MWL)	LoA	2	2	3.11	21	6	0	0	46	14	1	31	66	12.8	0.93	.093
2008	Daytona (FSL)	HiA	2	4	4.80	15	12	0	0	54	41	4	28	53	8.8	1.27	.212
	Tennessee (SL)	AA	2	1	2.08	22	0	0	9	30	26	2	14	42	12.5	1.32	.234
2009	Did Not Play—Injured																
2010	Greensboro (SAL)	LoA	0	0	4.50	7	0	0	0	8	7	2	1	5	5.6	1.00	.226
	Jacksonville (SL)	AA	4	1	1.39	27	0	0	6	32	18	2	20	45	12.5	1.18	.168
	Florida (NL)	MAJ	0	0	5.19	8	0	0	0	9	8	1	11	9	9.3	2.19	.242
2011	New Orleans (PCL)	AAA	3	1	1.36	36	0	0	24	40	30	1	13	53	12.0	1.08	.201
	Florida (NL)	MAJ	0	1	4.43	17	0	0	0	20	16	1	12	21	9.3	1.38	.211
2012	Did Not Play—Injured																
Major League Totals			0	1	4.66	25	0	0	0	29	24	2	23	30	9.3	1.62	.220
Minor League Totals			20	9	2.69	159	38	2	41	321	207	16	161	413	11.6	1.15	.183

28 DANNY BLACK, SS

BA GRADE
45
HIGH

Born: Aug. 19, 1988. **B-T:** L-R. **Ht.:** 6-2. **Wt.:** 170. **Drafted:** Oklahoma, 2010 (14th round). **Signed by:** Steve Taylor.

Unheralded out of high school, Black spent two years at Feather River (Calif.) JC raising his profile. He turned down the Yankees as a 42nd-round pick in 2009 and transferred to Oklahoma, where he helped the Sooners reach the College World Series in 2010. The Marlins signed him for $125,000 in the 14th round that June, and he was moving swiftly though the lower levels of the minors before a sprained right wrist ended his 2012 season in mid-July. Black projects as an average hitter who will make line-drive contact. He has no home run power, but he has enough strength that the bat won't get knocked out of his hands and he should collect his share of doubles. Black is adept enough to drop down bunts and has the plus speed to beat some of them out for hits. Once on base, he's an aggressive baserunner who generally gets a good first step. He could enhance his offensive value by drawing more walks. A solid defender with above-average range and arm strength at shortstop, he also can play second and third base. Black should open the year in Double-A.

Year	Club (League)	Class	AVG	G	AB	R	H	2B	3B	HR	RBI	BB	SO	SB	CS	OBP	SLG
2010	Jamestown (NYP)	SS	.271	43	181	32	49	8	8	0	15	17	45	8	1	.337	.403
2011	Greensboro (SAL)	LoA	.280	120	415	58	116	18	5	5	51	37	81	32	10	.338	.383
2012	Jupiter (FSL)	HiA	.314	78	293	38	92	16	4	0	30	27	68	17	7	.375	.396
	Jacksonville (SL)	AA	.265	8	34	5	9	3	0	0	2	3	11	2	1	.316	.353
Minor League Totals			.288	249	923	133	266	45	17	5	98	84	205	59	19	.349	.390

29 AUSTIN BARNES, 2B/C

BA GRADE
45
HIGH

Born: Dec. 28, 1989. **B-T:** R-R. **Ht.:** 5-10. **Wt.:** 190. **Drafted:** Arizona State, 2011 (9th round). **Signed by:** Scott Stanley.

The nephew of former big league utilityman Mike Gallego, Barnes shifted from infield to catcher when injuries created a need at Arizona State. Though he started the 2012 South Atlantic League all-star game at catcher, he spent most of the season at second base. His average bat profiles well at either spot. He consistently makes hard contact with a compact swing, peppering line drives all over the field, and has gap power geared more for doubles than for homers. He has a patient, disciplined approach with enough confidence to let the ball travel deep and take it the other way. An average runner, he shows good instincts on the bases. Fundamentally sound behind the plate, Barnes looked comfortable even playing there only once a week. He has quick feet and soft hands, and he blocks and receives well. His arm is a tick below average, but he has a quick, accurate release. Small for a full-time catcher, he needs to get stronger. He's athletic enough to play anywhere on the infield, though his arm is light for anything more than spot duty on the left side. The Marlins see him as a catcher and would like to get him more time behind the plate in high Class A this season.

Year	Club (League)	Class	AVG	G	AB	R	H	2B	3B	HR	RBI	BB	SO	SB	CS	OBP	SLG
2011	Jamestown (NYP)	SS	.288	57	219	33	63	13	0	1	19	25	22	6	1	.369	.361
2012	Greensboro (SAL)	LoA	.318	123	478	76	152	36	3	12	65	59	61	9	2	.401	.481
Minor League Totals			.308	180	697	109	215	49	3	13	84	84	83	15	3	.391	.443

30 BRENT KEYS, OF

BA GRADE
45
HIGH

Born: July 14, 1990. **B-T:** L-R. **Ht.:** 6-1. **Wt.:** 210. **Drafted:** HS—Simi Valley, Calif., 2009 (17th round). **Signed by:** Tim McDonnell.

A national Punt, Pass & Kick champion as a 15-year-old, Keys hasn't been able to fully show off his athleticism as a pro. Hampered by chronic hamstring injuries, he logged just 539 at-bats over his first three seasons. After devoting himself to strengthening his legs before the 2012 season, he stayed on the field long enough to capture the South Atlantic League batting crown (.335), though he again missed time with hamstring problems. An above-average hitter who manages his at-bats well, Keys keeps his swing short with little wasted movement. He gets the bat head through the hitting zone quickly and uses the entire field. He lacks the strength to turn on the ball and has little home run power. He profiles as a No. 2 hitter who's happy to take what the pitcher gives him and covers the plate well. He will take a walk, drop a bunt or spray the ball and run. When Keys' legs are healthy, he's a plus runner who can steal bases. An average center fielder, he has above-average range, gets good jumps and takes the right angles. His arm is solid. Keys is a dirtbag with great all-around instincts for the game. He'll advance to high Class A to begin 2013.

Year	Club (League)	Class	AVG	G	AB	R	H	2B	3B	HR	RBI	BB	SO	SB	CS	OBP	SLG
2009	Marlins (GCL)	R	.288	50	163	23	47	5	0	0	19	28	20	13	4	.395	.319
2010	Jamestown (NYP)	SS	.267	65	217	39	58	8	1	0	25	31	36	11	4	.360	.313
2011	Greensboro (SAL)	LoA	.208	17	53	6	11	0	0	0	5	10	14	5	1	.348	.208
	Jamestown (NYP)	SS	.340	26	106	13	36	2	0	1	12	2	9	6	2	.352	.387
2012	Greensboro (SAL)	LoA	.335	95	370	72	124	21	3	5	51	34	30	18	5	.394	.449
Minor League Totals			.304	253	909	153	276	36	4	6	112	105	109	53	16	.379	.372

Milwaukee Brewers

BY TOM HAUDRICOURT

When the Brewers were foundering in late July amid a bullpen crisis, general manager Doug Melvin decided it was time to trade Zack Greinke, who had spurned attempts to sign him to a contract extension.

Melvin figured it best to recoup some young talent after dealing Lorenzo Cain, Alcides Escobar, Jeremy Jeffress and Jake Odorizzi to acquire Greinke from the Royals in December 2010. The GM sent Greinke to the Angels for shortstop Jean Segura and righthanders Johnny Hellweg and Ariel Pena. Melvin would have traded other veteran pitchers too, but  Francisco Rodriguez and Randy Wolf were struggling too badly to attract interest and Shaun Marcum had an elbow injury.

A funny thing happened after the Brewers waved their white flag. They started winning. Milwaukee won 24 of 30 games to climb back into the National League wild-card race before being eliminated with three games left in the season. While they failed to make the playoffs, they did record consecutive winning seasons for just the second time in the last two decades.

The surge came with young players playing key roles. Righthander Mike Fiers had come up from Triple-A Nashville in late May to assume a starting role, and he was followed by Mark Rogers and Wily Peralta. Those pitchers performed so well that the Brewers began rethinking their plans for 2013, when they'll give all three of them the opportunity to win permanent jobs in the rotation.

Segura made the Brewers feel better about their shortstop situation, which was thrown into turmoil in early May when veteran Alex Gonzalez tore the anterior cruciate ligament in his right knee. The 22-year-old Segura came up from Double-A Huntsville just eight games after the trade and was thrust into a sink-or-swim situation. After taking on water early, he made adjustments and held his own down the stretch, and the Brewers are prepared to go with him at shortstop to open 2013.

Two other rookies made significant contributions to the lineup. After first baseman Mat Gamel went down in early May with a torn ACL in his right knee, Corey Hart moved from right field to first base and Japanese import Norichika Aoki took over in right and settled in as the leadoff hitter. The 30-year-old Aoki stole 30 bases in 38 attempts.

When Jonathan Lucroy broke his hand in late May and missed two months, Martin Maldonado proved

ED WOLFSTEIN

The Brewers landed shortstop Jean Segura from the Angels in a deal for Zack Greinke

he could handle everyday catching duties if necessary. When Lucroy returned, Milwaukee dealt George Kottaras to the Athletics and made Maldonado the backup.

After focusing on pitching in the 2011 draft, the Brewers used extra picks to stock up on hitters in 2012. They selected Washington high school catcher Clint Coulter and Georgia Southern outfielder Victor Roache in the first round, then followed with Cal Poly outfielder Mitch Haniger in the supplemental first. All three rank among Milwaukee's Top 10 Prospects.

The Brewers hope Coulter, Roache and Haniger will have an easier time getting acclimated to pro ball than the pitchers they took at the top of the 2011 draft. Taylor Jungmann, the 12th overall pick, didn't miss many bats when he went straight to high Class A. He had more success than 15th overall choice Jed Bradley, who got progressively worse on the same club before getting shut down in early August.

Second-rounder Jorge Lopez battled back problems and took a rare step back from the Rookie-level Arizona League to the Rookie-level Dominican Summer League. The silver lining from the 2011 draft crop of pitchers was that Drew Gagnon (third round) and David Goforth (seventh) helped Wisconsin win the low Class A Midwest League title.

THIS YEAR'S TOP 30

Player, Pos.		Grade
1.	Wily Peralta, rhp	60/High
2.	Tyler Thornburg, rhp	55/Medium
3.	Taylor Jungmann, rhp	50/Medium
4.	Hunter Morris, 1b	50/Medium
5.	Jimmy Nelson, rhp	55/High
6.	Johnny Hellweg, rhp	55/High
7.	Victor Roache, of	55/Extreme
8.	Scooter Gennett, 2b	50/Medium
9.	Clint Coulter, c	50/High
10.	Mitch Haniger, of	50/High
11.	Mark Rogers, rhp	50/High
12.	Jed Bradley, lhp	50/High
13.	Logan Schafer, of	45/Medium
14.	Hiram Burgos, rhp	45/Medium
15.	Tyrone Taylor, of	50/High
16.	Khris Davis, of	50/High
17.	Orlando Arcia, ss	55/Extreme
18.	Drew Gagnon, rhp	45/Medium
19.	David Goforth, rhp	50/High
20.	Nick Bucci, rhp	50/High
21.	Jesus Sanchez, rhp	45/Medium
22.	Ariel Pena, rhp	50/High
23.	Jorge Lopez, rhp	50/High
24.	Cody Scarpetta, rhp	45/High
25.	Yadiel Rivera, ss	50/Extreme
26.	Santo Manzanillo, rhp	50/Extreme
27.	Caleb Gindl, of	40/Low
28.	Kentrail Davis, of	45/High
29.	Kyle Heckathorn, rhp	45/High
30.	Josh Prince, of	45/High

LAST YEAR'S TOP 30

Player, Pos.		Status
1.	Wily Peralta, rhp	No. 1
2.	Taylor Jungmann, rhp	No. 3
3.	Jed Bradley, lhp	No. 12
4.	Tyler Thornburg, rhp	No. 2
5.	Scooter Gennett, 2b	No. 8
6.	Logan Schafer, of	No. 13
7.	Cody Scarpetta, rhp	No. 24
8.	Taylor Green, 3b/2b	Dropped out
9.	Jorge Lopez, rhp	No. 23
10.	Jimmy Nelson, rhp	No. 5
11.	Santo Manzanillo, rhp	No. 26
12.	Michael Fiers, rhp	Majors
13.	Caleb Gindl, of	No. 27
14.	Hunter Morris, 1b	No. 4
15.	Yadiel Rivera, ss	No. 25
16.	Kentrail Davis, of	No. 28
17.	David Goforth, rhp	No. 19
18.	Martin Maldonado, c	Majors
19.	Mark Rogers, rhp	No. 11
20.	Nick Bucci, rhp	No. 20
21.	D'Vontrey Richardson, of	Dropped out
22.	Orlando Arcia, ss	No. 17
23.	Dreg Gagnon, rhp	No. 18
24.	Michael Reed, of	Dropped out
25.	Brooks Hall, rhp	Dropped out
26.	Kyle Heckathorn, rhp	No. 29
27.	Eric Farris, 2b/ss	(Mariners)
28.	Nick Ramirez, 1b	Dropped out
29.	Khris Davis, of	No. 16
30.	Amaury Rivas, rhp	Dropped out

BEST TOOLS

Best Hitter for Average	Scooter Gennett
Best Power Hitter	Victor Roache
Best Strike-Zone Discipline	Jason Rogers
Fastest Baserunner	Edgardo Rivera
Best Athlete	Tyrone Taylor
Best Fastball	Johnny Hellweg
Best Curveball	Tyler Thornburg
Best Slider	Wily Peralta
Best Changeup	Hiram Burgos
Best Control	Drew Gagnon
Best Defensive Catcher	Adam Weisenburger
Best Defensive Infielder	Yadiel Rivera
Best Infield Arm	Hector Gomez
Best Defensive Outfielder	Logan Schafer
Best Outfield Arm	Mitch Haniger

PROJECTED 2016 LINEUP

Catcher	Jonathan Lucroy
First Base	Corey Hart
Second Base	Scooter Gennett
Third Base	Rickie Weeks
Shortstop	Jean Segura
Left Field	Ryan Braun
Center Field	Carlos Gomez
Right Field	Norichika Aoka
No. 1 Starter	Yovani Gallardo
No. 2 Starter	Wily Peralta
No. 3 Starter	Marco Estrada
No. 4 Starter	Tyler Thornburg
No. 5 Starter	Taylor Jungmann
Closer	John Axford

TOP PROSPECTS OF THE DECADE

Year	Player, Pos.	2012 Org.
2003	Brad Nelson, 1b	Rangers
2004	Rickie Weeks, 2b	Brewers
2005	Rickie Weeks, 2b	Brewers
2006	Prince Fielder, 1b	Tigers
2007	Yovani Gallardo, rhp	Brewers
2008	Matt LaPorta, of	Indians
2009	Alcides Escobar, ss	Royals
2010	Alcides Escobar, ss	Royals
2011	Mark Rogers, rhp	Brewers
2012	Wily Peralta, rhp	Brewers

TOP DRAFT PICKS OF THE DECADE

Year	Player, Pos.	2012 Org.
2003	Rickie Weeks, 2b	Brewers
2004	Mark Rogers, rhp	Brewers
2005	Ryan Braun, 3b	Brewers
2006	Jeremy Jeffress, rhp	Royals
2007	Matt LaPorta, of	Indians
2008	Brett Lawrie, c/3b	Blue Jays
2009	Eric Arnett, rhp	Brewers
2010	*Dylan Covey, rhp	U. of San Diego
2011	Taylor Jungmann, rhp	Brewers
2012	Clint Coulter, c	Brewers
*Did not sign.		

LARGEST BONUSES IN CLUB HISTORY

Rickie Weeks, 2003	$3,600,000
Taylor Jungmann, 2011	$2,525,000
Ben Sheets, 1999	$2,450,000
Ryan Braun, 2005	$2,450,000
Prince Fielder, 2002	$2,400,000

MILWAUKEE BREWERS

TOP 2013 ROOKIE: Wily Peralta, rhp. If he pitches in the spring as he did last September for the Brewers, he'll make the starting rotation.

BREAKOUT PROSPECT: Hiram Burgos, rhp. He soared through the system in 2012, finishing third in the minors with a 1.95 ERA while reaching Triple-A.

SLEEPER: Miguel de los Santos, lhp. If the deceptive reliever (and ex-Rangers farmhand) throws strikes, he could move quickly to the big leagues.

SOURCE OF TOP 30 TALENT			
Homegrown	27	Acquired	3
College	15	Trades	2
Junior college	0	Rule 5 draft	0
High school	9	Independent leagues	0
Draft-and-follow	0	Free agents/waivers	1
Nondrafted free agents	0		
International	3		

LF
Victor Roache (7)
Khris Davis (16)
Kentrail Davis (28)
Lee Haydel
Ben McMahan
Ruben Ozuna

CF
Logan Schafer (13)
Tyrone Taylor (15)
Josh Prince (30)
Michael Reed
Edgardo Rivera
Reggie Keen

RF
Mitch Haniger (10)
Caleb Gindl (27)
Max Walla
Jose Pena
Chad Stang

3B
Taylor Green
Michael Garza
Brandon Macias
Mike Walker
Jose Dicent

SS
Orlando Arcia (17)
Yadiel Rivera (25)
Jeff Bianchi
Angel Ortega
Hector Gomez
Nick Shaw
Carlos Belonis
Alfredo Rodriguez

2B
Scooter Gennett (8)
Chris McFarland
Greg Hopkins
Jose Sermo
Alejandro Mendoza

1B
Hunter Morris (4)
Adam Giacalone
Nick Ramirez
Cody Hawn
Brock Kjeldgaard
Jason Rogers
Sean Halton

C
Clint Coulter (9)
Anderson de la Rosa
Cameron Garfield
Rafael Neda
Adam Weisenburger
Tyler Roberts

LHP

LHSP	LHRP
Jed Bradley (12)	Miguel de los Santos
Will West	Brian Garman
Anthony Banda	Thomas Keeling
Taylor Wall	Alan Williams
David Otterman	Stephen Peterson
Juan Santiago	Mike Strong
	Brent Suter

RHP

RHSP	RHRP
Wily Peralta (1)	Johnny Hellweg (6)
Tyler Thornburg (2)	Jesus Sanchez (21)
Taylor Jungmann (3)	Santo Manzanillo (26)
Jimmy Nelson (5)	Kyle Heckathorn (29)
Mark Rogers (11)	Damien Magnifico
Hiram Burgos (14)	Fautino de los Santos
Drew Gagnon (18)	Michael Olmsted
David Goforth (19)	Arcenio Leon
Nick Bucci (20)	Darren Byrd
Ariel Pena (22)	Robert Wooten
Jorge Lopez (23)	Casey Medlen
Cody Scarpetta (24)	Tommy Toledo
Zach Quintana	Martin Viramontes
Tyler Wagner	R.J. Seidel
Josh Stinson	Seth Harvey
Brooks Hall	Eric Arnett
Chad Thompson	
Alex Lavandero	

2012

BEST PURE HITTER: OF Tyrone Taylor (2) has a line-drive stroke, good bat speed, plus running speed and athleticism, so the Brewers are confident he'll hit for average. Physical C Clint Coulter (1) has advanced plate discipline for a prep, and he has the strength and swing to take advantage.

BEST POWER HITTER: OF Victor Roache (1) missed most of the 2012 season with a wrist injury but led NCAA Division I with 30 homers in 2011. His was the first 30-homer season in D-I since 2002, and he did it with the less lively BBCOR bats. OF Mitch Haniger (1s) offers promising power as well.

FASTEST RUNNER: A raw all-around player, OF Edgardo Rivera (8) is a burner, turning in consistent 70 times on the 20-80 scouting scale and flashing 80 speed in sprints.

BEST DEFENSIVE PLAYER: Puerto Rican SS Angel Ortega (6) has smooth hands, infield actions and instincts to go with above-average arm strength and range. Taylor and Haniger, who has a well above-average arm, could be premium outfielders.

BEST FASTBALL: RHP Damien Magnifico (5) hits 100 mph as regularly as anyone in the 2012 draft, but he gets hit because the pitch lacks life and command. RHP Tyler Wagner (4) sits in the mid-90s at times.

BEST SECONDARY PITCH: Wagner's slider and RHP Zachary Quintana's (3) curveball are above-average breaking balls. Magnifico made huge progress with his slider in instructional league but must carry that over to games that matter.

BEST PRO DEBUT: Coulter hit .302/.349/.444 and led the Rookie-level Arizona League in on-base percentage. Taylor was dynamic in a short look, batting .387/.432/.667 with 14 extra-base hits and six steals in 18 games before a wrist injury sidelined him.

BEST ATHLETE: Taylor was a star running back and free safety as a prep. Rivera has the physique and athleticism to have been a wide receiver had he grown up in the United States.

MOST INTRIGUING BACKGROUND: OF Lance Roenicke's (25) father Ron is Milwaukee's manager. He played in the majors, as did Lance's uncle Gary and cousin Josh. RHP Austin Blaski (21) was MVP of the 2011 Division III World Series and helped Marietta (Ohio) repeat as national champion.

CLOSEST TO THE MAJORS: Haniger combines all-around tools and polish. His pro debut ended early when he tore the posterior cruciate ligament in his right knee.

BEST LATE-ROUND PICK: NAIA product 2B Jose Sermo (35) has strength and switch-hitting ability. He may not stay on the dirt but should hit his way into being a prospect. RHP Martin Viramontes (28), a fifth-year senior who was drafted for a third time, throws in the mid-90s but has a history of health problems.

THE ONE WHO GOT AWAY: Milwaukee thought it could work out a deal with big-bodied RHP Buck Farmer (15), a third-round talent who slid in the draft, but he returned to Georgia Tech.

ASSESSMENT: The Brewers focused on bats at the top of the draft and swung for the fences with raw, high-ceiling players in rounds 5-10. Getting an unpolished power arm such as Magnifico to come through would be a boon.

2011

Milwaukee had two of the top 15 picks and used them on RHP Taylor Jungmann (1) and LHP Jed Bradley (1), who haven't had as much initial success as expected. Neither has RHP Jorge Lopez (2).

GRADE: C

2010

When RHP Dylan Covey (1) learned he had diabetes, he opted not to sign. The Brewers recovered, however, landing RHPs Jimmy Nelson (2) and Tyler Thornburg (3) and 1B Hunter Morris (4) with their next three picks.

GRADE: B

2009

Milwaukee may not get much out of RHPs Eric Arnett (1) and Kyle Heckathorn (1s) or OF Kentrail Davis (1s). But it did find rotation help in RHP Michael Fiers (22) and a pair of sleepers in RHP Hiram Burgos (6) and 2B Scooter Gennett (16).

GRADE: B

2008

3B Brett Lawrie (1) looks like a future all-star and RHP Jake Odorizzi (1s) could be a solid No. 3 starter, though they were used in trades for Shaun Marcum and Zack Greinke. Two other players have reached the majors with other teams, OF Erik Komatsu (8) and LHP Lucas Luetge (21). The best player still in the organization is another big leaguer, OF Logan Schafer (3).

GRADE: A

Draft analysis by John Manuel (2012) and Jim Callis (2008-11).
Numbers in parentheses indicate draft rounds.

1 WILY PERALTA, RHP

Born: May 8, 1989. **B-T:** R-R. **Ht.:** 6-2. **Wt.:** 240. **Signed:** Dominican Republic, 2005. **Signed by:** Fausto Sosa Pena/Fernando Arango.

BA GRADE
60
HIGH

JOHN WILLIAMSON

Peralta's handlers in the Dominican Republic advertised him as an athletic outfielder with a promising power-speed combination when he became available on the international market in 2005. But the Brewers were more enamored with his strong, quick arm, and they signed him as a pitcher for $450,000. He lasted just one pro summer before blowing out his elbow, however, requiring Tommy John surgery that cost him the entire 2007 season. Back to full strength by 2009, Peralta began a steady climb through the system. In 2011, he led the Double-A Southern League with a 3.46 ERA and was so dominant in five late-season starts at Triple-A Nashville that Milwaukee expected him to return there last season and cruise. That didn't happen. He struggled with his mechanics, had trouble throwing strikes, pitched behind in the count too often and allowed hitters to sit on his fastball. Peralta allowed just four runs in his first three starts, but after a brief promotion to the Brewers—he gave up three hits and one run in his big league debut, a relief appearance on April 22—he returned to Nashville and couldn't get anyone out. His ERA swelled to 6.40 in late June, and his struggles cost him at least one chance to fill a hole in Milwaukee's rotation. Brewers officials were getting quite concerned. Peralta finally was able to make adjustments—a key was closing his front side instead of flying open in his delivery—and pitched well enough to get a September promotion to Milwaukee. He won his first big league start against the Marlins and two-hit the Mets for eight innings in his third.

When Peralta has his mechanics together, he pounds the bottom half of the strike zone with a heavy 93-95 mph fastball. He also has the ability to reach back for a little extra velocity when needed, topping out at 98. He throws two- and four-seamers, and he likes to jam hitters by pitching inside. During his September callup, he featured a devastating slider that gave righthanders fits with its deception and sharp bite. He also has a reliable changeup with splitter action. There's nothing wrong with Peralta's stuff, but he still needs to control and command it better. For a big-bodied pitcher, he's quite athletic, fielding his position well and controlling the running game with quick times to the plate. His confidence waned during his early-season struggles, but he worked his way back and displayed solid poise while in Milwaukee.

Peralta's September re-established his status as Milwaukee's top prospect and put him in position to make the major league rotation in spring training. He remains prone to bouts of wildness, but he profiles as at least a No. 2 starter. The Brewers haven't developed a pitcher this highly regarded since Yovani Gallardo, so a lot is riding on Peralta's success.

SCOUTING GRADES

Fastball: 70. **Control:** 55.
Slider: 60. **Command:** 50.
Changeup: 55.

Based on 20-80 scouting scale, where 50 represents major league average, and future projection rather than present tools.

Year	Club (League)	Class	W	L	ERA	G	GS	CG	SV	IP	H	HR	BB	SO	K/9	WHIP	AVG
2006	Brewers (AZL)	R	2	5	6.63	14	6	0	0	38	51	5	20	28	6.6	1.87	.319
2007	Did Not Play—Injured																
2008	Helena (PIO)	R	1	1	3.07	15	2	0	2	29	23	4	8	36	11.0	1.06	.209
	West Virginia (SAL)	LoA	0	1	10.80	2	2	0	0	5	6	0	3	3	5.4	1.80	.316
2009	Wisconsin (MWL)	LoA	4	4	3.47	27	15	0	1	104	91	5	46	118	10.2	1.32	.235
2010	Brevard County (FSL)	HiA	6	3	3.86	19	17	0	0	105	102	5	40	75	6.4	1.35	.253
	Huntsville (SL)	AA	2	3	3.61	8	8	0	0	42	43	5	24	29	6.2	1.58	.269
2011	Huntsville (SL)	AA	9	7	3.46	21	21	1	0	120	106	9	48	117	8.8	1.29	.243
	Nashville (PCL)	AAA	2	0	2.03	5	5	0	0	31	21	0	11	40	11.6	1.03	.193
2012	Nashville (PCL)	AAA	7	11	4.66	28	28	1	0	147	154	9	78	143	8.8	1.58	.275
	Milwaukee (NL)	MAJ	2	1	2.48	6	5	0	0	29	24	0	11	23	7.1	1.21	.242
Major League Totals			2	1	2.48	6	5	0	0	29	24	0	11	23	7.1	1.21	.242
Minor League Totals			33	35	3.99	139	104	2	3	621	597	42	278	589	8.5	1.41	.254

2 TYLER THORNBURG, RHP

Born: Sept. 29, 1988. **B-T:** R-R. **Ht.:** 5-11. **Wt.:** 185. **Drafted:** Charleston Southern, 2010 (3rd round). **Signed by:** Ryan Robinson.

The Brewers bounced Thornburg around in 2012. He was headed for the Southern League all-star game when they summoned him for an emergency start in mid-June. Then he went to Triple-A, where he sat for a couple of weeks with a sore wrist, before getting recalled again in late July and placed in an unfamiliar relief role. As a September callup, he mostly watched before getting a start after Milwaukee was eliminated from contention. Thornburg primarily works with a 91-94 mph fastball that hits 97 and an overhand curveball that buckles knees when he thows it for strikes. Scouts like his deceptive changeup more than his curve, though the latter was his best pitch in the majors. Thornburg has unorthodox mechanics, pinwheeling the ball to the plate a la Tim Lincecum and prompting some scouts to wonder if he'll be able to repeat his delivery enough to be a starter in the majors. He does throw strikes but needs to improve his command. He left his somewhat straight fastball up in the strike zone too often in the big leagues, and gave up eight homers in 22 innings. Thornburg likely will open 2013 in Nashville because the Brewers don't have any rotation openings. They still see him as a mid-rotation starter, though his future could be as a late-inning reliever.

BA GRADE
55
MEDIUM

Year	Club (League)	Class	W	L	ERA	G	GS	CG	SV	IP	H	HR	BB	SO	K/9	WHIP	AVG
2010	Helena (PIO)	R	1	0	1.93	9	6	0	1	23	15	2	11	38	14.7	1.11	.179
2011	Wisconsin (MWL)	LoA	7	0	1.57	12	12	2	0	69	49	3	25	76	10.0	1.08	.203
	Brevard County (FSL)	HiA	3	6	3.57	12	12	0	0	68	45	5	33	84	11.1	1.15	.186
2012	Huntsville (SL)	AA	8	1	3.00	13	13	0	0	75	57	6	24	71	8.5	1.08	.212
	Nashville (PCL)	AAA	2	3	3.58	8	8	0	0	38	38	1	13	42	10.0	1.35	.264
	Milwaukee (NL)	MAJ	0	0	4.50	8	3	0	0	22	24	8	7	20	8.2	1.41	.279
Major League Totals			0	0	4.50	8	3	0	0	22	24	8	7	20	8.2	1.41	.279
Minor League Totals			21	10	2.77	54	51	2	1	273	204	17	106	311	10.3	1.14	.208

3 TAYLOR JUNGMANN, RHP

Born: Dec. 18, 1989. **B-T:** R-R. **Ht.:** 6-6. **Wt.:** 220. **Drafted:** Texas, 2011 (1st round). **Signed by:** Jeremy Booth.

The 12th overall pick in the 2011 draft, Jungmann signed for $2,525,000, the second-largest bonus in club history. Sent to pitcher-friendly high Class A Brevard County for his pro debut, he had an up-and-down season. He didn't dominate as much as expected, but he made 26 starts and went 3-0, 1.66 in August. Jungmann is all about pounding the bottom of the strike zone with his 90-96 mph sinker and getting hitters to beat the ball into the ground. He uses his tall frame to pitch on a downward plane and get outs early in the count. When he stays on top of his slider, it's a solid pitch with sharp break. The Brewers are encouraging him to throw his changeup more, though it's still below-average. Jungmann doesn't walk a lot of batters, nor does he pile up high strikeout numbers. There were concerns about his delivery coming out of college, but he smoothed it out and displayed good command of his pitches in his first pro season. Jungmann will head to Double-A Huntsville in 2013 and could see Triple-A before season's end. He could join Milwaukee's rotation at some point the following year, with the club envisioning him as a future No. 2 or 3 starter.

BA GRADE
50
MEDIUM

Year	Club (League)	Class	W	L	ERA	G	GS	CG	SV	IP	H	HR	BB	SO	K/9	WHIP	AVG
2012	Brevard County (FSL)	HiA	11	6	3.53	26	26	1	0	153	159	7	46	99	5.8	1.34	.267
Minor League Totals			11	6	3.53	26	26	1	0	153	159	7	46	99	5.8	1.34	.267

4 HUNTER MORRIS, 1B

Born: Oct. 7, 1988. **B-T:** L-R. **Ht.:** 6-4. **Wt.:** 210. **Drafted:** Auburn, 2010 (4th round). **Signed by:** Joe Mason.

Morris had a breakthrough 2012 season, becoming the first Brewers farmhand named Southern League MVP since Corey Hart in 2003. He led the league in hits (158), extra-base hits (74), homers (28), RBIs (113), total bases (294) and slugging (.563). Managers rated him the best batting prospect and best defensive first baseman in the league, and Rawlings honored him with a Gold Glove as the minors' top defender at his position. Morris hits with power to all fields and has produced 57 homers in 337 pro games. He has an aggressive approach at the plate but improved his plate discipline last year. He drew more walks (40) than he had in his previous 201 pro games in the minors (38) and waited more patiently for pitches to drive. Morris also made dramatic strides in the field, enhancing his footwork and cutting his errors to six after making 19 in 2011. His

BA GRADE
50
MEDIUM

range remains average at best but he has good arm strength for the position. He gets no leg hits thanks to his below-average speed. The Brewers now believe Morris can be a big league regular. He'll move up to Triple-A and could be in position to start for Milwaukee in 2014, though winning a job will be more difficult if Corey Hart remains at first base.

Year	Club (League)	Class	AVG	G	AB	R	H	2B	3B	HR	RBI	BB	SO	SB	CS	OBP	SLG
2010	Wisconsin (MWL)	LoA	.251	71	291	38	73	19	4	9	44	20	58	7	2	.306	.436
2011	Huntsville (SL)	AA	.353	4	17	6	6	1	1	1	2	0	1	0	0	.353	.706
	Brevard County (FSL)	HiA	.271	126	501	75	136	28	5	19	67	18	84	7	3	.299	.461
2012	Huntsville (SL)	AA	.303	136	522	77	158	40	6	28	113	40	117	2	1	.357	.563
Minor League Totals			.280	337	1331	196	373	88	16	57	226	78	260	16	6	.324	.499

5 JIMMY NELSON, RHP

Born: June 5, 1989. **B-T:** R-R. **Ht.:** 6-6. **Wt.:** 245. **Drafted:** Alabama, 2010 (2nd round). **Signed by:** Joe Mason.

While 2011 first-rounders Taylor Jungmann and Jed Bradley had inconsistent seasons at Brevard County, Nelson dominated and earned a promotion by mid-June. His control was much more erratic in Double-A, probably the result of shoulder fatigue that prompted the Brewers to skip some of his starts. He recovered in time to get more innings in the Arizona Fall League, though the strike zone remained elusive there. An imposing figure on the mound, Nelson often overpowers hitters with a 92-94 mph fastball that he can run up to 96. He also throws an effective two-seamer in the low 90s that has good sink and induces weak groundouts. He has become more consistent with his sharp 84-86 mph slider, which he uses to shut down righthanders, and more confident with his fringy changeup. He also did a better job repeating his herky-jerky delivery last year until the shoulder fatigue set in. Nelson is a bulldog on the mound with a confident demeanor. The key to his development will be improving his control and command. Nelson likely will return to Huntsville in 2013, at least for the start of the season. He projects as a No. 3 starter and could find himself in Milwaukee's rotation before 2014 is done.

BA GRADE
55
HIGH

Year	Club (League)	Class	W	L	ERA	G	GS	CG	SV	IP	H	HR	BB	SO	K/9	WHIP	AVG
2010	Helena (PIO)	R	2	0	3.71	12	0	0	3	27	30	2	13	33	11.1	1.61	.268
2011	Wisconsin (MWL)	LoA	8	9	4.38	26	25	1	0	146	146	9	65	120	7.4	1.45	.266
2012	Brevard County (FSL)	HiA	4	4	2.21	13	13	1	0	81	63	3	25	77	8.5	1.08	.216
	Huntsville (SL)	AA	2	4	3.91	10	10	0	0	46	34	2	37	42	8.2	1.54	.206
Minor League Totals			16	17	3.66	61	48	2	3	300	273	16	140	272	8.2	1.38	.245

6 JOHNNY HELLWEG, RHP

Born: Oct. 29, 1988. **B-T:** R-R. **Ht.:** 6-9. **Wt.:** 210. **Drafted:** Florida CC, 2008 (16th round). **Signed by:** Tom Kotchman (Angels).

Once the Brewers saw that Zack Greinke had no interest in signing a contract extension, they sent him to the Angels last July for Jean Segura and hard-throwing righthanders Hellweg and Ariel Pena. Because Hellweg already had exceeded his previous career high for innings by 31, Milwaukee pitched him sparingly afterward. The Angels switched Hellweg from relieving to starting in 2011 to give him more innings in an attempt to help him repeat his delivery more consistently and improve his problematic command. He has made strides with locating his pitches, but his strikeout totals have dipped as he has dialed back his fastball to get ahead in the count. Hellweg still pitches regularly in the mid-90s with his fastball, which features late sink and has hit 100 mph when he came out of the bullpen. He can be tough to hit when he throws his slurvy breaking ball for strikes. His changeup is a work in progress. Tall and skinny, he can overpower hitters with the downward tilt on his fastball, but his long limbs also make it difficult to maintain his release point. When Hellweg throws all of his pitches for strikes, he looks like a potential No. 2 starter. But his lack of consistency could mean that his future will come as a late-inning reliever, possibly as a closer. He'll open 2013 in Triple-A.

BA GRADE
55
HIGH

Year	Club (League)	Class	W	L	ERA	G	GS	CG	SV	IP	H	HR	BB	SO	K/9	WHIP	AVG
2008	Angels (AZL)	R	1	0	4.98	14	3	0	0	22	19	1	38	25	10.4	2.63	.224
2009	Angels (AZL)	R	2	1	2.96	18	0	0	6	24	16	0	8	25	9.2	0.99	.186
	Cedar Rapids (MWL)	LoA	0	0	1.35	5	0	0	2	7	4	0	7	7	9.5	1.65	.160
2010	Cedar Rapids (MWL)	LoA	2	4	4.33	41	0	0	16	44	20	2	45	66	13.6	1.49	.133
2011	Inland Empire (CAL)	HiA	6	4	3.73	28	14	0	0	89	75	2	59	113	11.4	1.50	.229
2012	Arkansas (TL)	AA	5	10	3.38	21	21	1	0	120	105	6	60	88	6.6	1.38	.245
	Huntsville (SL)	AA	2	1	2.70	7	2	0	0	20	16	0	15	17	7.7	1.55	.222
Minor League Totals			18	20	3.60	134	40	1	24	325	255	13	232	341	9.4	1.50	.217

7 VICTOR ROACHE, OF

Born: Sept. 17, 1991. **B-T:** R-R. **Ht.:** 6-1. **Wt.:** 225. **Drafted:** Georgia Southern, 2012 (1st round). **Signed by:** Steve Smith.

The Brewers thought they got one of the steals of the 2012 draft when Roache fell to the 28th overall pick. After leading NCAA Division I with 30 homers in 2011, he broke his left wrist diving for a ball six games into his junior season. The injury required six screws, two pins and a metal plate to repair and he didn't play again for Georgia Southern or in the minors after signing for $1,525,000. Roache's calling card is his top-shelf power potential, the product of strength, bat speed and patience. Some scouts question his ability to recognize and handle breaking balls, and his swing can get stiff at times. He may not make enough contact to hit for a high average, but his power should be worth it. Roache has fringy speed and average arm strength, with the instincts to be an effective corner outfielder. Milwaukee praises his devotion to coming back from his injury as soon as possible, as he worked hard so he could take part in instructional league. The Brewers' medical reports indicate that Roache will make a complete recovery. With his track record of college success, he'll start his career at one of their Class A affiliates. It may take time for him to return to form, but he has the potential to be an impact offensive player.

BA GRADE 55 EXTREME

Year	Club (League)	Class	AVG	G	AB	R	H	2B	3B	HR	RBI	BB	SO	SB	CS	OBP	SLG
Did Not Play—Injured																	

8 SCOOTER GENNETT, 2B

Born: May 1, 1990. **B-T:** L-R. **Ht.:** 5-9. **Wt.:** 165. **Drafted:** HS—Sarasota, Fla., 2009 (16th round). **Signed by:** Tim McIlvaine.

Gennett did in 2012 what he's done at every level of the Brewers system—hit for a high average and make his league's all-star team. He also represented Milwaukee in the Futures Game and earned a spot on the 40-man roster. He continues to prove that his size won't stop him from succeeding and remains motivated by those who say he's too small to make it in the majors. Using an open stance and a level swing, Gennett hits line drives to all fields. He makes consistent contact and has surprising pop for his size, most of it coming with doubles to the gaps. He's a free swinger who doesn't take many pitches and draws few walks, resulting in relatively low on-base percentages considering how many hits he accumulates. Gennett has average speed and knows how to run the bases. A high school shortstop, he has worked hard to improve at second base but still has rough edges to smooth out. He has led his league's second basemen in errors in each of his three pro seasons. His arm and range are average. The next step for Gennett is Triple-A. If he succeeds there as he has at every other level, the Brewers will have to decide whether to keep incumbent Rickie Weeks at second base or move him to give Gennett a shot.

BA GRADE 50 MEDIUM

Year	Club (League)	Class	AVG	G	AB	R	H	2B	3B	HR	RBI	BB	SO	SB	CS	OBP	SLG
2010	Wisconsin (MWL)	LoA	.309	118	482	87	149	39	4	9	55	31	91	14	4	.354	.463
2011	Brevard County (FSL)	HiA	.300	134	556	74	167	20	6	9	51	27	69	11	10	.334	.406
2012	Huntsville (SL)	AA	.293	133	533	66	156	30	2	5	44	28	71	11	5	.330	.385
Minor League Totals			.300	385	1571	227	472	89	12	23	150	86	231	36	19	.339	.416

9 CLINT COULTER, C

Born: July 30, 1993. **B-T:** R-R. **Ht.:** 6-3. **Wt.:** 210. **Drafted:** HS—Camas, Wash., 2012 (1st round). **Signed by:** Shawn Whalen.

The Brewers fell in love with Coulter's offensive potential and quickly zeroed in on him as the first of their two first-round picks in 2012. He's a physical specimen who was a Washington state high school wrestling champion before turning his focus to baseball. After going 27th overall and signing for $1,675,000, he led the Rookie-level Arizona League in on-base percentage (.439). Coulter has considerable offensive upside. He's strong with good leverage in his quick swing, and he knows how to work counts to get pitches to drive, so he has above-average power potential. He doesn't get himself out at the plate. Though his high school coach was former big league catcher Tom Lampkin, Coulter is still raw defensively. He has solid arm strength but must improve his mechanics and agility after throwing out just 16 percent of basestealers and giving up 21 passed balls in 26 pro games. He has the leadership, desire and work ethic to remain behind the plate. He has below-average speed but good instincts and an aggressive nature on the bases. The Brewers will be patient with Coulter, who is just 19 and didn't play a lengthy high school schedule in the Pacific Northwest. Whether he

BA GRADE 50 HIGH

DAVE LAX

begins his first full pro season in low Class A Wisconsin depends on how he looks behind the plate in the spring.

Year	Club (League)	Class	AVG	G	AB	R	H	2B	3B	HR	RBI	BB	SO	SB	CS	OBP	SLG
2012	Brewers (AZL)	R	.302	49	169	37	51	3	3	5	33	37	40	3	5	.439	.444
Minor League Totals			.302	49	169	37	51	3	3	5	33	37	40	3	5	.439	.444

10 MITCH HANIGER, OF

Born: Dec. 23, 1990. **B-T:** R-R. **Ht.:** 6-2. **Wt.:** 213. **Drafted:** Cal Poly, 2012 (1st round supplemental). **Signed by:** Dan Huston.

As compensation for losing free agent Prince Fielder to the Tigers, the Brewers got the 27th (Clint Coulter) and 38th (Haniger) picks in the 2012 draft. Haniger headed to low Class A after signing for $1.2 million, but his pro debut ended after 14 games when he tore the posterior cruciate ligament in his right knee. That injury healed in time for Haniger to participate in instructional league. Milwaukee coveted Haniger for his power as well as his overall athleticism and arm. He improved his plate discipline as a junior at Cal Poly, taking pitches, drawing walks and doing a better job of handling offspeed stuff. Those upgrades and an adjustment to load his hands better in his swing allowed him to make better use of his above-average raw power. After totaling 13 homers in his first two seasons at Cal Poly, he hit 13 as a junior, and he could produce 25 or more on an annual basis. Haniger is a fringy runner and average defender in right field. His arm is a weapon, as his throws are not only strong but also accurate. He draws praise for his work ethic, poise and confidence. Because Haniger's pro debut was so brief, the Brewers probably will send him back to Wisconsin to begin 2013. They consider him an advanced player who can move quickly.

BA GRADE
50
HIGH

ANN MOLLICA

Year	Club (League)	Class	AVG	G	AB	R	H	2B	3B	HR	RBI	BB	SO	SB	CS	OBP	SLG
2012	Wisconsin (MWL)	LoA	.286	14	49	9	14	4	0	1	8	7	13	1	0	.379	.429
Minor League Totals			.286	14	49	9	14	4	0	1	8	7	13	1	0	.379	.429

11 MARK ROGERS, RHP

BA GRADE
50
HIGH

Born: Jan. 30, 1986. **B-T:** R-R. **Ht.:** 6-2. **Wt.:** 225. **Drafted:** HS—Mount Ararat, Maine, 2004 (1st round). **Signed by:** Tony Blengino.

The Brewers had no idea what to expect from Rogers in 2012. The fifth overall pick in the 2004 draft and recipient of a $2.2 million bonus, he had missed most of the 2011 season with carpal tunnel syndrome that required surgery on both wrists, as well as a 25-game suspension for testing positive for a banned stimulant. He struggled early on last year in Triple-A, battling command issues as he tried to scrape off the rust. He started throwing better by July, with the velocity on his fastball increasing to the mid-90s as he worked regularly. He got a better feel for his overhand curveball and threw more strikes with his slider. The timing was fortuitous, as he was ready to move into the major league rotation after Zack Greinke was traded to the Angels in late July. Rogers turned in several impressive starts, though erratic command boosted his pitch counts and led to early exits. He'll need more consistency to stick in the majors, but his comeback from a pair of shoulder surgeries that cost him the 2007 and 2008 seasons has been impressive. Milwaukee shut him down after seven big league starts to protect his arm but will give him every chance to make its rotation in the spring.

Year	Club (League)	Class	W	L	ERA	G	GS	CG	SV	IP	H	HR	BB	SO	K/9	WHIP	AVG
2004	Brewers (AZL)	R	0	3	4.73	9	6	0	0	27	30	0	14	35	11.8	1.65	.294
2005	West Virginia (SAL)	LoA	2	9	5.11	25	20	0	1	99	87	11	70	109	9.9	1.59	.238
2006	Brevard County (FSL)	HiA	1	2	5.07	16	16	0	0	71	68	6	53	96	12.2	1.70	.253
	Brewers (AZL)	R	0	0	2.25	3	3	0	0	4	5	0	2	5	11.3	1.75	.294
2007	Did Not Play—Injured																
2008	Did Not Play—Injured																
2009	Brevard County (FSL)	HiA	1	3	1.67	23	22	0	0	65	46	2	29	67	9.3	1.16	.201
2010	Nashville (PCL)	AAA	0	0	2.08	1	1	0	0	4	3	0	3	3	6.2	1.38	.188
	Huntsville (SL)	AA	6	8	3.71	24	24	0	0	112	86	3	69	111	8.9	1.39	.210
	Milwaukee (NL)	MAJ	0	0	1.80	4	2	0	0	10	2	0	3	11	9.9	0.50	.067
2011	Nashville (PCL)	AAA	0	2	13.20	5	5	0	0	15	21	1	22	12	7.2	2.87	.333
	Brevard County (FSL)	HiA	0	3	9.37	5	5	0	0	16	22	4	15	17	9.4	2.27	.301
	Brewers (AZL)	R	0	0	4.85	5	3	0	0	13	13	1	5	11	7.6	1.38	.250
2012	Nashville (PCL)	AAA	6	6	4.72	18	18	0	0	95	92	13	49	74	7.0	1.48	.258
	Milwaukee (NL)	MAJ	3	1	3.92	7	7	0	0	39	36	5	14	41	9.5	1.28	.243
Major League Totals			3	1	3.49	11	9	0	0	49	38	5	17	52	9.6	1.12	.213
Minor League Totals			16	36	4.60	134	123	0	1	521	473	41	331	540	9.3	1.54	.242

12 JED BRADLEY, LHP

BA GRADE

50
HIGH

Born: June 12, 1990. **B-T:** L-L. **Ht.:** 6-4. **Wt.:** 225. **Drafted:** Georgia Tech, 2011 (1st round). **Signed by:** Ryan Robinson.

Bradley saw his 2012 pro debut degenerate into a nightmare after signing for $2 million as the 15th overall pick the year before. His troubles began in spring training, where he sustained a groin strain that prevented him from getting on the mound and bothered him after he was assigned to high Class A. As he tried to compensate for his injury, his mechanics broke down, and his command was so bad that he rarely put pitches where he wanted to. Bradley looked like a far cry from the advanced pitcher he was at Georgia Tech. He was such a mess that the Brewers shut him down in early August and told him to focus on getting healthy and recouping his mechanics. He also had trouble adjusting to pro ball, often throwing too much between starts and generally failing to pace himself. Milwaukee hasn't lost faith in Bradley. When healthy and mechanically sound, he throws an 88-93 mph fastball with armside run and a mid-80s slider. He has good arm action and deception on his changeup. The Brewers didn't expect him to have physical or mechanical issues because he was a workhorse in college who was able to repeat his delivery consistently. They will likely send Bradley back to Brevard County in 2013 to get a fresh start.

Year	Club (League)	Class	W	L	ERA	G	GS	CG	SV	IP	H	HR	BB	SO	K/9	WHIP	AVG
2012	Brevard County (FSL)	HiA	5	10	5.53	20	20	1	0	107	136	9	43	60	5.0	1.67	.311
Minor League Totals			5	10	5.53	20	20	1	0	107	136	9	43	60	5.0	1.67	.311

13 LOGAN SCHAFER, OF

BA GRADE

45
MEDIUM

Born: Sept. 8, 1986. **B-T:** L-L. **Ht.:** 6-1. **Wt.:** 175. **Drafted:** Cal Poly, 2008 (3rd round). **Signed by:** Corey Rodriguez.

Schafer had a modest year statistically in 2012, but there was plenty of good news as he played a full season and finished it in the majors. He missed all but seven games in 2010 with a sports hernia and later a broken foot. A broken thumb in spring training cost him the first six weeks of the 2011 season. Schafer is at his best when sending line drives into the gaps with a simple, level swing. His plate discipline waned in Triple-A last year, but he did continue to make contact and showed decent pop—mostly to the gaps—considering his wiry frame. Schafer doesn't have blazing speed but runs the bases well. He also has great instincts in center field, getting good jumps and chasing down deep flies with ease. His arm is average but accurate, and he plays with confidence and poise. The Brewers were encouraged by Schafer's play during his September callup, as he got several big hits off the bench in the heat of a playoff race and played strong defense in center. He'll have every chance to make the big league club and back up Carlos Gomez in center.

Year	Club (League)	Class	AVG	G	AB	R	H	2B	3B	HR	RBI	BB	SO	SB	CS	OBP	SLG
2008	Helena (PIO)	R	.240	8	25	4	6	0	1	2	8	5	4	1	0	.355	.560
	West Virginia (SAL)	LoA	.276	43	181	25	50	13	2	0	20	8	42	3	8	.306	.370
2009	Huntsville (SL)	AA	.217	7	23	4	5	0	1	0	4	3	1	0	.379	.304
	Brevard County (FSL)	HiA	.313	113	457	76	143	31	6	6	58	38	53	16	8	.369	.446
2010	Brevard County (FSL)	HiA	.174	7	23	7	4	2	0	0	1	4	6	0	0	.286	.261
2011	Brevard County (FSL)	HiA	.306	9	36	4	11	0	0	0	1	5	4	1	1	.390	.306
	Huntsville (SL)	AA	.302	50	189	31	57	9	4	0	19	17	25	10	5	.368	.392
	Nashville (PCL)	AAA	.331	40	169	31	56	13	2	5	23	17	18	5	3	.401	.521
	Milwaukee (NL)	MAJ	.333	8	3	1	1	0	0	0	0	1	1	0	0	.500	.333
2012	Nashville (PCL)	AAA	.278	124	464	72	129	23	9	11	40	29	72	16	7	.332	.438
	Milwaukee (NL)	MAJ	.304	16	23	3	7	1	2	0	5	1	3	0	1	.320	.522
Major League Totals			.308	24	26	4	8	1	2	0	5	2	4	0	1	.345	.500
Minor League Totals			.294	401	1567	254	461	91	25	24	170	127	227	53	32	.354	.430

14 HIRAM BURGOS, RHP

BA GRADE

45
MEDIUM

Born: Aug. 4, 1987. **B-T:** R-R. **Ht.:** 6-0. **Wt.:** 210. **Drafted:** Bethune-Cookman, 2009 (6th round). **Signed by:** Tim McIlvaine.

No Brewers farmhand made a bigger leap forward in 2012 than Burgos. Sent back to repeat high Class A, he dominated Florida State League hitters and earned promotions to Double-A and Triple-A. He was pitching well enough at season's end that he could have been summoned to the majors had there been a need. He went 10-4, 1.95 overall, ranking third in the minors in ERA and leading the system with 153 strikeouts. Burgos doesn't wow with his stuff, throwing his fastball mainly at 88-91 mph, but it plays up because of his strong fastball command and his other pitches. He features a cutter, a changeup that can bottom out when at its best, a curveball and an occasional slider. He can throw each of them for strikes in any count. He varies his patterns, keeping hitters off balance, and consistently pounds the strike zone. Milwaukee compares him to Mike Fiers, another pitcher who succeeded at a somewhat advanced age by carving up hitters with deception and location. After adding him to their 40-man roster in November, the Brewers are anxious to see Burgos in his first major league camp in the spring. He'll probably open the season in the Nashville rotation.

Year	Club (League)	Class	W	L	ERA	G	GS	CG	SV	IP	H	HR	BB	SO	K/9	WHIP	AVG
2009	Helena (PIO)	R	3	2	5.62	14	7	0	0	58	75	7	14	53	8.3	1.54	.309
2010	Helena (PIO)	R	3	0	2.37	6	6	0	0	38	31	1	5	48	11.4	0.95	.215
	Wisconsin (MWL)	LoA	5	7	4.48	19	8	0	0	74	77	5	21	62	7.5	1.32	.271
2011	Brevard County (FSL)	HiA	6	8	4.89	24	22	0	0	120	142	13	35	80	6.0	1.48	.302
2012	Brevard County (FSL)	HiA	2	1	0.87	7	6	0	0	41	21	1	6	41	8.9	0.65	.150
	Huntsville (SL)	AA	6	1	1.94	13	13	1	0	83	68	3	28	77	8.3	1.15	.230
	Nashville (PCL)	AAA	2	2	2.91	8	8	0	0	46	39	4	15	35	6.8	1.17	.224
Minor League Totals			27	21	3.61	91	70	1	0	461	453	34	124	396	7.7	1.25	.259

15 TYRONE TAYLOR, OF

BA GRADE

50

HIGH

Born: Jan. 22, 1994. **B-T:** R-R. **Ht.:** 6-0. **Wt.:** 185. **Drafted:** HS—Torrance, Calif., 2012 (2nd round). **Signed by:** Dan Huston.

Taylor was a standout running back and safety for his high school football team, and he showed potential in baseball that figured to blossom when he focused on one sport. The Brewers loved his athleticism, taking him in the second round last June and signing him for $750,000. He put together a strong pro debut before a wrist injury cut his season short. Taylor has improved his mechanics at the plate and features a line-drive stroke with good bat speed. Some amateur scouts worried about the load in his swing, as he rocked back before moving forward, but he smoothed that out after signing. His power goes mostly to the gaps, though he has a chance to produce double-digit homers on an annual basis as he matures. Taylor has above-average speed that plays well in center field, where he shows good instincts, as well as the basepaths, where he's aggressive and gets good jumps. His all-around package of tools gives Taylor an ideal center-field profile if he hits. He'll move on to low Class A for his first full professional season.

Year	Club (League)	Class	AVG	G	AB	R	H	2B	3B	HR	RBI	BB	SO	SB	CS	OBP	SLG
2012	Brewers (AZL)	R	.389	8	36	11	14	5	3	0	6	1	3	3	1	.395	.694
	Helena (PIO)	R	.385	10	39	11	15	4	0	2	5	5	8	3	2	.467	.641
Minor League Totals			.387	18	75	22	29	9	3	2	11	6	11	6	3	.434	.667

16 KHRIS DAVIS, OF

BA GRADE

50

HIGH

Born: Dec. 21, 1987. **B-T:** R-R. **Ht.:** 5-11. **Wt.:** 190. **Drafted:** Cal State Fullerton, 2009 (7th round). **Signed by:** Josh Belovsky.

Davis strained his right calf early in 2012, tried to return too soon and re-injured his leg, costing him two months of the season. Determined to make up for lost time, he went on an offensive binge when he returned to Double-A and continued to rake following a promotion to Triple-A, hitting a combined .350/.451/.604 for the year. Davis' quick bat gives him 20-25 homer potential in the majors, and he can drive the ball out of the park to all fields. Sometimes his swing gets long, but he takes walks and doesn't get himself out as often as he did earlier in his career. Davis' biggest issue is where he'll play. He's a below-average runner who doesn't get great jumps, and his arm isn't strong either. He fits best in left field, where the Brewers have Ryan Braun signed for years to come. Davis has turned himself into a serviceable outfielder and has some experience in right field. After joining the 40-man roster in November, he'll return to Nashville and try to hit his way into big league consideration.

Year	Club (League)	Class	AVG	G	AB	R	H	2B	3B	HR	RBI	BB	SO	SB	CS	OBP	SLG
2009	Helena (PIO)	R	.000	1	1	0	0	0	0	0	0	0	0	0	0	.000	.000
	Brewers (AZL)	R	.243	10	37	7	9	0	2	2	8	6	11	4	0	.356	.514
2010	Wisconsin (MWL)	LoA	.280	128	457	86	128	26	4	22	72	77	120	17	10	.398	.499
2011	Brevard County (FSL)	HiA	.309	90	304	50	94	21	1	15	68	51	70	10	5	.415	.533
	Huntsville (SL)	AA	.210	35	124	10	26	7	1	2	16	10	23	0	0	.272	.331
2012	Huntsville (SL)	AA	.383	44	128	23	49	9	0	8	23	20	33	2	2	.484	.641
	Brewers (AZL)	R	.368	6	19	7	7	0	0	3	5	2	7	1	1	.455	.842
	Nashville (PCL)	AAA	.310	32	113	23	35	12	0	4	24	20	27	1	0	.414	.522
Minor League Totals			.294	346	1183	206	348	75	8	56	216	186	291	35	18	.400	.513

17 ORLANDO ARCIA, SS

BA GRADE

55

EXTREME

Born: Aug. 4, 1994. **B-T:** R-R. **Ht.:** 6-0. **Wt.:** 165. **Signed:** Venezuela, 2010. **Signed by:** Fernando Arango.

Following a strong showing in the Rookie-level Dominican Summer League in 2011, Arcia saw his U.S. debut end before it even began when he broke his ankle sliding into second base during extended spring training. The break was so severe that doctors inserted a metal plate to repair it. Arcia, whose older brother Oswaldo is a top prospect in the Twins system, recovered in time to participate in instructional league and got more action over the winter at the Brewers' Dominican academy. The good news is that Arcia is just 18 and still has plenty of time to make up for the lost season. He has the skills to be an outstanding defender at shortstop, with good range to both sides, solid footwork around the bag and plenty of arm strength. He also shows great instincts in the field. Milwaukee hopes Arcia will develop into an above-average offensive player. He shows contact ability and some surprising pop for his size, so he could hit for a solid average with gap power down the road. His speed is average at best, but he runs the bases well and shows good instincts there as well. The Brewers may consider sending Arcia to low Class A in 2013, though that might be pushing it considering his age and inexperience.

Year	Club (League)	Class	AVG	G	AB	R	H	2B	3B	HR	RBI	BB	SO	SB	CS	OBP	SLG
2011	Brewers (DSL)	R	.294	64	218	47	64	16	1	6	36	30	20	13	4	.386	.459
2012	Did Not Play—Injured																
Minor League Totals			.294	64	218	47	64	16	1	6	36	30	20	13	4	.386	.459

18 DREW GAGNON, RHP

BA GRADE

45

MEDIUM

Born: June 26, 1990. **B-T:** R-R. **Ht.:** 6-4. **Wt.:** 195. **Drafted:** Long Beach State, 2011 (3rd round). **Signed by:** Josh Belovsky.

Ten former Long Beach State pitchers saw big league action in 2012, and Gagnon is on his way to joining their ranks. He went through a dead-arm stage after signing for $340,000 as a third-round pick in 2011 and got roughed up in Rookie ball. He threw much better in instructional league that fall and found his groove last season at two Class A stops. Gagnon pounds the strike zone, walking few hitters and inducing early count outs. He has good life on an 88-92 mph fastball and has the ability to reach back for a little extra velocity when needed. He has abandoned a slider to go with a more conventional curveball that he regularly throws for strikes. His changeup still needs work but he delivers it with good arm speed, and he dabbles with a cutter that can be effective. Gagnon has a strong mound presence and knows how to set up hitters. He continued to perform after a midseason promotion to Brevard County and could be ready for Double-A in 2013. His lack of a plus pitch limits his ceiling, but he could be a very solid back-of-the-rotation starter in the big leagues.

Year	Club (League)	Class	W	L	ERA	G	GS	CG	SV	IP	H	HR	BB	SO	K/9	WHIP	AVG
2011	Helena (PIO)	R	0	3	8.05	8	7	0	1	19	25	1	10	27	12.8	1.84	.321
2012	Wisconsin (MWL)	LoA	6	1	2.83	14	14	0	0	83	67	6	19	65	7.1	1.04	.219
	Brevard County (FSL)	HiA	1	2	2.82	11	11	1	0	67	56	3	18	49	6.6	1.10	.229
Minor League Totals			7	6	3.42	33	32	1	1	169	148	10	47	141	7.5	1.16	.235

19 DAVID GOFORTH, RHP

BA GRADE

50

HIGH

Born: Oct. 11, 1988. **B-T:** R-R. **Ht.:** 6-0. **Wt.:** 186. **Drafted:** Mississippi, 2011 (7th round). **Signed by:** Joe Mason.

The Brewers used Goforth in relief after signing him for $100,000 in 2011, then moved him into the rotation at Wisconsin last season. The idea was to get the hard-throwing righty to work on his secondary pitches because there is no question about his ability to throw fastballs past hitters. Goforth regularly pitches in the mid-90s and can reach 98 mph. His fastball straightens out when it's up in the strike zone, leaving him vulnerable to home runs, however. He made some progess with his curveball, cutter and changeup in 2012, but they remain average at best. He loses his mechanics at times, resulting in walks and wild pitches, and is learning to pace himself as a starter. He did pitch better in the second half of last season and won two playoff starts (including a shutout against Burlington) as the Timber Rattlers won the Midwest League crown. Goforth still profiles better as a reliever in the majors, which would allow him to unleash his fastball with more fury and pitch in shorter bursts. The Brewers may keep him in the rotation in 2013 to get more innings while refining his pitches and command.

Year	Club (League)	Class	W	L	ERA	G	GS	CG	SV	IP	H	HR	BB	SO	K/9	WHIP	AVG
2011	Helena (PIO)	R	0	4	4.43	19	0	0	2	41	44	5	10	42	9.3	1.33	.277
2012	Wisconsin (MWL)	LoA	10	8	4.66	28	28	0	0	151	154	16	63	93	5.6	1.44	.269
Minor League Totals			10	12	4.61	47	28	0	2	191	198	21	73	135	6.4	1.42	.270

20 NICK BUCCI, RHP

BA GRADE

50

HIGH

Born: Aug. 16, 1990. **B-T:** R-R. **Ht.:** 6-2. **Wt.:** 180. **Drafted:** HS—Sarnia, Ont., 2008 (18th round). **Signed by:** Jay Lapp.

The Brewers had high expectations for Bucci in 2012, but he severely strained his shoulder in spring training. It took him most of the season to rehab it and get ready to pitch again. He was impressive in six starts at Brevard County, including an eight-inning outing to close the season. Bucci features a fastball that sits at 90-92 mph and touches 94, uses it on both sides of the plate and isn't afraid to pitch inside. His secondary pitches include a cutter, sharp-breaking curveball and changeup, all of which have a chance to be at least average. He shows a good feel for pitching and repeats his delivery well. Last year's shoulder issue notwithstanding, his frame and athleticism should lend themselves to durability. Milwaukee loves his competitiveness on the mound, which he developed during his time with Canada's national teams. He was part of bronze-medal winners at the 2009 and 2011 World Cups and a gold-medal squad at the 2011 Pan American Games. Though he missed much of last season, Bucci has plenty of time to develop into a middle-of-the-rotation starter. Protected on the 40-man roster in November, he'll make the jump to Double-A.

Year	Club (League)	Class	W	L	ERA	G	GS	CG	SV	IP	H	HR	BB	SO	K/9	WHIP	AVG
2008	Brewers (AZL)	R	0	3	7.36	5	4	0	0	11	12	2	2	14	11.5	1.27	.273
2009	Huntsville (SL)	AA	1	0	6.75	3	0	0	0	4	3	2	2	3	6.8	1.25	.231
	Helena (PIO)	R	6	3	4.41	13	12	0	0	69	59	7	21	66	8.6	1.15	.231
2010	Wisconsin (MWL)	LoA	6	7	3.51	26	20	0	1	121	96	12	68	100	7.5	1.36	.220
2011	Brevard County (FSL)	HiA	8	11	3.84	26	25	1	0	150	143	12	51	119	7.1	1.29	.247
2012	Brewers (AZL)	R	1	1	1.64	4	4	0	0	11	7	1	0	7	5.7	0.64	.179
	Brevard County (FSL)	HiA	2	2	1.99	6	6	0	0	32	25	3	15	37	10.5	1.26	.210
Minor League Totals			24	27	3.76	83	71	1	1	398	345	39	159	346	7.8	1.27	.232

21 JESUS SANCHEZ, RHP

BA GRADE

45

MEDIUM

Born: Sept. 24, 1987. **B-T:** R-R. **Ht.:** 5-11. **Wt.:** 206. **Signed:** Venezuela, 2004. **Signed by:** Hector Rincones/Ricardo Finol (Yankees).

Originally signed by the Yankees as a catcher in 2004, Sanchez was traded two years later to the Phillies in the Bobby Abreu/Cory Lidle deal. When it became apparent Sanchez wasn't going to hit enough, Philadelphia decided to take advantage of his arm strength and shifted him to pitching. He posted two solid seasons in Class A before the Phillies released him after the 2010 season. The Brewers signed him two weeks later and moved him to the bullpen in mid-2011. He has thrived in his new role, reaching Triple-A last year and claiming a spot on the 40-man roster. As a reliever, Sanchez can focus on two pitches, a 94-97 mph fastball that he commands well and a developing slider that improved considerably last season. He throws strikes and keeps the ball down in the zone. Sanchez will get a good look in spring training and should have a chance to join a retooled Milwaukee relief corps.

Year	Club (League)	Class	AVG	G	AB	R	H	2B	3B	HR	RBI	BB	SO	SB	CS	OBP	SLG
2005	Yankees1 (DSL)	R	.165	37	115	11	19	4	1	0	5	8	38	0	2	.267	.217
2006	Yankees (GCL)	R	.269	24	93	10	25	5	0	0	10	9	19	3	0	.346	.323
	Phillies (GCL)	R	.192	8	26	1	5	2	0	0	1	1	8	1	0	.241	.269
2007	Clearwater (FSL)	HiA	1.000	1	1	0	1	0	0	0	0	0	0	0	0	1.000	1.000
	Phillies (GCL)	R	.208	34	96	12	20	4	0	0	3	15	29	3	1	.315	.250
Minor League Totals			.202	191	456	48	92	18	1	1	28	39	122	8	3	.280	.252

Year	Club (League)	Class	W	L	ERA	G	GS	CG	SV	IP	H	HR	BB	SO	K/9	WHIP	AVG
2008	Phillies (GCL)	R	0	0	0.00	1	0	0	0	1	0	0	1	0	0.00	1.00	.000
2009	Lakewood (SAL)	LoA	10	6	3.44	26	26	0	0	136	137	4	42	120	7.9	1.32	.265
2010	Clearwater (FSL)	HiA	9	7	2.99	23	22	1	0	129	109	9	33	84	5.8	1.10	.230
2011	Huntsville (SL)	AA	4	7	4.91	30	14	0	1	99	104	13	47	66	6.0	1.53	.271
2012	Huntsville (SL)	AA	3	2	1.59	32	0	0	11	45	34	2	13	41	8.1	1.04	.213
	Nashville (PCL)	AAA	4	1	1.71	20	0	0	0	26	23	0	9	23	7.9	1.22	.242
Minor League Totals			30	23	3.34	132	62	1	12	437	407	28	145	334	6.9	1.26	.249

22 ARIEL PENA, RHP

BA GRADE

50

HIGH

Born: May 20, 1989. **B-T:** R-R. **Ht.:** 6-3. **Wt.:** 190. **Signed:** Dominican Republic, 2007. **Signed by:** Freddy Rodriguez (Angels).

Pena's performance after his acquisition from the Angels in the Zack Greinke trade last July wasn't what the Brewers had in mind. They knew he was rough around the edges, as evidenced by his Futures Game turn just before the deal. Pena hit 94-95 mph in the prospect all-star game but fooled no one, giving up eight runs on seven hits, a walk and a sacrifice fly. He wasn't the same afterward, making just three quality starts the rest of the year as his control and command disintegrated. Velocity isn't an issue. Pena pitches regularly at 92-94 mph with his sinker and can reach 98 with his four-seamer. He throws a hard slider that breaks late and sits at 82-86 mph. His 85-88 mph changeup is too firm and mostly just a show-me pitch. Though he has good size and obvious arm strength, Pena is so erratic with his command that many scouts figure he'll have to pitch in relief. He loses his mechanics too easily and often drags his arm behind his body, leaving pitches up in the strike zone. His problems persisted in a short winter ball stint in the Dominican Republic. Pena will try to make a better impression on his new organization when he returns to Double-A this year.

Year	Club (League)	Class	W	L	ERA	G	GS	CG	SV	IP	H	HR	BB	SO	K/9	WHIP	AVG
2007	Angels (DSL)	R	10	2	2.26	14	14	2	0	80	62	1	32	54	6.1	1.18	.212
2008	Angels (DSL)	R	7	3	1.86	15	15	0	0	97	73	0	26	110	10.2	1.02	.208
2009	Angels (AZL)	R	5	4	3.83	14	6	0	0	49	46	2	15	47	8.6	1.24	.247
2010	R. Cucamonga (CAL)	HiA	0	1	8.71	3	3	0	0	10	10	0	13	8	7.0	2.23	.270
	Cedar Rapids (MWL)	LoA	7	5	3.76	18	18	1	0	103	93	7	60	88	7.7	1.49	.242

Year	Club (League)	Class	W	L	ERA	G	GS	CG	SV	IP	H	HR	BB	SO	K/9	WHIP	AVG
2011	Inland Empire (CAL)	HiA	10	6	4.45	27	27	1	0	152	154	10	81	180	10.7	1.55	.264
	Salt Lake (PCL)	AAA	0	0	2.25	1	1	0	0	4	7	0	4	3	6.8	2.75	.389
2012	Arkansas (TL)	AA	6	6	2.99	19	19	1	0	114	95	14	42	111	8.7	1.20	.222
	Huntsville (SL)	AA	0	2	7.24	7	7	0	0	32	40	5	23	29	8.1	1.95	.336
Minor League Totals			45	29	3.56	118	110	5	0	641	580	39	296	630	8.8	1.37	.242

23 JORGE LOPEZ, RHP

BA GRADE
50
HIGH

Born: Feb. 10, 1993. **B-T:** R-R. **Ht.:** 6-4. **Wt.:** 175. **Drafted:** HS—Cayey, P.R., 2011 (2nd round). **Signed by:** Charlie Sullivan/Manolo Hernandez.

The Brewers wanted to restock their pitching with the 2011 draft, and they were excited to land Lopez in the second round and sign him for $690,000. The returns from his first full pro season were disappointing, however. He experienced some back issues in the early part of 2012 and didn't perform well in the Arizona League, before making an unusual move to the Rookie-level Dominican Summer League to work with instructors there. The good news was that Lopez looked better in instructional league, touching 95 mph and throwing a hammer curveball that buckled hitters' knees. He works around 90-91 mph with his fastball but should throw harder as he gets stronger. He has good feel for a breaking ball and uses it as a strikeout pitch when ahead in the count. Lopez continues to work on a changeup as his third pitch. He got better at repeating his loose delivery, which bodes well for improving his control and command. Still a teenager, Lopez has a long way to go but has No. 3 starter's upside. He probably will go to low Class A to begin 2013.

Year	Club (League)	Class	W	L	ERA	G	GS	CG	SV	IP	H	HR	BB	SO	K/9	WHIP	AVG
2011	Brewers (AZL)	R	0	0	2.25	4	4	0	0	12	13	0	3	10	7.5	1.33	.265
2012	Brewers (AZL)	R	1	3	5.33	7	3	0	2	25	27	2	12	20	7.1	1.54	.270
	Brewers (DSL)	R	0	1	4.76	5	3	0	0	23	22	0	10	26	10.3	1.41	.256
Minor League Totals			1	4	4.50	16	10	0	2	60	62	2	25	56	8.4	1.45	.264

24 CODY SCARPETTA, RHP

BA GRADE
45
HIGH

Born: Aug. 25, 1988. **B-T:** R-R. **Ht.:** 6-3. **Wt.:** 240. **Drafted:** HS—Guilford, Ill., 2007 (11th round). **Signed by:** Harvey Kuenn Jr.

The 2012 season figured to be a big one for Scarpetta. His original $325,000 deal was voided because he needed finger surgery after the Brewers made him an 11th-round pick in 2007, so Milwaukee had to place him on the 40-man roster when the club re-signed him. As a result, he ran out of minor league options last year, meaning he needed to get as close to big league-ready as possible to make Milwaukee feel good about keeping him. All of that went up in smoke when Scarpetta injured his elbow during spring training and had Tommy John surgery in May, and the Brewers removed him from the 40-man roster after the season. He probably won't be ready to pitch again until mid-2013, but at age 24 he's young enough to bounce back and still make it to the majors. When healthy, Scarpetta has a 90-94 mph fastball and a sharp-breaking curveball. His third pitch is a changeup that still needs work. He sometimes has trouble with his mechanics, which contributes to inconsistent control and may have led to his elbow trouble. Slated to pitch in Triple-A last year, Scarpetta probably will break in at a lower level when he returns to action. If he can stay healthy, the Brewers still see some upside as a No. 3 or 4 starter, but he also could be pegged for bullpen action.

Year	Club (League)	Class	W	L	ERA	G	GS	CG	SV	IP	H	HR	BB	SO	K/9	WHIP	AVG
2008	Brewers (AZL)	R	1	0	0.57	6	5	0	0	16	8	0	8	27	15.5	1.02	.154
	Helena (PIO)	R	1	0	3.48	6	3	0	0	21	18	2	8	31	13.5	1.26	.237
2009	Wisconsin (MWL)	LoA	4	11	3.43	26	18	0	0	105	83	5	55	116	9.9	1.31	.217
	Huntsville (SL)	AA	0	0	5.40	1	1	0	0	5	5	1	1	1	1.8	1.20	.263
2010	Brevard County (FSL)	HiA	7	12	3.87	27	27	1	0	128	120	4	67	142	10.0	1.46	.247
2011	Huntsville (SL)	AA	8	5	3.85	23	23	0	0	117	100	8	61	98	7.5	1.38	.234
2012	Did Not Play—Injured																
Minor League Totals			21	28	3.61	89	77	1	0	391	334	20	200	415	9.5	1.36	.231

25 YADIEL RIVERA, SS

BA GRADE
50
EXTREME

Born: May 1, 1992. **B-T:** R-R. **Ht.:** 6-3. **Wt.:** 180. **Drafted:** HS—Caguas, P.R., 2010 (9th round). **Signed by:** Charlie Sullivan.

The Brewers have no doubt that Rivera is a major league-quality defender at shortstop, but they haven't resolved the question of whether he'll hit enough to be an everyday player. The smooth shortstop makes highlight-reel plays with above-average range and a strong arm. He has sure hands and good lateral movement. Rivera made some strides at the plate in his second shot at low Class A in 2012, but he remains a free swinger with little plate discipline and a propensity to strike out. His .274 career on-base percentage indicates his lack of offensive polish. Rivera does have some home run power in his lanky frame, but he needs to focus on making contact and getting on base. He gets too long with his swing and too pull-conscious, especially after hitting a home run, and pitchers easily carve him up with breaking balls. He has average speed at best and isn't a basestealing threat. Rivera profiles as at least a utility player thanks to his defense, though he could develop into a regular if he can make some strides at the plate. High Class A could be a challenge for him in 2013.

Year	Club (League)	Class	AVG	G	AB	R	H	2B	3B	HR	RBI	BB	SO	SB	CS	OBP	SLG
2010	Brewers (AZL)	R	.209	49	206	22	43	8	1	0	23	9	72	6	2	.243	.257
2011	Wisconsin (MWL)	LoA	.194	32	103	6	20	2	1	1	5	4	34	0	0	.224	.262
	Helena (PIO)	R	.248	74	330	47	82	14	7	8	38	14	91	7	3	.285	.406
2012	Wisconsin (MWL)	LoA	.247	127	465	60	115	26	5	12	49	26	119	7	3	.290	.402
Minor League Totals			.236	282	1104	135	260	50	14	21	115	53	316	20	8	.274	.363

26 SANTO MANZANILLO, RHP

BA GRADE

50

EXTREME

Born: Sept. 20, 1988. **B-T:** R-R. **Ht.:** 6-1. **Wt.:** 220. **Signed:** Dominican Republic, 2005. **Signed by:** Fernando Arango/Fausto Sosa Pena.

When Manzanillo dislocated his shoulder and injured his scapula in a serious auto accident in the Dominican Republic after the 2011 season, he appeared to make a speedy recovery and was active in spring training. He told Milwaukee's training staff that his shoulder felt fine, but as it turned out, that wasn't the case. It quickly became evident he wasn't the same pitcher who had a breakout season in 2011. The Brewers pulled the plug after 12 mostly dreadful relief outings in Double-A, sending Manzanillo to Arizona to rehab a strained right rotator cuff. He returned to the mound in mid-August but didn't pitch well in the minors or the Arizona Fall League. Before he got hurt, Manzanillo regularly threw in the mid-90s and topped out at 99 mph, but his fastball velocity diminished significantly in 2012. His formerly mid-80s slider also lost some power, and his control diminished as well. He also throws a changeup that has become more effective. If Manzanillo can get back to where he was in 2011, he could help Milwaukee as a set-up man and perhaps even as a closer.

Year	Club (League)	Class	W	L	ERA	G	GS	CG	SV	IP	H	HR	BB	SO	K/9	WHIP	AVG
2006	Brewers (AZL)	R	0	0	13.22	14	0	0	0	16	14	1	47	13	7.2	3.73	.230
2007	Brewers (AZL)	R	4	4	3.90	14	0	0	1	28	22	1	29	18	5.9	1.84	.214
2008	Helena (PIO)	R	0	1	9.28	13	6	0	1	32	41	3	26	27	7.6	2.09	.318
2009	Did Not Play—Injured																
2010	Wisconsin (MWL)	LoA	1	1	5.77	26	0	0	0	53	58	3	30	40	6.8	1.66	.279
2011	Brevard County (FSL)	HiA	1	0	1.52	28	0	0	10	41	31	2	14	43	9.4	1.09	.200
	Huntsville (SL)	AA	1	1	2.21	20	0	0	7	20	13	2	12	19	8.4	1.23	.181
2012	Huntsville (SL)	AA	0	4	6.08	12	0	0	1	13	13	2	10	10	6.8	1.73	.260
	Brewers (AZL)	R	0	1	10.13	2	0	0	0	3	4	0	0	2	6.8	1.50	.333
	Wisconsin (MWL)	LoA	2	1	7.50	4	0	0	0	6	5	1	5	2	3.0	1.67	.263
Minor League Totals			8	13	5.59	133	6	0	20	213	201	15	173	174	7.4	1.76	.248

27 CALEB GINDL, OF

BA GRADE

40

LOW

Born: Aug. 31, 1988. **B-T:** L-L. **Ht.:** 5-9. **Wt.:** 185. **Drafted:** HS—Milton, Fla., 2007 (5th round). **Signed by:** Doug Reynolds.

Gindl played through nagging injuries in 2012, including a lower back issue that cost him a September callup, and turned in the worst offensive performance of his six-year pro career. His grinder mentality kept him in the lineup when others might have begged out, but in the end that did him little good. With a squatty build and limited athleticism, Gindl must hit to play in the majors. Before last year, he had established his credentials as a solid hitter with gap power, though his patience slipped when he repeated Triple-A. He's a below-average runner with fringy arm strength who fits best in left field, though he has played in all three outfield spots. That versatility should help him as he now looks like an extra outfielder and lefthanded bat off the bench in the Laynce Nix mold. If Gindl can get his bat going again, he could fill that role in Milwaukee this year.

Year	Club (League)	Class	AVG	G	AB	R	H	2B	3B	HR	RBI	BB	SO	SB	CS	OBP	SLG
2007	Helena (PIO)	R	.372	55	207	40	77	22	3	5	42	20	38	4	4	.420	.580
2008	West Virginia (SAL)	LoA	.307	137	508	86	156	38	4	13	81	63	144	14	5	.388	.474
2009	Brevard County (FSL)	HiA	.277	112	394	61	109	15	3	17	71	57	92	18	4	.363	.459
2010	Huntsville (SL)	AA	.272	128	463	61	126	33	1	9	60	55	78	10	5	.352	.406
2011	Nashville (PCL)	AAA	.307	126	472	84	145	23	5	15	60	63	93	6	5	.390	.472
2012	Nashville (PCL)	AAA	.261	127	452	54	118	27	5	12	50	37	98	4	1	.317	.423
Minor League Totals			.293	685	2496	386	731	158	21	71	364	295	543	56	24	.368	.458

28 KENTRAIL DAVIS, OF

BA GRADE

45

HIGH

Born: June 29, 1988. **B-T:** L-R. **Ht.:** 5-9. **Wt.:** 195. **Drafted:** Tennessee, 2009 (1st round supplemental). **Signed by:** Joe Mason.

The Brewers keep waiting for Davis to live up to the potential he showed as one of the best college hitters in the 2009 draft class, and to the $1.2 million bonus he received that summer as the 39th overall pick. He has the compact swing and bat speed to hit for average and power, but he has yielded modest production as a pro. He drew more walks in 2012 but also struck out more than ever, as he often got tied up by a small hitch in his swing. He has yet to show he'll have better than average power at best or enough to play on an outfield corner in the majors. Davis has battled leg issues that have hampered him on the bases and in the outfield. Whether he has the instincts to play center field on a regular basis is open for debate, and his fringy arm strength may relegate him to left field. His pure speed rates as above-average, but he doesn't get good jumps on the bases. Milwaukee declined to protect Davis on its 40-man roster this offseason, and no team deemed him worthy of selection in the Rule 5 draft. He'll move up to Triple-A in 2013.

Year	Club (League)	Class	AVG	G	AB	R	H	2B	3B	HR	RBI	BB	SO	SB	CS	OBP	SLG
2010	Brevard County (FSL)	HiA	.244	33	123	20	30	2	5	0	17	17	28	8	2	.380	.341
	Wisconsin (MWL)	LoA	.335	64	245	44	82	26	5	3	46	31	36	3	1	.421	.518
2011	Brevard County (FSL)	HiA	.245	132	507	76	124	19	8	8	46	37	97	33	8	.317	.361
2012	Huntsville (SL)	AA	.274	122	438	55	120	22	7	7	41	54	121	19	11	.357	.404
Minor League Totals			.271	351	1313	195	356	69	25	18	150	139	282	63	22	.357	.403

29 KYLE HECKATHORN, RHP

BA GRADE
45
HIGH

Born: June 17, 1988. **B-T:** R-R. **Ht.:** 6-6. **Wt.:** 235. **Drafted:** Kennesaw State, 2009 (1st round supplemental). **Signed by:** Ryan Robinson.

When Heckathorn was drafted 47th overall and signed for $776,000 in 2009, many scouts considered him a better fit as a late-inning power reliever than a starter. The Brewers wanted to give him a chance to start, however, and he continued to do so until midway through 2012, when Milwaukee finally shifted him to the bullpen. He couldn't maintain consistency through the course of a game as a starter, and the move gave him the chance to go all-out in brief stints. He posted a 3.68 ERA in 18 bullpen appearances for Huntsville, compared to his 5.10 ERA in 17 starts, though he had just 17 strikeouts in his 29 relief innings. Heckathorn's fastball improved from 88-91 mph to 91-94 with his new job description, and he continued to rely on movement and sink to get groundouts rather than whiffs. His slider got a similar boost into the mid-80s. Heckathorn's changeup can be effective when hitters sit on his hard stuff. He has a bulldog approach, which plays better in shorter bursts out of the bullpen. He does a good job of filling the strike zone, but it remains to be seen if he's more of a middle reliever than a set-up man. Milwaukee left him off its 40-man roster but will promote him to Triple-A in 2013.

Year	Club (League)	Class	W	L	ERA	G	GS	CG	SV	IP	H	HR	BB	SO	K/9	WHIP	AVG
2009	Helena (PIO)	R	0	1	6.04	6	5	0	0	22	30	4	4	15	6.0	1.52	.326
2010	Wisconsin (MWL)	LoA	6	6	2.96	17	13	1	0	85	82	2	23	67	7.1	1.24	.246
	Brevard County (FSL)	HiA	4	0	3.00	8	8	1	0	39	40	1	10	23	5.3	1.28	.265
2011	Brevard County (FSL)	HiA	5	6	3.95	15	15	1	0	80	82	8	21	65	7.3	1.29	.267
	Huntsville (SL)	AA	0	4	7.18	7	7	0	0	36	45	7	17	24	5.9	1.71	.296
2012	Huntsville (SL)	AA	5	11	4.75	35	17	0	0	119	127	7	38	88	6.6	1.38	.275
Minor League Totals			20	28	4.32	88	65	3	0	382	406	29	113	282	6.6	1.36	.271

30 JOSH PRINCE, OF

BA GRADE
45
HIGH

Born: Jan. 26, 1988. **B-T:** R-R. **Ht.:** 6-1. **Wt.:** 190. **Drafted:** Tulane, 2009 (3rd round). **Signed by:** Jeremy Booth.

Drafted as a shortstop, Prince played that position for three pro seasons before moving to center field in 2012. His best tool is his above-average speed, which he used to tie for the NCAA Division I lead with 48 steals in 2009. He continues to cause havoc with his aggressiveness on the bases, stealing 147 bases in 385 pro games. But he's not a pure burner and must improve his basestealing efficiency after getting caught in 25 percent of his pro attempts. Prince is a contact hitter with little pop, using a level swing to put the ball in play and get on base. He improved his plate discipline considerably in 2012. His athleticism allowed him to make the transition to center field, where he's still learning the proper reads and routes but can run down balls. He has an average arm. The Brewers like Prince's confidence and feel for the game. While he doesn't have fluid infield actions, he profiles as a utilityman who can play almost anywhere on the diamond. After he hit .404 in the Arizona Fall League, Milwaukee decided not to expose him to the Rule 5 draft and protected him on its 40-man roster. He'll be on call in Triple-A this year.

Year	Club (League)	Class	AVG	G	AB	R	H	2B	3B	HR	RBI	BB	SO	SB	CS	OBP	SLG
2009	Helena (PIO)	R	.298	36	141	32	42	5	1	0	8	33	25	26	7	.426	.348
	Wisconsin (MWL)	LoA	.221	31	122	18	27	5	0	1	10	15	21	12	5	.307	.287
2010	Brevard County (FSL)	HiA	.233	106	408	62	95	13	2	1	19	32	80	44	11	.287	.282
2011	Brevard County (FSL)	HiA	.281	75	249	41	70	11	0	5	24	17	37	24	8	.332	.386
2012	Huntsville (SL)	AA	.251	137	505	74	127	28	3	7	55	74	107	41	18	.346	.360
Minor League Totals			.253	385	1425	227	361	62	6	14	116	171	270	147	49	.333	.335

Minnesota Twins

BY JOHN MANUEL

Losing has become the norm again for the Twins. Minnesota followed its 99-loss 2011 debacle with a 96-loss snore of a season that was over in April, when it lost its first four games and 15 of its first 20.

The team's pitching imploded almost immediately and the season became an audition for young players, some of whom responded. Recent farm products such as Trevor Plouffe (24 homers, second on the team), Ben Revere (.333 OBP, 40 steals) and Chris Parmelee (.755 OPS in his final 26 games) showed signs they could be low-cost contributors. Former Rule 5 draftee

Scott Diamond turned out to be the team's top starter at 12-9, 3.54.

Other than strong seasons by Joe Mauer and free-agent signee Josh Willingham, though, that was about it for the good news in the Twin Cities. The team dropped 90 games in consecutive seasons for the first time in 12 years.

When that happened in 1999-2000, the Twins had the lowest payroll in baseball. This time, they had the highest (2011) and third-highest (2012) payrolls in franchise history, totaling more than $210 million. The losing has taken a hit on attendance at Target Field, which dropped nearly 400,000 to 2.8 million fans in 2011.

Terry Ryan had been brought back as general manager—technically on an interim basis, though that tag was removed in October—in an attempt to right the ship. Farm director Jim Rantz retired following the season, after drawing a paycheck from the organization for 52 years. Five major league coaches were fired or reassigned, and several changes were made in the scouting department. Manager Ron Gardenhire wasn't given an extension, meaning the 2013 season is the last on his current contract.

Minnesota's problems start on the mound. Twins starters posted a 5.40 ERA, worst in the American League, and Diamond's 173 innings led the club by a startling 64 frames. Twelve pitchers made five or more starts, and only Diamond and perhaps Cole DeVries earned spots in the 2013 rotation.

The picture wasn't much prettier on the mound in the minors, where Minnesota has suffered from a succession of injuries and flameouts by top draft picks. Its top pitching prospect, Kyle Gibson, made his way back from Tommy John surgery and could factor into the 2013 big league rotation after a strong performance in the Arizona Fall League.

Josh Willingham had a career year in 2012, but the Twins really needed more pitching

Low in power arms, the Twins made them a priority in the draft and added several. However, other than supplemental first-rounders J.O. Berrios and Luke Bard, most of them project as relievers. Berrios represents the highest the organization has reached to draft a high school pitcher since 2004.

To remedy this, the Twins acted boldly in the offseason, trading two center fielders for three pitchers, including a pair of power arms. First, they dealt Denard Span to the Nationals for hard-throwing righthander Alex Meyer. Then they sent Ben Revere to the Phillies for big league righty Vance Worley and minor leaguer Trevor May.

In the first year of baseball's new draft system, Minnesota had the largest signing pool for the first 10 rounds at $12.4 million and spent nearly half of that on its top pick, outfielder Byron Buxton. The No. 2 overall selection got the largest bonus in franchise history and in the entire 2012 draft at $6 million and made an immediate impact, helping lead Elizabethton to the Rookie-level Appalachian League title.

Buxton is part of a passel of exciting hitting prospects who give the Twins hope for the future, starting with third baseman Miguel Sano. That group also includes outfielders Oswaldo Arcia and Aaron Hicks and second baseman/outfielder Eddie Rosario.

THIS YEAR'S TOP 30

Player, Pos.		Grade
1.	Miguel Sano, 3b	70/High
2.	Byron Buxton, of	70/High
3.	Oswaldo Arcia, of	60/Medium
4.	Alex Meyer, rhp	60/High
5.	Kyle Gibson, rhp	55/Medium
6.	Aaron Hicks, of	55/Medium
7.	J.O. Berrios, rhp	55/High
8.	Eddie Rosario, 2b/of	55/High
9.	Trevor May, rhp	55/High
10.	Max Kepler, of	50/High
11.	Daniel Santana, ss/2b	50/High
12.	Luke Bard, rhp	50/High
13.	Mason Melotakis, lhp	50/High
14.	Jorge Polanco, 2b/ss	50/High
15.	J.T. Chargois, rhp	50/High
16.	Levi Michael, 2b/ss	50/High
17.	Travis Harrison, 3b	50/High
18.	Chris Herrmann, c/of	45/Medium
19.	Joe Benson, of	50/High
20.	B.J. Hermsen, rhp	45/Medium
21.	Angel Mata, rhp	50/High
22.	Madison Boer, rhp	45/Medium
23.	Tyler Jones, rhp	50/High
24.	Felix Jorge, rhp	50/High
25.	Jason Wheeler, lhp	45/High
26.	Niko Goodrum, ss	50/Extreme
27.	Adrian Salcedo, rhp	45/High
28.	Michael Tonkin, rhp	45/High
29.	Kennys Vargas, 1b	50/Extreme
30.	Matt Summers, rhp	45/High

LAST YEAR'S TOP 30

Player, Pos.		Status
1.	Miguel Sano, 3b/ss	No. 1
2.	Joe Benson, of	No. 19
3.	Eddie Rosario, 2b/of	No. 8
4.	Aaron Hicks, of	No. 6
5.	Oswaldo Arcia, of	No. 3
6.	Levi Michael, ss/2b	No. 16
7.	Liam Hendriks, rhp	Majors
8.	Kyle Gibson, rhp	No. 5
9.	Chris Parmelee, 1b/of	Majors
10.	Brian Dozier, ss/2b	Majors
11.	Travis Harrison, 3b/1b	No. 17
12.	Madison Boer, rhp	No. 22
13.	Corey Williams, lhp	Dropped out
14.	Chris Herrmann, c/of	No. 18
15.	Deolis Guerra, rhp	Dropped out
16.	Adrian Salcedo, rhp	No. 27
17.	Carlos Gutierrez, rhp	(Cubs)
18.	Hudson Boyd, rhp	Dropped out
19.	Niko Goodrum, ss	No. 26
20.	Max Kepler, of	No. 10
21.	Matt Summers, rhp	No. 30
22.	Logan Darnell, lhp	Dropped out
23.	Manuel Soliman, rhp	Dropped out
24.	Tom Stuifbergen, rhp	Dropped out
25.	Alex Wimmers, rhp	Dropped out
26.	Lester Oliveros, rhp	Dropped out
27.	B.J. Hermsen, rhp	No. 20
28.	Jorge Polanco, inf/of	No. 14
29.	Angel Mata, rhp	No. 21
30.	Terry Doyle, rhp	(Red Sox)

BEST TOOLS

Best Hitter for Average	Eddie Rosario
Best Power Hitter	Miguel Sano
Best Strike-Zone Discipline	Aaron Hicks
Fastest Baserunner	Byron Buxton
Best Athlete	Byron Buxton
Best Fastball	Alex Meyer
Best Curveball	Josh Burris
Best Slider	Alex Meyer
Best Changeup	Deolis Guerra
Best Control	B.J. Hermsen
Best Defensive Catcher	Chris Herrmann
Best Defensive Infielder	Levi Michael
Best Infield Arm	Miguel Sano
Best Defensive Outfielder	Aaron Hicks
Best Outfield Arm	Aaron Hicks

PROJECTED 2016 LINEUP

Catcher	Joe Mauer
First Base	Chris Parmelee
Second Base	Eddie Rosario
Third Base	Miguel Sano
Shortstop	Daniel Santana
Left Field	Oswaldo Arcia
Center Field	Byron Buxton
Right Field	Aaron Hicks
Designated Hitter	Justin Morneau
No. 1 Starter	Alex Meyer
No. 2 Starter	Kyle Gibson
No. 3 Starter	J.O. Berrios
No. 4 Starter	Scott Diamond
No. 5 Starter	Vance Worley
Closer	Glen Perkins

TOP PROSPECTS OF THE DECADE

Year	Player, Pos.	2012 Org.
2003	Joe Mauer, c	Twins
2004	Joe Mauer, c	Twins
2005	Joe Mauer, c	Twins
2006	Francisco Liriano, lhp	White Sox
2007	Matt Garza, rhp	Cubs
2008	Nick Blackburn, rhp	Twins
2009	Aaron Hicks, of	Twins
2010	Aaron Hicks, of	Twins
2011	Kyle Gibson, rhp	Twins
2012	Miguel Sano, 3b	Twins

TOP DRAFT PICKS OF THE DECADE

Year	Player, Pos.	2012 Org.
2003	Matt Moses, 3b	Out of baseball
2004	Trevor Plouffe, ss	Twins
2005	Matt Garza, rhp	Cubs
2006	Chris Parmelee, of/1b	Twins
2007	Ben Revere, of	Twins
2008	Aaron Hicks, of	Twins
2009	Kyle Gibson, rhp	Twins
2010	Alex Wimmers, rhp	Twins
2011	Levi Michael, ss	Twins
2012	Byron Buxton, of	Twins

LARGEST BONUSES IN CLUB HISTORY

Byron Buxton, 2012	$6,000,000
Joe Mauer, 2001	$5,150,000
Miguel Sano, 2009	$3,150,000
B.J. Garbe, 1999	$2,750,000
Adam Johnson, 2000	$2,500,000

MINNESOTA TWINS

TOP 2013 ROOKIE: Kyle Gibson, rhp. The Twins intend to give him as many big league innings as possible.

BREAKOUT PROSPECT: Angel Mata, rhp. He shows flashes of three solid pitches and has limited pro hitters to a .199 average.

SLEEPER: Adam Brett Walker, of. Minnesota thought he had more power than anyone in the 2012 draft, and he slugged 14 homers in his pro debut.

SOURCE OF TOP 30 TALENT

Homegrown	28	Acquired	2
College	10	Trades	2
Junior college	0	Rule 5 draft	0
High school	9	Independent leagues	0
Nondrafted free agents	1	Free agents/waivers	0
International	8		

LF
Max Kepler (10)
Nate Roberts
Danny Ortiz
JaDamion Williams
Romy Jimenez
Evan Bigley
Zach Larson

CF
Byron Buxton (2)
Aaron Hicks (6)
Angel Morales
Jake Proctor

RF
Oswaldo Arcia (3)
Joe Benson (19)
Adam Brett Walker
Dereck Rodriguez

3B
Miguel Sano (1)
Travis Harrison (17)
Deibinson Romero
Mark Sobolewski

SS
Daniel Santana (11)
Levi Michael (16)
Niko Goodrum (26)
Amaurys Minier
James Beresford
Will Hurt

2B
Eddie Rosario (8)
Jorge Polanco (14)
Aderlin Mejia

1B
Kennys Vargas (29)
Chris Colabello
Lance Ray
D.J. Hicks

C
Chris Herrmann (18)
Josmil Pinto
Matt Koch
Jorge Fernandez

LHP

LHSP	LHRP
Jason Wheeler (25)	Mason Melotakis (13)
Pedro Hernandez	Corey Williams
Logan Darnell	Caleb Thielbar
Pat Dean	Brett Lee
Taylor Rogers	Josue Montanez
Randy Rosario	
Hein Robb	
Anthony Albers	
Steven Gruver	
Andre Martinez	

RHP

RHSP	RHRP
Alex Meyer (4)	J.T. Chargois (15)
Kyle Gibson (5)	Tyler Jones (23)
J.O. Berrios (7)	Michael Tonkin (28)
Trevor May (9)	Matt Summers (30)
Luke Bard (12)	Zack Jones
B.J. Hermsen (20)	Ryan Pressly
Angel Mata (21)	Bruce Pugh
Madison Boer (22)	Dakota Watts
Felix Jorge (24)	Matt Hauser
Adrian Salcedo (27)	Deolis Guerra
Hudson Boyd	Lester Oliveros
D.J. Baxendale	A.J. Achter
Tyler Duffey	Daniel Turpen
Yorman Landa	Josh Burris
Kuo Hua Lo	Christian Powell
Manuel Soliman	Alex Muren

2012   BONUSES: $12.6 MILLION

BEST PURE HITTER: OF Byron Buxton (1) has a loose, easy swing and should be a line-drive machine. A top-of-the scale runner, he'll also leg out plenty of infield and bunt hits to boost his batting average.

BEST POWER HITTER: OF Adam Brett Walker (3) hits them far and frequently. He'll always have some swing-and-miss issues, but Twins scouts thought he had the best raw power in the draft. Buxton has at least plus raw power.

FASTEST RUNNER: Buxton is a true burner, posting sub-4.0-second times from the right side of the plate to first base. His speed plays on the bases and in center field.

BEST DEFENSIVE PLAYER: Buxton has everything needed to be a Gold Glover, including a top-shelf arm that delivered 94-mph fastballs off the mound in high school.

BEST FASTBALL: Velocity was a focus for Minnesota. RHP Zack Jones (4) hit 100 mph in instructional league. RHP J.O. Berrios (1s) pitches at 92-95 mph as a starter, while relievers LHP Mason Melotakis (2) and RHP J.T. Chargois (2), taken nine spots apart, both reach 97.

BEST SECONDARY PITCH: RHP Luke Bard (1s) showed one of the draft's best sliders, an 86-88 mph breaker with tilt. He missed the second half of the spring with a torn lat muscle and a minor setback cut short his instructional league. Chargois' hybrid breaking ball can be a plus-plus pitch at times.

BEST PRO DEBUT: Including two playoff starts that helped Elizabethton win the Appalachian League championship, Berrios went 4-0, 0.88 with a 63-9 K-BB ratio in 41 innings between two Rookie leagues. LHP Taylor Rogers (11) reached low Class A Beloit and went 4-3, 2.27 with 74 strikeouts in 63 innings. Walker tied for the Appy League home run title with 14, then hit three more in the playoffs. Jones (2.25 ERA, 15.3 K/9), Melotakis (1.88 ERA, 12.8 K/9) and RHP D.J. Baxendale (10; 0.96 ERA, 15.0 K/9) all dominated and joined Rogers in Beloit.

BEST ATHLETE: Buxton had the best combination of power, speed and baseball ability in the entire draft.

MOST INTRIGUING BACKGROUND: Unsigned OF Timmy Robinson's (31) half-brother Alex Burnett pitches for the Twins. Bard's brother Daniel and OF Jonathan Murphy's (19) brother Daniel are also active big leaguers. Unsigned 2B L.J. Mazzilli's (9) father Lee played and managed in the majors. Walker's family ties include his father Adam Brett, a former NFL replacement player; his mother Glynis, a college national champion in the high jump; and cousin Damion Easley, a big league all-star.

CLOSEST TO THE MAJORS: Relievers Chargois, Jones and Melotakis will compete with each other, with Jones taking a lead by making progress on his slider in instructional league.

BEST LATE-ROUND PICK: Rogers fits Minnesota's pitchability mold.

THE ONE WHO GOT AWAY: Mazzilli, who returned to Connecticut as a senior, and RHP James Marvel (37), who honored his Duke commitment despite a coaching change.

ASSESSMENT: Despite their need for pitching, the Twins couldn't pass up Buxton with the second overall pick. They used much of the draft's largest bonus pool to stock up on power arms, with Barrios and Bard the key selections.

2011   BONUSES: $5.9 MILLION

2B/SS Levi Michael (1) and RHP Hudson Boyd (1s) were less than dynamic in their 2012 pro debuts, though 3B Travis Harrison (1s) showed the bat that got him taken 50th overall. Unsigned OF James Ramsey (22) became a first-rounder a year later.

GRADE: C

2010   BONUSES: $3.5 MILLION

2B/OF Eddie Rosario (4) has hit everywhere he has played. RHP Alex Wimmers (1) had a major control meltdown in 2011, then succumbed to Tommy John surgery last year.

GRADE: C

2009   BONUSES: $4.7 MILLION

RHP Kyle Gibson (1) has come back from Tommy John surgery and is on the verge of claiming a rotation spot in Minnesota. C/OF Chris Herrmann (6) and SS Brian Dozier (8) have surfaced in the majors and project as role players. Oft-injured RHP Matt Bashore (1s) worked 19 innings in three seasons before getting released.

GRADE: C+

2008   BONUSES: $7.3 MILLION

OF Aaron Hicks (1) took a leap forward last year in terms of translating his considerable tools into skills. RHPs Carlos Gutierrez (1) and Shooter Hunt (1s) are no longer in the organization. Worse, three unsigned players became 2011 first-rounders: 2B Kolten Wong (16), OF George Springer (48) and LHP Tyler Anderson (50).

GRADE: C+

Draft analysis by John Manuel (2012) and Jim Callis (2008-11). Numbers in parentheses indicate draft rounds.

1 MIGUEL SANO, 3B

Born: May 11, 1993. **B-T:** R-R. **Ht.:** 6-3. **Wt.:** 232.
Signed: Dominican Republic, 2009. **Signed by:** Fred Guerrero.

Whether Sano is actually 19 or not almost seems immaterial at this point. The Twins signed him to a $3.15 million bonus (their largest ever for an international player) after a lengthy Major League Baseball investigation process, which confirmed his identity but not necessarily his age. Sano has been under the microscope for years. Already part of one documentary, the Bobby Valentine-produced "Pelotero" that began filming him at age 15, Sano now is involved in the follow-up. He has thrived in pro ball, ranking as the No. 2 prospect in the Rookie-level Gulf Coast League, No. 1 in the Rookie-level Appalachian League and No. 2 in the low Class A Midwest League the last three seasons. He led the MWL in homers (28), RBIs (100), total bases (238) and extra-base hits (60) while ranking second in walks (80) and third in slugging (.521).

Sano has enough juice to earn comparisons to Giancarlo Stanton, the only righthanded hitter in the game who matches his 80 raw power on the 20-80 scouting scale. He's strong enough to hit the ball out to any part of any park and he uses his lower half well. Minnesota envisions him as a future cleanup hitter thanks to his present power, improved patience and pitch recognition. Sano is learning to lay off breaking balls out of the strike zone and pound pitches in his hitting zone. When he slows the game down, he keeps his fast hands back and waits on pitches. He made adjustments as 2012 went on, pulling out of a June swoon to hit .291/.398/.564 in his final 51 games.

His bat attracts attention, but his glove does as well, usually for the wrong reasons. His defensive ability and where he'll play are the biggest questions facing Sano, who is large but moves well for his size. He has easy arm strength for third base, earning some 80 grades, and his errors come more frequently from lack of focus than ability. He made 42 miscues in 2012, the fourth-highest total in the minors. He did improve defensively as the year progressed, developing better instincts as he got more reps at third base after primarily playing shortstop in the past. Sano's hands remain hard, though, and he'll have to improve his footwork to get better hops and make more accurate throws. He's a below-average runner out of the box who's closer to average once he's underway. In addition to his playing ability, he also excites the Twins by showing leadership skills, even throwing in a dugout speech or two in his second language.

With continued maturity and repetitions at third, Sano should be able to stay on the dirt. He is headed for high Class A Fort Myers in 2013, and the Twins believe their step-by-step approach will serve him well as he learns to become more consistent. He should reach Minnesota by 2015.

BA GRADE
70
HIGH

MIKE JANES

SCOUTING GRADES

Batting: 55. **Defense:** 40.
Power: 80. **Arm:** 75.
Speed: 40.

Based on 20-80 scouting scale, where 50 represents major league average, and future projection rather than present tools.

Year	Club (League)	Class	AVG	G	AB	R	H	2B	3B	HR	RBI	BB	SO	SB	CS	OBP	SLG
2010	Twins (DSL)	R	.344	20	64	11	22	2	1	3	10	14	17	2	1	.463	.547
	Twins (GCL)	R	.291	41	148	23	43	14	0	4	19	10	43	2	2	.338	.466
2011	Elizabethton (APP)	R	.292	66	267	58	78	18	7	20	59	23	77	5	4	.352	.637
2012	Beloit (MWL)	LoA	.258	129	457	75	118	28	4	28	100	80	144	8	3	.373	.521
Minor League Totals			.279	256	936	167	261	62	12	55	188	127	281	17	10	.368	.547

2 BYRON BUXTON, OF

Born: Dec. 18, 1993. **B-T:** R-R. **Ht.:** 6-2. **Wt.:** 190. **Drafted:** HS—Baxley, Ga., 2012 (1st round). **Signed by:** Jack Powell.

Baseball America's 2012 High School Player of the Year, Buxton led Appling County High to the Georgia state 2-A championship, tossing a complete game with 18 strikeouts in the clincher. He was still throwing 91 mph in the seventh and final inning. BA's top-rated prospect and the No. 2 overall pick in the draft, he signed for a franchise-record $6 million and helped Rookie-level Elizabethton win the Appalachian League championship. If his blazing bat speed translates into power down the line, Buxton will be a true five-tool player. He'll need repetitions at the plate against better pitching, but his swing path keeps the bat in the hitting zone a long time. He'll have to learn to backspin balls a bit more down the line to have plus power, but many scouts think he'll get there. He's a top-of-the-scale runner who gets from the right side of the plate to first base in 3.9 seconds, with easy plus range and well above-average arm strength in center field. Buxton plays with confidence and has a chance to be a superstar along the lines of Andrew McCutchen. The Twins preach patience but know he's ready for full-season ball in 2013 with an assignment to their new low Class A Cedar Rapids affiliate.

BA GRADE 70 HIGH

Year	Club (League)	Class	AVG	G	AB	R	H	2B	3B	HR	RBI	BB	SO	SB	CS	OBP	SLG
2012	Twins (GCL)	R	.216	27	88	17	19	4	3	4	14	11	26	4	3	.324	.466
	Elizabethton (APP)	R	.286	21	77	16	22	6	1	1	6	8	15	7	0	.368	.429
Minor League Totals			.248	48	165	33	41	10	4	5	20	19	41	11	3	.344	.448

3 OSWALDO ARCIA, OF

Born: May 9, 1991. **B-T:** L-R. **Ht.:** 6-0. **Wt.:** 210. **Signed:** Venezuela, 2007. **Signed by:** Jose Leon.

The Appalachian League MVP in 2012, Arcia has a younger brother, Orlando, in the Brewers system. Oswaldo missed two months of 2011 with a right elbow injury, but was healthy last season. Arcia's supreme confidence in his hitting ability rankles opponents at times, probably because they find it hard to get him out. He walks the line between patience and aggressiveness well, pounding mistakes and showing plenty of bat speed to turn on good fastballs. He has improved his ability to lay off pitches out of the strike zone, and he stays back and balanced against lefthanders and offspeed stuff in general. He has lost some speed but runs well enough to stay in right field, where his strong, accurate arm is an asset. Arcia fits the right-field profile well, as he's shown the ability to hit for average and power. He will start 2013 season back in Double-A New Britain but could push for a spot in Triple-A Rochester, and Minnesota's outfield shakeup could speed his timetable.

BA GRADE 60 MEDIUM

Year	Club (League)	Class	AVG	G	AB	R	H	2B	3B	HR	RBI	BB	SO	SB	CS	OBP	SLG
2008	Twins (DSL)	R	.293	61	229	38	67	12	4	4	36	16	27	8	7	.343	.432
2009	Twins (GCL)	R	.275	44	167	20	46	11	2	5	24	15	18	8	0	.337	.455
2010	Elizabethton (APP)	R	.375	64	259	47	97	21	7	14	51	19	67	4	4	.424	.672
2011	Beloit (MWL)	LoA	.352	20	71	18	25	8	1	5	18	9	16	2	2	.420	.704
	Twins (GCL)	R	.500	2	8	1	4	1	1	0	1	0	1	0	0	.500	.875
	Fort Myers (FSL)	HiA	.263	59	213	27	56	14	2	8	32	9	53	1	1	.300	.460
2012	Fort Myers (FSL)	HiA	.309	55	207	22	64	16	3	7	31	23	45	1	3	.376	.517
	New Britain (EL)	AA	.328	69	262	54	86	20	5	10	67	28	62	3	2	.398	.557
Minor League Totals			.314	374	1416	227	445	103	25	53	260	119	289	27	19	.371	.535

4 ALEX MEYER, RHP

Born: Jan. 3, 1990. **B-T:** R-R. **Ht.:** 6-9. **Wt.:** 220. **Drafted:** Kentucky, 2011 (1st round). **Signed by:** Reed Dunn (Nationals).

In his first professional season, Meyer showed the talent that had prompted the Red Sox to offer him $2 million out of high school and the Nationals to sign him for the same amount three years later after drafting him 23rd overall in 2011. He made his pro debut in 2012, ranking second among Washington farmhands in ERA (2.86) and strikeouts (139) while pitching at two Class A stops and earning a trip to the Futures Game. The Nationals had been looking for a center fielder and the Twins desperately needed pitching, so they swapped Meyer for Denard Span in November. Like many tall pitchers, Meyer struggled to repeat his mechanics consistently in college, but he did a good job staying tall and creating more downward angle last season, improving his fastball command. He also learned to trust his electric stuff and to avoid overthrowing. Meyer's best pitch is a 95-97 mph four-seam fastball that bumps 99 mph, and he mixes in a 92-95 mph two-seamer

BA GRADE 60 HIGH

with good armside run and sink at times. He throws a power slider with a knuckle-curve grip at 84-87 mph, getting good depth and late, hard finish. His slider has a chance to be a plus-plus pitch, though it still flattens out occasionally. His straight changeup needs more consistency, but it has good sinking action and a chance to become an above-average offering. Meyer has solid control, but it remains to be seen if he'll develop the command to be a frontline starter. His size, stuff and improvement make him a key piece for the pitching-poor Twins, who will send him to Double-A.

Year	Club (League)	Class	W	L	ERA	G	GS	CG	SV	IP	H	HR	BB	SO	K/9	WHIP	AVG
2012	Hagerstown (SAL)	LoA	7	4	3.10	18	18	1	0	90	68	4	34	107	10.7	1.13	.210
	Potomac (CAR)	HiA	3	2	2.31	7	7	0	0	39	29	2	11	32	7.4	1.03	.213
Minor League Totals			10	6	2.86	25	25	1	0	129	97	6	45	139	9.7	1.10	.211

5 KYLE GIBSON, RHP

BA GRADE
55
MEDIUM

Born: Oct. 23, 1987. **B-T:** R-R. **Ht.:** 6-6. **Wt.:** 207. **Drafted:** Missouri, 2009 (1st round). **Signed by:** J.R. DiMercurio/Mike Ruth.

Gibson turned down the Phillies in the 36th round as an Indiana high schooler and became a first-rounder out of Missouri in 2009, signing for $1.85 million. His stock fell late that spring due to forearm tightness, and though he remained healthy in 2010, he needed Tommy John surgery in September 2011. He returned in 2012 with 13 appearances of no more than four innings before a stint in the Arizona Fall League. Gibson's stuff has returned after his elbow reconstruction. He threw his four-seam fastball at 92-94 mph in the regular season and the AFL, where he started in the Rising Stars Game and ranked third in strikeouts. He also threw strikes with his two-seamer and his plus changeup with sink that he long has used as an out pitch. While the velocity (80-84 mph) and good bite on his slider are back, he was still searching for his feel for the pitch in the AFL. The Twins are desperate for starting pitching, and Gibson is the closest candidate their system has to offer. Minnesota's offseason moves will determine whether he gets the chance to open 2013 in the big leagues or gets more time in the minors. He's already 25 but can become a No. 2 or 3 starter.

Year	Club (League)	Class	W	L	ERA	G	GS	CG	SV	IP	H	HR	BB	SO	K/9	WHIP	AVG
2010	Fort Myers (FSL)	HiA	4	1	1.87	7	7	1	0	43	33	2	12	40	8.3	1.04	.213
	New Britain (EL)	AA	7	5	3.68	16	16	1	0	93	91	5	22	77	7.5	1.22	.259
	Rochester (IL)	AAA	0	0	1.72	3	3	0	0	16	12	0	5	9	5.2	1.09	.214
2011	Rochester (IL)	AAA	3	8	4.81	18	18	0	0	95	109	11	27	91	8.6	1.43	.282
2012	Twins (GCL)	R	0	0	2.45	9	7	0	0	15	9	1	4	16	9.8	0.89	.176
	Fort Myers (FSL)	HiA	0	0	2.57	2	2	0	0	7	6	1	1	7	9.0	1.00	.231
	Rochester (IL)	AAA	0	2	9.45	2	2	0	0	7	11	1	1	10	13.5	1.80	.367
Minor League Totals			14	16	3.72	57	55	2	0	276	271	21	72	250	8.2	1.24	.257

6 AARON HICKS, OF

BA GRADE
55
MEDIUM

Born: Oct. 2, 1989. **B-T:** B-R. **Ht.:** 6-2. **Wt.:** 185. **Drafted:** HS—Long Beach, 2008 (1st round). **Signed by:** John Leavitt.

Hicks may still have the best fastball in the Twins system, though he hasn't pitched since signing for $1.78 million in 2008. The Athletics wanted to draft him 12th overall as a pitcher, but he wanted to hit and the Twins were the first team to agree, picking him 14th overall. A tremendous amateur golfer, he put a poor 2011 season behind him by setting career bests for homers (13), steals (32) and full-season OPS (.844) in 2012. Hicks remains an above-average athlete whose skills are starting to catch up to his tools. He listened to Minnesota coaches and stopped swinging big for power from the left side, shortening up and improving his ability to make contact. He improved from a .228/.357/.348 performance against righthanders in 2011 to .287/.394/.434 in 2012. He's still more natural and rhythmic as a righty, batting .283/.359/.522 last season. A gliding runner, he has improved his basestealing reads and possesses plenty of range in center field. Once capable of throwing 97-mph fastballs on the mound, he retains a well above-average arm. Scouts who like Hicks believe he's developing into a top-of-the-order tablesetter, while others consider him more of a solid regular who'll hit sixth or seventh on a good team while providing premium defense in center. After playing winter ball in Venezuela, he'll head to Triple-A.

Year	Club (League)	Class	AVG	G	AB	R	H	2B	3B	HR	RBI	BB	SO	SB	CS	OBP	SLG
2008	Twins (GCL)	R	.318	45	173	32	55	10	4	4	27	28	32	12	2	.409	.491
2009	Beloit (MWL)	LoA	.251	67	251	43	63	15	3	4	29	40	55	10	8	.353	.382
2010	Beloit (MWL)	LoA	.279	115	423	86	118	27	6	8	49	88	112	21	11	.401	.428
2011	Fort Myers (FSL)	HiA	.242	122	443	79	107	31	5	5	38	78	110	17	9	.354	.368
2012	New Britain (EL)	AA	.286	129	472	100	135	21	11	13	61	79	116	32	11	.384	.460
Minor League Totals			.271	478	1762	340	478	104	29	34	204	313	425	92	41	.379	.421

7 J.O. BERRIOS, RHP

Born: May 27, 1994. **B-T:** R-R. **Ht.:** 6-0. **Wt.:** 189. **Drafted:** HS—Bayamon, P.R., 2012 (1st round supplemental). **Signed by:** Hector Otero.

Berrios boosted his draft stock with an April no-hitter against a Puerto Rican all-star team featuring No. 1 overall pick Carlos Correa, helping him become the 32nd overall pick and the highest-drafted pitcher ever out of Puerto Rico. After signing for $1.55 million, he helped Elizabethton to the Appy League title with 36 strikeouts in 24 innings (counting the postseason). Berrios has the best fastball of any Twins farmhand who profiles as a starter. He can sit at 92-95 mph while throwing strikes to both sides of the plate, and his strong frame helps him maintain his velocity. He commands a changeup with fade that's already solid and should become a plus pitch in time. His slider has its moments as well, showing power and sharpness at 78-81 mph. At times his slider flattens out, and Berrios will have to be diligent about staying tall in his delivery to create plane and angle with his pitches. He needs to mix his pitches better, too. He has the arm action and delivery to project average or better command down the line. Confident to the point of being cocky, Berrios will be on Minnesota's idea of a fast track. He'll open his first full season in low Class A and has the upside of a No. 2 starter.

Year	Club (League)	Class	W	L	ERA	G	GS	CG	SV	IP	H	HR	BB	SO	K/9	WHIP	AVG
2012	Twins (GCL)	R	1	0	1.08	8	1	0	4	17	7	0	3	27	14.6	0.60	.121
	Elizabethton (APP)	R	2	0	1.29	3	3	0	0	14	8	1	1	22	14.1	0.64	.163
Minor League Totals			3	0	1.17	11	4	0	4	31	15	1	4	49	14.4	0.62	.140

8 EDDIE ROSARIO, 2B/OF

Born: Sept. 28, 1991. **B-T:** L-R. **Ht.:** 6-0. **Wt.:** 180. **Drafted:** HS—Guayama, P.R., 2010 (4th round). **Signed by:** Hector Otero.

Rosario led the Appalachian League with 21 homers in 2011 and won co-MVP honors as an outfielder. The Twins tried him at second base that fall in instructional league, and he played 67 of his 86 games in the field there in 2012. He missed nearly seven weeks after a batting-practice line drive hit him in the face in mid-June, requiring the insertion of a plate above his lip, but he played well after his return. Rosario uses his hands well in his swing and has excellent plate coverage. His hands are low in his set-up but quick through the hitting zone. Though he has slugged .538 in the lower minors, scouts and club officials expect him to settle in around 10-15 homers at higher levels because he has a line-drive swing and gap-to-gap approach. Rosario's average speed and range are less than ideal for center field, and scouts question whether his hands and throwing are good enough for second base. Minnesota has had him focus on making the routine play and turning the double play, but he'll need more work to be an average defender. Rosario will stay in the infield as he moves up to high Class A. He's a bit of a tweener if he has to go back to the outfield, so the Twins will give him every chance to remain at second base.

Year	Club (League)	Class	AVG	G	AB	R	H	2B	3B	HR	RBI	BB	SO	SB	CS	OBP	SLG
2010	Twins (GCL)	R	.294	51	194	34	57	9	2	5	26	16	28	22	5	.343	.438
2011	Elizabethton (APP)	R	.337	67	270	71	91	9	9	21	60	27	60	17	6	.397	.670
2012	Twins (GCL)	R	.368	5	19	2	7	3	0	1	4	1	2	0	0	.400	.684
	Beloit (MWL)	LoA	.296	95	392	60	116	32	4	12	70	31	69	11	11	.345	.490
Minor League Totals			.310	218	875	167	271	53	15	39	160	75	159	50	22	.362	.538

9 TREVOR MAY, RHP

Born: Sept. 23, 1989. **B-T:** R-R. **Ht.:** 6-5. **Wt.:** 215. **Drafted:** HS—Kelso, Wash., 2008 (4th round). **Signed by:** Dave Ryles (Phillies).

May's development path has been anything but linear since he signed for $375,000 as a fourth-round pick in 2008, when he ranked as the top prep prospect in Washington. He repeated both the low Class A and high Class A levels before ranking as the Phillies' No. 1 prospect after the 2011 season, then struggled with his consistency in Double-A last year. In need of a center fielder, Philadelphia packaged him and Vance Worley to get Ben Revere from the Twins in December. May has swing-and-miss stuff but runs into trouble because he doesn't work down in the strike zone with his fastball or throw his secondary stuff for quality strikes. He works with a 90-94 mph fastball that features two-seam run at its lower velocities. His 76-78 mph downer curveball had been his best secondary pitch, but last year it blended together with his 82-85 mph slider. He also throws an 81-84 mph changeup that can become an average offering. May won't reach his upside of a No. 2 or 3 starter if he can't improve his below-average control and command. More advanced hitters won't chase his high fastballs as much as lower-level batters did. His inconsistency leads his detractors to suggest he'll be no more than a late-inning reliever. May will repeat Double-A to start 2013, with Minnesota hoping he can provide some rotation help in the near future.

10 MAX KEPLER, OF

Born: Feb. 10, 1993. **B-T:** L-L. **Ht.:** 6-4. **Wt.:** 207. **Signed:** Germany, 2009. **Signed by:** Mike Radcliff.

The son of American and Polish ballet dancers, Kepler is the best prospect ever born and raised in Germany. He signed for $800,000 in 2009, the largest bonus ever for a European position player, then finished high school in Fort Myers, Fla., while participating in instructional league. Repeating the Appalachian League in 2012, he led the circuit in slugging (.539) and total bases (125) before going 2-for-14 for Germany in a World Baseball Classic qualifier. The Twins long have believed in Kepler's athleticism, and he added maturity and strength to his game in 2012. He has put on 17 pounds since signing and now has the physicality to drive the ball to all fields. He has a sound, balanced swing, doesn't mind going deep in counts and has a decent two-strike approach for his experience level. He's getting better as he sees more quality pitching, and his next step will be hitting for more power against lefthanders. A plus runner when he signed, Kepler is more of an average

BA GRADE
50
HIGH

runner now and moved from center to left field when Byron Buxton arrived in Elizabethton. Kepler's fringy arm fits better in left than in right, and he also has gotten work at first base. Kepler is ready for full-season ball at age 20. He'll join Buxton and 2012 draftee Adam Brett Walker in a power-packed Cedar Rapids outfield in 2013.

Year	Club (League)	Class	AVG	G	AB	R	H	2B	3B	HR	RBI	BB	SO	SB	CS	OBP	SLG
2010	Twins (GCL)	R	.286	37	140	15	40	6	1	0	11	13	27	6	1	.346	.343
2011	Elizabethton (APP)	R	.262	50	191	29	50	11	3	1	24	23	54	1	1	.347	.366
2012	Elizabethton (APP)	R	.297	59	232	40	69	16	5	10	49	27	33	7	0	.387	.539
Minor League Totals			.282	146	563	84	159	33	9	11	84	63	114	14	2	.363	.432

11 DANIEL SANTANA, SS/2B

BA GRADE
50
HIGH

Born: Nov. 7, 1990. **B-T:** B-R. **Ht.:** 5-11. **Wt.:** 174. **Signed:** Dominican Republic, 2007. **Signed by:** Fred Guerrero.

With his bat slow to develop, Santana fell into a utility role in 2011, spending time in center field as well as the middle infield. In his fifth season as a pro, he broke through in 2012. He alternated series between second base and shortstop for most of the season with 2011 first-round pick Levi Michael, but Santana outperformed him and finished the season as Fort Myers' regular shortstop. Santana's best tools are his speed and his throwing arm. He needs to polish his baserunning skills, but he's a plus runner down the line and has well above-average speed once under way. His throws have plenty of carry and he has become a more consistent defender as he has matured, though he still tends to botch more routine plays than he should. A switch-hitter, Santana has good swings from both sides of the plate that are geared for contact. He has little home run power as a lefty but more pop as a natural righty. He put together more consistent at-bats in 2012, tempering his aggressiveness somewhat. His lack of plate discipline could limit him to the bottom of a big league batting order. Santana reminds some scouts of Pedro Florimon, the light-hitting minor league veteran who finished the year as Minnesota's regular shortstop. The Twins believe Santana, who was added to the 40-man roster in November, has more offensive upside. They will send him to Double-A in 2013.

Year	Club (League)	Class	AVG	G	AB	R	H	2B	3B	HR	RBI	BB	SO	SB	CS	OBP	SLG
2008	Twins (DSL)	R	.274	51	190	37	52	6	10	1	27	20	38	15	4	.343	.426
2009	Twins (GCL)	R	.265	44	170	30	45	7	5	3	25	8	27	12	1	.302	.418
2010	Elizabethton (APP)	R	.264	30	140	23	37	8	1	4	16	3	30	5	4	.285	.421
	Beloit (MWL)	LoA	.238	40	130	14	31	4	3	0	11	7	40	10	4	.289	.315
2011	Beloit (MWL)	LoA	.247	104	365	55	90	15	5	7	41	25	98	24	15	.298	.373
2012	Fort Myers (FSL)	HiA	.286	121	507	70	145	21	9	8	60	29	77	17	11	.329	.410
Minor League Totals			.266	390	1502	229	400	61	33	23	180	92	310	83	39	.313	.397

12 LUKE BARD, RHP

BA GRADE
50
HIGH

Born: Nov. 13, 1990. **B-T:** R-R. **Ht.:** 6-3. **Wt.:** 195. **Drafted:** Georgia Tech, 2012 (1st round supplemental). **Signed by:** Jack Powell.

Like his big league brother Daniel, Bard struggled with a shift from relieving to starting in 2012. While Daniel couldn't find the strike zone, Luke tore a lat muscle on March 31, ending his junior season at Georgia Tech. After signing for $1,227,000 as the 42nd overall pick in the 2012 draft, he pitched seven pro innings before reaggravating the injury in instructional league. While he doesn't have his brother's easy gas, Bard pitches off his fastball and has above-average velocity. He sat as high as 93-95 mph as a starter in college and touched 97 as a reliever. His slider made significant progress in 2012, showing more consistency, depth and late bite. It's a well above-average pitch when at its best. He flashes an average changeup that needs more consistency. Bard has the clean arm action and sound delivery to become a full-time starter. He'll need to learn to sequence his pitches better and prove he can hold up in that role. If healthy, Bard will open his first full pro season in the rotation of one of the Twins' Class A affiliates. At best, he'll be a No. 3 starter. At worst, he should be one of the best relievers from the entire 2012 draft class.

Year	Club (League)	Class	W	L	ERA	G	GS	CG	SV	IP	H	HR	BB	SO	K/9	WHIP	AVG
2012	Twins (GCL)	R	0	0	6.75	3	1	0	0	4	3	0	5	3	6.8	2.00	.231
	Elizabethton (APP)	R	0	0	0.00	4	0	0	1	3	2	0	2	4	12.0	1.33	.200
Minor League Totals			0	0	3.86	7	1	0	1	7	5	0	7	7	9.0	1.71	.217

13 MASON MELOTAKIS, LHP

BA GRADE
50
HIGH

Born: June 28, 1991. **B-T:** L-L. **Ht.:** 6-2. **Wt.:** 204. **Drafted:** Northwestern State, 2012 (2nd round). **Signed by:** Greg Runser.

Melotakis is trying to join the likes of Lee Smith and Brian Lawrence as big league alumni from Northwestern State. Melotakis made just nine starts in college and had more success as a reliever, notching 12 saves in two seasons and dominating at times, such as a 10-strikeout effort in 4 1/3 innings against Louisiana State as a sophomore. He shined after signing for $750,000 in the second round last June, averaging 12.8 strikeouts per nine innings in his debut. Melotakis has impressive stuff for a lefthander, beginning with a fastball that sits at 94-96 mph and touches 97. He gets tremendous spin on his 81-84 mph slider, which has power and depth. He doesn't always command it, however, and he has to have a catcher who can block balls in the dirt, because his slider ends up there a lot. Melotakis has an unconventional short arm stroke that makes most scouts consider him a reliever, and he struggled to maintain his stuff when he started as an amateur. He has the physicality to work out of a rotation and wants to give it a try as a pro. The Twins have put out a casting call for starters among the system's pitchers and intend to take him up on his offer, with relieving a strong fallback position. He'll return to low Class A to begin 2013.

Year	Club (League)	Class	W	L	ERA	G	GS	CG	SV	IP	H	HR	BB	SO	K/9	WHIP	AVG
2012	Elizabethton (APP)	R	1	1	1.35	7	0	0	0	7	2	0	2	10	13.5	0.60	.091
	Beloit (MWL)	LoA	3	1	2.08	13	0	0	1	17	15	3	4	24	12.5	1.10	.221
Minor League Totals			4	2	1.88	20	0	0	1	24	17	3	6	34	12.8	0.96	.189

14 JORGE POLANCO, 2B/SS

BA GRADE
50
HIGH

Born: 5-11. **B-T:** B-R. **Ht.:** 5-11. **Wt.:** 185. **Signed:** Dominican Republic, 2009. **Signed by:** Fred Guerrero.

Polanco finally may be ready to make his full-season debut in his fourth pro season. Despite his slow path, he made major strides in 2012 and added much-needed strength. He made the jump to Elizabethton and had his best season after sliding to second base, in part so the Twins could evaluate Niko Goodrum at shortstop. He's a more reliable defender than Goodrum, with good actions and hands, sound footwork and impressive consistency for a teenager. Polanco has put on 20 pounds since signing, giving him the strength to drive the ball and break out offensively. He finished sixth in the Appalachian League in batting (.318), fifth in on-base percentage (.388) and even fourth in slugging (.514). He has a solid swing from both sides of the plate and makes solid contact. With his physical maturation, Polanco got too tight and lost a step. He's now a fringy runner and his range is just adequate at shortstop—where he made four errors in 14 starts—leaving him better suited for second base. Minnesota likes his grinder attitude and makeup. After batting ninth most of the year for Elizabethton, Polanco has raised expectations. With a good spring, he should earn the everyday second-base job at Cedar Rapids for 2013.

Year	Club (League)	Class	AVG	G	AB	R	H	2B	3B	HR	RBI	BB	SO	SB	CS	OBP	SLG
2010	Twins (DSL)	R	.250	18	60	5	15	2	0	0	7	6	9	1	3	.309	.283
	Twins (GCL)	R	.223	34	103	12	23	5	0	1	12	12	9	2	4	.299	.301
2011	Twins (GCL)	R	.250	51	172	21	43	8	3	1	16	15	24	6	4	.319	.349
2012	Elizabethton (APP)	R	.318	51	173	35	55	15	2	5	27	20	26	6	3	.388	.514
Minor League Totals			.268	154	508	73	136	30	5	7	62	53	68	15	14	.338	.388

15 J.T. CHARGOIS, RHP

BA GRADE
50
HIGH

Born: Dec. 3, 1990. **B-T:** B-R. **Ht.:** 6-3. **Wt.:** 198. **Drafted:** Rice, 2012 (2nd round). **Signed by:** Greg Runser.

A two-way player at Rice, the switch-hitting Chargois hit .308 for the Owls but lacked the power at the plate that he provides on the mound. He blossomed as a closer in the Cape Cod League in 2011 after throwing just seven innings as a sophomore that spring. He's still fairly new to pitching and has a fresh arm after working just 72 innings in three seasons at Rice. Signed for $712,600 as a second-round pick in June, Chargois can run his fastball as high as 97 mph with explosive sink at times. At others, his velocity will back up into the low 90s. His arm got a little tender during Elizabethton's run to the Appalachian League title, though he returned for five scoreless playoff innings while sitting at 94-95 mph with his heater. Chargois' hard breaking ball, alternately described as a curveball and a slider, is similarly inconsistent but earns plus-plus grades from some Twins scouts. It's a low-80s hybrid with depth and power. His arm action and high-effort delivery, as well as his overall inexperience as a pitcher, make it unlikely that Minnesota will try to shift him to starting. Instead, he could jump to high Class A as a reliever and get on the fast track if he stays healthy.

Year	Club (League)	Class	W	L	ERA	G	GS	CG	SV	IP	H	HR	BB	SO	K/9	WHIP	AVG
2012	Elizabethton (APP)	R	0	0	1.69	12	0	0	5	16	10	0	5	22	12.4	0.94	.182
Minor League Totals			0	0	1.69	12	0	0	5	16	10	0	5	22	12.4	0.94	.182

16 LEVI MICHAEL, 2B/SS

BA GRADE

50

HIGH

Born: Feb. 9, 1991. **B-T:** B-R. **Ht.:** 5-11. **Wt.:** 183. **Drafted:** North Carolina, 2011 (1st round). **Signed by:** Ricky Taylor.

Minnesota expected more from its 2011 first-round pick than 20 extra-base hits, and it hopes for more return on its $1.175 million investment in Michael in the future. Assigning him to high Class A for his pro debut last year was a surprise on multiple levels: Michael enrolled at North Carolina a semester early and was just 20 when drafted, and injuries to his lower half prompted him to struggle as a North Carolina junior and fall to the 30th overall selection. His injuries to his groin and, according to the Twins, virtually every joint below his waist kept him from playing even in instructional league in 2011, making it even more curious that the traditionally patient organization pushed him. Michael's polished plate approach and defensive ability prompted the decision, and his .339 on-base percentage exceeded the Florida State League average. However, he lacked the burst he'd shown when healthy in college—in his swing, on the bases and on his throws. Scouts consistently commented that Michael didn't stand out physically, and the Twins agree. In the past, Michael was a plus runner with the arm and range for shortstop and pop from both sides of the plate. He looked better after taking a couple of weeks off and getting back in action in instructional league, where club officials say he ran and threw better than he had since signing. If Michael doesn't hit, though, he'll be relegated to a ceiling as a utilityman. He figures to return to Fort Myers in 2013.

Year	Club (League)	Class	AVG	G	AB	R	H	2B	3B	HR	RBI	BB	SO	SB	CS	OBP	SLG
2012	Fort Myers (FSL)	HiA	.246	117	431	58	106	14	4	2	38	56	82	6	0	.339	.311
Minor League Totals			.246	117	431	58	106	14	4	2	38	56	82	6	0	.339	.311

17 TRAVIS HARRISON, 3B

BA GRADE

50

HIGH

Born: Oct. 17, 1992. **B-T:** R-R. **Ht.:** 6-2. **Wt.:** 215. **Drafted:** HS—Tustin, Calif., 2011 (1st round supplemental). **Signed by:** John Leavitt.

The 50th overall pick in the 2011 draft, Harrison signed late for $1.05 million and made his pro debut last summer at Elizabethton. Taken for his bat, he finished eighth in the Appalachian League in hitting (.301) and settled in as a consistent complement to college-drafted sluggers Adam Brett Walker and D.J. Hicks. Harrison has a strong upper body to go with natural rhythm and hitting. His swing is more line-drive oriented now, but he should tap into his plus raw power as he learns his strike zone. He has started using the whole field more after being too pull-conscious as an amateur. Harrison improved greatly at third base last season, shortening his arm stroke to have a consistently average, accurate arm. He isn't the most graceful athlete and lacks ideal first-step or lateral quickness, so his footwork never will be a plus. Some scouts think he'll hit enough for his defense at third to be playable. He's a fringy runner who could wind up in left field or first base. Harrison has to produce at the plate to make an impact. He'll head to Cedar Rapids in 2013.

Year	Club (League)	Class	AVG	G	AB	R	H	2B	3B	HR	RBI	BB	SO	SB	CS	OBP	SLG
2012	Elizabethton (APP)	R	.301	60	219	39	66	12	4	5	27	24	51	3	0	.383	.461
Minor League Totals			.301	60	219	39	66	12	4	5	27	24	51	3	0	.383	.461

18 CHRIS HERRMANN, C/OF

BA GRADE

45

MEDIUM

Born: Nov. 24, 1987. **B-T:** L-L. **Ht.:** 6-0. **Wt.:** 200. **Drafted:** Miami, 2009 (6th round). **Signed by:** Hecter Otero.

The system's lone true prospect behind the plate, Herrmann had a career-best season at Double-A in 2012, ranking third in the Eastern League in runs (91) and reaching double figures in homers for the first time. He got his first big league promotion in September and recorded his first big league hit off Cody Eppley. Herrmann has become the system's best defensive catcher through hard work. He's a good athlete for a catcher and has a loose arm with solid arm strength. He has quickened his release and led the EL by throwing out 44 percent of basestealers. He's agile and does a good job of staying low behind the plate. Herrmann's power has improved as he continues to learn when to take advantage of pitches in his hitting zone, rather than just trying to work walks. When he's not ahead in the count, he generally employs a contact-oriented swing that serves him well against lefthanders, whom he hit at a .325/.396/.415 clip in Double-A. He's an average runner who can fill in on the infield and outfield corners. That's useful considering Joe Mauer's presence in Minnesota. Herrmann figures to be the regular catcher at Rochester this season, and he could settle in as Mauer's backup/caddy as the Twins try to keep their star's legs fresh.

Year	Club (League)	Class	AVG	G	AB	R	H	2B	3B	HR	RBI	BB	SO	SB	CS	OBP	SLG
2009	Elizabethton (APP)	R	.297	59	236	45	70	14	1	7	30	33	40	2	2	.391	.453
2010	Fort Myers (FSL)	HiA	.219	107	356	34	78	17	3	2	30	41	74	3	2	.310	.301
2011	Fort Myers (FSL)	HiA	.310	24	87	14	27	5	1	1	16	15	6	1	0	.404	.425
	New Britain (EL)	AA	.258	97	337	53	87	14	5	7	46	64	68	9	3	.380	.392
2012	New Britain (EL)	AA	.276	127	490	91	135	25	1	10	61	58	89	2	1	.350	.392
	Minnesota (AL)	MAJ	.056	7	18	0	1	0	0	0	1	1	5	0	0	.105	.056
Major League Totals			.056	7	18	0	1	0	0	0	1	1	5	0	0	.105	.056
Minor League Totals			.264	414	1506	237	397	75	11	27	183	211	277	17	8	.357	.382

19 JOE BENSON, OF

BA GRADE
50
HIGH

Born: March 5, 1988. **B-T:** R-R. **Ht.:** 6-1. **Wt.:** 215. **Drafted:** HS—Joliet, Ill., 2006 (2nd round). **Signed by:** Billly Milos.

Benson has been on this list every year since being drafted in the second round in 2006, twice ranking No. 2 overall. He seemed to put it all together in 2011, posting an .883 OPS in Double-A and earning his first big league promotion. His 2012 was a disaster, however, beginning with a .179 start in Triple-A. After a demotion, he missed six weeks with broken hamate bone in his left hand, and he was in a 1-for-35 slump when he was shut down with a left knee injury in mid-August. He not only needed bone chips removed but also had cartilage damage, and knee surgery scrubbed him from the Arizona Fall League. Benson had injury issues in the past (fractured vertebra in 2008, broken right hand in 2009), but had stayed healthy the previous two seasons. A former Purdue football recruit, he remains one of the system's best athletes. He has plus speed and raw power, a cannon arm and the defensive chops to play center field. The problem is that he's not a pure hitter despite his fast hands. He never got into a rhythm in 2012, striking out in 29 percent of his at-bats—up from 22 percent the year before. Minnesota no longer is counting on Benson, and the system's outfield depth is catching up to him. With both Denard Span and Ben Revere traded in the offseason, Benson has his chance. His strong defense and a hot spring training could push him past the likes of Darin Mastroianni for the big league center-field job. Otherwise, he'll head back to Rochester to try to get back on track.

Year	Club (League)	Class	AVG	G	AB	R	H	2B	3B	HR	RBI	BB	SO	SB	CS	OBP	SLG
2006	Twins (GCL)	R	.260	52	196	30	51	11	5	5	28	21	41	9	10	.335	.444
	Beloit (MWL)	LoA	.263	8	19	2	5	0	0	0	1	0	6	1	0	.263	.263
2007	Beloit (MWL)	LoA	.255	122	432	73	110	18	8	5	38	49	124	18	16	.347	.368
2008	Beloit (MWL)	LoA	.248	69	254	39	63	16	3	4	27	24	73	17	11	.326	.382
2009	Twins (GCL)	R	.200	2	5	1	1	0	0	0	0	2	0	1	1	.429	.200
	Fort Myers (FSL)	HiA	.285	80	263	46	75	10	3	5	29	46	74	14	7	.414	.403
2010	Fort Myers (FSL)	HiA	.294	21	85	16	25	11	1	4	13	8	21	5	0	.375	.588
	New Britain (EL)	AA	.251	102	374	65	94	20	7	23	49	39	115	14	9	.336	.527
2011	Twins (GCL)	R	.222	3	9	2	2	1	0	0	0	2	2	1	1	.364	.333
	New Britain (EL)	AA	.285	111	400	69	114	28	4	16	67	56	109	13	9	.388	.495
	Minnesota (AL)	MAJ	.239	21	71	3	17	6	1	0	2	3	21	2	2	.270	.352
2012	Rochester (IL)	AAA	.179	28	95	9	17	3	2	2	8	11	27	4	0	.269	.316
	New Britain (EL)	AA	.184	37	141	13	26	6	1	3	20	13	43	4	3	.268	.305
	Twins (GCL)	R	.375	3	8	1	3	1	0	0	0	1	2	1	1	.444	.500
	Fort Myers (FSL)	HiA	.303	8	33	7	10	3	0	1	8	5	9	4	0	.395	.485
Major League Totals			.239	21	71	3	17	6	1	0	2	3	21	2	2	.270	.352
Minor League Totals			.258	646	2314	373	596	128	34	68	288	277	646	106	68	.351	.430

20 B.J. HERMSEN, RHP

BA GRADE
45
MEDIUM

Born: Dec. 1, 1989. **B-T:** R-R. **Ht.:** 6-5. **Wt.:** 235. **Drafted:** HS—Manchester, Iowa, 2008 (6th round). **Signed by:** Mark Wilson.

Hermsen's timing might get him to the big leagues, as the Twins are desperate for starters in the majors and he's coming off his best season. Signed for $650,000 as a 2008 sixth-rounder, he won the organization's minor league pitcher of the year award in 2012 after leading the system in innings (163) and ERA (2.88) with an Eastern League-best 1.6 walks per nine innings. His big frame makes him a durable workhorse, but despite his size he's no power pitcher. Instead, Hermsen works off his sinker and slider to get groundballs. His fastball velocity improved over the course of last season, from 85-89 mph early on to 88-90 mph with a high of 92. While the pitch has sink, it succeeds more because Hermsen locates it well and throws it with good downhill plane. His slider lacks depth and is more of a cutter at 83-85 mph. His sinking changeup has the potential to be an average pitch, though he tends to tip it off by slowing his arm speed. A high school quarterback, Hermsen nevertheless is a below-average athlete with a deliberate delivery that makes it tough to control the running game. Armed with good fastball command, he should start 2013 in the Triple-A rotation and could earn innings in Minnesota. Added to the 40-man roster in November, he has a ceiling of a fifth starter.

Year	Club (League)	Class	W	L	ERA	G	GS	CG	SV	IP	H	HR	BB	SO	K/9	WHIP	AVG
2009	Twins (GCL)	R	6	2	1.35	10	10	1	0	53	32	0	4	42	7.1	0.68	.171
2010	Beloit (MWL)	LoA	4	6	5.00	12	12	1	0	72	85	6	15	46	5.8	1.39	.295
	Elizabethton (APP)	R	2	2	3.32	8	6	0	0	38	39	2	4	39	9.2	1.13	.257
2011	Beloit (MWL)	LoA	11	7	3.10	21	20	1	0	125	131	10	31	81	5.8	1.30	.271
	Fort Myers (FSL)	HiA	2	1	4.39	5	5	0	0	27	34	1	6	20	6.8	1.50	.312
2012	Fort Myers (FSL)	HiA	1	0	0.78	4	4	0	0	23	16	1	5	12	4.7	0.91	.190
	New Britain (EL)	AA	11	6	3.22	22	22	1	0	140	145	12	25	75	4.8	1.22	.269
Minor League Totals			37	24	3.21	82	79	4	0	477	482	32	90	315	5.9	1.20	.261

21 ANGEL MATA, RHP

BA GRADE
50
HIGH

Born: Dec. 3, 1992. **B-T:** R-R. **Ht.:** 6-2. **Wt.:** 227. **Signed:** Venezuela, 2010. **Signed by:** Jose Leon.

Mata lacked the pitch efficiency to last more than five innings in any of his starts at Elizabethton last summer, but he worked five scoreless innings on four occasions. He also turned in five strong innings in a playoff start and held Appalachian League hitters to a .171 average. Mata shows flashes of two average to plus pitches. He fastball usually sits at 88-92 mph and touches 94. His slurvy curveball, thrown with power in the upper 70s and reaching 80 mph at times, remains inconsistent. When he throws strikes with his fastball and curve, he dominates. He throws a changeup that also has its moments, though it's clearly a third pitch at this stage. Mata has good size and will need to work hard to maintain his fitness and master a consistent between-starts routine. He doesn't repeat his delivery enough and lacks maturity when calls don't go his way, helping lead to 5.7 walks per nine innings last year. He has the size and stuff to start but still is figuring out the command. Mata continued to get swings and misses pitching out of the bullpen in the Venezuelan League. He'll have to build off his strong winter to earn a rotation spot in low Class A this spring.

Year	Club (League)	Class	W	L	ERA	G	GS	CG	SV	IP	H	HR	BB	SO	K/9	WHIP	AVG
2010	Twins (DSL)	R	1	5	2.12	13	10	1	0	59	50	0	15	54	8.2	1.10	.230
2011	Twins (GCL)	R	0	1	1.46	12	11	0	0	37	23	0	19	30	7.3	1.14	.184
2012	Elizabethton (APP)	R	4	3	3.38	13	13	0	0	53	31	7	34	55	9.3	1.22	.171
Minor League Totals			5	9	2.41	38	34	1	0	150	104	7	68	139	8.4	1.15	.199

22 MADISON BOER, RHP

BA GRADE
45
MEDIUM

Born: Nov. 9, 1989. **B-T:** R-R. **Ht.:** 6-3. **Wt.:** 228. **Drafted:** Oregon, 2011 (2nd round). **Signed by:** Trevor Brown.

Among the legion of Twins relievers-turned-starters, Boer had the roughest 2012 season, giving up 173 hits and posting a 5.84 ERA. Minnesota challenged the former Oregon closer with a promotion to high Class A in May of his first full pro season. He promptly went 0-6, 11.22 in his first six starts at Fort Myers. He did finish with seven quality starts in his last 11 outings as he gradually adjusted to the better competition, the new role and the reduced quality of stuff that came with it. A Minnesota native, Boer has the size and arm action to start, as well as a four-pitch mix. His fastball tends to straighten out, which became a problem when he averaged 90-92 mph as a starter. He hit 95-96 regularly in relief, so he got away with less movement. Now he's working to add cut action and armside run to his fastball, which has tailing action. He has an average slider that touches 86 mph, and he throws a fringy changeup and get-me-over curveball. Boer's arm tended to drag last year as he rushed through his delivery, making his pitches flatter, but he did make late-season adjustments. His lack of a putaway pitch was evident in his 2012, though he did handle a starter's workload well and always can fall back on relieving. Despite his ugly numbers, he'll move up to Double-A in 2013.

Year	Club (League)	Class	W	L	ERA	G	GS	CG	SV	IP	H	HR	BB	SO	K/9	WHIP	AVG
2011	Elizabethton (APP)	R	2	1	2.60	15	0	0	9	17	13	1	2	31	16.1	0.87	.203
	Beloit (MWL)	LoA	0	0	6.75	8	0	0	2	8	12	0	1	12	13.5	1.63	.343
2012	Beloit (MWL)	LoA	2	2	3.58	5	5	0	0	28	26	1	10	20	6.5	1.30	.252
	Fort Myers (FSL)	HiA	7	10	6.41	22	19	0	0	111	147	15	32	66	5.4	1.61	.322
Minor League Totals			11	13	5.54	50	24	0	11	164	198	17	45	129	7.1	1.48	.301

23 TYLER JONES, RHP

BA GRADE
50
HIGH

Born: Sept. 5, 1989. **B-T:** R-R. **Ht.:** 6-4. **Wt.:** 247. **Drafted:** Louisiana State, 2011 (11th round). **Signed by:** Greg Runser.

Jones led his Madison (Wis.) JC team to the Division II Junior College World Series and was drafted in the 21st round by the White Sox in 2010 but headed to Louisiana State rather than turning pro. He missed a season-opening series as punishment for a misdemeanor shoplifting charge and never earned consistent rotation time, going 4-0, 5.21. The Twins still drafted him in the 11th round and paid him $105,000 because he had flashed a 95-96 mph fastball as a reliever. Jones continues to throw hard, working at 90-94 mph and touching 95 with his fastball, which has average life with cut and sink. It helped him lead Minnesota's minor league starters with 10.6 strikeouts per nine innings in his first full pro season. His slider gives him another swing-and-miss pitch with depth at times; at others it's more of a hard cutter in the upper 80s. His curveball and changeup are just show-me pitches. His arm action has a stab in it that makes it hard for Jones to repeat his release point, and his lack of command leads to too many hitter's counts. He's headed for the Fort Myers rotation in 2013 but could move to the bullpen sooner rather than later.

Year	Club (League)	Class	W	L	ERA	G	GS	CG	SV	IP	H	HR	BB	SO	K/9	WHIP	AVG
2011	Elizabethton (APP)	R	0	0	12.86	4	1	0	0	7	16	2	2	8	10.3	2.57	.432
2012	Beloit (MWL)	LoA	5	5	4.67	18	16	0	0	87	90	5	35	102	10.6	1.44	.263
Minor League Totals			5	5	5.28	22	17	0	0	94	106	7	37	110	10.6	1.53	.280

24 FELIX JORGE, RHP

Born: Jan. 2, 1994. **B-T:** R-R. **Ht.:** 6-2. **Wt.:** 170. **Signed:** Dominican Republic, 2011. **Signed by:** Fred Guerrero.

Jorge entered 2010 as one of the top pitchers in the Dominican amateur market, and the Twins stuck with him even after his velocity dipped close to the July 2 signing date. They signed him the following February for $250,000. In his U.S. debut last year, he was the best pitching prospect on a Gulf Coast League Twins staff that led the league with a 2.75 ERA. That group also includes slender lefty Yorman Landa, strike-throwing Taiwan import Kuo Hua Lo and hard-throwing lefty Randy Rosario. Jorge showed off his advanced pitchability by going 23 2/3 consecutive innings without allowing an earned run. His fastball currently ranges from 89-92 mph and touches 94. His curveball shows signs of becoming an average pitch, with some snap and downer action. His arm works well with an easy delivery. Jorge has room to add 30 or more pounds to his projectable frame, so he's far from a finished product. He'll advance to Elizabethon this year and make his full-season debut in 2014.

Year	Club (League)	Class	W	L	ERA	G	GS	CG	SV	IP	H	HR	BB	SO	K/9	WHIP	AVG
2011	Twins (DSL)	R	2	1	2.67	9	5	0	1	27	19	0	9	26	8.7	1.04	.192
2012	Twins (GCL)	R	0	3	2.34	12	7	0	1	35	30	0	12	37	9.6	1.21	.221
Minor League Totals			2	4	2.48	21	12	0	2	62	49	0	21	63	9.2	1.14	.209

25 JASON WHEELER, LHP

Born: Oct. 27, 1990. **B-T:** L-L. **Ht.:** 6-8. **Wt.:** 265. **Drafted:** Loyola Marymount, 2011 (8th round). **Signed by:** Mike Eaglin.

Wheeler's older brother Ryan was his teammate at Loyola Marymount and made his big league debut in 2012 with the Diamondbacks before being traded in November to the Rockies. Jason is quite different from his brother, as he's lefthanded and huge. After signing for $132,500 as a 2011 eighth-rounder, he led the Midwest League with 14 wins and the Twins system with 115 strikeouts in his pro debut last year. Wheeler pitches at 88-90 mph with his fastball, and uses his height and high three-quarters arm slot to pitch downhill and get early-count outs. He's hittable but gets his share of groundballs and generally keeps the ball in the park. He holds his velocity well and is exceptional at stopping the running game, with 16 of 28 basestealers caught on his watch in 2012. Wheeler's secondary stuff is nothing special. His changeup has sink and his cutter-type slider helps him give lefthanders a different look. He'll also drop in an early-count curveball that has its moments. Wheeler's durability and feel for pitching make him one of Minnesota' better starting pitching prospects, though he may not be more than a No. 5 starter. He could skip a level to Double-A this year.

Year	Club (League)	Class	W	L	ERA	G	GS	CG	SV	IP	H	HR	BB	SO	K/9	WHIP	AVG
2012	Beloit (MWL)	LoA	14	6	3.45	27	27	0	0	157	170	12	43	115	6.6	1.36	.281
Minor League Totals			14	6	3.45	27	27	0	0	157	170	12	43	115	6.6	1.36	.281

26 NIKO GOODRUM, SS

Born: Feb. 28, 1992. **B-T:** B-R. **Ht.:** 6-4. **Wt.:** 190. **Drafted:** HS—Fayetteville, Ga., 2010 (2nd round). **Signed by:** Jack Powell.

Goodrum repeated the Appalachian League and saw his batting average drop 33 points in 2012, not what an organization wants to see from a prospect. However, every indicator other than batting average was positive for Goodrum, who moved from a second base/utility role in 2011 to an everyday shortstop job. While he has added 15 pounds since signing, Goodrum is still built like a young colt, long-legged and high-waisted. The added strength helped him drive the ball with more consistency last season. He doubled his home run total from 2011 and led the Appalachian League with eight triples and 38 walks. He has fast hands that work on both sides of the plate as well as in the field. Goodrum is an above-average runner whose first-step quickness gives him range in the middle infield. He also has plus arm strength and an energetic style of play. He remains unpolished defensively, though, thanks to inconsistent footwork and focus, and some scouts think he's headed for the outfield as his body fills out. Goodrum profiles as a utility infielder unless he develops more physically and adds power. He's slated to finally break through to full-season ball in 2013, his fourth pro season.

Year	Club (League)	Class	AVG	G	AB	R	H	2B	3B	HR	RBI	BB	SO	SB	CS	OBP	SLG
2010	Twins (GCL)	R	.161	36	118	10	19	4	0	0	5	9	34	4	2	.219	.195
2011	Elizabethton (APP)	R	.275	59	204	39	56	10	3	2	20	21	56	8	1	.352	.382
2012	Elizabethton (APP)	R	.242	58	227	38	55	12	8	4	38	38	56	6	3	.349	.419
Minor League Totals			.237	153	549	87	130	26	11	6	63	68	146	18	6	.324	.357

27 ADRIAN SALCEDO, RHP

BA GRADE
45
HIGH

Born: Feb. 5, 1991. **B-T:** R-R. **Ht.:** 6-4. **Wt.:** 196. **Signed:** Dominican Republic, 2007. **Signed by:** Fred Guerrero.

Salcedo remains one of the Twins' hardest workers, a slender righthander who keeps himself in excellent physical shape. He had a strong spring training and seemed ready to move back up this list. An avid runner, he finally added weight to his slender 6-foot-4 frame while also better incorporating his lower half into his delivery. His velocity spiked as a result, as his fastball touched 96 in the spring. However, Salcedo's arm apparently wasn't ready for the extra velocity and he had an injury-plagued season. He went on the disabled list in May with an elbow strain, and working his way back to the mound for only four more outings before tightness in his shoulder capsule ended his season. He didn't have surgery, but he still had trouble getting loose and remained in rehab mode throughout instructional league. When healthy, Salcedo pounds the strike zone with a fastball that usually sits at 90-93 mph and two inconsistent breaking balls, a slider and a curveball he struggles to separate. His fastball and solid changeup both feature sink. A healthy Salcedo would be a boon to Minnesota's thin pitching ranks, though the team opted not to protect him on its 40-man roster this offseason.

Year	Club (League)	Class	W	L	ERA	G	GS	CG	SV	IP	H	HR	BB	SO	K/9	WHIP	AVG
2008	Twins (DSL)	R	4	4	1.65	12	12	0	0	65	47	1	8	50	6.9	0.84	.198
2009	Twins (GCL)	R	3	2	1.46	11	10	0	0	62	60	1	3	58	8.5	1.02	.241
2010	Fort Myers (FSL)	HiA	1	3	6.26	6	6	0	0	27	42	3	8	16	5.3	1.83	.378
	Elizabethton (APP)	R	4	3	3.27	16	8	0	1	66	55	3	10	65	8.9	0.98	.230
2011	Beloit (MWL)	LoA	6	6	2.93	29	20	1	0	135	131	4	27	92	6.1	1.17	.252
2012	Fort Myers (FSL)	HiA	0	1	6.39	8	7	0	0	25	33	1	15	14	5.0	1.89	.314
	Twins (GCL)	R	0	1	3.38	3	2	0	0	5	7	0	1	4	6.8	1.50	.292
Minor League Totals			18	20	3.01	85	65	1	1	386	375	13	72	299	7.0	1.16	.253

28 MICHAEL TONKIN, RHP

BA GRADE
45
HIGH

Born: Nov. 19, 1989. **B-T:** R-R. **Ht.:** 6-7. **Wt.:** 220. **Drafted:** HS—Palmdale, Calif., 2008 (30th round). **Signed by:** Dan Cox.

Tonkin's sister is married to former Twins outfielder Jason Kubel, now with the Diamondbacks. Signed for $230,000 as a 30th-round pick in 2008, Tonkin seemed like a longshot to ever join Kubel in the majors until he finally found his footing in a full-time relief role last year. He led the system's relievers in strikeout rate (12.6 per nine innings), picking up 12 saves while finally getting out of low Class A, where he spent parts of three seasons. His development landed him a spot on Minnesota's 40-man roster. Tonkin uses a three-quarters arm slot and generates one of the system's hardest fastballs, working at 91-94 mph, hitting 96 regularly and touching 97 in the Midwest League all-star game. He has a strong body with some effort in his delivery, though some scouts said improved direction to the plate was what helped him take off. His solid slider has power in the low 80s and made significant improvement as well in 2012. For Tonkin to become a big league closer or set-up man, he'll have to make his slider more of a swing-and-miss pitch in the strike zone, not just a chase pitch. He continued to throw well in the Arizona Fall League as well and could move quickly now that he's found confidence. He'll start 2013 in Double-A.

Year	Club (League)	Class	W	L	ERA	G	GS	CG	SV	IP	H	HR	BB	SO	K/9	WHIP	AVG
2008	Twins (GCL)	R	0	1	3.27	6	1	0	0	11	10	0	3	8	6.5	1.18	.244
2009	Twins (GCL)	R	3	4	3.62	11	9	0	0	55	55	2	9	60	9.9	1.17	.258
2010	Beloit (MWL)	LoA	3	6	4.29	13	12	0	0	65	76	7	18	40	5.5	1.45	.287
	Elizabethton (APP)	R	1	0	1.08	10	0	0	1	25	18	1	4	26	9.4	0.88	.196
2011	Beloit (MWL)	LoA	4	3	3.87	48	3	0	2	77	82	3	24	69	8.1	1.38	.271
2012	Beloit (MWL)	LoA	3	0	1.38	22	0	0	6	39	29	1	9	53	12.2	0.97	.206
	Fort Myers (FSL)	HiA	1	1	2.97	22	0	0	6	30	24	2	11	44	13.1	1.15	.212
Minor League Totals			15	15	3.25	132	25	0	15	302	294	16	78	300	9.0	1.23	.252

29 KENNYS VARGAS, 1B

BA GRADE
50
EXTREME

Born: Aug. 1, 1990. **B-T:** B-R. **Ht.:** 6-5. **Wt.:** 272. **Signed:** HS—Canovanas, P.R., NDFA 2009. **Signed by:** Hector Otero.

Led by area scout Hector Otero, the Twins have been one of the most active organizations in Puerto Rico in recent years. The club didn't retain Otero after the season, though several of his signees (Eddie Rosario, Chris Herrman and Vargas) made real progress in 2012. Vargas was a 215-pound third baseman when Otero worked him out and the Twins signed him in February 2009 as a nondrafted free agent. Vargas has grown significantly since then—and not in a positive way. He tipped the scales at a massive 272 pounds in instructional league. His calling card is power and he clubbed 11 homers in just 41 games in low Class A last year, including a monster shot over the batter's eye in Cedar Rapids. He has a surprising feel for the barrel as well. Besides his weight, pitch recognition stemming from his lack of experience is his biggest obstacle to overcome as a hitter. Vargas was suspended for 50 games late in 2011 after testing positive for a performance-enhancing drug, which may have been related to a weight-loss product. Because he was busted in the Appalachian League, he had to wait for Appy League season to start before his suspension clock restarted in 2012. He has arm strength, but he's a well below-average runner and defender at first base. He played a game at third base to give Miguel Sano a breather last summer, and Vargas may return there if he drops some pounds. If he can trim up and stay on the field, he could have a breakout season in high Class A.

Year	Club (League)	Class	AVG	G	AB	R	H	2B	3B	HR	RBI	BB	SO	SB	CS	OBP	SLG
2009	Twins (GCL)	R	.257	35	109	12	28	7	0	3	18	17	34	2	0	.369	.404
2010	Twins (GCL)	R	.324	39	142	24	46	15	1	3	26	13	40	1	0	.388	.507
2011	Elizabethton (APP)	R	.322	44	174	27	56	11	0	6	33	15	50	0	0	.377	.489
2012	Beloit (MWL)	LoA	.318	41	154	22	49	10	1	11	36	28	41	0	0	.419	.610
Minor League Totals			.309	159	579	85	179	43	2	23	113	73	165	3	0	.390	.509

30 MATT SUMMERS, RHP

BA GRADE
45
HIGH

Born: Aug. 17, 1989. **B-T:** L-R. **Ht.:** 6-1. **Wt.:** 200. **Drafted:** UC Irvine, 2011 (4th round). **Signed by:** John Leavitt.

Like many of the Twins' pitching prospects, Summers was a college closer, helping UC Irvine get within an out of the 2010 College World Series. He moved to the rotation as a junior in 2011, returned to the bullpen after signing for $171,900 as a fourth-round pick that summer, then started again in his first full pro season. In the system, only 2012 draftee Mason Melotakis rivals Summers' unconventionally short arm action. He worked with a 92-95 mph fastball that touched 98 as a college closer, but he pitched with an average 90 mph fastball as a pro. It still gets outs because he has a knack for throwing strikes low and away to righthanders. He also throws a slider, curveball and changeup. His low-80s slider has the best chance to give him a plus secondary pitch, though his changeup has its moments as well. When Summers is on, he generates a lot of weak contact. He grinded his way to high Class A by the end of 2012 despite not having a consistent above-average offering. His arm action and high-effort delivery have most scouts convinced he'll wind up back in the bullpen, but he'll begin 2013 back in the Fort Myers rotation.

Year	Club (League)	Class	W	L	ERA	G	GS	CG	SV	IP	H	HR	BB	SO	K/9	WHIP	AVG
2011	Elizabethton (APP)	R	1	1	0.87	20	0	0	6	21	11	0	5	36	15.7	0.77	.153
2012	Beloit (MWL)	LoA	9	4	3.55	19	18	1	0	109	103	9	34	71	5.9	1.26	.249
	Fort Myers (FSL)	HiA	2	3	4.81	9	8	0	0	39	46	7	25	26	5.9	1.81	.307
Minor League Totals			12	8	3.51	48	26	1	6	169	160	16	64	133	7.1	1.33	.252

New York Mets

BY MATT EDDY

Even as individual Mets players achieve franchise milestones, the club has remained mired in fourth place in the National League East for the past four seasons. Win totals have diminished each year since 2010, dropping from 79 to 77 down to 74.

New York's salary expenditures and attendance continue to drop as well. Its Opening Day payroll has plummeted from $149 million in 2009 to $93 million in 2012, while Citi Field attendance has fallen from 3.2 million to 2.2 million in the same period.

The Mets may begin bidding for impact free agents again following the 2013 season, after which Jason

Bay and Johan Santana come off the books. Then again, they may not, given the financial difficulties faced by owner Fred Wilpon, who took a $162 million hit because of his involvement with Ponzi schemer Bernie Madoff.

Amid the gloom, Mets players delivered a number of high points in 2012.

Santana threw the first no-hitter in the 51-year history of the franchise on June 1, though it required 134 pitches and he was ineffective afterward.

Signed as a minor league free agent in 2009, R.A. Dickey tossed back-to-back one-hitters in June, led the NL in strikeouts (230) and innings (234), and became the first knuckleballer to win a Cy Young Award.

David Wright, the last impact player developed by the Mets, established franchise career marks for runs, hits, RBIs and walks. He'll add more records after the club signed him to an eight-year, $138 million extension in December.

The arrival of 23-year-old Matt Harvey in late July served as perhaps the brightest spot for the Mets' future. The seventh overall pick in the 2010 draft, Harvey struck out 11 Diamondbacks over 5⅓ shutout innings in his debut.

He ranked as the No. 1 prospect in the Triple-A International League—and might have done the same on this list had he still qualified—and ranked fourth among major league starters in fastball velocity (94.7 mph) and first in slider velocity (88.4 mph) among those with at least 50 innings.

The Mets have several holes to fill after ranking 12th in the NL in scoring and 10th in runs allowed in 2012. They have hope on the mound if Harvey and righthander Zack Wheeler, the system's best prospect, fulfill their potential as frontline starters.

A lack of blue-chip position prospects clouds New

Rookie Matt Harvey put Triple-A behind him by striking out 70 in 59 big league innings

York's future lineup possibilities, however. Its best upper-level hitter is infielder Wilmer Flores, but he may not have enough power or defensive chops to profile as a long-term starter at any position.

Mets domestic farm clubs finished with a cumulative winning record for the third straight season, with the pitching staffs at high Class A St. Lucie, low Class A Savannah and short-season Brooklyn serving as particular highlights. All three units led their leagues in ERA, WHIP and K-BB ratio while featuring the bulk of the system's most promising arms, including Luis Mateo, Rafael Montero and Michael Fulmer.

The Mets sought to cut costs by going without an entry in the Rookie-level Gulf Coast League in 2012, though they'll reverse course in 2013 and continue to invest in player development. For the second straight year, New York set a new franchise record for draft bonuses, upping the mark to $7 million. It also signed Dominican shortstop Amed Rosario for $1.75 million, the highest bonus it ever has paid for an international amateur.

All was not rosy on the minor league front, however. Buffalo opted not to renew its Player Development Contract with the Mets, aligning instead with the Blue Jays and forcing New York to take Toronto's vacated Triple-A affiliate in Las Vegas.

THIS YEAR'S TOP 30

Player, Pos.		Grade
1.	Zack Wheeler, rhp	65/Medium
2.	Gavin Cecchini, ss	55/High
3.	Brandon Nimmo, of	55/Extreme
4.	Luis Mateo, rhp	50/High
5.	Rafael Montero, rhp	50/High
6.	Wilmer Flores, 3b/2b	50/High
7.	Michael Fulmer, rhp	50/High
8.	Jeurys Familia, rhp	45/Medium
9.	Domingo Tapia, rhp	50/High
10.	Cory Mazzoni, rhp	50/High
11.	Jake deGrom, rhp	50/High
12.	Hansel Robles, rhp	50/High
13.	Wilfredo Tovar, ss	50/High
14.	Cory Vaughn, of	50/High
15.	Matt den Dekker, of	45/Medium
16.	Phillips Evans, ss	50/High
17.	Robert Carson, lhp	45/Medium
18.	Cesar Puello, of	50/High
19.	Aderlin Rodriguez, 3b/1b	50/High
20.	Gabriel Ynoa, rhp	50/High
21.	Kevin Plawecki, c	50/High
22.	Jack Leathersich, lhp	45/Medium
23.	Matt Reynolds, ss	50/High
24.	Collin McHugh, rhp	45/Medium
25.	Tyler Pill, rhp	45/Medium
26.	Logan Verrett, rhp	45/Medium
27.	Darrell Ceciliani, of	45/Medium
28.	Amed Rosario, ss	50/Extreme
29.	Steve Matz, lhp	50/Extreme
30.	Cam Maron, c	45/High

LAST YEAR'S TOP 30

Player, Pos.		Status
1.	Zack Wheeler, rhp	No. 1
2.	Matt Harvey, rhp	Majors
3.	Brandon Nimmo, of	No. 3
4.	Jeurys Familia, rhp	No. 8
5.	Cesar Puello, of	No. 18
6.	Jenrry Mejia, rhp	Majors
7.	Kirk Nieuwenhuis, of	Majors
8.	Michael Fulmer, rhp	No. 7
9.	Reese Havens, 2b	Dropped out
10.	Wilmer Flores, ss	No. 6
11.	Jordany Valdespin, ss/2b	Majors
12.	Matt den Dekker, of	No. 15
13.	Cory Mazzoni, rhp	No. 10
14.	Aderlin Rodriguez, 3b	No. 19
15.	Cory Vaughn, of	No. 14
16.	Zach Lutz, 3b/1b	Dropped out
17.	Domingo Tapia, rhp	No. 9
18.	Juan Urbina, lhp	Dropped out
19.	Darrell Ceciliani, of	No. 27
20.	Darin Gorski, lhp	Dropped out
21.	Phillip Evans, ss	No. 16
22.	Juan Lagares, of	Dropped out
23.	Josh Edgin, lhp	Majors
24.	Chris Schwinden, rhp	Dropped out
25.	Bradley Marquez, of	Dropped out
26.	Logan Verrett, rhp	No. 26
27.	Jack Leathersich, lhp	No. 22
28.	Robert Carson, lhp	No. 17
29.	Josh Satin, 3b/2b	Dropped out
30.	Danny Muno, ss	Dropped out

BEST TOOLS

Best Hitter for Average	Wilmer Flores
Best Power Hitter	Aderlin Rodriguez
Best Strike-Zone Discipline	Danny Muno
Fastest Baserunner	Alonzo Harris
Best Athlete	Bradley Marquez
Best Fastball	Domingo Tapia
Best Curveball	Zack Wheeler
Best Slider	Luis Mateo
Best Changeup	Darin Gorski
Best Control	Rafael Montero
Best Defensive Catcher	Albert Cordero
Best Defensive Infielder	Wilfredo Tovar
Best Infield Arm	Aderlin Rodriguez
Best Defensive Outfielder	Matt den Dekker
Best Outfield Arm	Cesar Puello

PROJECTED 2016 LINEUP

Catcher	Kevin Plawecki
First Base	Ike Davis
Second Base	Gavin Cecchini
Third Base	David Wright
Shortstop	Ruben Tejada
Left Field	Wilmer Flores
Center Field	Brandon Nimmo
Right Field	Cory Vaughn
No. 1 Starter	Zack Wheeler
No. 2 Starter	Matt Harvey
No. 3 Starter	R.A. Dickey
No. 4 Starter	Jonathon Niese
No. 5 Starter	Rafael Montero
Closer	Luis Mateo

TOP PROSPECTS OF THE DECADE

Year	Player, Pos.	2012 Org.
2003	Jose Reyes, ss	Marlins
2004	Kazuo Matsui, ss	Rakuten (Japan)
2005	Lastings Milledge, of	Yakult (Japan)
2006	Lastings Milledge, of	Yakult (Japan)
2007	Mike Pelfrey, rhp	Mets
2008	Fernando Martinez, of	Astros
2009	Fernando Martinez, of	Astros
2010	Jenrry Mejia, rhp	Mets
2011	Jenrry Mejia, rhp	Mets
2012	Zack Wheeler, rhp	Mets

TOP DRAFT PICKS OF THE DECADE

Year	Player, Pos.	2012 Org.
2003	Lastings Milledge, of	Yakult (Japan)
2004	Philip Humber, rhp	White Sox
2005	Mike Pelfrey, rhp	Mets
2006	Kevin Mulvey, rhp (2nd round)	Mets
2007	Eddie Kunz, rhp (1st round supp.)	Padres
2008	Ike Davis, 1b	Mets
2009	Steve Matz, lhp (2nd round)	Mets
2010	Matt Harvey, rhp	Mets
2011	Brandon Nimmo, of	Mets
2012	Gavin Cecchini, ss	Mets

LARGEST BONUSES IN CLUB HISTORY

Mike Pelfrey, 2005	$3,550,000
Philip Humber, 2004	$3,000,000
Matt Harvey, 2010	$2,525,000
Gavin Cecchini, 2012	$2,300,000
Scott Kazmir, 2002	$2,150,000

NEW YORK METS

TOP 2013 ROOKIE: Zack Wheeler, rhp. The system's top prospect could make a Matt Harvey-like debut in the second half and possibly sooner.

BREAKOUT PROSPECT: Gabriel Ynoa, rhp. Command, pitchability and stuff give him a chance to break out like Rafael Montero did in 2012.

SLEEPER: Matt Koch, rhp. The 2012 third-rounder shows 96-mph velocity in short bursts.

SOURCE OF TOP 30 TALENT			
Homegrown	29	Acquired	1
College	10	Trades	1
Junior college	1	Rule 5 draft	0
High school	7	Independent leagues	0
Nondrafted free agents	0	Free agents/waivers	0
International	11		

LF
Vicente Lupo
Travis Taijeron
Dustin Lawley
Stefan Sabol

CF
Brandon Nimmo (3)
Matt den Dekker (15)
Darrell Ceciliani (27)
Bradley Marquez
Gilbert Gomez

RF
Cory Vaughn (14)
Cesar Puello (18)
Juan Lagares
Eudy Pina

3B
Wilmer Flores (6)
Matt Reynolds (23)
Zach Lutz
Jefry Marte
Jhoan Urena

SS
Gavin Cecchini (2)
Wilfredo Tovar (13)
Phillip Evans (16)
Amed Rosario (28)
Brandon Hicks
Anthony Chavez

2B
Reese Havens
Danny Muno
Branden Kaupe
T.J. Rivera
Richie Rodriguez

1B
Aderlin Rodriguez (19)
Josh Satin
Jayce Boyd

C
Kevin Plawecki (21)
Cam Maron (30)
Jose Garcia
Anthony Recker
Blake Forsythe
Juan Torres
Tomas Nido

LHP

LHSP	LHRP
Steve Matz (29)	Robert Carson (17)
Darin Gorski	Jack Leathersich (22)
Alex Panteliodis	Chase Huchingson
	Juan Urbina

RHP

RHSP	RHRP
Zack Wheeler (1)	Jeurys Familia (8)
Luis Mateo (4)	Elvin Ramirez
Rafael Montero (5)	Gonzalez Germen
Michael Fulmer (7)	Ryan Fraser
Domingo Tapia (9)	Adrian Rosario
Cory Mazzoni (10)	Armando Rodriguez
Jake deGrom (11)	Brad Holt
Hansel Robles (13)	Akeel Morris
Gabriel Ynoa (20)	Taylor Whitenton
Collin McHugh (24)	Jeff Walters
Tyler Pill (25)	John Church
Logan Verrett (26)	Logan Taylor
Rainy Lara	Matt Bowman
Matt Koch	Tim Peterson
Erik Goeddel	
Chris Schwinden	
Greg Peavey	
Chris Flexen	
Miller Diaz	
Corey Oswalt	
Luis Cessa	
Julian Hilario	
Brandon Welch	

2012

BEST PURE HITTER: SS Matt Reynolds (2) has a short stroke and advanced plate discipline. His swing and approach should allow him to be a line-drive machine and post solid on-base percentages. SS Gavin Cecchini (1) has a polished approach and handles the bat well. C Kevin Plawecki (1s) utilizes a compact swing to make consistent contact, striking out just 29 times in three seasons at Purdue.

BEST POWER HITTER: C Tomas Nido (8) has well above-average raw power but is still raw at the plate. Plawecki has plus raw pop to his pull side and is more of a doubles hitter when he goes the other way.

FASTEST RUNNER: 2B Brandon Kaupe (4) was one of the biggest surprise picks in the draft, but he's a tightly wound, energetic player whose best tool is his 65 speed on the 20-80 scouting scale.

BEST DEFENSIVE PLAYER: Cecchini is a steady shortstop with a solid, accurate arm and a better chance to stay at the position than Reynolds, who could be an above-average defender at third base. Plawecki shows soft hands and quick feet behind the plate, helping his fringy arm play up.

BEST FASTBALL: RHP Matt Koch (3) shows the best pure velocity, running his fastball up to 96 mph. RHP Logan Taylor (11) isn't far behind, topping out at 94 and throwing his fastball on a steeper plane to the plate.

BEST SECONDARY PITCH: RHP Brandon Welch (5) throws a filthy slider with tight tilt at 84-85 mph. He has the feel to manipulate the pitch, change its shape and throw it for strikes.

BEST PRO DEBUT: A $1,000 senior sign, crafty RHP Paul Sewald (10) posted a 1.88 ERA and 35-2 K-BB ratio in 29 innings at short-season Brooklyn. Plawecki led Brooklyn with seven homers and threw out 32 percent of basestealers.

BEST ATHLETE: Cecchini's sum is greater than his parts, as his tools play up because of his instincts and work ethic. He's a solid athlete who can impact the game from the batter's box, in the field or on the basepaths.

MOST INTRIGUING BACKGROUND: Cecchini's brother Garin is a blue-chip prospect in the Red Sox system. Unsigned C Benny Distefano's (37) father, also named Benny, played parts of five seasons in the majors. Kaupe is the highest-drafted Hawaiian prep since the Blue Jays took Brandon League in the second round in 2001.

CLOSEST TO THE MAJORS: Reynolds is polished after spending three years in the Southeastern Conference and was the only Mets pick to start out in a full-season league.

BEST LATE-ROUND PICK: In addition to owning a plus fastball, Taylor can throw his tight curveball for strikes. RHP Chris Flexen (14) has a pair of potential above-average pitches in his fastball and curve.

THE ONE WHO GOT AWAY: The Mets never offered RHP Teddy Stankiewicz (2) the full value for his draft slot. Originally committed to Arkansas, he opted to attend Seminole State (Okla.) JC so he'd be draft-eligible in 2013.

ASSESSMENT: The Mets added three solid up-the-middle players at the top of their draft. On the downside, Stankewicz was the highest-selected prep pick in the entire draft not to sign.

2011

The Mets set a franchise record for draft spending (which they broke again in 2012) and came away with several promising prospects, including OF Brandon Nimmo (1), RHPs Michael Fulmer (1s) and Cory Mazzoni (2) and SS Phillip Evans (15).

GRADE: C+

2010

RHP Matt Harvey (1) was spectacular at times in his big league debut last summer. LHP Josh Edgin (30) also raced to Citi Field, and OFs Cory Vaughn (4) and Matt den Dekker (5) and RHP Jake deGrom (9) could get there as well.

GRADE: B+

2009

New York didn't have a first-round pick and its top two choices, LHP Steve Matz (2) and SS Robbie Shields (3), were sidetracked by Tommy John surgery. There may not be a big leaguer in this bunch.

GRADE: F

2008

With three picks before the second round, the Mets found one regular (1B Ike Davis, 1) but whiffed on oft-injured 2B Reese Havens (1) and RHP Brad Holt (1s). In later rounds, they grabbed four complementary big leaguers in OF Kirk Nieuwenhuis (3), 1B/2B Josh Satin (6) and RHPs Collin McHugh (18) and Chris Schwinden (22).

GRADE: B

Draft analysis by Conor Glassey (2012) and Jim Callis (2008-11).
Numbers in parentheses indicate draft rounds.

1 ZACK WHEELER, RHP

Born: May 30, 1990. **B-T:** R-R. **Ht.:** 6-4. **Wt.:** 185.
Drafted: HS—Dallas, Ga., 2009 (1st round). **Signed by:** Sean O'Connor (Giants).

BA GRADE
65
MEDIUM

MIKE JANES

The Giants know a thing or three about drafting high school pitchers in the first round. Matt Cain (25th overall, 2002) and Madison Bumgarner (10th overall, 2007) have helped pitch San Francisco to World Series titles in two of the past three seasons. Taken sixth overall in 2009 out of East Paulding High in the metro Atlanta area, Wheeler might have joined that duo in the Giants rotation had he not been sent to the Mets for Carlos Beltran at the 2011 trade deadline. Shortly before the deal, Wheeler reverted to his high school pitching mechanics—highlighted by a higher kick and faster tempo—and began to rein in the high walk rate that had plagued him as a pro. He dominated Double-A competition with Binghamton in 2012, leading Eastern League starters by striking out 25 percent of batters faced while ranking fourth in both opponent average (.225) and WHIP (1.16). Though his control regressed following an August promotion to Triple-A Buffalo, Wheeler continued to miss bats and keep the ball in the park, allowing just four homers in 25 starts on the year.

Since his trade to the Mets, Wheeler has blossomed into one of the top pitching prospects in the game. His fastball sits at 94-95 mph and tops out at 98, playing up thanks to an easy arm action and late life that often causes batters to take defensive swings. He throws downhill from a lanky 6-foot-4 frame, making it difficult—particularly for righthanders—to lift the ball. Righties batted just .204/.259/.271 against him last season. He shows a good feel for changing speeds on his fastball and for mixing in a two-seamer that runs away from lefties. Wheeler owes his breakthrough success largely to growth in three areas: health, control and repertoire. He learned to manage the persistent soreness in the middle finger of his pitching hand—caused by a fingernail avulsion—and established a career high with 149 innings in 2012. His walk rate has decreased from 5.2 per nine innings in the Giants system to 3.3 with the Mets, and he has added a slider and a changeup. Wheeler relied more on a power curveball as a Giant, but he now turns equally to an upper-80s slider with plus potential. He still mixes in a sharp high-70s curve that bottoms out, and he also has the makings of an average changeup for which he's trying to find the perfect grip. He's remarkably efficient for a young power pitcher, averaging six innings per start in 2012, and he also excels at holding runners. Just eight of 19 basestealers succeeded against him last season.

Matt Harvey electrified Mets observers with a power arsenal during his rookie season in 2012, and Wheeler could produce similar results when he makes his big league debut in 2013. He may get some more time in Triple-A first. He has a classic No. 2 starter profile with a plus fastball and breaking ball, and at least an average third pitch and average command. Health permitting, he and Harvey could front New York's rotation as soon as 2014.

SCOUTING GRADES

Fastball: 70.   **Control:** 60.
Slider: 60.   **Command:** 55.
Changeup: 50.

Based on 20-80 scouting scale, where 50 represents major league average, and future projection rather than present tools.

Year	Club (League)	Class	W	L	ERA	G	GS	CG	SV	IP	H	HR	BB	SO	K/9	WHIP	AVG
2010	Augusta (SAL)	LoA	3	3	3.99	21	13	0	0	59	47	0	38	70	10.7	1.45	.218
2011	San Jose (CAL)	HiA	7	5	3.99	16	16	0	0	88	74	7	47	98	10.0	1.38	.224
	St. Lucie (FSL)	HiA	2	2	2.00	6	6	0	0	27	26	0	5	31	10.3	1.15	.252
2012	Binghamton (EL)	AA	10	6	3.26	19	19	1	0	116	92	2	43	117	9.1	1.16	.225
	Buffalo (IL)	AAA	2	2	3.27	6	6	1	0	33	23	2	16	31	8.5	1.18	.205
Minor League Totals			24	18	3.49	68	60	2	0	323	262	11	149	347	9.7	1.27	.224

2 GAVIN CECCHINI, SS

TONY FARLOW

Born: Dec. 22, 1993. **B-T:** R-R. **Ht.:** 6-1. **Wt.:** 180. **Drafted:** HS—Lake Charles, La., 2012 (1st round). **Signed by:** Tommy Jackson.

Cecchini got $2.3 million as the 12th overall pick in the 2012 draft, going three rounds earlier than his brother Garin went to the Red Sox in 2010. Their father Glenn coached both brothers at Barbe High in Lake Charles, La. An errant pitch broke the tip of Gavin's right middle finger on Aug. 1, forcing him to DH for the rest of his pro debut. A strong fundamental player and intense competitor, Cecchini possesses the footwork, hands and range to be a solid shortstop, but he'll need to further develop his average (though accurate) arm to seal the deal. The coordination and footwork he displays in the field help him in the batter's box, where he's a line-drive hitter with a middle-of-the-field approach and feel for contact. Some evaluators would like to see Cecchini tone down the moving parts in his swing to get in better position to hit. Some believe he'll hit for more power as his body matures, perhaps topping out near 10 homers annually. He has average speed and makes smart decisions on the bases. Cecchini's work habits and passion made him attractive to the Mets, who see him as a starting shortstop and top-of-the-lineup hitter. His maturity makes him a strong candidate to open his first full pro season at low Class A Savannah.

BA GRADE
55
HIGH

Year	Club (League)	Class	AVG	G	AB	R	H	2B	3B	HR	RBI	BB	SO	SB	CS	OBP	SLG
2012	Kingsport (APP)	R	.246	53	191	21	47	9	2	1	22	18	43	5	4	.311	.330
	Brooklyn (NYP)	SS	.000	5	5	2	0	0	0	0	0	0	1	0	0	.167	.000
Minor League Totals			.240	58	196	23	47	9	2	1	22	18	44	5	4	.307	.321

3 BRANDON NIMMO, OF

Born: March 27, 1993. **B-T:** L-R. **Ht.:** 6-3. **Wt.:** 185. **Drafted:** HS—Cheyenne, Wyo., 2011 (1st round). **Signed by:** Jim Reeves.

The first Wyoming high school player ever selected in the first round, Nimmo signed for $2.1 million as the 13th pick in the 2011 draft. He showed promise in the short-season New York-Penn League last summer, ranking second with 46 walks and third with 28 extra-base hits, but also ample rawness, finishing second with 78 strikeouts. Scouts who saw Nimmo at the very beginning or end of the NY-P season might have come away unimpressed, but he hit .309/.402/.494 over a 41-game midseason stretch while showcasing premium bat speed and a discerning approach. In fact, he may let too many hittable pitches pass at this stage. Though he swings and misses too much—especially versus lefties—his command of the strike zone gives him a chance to hit for solid average and at least plus power. Despite leading NY-P outfielders with 152 putouts, Nimmo showed fringy speed down the line, stole only one base and didn't make great reads off the bat in center field. He throws OK and could handle right field if his instincts don't improve with experience. The Mets rave about Nimmo's preparation and mental toughness, and they envision him as a center-field regular with average to plus tools across the board. He's ready for a full-season assignment in low Class A.

BA GRADE
55
EXTREME

Year	Club (League)	Class	AVG	G	AB	R	H	2B	3B	HR	RBI	BB	SO	SB	CS	OBP	SLG
2011	Mets (GCL)	R	.241	7	29	5	7	0	0	2	4	3	9	0	0	.313	.448
	Kingsport (APP)	R	.111	3	9	0	1	0	0	0	0	3	5	0	0	.333	.111
2012	Brooklyn (NYP)	SS	.248	69	266	41	66	20	2	6	40	46	78	1	5	.372	.406
Minor League Totals			.243	79	304	46	74	20	2	8	44	52	92	1	5	.365	.401

4 LUIS MATEO, RHP

Born: March 22, 1990. **B-T:** R-R. **Ht.:** 6-3. **Wt.:** 185. **Signed:** Dominican Republic, 2011. **Signed by:** Rafael Perez/Ismael Cruz/Sandy Rosario.

Contracts Mateo signed with the Giants ($625,000 in 2008) and Padres ($300,000 later that year) were dissolved following revelations of, respectively, bone chips in his elbow and a falsified age. MLB suspended Mateo for one year when it learned he was two years older than initially believed. The Mets signed him for $150,000 in April 2011, shortly after his reinstatement. He has been old for his leagues after missing three seasons while sorting out his affairs, but he led the New York-Penn League with 85 strikeouts and finished second with a 0.90 WHIP in 2012. Mateo brandishes two pitches that project as plus weapons. He tops out near 97 mph and typically ranges from 92-95 with a fastball he leverages down in the zone. His slider is his best pitch, touching 90 mph and featuring tight, late break. His athleticism allows him to find the strike zone regularly—he walked nine batters in 12 starts—and he'll need to rely on it to help him refine a fringy changeup that he doesn't throw much at this stage. Mateo's combination of uncommon arm strength and control give him a

BA GRADE
50
HIGH

legitimate shot to develop into a mid-rotation starter or shutdown closer. He'll remain a starter in 2013, when the Mets may begin to push him more aggressively considering he's 23. He figures to open the season in low Class A.

Year	Club (League)	Class	W	L	ERA	G	GS	CG	SV	IP	H	HR	BB	SO	K/9	WHIP	AVG
2011	Mets1 (DSL)	R	6	1	2.00	13	13	0	0	63	44	1	5	80	11.4	0.78	.194
2012	Brooklyn (NYP)	SS	4	5	2.45	12	12	0	0	73	57	2	9	85	10.4	0.90	.210
Minor League Totals			10	6	2.24	25	25	0	0	136	101	3	14	165	10.9	0.84	.202

5 RAFAEL MONTERO, RHP

Born: Oct. 17, 1990. **B-T:** R-R. **Ht.:** 6-0. **Wt.:** 170. **Signed:** Dominican Republic, 2011. **Signed by:** Rafael Perez/Ismael Cruz/Gerardo Cabrera.

Since turning pro at an older age (20) than most Dominican signees, Montero has moved quickly. In his introduction to full-season ball in 2012, he mastered two Class A levels and ranked second in the minors in WHIP (0.94), fifth in K-BB ratio (5.8) and eighth in ERA (2.36). The Mets shut Montero down following his Aug. 7 start after he reached his innings limit. Montero has good stuff across the board and even better command, making him a starter prospect despite a small, thin frame. He pitches at 90-93 mph and rears back for 95 when he needs it, locating his running fastball wherever he wants thanks to a simple, repeatable delivery. Montero pitches backward at times because he trusts his slider and changeup. His breaking ball sweeps across the zone and features hard break at 82-84 mph. His mid-80s changeup has fade and usually grades as average. He shows dogged determination to improve the pitch, throwing it each time out. The Mets rave about his even demeanor. New York bypassed Matt Harvey and Zack Wheeler to name Montero their minor league pitcher of the year in 2012, indicating the faith they have in his feel for pitching and capacity to improve. Scouts see his upside as a No. 3 starter or quality reliever. He'll reach Double-A at some point in 2013.

Year	Club (League)	Class	W	L	ERA	G	GS	CG	SV	IP	H	HR	BB	SO	K/9	WHIP	AVG
2011	Mets1 (DSL)	R	1	1	1.00	4	4	0	0	18	7	1	0	20	10.0	0.39	.119
	Mets (GCL)	R	1	2	1.45	7	4	0	1	31	28	0	6	32	9.3	1.10	.228
	Kingsport (APP)	R	2	1	4.24	4	4	0	0	17	17	2	6	9	4.8	1.35	.258
	Brooklyn (NYP)	SS	1	0	3.60	2	0	0	0	5	3	1	1	5	9.0	0.80	.176
2012	Savannah (SAL)	LoA	6	3	2.52	12	12	0	0	71	61	4	8	54	6.8	0.97	.223
	St. Lucie (FSL)	HiA	5	2	2.13	8	8	1	0	51	35	2	11	56	9.9	0.91	.196
Minor League Totals			16	9	2.28	37	32	1	1	193	151	10	32	176	8.2	0.95	.210

6 WILMER FLORES, 3B/2B

Born: Aug. 6, 1991. **B-T:** R-R. **Ht.:** 6-3. **Wt.:** 190. **Signed:** Venezuela, 2007. **Signed by:** Sandy Johnson, Ismael Cruz/Robert Alfonzo.

A fixture on this list (peak chart position: No. 2 after the 2008-10 seasons) since signing out of Venezuela for $750,000 in 2007, Flores turned in his best season yet in 2012. He finished the year in Double-A and established career highs for homers (18) and OPS (.827). Flores' supreme hand-eye coordination and ability to let the ball travel deep typically yield high batting averages and contact rates, as well as a natural power stroke to right-center field. He has learned to turn on more inner-half fastballs with experience, pulling 15 of his 18 homers last season to left field. Developing a more patient approach resulted in more fastballs in hitter's counts in 2012, as well as the best walk and strikeout rates of his career. Despite well below-average speed, Flores played exclusively at shortstop through his first four seasons, but he spent most of his time at third base in 2012. He has sure hands and a strong arm, but his lack of first-step quickness will be an issue wherever he plays. Flores can hit for average, but he may stop short of having profile power for first base or acceptable quickness to play third base or left field. With a strong showing at the Mets' new Triple-A Las Vegas affiliate, he could get his first taste of the majors in 2013.

Year	Club (League)	Class	AVG	G	AB	R	H	2B	3B	HR	RBI	BB	SO	SB	CS	OBP	SLG
2008	Kingsport (APP)	R	.310	59	245	36	76	12	4	8	41	12	28	2	1	.352	.490
	Savannah (SAL)	LoA	.400	1	5	1	2	0	0	0	0	0	2	0	0	.400	.400
	Brooklyn (NYP)	SS	.267	8	30	3	8	1	0	0	1	1	7	0	0	.290	.300
2009	Savannah (SAL)	LoA	.264	125	488	44	129	20	2	3	36	22	72	3	3	.305	.332
2010	Savannah (SAL)	LoA	.278	66	277	30	77	18	2	7	44	23	37	2	1	.342	.433
	St. Lucie (FSL)	HiA	.300	67	277	32	83	18	1	4	40	9	40	2	4	.324	.415
2011	St. Lucie (FSL)	HiA	.269	133	516	52	139	26	2	9	81	27	68	2	2	.309	.380
2012	St. Lucie (FSL)	HiA	.289	64	242	31	70	12	0	10	42	18	30	3	2	.336	.463
	Binghamton (EL)	AA	.311	66	251	37	78	18	2	8	33	20	30	0	0	.361	.494
Minor League Totals			.284	589	2331	266	662	125	13	49	318	132	314	14	13	.327	.412

7 MICHAEL FULMER, RHP

Born: March 15, 1993. **B-T:** R-R. **Ht.:** 6-3. **Wt.:** 200. **Drafted:** HS—Edmond, Okla., 2011 (1st round supplemental). **Signed by:** Steve Gossett.

Fulmer pitched just five innings in the Gulf Coast League after signing for $937,500 in the 2011 draft, but he had no trouble adjusting to a pro routine in 2012. He spent all season in the low Class A Savannah rotation, notching a 2.20 ERA with 57 strikeouts in 57 innings during the second half. Fulmer's power approach plays exceptionally well when he keeps the ball down in the strike zone. His 92-93 mph fastball features heavy life and tailing action, and his slider could be a plus pitch based on its tight rotation and depth. He is learning to trust his changeup, which is too firm in the mid-80s. Though Fulmer tops out near 95 mph and holds his velocity, he gets in trouble when he leaves the ball out over the plate. Scouts are mixed as to whether he'll refine his delivery enough to develop more than fringy command. He presently throws slightly across his body and off a stiff front side. Concerns about Fulmer's direction to the plate and his soft-bodied physique lead some evaluators to project him as a reliever. The Mets are committed to developing him as a starter and will send him to high Class A St. Lucie.

BA GRADE

50

HIGH

Year	Club (League)	Class	W	L	ERA	G	GS	CG	SV	IP	H	HR	BB	SO	K/9	WHIP	AVG
2011	Mets (GCL)	R	0	1	10.13	4	3	0	0	5	9	0	4	10	16.9	2.44	.346
2012	Savannah (SAL)	LoA	7	6	2.74	21	21	1	0	108	92	6	38	101	8.4	1.20	.227
Minor League Totals			7	7	3.09	25	24	1	0	114	101	6	42	111	8.8	1.26	.234

8 JEURYS FAMILIA, RHP

Born: Oct. 10, 1989. **B-T:** R-R. **Ht.:** 6-4. **Wt.:** 230. **Signed:** Dominican Republic, 2007. **Signed by:** Ismael Cruz/Marcelino Vallejo.

An unheralded international signee in 2007, Familia broke out by winning Mets minor league pitcher of the year honors in 2009. He reached New York three years later, earning a September callup and maxing out at 98 mph in a relief role. Though he led the Triple-A International League with 28 starts in 2012, he averaged fewer than five innings per turn and ranked third with 73 walks. Familia holds steady 94-95 mph velocity and touches triple digits with his fastball deep into starts, but a hard-to-repeat delivery and below-average control mean a bullpen role is most likely in the majors. He previewed coming attractions by relying on his fastball and a mid-80s slider with short break as a reliever in New York. He has a sinking changeup but didn't throw it much in relief. Some scouts wonder if he'll need to add a splitter to combat lefties. He's slow to the plate and easy to run on. With a pair of major league-caliber offerings, Familia could grow into a late-game relief option for the Mets. He has ample time to figure things out in Triple-A if he doesn't make the club out of spring training.

BA GRADE

45

MEDIUM

Year	Club (League)	Class	W	L	ERA	G	GS	CG	SV	IP	H	HR	BB	SO	K/9	WHIP	AVG
2008	Mets (GCL)	R	2	2	2.79	11	11	0	0	52	46	2	13	38	6.6	1.14	.232
2009	Savannah (SAL)	LoA	10	6	2.69	24	23	0	0	134	109	3	46	109	7.3	1.16	.221
2010	St. Lucie (FSL)	HiA	6	9	5.58	24	24	0	0	121	117	7	74	137	10.2	1.58	.257
2011	St. Lucie (FSL)	HiA	1	1	1.49	6	6	0	0	36	21	1	8	36	8.9	0.80	.171
	Binghamton (EL)	AA	4	4	3.49	17	17	0	0	88	85	10	35	96	9.9	1.37	.249
2012	Buffalo (IL)	AAA	9	9	4.73	28	28	1	0	137	145	8	73	128	8.4	1.59	.267
	New York (NL)	MAJ	0	0	5.84	8	1	0	0	12	10	0	9	10	7.3	1.54	.233
Major League Totals			0	0	5.84	8	1	0	0	12	10	0	9	10	7.3	1.54	.233
Minor League Totals			32	31	3.85	110	109	1	0	568	523	31	249	544	8.6	1.36	.243

9 DOMINGO TAPIA, RHP

Born: Dec. 16, 1991. **B-T:** R-R. **Ht.:** 6-4. **Wt.:** 190. **Signed:** Dominican Republic, 2009. **Signed by:** Rafael Perez/Ismael Cruz/Camilo Pina/Sandy Rosario.

Signed in February 2009, Tapia got a late start to his career while sorting through a visa issue. He first attracted attention when he flashed triple-digit velocity in the Rookie-level Gulf Coast League during his 2010 pro debut. He showed as much arm strength as any pitcher in the low Class A South Atlantic League in 2012, and for the first time his strikeout rate (8.4 per nine innings) matched his radar-gun readings. Tapia's fastball sits at 95 mph, tops out at 98 and features armside run and sink that completely ties up righthanders, who hit just .204/.279/.283 against him last season. He loves to throw his fastball, but he also has confidence in a high-80s sinking changeup that could be a consistent plus pitch in time. Because of his low three-quarters arm slot, Tapia struggles to stay on top of his low-80s slider. It's typically a below-average pitch that spins rather than

BA GRADE

50

HIGH

bites though the strike zone. His long arm action doesn't prevent him from throwing strikes, but it does make him slow to the plate and vulnerable to basestealers. Scouts love Tapia's arm strength and 6-foot-4 physique, but unless he refines his slider, he may profile better as a late-inning reliever than as a starter. He'll continue gaining innings and experience in the St. Lucie rotation in 2013.

Year	Club (League)	Class	W	L	ERA	G	GS	CG	SV	IP	H	HR	BB	SO	K/9	WHIP	AVG
2010	Mets1 (DSL)	R	0	1	3.09	3	3	0	0	12	8	0	5	5	3.9	1.11	.195
	Mets (GCL)	R	4	3	3.45	10	10	0	0	47	49	0	10	29	5.6	1.26	.269
2011	Kingsport (APP)	R	5	5	3.78	11	11	0	0	50	50	3	16	30	5.4	1.32	.258
	Brooklyn (NYP)	SS	1	0	0.00	1	1	0	0	6	5	0	0	6	9.0	0.83	.227
2012	Savannah (SAL)	LoA	6	5	3.98	20	19	0	0	109	92	2	32	101	8.4	1.14	.227
Minor League Totals			16	14	3.67	45	44	0	0	223	204	5	63	171	6.9	1.20	.241

10 CORY MAZZONI, RHP

Born: Oct. 19, 1989. **B-T:** R-R. **Ht.:** 6-1. **Wt.:** 190. **Drafted:** North Carolina State, 2011 (2nd round). **Signed by:** Marlin McPhail.

Mets scouts saw the quality of Mazzoni's stuff improve throughout his junior year at North Carolina State, leading to his selection in the second round of the 2011 draft. He showed an explosive two-pitch mix as a reliever in his pro debut, then had little trouble returning to the rotation in 2012. He was spectacular at times after reaching Double-A in June. At his best, Mazzoni unleashes 93-95 mph fastballs with tailing action and mid-80s sliders with depth and late break. He has made strides with a splitter that he uses as a changeup, but he'll have to show continued growth after allowing Double-A lefthanders to hit .342/.385/.541 against him. While Mazzoni has above-average control of his stuff, he struggles to locate the ball with precision due to the effort in his delivery. His fastball drops in velocity and his slider loses crispness the further he works in a game, leading many scouts to project him as reliever. Mazzoni is moving quickly through the minors, but he'll need to improve his third pitch and command to profile as a starter. Failing that, he has a future in the big leagues as a late-game reliever. He's on track to make his big league debut in 2014.

BA GRADE
50
HIGH

Year	Club (League)	Class	W	L	ERA	G	GS	CG	SV	IP	H	HR	BB	SO	K/9	WHIP	AVG
2011	Brooklyn (NYP)	SS	1	0	0.00	6	1	0	0	6	5	0	2	10	15.0	1.17	.238
	St. Lucie (FSL)	HiA	1	1	2.57	6	0	0	0	7	7	1	1	8	10.3	1.14	.250
2012	St. Lucie (FSL)	HiA	5	1	3.25	12	12	0	0	64	64	3	16	48	6.8	1.26	.264
	Binghamton (EL)	AA	5	5	4.46	14	14	2	0	81	90	9	20	56	6.2	1.36	.281
Minor League Totals			12	7	3.72	38	27	2	0	157	166	13	39	122	7.0	1.30	.272

11 JAKE DeGROM, RHP

BA GRADE
50
HIGH

Born: June 19, 1988. **B-T:** L-R. **Ht.:** 6-4. **Wt.:** 185. **Drafted:** Stetson, 2010 (9th round). **Signed by:** Steve Nichols.

DeGrom began his college career at Stetson as the starting shortstop, but he finished his time with the Hatters as the club's No. 1 starter. He first took the mound during his junior year, beginning as closer but moving into the rotation down the stretch out of necessity. He had Tommy John surgery just a few months after signing for $95,000 as a ninth-rounder in 2010 and missed all of the following season. DeGrom appeared no worse for the time off while making his full-season debut in 2012. His athleticism and clean arm action encourage scouts that he can refine his secondary pitches and stay in a starting role. His fastball is plenty good already. DeGrom carries 93-95 mph velocity through six innings, tops out at 98 and features solid sinking life. He creates good angle and plane and has no trouble throwing strikes, as evidenced by his rate of 1.6 walks per nine innings last year. His slider could develop into a plus weapon if he succeeds in getting more lateral break on the pitch. That's a possibility because he generates plenty of tight spin now. He'll need to continue honing his feel for a changeup. Though he's much less experienced than the typical 24-year-old pitching prospect, deGrom's feel for a sinker and slider make him a potential No. 3 or 4 starter. He may begin 2013 in high Class A, but look for him to receive ample Double-A experience during the year.

Year	Club (League)	Class	W	L	ERA	G	GS	CG	SV	IP	H	HR	BB	SO	K/9	WHIP	AVG
2010	Kingsport (APP)	R	1	1	5.19	6	6	0	0	26	35	2	6	22	7.6	1.58	.324
2011	Did Not Play—Injured																
2012	Savannah (SAL)	LoA	6	3	2.51	15	15	0	0	90	77	3	14	78	7.8	1.01	.225
	St. Lucie (FSL)	HiA	3	0	2.08	4	4	0	0	22	14	1	6	18	7.5	0.92	.177
Minor League Totals			10	4	2.95	25	25	0	0	137	126	6	26	118	7.7	1.11	.238

12 HANSEL ROBLES, RHP

BA GRADE
50
HIGH

Born: Aug. 13, 1990. **B-T:** R-R. **Ht.:** 5-11. **Wt.:** 185. **Signed:** Dominican Republic, 2008. **Signed by:** Ramon Pena/Ismael Cruz/Marciano Alvarez.

None of the Mets' top Dominican pitching prospects signed at age 16. Robles turned pro as an 18-year-old and spent four years in short-season ball. His development took a quantum leap forward in 2012, when he led the New York-Penn League in ERA (1.11) and WHIP (0.78). He finished the year by authoring 45 straight innings without allowing an earned run, including a four-hit shutout of Hudson Valley in the playoffs. Robles shows supreme fastball command, and the pitch features more sinking life than any other fastball in the system. He ranges from 92-96 mph, throwing the ball to both sides of the plate. Robles repeats his simple delivery and quick arm action, yet he doesn't always get the results with his secondary stuff that one would expect from clean mechanics. His mid-80s slider features more slurvy break than hard tilt, but it plays up because he busts righties inside so well with his heater. He throws a firm, mid-80s changeup that probably will be solid in time. Despite his short stature, he profiles as a starter because of his command and ability to read opposing hitters. The Mets hope Robles shows the same confidence in 2013 that he did down the stretch last year. If he does, he could skip a level and begin the season in high Class A.

Year	Club (League)	Class	W	L	ERA	G	GS	CG	SV	IP	H	HR	BB	SO	K/9	WHIP	AVG
2009	Mets (DSL)	R	5	4	2.91	15	9	0	0	59	47	0	16	60	9.2	1.07	.216
2010	Mets1 (DSL)	R	3	3	3.09	14	12	0	1	67	64	1	13	51	6.9	1.15	.257
2011	Kingsport (APP)	R	3	1	2.68	15	0	0	1	37	28	2	16	42	10.2	1.19	.211
2012	Brooklyn (NYP)	SS	6	1	1.11	12	12	0	0	73	47	0	10	66	8.2	0.78	.184
Minor League Totals			17	9	2.37	56	33	0	2	235	186	3	55	219	8.4	1.02	.217

13 WILFREDO TOVAR, SS

BA GRADE
50
HIGH

Born: Aug. 11, 1991. **B-T:** R-R. **Ht.:** 5-10. **Wt.:** 160. **Signed:** Venezuela, 2007. **Signed by:** Ismael Cruz/Robert Alfonzo.

Evaluators agree that Tovar can field the shortstop position at a major league level of efficiency and skill. The system's best defensive infielder for three years running, he earned a place on the 40-man roster after hitting a career-high .270 and reaching Double-A in the second half of 2012. Thick-legged but not very physical, Tovar ranges well to both sides, plays the right hop with regularity and showcases soft hands. He makes strong, accurate throws to first base and is an above-average defender overall, though—much like Mets regular Ruben Tejada—he's not flashy. Tovar can manipulate the barrel to hit different pitch types and use all fields, but he offers minimal power. He bunts and moves runners well, and he has average speed, so he would fit best as a contact-oriented hitter in the No. 2 spot or at the bottom of the order. Tovar may not have as high a ceiling as Tejada, but he could be ready for a big league cameo in 2013 if needed. If not, Tovar ought to get to Triple-A by midseason at the latest.

Year	Club (League)	Class	AVG	G	AB	R	H	2B	3B	HR	RBI	BB	SO	SB	CS	OBP	SLG
2008	Mets (VSL)	R	.203	49	153	16	31	7	1	2	11	12	23	7	4	.269	.301
2009	Mets (VSL)	R	.289	12	38	3	11	3	1	0	2	5	3	1	1	.364	.421
	Mets (GCL)	R	.243	38	148	21	36	5	3	0	14	8	19	16	8	.294	.318
2010	St. Lucie (FSL)	HiA	.246	30	118	14	29	5	1	0	6	3	22	4	3	.276	.305
	Savannah (SAL)	LoA	.281	44	160	12	45	10	0	0	17	8	12	4	5	.327	.344
	Brooklyn (NYP)	SS	.265	18	68	11	18	2	1	0	6	2	9	4	3	.311	.324
2011	Savannah (SAL)	LoA	.251	131	491	70	123	21	3	2	41	44	53	15	9	.318	.318
2012	St. Lucie (FSL)	HiA	.284	65	218	31	62	17	1	1	23	29	17	12	7	.377	.385
	Binghamton (EL)	AA	.254	57	193	20	49	11	2	0	27	11	22	2	1	.308	.332
Minor League Totals			.255	444	1587	198	404	81	13	5	147	122	180	65	41	.317	.331

14 CORY VAUGHN, OF

BA GRADE
50
HIGH

Born: May 1, 1989. **B-T:** R-R. **Ht.:** 6-3. **Wt.:** 225. **Drafted:** San Diego State, 2010 (4th round). **Signed by:** Fred Mazuca.

The son of four-time all-star slugger Greg Vaughn, Cory has exhibited obvious potential since he was a teenager, and he has made steady if slow progress as a pro. He smacked a career-high 23 homers for St. Lucie in 2012, a total that ranked second in the Florida State League. He also ranked third in the FSL with 51 extra-base hits and fourth with 65 walks, and few question whether he has the raw power and bat speed to profile as a corner regular. Concern stems from how playable Vaughn's power will be if he doesn't tone down his pull-happy approach and begin incorporating his lower half in his swing. Observers reported a more straightaway hitting approach in the second half of the season, when he hit .265/.373/.496. He probably always will strike out liberally against righthanders with good breaking balls, diminishing his chance to hit for a high average. Vaughn plays an efficient right field and can handle center in a pinch despite fringy speed. He has a strong, accurate arm. Scouts love his athletic build and high energy, and his diabetes hasn't slowed him in the least. Vaughn will try to clear the Double-A hurdle in 2013.

Year	Club (League)	Class	AVG	G	AB	R	H	2B	3B	HR	RBI	BB	SO	SB	CS	OBP	SLG
2010	Brooklyn (NYP)	SS	.307	72	264	45	81	14	5	14	56	34	63	12	5	.396	.557
2011	Savannah (SAL)	LoA	.286	68	245	33	70	14	2	4	30	36	64	8	5	.405	.408
	St. Lucie (FSL)	HiA	.219	63	210	29	46	8	1	9	29	23	53	2	3	.308	.395
2012	St. Lucie (FSL)	HiA	.243	126	456	73	111	25	3	23	69	65	114	21	4	.351	.463
Minor League Totals			.262	329	1175	180	308	61	11	50	184	158	294	43	17	.366	.460

15 MATT DEN DEKKER, OF

BA GRADE

45

MEDIUM

Born: Aug. 10, 1987. **B-T:** L-L. **Ht.:** 6-1. **Wt.:** 205. **Drafted:** Florida, 2010 (5th round). **Signed by:** Les Parker.

A $110,000 senior sign out of Florida in 2010, den Dekker reached Double-A in his first full pro campaign but struggled to find hits at the Triple-A level in his second. He has ranked as the system's top defensive outfielder since turning pro. Graceful actions, plus range and good routes in center field make him a favorite of scouts, who grade him as at least a 60 defender on the 20-80 scouting scale. An average and accurate arm allowed him to rack up 11 outfield assists in 2012. Den Dekker runs average times to first base, so he's not a big basestealing threat, but he has plus speed under way in the outfield. At the plate, he can turn on fastballs and drive them for power with a fluid lefty stroke, but he struggles to identify offspeed pitches or hit southpaws, so high strikeout totals and low batting averages will be par for the course. With consecutive 150-strikeout seasons on his résumé, den Dekker looks less like an everyday option and more like an extra outfielder. His glove, speed and power could make him a valuable reserve, a role he may begin filling in the second half of 2013 if he makes a better showing against Triple-A pitchers.

Year	Club (League)	Class	AVG	G	AB	R	H	2B	3B	HR	RBI	BB	SO	SB	CS	OBP	SLG
2010	Mets (GCL)	R	.278	5	18	2	5	2	0	0	5	2	5	0	0	.350	.389
	Savannah (SAL)	LoA	.346	27	104	21	36	13	0	0	15	9	28	3	0	.404	.471
2011	St. Lucie (FSL)	HiA	.296	67	267	54	79	19	8	6	36	24	65	12	5	.362	.494
	Binghamton (EL)	AA	.235	72	272	49	64	13	3	11	32	27	91	12	5	.312	.426
2012	Binghamton (EL)	AA	.340	58	238	47	81	21	4	8	29	20	64	10	7	.397	.563
	Buffalo (IL)	AAA	.220	77	295	37	65	10	4	9	47	14	90	11	2	.256	.373
Minor League Totals			.276	306	1194	210	330	78	19	34	164	96	343	48	19	.336	.459

16 PHILLIP EVANS, SS

BA GRADE

50

HIGH

Born: Sept. 10, 1992. **B-T:** R-R. **Ht.:** 5-10. **Wt.:** 180. **Drafted:** HS—Carlsbad, Calif., 2011 (15th round). **Signed by:** Fred Mazuca.

A projected top-three-rounds pick entering 2011, Evans fell all the way to the 15th round following a flop of a senior high school season. The Mets ponied up $650,000 to sign him away from San Diego State. Evans generates gap power with a strong righthanded stroke, but he's maxed out physically so he must work with what he has. He controls the strike zone well for a teenager and could grow into a solid hitter, though he's a below-average runner and basestealer. Evans rewrote his scouting report with short-season Brooklyn last year, working with infield coordinator Kevin Morgan to improve his lateral quickness and arm strength while showing fluid actions at shortstop. Amateur scouts had pegged him as a future second baseman because of his squat body and fringy range, but now most evaluators give him a chance to stay at shortstop—with average range and an above-average arm—at least in the short term. He may have to share shortstop with Gavin Cecchini if the two wind up at Savannah this spring.

Year	Club (League)	Class	AVG	G	AB	R	H	2B	3B	HR	RBI	BB	SO	SB	CS	OBP	SLG
2011	Mets (GCL)	R	.333	4	15	3	5	2	0	0	1	2	3	0	1	.412	.467
	Kingsport (APP)	R	.364	3	11	3	4	2	0	0	3	1	2	0	0	.417	.545
	Brooklyn (NYP)	SS	.125	2	8	1	1	0	0	0	0	0	0	0	0	.125	.125
2012	Brooklyn (NYP)	SS	.252	73	294	32	74	8	1	5	29	31	48	2	0	.328	.337
Minor League Totals			.256	82	328	39	84	12	1	5	33	34	53	2	1	.331	.345

17 ROBERT CARSON, LHP

BA GRADE

45

MEDIUM

Born: Jan. 23, 1989. **B-T:** L-L. **Ht.:** 6-4. **Wt.:** 240. **Drafted:** HS—Hattiesburg, Miss., 2007 (14th round). **Signed by:** Benny Latino.

Carson's uncommon arm strength from the left side earned him a rapid promotion to Double-A in July 2010, after just a season and a half at the Class A level. He wasn't ready for the jump, and his performance didn't improve much in 2012 after switching from starter to closer at Binghamton. Still, Carson earned his first callup to New York on Aug. 21 following a 10-game stopover in Triple-A, and big league hitters proved not so eager to chase his fastball or slider out of the zone. He didn't strike out any of the 25 righty batters he faced. Tall and broad-shouldered, Carson doesn't do it easy, stabbing with his arm in back and throwing across his body, but he sits at 93-95 mph with sinking and tailing action on his fastball. He throws a slider that shows signs of becoming an average pitch. The combination of pitches served him well versus minor league lefties, who went 11-for-51 (.216) with one extra-base hit against him in 2012, and situational work would seem to be his surest path to success in the majors. He could ride the Triple-A shuttle in 2012, earning big league experience and battle scars in Las Vegas.

Year	Club (League)	Class	W	L	ERA	G	GS	CG	SV	IP	H	HR	BB	SO	K/9	WHIP	AVG
2007	Mets (GCL)	R	1	0	5.00	4	1	0	0	9	8	1	5	9	9.0	1.44	.216
2008	Mets (GCL)	R	1	0	1.57	5	5	0	0	23	11	0	6	25	9.8	0.74	.143
	Kingsport (APP)	R	2	3	1.76	6	6	0	0	31	29	1	18	21	6.2	1.53	.274
2009	Savannah (SAL)	LoA	8	10	3.21	25	25	2	0	132	139	4	45	90	6.2	1.40	.270
2010	St. Lucie (FSL)	HiA	7	5	4.17	17	16	0	0	86	98	5	33	69	7.2	1.52	.287
	Binghamton (EL)	AA	1	6	8.32	10	10	0	0	49	68	7	23	30	5.5	1.87	.343
2011	Binghamton (EL)	AA	4	11	5.05	25	24	0	0	128	154	14	55	91	6.4	1.63	.299
2012	Binghamton (EL)	AA	1	2	4.79	31	0	0	9	36	45	2	15	37	9.3	1.68	.300
	Buffalo (IL)	AAA	0	0	1.72	10	0	0	1	16	16	1	6	15	8.6	1.40	.276
	New York (NL)	MAJ	0	0	4.73	17	0	0	0	13	13	2	4	5	3.4	1.28	.260
Major League Totals			0	0	4.73	17	0	0	0	13	13	2	4	5	3.4	1.28	.260
Minor League Totals			25	37	4.26	133	87	2	10	509	568	35	206	387	6.8	1.52	.285

18 CESAR PUELLO, OF

BA GRADE

50

HIGH

Born: April 1, 1991. **B-T:** R-R. **Ht.:** 6-2. **Wt.:** 195. **Signed:** Dominican Republic, 2007. **Signed by:** Ismael Cruz/Marciano Alvarez.

Like clockwork, Puello performed better in the second half of 2012 (.786 OPS) than he had in in the first (.721), just as he had in 2010 (an increase of 216 points) and 2011 (an increase of 158). This time, however, he fought to redeem a lost year rather than earn a promotion or buttress his prospect standing. A chronic hamstring injury followed by a fractured hamate bone in his left hand knocked him out for six weeks at midseason, and he wound up playing in just 66 games as he repeated high Class A. Evaluators still admire Puello's raw tools, though he hasn't yet made the adjustments to get the most out of his plus raw power. A consistent approach would go a long way. Early in games he tries to do too much, offering at pitcher's pitches and pulling off the ball before toning down his swing in later innings. Puello played more games in center field than in right for the first time in 2012, and he shows solid range at the position. His above-average arm strength and a strong physique still lead many to project him as a right fielder, however. He runs well and stole 19 bases in 21 tries last season, the best success rate of his career. Puello will be tested at Double-A in 2013, and he has two option years remaining to prove he can hit enough to be a big league corner player.

Year	Club (League)	Class	AVG	G	AB	R	H	2B	3B	HR	RBI	BB	SO	SB	CS	OBP	SLG
2008	Mets (GCL)	R	.305	40	151	24	46	6	0	1	17	5	32	13	5	.350	.364
2009	Kingsport (APP)	R	.296	49	196	37	58	10	0	5	23	10	51	15	5	.373	.423
2010	Savannah (SAL)	LoA	.292	109	404	80	118	22	1	1	34	32	82	45	10	.375	.359
2011	St. Lucie (FSL)	HiA	.259	117	441	67	114	21	5	10	50	18	103	19	9	.313	.397
2012	St. Lucie (FSL)	HiA	.260	66	227	36	59	17	4	4	21	7	58	19	2	.328	.423
Minor League Totals			.278	381	1419	244	395	76	10	21	145	72	326	111	31	.346	.390

19 ADERLIN RODRIGUEZ, 3B/1B

BA GRADE

50

HIGH

Born: Nov. 18, 1991. **B-T:** R-R. **Ht.:** 6-3. **Wt.:** 225. **Signed:** Dominican Republic, 2008. **Signed by:** Ismael Cruz/Marcelino Vallejo.

The Mets ponied up $600,000 to sign Rodriguez in 2008, but he hasn't lived up to the price tag or made it out of Class A yet. Only older college players like Cory Vaughn and Zach Lutz can challenge the 21-year-old Rodriguez's raw power among Mets farmhands, however, so that's why he's still worth monitoring. A year after bashing 17 home runs at Savannah, he hit 16 in 83 games there in 2012, then added eight more for St. Lucie to give him an organization-best 24 on the year. Getting to that raw power can be a challenge for Rodriguez, who sometimes goes to the plate seemingly determined to swing at the first pitch no matter what. He likes to jerk the inside pitch to left field, so he struggles against lefties who can locate away, batting .210/.252/.387 against southpaws last season. Though he has the best infield arm in the system, Rodriguez's thick lower half, bottom-of-the-scale speed and general inefficiency (.897 fielding percentage) portend a shift to first base, and that's where New York had him focus his attention in instructional league. He wasn't added to the 40-man roster or taken in the Rule 5 draft, so he'll likely be St. Lucie's first baseman in 2013.

Year	Club (League)	Class	AVG	G	AB	R	H	2B	3B	HR	RBI	BB	SO	SB	CS	OBP	SLG
2009	Mets (GCL)	R	.290	17	62	5	18	3	0	1	10	9	15	1	1	.389	.387
2010	Kingsport (APP)	R	.312	61	250	44	78	22	0	13	48	15	43	3	1	.352	.556
	Savannah (SAL)	LoA	.200	8	30	3	6	1	0	1	11	6	10	0	0	.333	.333
2011	Savannah (SAL)	LoA	.221	131	516	59	114	23	2	17	78	29	106	2	1	.265	.372
2012	Savannah (SAL)	LoA	.274	83	318	41	87	21	1	16	59	29	71	1	0	.336	.497
	St. Lucie (FSL)	HiA	.242	42	153	19	37	5	0	8	24	8	30	1	0	.288	.431
Minor League Totals			.256	342	1329	171	340	75	3	56	230	96	275	8	3	.309	.443

20 GABRIEL YNOA, RHP

BA GRADE
50
HIGH

Born: May 26, 1993. **B-T:** R-R. **Ht.:** 6-2. **Wt.:** 160. **Signed:** Dominican Republic, 2009. **Signed by:** Rafael Perez/Ismael Cruz/Modesto Abreu.

Though he didn't post strikeout rates as gaudy as those of Brooklyn teammates Luis Mateo, Rainy Lara and Hansel Robles last year, Ynoa was the youngest of the bunch (19 all season) and shows the most room for growth. One Mets official said Ynoa has the smoothest, most efficient delivery in the system, while scouts laud him for strong control that could grade as well above-average one day. A lean 6-foot-2, he has plenty of room to fill out and add velocity to his sinking 88-92 mph fastball. Using a high three-quarters arm slot, Ynoa works the ball down to both sides of the plate to generate weak contact early in counts. His average changeup keeps batters off his fastball. His below-average slider needs to be tightened, and he has the aptitude to make it happen. He's attentive and shows an advanced ability to attack batters' weak spots. Given his control and room for improvement, Ynoa might be the system's top sleeper pitching prospect. He has mid-rotation potential and will get his first taste of full-season ball with Savannah in April.

Year	Club (League)	Class	W	L	ERA	G	GS	CG	SV	IP	H	HR	BB	SO	K/9	WHIP	AVG
2010	Mets2 (DSL)	R	5	3	1.99	14	12	1	0	72	63	1	8	35	4.4	0.98	.243
2011	Mets (GCL)	R	2	3	3.00	10	7	0	0	48	51	1	4	21	3.9	1.15	.277
	Kingsport (APP)	R	0	0	4.50	2	0	0	1	8	6	4	0	6	6.8	0.75	.207
2012	Brooklyn (NYP)	SS	5	2	2.23	13	13	0	0	77	61	1	10	64	7.5	0.93	.213
Minor League Totals			12	8	2.41	39	32	1	1	205	181	7	22	126	5.5	0.99	.239

21 KEVIN PLAWECKI, C

BA GRADE
50
HIGH

Born: Feb. 26, 1991. **B-T:** R-R. **Ht.:** 6-2. **Wt.:** 215. **Drafted:** Purdue, 2012 (1st round supplemental). **Signed by:** Scott Trcka.

Plawecki intrigued teams in the 2012 draft as an offensive-minded catcher with barrel awareness and strike-zone discipline. He struck out just 29 times in three seasons at Purdue. The Mets tabbed him with the 35th overall pick—compensation for the free-agent departure of Jose Reyes—and signed him for $1.4 million. He led Brooklyn with seven home runs and faced an even bigger challenge on defense, where he caught perhaps the best pitching staff in the league. The rotation's heavy Latin American flavor was a world removed from the Big Ten Conference, though Plawecki made great strides and won over his staff with his natural leadership skills. His receiving is fine, and his feet and transfer are quick, though he sabotages fringy arm strength with tailing throws brought on by a low arm slot. He threw out 32 percent of basestealers. Plawecki can be tough to pitch to because he has home run power to his pull side, and he's not afraid to take the ball to the opposite field when pitchers work him away. He also has good hit-and-run skills. Scouts who like Plawecki see a future .270 hitter with on-base ability and maybe 10 homers in his best years. He has a chance to move quickly in a system sorely lacking in impact catching talent.

Year	Club (League)	Class	AVG	G	AB	R	H	2B	3B	HR	RBI	BB	SO	SB	CS	OBP	SLG
2012	Brooklyn (NYP)	SS	.250	61	216	26	54	8	0	7	27	25	24	0	0	.345	.384
Minor League Totals			.250	61	216	26	54	8	0	7	27	25	24	0	0	.345	.384

22 JACK LEATHERSICH, LHP

BA GRADE
45
MEDIUM

Born: July 14, 1990. **B-T:** R-L. **Ht.:** 5-11. **Wt.:** 205. **Drafted:** Massachusetts-Lowell, 2011 (5th round). **Signed by:** Art Pontarelli.

As a starter at Massachusetts-Lowell, Leathersich ranked second among all NCAA Division II pitchers with 12.7 strikeouts per nine innings in 2011. As a pro, he has raised that mark to 14.8 per nine working in relief. After breezing through two levels of Class A ball in 2012, he isn't going back to the rotation. Where many lefty relievers rack up whiffs with breaking balls or changeups, Leathersich generates most of his swings and misses with a 91-94 mph fastball he throws downhill with tailing life. He throws slightly across his body and hides the ball until the last instant, which proved to be a tough look for righthanded batters in 2012. They hit just .162/.276/.237 with 83 strikeouts in 205 at-bats. Leathersich sometimes shows tight rotation on an above-average curveball, and he can improve the consistency and finish on the pitch by staying back in his delivery. He'll need to refine a fringy changeup to give him a weapon to combat righties as the level of competition improves. He already has a memorable Twitter handle (@LeatherRocket), and with improved control Leathersich one day could be remembered as a quality reliever.

Year	Club (League)	Class	W	L	ERA	G	GS	CG	SV	IP	H	HR	BB	SO	K/9	WHIP	AVG
2011	Brooklyn (NYP)	SS	0	0	0.71	9	0	0	1	13	6	0	3	26	18.5	0.71	.136
2012	Savannah (SAL)	LoA	0	1	0.75	12	0	0	1	24	10	0	8	37	13.9	0.75	.132
	St. Lucie (FSL)	HiA	2	5	4.13	26	0	0	1	48	41	3	24	76	14.3	1.35	.224
Minor League Totals			2	6	2.66	47	0	0	3	85	57	3	35	139	14.8	1.09	.188

23 MATT REYNOLDS, SS

BA GRADE
50
HIGH

Born: Dec. 3, 1990. **B-T:** R-R. **Ht.:** 6-1. **Wt.:** 200. **Drafted:** Arkansas, 2012 (2nd round). **Signed by:** Steve Gossett.

The Mets prioritized makeup, contact ability and strike-zone discipline when selecting position players at the top of the 2012 draft, and Gavin Cecchini, Kevin Plawecki and Reynolds all fit the description. A torn thumb ligament forced Reynolds off shortstop as an Arkansas freshman, and he wound up playing mostly third base in college. After signing him for $525,000 in the second round, New York shifted him back to shortstop and jumped him to Savannah, bypassing Cecchini in Rookie-level Kingsport and Phillip Evans in Brooklyn. Reynolds draws below-average grades for power, as he's more of a line-drive, gap-to-gap hitter, as well as his speed. One scout timed him at 4.5 seconds to first base, good for a 30 grade on the 20-80 scale. The Mets love his short stroke, strike-zone control and defensive actions. "He's a cool customer," said one club official, "He takes a cerebral, low-key approach to hitting. He's not an anxious hitter—he's just a hitter." Reynolds adjusted after a slow start at the plate and applies instruction well, drawing comparisons to a young Aaron Hill. His lack of quickness might not make him a safe bet at shortstop, though his above-average arm, soft hands and sure feet would fit at second or third base. The Mets expect him to be ready for high Class A in his first full pro season.

Year	Club (League)	Class	AVG	G	AB	R	H	2B	3B	HR	RBI	BB	SO	SB	CS	OBP	SLG
2012	Savannah (SAL)	LoA	.259	42	158	18	41	8	0	3	13	12	26	5	1	.335	.367
Minor League Totals			.259	42	158	18	41	8	0	3	13	12	26	5	1	.335	.367

24 COLLIN McHUGH, RHP

BA GRADE
45
MEDIUM

Born: June 19, 1987. **B-T:** R-R. **Ht.:** 6-2. **Wt.:** 195. **Drafted:** Berry (Ga.), 2008 (18th round). **Signed by:** Marlin McPhail.

When McHugh made his major league debut on Aug. 23, he joined a growing list of Mets big league pitchers drafted in the later rounds from college programs outside the national spotlight. The 2007 draft delivered Dillon Gee (21st round, Texas-Arlington); McHugh (18th) and Chris Schwinden (22nd, Fresno Pacific) hail from the 2008 draft; and Josh Edgin (30th, Francis Marion) is a product of the 2010 draft. McHugh shares a few similarities with Gee in that he mixes and matches four pitches and seldom strays from the strike zone. Where Gee's best pitch is a changeup, McHugh throws with a bit more velocity, as his fastball sits at 91-92 mph with tailing action. He spots the ball to both sides of the plate, forcing batters to consider inside/outside as well as up/down. McHugh's changeup features reliable sinking action, while he induces some righthanders to chase a mid-80s slider that breaks horizontally. Righties hit .202/.259/.320 against him in the minors last year. A slow 11-to-5 curveball functions more as a surprise pitch and is his weakest offering. Though he'll probably begin 2013 in Triple-A, McHugh could capably fill in as a No. 5 starter or middle reliever as needed.

Year	Club (League)	Class	W	L	ERA	G	GS	CG	SV	IP	H	HR	BB	SO	K/9	WHIP	AVG
2008	Kingsport (APP)	R	0	0	4.17	12	8	0	1	41	47	5	16	41	9.0	1.54	.285
2009	Brooklyn (NYP)	SS	8	2	2.76	14	14	1	0	75	61	1	21	79	9.5	1.09	.219
2010	Savannah (SAL)	LoA	7	8	3.33	28	20	0	1	132	139	7	38	129	8.8	1.34	.268
2011	St. Lucie (FSL)	HiA	1	2	6.31	9	6	0	1	36	47	3	14	39	9.8	1.71	.318
	Binghamton (EL)	AA	8	2	2.89	18	16	1	2	93	78	2	32	100	9.6	1.18	.223
2012	Binghamton (EL)	AA	5	5	2.41	12	12	0	0	75	63	4	17	65	7.8	1.07	.228
	Buffalo (IL)	AAA	2	4	3.42	13	13	0	0	74	60	8	29	70	8.6	1.21	.216
	New York (NL)	MAJ	0	4	7.59	8	4	0	0	21	27	5	8	17	7.2	1.64	.314
Major League Totals			0	4	7.59	8	4	0	0	21	27	5	8	17	7.2	1.64	.314
Minor League Totals			31	23	3.32	106	89	2	5	526	495	30	167	523	9.0	1.26	.246

25 TYLER PILL, RHP

BA GRADE
45
MEDIUM

Born: May 29, 1990. **B-T:** R-R. **Ht.:** 6-1. **Wt.:** 185. **Drafted:** Cal State Fullerton, 2011 (4th round). **Signed by:** Fred Mazuca.

Pill's older brother Brett plays first base in the Giants system and has logged 63 games for San Francisco. Both starred at Cal State Fullerton, with Tyler doing so as a two-way player. In that regard, he's similar to fellow Mets prospects Jake deGrom and Chase Huchingson as pro pitchers with backgrounds as college position players. Pill showed remarkable progress in his first season spent exclusively on the mound, going 9-5, 2.31 at two Class A stops and ranking seventh in the minors in ERA. He reminded scouts of Ian Kennedy in college because of his short but athletic build and command of the strike zone, and that comparison fit like a glove last season, as he threw any pitch in any count to keep hitters off balance. Pill works all four quadrants with an 88-90 mph fastball that bumps 92, with the improvement of his secondary pitches helping his fastball play up. He throws opponents off stride with a downer curveball and changeup, both of which grade as solid-average and serve as finishing pitches. He gets in the kitchen of lefties with an 87-88 mph cutter. If Pill develops more velocity, he might make it as a mid-rotation starter, and if not he could have a future at the back of a rotation or in the bullpen.

Year	Club (League)	Class	W	L	ERA	G	GS	CG	SV	IP	H	HR	BB	SO	K/9	WHIP	AVG
2011	Mets (GCL)	R	0	0	4.50	2	0	0	0	2	3	0	0	1	4.5	1.50	.375
	Brooklyn (NYP)	SS	1	0	3.86	7	1	0	0	7	4	0	3	9	11.6	1.00	.174
2012	Savannah (SAL)	LoA	3	4	2.61	9	9	0	0	52	56	3	8	54	9.4	1.24	.279
	St. Lucie (FSL)	HiA	6	1	2.05	11	10	0	0	61	53	2	14	51	7.5	1.09	.240
Minor League Totals			10	5	2.43	29	20	0	0	122	116	5	25	115	8.5	1.16	.256

26 LOGAN VERRETT, RHP

BA GRADE 45 MEDIUM

Born: June 19, 1990. **B-T:** R-R. **Ht.:** 6-2. **Wt.:** 180. **Drafted:** Baylor, 2011 (3rd round). **Signed by:** Max Semler.

Verrett pitched his way out of first-round consideration with a so-so junior year at Baylor, though his performance as a pro has encouraged other clubs to ask about him in trade talks. Like Rafael Montero, Jake deGrom and Tyler Pill, Verrett graduated from Savannah to St. Lucie during the 2012 season and continued to thrive. His slider stands as his best pitch, a well above-average offering at its peak. Verrett throws his slider anywhere from 79-85 mph and shows such feel that he can run it hard in under the hands of lefties or land it away against righties. He tends to fall in love with the slider, pitching backward because the rest of his repertoire is nothing special. Verrett sits at 89 mph and ranges from 86-92 with his fastball, spotting it with precision while mixing in an average curveball and changeup. Scouts can't shake the feeling that he profiles best as a reliever, based on durability concerns stemming from a lanky build (he worked through a shoulder impingement in April), below-average fastball velocity and a heavy reliance on his slider. He'll continue to build innings in the rotation in 2013, perhaps in Double-A to start the season.

Year	Club (League)	Class	W	L	ERA	G	GS	CG	SV	IP	H	HR	BB	SO	K/9	WHIP	AVG
2012	Savannah (SAL)	LoA	3	2	3.06	11	11	1	0	65	57	7	9	67	9.3	1.02	.228
	St. Lucie (FSL)	HiA	2	0	2.09	6	6	1	0	39	30	4	4	26	6.1	0.88	.205
Minor League Totals			5	2	2.70	17	17	2	0	103	87	11	13	93	8.1	0.97	.220

27 DARRELL CECILIANI, OF

BA GRADE 45 MEDIUM

Born: June 22, 1990. **B-T:** L-L. **Ht.:** 6-1. **Wt.:** 220. **Drafted:** Columbia Basin (Wash.) CC, 2009 (4th round). **Signed by:** Jim Reeves.

Ceciliani represents the best chance the Mets have to redeem their 2009 draft. The club lacked a first-round pick that year after signing free agent Francisco Rodriguez, and second-rounder Steve Matz and third-rounder Robbie Shields had Tommy John surgery shortly after turning pro. Ceciliani reached high Class A last year before succumbing to the injury bug. He appeared in just 23 games for St. Lucie (plus 18 more in the Arizona Fall League) between disabled-list stints stemming from a hamstring injury. The same affliction cut into his 2011 season as well. When healthy, Ceciliani continued to improve at the plate, making more contact, drawing more walks and driving the ball more frequently. His swing path is geared more for singles and doubles than homers, though scouts believe double-digit home run totals are possible. Though he lacks true plus speed, Ceciliani displays strong instincts in center field and a fringy arm that would preclude a future in right. New York gained an extra year to evaluate Ceciliani for the 40-man roster because he was drafted at age 18. That additional shot of youth ensures that he'll be right on time when he reaches Double-A in 2013, whether he arrives in April or July.

Year	Club (League)	Class	AVG	G	AB	R	H	2B	3B	HR	RBI	BB	SO	SB	CS	OBP	SLG
2009	Kingsport (APP)	R	.234	42	158	29	37	6	0	2	13	13	31	14	2	.313	.310
2010	Brooklyn (NYP)	SS	.351	68	271	56	95	19	12	2	35	24	56	21	14	.410	.531
2011	Savannah (SAL)	LoA	.259	109	421	62	109	23	4	4	40	52	96	25	8	.351	.361
2012	St. Lucie (FSL)	HiA	.329	23	85	19	28	6	1	1	10	10	13	2	0	.402	.459
Minor League Totals			.288	242	935	166	269	54	17	9	98	99	196	62	24	.366	.411

28 AMED ROSARIO, SS

BA GRADE 50 EXTREME

Born: Nov. 20, 1995. **B-T:** R-R. **Ht.:** 6-2. **Wt.:** 175. **Signed:** Dominican Republic, 2012. **Signed by:** Chris Becerra/Gerardo Cabrera.

Under previous GM Omar Minaya, the Mets never shied away from opening the checkbook for international amateurs such as Fernando Martinez and Deolis Guerra (2005), Francisco Pena (2006), Wilmer Flores (2007), Aderlin Rodriguez (2008) and Juan Urbina (2009). Yet none of them received a larger bonus than than Rosario, who signed for $1.75 million on July 2. As an amateur, he teamed with Rangers outfield prospect Nomar Mazara in the La Javilla youth league in their native Santo Domingo. The Mets love Rosario's makeup. He graduated from high school prior to signing, and his father is a lawyer in the Dominican Republic. He shone in instructional league, with true shortstop actions, wicked bat speed and noteworthy aptitude for a teenager. He has strong wrists and hands, and the ball jumps off his bat. He already generates occasional home run power from his long, lanky frame. Defensively, his footwork is sound and his arm is above average. He's just an average runner, and he may move to third base after he fills out. The Mets previously dropped big money on switch-hitting Venezuelan catcher Jose Garcia, signing him for $800,000 in 2011, but Garcia had a pedestrian debut in the Dominican Summer League in 2012 and didn't attend instructional league. So both he and Rosario could make their U.S. debuts in the Gulf Coast League in June.

Year	Club (League)	Class	AVG	G	AB	R	H	2B	3B	HR	RBI	BB	SO	SB	CS	OBP	SLG
Did Not Play—Signed 2013 Contract																	

29 STEVE MATZ, LHP

BA GRADE
50
EXTREME

Born: May 29, 1991. **B-T:** R-L. **Ht.:** 6-2. **Wt.:** 192. **Drafted:** HS—East Setauket, N.Y., 2009 (2nd round). **Signed by:** Larry Izzo Jr.

Matz began and ended the 2012 season on the sidelines, rehabbing from injury setbacks, but in between he made six electric starts for Rookie-level Kingsport. That he pitched at all was the real news, for the fourth-year pro hadn't pitched in a game that counted since high school. The top Northeast pitching prospect in the 2009 draft, Matz was the Mets' top pick (second round) and signed for $895,000. Plagued by elbow soreness the following spring, he had Tommy John surgery in May 2010 and missed the season. He missed the 2011 season, too, with lingering soreness. More soreness in 2012 necessitated an MRI in May, which revealed only scar tissue breaking apart, so he reported to Kingsport in June with an 80-pitch limit. After feeling his way through three starts, Matz blazed a trail through Appalachian League competition in July, throwing six scoreless innings in three consecutive starts, notching 23 strikeouts against eight walks and five hits. At his peak, he topped out at 96 mph with explosive life on his fastball while mixing in an average curveball and changeup. The run came to an end following his July 26 start, when a bout of shoulder tendinitis landed him back on the disabled list. He spent his time rehabbing during instructional league. New York says Matz has the best lefthanded stuff in the system—with a pie-in-the-sky ceiling of No. 2 starter—but he obviously has much to prove.

Year	Club (League)	Class	W	L	ERA	G	GS	CG	SV	IP	H	HR	BB	SO	K/9	WHIP	AVG
2010	Did Not Play—Injured																
2011	Did Not Play—Injured																
2012	Kingsport (APP)	R	2	1	1.55	6	6	0	0	29	16	1	17	34	10.6	1.14	.158
Minor League Totals			2	1	1.55	6	6	0	0	29	16	1	17	34	10.6	1.14	.158

30 CAM MARON, C

BA GRADE
45
HIGH

Born: Jan. 20, 1991. **B-T:** L-R. **Ht.:** 6-0. **Wt.:** 190. **Drafted:** HS—Hicksville, N.Y., 2009 (34th round). **Signed by:** Larry Izzo Jr.

The Mets looked to Long Island high schools twice in the 2009 draft, selecting lefty Steve Matz with their top pick (second round) and Maron in the 34th round. A Mets fan growing up, Maron has performed well at the plate as a pro with a strong walk-strikeout ratio and high-energy approach. A lefty-hitting grinder, he refuses to give up at-bats, and he led South Atlantic League catchers (minimum 300 plate appearances) in walk rate (13 percent) and on-base percentage (.403) last year. He shows solid raw power in batting practice but doesn't bring it into games, instead focusing on hitting the ball where it's pitched. He keeps his hands inside the ball well and keeps the bat head in the hitting zone a long time, giving him a chance to hit for average as he advances. Some in the organization deem him the system's top hitter for average. Given Maron's approach, his power production figures to be below average, which makes him a tough sell at any position but catcher. He needs to clean up his footwork behind the plate, as SAL basestealers ran at will against him and succeeded 88 percent of the time. Clunky feet and slow glove-to-hand transfers led to consistently poor times on throws to second base. His solid arm strength is fine, and he blocks and receives well enough, but he'll have to coordinate his upper and lower halves to stick behind the plate. He's ready for high Class A, the level at which Josh Thole, a player with a similar profile, first blossomed in 2008.

Year	Club (League)	Class	AVG	G	AB	R	H	2B	3B	HR	RBI	BB	SO	SB	CS	OBP	SLG
2009	Mets (GCL)	R	.293	12	41	8	12	2	0	1	7	7	7	1	0	.408	.415
2010	Mets (GCL)	R	.313	20	48	8	15	1	1	1	7	7	8	0	0	.411	.438
2011	Kingsport (APP)	R	.318	58	201	38	64	8	1	3	24	38	34	4	2	.434	.413
	Savannah (SAL)	LoA	.250	1	4	0	1	0	0	0	0	0	2	0	0	.250	.250
2012	Savannah (SAL)	LoA	.300	93	343	48	103	18	2	5	47	53	73	2	1	.403	.408
Minor League Totals			.306	184	637	102	195	29	4	10	85	105	124	7	3	.413	.411

New York Yankees

BY JOHN MANUEL

Will 2012 be the turning point in recent Yankees history, the year where the heroes of teams that have reached the postseason in 17 of the last 18 seasons fade into the past and force the franchise to forge a new identity?

Derek Jeter and Mariano Rivera have been the two constants in New York, both making their major league debuts when the club started its playoff run in 1995. The two future first-ballot Hall of Famers have aged gracefully, maintaining high levels of play while remaining remarkably durable—until this past season.

Rivera tore the anterior cruciate ligament in his

right knee in May while shagging balls during batting practice in Kansas City, costing him the rest of the season. Jeter fared better, leading the majors in hits for the second time and moved into 11th place on the all-time list. But he fractured his left ankle while trying to make a defensive play during the American League Championship Series, and the Tigers went on to sweep a listless Yankees club that looked very old.

While Jeter's career doesn't figure to be over, there's reason to wonder how well a 38-year-old shortstop will recover from such an injury. The same is true of Rivera, who re-signed as a free agent and will be 43 when he tries to come back in 2013. And Alex Rodriguez's situation became more complicated with the postseason news that he required another hip surgery, clouding his availability for 2013.

The Yankees spent $12 million on a one-year deal for former foe Kevin Youkilis as a stop-gap replacement for Rodriguez. At best, Eduardo Nunez would be a short-term replacement for Jeter. Rafael Soriano filled in capably for Rivera, though he exercised the opt-out clause in his contract after the season. The farm system isn't in position to provide any immediate help, as many of the Yankees' top prospects took a step backwards.

That was especially true of Manny Banuelos and Dellin Betances, who entered the year as New York's best pitching prospects. Banuelos blew out his elbow and required Tommy John surgery, while Betances was bumped down to Double-A and is no longer counted on by the organization.

Yankees pitching took two more hits when big leaguer Michael Pineda missed the entire season with a shoulder tear and 20-year-old Jose Campos worked just 25 innings before being shut down with elbow issues. Both were acquired from the Mariners

The Yankees need 38-year-old Derek Jeter to return from his ankle injury at full strength

in January for New York's previous No. 1 prospect, Jesus Montero.

Recent top draft picks Cito Culver (2010) and Dante Bichette (2011) also floundered, but other position prospects flourished while playing together in Class A. Outfielders Mason Williams, Slade Heathcott and Tyler Austin and catcher Gary Sanchez need more time to develop, but all are candidates to become the first homegrown Yankees to crack the big league lineup on a consistent basis since Brett Gardner in 2008. Another candidate is oft-injured catcher Austin Romine, who may get a shot after Russell Martin's free-agent departure.

Owner Hal Steinbrenner has said he doesn't want to exceed the $189 million luxury-tax threshold in 2014, but that will be difficult. New York spent roughly $222 million on payroll in 2012, and it carries unenviable contracts for declining players such as Rodriguez ($114 million through 2017) and Mark Teixeira ($93 million through 2016). Its top player, Robinson Cano, is a year away from free agency.

The Yankees have signed and developed young core players in recent years, but they traded Austin Jackson and Montero. The end of the 2012 season made it clear that a new nucleus will have to be developed, and soon.

THIS YEAR'S TOP 30

Player, Pos.	Grade
1. Mason Williams, of	65/High
2. Slade Heathcott, of	60/High
3. Gary Sanchez, c	60/High
4. Tyler Austin, of	60/High
5. Jose Campos, rhp	60/Extreme
6. Brett Marshall, rhp	50/Medium
7. Angelo Gumbs, 2b	55/High
8. Manny Banuelos, lhp	55/High
9. Ty Hensley, rhp	55/High
10. Rafael DePaula, rhp	55/Extreme
11. Mark Montgomery, rhp	50/Medium
12. Ramon Flores, of	50/High
13. Bryan Mitchell, rhp	55/Extreme
14. Nik Turley, lhp	50/High
15. J.R. Murphy, c	50/High
16. Jose Ramirez, rhp	50/High
17. Austin Romine, c	45/Medium
18. Melky Mesa, of	45/Medium
19. Dellin Betances, rhp	50/High
20. Austin Aune, ss	50/High
21. Dante Bichette Jr., 3b	50/High
22. Greg Bird, 1b	50/High
23. David Adams, 2b/3b	45/Medium
24. Adam Warren, rhp	45/Medium
25. Corey Black, rhp	50/High
26. Matt Tracy, lhp	50/High
27. Corban Joseph, 2b	45/Medium
28. Tommy Kahnle, rhp	45/Medium
29. Cito Culver, ss	45/High
30. Gabe Encinas, rhp	50/Extreme

LAST YEAR'S TOP 30

Player, Pos.	Status
1. Jesus Montero, c	(Mariners)
2. Manny Banuelos, lhp	No. 8
3. Dellin Betances, rhp	No. 19
4. Gary Sanchez, c	No. 3
5. Mason Williams, of	No. 1
6. Dante Bichette Jr., 3b	No. 21
7. Ravel Santana, of	Dropped out
8. Austin Romine, c	No. 17
9. J.R. Murphy, c/3b	No. 15
10. Slade Heathcott, of	No. 2
11. Brett Marshall, rhp	No. 6
12. Cito Culver, ss	No. 28
13. Ramon Flores, of/1b	No. 12
14. Angelo Gumbs, 2b	No. 7
15. Adam Warren, rhp	No. 24
16. D.J. Mitchell, rhp	(Mariners)
17. Bryan Mitchell, rhp	No. 13
18. Brandon Laird, 3b/of	(Astros)
19. Zoilo Almonte, of	Dropped out
20. Tyler Austin, 3b/1b	No. 4
21. David Phelps, rhp	Majors
22. Zach Nuding, rhp	Dropped out
23. Mark Montgomery, rhp	No. 11
24. Jake Cave, of	Dropped out
25. Claudio Custodio, ss	Dropped out
26. David Adams, 2b	No. 23
27. Nik Turley, lhp	No. 14
28. Greg Bird, c/1b	No. 22
29. Chase Whitley, rhp	Dropped out
30. Branden Pinder, rhp	Dropped out

BEST TOOLS

Best Hitter for Average	Tyler Austin
Best Power Hitter	Gary Sanchez
Best Strike-Zone Discipline	Taylor Dugas
Fastest Baserunner	Mason Williams
Best Athlete	Mason Williams
Best Fastball	Jose Ramirez
Best Curveball	Bryan Mitchell
Best Slider	Mark Montgomery
Best Changeup	Brett Marshall
Best Control	Vidal Nuno
Best Defensive Catcher	Austin Romine
Best Defensive Infielder	Cito Culver
Best Infield Arm	Cito Culver
Best Defensive Outfielder	Mason Williams
Best Outfield Arm	Slade Heathcott

PROJECTED 2016 LINEUP

Catcher	Gary Sanchez
First Base	Tyler Austin
Second Base	Angelo Gumbs
Third Base	Robinson Cano
Shortstop	Eduardo Nunez
Left Field	Curtis Granderson
Center Field	Mason Williams
Right Field	Slade Heathcott
Designated Hitter	Mark Teixeira
No. 1 Starter	CC Sabathia
No. 2 Starter	Phil Hughes
No. 3 Starter	Ivan Nova
No. 4 Starter	Jose Campos
No. 5 Starter	Brett Marshall
Closer	David Robertson

TOP PROSPECTS OF THE DECADE

Year	Player, Pos.	2012 Org.
2003	Jose Contreras, rhp	Phillies
2004	Dioner Navarro, c	Reds
2005	Eric Duncan, 3b	Royals
2006	Phil Hughes, rhp	Yankees
2007	Phil Hughes, rhp	Yankees
2008	Joba Chamberlain, rhp	Yankees
2009	Austin Jackson, of	Tigers
2010	Jesus Montero, c	Mariners
2011	Jesus Montero, c	Mariners
2012	Jesus Montero, c	Mariners

TOP DRAFT PICKS OF THE DECADE

Year	Player, Pos.	2012 Org.
2003	Eric Duncan, 3b	Royals
2004	Phil Hughes, rhp	Yankees
2005	C.J. Henry, ss	Out of baseball
2006	Ian Kennedy, rhp	Diamondbacks
2007	Andrew Brackman, rhp	Reds
2008	*Gerrit Cole, rhp	Pirates
2009	Slade Heathcott, of	Yankees
2010	Cito Culver, ss	Yankees
2011	Dante Bichette Jr., 3b (1st round supp.)	Yankees
2012	Ty Hensley, rhp	Yankees

*Did not sign.

LARGEST BONUSES IN CLUB HISTORY

Hideki Irabu, 1997	$8,500,000
Jose Contreras, 2002	$6,000,000
Andrew Brackman, 2007	$3,350,000
Gary Sanchez, 2009	$3,000,000
Wily Mo Pena, 1999	$2,440,000

NEW YORK YANKEES

TOP 2013 ROOKIE: Mark Montgomery, rhp. His devastating slider gives him a chance to contribute in the bullpen.

BREAKOUT PROSPECT: Greg Bird, 1b. If he leaves catching behind, he should stay healthier and take off offensively.

SLEEPER: Rony Bautista, lhp. The towering 6-foot-8 southpaw will have big stuff if he can keep his delivery together.

SOURCE OF TOP 30 TALENT

Homegrown	29	Acquired	1
College	6	Trades	1
Junior college	0	Rule 5 draft	0
High school	17	Independent leagues	0
Draft-and-follow	0	Free agents/waivers	0
Nondrafted free agents	0		
International	6		

LF
Ramon Flores (12)
Ben Gamel
Daniel Aldrich
Ronnier Mustelier

CF
Mason Williams (1)
Slade Heathcott (2)
Austin Aune (20)
Abe Almonte
Taylor Dugas
Adonis Garcia
Daniel Lopez
Mikeson Oliberto

RF
Tyler Austin (4)
Melky Mesa (18)
Ravel Santana
Zoilo Almonte
Robert Refsnyder
Jake Cave
Alexander Palma
Yeicok Calderon
Kelvin DeLeon

3B
Dante Bichette Jr. (21)
David Adams (23)
Miguel Andujar
Addison Maruszak

SS
Cito Culver (29)
Claudio Custodio

2B
Angelo Gumbs (7)
Corban Joseph (27)
Jose Rosario

1B
Greg Bird (22)
Kyle Roller
Saxon Butler
Matt Duran
Nathan Mikolas

C
Gary Sanchez (3)
J.R. Murphy (15)
Austin Romine (17)
Peter O'Brien
Luis Torrens
Dalton Smith

LHP

LHSP	LHRP
Manny Banuelos (8)	Francisco Rondon
Nik Turley (14)	Cesar Cabral
Matt Tracy (26	James Pazos
Rony Bautista	
Daniel Camarena	
Omar Luis	
Vidal Nuno	
Evan Rutckyj	
Caleb Frare	
Shaffer Hall	

RHP

RHSP	RHRP
Jose Campos (5)	Mark Montgomery (11)
Brett Marshall (6)	Dellin Betances (19)
Ty Hensley (9)	Tommy Kahnle (28)
Rafael DePaula (10)	Zach Nuding
Bryan Mitchell (13)	Nick Goody
Jose Ramirez (16)	Branden Pinder
Adam Warren (24)	Daniel Burawa
Corey Black (25)	Chase Whitley
Gabe Encinas (30)	Stefan Lopez
Caleb Cotham	Jose Mesa Jr.
Jordan Cote	
Rookie Davis	
Andrew Benak	
Dayton Dawe	
Brady Lail	
Taylor Morton	
Luis Niebla	
Cesar Vargas	
Hayden Sharp	

2012

BEST PURE HITTER: OF Robert Refsnyder (5) hit .364 to earn Most Outstanding Player honors at the 2012 College World Series. He's short to the ball with a consistent, strong swing.

BEST POWER HITTER: C Peter O'Brien (2) has solid bat speed and tremendous leverage and strength at 6-foot-3 and 215 pounds. He's not a pretty defender but fits the Yankees' hit-first catcher mold.

FASTEST RUNNER: SS Austin Aune (2) adds plus speed to an athletic overall frame. He covers 60 yards in 6.5-6.6 seconds.

BEST DEFENSIVE PLAYER: OF Taylor Dugas (8) earns Sam Fuld comparisons for his modest size, all-out style and defensive instincts in center field. He's a solid runner with good range and a playable arm.

BEST FASTBALL: After transferring from San Diego State to Faulkner (Ala.), RHP Corey Black (4) showcased a big arm despite being 5-foot-11 and 170 pounds. He worked at 94-96 mph in the spring and hit 100 mph in pro ball. RHP Ty Hensley (1) sits at 92-95 mph and touches 97. New York reduced his bonus from $1.6 million to $1.2 million after a physical revealed shoulder concerns, though he hasn't had any health issues.

BEST SECONDARY PITCH: Hensley had one of the entire draft's best curveballs, an upper-70s breaker that he locates well. RHP Brady Lail (18) spins an above-average curve as well.

BEST PRO DEBUT: RHP Nick Goody (6) posted a 1.12 ERA, seven saves and a 52-9 K-BB ratio in 32 innings while getting to high Class A. Dugas led the short-season New York-Penn League in walks (51) and on-base percentage (.465). 1B Saxon Butler (33) tied for the NY-P lead with 10 homers, then hit three more after a promotion to low Class A.

BEST ATHLETE: Aune had a football scholarship to play quarterback at Texas Christian. With speed, strength and a plus arm, he'll stay at shortstop until he plays his way off. Hensley is an impressive athlete for a pitcher.

MOST INTRIGUING BACKGROUND: 1B Matt Snyder's (10) father Brian and brother Brandon played in the majors, and the Angels drafted his twin Mike in the 23rd round. RHP Jose Mesa Jr. (24) is the son of the former all-star closer. Hensley's father Mike was a third-round pick out of high school in 1985 and a second-rounder in 1988 out of Oklahoma.

CLOSEST TO THE MAJORS: As a short college righthander, Goody could follow the David Robertson playbook. He has natural deception and gets swings and misses with his 90-91 mph fastball and short, sharp slider. Black also could move quickly, especially if he moves to the bullpen.

BEST LATE-ROUND PICK: Lail needs to add strength but has a chance for three average to plus pitches. Athletic RHP Dayton Dawe (15) has a clean delivery and a chance for a four-pitch mix.

THE ONE WHO GOT AWAY: The Yankees loved OF Ty Moore's (25) bat but couldn't pry him away from UCLA.

ASSESSMENT: Assuming Hensley's shoulder is fine, he and Aune give the Yankees a pair of athletic prep prospects. Black and Goody could be the first major league contributors, with the chance to move quickly as relievers.

2011

The Yankees didn't have a first-rounder and failed to sign LHP Sam Stafford (2). But RHP Mark Montgomery (11) is speeding to the majors, and New York likes the offensive upside of two high schoolers, 3B Dante Bichette Jr. (1s) and 1B Greg Bird (5).

GRADE: C

2010

OF Mason Williams (4) is the system's top prospect, and 2B Angelo Gumbs (2) and OF Tyler Austin (13) are two more high-ceiling prep bats. SS Cito Culver (1), a surprise first-rounder, hasn't hit.

GRADE: B

2009

OF Slade Heathcott (1) and RHP Bryan Mitchell (16) have two of the highest ceilings in the system, and just need health and consistency. C J.R. Murphy (2) also is intriguing, while RHP Adam Warren (4) reached the big leagues in 2012.

GRADE: C+

2008

The Yankees didn't sign RHPs Gerrit Cole (1), who became the No. 1 overall pick in 2011, or Scott Bittle (2). LHP Jeremy Bleich (1s), the top signee, can't stay healthy. RHP David Phelps (14) did contribute in New York as a rookie last year, and RHP D.J. Mitchell (10) appeared briefly before becoming part of the Ichiro Suzuki trade.

GRADE: C

Draft analysis by John Manuel (2012) and Jim Callis (2008-11). Numbers in parentheses indicate draft rounds.

1 MASON WILLIAMS, OF

Born: Aug. 21, 1991. **B-T:** L-R. **Ht.:** 6-0. **Wt.:** 150.
Drafted: HS—Winter Garden, Fla., 2010 (4th round).
Signed by: Jeff Deardorff.

BA GRADE
65
HIGH

MIKE JANES

Williams has athletic bloodlines. His father Derwin made it to the National Football League, playing wide receiver for three seasons for the New England Patriots, including on their 1985 team that lost to the Bears in the Super Bowl. Raised in Rhode Island, Mason and his family moved to Florida in part so he could face better competition, and he became a standout at West Orange High in Winter Garden, where he was a teammate of 2012 Astros second-round pick Nolan Fontana. Williams bypassed a commitment to South Carolina after the Yankees drafted him in the fourth round and gave him a $1.45 million bonus, the largest in their 2010 draft class. After earning No. 1 prospect honors in the New York-Penn League in 2011, he broke out in 2012, a season that ended when he dislocated his left shoulder trying to make a diving catch in late July.

Despite a thin frame that has earned him Doug Glanville comparisons, Williams has surprising, wiry strength. He has explosive offensive ability, thanks to a special combination of quick-twitch athleticism, excellent running speed, above-average bat speed and snap in his wrists and forearms. He doesn't look like a power hitter, and at times he doesn't get his legs under him and employs a slap approach. When he stays balanced, though, he can drive the ball to any part of the ballpark, and Yankees officials expect him to hit 20 or more homers annually as he learns to hit from a more consistent, solid base. He has shown the ability to backspin the ball and has some loft in his swing. He has a loose, handsy stroke and excellent bat-to-ball skills. He's a plus-plus runner down the line but his baserunning skills need polish. He was caught 13 times in 33 steal attempts in 2012. Williams is capable of spectacular plays in the field. He touched 91 mph as a high school pitcher, and his arm strength rates as average despite inconsistent throwing mechanics. Aside from inexperience, his greatest weakness is immaturity. One pro scout who saw him in the South Atlantic League in 2012 said he "needed to be humbled," and New York benched him several times for

SCOUTING GRADES

Batting: 60.   **Defense:** 70.
Power: 60.   **Arm:** 50.
Speed: 70.

Based on 20-80 scouting scale, where 50 represents major league average, and future projection rather than present tools.

not running balls out. One club official chalked it up to Williams' being too hard on himself and expressing his frustration with poor at-bats by not giving full effort. He plays the game with flair, which some scouts see as a manifestation of his confidence.

Williams believes he's good and has played like it as a pro. One club official likened him to a more athletic version of former Yankees No. 1 prospect Austin Jackson, combining premium speed and tools with Jackson's swagger and playmaking ability. Williams will return to high Class A Tampa at age 21. New York expects more emotional and physical maturity in 2013. That would help him make the leap to Double-A Trenton during the season, where he could team with the similarly athletic Slade Heathcott in a glimpse of the Yankees' outfield of the future. Williams will race Heathcott to be ready to make the leap to New York if Curtis Granderson becomes a free agent after the 2013 season.

Year	Club (League)	Class	AVG	G	AB	R	H	2B	3B	HR	RBI	BB	SO	SB	CS	OBP	SLG
2010	Yankees (GCL)	R	.222	5	18	0	4	0	0	0	0	1	4	1	2	.263	.222
2011	Staten Island (NYP)	SS	.349	68	269	42	94	11	6	3	31	20	41	28	12	.395	.468
2012	Charleston, SC (SAL)	LoA	.304	69	276	55	84	19	4	8	28	21	33	19	9	.359	.489
	Tampa (FSL)	HiA	.277	22	83	13	23	3	0	3	7	3	14	1	4	.302	.422
Minor League Totals			.317	164	646	110	205	33	10	14	66	45	92	49	27	.364	.464

2 SLADE HEATHCOTT, OF

Born: Sept. 28, 1990. **B-T:** L-L. **Ht.:** L-L. **Wt.:** 197. **Drafted:** HS—Texarkana, Texas, 2009 (1st round). **Signed by:** Mark Batchko/Tim Kelly.

An alcohol problem and troubled home life helped drive Heathcott down draft boards in 2009, but New York took him 29th overall and signed him for $2.2 million. He sought treatment for his alcohol issues after the 2010 season. He has yet to accrue 300 at-bats in a single season thanks to a pair of left shoulder injuries that have required two surgeries. The second operation, on his labrum, kept him out until June in 2012, but he made his time count in high Class A and in the Arizona Fall League. Heathcott plays with explosive tools and effort. He's a consistent 70 runner with a strong frame who's developing above-average power. He has two more plus tools with his center-field defense and a throwing arm that's returning to close to full strength. Heathcott's future depends most on his bat. He gets too rotational, spins off pitches and doesn't keep his bat in the hitting zone long enough. His resulting choppy swing reduces his contact rate, but when he connects, he drives the ball. His all-out style has helped lead to injuries. He will head to Double-A in 2013 to work on his swing issues.

BA GRADE

60

HIGH

Year	Club (League)	Class	AVG	G	AB	R	H	2B	3B	HR	RBI	BB	SO	SB	CS	OBP	SLG
2009	Yankees (GCL)	R	.100	3	10	0	1	0	0	0	0	1	2	0	0	.182	.100
2010	Charleston (SAL)	LoA	.258	76	298	48	77	16	3	2	30	42	101	15	10	.359	.352
2011	Charleston (SAL)	LoA	.271	52	210	36	57	11	4	4	16	19	57	6	7	.342	.419
	Tampa (FSL)	HiA	.600	1	5	2	3	0	0	1	1	0	1	0	0	.600	1.200
2012	Yankees (GCL)	R	.235	5	17	3	4	2	0	0	2	5	4	2	0	.409	.353
	Tampa (FSL)	HiA	.307	60	215	38	66	16	2	5	27	20	66	17	4	.378	.470
Minor League Totals			.275	197	755	127	208	45	9	12	76	87	231	40	21	.360	.407

3 GARY SANCHEZ, C

Born: Dec. 2, 1992. **B-T:** R-R. **Ht.:** 6-2. **Wt.:** 220. **Signed:** Dominican Republic, 2009. **Signed by:** Victor Mata/Raymon Sanchez.

Signed for $3 million, Sanchez hit 18 home runs in 2012 and earned a spot on Baseball America's minor league all-star first team. Sanchez has well above-average raw power as well as a fundamentally sound swing, and he improved his two-strike approach late in the season. With plus-plus raw arm strength to go with solid athleticism and receiving skills, Sanchez has the tools to remain a catcher. He's an erratic defender prone to lapses in receiving, but he made progress in 2012 while throwing out 30 percent of basestealers. As his English improves, he'll be able to take charge more behind the plate. He also needs more experience calling his own pitches. Though he's a below-average runner, he stole 15 bases in 19 attempts in 2012. He played harder and showed none of the lapses in judgment that prompted a two-week suspension in May 2011. Sanchez will return to high Class A to start 2013 and has a clear path to the Bronx if he continues to make progress.

BA GRADE

60

HIGH

Year	Club (League)	Class	AVG	G	AB	R	H	2B	3B	HR	RBI	BB	SO	SB	CS	OBP	SLG
2010	Yankees (GCL)	R	.353	31	119	25	42	11	0	6	36	11	28	1	1	.419	.597
	Staten Island (NYP)	SS	.278	16	54	8	15	2	0	2	7	3	16	1	1	.333	.426
2011	Charleston (SAL)	LoA	.256	82	301	49	77	16	1	17	52	36	93	2	1	.335	.485
2012	Charleston (SAL)	LoA	.297	68	263	44	78	19	0	13	56	22	65	11	4	.353	.517
	Tampa (FSL)	HiA	.279	48	172	21	48	10	1	5	29	10	41	4	0	.330	.436
Minor League Totals			.286	245	909	147	260	58	2	43	180	82	243	19	7	.350	.496

4 TYLER AUSTIN, OF

Born: Sept. 6, 1991. **B-T:** R-R. **Ht.:** 6-2. **Wt.:** 200. **Drafted:** HS—Conyers, Ga., 2010 (13th round). **Signed by:** Darryl Monroe.

Austin was diagnosed with testicular cancer the summer after his junior year in high school, which led to a poor senior season. He fell to the 13th round, where the Yankees stole him and signed him for $130,000 in 2010. Austin had a breakout year in his first try at full-season ball in 2012. Shrugging off a mild concussion that kept him out of the Futures Game, he batted .322/.400/.559 and reached Double-A. He homered in a losing cause in Trenton's Eastern League finals loss. The Yankees' most advanced young hitter, Austin mixes physical maturity with athleticism. He has a short, quick swing and good balance at the plate, usually staying back and trusting his fast hands. His relatively flat stroke limits his home run potential to an extent, but some scouts believe he'll tap into solid power down the line. Though just an average runner, he has the quick first step and

BA GRADE

60

HIGH

savvy to steal 10-15 bags annually in the big leagues. A corner infielder in his first two seasons, Austin found a home in right field in 2012, exhibiting solid range and a plus arm. The game is probably too fast for him at third base, though he'd make a fine first baseman. Austin will begin 2013 back in Double-A. The lack of a young, righthanded bat in New York will open an opportunity for him to move fast if he continues to hit.

Year	Club (League)	Class	AVG	G	AB	R	H	2B	3B	HR	RBI	BB	SO	SB	CS	OBP	SLG
2010	Yankees (GCL)	R	.000	2	2	0	0	0	0	0	0	0	1	0	0	.500	.000
2011	Yankees (GCL)	R	.390	20	82	13	32	8	1	3	22	5	16	11	0	.438	.622
	Staten Island (NYP)	SS	.323	27	96	16	31	10	1	3	14	10	23	7	0	.402	.542
2012	Charleston (SAL)	LoA	.320	70	266	69	85	22	5	14	54	37	68	17	2	.405	.598
	Yankees (GCL)	R	.500	2	6	1	3	0	0	1	2	1	1	0	0	.571	1.000
	Tampa (FSL)	HiA	.321	36	134	20	43	13	1	2	23	12	28	6	0	.385	.478
	Trenton (EL)	AA	.286	2	7	2	2	0	0	0	1	1	1	0	0	.375	.286
Minor League Totals			.331	159	593	121	196	53	8	23	116	66	138	41	2	.406	.563

5 JOSE CAMPOS, RHP

Born: July 27, 1992. **B-T:** R-R. **Ht.:** 6-4. **Wt.:** 195. **Signed:** Venezuela, 2009. **Signed by:** Emilio Carrasquel/Patrick Guerrero (Mariners).

Campos led the short-season Northwest League in ERA (2.32) and strikeouts (85) as an 18-year-old making his U.S. debut in 2011. The Yankees targeted him in trade talks with the Mariners, acquiring him in January 2012 along with Michael Pineda in exchange for former No. 1 prospect Jesus Montero and Hector Noesi. Five starts into the season, though, the Yankees shut Campos down with what they termed elbow inflammation. Campos gave up one hit in his first 11 innings at low Class A Charleston, and his stuff was electric. When healthy, he pitches at 94-95 mph with his fastball, throwing plenty of strikes and showing late life. For a youngster who throws that hard, he has excellent command of the pitch. At times he wipes out hitters with a power curveball in the upper 70s, and his changeup shows flashes of becoming an above-average offering as well. He needs more innings to refine his secondary pitches and polish up details such as controlling the running game. He didn't throw in any games in instructional league, and one club official said "hopefully" Campos will be ready for spring training. That's hardly a ringing endorsement of health for the Yankees' pitching prospect with the most upside. He likely will work his way back in extended spring training and move up to high Class A in 2013.

BA GRADE 60 EXTREME

Year	Club (League)	Class	W	L	ERA	G	GS	CG	SV	IP	H	HR	BB	SO	K/9	WHIP	AVG
2009	Mariners (VSL)	R	1	3	5.73	13	4	0	1	33	38	3	16	23	6.3	1.64	.297
2010	Mariners (VSL)	R	8	2	3.16	13	12	1	0	57	49	0	19	59	9.3	1.19	.231
2011	Everett (NWL)	SS	5	5	2.32	14	14	0	0	81	66	4	13	85	9.4	0.97	.214
2012	Charleston (SAL)	LoA	3	0	4.01	5	5	0	0	25	20	2	8	26	9.5	1.14	.213
Minor League Totals			17	10	3.35	45	35	1	1	196	173	9	56	193	8.9	1.17	.236

6 BRETT MARSHALL, RHP

Born: March 22, 1990. **B-T:** R-R. **Ht.:** 5-11. **Wt.:** 200. **Drafted:** HS—Baytown, Texas, 2008 (6th round). **Signed by:** Steve Boros.

When the Yankees didn't sign first-rounder Gerrit Cole in 2008, Marshall wound up with the largest bonus in their draft class—$850,000 in the sixth round. He struggled mightily before having Tommy John in surgery 2009, but he hasn't missed a start and has gone 26-16, 3.41 since returning. He led Trenton to the Eastern League finals in 2012, topping the system with 13 wins and ranking fourth with 120 strikeouts. New York originally wanted Marshall to pitch off his fastball and curveball. Since his elbow reconstruction, he has found a consistent high three-quarters slot and pounded the strike zone with a 90-94 mph fastball and the system's best changeup. Both pitches have similar sinking action and come from the same release point. His changeup arrives at 77-80 mph and made him more effective against lefthanders (.677 OPS) than righthanders (.724) in 2012. A fairly long arm action makes it hard for Marshall to maintain the release point on

BA GRADE 50 MEDIUM

DAVID SCHOFIELD

his two breaking balls. He still throws a show-me curve early in counts, but his mid-80s slider has more potential. It lacks consistency but flashes occasional bite. It's an average pitch that helps him get grounders rather than strikeouts. Marshall profiles as a durable, sinkerballing No. 4 starter—not the Yankees' prototype prospect but a useful trade chip. He's slated to see his first Triple-A action at Scranton/Wilkes-Barre in 2013.

Year	Club (League)	Class	W	L	ERA	G	GS	CG	SV	IP	H	HR	BB	SO	K/9	WHIP	AVG
2008	Yankees (GCL)	R	0	0	0.00	3	3	0	0	6	2	0	2	8	12.0	0.67	.087
2009	Charleston (SAL)	LoA	3	6	5.56	17	17	0	0	87	98	7	37	60	6.2	1.55	.290
2010	Yankees (GCL)	R	0	0	2.25	2	1	0	0	8	6	0	4	8	9.0	1.25	.194

			W	L	ERA	G	GS	CG	SV	IP	H	HR	BB	SO	K/9	WHIP	AVG
	Charleston (SAL)	LoA	4	2	2.50	13	13	1	0	72	52	2	22	56	7.0	1.03	.199
	Tampa (FSL)	HiA	0	0	4.50	1	1	0	0	4	5	0	0	6	13.5	1.25	.294
2011	Tampa (FSL)	HiA	9	7	3.78	27	26	0	0	140	142	6	48	114	7.3	1.35	.271
2012	Trenton (EL)	AA	13	7	3.52	27	27	0	0	158	151	15	53	120	6.8	1.29	.255
Minor League Totals			29	22	3.76	90	88	1	0	476	456	30	166	372	7.0	1.31	.255

7 ANGELO GUMBS, 2B

BA GRADE 55 HIGH

Born: Oct. 13, 1992. **B-T:** R-R. **Ht.:** 6-0. **Wt.:** 175. **Drafted:** HS—Torrance, Calif., 2010 (2nd round). **Signed by:** Dave Keith.

The Yankees have paired Gumbs with 2010 first-rounder Cito Culver for three seasons, and the converted prep outfielder/shortstop has surpassed his double-play partner as a prospect. Gumbs shook off a slow start and was heating up in low Class A when his 2012 season ended in June with a torn ligament in his left elbow that didn't require surgery. Gumbs still hasn't completely tapped into his offensive potential because his excessive pre-swing movement negates his premium bat speed. With some easy mechanical adjustments, such as a wider base and calming down his leg kick and bat waggle, he should be able to trust his hands and stay back on offspeed pitches better. He crushes fastballs, lashing line drives from gap to gap. He's also a plus runner and the system's best basestealer. Gumbs has made significant growth defensively and is beginning to take advantage of his plus arm and range. He still has some stiffness and hardness to his hands, but as his footwork improves with repetition, he should be a solid defender at second base. Gumbs' aptitude will determine how quickly he moves. He has made defensive progress and now must do the same offensively to develop into the most well-rounded infielder in the system. He'll start 2013 in high Class A.

Year	Club (League)	Class	AVG	G	AB	R	H	2B	3B	HR	RBI	BB	SO	SB	CS	OBP	SLG
2010	Yankees (GCL)	R	.192	7	26	1	5	1	0	0	1	3	3	0	.222	.231
2011	Staten Island (NYP)	SS	.264	51	197	32	52	11	4	3	29	20	57	11	7	.332	.406
2012	Charleston (SAL)	LoA	.272	67	257	40	70	14	3	7	36	18	60	26	3	.320	.432
Minor League Totals			.265	125	480	73	127	26	7	10	65	39	120	40	10	.320	.410

8 MANNY BANUELOS, LHP

BA GRADE 55 HIGH

Born: March 13, 1991. **B-T:** L-L. **Ht.:** 5-11. **Wt.:** 200. **Signed:** Mexico, 2008. **Signed by:** Lee Sigman.

Banuelos was the Yankees' best southpaw prospect since Andy Pettitte. He nearly made the Yankees with a dominant performance in big league camp in 2011, but instead made a career-best 27 minor league starts as his control regressed. He began 2012 in a prospect-laden Triple-A rotation but made just six starts before getting shut down with elbow pain. He had Tommy John surgery in early October. A command-oriented pitcher when he signed, Banuelos saw his fastball touch 94 at the end of the 2009 season in relief. He maintained his velocity spike in 2010 as a starter, but has had difficulty either staying healthy or throwing strikes since. Before he got hurt, his fastball sat at 91-94 mph and touched 96, with good tailing life at the lower end of that velocity range. He also threw a sharp curveball in the upper 70s and a tumbling changeup, giving him two above-average secondary pitches at his best. He had trouble harnessing his livelier stuff and was unable to make adjustments to throw quality strikes prior to his injury. The track record for elbow reconstruction is good, and the Yankees added him to the 40-man roster in November. Banuelos will be just 23 when he returns to minor league action in 2014. If his stuff returns and he learns to command it, he could develop into a No. 2 starter.

Year	Club (League)	Class	W	L	ERA	G	GS	CG	SV	IP	H	HR	BB	SO	K/9	WHIP	AVG
2008	Yankees (GCL)	R	4	1	2.57	12	3	0	0	42	32	3	13	37	7.9	1.07	.208
2009	Charleston (SAL)	LoA	9	5	2.67	25	19	0	0	108	88	4	28	104	8.7	1.07	.219
	Tampa (FSL)	HiA	0	0	0.00	1	1	0	0	1	0	0	0	2	18.0	0.00	.000
2010	Yankees (GCL)	R	0	0	1.80	2	2	0	0	5	1	0	3	6	10.8	0.80	.063
	Tampa (FSL)	HiA	0	3	2.23	10	10	0	0	44	38	1	14	62	12.6	1.17	.230
	Trenton (EL)	AA	0	1	3.52	3	3	0	0	15	15	2	8	17	10.0	1.50	.273
2011	Trenton (EL)	AA	4	5	3.59	20	20	0	0	95	94	7	52	94	8.9	1.53	.263
	Scranton/W-B (IL)	AAA	2	2	4.19	7	7	1	0	34	36	2	19	31	8.1	1.60	.277
2012	Scranton/W-B (IL)	AAA	0	2	4.50	6	6	0	0	24	29	2	10	22	8.3	1.63	.299
Minor League Totals			19	19	3.12	86	70	1	0	369	333	21	147	375	9.1	1.30	.237

9 TY HENSLEY, RHP

USA BASEBALL

Born: July 30, 1993. **B-T:** B-R. **Ht.:** 6-5. **Wt.:** 220. **Drafted:** HS—Edmond, Okla., 2012 (1st round). **Signed by:** Lloyd Simmons/Dennis Woody.

Hensley's father Mike was drafted 66th overall out of high school and 53rd overall out of Oklahoma in 1988 before pitching three seasons in the Cardinals system. The Yankees hope to have more success with his son, who gave up football to focus on baseball. The 30th overall pick in June, he originally signed for $1.6 million but had his bonus reduced to $1.2 million after a physical revealed some shoulder abnormalities. He hasn't had any health issues, however. New York favors curveballs over sliders, and Hensley had one of the best curves in the entire draft, a 12-to-6 breaker in the upper 70s. He has size, athleticism and hand speed, all of which allow him to spin the ball and maintain a 92-95 mph fastball that peaks at 97. He didn't need a changeup much as an amateur and worked on one during instructional league. Hensley still is growing into his frame and needs to add some strength to maintain his delivery and find a consistent release point, which would improve his command. He tends to elevate his fastball and work up and down in the strike zone. The Yankees sent Hensley to their Dominican instructional camp so he could continue working with pitching coordinator Nardi Contreras. Hensley will focus on improving his fastball command and his changeup in 2013, possibly in low Class A.

BA GRADE

55

HIGH

Year	Club (League)	Class	W	L	ERA	G	GS	CG	SV	IP	H	HR	BB	SO	K/9	WHIP	AVG
2012	Yankees (GCL)	R	1	2	3.00	5	4	0	0	12	8	1	7	14	10.5	1.25	.174
Minor League Totals			1	2	3.00	5	4	0	0	12	8	1	7	14	10.5	1.25	—

10 RAFAEL DePAULA, RHP

PINSTRIPE PROSPECTS

Born: March 24, 1991. **B-T:** R-R. **Ht.:** 6-2. **Wt.:** 212. **Signed:** Dominican Republic, 2012. **Signed by:** Arturo Pena.

DePaula has presented different versions of his name and several different birthdates over the years, leading to a one-year suspension from MLB in May 2009, before he ever even signed a professional contract. DePaula agreed to a $500,000 bonus with the Yankees in November 2010, and MLB took 16 months to approve the deal while it investigated. He worked out at the Yankees' Dominican Republic academy while in limbo and finally acquired a visa in March 2012, passed his physical and signed with New York. He made his pro debut with their Rookie-level Dominican Summer League affiliate. He led the DSL with 12.4 strikeouts per nine innings. Most 21-year-olds in a Latin American complex league aren't prospects, but DePaula is different. His fastball sits in the mid-90s and touches 98 as a starter. Scouts also like his hard curveball, which projects as an above-average or better pitch. He hasn't needed it much, but he has flashed a promising changeup as well. DePaula's secondary stuff was inconsistent in his debut, due in part to his lack of experience. But he's physical with a strong, strapping frame, has a clean arm action and repeats his delivery, allowing him to throw consistent strikes. He has big hands and long arms, and he has shown a feel for manipulating the baseball. Club officials are excited about his work ethic and makeup. DePaula is the biggest X-factor in the system and his ceiling is as high as any Yankees minor league pitcher. He's expected to make an aggressive jump from the DSL to high Class A.

BA GRADE

55

EXTREME

Year	Club (League)	Class	W	L	ERA	G	GS	CG	SV	IP	H	HR	BB	SO	K/9	WHIP	AVG
2012	Yankees 1 (DSL)	R	8	2	1.46	14	14	1	0	62	35	2	18	85	12.4	0.86	.162
Minor League Totals			8	2	1.46	14	14	1	0	62	35	2	18	85	12.4	0.86	.162

11 MARK MONTGOMERY, RHP

BA GRADE

50

MEDIUM

Born: Aug. 30, 1990. **B-T:** R-R. **Ht.:** 5-11. **Wt.:** 205. **Drafted:** Longwood, 2011 (11th round). **Signed by:** Scott Lovekamp.

Montgomery wasn't heavily recruited out of a Williamsburg, Va., high school as a position player who pitched a little, so he headed to Longwood, a small Division I school in the middle of the state. He became the team's top reliever, and after the Yankees signed him for $65,000 as an 11th-rounder in 2011, he jumped on the fast track. He finished his first pro season in Double-A and didn't give up his first home run until Manny Machado took him deep on Aug. 4. Montgomery had the system's best slider the day he signed, and some scouts give it plus-plus grades at times. It has uncommon depth to go with low- to mid-80s power, and it gives him the consistent swing-and-miss pitch that closers need. He ranked seventh in the minors among full-season relievers with 13.8 strikeouts per nine innings last year, and not just because of his slider. He has deception in his crossfire delivery, giving his 90-93 mph fastball good running life. He has better control than might be expected for a reliever with length in his arm action. He throws a fringy changeup to help him against lefthanders, but usually his slider and fastball are enough. Montgomery could crack New York's bullpen in 2013.

Year	Club (League)	Class	W	L	ERA	G	GS	CG	SV	IP	H	HR	BB	SO	K/9	WHIP	AVG
2011	Staten Island (NYP)	SS	0	0	2.25	4	0	0	1	4	3	0	2	10	22.5	1.25	.200
	Charleston (SAL)	LoA	0	0	1.85	22	0	0	14	24	17	0	11	41	15.2	1.15	.183
2012	Tampa (FSL)	HiA	4	1	1.34	31	0	0	14	40	23	0	16	61	13.6	0.97	.165
	Trenton (EL)	AA	3	1	1.88	15	0	0	1	24	12	1	6	38	14.3	0.75	.143
Minor League Totals			7	2	1.65	72	0	0	30	93	55	1	35	150	14.6	0.97	.185

12 RAMON FLORES, OF

BA GRADE
50
HIGH

Born: March 26, 1992. **B-T:** L-L. **Ht.:** 5-11. **Wt.:** 190. **Signed:** Venezuela, 2008. **Signed by:** Ricardo Finol.

The Yankees' outfield depth makes Flores a bit of a stealth prospect, but scouts inside and outside of the organization agree he can hit. Some club officials consider him the system's best pure hitter. Flores got off to a rough start last April before hitting his way onto Trenton's playoff roster. He's a disciplined hitter with a good sense of the strike zone. Even scouts who see Flores as an extra outfielder rather than a regular consider him an above-average hitter with feel for his swing. Opinions are mixed on his power, as some see him as a contact-first hitter with fringy pop, while others project him to grow into more power, citing his size 14 feet as evidence of coming physicality. His supporters envision him producing 15-20 homers annually. Flores is an average runner with average arm strength that plays up thanks to a quick transfer and accuracy. A first baseman earlier in his career, he has moved up the defensive spectrum, spending 33 games in center field in 2012 and is well suited for left on a regular basis. After getting added to the 40-man roster in November, Flores should return to Double-A for 2013. He'll likely will play left field, deferring to Slade Heathcott and Mason Williams.

Year	Club (League)	Class	AVG	G	AB	R	H	2B	3B	HR	RBI	BB	SO	SB	CS	OBP	SLG
2009	Yankees 2 (DSL)	R	.256	11	39	8	10	0	3	1	5	11	5	0	1	.423	.487
	Yankees (GCL)	R	.196	51	158	14	31	5	1	0	14	22	35	7	5	.303	.241
2010	Tampa (FSL)	HiA	.250	8	28	0	7	0	0	0	2	0	5	0	0	.250	.250
	Yankees (GCL)	R	.329	43	158	33	52	10	4	2	22	28	22	4	1	.436	.481
	Charleston (SAL)	LoA	.250	14	48	3	12	3	0	0	2	3	15	1	0	.294	.313
2011	Charleston (SAL)	LoA	.265	125	468	59	124	26	2	11	59	61	93	13	2	.353	.400
2012	Tampa (FSL)	HiA	.302	131	517	83	156	29	7	6	39	54	85	24	9	.370	.420
	Trenton (EL)	AA	.400	1	5	2	2	0	0	1	2	0	0	0	0	.400	1.000
Minor League Totals			.277	384	1421	202	394	73	17	21	145	179	260	49	18	.362	.397

13 BRYAN MITCHELL, RHP

BA GRADE
55
EXTREME

Born: April 19, 1991. **B-T:** L-R. **Ht.:** 6-2. **Wt.:** 175. **Drafted:** HS—Hamlet, N.C., 2009 (16th round). **Signed by:** Scott Lovekamp.

The Yankees lured Mitchell away from a North Carolina scholarship with an $800,000 bonus in 2009. He had second thoughts about signing the deal, so New York had fellow righthander and UNC alumnus Adam Warren shepherd him through his first days in the organization. He didn't make his full-season debut until 2012, and his maturity remains a question. But no one questions his arm. He was wild but electric for Charleston and was the team's best pitching prospect after Jose Campos' elbow injury. One club official compares his stuff to that of former Yankee A.J. Burnett, and scouts give Mitchell future plus-plus grades for both his fastball and curveball. Both are swing-and-miss pitches, with the fastball ranging from 92-94 mph and the power curve reaching 81 mph. Mitchell's changeup is still in its early stages, and New York is more concerned with straightening out his mechanics and improving his control at this point anyway. He has a quick arm but doesn't finish his pitches consistently. He overthrows and tends to lose his release point. He's getting stronger physically and needs to get stronger mentally. He made every start last season and more than doubled his career innings total, earning a spot on the 40-man roster in November. He should graduate to high Class A in 2013.

Year	Club (League)	Class	W	L	ERA	G	GS	CG	SV	IP	H	HR	BB	SO	K/9	WHIP	AVG
2010	Yankees (GCL)	R	2	1	3.67	10	9	0	0	42	28	2	22	36	7.8	1.20	.190
	Staten Island (NYP)	SS	0	1	6.75	1	1	0	0	4	7	0	1	3	6.8	2.00	.368
2011	Staten Island (NYP)	SS	1	3	4.09	14	14	0	0	62	65	5	31	59	8.6	1.56	.275
2012	Charleston (SAL)	LoA	9	11	4.58	27	26	0	0	120	107	7	72	121	9.1	1.49	.240
Minor League Totals			12	16	4.32	52	50	0	0	227	207	14	126	219	8.7	1.46	.249

14 NIK TURLEY, LHP

BA GRADE
50
HIGH

Born: Sept. 11, 1989. **B-T:** L-L. **Ht.:** 6-6. **Wt.:** 230. **Drafted:** HS—Studio City, Calif., 2008 (50th round). **Signed by:** Stuart Smothers.

Signed for $125,000 as the third-to-last player picked in the 2008 draft, Turley has made a place for himself in the organization and had his best season in 2012. He battled through blister issues that landed him on the disabled list in May to pitch more than 100 innings for the first time, and made two starts in the Double-A Eastern League playoffs. He has a big, physical frame and delivery reminiscent of Andy Pettitte's. Turley doesn't have the same upside or raw arm strength, but he does have a fastball that sits at 88-91 mph and touches 92 on good nights. He'll cut his fastball and sink it, and his changeup has similar downward movement. He limited righthanders to a .228 average last season. His curveball has solid depth and good shape, showing flashes of becoming a plus pitch. Turley needs to command his fastball better and get ahead so he can use his secondary stuff effectively. He handles the running game well, giving up just 13 steals in 26 tries last year. Turley earned a place on New York's 40-man roster in November. and will open 2013 in Double-A.

Year	Club (League)	Class	W	L	ERA	G	GS	CG	SV	IP	H	HR	BB	SO	K/9	WHIP	AVG
2008	Yankees (GCL)	R	2	1	1.13	4	1	0	0	8	6	0	0	13	14.6	0.75	.207
2009	Yankees (GCL)	R	2	3	2.82	11	10	0	0	54	45	1	23	46	7.6	1.25	.228
2010	Yankees (GCL)	R	0	2	0.84	3	2	0	0	11	11	0	2	9	7.6	1.22	.239
	Staten Island (NYP)	SS	4	4	4.38	12	12	1	0	62	57	0	29	47	6.9	1.39	.259
2011	Charleston (SAL)	LoA	4	6	2.51	15	15	0	0	82	70	8	21	82	9.0	1.11	.224
	Tampa (FSL)	HiA	0	0	6.14	2	2	0	0	7	11	1	1	5	6.1	1.64	.344
2012	Tampa (FSL)	HiA	9	5	2.89	23	21	1	0	112	97	7	44	116	9.3	1.26	.235
	Trenton (EL)	AA	1	0	5.40	1	1	0	0	5	8	0	1	1	1.8	1.80	.381
Minor League Totals			22	21	3.06	71	64	2	0	341	305	17	121	319	8.4	1.25	.239

15 J.R. MURPHY, C

Born: May 13, 1991. **B-T:** R-R. **Ht.:** 5-11. **Wt.:** 195. **Drafted:** HS—Bradenton, Fla., 2009 (2nd round). **Signed by:** Jeff Deardorff/Brian Barber.

BA GRADE
50
HIGH

Murphy made the full transformation into a catcher in 2012, working a career-high 97 games behind the plate and only one game at third base. His offensive production suffered as he spent more time catching, but he generally stayed healthy and still showed potential with the bat. Murphy has made significant progress behind the plate, particularly with his throwing. He threw out 32 percent of basestealers last year after erasing just 23 percent in his first three pro seasons. He has an average arm that usually delivers the ball to second base in about 2.0 seconds. His receiving could use polish, as could his game-calling, and he's still learning how to bring consistent energy and leadership behind the plate. Murphy long has impressed the Yankees with his balanced, easy swing. He's starting to show more pull power, though he's at his best going gap to gap. The Yankees have Austin Romine ahead of him and Gary Sanchez coming up behind him, so Murphy will have to put offense and defense together in one season, perhaps at Trenton in 2013, to establish himself as a future regular.

Year	Club (League)	Class	AVG	G	AB	R	H	2B	3B	HR	RBI	BB	SO	SB	CS	OBP	SLG
2009	Yankees (GCL)	R	.333	9	33	4	11	2	0	1	7	3	8	0	0	.405	.485
2010	Charleston (SAL)	LoA	.255	87	330	46	84	15	2	7	54	36	64	4	5	.327	.376
2011	Charleston (SAL)	LoA	.297	63	256	31	76	23	0	6	32	19	38	2	0	.343	.457
	Tampa (FSL)	HiA	.259	23	85	8	22	6	0	1	14	2	9	0	0	.270	.365
2012	Tampa (FSL)	HiA	.257	67	265	39	68	14	1	5	28	26	41	4	3	.322	.374
	Trenton (EL)	AA	.231	43	147	23	34	12	1	4	16	16	32	0	0	.306	.408
Minor League Totals			.264	292	1116	151	295	72	4	24	151	102	192	10	8	.325	.401

16 JOSE RAMIREZ, RHP

Born: Jan. 21, 1990. **B-T:** R-R. **Ht.:** 6-3. **Wt.:** 180. **Signed:** Dominican Republic, 2007. **Signed by:** Victor Mata.

BA GRADE
50
HIGH

Ramirez was starting to emerge as one of the Yankees' better pitching prospects before stumbling in 2011 in high Class A. He did better in his second shot in 2012, shaking off a rough start to go 6-2, 2.11 with 73 strikeouts in as many innings over the final four months. He missed five weeks in May and June with a lat strain but bounced back fine. While growing by at least an inch or two and adding 25 pounds, Ramirez also has picked up fastball velocity, sitting at 93-96 and hitting 97 regularly. He's the most consistent hard-thrower in the system, and his fastball has decent life as well. Ramirez has made progress with his slider. It's inconsistent, but at times he'll throw above-average breaking balls that reach 87 mph and have tilt. Ramirez's changeup is his most reliable secondary pitch, as it has sink and at times resembles a splitter. Ramirez can be hittable because he lacks deception and fastball command, and more scouts believe he's headed to the bullpen, a role he filled in the Dominican League this winter. Added to the 40-man roster, he'll make his Double-A debut in 2013.

Year	Club (League)	Class	W	L	ERA	G	GS	CG	SV	IP	H	HR	BB	SO	K/9	WHIP	AVG
2008	Yankees 2 (DSL)	R	0	3	4.15	12	10	0	0	39	35	2	18	39	9.0	1.36	.238
2009	Yankees (GCL)	R	6	0	1.48	11	10	0	0	61	33	5	16	53	7.8	0.80	.159
	Tampa (FSL)	HiA	0	0	0.00	1	0	0	0	3	1	0	0	2	6.0	0.33	.100
2010	Charleston (SAL)	LoA	6	5	3.60	22	21	0	0	115	106	3	42	105	8.2	1.29	.239
2011	Tampa (FSL)	HiA	0	5	8.14	6	6	0	0	24	35	3	11	25	9.2	1.89	.337
	Charleston (SAL)	LoA	5	7	4.90	15	15	0	0	79	84	9	32	74	8.4	1.47	.276
2012	Tampa (FSL)	HiA	7	6	3.19	21	18	0	0	99	92	7	30	94	8.6	1.24	.239
Minor League Totals			24	26	3.73	88	80	0	0	420	386	29	149	392	8.4	1.27	.242

17 AUSTIN ROMINE, C

BA GRADE
45
MEDIUM

Born: Nov. 22, 1988. **B-T:** R-R. **Ht.:** 6-0. **Wt.:** 220. **Drafted:** HS—Lake Forest, Calif, 2007 (2nd round). **Signed by:** David Keith.

Romine became the third member of his family to reach the major leagues in 2011, joining father Kevin and brother Andrew. He also had a concussion and back issues that year, and the back problem lingered into 2012, when he played just 31 games. Clubs officials said Romine didn't work on his conditioning the way he needed last offseason, and scouts inside and outside the organization are starting to wonder if he'll reach his ceiling. Romine has tempered his high leg kick in an attempt to get more consistent with his timing at the plate. Scouts used to project him to hit 15-20 homers annually due to his raw power but didn't see the same snap in his bat in 2012. He has lost some athleticism but still rates well in that regard for a catcher. Romine has a strong arm yet threw out just 24 percent of basestealers last year, matching his career rate. His receiving has been solid in the past, though he wasn't as sharp while getting much-needed reps in the Arizona Fall League. He also hit just .222/.342/.286 in the AFL. With Russell Martin gone, Romine will compete with Francisco Cervelli and Chris Stewart if the Yankees choose to use an in-house replacement. Otherwise, he's headed for Triple-A.

Year	Club (League)	Class	AVG	G	AB	R	H	2B	3B	HR	RBI	BB	SO	SB	CS	OBP	SLG
2007	Yankees (GCL)	R	.500	1	2	2	1	1	0	0	1	1	1	0	0	.667	1.000
2008	Charleston (SAL)	LoA	.300	104	407	66	122	24	1	10	49	25	56	3	0	.344	.437
2009	Tampa (FSL)	HiA	.276	118	442	61	122	28	3	13	72	29	78	11	5	.322	.441
2010	Trenton (EL)	AA	.268	115	455	61	122	31	0	10	69	37	94	2	0	.324	.402
2011	Trenton (EL)	AA	.286	85	336	43	96	13	0	6	47	32	60	2	2	.351	.378
	Scranton/W-B (IL)	AAA	.133	4	15	1	2	0	0	0	1	0	3	0	0	.133	.133
	New York (AL)	MAJ	.158	9	19	2	3	0	0	0	0	1	5	0	0	.200	.158
2012	Yankees (GCL)	R	.208	9	24	3	5	3	0	0	5	5	3	0	0	.367	.333
	Tampa (FSL)	HiA	.389	5	18	2	7	0	0	1	1	1	3	0	0	.421	.556
	Scranton/W-B (IL)	AAA	.213	17	61	6	13	2	0	3	9	8	10	0	0	.296	.393
Major League Totals			.158	9	19	2	3	0	0	0	0	1	5	0	0	.200	.158
Minor League Totals			.278	458	1760	245	490	102	4	43	254	138	308	18	7	.333	.414

18 MELKY MESA, OF

BA GRADE
45
MEDIUM

Born: Jan. 31, 1987. **B-T:** R-R. **Ht.:** 6-1. **Wt.:** 190. **Signed:** Dominican Republic, 2003. **Signed by:** Victor Mata/Carlos Rios.

Mesa didn't make it to full-season ball until 2009, his sixth pro campaign. His ninth pro season ended in the major leagues, as he earned a September callup and got his first big league hit after setting career highs in home runs (23) and slugging percentage (.480). Consistent contact has been Mesa's biggest problem over the years, though he shaved his strikeout rate to 26 percent last season, down from 33 percent in 2011. He has tinkered with gimmicky stances in the past but stayed with one basic approach in 2012, allowing him to see the ball better and stay consistent. Breaking balls still vex him at times, but he's less pull-happy and makes better use of the whole field now. He has plus raw power, though he'll likely never be a first-division regular because of his lack of plate discipline. Mesa, who shook off a shoulder injury during the season, is a plus runner and a fine defender in center field. His above-average arm makes him an even better fit in right, and he can handle all three spots. Veteran Andruw Jones signed to play in Japan, so Mesa could provide a younger, cheaper, much faster alternative for the Yankees' lefty-heavy outfield. Otherwise, he's ticketed for Triple-A.

Year	Club (League)	Class	AVG	G	AB	R	H	2B	3B	HR	RBI	BB	SO	SB	CS	OBP	SLG
2004	Yankees2 (DSL)	R	.146	49	144	13	21	5	0	3	10	12	67	2	2	.279	.243
2005	Yankees1 (DSL)	R	.304	8	23	3	7	2	0	2	6	3	7	1	0	.407	.652
2006	Yankees (GCL)	R	.207	40	145	20	30	7	2	3	22	11	45	3	3	.266	.345
2007	Yankees (GCL)	R	.235	49	153	27	36	10	2	3	13	9	55	5	3	.293	.386
2008	Staten Island (NYP)	SS	.221	46	122	19	27	5	2	7	23	4	38	4	1	.252	.467
2009	Charleston (SAL)	LoA	.225	133	497	76	112	24	7	20	74	51	168	18	6	.309	.423
2010	Tampa (FSL)	HiA	.260	121	446	81	116	21	9	19	74	44	129	31	9	.338	.475
2011	Tampa (FSL)	HiA	.167	4	12	1	2	1	0	0	1	3	4	1	0	.412	.250
	Trenton (EL)	AA	.251	105	386	58	97	24	4	9	46	36	129	18	13	.329	.404
2012	Trenton (EL)	AA	.277	88	332	60	92	18	1	14	46	29	75	17	3	.344	.464
	Scranton/W-B (IL)	AAA	.230	33	126	19	29	8	1	9	21	7	43	5	1	.271	.524
	New York (AL)	MAJ	.500	3	2	0	1	0	0	0	1	0	0	0	0	.500	.500
Major League Totals			.500	3	2	0	1	0	0	0	1	0	0	0	0	.500	.500
Minor League Totals			.238	676	2386	377	569	125	28	89	336	209	760	105	41	.314	.426

19 DELLIN BETANCES, RHP

BA GRADE
50
HIGH

Born: March 23, 1988. **B-T:** R-R. **Ht.:** 6-8. **Wt.:** 260. **Drafted:** HS—New York, 2006 (8th round). **Signed by:** Cesar Presbott/Brian Barber.

Unless he figures out a new role, Betances' big league cameo at the end of the 2011 season will be the pinnacle of his career. Signed for $1 million, at the time a record for the eighth round, he always has been a behemoth whose frequent bouts of wildness have negated his premium stuff. Betances still throws two plus pitches at times, with a fastball that peaks at 97 mph to go with a power curveball in the low 80s. His changeup developed into an erratic pitch, average at times and playable when he threw strikes. Betances never has done so consistently, both prior to 2009 surgery to reinforce an elbow ligament and since then. Triple-A hitters wouldn't chase his pitches last year, and a demotion to Trenton didn't help. Betances lacks the athleticism to repeat the release point in his stiff delivery and doesn't have enough savvy to make adjustments. The Yankees hope his power repertoire and intimidating size can translate into success in shorter relief stints. He worked out of the bullpen in the Arizona Fall League but continued to get hit hard.

Year	Club (League)	Class	W	L	ERA	G	GS	CG	SV	IP	H	HR	BB	SO	K/9	WHIP	AVG
2006	Yankees (GCL)	R	0	1	1.16	7	7	0	0	23	14	1	7	27	10.4	0.90	.173
2007	Staten Island (NYP)	SS	1	2	3.60	6	6	0	0	25	24	0	17	29	10.4	1.64	.255
2008	Yankees (GCL)	R	0	1	8.53	3	2	0	0	6	13	0	3	6	8.5	2.53	.406
	Charleston (SAL)	LoA	9	4	3.67	22	22	0	0	115	87	9	59	135	10.5	1.27	.208
2009	Tampa (FSL)	HiA	2	5	5.48	11	11	0	0	44	48	2	27	44	8.9	1.69	.277
2010	Tampa (FSL)	HiA	8	1	1.77	14	14	0	0	71	43	1	19	88	11.2	0.87	.169
	Trenton (EL)	AA	0	0	3.77	3	3	0	0	14	10	3	3	20	12.6	0.91	.200
2011	Trenton (EL)	AA	4	6	3.42	21	21	0	0	105	86	7	55	115	9.8	1.34	.219
	Scranton/W-B (IL)	AAA	0	3	5.14	4	4	1	0	21	16	2	15	27	11.6	1.48	.208
	New York (AL)	MAJ	0	0	6.75	2	1	0	0	3	1	0	6	2	6.8	2.63	.125
2012	Scranton/W-B (IL)	AAA	3	5	6.39	16	16	0	0	75	71	9	69	71	8.6	1.88	.250
	Trenton (EL)	AA	3	4	6.51	11	10	0	0	57	73	4	30	53	8.4	1.82	.319
Major League Totals			0	0	6.75	2	1	0	0	3	1	0	6	2	6.8	2.63	.125
Minor League Totals			30	32	4.18	118	116	1	0	557	485	38	304	615	9.9	1.42	.217

20 AUSTIN AUNE, SS

BA GRADE

50
HIGH

Born: Sept. 6, 1993. **B-T:** L-R. **Ht.:** 6-2. **Wt.:** 190. **Drafted:** HS—Argyle, Texas, 2012 (2nd round). **Signed by:** Steve Boros/Mark Batchko.

As a senior quarterback, Aune accounted for 3,949 yards and 42 touchdowns while leading Argyle High to the Texas 3-A title game. He had a football scholarship from Texas Christian but passed it up to sign with the Yankees for a $1 million bonus. His two-sport background makes him raw from a baseball standpoint. His inexperience showed after signing, as the speed of the game exposed his footwork defensively. His athleticism and natural hitting ability also showed, and he held his own at the plate and showed plus speed. Aune has good balance and plus raw power. He needs to refine his basestealing skills but has a chance to become a top-of-the-order hitter. One club official compares Aune to Shawn Green for his lean, athletic frame and lefthanded swing. It will be a long time before Aune can earn Green comparisons as a hitter, however, so the Yankees will have to be patient. They intend to leave him at shortstop as long as possible, with second base and center field possible future positions. His range and arm strength are solid, but he may not have the hands to stay in the dirt. He will start 2013 in extended spring training before heading to short-season Staten Island in June.

Year	Club (League)	Class	AVG	G	AB	R	H	2B	3B	HR	RBI	BB	SO	SB	CS	OBP	SLG
2012	Yankees (GCL)	R	.273	39	139	19	38	10	3	1	20	19	45	6	4	.358	.410
Minor League Totals			.273	39	139	19	38	10	3	1	20	19	45	6	4	.358	.410

21 DANTE BICHETTE JR., 3B

BA GRADE

50
HIGH

Born: Sept. 26, 1992. **B-T:** R-R. **Ht.:** 6-1. **Wt.:** 215. **Drafted:** HS—Orlando, 2011 (1st round supplemental). **Signed by:** Jeff Deardorff.

Bichette's father Dante made four all-star teams despite struggling early in his minor league career, posting a .688 OPS in low Class A in 1985 as a 21-year-old. Two years younger at the same level in 2012, Dante Jr. grinded his way to a .653 OPS. That was a far cry from his pro debut after he signed for $750,000 as New York's top draft pick in 2011, when he ranked as the No. 1 prospect and earned MVP honors in the Rookie-level Gulf Coast League. Bichette struggled with the heavier diet of breaking balls he saw in low Class A, making lots of weak contact. His bat-to-ball skills kept him from striking out more, and when he did connect, the ball often was swallowed up at spacious Riley Park in Charleston. He posted a .591 OPS at home, compared to a more respectable .713 on the road. Bichette has solid raw power with good bat speed and the ability to put backspin on the ball. His defense made significant progress as he became more comfortable with third base. His quickness, range and arm are all fringy to average, so he's not a lock to stay at the hot corner. He'll likely start 2013 back in Charleston.

Year	Club (League)	Class	AVG	G	AB	R	H	2B	3B	HR	RBI	BB	SO	SB	CS	OBP	SLG
2011	Yankees (GCL)	R	.342	52	196	33	67	17	3	3	47	30	41	3	3	.446	.505
	Staten Island (NYP)	SS	.143	2	7	1	1	0	0	1	1	1	2	0	1	.250	.571
2012	Charleston (SAL)	LoA	.248	122	471	67	117	24	3	3	46	44	94	3	4	.322	.331
Minor League Totals			.274	176	674	101	185	41	6	7	94	75	137	6	8	.360	.384

22 GREG BIRD, 1B/C

Born: Nov. 9, 1992. **B-T:** L-R. **Ht.:** 6-3. **Wt.:** 215. **Drafted:** HS—Aurora, Colo., 2011 (4th round). **Signed by:** Steve Kmetko.

BA GRADE
50
HIGH

The Yankees surprised the industry by signing Bird for $1.1 million after drafting him in the fifth round in 2011. The high school catcher for Kevin Gausman, who became the No. 4 overall pick in the 2012 draft, Bird was considered too stiff and too big to stay behind the plate, but the Yankees were buying the bat, and they're all in on Bird's. They did intend to give Bird a shot to catch, but nagging back pain and weakness in the spring lasted into extended spring training, and he went on the disabled list after playing four games in June. He returned in August as a first baseman/DH and mashed, so he's probably there to stay. He hit his way up to Staten Island, where he finished with a flourish and homered in his last game, and he continued to hit well in instructional league. The Yankees are high on his hitting instincts, bat speed and plus raw power. He has the ability to put backspin on the ball and should hit for enough power to profile at first base. He has a strong arm but lacks athleticism, agility and speed. New York praises Bird's makeup, and he should help anchor the Charleston lineup in 2013.

Year	Club (League)	Class	AVG	G	AB	R	H	2B	3B	HR	RBI	BB	SO	SB	CS	OBP	SLG
2011	Yankees (GCL)	R	.083	4	12	0	1	0	0	0	0	1	4	0	0	.154	.083
2012	Yankees (GCL)	R	.286	17	49	9	14	2	1	0	5	11	13	0	0	.419	.367
	Staten Island (NYP)	SS	.400	11	40	4	16	4	0	2	8	6	10	0	0	.489	.650
Minor League Totals			.307	32	101	13	31	6	1	2	13	18	27	0	0	.418	.446

23 DAVID ADAMS, 3B/2B

Born: May 15, 1987. **B-T:** R-R. **Ht.:** 6-1. **Wt.:** 205. **Drafted:** Virginia, 2008 (3rd round). **Signed by:** Scott Lovekamp.

BA GRADE
45
MEDIUM

Adams injured his right ankle in May 2010, which threw a wrench into the Yankees' proposed acquisition of Cliff Lee from the Mariners. As New York and Seattle tried to rework the deal, the Rangers swooped in and scooped up Lee. What was originally diagnosed as a high ankle sprain proved to be a fracture that proved frustratingly slow to heal. Adams missed the rest of 2010 and played in just 27 games in 2011. He wound up spending another month on the disabled list with a neck injury, but was healthy from mid-May on. Adams has a plan at the plate, works counts and has an effective two-strike approach. He has the solid power to produce 15-20 homers a season. Never fast, Adams now has well below-average speed. He has lost the quickness to play second base and played almost exclusively at the hot corner in the final six weeks of the season. He has enough arm strength and had played there a bit before getting hurt. His intangibles are a positive. With Alex Rodriguez's Yankees future in doubt, Adams could be an stopgap solution. He's headed for Triple-A in 2013 and will be on call if free-agent signee Kevin Youkilis—who hasn't played 130 games in a season since 2009—gets banged up.

Year	Club (League)	Class	AVG	G	AB	R	H	2B	3B	HR	RBI	BB	SO	SB	CS	OBP	SLG
2008	Staten Island (NYP)	SS	.257	67	257	45	66	19	2	4	31	32	57	8	2	.350	.393
2009	Charleston (SAL)	LoA	.290	67	259	32	75	23	2	0	34	35	49	8	4	.385	.394
	Tampa (FSL)	HiA	.281	65	231	37	65	17	6	7	41	26	39	3	4	.360	.498
2010	Trenton (EL)	AA	.309	39	152	31	47	15	3	3	32	18	31	5	2	.393	.507
2011	Yankees (GCL)	R	.429	17	56	13	24	9	0	1	11	5	10	2	1	.469	.643
2012	Tampa (FSL)	HiA	.308	12	52	6	16	3	0	0	4	4	8	0	2	.368	.365
	Trenton (EL)	AA	.306	86	327	44	100	23	0	8	48	38	53	3	1	.385	.450
Minor League Totals			.295	353	1334	208	393	109	13	23	201	158	247	29	16	.378	.448

24 ADAM WARREN, RHP

Born: Aug. 25, 1987. **B-T:** R-R. **Ht.:** 6-2. **Wt.:** 225. **Drafted:** North Carolina, 2009 (4th round). **Signed by:** Scott Lovekamp.

BA GRADE
45
MEDIUM

Warren started 2012 as part of a highly touted Triple-A rotation, and he was the only prospect left when the playoffs rolled around, as Manny Banuelos got hurt, Dellin Betances got demoted, D.J. Mitchell got traded and David Phelps spent most of the season in New York. Warren joined him in late June, failed to make it out of the third inning against the White Sox and quickly found himself back in Triple-A. Warren is a durable, physical veteran whose fastball sits at 90-93 mph and touches 94-95. He pitches off his four-seamer and mixes in a two-seamer at times, then goes to his curveball, slider and changeup. More often than not, the slider is his best secondary pitch, though it's really more of a cutter. He's not overpowering but throws strikes and usually gives his team a chance to win. Warren didn't get a second chance in 2012 after Chicago shellacked him, but he remains on the 40-man roster and will head back to Triple-A as big league rotation insurance.

Year	Club (League)	Class	W	L	ERA	G	GS	CG	SV	IP	H	HR	BB	SO	K/9	WHIP	AVG
2009	Staten Island (NYP)	SS	4	2	1.43	12	12	0	0	57	49	1	10	50	7.9	1.04	.236
2010	Tampa (FSL)	HiA	7	5	2.22	15	15	1	0	81	72	2	17	67	7.4	1.10	.235

NEW YORK YANKEES

Year	Club (League)	Class	W	L	ERA	G	GS	CG	SV	IP	H	HR	BB	SO	K/9	WHIP	AVG
	Trenton (EL)	AA	4	2	3.15	10	10	0	0	54	49	2	16	59	9.8	1.20	.232
2011	Scranton/W-B (IL)	AAA	6	8	3.60	27	27	1	0	152	145	13	53	111	6.6	1.30	.249
2012	New York (AL)	MAJ	0	0	23.14	1	1	0	0	2	8	2	2	1	3.9	4.29	.533
	Scranton/W-B (IL)	AAA	7	8	3.71	26	26	2	0	153	167	11	46	107	6.3	1.40	.276
Major League Totals			0	0	23.14	1	1	0	0	2	8	2	2	1	3.9	4.29	—
Minor League Totals			28	25	3.11	90	90	4	0	497	482	29	142	394	7.1	1.26	.241

25 COREY BLACK, RHP

BA GRADE
50
HIGH

Born: Aug. 4, 1991. **B-T:** R-R. **Ht.:** 5-11. **Wt.:** 175. **Drafted:** Faulkner (Ala.), 2012 (4th round). **Signed by:** D.J. Svihlik.

Black had Tommy John surgery as a high school junior in San Diego and wound up attending San Diego State. A dispute with the coaching staff prompted him to transfer to Faulkner (Ala.), an NAIA school where he could pitch immediately in 2012 rather than sit out a year. He went 11-2, 1.53 there, prompting the Yankees to draft him in the fourth round and sign him for a below-slot $215,000. He had one of the better pro debuts in New York's draft class, and Black's quick arm has impressed the Yankees' pro staff. He touched 100 mph and never dipped below 94 during instructional league. With a week of rest as an amateur, his sinking fastball sat at 95-98 at its best, and he worked around 95 in pro ball. His athleticism helps him repeat his release point and allowed him to adjust his delivery as a pro, eliminating a head whack that worried scouts. Black throws an average changeup and improved 83-85 mph slider to go with an early-count, fringy curve. Black could open his first full pro season in high Class A, and New York will keep developing him as a starter.

Year	Club (League)	Class	W	L	ERA	G	GS	CG	SV	IP	H	HR	BB	SO	K/9	WHIP	AVG
2012	Yankees (GCL)	R	0	0	6.75	1	1	0	0	1	2	0	2	0	0.0	3.00	.333
	Staten Island (NYP)	SS	0	0	2.28	6	6	0	0	28	22	1	8	21	6.8	1.08	.222
	Charleston (SAL)	LoA	2	2	3.80	5	5	0	0	24	18	0	5	29	11.0	0.97	.214
Minor League Totals			2	2	3.08	12	12	0	0	53	42	1	15	50	8.5	1.08	—

26 MATT TRACY, LHP

BA GRADE
50
HIGH

Born: Nov. 26, 1988. **B-T:** L-L. **Ht.:** 6-3. **Wt.:** 212. **Drafted:** Mississippi, 2011 (24th round). **Signed by:** Andy Cannizaro.

Tracy got as much playing time in the outfield as on the mound at Mississippi. The Yankees liked his physical frame and fresh arm, waited until the 24th round to draft him in 2011, and signed him for just $2,000. Hitting 94 mph with his fastball, he pitched his way into the Staten Island rotation in his pro debut and continued to impress during instructional league. He jumped to Tampa for his first full pro season, but he strained his right hamstring in spring training and had an inconsistent 2012. Tracy's arm strength and size are his best traits. His fastball sits at 89-92 mph and he has a feel for locating it inside against righthanders, making them uncomfortable. His curveball and changeup also have their moments. New York worked with him in instructional league on getting better snap on his curve, altering his grip. A wrist wrap in his arm action makes it tougher for him to repeat his breaking ball's release point. He also could use better control and command. He'll join forces again with Nik Turley in 2013, this time in Double-A.

Year	Club (League)	Class	W	L	ERA	G	GS	CG	SV	IP	H	HR	BB	SO	K/9	WHIP	AVG
2011	Staten Island (NYP)	SS	1	2	3.04	17	6	0	0	47	41	1	16	48	9.1	1.20	.232
2012	Tampa (FSL)	HiA	5	7	3.27	18	18	2	0	99	88	3	39	64	5.8	1.28	.249
	Scranton/W-B (IL)	AAA	1	0	1.80	1	1	0	0	5	3	0	3	4	7.2	1.20	.167
Minor League Totals			7	9	3.15	36	25	2	0	151	132	4	58	116	6.9	1.26	.232

27 CORBAN JOSEPH, 2B

BA GRADE
45
MEDIUM

Born: Oct. 28, 1988. **B-T:** L-R. **Ht.:** 6-0. **Wt.:** 180. **Drafted:** HS—Franklin, Tenn., 2008 (4th round). **Signed by:** D.J. Svihlik.

The younger brother of Orioles minor league catcher Caleb Joseph, Corban reached Triple-A for the first time in 2012 and posted career bests in home runs (15), slugging (.465) and OPS (.840). Joseph has an easy line-drive stroke, swings at strikes and draws walks. Scouts fret about the movement in his hands before he swings, yet he makes consistent hard contact and added loft power last season. He has significant limitations, though, and doesn't run well, with fringy range and fair footwork. Most scouts consider him a below-average defender at second base. New York has worked him at third base, including in big league camp last spring, and he has taken fly balls in the outfield during pregame drills as well. If Joseph maintains his power production, he could hit enough to be a regular. Otherwise, his bat could make him a useful utilityman.

Year	Club (League)	Class	AVG	G	AB	R	H	2B	3B	HR	RBI	BB	SO	SB	CS	OBP	SLG
2008	Yankees (GCL)	R	.277	49	159	25	44	15	2	2	18	20	24	2	5	.359	.434
2009	Charleston (SAL)	LoA	.300	100	380	39	114	17	8	4	57	49	61	8	5	.381	.418

Year	Club (League)	Class	AVG	G	AB	R	H	2B	3B	HR	RBI	BB	SO	SB	CS	OBP	SLG
2010	Tampa (FSL)	HiA	.302	98	381	52	115	27	3	6	52	43	74	5	8	.378	.436
	Trenton (EL)	AA	.216	31	111	11	24	6	4	0	13	15	33	1	0	.305	.342
2011	Trenton (EL)	AA	.277	131	499	75	138	38	8	5	58	59	104	4	3	.353	.415
2012	Trenton (EL)	AA	.314	23	86	9	27	4	0	2	6	15	13	0	0	.412	.430
	Scranton/W-B (IL)	AAA	.266	84	327	50	87	25	2	13	56	53	57	0	1	.366	.474
Minor League Totals			.283	516	1943	261	549	132	27	32	260	254	366	20	22	.366	.428

28 CITO CULVER, SS

BA GRADE
45
MEDIUM

Born: Aug. 26, 1992. **B-T:** B-R. **Ht.:** 6-0. **Wt.:** 185. **Drafted:** HS—Rochester, N.Y., 2010 (1st round). **Signed by:** Matt Hyde.

The Yankees drafted Culver with their top pick and signed him for $954,000 in 2010. New York knew he would need time, but he's behind where the franchise hoped he would be. He posted the fifth-lowest OPS (.604) among South Atlantic League batting qualifiers. Culver faces several offensive challenges, starting with switch-hitting. Because he's just an average or slightly above-average runner and not a burner, there's no major advantage to having him switch-hit, and some club officials want him to bat solely righthanded. Culver has a good idea of the strike zone and recognizes pitches, but he can't hit them with authority from the left side, and his righthanded swing gets long and mechanical. Culver can make highlight plays from the hole with good footwork and an above-average arm, and he was fairly reliable in 2012, making just 22 errors. Culver's bat has to improve for him to be a future regular and not a utilityman. He's likely to return to Charleston in 2013.

Year	Club (League)	Class	AVG	G	AB	R	H	2B	3B	HR	RBI	BB	SO	SB	CS	OBP	SLG
2010	Yankees (GCL)	R	.269	41	160	21	43	7	1	2	18	13	41	6	3	.320	.363
	Staten Island (NYP)	SS	.186	15	43	2	8	1	0	0	8	10	1	1		.340	.209
2011	Staten Island (NYP)	SS	.250	69	276	40	69	14	2	2	33	30	57	10	0	.323	.337
2012	Charleston (SAL)	LoA	.215	122	466	66	100	14	6	2	40	71	104	22	11	.321	.283
Minor League Totals			.233	247	945	129	220	36	9	6	91	122	212	39	15	.322	.309

29 TOMMY KAHNLE, RHP

BA GRADE
45
MEDIUM

Born: Aug. 7, 1989. **B-T:** R-R. **Ht.:** 6-1. **Wt.:** 220. **Drafted:** Lynn (Fla.), 2010 (4th round). **Signed by:** Jeff Deardorff.

A native of upstate New York, Kahnle helped Lynn (Fla.) win the 2009 NCAA Division II national championship. In 2012, he earned a late promotion to Double-A and pitched in the Eastern League playoffs, after a shoulder strain pushed his debut back to May. He pumps his fastball into the high 90s, touching 98 mph, and threw more strikes with it last year. Kahnle has effort in his delivery and favors power over precision, attacking with the fastball and using his changeup and improved slider as chase pitches. His changeup has splitter action at its best and helps him neutralize lefthanders, who hit .161 against him in 2012. As the season progressed, Kahnle improved at locating his fastball in the inner half. His control got better as well, as he issued 12 walks in May and 12 more for the rest of the season. Kahnle isn't a great athlete and has spent time on the disabled list in each of his two full pro seasons. He projects as a set-up man and will return to Double-A to begin 2013.

Year	Club (League)	Class	W	L	ERA	G	GS	CG	SV	IP	H	HR	BB	SO	K/9	WHIP	AVG
2010	Staten Island (NYP)	SS	0	0	0.56	11	0	0	3	16	3	0	5	25	14.1	0.50	.061
2011	Charleston (SAL)	LoA	3	5	4.22	40	0	0	2	81	69	1	49	112	12.4	1.46	.223
2012	Tampa (FSL)	HiA	2	1	2.45	30	0	0	6	55	30	3	24	72	11.8	0.98	.158
	Trenton (EL)	AA	0	0	0.00	1	0	0	0	2	2	0	0	2	9.0	1.00	.250
Minor League Totals			5	6	3.16	82	0	0	11	154	104	4	78	211	12.3	1.18	.201

30 GABE ENCINAS, RHP

BA GRADE
50
EXTREME

Born: Dec. 21, 1991. **B-T:** R-R. **Ht.:** 6-3. **Wt.:** 195. **Drafted:** HS—Santa Fe Springs, Calif., 2010 (6th round). **Signed by:** Jeff Patterson.

While the Yankees focused mainly on hitters in the 2010 draft, they spent $1.25 million on a trio of prep pitchers. Encinas ($300,000) has emerged as the best of the lot, surpassing lefthander Evan Rutckyj ($500,000) and righty Taylor Morton ($450,000). He hasn't put up big numbers as a pro yet because he's still learning to harness his newfound power stuff. He sat at 90-92 mph with his fastball in high school and has added velocity since signing, at times reaching 97 with his two-seamer and working at 92-95. At times Encinas loses his release point, resulting in 5.0 walks per nine innings last season. As his arm slot wanders, so does the consistency of his curveball. His changeup has its moments but remains inconsistent. Encinas encouraged the club with his progress in instructional league. He's slated for his first full-season assignment at Charleston in 2013.

Year	Club (League)	Class	W	L	ERA	G	GS	CG	SV	IP	H	HR	BB	SO	K/9	WHIP	AVG
2011	Yankees (GCL)	R	3	0	5.08	12	11	0	0	51	57	3	18	46	8.1	1.46	.284
2012	Staten Island (NYP)	SS	3	7	4.97	16	15	0	0	71	73	8	39	48	6.1	1.58	.266
Minor League Totals			6	7	5.02	28	26	0	0	122	130	11	57	94	6.9	1.53	.284

Oakland Athletics

BY JIM SHONERD

The Athletics were supposed to be an afterthought in 2012. Instead, they won 94 regular season games, their most in nine years, and authored a memorable season. Oakland surged in the second half, coming out of nowhere to shock the Rangers by winning the American League West on the last day of the regular season, then pushing the eventual AL champion Tigers to five games in the Division Series.

There was little reason to expect these results after the A's traded away their last three all-stars—Andrew Bailey, Trevor Cahill and Gio Gonzalez—for prospects during the offseason. Their  Opening Day payroll of $55.4 million ranked 29th among the 30 major league teams. It looked like general manager Billy Beane was hitting the reset button once again, and his team was just 37-42 and 13 games behind the Rangers at the end of June.

Instead of fading away, however, Oakland caught fire. It won 16 of its first 18 games in July and stayed hot the rest of the way, erasing a five-game deficit with nine to play and snatching the division title by sweeping Texas in the final series of the year. Justin Verlander put an end to the fairy tale, beating the A's twice in the ALDS, but that did little to dampen the glow of the season.

There may never have been a contender that relied on rookies as much as Oakland, which carried a record 12 on its ALDS roster. At times down the stretch, the A's went with an all-rookie rotation that included Jarrod Parker and Tommy Milone—key pieces obtained in the Cahill and Gonzalez trades—and homegrown products A.J. Griffin and Dan Straily. Derek Norris, another product of the Gonzalez deal with the Nationals, did most of the catching down the stretch.

Yet the best rookie was Cuban defector Yoenis Cespedes, who belted 23 homers and led the team in all three slash categories at .292/.356/.505. Oakland won a spirited competition to sign Cespedes in March with a four-year, $36 million contract. Along with Cespedes and Norris, other rookies in the A's lineup were players like Chris Carter and Josh Donaldson, who both finally broke through to contribute in the major leagues after their careers seemingly stalled in Triple-A.

While the A's were enjoying their first winning season and playoff appearance since 2006, their farm system also took on a much different look. Not only

Yoenis Cespedes and a cast of rookies led the A's to their first playoff trip since 2006

did several players graduate to the majors, but many new faces came in via trades and the draft. Along with Milone and Norris, Oakland also acquired righthanders Brad Peacock and A.J. Cole from Washington for Gonzalez. They're two of the system's best prospects, as is corner infielder Miles Head, who was part of the Bailey trade with the Red Sox (as was non-rookie Josh Reddick, who slugged 32 homers in his first full season as a big leaguer).

In a departure from its "Moneyball" history of eschewing high school players, Oakland took prepsters with each of its three 2012 draft picks before the second round. The A's hadn't used their top choice on a high schooler since taking Cahill in the second round in 2006, and hadn't expended a first-rounder on one since selecting Jeremy Bonderman 26th overall in 2001.

Shortstop Addison Russell was the 11th overall pick and the highest-drafted A's prepster since Eric Chavez at No. 10 in 1996, and he already ranks as the organization's No. 1 prospect after hitting .369/.432/.594 and reaching low Class A in his pro debut. Shortstop/third baseman Daniel Roberston and first baseman Matt Olson, both supplemental first-rounders last June, are two of the system's most promising young hitters.

THIS YEAR'S TOP 30

Player, Pos.		Grade
1.	Addison Russell, ss	60/High
2.	Michael Choice, of	55/High
3.	A.J. Cole, rhp	55/High
4.	Brad Peacock, rhp	55/High
5.	Sonny Gray, rhp	55/High
6.	Dan Straily, rhp	50/Medium
7.	Miles Head, 3b/1b	50/High
8.	Grant Green, of/inf	45/Medium
9.	Daniel Robertson, ss/3b	50/High
10.	Matt Olson, 1b	50/High
11.	Nolan Sanburn, rhp	50/High
12.	Renato Nunez, 3b	55/Extreme
13.	Pedro Figueroa, lhp	45/Medium
14.	Max Stassi, c	50/High
15.	Michael Taylor, of	45/Medium
16.	Max Muncy, 1b	50/High
17.	B.A. Vollmuth, 3b/1b	50/High
18.	Michael Ynoa, rhp	55/Extreme
19.	Beau Taylor, c	45/Medium
20.	Chris Bostick, 2b/ss	50/High
21.	Seth Streich, rhp	50/High
22.	B.J. Boyd, of	50/High
23.	Bruce Maxwell, c	45/High
24.	Aaron Shipman, of	50/Extreme
25.	Bobby Crocker, of	45/High
26.	Raul Alcantara, rhp	40/Medium
27.	Stephen Parker, 3b	40/Medium
28.	Andrew Carignan, rhp	45/High
29.	Arnold Leon, rhp	45/High
30.	Josh Bowman, rhp	45/High

LAST YEAR'S TOP 30

Player, Pos.		Status
1.	Jarrod Parker, rhp	Majors
2.	Sonny Gray, rhp	No. 5
3.	Michael Choice, of	No. 2
4.	Grant Green, of/ss	No. 8
5.	Jermaine Mitchell, of	(Free agent)
6.	Michael Taylor, of	No. 15
7.	Chris Carter, 1b	Majors
8.	Aaron Shipman, of	No. 24
9.	B.A. Vollmuth, 3b	No. 17
10.	Bobby Crocker, of	No. 25
11.	Collin Cowgill, of	Majors
12.	Adrian Cardenas, of/2b/3b	(Free agent)
13.	A.J. Griffin, rhp	Majors
14.	Max Stassi, c	No. 14
15.	Yordy Cabrera, ss	(Marlins)
16.	Stephen Parker, 3b/1b	No. 27
17.	Andrew Carignan, rhp	No. 28
18.	Ryan Cook, rhp	Majors
19.	Blake Treinen, rhp	Dropped out
20.	Josh Donaldson, c/3b	Majors
21.	Rob Gilliam, rhp	(Nationals)
22.	Eric Sogard, ss/3b	Majors
23.	Justin Souza, rhp	(Free agent)
24.	Chris Bostick, ss/2b	No. 20
25.	Chih-Fang Pan, 2b	Dropped out
26.	Renato Nunez, 3b	No. 12
27.	Michael Ynoa, rhp	No. 18
28.	Ryan Ortiz, c	Dropped out
29.	Ian Krol, lhp	Dropped out
30.	Beau Taylor, c	No. 19

BEST TOOLS

Best Hitter for Average	Addison Russell
Best Power Hitter	Michael Choice
Best Strike-Zone Discipline	Connor Crumbliss
Fastest Baserunner	B.J Boyd
Best Athlete	Addison Russell
Best Fastball	Pedro Figueroa
Best Curveball	Sonny Gray
Best Slider	Dan Straily
Best Changeup	Dan Straily
Best Control	A.J. Cole
Best Defensive Catcher	Max Stassi
Best Defensive Infielder	Addison Russell
Best Infield Arm	B.A. Vollmuth
Best Defensive Outfielder	Jermaine Mitchell
Best Outfield Arm	Jeremy Barfield

PROJECTED 2016 LINEUP

Catcher	Derek Norris
First Base	Miles Head
Second Base	Jemile Weeks
Third Base	Daniel Robertson
Shortstop	Addison Russell
Left Field	Michael Choice
Center Field	Chris Young
Right Field	Josh Reddick
Designated Hitter	Yoenis Cespedes
No. 1 Starter	Jarrod Parker
No. 2 Starter	Brett Anderson
No. 3 Starter	A.J. Cole
No. 4 Starter	Brad Peacock
No. 5 Starter	Sonny Gray
Closer	Ryan Cook

TOP PROSPECTS OF THE DECADE

Year	Player, Pos.	2012 Org.
2003	Rich Harden, rhp	Out of baseball
2004	Bobby Crosby, ss	Out of baseball
2005	Nick Swisher, of	Yankees
2006	Daric Barton, 1b	Athletics
2007	Travis Buck, of	Astros
2008	Daric Barton, 1b	Athletics
2009	Brett Anderson, lhp	Athletics
2010	Chris Carter, 1b/of	Athletics
2011	Grant Green, ss	Athletics
2012	Jarrod Parker, rhp	Athletics

TOP DRAFT PICKS OF THE DECADE

Year	Player, Pos.	2012 Org.
2003	Brad Sullivan, rhp	Out of baseball
2004	Landon Powell, c	Astros
2005	Cliff Pennington, ss	Athletics
2006	Trevor Cahill, rhp (2nd round)	Diamondbacks
2007	James Simmons, rhp	Athletics
2008	Jemile Weeks, 2b	Athletics
2009	Grant Green, ss	Athletics
2010	Michael Choice, of	Athleitcs
2011	Sonny Gray, rhp	Athletics
2012	Addison Russell, ss	Athletics

LARGEST BONUSES IN CLUB HISTORY

Michael Ynoa, 2008	$4,250,000
Mark Mulder, 1998	$3,200,000
Grant Green, 2009	$2,750,000
Addison Russell, 2012	$2,625,000
Renato Nunez, 2010	$2,200,000

OAKLAND ATHLETICS

TOP 2013 ROOKIE: Dan Straily, rhp. The minors' reigning strikeout king was an effective starter down the stretch for Oakland.

BREAKOUT PROSPECT: Nolan Sanburn, rhp. The former Arkansas reliever will look to take his big-time stuff into a starting role in his first full pro season.

SLEEPER: Josh Whitaker, of. A find in the 25th round of the 2010 draft, he has real power potential and hit 20 homers in high Class A last year.

SOURCE OF TOP 30 TALENT			
Homegrown	25	Acquired	5
College	14	Trades	5
Junior college	0	Rule 5 draft	0
High school	7	Independent leagues	0
Nondrafted free agents	0	Free agents/waivers	0
International	4		

LF
Josh Whitaker
Shane Peterson
Luis Barrera
Ryan Mathews

CF
Michael Choice (2)
B.J. Boyd (22)
Aaron Shipman (24)
Bobby Crocker (25)
Chad Oberacker
Brett Vertigan

RF
Michael Taylor (15)
Dusty Robinson
Rashun Dixon
Jeremy Barfield
Vicmal de la Cruz

3B
Miles Head (7)
Daniel Robertson (9)
Renato Nunez (12)
B.A. Vollmuth (17)
Stephen Parker (27)
Tommy Mendonca
Wade Kirkland

SS
Addison Russell (1)
Dusty Coleman
Wilfredo Solano
Sean Jamieson

2B
Grant Green (8)
Chris Bostick (20)
Conner Crumbliss
Chih-Fang Pan
Josh Horton

1B
Matt Olson (10)
Max Muncy (16)
Steve Hill
Tony Thompson

C
Max Stassi (14)
Beau Taylor (19)
Bruce Maxwell (23)
David Freitas
Ryan Ortiz

LHP

LHSP
Andrew Werner
Ian Krol

LHRP
Pedro Figueroa (13)
Omar Duran

RHP

RHSP
A.J. Cole (3)
Brad Peacock (4)
Sonny Gray (5)
Dan Straily (6)
Nolan Sanburn (11)
Michael Ynoa (18)
Seth Streich (21)
Raul Alcantara (26)
Josh Bowman (30)
Blake Treinen
Bruce Billings
Dakota Bacus
Drew Granier
Tyler Vail
Blake Hassebrock
Sean Murphy
Tanner Peters

RHRP
Andrew Carignan (28)
Arnold Leon (29)
Jose Macias
T.J. Walz
Kris Hall
Austin House
Connor Hoehn
Stuart Pudenz
Cody Kurz

2012

BEST PURE HITTER: SS Addison Russell's (1) swing doesn't look pure, but he has a knack for centering balls and explosiveness in his hands. SS/3B Daniel Robertson (1s) has a sweet stroke and reminds the Athletics of David Wright. 1B Max Muncy (5) has a short swing and controls the strike zone well.

BEST POWER HITTER: Russell's bat speed and barrel awareness give him the edge here as well. 1B Matt Olson (1s) has a prototypical power hitter's frame and a smooth lefthanded swing. C Bruce Maxwell (2) has big lefty power and led NCAA Division III with 15 homers and a .918 slugging percentage in the spring.

FASTEST RUNNER: After shedding nearly 30 pounds heading into his senior season, Russell showed above-average speed. OF B.J. Boyd (4) is also a plus runner and covers a lot of ground in center field.

BEST DEFENSIVE PLAYER: Russell's improved athleticism also helped him at shortstop. Just like at the plate, his actions aren't always fluid, but he covers ground, makes plays and has a strong arm.

BEST FASTBALL: RHP Nolan Sanburn (2) reached 99 mph in the spring at Arkansas and settled into the mid-90s as a pro. RHP Seth Streich (6) peaks at 95 and may add velocity after being a two-way player at Ohio.

BEST SECONDARY PITCH: Sanburn's power curveball shows flashes of being an out pitch with downer movement. RHP Kris Hall (8) owns a hard slider.

BEST PRO DEBUT: Russell scorched the Rookie-level Arizona League, hitting .415/.488/.717 in 106 at-bats before continuing to rake in brief stops in short-season Vermont and low Class A Burlington. RHP Dakota Bacus (9) joined him on the AZL all-star team by going 3-0, 1.20 with seven saves, a 35-5 K-BB ratio and a .121 opponent average in 30 innings.

BEST ATHLETE: Russell has quick-twitch athleticism and can do backflips on command. Boyd drew college football interest as a running back/wide receiver.

MOST INTRIGUING BACKGROUND: At No. 62 overall, Maxwell was the highest-drafted Division III player since the Astros took Jason Hirsch with the 59th pick in 2003. Oakland drafted Streich's brother Tobias in the 26th round in 2007, and he signed as a Twins fifth-rounder two years later.

CLOSEST TO THE MAJORS: Sanburn is an obvious choice if the A's develop him as a reliever, though they plan on trying him as a starter. Don't count out Russell, who handled everything thrown at him in his pro debut.

BEST LATE-ROUND PICK: RHP Austin House (14) was a bit of an enigma for scouts at New Mexico, but he pitched well out of Vermont's bullpen. He features a 93-95 mph four-seam fastball and an 89-90 mph sinker.

THE ONE WHO HOT AWAY: LHP Kyle Twomey (3) has a great feel for pitching along with plenty of projection remaining in his slender frame, but Oakland couldn't buy him away from his commitment to Southern California.

ASSESSMENT: For the first time since 1978, the A's used their first three picks on high school players. Early returns are positive, and Russell, Robertson and Olson all have star potential.

2011

The A's were thrilled to grab RHP Sonny Gray (1) with the 18th overall selection, though he did have a lackluster first full pro season. The same is true of most members of this crop, such as 3B/1B B.A. Vollmuth (2).

GRADE: C+

2010

RHP A.J. Griffin (13) shot to the majors and played a role in Oakland's surprising 2012 division title. OF Michael Choice (1) is the system's top power prospect.

GRADE: B

2009

RHP Dan Straily (24) led the minors in strikeouts and was a crucial addition to the A's rotation late last season. His emergence helps take the edge off the slower-than-expected development of OF/INF Grant Green (1) and C Max Stassi (4). Oakland failed to sign big league RHP Sam Dyson (10) or C Mike Zunino (29), who went No. 3 overall in 2012.

GRADE: C+

2008

After a promising 2011 rookie season, 2B Jemile Weeks (1) lost his job last year. RHP Tyson Ross (2) regressed significantly as well. This group includes three other major leaguers in RHP Mickey Storey (31), who was traded, and LHPs Chris Rusin (23) and Nick Maronde (43), who didn't sign.

GRADE: C

Draft analysis by Conor Glassey (2012) and Jim Callis (2008-11). Numbers in parentheses indicate draft rounds.

1 ADDISON RUSSELL, SS

Born: Jan. 23, 1994. **B-T:** R-R. **Ht.:** 6-0. **Wt.:** 185.
Drafted: HS—Pace, Fla., 2012 (1st round). **Signed by:**
Kelcey Mucker.

BA GRADE
60
HIGH

BILL MITCHELL

Before Russell became the Athletics' 2012 first-round pick and top prospect, he had to transform himself. The starting shortstop for Pace (Fla.) High since he was a freshman, he bulked up to add power but scouts started comparing him to Juan Uribe. Getting moved from short to third base while playing for Team USA's 18-and-under team in the summer of 2011 lit a fire under him to shed the extra weight, and he dropped nearly 30 pounds between then and the spring of 2012. Along the way, Russell earned back the shortstop job with Team USA and caught Oakland's attention at the 18-and-under Pan Am Championship in Colombia in November 2011. He belted a grand slam in the gold medal game and hit .364/.481/.614 for the tournament. Despite a solid but somewhat modest high school senior season, Russell went 11th overall in the 2012 draft and gave up an Auburn commitment for a bonus of $2.625 million. He excelled in his pro debut, batting .415 in the Rookie-level Arizona League and getting all the way to low Class A Burlington by the end of the summer.

When scouts describe Russell, the adjectives that come up the most are "aggressive" and "explosive." He combines quick hands with tremendous barrel accuracy, enabling him to make consistent hard contact. He hits line drives all over the field with projectable power. It's more like sneaky power right now, though one club official compares Russell's home run upside to that of Nationals shortstop Ian Desmond, who went deep 25 times in 2012. Russell goes to the plate looking to attack the ball. He's vulnerable to chasing breaking pitches away from him, like most young hitters, but his hand-eye coordination and swing should allow him to hit for high averages as he learns to lay off those pitches. Once a kid with a softer body, he now has a leaner, stronger frame and above-average speed. From home to first base, some scouts have graded him as a 70 runner on the 20-80 scouting scale. As aggressive on the bases as he is at the plate, he stole 16 bases in 18 tries in his pro debut. Once he learns the nuances

of basestealing, he could develop into a threat to swipe 20-30 bags annually in the major leagues. Russell has eliminated questions about whether he can stay at shortstop. He's a quality athlete with good range, particularly to his left. His actions could stand to be a little cleaner, but he's already a reliable defender who made just 10 errors in his first 48 pro games last summer. He has solid arm strength and a quick release. In addition to all of his physical tools, the A's also love Russell's makeup. He's focused and driven to succeed.

Russell has the makings of a big-time shortstop who can affect a game in multiple ways with his power, speed and defense. The A's believe he could advance through the system quickly after seeing how well he handled two promotions in his pro debut, though he'll still likely be ticketed for Oakland's new low Class A Beloit affiliate to start the 2013 season, where he should be joined by fellow premium high school picks Daniel Robertson and Matt Olson. He may only need a couple of years in the minors and could be the franchise's best shortstop since former American League MVP Miguel Tejada.

SCOUTING GRADES

Batting: 60.   **Defense:** 55.
Power: 60.   **Arm:** 55.
Speed: 60.

Based on 20-80 scouting scale, where 50 represents major league average, and future projection rather than present tools.

Year	Club (League)	Class	AVG	G	AB	R	H	2B	3B	HR	RBI	BB	SO	SB	CS	OBP	SLG
2012	Athletics (AZL)	R	.415	26	106	29	44	4	5	6	29	14	23	9	1	.488	.717
	Vermont (NYP)	SS	.340	13	53	9	18	2	2	1	7	4	13	2	0	.386	.509
	Burlington (MWL)	LoA	.310	16	58	8	18	4	2	0	9	5	12	5	1	.369	.448
Minor League Totals			.369	55	217	46	80	10	9	7	45	23	48	16	2	.432	.594

2 MICHAEL CHOICE, OF

Born: Nov. 10, 1989. **B-T:** R-R. **Ht.:** 6-0. **Wt.:** 220. **Drafted:** Texas-Arlington, 2010 (1st round). **Signed by:** Armann Brown.

After setting a Texas-Arlington record with 34 career home runs, Choice became the highest-drafted player in school history when he went 10th overall in 2010. Signed for $2 million, he led the high Class A California League with 30 homers in his first full pro season. He started slowly in 2012 while making adjustments to his swing. He was heating up before an errant pitch broke his left hand on July 21, ending his season. Choice has plenty of strength, and his quick wrists generate blinding bat speed and towering home runs. He's capable of hitting balls out to any part of the park. He has worked diligently to cut down on excess movement in his swing, shortening his stroke and creating a better bat path. He still has trouble with breaking pitches and may strike out too much to hit for a high average. Choice isn't a burner, but he's a solid runner who gets the job done in center field thanks to his good reads and jumps. If he has to move, he'd slide over to left field because he has fringy arm strength. Choice may start 2013 back in Double-A Midland but could advance to Triple-A Sacramento quickly if things go well. He could force his way into Oakland's outfield plans for 2014.

BA GRADE

55

HIGH

Year	Club (League)	Class	AVG	G	AB	R	H	2B	3B	HR	RBI	BB	SO	SB	CS	OBP	SLG
2010	Athletics (AZL)	R	.000	3	7	1	0	0	0	0	0	2	2	0	0	.222	.000
	Vancouver (NWL)	SS	.284	27	102	20	29	10	2	7	26	15	43	6	1	.388	.627
2011	Stockton (CAL)	HiA	.285	118	467	79	133	28	1	30	82	61	134	9	5	.376	.542
2012	Midland (TL)	AA	.287	91	359	59	103	15	2	10	58	33	88	5	1	.356	.423
Minor League Totals			.283	239	935	159	265	53	5	47	166	111	267	20	7	.369	.502

3 A.J. COLE, RHP

Born: Jan. 5, 1992. **B-T:** R-R. **Ht.:** 6-4. **Wt.:** 180. **Drafted:** HS—Oviedo, Fla., 2010 (4th round). **Signed by:** Paul Tinnell (Nationals).

A potential first-rounder going into 2010, Cole slid but still netted a fourth-round-record $2 million bonus from the Nationals. After coming to Oakland in the Gio Gonzalez trade last offseason, Cole ranked last in the California League with a 7.82 ERA before he was demoted to low Class A in May. Following a rough first start, he smoothed out his mechanics in Burlington and would have led the Midwest League in ERA (2.07) if he had logged enough innings to qualify. Cole's fastball ranges from 92-97 mph with some sinking and cutting action. His slurvy curveball lacks consistency because he keeps tinkering with grips for it, but it shows good bite when it's on and he tightened its rotation in instructional league. He has nice feel for his changeup, which has some fade and improved after his demotion. Cole's Cal League problems came because he opened up too quickly in his delivery, dragged his arm and over-rotated, and left pitches up in the strike zone. The A's like how he comes after hitters. With his power arm, Cole has more upside than any A's pitching prospect and projects as a possible frontline starter. He'll get another crack at Stockton to open 2013.

BA GRADE

55

HIGH

Year	Club (League)	Class	W	L	ERA	G	GS	CG	SV	IP	H	HR	BB	SO	K/9	WHIP	AVG
2010	Vermont (NYP)	SS	0	0	0.00	1	0	0	0	1	1	0	1	1	9.0	2.00	.333
2011	Hagerstown (SAL)	LoA	4	7	4.04	20	18	0	0	89	87	6	24	108	10.9	1.25	.251
2012	Stockton (CAL)	HiA	0	7	7.82	8	8	0	0	38	60	7	10	31	7.3	1.84	.364
	Burlington (MWL)	LoA	6	3	2.07	19	19	0	0	96	78	7	19	102	9.6	1.01	.222
Minor League Totals			10	17	3.82	48	45	0	0	224	226	20	54	242	9.7	1.25	.261

4 BRAD PEACOCK, RHP

Born: Feb. 2, 1988. **B-T:** R-R. **Ht.:** 6-1. **Wt.:** 175. **Drafted:** Palm Beach (Fla.) CC, D/F 2006 (41st round). **Signed by:** Tony Arango (Nationals).

A high school shortstop drafted as a catcher, Peacock signed for $110,000 as a draft-and-follow pitcher in 2007. He broke out in 2011, when he was the Double-A Eastern League's pitcher of the year and made his big league debut with the Nationals. Part of the package for Gio Gonzalez, Peacock had his worst pro season in 2012. Peacock pitched up in the zone too frequently in 2012. The A's tried to remedy the issue by having him keep his shoulders more level and eliminate a tilt in his delivery, but the changes didn't have the desired effect and he went back to his old mechanics. When he's going well, he still shows three quality pitches. Peacock's fastball works at 91-95 mph but lacks movement, underscoring the need for better command. He also flashes a sharp curveball and a changeup with depth. He has added a slider/cutter hybrid to help induce weak contact,

BA GRADE

55

HIGH

but it remains a work in progress. The A's consider 2012 a transition year for Peacock, who may have put too much pressure on himself while a parade of other young pitchers made it to Oakland. They still expect big things from him, though he'll likely be back in Triple-A to open 2013.

Year	Club (League)	Class	W	L	ERA	G	GS	CG	SV	IP	H	HR	BB	SO	K/9	WHIP	AVG
2007	Nationals (GCL)	R	1	1	3.89	13	7	0	0	39	38	1	15	34	7.8	1.35	.242
2008	Hagerstown (SAL)	LoA	0	5	9.09	8	8	0	0	34	38	8	21	23	6.1	1.75	.284
	Vermont (NYP)	SS	4	7	3.12	14	14	2	0	75	67	3	27	54	6.5	1.25	.235
2009	Hagerstown (SAL)	LoA	5	8	4.05	19	17	0	0	100	104	10	32	77	6.9	1.36	.272
	Potomac (CAR)	HiA	3	3	4.34	8	7	0	0	48	46	4	10	27	5.1	1.17	.253
2010	Potomac (CAR)	HiA	4	9	4.44	19	18	1	0	103	109	11	25	118	10.3	1.30	.268
	Harrisburg (EL)	AA	2	2	4.66	7	7	0	0	39	33	5	22	30	7.0	1.42	.234
2011	Harrisburg (EL)	AA	10	2	2.01	16	14	1	0	99	62	4	23	129	11.8	0.86	.179
	Syracuse (IL)	AAA	5	1	3.19	9	9	0	0	48	36	5	24	48	9.0	1.25	.205
	Washington (NL)	MAJ	2	0	0.75	3	2	0	0	12	7	0	6	4	3.0	1.08	.167
2012	Sacramento (PCL)	AAA	12	9	6.01	28	25	0	0	135	147	16	66	139	9.3	1.58	.275
Major League Totals			2	0	0.75	3	2	0	0	12	7	0	6	4	3.0	1.08	.167
Minor League Totals			46	47	4.32	141	126	4	0	719	680	67	265	679	8.5	1.31	.248

5 SONNY GRAY, RHP

Born: Nov. 7, 1989. **B-T:** R-R. **Ht.:** 5-11. **Wt.:** 200. **Drafted:** Vanderbilt, 2011 (1st round). **Signed by:** Matt Ranson.

Gray is accustomed to success, having led Smyrna (Tenn.) High to state baseball and football championships and Vanderbilt to its first-ever College World Series in 2011. But after signing for $1.54 million as the 18th overall pick that June, he struggled for most of his first full pro season. Gray tends to spin off as he finishes his delivery, so the A's tried to get him more on line to the plate. His command suffered and his pitches flattened out, leading him to return to his old mechanics in the second half. His pure stuff isn't a problem, as he has a 91-95 mph fastball that reaches 97 and features some sink and natural cutting action. He also has a knockout curveball, and he can vary both its velocity (76-84 mph) and shape. His changeup has depth but he still doesn't fully trust it. He needs to do a better job of setting hitters up. Gray did finish last season on a solid note, pitching well in a Triple-A playoff game. He'll go back to Sacramento to open 2013 and still can reach his ceiling of a No. 2 starter as long as he irons out his command.

BA GRADE
55
HIGH

Year	Club (League)	Class	W	L	ERA	G	GS	CG	SV	IP	H	HR	BB	SO	K/9	WHIP	AVG
2011	Athletics (AZL)	R	0	1	4.50	1	1	0	0	2	4	0	0	2	9.0	2.00	.444
	Midland (TL)	AA	1	0	0.45	5	5	0	0	20	15	0	6	18	8.1	1.05	.214
2012	Midland (TL)	AA	6	9	4.14	26	26	1	0	148	148	8	57	97	5.9	1.39	.263
	Sacramento (PCL)	AAA	0	0	9.00	1	1	0	0	4	10	0	1	2	4.5	2.75	.500
Minor League Totals			7	10	3.83	33	33	1	0	174	177	8	64	119	6.2	1.39	.268

6 DAN STRAILY, RHP

Born: Dec. 1, 1988. **B-T:** R-R. **Ht.:** 6-2. **Wt.:** 215. **Drafted:** Marshall, 2009 (24th round). **Signed by:** Matt Ranson.

Straily was once cut from his high school team and received only one offer to play Division I baseball, from Marshall. Signed for $12,500 as a 24th-rounder in 2009, he didn't emerge on the prospect radar until 2012, when he took the minors by storm. He led all minor leaguers with 190 strikeouts in 152 innings and reached the majors in August, making seven solid starts. Straily's greatest strength is his command of four pitches. He mixes them well and can locate them to every part of the strike zone. His fastball doesn't overpower hitters, but he maintains his 91-92 mph velocity deep into games and touches 95. Straily's slider and changeup are his two best offerings and account for the bulk of his strikeouts. His slider has good depth, while his changeup is a weapon against lefthanders with its armside run and his deceptive arm speed. His curveball is below-average, though it's still useful as an early-count offering. Since turning pro, he has gotten better at staying on line to the plate and maintaining his conditioning. Though Straily's stuff may not be loud enough for a frontline starter, he can be a dependable mid-rotation presence. He has the inside track on a big league job in 2013.

BA GRADE
50
MEDIUM

Year	Club (League)	Class	W	L	ERA	G	GS	CG	SV	IP	H	HR	BB	SO	K/9	WHIP	AVG
2009	Vancouver (NWL)	SS	5	3	4.12	16	11	0	0	59	66	5	18	66	10.1	1.42	.286
2010	Kane County (MWL)	LoA	10	7	4.32	28	28	0	0	148	138	13	61	149	9.1	1.34	.254
2011	Stockton (CAL)	HiA	11	9	3.87	28	26	0	0	161	160	10	40	154	8.6	1.24	.260
2012	Midland (TL)	AA	3	4	3.38	14	14	0	0	85	70	6	23	108	11.4	1.09	.224
	Sacramento (PCL)	AAA	6	3	2.03	11	11	0	0	67	40	3	19	82	11.1	0.89	.172
	Oakland (AL)	MAJ	2	1	3.89	7	7	0	0	39	36	11	16	32	7.3	1.32	.237
Major League Totals			2	1	3.89	7	7	0	0	39	36	11	16	32	7.3	1.32	.237
Minor League Totals			35	26	3.71	97	90	0	0	520	474	37	161	559	9.7	1.22	.245

7 MILES HEAD, 3B/1B

BA GRADE

50

HIGH

Born: May 2, 1991. **B-T:** R-R. **Ht.:** 6-0. **Wt.:** 215. **Drafted:** HS—Fayetteville, Ga., 2009 (26th round). **Signed by:** Tim Hyers (Red Sox).

The best pure hitter in the 2009 Georgia high school class, Head signed for an above-slot $335,000 as Boston's 26th-round pick. The Red Sox sent him, Josh Reddick and righthander Raul Alcantara to the A's for Andrew Bailey in December 2011. Head led Oakland farmhands in hitting (.333) and RBIs (84) while finishing second in homers (23) in his first season in the system. Head's swing isn't graceful, but it's quick and compact. He has outstanding bat control and the ability to barrel pitches in all parts of the strike zone. He has strong wrists and great bat speed, giving him the power to profile on a corner. Head played first base for the Red Sox but the A's shifted him to third base, his high school position. He has enough arm and can make routine plays at the hot corner, but his lack of range and athleticism leave his ability to stick there in question. He's a well below-average runner. The A's will soldier on with Head at third base after having him work on speed and quickness during the offseason. He planned on playing in the Arizona Fall League but left after one game when he strained his left shoulder taking a swing. He was too aggressive and less productive after his promotion to Double-A, so he'll return there to begin 2013.

Year	Club (League)	Class	AVG	G	AB	R	H	2B	3B	HR	RBI	BB	SO	SB	CS	OBP	SLG
2009	Red Sox (GCL)	R	.103	10	29	1	3	0	0	0	0	3	8	0	0	.188	.103
2010	Lowell (NYP)	SS	.240	65	229	21	55	16	2	1	35	30	36	1	1	.328	.341
2011	Greenville (SAL)	LoA	.338	66	263	61	89	25	1	15	53	30	53	4	2	.409	.612
	Salem (CAR)	HiA	.254	63	232	27	59	12	1	7	29	20	56	0	2	.328	.405
2012	Stockton (CAL)	HiA	.382	67	267	57	102	23	6	18	56	23	55	3	0	.433	.715
	Midland (TL)	AA	.272	57	213	25	58	9	2	5	28	16	75	0	1	.338	.404
Minor League Totals			.297	328	1233	192	366	85	12	46	201	122	283	8	6	.366	.497

8 GRANT GREEN, 2B/OF

BA GRADE

45

MEDIUM

Born: Sept. 27, 1987. **B-T:** R-R. **Ht.:** 6-3. **Wt.:** 180. **Drafted:** Southern California, 2009 (1st round). **Signed by:** J.T. Stotts.

Green has had no issues at the plate since Oakland signed him for $2.75 million as the 13th overall pick in 2009, batting .302/.348/.461 in the minors. But he has journeyed all over the diamond in a quest to find a defensive home. He started as a shortstop and played five different positions in 2012 before settling on second base. Green is a pure hitter who can recognize and square up a variety of pitches. He has an easy, line-drive stroke and makes contact to all fields. The A's looked to get him to drive more balls by widening his stance after the 2011 season, and while that helped, his power still won't be better than average. Green looked more comfortable than he had through his series of position changes. His arm was a question mark at shortstop but is fine at second base, and he has good hands, enough range and solid instincts for turning the double play. He's an average runner. With Cliff Pennington departing in a trade for Chris Young, Green will compete with Jemile Weeks for the A's second-base job in spring training. Oakland added Green to its 40-man roster in November. While he may not have an impact bat, he'll provide enough offense to be a solid regular.

Year	Club (League)	Class	AVG	G	AB	R	H	2B	3B	HR	RBI	BB	SO	SB	CS	OBP	SLG
2009	Stockton (CAL)	HiA	.316	5	19	2	6	1	0	0	3	1	5	1	0	.350	.368
2010	Stockton (CAL)	HiA	.318	131	548	107	174	39	6	20	87	38	117	9	5	.363	.520
2011	Midland (TL)	AA	.291	127	530	76	154	33	1	9	62	39	119	6	8	.343	.408
2012	Sacramento (PCL)	AAA	.296	125	524	73	155	28	6	15	75	33	75	13	9	.338	.458
Minor League Totals			.302	388	1621	258	489	101	13	44	227	111	316	29	22	.348	.461

9 DANIEL ROBERTSON, SS/3B

Born: March 22, 1994. **B-T:** R-R. **Ht.:** 6-0. **Wt.:** 190. **Drafted:** HS—Upland, Calif., 2012 (1st round supplemental). **Signed by:** Eric Martins.

The second of the three high schoolers Oakland took at the top of its 2012 draft, Robertson signed for $1.5 million as the 34th overall pick. In his debut, he hit well in the Arizona League and earned a promotion to short-season Vermont, but he ran out of gas in August and tailed off markedly. Robertson stands out as an instinctive hitter who's advanced for his age. He has a fluid swing with natural timing and rhythm. He mostly has gap power for now, but he shows flashes of something more. Some scouts believe he could have above-average power in time. He projects as a third baseman, though the A's gave him some time at shortstop when he wasn't playing alongside 2012 first-rounder Addison Russell. Robertson has reliable hands and solid arm strength, but his lack of speed makes him a better fit at the hot corner. Robertson is comfortable at third and should spend most of his time there when he teams with Russell in low Class A in 2013.

BA GRADE
50
HIGH

Year	Club (League)	Class	AVG	G	AB	R	H	2B	3B	HR	RBI	BB	SO	SB	CS	OBP	SLG
2012	Athletics (AZL)	R	.297	29	101	25	30	10	2	4	22	16	15	2	0	.405	.554
	Vermont (NYP)	SS	.181	26	94	9	17	2	0	1	8	7	31	1	1	.238	.234
Minor League Totals			.241	55	195	34	47	12	2	5	30	23	46	3	1	.330	.400

10 MATT OLSON, 1B

Born: March 29, 1994. **B-T:** L-R. **Ht.:** 6-4. **Wt.:** 236. **Drafted:** HS—Lilburn, Ga., 2012 (1st round supplemental). **Signed by:** Matt Ranson.

Olson hit 17 homers as a junior at Parkview High (Lilburn, Ga.) and 11 more as a senior in 2012, including one off Max Fried, the seventh overall pick in the draft. After leading Parkview to the No. 1 national ranking—he won the first game of the Georgia 5-A state finals as a pitcher and the second with a homer—Olson went 40 picks after Fried and signed for $1,079,700. Olson offers a premium blend of power and natural hitting ability. He has a short, easy lefthanded swing and has shown he can get around on quality inside fastballs. With a big, physical frame, he should have above-average usable power. In high school, his stroke was flatter and most of his homers were line drives. Since signing, he has added more leverage to his swing and looked to loft more balls. Olson is a below-average runner but shows good reactions and hands on defense, leading the A's to believe he can be a plus defender at first base. He also pitched in high school and would have been a two-way player at Vanderbilt, so his arm is solid. The A's see Olson as a future middle-of-the-order hitter. He'll form part of talented Beloit infield with Addison Russell and Daniel Robertson in 2013.

BA GRADE
50
HIGH

Year	Club (League)	Class	AVG	G	AB	R	H	2B	3B	HR	RBI	BB	SO	SB	CS	OBP	SLG
2012	Athletics (AZL)	R	.282	46	177	29	50	16	1	8	41	16	46	0	0	.345	.520
	Vermont (NYP)	SS	.273	4	11	3	3	0	0	1	4	3	4	0	0	.438	.545
Minor League Totals			.282	50	188	32	53	16	1	9	45	19	50	0	0	.352	.521

11 NOLAN SANBURN, RHP

BA GRADE
50
HIGH

Born: July 21, 1991. **B-T:** R-R. **Ht.:** 6-0. **Wt.:** 175. **Drafted:** Arkansas, 2012 (2nd round). **Signed by:** Yancy Ayres.

Mainly a position player in high school, Sanburn was a fringy prospect as a hitter but started showing the makings of a big fastball at the East Coast Pro Showcase in 2009. He turned down the Tigers as a 34th-round pick out of high school and went to Arkansas, where he pitched out of the bullpen before the A's made him a second-round pick and signed him for $710,000 as an eligible sophomore in 2012. Though he was a reliever in college, Oakland looks at his four-pitch mix and efficient delivery and sees a starter. Sanburn works his fastball at 93-97 mph and can touch 99. He backs up his heater with a hard 12-to-6 curveball that's another plus pitch. He has shown feel for a changeup with downward action. The A's are working to turn his slider into more of a cutter, and the pitch shows promise operating in the mid-80s. Sanburn still has much to learn about being a starter, though. He pitches with a closer's intensity, sometimes getting too amped up. His fastball command has to get better, as he's not efficient enough with his pitches to work deep into games. While Sanburn lacks experience pitching in a rotation, the bright side is that he has low mileage on his arm. Oakland believes he has the upside of a frontline starter. He'll go to low Class A for his first full pro season, with a target of 100-120 innings.

Year	Club (League)	Class	W	L	ERA	G	GS	CG	SV	IP	H	HR	BB	SO	K/9	WHIP	AVG
2012	Vermont (NYP)	SS	0	1	3.86	7	7	0	0	19	23	2	6	19	9.2	1.55	.299
Minor League Totals			0	1	3.86	7	7	0	0	19	23	2	6	19	9.2	1.55	.299

12 RENATO NUNEZ, 3B

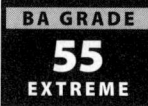

BA GRADE
55
EXTREME

Born: April 4, 1994. **B-T:** R-R. **Ht.:** 6-1. **Wt.:** 185. **Signed:** Venezuela, 2010. **Signed by:** Julio Franco.

The A's kept a watchful eye on Nunez since he was 13 and signed him for $2.2 million as soon as he was eligible as a 16-year-old on July 2, 2010. After an underwhelming pro debut in the Rookie-level Dominican Summer League in 2011, he had a big summer in the Arizona League in his 2012 U.S. debut, tying for second in the league in RBIs (42) and ranking fifth in slugging (.550). Nunez has a chance to have an impact bat, displaying above-average bat speed with the torque and leverage in his swing for power potential. He doesn't get cheated either, taking aggressive hacks. He did make progress last year with shortening his swing and not flying open, and he shows feel for hitting. Nunez is a below-average runner and defender. He works hard on his third base play and has shown improvement. His arm is strong and accurate enough to keep him at the hot corner, but he makes too many careless errors and has to focus better. Nunez should step up to Vermont in 2013.

Year	Club (League)	Class	AVG	G	AB	R	H	2B	3B	HR	RBI	BB	SO	SB	CS	OBP	SLG
2011	Athletics (DSL)	R	.268	53	194	20	52	12	0	5	28	6	42	1	2	.301	.407
2012	Athletics (AZL)	R	.325	42	160	31	52	18	3	4	42	17	32	4	0	.403	.550
Minor League Totals			.294	95	354	51	104	30	3	9	70	23	74	5	2	.349	.472

13 PEDRO FIGUEROA, LHP

BA GRADE
45
MEDIUM

Born: Nov. 23, 1985. **B-T:** L-L. **Ht.:** 6-0. **Wt.:** 215. **Signed:** Dominican Republic, 2003. **Signed by:** Juan Carlos de la Cruz.

Figueroa was rated Oakland's best pitching prospect entering the 2010 season, but his slow development ground to a halt when he needed Tommy John surgery that June. He missed the second half of 2010 and almost all of 2011. When he resurfaced last season, the A's made him a reliever to keep him healthy. He found his old form, excelling in Triple-A and reaching the majors. He made Oakland's postseason roster but didn't pitch in the Division Series. Figueroa throws harder than most lefthanders, with a fastball that sits at 96-97 mph and touches 99 when he comes out of the bullpen. He has a second quality pitch in his hard, late-breaking slider, and he throws a changeup with some armside run. Figueroa whips the ball with a slingshot arm action. He has average control and fringy command, getting into trouble when he pitches up in the strike zone and falls behind in the count. The A's still are considering giving him another chance at starting, though his health and their needs will dictate his role. He could open 2013 in Oakland's bullpen or Sacramento's rotation.

Year	Club (League)	Class	W	L	ERA	G	GS	CG	SV	IP	H	HR	BB	SO	K/9	WHIP	AVG
2004	Athletics2 (DSL)	R	2	2	2.90	15	2	0	1	50	52	3	11	40	7.2	1.27	.261
2005	Athletics2 (DSL)	R	3	0	2.27	13	3	0	1	36	29	0	12	25	6.3	1.15	.215
2006	Athletics1 (DSL)	R	1	0	4.50	1	1	0	0	6	5	1	1	1	1.00	.227
	Athletics (AZL)	R	1	6	6.07	13	8	0	0	43	59	4	11	27	5.7	1.63	.321
2007	Vancouver (NWL)	SS	2	2	4.30	17	7	0	1	44	41	2	31	35	7.2	1.64	.252
2008	Vancouver (NWL)	SS	2	5	3.93	15	15	0	0	69	62	3	32	77	10.1	1.37	.238
2009	Kane County (MWL)	LoA	10	2	3.23	16	16	0	0	86	89	6	31	78	8.1	1.39	.267
	Stockton (CAL)	HiA	3	4	3.56	11	11	0	0	66	62	3	35	67	9.2	1.48	.251
2010	Midland (TL)	AA	1	6	5.30	13	13	0	0	71	84	6	29	57	7.2	1.58	.295
2011	Athletics (AZL)	R	0	0	4.50	2	2	0	0	2	3	0	0	6	27.0	1.50	.300
2012	Sacramento (PCL)	AAA	0	2	2.62	32	0	0	1	45	35	1	18	40	8.1	1.19	.212
	Oakland (AL)	MAJ	0	0	3.32	19	0	0	0	22	16	2	15	14	5.8	1.43	.216
Major League Totals			0	0	3.32	19	0	0	0	22	16	2	15	14	5.8	1.43	.216
Minor League Totals			25	29	3.85	148	78	0	4	517	521	29	211	453	7.9	1.42	.260

14 MAX STASSI, C

BA GRADE
50
HIGH

Born: March 15, 1991. **B-T:** R-R. **Ht.:** 5-10. **Wt.:** 205. **Drafted:** HS—Yuba City, Calif., 2009 (4th round). **Signed by:** Jermaine Clark.

Stassi's baseball bloodlines go back to his great-great uncle Myril Hoag, who played 13 seasons in the majors in the 1930s and '40s. His father Jim reached Triple-A with the Giants and his brother Brock is a first baseman in the Phillies system. Max netted a $1.5 million bonus in 2009, but injuries have slowed his pro career. He put two years of right shoulder problems behind him with surgery in May 2011, then missed time last year with ankle and oblique maladies. Stassi has a simple swing with few moving parts and a short load and stride. His pitch recognition and the quality of his at-bats have improved, but he still tends to press and is susceptible to chasing pitches up in the strike zone or down and away. Oakland believes there's enough power in his bat to hit 15-20 home runs a season. Stassi's defense always has been advanced for his age, and he continues to receive high marks for his receiving and ability to handle pitchers. He has an accurate arm and its strength has continued getting better since his injuries, rating close to average. He threw out 24 percent of basestealers in 2012. After a stint in the Arizona Fall League, Stassi has positioned himself to move up to Double-A in 2013.

Year	Club (League)	Class	AVG	G	AB	R	H	2B	3B	HR	RBI	BB	SO	SB	CS	OBP	SLG
2009	Athletics (AZL)	R	.000	1	1	0	0	0	0	0	0	1	1	0	0	.500	.000
	Vancouver (NWL)	SS	.286	13	49	3	14	4	0	0	8	2	11	0	0	.340	.367
2010	Kane County (MWL)	LoA	.229	110	411	54	94	21	1	13	51	45	141	3	3	.310	.380
2011	Stockton (CAL)	HiA	.231	31	121	22	28	6	0	2	19	16	22	1	1	.331	.331
2012	Stockton (CAL)	HiA	.268	84	314	48	84	18	0	15	45	27	83	3	1	.331	.468
Minor League Totals			.246	239	896	127	220	49	1	30	123	91	258	7	5	.322	.403

15 MICHAEL TAYLOR, OF

BA GRADE
45
MEDIUM

Born: Dec. 19, 1985. **B-T:** R-R. **Ht.:** 6-5. **Wt.:** 255. **Drafted:** Stanford, 2007 (5th round). **Signed by:** Joey Davis (Phillies).

Taylor has racked up 1,372 Triple-A at-bats in the last four seasons as he has been unable to break through to the majors for any significant time. The Phillies sent him, Travis d'Arnaud and Kyle Drabek to the Blue Jays for Roy Halladay in December 2009, and Toronto immediately spun Taylor to the Athletics for Brett Wallace. Taylor did establish personal Triple-A bests for batting average (.287) and on-base percentage (.405) while leading the Pacific Coast League in walks (86) in 2012. He still cuts an imposing figure and can put on a show in batting practice, but those displays are a tease. After trying to hit for more power the previous two seasons, he reverted to more of a line-drive approach last year. He got himself in a better position to hit and started his swing earlier. His pitch recognition got better and he generally put together quality at-bats. Though Taylor's not a fast runner, he gets outstanding reads and jumps on balls and is a quality outfielder. He could play center field in a pinch, and his arm is strong enough to keep him in right. He's still in the conversation for an outfield job with the A's, but he's buried on the depth chart and destined for another trip to Sacramento.

Year	Club (League)	Class	AVG	G	AB	R	H	2B	3B	HR	RBI	BB	SO	SB	CS	OBP	SLG
2007	Williamsport (NYP)	SS	.227	66	233	30	53	14	0	6	33	23	53	8	2	.300	.365
2008	Lakewood (SAL)	LoA	.361	67	249	40	90	12	3	10	50	31	43	10	3	.441	.554
	Clearwater (FSL)	HiA	.329	65	243	36	80	27	1	9	38	19	46	5	6	.380	.560
2009	Reading (EL)	AA	.333	86	318	59	106	22	4	15	65	35	51	18	4	.408	.569
	Lehigh Valley (IL)	AAA	.282	30	110	15	31	6	1	5	19	13	19	3	1	.359	.491
2010	Sacramento (PCL)	AAA	.272	127	464	79	126	26	6	6	78	51	92	16	5	.348	.392
2011	Sacramento (PCL)	AAA	.272	93	349	51	95	16	0	16	64	46	80	14	5	.360	.456
	Oakland (AL)	MAJ	.200	11	30	4	6	0	0	1	1	5	11	0	0	.314	.300
2012	Oakland (AL)	MAJ	.143	6	21	2	3	1	0	0	0	0	10	0	0	.143	.190
	Sacramento (PCL)	AAA	.287	120	449	81	129	31	1	12	67	86	105	18	3	.405	.441
Major League Totals			.176	17	51	6	9	1	0	1	1	5	21	0	0	.250	.255
Minor League Totals			.294	654	2415	391	710	154	16	79	414	304	489	92	29	.377	.469

16 MAX MUNCY, 1B

BA GRADE
50
HIGH

Born: Aug. 25, 1990. **B-T:** L-R. **Ht.:** 6-1. **Wt.:** 205. **Drafted:** Baylor, 2012 (5th round). **Signed by:** Armann Brown.

Muncy passed on signing with the Indians as a 41st-round pick out of high school in 2009 to attend Baylor, emerging as a fifth-round pick three years later. Signed for $240,000, he held his own after going straight to low Class A. There's little question about Muncy's pure hitting ability. His pitch-recognition skills already rank among the system's best, and his short swing helps him find the barrel consistently. He's regarded as a heady player who should have high on-base percentages, though how much power he'll produce remains in question. The A's felt he did a better job of staying through the ball in instructional league, though scouts who watched him in college didn't project more than average pop. Muncy has good hands at first base and enough athleticism to perhaps play on an outfield corner or third base, though Oakland has no plans to move him. He's a below-average runner but not a baseclogger. How much power Muncy develops will determine how high his ceiling ultimately is, but he should advance quickly. He'll get a chance to open his first full season in high Class A.

Year	Club (League)	Class	AVG	G	AB	R	H	2B	3B	HR	RBI	BB	SO	SB	CS	OBP	SLG
2012	Burlington (MWL)	LoA	.275	64	229	34	63	20	2	4	23	41	37	3	1	.383	.432
Minor League Totals			.275	64	229	34	63	20	2	4	23	41	37	3	1	.383	.432

17 B.A. VOLLMUTH, 3B/1B

BA GRADE
50
HIGH

Born: Dec. 23, 1989. **B-T:** R-R. **Ht.:** 6-3. **Wt.:** 215. **Drafted:** Southern Mississippi, 2011 (3rd round). **Signed by:** Kelcey Mucker.

As a freshman in 2009, Vollmuth homered six times in NCAA tournament play to lead Southern Mississippi to its first College World Series appearance. He went on to lead the Golden Eagles in homers in each of the next two seasons before landing $304,200 as a 2011 third-round pick. He hit .261/.336/.405 while reaching high Class A in his first full pro season, though his performance was a bit underwhelming.

Vollmuth has always had issues with streakiness and handling breaking pitches. When he's in rhythm, he has a short bat path that can produce above-average power to all fields. He has a willingness to use the middle of the field and patience as well. A shortstop in college, Vollmuth has a strong arm and good hands at third base, but he tends to lose focus and make careless errors. He's still learning the position in terms of reading balls and playing the proper angles. Vollmuth can profile as a corner player, but he'll have to prove he can produce against quality pitching. The A's would like to get him to Double-A in 2013, though a return to Stockton is a possibility.

Year	Club (League)	Class	AVG	G	AB	R	H	2B	3B	HR	RBI	BB	SO	SB	CS	OBP	SLG
2011	Athletics (AZL)	R	.148	8	27	3	4	0	0	1	2	3	6	0	0	.281	.259
	Vermont (NYP)	SS	.500	4	14	8	7	4	1	0	6	2	3	0	1	.588	.929
2012	Burlington (MWL)	LoA	.260	67	265	37	69	17	1	7	44	29	74	7	1	.337	.411
	Stockton (CAL)	HiA	.261	65	264	45	69	15	0	7	29	27	70	0	2	.336	.398
Minor League Totals			.261	144	570	93	149	36	2	15	81	61	153	7	4	.340	.411

18 MICHAEL YNOA, RHP

BA GRADE
55
EXTREME

Born: Sept. 24, 1991. **B-T:** R-R. **Ht.:** 6-7. **Wt.:** 210. **Signed:** Dominican Republic, 2008. **Signed by:** Raymond Abreu.

Ynoa stood 6-foot-4 when he 13 years old, and some international scouts labeled him a once-in-a-generation talent leading up to his signing in 2008. At the time, his $4.25 million bonus was the largest ever given to a Latin American amateur. Injuries have stymied his pro career, knocking him out for all of 2009 (elbow tendinitis) and 2011 (recovering from Tommy John surgery). Ynoa pitched meaningful innings for the first time in 2012, and the fact that he stayed healthy mattered more to the A's than his unimpressive statistics. By the end of instructional league, he finally felt comfortable enough to completely let loose on the mound. Ynoa's talent is still apparent. He has a smooth delivery and his fastball jumps out of his hand at 93-95 mph. He has a sharp 12-to-6 curveball with good rotation. He needs to hone his fastball command and refine a changeup that features promising depth. Oakland still believes in his potential and protected him on its 40-man roster in November. He'll head to full-season ball for the first time in 2013, with a goal of working 120 innings at Beloit.

Year	Club (League)	Class	W	L	ERA	G	GS	CG	SV	IP	H	HR	BB	SO	K/9	WHIP	AVG
2009	Did Not Play—Injured																
2010	Athletics (AZL)	R	0	1	5.00	3	3	0	0	9	6	1	4	11	11.0	1.11	.188
2011	Did Not Play—Injured																
2012	Athletics (AZL)	R	0	1	5.40	6	6	0	0	10	11	1	9	6	5.4	2.00	.282
	Vermont (NYP)	SS	1	3	6.97	8	6	0	0	21	20	2	16	19	8.3	1.74	.247
Minor League Totals			1	5	6.13	17	15	0	0	40	37	4	29	36	8.2	1.66	.243

19 BEAU TAYLOR, C

BA GRADE
45
MEDIUM

Born: Feb. 13, 1990. **B-T:** L-R. **Ht.:** 6-0. **Wt.:** 200. **Drafted:** Central Florida, 2011 (5th round). **Signed by:** Trevor Schaffer.

Taylor has advanced quickly since signing for $147,600 as a fifth-round pick in 2011. He spent most of his pro debut in low Class A and finished his first full season in Double-A. He didn't take up catching full-time until he got to Central Florida, and his bat remains ahead of his defense. Taylor utilizes a contact-oriented, line-drive approach. He has a simple swing and a knack for barreling balls, though his power is limited beyond hitting balls to the gaps. His swing can get long at times but he usually puts together quality at-bats. Taylor has a strong throwing arm and the footwork to help it play up, though he threw out just 23 percent of basestealers in 2012. His defense is rough around the edges and he struggles with his receiving at times. He's still learning about calling games, though the A's were encouraged by how he ran the Double-A staff as a first-year pro. He doesn't have much speed, but his baserunning instincts are good. Taylor's ability to improve his power and defense will determine whether he'll be a regular or backup at the major league level. He'll head back to Midland to start 2013.

Year	Club (League)	Class	AVG	G	AB	R	H	2B	3B	HR	RBI	BB	SO	SB	CS	OBP	SLG
2011	Vermont (NYP)	SS	.111	5	18	1	2	0	0	0	1	0	4	0	0	.111	.111
	Burlington (MWL)	LoA	.293	43	147	16	43	7	2	0	17	18	34	1	3	.367	.367
2012	Stockton (CAL)	HiA	.328	52	195	25	64	10	2	3	34	28	29	0	2	.412	.446
	Midland (TL)	AA	.233	36	120	13	28	5	0	0	10	11	36	0	0	.303	.275
Minor League Totals			.285	136	480	55	137	22	4	3	62	57	103	1	5	.362	.367

20 CHRIS BOSTICK, 2B/SS

BA GRADE
50
HIGH

Born: March 24, 1993. **B-T:** R-R. **Ht.:** 5-11. **Wt.:** 185. **Drafted:** HS—Rochester, N.Y., 2011 (44th round). **Signed by:** Matt Higginson.

The Athletics took high schoolers with their first three picks in the 2012 draft, a radical departure from the year before, when Bostick was the lone prep player they signed. Oakland spent $125,000 to buy him out of a St. John's commitment. Bostick's swing is direct to the ball and he has a feel for the barrel of the bat. The A's would like to see him hit more line drives and fewer balls in the air, though the strength in his wrists and forearms gives him sneaky power. He already shows a willingness to use the whole field. Drafted as a short-stop, Bostick has shifted to second base already, though the move was partly in deference to Addison Russell's arrival at Vermont last summer. Bostick is a good athlete with plenty of arm for second base, and Oakland thinks he has the tools to play anywhere in the infield. He needs to clean up his infield actions, though, as his 13 errors were the second-most among New York-Penn League second basemen last year. While Bostick's versatility is an asset, his bat looks to have enough potential for him to be more than a utilityman. He held his own against older competition with Vermont, and he'll be in for a similar challenge as he moves up to low Class A in 2013.

Year	Club (League)	Class	AVG	G	AB	R	H	2B	3B	HR	RBI	BB	SO	SB	CS	OBP	SLG
2011	Athletics (AZL)	R	.442	14	52	13	23	6	1	1	5	3	12	4	0	.482	.654
2012	Vermont (NYP)	SS	.251	70	279	41	70	16	4	3	29	27	66	12	5	.325	.369
Minor League Totals			.281	84	331	54	93	22	5	4	34	30	78	16	5	.349	.414

21 SETH STREICH, RHP

BA GRADE
50
HIGH

Born: Feb. 19, 1991. **B-T:** L-R. **Ht.:** 6-3. **Wt.:** 210. **Drafted:** Ohio, 2012 (6th round). **Signed by:** Rich Sparks.

Streich was a two-way player for Ohio, pitching in the weekend rotation and doubling as a first baseman and DH. Hampered by hamstring and oblique injuries in 2012, he went just 4-7, 4.42, but the A's had seen enough to give him $183,500 in the sixth round. They also once drafted Streich's older brother Tobias in the 26th round in 2007, though they didn't sign him. The younger Streich uses a simple delivery that looks like he's just playing catch, and he pounds the zone with a low-90s fastball that reaches 95 mph. He also possesses a promising changeup with splitter-like action. Oakland felt Streich's slider tended to get too flat, so he went to work on tweaking his grips and finding more angle in instructional league. By the end of the fall, he had developed both a solid 76-77 mph curveball with tight rotation and a cutter. The A's believe both pitches can become weapons. After pitching well in his debut and building on that momentum in instructional league, Streich will open his first full pro season in low Class A. He has the mix to be a mid-rotation starter.

Year	Club (League)	Class	W	L	ERA	G	GS	CG	SV	IP	H	HR	BB	SO	K/9	WHIP	AVG
2012	Athletics (AZL)	R	0	0	3.38	2	0	0	0	3	1	0	1	6	20.3	0.75	.111
	Vermont (NYP)	SS	4	1	2.60	15	4	0	0	35	26	1	17	42	10.9	1.24	.206
Minor League Totals			4	1	2.65	17	4	0	0	37	27	1	18	48	11.6	1.21	.200

22 B.J. BOYD, OF

BA GRADE
50
HIGH

Born: July 16, 1993. **B-T:** L-R. **Ht.:** 5-10. **Wt.:** 190. **Drafted:** HS—Palo Alto, Calif., 2012 (4th round). **Signed by:** Jermaine Clark.

Boyd attracted football recruiters as a running back/wide receiver, racking up 1,108 yards and 17 touchdowns as a senior at Palo Alto (Calif.) High. He preferred baseball, though, and signed for $300,000 as a fourth-round pick last June. Like many multisport athletes, Boyd is raw because he hasn't focused on baseball, but he does have some instincts to go with his explosive tools. He shows a good eye at the plate and a quick bat, though the A's worked on refining his swing during instructional league. They believe he has the raw power for 10-15 homers annually, but he had a flat stroke and tended to let pitches travel almost too deep. Oakland wants him to start his swing earlier and add loft to it. He often just shoots balls the other way and the A's would like to see him turn on more pitches. Boyd has plus speed and knows how to use it, stealing 16 bases in 39 pro games. His reads and angles in center field aren't ideal, but his quickness helps him make up for most of his mistakes. His arm is below-average. Boyd has the components to be a future leadoff hitter. He could get a shot to open his first full year in low Class A with the rest of Oakland's premium 2012 high school picks, though it's more likely he'll stay in extended spring training to keep honing his swing before heading to Vermont.

Year	Club (League)	Class	AVG	G	AB	R	H	2B	3B	HR	RBI	BB	SO	SB	CS	OBP	SLG
2012	Athletics (AZL)	R	.301	39	143	37	43	8	4	1	20	23	36	16	4	.401	.434
Minor League Totals			.301	39	143	37	43	8	4	1	20	23	36	16	4	.401	.434

23 BRUCE MAXWELL, C

BA GRADE
45
HIGH

Born: Dec. 20, 1990. **B-T:** L-R. **Ht.:** 6-2. **Wt.:** 235. **Drafted:** Birmingham-Southern, 2012 (2nd round). **Signed by:** Kelcey Mucker.

Maxwell topped NCAA Division III in both home runs (15) and slugging percentage (.918) last spring en route to being the highest drafted D-III player, at 62nd overall, since Jason Hirsh went 59th overall in 2003. He signed for $700,000. If he can stick behind the plate, he makes for an intriguing package as a lefthanded-hitting catcher with power. Maxwell has a physical frame and hits home runs without selling out. He uses a level, efficient swing with an up-the-middle approach. The A's worked with him in instructional league to utilize his legs more, and they hope to see him pull more balls with authority. He didn't go deep in his pro debut but they know the power is there. Maxwell played both first base and catcher in college, and he has a long way to go behind the plate. He committed 18 passed balls in 41 pro games, a testament to how raw he is as a receiver. The A's have revamped his set-up and the positioning of his mitt. He does have a solid arm and threw out 33 percent of basestealers. His lack of agility and speed make first base his only other defensive option. Maxwell could spend his first full pro season in low Class A, giving him a chance to improve his defense and get his bat going.

Year	Club (League)	Class	AVG	G	AB	R	H	2B	3B	HR	RBI	BB	SO	SB	CS	OBP	SLG
2012	Athletics (AZL)	R	.524	6	21	8	11	4	0	0	4	5	3	0	0	.615	.714
	Vermont (NYP)	SS	.254	61	228	22	58	14	0	0	22	26	35	1	0	.329	.316
Minor League Totals			.277	67	249	30	69	18	0	0	26	31	38	1	0	.356	.349

24 AARON SHIPMAN, OF

BA GRADE

50

EXTREME

Born: Jan. 27, 1992. **B-T:** L-L. **Ht.:** 6-0. **Wt.:** 175. **Drafted:** HS—Quitman, Ga., 2010 (3rd round). **Signed by:** Matt Ranson.

Shipman flew under the radar for most of his high school career, playing for a small school in south Georgia, before zooming up draft boards leading up to the 2010 draft. Shipman's father Robert was a Tigers 10th-round pick in 1987, and the A's made Aaron their 2010 third-rounder and signed him for $500,000. He has some of the most enticing tools in the system, but his performance hasn't shown it yet. Shipman has a short swing, good bat control and a discerning eye, though his selectivity can work to his detriment. While it's laudable that he works deep in counts, he gets overly passive. The A's have pushed him to attack hittable pitches earlier in at-bats, and he has struggled to find a happy medium. There was hope he could develop average power when he came out of high school, but those projections have dropped as he has yet to homer as a pro. Shipman can be an elite defender in center field, with above-average speed and an arm that was capable of throwing 90-91 mph fastballs in high school. He's fast enough to be a basestealing threat, though he succeeded in just 11 of 22 attempts last season. Shipman's potential as a leadoff hitter remains. He could repeat low Class A in 2013, though a promotion to the more hitter-friendly California League might help him get going.

Year	Club (League)	Class	AVG	G	AB	R	H	2B	3B	HR	RBI	BB	SO	SB	CS	OBP	SLG
2010	Athletics (AZL)	R	.118	4	17	2	2	0	0	0	2	0	6	3	0	.118	.118
2011	Vermont (NYP)	SS	.254	63	201	34	51	8	1	0	19	42	39	17	3	.385	.303
2012	Burlington (MWL)	LoA	.206	108	360	40	74	12	4	0	32	60	86	11	11	.319	.261
Minor League Totals			.220	175	578	76	127	20	5	0	53	102	131	31	14	.338	.272

25 BOBBY CROCKER, OF

BA GRADE

45

HIGH

Born: May 1, 1990. **B-T:** R-R. **Ht.:** 6-3. **Wt.:** 220. **Drafted:** Cal Poly, 2011 (4th round). **Signed by:** Jermaine Clark.

The Athletics couldn't sign Crocker on their first pass, when they took him in the 38th round out of high school in 2008, but they landed him for $198,000 as a fourth-rounder three years later. He's one of the system's better athletes and has a physical build, but his power production never has lived up to its solid potential. He hit just 13 homers in three years at Cal Poly and six in his first full pro season. That led the A's to retool his swing, which lacked fluidity and was too geared for the opposite field. During instructional league, he made adjustments to develop a looser stroke that should free up his wrists and his hands. He also started turning on more pitches. He needs to refine his approach, as he'll chase pitches out of the strike zone and not offer at ones he should mash. Crocker has the potential for solid tools across the board, outside of his below-average arm, so his upside is intriguing if the swing adjustments have the desired results. He's an energetic player who runs well enough to perhaps stay in center field. His arm would dictate a move to left field if he can't remain in center. He'll go to high Class A in 2013, hoping to turn a corner in the California League.

Year	Club (League)	Class	AVG	G	AB	R	H	2B	3B	HR	RBI	BB	SO	SB	CS	OBP	SLG
2011	Athletics (AZL)	R	.261	24	88	14	23	4	3	0	4	5	22	2	2	.316	.375
	Vermont (NYP)	SS	.322	32	118	19	38	5	0	3	15	8	22	6	1	.367	.441
2012	Burlington (MWL)	LoA	.268	112	406	56	109	19	2	6	53	39	109	17	10	.347	.369
Minor League Totals			.278	168	612	89	170	28	5	9	72	52	153	25	13	.346	.384

26 RAUL ALCANTARA, RHP

BA GRADE

50

EXTREME

Born: Dec. 4, 1992. **B-T:** R-R. **Ht.:** 6-3. **Wt.:** 180. **Signed:** Dominican Republic, 2009. **Signed by:** Manny Nanita (Red Sox).

Alcantara was named the Rookie-level Gulf Coast League pitcher of the year in 2011 before the Red Sox packaged him with Josh Reddick and Miles Head to acquire Andrew Bailey that December.

Pitching at age 19 in low Class A last year, Alcantara was hit hard in his first exposure to full-season hitters and didn't show much mound presence. Nevertheless, the A's thought he made progress. He sharpened the command of his 90-95 mph fastball, though the pitch needs more movement. He has a quality changeup with depth and armside run. His hard slider shows promise but gets slurvy at times, and he needs to locate it better. He'll even mix in a mid-70s curveball early in the count. Alcantara throws with a balanced, easy motion, and the ball jumps out of his hand. He already throws strikes but must improve his command. After limiting him to 100 innings last year, Oakland will look to build him up further in high Class A.

Year	Club (League)	Class	W	L	ERA	G	GS	CG	SV	IP	H	HR	BB	SO	K/9	WHIP	AVG
2010	Red Sox (DSL)	R	5	3	3.28	13	13	1	0	60	61	1	8	34	5.1	1.14	.260
2011	Red Sox (GCL)	R	1	1	0.75	9	9	0	0	48	23	0	6	36	6.8	0.60	.147
	Lowell (NYP)	SS	0	3	6.23	4	4	0	0	17	25	0	6	14	7.3	1.79	.333
2012	Burlington (MWL)	LoA	6	11	5.08	27	17	0	0	103	119	12	38	57	5.0	1.53	.304
Minor League Totals			12	18	3.78	53	43	1	0	228	228	13	58	141	5.6	1.25	.266

27 STEPHEN PARKER, 3B

Born: Sept. 3, 1987. **B-T:** L-R. **Ht.:** 6-2. **Wt.:** 200. **Drafted:** Brigham Young, 2009 (5th round). **Signed by:** Jeremy Schied.

BA GRADE
40
MEDIUM

Parker breezed through his first three pro seasons before having an up-and-down 2012 campaign at Sacramento. He hit 21 homers in high Class A in 2010 but has gone deep just 17 times over the last two seasons, including just once in the second half of 2012. His questionable power diminishes his prospect status. Parker has tried to generate more pop, but he's a contact-first hitter with a natural, easy approach. He has a good eye at the plate and one of the purer swings in the system, a short stroke that allows him to spray balls all over the field. Scouts can see him hitting for average power if he learns to drive more pitches. Parker has developed into an adequate third baseman, though his defense doesn't stand out either. He has solid hands and can make the routine plays, showing improved reactions and using better angles last season. He still made 14 errors in 88 games at the hot corner, however. He had an unusual throwing motion in college but has smoothed that out and now shows an average arm. He has below-average speed with decent baserunning instincts. If Parker is going to make a bid for Oakland's third-base job, he'll need to do it quickly with Miles Head coming up behind him. The A's opted not to protect Parker on their 40-man roster this offseason and likely will send him back to Sacramento to open 2013.

Year	Club (League)	Class	AVG	G	AB	R	H	2B	3B	HR	RBI	BB	SO	SB	CS	OBP	SLG
2009	Athletics (AZL)	R	.214	3	14	2	3	2	0	0	2	1	6	0	0	.267	.357
	Kane County (MWL)	LoA	.244	70	254	27	62	11	2	5	39	25	55	1	4	.312	.362
2010	Stockton (CAL)	HiA	.296	139	524	102	155	38	5	21	98	84	105	3	1	.392	.508
2011	Midland (TL)	AA	.286	132	504	72	144	30	2	10	74	69	107	1	1	.373	.413
	Sacramento (PCL)	AAA	.320	5	25	4	8	0	0	0	2	2	6	0	0	.370	.320
2012	Sacramento (PCL)	AAA	.256	99	328	43	84	13	5	7	47	32	93	5	1	.327	.390
Minor League Totals			.277	448	1649	250	456	94	14	43	262	213	372	10	7	.361	.429

28 ANDREW CARIGNAN, RHP

Born: July 23, 1986. **B-T:** R-R. **Ht.:** 5-11. **Wt.:** 235. **Drafted:** North Carolina, 2007 (5th round). **Signed by:** Neil Avent.

BA GRADE
45
HIGH

Carignan looked like he was on his way to establishing himself in the major league bullpen after he made four straight scoreless appearances following a May callup. But injuries have dogged him throughout his pro career, and his latest setback was his most serious as he tore an elbow ligament and needed Tommy John surgery. He previously had missed most of the 2009 season with forearm problems, followed by surgery to remove bone spurs from his elbow. When healthy, Carignan features a lively 93-97 mph fastball and a hard, sharp slider. The A's have toyed with having him throw a curveball, but he prefers the slider. He also has a usable changeup but employs it sparingly. Carignan had made progress with calming the violence in his delivery, which improved the command of his pitches but didn't keep him healthy. He has the upside of a late-inning reliever, but the A's will have to see how well his stuff comes back. They outrighted him off the 40-man roster in November. Carignan should get back on the mound by mid-2013 if his rehab stays on schedule.

Year	Club (League)	Class	W	L	ERA	G	GS	CG	SV	IP	H	HR	BB	SO	K/9	WHIP	AVG
2007	Kane County (MWL)	LoA	1	1	2.03	12	0	0	4	13	6	0	11	19	12.8	1.28	.136
2008	Stockton (CAL)	HiA	1	1	0.90	9	0	0	4	10	5	0	5	17	15.3	1.00	.147
	Midland (TL)	AA	3	3	2.22	46	0	0	24	53	36	4	39	67	11.4	1.42	.196
2009	Stockton (CAL)	HiA	0	0	4.50	2	0	0	0	2	1	0	3	2	9.0	2.00	.167
2010	Stockton (CAL)	HiA	3	3	6.27	30	0	0	0	33	28	2	34	44	12.0	1.88	.228
2011	Stockton (CAL)	HiA	1	0	0.00	9	0	0	5	11	4	0	2	12	9.8	0.55	.108
	Midland (TL)	AA	1	1	3.18	11	0	0	3	11	10	1	3	15	11.9	1.15	.238
	Sacramento (PCL)	AAA	0	0	2.16	13	0	0	0	17	11	1	7	19	10.3	1.08	.186
	Oakland (AL)	MAJ	0	0	4.26	6	0	0	0	6	8	1	2	5	7.1	1.58	.276

2012	Sacramento (PCL)	AAA	2	0	2.70	9	0	0	1	13	9	0	1	21	14.2	0.75	.184
	Oakland (AL)	MAJ	1	1	4.66	11	0	0	0	10	8	0	10	8	7.4	1.86	.242
Major League Totals			1	1	4.50	17	0	0	0	16	16	1	12	13	7.3	1.75	.258
Minor League Totals			11	8	2.92	141	0	0	41	163	110	8	105	216	11.9	1.32	.190

29 ARNOLD LEON, RHP

BA GRADE 45 HIGH

Born: Sept. 6, 1988. **B-T:** R-R. **Ht.:** 6-1. **Wt.:** 205. **Signed:** Mexico, 2007. **Signed by:** Randy Johnson/Craig Weissmann.

The A's signed Leon out of the Mexican League in 2007, and he looked to be on the rise after a solid 2009 season in Double-A. His career went off the rails when he went down after just three appearances in 2010, needed Tommy John surgery and essentially missed two full years. Oakland had harbored hopes of making him a starter, but he had been a reliever throughout his career in Mexico and returned to the bullpen once he finally pitched meaningful innings again last season. Leon put himself back on the team's radar with strong showings in the upper minors, earning a spot on the A's 40-man roster. His low 90s fastball has returned and he touches 95 mph from an easy, effortless delivery. His heater is fairly straight, but he does a good job of keeping it down in the strike zone. Leon's fading changeup is his go-to secondary pitch, and he mixes in a slow curveball. Oakland hasn't completely abandoned the idea of turning Leon into a starter, but with its glut of young pitchers, his path the big leagues looks to be as a reliever. He's a longshot to earn a job in big league camp, and if that doesn't happen he'll head back to Triple-A to begin the season.

Year	Club (League)	Class	W	L	ERA	G	GS	CG	SV	IP	H	HR	BB	SO	K/9	WHIP	AVG
2006	Saltillo (MEX)	AAA	0	0	2.70	4	0	0	0	3	2	0	2	2	5.4	1.20	.167
2007	Saltillo (MEX)	AAA	3	0	1.94	35	0	0	1	42	31	2	24	38	8.2	1.32	.217
2008	Stockton (CAL)	HiA	0	0	2.86	20	0	0	2	28	25	1	9	28	8.9	1.20	.238
	Saltillo (MEX)	AAA	2	1	4.30	13	0	0	0	15	12	0	2	21	12.9	0.95	.235
2009	Midland (TL)	AA	2	3	3.51	33	7	0	1	74	71	3	28	63	7.6	1.33	.247
2010	Midland (TL)	AA	0	0	6.23	3	0	0	0	4	6	1	3	1	2.1	2.08	.333
2011	Athletics (AZL)	R	0	1	8.53	5	5	0	0	6	6	0	4	8	11.4	1.58	.273
2012	Stockton (CAL)	HiA	0	1	5.28	12	0	0	0	15	26	1	5	25	14.7	2.02	.366
	Midland (TL)	AA	1	0	2.30	10	0	0	1	16	17	0	3	18	10.3	1.28	.288
	Sacramento (PCL)	AAA	3	0	1.77	22	0	0	0	36	26	4	15	31	7.8	1.15	.208
Minor League Totals			11	6	3.15	157	12	0	5	240	222	12	95	235	8.8	1.32	.258

30 JOSH BOWMAN, RHP

BA GRADE 45 HIGH

Born: Sept. 9, 1988. **B-T:** R-R. **Ht.:** 6-2. **Wt.:** 195. **Drafted:** Tampa, 2010 (10th round). **Signed by:** Trevor Schaffer.

Like Bobby Crocker, Bowman turned down the A's out of high school before signing with them three years later. A 49th-round pick in 2007, he pitched three seasons at NCAA Division II Tampa before turning pro for $75,000 as a 10th-rounder. After an unspectacular first full pro season and a 5.56 ERA in the first two months last year, he turned a corner. Bowman posted the California League's lowest ERA (2.75) in the final three months of the season, earning a cameo in Double-A. Former A's pitching coordinator Gil Patterson (who left after last season to become director of pitching for the Yankees) is a major proponent of the cutter, and that's the pitch that made the difference for Bowman. His high-80s cutter has sharp, late movement, giving him a weapon to play off his sinker, which tops out at 92 mph. He has good balance and direction in his delivery, helping him maintain solid command of both pitches. He also can mix in a 12-to-6 curveball and a changeup that has depth. Bowman doesn't profile to be more than a back-of-the-rotation starter, but he could be the next under-the-radar Oakland pitching prospect to take off, a la A.J. Griffin and Dan Straily. Bowman will return to Midland in 2013.

Year	Club (League)	Class	W	L	ERA	G	GS	CG	SV	IP	H	HR	BB	SO	K/9	WHIP	AVG
2010	Athletics (AZL)	R	0	0	0.00	1	0	0	0	1	0	0	0	2	18.0	0.00	.000
	Vancouver (NWL)	SS	0	2	3.74	14	0	0	0	22	29	2	5	23	9.6	1.57	.302
2011	Burlington (MWL)	LoA	8	6	3.55	28	28	0	0	155	148	9	44	98	5.7	1.24	.253
2012	Stockton (CAL)	HiA	6	10	3.62	25	25	0	0	147	157	14	33	127	7.8	1.30	.270
	Midland (TL)	AA	0	1	5.40	1	1	0	0	5	7	0	2	3	5.4	1.80	.333
Minor League Totals			14	19	3.61	69	54	0	0	329	341	25	84	253	6.9	1.29	.265

Philadelphia Phillies

BY MATT FORMAN

For different reasons, the Phillies' last two seasons have ended in disappointment. In 2011, the playoff run that had become an annual expectation in Philadelphia ended too early. In 2012, there was no postseason baseball in Philadelphia at all, for the first time in six years.

The Phillies expected their season to start slowly because of lingering injuries to Ryan Howard and Chase Utley, but it never really got on its projected course, at least until it was too late. The Phillies finished 81-81, their worst record since 2002, and needed a late-season blitz just to break even after falling 14 games under .500 at one point. Philadelphia lost several more players for significant time to injuries, including Jose Contreras, Freddy Galvis, Roy Halladay, Placido Polanco, Mike Stutes and Vance Worley.

As a result, the Phillies were sellers on the trade market for the first time since 2006. One year after acquiring Hunter Pence, general manager Ruben Amaro Jr. shipped him to the Giants for Nate Schierholtz and a pair of prospects (catcher Tommy Joseph and righthander Seth Rosin). Amaro also sent Joe Blanton and Shane Victorino to the Dodgers in separate deals for Josh Lindblom and righthanders Ethan Martin and Ryan O'Sullivan.

The big league struggles gave Philadelphia a chance to evaluate its system, as eight rookies debuted in the majors, the most since it had 15 in 1996. Along with the unexpected development of a few prospects, that ensured the last two months of the season weren't completely irrelevant.

Once considered an organization player, first baseman/outfielder Darin Ruf blasted 20 homers in Double-A in August, the most in United States professional baseball since Sammy Sosa in 1998, then hit three more during a September callup. Tyler Cloyd, a soft-tossing righty who's short on stuff but strong on pitching sense, made his major league debut in August and won two of his six starts. Longtime minor league veteran Eric Kratz showed some pop, while Phillippe Aumont flashed his plus stuff out of the bullpen. In varying capacities, they all figure to contribute in 2013.

Meanwhile, the Phillies' .500 finish secured them a higher first-round pick than any in recent memory, as long as they don't sign a free agent who requires compensation. They're slated to select 16th, their highest selection since they took Gavin Floyd fourth

Ryan Howard played just 71 games in 2012 coming back from his torn Achilles tendon

ANDREW WOOLLEY

overall in 2001.

Philadelphia has stuck with its philosophy of drafting high-upside athletes, with scouting director Marti Wolever preferring lefthanded pitching and speed. That's reflected on this list, which begins with a southpaw (Jesse Biddle) and a fleet-footed shortstop (Roman Quinn). Quinn is one of several members of a talented 2011 draft class who took a big step forward in their first full pro seasons, a group that also included lefthander Adam Morgan, third baseman Cody Asche and flamethrowing reliever Kenny Giles.

Most of the Phillies' best prospects are at least a year or two away from being ready for Citizens Bank Park, so Amaro swung two trades for veteran offensive help in December. He acquired Ben Revere from the Twins for Vance Worley and enigmatic righthander Trevor May, then dispatched Lindblom and righty Lisalverto Bonilla to get Michael Young from the Rangers. The Phillies then signed John Lannan and Mike Adams to fill gaps in the bullpen and starting rotation.

It's not all doom and gloom for the Phillies, who will return several significant players from their 2007-11 National League East championship clubs in 2013. If they can stay healthy—certainly not a guarantee given the age of many of the players—their season could have a happier ending.

THIS YEAR'S TOP 30

Player, Pos.		Grade
1.	Jesse Biddle, lhp	55/High
2.	Roman Quinn, ss	60/Extreme
3.	Tommy Joseph, c/1b	50/Medium
4.	Jonathan Pettibone, rhp	50/Medium
5.	Adam Morgan, lhp	55/High
6.	Ethan Martin, rhp	55/High
7.	Cody Asche, 3b	50/Medium
8.	Maikel Franco, 3b	55/High
9.	Darin Ruf, 1b/of	45/Low
10.	Carlos Tocci, of	55/Extreme
11.	Larry Greene, of	55/Extreme
12.	Shane Watson, rhp	50/High
13.	Phillippe Aumont, rhp	50/High
14.	Sebastian Valle, c	50/High
15.	Cesar Hernandez, 2b	45/Medium
16.	Mitchell Walding, 3b	50/High
17.	Mitch Gueller, rhp	50/High
18.	Austin Wright, lhp	50/High
19.	Kenny Giles, rhp	50/High
20.	Justin DeFratus, rhp	45/Medium
21.	Tyler Cloyd, rhp	40/Low
22.	Cameron Rupp, c	45/Medium
23.	Brody Colvin, rhp	45/High
24.	Zach Collier, of	45/High
25.	Aaron Altherr, of	45/High
26.	Tyson Gillies, of	45/High
27.	Dylan Cozens, of	50/Extreme
28.	Andrew Pullin, of/2b	45/High
29.	Kyrell Hudson, of	50/Extreme
30.	Kyle Simon, rhp	45/High

LAST YEAR'S TOP 30

Player, Pos.		Status
1.	Trevor May, rhp	(Twins)
2.	Jesse Biddle, c	No. 1
3.	Sebastian Valle, c	No. 14
4.	Jonathan Pettibone, rhp	No. 4
5.	Phillippe Aumont, rhp	No. 13
6.	Freddy Galvis, ss	Majors
7.	Justin DeFratus, rhp	No. 20
8.	Brody Colvin, rhp	No. 23
9.	Jiwan James, of	Dropped out
10.	Maikel Franco, 3b	No. 8
11.	Roman Quinn, ss	No. 2
12.	Lisalverto Bonilla, rhp	(Rangers)
13.	Carlos Tocci, of	No. 10
14.	Cesar Hernandez, 2b	No. 15
15.	Aaron Altherr, of	No. 25
16.	Ervis Manzanillo, lhp	Dropped out
17.	Julio Rodriguez, rhp	Dropped out
18.	Kyrell Hudson, of	No. 29
19.	Harold Garcia, 2b	Dropped out
20.	Larry Greene, of	No. 11
21.	Perci Garner, rhp	Dropped out
22.	Austin Hyatt, rhp	Dropped out
23.	Mitchell Walding, 3b	No. 16
24.	Leandro Castro, of	Dropped out
25.	Joe Savery, lhp	Dropped out
26.	Austin Wright, lhp	No. 18
27.	Zach Collier, of	No. 24
28.	J.C. Ramirez, rhp	Dropped out
29.	Adam Morgan, lhp	No. 5
30.	Michael Schwimer, rhp	Majors

BEST TOOLS

Best Hitter for Average	Cody Asche
Best Power Hitter	Darin Ruf
Best Strike-Zone Discipline	Darin Ruf
Fastest Baserunner	Roman Quinn
Best Athlete	Roman Quinn
Best Fastball	Kenny Giles
Best Curveball	Jesse Biddle
Best Slider	Adam Morgan
Best Changeup	Jonathan Pettibone
Best Control	Jonathan Pettibone
Best Defensive Catcher	Sebastian Valle
Best Defensive Infielder	Cesar Hernandez
Best Infield Arm	Maikel Franco
Best Defensive Outfielder	Tyson Gillies
Best Outfield Arm	Kyrell Hudson

PROJECTED 2017 LINEUP

Catcher	Tommy Joseph
First Base	Ryan Howard
Second Base	Chase Utley
Third Base	Cody Asche
Shortstop	Roman Quinn
Left Field	Darin Ruf
Center Field	Ben Revere
Right Field	Domonic Brown
No. 1 Starter	Cole Hamels
No. 2 Starter	Cliff Lee
No. 3 Starter	Roy Halladay
No. 4 Starter	Jesse Biddle
No. 5 Starter	Jonathan Pettibone
Closer	Jonathan Papelbon

TOP PROSPECTS OF THE DECADE

Year	Player, Pos.	2012 Org.
2003	Gavin Floyd, rhp	White Sox
2004	Cole Hamels, lhp	Phillies
2005	Ryan Howard, 1b	Phillies
2006	Cole Hamels, lhp	Phillies
2007	Carlos Carrasco, rhp	Indians
2008	Carlos Carrasco, rhp	Indians
2009	Domonic Brown, of	Phillies
2010	Domonic Brown, of	Phillies
2011	Domonic Brown, of	Phillies
2012	Trevor May, rhp	Phillies

TOP DRAFT PICKS OF THE DECADE

Year	Player, Pos.	2012 Org.
2003	Tim Moss, 2b (3rd round)	Out of baseball
2004	Greg Golson, of	Yankees
2005	Mike Costanzo, 3b (2nd round)	Reds
2006	Kyle Drabek, rhp	Blue Jays
2007	Joe Savery, lhp	Phillies
2008	Anthony Hewitt, 3b/of	Phillies
2009	Kelly Dugan, of (2nd round)	Phillies
2010	Jesse Biddle, lhp	Phillies
2011	Larry Greene, of (1st round supp.)	Phillies
2012	Shane Watson, rhp (1st round supp.)	Phillies

LARGEST BONUSES IN CLUB HISTORY

Gavin Floyd, 2001	$4,200,000
Pat Burrell, 1998	$3,150,000
Brett Myers, 1999	$2,050,000
Cole Hamels, 2002	$2,000,000
Chase Utley, 2000	$1,780,000

PHILADELPHIA PHILLIES

TOP 2013 ROOKIE: Darin Ruf, 1b/of. Manager Charlie Manuel likes power bats, and Ruf will be given a chance to win the left-field job after leading the minors with 38 homers.

BREAKOUT PROSPECT: Mitchell Walding, 3b. His pro debut didn't go according to plan, but he has all the tools to be an everyday third baseman, including solid power and defense.

SLEEPER: Yoel Mecias, lhp. A lanky lefty from Venezuela, he runs his fastball up to the mid-90s.

SOURCE OF TOP 30 TALENT			
Homegrown	25	Acquired	5
College	6	Trades	5
Junior college	2	Rule 5 draft	0
High school	13	Independent leagues	0
Nondrafted free agents	0	Free agents/waivers	0
International	4		

LF
Larry Greene (11)

CF
Carlos Tocci (10)
Zach Collier (24)
Aaron Altherr (25)
Tyson Gillies (26)
Kyrell Hudson (29)
Ender Inciarte
Jiwan James
Steven Golden

RF
Dylan Cozens (27)
Leandro Castro
Jose Pujols
Anthony Hewitt

3B
Cody Asche (7)
Maikel Franco (8)
Mitchell Walding (16)
Zach Green
Cameron Perkins
Harold Martinez

SS
Roman Quinn (2)
Troy Hanzawa
Edgar Duran

2B
Cesar Hernandez (15)
Andrew Pullin (28)
Angelo Mora

1B
Darin Ruf (9)
Chris Serritella
William Carmona
Kelly Dugan

C
Tommy Joseph (3)
Sebastian Valle (14)
Cameron Rupp (22)
Deivi Grullon
Gabriel Lino
Logan Moore

LHP

LHSP	LHRP
Jesse Biddle (1)	James Birmingham
Adam Morgan (5)	Brendan Lafferty
Austin Wright (18)	Jay Johnson
Ethan Stewart	Cesar Jimenez
Yoel Mecias	
Hoby Milner	
Ervis Manzanillo	
Franklyn Vargas	

RHP

RHSP	RHRP
Jonathan Pettibone (4)	Phillippe Aumont (13)
Ethan Martin (6)	Kenny Giles (19)
Shane Watson (12)	Justin DeFratus (20)
Mitch Gueller (17)	Kyle Simon (30)
Tyler Cloyd (21)	B.J. Rosenberg
Brody Colvin (23)	Tyler Knigge
Julio Rodriguez	Juan Sosa
Perci Garner	Colby Shreve
Kevin Brady	J.C. Ramirez
Colin Kleven	Colton Murray
Seth Rosin	Zach Cooper
David Buchanan	Ryan Duke
Ricky Bielski	Gabriel Arias
Drew Anderson	Hector Neris

DRAFT ANALYSIS

2012   BONUSES: $4.8 MILLION

BEST PURE HITTER: OF/2B Andrew Pullin (5) has an unorthodox stance and set-up, but once he loads his hands and gets his swing going, everything is in the right place and his bat stays in the hitting zone a long time. 1B/3B/OF Cameron Perkins (6) combines a fast bat and aggressive approach, and he has a consistent track record of producing at the plate.

BEST POWER HITTER: OF Dylan Cozens (2) wasn't a consensus early-round pick because of questions about his defense and hitting ability, but there's no doubting his top-of-the-scale raw power. 1B Chris Serritella (4) has plus pop.

FASTEST RUNNER: The Phillies didn't draft any burners, but OF Steven Golden (13) is a good athlete with above-average speed.

BEST DEFENSIVE PLAYER: 3B Zach Green (3) was a shortstop in high school, but his size and range make him a better fit at the hot corner. He's a baseball rat with good instincts, soft hands and a strong arm.

BEST FASTBALL: RHP Mitch Gueller (1s) uses an athletic frame to generate a 90-93 mph fastball that tops out at 95. RHPs Shane Watson (1s), Kevin Brady (10) and Zach Cooper (15) also can get to 95.

BEST SECONDARY PITCH: Watson has a true hammer curveball. He discovered that he has diabetes after being drafted.

BEST PRO DEBUT: LHP Hoby Milner (7) went 7-3, 2.50 with 54 strikeouts in 68 innings, including 12 starts in low Class A.

BEST ATHLETE: Cozens has a good combination of size and strength, and if he had gone to Arizona he planned to play baseball and defensive end for the football team. His father Randy also was a defensive end, and he was selected by the Denver Broncos in the 1976 NFL draft.

MOST INTRIGUING BACKGROUND: Before standing out as a position player, Pullin was known as an ambidextrous pitcher. Milner's father Brian went straight from high school to the big leagues in 1978 as a Blue Jays bonus baby. C Darrell Miller Jr.'s (34) dad spent five years in the majors and now works for Major League Baseball. Miller's aunt Cheryl and uncle Reggie are basketball Hall of Famers. RHP Chris Nichols' (31) father Rod pitched in the big leagues and is Philadelphia's bullpen coach.

CLOSEST TO THE MAJORS: Coming out of Texas, Milner shows advanced polish and feel for pitching.

BEST LATE-ROUND PICK: RHP Drew Anderson (21) opened eyes in instructional league, showing the potential for a solid fastball and plus breaking ball.

THE ONE WHO GOT AWAY: RHP Alec Rash (2) didn't pitch well during his summer high school season in Iowa and wound up at Missouri. Philadelphia made a bigger run at RHP David Hill (17), who has more upside and is now at Long Beach State.

ASSESSMENT: Despite forfeiting their first-round pick by signing Jonathan Papelbon, the Phillies added a pair of promising high school pitchers with supplemental picks they got for losing Raul Ibanez and Ryan Madson.

2011   BONUSES: $4.7 MILLION

Even without a first-round pick, the Phillies found seven intriguing prospects in the first seven rounds in OF Larry Greene (1s), SS Roman Quinn (2), LHPs Adam Morgan (3) and Austin Wright (8), 3Bs Cody Asche (4) and Mitchell Walding (5) and RHP Kenny Giles (7).

GRADE: B

2010   BONUSES: $3.9 MILLION

LHP Jesse Biddle (1), a hometown prep product, is the system's No. 1 prospect. But there's not another standout in this crop.

GRADE: C+

2009   BONUSES: $3.2 MILLION

In another year without a first-rounder, Philadelphia discovered a couple of slugging 1B/OFs in the later rounds in Jonathan Singleton (8) and Darin Ruf (20). Singleton went to the Astros in a 2011 trade for Hunter Pence. Ruf led the minors with 38 homers last year and made his big league debut, as did unsigned RHP A.J. Griffin (34).

GRADE: B+

2008   BONUSES: $6.7 MILLION

It's not easy having a deep draft despite missing on three of your top four picks, but the Phillies did just that. OFs Anthony Hewitt (1) and Zach Collier (1s) have scuffled, while RHP Jason Knapp (2) can't stay healthy. But OF Anthony Gose (2) and RHPs Vance Worley (3), Mike Stutes (11), B.J. Rosenberg (13), Michael Schwimer (14) and Tyler Cloyd (18) all have played in the majors, and RHPs Jonathan Pettibone (3s), Trevor May (4) and Jarred Cosart (38) should join them in he near future. Gose (Roy Halladay), Knapp (Cliff Lee), Worley and May (Ben Revere), and Cosart (Pence) all were used in significant trades.

GRADE: B+

Draft analysis by Conor Glassey (2012) and Jim Callis (2008-11). Numbers in parentheses indicate draft rounds.

1 JESSE BIDDLE, LHP

Born: Oct. 22, 1991. **B-T:** L-L. **Ht.:** 6-4. **Wt.:** 225.
Drafted: HS—Philadelphia, 2010 (1st round). **Signed by:** Eric Valent.

BA GRADE
55
HIGH

CLIFF WELCH

The Phillies were enamored with two high school players, California outfielder Christian Yelich and local lefty Jesse Biddle, in the 2010 draft. When the Marlins took Yelich four picks prior to Philadelphia's selection at No. 27, that made the decision for them. They were thrilled to get Biddle, a lifelong Phillies fan who was in the stands at Citizens Bank Park for the Game Five clincher in the 2008 World Series. After seeing him shine at the East Coast Pro Showcase in the summer of 2011, Philadelphia targeted Biddle, who had thrown only 33 innings as a junior at Germantown Friends School—13 miles north of the Phillies' ballpark. Area scout Eric Valent went to nearly every one of his starts as a senior, and various club officials including general manager Ruben Amaro Jr. and senior adviser Pat Gillick also scouted him. Biddle sealed the deal by impressing in a private predraft workout at Citizens Bank Park. He gave up an Oregon commitment to sign quickly for $1.16 million. He has progressed steadily, leading the high Class A Florida State League with 151 strikeouts in 2012. He pitched the entire season at age 20 and was the FSL's second-youngest ERA qualifier behind Pirates righthander Jameson Taillon. Biddle ranked No. 8 and No. 2 on this list after his first two pro seasons before ascending to the top spot.

Biddle has drawn comparisons to Andy Pettitte for his frame, four-pitch mix and tough three-quarters arm angle that induces whiffs and weak contact. Pitching once a week as an amateur, Biddle worked at 92-94 mph with his fastball. He now operates more at 88-93 mph, but his fastball sneaks up on hitters and plays as a plus pitch because of his crossfire deception and leverage on the mound. He can also get swings and misses with a sweeping 72-75 mph curveball that features good shape and arc. He struggled to control its depth and throw it for strikes in the past, but he was much more consistent with his curve in 2012 and it now projects as a future above-average offering. His 78-80 mph tumbling changeup continues to progress

SCOUTING GRADES

Fastball: 60.   **Control:** 55.
Curveball: 60.   **Command:** 50.
Changeup: 50.

Based on 20-80 scouting scale, where 50 represents major league average, and future projection rather than present tools.

and could develop into an average pitch. Biddle added two new weapons in 2012. The Phillies reintroduced the slider that he threw in high school, and they also worked with him on picking up a two-seam fastball to get more outs early in the count. Biddle has cut his walk rate every year since signing, and did a better job of pitching to both sides of the plate in the FSL. He has a smooth delivery and arm swing, so he could continue to improve his control and command. He also earns praise for his maturity, competitiveness, aptitude and work ethic.

The safe projection would be to call Biddle a solid No. 3 starter who can eat innings in the middle of a contender's rotation. But he could have more upside if he continues to get better like he has throughout his young pro career. He benefited from pitching alongside college draftees and fellow lefties Adam Morgan and Austin Wright in Clearwater, and the trio could stick together in 2013 at Double-A Reading.

Year	Club (League)	Class	W	L	ERA	G	GS	CG	SV	IP	H	HR	BB	SO	K/9	WHIP	AVG
2010	Phillies (GCL)	R	3	1	4.32	9	9	1	0	33	35	2	9	41	11.1	1.32	.263
	Williamsport (NYP)	SS	1	0	2.61	3	3	0	0	10	5	0	11	9	7.8	1.55	.152
2011	Lakewood (SAL)	LoA	7	8	2.98	25	24	0	0	133	104	5	66	124	8.4	1.28	.219
2012	Clearwater (FSL)	HiA	10	6	3.22	26	26	1	0	143	129	10	54	151	9.5	1.28	.237
Minor League Totals			21	15	3.21	63	62	2	0	319	273	17	140	325	9.2	1.29	.230

2 ROMAN QUINN, SS

DAVID SCHOFIELD

Born: May 14, 1993. **B-T:** B-R. **Ht.:** 5-10. **Wt.:** 170. **Drafted:** HS—Port St. Joe, Fla., 2011 (2nd round). **Signed by:** Aaron Jersild.

The fastest player in the 2011 draft, Quinn signed for $775,000 hours before the Aug. 15 deadline. He made his pro debut in 2012 and led the short-season New York-Penn League in runs (56), triples (11) and steals (30). A true 80 runner on the 20-80 scouting scale, Quinn impacts all phases of the game with his speed. After toying with switch-hitting as an amateur, he committed to it after signing and he projects to be a solid hitter from both sides. He has a simple, fast stroke and more pop than his size would suggest, but he won't be a home run threat and will need to cut down on his strikeouts. A center fielder in high school, Quinn is learning the intricacies of shortstop. He must do a better job at positioning and gathering his feet before throwing after making 27 errors in 66 games at Williamsport. He has elite first-step quickness and tremendous range to go along with a plus arm. All the pieces are in place for Quinn to become a top-of-the-order, middle-of-the-diamond catalyst. He inevitably draws comparisons to Jimmy Rollins, but he runs faster and has a better arm than Rollins did at the same stage. Quinn will advance to low Class A Lakewood in 2013.

BA GRADE

60

EXTREME

Year	Club (League)	Class	AVG	G	AB	R	H	2B	3B	HR	RBI	BB	SO	SB	CS	OBP	SLG
2012	Williamsport (NYP)	SS	.281	66	267	56	75	9	11	1	23	28	61	30	6	.370	.408
Minor League Totals			.281	66	267	56	75	9	11	1	23	28	61	30	6	.370	.408

3 TOMMY JOSEPH, C/1B

Born: July 16, 1991. **B-T:** R-R. **Ht.:** 6-1. **Wt.:** 215. **Drafted:** HS—Scottsdale, Ariz., 2009 (2nd round). **Signed by:** Chuck Hensley (Giants).

A power-hitting Arizona prep product who moved behind the plate full-time as a senior, Joseph signed for $712,500 as a Giants second-round pick in 2009. He was the primary piece in the Hunter Pence deal, coming to the Phillies along with Nate Schierholtz and minor league righthander Seth Rosin last July. With Double-A Eastern League affiliate Richmond playing Reading, Joseph literally switched dugouts the night of the trade. Joseph is thick, strong and durable, especially in his lower half. His direct swing produces natural backspin, yielding plus raw power to all fields, and he's at his best when he's hitting the ball gap to gap. He projects as an average hitter, though he runs into trouble when his bat wraps and barrels the ball late. There were questions about Joseph's ability to remain behind the plate early in his pro career, but the Phillies believe in him. He has soft hands and plus arm strength, and he threw out 40 percent of basestealers in 2012. He's still working on positioning and blocking balls in the dirt. He's a below-average runner but has some instincts on the bases. Joseph is Philadelphia's backstop of the future, and Carlos Ruiz is signed through only 2013. Joseph should spend the season at Triple-A Lehigh Valley splitting time with Sebastian Valle, who along with Cameron Rupp gives the system strong catching depth.

BA GRADE

50

MEDIUM

Year	Club (League)	Class	AVG	G	AB	R	H	2B	3B	HR	RBI	BB	SO	SB	CS	OBP	SLG
2010	Augusta (SAL)	LoA	.236	117	436	46	103	22	1	16	68	26	116	0	0	.290	.401
2011	San Jose (CAL)	HiA	.270	127	514	80	139	33	2	22	95	29	102	1	0	.317	.471
2012	Richmond (EL)	AA	.260	80	304	32	79	16	0	8	38	25	64	0	3	.313	.391
	Reading (EL)	AA	.250	28	100	12	25	8	0	3	10	9	32	0	1	.327	.420
Minor League Totals			.256	352	1354	170	346	79	3	49	211	89	314	1	4	.308	.427

4 JONATHAN PETTIBONE, RHP

DAVID SCHOFIELD

Born: July 19, 1990. **B-T:** L-R. **Ht.:** 6-5. **Wt.:** 200. **Drafted:** HS—Yorba Linda, Calif., 2008 (3rd round supplemental). **Signed by:** Darrell Conner.

The son of former big league pitcher Jay Pettibone, Jonathan signed for $500,000 in 2008. He has climbed steadily through the system and claimed a spot on the 40-man roster. Pettibone doesn't have the highest ceiling among Phillies farmhands, but he might have the lowest floor. Aside from his youth, he has several attributes working in his favor—a tall frame that allows him to work downhill easily, a solid three-pitch mix, durability and a track record or performance. Pettibone works quickly and establishes tempo with a 90-92 mph sinker that touches 94, and he effectively pitches to both sides of the plate. He also throws an above-average changeup at 80-84 mph with good arm speed. He started throwing an 83-86 mph cutter late in 2012. His cutter is firmer and breaks later than his low-80s slider, giving him an added weapon against lefthanders. He has an effortless, repeatable delivery that looks like he's playing catch, and he has the

BA GRADE

50

MEDIUM

system's best command. Though Pettibone doesn't have a true swing-and-miss pitch, his stuff plays up because of his command. He profiles as a mid-rotation, innings-eating starter, and he needs little more seasoning before contributing in the big leagues. He could be the first starter promoted to Philadelphia in 2013.

Year	Club (League)	Class	W	L	ERA	G	GS	CG	SV	IP	H	HR	BB	SO	K/9	WHIP	AVG
2008	Phillies (GCL)	R	0	1	0.00	1	1	0	0	1	3	0	1	0	0.0	4.00	.600
2009	Williamsport (NYP)	SS	2	4	5.35	9	8	0	0	35	37	0	16	36	9.2	1.50	.261
2010	Lakewood (SAL)	LoA	8	6	3.49	24	23	1	0	131	114	10	41	84	5.8	1.18	.237
2011	Clearwater (FSL)	HiA	10	11	2.96	27	27	0	0	161	149	5	34	115	6.4	1.14	.248
2012	Reading (EL)	AA	9	7	3.30	19	19	1	0	117	115	9	27	81	6.2	1.21	.257
	Lehigh Valley (IL)	AAA	4	1	2.55	7	7	1	0	42	31	0	22	32	6.8	1.25	.204
Minor League Totals			33	30	3.32	87	85	3	0	488	449	24	141	348	6.4	1.21	.246

5 ADAM MORGAN, LHP

Born: Feb. 27, 1990. **B-T:** L-L. **Ht.:** 6-1. **Wt.:** 195. **Drafted:** Alabama, 2011 (3rd round). **Signed by:** Mike Stauffer.

Inconsistent during three years as a weekend starter at Alabama, Morgan signed with the Phillies for $250,000 as a third-round pick in 2011. Following a strong spring training, he skipped a level to high Class A for his first full pro season and led the Florida State League in strikeouts per nine innings (10.2) and WHIP (1.07). He finished the year by winning four of his six Double-A starts. Morgan's stuff took a significant step forward in 2012. He did a better job of establishing his 91-94 mph fastball, especially on the inner half of the plate, making the rest of his arsenal more effective. His 81-84 mph sharp slider flashes plus potential and is more consistent than in the past, while managers rated his 78-80 mph changeup the FSL's best. He also throws a 76-78 mph show-me curveball. Morgan has above-average control. His smooth delivery, high three-quarters arm action, burrowing glove tuck, strike-throwing ability and competitiveness all evoke comparisons

BA GRADE

55

HIGH

to Cliff Lee, though he doesn't quite have Lee's arsenal. With the boost in stuff, Morgan profiles as a mid-rotation starter and possibly more, given the development of his secondary offerings. He could earn an aggressive assignment to Triple-A in 2013, though a brief return to Reading isn't out of the question.

Year	Club (League)	Class	W	L	ERA	G	GS	CG	SV	IP	H	HR	BB	SO	K/9	WHIP	AVG
2011	Williamsport (NYP)	SS	3	3	2.01	11	11	0	0	54	42	2	14	43	7.2	1.04	.206
2012	Clearwater (FSL)	HiA	4	10	3.29	21	20	1	0	123	103	7	28	140	10.2	1.07	.227
	Reading (EL)	AA	4	1	3.53	6	6	0	0	36	34	2	11	29	7.3	1.26	.260
Minor League Totals			11	14	3.01	38	37	1	0	212	179	11	53	212	9.0	1.09	.227

6 ETHAN MARTIN, RHP

Born: June 6, 1989. **B-T:** R-R. **Ht.:** 6-2. **Wt.:** 195. **Drafted:** HS—Toccoa, Ga., 2008 (1st round). **Signed by:** Lon Joyce (Dodgers).

The first high school pitcher selected in the 2008 draft, Martin went 15th overall and signed for $1.73 million. He had sporadic success in four years in the Dodgers system, but made strides in 2012 before coming to the Phillies along with Josh Lindblom in a July deal for Shane Victorino. After splitting time between the rotation and bullpen in the past, Martin was exclusively a starter last season. Athletic yet unrefined, Martin has an effortless delivery, a loose arm action and the potential for three plus pitches. He operates anywhere from 91-97 mph with his fastball, mostly sitting at 93-95 with late two-seam life. His best secondary pitch is an 85-88 mph slider that's almost like a cutter. He didn't use his 72-75 mph curveball much in relief, so it's still developing, but it has sharp, late

DAVID SCHOFIELD

BA GRADE

55

HIGH

break. He also shows feel for an 82-84 mph fading changeup. Martin has average-at-best control and even shakier command. He gets in trouble with high pitch counts, though his 2012 walk rate (4.5 per nine innings) was a career best. With his variety of weapons and a history of durability, Martin has the ceiling of a solid mid-rotation starter, but his struggles to throw consistent strikes could push him to the bullpen. Placed on the 40-man roster in November, he should spend 2013 in Triple-A.

Year	Club (League)	Class	W	L	ERA	G	GS	CG	SV	IP	H	HR	BB	SO	K/9	WHIP	AVG
2009	Great Lakes (MWL)	LoA	6	8	3.87	27	19	0	1	100	85	4	61	120	10.8	1.46	.232
2010	Inland Empire (CAL)	HiA	9	14	6.35	25	22	1	0	113	120	10	81	105	8.3	1.77	.279
2011	R. Cucamonga (CAL)	HiA	4	4	7.36	16	9	0	0	55	65	8	37	61	10.0	1.85	.291
	Chattanooga (SL)	AA	5	3	4.02	21	3	0	2	40	31	3	29	43	9.6	1.49	.215
2012	Chattanooga (SL)	AA	8	6	3.58	20	20	0	0	118	89	5	61	112	8.5	1.27	.214
	Reading (EL)	AA	5	0	3.18	7	7	0	0	40	29	3	18	35	7.9	1.18	.206
Minor League Totals			37	35	4.77	116	80	1	3	466	419	33	287	476	9.2	1.51	.244

7 CODY ASCHE, 3B

Born: June 30, 1990. **B-T:** L-R. **Ht.:** 6-1. **Wt.:** 180. **Drafted:** Nebraska, 2011 (4th round). **Signed by:** David Seifert.

Asche posted potent power numbers at Nebraska and signed for $168,300 in 2011, but he batted just .192 with little pop in his pro debut. The Phillies weren't sure what to make of his struggles, but then he hit .324/.369/.481 and reached Double-A in his first full pro season. Asche has the hands, bat speed and plate discipline to hit. Adding a better load to his swing during instructional league in 2011 allowed him to better tap into his power. His short stroke and strong finish create loft off the barrel, though some scouts wonder if he'll have enough pop to profile as a regular at third base. He gets a tad overly aggressive at times, but he goes to the plate with a good plan. Asche grades as average with the glove, and managers named him the Florida State League's best defensive third baseman in 2012. He has a solid arm and good hands, and he has improved his positioning and footwork. He's an average runner who's quicker under way. He's not a prototypical power-hitting, slick-fielding third baseman, but Asche should hit enough to have a regular big league role. He could start 2013 in Triple-A and be in line to take over for Michael Young when Young becomes a free agent after the season.

BA GRADE
50
MEDIUM

Year	Club (League)	Class	AVG	G	AB	R	H	2B	3B	HR	RBI	BB	SO	SB	CS	OBP	SLG
2011	Williamsport (NYP)	SS	.192	68	239	14	46	11	0	2	19	24	50	0	3	.273	.264
2012	Clearwater (FSL)	HiA	.349	62	255	31	89	13	3	2	25	12	37	10	2	.378	.447
	Reading (EL)	AA	.300	68	263	42	79	20	3	10	47	22	56	1	1	.360	.513
Minor League Totals			.283	198	757	87	214	44	6	14	91	58	143	11	6	.338	.412

8 MAIKEL FRANCO, 3B

DAVID SCHOFIELD

Born: Aug. 26, 1992. **B-T:** R-R. **Ht.:** 6-1. **Wt.:** 180. **Signed:** Dominican Republic, 2010. **Signed by:** Sal Agostinelli.

His 7.7-second 60-yard dash times scared scouts off Franco in showcase settings, but Koby Perez closely followed him and suggested to Phillies international supervisor Sal Agostinelli that Franco could move behind the plate. That never came to pass, but Philadelphia has been pleased with his progress since signing him for $100,000. He hit .346/.395/.530 in the second half of 2012 as a 19-year-old in low Class A. Franco has an unconventional arm-bar swing and pre-pitch movement that make his stroke long at times, but he has quick hands and good feel for the barrel. He has well above-average raw power and puts on a show in batting practice, though he doesn't always get to his pop during games. Early in 2012, he struggled with soft stuff away, got pull-happy and didn't have much of a two-strike approach. He found success when he worked the middle of the diamond in the second half. Despite being a 20 runner on the 20-80 scouting scale, Franco projects as a solid third baseman with a strong arm and soft hands. He has a thick lower half and will need to keep his body in check. Franco has a ceiling of a power-hitting corner infielder, but he'll have to continue to make offensive adjustments, especially in recognizing offspeed stuff. He'll make the jump to high Class A in 2013.

BA GRADE
55
HIGH

Year	Club (League)	Class	AVG	G	AB	R	H	2B	3B	HR	RBI	BB	SO	SB	CS	OBP	SLG
2010	Phillies (GCL)	R	.222	51	194	23	43	11	2	2	29	16	46	0	0	.292	.330
2011	Lakewood (SAL)	LoA	.123	17	65	6	8	2	0	1	6	1	15	0	0	.149	.200
	Williamsport (NYP)	SS	.287	54	202	19	58	17	1	2	38	25	30	0	0	.367	.411
2012	Lakewood (SAL)	LoA	.280	132	503	70	141	32	3	14	84	38	80	3	1	.336	.439
Minor League Totals			.259	254	964	118	250	62	6	19	157	80	171	3	1	.322	.395

9 DARIN RUF, 1B/OF

Born: July 28, 1986. **B-T:** R-R. **Ht.:** 6-3. **Wt.:** 220. **Drafted:** Creighton, 2009 (20th round). **Signed by:** David Seifert.

Signed for just $2,500 as a 20th-round pick in 2009, Ruf wasn't in the Phillies' future plans until he mashed 20 homers in August, the most since Sammy Sosa in 1998. He finished the year with a minor league-high 38 homers, smacked three during a September callup and added 10 more in the Venezuelan League. Ruf always has hit, batting .290 or better in each of his four pro seasons. Though he didn't break out until he turned 26, Philadelphia believes his home run binge is the result of maturing at the plate. He has plenty of raw strength and started tapping into it when he added loft to his swing and identified which pitches he can drive. He's a good fastball hitter, and he had success against soft stuff in his short stint in the big leagues. Ruf is a well below-average runner and a fringy defender at first base, his natural position. He started taking flyballs in left field last July and isn't pretty in the outfield, though he catches what he gets to. His arm

BA GRADE
45
LOW

is playable. He's blocked at first base by Ryan Howard, but the Phillies want to get his bat in their lineup. He could be their everyday left fielder in 2013, a scenario unimaginable in the middle of last season. At worst, he should be a power bat off the bench.

Year	Club (League)	Class	AVG	G	AB	R	H	2B	3B	HR	RBI	BB	SO	SB	CS	OBP	SLG
2009	Phillies (GCL)	R	.326	20	43	5	14	3	0	0	6	3	8	0	0	.400	.395
	Williamsport (NYP)	SS	.301	37	133	17	40	17	0	3	24	14	22	0	1	.377	.496
2010	Lakewood (SAL)	LoA	.330	32	115	25	38	7	3	4	17	21	23	3	2	.443	.548
	Clearwater (FSL)	HiA	.277	97	368	45	102	34	2	5	50	26	87	2	2	.335	.421
2011	Clearwater (FSL)	HiA	.308	133	484	72	149	43	1	17	82	56	95	0	1	.388	.506
2012	Reading (EL)	AA	.317	139	489	93	155	32	1	38	104	65	102	2	0	.408	.620
	Philadelphia (NL)	MAJ	.333	12	33	4	11	2	1	3	10	2	12	0	0	.351	.727
Major League Totals			.333	12	33	4	11	2	1	3	10	2	12	0	0	.351	.727
Minor League Totals			.305	458	1632	257	498	136	7	67	283	185	337	7	6	.386	.520

10 CARLOS TOCCI, OF

Born: Aug. 23, 1995. **B-T:** R-R. **Ht.:** 6-2. **Wt.:** 160. **Signed:** Venezuela, 2011. **Signed by:** Sal Agostinelli.

Tocci attracted one of the largest bonuses that international supervisor Sal Agostinelli's budget-conscious staff ever has given an international amateur, signing for $759,000 as soon as he turned 16 in 2011. Though the Phillies have an academy in his native Venezuela, they aggressively assigned him to the Rookie-level Gulf Coast League for his 2012 pro debut. He held his own as the GCL's lone 16-year-old. Tocci has a stick-figure frame, so Philadelphia closely monitored his physical wear and tear during the summer. Other than strength and corresponding power, he has all the tools the scouts look for, as well as uncanny instincts. He's a plus-plus runner who picks his spots to steal. He glides in center field, has a plus arm and could be a top-flight defender. Tocci has a good idea of the strike zone, consistently barrels the ball and uses the whole field. He projects as an above-average hitter, though it's uncertain if he'll ever have much power. He has narrow

BA GRADE

55

EXTREME

shoulders and may not fill out much. While he has an intriguing ceiling, Tocci also will need plenty of time to develop his tools and add strength. He might be able to handle an assignment to low Class A in 2013, but the safer play would be to keep him in extended spring training and send him to Williamsport in June.

Year	Club (League)	Class	AVG	G	AB	R	H	2B	3B	HR	RBI	BB	SO	SB	CS	OBP	SLG
2012	Phillies (GCL)	R	.278	38	97	13	27	2	0	0	9	6	18	9	2	.330	.299
Minor League Totals			.278	38	97	13	27	2	0	0	9	6	18	9	2	.330	.299

11 LARRY GREENE, OF

BA GRADE

55

EXTREME

Born: Feb. 10, 1993. **B-T:** L-R. **Ht.:** 6-0. **Wt.:** 235. **Drafted:** HS—Nashville, Ga., 2011 (1st round supplemental). **Signed by:** Aaron Jersild.

A physically imposing presence with a barrel chest and thick lower half, Greene attracted the attention of Alabama football coach Nick Saban as a linebacker. But Greene knew his future was in baseball, and after breaking his ankle on the gridiron the year before, he didn't play football as a high school senior. The Phillies took him 39th overall in 2011 and signed him away from a commitment to Chipola (Fla.) JC for $1 million. A groin tweak delayed his debut, and Greene didn't prepare himself physically for the demands of pro baseball last spring. After getting in shape in extended spring training, he spent the summer with Williamsport. Greene's value is mostly tied to his power bat. He has worked on shortening his path to the ball and using the middle of the diamond. Though he struck out 78 times in 70 games, he's not a free swinger. He's learning to identify secondary pitches, but he's not afraid to work deep counts and also drew 41 walks. The Phillies were pleased with the progress Greene made defensively in left field last summer. He's an average runner with an average arm, and he moves well for his size. He'll make the jump to low Class A in 2013.

Year	Club (League)	Class	AVG	G	AB	R	H	2B	3B	HR	RBI	BB	SO	SB	CS	OBP	SLG
2012	Williamsport (NYP)	SS	.272	70	257	36	70	22	0	2	26	41	78	1	2	.373	.381
Minor League Totals			.272	70	257	36	70	22	0	2	26	41	78	1	2	.373	.381

12 SHANE WATSON, RHP

BA GRADE

50

HIGH

Born: Aug. 13, 1993. **B-T:** R-R. **Ht.:** 6-4. **Wt.:** 200. **Drafted:** HS—Lakewood, Calif., 2012 (1st round supplemental). **Signed by:** Demerius Pittman.

The first of two Phillies supplemental first-round picks in 2012, Watson attended Lakewood (Calif.) High, the alma mater of Travis d'Arnaud, the star catcher prospect whom Philadelphia included in the Roy Halladay deal in December 2009. In one of the most highly anticipated and scouted high school games last spring, Watson outdueled Chase DeJong in a matchup of Southern California recruits. After signing with the Phillies for $1,291,300, Watson lost about 30 pounds as he dealt with vomiting and tingling in his hands. Diagnosed with Type 1 diabetes, he made five pro appearances once everything was under control and looked back to full strength in instructional league. For his frame, aggressiveness on the mound and power curveball, Watson reminds club officials of Phillies 1999 first-rounder Brett Myers. He also drew comparisons as an amateur to Brian Wilson. Watson runs his fastball from 89-95 mph. His curveball has bite and already is a plus offering, and his changeup is a work in progress. He doesn't have a classic arm action, and Philadelphia will work to refine his delivery, which should help his command. Watson projects as a mid-rotation starter and possibly more. He could make the jump to low Class A for his first full pro season.

Year	Club (League)	Class	W	L	ERA	G	GS	CG	SV	IP	H	HR	BB	SO	K/9	WHIP	AVG
2012	Phillies (GCL)	R	0	1	1.29	5	3	0	0	7	5	0	1	8	10.3	0.86	.200
Minor League Totals			0	1	1.29	5	3	0	0	7	5	0	1	8	10.3	0.86	.200

13 PHILLIPPE AUMONT, RHP

Born: Jan. 7, 1989 **B-T:** L-R. **Ht.:** 6-7. **Wt.:** 260. **Drafted:** HS—Gatineau, Quebec, 2007 (1st round). **Signed by:** Wayne Norton (Mariners).

Nearly three years after being acquired with outfielder Tyson Gillies and righthander J.C. Ramirez in the December 2009 deal that sent Cliff Lee to the Mariners, Aumont made his big league debut last August. The centerpiece of that deal, Aumont signed for $1.9 million as the 11th overall pick in the 2007 draft. He took a long road to the majors, bouncing between the bullpen and rotation while struggling with command, consistency and composure. Aumont still has the size and stuff that get scouts excited, and some project him as a future closer. In the last two years he has embraced his role in the bullpen. He has the best two-pitch combination in the system, a heavy 93-97 mph fastball with sink and a high-breaking curveball. They both induce feeble swings and whiffs. Fastball command will be critical to his future success, and he doesn't have a track record of consistently throwing strikes. He also needs to stay on top of his curveball, which can get slurvy at times. Aumont should have an inside track for a spot in Philadephia's bullpen to open 2013.

Year	Club (League)	Class	W	L	ERA	G	GS	CG	SV	IP	H	HR	BB	SO	K/9	WHIP	AVG
2008	Wisconsin (MWL)	LoA	4	4	2.75	15	8	0	2	56	46	4	19	50	8.1	1.17	.224
2009	High Desert (CAL)	HiA	1	2	3.24	29	0	0	12	33	24	3	12	35	9.5	1.08	.195
	West Tenn (SL)	AA	1	4	5.09	15	0	0	4	18	21	1	11	24	12.2	1.81	.292
2010	Reading (EL)	AA	1	6	7.43	11	11	0	0	50	55	4	38	38	6.9	1.87	.284
	Clearwater (FSL)	HiA	2	5	4.48	16	10	1	1	72	74	6	42	77	9.6	1.60	.270
2011	Reading (EL)	AA	1	5	2.32	25	0	0	4	31	23	2	11	41	11.9	1.10	.195
	Lehigh Valley (IL)	AAA	1	0	3.18	18	0	0	3	23	21	0	14	37	14.7	1.54	.244
2012	Lehigh Valley (IL)	AAA	3	1	4.26	41	0	0	15	44	34	3	34	59	12.0	1.53	.209
	Philadelphia (NL)	MAJ	0	1	3.68	18	0	0	2	15	10	0	9	14	8.6	1.30	.189
Major League Totals			0	1	3.68	18	0	0	2	15	10	0	9	14	8.6	1.30	.189
Minor League Totals			14	27	4.22	170	29	1	41	327	298	23	181	361	9.9	1.47	.241

14 SEBASTIAN VALLE, C

Born: July 24, 1990. **B-T:** R-R. **Ht.:** 6-1. **Wt.:** 205. **Signed:** Mexico, 2006. **Signed by:** Sal Agostinelli.

Valle signed as a 16-year-old for $30,000 out of Los Mochis, Mexico, where he impressed international supervisor Sal Agostinelli in a private workout. Valle moved up the ladder one level per year, catching staffs full of hard throwers, then moved up to Triple-A when the Phillies acquired backstop Tommy Joseph in the Hunter Pence deal last July. Valle generates above-average raw power thanks to quick hands and explosive wrists, but he has poor plate discipline. He has an overly aggressive hitting approach and his instinct is to cheat on inner-half fastballs, which leaves him susceptible to breaking stuff. Valle should be at least average defensively. He moves well laterally, is a sure-handed receiver and has plus arm strength, though he doesn't consistently get his feet underneath him on stolen-base attempts. He threw out 26 percent of basestealers last season. Valle runs well for a catcher and has taken ground balls at third base in the past, and one scout suggested that trying him there again might give him a different perspective at the plate. He should return to Lehigh Valley to open 2013.

Year	Club (League)	Class	AVG	G	AB	R	H	2B	3B	HR	RBI	BB	SO	SB	CS	OBP	SLG
2007	Phillies (DSL)	R	.284	54	176	29	50	13	1	2	25	29	26	4	4	.398	.403
2008	Phillies (GCL)	R	.281	48	167	27	47	15	0	2	18	12	31	0	0	.341	.407
2009	Lakewood (SAL)	LoA	.223	45	157	16	35	12	1	1	15	16	37	1	2	.313	.331
	Williamsport (NYP)	SS	.307	50	192	25	59	15	5	6	40	11	41	0	0	.335	.531
2010	Lakewood (SAL)	LoA	.255	117	447	51	114	28	1	16	74	27	101	3	2	.298	.430
2011	Clearwater (FSL)	HiA	.284	91	348	34	99	19	2	5	40	13	84	0	0	.312	.394
2012	Reading (EL)	AA	.261	83	310	31	81	13	1	13	45	11	83	0	2	.280	.435
	Lehigh Valley (IL)	AAA	.218	22	78	7	17	2	0	4	13	2	31	0	1	.232	.397
Minor League Totals			.268	510	1875	220	502	117	11	49	270	120	434	8	11	.314	.420

15 CESAR HERNANDEZ, 2B

BA GRADE

45
MEDIUM

Born: May 23, 1990. **B-T:** B-R. **Ht.:** 5-10. **Wt.:** 160. **Signed:** Venezuela, 2006. **Signed by:** Sal Agostinelli.

Hernandez is often mentioned with fellow switch-hitting Venezuelan infielder Freddy Galvis, as they both signed on July 2, 2006. Galvis made his major league debut in 2012, while Hernandez reached Triple-A two seasons after being added to the 40-man roster. He doesn't quite have Galvis' arm or defensive ability, but he has flashy actions at the keystone sack and managers rated him the Eastern League's best defensive second baseman in 2012. He has a solid arm and good hands. Hernandez packs more punch at the plate than Galvis, though he still has below-average power, and is a better runner. He has good bat-to-ball ability and a line-drive mentality, though pre-pitch hand movement sometimes causes him to get to the ball late. His approach is somewhat undisciplined. Hernandez still needs to learn the intricacies of stealing bases, though he covers 60 yards in 6.6 seconds. He would benefit from adding strength to his slight frame. The Phillies have also worked to make sure he remains focused pitch-to-pitch and inning-to-inning. Scouts are divided on whether Hernandez will hit enough to be an everyday player. He'll get more Triple-A seasoning in 2013.

Year	Club (League)	Class	AVG	G	AB	R	H	2B	3B	HR	RBI	BB	SO	SB	CS	OBP	SLG
2007	Phillies (VSL)	R	.276	54	181	32	50	7	8	2	21	11	30	6	4	.328	.436
2008	Phillies (VSL)	R	.315	60	197	31	62	7	6	1	24	33	22	19	7	.412	.426
2009	Phillies (GCL)	R	.267	41	150	21	40	5	1	0	18	17	20	13	5	.351	.313
2010	Williamsport (NYP)	SS	.325	65	255	36	83	13	2	0	23	26	27	32	6	.390	.392
2011	Clearwater (FSL)	HiA	.268	119	421	47	113	7	4	4	37	23	80	23	10	.306	.333
2012	Reading (EL)	AA	.304	103	411	50	125	26	11	2	51	27	67	16	12	.345	.436
	Lehigh Valley (IL)	AAA	.248	30	121	13	30	4	1	0	6	4	11	5	3	.270	.298
Minor League Totals			.290	472	1736	230	503	69	33	9	180	141	257	114	47	.345	.383

16 MITCHELL WALDING, 3B

BA GRADE

50
HIGH

Born: Sept. 10, 1992. **B-T:** L-R. **Ht.:** 6-3. **Wt.:** 195. **Drafted:** HS—Stockton, Calif., 2011 (5th round). **Signed by:** Joey Davis.

A two-sport high school star from Northern California, Walding slipped under the radar as an amateur. He didn't play in many summer showcases because of football, and he missed time in his senior baseball season with a broken bone in his foot. Area scout Joey Davis liked what he saw of Walding, however. The Phillies took him in the fifth round in 2011, followed him closely in a summer collegiate league and then signed him away from an Oregon commitment for $800,000. He made his pro debut last year, and after hitting .383/.420/.532 in June at Williamsport, he ran into some struggles that snowballed as he got down on himself. Walding is learning how to translate his tools into baseball ability, but his upside is significant. He has a sweet lefthanded swing that generates natural backspin, and he projects to have above-average raw power as he grows into his broad-shouldered frame. He would benefit from being more aggressive at the plate, and he must better identify secondary pitches as he moves up the ladder. His lack of baseball experience works against him in that regard. Walding played shortstop as an amateur, and while he's still learning third base, he has a plus arm, good hands and moves well for his size. He's an average runner. Walding will make the jump to full-season ball with Lakewood in 2013.

Year	Club (League)	Class	AVG	G	AB	R	H	2B	3B	HR	RBI	BB	SO	SB	CS	OBP	SLG
2012	Williamsport (NYP)	SS	.233	69	253	33	59	10	3	1	31	31	66	5	2	.326	.308
Minor League Totals			.233	69	253	33	59	10	3	1	31	31	66	5	2	.326	.308

17 MITCH GUELLER, RHP

HIGH

Born: Nov. 10, 1993. **B-T:** R-R. **Ht.:** 6-3. **Wt.:** 210. **Drafted:** HS—Rochester, Wash., 2012 (1st round supplemental). **Signed by:** Rick Jacques.

The Phillies had two supplemental first-round picks in 2012 after losing Raul Ibanez and Ryan Madson to free agency, and they used them both on projectable high school righthanders, taking Gueller 14 picks after Shane Watson. Arguably the Pacific Northwest's best athlete in the 2012 draft, Gueller guided his high school football team to the Washington state semifinals as a quarterback, and averaged 13.5 points a game as a forward on the basketball team. Some scouts liked the strength in his bat enough to make him a position player, but the Phillies prefer him as a pitcher and say he reminds them of fellow Evergreen State product Trevor May, whom they traded away this offseason. Gueller isn't as advanced as Watson, but he has more upside and a better chance to stay in the rotation because of his athleticism. His fastball sits at 90-93 mph and touches 95. He shows flashes of a slurvy, low-80s breaking ball that could develop into a good slider with time, and he has feel for a changeup. His delivery will need to be smoothed out, which would help with his command, and his aptitude during instructional league impressed Philadelphia. An aggressive assignment to low Class A isn't out of the question for his first full pro season, but he likely will start the year in extended spring training.

Year	Club (League)	Class	W	L	ERA	G	GS	CG	SV	IP	H	HR	BB	SO	K/9	WHIP	AVG
2012	Phillies (GCL)	R	1	5	5.27	8	6	0	0	27	26	0	12	19	6.3	1.39	.255
Minor League Totals			1	5	5.27	8	6	0	0	27	26	0	12	19	6.3	1.39	.255

18 AUSTIN WRIGHT, LHP

BA GRADE
50
HIGH

Born: Sept. 26, 1989. **B-T:** L-L. **Ht.:** 6-4. **Wt.:** 235. **Drafted:** Mississippi, 2011 (8th round). **Signed by:** Mike Stauffer.

Wright was considered somewhat of a tease as an amateur. His arm strength from the left side always piqued scouts' interest, but they were concerned about his command and makeup. The Pirates drafted him out of an Illinois high school in 2008 and the Red Sox took him out of Chipola (Fla.) JC in 2010, but he declined to sign and went to Mississippi. The Phillies signed him for $125,000 as an eighth-rounder in 2011. Wright has exceeded expectations so far, jumping to high Class A in his first full pro season and winning Florida State League pitcher of the year honors. Wright's fastball sits at 90-94 mph but seems harder thanks to his quirky, up-tempo delivery with a short, quick arm circle. He has one of the system's best curveballs, a 77-80 mph late-breaking downer. He too frequently guides his changeup, but it shows above-average potential, especially when he lets it loose. Wright often gets strikeout-happy and piles up hefty pitch and walk totals, and he would benefit from being more aggressive early in the count. His iffy command led to 17 wild pitches, tops in the FSL. The Phillies will continue developing him as a starter, though he might be best served as a multi-inning reliever who can get outs against both lefties and righties. He'll move to Double-A in 2013.

Year	Club (League)	Class	W	L	ERA	G	GS	CG	SV	IP	H	HR	BB	SO	K/9	WHIP	AVG
2011	Williamsport (NYP)	SS	3	1	3.38	8	7	1	0	35	30	1	13	44	11.4	1.24	.231
	Lakewood (SAL)	LoA	1	2	2.67	7	7	0	0	34	29	2	9	41	11.0	1.13	.238
2012	Clearwater (FSL)	HiA	11	5	3.47	27	25	0	0	148	147	11	60	133	8.1	1.40	.259
Minor League Totals			15	8	3.33	42	39	1	0	216	206	14	82	218	9.1	1.33	.252

19 KENNY GILES, RHP

BA GRADE
50
HIGH

Born: Sept. 20, 1990. **B-T:** R-R. **Ht.:** 6-2. **Wt.:** 190. **Drafted:** Yavapai (Ariz.) JC, 2011 (7th round). **Signed by:** Brad Holland.

Giles didn't pitch much as an amateur, missing his high school senior season with elbow tendinitis and throwing 11 innings for New Mexico JC in 2010. He struck out 67 in 38 innings as a sophomore at Yavapai (Ariz.) JC, and the Phillies saw enough arm strength to take him in the seventh round and sign him for $250,000. He reached high Class A in his first full season while striking out 12.2 batters per nine innings across two levels. Giles lights up radar guns with a 94-98 mph fastball that routinely touches triple digits, making it a plus-plus offering despite modest life. There's some effort in his delivery, and he runs into trouble with command and control when he overthrows. He's much better off when he allows his lower half to get out in front and his arm to follow. His slider grades as solid and has plus potential, and it drastically improved after Philadelphia shelved his curveball and splitter. He could add back the extra secondary offerings down the line, but his future is in the bullpen and he has an effective two-pitch combo. Scouts like Giles' intense demeanor, which evokes Jonathan Papelbon, and he could move quickly after opening 2013 in Double-A.

Year	Club (League)	Class	W	L	ERA	G	GS	CG	SV	IP	H	HR	BB	SO	K/9	WHIP	AVG
2011	Phillies (GCL)	R	1	1	5.79	3	0	0	0	5	6	1	3	7	13.5	1.93	.333
2012	Lakewood (SAL)	LoA	3	3	3.61	29	6	0	5	67	54	5	44	86	11.5	1.46	.215
	Clearwater (FSL)	HiA	1	0	3.07	10	0	0	3	15	10	1	6	25	15.3	1.09	.182
Minor League Totals			5	4	3.63	42	6	0	8	87	70	7	53	118	12.3	1.42	.216

20 JUSTIN DeFRATUS, RHP

BA GRADE
45
MEDIUM

Born: Oct. 21, 1987. **B-T:** B-R. **Ht.:** 6-4. **Wt.:** 215. **Drafted:** Ventura (Calif.) JC, 2007 (11th round). **Signed by:** Tim Kissner.

DeFratus had been on an accelerated path to Philadelphia ever since moving to the bullpen full-time in 2010. He made five big league relief appearances at the end of 2011 and seemed primed to make an impact with the Phillies last year, but he had an injury-plagued campaign. He strained his right elbow while working out in the offseason and went to the disabled list in spring training, and he didn't return to full health until mid-July. After spending most of the year in Triple-A, DeFratus returned to the majors in September. His fastball sits at 91-95 mph with slight sink, and he backs it up with a swing-and-miss slider and a fringy changeup. A raw junior-college find, he has benefited from professional coaching and the daily routine of pro ball. Scouts laud his competitiveness and aggressiveness on the mound, and some compare him to Brad Lidge. DeFratus figures to spend 2013 in Philadelphia's bullpen, and he has the upside of a set-up man.

Year	Club (League)	Class	W	L	ERA	G	GS	CG	SV	IP	H	HR	BB	SO	K/9	WHIP	AVG
2007	Phillies (GCL)	R	2	3	4.30	10	8	0	0	46	51	1	3	34	6.7	1.17	.273
2008	Williamsport (NYP)	SS	6	5	3.67	14	14	1	0	83	87	1	25	74	8.0	1.34	.260

Year	Club (League)	Class	W	L	ERA	G	GS	CG	SV	IP	H	HR	BB	SO	K/9	WHIP	AVG
2009	Lakewood (SAL)	LoA	5	6	3.19	36	12	0	3	110	108	3	16	101	8.3	1.13	.258
2010	Clearwater (FSL)	HiA	2	0	1.79	29	0	0	15	40	31	1	11	43	9.6	1.04	.215
	Reading (EL)	AA	1	0	2.19	20	0	0	6	25	17	2	5	28	10.2	0.89	.195
2011	Reading (EL)	AA	4	0	2.10	23	0	0	8	34	28	1	14	43	11.3	1.22	.224
	Lehigh Valley (IL)	AAA	2	3	3.73	28	0	0	7	41	35	3	11	56	12.3	1.12	.230
	Philadelphia (NL)	MAJ	1	0	2.25	5	0	0	0	4	1	0	3	3	6.8	1.00	.083
2012	Phillies (GCL)	R	0	0	0.00	2	1	0	0	2	1	0	0	3	13.5	0.50	.143
	Clearwater (FSL)	HiA	0	0	0.00	2	1	0	0	2	2	0	0	1	4.5	1.00	.286
	Lehigh Valley (IL)	AAA	0	1	2.49	17	0	0	3	22	15	2	3	22	9.1	0.83	.203
	Philadelphia (NL)	MAJ	0	0	3.38	13	0	0	0	11	7	0	5	8	6.8	1.13	.179
Major League Totals			1	0	3.07	18	0	0	0	15	8	0	8	11	6.8	1.09	.157
Minor League Totals			22	18	3.11	181	36	1	42	405	375	14	88	405	9.0	1.14	.244

21 TYLER CLOYD, RHP

Born: May 16, 1987. **B-T:** R-R. **Ht.:** 6-3. **Wt.:** 190. **Drafted:** Nebraska-Omaha (18th round), 2008. **Signed by:** Jerry Lafferty.

If Darin Ruf's emergence was the most surprising Phillies prospect story in 2012, Cloyd's progress was a close second. The Phillies took a flier on him in the 18th round in 2008 at the suggestion of Nebraska-Omaha pitching coach Dan McGinn, even though Cloyd didn't pitch as a sophomore because of an academic suspension and spent the ensuing summer playing slow-pitch softball. Signed for $15,000, he moved slowly in pro ball until 2012. Slated to open the season in Double-A, he made an emergency appearance at Lehigh Valley and tossed six perfect innings while striking out eight. He was named International League pitcher of the week but still headed back to Reading. A month later he returned for good, earning IL pitcher of the year honors after leading the league in ERA (2.35) and WHIP (1.01) before getting called up for six major league starts at the end of the year. Cloyd knows who he is and what he's got, and he thrives not on stuff but on pitchability and command—the best in the system. His fastball sits at 85-89 mph, and he relies heavily on an 83-87 mph cutter. He also throws a changeup and curveball. Cloyd's margin for error is minimal. He has a ceiling of a poor man's Kyle Kendrick, and a chance to be No. 5 starter. Philadelphia will give him a chance to win a big league job out of spring training.

Year	Club (League)	Class	W	L	ERA	G	GS	CG	SV	IP	H	HR	BB	SO	K/9	WHIP	AVG
2008	Phillies (GCL)	R	2	0	0.00	2	1	0	0	11	5	0	1	11	9.0	0.55	.139
	Williamsport (NYP)	SS	5	4	4.57	12	12	0	0	65	76	8	21	58	8.0	1.49	.298
2009	Lakewood (SAL)	LoA	7	3	3.05	14	14	1	0	89	90	3	19	77	7.8	1.23	.268
	Clearwater (FSL)	HiA	5	6	4.11	13	12	0	0	77	83	4	23	39	4.6	1.38	.274
2010	Clearwater (FSL)	HiA	4	3	5.32	35	4	0	0	69	85	8	16	67	8.7	1.46	.299
	Reading (EL)	AA	1	1	4.00	2	1	0	0	9	5	3	1	6	6.0	0.67	.152
2011	Clearwater (FSL)	HiA	3	1	2.75	13	5	0	0	39	31	3	7	39	8.9	0.97	.212
	Reading (EL)	AA	6	3	2.78	18	17	0	0	107	101	7	15	99	8.4	1.09	.250
2012	Reading (EL)	AA	3	0	1.80	4	4	0	0	25	22	1	3	20	7.2	1.00	.239
	Lehigh Valley (IL)	AAA	12	1	2.35	22	22	1	0	142	105	14	38	93	5.9	1.01	.210
	Philadelphia (NL)	MAJ	2	2	4.91	6	6	0	0	33	33	8	7	30	8.2	1.21	.260
Major League Totals			2	2	4.91	6	6	0	0	33	33	8	7	30	8.2	1.21	.260
Minor League Totals			48	22	3.27	135	92	2	0	633	603	51	144	509	7.2	1.18	.252

22 CAMERON RUPP, C

Born: Sept. 28, 1988. **B-T:** R-R. **Ht.:** 6-1. **Wt.:** 240. **Drafted:** Texas, 2010 (3rd round). **Signed by:** Steve Cohen.

Rupp generated first-round talk before his junior season at Texas, and though he didn't hit enough to go that early, the Phillies took him in the third round and signed him for $287,000. He improved significantly last year and put himself in the organization's plans with a strong performance in high Class A, where he managed a prospect-laden staff with aplomb. Rupp's 2012 season started in mid-January, when he reported early to spring training and caught bullpens from Roy Halladay. He also lost 15 pounds, which helped him play with more energy. Rupp has a long arm bar in his swing but got to fastballs on the inner half more frequently than he had previously. He has impressed with plus raw power since he won a high school home run derby in 2006, and he knocked 33 extra-base hits last season in a tough hitter's environment. Rupp is a solid defensive catcher, offering a wide target and smothering balls in the dirt. He has plus arm strength and has worked to shorten his release, leading to 1.9-second pop times and a 34 percent caught-stealing rate last season. He's a well below-average runner. Rupp doesn't have huge upside but should have a big league future. He'll advance to Double-A in 2013.

Year	Club (League)	Class	AVG	G	AB	R	H	2B	3B	HR	RBI	BB	SO	SB	CS	OBP	SLG
2010	Williamsport (NYP)	SS	.218	55	193	20	42	16	0	5	28	25	51	0	0	.318	.378
2011	Lakewood (SAL)	LoA	.272	99	324	33	88	19	1	4	44	31	96	0	0	.346	.373
2012	Clearwater (FSL)	HiA	.267	104	344	32	92	22	1	10	49	40	77	0	0	.345	.424
Minor League Totals			.258	258	861	85	222	57	2	19	121	96	224	0	0	.339	.395

23 BRODY COLVIN, RHP

BA GRADE
45
HIGH

Born: Aug. 14, 1990. **B-T:** R-R. **Ht.:** 6-4. **Wt.:** 195. **Drafted:** HS—Lafayette, La., 2009 (7th round). **Signed by:** Mike Stauffer.

Rated as a sandwich-round talent in the 2009 draft, Colvin dropped to the seventh round because of his strong commitment to Louisiana State but signed for $900,000, considerably more money than any other Phillies draftee in that class. He ranked as Philadelphia's top pitching prospect entering the 2011 season, but his development has slowed the last two years. He still has the pure stuff and big body to get back on track, but he struggles with consistency and hasn't allayed concerns about his makeup. Colvin's fastball sits at 90-94 mph with sink, and he throws a power curveball and an average changeup. Fastball command has been his Achilles' heel throughout his career, mostly because he has an inconsistent release point. He has a long arm circle with a hook and wrap in the back, and he throws across his body. Colvin seemed to panic in the rotation last year, and the Phillies tried to clear his mind by letting him work out of the bullpen. Pitching in relief might best suit his delivery and mentality, though he still has starter stuff. He should return to Double-A this year, with his role to be determined.

Year	Club (League)	Class	W	L	ERA	G	GS	CG	SV	IP	H	HR	BB	SO	K/9	WHIP	AVG
2009	Phillies (GCL)	R	0	0	0.00	1	0	0	0	2	0	0	1	2	9.0	0.50	.000
2010	Lakewood (SAL)	LoA	6	8	3.39	27	27	0	0	138	138	7	42	120	7.8	1.30	.258
2011	Clearwater (FSL)	HiA	3	8	4.71	22	21	0	0	117	131	10	42	78	6.0	1.48	.289
2012	Clearwater (FSL)	HiA	5	6	4.27	23	18	0	0	105	113	5	51	93	7.9	1.56	.285
	Reading (EL)	AA	1	4	11.02	7	7	0	0	33	43	6	23	16	4.4	2.02	.328
Minor League Totals			15	26	4.63	80	73	0	0	395	425	28	159	309	7.0	1.48	.279

24 ZACH COLLIER, OF

BA GRADE
45
HIGH

Born: Aug. 27, 1989. **B-T:** L-L. **Ht.:** 6-2. **Wt.:** 185. **Drafted:** HS—Chino Hills, Calif., 2008 (1st round supplemental). **Signed by:** Darrell Conner.

Collier has been slowed by injuries and a suspension since signing for $1.02 million as the 34th overall pick in 2008, though he did show promise last season. He missed all of 2010 after having two surgeries on his right hand, and his 2011 comeback was short-circuited by a 50-game suspension for testing positive for Adderall, a prescription amphetamine. Despite a late start last year, Collier stood out in high Class A and made up for lost time in the Arizona Fall League. Scouts came away seeing the tools of a prototype center fielder, with everything except power, and compared him to Denard Span. Collier is a plus runner with good range and a solid arm. He has a quick swing and the ball jumps off his bat. He's working to better incorporate his lower half at the plate. He was considered a polished hitter coming out of high school, and he still has a solid approach. Added to the 40-man roster in November, Collier just needs to play, and 2013 will be an important developmental year for him as he moves to Double-A.

Year	Club (League)	Class	AVG	G	AB	R	H	2B	3B	HR	RBI	BB	SO	SB	CS	OBP	SLG
2008	Phillies (GCL)	R	.271	37	129	15	35	9	1	0	19	17	28	5	0	.347	.357
2009	Lakewood (SAL)	LoA	.218	82	298	40	65	16	7	0	32	23	80	13	7	.275	.319
	Williamsport (NYP)	SS	.226	34	137	21	31	10	1	1	13	9	42	7	0	.280	.336
2010	Did Not Play—Injured																
2011	Lakewood (SAL)	LoA	.255	112	416	50	106	24	6	1	36	40	99	35	13	.328	.349
2012	Clearwater (FSL)	HiA	.269	78	283	39	76	13	3	6	32	26	60	11	3	.333	.399
Minor League Totals			.248	343	1263	165	313	72	18	8	132	115	309	71	23	.314	.352

25 AARON ALTHERR, OF

BA GRADE
45
HIGH

Born: Jan. 14, 1991. **B-T:** R-R. **Ht.:** 6-5. **Wt.:** 190. **Drafted:** HS—Buckeye, Ariz., 2009 (9th round). **Signed by:** Brad Holland.

An outfielder who fits the high-upside, athletic profile the Phillies like, Altherr signed for $150,000 after being taken in the ninth round in 2009. An assignment to low Class A proved too big a jump in 2011, but he repeated the level last year and held his own. He finished the year playing for Germany (where he was born) in a World Baseball Classic qualifier. Altherr is still learning to translate his tools into baseball talent, and his potential is tied to projection more than performance. Tall and lanky, he has a racehorse frame and is still growing into his body. He has a short, smooth swing, especially for someone with such long limbs, but he's susceptible to pitches on the outer half. He has a line-drive swing that gets occasional loft, and he has a chance for average power as he adds strength. With his skill set, Altherr will have to cut down on his swings and misses. As a center fielder, he coasts gracefully and covers a lot of ground. His solid arm will play anywhere in the outfield. He's a plus runner with good basestealing ability, though he doesn't always play at full speed and posts average times down the line to first base. Altherr has time on his side and plenty of tools, but at some point his production will have to catch up. He'll play 2013 in high Class A.

Year	Club (League)	Class	AVG	G	AB	R	H	2B	3B	HR	RBI	BB	SO	SB	CS	OBP	SLG
2009	Phillies (GCL)	R	.214	28	84	10	18	3	0	1	11	8	15	6	1	.283	.286
2010	Phillies (GCL)	R	.304	27	115	12	35	6	1	1	15	3	22	10	3	.331	.400
	Williamsport (NYP)	SS	.287	28	94	11	27	7	3	0	10	8	13	2	3	.350	.426
2011	Lakewood (SAL)	LoA	.211	41	147	20	31	6	0	1	15	11	47	12	0	.272	.272
	Williamsport (NYP)	SS	.260	71	269	41	70	12	2	5	31	13	52	25	4	.302	.375
2012	Lakewood (SAL)	LoA	.252	110	420	65	106	27	6	8	50	38	102	25	8	.319	.402
Minor League Totals			.254	305	1129	159	287	61	12	16	132	81	251	80	19	.310	.372

26 TYSON GILLIES, OF

BA GRADE
45
HIGH

Born: Oct. 31, 1988. **B-T:** L-R. **Ht.:** 6-2. **Wt.:** 195. **Drafted:** Iowa Western CC, D/F 2006 (25th round). **Signed by:** Wayne Norton (Mariners).

It has been a long, strange journey for Gillies, acquired from the Mariners in the December 2009 Cliff Lee trade. Gillies, who is legally deaf, played only 31 games in his first two seasons in the organization as he dealt with injuries and off-the-field difficulties. When rehabbing a nagging hamstring injury in 2010, he was arrested on charges of cocaine possession, which were later dropped. The hamstring issues lingered into 2011, when he played just three games. He missed about half the 2012 season due to a concussion, hamstring problems and a suspension after an altercation with a team bus driver, but he finally showed signs of the talent that got him selected for the 2009 Futures Game. He's an exciting, toolsy center fielder who's a plus-plus runner, gliding defender and top-of-the-order catalyst. He has a quick, strong swing and makes solid contact, though he occasionally gets pull-happy. Depending on the situation, Gillies will bunt or employ a slap-and-run approach to get on base. He has the tools to project as a regular in center field, though he has to answer questions about his health and makeup. Gillies played for Canada in September's World Baseball Classic qualifier in Germany. He'll start 2013 in Triple-A and could contribute in Philadelphia later in the year.

Year	Club (League)	Class	AVG	G	AB	R	H	2B	3B	HR	RBI	BB	SO	SB	CS	OBP	SLG
2007	Mariners (AZL)	R	.221	35	86	20	19	3	2	0	6	6	23	9	6	.337	.302
	Everett (NWL)	SS	.625	4	8	3	5	0	0	0	2	0	1	2	0	.625	.625
2008	High Desert (CAL)	HiA	.233	11	30	4	7	0	1	0	1	1	6	1	1	.281	.300
	Everett (NWL)	SS	.313	61	192	36	60	6	5	2	22	35	46	24	7	.439	.427
2009	High Desert (CAL)	HiA	.341	124	498	104	170	17	14	9	42	60	81	44	19	.430	.486
2010	Reading (EL)	AA	.238	26	105	15	25	2	1	2	6	5	24	2	2	.286	.333
	Phillies (GCL)	R	.500	2	2	3	1	0	0	0	1	2	0	0	0	.750	.500
2011	Clearwater (FSL)	HiA	.154	3	13	1	2	2	0	0	0	0	1	0	0	.154	.308
2012	Lakewood (SAL)	LoA	.400	2	5	2	2	0	0	0	0	2	0	0	0	.625	.400
	Clearwater (FSL)	HiA	.176	5	17	1	3	1	0	0	0	0	7	1	0	.263	.235
	Reading (EL)	AA	.304	68	276	59	84	13	8	4	24	18	52	8	6	.369	.453
Minor League Totals			.307	341	1232	248	378	44	31	17	104	129	241	91	41	.395	.434

27 DYLAN COZENS, OF

BA GRADE
50
EXTREME

Born: May 31, 1994. **B-T:** L-L. **Ht.:** 6-6. **Wt.:** 235. **Drafted:** HS—Scottsdale, Ariz., 2012 (2nd round). **Signed by:** Brad Holland.

Cozens' limited baseball experience and background scared off some teams prior to the 2012 draft, but the Phillies took him in the second round and signed him for $659,800 after he smashed 10 homers in a private workout at Citizen's Bank Park. The son of Randy Cozens, a defensive end drafted in 1976 by the NFL's Denver Broncos, Dylan committed to Arizona to play both football and baseball. He was kicked off Desert Mountain High's (Scottsdale, Ariz.) team and missed much of his junior year, with the circumstances around his dismissal causing questions about his makeup. He transferred to Chaparral High (Scottsdale) and broke Paul Konerko's school record with 19 homers in 2012, including a walkoff shot in the Arizona Division I state championship game. Philadelphia, which has a former CIA agent on staff, did its homework on Cozens. He has a lot to learn but he has a tremendous ceiling. Cozens generates extraordinary raw power to all fields, possibly the most in the system, by leveraging his massive frame. His swing is stiff, so it's unclear if his power will translate or if his bat will progress. He also needs to develop an approach at the plate. Cozens is a good athlete who moves well for his size. He has a strong arm and played right field in his pro debut, and he'll either play an outfield corner or move to first base. He likely will open 2013 in extended spring training.

Year	Club (League)	Class	AVG	G	AB	R	H	2B	3B	HR	RBI	BB	SO	SB	CS	OBP	SLG
2012	Phillies (GCL)	R	.255	50	161	24	41	11	2	5	24	21	44	8	2	.341	.441
Minor League Totals			.255	50	161	24	41	11	2	5	24	21	44	8	2	.341	.441

28 ANDREW PULLIN, OF/2B

BA GRADE
45
HIGH

Born: Sept. 25, 1993. **B-T:** L-R. **Ht.:** 6-0. **Wt.:** 190. **Drafted:** HS—Centralia, Wash., 2012 (5th round). **Signed by:** Rick Jacques.

The Phillies have had success mining the Pacific Northwest in recent years, and they think they've found another gem in Pullin, whom they took four rounds after fellow South Sound native Mitch Gueller last June. Much like fellow Washington resident Drew Vettleson, now with the Rays, Pullin is a former switch-pitcher who became a prospect as a position player. Area scout Rick Jacques and special assistant Pat Gillick worked out Pullin at second base before the draft and liked what they saw, so they signed him away from an Oregon commitment for $203,900. Pullin played mostly left field in his pro debut and started the conversion to second base during instructional league, and early returns were positive. He has a solid arm. Pullin's potential is mostly tied to his bat, and he has advanced instincts at the plate. He uses a crouched set-up, almost like Pete Rose, with his bat pointed back toward the backstop. He has a smooth, line-drive stroke and good bat speed. His barrel stays in the hitting zone for a long time, and his high finish resembles that of Johnny Damon. Pullin has shown flashes of average power and has average speed. He might be able to handle a full-season assignment to low Class A this year.

Year	Club (League)	Class	AVG	G	AB	R	H	2B	3B	HR	RBI	BB	SO	SB	CS	OBP	SLG
2012	Phillies (GCL)	R	.321	41	140	16	45	10	0	2	13	12	32	3	5	.403	.436
Minor League Totals			.321	41	140	16	45	10	0	2	13	12	32	3	5	.403	.436

29 KYRELL HUDSON, OF

BA GRADE

50

EXTREME

Born: Dec. 6, 1990. **B-T:** R-R. **Ht.:** 6-1. **Wt.:** 185. **Drafted:** HS—Vancouver, Wash., 2009 (3rd round). **Signed by:** Tim Kissner.

Concerns about Hudson's inconsistent effort, makeup and commitment to Oregon State, where he also would have played wide receiver for the football team, drove him down draft boards in 2009. But then-Phillies area scout Tim Kissner (now Mariners director of international operations) followed Hudson closely, and scouting director Marti Wolever saw his athleticism on display in an impressive spring showing. Hudson hadn't played much baseball when he signed for $475,000 as a third-round pick, and his development has been slow. Season-ending surgery last July to repair torn tendons in his right wrist didn't help. Still, Hudson's raw tools make him hard to write off. A plus-plus defender in center field, Hudson could play in the big leagues now defensively. He glides to balls in the gaps and he has the best outfield arm in the system. Though he doesn't get out of the box well, Hudson can fly—he ran a 6.5-second 60-yard dash in spring training—and he's aggressive on the basepaths. A good swing path and bat speed produce power in batting practice, but Hudson lacks feel for hitting and he swings and misses frequently. Even if his bat progresses, Hudson is a longshot to be more than a fourth outfielder. He likely will return to Lakewood to begin 2013.

Year	Club (League)	Class	AVG	G	AB	R	H	2B	3B	HR	RBI	BB	SO	SB	CS	OBP	SLG
2009	Phillies (GCL)	R	.162	10	37	3	6	2	0	0	6	3	9	2	0	.225	.216
2010	Williamsport (NYP)	SS	.173	49	156	13	27	5	0	0	15	5	45	11	3	.205	.205
2011	Williamsport (NYP)	SS	.275	68	269	31	74	11	4	1	18	18	63	28	11	.322	.357
2012	Lakewood (SAL)	LoA	.224	64	219	28	49	11	1	1	21	10	73	23	7	.277	.297
Minor League Totals			.229	191	681	75	156	29	5	2	60	36	190	64	21	.276	.295

30 KYLE SIMON, RHP

BA GRADE

45

HIGH

Born: Aug. 18, 1990. **B-T:** R-R. **Ht.:** 6-5. **Wt.:** 225. **Drafted:** Arizona, 2011 (4th round). **Signed by:** John Gillette (Orioles).

Acquired with catcher Gabriel Lino in the June deal that sent Jim Thome to the Orioles, Simon rejoined Phillies farm director Joe Jordan. Formerly Baltimore's scouting director, Jordan liked Simon's size and sinker enough to sign him in the fourth round of the 2011 draft for $231,300. He struggled at the outset of his first full pro season while working as a starter in high Class A, but he took off after the trade when Jordan put him in the bullpen, which best suits Simon's mentality. He quickly advanced to Double-A before ending the year in the Arizona Fall League. Working from a deceptive low three-quarters arm slot, Simon throws a heavy 89-92 mph sinker that Jordan says "hunts ground." He can get consistent groundouts in the minors with just that one pitch. The Phillies sent Simon to the AFL to get him more innings to develop his short, sweeping slider and his changeup, both of which are fringy offerings. Simon should advance to Triple-A in 2013, and his future is in middle relief.

Year	Club (League)	Class	W	L	ERA	G	GS	CG	SV	IP	H	HR	BB	SO	K/9	WHIP	AVG
2011	Aberdeen (NYP)	SS	1	0	0.00	6	0	0	1	8	3	0	3	2	2.3	0.75	.120
	Delmarva (SAL)	LoA	0	2	4.15	8	0	0	0	9	6	1	2	7	7.3	0.92	.194
2012	Frederick (CAR)	HiA	2	8	3.96	14	14	0	0	73	86	8	21	49	6.1	1.47	.293
	Clearwater (FSL)	HiA	3	0	1.26	7	0	0	1	14	10	1	1	14	8.8	0.77	.208
	Reading (EL)	AA	1	0	1.42	13	0	0	2	25	12	0	5	21	7.5	0.67	.133
Minor League Totals			7	10	2.93	48	14	0	4	129	117	10	32	93	6.5	1.16	.240

Pittsburgh Pirates

BY JOHN PERROTTO

Halfway through the 2012 season, things were finally looking up for the Pirates. They went into the all-star break in first place in the National League Central and 11 games above .500, and it finally appeared that the longest streak of futility in North American professional sports history would end.

Little went right after that.

Pittsburgh beat the Diamondbacks on Aug. 8 to improve to 63-47 and peak at 16 games above .500. But it went just 16-36 the rest of the way to finish at 79-83, its 20th straight losing season. It was a second straight collapse for the Pirates, who have gone a combined 38-77 during the final two months of the last two seasons.

The news wasn't any better on the scouting and player-development fronts, where the organization says it must be strong to be successful. In the draft, Pittsburgh gambled on Stanford righthander Mark Appel, a candidate for the No. 1 pick who slid because of questions about his asking price.

The Pirates took Appel at No. 8 without gauging exactly what his price tag would be. They offered $3.8 million—the most they could without losing future first-round picks under the new draft rules—but never came close to signing him. Pittsburgh will get the ninth overall pick this year as compensation, but the failure to sign Appel was a big hit to the 2012 draft class.

The organization also found itself scorned for its player-development approach. The Pittsburgh Tribune-Review and Yahoo! Sports ran a series of articles revealing that the Pirates were using Navy SEAL training techniques for players during extended spring training and instructional league. Most disturbing were reports that two of their best prospects, righthander Jameson Taillon (knee) and outfielder Gregory Polanco (ankle), sustained minor injuries while participating in the drills.

An e-mail from assistant GM Kyle Stark to members of Pittsburgh's player-development staff also got leaked to the media, featuring statements that could generously be called unconventional. In it, Stark said he wanted to develop players who had the creativity of hippies and the brotherhood of Hell's Angels, and he concluded the e-mail with the phrase, "Hoka Hey," a battle cry used by Sitting Bull. While the spirit of the statement is that if you give a complete effort, you can be satisfied no matter the outcome, the literal transla-

The Pirates failed to sign top pick Mark Appel, and the bad news didn't end there

tion of the phrase is, "It's a good day to die."

The collapse and controversy prompted usually reclusive Pirates owner Bob Nutting to conduct his own inquiry into the state of the baseball operation after the season. In the end, he decided the team was on the right course and kept the staff in place, though he ordered Stark's military-style training methods to stop.

The news in the minor leagues wasn't all bad. Blue-chip pitching prospects Gerrit Cole, Taillon and Luis Heredia took steps forward in their development, while Polanco and shortstop Alen Hanson had breakout seasons in low Class A. The Rookie-level Gulf Coast League team won its first league title—in its 42nd year of existence—and Triple-A Indianapolis captured a division title and had the International League's best record.

Pittsburgh created more acrimony in its home state when it broke off its affiliation with State College in the short-season New York-Penn League. Medlar Field at Lubrano Park was built with the same dimensions as PNC Park, with the idea that the Pirates and State College would have a long-term relationship, but the Bucs bolted for Jamestown after six years. State College management claimed the parent club never returned phone calls about renewing the agreement.

THIS YEAR'S TOP 30

Player, Pos.	Grade
1. Gerrit Cole, rhp	70/Medium
2. Jameson Taillon, rhp	65/Medium
3. Luis Heredia, rhp	60/High
4. Gregory Polanco, of	60/High
5. Alen Hanson, ss	60/High
6. Josh Bell, of	60/High
7. Kyle McPherson, rhp	50/Medium
8. Justin Wilson, lhp	50/Medium
9. Barrett Barnes, of	50/High
10. Clay Holmes, rhp	50/High
11. Alex Dickerson, 1b	50/High
12. Tony Sanchez, c	45/Medium
13. Andy Oliver, lhp	45/Medium
14. Bryan Morris, rhp	45/Medium
15. Wyatt Mathisen, c	50/High
16. Vic Black, rhp	50/High
17. Nick Kingham, rhp	50/High
18. Willy Garcia, of	50/High
19. Tyler Glasnow, rhp	50/High
20. Dilson Herrera, 2b	50/High
21. Adrian Sampson, rhp	50/High
22. Brock Holt, ss/2b	45/Medium
23. Matt Curry, 1b	45/Medium
24. Jose Osuna, 1b	50/High
25. Brandon Cumpton, rhp	45/Medium
26. Duke Welker, rhp	45/Medium
27. Jin-De Jhang, c	50/Extreme
28. Harold Ramirez, of	50/Extreme
29. Clint Robinson, 1b	40/Low
30. Gift Ngoepe, ss	45/High

LAST YEAR'S TOP 30

Player, Pos.	Status
1. Gerrit Cole, rhp	No. 1
2. Jameson Taillon, rhp	No. 2
3. Josh Bell, of	No. 6
4. Starling Marte, of	Majors
5. Luis Heredia, rhp	No. 3
6. Kyle McPherson, rhp	No. 7
7. Tony Sanchez, c	No. 12
8. Robbie Grossman, of	(Astros)
9. Stetson Allie, rhp	Dropped out
10. Jeff Locke, lhp	Majors
11. Alex Dickerson, 1b	No. 11
12. Bryan Morris, rhp	No. 14
13. Colton Cain, lhp	(Astros)
14. Nick Kingham, rhp	No. 17
15. Clay Holmes, rhp	No. 10
16. Rudy Owens, lhp	(Astros)
17. Justin Wilson, lhp	No. 8
18. Jarek Cunningham, 2b	Dropped out
19. Vic Black, rhp	No. 16
20. Gorkys Hernandez, of	(Marlins)
21. Zack Von Rosenberg, rhp	Dropped out
22. Ramon Cabrera, c	(Tigers)
23. Zack Dodson, lhp	Dropped out
24. Yamaico Navarro, inf/of	(Orioles)
25. Matt Curry, 1b	No. 23
26. Evan Chambers, of	Dropped out
27. Alen Hanson, ss	No. 5
28. Brandon Cumpton, rhp	No. 25
29. Mel Rojas Jr., of	Dropped out
30. Jose Osuna, 1b	No. 24

BEST TOOLS

Best Hitter for Average	Gregory Polanco
Best Power Hitter	Josh Bell
Best Strike-Zone Discipline	Clint Robinson
Fastest Baserunner	Harold Ramirez
Best Athlete	Gregory Polanco
Best Fastball	Gerrit Cole
Best Curveball	Jameson Taillon
Best Slider	Gerrit Cole
Best Changeup	Nathan Baker
Best Control	Kyle McPherson
Best Defensive Catcher	Tony Sanchez
Best Defensive Infielder	Gift Ngoepe
Best Infield Arm	Kirk Singer
Best Defensive Outfielder	Gregory Polanco
Best Outfield Arm	Willy Garcia

PROJECTED 2016 LINEUP

Catcher	Russell Martin
First Base	Alex Dickerson
Second Base	Neil Walker
Third Base	Pedro Alvarez
Shortstop	Alen Hanson
Left Field	Josh Bell
Center Field	Andrew McCutchen
Right Field	Gregory Polanco
No. 1 Starter	Gerrit Cole
No. 2 Starter	Jameson Taillon
No. 3 Starter	Luis Heredia
No. 4 Starter	James McDonald
No. 5 Starter	Kyle McPherson
Closer	Joel Hanrahan

TOP PROSPECTS OF THE DECADE

Year	Player, Pos.	2012 Org.
2003	John Van Benschoten, rhp	Out of baseball
2004	John Van Benschoten, rhp	Out of baseball
2005	Zach Duke, lhp	Nationals
2006	Neil Walker, c	Pirates
2007	Andrew McCutchen, of	Pirates
2008	Andrew McCutchen, of	Pirates
2009	Pedro Alvarez, 3b	Pirates
2010	Pedro Alvarez, 3b	Pirates
2011	Jameson Taillon, rhp	Pirates
2012	Gerrit Cole, rhp	Pirates

TOP DRAFT PICKS OF THE DECADE

Year	Player, Pos.	2012 Org.
2003	Paul Maholm, lhp	Braves
2004	Neil Walker, c	Pirates
2005	Andrew McCutchen, of	Pirates
2006	Brad Lincoln, rhp	Blue Jays
2007	Daniel Moskos, lhp	White Sox
2008	Pedro Alvarez, 3b	Pirates
2009	Tony Sanchez, c	Pirates
2010	Jameson Taillon, rhp	Pirates
2011	Gerrit Cole, rhp	Pirates
2012	*Mark Appel, rhp	Stanford U.

*Did not sign.

LARGEST BONUSES IN CLUB HISTORY

Gerrit Cole, 2011	$8,000,000
Jameson Taillon, 2010	$6,500,000
Pedro Alvarez, 2008	$6,000,000
Josh Bell, 2011	$5,000,000
Bryan Bullington, 2002	$4,000,000

PITTSBURGH PIRATES

TOP 2013 ROOKIE: Kyle McPherson, rhp. He'll get a chance to win a rotation spot after showing great poise in a September callup last season.

BREAKOUT PROSPECT: Tyler Glasnow, rhp. He's still growing into his body and starting to hit 96 mph with his fastball.

SLEEPER: Kevin Ross, 3b. A possible steal as a 2012 eighth-rounder, he offers plus raw power and arm strength.

SOURCE OF TOP 30 TALENT

Homegrown	27	Acquired	3
College	11	Trades	3
Junior college	1	Rule 5 draft	0
High school	6	Independent leagues	0
Nondrafted free agents	0	Free agents/waivers	0
International	9		

LF
Quincy Latimore

CF
Gregory Polanco (4)
Barrett Barnes (9)
Harold Ramirez (28)
Mel Rojas Jr.
Elvis Escobar

RF
Josh Bell (6)
Willy Garcia (18)
Adalberto Santos
Andrew Lambo
Tyler Gaffney

3B
Kevin Ross
Eric Wood
Eric Avila
D.J. Crumlich

SS
Alen Hanson (5)
Gift Ngoepe (30)
Jordy Mercer
Max Moroff
Chris Diaz
Drew Maggi

2B
Dilson Herrera (20)
Brock Holt (22)
Dan Gamache

1B
Alex Dickerson (11)
Matt Curry (23)
Jose Osuna (24)
Clint Robinson (29)
Matt Hague

C
Tony Sanchez (12)
Wyatt Mathisen (15)
Jin-De Jhang (27)
Jacob Stallings

LHP

LHSP	LHRP
Justin Wilson (8)	Philippe Valiquette
Andy Oliver (13)	Jhonathan Ramos
Nate Baker	Eliecer Navarro
	Dalton Friend

RHP

RHSP	RHRP
Gerrit Cole (1)	Bryan Morris (14)
Jameson Taillon (2)	Vic Black (16)
Luis Heredia (3)	Brandon Crumpton (25)
Kyle McPherson (7)	Duke Welker (26)
Clay Holmes (10)	Chad Beck
Nick Kingham (17)	Zach Thornton
Tyler Glasnow (19)	John Kuchno
Adrian Sampson (21)	Kyle Haynes
Zack Von Rosenberg	Emmanuel DeLeon
Tyler Waldron	Jason Townsend
Casey Sadler	
Phil Irwin	
Robby Rowland	
Hunter Strickland	
Hayden Hurst	
Jon Sandfort	
Quinton Miller	
Jake Burnette	
Joely Rodriguez	
Jason Creasey	

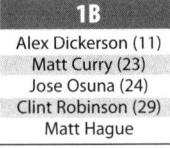

2012

BONUSES: $3.8 MILLION

BEST PURE HITTER: SS Max Moroff (16) has a line-drive swing from both sides of the plate and controls the strike zone well for his age. 3B Eric Wood (6) went to junior college as a pitcher, but his sound righthanded stroke made him an everyday player.

BEST POWER HITTER: OF Barrett Barnes (1s) has excellent bat speed and works counts, allowing him to get to his plus power. He led Pirates draft picks with five homers after signing.

FASTEST RUNNER: Barnes has plus straight-line speed, though he's still learning to steal bases. OF Tyler Gaffney (24) also is an above-average runner who needs to polish his baserunning skills, thanks to his lack of baseball experience.

BEST DEFENSIVE PLAYER: Polished collegians C Jacob Stallings (7), a durable receiver with a plus arm, and SS Chris Diaz (11), who has solid hands and range. Barnes and C Wyatt Mathisen (2) have the tools to play well up the middle with more experience.

BEST FASTBALL: RHP Adrian Sampson (5) pitches at 91 mph and touches 94, commanding his fastball well while maintaining sinking life. RHPs Hayden Hurst (17), John Kuchno (18) and Kyle Haynes (20) have reached the mid-90s.

BEST SECONDARY PITCH: Hurst and Sampson both throw curveballs with power. Sampson also has a solid changeup.

BEST PRO DEBUT: Sampson used his three-pitch mix to post a 2.95 ERA and 44 strikeouts in 43 innings at short-season State College. Gaffney hit .297/.483/.441 for the same club, while Moroff batted .343/.476/.433 in a brief stint in the Rookie-level Gulf Coast League.

BEST ATHLETE: Barnes and Gaffney. The latter played three seasons of football at Stanford, rushing for 791 yards and 12 touchdowns. He's a grinder who has to refine a stiff, somewhat awkward swing.

MOST INTRIGUING BACKGROUND: Stallings' father Kevin is the basketball coach at Vanderbilt. Barnes is the nephew of former big leaguer Anthony Young. Unsigned 2B Tommy Mirabelli's (28) dad John is vice president of scouting operations for the Indians. Kuchno pitched one season of high school baseball and walked on at Wake Forest before emerging as a redshirt sophomore at Ohio State.

CLOSEST TO THE MAJORS: Barnes, though there's no true fast-track player in this class.

BEST LATE-ROUND PICK: Gaffney or Moroff.

THE ONE WHO GOT AWAY: The two best college players and top high schooler who didn't sign in the entire draft were all Pittsburgh picks. RHP Mark Appel (1) was the consensus choice to go No. 1 overall to the Astros, but when he didn't, he slid to No. 8. The Pirates ultimately couldn't pay him more than $3.8 million without forfeiting a 2013 first-round pick, and he opted to return to Stanford. Pittsburgh's top backup plan for Appel was RHP Walker Buehler (14), who decided to attend Vanderbilt. Athletic OF Brandon Thomas (4) turned down Pittsburgh to go back to Georgia Tech.

ASSESSMENT: Pursuing Appel was a worthwhile gamble, but it led the Pirates to scrap a predraft deal with David Dahl, who starred in the Rockies system after going 10th overall. It's hard to have a good draft without signing first- and fourth-round picks.

2011

BONUSES: $17.0 MILLION

The Pirates gave round-record bonuses to RHPs Gerrit Cole (1, $8 million) and Clay Holmes (9, $1.2, million) and OF Josh Bell (2, $5 million), and have no reason to regret doing so. 1B Alex Dickerson (3) is one of the system's best hitters.

GRADE: A

2010

BONUSES: $11.9 MILLION

RHP Jameson Taillon (1) has been everything he was supposed to be as the No. 2 overall pick, but $2.25 million 1B Stetson Allie (2) has been moved off the mound after posting a 7.76 ERA and 37 walks in 27 pro innings.

GRADE: B+

2009

BONUSES: $8.9 MILLION

Pittsburgh overdrafted C Tony Sanchez (1) at No. 4 to save money to sign Dominican slugger Miguel Sano, then lost out on Sano to the Twins and watched Sanchez stall in the upper minors. SS/2B Brock Holt (9) batted .344 and reached the majors last year.

GRADE: D

2008

BONUSES: $9.8 MILLION

3B Pedro Alvarez (1) hasn't been a picture of consistency, but he did slam 30 homers in 2012. The rest of their top five picks—unsigned RHP Tanner Scheppers (2), INF Jordy Mercer (3), SS Chase d'Arnaud (4), LHP Justin Wilson (5)—also have made it to the big leagues, as has 1B/3B Matt Hague (9).

GRADE: B+

Draft analysis by John Manuel (2012) and Jim Callis (2008-11). Numbers in parentheses indicate draft rounds.

1 GERRIT COLE, RHP

Born: Sept. 8, 1990. **B-T:** R-R. **Ht.:** 6-4. **Wt.:** 220.
Drafted: UCLA, 2011 (1st round). **Signed by:** Rick
Allen.

Cole was a big Yankees fan as a kid growing up in Southern California. In fact, a picture of an 11-year-old Cole appeared on the front page of the Newark Star-Ledger during the 2001 World Series that showed him holding a sign before Game Six that read "Yankee Fan Today Tomorrow Forever." However, he didn't even negotiate with the Yankees when they took him with the 28th overall pick in 2008 following his senior season at Orange (Calif.) Lutheran High. He and his parents felt he would be better served by going to UCLA, where he could mature both physically and socially. He did just that and helped the Bruins reach the finals of the 2010 College World Series. His decision paid off in 2011, as the Pirates made Cole the No. 1 overall selection. Cole signed at the Aug. 15 deadline for a draft-record $8 million bonus and played in the Arizona Fall League before making his official pro debut in 2012. He reached Triple-A Indianapolis and pitched in the Futures Game along the way.

Cole is a power pitcher with a pair of devastating offerings. He can effortlessly throw his four-seam fastball up to 101 mph, sitting at 96-98 mph and carrying that velocity deep into games. He also throws a two-seamer with sink at 93-95. His slider is a wipeout pitch with very hard tilt and he typically throws it at 88-90 mph, topping out as high as 93. When he stays on top of the slider, it's almost unhittable for right-handers. He also has a solid upper-80s changeup that keeps improving, and he'll mix in an occasional slow curveball for show. In order to become a true ace, Cole will have to make some adjustments. He'll have to keep working on taking a little more off his changeup, which would slow down hitters' bats. He also needs to fine-tune his command. He throws strikes fairly consistently, but he gets hit more than he should considering the quality of his stuff because he doesn't locate his pitches with enough precision. Hitters also seem to see the ball well out of Cole's hand. Some scouts are concerned that he has a tendency to drift away from the rubber during his

delivery. He's athletic and intelligent, so he should be able to make the necessary mechanical refinements.

Cole got a taste of Triple-A at the end of last season, pitching once in the regular season and once in the International League playoffs. He'll start the 2013 season back at Indianapolis but it would be no surprise to see him in Pittsburgh's rotation by the all-star break—and probably a bit of a disappointment if he isn't. Cole draws comparisons to Justin Verlander and certainly has the look of a No. 1 starter who could anchor their rotation with 2010 first-rounder Jameson Taillon for years.

SCOUTING GRADES

Fastball: 80.   **Control:** 55.
Slider: 70.   **Command:** 50.
Changeup: 60.

Based on 20-80 scouting scale, where 50 represents major league average, and future projection rather than present tools.

Year	Club (League)	Class	W	L	ERA	G	GS	CG	SV	IP	H	HR	BB	SO	K/9	WHIP	AVG
2012	Bradenton (FSL)	HiA	5	1	2.55	13	13	0	0	67	53	5	21	69	9.3	1.10	.217
	Altoona (EL)	AA	3	6	2.90	12	12	0	0	59	54	2	23	60	9.2	1.31	.239
	Indianapolis (IL)	AAA	1	0	4.50	1	1	0	0	6	6	0	1	7	10.5	1.17	.273
Minor League Totals			9	7	2.80	26	26	0	0	132	113	7	45	136	9.3	1.20	.230

BA GRADE
70
MEDIUM

TOMASSO DeROSA

2 JAMESON TAILLON, RHP

Born: Nov. 18, 1991. **B-T:** R-R. **Ht.:** 6-6. **Wt.:** 225. **Drafted:** HS—The Woodlands, Texas, 2010 (1st round). **Signed by:** Trevor Haley.

Taillon's ceiling is so high that the Pirates rated him ahead of Bryce Harper on their 2010 draft board and took him second overall even though GM Neal Huntington doesn't believe in drafting prep righthanders in the first round. Taillon had a 3.85 grade-point average in high school and planned to attend Rice until Pittsburgh changed those plans with a $6.5 million bonus. With stuff, command and smarts, Taillon has the total package for a frontline starter. His four-seam fastball sits at 94-96 mph and hits 99 with boring action, and he'll mix in a two-seamer with more sink. His curveball is an excellent pitch that breaks so late and so sharply that it can be confused for a slider. He's still refining his changeup but it should become at least an average pitch. Taillon went through a crisis of confidence for a stretch early last season where he questioned his pitch selection and stopped pitching aggressively. However, he regained his killer instinct in the second half and finished strong after a late-season promotion to Double-A Altoona. Taillon would be the future No. 1 starter for most organizations but likely will slot in at No. 2 behind Gerrit Cole with the Pirates. Taillon will begin 2013 back in Double-A but could see Pittsburgh before season's end.

BA GRADE

65

MEDIUM

Year	Club (League)	Class	W	L	ERA	G	GS	CG	SV	IP	H	HR	BB	SO	K/9	WHIP	AVG
2011	West Virginia (SAL)	LoA	2	3	3.98	23	23	0	0	93	89	9	22	97	9.4	1.20	.249
2012	Bradenton (FSL)	HiA	6	8	3.82	23	23	2	0	125	109	10	37	98	7.1	1.17	.230
	Altoona (EL)	AA	3	0	1.59	3	3	0	0	17	11	0	1	18	9.5	0.71	.183
Minor League Totals			11	11	3.72	49	49	2	0	235	209	19	60	213	8.2	1.15	.234

3 LUIS HEREDIA, RHP

Born: Aug. 10, 1994. **B-T:** R-R. **Ht.:** 6-6. **Wt.:** 205. **Signed:** Mexico, 2010. **Signed by:** Rene Gayo/Chino Valdez.

Heredia represented Pittsburgh's first big international strike when he signed out of Mexico for $2.6 million in 2010. He was considered the best foreign amateur pitcher available that summer, and the Pirates had developed a relationship with him since he was 13. Extremely advanced for his age, he was the youngest in the short-season New York-Penn League last year, pitching most of the summer at 17. Heredia offers a lot of projection as a 6-foot-6 teenager, but there's also a lot to like about him in the present. He throws his fastball at 91-94 mph with good movement, with the promise of more velocity as he gets stronger. He threw a slow curveball when he first came to the United States but has added power to it. He has a good feel for his changeup, though he needs to subtract some velocity from it. Heredia can throw his secondary pitches for strikes consistently and is becoming adept at keeping the ball down in the strike zone. Pittsburgh praises his work ethic. Heredia could develop three plus pitches, giving the Pirates a third potential frontline starter. The Pirates are trying to manage his workload, so they may keep him in extended spring training for a month before sending him to low Class A West Virginia. He could reach the majors sometime around his 21st birthday in 2015.

BA GRADE

60

HIGH

Year	Club (League)	Class	W	L	ERA	G	GS	CG	SV	IP	H	HR	BB	SO	K/9	WHIP	AVG
2011	Pirates (GCL)	R	1	2	4.75	12	11	0	0	30	28	3	19	23	6.8	1.55	.257
2012	State College (NYP)	SS	4	2	2.71	14	14	0	0	66	53	2	20	40	5.4	1.10	.224
Minor League Totals			5	4	3.35	26	25	0	0	97	81	5	39	63	5.9	1.24	.234

4 GREGORY POLANCO, OF

Born: Sept. 14, 1991. **B-T:** L-L. **Ht.:** 6-4. **Wt.:** 170. **Signed:** Dominican Republic, 2009. **Signed by:** Rene Gayo/Ellis Pena.

After hitting a combined .218/.288/.322 in the previous two seasons in the Rookie-level Gulf Coast League, Polanco clearly was the system's breakout player in 2012. He led Pirates farmhands in steals (40) while ranking second in all three slash stats (.325/.388/.522) as well as homers (16) and RBIs (85). Signed for $175,000 out of the Dominican Republic in 2009, he's starting to look like a bargain. Polanco has blossomed into a five-tool talent now that he has improved his plate discipline and ability to drive the ball. His swing can get long and he can get pull-happy, but he makes consistent hard contact and good adjustments at the plate. He projects to hit for at least solid average and power. Polanco is a quality center fielder with plenty of range and a strong arm. He also projects as a high-volume basestealer, though he needs refinement in that area. Polanco played so well last season that it's not a stretch to think he could be a 30/30 player in

BA GRADE

60

HIGH

Pittsburgh. While he must prove he's more than a one-year wonder, the tools are there for him to be a star. He'll move up to high Class A at age 21 and is at least two full minor league seasons away from being ready for the majors.

Year	Club (League)	Class	AVG	G	AB	R	H	2B	3B	HR	RBI	BB	SO	SB	CS	OBP	SLG
2009	Pirates (DSL)	R	.267	63	221	34	59	8	6	0	24	33	50	12	4	.370	.357
2010	Pirates (GCL)	R	.202	53	188	21	38	5	1	3	23	9	41	19	2	.245	.287
2011	Pirates (GCL)	R	.237	48	169	34	40	4	4	3	34	24	33	18	0	.333	.361
	State College (NYP)	SS	.100	3	10	0	1	0	0	0	1	0	2	0	0	.100	.100
2012	West Virginia (SAL)	LoA	.325	116	437	84	142	26	6	16	85	44	64	40	15	.388	.522
Minor League Totals			.273	283	1025	173	280	43	17	22	167	110	190	89	21	.347	.413

5 ALEN HANSON, SS

Born: Oct. 22, 1992. **B-T:** B-R. **Ht.:** 5-11. **Wt.:** 152. **Signed:** Dominican Republic, 2009. **Signed by:** Rene Gayo/Ellis Pena.

BA GRADE

60

HIGH

Hanson's low Class A performance was just as spectacular as Gregory Polanco's last year. Hanson, who had a better track record of success in Rookie ball, had extremely similar numbers and led the South Atlantic League in runs (99), triples (13) and total bases (258). Hanson is developing into quite a hitter for a lithe shortstop. He has gap power from both sides of the plate and enough strength to pull mistakes on the inner half over the fence. He also can inside-out the ball for opposite-field hits or lay down a bunt to use his plus speed. His quickness puts pressure on opponents, though he needs to hone his baserunning and basestealing skills. The biggest question about Hanson is his defense. He has the range to play shortstop but his arm is average at best and he's inconsistent, as evidenced by his 40 errors in 103 games last year. Some scouts feel he projects as a second baseman, a position he has played in the past. He brings energy to the ballpark every day. Hanson has a chance to provide an impact bat at a middle-infield position. He'll stay at shortstop when he plays at high Class A Bradenton at age 20 this year. Like Polanco, he doesn't figure to surface in Pittsburgh before the second half of 2015.

Year	Club (League)	Class	AVG	G	AB	R	H	2B	3B	HR	RBI	BB	SO	SB	CS	OBP	SLG
2010	Pirates (DSL)	R	.324	68	244	48	79	10	7	2	28	22	37	20	8	.383	.447
2011	Pirates (GCL)	R	.263	52	198	42	52	13	7	2	35	21	34	24	6	.352	.429
	State College (NYP)	SS	.200	3	10	1	2	0	0	0	0	1	2	0	0	.273	.200
2012	West Virginia (SAL)	LoA	.309	124	489	99	151	33	13	16	62	55	105	35	19	.381	.528
Minor League Totals			.302	247	941	190	284	56	27	20	125	99	178	79	33	.374	.482

6 JOSH BELL, OF

Born: Aug. 14, 1992. **B-T:** B-R. **Ht.:** 6-4. **Wt.:** 195. **Drafted:** HS—Dallas, 2011 (2nd round). **Signed by:** Mike Leuzinger.

BA GRADE

60

HIGH

The Pirates stunned the industry when they landed the thought-to-be-unsignable Bell for $5 million at the 2011 deadline. He had written all 30 teams and asked them not to select him because he was committed to attending Texas, but Pittsburgh had him ranked sixth on its draft board and popped him at No. 61 overall. His 2012 pro debut ended quickly, as he had surgery April 26 after tearing the meniscus in his left knee while running the bases. He was supposed to return for instructional league but persistent swelling in the knee scuttled that plan. Bell has big-time power potential from both sides of the plate. With his bat speed, strike-zone discipline and mature approach, he also should hit for average. He had average speed before he got hurt, and there's some fear that he might lose a step after his knee injury. Bell projects as a right fielder with average range and solid arm strength. Bell has the makings of a No. 3 or 4 hitter in a contender's lineup. Though he essentially lost a full season, he's will be just 20 when he returns to low Class A. The Pirates are anxious to see how he bounces back from his injury, and he has the bat to move fast once he gets going.

Year	Club (League)	Class	AVG	G	AB	R	H	2B	3B	HR	RBI	BB	SO	SB	CS	OBP	SLG
2012	West Virginia (SAL)	LoA	.274	15	62	6	17	5	0	1	11	2	21	1	0	.288	.403
Minor League Totals			.274	15	62	6	17	5	0	1	11	2	21	1	0	.288	.403

7 KYLE McPHERSON, RHP

Born: Nov. 11, 1987. **B-T:** R-R. **Ht.:** 6-4. **Wt.:** 220. **Drafted:** Mobile (Ala.), 2007 (14th round). **Signed by:** Darren Mazeroski.

McPherson was primarily a shortstop at Mobile (Ala.), an NAIA program, and compiled a 6.02 ERA primarily mopping up in blowouts. Pirates scout Darren Mazeroski, the son of Hall of Fame second baseman Bill, glimpsed big league mound potential in McPherson and signed him for $30,000. Mazeroski was proven right when Pittsburgh called McPherson up last August, and he shut out the Reds for six innings in his final start. McPherson doesn't have overwhelming stuff, though he's not a soft-tosser either. His fastball sits at 90-92 mph and can reach 95 on occasion. He can locate his fastball wherever he wants and commands all of his pitches. His best offering might be his changeup, which he throws with deceptive arm speed. His curveball is average at times, though he must guard against flattening it out by overthrowing. McPherson isn't afraid to pitch inside and likes to use his changeup when behind in the count to disrupt hitters' timing. Though he spent the first 10 weeks of last season on the disabled list with shoulder tendinitis, he otherwise has been durable through six pro seasons. While he has the stuff of a No. 4 starter, McPherson's moxie gives him a chance to play up to a No. 3 who can eat innings. He'll get an opportunity to win a spot in Pittsburgh's rotation this spring.

BA GRADE

50

MEDIUM

Year	Club (League)	Class	W	L	ERA	G	GS	CG	SV	IP	H	HR	BB	SO	K/9	WHIP	AVG
2007	Pirates (GCL)	R	4	2	2.61	12	10	0	0	52	47	3	10	35	6.1	1.10	.246
	State College (NYP)	SS	0	1	6.28	3	3	0	0	14	20	1	3	6	3.8	1.60	.323
2008	State College (NYP)	SS	1	3	4.37	15	7	0	1	56	52	10	5	41	6.6	1.02	.240
2009	West Virginia (SAL)	LoA	5	2	4.94	13	8	0	0	51	53	3	6	32	5.6	1.16	.269
	State College (NYP)	SS	4	3	2.99	13	13	0	0	75	70	5	11	57	6.8	1.08	.248
2010	West Virginia (SAL)	LoA	9	9	3.59	26	21	0	0	118	96	14	31	124	9.5	1.08	.216
	Bradenton (FSL)	HiA	0	0	0.00	2	0	0	0	4	2	0	0	7	15.8	0.50	.133
2011	Bradenton (FSL)	HiA	4	1	2.89	12	12	1	0	72	62	4	6	60	7.5	0.95	.227
	Altoona (EL)	AA	8	5	3.02	16	16	0	0	89	75	7	21	82	8.3	1.07	.226
2012	Altoona (EL)	AA	3	5	4.07	9	9	0	0	49	54	5	5	46	8.5	1.21	.278
	Indianapolis (IL)	AAA	0	1	0.98	3	3	0	0	18	11	1	4	17	8.3	0.82	.172
	Pittsburgh (NL)	MAJ	0	2	2.73	10	3	0	0	26	24	3	7	21	7.2	1.18	.247
Major League Totals			0	2	2.73	10	3	0	0	26	24	3	7	21	7.2	1.18	.247
Minor League Totals			38	32	3.45	124	102	1	1	598	542	53	102	507	7.6	1.08	.239

8 JUSTIN WILSON, LHP

Born: Aug. 18, 1987. **B-T:** L-L. **Ht.:** 6-2. **Wt.:** 221. **Drafted:** Fresno State, 2008 (5th round). **Signed by:** Sean Campbell.

Wilson etched his name in College World Series lore by winning the championship game for Fresno State in 2008. He had the distinction of being part of two no-hitters last season at Indianapolis, pitching 7 ⅓ innings of a combined effort against Durham on April 29 and a rain-shortened, eight-inning gem versus Charlotte on Aug. 9. He led the International League in opponent average (.189) and ranked second in strikeouts (138). Wilson throws harder than most lefthanders, working with a 92-94 mph and reaching 96. His peak velocity spiked to 99 mph when he worked in a relief role in Triple-A late in each of the last two seasons, though he didn't throw that hard while coming out of the bullpen during his first big league callup last September. Wilson's curveball, slider and changeup all can be average pitches, but his command of his entire arsenal is spotty. That's why the Pirates have looked at him in relief. Pittsburgh still hasn't decided if Wilson's long-term future is as a starter or a reliever, though the latter seems more likely in the long run. He'll get a chance to win a job in the major league bullpen during spring training. If he doesn't make the Pirates, he may continue starting at Indianapolis to give him more innings to work on his command.

BA GRADE

50

MEDIUM

Year	Club (League)	Class	W	L	ERA	G	GS	CG	SV	IP	H	HR	BB	SO	K/9	WHIP	AVG
2009	Lynchburg (CAR)	HiA	6	8	4.50	26	26	0	0	116	118	14	55	94	7.3	1.49	.262
2010	Altoona (EL)	AA	11	8	3.09	27	26	0	0	143	109	4	71	134	8.5	1.26	.215
2011	Indianapolis (IL)	AAA	10	8	4.13	30	21	0	3	124	121	12	67	94	6.8	1.51	.254
2012	Indianapolis (IL)	AAA	9	6	3.78	29	25	1	0	136	91	12	66	138	9.2	1.16	.189
	Pittsburgh (NL)	MAJ	0	0	1.93	8	0	0	0	5	10	0	3	7	13.5	2.79	.455
Major League Totals			0	0	1.93	8	0	0	0	5	10	0	3	7	13.5	2.79	.455
Minor League Totals			36	30	3.83	112	98	1	3	519	439	42	259	460	8.0	1.35	.229

9 BARRETT BARNES, OF

Born: July 29, 1991. **B-T:** R-R. **Ht.:** 6-1. **Wt.:** 195. **Drafted:** Texas Tech, 2012 (1st round supplemental). **Signed by:** Mike Leuzinger.

When first-rounder Mark Appel decided to return to Stanford, Barnes became the Pirates' top signee in the 2012 draft. The nephew of Anthony Young, who lost a major league-record 27 straight decisions with the Mets in 1992-93, Barnes went 45th overall and signed for $1 million. He earned New York-Penn League all-star recognition before a stress-related shin injury ended his pro debut a month early. Barnes has the potential to do it all offensively. He has a quick bat, good plate discipline, plus raw power and above-average speed. He's willing to work the count more than most young hitters. He has trouble with breaking pitches and gets pull-conscious at times, which may limit his ability to hit for average. Barnes is still learning to steal bases after getting caught in six of his 16 attempts as a pro. He may be able to stick in center field if he can improve his jumps with more experience. His arm is fringy. Barnes obviously will have more value if he can remain in center field, but he should have enough power to profile as a regular if he has to move to left field. He should reach high Class A at some point during his first full pro season and may not need much more than two years of minor league seasoning.

BA GRADE
50
HIGH

Year	Club (League)	Class	AVG	G	AB	R	H	2B	3B	HR	RBI	BB	SO	SB	CS	OBP	SLG
2012	State College (NYP)	SS	.288	38	125	16	36	6	0	5	24	17	21	10	6	.401	.456
Minor League Totals			.288	38	125	16	36	6	0	5	24	17	21	10	6	.401	.456

10 CLAY HOLMES, RHP

Born: March 27, 1993. **B-T:** R-R. **Ht.:** 6-5. **Wt.:** 230. **Drafted:** HS—Slocomb, Ala., 2011 (9th round). **Signed by:** Darren Mazeroski.

Holmes was the valedictorian of his high school class and the Alabama coaches association student-athlete of the year in 2011. He was part of the Pirates' draft binge that year, when they set bonus records for the first (Gerrit Cole, $8 million), second (Josh Bell, $5 million) and ninth (Holmes, $1.2 million) rounds. In his 2012 pro debut, he limited more advanced hitters to a .176 average, which would have ranked second in the New York-Penn League if he hadn't missed qualifying by two innings. Holmes uses his big frame and quick arm to throw 90-95 mph fastballs on a steep downward plane. He can pound the bottom of the strike zone when his mechanics are in sync, but he's still learning to consistently control all of his pitches. He also throws a hard three-quarters breaking ball and is working to add a changeup. Holmes is a good athlete for his size, which bodes well for his ability to repeat his delivery and throw more strikes. He's built for durability and gets high marks for his maturity and competitiveness. Holmes' arm strength and smarts give him the upside of a No. 3 starter, though he's still a long ways from reaching that ceiling. He's ready to advance to low Class A in 2013.

BA GRADE
50
HIGH

Year	Club (League)	Class	W	L	ERA	G	GS	CG	SV	IP	H	HR	BB	SO	K/9	WHIP	AVG
2012	State College (NYP)	SS	5	3	2.28	13	13	0	0	59	35	1	29	34	5.2	1.08	.176
Minor League Totals			5	3	2.28	13	13	0	0	59	35	1	29	34	5.2	1.08	.176

11 ALEX DICKERSON, 1B

BA GRADE
50
HIGH

Born: May 26, 1990. **B-T:** L-L. **Ht.:** 6-3. **Wt.:** 235. **Drafted:** Indiana, 2011 (3rd round). **Signed by:** Jerry Jordan.

Dickerson won the Big Ten Conference triple crown as a sophomore in 2010, before his numbers fell off somewhat the next year—as they did throughout college baseball because of the use of toned-down bats. The Pirates still were attracted to his all-around hitting ability and drafted him in the third round, and he repaid their faith by going to high Class A in his first full pro season and winning the league MVP award. Dickerson uses the whole field and doesn't try to pull everything. He has the raw strength to have at least average power once he gets more comfortable turning on inside pitches. Dickerson was a left fielder in college, but Pittsburgh immediately moved him to first base because he has below-average speed and arm strength. He made nice strides in the field last season, though his hands a little stiff. Dickerson will make the jump to Double-A in 2013. If he develops more power, he could get to the major leagues in 2014 because the Pirates don't have many longball hitters.

Year	Club (League)	Class	AVG	G	AB	R	H	2B	3B	HR	RBI	BB	SO	SB	CS	OBP	SLG
2011	State College (NYP)	SS	.313	41	150	25	47	16	1	3	19	16	28	0	0	.393	.493
2012	Bradenton (FSL)	HiA	.295	129	488	65	144	31	3	13	90	39	93	12	7	.353	.451
Minor League Totals			.299	170	638	90	191	47	4	16	109	55	121	12	7	.362	.461

12 TONY SANCHEZ, C

Born: May 20, 1988. **B-T:** R-R. **Ht.:** 6-0. **Wt.:** 225. **Drafted:** Boston College, 2009 (1st round). **Signed by:** Chris Kline.

Pittsburgh took plenty of heat for selecting Sanchez with the fourth overall pick in the 2009 draft and signing him for a below-slot $2.5 million. The Pirates' strategy was to use the savings toward signing Dominican slugger Miguel Sano, but they lost Sano to the Twins. After four pro seasons, Sanchez hasn't done much on his part to justify the selection. Sanchez was supposed to be close to major league-ready defensively when he was drafted, but he has struggled behind the plate and shown signs of the yips when throwing the ball back to the pitcher. He has a strong arm but lacks consistent accuracy on his throws, which is why he has thrown out just 24 percent of basestealers in pro ball. To his credit, he has become a good receiver and learned how to work better with pitchers. There are questions about whether Sanchez will develop enough offensively to be a major league regular. His swing gets long and he becomes too pull-conscious when he tries to hit for power, and his average dipped to .233 last year in Triple-A. A realistic expectation would be for him to become an average hitter with moderate power. He's a well below-average runner. It's too early to write Sanchez off as a starter, though Pittsburgh planned on him being their regular catcher by now. Instead, the Pirates signed Russell Martin as a free agent this offseason and will send Sanchez back to Indianapolis. They did protect him on the 40-man roster in November.

Year	Club (League)	Class	AVG	G	AB	R	H	2B	3B	HR	RBI	BB	SO	SB	CS	OBP	SLG
2009	State College (NYP)	SS	.308	4	13	2	4	1	0	0	1	1	2	0	0	.357	.385
	West Virginia (SAL)	LoA	.316	41	155	29	49	15	1	7	46	21	34	1	0	.415	.561
	Lynchburg (CAR)	HiA	.200	3	10	2	2	2	0	0	1	1	4	0	0	.385	.400
2010	Bradenton (FSL)	HiA	.314	59	207	31	65	17	0	4	35	28	41	2	1	.416	.454
2011	Altoona (EL)	AA	.241	118	402	46	97	14	1	5	44	47	76	5	5	.340	.318
2012	Altoona (EL)	AA	.277	40	141	22	39	14	1	0	17	18	33	1	1	.370	.390
	Indianapolis (IL)	AAA	.233	62	206	21	48	12	0	8	26	23	46	0	0	.316	.408
Minor League Totals			.268	327	1134	153	304	75	3	24	170	139	236	9	7	.365	.403

13 ANDY OLIVER, LHP

Born: Dec. 3, 1987. **B-T:** L-L. **Ht.:** 6-3. **Wt.:** 210. **Drafted:** Oklahoma State, 2009 (2nd round). **Signed by:** Chris Wimmer (Tigers).

Oliver sued the NCAA in 2008 after it suspended him for having an adviser while negotiating with the Twins when they drafted him out of high school. Reinstated after winning the lawsuit, he received a $750,000 settlement and signed with the Tigers for $1,495,000 as a second-round pick in 2009. Oliver saw time in the big leagues in 2010 and 2011, but spent 2012 exclusively at the Triple-A level. He had the worst year of his pro career and led the International League with 88 walks, after which Detroit traded him to Pittsburgh for catcher Ramon Cabrera during the Winter Meetings. Oliver still has a quality fastball that sits at 92-94 mph and tops out at 96. After alternating between a curveball and a slider in the past, he's focusing on a curve that still gets slurvy at times. He also throws an inconsistent changeup but mostly relies on his fastball and curve. Oliver has averaged 5.0 walks per nine innings in the minors, wildness that's attributed to him having static hands in his delivery, which leads to an inconsistent release point. The Tigers worked with him to get more rhythm and flow into his mechanics. Oliver went on the disabled list in the middle of the season with shoulder fatigue and mostly pitched out of the bullpen in the second half. Some scouts still believe he could develop into a mid-rotation starter. If he can't cut his walks down, his more likely destination is in the bullpen as a power-armed lefthanded reliever—though he hasn't shown a significant platoon advantage in that regard.

Year	Club (League)	Class	W	L	ERA	G	GS	CG	SV	IP	H	HR	BB	SO	K/9	WHIP	AVG
2010	Erie (EL)	AA	6	4	3.61	14	14	0	0	77	74	7	25	70	8.1	1.28	.253
	Detroit (AL)	MAJ	0	4	7.36	5	5	0	0	22	26	3	13	18	7.4	1.77	.310
	Toledo (IL)	AAA	3	4	3.23	9	9	0	0	53	43	6	25	49	8.3	1.28	.226
2011	Detroit (AL)	MAJ	0	1	6.52	2	2	0	0	10	11	3	8	5	4.7	1.97	.289
	Toledo (IL)	AAA	8	12	4.71	26	26	0	0	147	149	15	80	143	8.8	1.56	.272
2012	Toledo (IL)	AAA	5	9	4.88	28	19	0	0	118	103	7	88	112	8.5	1.62	.235
Major League Totals			0	5	7.11	7	7	0	0	32	37	6	21	23	6.5	1.83	.303
Minor League Totals			22	29	4.35	77	68	0	0	395	369	35	218	374	8.5	1.48	.251

14 BRYAN MORRIS, RHP

Born: March 28, 1987. **B-T:** L-R. **Ht.:** 6-3. **Wt.:** 220. **Drafted:** Motlow State (Tenn.) CC, 2006 (1st round). **Signed by:** Marty Lamb (Dodgers).

More than six years after being drafted in the first round by the Dodgers, Morris finally completed his long journey to the major leagues last season with a September callup.

Morris had Tommy John surgery in 2007 and also has battled shoulder, toe and oblique problems in his professional career. He's the last player remaining with the organization from the three-team Jason Bay/Manny Ramirez trade in July 2008, as Craig Hansen, Andy LaRoche and Brandon Moss all washed out of Pittsburgh. The Pirates moved him to the bullpen at Altoona midway through the 2011 season, and that revived his career. Morris has stayed healthy in a relief role, and his fastball now sits at 92-94 mph and peaks at 96. He has a plus curveball for a second pitch and no longer has to worry about an inconsistent changeup. He has had high groundball rates throughout his career and significantly improved his control in 2012. It's not out of the question to project Morris as a major league closer, but his realistic ceiling is as a set-up man. He figures to make Pittsburgh's Opening Day roster because he's out of minor league options.

Year	Club (League)	Class	W	L	ERA	G	GS	CG	SV	IP	H	HR	BB	SO	K/9	WHIP	AVG
2006	Ogden (PIO)	R	4	5	5.13	14	14	0	0	60	64	3	40	79	11.9	1.74	.267
2007	Did Not Play—Injured																
2008	Great Lakes (MWL)	LoA	2	4	3.20	17	17	1	0	82	74	5	31	72	7.9	1.29	.247
	Hickory (SAL)	LoA	0	2	5.02	3	3	0	0	14	17	2	12	11	6.9	2.02	.288
2009	Lynchburg (CAR)	HiA	4	9	5.57	15	15	0	0	73	87	2	34	32	4.0	1.67	.295
2010	Bradenton (FSL)	HiA	3	0	0.60	8	8	0	0	45	37	0	7	40	8.1	0.99	.220
	Altoona (EL)	AA	6	4	4.25	19	16	0	0	89	87	9	31	84	8.5	1.33	.258
2011	Altoona (EL)	AA	3	4	3.35	35	6	0	3	78	72	2	33	64	7.4	1.35	.252
2012	Indianapolis (IL)	AAA	2	2	2.67	46	0	0	5	81	76	8	17	79	8.8	1.15	.240
	Pittsburgh (NL)	MAJ	0	0	1.80	5	0	0	0	5	2	0	2	6	10.8	0.80	.125
Major League Totals			0	0	1.80	5	0	0	0	5	2	0	2	6	10.8	0.80	.125
Minor League Totals			24	30	3.70	157	79	1	8	521	514	31	205	461	8.0	1.38	.257

15 WYATT MATHISEN, C

BA GRADE
50
HIGH

Born: Dec. 30, 1993. **B-T:** R-R. **Ht.:** 6-1. **Wt.:** 205. **Drafted:** HS—Corpus Christi, Texas, 2012 (2nd round). **Signed by:** Trevor Haley.

Baseball America rated Mathisen as the top high school catcher in last year's draft, but some teams were leery because he played much more at shortstop than behind the plate as an amateur. The Pirates saw enough of him at catcher to think he could play there, and they believed Gulf Coast League manager Tom Prince, who had a 20-year pro career as a catcher, could help him make the transition to full-time backstop. After Mathisen signed for $746,300 as a second-round pick, he made nice strides behind the plate in his pro debut, showing a strong arm and throwing out 36 percent of basestealers. He's somewhat stiff receiving the ball and flinches on some pitches, but he should eliminate those problems in time. Mathisen has a quick bat with line-drive power and possesses good plate discipline for a young hitter. He should develop at least average home run pop as his body matures. He's more athletic than most catchers and has close to average speed, though he'll slow down as he spends more time behind the plate. He'll spend his first full pro season in low Class A.

Year	Club (League)	Class	AVG	G	AB	R	H	2B	3B	HR	RBI	BB	SO	SB	CS	OBP	SLG
2012	Pirates (GCL)	R	.295	45	139	24	41	8	0	1	15	16	19	10	8	.388	.374
Minor League Totals			.295	45	139	24	41	8	0	1	15	16	19	10	8	.388	.374

16 VIC BLACK, RHP

BA GRADE
50
HIGH

Born: May 23,1988. **B-T:** R-R. **Ht.:** 6-3. **Wt.:** 185. **Drafted:** Dallas Baptist, 2009 (1st round supplemental). **Signed by:** Mike Leuzinger.

One of the hardest throwers in the 2009 draft, Black went 49th overall and signed for $717,000. He began his pro career as a starter but was plagued by control problems and continual bouts of biceps tendinitis. The Pirates decided to convert him into a reliever in 2011 and he continued to struggle with his control, then started putting it all together last year in Double-A. He led Eastern League relievers in opponent average (.189) and strikeouts per nine innings (12.8). Black racks up whiffs with a fastball that has been clocked as high as 101 mph and sits at 95-97. He mixes in a hard slider and has all but junked his changeup, which was never effective. In the Arizona Fall League, he worked on learning a two-seam fastball to give hitters a different look. Black still walks too many hitters, but if he can keep making strides like he did last year, he has the stuff to close in the major leagues. Even with spotty control, he's good enough to work in the late innings. Pittsburgh added him to the 40-man roster in November and likely will give him his first big league opportunity in 2013, though he figures to start the year in Triple-A.

Year	Club (League)	Class	W	L	ERA	G	GS	CG	SV	IP	H	HR	BB	SO	K/9	WHIP	AVG
2009	State College (NYP)	SS	1	2	3.45	13	7	0	1	31	26	0	15	33	9.5	1.31	.213
2010	West Virginia (SAL)	LoA	0	0	9.64	2	2	0	0	5	3	1	5	8	15.4	1.71	.176
2011	West Virginia (SAL)	LoA	2	1	5.28	22	0	0	1	29	30	0	16	23	7.1	1.59	.268
	Bradenton (FSL)	HiA	1	0	4.05	5	0	0	0	7	8	1	4	5	6.8	1.80	.333
2012	Altoona (EL)	AA	2	3	1.65	51	0	0	13	60	40	2	29	85	12.8	1.15	.189
Minor League Totals			6	6	3.28	93	9	0	15	132	107	4	69	154	10.5	1.34	.220

17 NICK KINGHAM, RHP

BA GRADE
50
HIGH

Born: Nov. 8, 1991. **B-T:** R-R. **Ht.:** 6-5. **Wt.:** 220. **Drafted:** HS—Las Vegas, 2010 (4th round). **Signed by:** Larry Broadway.

Kingham pitched in the large shadow of Bryce Harper during his high school years in Las Vegas, but he didn't escape the notice of area scout Larry Broadway, who is now the Pirates' farm director. Pittsburgh selected Kingham in the fourth round in 2010, higher than many organizations had him on their boards, and signed him for $480,000. He has a big, projectable body that has yet to fill out. He works at 90-92 mph with his fastball, touches 95 and could gain more velocity as he gets stronger. His big-breaking curveball has the makings of a plus pitch but is erratic. He's also working to improve his changeup. Kingham also needs better control and consistency. He'll have stretches when he dominates, like when he posted a 1.68 ERA in his final nine starts for West Virginia last season, but also stretches when he struggles. He'll have to do a better job of damage control, as he has a tendency to give up big innings. Kingham has the body and stuff to be a dependable mid-rotation starter down the road. He'll move up to high Class A this season.

Year	Club (League)	Class	W	L	ERA	G	GS	CG	SV	IP	H	HR	BB	SO	K/9	WHIP	AVG
2010	Pirates (GCL)	R	0	0	0.00	2	0	0	0	3	3	0	0	2	6.0	1.00	.273
2011	State College (NYP)	SS	6	2	2.15	15	15	0	0	71	63	5	15	47	6.0	1.10	.238
2012	West Virginia (SAL)	LoA	6	8	4.39	27	27	0	0	127	115	15	36	117	8.3	1.19	.243
Minor League Totals			12	10	3.54	44	42	0	0	201	181	20	51	166	7.4	1.15	.242

18 WILLY GARCIA, OF

BA GRADE
50
HIGH

Born: Sept. 4, 1992. **B-T:** R-R. **Ht.:** 6-3. **Wt.:** 180. **Signed:** Dominican Republic, 2010. **Signed by:** Rene Gayo/Marino Tejada.

The Pirates were excited to sign Garcia as an international amateur free agent in 2010, though he was overshadowed by the signing of Mexican righthander Luis Heredia for $2.6 million. Garcia remains raw but he led the system with 18 homers in 2012, when he got his first taste of full-season ball as a teenager in low Class A. He has above-average pull power and the strength to hit the ball hard the other way. To hit for average, he'll need to tone down an uppercut swing, a tendency to pull everything and an overly aggressive approach. Garcia has average speed and is still learning how to run the bases and play the outfield corners. He recorded 12 outfield assists last year and has enough arm strength to handle right field. Garcia is just 20, so the Pirates are considering having him repeat low Class A, fearing that more advanced pitchers might exploit his free-swinging ways and damage his confidence. He has a chance to be a middle-of-the-order hitter in the major leagues, but he's too unpolished to count on him reaching that ceiling right now.

Year	Club (League)	Class	AVG	G	AB	R	H	2B	3B	HR	RBI	BB	SO	SB	CS	OBP	SLG
2010	Pirates (DSL)	R	.250	51	168	27	42	11	0	1	22	14	29	8	5	.333	.333
2011	Pirates (GCL)	R	.266	47	177	26	47	9	4	5	35	11	49	7	5	.323	.446
	State College (NYP)	SS	.286	3	7	1	2	0	0	0	0	0	0	0	0	.286	.286
2012	West Virginia (SAL)	LoA	.240	122	459	57	110	17	2	18	77	32	131	10	8	.286	.403
Minor League Totals			.248	223	811	111	201	37	6	24	134	57	209	25	18	.305	.397

19 TYLER GLASNOW, RHP

BA GRADE
50
HIGH

Born: Aug, 23, 1993. **B-T:** L-R. **Ht.:** 6-7. **Wt.:** 195. **Drafted:** HS—Santa Clarita, Calif., 2011 (5th round). **Signed by:** Rick Allen.

Until new draft rules went into effect in 2012, the Pirates' draft approach under GM Neal Huntington was to sign projectable high school pitchers to over-slot bonuses in later rounds. Glasnow was one of the last beneficiaries, getting $600,000 as a fifth-round pick in 2011, with one club official boldly predicting he would be the system's top prospect by the end of 2013. A gangly righthander who wears a size-17 shoe, he's still growing into his body after shooting up eight inches as a sophomore in high school. His fastball velocity is on the rise as well, reaching 96 mph last summer after sitting at 90-93 for most of the spring. His big-breaking curveball shows flashes of becoming a plus pitch, and his changeup is rudimentary at this point. Glasnow has athletic bloodlines, as his father was a decathlete at Notre Dame and his mother was a gymnast. He'll need to lean on his athleticism as he learns to repeat his delivery and improve his command. Glasnow is certainly someone to dream on, a potential frontline starter if things break right. For now, Pittsburgh must decide whether to hold him back in extended spring training or challenge him with a promotion to low Class A.

Year	Club (League)	Class	W	L	ERA	G	GS	CG	SV	IP	H	HR	BB	SO	K/9	WHIP	AVG
2012	Pirates (GCL)	R	0	3	2.10	11	10	0	0	34	19	3	16	40	10.5	1.02	.156
	State College (NYP)	SS	0	0	0.00	1	1	0	0	4	4	0	1	4	9.0	1.25	.267
Minor League Totals			0	3	1.88	12	11	0	0	38	23	3	17	44	10.3	1.04	.168

20 DILSON HERRERA, 2B

BA GRADE
50
HIGH

Born: March 3, 1994. **B-T:** R-R. **Ht.:** 5-10. **Wt.:** 150. **Signed:** Colombia, 2010. **Signed by:** Rene Gayo/Orlando Covo.

Latin American scouting director Rene Gayo has developed a pipeline into Colombia thanks to a strong relationship with Con Familiar, a youth baseball program there. Those ties helped the Pirates sign Herrera for $220,000 in 2010. He made a strong U.S. debut last season, leading the Gulf Coast League in runs (41), extra-base hits (22) and total bases (96). Herrera has few holes in his swing and makes consistent contact to all fields while showing surprising power for a smaller player. He also has plus speed that makes him a potential stolen-base threat. Herrera played shortstop as an amateur and some third base in the Rookie-level Venezuelan Summer League in 2011, but his lack of arm strength limits him to second base. He has the range to be above-average at the keystone and showed improvement in turning the double play last season. He'll make his full-season debut in low Class A this season.

Year	Club (League)	Class	AVG	G	AB	R	H	2B	3B	HR	RBI	BB	SO	SB	CS	OBP	SLG
2011	Pirates (VSL)	R	.308	65	214	42	66	19	5	2	27	32	40	16	8	.413	.472
2012	Pirates (GCL)	R	.281	53	199	41	56	11	4	7	27	18	41	11	4	.341	.482
	State College (NYP)	SS	.321	7	28	7	9	1	1	1	2	1	6	1	0	.345	.536
Minor League Totals			.297	125	441	90	131	31	10	10	56	51	87	28	12	.378	.481

21 ADRIAN SAMPSON, RHP

BA GRADE
50
HIGH

Born: Oct. 7, 1991. **B-T:** R-R. **Ht.:** 6-3. **Wt.:** 200. **Drafted:** Bellevue (Wash.) CC, 2012 (5th round). **Signed by:** Greg Hopkins.

Sampson was one of the top high school players in Washington going into 2010, but he tore an elbow ligament and missed his senior season following Tommy John surgery. He had committed to play at Oregon before his elbow reconstruction, then decided to stay close to home and attend Bellevue (Wash.) CC. He spurned the Marlins after they selected him in the 16th round of the 2011 draft before signing with the Pirates for $250,000 as a fifth-round pick last summer. At his best, Sampson has three solid pitches. His sinking fastball usually sits at 91 mph and tops out at 94, though at times it will dip to 87-91. His curveball has good depth and break and often is his best pitch. His changeup is effective as well. Sampson came with a reputation for controlling and commanding his pitches, though he wasn't as sharp in his pro debut. He has the upside of a mid-rotation starter and will head to low Class A for his first full pro season.

Year	Club (League)	Class	W	L	ERA	G	GS	CG	SV	IP	H	HR	BB	SO	K/9	WHIP	AVG
2012	State College (NYP)	SS	0	1	2.95	11	9	0	0	43	38	2	17	44	9.3	1.29	.241
Minor League Totals			0	1	2.95	11	9	0	0	43	38	2	17	44	9.3	1.29	.241

22 BROCK HOLT, SS/2B

BA GRADE
45
MEDIUM

Born: June 11, 1988. **B-T:** L-R. **Ht.:** 5-10. **Wt.:** 170. **Drafted:** Rice, 2009 (9th round). **Signed by:** Trevor Haley.

Holt did not receive any Division I scholarship offers as a high school senior in Stephenville, Texas, so he spent two seasons playing shortstop at Navarro (Texas) JC. He got a shot at big-time college baseball at Rice, where he played his way into the ninth round of the 2009 draft. He was hitting .351 in high Class A during his first full pro season when he injured his left knee in a June collision with a teammate, ending his season. After an unremarkable Double-A season in 2011, he broke out last year by ranking sixth in the minors with a .344 batting average and then batting .292 during a September callup. Holt has shown the ability to make consistent contact and get on base throughout his minor league career. He understands he has to play the little man's game and doesn't let his swing get very big. He has little home run power, though he can surprise and occasionally drive a ball in the gaps if a pitcher gets careless. Holt's range and arm are a bit light for him to be a regular shortstop in the major leagues, though he compensates with a quick first step and a fast release on his throws. He's an average runner with fine instincts on the bases. Holt will get a chance to win a reserve job in Pittsburgh, but he'll likely wind up opening the season in Triple-A.

Year	Club (League)	Class	AVG	G	AB	R	H	2B	3B	HR	RBI	BB	SO	SB	CS	OBP	SLG
2009	State College (NYP)	SS	.299	66	254	45	76	14	3	6	33	26	31	9	0	.361	.449
2010	Bradenton (FSL)	HiA	.351	47	194	31	68	12	1	1	27	19	30	6	6	.410	.438
2011	Altoona (EL)	AA	.288	132	511	62	147	30	9	1	40	50	85	18	10	.356	.387
2012	Altoona (EL)	AA	.322	102	382	52	123	24	6	2	43	40	51	11	11	.389	.432
	Indianapolis (IL)	AAA	.432	24	95	13	41	7	0	1	7	9	9	5	2	.476	.537
	Pittsburgh (NL)	MAJ	.292	24	65	6	19	2	1	0	3	4	14	0	0	.329	.354
Major League Totals			.292	24	65	6	19	2	1	0	3	4	14	0	0	.329	.354
Minor League Totals			.317	371	1436	203	455	87	19	11	150	144	206	49	29	.381	.427

23 MATT CURRY, 1B

BA GRADE
45
MEDIUM

Born: July 27, 1988. **B-T:** L-R. **Ht.:** 6-1. **Wt.:** 225. **Drafted:** Texas Christian, 2010 (16th round). **Signed by:** Mike Leuzinger.

The Pirates drafted Curry in 2008 after he hit 60 doubles and 30 homers in two seasons at Howard (Texas) JC, but he opted to attend Texas Christian instead. They drafted him again in 2010 after he helped lead the Horned Frogs to the College World Series, signing him for $2,000 in the 16th round. Power is his calling card and ultimately will determine his future. Curry has hit 33 homers in 304 pro games while playing mostly in pitcher's parks that have kept his numbers down. He has solid pop, though he tends to get pull-happy and swing through some pitches. He has hit just .266 in Double-A after batting .327 in the lower minors. Curry has below-average speed and defensive ability, limiting him to first base, so he'll have to produce homers to have a big league future. He does have some of the best power potential in a system short on power hitters, giving him an opportunity. Pittsburgh will send him to another pitcher's park in Indianapolis and may give him a major league look late in the summer.

Year	Club (League)	Class	AVG	G	AB	R	H	2B	3B	HR	RBI	BB	SO	SB	CS	OBP	SLG
2010	State College (NYP)	SS	.299	58	197	36	59	14	0	7	29	39	47	7	5	.421	.477
2011	West Virginia (SAL)	LoA	.361	46	155	39	56	15	3	9	34	35	29	6	2	.477	.671
	Altoona (EL)	AA	.242	87	302	38	73	16	3	6	39	33	91	1	1	.320	.374
2012	Altoona (EL)	AA	.285	111	396	53	113	34	5	11	76	44	107	4	4	.352	.480
	Indianapolis (IL)	AAA	.400	2	5	0	2	0	0	0	2	1	1	0	1	.500	.400
Minor League Totals			.287	304	1055	166	303	79	11	33	180	152	274	18	13	.377	.477

24 JOSE OSUNA, 1B

BA GRADE
50
HIGH

Born: Dec. 12, 1992. **B-T:** R-R. **Ht.:** 6-2. **Wt.:** 213. **Signed:** Venezuela, 2009. **Signed by:** Rene Gayo/Rodolfo Petit.

Osuna was one of the top pitching prospects in Venezuela until he mysteriously started losing velocity on his fastball as a 15-year-old. Most clubs backed away, but the Pirates were intrigued by his power-hitting potential and signed him as a first baseman for $250,000 in 2009. The sturdily built Osuna's value is wrapped up entirely in his bat. He doesn't run well and is a poor defender, but he can hit the ball a long way. He has above-average power potential and a willingness to work counts to get pitches to drive. He's a streaky hitter who almost always looks to pull the ball. Osuna's lack of speed and arm strength limit him strictly to first base. How well he handles high Class A pitching as a 20-year-old will say a lot about his ultimate ceiling.

Year	Club (League)	Class	AVG	G	AB	R	H	2B	3B	HR	RBI	BB	SO	SB	CS	OBP	SLG
2010	Pirates (VSL)	R	.251	64	215	33	54	14	0	10	43	19	35	2	4	.325	.465
2011	Pirates (GCL)	R	.331	48	178	28	59	14	3	4	32	18	21	3	2	.400	.511
	State College (NYP)	SS	.250	2	8	2	2	1	0	0	1	1	0	0	0	.333	.375
2012	West Virginia (SAL)	LoA	.280	126	482	68	135	36	0	16	72	31	82	4	4	.324	.454
Minor League Totals			.283	240	883	131	250	67	3	30	148	69	138	9	10	.340	.468

25 BRANDON CUMPTON, RHP

BA GRADE
45
MEDIUM

Born: Nov. 16, 1988. **B-T:** R-R. **Ht.:** 6-2. **Wt.:** 198. **Drafted:** Georgia Tech, 2010 (9th round). **Signed by:** Greg Schilz.

Cumpton was 31-3 as a high school pitcher in Georgia, winning 4-A state titles in his junior and senior seasons, but was inconsistent during his time at Georgia Tech and has put up middling numbers as a pro. He has a 90-92 mph fastball that occasionally gets up to 94, along with a decent slider. He showed improved command of those pitches last season in Double-A, but his changeup remained inconsistent. Used almost solely as a starter in pro ball, Cumpton posted a 2.57 ERA in 11 relief appearances in the Arizona Fall League. He may be better suited for the bullpen because he's able to get his fastball up to 96 mph in short bursts and doesn't have to worry about throwing the changeup. He has no problem finding the strike zone, but he has yet to show he can miss bats in either role. Cumpton gave the Pirates food for thought with his AFL performance, and they'll decide in the spring whether he returns to the Altoona rotation or jumps to the Indianapolis bullpen.

Year	Club (League)	Class	W	L	ERA	G	GS	CG	SV	IP	H	HR	BB	SO	K/9	WHIP	AVG
2010	State College (NYP)	SS	0	1	2.53	4	3	0	0	11	8	0	5	6	5.1	1.22	.200
2011	West Virginia (SAL)	LoA	7	4	4.30	13	12	0	0	67	60	6	18	48	6.4	1.16	.240
	Bradenton (FSL)	HiA	3	3	3.66	13	12	0	0	66	73	6	12	42	5.7	1.28	.280
2012	Altoona (EL)	AA	12	11	3.84	27	27	0	0	152	149	9	46	88	5.2	1.28	.261
Minor League Totals			22	19	3.86	57	54	0	0	296	290	21	81	184	5.6	1.25	.258

26 DUKE WELKER, RHP

Born: Feb. 10, 1986. **B-T:** L-R. **Ht.:** 6-7. **Wt.:** 260. **Drafted:** Arkansas, 2007 (2nd round). **Signed by:** Mike Leuzinger.

BA GRADE
45
MEDIUM

Welker may be setting a record by returning to the Prospect Handbook following a five-year absence. He was No. 9 on this list following the 2007 season, when he made his pro debut as a second-round pick. He then dropped off the prospect radar because of a combination of poor performance and minor injuries. Becoming a full-time reliever in 2010 turned his career around, as his heavy fastball rose to a steady 94-96 mph and a peak of 98. His second pitch is an 83-85 mph slider that breaks a bit early but has nice bite. He has control problems at times but generally is hard to hit. If Welker can get more consistent with his slider and his strike-throwing ability, he could become a set-up man for the Pirates. He'll open this season in Triple-A and could finally get to the majors sometime after the all-star break.

Year	Club (League)	Class	W	L	ERA	G	GS	CG	SV	IP	H	HR	BB	SO	K/9	WHIP	AVG
2007	State College (NYP)	SS	2	2	2.35	7	7	0	0	31	29	2	10	27	7.9	1.27	.259
2008	Hickory (SAL)	LoA	4	13	5.51	24	24	0	0	116	142	7	48	72	5.6	1.64	.307
2009	West Virginia (SAL)	LoA	0	11	5.79	31	15	0	2	101	96	7	67	69	6.1	1.61	.253
2010	West Virginia (SAL)	LoA	1	1	3.63	20	0	0	5	22	16	0	24	25	10.1	1.79	.198
	Bradenton (FSL)	HiA	0	1	3.70	20	0	0	0	24	16	2	23	20	7.4	1.60	.182
2011	Bradenton (FSL)	HiA	3	5	2.25	36	0	0	6	52	33	2	25	41	7.1	1.12	.186
	Altoona (EL)	AA	1	0	5.40	8	0	0	0	10	11	0	1	9	8.1	1.20	.256
2012	Altoona (EL)	AA	2	1	2.31	15	0	0	5	23	19	0	7	19	7.3	1.11	.221
	Indianapolis (IL)	AAA	0	1	2.27	26	0	0	0	32	24	1	18	30	8.5	1.33	.214
Minor League Totals			13	35	4.29	187	46	0	18	411	386	21	223	312	6.8	1.48	.250

27 JIN-DE JHANG, C

Born: May 17, 1993. **B-T:** L-R. **Ht.:** 5-11. **Wt.:** 220. **Signed:** Taiwan, 2011. **Signed by:** Fu Chun Chiang.

BA GRADE
50
EXTREME

The Pirates haven't made too many forays into the Far East amateur free agent market but found an intriguing prospect in Jhang, whom they signed for $250,000 out of Taiwan in 2011. In his pro debut, he split catching duties with second-round pick Wyatt Mathisen in the Gulf Coast League, showing the ability to hit for average and command the strike zone. He recognizes pitches well and uses the whole field. Though he homered just once in 128 at-bats, he has the bat speed and strength to grow into average power. Jhang has a thick lower half and doesn't run well, but he's a good defensive catcher. He receives well and makes strong, accurate throws. He erased 29 percent of basestealers last year. He'll have to watch his weight so he doesn't lose any agility behind the plate. While Mathisen will head to low Class A in 2013, Jhang probably will start the year in extended spring training before going to Jamestown in June.

Year	Club (League)	Class	AVG	G	AB	R	H	2B	3B	HR	RBI	BB	SO	SB	CS	OBP	SLG
2012	Pirates (GCL)	R	.305	43	128	12	39	5	2	1	23	14	16	1	1	.382	.398
Minor League Totals			.305	43	128	12	39	5	2	1	23	14	16	1	1	.382	.398

28 HAROLD RAMIREZ, OF

Born: Sept. 6, 1994. **B-T:** R-R. **Ht.:** 5-11. **Wt.:** 170. **Signed:** Colombia, 2011. **Signed by:** Rene Gayo/Orlando Covo.

BA GRADE
50
EXTREME

The Pirates signed Ramirez for $1.05 million in 2011, the second-highest bonus they have given an international free agent behind Luis Heredia's $2.6 million in 2010. They aggressively brought him straight to the United States for his pro debut last summer in the Gulf Coast League at age 17. He hit .319 in his first month in pro ball before wearing down and slumping afterward. Ramirez's top-of-the-scale speed will make him a valuable tablesetter at the top of the lineup if he develops enough plate discipline to get on base consistently. Pittsburgh expects him to develop respectable power, but scouts from other organizations question whether he'll ever drive the ball. In either case, he needs to focus on making contact and keeping the ball on the ground to take advantage of his quickness. He has more than enough speed to cover ground in center field, but Ramirez's defense is a work in progress and he played left field in the GCL. He runs poor routes and his arm is somewhat scattershot. Ramirez will try to refine his overall game in extended spring training before playing at short-season Jamestown in 2013.

Year	Club (League)	Class	AVG	G	AB	R	H	2B	3B	HR	RBI	BB	SO	SB	CS	OBP	SLG
2012	Pirates (GCL)	R	.259	39	135	18	35	5	1	1	12	6	20	9	5	.310	.333
Minor League Totals			.259	39	135	18	35	5	1	1	12	6	20	9	5	.310	.333

29 CLINT ROBINSON, 1B

BA GRADE

40

LOW

Born: Feb. 16, 1985. **B-T:** L-L. **Ht.:** 6-5. **Wt.:** 225. **Drafted:** Troy, 2007 (25th round). **Signed by:** Max Semler (Royals).

Robinson has blown away expectations for a college senior sign who got a $1,000 bonus as a 25th-round pick. He has hit .308/.382/.520 in six minor league seasons, won the triple crown in the Double-A Texas League in 2010 and got his first four big league at-bats last summer with Kansas City. He was the first Troy product to make it to the majors since Mike Rivera in 2001. The Royals didn't need Robinson with Eric Hosmer at first base and Billy Butler at DH, so they traded him and Vin Mazzaro to the Pirates for young Dominican pitchers Luis Rico and Luis Santos in November. Robinson projects as a solid hitter with average power. He doesn't strike out much and gets on base, but his value is limited because he's a 20 runner on the 20-80 scouting scale and is a below-average defender at first base. Though he throws well enough to play left field, he doesn't have enough range to pull it off. Pittsburgh has Garrett Jones and Gaby Sanchez as its primary first-base option for 2013 but will give Robinson a chance to make the team in a reserve role.

Year	Club (League)	Class	AVG	G	AB	R	H	2B	3B	HR	RBI	BB	SO	SB	CS	OBP	SLG
2007	Idaho Falls (PIO)	R	.336	67	253	39	85	18	1	15	66	19	42	2	0	.388	.593
2008	Burlington (MWL)	LoA	.226	106	379	53	100	22	3	17	64	37	67	0	3	.333	.472
2009	Wilmington (CAR)	HiA	.298	124	436	65	130	31	1	13	57	35	79	4	3	.356	.463
2010	NW Arkansas (TL)	AA	.335	129	477	90	160	41	5	29	98	58	86	4	3	.410	.625
2011	Omaha (PCL)	AAA	.326	134	503	86	164	35	0	23	100	58	88	2	1	.399	.533
2012	Kansas City (AL)	MAJ	.000	4	4	0	0	0	0	0	0	0	2	0	0	.000	.000
	Omaha (PCL)	AAA	.292	131	487	70	142	37	1	13	67	79	65	1	0	.393	.452
Major League Totals			.000	4	4	0	0	0	0	0	0	0	2	0	0	.000	.000
Minor League Totals			.308	691	2535	403	781	184	11	110	452	286	427	13	10	.382	.520

30 GIFT NGOEPE, SS

BA GRADE

45

HIGH

Born: Jan. 18, 1990. **B-T:** B-R. **Ht.:** 5-10. **Wt.:** 165. **Signed:** South Africa, 2008. **Signed by:** Tom Randolph.

Ngoepe is proving to be more than a great story. The Pirates signed him for $15,000 in 2008 after seeing him play at Major League Baseball's academy in Italy, and his tale of becoming the first black South African ever signed by a big league organization was prominently featured in Sports Illustrated in 2009. Ngoepe has made huge strides in going from a raw athlete to an above-average defender with outstanding range and a strong arm. Managers rated him as the Florida State League's top defensive shortstop last year. His speed is a tick above-average and he has improved his instincts on the bases, though he still has more work to do in that regard. Ngoepe's bat is still a major question mark. He hit just .232 in high Class A in 2012, and he must make more contact from both sides of the plate and learn to use the whole field. After hitting just four homers in his first three pro seasons, he went deep nine times last year, and he has enough strength in his wrists to develop decent power for a middle infielder. Ngoepe has the defensive ability to play shortstop in the major leagues, but his bat will dictate whether he gets there. Double-A will provide a stern test for him in 2013.

Year	Club (League)	Class	AVG	G	AB	R	H	2B	3B	HR	RBI	BB	SO	SB	CS	OBP	SLG
2009	Pirates (GCL)	R	.238	47	160	24	38	4	0	1	9	21	52	13	9	.341	.281
2010	Bradenton (FSL)	HiA	.250	2	4	0	1	0	0	0	0	1	2	0	0	.400	.250
	State College (NYP)	SS	.205	64	229	30	47	13	5	1	20	36	68	11	7	.315	.319
2011	West Virginia (SAL)	LoA	.306	25	85	14	26	5	1	2	5	7	14	3	3	.359	.459
	Pirates (GCL)	R	.167	2	6	0	1	0	0	0	0	0	1	0	0	.286	.167
2012	Bradenton (FSL)	HiA	.232	124	456	66	106	11	5	9	36	63	131	22	14	.330	.338
Minor League Totals			.233	264	940	134	219	33	11	13	70	128	268	49	33	.331	.333

St. Louis Cardinals

BY DERRICK GOOLD

Trevor Rosenthal displayed an overpowering fastball during the Cardinals' postseason run

When the Cardinals took the field for Game Five of the National League Championship Series with hopes of a second consecutive trip to the World Series, starting pitcher Lance Lynn was one of six players on the lineup card who was drafted and developed by the organization. Eleven of the 15 players who appeared in the game were homegrown, and third baseman David Freese has spent most of his career with St. Louis after arriving as a minor leaguer via trade.

This wasn't a fluke. This is the future.

"For us to have sustained success we have to be able to produce players internally," general manager John Mozeliak said. "We knew without that it was going to be hard to be successful because the free-agent market was not a place we wanted to be using resources."

The Cardinals lost Game Five and squandered a 3-1 lead in the best-of-seven series against the Giants to fall one win shy of defending their NL pennant. But while 2012 ended in disappointment, it also marked a positive move in the first year after the departures of Albert Pujols and Tony La Russa.

Though Lynn won 18 games and was picked as an all-star in his first season as a starter, he'll be welcomed to spring training by three challengers for his spot in the rotation: Joe Kelly, Trevor Rosenthal and Shelby Miller, not one of whom will be older than 24. Also poised to join the major league mix at some point in 2013 is outfielder Oscar Taveras, arguably the game's top hitting prospect, and second baseman Kolten Wong, a first-round pick in 2011.

The emergence of Kelly, Rosenthal and Miller affirmed the organization's optimism about its pitching depth. Taveras and Wong both played for a Double-A Springfield squad that won the Texas League championship and Baseball America's Minor League Team of the Year award. They were kept together to benefit from the postseason run, and it was the third league title in three yeas for Taveras, the TL MVP.

Mike Matheny, who hadn't managed at any professional level before replacing La Russa for 2012, was every bit the steward of young talent and established players the front office had imagined. Nine Cardinals made their major league debuts in 2012. Matheny's staff also becomes an extension of development, as John Mabry was promoted from assistant hitting coach to hitting coach when Mark McGwire departed

to be the Dodgers' hitting coach and Blaise Ilsley moved from Triple-A pitching coach to big league bullpen coach.

St. Louis took advantage of an opportunity to fortify its talent base with six of the first 86 picks in the 2012 draft. The Cardinals selected right-hander Michael Wacha at No. 18, then followed with five position players: outfielder James Ramsey; third basemen Stephen Piscotty, Patrick Wisdom and Carson Kelly; and catcher Steve Bean. Wacha raced to Double-A in his first pro summer and may not need much more than another full season in the minors before making his major league debut.

Upon their entry into pro ball, each of those players received a handbook called "The Cardinal Way." It details rules, cutoff plays and the general ethos of the organization, one reflected by the team's seventh appearance in the NLCS in 13 seasons.

"It was instilled in us at the beginning," homegrown outfielder Jon Jay says, "that it is about winning."

After making two trades involving 10 players in July 2011, the Cardinals weren't as active on the trade market in 2012, dealing 2010 first-rounder Zack Cox to the Marlins for bullpen righty Edward Mujica at the trading deadline.

THIS YEAR'S TOP 30

Player, Pos.		Grade
1.	Oscar Tavares, of	70/Low
2.	Shelby Miller, rhp	70/Medium
3.	Carlos Martinez, rhp	65/High
4.	Trevor Rosenthal, rhp	55/Low
5.	Kolten Wong, 2b	55/Medium
6.	Michael Wacha, rhp	55/Medium
7.	Matt Adams, 1b	50/Low
8.	Tyrell Jenkins, rhp	55/Extreme
9.	Carson Kelly, 3b	55/Extreme
10.	Stephen Piscotty, of/3b	50/High
11.	Patrick Wisdom, 3b	50/High
12.	James Ramsey, of	50/High
13.	Pete Kozma, ss/2b	45/Medium
14.	Kevin Siegrist, lhp	50/High
15.	Ryan Jackson, ss/2b	45/Medium
16.	Victor DeLeon, rhp	50/High
17.	C.J. McElroy, of	50/High
18.	Jordan Swagerty, rhp	50/High
19.	Charlie Tilson, of	50/High
20.	Steve Bean, c	50/High
21.	Eric Fornataro, rhp	45/Medium
22.	Sam Freeman, lhp	45/Medium
23.	Seth Maness, rhp	45/Medium
24.	Jorge Rondon, rhp	45/Medium
25.	Tim Cooney, lhp	50/High
26.	John Gast, lhp	45/Medium
27.	Maikel Cleto, rhp	45/Medium
28.	Mike O'Neill, of	40/Low
29.	Keith Butler, rhp	45/Medium
30.	Seth Blair, rhp	50/Extreme

LAST YEAR'S TOP 30

Player, Pos.		Status
1.	Shelby Miller, rhp	No. 2
2.	Carlos Martinez, rhp	No. 3
3.	Oscar Taveras, of	No. 1
4.	Zack Cox, 3b	(Marlins)
5.	Kolten Wong, 2b	No. 5
6.	Tyrell Jenkins, rhp	No. 8
7.	Lance Lynn, rhp	Majors
8.	Eduardo Sanchez, rhp	Majors
9.	Matt Adams, 1b	No. 7
10.	Jordan Swagerty, rhp	No.18
11.	Trevor Rosenthal, rhp	No. 4
12.	Matt Carpenter, 3b	Majors
13.	Ryan Jackson, ss	No. 15
14.	Maikel Cleto, rhp	No. 27
15.	Charlie Tilson, of	No. 19
16.	Joe Kelly, rhp	Majors
17.	John Gast, lhp	No. 26
18.	C.J. McElroy, of	No. 17
19.	Adron Chambers, of	Dropped out
20.	Tony Cruz, c	Majors
21.	Adam Reifer, rhp	Dropped out
22.	Brandon Dickson, rhp	(Orix/Japan)
23.	David Kopp, rhp	(Tigers)
24.	Cody Stanley, c	Dropped out
25.	Victor DeLeon, rhp	No. 16
26.	Adam Ottavino, rhp	(Rockies)
27.	Boone Whiting, rhp	Dropped out
28.	Seth Blair, rhp	No. 30
29.	Lance Jeffries, of	Dropped out
30.	Sam Freeman, lhp	No. 22

BEST TOOLS

Best Hitter for Average	Oscar Taveras
Best Power Hitter	Matt Adams
Best Strike-Zone Discipline	Mike O'Neill
Fastest Baserunner	C.J. McElroy
Best Athlete	Tyrell Jenkins
Best Fastball	Trevor Rosenthal
Best Curveball	Carlos Martinez
Best Slider	Jorge Rondon
Best Changeup	Michael Wacha
Best Control	Seth Maness
Best Defensive Catcher	Steve Bean
Best Defensive Infielder	Pete Kozma
Best Infield Arm	Patrick Wisdom
Best Defensive Outfielder	Charlie Tilson
Best Outfield Arm	Stephen Piscotty

PROJECTED 2016 LINEUP

Catcher	Yadier Molina
First Base	Allen Craig
Second Base	Kolten Wong
Third Base	David Freese
Shortstop	Pete Kozma
Left Field	Matt Holliday
Center Field	Jon Jay
Right Field	Oscar Taveras
No. 1 Starter	Adam Wainwright
No. 2 Starter	Shelby Miller
No. 3 Starter	Jaime Garcia
No. 4 Starter	Lance Lynn
No. 5 Starter	Carlos Martinez
Closer	Jason Motte

TOP PROSPECTS OF THE DECADE

Year	Player, Pos.	2012 Org.
2003	Dan Haren, rhp	Angels
2004	Blake Hawksworth, rhp	Dodgers
2005	Anthony Reyes, rhp	Padres
2006	Anthony Reyes, rhp	Padres
2007	Colby Rasmus, of	Blue Jays
2008	Colby Rasmus, of	Blue Jays
2009	Colby Rasmus, of	Blue Jays
2010	Shelby Miller, rhp	Cardinals
2011	Shelby Miller, rhp	Cardinals
2012	Shelby Miller, rhp	Cardinals

TOP DRAFT PICKS OF THE DECADE

Year	Player, Pos.	2012 Org.
2003	Daric Barton, 1b	Athletics
2004	Chris Lambert, rhp	Out of baseball
2005	Colby Rasmus, of	Blue Jays
2006	Adam Ottavino, rhp	Rockies
2007	Pete Kozma, ss	Cardinals
2008	Brett Wallace, 1b	Astros
2009	Shelby Miller, rhp	Cardinals
2010	Zack Cox, 3b	Marlins
2011	Kolten Wong, 2b	Cardinals
2012	Michael Wacha, rhp	Cardinals

LARGEST BONUSES IN CLUB HISTORY

J.D. Drew, 1998	$3,000,000
Shelby Miller, 2009	$2,875,000
Rick Ankiel, 1999	$2,500,000
Chad Hutchinson, 1998	$2,300,000
Zack Cox, 2010	$2,000,000

MINOR LEAGUE DEPTH CHART

ST. LOUIS CARDINALS

TOP 2013 ROOKIE: Trevor Rosenthal, rhp. He routinely hit 99 mph as a reliever in the playoffs for the Cardinals, and has the stuff to start if given the opportunity.

BREAKOUT PROSPECT: Jordan Swagerty, rhp. Derailed by Tommy John surgery in 2012, he has the fastball-curveball combination to surge through the minors once he regains his health.

SOURCE OF TOP 30 TALENT			
Homegrown	29	Acquired	1
College	14	Trades	1
Junior college	4	Rule 5 draft	0
High school	7	Independent leagues	0
Nondrafted free agents	0	Free agents/waivers	0
International	4		

SLEEPER: Colin Walsh, of/2b. The switch-hitting Stanford alum finished among the system's leaders in on-base percentage (.413) and slugging (.521) while showing promise at second base.

LF
Mike O'Neill (28)
Anthony Garcia
Adam Melker
Virgil Hill
Nick Martini

CF
James Ramsey (12)
C. J. McElroy (17)
Charlie Tilson (19)
Lance Jeffries
Adron Chambers
Tommy Pham
Yeonny Gonzalez

RF
Oscar Taveras (1)
Stephen Piscotty (10)
Chris Swauger
Nick Longmire
Michael Swinson

3B
Carson Kelly (9)
Patrick Wisdom (11)
Tyler Rahmatulla
Jermaine Curtis
Matt Cerda

SS
Pete Kozma (13)
Ryan Jackson (15)
Greg Garcia
Alex Mejia
Matt Williams
Kenny Peoples
Ronny Gil

2B
Kolten Wong (5)
Colin Walsh
Breyvic Valera
Starlin Rodriguez
Bruce Caldwell
Jacob Wilson

1B
Matt Adams (7)
Xavier Scruggs
Jonathan Rodriguez
Roberto de la Cruz

C
Steve Bean (20)
Cody Stanley
Adam Ehrlich
Audry Perez
Nick Derba
Rowan Wick

LHP

LHSP	LHRP
Kevin Siegrist (14)	Sam Freeman (22)
Tim Cooney (25)	Barret Browning
John Gast (26)	Nick Greenwood
Tyler Lyons	Justin Wright
Kyle Hald	Danny Miranda
Max Foody	Lee Stoppelman
Nick Additon	Jay Voss
Anthony Ferrara	
Hector Hernandez	

RHP

RHSP	RHRP
Shelby Miller (2)	Jordan Swagerty (18)
Carlos Martinez (3)	Eric Fornataro (21)
Trevor Rosenthal (4)	Jorge Rondon (24)
Michael Wacha (6)	Maikel Cleto (27)
Tyrell Jenkins (8)	Keith Butler (29)
Victor DeLeon (16)	Sam Tuivailala
Seth Maness (23)	Kyle Barraclough
Seth Blair (30)	Adam Reifer
Boone Whiting	Michael Blazek
Scott Gorgen	Dixon Llorens
Kurt Heyer	Richard Castillo
Cory Jones	Ronnie Shaban

2012

BEST PURE HITTER: OF/3B Stephen Piscotty's (1s) pitch recognition and approach are ahead of the curve, his swing is efficient and he has the strength to drive the ball from gap to gap.

BEST POWER HITTER: 3B Carson Kelly's (2) power gives him the highest ceiling in this draft class and earned him a $1.6 million bonus. Just 17 when he signed, he hit nine homers in the Rookie-level Appalachian League, more than any other 2012 prep draftee.

FASTEST RUNNER: OF Yoenny Gonzalez (8) ran a 6.3-second 60-yard dash in a predraft workout, but he's raw and his speed doesn't play at that level. OF James Ramsey (1) turns in plus-plus times down the line, with sub-4.0-second times from the left side.

BEST DEFENSIVE PLAYER: Ramsey, 3B Patrick Wisdom (1s) and SS Alex Mejia (4) are all polished college defenders. A torn left ACL cut Mejia's debut short. C Steve Bean (1s) has a cannon arm and projects as an above-average defender.

BEST FASTBALL: RHP Michael Wacha (1) mowed his way to Double-A pitching off his fastball, touching 97 mph and sitting at 94-95 in short stints. He pitched at 90-93 as a starter in the spring. RHP Kyle Barraclough (7) reached 97 mph this summer as a reliever and will remain in that role. RHP Cory Jones (5) sits in the mid-90s when he's at his best.

BEST SECONDARY PITCH: Wacha had the best changeup in the entire draft. RHP Dixon Llorens (25) owns a wipeout slider.

BEST PRO DEBUT: Wacha gave up just two runs in 24 innings (counting the Texas League playoffs) and rolled up a 45-4 K-BB ratio. Llorens went 2-1, 2.25 with 62 strikeouts in 36 innings while reaching low Class A. LHP Lee Stoppelman (24) had a 0.79 ERA and 49 strikeouts in 34 innings at short-season Batavia.

BEST ATHLETE: Ramsey has present strength, speed and all-around skills.

MOST INTRIGUING BACKGROUND: Ramsey was president of Florida State's student-athlete advisory council, won an award for his community service and charity work, and was a Rhodes Scholar nominee. LHP Max Foody (12) lost the tip of his left middle finger in a childhood accident. Unsigned OF Tate Matheny's (23) father Mike manages the Cardinals and won four Gold Gloves as a catcher. Unsigned 3B Trey Williams' (11) dad Eddie and unsigned OF Derrick May Jr.'s (37) father were top-10 overall picks who played in the majors.

CLOSEST TO THE MAJORS: Wacha.

BEST LATE-ROUND PICK: Stoppelman throws three pitches for strikes, including a 90-92 mph fastball.

THE ONE WHO GOT AWAY: The Cardinals drafted Williams as insurance in case one of their top picks didn't sign. He wound up at JC of the Canyons (Calif.).

ASSESSMENT: Saving money on several of their early picks allowed the Cardinals to find enough cash to sign Kelly. They landed plenty of premium defenders and potential impact bats, and several had strong debuts.

2011

2B Kolten Wong (1) may be starting in St. Louis at some point this season. Speedy OFs Charlie Tilson (2) and C.J. McElroy (3) are two of the best athletes in the system.

GRADE: B

2010

The Cardinals used 3B Zack Cox (1) in a mid-2012 trade for Edward Mujica but he hasn't lived up to his advance billing so far. Neither have RHPs Seth Blair (1s) and Tyrell Jenkins (1s), while RHP Jordan Swaggerty had Tommy John surgery.

GRADE: C

2009

RHPs Shelby Miller (1), Joe Kelly (3) and Trevor Rosenthal (21) all starred in St. Louis' bullpen during the playoffs, and Miller and Rosenthal could be frontline starters in the future. 1B Matt Adams (23) reached the majors in 2012 and has enough bat to be a regular. SS/2B Ryan Jackson (5) and 1B/3B/OF Matt Carpenter (13) are two more big leaguers.

GRADE: A

2008

RHP Lance Lynn (1s) got picked for the 2012 All-Star Game in his first full season in the majors. 1B Brett Wallace (1) hasn't provided much offensive impact, but the Cardinals included him and OF Shane Peterson (2) in a trade for Matt Holliday. They also got Rafael Furcal in a deal for OF/2B/3B Alex Castellanos (10), who made his big league debut last year, as did LHP Sam Freeman (32).

GRADE: B

Draft analysis by John Manuel (2012) and Jim Callis (2008-11). Numbers in parentheses indicate draft rounds.

1 OSCAR TAVERAS, OF

Born: June 19, 1992. **B-T:** L-L. **Ht.:** 6-2. **Wt.:** 185.
Signed: Dominican Republic, 2008. **Signed by:** Juan Mercado.

BA GRADE
70
LOW

JOHN WILLIAMSON

When Taveras arrived at spring training last year, he was brought into meetings with club officials, including big league manager Mike Matheny. They presented him a challenge. His bat was fit for Double-A Springfield, but to skip high Class A Palm Beach he'd have to show his fielding and baserunning were ready, too. He did that, leapfrogged a level and continued a meteoric ascent. Taveras earned Texas League MVP honors one year after winning the low Class A Midwest League batting title with a .386 average. He led the TL in batting (.321), doubles (37), extra-base hits (67) and total bases (270) while leading his team to a league title for a third consecutive year. General manager John Mozeliak calls him the organization's top hitting prospect since Albert Pujols. Signed for $145,000 out of the Dominican Republic in 2008, Taveras has batted .321/.381/.525 in four pro seasons.

Taveras has an innate ability to barrel pitches. Credit superb hand-eye coordination and the natural balance of his swing for the preternatural ease he brings to the plate. He's an aggressive hitter with a quick bat and the confidence he can drive any pitch he can reach within the strike zone—because he so often does. But he's not undisciplined, doesn't strike out often and has proven to be an effective bad-ball hitter. Taveras saw a spike in walks as his projected power blossomed in Double-A. He set career highs with 23 homers and 37 doubles, harbingers of more power ahead. The elements of Taveras' game that once lagged behind his offense started to keep pace in 2012. He improved enough in the field for St. Louis to consider him a center fielder going forward. He finished the Futures Game in center, earning praise from his manager, former Gold Glove winner Bernie Williams. Taveras has enough speed to be an average baserunner and provide average range in center. He probably fits best in right field, where his bat and strong arm profile well. His effort and atten-

SCOUTING GRADES

Batting: 75.   **Defense:** 55.
Power: 60.   **Arm:** 55.
Speed: 50.

Based on 20-80 scouting scale, where 50 represents major league average, and future projection rather than present tools.

tion waned at times in low Class A, and he has been benched a couple times for lapses. The Cardinals tied such moments to frustrations he had at the plate rather than apathy or a lackadaisical attitude, and he has acknowledged his need to eliminate them completely.

St. Louis discussed bringing Taveras to the majors last September but opted not to push him without guaranteed playing time. He'll come to major league spring training with a chance to make an impression. He's positioned to replace Carlos Beltran in right field when the veteran's contract expires after 2013, but proving proficient in center could open a swifter route to the majors. The Cardinals want him to play regularly at the start of the year, and that could mean some seasoning in Triple-A Memphis.

Year	Club (League)	Class	AVG	G	AB	R	H	2B	3B	HR	RBI	BB	SO	SB	CS	OBP	SLG
2009	Cardinals (DSL)	R	.257	65	237	35	61	13	8	1	42	28	36	9	4	.338	.392
2010	Cardinals (GCL)	R	.167	7	30	1	5	1	0	0	2	1	5	1	0	.194	.200
	Johnson City (APP)	R	.322	53	211	39	68	13	3	8	43	12	41	8	5	.362	.526
2011	Quad Cities (MWL)	LoA	.386	78	308	52	119	27	5	8	62	32	52	1	4	.444	.584
2012	Springfield (TL)	AA	.321	124	477	83	153	37	7	23	94	42	56	10	1	.380	.572
Minor League Totals			.321	327	1263	210	406	91	23	40	243	115	190	29	14	.381	.525

2 SHELBY MILLER, RHP

Born: Oct. 10, 1990. **B-T:** R-R. **Ht.:** 6-3. **Wt.:** 195. **Drafted:** HS—Brownwood, Texas, 2009 (1st round). **Signed by:** Ralph Garr Jr.

The 19th overall pick in 2009, Miller signed for $2,875,000. He struggled for the first time as a pro last year, going 4-8, 6.17 in his first 17 Triple-A starts before resetting his mechanics and getting told he couldn't shake off his catcher. He went 7-2, 2.88 with a 70-7 K-BB ratio in 57 second-half innings and rode that success into a September callup and postseason role. Miller has an overpowering fastball that averaged 94 mph in the playoffs and can touch 97. It has late, heavy movement. He learned in 2012 that his heater is more effective when he utilizes his plus curveball and developing changeup. His control and command improved late in the year as well. St. Louis was concerned that he adopted a diet and workout plan that cost him muscle, so the team helped him choose a different approach to add strength and stamina. A potential No. 1 starter, Miller will come to spring training with a chance to win a spot in the rotation.

BA GRADE

70

MEDIUM

Year	Club (League)	Class	W	L	ERA	G	GS	CG	SV	IP	H	HR	BB	SO	K/9	WHIP	AVG
2009	Quad Cities (MWL)	LoA	0	0	6.00	2	2	0	0	3	5	0	2	2	6.0	2.33	.357
2010	Quad Cities (MWL)	LoA	7	5	3.62	24	24	0	0	104	97	7	33	140	12.1	1.25	.243
2011	Palm Beach (FSL)	HiA	2	3	2.89	9	9	0	0	53	40	2	20	81	13.8	1.13	.204
	Springfield (TL)	AA	9	3	2.70	16	16	0	0	87	72	2	33	89	9.2	1.21	.229
2012	Memphis (PCL)	AAA	11	10	4.74	27	27	0	0	137	138	24	50	160	10.5	1.38	.260
	St. Louis (NL)	MAJ	1	0	1.32	6	1	0	0	14	9	0	4	16	10.5	0.95	.184
Major League Totals			1	0	1.32	6	1	0	0	14	9	0	4	16	10.5	0.95	.184
Minor League Totals			29	21	3.73	78	78	0	0	384	352	35	138	472	11.1	1.28	.242

3 CARLOS MARTINEZ, RHP

Born: Sept. 21, 1991. **B-T:** R-R. **Ht.:** 6-0. **Wt.:** 165. **Signed:** Dominican Republic, 2010. **Signed by:** Juan Mercado.

Then known as Carlos Matias, Martinez was suspended for a year by MLB when he couldn't present the paperwork needed to finalize a $160,000 deal with the Red Sox in 2009. The Cardinals spent weeks piecing together the proof needed to sign him for $1.5 million in 2010, with most of the legwork done by scout Aaron Rodriguez. Martinez has blistered opponents ever since, shaking off shoulder tendinitis early last year to reach Double-A at age 20 and throw seven shutout innings in the Texas League championship series. He is an aggressive pitcher with a fastball that regularly hums at 94-98 mph and hit 100 in his first Springfield appearance. He has a biting curveball and a changeup that's more effective when he doesn't throw it too hard. Both could develop into plus pitches. Martinez has a natural delivery but sometimes strays from it and his command wobbles. Some scouts see him as too small to handle starting, but he has wiry strength and his efficient mechanics will help. Martinez is set to return to Double-A in 2013 with a chance to advance to Triple-A.

BA GRADE

65

HIGH

Year	Club (League)	Class	W	L	ERA	G	GS	CG	SV	IP	H	HR	BB	SO	K/9	WHIP	AVG
2010	Cardinals (DSL)	R	3	2	0.76	12	12	1	0	59	28	1	14	78	11.9	0.71	.144
2011	Quad Cities (MWL)	LoA	3	2	2.33	8	8	0	0	39	27	1	14	50	11.6	1.06	.196
	Palm Beach (FSL)	HiA	3	3	5.28	10	10	0	0	46	49	2	30	48	9.4	1.72	.269
2012	Palm Beach (FSL)	HiA	2	2	3.00	7	7	0	0	33	29	0	10	34	9.3	1.18	.236
	Springfield (TL)	AA	4	3	2.90	15	14	0	0	71	62	6	22	58	7.3	1.18	.237
Minor League Totals			15	12	2.76	52	51	1	0	248	195	10	90	268	9.7	1.15	.217

4 TREVOR ROSENTHAL, RHP

Born: May 29, 1990. **B-T:** R-R. **Ht.:** 6-2. **Wt.:** 190. **Drafted:** Cowley County (Kan.) CC, 2009 (21st round). **Signed by:** Aaron Looper.

Area scout Aaron Looper advocated selecting Rosenthal in the 21st round of the 2009 draft after seeing him throw all of one inning, believing the athletic righthander personified the gut-feeling picks the Cardinals encourage their evaluators to make. A shortstop at the start of his Cowley County (Kan.) CC career, he signed for $65,000 and emerged as a prospect when he struck out 11 in his first full-season start in 2011. He skipped a level last year, advanced from Double-A to the majors and became St. Louis' shutdown middle reliever in the playoffs. Rosenthal was a revelation in the postseason, with half of his fastballs in October clocked at 99 mph or faster. He works in the mid-90s as a starter and consistently hits 98 and tops out at 101 as a reliever. He spots his fastball low in the strike zone. Rosenthal also has a hard curveball and a solid changeup, pitches the Cardinals

BA GRADE

55

LOW

believe will allow him to be a big league starter. The key for him will be able to maintain the improved command he showed late in the year. Like Shelby Miller, Rosenthal will come to spring training with the opportunity to take a spot in the rotation. If he doesn't win one, he'll slide easily into a late-inning relief role.

Year	Club (League)	Class	W	L	ERA	G	GS	CG	SV	IP	H	HR	BB	SO	K/9	WHIP	AVG
2009	Cardinals (GCL)	R	4	1	4.88	14	0	0	0	24	25	0	10	26	9.8	1.46	.269
2010	Johnson City (APP)	R	3	0	2.25	10	6	0	1	32	23	1	7	30	8.4	0.94	.200
2011	Quad Cities (MWL)	LoA	7	7	4.11	22	22	1	0	120	111	7	39	133	9.9	1.25	.247
2012	Springfield (TL)	AA	8	6	2.78	17	17	0	0	94	67	6	37	83	7.9	1.11	.202
	Memphis (PCL)	AAA	0	0	4.20	3	3	0	0	15	11	1	5	21	12.6	1.07	.208
	St. Louis (NL)	MAJ	0	2	2.78	19	0	0	0	23	14	2	7	25	9.9	0.93	.175
Major League Totals			0	2	2.78	19	0	0	0	23	14	2	7	25	9.9	0.93	.175
Minor League Totals			22	14	3.53	66	48	1	1	285	237	15	98	293	9.2	1.17	.227

5 KOLTEN WONG, 2B

Born: Oct. 10, 2010. **B-T:** L-R. **Ht.:** 5-9. **Wt.:** 190. **Drafted:** Hawaii, 2011 (1st round). **Signed by:** Matt Swanson.

The Cardinals hadn't drafted a second baseman in the first round in 25 years (Luis Alicea) before taking Wong 22nd overall in 2011. Since singing for $1.3 million, Wong has hit .300, reached Double-A, played in the Futures Game and won two league championships. He slumped late in the season due to fatigue, but went to the Arizona Fall League and batted .324. Wong springs from a compact stance to deliver consistent sharp contact. He has surprising power for his size, mostly to the gaps but also the potential for double-digit home run totals. He's so proficient at bunting that Texas League opponents had to reposition their defenses against him. Wong doesn't walk a lot, but he has a keen sense of the strike zone and enjoys a slash-and-attack approach as a leadoff hitter. His arm is fit for second base and his instincts have improved, making him a solid fielder. He has average speed and good baserunning sense. Wong will bring some stability to the position in the near future, and he'll get a chance to audition for the starting job this spring. He figures to open the season in Triple-A and arrive in St. Louis during the summer.

BA GRADE
55
MEDIUM

Year	Club (League)	Class	AVG	G	AB	R	H	2B	3B	HR	RBI	BB	SO	SB	CS	OBP	SLG
2011	Quad Cities (MWL)	LoA	.335	47	194	39	65	15	2	5	25	21	24	9	5	.401	.510
2012	Springfield (TL)	AA	.287	126	523	79	150	23	6	9	52	44	74	21	11	.348	.405
Minor League Totals			.300	173	717	118	215	38	8	14	77	65	98	30	16	.363	.434

6 MICHAEL WACHA, RHP

Born: July 1, 1991. **B-T:** R-R. **Ht.:** 6-6. **Wt.:** 195. **Drafted:** Texas A&M, 2012 (1st round). **Signed by:** Ralph Garr Jr.

Wacha and Shelby Miller were the jewels of Texas A&M's 2009 recruiting class. While Miller signed out of high school, Wacha went 27-7 in three years with the Aggies before turning pro for $1.9 million as the 19th overall pick in the 2012 draft. The Cardinals eased him into pro ball as a reliever, and he responded by striking out 45 in 24 innings (including the Texas League playoffs). Wacha pitches with a 90-93 mph sinking fastball as a starter, though he worked from 94-97 while coming out of the bullpen in his pro debut. What makes his fastball devastating is his changeup, the best available in the 2012 draft. He uses a circle grip and throws it with deception and a late fade. Wacha would have gone toward the top of the draft if he had a better breaking pitch. His slider shows more promise than his curveball, though neither figures to become better than average. His command and competitiveness are two more pluses in his favor. After reaching Double-A in his pro debut, Wacha will return to Springfield in 2013, this time as a starter. It's easy to project him as a mid-rotation starter, and he could turn into something more if he finds a reliable breaking ball.

BA GRADE
55
MEDIUM

Year	Club (League)	Class	W	L	ERA	G	GS	CG	SV	IP	H	HR	BB	SO	K/9	WHIP	AVG
2012	Cardinals (GCL)	R	0	0	1.80	3	2	0	0	5	4	1	0	7	12.6	0.80	.222
	Palm Beach (FSL)	HiA	0	0	0.00	4	0	0	0	8	1	0	1	16	18.0	0.25	.040
	Springfield (TL)	AA	0	0	1.13	4	0	0	0	8	3	0	3	17	19.1	0.75	.111
Minor League Totals			0	0	0.86	11	2	0	0	21	8	1	4	40	17.1	0.57	.114

7 MATT ADAMS, 1B

Born: Aug. 31, 1988. **B-T:** L-R. **Ht.:** 6-3. **Wt.:** 230. **Drafted:** Slippery Rock (Pa.), 2009 (23rd round). **Signed by:** Brian Hopkins.

Like Trevor Rosenthal, Adams has become an emblem of the Cardinals' ongoing success in later rounds of the draft. He signed for $25,000 as a 23rd-round pick in 2009 after leading NCAA Division II in hitting (.495). He has continued to rake, hitting 74 homers in the last three years, including two for St. Louis last summer. Adams has a muscular, stout frame, but his light-tower power doesn't come from his physique alone. He has a compact, spring-loaded swing that means he doesn't need a loop or uppercut to generate distance. A coach called his stroke foolproof, one that should allow him to hit for power and average. He's an adequate defender at first base, but his well below-average speed makes playing left field a stretch. Adams missed the final month of the season to have bone chips removed from his right elbow, a condition that had bothered him for more than a year. He should be healthy for spring training. Though he has nothing left to prove in the minors, he's blocked by Allen Craig and has no apparent path to a starting job with the Cardinals.

BA GRADE
50
LOW

Year	Club (League)	Class	AVG	G	AB	R	H	2B	3B	HR	RBI	BB	SO	SB	CS	OBP	SLG
2009	Johnson City (APP)	R	.365	32	115	15	42	6	0	6	25	9	20	0	0	.406	.574
	Batavia (NYP)	SS	.346	31	130	16	45	11	0	4	27	11	21	0	0	.394	.523
2010	Quad Cities (MWL)	LoA	.310	121	464	71	144	41	0	22	88	33	78	5	1	.355	.541
2011	Springfield (TL)	AA	.300	115	463	80	139	23	2	32	101	40	90	0	1	.357	.566
2012	St. Louis (NL)	MAJ	.244	27	86	8	21	6	0	2	13	5	24	0	0	.286	.384
	Memphis (PCL)	AAA	.329	67	258	41	85	22	0	18	50	15	57	3	1	.362	.624
Major League Totals			.244	27	86	8	21	6	0	2	13	5	24	0	0	.286	.384
Minor League Totals			.318	366	1430	223	455	103	2	82	291	108	266	8	3	.365	.565

8 TYRELL JENKINS, RHP

Born: July 20, 1992. **B-T:** R-R. **Ht.:** 6-4. **Wt.:** 192. **Drafted:** HS—Henderson, Texas, 2010 (1st round supplemental). **Signed by:** Ralph Garr Jr.

The Cardinals wooed Jenkins from a football commitment to Baylor by paying him $1.3 million in 2010. They knew his development would require patience and didn't give him a full-season assignment until 2012. He missed a month with shoulder soreness and two weeks with a strained lat muscle at low Class A Quad Cities, and he was inconsistent when he took the mound. Jenkins has a long, lithe frame that made him a successful quarterback and sprinter in high school. It creates the leverage to unleash 93-96 mph fastballs and the strength to maintain velocity throughout his starts. He'll develop more power as he matures and more command as he tames his delivery. He has ditched an exaggerated leg kick and has sought to settle on more fluid mechanics that he can repeat. Jenkins gets depth on his curveball, but he doesn't always throw it with enough power. He's developing a solid changeup. A spot in the high Class A rotation awaits Jenkins in 2013, when a mix of maturity and pitcher-friendly Florida State League parks could elicit the breakout the Cardinals are hoping for.

BA GRADE
55
EXTREME

Year	Club (League)	Class	W	L	ERA	G	GS	CG	SV	IP	H	HR	BB	SO	K/9	WHIP	AVG
2010	Johnson City (APP)	R	0	0	0.00	2	2	0	0	3	2	0	2	2	6.0	1.33	.200
2011	Johnson City (APP)	R	4	2	3.86	11	11	0	0	56	63	3	13	55	8.8	1.36	.296
2012	Quad Cities (MWL)	LoA	4	4	5.14	19	19	0	0	82	84	5	36	80	8.7	1.46	.267
Minor League Totals			8	6	4.52	32	32	0	0	141	149	8	51	137	8.7	1.42	.277

9 CARSON KELLY, 3B

Born: July 14, 1994. **B-T:** R-R. **Ht.:** 6-2. **Wt.:** 200. **Drafted:** HS—Portland, Ore., 2012 (2nd round). **Signed by:** Matt Swanson.

Though he was the Cardinals' sixth pick (second round) in 2012, Kelly tied for the second-highest bonus ($1.6 million) in their draft class. The highest-drafted Oregon prep player since 1996, he drew some interest as a pitcher with a low-90s fastball. St. Louis coveted his power at the plate, which he showed off by hitting nine homers at Rookie-level Johnson City. Kelly has a sturdy build and has already matured into muscle. He has a calm, quiet stance at the plate and an easy, balanced swing that creates natural carry. His batting average sagged as he struggled with quality secondary pitches and the overall speed of the pro game, but he has the tools to develop into a solid hitter. Kelly has a strong arm and reliable hands at third base. He doesn't run well and will have to enhance his lateral movement to remain at the hot corner. Kelly won't turn 19 until the middle of his first

BA GRADE
50
HIGH

full pro season and there's no need to rush him. Patrick Wisdom, a 2012 supplemental first-rounder, is ticketed for third base at the Cardinals' new low Class A Peoria affiliate, so Kelly likely will head to short-season State College. He could make his full-season debut by the end of the year.

Year	Club (League)	Class	AVG	G	AB	R	H	2B	3B	HR	RBI	BB	SO	SB	CS	OBP	SLG
2012	Johnson City (APP)	R	.225	56	213	24	48	10	0	9	25	10	33	0	0	.263	.399
Minor League Totals			.225	56	213	24	48	10	0	9	25	10	33	0	0	.263	.399

10 STEPHEN PISCOTTY, OF/3B

Born: Jan. 14, 1991. **B-T:** R-R. **Ht.:** 6-3. **Wt.:** 210. **Drafted:** Stanford, 2012 (1st round supplemental). **Signed by:** Matt Swanson.

Even with a new scouting director, Dan Kantrovitz, helming their draft, the Cardinals continued to load up on polished college performers in 2012. They used the 36th overall pick on Piscotty, who won the 2011 Cape Cod League batting title (.349) and hit .340 in three seasons at Stanford. After signing for $1,430,400, he immediately went to low Class A, where he impressed observers with an .824 OPS and a big league approach. Piscotty has a seasoned sense of the strike zone and a good read on pitches. His line-drive swing is built more for high batting averages with plenty of doubles. The soft spots in his robust résumé that kept him from being a first-round pick followed him into pro ball. Piscotty lacks true home run power and went deep just four times in 210 at-bats. Though he has a strong arm, he lacks the hands and range to play a good third base and made 22 errors in 36 pro games there. St. Louis will move Piscotty to right field and advance him to high Class A in 2013. The position change will put even more pressure on him to add more home run power. His ability to do so will determine if he emerges as an everyday outfielder or a high-average utility cornerman.

BA GRADE
50
HIGH

Year	Club (League)	Class	AVG	G	AB	R	H	2B	3B	HR	RBI	BB	SO	SB	CS	OBP	SLG
2012	Quad Cities (MWL)	LoA	.295	55	210	29	62	18	1	4	27	18	25	3	0	.376	.448
Minor League Totals			.295	55	210	29	62	18	1	4	27	18	25	3	0	.376	.448

11 PATRICK WISDOM, 3B

BA GRADE
50
HIGH

Born: Aug. 27, 1991. **B-T:** R-R. **Ht.:** 6-2. **Wt.:** 210. **Drafted:** St. Mary's, 2012 (1st round supplemental). **Signed by:** Matt Swanson.

Wisdom had a breakout sophomore season at St. Mary's in 2011 before posting a .925 OPS in the Alaska League, a wood-bat college summer circuit. But he didn't live up to expectations last spring, batting .262/.385/.476 as a junior. That slump allowed the Cardinals to grab him with the 52nd overall pick and sign him for a discounted $678,790 in June—a savings that helped them pay fellow third-base prospect Carson Kelly $1.6 million in the second round. Wisdom's numbers with wood in his pro debut nearly matched his college numbers with metal, hinting at his raw power. He has a workable swing and could be an average hitter once he lets his pop come naturally, instead of sabotaging his approach by trying to force it and pull everything. Wisdom is a fringy runner with good athleticism that really emerges in the field. He has good instincts for third base and a strong, accurate arm. A quick first step gives him above-average range. One evaluator called him the best defensive prospect St. Louis has had at the hot corner in more than a decade. Widsom will start his first full pro season in low Class A, and his offensive improvement and adjustments will dictate how quickly he rises.

Year	Club (League)	Class	AVG	G	AB	R	H	2B	3B	HR	RBI	BB	SO	SB	CS	OBP	SLG
2012	Batavia (NYP)	SS	.282	65	241	40	68	16	5	6	32	31	58	2	1	.373	.465
Minor League Totals			.282	65	241	40	68	16	5	6	32	31	58	2	1	.373	.465

12 JAMES RAMSEY, OF

BA GRADE
50
HIGH

Born: Dec. 19, 1989. **B-T:** L-R. **Ht.:** 6-0. **Wt.:** 190. **Drafted:** Florida State, 2012 (1st round). **Signed by:** Rob Fidler.

Ramsey was the Tim Tebow of college baseball for his combination of leadership, charisma and Christian faith. The label also fit the divergent views of his potential. To some, Ramsey is a talented player and a standup individual with no standout tool. To others, he's a potential starter in center field who could hit near the top of a big league order while galvanizing a clubhouse. Count the Cardinals among the latter after they drafted him 23rd overall in June and signed him for $1.6 million, the fifth-highest bonus ever for a college senior. He turned in a first-team All-America season last spring, batting .378/.513/.652 and leading Florida State to the College World Series after turning down second-round money from the Twins as a 22nd-round pick in 2011. In an aggressive move, St. Louis pushed Ramsey to high Class A for his pro debut and he struggled. His 59 strikeouts in 56 games were attributed to a mechanical glitch in his swing, one coaches think he can correct with experience. Most scouts agree that he can hit for a solid average, but many wonder if he'll have even average power. Ramsey has above-average speed and puts it to good use in center and on the bases. He'll turn in plus-plus times down the first-base line, a tribute to his constant energy and effort. His arm is average. There's no doubt about his stellar makeup, as Ramsey was the first Seminole to wear a captain's "C" on his uniform, won an award for his community service and was both president of Florida State's student-athlete advisory council and a Rhodes Scholar nominee. He'll return to Palm Beach to start 2013.

Year	Club (League)	Class	AVG	G	AB	R	H	2B	3B	HR	RBI	BB	SO	SB	CS	OBP	SLG
2012	Palm Beach (FSL)	HiA	.229	56	210	36	48	9	3	1	14	33	59	10	2	.333	.314
Minor League Totals			.229	56	210	36	48	9	3	1	14	33	59	10	2	.333	.314

13 PETE KOZMA, SS/2B

BA GRADE
45
MEDIUM

Born: April 11, 1988. **B-T:** R-R. **Ht.:** 6-0. **Wt.:** 180. **Drafted:** HS—Owasso, Okla., 2007 (1st round). **Signed by:** Steve Gossett.

No Cardinals farmhand more radically altered his standing in the organization than Kozma did in 2012. He has a .652 career OPS in the minors but was thrust into a starting job at shortstop in August when Rafael Furcal went down with an elbow injury. Kozma helped propel St. Louis into the postseason by hitting .333/.383/.569 in 26 games, and his 14 RBIs were the most by a Cardinals rookie in September since Albert Pujols. Kozma's success carried into the playoffs, where he drove in the National League Division Series-winning runs in the ninth inning of Game Five. Before his stunning breakout, he spent most of the season at Triple-A, where he was replaced at shortstop by Ryan Jackson and told to prepare for a utility role in the majors. Necessity made him more. When Kozma signed for $1,395,000, his tools were described as average across the board. His solid defense and strong arm carried him, as his bat didn't develop as expected—until St. Louis needed it most. His realistic offensive ceiling is as an average hitter with gap power and decent speed. Almost removed from the 40-man roster several times in 2012, Kozma enters this year with a shot at the big league bench.

Year	Club (League)	Class	AVG	G	AB	R	H	2B	3B	HR	RBI	BB	SO	SB	CS	OBP	SLG
2007	Cardinals (GCL)	R	.154	4	13	4	2	0	0	0	0	2	2	0	0	.267	.154
	Johnson City (APP)	R	.264	30	106	16	28	8	0	2	9	12	21	3	2	.350	.396
	Batavia (NYP)	SS	.148	8	27	1	4	0	1	0	2	1	7	1	1	.179	.222
2008	Quad Cities (MWL)	LoA	.284	99	377	58	107	20	4	5	40	45	69	12	5	.363	.398
	Palm Beach (FSL)	HiA	.130	24	77	4	10	4	0	0	10	10	27	0	1	.231	.182
2009	Palm Beach (FSL)	HiA	.315	18	73	8	23	5	0	0	8	8	16	1	0	.381	.384
	Springfield (TL)	AA	.216	113	407	52	88	15	3	6	37	42	88	4	2	.288	.312
2010	Springfield (TL)	AA	.243	132	503	69	122	28	2	13	72	56	111	13	2	.318	.384
2011	St. Louis (NL)	MAJ	.176	16	17	2	3	1	0	0	1	4	4	0	0	.333	.235
	Memphis (PCL)	AAA	.214	112	398	48	85	17	2	3	47	36	91	2	2	.280	.289
2012	Memphis (PCL)	AAA	.232	131	448	61	104	16	3	11	63	41	74	7	4	.292	.355
	St. Louis (NL)	MAJ	.333	26	72	11	24	5	3	2	14	7	19	2	0	.383	.569
Major League Totals			.303	42	89	13	27	6	3	2	15	11	23	2	0	.373	.506
Minor League Totals			.236	671	2429	321	573	113	15	40	288	253	506	43	19	.308	.344

14 KEVIN SIEGRIST, LHP

BA GRADE
50
HIGH

Born: July 20, 1989. **B-T:** L-L. **Ht.:** 6-5. **Wt.:** 190. **Drafted:** Palm Beach (Fla.) CC, 2008 (41st round). **Signed by:** Charlie Gonzalez.

Siegrist has all of the ingredients to be a big league lefty, though health has eluded him since he signed for $85,000 as a 41st-round pick in 2008. His development has been hampered by neck pain, lower-back stiffness and a right (non-throwing) shoulder strain that landed him on the disabled list last summer, though he has avoided surgery each time. He returned in time to pitch in the Texas League playoffs and then broke through in the Arizona Fall League, where he went 2-1, 2.39 with 27 strikeouts in 19 innings. When healthy, Siegrist is hard to hit thanks to a 91-93 mph fastball, solid curveball and developing changeup. He throws them all from a low three-quarters slot, and that coupled with his frame adds deception. His command has improved with increased innings. Siegrist has enough promise and stuff to remain a starter, but the Cardinals have an immediate need for lefty relief. Added to the 40-man roster, he's earmarked for Triple-A, where he'll continue to start until the big league club requires another lefty reliever.

Year	Club (League)	Class	W	L	ERA	G	GS	CG	SV	IP	H	HR	BB	SO	K/9	WHIP	AVG
2008	Cardinals (GCL)	R	0	0	1.38	7	2	0	0	13	3	0	3	11	7.6	0.46	.070
2009	Batavia (NYP)	SS	1	0	3.86	10	4	0	0	28	30	4	11	23	7.4	1.46	.273
2010	Batavia (NYP)	SS	0	1	7.29	7	4	0	0	21	24	1	16	14	6.0	1.90	.282
	Johnson City (APP)	R	4	3	1.93	7	5	0	0	33	28	3	6	31	8.5	1.04	.237
2011	Quad Cities (MWL)	LoA	8	1	1.15	9	8	0	0	55	38	1	15	34	5.6	0.97	.194
	Palm Beach (FSL)	HiA	0	3	3.42	11	11	0	0	53	44	3	30	45	7.7	1.41	.232
2012	Palm Beach (FSL)	HiA	6	0	2.28	10	10	0	0	55	33	3	22	41	6.7	0.99	.173
	Springfield (TL)	AA	1	2	3.62	8	5	0	0	32	26	4	9	27	7.5	1.08	.218
Minor League Totals			20	10	2.86	69	49	0	2	290	226	19	112	226	7.0	1.17	.215

15 RYAN JACKSON, SS/2B

Born: May 10, 1988. **B-T:** R-R. **Ht.:** 6-3. **Wt.:** 180. **Drafted:** Miami, 2009 (5th round). **Signed by:** Mike Elias.

BA GRADE
45
MEDIUM

The Cardinals cleared the way for Jackson to be the starting shortstop at Memphis last summer by shifting Pete Kozma into a utility role. By the time Rafael Furcal hurt his elbow and St. Louis needed a replacement at shortstop, the roles had reversed. Jackson's playing time had all but vanished, a sudden and curious development for the young infielder who remains one of the best gloves in the system. He was considered the finest college shortstop in the 2009 draft and has validated that reputation as a pro. He has a strong and accurate arm, high baseball intelligence and enough first-step quickness to overcome fringy speed. Jackson has decent bat speed and plate discipline and projects as maybe an average hitter with some gap power, especially against lefthanders. He struggled at the plate in his big league cameo and had a difficult game at second base in Philadelphia that seemed to secure his bench status. Jackson will come to spring training with a chance to erase that first impression, win a utility job and battle Kozma to reclaim the role as Furcal's potential successor in 2014.

Year	Club (League)	Class	AVG	G	AB	R	H	2B	3B	HR	RBI	BB	SO	SB	CS	OBP	SLG
2009	Batavia (NYP)	SS	.216	67	245	29	53	4	1	0	14	29	37	4	3	.297	.241
2010	Quad Cities (MWL)	LoA	.272	84	302	47	82	13	2	2	27	48	63	6	7	.366	.348
	Palm Beach (FSL)	HiA	.291	41	148	14	43	10	1	1	8	11	21	3	2	.342	.392
2011	Springfield (TL)	AA	.278	135	533	65	148	34	3	11	73	44	91	2	0	.334	.415
2012	Memphis (PCL)	AAA	.272	117	445	60	121	23	1	10	47	43	75	2	0	.334	.396
	St. Louis (NL)	MAJ	.118	13	17	2	2	0	0	0	0	1	3	0	0	.167	.118
Major League Totals			.118	13	17	2	2	0	0	0	0	1	3	0	0	.167	.118
Minor League Totals			.267	444	1673	215	447	84	8	24	169	175	287	17	12	.335	.370

16 VICTOR DeLEON, RHP

Born: April 19, 1992. **B-T:** R-R. **Ht.:** 6-2. **Wt.:** 190. **Signed:** Dominican Republic, 2009. **Signed by:** Juan Mercado.

BA GRADE
50
HIGH

When the major league workouts were over one day last spring, the coaches drifted to the back fields to see some of the Cardinals' youngest pitching prospects. One stood out. Well built and gifted with raw velocity, DeLeon drew the coaches toward his bullpen session. He can hit 98 mph with his fastball, and he sits at 92-95 mph as a starter. His low-80s slider improved last season, and he continues to tinker with a changeup. He shows good instincts for pitching and because he's able to repeat his delivery, the command should come. He made significant progress in 2012, which he finished with a strong seven-inning, no-walk start in the Rookie-level Appalachian League playoffs. St. Louis will push him to full-season ball as a 21-year-old in 2013. The plan is to get him innings as a starter to see if he can develop consistent secondary pitches. If that doesn't work out, he could be a late-inning lightning bolt from the bullpen.

Year	Club (League)	Class	W	L	ERA	G	GS	CG	SV	IP	H	HR	BB	SO	K/9	WHIP	AVG
2010	Cardinals (DSL)	R	4	3	2.76	14	8	1	0	49	39	5	26	40	7.3	1.33	.225
2011	Cardinals (GCL)	R	0	6	4.47	10	9	0	0	50	56	2	24	30	5.4	1.59	.290
2012	Johnson City (APP)	R	3	0	3.25	10	10	0	0	44	39	1	20	42	8.5	1.33	.236
Minor League Totals			7	9	3.51	34	27	1	0	144	134	8	70	112	7.0	1.42	.252

17 C.J. McELROY, OF

Born: May 29, 1993. **B-T:** R-R. **Ht.:** 5-10. **Wt.:** 180. **Drafted:** HS—League City, Texas, 2011 (3rd round). **Signed by:** Ralph Garr Jr.

BA GRADE
50
HIGH

Even during the lengthy bus trips in the Appalachian League, McElroy didn't feel regret for walking away from a football scholarship to play wide receiver at Houston. The son of former major league reliever Chuck McElroy and nephew of former all-star Cecil Cooper, C.J. signed for $510,000 as a 2011 third-rounder. The swiftest player in the system, he stole 24 bases for Rookie-level Johnson City, becoming more aggressive as coaches worked with him on getting a quality lead instead of just relying on his feet. His speed earns 80 grades on the 20-80 scale from some scouts, and the Cardinals clocked him at 6.37 seconds in a 60-yard dash. Stealing second base wasn't the issue, however; getting to first was. McElroy drew just two walks in his final 31 games because he was determined to enact improvements to his swing. He lowered his back elbow to create fewer grounders and popups. He has little power, so his focus is getting on base. He should develop into a plus defender in center field, though his arm is below-average. During instructional league, McElroy worked on switch-hitting, a new skill he'll continue to refine during spring training. His first full-season assignment awaits in April.

Year	Club (League)	Class	AVG	G	AB	R	H	2B	3B	HR	RBI	BB	SO	SB	CS	OBP	SLG
2011	Cardinals (GCL)	R	.228	23	79	10	18	2	1	0	7	7	15	8	2	.303	.278
2012	Johnson City (APP)	R	.271	61	247	40	67	11	2	0	22	15	42	24	5	.314	.332
Minor League Totals			.261	84	326	50	85	13	3	0	29	22	57	32	7	.312	.319

18 JORDAN SWAGERTY, RHP

Born: July 14,1989. **B-T:** R-R. **Ht.:** 6-2. **Wt.:** 175. **Drafted:** Arizona State, 2010 (2nd round). **Signed by:** Aaron Krawiec.

After reaching Double-A in his 2011 pro debut, Swagerty arrived in big league camp last spring with a chance to lay the groundwork for a big league promotion later in the season. He left knowing he wouldn't throw a pitch at all in 2012. Pain radiating from bone spurs in his elbow led to Tommy John surgery, a proactive move to repair a ligament that would have unraveled at some point. When at full strength, Swagerty has a 92-94 mph fastball that climbs to 96. The Cardinals graded his curveball as the best available in the 2010 draft, and it's a classic knee-buckler. They broke him into pro ball as a starter so he could get innings to refine a third pitch and improve his command, and he showed promise in that role. But a return to relief could be a compromise St. Louis makes to monitor Swagerty's innings and put him back on his quick climb toward the majors. Reports from his rehab were encouraging and he still has a ceiling as a closer.

Year	Club (League)	Class	W	L	ERA	G	GS	CG	SV	IP	H	HR	BB	SO	K/9	WHIP	AVG
2011	Quad Cities (MWL)	LoA	3	1	1.50	5	5	0	0	30	18	2	2	30	9.0	0.67	.178
	Palm Beach (FSL)	HiA	2	2	1.82	22	7	0	5	54	42	1	16	52	8.6	1.07	.214
	Springfield (TL)	AA	0	0	2.89	9	0	0	3	9	8	1	5	7	6.8	1.39	.222
2012	Did Not Play—Injured																
Minor League Totals			5	3	1.83	36	12	0	8	94	68	4	23	89	8.6	0.97	.204

19 CHARLIE TILSON, OF

Born: Dec. 2, 1992. **B-T:** L-L. **Ht.:** 5-11. **Wt.:** 175. **Drafted:** HS—Winnetka, Ill, 2011 (2nd round). **Signed by:** Kris Gross.

What should have been Tilson's first full pro season ended before it began. During a scrimmage in extended spring training, he separated his right (non-throwing) shoulder and tore his labrum while attempting a diving catch. Surgery followed and the summer was a loss. He returned in time for instructional league, where he impressed coaches with solid production while regaining his strength. The Chicagoland prep star caught the Cardinals' eye and improved his draft stock with his performance at the 2010 Area Code Games, and the Cardinals signed him the next summer for $1,275,000 as a second-rounder. Tilson is a contact hitter with a line-drive swing and the potential to hit for a solid average. Speed is where his extra-base hits will come from, as he rates as a 65 runner on the 20-80 scouting scale but has below-average raw power. His injury puts him behind fellow 2011 high school center fielder C.J. McElroy, but Tilson will get priority playing time in center because St. Louis believes his speed, arm and instincts fit the position. A jump to a full-season club at some point in 2013 is likely, though probably not to start the season because he has just 27 pro at-bats.

Year	Club (League)	Class	AVG	G	AB	R	H	2B	3B	HR	RBI	BB	SO	SB	CS	OBP	SLG
2011	Cardinals (GCL)	R	.167	4	12	2	2	0	0	0	1	2	3	1	0	.286	.167
	Johnson City (APP)	R	.467	4	15	2	7	2	0	0	4	1	1	0	0	.500	.600
2012	Did Not Play—Injured																
Minor League Totals			.333	8	27	4	9	2	0	0	5	3	4	1	0	.400	.407

20 STEVE BEAN, C

Born: Sept. 15, 1993. **B-T:** L-R. **Ht.:** 6-2. **Wt.:** 190. **Drafted:** HS—Rockwall, Texas, 2012 (1st round supplemental). **Signed by:** Aaron Looper.

The initial plan to push Bean to Johnson City proved a little daunting and perhaps unfair for the prep catcher whom the Cardinals took with the 66th overall pick last June. He struck out 32 times in 80 at-bats in the Appalachian League but rallied to hit .320/.424/.400 after he was drawn back to the Rookie-level Gulf Coast League. Bean had committed to Texas before a $700,000 bonus lured him to pro ball, where he instantly became the system's best defensive catcher. His arm rates a 65 on the 20-80 scouting scale, and he threw out 37 percent of basestealers in his pro debut. Despite some youthful hiccups, he's a nimble and sound receiver who should grow with experience. Bean doesn't hit for much power now, but his developing strength hints at more down the road. He has a feel for the strike zone and a quick bat. He does have excess movement at the plate that makes him vulnerable against quality pitching, so St. Louis will try to quiet that down. He's a below-average runner but plays with more athleticism and energy than most catchers. Given his initial struggles, Bean may open his first full pro season in extended spring training before going to State College in June.

Year	Club (League)	Class	AVG	G	AB	R	H	2B	3B	HR	RBI	BB	SO	SB	CS	OBP	SLG
2012	Johnson City (APP)	R	.125	24	80	6	10	4	0	1	5	15	32	2	0	.263	.213
	Cardinals (GCL)	R	.320	15	50	8	16	4	0	0	7	8	11	0	0	.424	.400
Minor League Totals			.200	39	130	14	26	8	0	1	12	23	43	2	0	.325	.285

21 ERIC FORNATARO, RHP

Born: Jan. 2, 1988. **B-T:** R-R. **Ht.:** 6-1. **Wt.:** 215. **Drafted:** Miami Dade JC, 2008 (6th round). **Signed by:** Charlie Gonzalez.

A burly righty with an aggressive demeanor on the mound, Fornataro is a late comer to the prospect tag and arrives without the usual trappings. He was a sixth-round pick in 2008 who received a $150,000 bonus and had suitable but not sizzling early success. It all changed when he moved to the bullpen and blossomed as Springfield's surefire set-up man in 2012. Instead of trying to shoulder the innings of a starter, Fornataro was able to let loose in short bursts. The result was a fastball that jumped to elite status, sitting at 96-98 mph and hitting 99. His hard curveball has good rotation and power in the low 80s, giving him a plus second pitch, and his splitter has late drop. Fornataro still is learning to harness and use his newfound stuff, as his strikeout rate actually dipped to a pedestrian 5.5 per nine innings last season despite his jump in stuff. He keeps the ball in the park and gets plenty of groundballs when he's on. The Cardinals added Fornataro to the 40-man roster in November and think he'll contribute in the major league bullpen soon. That depends on whether he can maintain his progress in Triple-A this year.

Year	Club (League)	Class	W	L	ERA	G	GS	CG	SV	IP	H	HR	BB	SO	K/9	WHIP	AVG
2008	Cardinals (GCL)	R	2	2	1.74	9	3	0	0	31	27	1	6	19	5.5	1.06	.227
	Johnson City (APP)	R	0	1	2.57	2	1	0	1	7	5	0	3	6	7.7	1.14	.172
2009	Batavia (NYP)	SS	4	0	2.15	8	5	0	0	38	23	0	6	14	3.3	0.77	.177
	Quad Cities (MWL)	LoA	0	5	5.24	7	6	0	0	34	42	2	11	11	2.9	1.54	.302
2010	Quad Cities (MWL)	LoA	7	15	5.26	28	28	0	0	140	161	13	59	100	6.4	1.57	.290
2011	Palm Beach (FSL)	HiA	7	13	3.67	24	24	1	0	145	150	7	50	116	7.2	1.38	.265
2012	Springfield (TL)	AA	3	3	2.39	57	0	0	5	68	55	1	17	41	5.5	1.06	.226
Minor League Totals			23	39	3.81	135	67	1	6	463	463	24	152	307	6.0	1.33	.260

22 SAM FREEMAN, LHP

Born: June 24, 1987. **B-T:** R-L. **Ht.:** 5-11. **Wt.:** 170. **Drafted:** Kansas, 2008 (32nd round). **Signed by:** Joe Almaraz.

After losing the 2010 season while recovering from Tommy John surgery, Freeman made his major league debut last June and scored a place on the Cardinals' wild-card playoff roster. Primarily an outfielder at North Central Texas CC, he became a full-time pitcher at Kansas in 2008, recording an 8.53 ERA before signing for $10,000 as a 32nd-round pick. Still relatively inexperienced on the mound, Freeman has a slight frame that belies his velocity and stamina, which result from being one of the best athletes in the system. He regularly throws 94-95 mph with his four-seam fastball, mixes in a low-90s sinker and owns a decent 78-82 slurve. He has worked to correct his habit of slowing his arm when delivering his breaking ball or fringy changeup. Freeman still doesn't dominate lefties as much as he should because he doesn't command his pitches. St. Louis sent him to the Arizona Fall League instead of keeping him on its playoff roster for the next two rounds, but he came down with a sore shoulder. The Cardinals signed veteran Randy Choate to a three-year deal, which will put Freeman back in Triple-A to start 2013 but not out of mind when another lefty is needed.

Year	Club (League)	Class	W	L	ERA	G	GS	CG	SV	IP	H	HR	BB	SO	K/9	WHIP	AVG
2008	Johnson City (APP)	R	4	1	3.70	20	0	0	2	24	23	2	12	34	12.6	1.44	.250
	Palm Beach (FSL)	HiA	0	0	0.00	1	0	0	0	2	0	0	1	4	18.0	0.50	.000
2009	Palm Beach (FSL)	HiA	2	1	1.64	26	0	0	1	33	18	0	13	30	8.2	0.94	.157
	Springfield (TL)	AA	0	1	3.52	15	0	0	1	23	19	6	14	17	6.7	1.43	.241
2010	Did Not Play—Injured																
2011	Palm Beach (FSL)	HiA	0	0	4.00	7	0	0	0	9	8	0	4	7	7.0	1.33	.258
	Springfield (TL)	AA	2	2	3.03	52	0	0	3	59	53	5	28	52	7.9	1.37	.240
2012	Springfield (TL)	AA	1	3	1.56	15	0	0	1	17	12	1	4	12	6.2	0.92	.190
	Memphis (PCL)	AAA	2	2	2.08	27	0	0	0	30	25	3	12	27	8.0	1.22	.227
	St. Louis (NL)	MAJ	0	2	5.40	24	0	0	0	20	17	2	10	18	8.1	1.35	.230
Major League Totals			0	2	5.40	24	0	0	0	20	17	2	10	18	8.1	1.35	.230
Minor League Totals			11	10	2.68	163	0	0	8	198	158	17	88	183	8.3	1.24	.220

23 SETH MANESS, RHP

Born: Oct. 14, 1988. **B-T:** R-R. **Ht.:** 6-0. **Wt.:** 180. **Drafted:** East Carolina, 2011 (11th round). **Signed by:** Nick Brannon.

By his own admission, Maness' fastball isn't overpowering, but he has the uncanny ability to put it wherever he wants. Signed for $1,000 as an 11th-round college senior in 2011, he went 42 innings into his first full pro season before he walked a batter. He led the minors with 0.5 walks per nine innings last year, a rate that was less than half of his closest competitor. Maness knows he has to rely on movement and pitch to contact, which he does by pinpointing an 89-91 mph sinker to both sides of the plate. Some scouts give him 70 command on the 20-80 scale. He relentlessly throws strikes and mixes in a slider and a changeup that both have a chance to be average. Maness started his East Carolina career as a two-way player before shifting to the mound full-time and setting school records for career wins (38) and strikeouts (334). He uses a lot of upper body in his delivery, though he's consistent with his mechanics and his arm speed. The Cardinals have a lot of talented pitchers in the high minors, but Maness' reliability could be enough to earn a spot in the Triple-A rotation this year.

Year	Club (League)	Class	W	L	ERA	G	GS	CG	SV	IP	H	HR	BB	SO	K/9	WHIP	AVG
2011	Batavia (NYP)	SS	0	1	0.91	10	7	0	0	40	27	0	3	31	7.0	0.76	.185
	Palm Beach (FSL)	HiA	1	0	4.32	3	0	0	0	8	7	0	2	8	8.6	1.08	.219
	Quad Cities (MWL)	LoA	1	0	1.80	2	0	0	0	5	4	0	0	3	5.4	0.80	.222
2012	Palm Beach (FSL)	HiA	3	1	2.15	7	7	0	0	46	45	5	1	29	5.7	1.00	.256
	Springfield (TL)	AA	11	3	3.27	20	20	1	0	124	122	13	9	83	6.0	1.06	.253
Minor League Totals			16	5	2.63	42	34	1	0	223	205	18	15	154	6.2	0.99	.240

24 JORGE RONDON, RHP

Born: Sept. 16, 1988. **B-T:** R-R. **Ht.:** 6-1. **Wt.:** 175. **Signed:** Venezuela, 2006. **Signed by:** Bobby Diaz.

BA GRADE
45
MEDIUM

A year after the undersized righty with the oversized fastball emerged as a closer in Springfield, Rondon asserted his place as a rising power arm in a system that's increasingly flush with them. He joined Carlos Martinez, Trevor Rosenthal and Maikel Cleto as 100-mph flamethrowers when he tripped triple digits in the middle of the season. Rondon averages 95 mph with his fastball and did so with increasing command in 2012, though he still needs to get better in that regard. He maximizes his mechanics to gain velocity, but when he muscles his pitches he sacrifices location. He complements his fastball with a hard slider that can get swings and misses when it's on. Already a veteran of seven pro seasons, Rondon went unclaimed in the 2010-11 Rule 5 drafts before the Cardinals protected him on the 40-man roster this offseason. They likened him to Eduardo Sanchez, another small but hard-throwing righty who has helped them in the majors. Rondon spent the winter pitching in the Venezuelan League and is headed back to Triple-A.

Year	Club (League)	Class	W	L	ERA	G	GS	CG	SV	IP	H	HR	BB	SO	K/9	WHIP	AVG
2006	Cardinals (VSL)	R	0	1	6.46	10	1	0	1	15	20	1	6	12	7.0	1.70	.317
2007	Cardinals (VSL)	R	1	6	4.74	17	9	0	2	63	80	5	18	27	3.9	1.56	.321
2008	Johnson City (APP)	R	2	2	4.03	21	0	0	6	22	28	1	8	21	8.5	1.61	.308
	Quad Cities (MWL)	LoA	1	0	3.24	8	0	0	0	8	11	0	3	5	5.4	1.68	.367
2009	Palm Beach (FSL)	HiA	0	1	7.71	8	2	0	0	16	24	1	10	11	6.1	2.08	.338
	Quad Cities (MWL)	LoA	1	5	4.27	10	10	0	0	53	59	7	13	37	6.3	1.37	.278
2010	Quad Cities (MWL)	LoA	4	8	5.30	29	19	0	0	109	121	6	65	76	6.3	1.71	.287
2011	Palm Beach (FSL)	HiA	1	5	4.05	21	0	0	6	27	29	1	13	27	9.1	1.58	.302
	Springfield (TL)	AA	1	8	9.16	37	0	0	7	37	43	4	33	30	7.2	2.04	.295
2012	Springfield (TL)	AA	2	3	3.44	33	0	0	4	34	29	1	16	30	7.9	1.32	.238
	Memphis (PCL)	AAA	0	1	3.60	13	0	0	1	15	12	1	8	20	12.0	1.33	.214
Minor League Totals			13	38	5.16	207	41	0	27	399	456	28	193	296	6.7	1.63	.293

25 TIM COONEY, LHP

Born: Dec. 19, 1990. **B-T:** L-L. **Ht.:** 6-3. **Wt.:** 195. **Drafted:** Wake Forest, 2012 (3rd round). **Signed by:** Matt Blood.

BA GRADE
50
HIGH

The same fickle winds that carried Cooney to prominence after his strong showing in the Cape Cod League in 2011 slowed when inconsistency took hold in his junior year at Wake Forest. When he reached pro ball after signing for $404,400 as a third-rounder in June, performance finally took over. Cooney had far and away the best stuff on the short-season Batavia staff, according to one evaluator. His solid debut reflected the pitcher the Cardinals saw on the Cape, not the one challenged by flighty command. Cooney's fastball darts from 87-93 mph, sitting around 90. He pitches assertively with his cutter and mixes in an erratic curveball. At its best, his changeup can elicit swings and misses from righthanders. Cooney's control can unravel when he overthrows, but he avoided that at Batavia and issued just eight walks in 56 innings. A potential quick riser, he could advance to high Class A in his first full year as a pro.

Year	Club (League)	Class	W	L	ERA	G	GS	CG	SV	IP	H	HR	BB	SO	K/9	WHIP	AVG
2012	Batavia (NYP)	SS	3	3	3.40	13	11	1	0	56	56	4	8	43	7.0	1.15	.268
Minor League Totals			3	3	3.40	13	11	1	0	56	56	4	8	43	7.0	1.15	.268

26 JOHN GAST, LHP

Born: Feb. 16, 1989. **B-T:** L-L. **Ht.:** 6-1. **Wt.:** 195. **Drafted:** Florida State, 2010 (6th round). **Signed by:** Mike Elias.

BA GRADE
45
MEDIUM

Gast was a Rangers fifth-round pick out of high school in 2007, but he opted to have Tommy John surgery and try to enhance his stock at Florida State. That didn't quite happen, and the Cardinals were able to get him with a sixth-round pick and $140,000 bonus in 2010. He advanced to Double-A in his first full pro season, but Triple-A hitters took advantage of his spotty command last year. He fought shoulder troubles in the second half that complicated his control issues and landed him on the disabled list. Gast has a deceptive, whippy release that gives him the system's best pickoff move and helps his stuff play up. His fastball usually ranges from 87-91 mph, and he also has a solid changeup and average curveball. When he's unable to control his fastball, he slips behind in the count and into trouble. Gast lacks the standout breaking ball to be a lefthanded specialist, so he'll continue to develop as a starter in Memphis.

Year	Club (League)	Class	W	L	ERA	G	GS	CG	SV	IP	H	HR	BB	SO	K/9	WHIP	AVG
2010	Batavia (NYP)	SS	6	0	1.54	8	6	0	0	35	27	1	8	36	9.3	1.00	.227
2011	Palm Beach (FSL)	HiA	5	4	3.95	13	12	1	0	82	85	7	28	59	6.5	1.38	.272
	Springfield (TL)	AA	4	4	4.08	13	13	1	0	79	80	9	33	54	6.1	1.42	.266
2012	Springfield (TL)	AA	4	2	1.93	8	8	0	0	51	38	5	13	41	7.2	0.99	.211
	Memphis (PCL)	AAA	9	5	5.10	20	20	0	0	109	124	10	42	86	7.1	1.52	.286
Minor League Totals			28	15	3.81	62	59	2	0	357	354	32	124	276	7.0	1.34	.263

27 MAIKEL CLETO, RHP

BA GRADE 45 MEDIUM

Born: May 1, 1989. **B-T:** R-R. **Ht.:** 6-3. **Wt.:** 235. **Signed:** Dominican Republic, 2006. **Signed by:** Ramon Pena (Mets).

Originally signed by the Mets, Cleto went to the Mariners in a three-team trade that also sent Franklin Gutierrez to Seattle and J.J Putz to New York in December 2008, then came to the Cardinals prior to the 2011 season in exchange for Brendan Ryan. The hulking righthander has pitched briefly in St. Louis in each of the last two seasons, showing just enough raw power to intrigue and just enough inconsistency to merit a return to the minors. He posted the best K-BB ratio (3.0) of his career in 2012, he also had his worst ERA (5.37) since pitching for high Class A High Desert, one of the minors' toughest pitcher's parks. Heat is Cleto's game. He has hit 102 mph as a starter in the past and has topped 100 mph several times. Recast as a full-time reliever last year, he kept the velocity and maintained more consistency with his flamboyant, max-effort delivery. His fastball sits from 95-99 mph and he complements it with an exaggerated, mid-80s slider that can slip away from him at times. His changeup is more of a 91-mph sinker that he uses judiciously. Cleto is destined to open 2013 back in Triple-A, but the strides he made with his control have him in line for another big league promotion.

Year	Club (League)	Class	W	L	ERA	G	GS	CG	SV	IP	H	HR	BB	SO	K/9	WHIP	AVG
2007	Mets (GCL)	R	1	2	5.03	11	4	0	1	34	34	2	25	28	7.4	1.74	.270
2008	Savannah (SAL)	LoA	5	11	4.25	25	22	1	0	136	140	8	34	81	5.4	1.28	.268
	St. Lucie (FSL)	HiA	0	1	9.00	1	1	0	0	5	5	1	2	1	1.8	1.40	.278
2009	Mariners (AZL)	R	0	1	13.50	1	0	0	0	1	3	0	1	1	13.5	6.00	.500
	Clinton (MWL)	LoA	0	3	5.33	8	8	0	0	25	35	4	11	24	8.5	1.82	.321
2010	High Desert (CAL)	HiA	4	9	6.16	23	21	0	0	102	125	10	44	83	7.3	1.65	.305
2011	Palm Beach (FSL)	HiA	1	1	2.48	5	5	0	0	29	20	2	10	33	10.2	1.03	.190
	Springfield (TL)	AA	2	2	3.93	7	6	0	0	34	40	2	12	36	9.4	1.51	.301
	Memphis (PCL)	AAA	5	3	4.29	13	13	0	0	71	57	6	43	66	8.3	1.40	.218
	St. Louis (NL)	MAJ	0	0	12.46	3	0	0	0	4	7	2	4	6	12.5	2.54	.333
2012	Memphis (PCL)	AAA	3	2	5.37	45	0	0	2	54	51	4	22	66	11.1	1.36	.254
	St. Louis (NL)	MAJ	0	0	7.00	9	0	0	0	9	13	4	2	15	15.0	1.67	.342
Major League Totals			0	0	8.78	12	0	0	0	13	20	6	6	21	14.2	1.95	.339
Minor League Totals			21	35	4.82	139	80	1	3	491	510	39	204	419	7.7	1.45	.270

28 MIKE O'NEILL, OF

BA GRADE 40 LOW

Born: Feb. 12, 1988. **B-T:** L-L. **Ht.:** 5-9. **Wt.:** 170. **Drafted:** Southern California, 2010 (31st round). **Signed by:** Jamal Strong.

An afterthought as a $1,000 senior sign in the 31st round of the 2010 draft, O'Neill had a spectacular 2012 season. Bouncing back from a knee injury the year before, he led the minors in on-base percentage (.458) and ranked second in hitting (.359), won the Florida State League batting title (.342) and helped Springfield capture the Texas League championship. He also starred in the Arizona Fall League, batting .368/.463/.397. O'Neill relishes his role as a tablesetter, exhibiting a keen sense of the strike zone and unwavering patience. His swing is built for contact at the expense of power, which limits his ceiling. He has just one homer in 683 pro at-bats, which makes it difficult to profile him as a big league regular. Though he has played all three outfield spots and has good defensive instincts, his average speed and fringy arm strength fit best in left field—a position with a premium on pop. O'Neill will try to keep exceeding expectations when he returns to Double-A, where he hit .563 in 13 games last year, and eventually could carve out a big league role as a fourth outfielder and bat off the bench.

Year	Club (League)	Class	AVG	G	AB	R	H	2B	3B	HR	RBI	BB	SO	SB	CS	OBP	SLG
2010	Batavia (NYP)	SS	.283	40	92	23	26	5	2	0	9	18	13	5	1	.393	.380
2011	Batavia (NYP)	SS	.290	25	93	18	27	9	0	1	8	22	10	3	1	.432	.419
	Quad Cities (MWL)	LoA	.338	25	80	15	27	8	0	0	10	13	13	1	0	.430	.438
2012	Palm Beach (FSL)	HiA	.342	108	386	56	132	19	5	0	35	70	24	12	10	.442	.417
	Springfield (TL)	AA	.563	13	32	8	18	5	0	0	5	8	2	3	0	.643	.719
Minor League Totals			.337	211	683	120	230	46	7	1	67	131	62	24	12	.443	.429

29 KEITH BUTLER, RHP

BA GRADE 45 MEDIUM

Born: Jan. 30, 1989. **B-T:** R-R. **Ht.:** 6-0. **Wt.:** 180. **Drafted:** Wabash Valley (Ill.) CC, 2009 (24th round). **Signed by:** Rob Fidler.

Some scouts see it and think it's slow enough to be a curve. Catchers decline to commit and call it a breaking ball. Some coaches term it a slurve. And Butler insists it's a slider. By any name, his breaking ball is effective. He can throw it at different speeds with different breaks, ranging from a Frisbee slider to a downer curve, using it for strikes or as a chase pitch. It's the main reason he has held opponents to a .203 average in four years of pro ball. Signed for $25,000 as a 24th-rounder in 2009, he contributed 25 saves to Springfield's march toward the 2012 Texas League championship. Though unimposing on the mound, Butler has a quick delivery and throws from a low arm angle, a tick above sidearm. His lively fastball arrives at 90-93 mph, his breaking ball runs in the low 80s and his changeup drops into the 70s. There are innings when he'll only throw changeups and variations of his breaking pitch, so hitters often are surprised when he uses his fastball and they take it for strikes. Josh Kinney turned a similar breaking ball into a ticket to the majors, and Butler could do the same after joining the 40-man roster in November.

Year	Club (League)	Class	W	L	ERA	G	GS	CG	SV	IP	H	HR	BB	SO	K/9	WHIP	AVG
2009	Cardinals (GCL)	R	1	1	2.22	21	0	0	6	28	18	0	12	34	10.8	1.06	.182
	Johnson City (APP)	R	0	0	0.00	2	0	0	0	2	0	0	1	4	18.0	0.50	.000
2010	Batavia (NYP)	SS	0	3	2.93	27	0	0	5	31	29	1	15	50	14.7	1.43	.242
2011	Quad Cities (MWL)	LoA	0	1	1.17	12	0	0	5	15	7	0	5	16	9.4	0.78	.135
	Palm Beach (FSL)	HiA	1	0	1.25	34	0	0	12	36	19	1	18	52	13.0	1.03	.151
2012	Springfield (TL)	AA	5	1	2.76	53	0	0	25	59	53	5	23	59	9.1	1.30	.242
Minor League Totals			7	6	2.21	149	0	0	53	171	126	7	74	215	11.3	1.17	.203

30 SETH BLAIR, RHP

BA GRADE 50 EXTREME

Born: March 3, 1989. **B-T:** R-R. **Ht.:** 6-2. **Wt.:** 185. **Drafted:** Arizona State, 2010 (1st round supplemental). **Signed by:** Aaron Krawiec.

Before Blair ever had a chance last year to reclaim his spot with the system's other high-round, high-expectations pitchers, he felt a recurring and crippling pain in his right hand. An MRI revealed an enchondroma tumor nestled into the knuckle on his middle finger. The tumor had caused microfractures that radiated out from his knuckle and required surgery that kept him off the mound until late July. The 46th overall selection in 2010, Blair salvaged 20 innings in the regular season and another 20 in the Arizona Fall League. It wasn't the bounceback he imagined but it did halt a downward spiral that began with a total loss of control and a suspension in 2011. The Cardinals were drawn to Blair because of his consistency at Arizona State, a trait that failed him in his pro debut. Rehab gave him a chance to reset. When Blair is right, he works with a 92-94 mph sinker and a curveball that could become a plus pitch. He has some feel for his changeup, giving it a chance to become effective. Blair has fallen behind pitchers drafted after him, but he'll compete for a spot in the Double-A rotation this year and try to regain lost ground.

Year	Club (League)	Class	W	L	ERA	G	GS	CG	SV	IP	H	HR	BB	SO	K/9	WHIP	AVG
2011	Quad Cities (MWL)	LoA	6	3	5.29	21	21	0	0	82	79	9	62	70	7.7	1.73	.259
2012	Cardinals (GCL)	R	0	0	0.00	2	1	0	0	3	1	0	2	1	3.0	1.00	.167
	Palm Beach (FSL)	HiA	1	3	5.40	5	5	0	0	17	18	1	14	12	6.5	1.92	.273
Minor League Totals			7	6	5.15	28	27	0	0	101	98	10	78	83	7.4	1.74	.260

San Diego Padres

BY MATT EDDY

The Padres opened the 2012 season with a $55.2 million payroll, the lowest in the game. But Josh Byrnes, in his first year as the team's general manager, had every reason to expect in-season improvement as a young roster gained experience and San Diego's abundance of upper-level pitching prospects made their way to Petco Park.

After all, the Athletics followed a similar course all the way to a division crown over in the American League.

In fact, the Padres did improve in the second half, going 47-36 in the final three months of the season. But a miserable first half condemned them to their fourth second-division finish in the last five years. Worse, their on-the-cusp pitching prospects turned out to be on-the-shelf bystanders, with the four brightest plagued by arm injuries.

Righthanders Casey Kelly and Joe Wieland and lefties Robbie Erlin and Juan Oramas had pitched Double-A San Antonio to the Texas League title in 2011. San Diego hoped that quartet, following additional seasoning in Triple-A, would provide rotation support in the second half of 2012. Instead, Wieland and Oramas had Tommy John surgery in the summer, while lesser elbow injuries sidelined Kelly for three months and Erlin for nearly that long.

Even young big league pitchers weren't immune to the injury bug. Cory Luebke had Tommy John surgery, while Andrew Cashner, the key piece acquired in an offseason trade that sent young slugger Anthony Rizzo to the Cubs, missed half the season with a strained lat muscle.

Kelly recovered in time to make his big league debut on Aug. 27, throwing six scoreless innings against the Braves. He turned in only one more quality start in his next five turns, though he showed enough promise to rank No. 1 on this list.

Two other rookies, both acquired from the Reds in an offseason deal for Mat Latos, provided ample hope for the future. First baseman Yonder Alonso played 155 games, batted .273/.348/.393 and led all big league rookies with 39 doubles. He improved in the second half, swatting seven of nine homers to go with a .800 OPS from July 1 onward.

Catcher Yasmani Grandal homered from both sides of the plate for his first two big league hits on June 30 and batted .297/.394/.469 in 60 contests. Grandal won't be available to San Diego for the first 50 games of 2013, however. He must sit out after a drug test

Yonder Alonso's 39 doubles led all rookies, and he put up an .800 OPS in the second half

turned up elevated levels of testosterone.

While Alonso, Grandal and Kelly may form the core of the next successful Padres club, Chase Headley may be suiting up for another team by then. The 2005 second-rounder drew significant trade interest after he turned in a career year in 2012, swatting 31 homers and leading the National League with 115 RBIs.

For the second year in a row, San Diego invested $11 million in the draft. It dropped a combined $5 million on a pair of prep pitchers, Max Fried and Walker Weickel, one year after spending $5.75 million to sign another high school duo, righthander Joe Ross and catcher Austin Hedges.

Jaron Madison, the scouting director who ran both of those drafts, left in August to take the same job with the Cubs, following former Padres GM Jed Hoyer and vice president of scouting and player development Jason McLeod to Chicago. The Padres promoted national crosschecker Billy Gasparino to replace Madison.

Led by Hedges, Ross and other 2011 draft picks such as shortstop Jace Peterson and righthander Matt Wisler, low Class A Fort Wayne advanced to the Midwest League finals. But in terms of overall minor league winning percentage, only the Reds and Angels fared more poorly than the Padres (.455) last season.

THIS YEAR'S TOP 30

Player, Pos.		Grade
1.	Casey Kelly, rhp	55/Medium
2.	Max Fried, lhp	60/High
3.	Jedd Gyorko, 3b/2b	55/Medium
4.	Austin Hedges, c	60/High
5.	Rymer Liriano, of	55/High
6.	Matt Wisler, rhp	50/High
7.	Cory Spangenberg, 2b	50/High
8.	Joe Wieland, rhp	50/High
9.	Adys Portillo, rhp	50/High
10.	Robbie Erlin, lhp	50/High
11.	Jace Peterson, ss	50/High
12.	Walker Weickel, rhp	50/High
13.	Keyvius Sampson, rhp	50/High
14.	Joe Ross, rhp	55/Extreme
15.	Brad Boxberger, rhp	45/Low
16.	Zach Eflin, rhp	50/High
17.	Fernando Perez, 3b	50/High
18.	James Darnell, 3b/of	45/Medium
19.	Donn Roach, rhp	45/Medium
20.	Matt Andriese, rhp	50/High
21.	Travis Jankowski, of	50/High
22.	Burch Smith, rhp	50/High
23.	Jaff Decker, of	45/Medium
24.	Yeison Asencio, of	50/High
25.	Miles Mikolas, rhp	45/Medium
26.	Juan Oramas, lhp	50/High
27.	Matt Stites, rhp	45/Medium
28.	Mallex Smith, of	50/High
29.	Kevin Quackenbush, rhp	45/Medium
30.	Johnny Barbato, rhp	45/High

LAST YEAR'S TOP 30

Player, Pos.		Status
1.	Anthony Rizzo, 1b	(Cubs)
2.	Rymer Liriano, of	No. 5
3.	Casey Kelly, rhp	No. 1
4.	Cory Spangenberg, 2b	No. 7
5.	Austin Hedges, c	No. 4
6.	Jedd Gyorko, 3b	No. 3
7.	Joe Wieland, rhp	No. 8
8.	Robbie Erlin, lhp	No. 10
9.	Joe Ross, rhp	No. 14
10.	Keyvius Sampson, rhp	No. 13
11.	Jaff Decker, of	No. 23
12.	Juan Oramas, lhp	No. 26
13.	James Darnell, 3b/of	No. 18
14.	Simon Castro, rhp	(White Sox)
15.	Blake Tekotte, of	(White Sox)
16.	Miles Mikolas, rhp	No. 25
17.	Jace Peterson, ss	No. 11
18.	Reymond Fuentes, of	Dropped out
19.	Edinson Rincon, 3b	Dropped out
20.	Jason Hagerty, c	Dropped out
21.	Matt Lollis, rhp	Dropped out
22.	Donavan Tate, of	Dropped out
23.	Pedro Hernandez, lhp	(Twins)
24.	Jeudy Valdez, ss	Dropped out
25.	Jose DePaula, lhp	Dropped out
26.	Adys Portillo, rhp	No. 9
27.	Mike Kelly, rhp	Dropped out
28.	Anthony Bass, rhp	Majors
29.	Brad Brach, rhp	Majors
30.	Vince Belnome, 2b/1b	Dropped out

BEST TOOLS

Best Hitter for Average	Jedd Gyorko
Best Power Hitter	Rymer Liriano
Best Strike-Zone Discipline	Jaff Decker
Fastest Baserunner	Mallex Smith
Best Athlete	Brian Adams
Best Fastball	Adys Portillo
Best Curveball	Max Fried
Best Slider	Matt Wisler
Best Changeup	Keyvius Sampson
Best Control	Joe Wieland
Best Defensive Catcher	Austin Hedges
Best Defensive Infielder	Stephen Carmon
Best Infield Arm	Edinson Rincon
Best Defensive Outfielder	Rico Noel
Best Outfield Arm	Yeison Asencio

PROJECTED 2016 LINEUP

Catcher	Yasmani Grandal
First Base	Yonder Alonso
Second Base	Cory Spangenberg
Third Base	Chase Headley
Shortstop	Jace Peterson
Left Field	Jedd Gyorko
Center Field	Cameron Maybin
Right Field	Rymer Liriano
No. 1 Starter	Casey Kelly
No. 2 Starter	Max Fried
No. 3 Starter	Cory Luebke
No. 4 Starter	Matt Wisler
No. 5 Starter	Joe Wieland
Closer	Andrew Cashner

TOP PROSPECTS OF THE DECADE

Year	Player, Pos.	2012 Org.
2003	Xavier Nady, of	Giants
2004	Josh Barfield, 2b	Orioles
2005	Josh Barfield, 2b	Orioles
2006	Cesar Carrillo, rhp	Tigers
2007	Cedric Hunter, of	Cardinals
2008	Chase Headley, 3b	Padres
2009	Kyle Blanks, 1b	Padres
2010	Donavan Tate, of	Padres
2011	Casey Kelly, rhp	Padres
2012	Anthony Rizzo, 1b	Cubs

TOP DRAFT PICKS OF THE DECADE

Year	Player, Pos.	2012 Org.
2003	Tim Stauffer, rhp	Padres
2004	Matt Bush, ss	Rays
2005	Cesar Carrillo, rhp	Tigers
2006	Matt Antonelli, 3b	Yankees
2007	Nick Schmidt, lhp	Rockies
2008	Allan Dykstra, 1b	Mets
2009	Donavan Tate, of	Padres
2010	*Karsten Whitson, rhp	U. of Florida
2011	Cory Spangenberg, 2b	Padres
2012	Max Fried, lhp	Padres

*Did not sign.

LARGEST BONUSES IN CLUB HISTORY

Donavan Tate, 2009	$6,250,000
Matt Bush, 2004	$3,150,000
Austin Hedges, 2011	$3,000,000
Max Fried, 2012	$3,000,000
Joe Ross, 2011	$2,750,000

MINOR LEAGUE DEPTH CHART

SAN DIEGO PADRES

TOP 2013 ROOKIE: Casey Kelly, rhp. He has the stuff and the control to succeed, so all he needs is to command the ball better to halve his 6.21 ERA from 2012.

BREAKOUT PROSPECT: Fernando Perez, 3b. The Padres rave about the lefty hitter's rhythm and balance at the plate.

SLEEPER: Tayron Guerrero, rhp. The 6-foot-7 Colombian touched 100 mph in instructional league and does it easy.

SOURCE OF TOP 30 TALENT			
Homegrown	21	Acquired	9
College	9	Trades	5
Junior college	3	Rule 5 draft	0
High school	9	Independent leagues	0
Draft-and-follow	0	Free agents/waivers	0
Nondrafted free agents	0	International	4

LF
James Darnell (18)
Jeremy Baltz
Donavan Tate
Everett Williams
Luis Domoromo

CF
Travis Jankowski (21)
Mallex Smith (28)
Reymond Fuentes
Rico Noel
Alberth Martinez

RF
Rymer Liriano (5)
Jaff Decker (23)
Yeison Asencio (24)
Brian Adams

3B
Jedd Gyorko (3)
Fernando Perez (17)
Vince Belnome
Duanel Jones
Gabriel Quintana

SS
Jace Peterson (11)
Beamer Weems
Stephen Carmon

2B
Cory Spangenberg (7)
Jeudy Valdez
Jonathan Galvez
Jalen Goree
River Stevens
Maxx Tissenbaum

1B
Matt Clark
Edinson Rincon
Cody Decker
Lee Orr
Tommy Medica

C
Austin Hedges (4)
Jason Hagerty
Dane Phillips
Rodney Daal

LHP	
LHSP	**LHRP**
Max Fried (2)	Tommy Layne
Robbie Erlin (10)	Chris Nunn
Juan Oramas (26)	Drew Harrelson
Jose DePaula	Christian Miller
Frank Garces	Griffin Russell
Brandon Alger	

RHP	
RHSP	**RHRP**
Casey Kelly (1)	Adys Portillo (9)
Matt Wisler (6)	Brad Boxberger (15)
Joe Wieland (8)	Burch Smith (22)
Walker Weickel (12)	Miles Mikolas (25)
Keyvius Sampson (13)	Matt Stites (27)
Joe Ross (14)	Kevin Quackenbush (29)
Zach Eflin (16)	Johnny Barbato (30)
Donn Roach (19)	Genison Reyes
Matt Andriese (20)	Nick Vincent
Cody Hebner	Roman Madrid
Tayron Guerrero	Matt Lollis
Mike Kelly	Luis de la Cruz
Walker Lockett	James Needy
Justin Hancock	Cory Bostjancic
Colin Rea	Cam Stewart
	Corey Kimber

2012   BONUSES: $11.0 MILLION

BEST PURE HITTER: OF Travis Jankowski (1s) makes easy line-drive contact with his handsy swing. He batted .414 and led NCAA Division I with 110 hits in the spring, fueling Stony Brook's surprise run to the College World Series.

BEST POWER HITTER: OF Brian Adams (8) has plus raw power but is still figuring out how to unlock it after playing sparingly at Kentucky.

FASTEST RUNNER: The Padres loaded up on speed, starting with OF Mallex Smith (5), an 80 runner on the 20-80 scouting scale. Jankowski and Adams are 70 runners, while SS/2B Jalen Goree (6) grades as a 60.

BEST DEFENSIVE PLAYER: Jankowski is a potential Gold Glover in center, and Smith could become one with more refinement. SS Stephen Carmon (10) already ranks as the system's top infield defender.

BEST FASTBALL: RHP Cory Bostjancic (15) opened eyes by throwing 96-98 mph with heavy life during instructional league. LHP Max Fried (1) has more history and more aptitude with a quality fastball, operating in the low 90s and peaking at 96. RHPs Zach Eflin (1s) and Walker Weickel (1s) can run their heaters into the mid-90s.

BEST SECONDARY PITCH: Fried's downer curveball is a plus-plus pitch at its best. Eflin has an above-average changeup and RHP Roman Madrid (7) has a plus cutter/slider.

BEST PRO DEBUT: Madrid, who also owns a 91-94 mph fastball, had a short-season Northwest League-best 14 saves and 44 strikeouts in 37 innings. LHP Chris Nunn (24) joined him on the NWL all-star team after posting a 0.81 ERA and 49 whiffs in 33 innings. Nunn has a low-90s fastball but thrives more on the deception provided by his funky delivery.

BEST ATHLETE: Adams easily has the best strength among the Padres' speedsters. He also played wide receiver at Kentucky. LHP Terrance Owens (40) is a Toledo quarterback with the potential for an NFL career.

MOST INTRIGUING BACKGROUND: Owens hasn't played baseball since he was a high school freshman in 2006, but San Diego took a flier on him because it liked his athleticism and arm action. Fried and Lucas Giolito (Nationals) became the seventh pair of high school teammates selected in the first round of the same draft. C Chris O'Dowd's (23) father Dan is GM of the Rockies. LHP Kyle Ottoson (34) is a cousin of former Padres all-star Mark Loretta.

CLOSEST TO THE MAJORS: Madrid has the weapons to advance quickly as a reliever. Fried is exceptionally gifted for a high school lefthander and could speed through the minors in the same fashion as Cole Hamels and Clayton Kershaw.

BEST LATE-ROUND PICK: San Diego managed to sign six high school arms after the 10th round. The best may be athletic and projectable LHP Drew Harrelson (12), who has an 87-90 mph fastball and a promising curveball.

THE ONE WHO GOT AWAY: RHP Kevin McCanna (22) has solid stuff and lots of polish but couldn't be diverted from attending Rice.

ASSESSMENT: The Padres may have gotten the best pitcher in the draft with Fried with the seventh overall pick. They followed up with several arms and speedsters tailor-made for Petco Park.

2011   BONUSES: $11.0 MILLION

San Diego found plenty of depth, including five of its current top 15 prospects in 2B Cory Spangenberg (1), RHPs Joe Ross (1) and Matt Wisler (7), SS Jace Peterson (1s) and C Austin Hedges (2). Hedges makes up for the inability to sign C Brett Austin (1s).

GRADE: B+

2010   BONUSES: $4.3 MILLION

3B/2B Jedd Gyorko (2) is one of the better hitters in the entire minors, and since-waived LHP Josh Spence (9) was the second player from the 2010 draft to reach the majors. The Padres didn't get much else and couldn't sign RHP Karsten Whitson (1).

GRADE: C+

2009   BONUSES: $9.1 MILLION

OFs Donavan Tate (1), who landed a $6.25 million bonus, and Everett Williams (2) have been huge busts. That leaves RHPs Keyvious Sampson (4) and Miles Mikolas (5) as the cream of this crop. Mikolas joined the San Diego bullpen last summer.

GRADE: C+

2008   BONUSES: $5.4 MILLION

The Padres blew their top pick on since-traded 1B Allan Dykstra (1) but still selected seven big leaguers. That group includes starting 2B Logan Forsythe (1s), 3B/OF James Darnell (2) and RHPs Anthony Bass (5), Nick Vincent (18) and Brad Brach (29). OF Blake Tekotte (3) was traded this offseason, but the best player was the one who didn't sign—2B Jason Kipnis (4).

GRADE: C+

Draft analysis by Jim Callis. Numbers in parentheses indicate draft rounds.

1 CASEY KELLY, RHP

Born: Oct. 4, 1989. **B-T:** R-R. **Ht.:** 6-3. **Wt.:** 195.
Drafted: HS—Sarasota, Fla., 2008 (1st round).
Signed by: Anthony Turco (Red Sox).

BA GRADE
55
MEDIUM

BILL MITCHELL

When the Padres traded Adrian Gonzalez, their best player of the last decade, they received Kelly, Anthony Rizzo and outfielder Reymond Fuentes from the Red Sox in December 2010. San Diego subsequently turned Rizzo into Andrew Cashner and Fuentes has faded, leaving Kelly as the most prominent direct link to Gonzalez. Kelly entered pro ball as the 30th pick in the 2008 draft, the recipient of a Boston draft-record $3 million bonus. At the time he viewed himself as a shortstop, and though the Red Sox preferred him on the mound, they acceded to his wishes so he'd give up a football scholarship to play quarterback at Tennessee. But after hitting .219 over two seasons he committed to pitching full-time in 2010, zooming to Double-A as a 20-year-old and getting traded that offseason. Kelly hit the ground running with Triple-A Tucson in 2012, tallying 14 strikeouts, no walks and just three runs allowed through his first two starts—but that's when his elbow started barking. He missed three months as he recovered from a strained ligament. Once healthy, Kelly resumed his march to the majors and debuted with San Diego on Aug. 27, tossing six scoreless innings against the Braves.

The sinking action Kelly generates on his fastball enables it to play up as a plus offering, even at his typical velocity range of 90-92 mph. At its best, the pitch features plus armside run and veers away from the barrel of lefthanders. He'll bump his four-seam fastball up to 95 mph at times, but his sinker and ability to consistently locate down and to both corners remain his strongest attributes. In his six starts with San Diego, he generated grounders on nearly 56 percent of balls put into play against him—well above the major league average of 45 percent. Kelly throws his curveball with more power now than he did two years ago. He tops out near 80 mph and generating

SCOUTING GRADES

Fastball: 60.   **Control:** 60.
Curveball: 60.   **Command:** 55.
Changeup: 55.

Based on 20-80 scouting scale, where 50 represents major league average, and future projection rather than present tools.

12-to-6 break that induces awkward swings and misses, especially when he throws it as a chase pitch ahead in the count. He must develop consistency with his mid-80s changeup, but his clean, compact delivery and athleticism auger well for improvement. Scouts think the changeup could become above average because lefties swing right over the top of the best ones.

Kelly shined on occasion during his first tour of duty in the big leagues, but he still finished with a 6.21 ERA. He found the strike zone frequently enough, though his command appeared rusty at times, a byproduct of making just 11 non-rehab starts in 2012. He could grow into a No. 2 starter and should be a safe bet to be at least a No. 3. He has pitched just 41 innings above Double-A, so San Diego may give him more time at Tucson to begin 2013.

Year	Club (League)	Class	W	L	ERA	G	GS	CG	SV	IP	H	HR	BB	SO	K/9	WHIP	AVG
2009	Salem (CAR)	HiA	1	4	3.09	8	8	0	0	47	33	4	7	35	6.8	0.86	.196
	Greenville (SAL)	LoA	6	1	1.12	9	9	0	0	48	32	0	9	39	7.3	0.85	.184
2010	Portland (EL)	AA	3	5	5.31	21	21	0	0	95	118	10	35	81	7.7	1.61	.307
2011	San Antonio (TL)	AA	11	6	3.98	27	27	0	0	142	153	8	46	105	6.6	1.40	.278
2012	Tucson (PCL)	AAA	0	0	2.25	2	2	0	0	12	12	0	0	14	10.5	1.00	.261
	Padres (AZL)	R	0	1	4.00	3	3	0	0	9	10	0	0	7	7.0	1.11	.250
	San Antonio (TL)	AA	0	1	3.78	3	3	0	0	17	11	1	3	18	9.7	0.84	.190
	San Diego (NL)	MAJ	2	3	6.21	6	6	0	0	29	39	5	10	26	8.1	1.69	.322
Major League Totals			2	3	6.21	6	6	0	0	29	39	5	10	26	8.1	1.69	.322
Minor League Totals			21	18	3.77	73	73	0	0	370	369	23	100	299	7.3	1.27	.260

2 MAX FRIED, LHP

BA GRADE
60
HIGH

Born: Jan. 18, 1994. **B-T:** L-L. **Ht.:** 6-4. **Wt.:** 185. **Drafted:** HS—Studio City, Calif., 2012 (1st round). **Signed by:** Brent Mayne.

Fried transferred to the Harvard-Westlake School for his 2012 senior season when his previous high school eliminated its athletic program. There he teamed briefly with righty Lucas Giolito before a strained elbow ligament sidelined Giolito in March. Regardless, Fried (seventh overall) and Giolito (16th, Nationals) became the seventh pair of prep teammates selected in the first round of the same draft. Fried gave up a UCLA commitment for $3 million. Fried's arm action, projectable frame and steady 90-94 mph fastball from the left side would have made him a first-round pick. The quality of his breaking ball coupled with his athleticism and work ethic made him the top high school pitcher in his draft class, a Clayton Kershaw with less power or a Tyler Skaggs with firmer stuff. The Padres have clocked Fried as high as 96 mph, but they're equally impressed with his ability to two-seam his fastball at 90-91 and command it to his arm side. His curveball sits in the mid-70s now with top-to-bottom spin and plus depth, and scouts expect plus-plus grades and steady high-70s readings down the line. Like most prep pitchers, he has the least feel for his changeup, though he already gets average separation from his fastball. Improving his changeup and stamina will be focal points for Fried as he embarks on his first full pro season, probably with low Class A Fort Wayne.

Year	Club (League)	Class	W	L	ERA	G	GS	CG	SV	IP	H	HR	BB	SO	K/9	WHIP	AVG
2012	Padres (AZL)	R	0	1	3.57	10	9	0	0	18	14	1	6	17	8.7	1.13	.215
Minor League Totals			0	1	3.57	10	9	0	0	18	14	1	6	17	8.7	1.13	.215

3 JEDD GYORKO, 3B/2B

BA GRADE
55
MEDIUM

Born: Sept. 23, 1988. **B-T:** R-R. **Ht.:** 5-10. **Wt.:** 195. **Drafted:** West Virginia, 2010 (2nd round). **Signed by:** Andrew Salvo.

The top draft pick (second round) signed by the Padres in 2010, Gyorko has developed into one of the top performance prospects in the minors. He led the minors with 192 hits and ranked second with 114 RBIs in 2011. and for an encore, he blasted 30 homers (fourth in the minors) and drove in 100 runs while spending most of 2012 in Triple-A. Most everybody agrees that Gyorko will hit for average in the big leagues, perhaps .300 in his best seasons, with his short righty stroke and plate discipline. Barrel awareness and the ability to hit the ball where he wants makes him especially dangerous as a situational hitter. He has solid power and ought to be good for 40 doubles in Petco Park's spacious outfield. A below-average runner with poor lateral range, Gyorko has sufficient footwork, hands and arm strength to play a solid third base. He's more athletic than his stocky body suggests, and he played capably at second base in 47 games there last year. He may begin 2013 in Triple-A, but Gyorko will be up as soon as San Diego can give him regular at-bats.

Year	Club (League)	Class	AVG	G	AB	R	H	2B	3B	HR	RBI	BB	SO	SB	CS	OBP	SLG
2010	Eugene (NWL)	SS	.330	26	106	16	35	6	0	5	18	9	26	1	1	.383	.528
	Fort Wayne (MWL)	LoA	.284	42	162	19	46	11	0	2	23	19	31	1	0	.366	.389
2011	Lake Elsinore (CAL)	HiA	.365	81	340	78	124	35	2	18	74	38	64	11	3	.429	.638
	San Antonio (TL)	AA	.288	59	236	41	68	12	0	7	40	26	50	1	0	.358	.428
2012	San Antonio (TL)	AA	.262	34	130	18	34	4	0	6	17	17	27	1	1	.356	.431
	Tucson (PCL)	AAA	.328	92	369	62	121	24	0	24	83	34	68	4	3	.380	.588
Minor League Totals			.319	334	1343	234	428	92	2	62	255	143	266	19	8	.385	.529

4 AUSTIN HEDGES, C

BA GRADE
60
HIGH

Born: Aug. 18, 1992. **B-T:** R-R. **Ht.:** 6-1. **Wt.:** 190. **Drafted:** HS—San Juan Capistrano, Calif., 2011 (2nd round). **Signed by:** Josh Emmerick.

No Padres 2011 draft pick received a higher bonus than Hedges, who signed for $3 million as a second-rounder. High school catchers are notoriously risky picks, but amateur scouts had few reservations about his defensive potential. Pro scouts joined the chorus of supporters based on his all-around showing as a teenager in low Class A in 2012. Hedges shows remarkable arm strength and accuracy for a young catcher. He gunned down 32 percent of Midwest League basestealers, showing consistent off-the-charts pop times of 1.85 seconds. He has soft hands and solid blocking technique, and he successfully worked to eliminate excess movement in his setup and in his throwing motion during the season. Hedges lines the ball to all fields and projects to hit for average with a compact swing and discerning eye. His power has come as advertised, and he could hit 15 or more homers annually based on his frequency of hard contact and loft in his swing. He has below-average speed but runs the bases aggressively. Given that the Padres have Yasmani Grandal and Nick Hundley in the big leagues, they can afford to be patient with Hedges. He still shouldn't require much more than two full seasons in the minors, and they wouldn't be surprised if he finished 2013 in Double-A.

Year	Club (League)	Class	AVG	G	AB	R	H	2B	3B	HR	RBI	BB	SO	SB	CS	OBP	SLG
2011	Padres (AZL)	R	.313	5	16	3	5	0	0	1	4	5	1	1	0	.500	.500
	Eugene (NWL)	SS	.100	4	10	0	1	1	0	0	0	2	3	0	0	.250	.200
2012	Fort Wayne (MWL)	LoA	.279	96	337	44	94	28	0	10	56	23	62	14	9	.334	.451
Minor League Totals			.275	105	363	47	100	29	0	11	60	30	66	15	9	.341	.446

5 RYMER LIRIANO, OF

Born: June 20, 1991. **B-T:** R-R. **Ht.:** 6-0. **Wt.:** 210. **Signed:** Dominican Republic, 2007. **Signed by:** Randy Smith/Felix Francisco.

BA GRADE
55
HIGH

Liriano took another step toward San Diego in his fifth season since signing for $300,000 as a 16-year-old out of the Dominican Republic. He mastered high Class A—following an aborted assignment there in 2011—and reached Double-A for first time, where he hit .322/.408/.444 over his final 26 games. He shined in the Arizona Fall League, batting .319/.376/.505. Built like a running back, Liriano features a similar explosiveness to his game. He showcases all five tools at various points, highlighted by plus power, arm strength and range in right field. While he hasn't topped 12 homers in any one season, he can take the ball out to any part of the park. His contact rate ultimately will dictate whether his power plays as plus or merely average. Distant left-center power alleys in high Class A Lake Elsinore forced Liriano to use the middle of the field in 2012, which coupled with a more discerning eye made him a better hitter. He's not immune to chasing pitches out of the zone when he falls behind in the count, however. A solid runner, he swiped 32 bases in 2012 after registering 66 the year before, and those totals will continue to dwindle as he fills out. Liriano has 20-20 potential if he puts everything together. The Padres are counting on their upper-level corner prospects, such as Liriano and Jedd Gyorko, because the cost of acquiring established run producers is prohibitive.

Year	Club (League)	Class	AVG	G	AB	R	H	2B	3B	HR	RBI	BB	SO	SB	CS	OBP	SLG
2008	Padres (DSL)	R	.198	67	232	34	46	13	1	9	37	28	106	9	5	.296	.379
2009	Padres (AZL)	R	.350	50	197	44	69	8	1	8	44	15	52	14	5	.398	.523
2010	Fort Wayne (MWL)	LoA	.191	50	188	21	36	11	1	2	20	10	54	11	6	.234	.293
	Eugene (NWL)	SS	.271	53	203	35	55	13	6	0	12	17	53	17	7	.335	.394
	Lake Elsinore (CAL)	HiA	.220	14	50	3	11	2	0	1	6	5	12	3	0	.291	.320
2011	Lake Elsinore (CAL)	HiA	.127	15	55	8	7	1	1	0	6	6	13	1	1	.213	.182
	Fort Wayne (MWL)	LoA	.319	116	455	81	145	30	8	12	62	47	95	65	20	.383	.499
2012	Lake Elsinore (CAL)	HiA	.298	74	282	41	84	22	2	5	41	21	69	22	7	.360	.443
	San Antonio (TL)	AA	.251	53	183	24	46	10	2	3	20	20	50	10	1	.335	.377
Minor League Totals			.270	492	1845	291	499	110	22	40	248	169	504	152	52	.338	.419

6 MATT WISLER, RHP

Born: Sept. 12, 1992. **B-T:** R-R. **Ht.:** 6-3. **Wt.:** 175. **Drafted:** HS—Bryan, Ohio, 2011 (7th round). **Signed by:** Mark Conner.

BA GRADE
50
HIGH

Ohio's top high school prospect in the 2011 draft, Wisler lasted until the seventh round because of a strong commitment to Ohio State. The Padres persuaded him to sign for $500,000 bonus, believing he'd regain his stuff after he tailed off as a senior. He did just that in 2012, wowing Midwest League observers with premium velocity and a hammer curveball. Wisler pitches with a 91-93 mph fastball that tops out at 96 with heavy sink down in the zone, while showing a feel for when to deploy two strong secondary offerings. He found the zone more often as the year progressed with both a 75-79 mph curveball and a low-80s, fading changeup that he sells with solid arm speed. Wisler's athleticism and clean arm action help him command both pitches, and he completely owned Midwest League righties, notching 71 strikeouts against five walks in 242 plate appearances. He led the minors in home run rate (one in 114 innings), a testament to his skill at working down in the zone. Wisler's stuff could make him a mid-rotation starter or better, and the Padres are equally excited about his command and work ethic. He'll need both to survive the rigors of the California League in 2013.

Year	Club (League)	Class	W	L	ERA	G	GS	CG	SV	IP	H	HR	BB	SO	K/9	WHIP	AVG
2011	Padres (AZL)	R	0	0	--	1	0	0	0	0	2	0	2	0	--	--	1.000
2012	Fort Wayne (MWL)	LoA	5	4	2.53	24	23	1	0	114	95	1	28	113	8.9	1.08	.227
Minor League Totals			5	4	2.84	25	23	1	0	114	97	1	30	113	8.9	1.11	.231

7 CORY SPANGENBERG, 2B

Born: March 16, 1991. **B-T:** L-R. **Ht.:** 6-0. **Wt.:** 185. **Drafted:** Indian River (Fla.) JC, 2011 (1st round). **Signed by:** Willie Bosque.

The 10th overall pick in the 2011 draft, Spangenberg signed quickly for $1.863 million and ranked as the top position prospect in the short-season Northwest League before zooming to low Class A Fort Wayne, where he hit .381 that August. He broke camp with Lake Elsinore in 2012 and made the California League all-star team, but he suffered a concussion right after the break when struck in the head by a ball during practice. He hit his head on the ground diving for a ball in his first game back, wound up missing six weeks and batted just .224/.303/.267 in the second half. Spangenberg's double-plus speed, bunting skill and ability to use all fields make him difficult to defend. He gets down the first-base line in four seconds flat and can hit the ball hard in different parts of the zone, though he'll need to soften his stride to barrel offspeed pitches more frequently. His swing won't translate into many homers, but he could hit his share of doubles while adding 30-40 extra bases via steals. His raw speed and quick first step give him plus range around the keystone, though he still appears rigid when backhanding balls and charging grounders. Spangenberg hit .345 and recovered some of his timing in a brief Arizona Fall League stint, so the Padres have him penciled in for Double-A San Antonio this year. If Jedd Gyorko can't stick at second base, Spangenberg could man the position for San Diego by mid-2014.

BA GRADE

50

HIGH

Year	Club (League)	Class	AVG	G	AB	R	H	2B	3B	HR	RBI	BB	SO	SB	CS	OBP	SLG
2011	Eugene (NWL)	SS	.384	25	86	20	33	10	0	1	20	31	15	10	4	.545	.535
	Fort Wayne (MWL)	LoA	.286	47	189	35	54	7	1	2	24	14	42	15	4	.345	.365
2012	Lake Elsinore (CAL)	HiA	.271	98	384	53	104	12	8	1	40	26	72	27	9	.324	.352
Minor League Totals			.290	170	659	108	191	29	9	4	84	71	129	52	17	.365	.379

8 JOE WIELAND, RHP

Born: Jan. 21, 1990. **B-T:** R-R. **Ht.:** 6-3. **Wt.:** 195. **Drafted:** HS—Reno, Nev., 2008 (4th round). **Signed by:** Butch Metzger (Rangers).

The Padres' trades of Adrian Gonzalez and Mat Latos yielded prospects such as Casey Kelly and Yonder Alonso, but the July 2011 swap that sent reliever Mike Adams to the Rangers could provide the greatest quantity of innings. But that's only if Wieland and lefty Robbie Erlin can regain their form after suffering elbow injuries in 2012. Wieland made his big league debut on April 14 but made just five stats for San Diego before straining an elbow ligament. He unsuccessfully tried to rehab the injury before submitting to Tommy John surgery in late July. Wieland doesn't light up radar guns, but his stuff worked against big leaguers because he has plus command. He relies on precise location of a 90-91 mph fastball that peaks at 94 with late life. He uses his fastball to set up a big-breaking curveball that touches 80 mph and a low-80s changeup that sinks and fades. He threw more sliders in 2012 because they're easier to get over the plate than his curve, and it's a solid fourth offering. The Padres won't have Wieland back in game action until the second half of 2013. If he makes a full recovery, he's a strong No. 4 starter candidate who might pitch like a No. 3 in Petco Park.

BA GRADE

50

HIGH

Year	Club (League)	Class	W	L	ERA	G	GS	CG	SV	IP	H	HR	BB	SO	K/9	WHIP	AVG
2008	Rangers (AZL)	R	5	1	1.44	13	7	0	0	44	32	2	8	41	8.5	0.92	.200
2009	Hickory (SAL)	LoA	4	6	5.31	19	18	0	0	83	102	7	24	73	7.9	1.52	.299
2010	Hickory (SAL)	LoA	7	4	3.34	15	15	2	0	89	84	4	15	71	7.2	1.11	.251
	Bakersfield (CAL)	HiA	4	3	5.19	11	10	0	0	59	67	6	10	62	9.5	1.31	.283
2011	Myrtle Beach (CAR)	HiA	6	3	2.10	14	13	1	0	86	78	7	4	96	10.1	0.96	.240
	Frisco (TL)	AA	4	0	1.23	7	7	1	0	44	35	2	11	36	7.4	1.05	.217
	San Antonio (TL)	AA	3	1	2.77	5	5	0	0	26	23	0	6	18	6.2	1.12	.240
2012	Tucson (PCL)	AAA	0	1	3.52	2	2	0	0	8	10	0	2	11	12.9	1.57	.313
	San Diego (NL)	MAJ	0	4	4.55	5	5	0	0	28	26	5	9	24	7.8	1.27	.245
Major League Totals			0	4	4.55	5	5	0	0	28	26	5	9	24	7.8	1.27	.245
Minor League Totals			33	19	3.29	86	77	4	0	438	431	28	80	408	8.4	1.17	.255

9 ADYS PORTILLO, RHP

Born: Dec. 21, 1991. **B-T:** R-R. **Ht.:** 6-2. **Wt.:** 240. **Signed:** Venezuela, 2008. **Signed by:** Yfrain Linares/Felix Feliz/Randy Smith.

Four years after signing out of Venezuela for $2 million in 2008, Portillo finally had sustained success. While repeating low Class A, he slashed his walk rate (4.4 per nine innings, compared to 6.0 in 2011) and increased his pitch efficiency without sacrificing velocity. The Padres promoted him to Double-A in late July and added him to the 40-man roster in November. Portillo has added more than 50 pounds to his 6-foot-2 frame since signing—mostly filling out his lower half—and now sits at 94-96 mph while touching 99 with heavy life. The quality of his breaking ball improved dramatically after he applied tweaks to his delivery in 2011 instructional league. He now stresses balance over the rubber and a quicker tempo between pitches, resulting in a more consistent arm slot. Where once he threw a traditional curveball, he learned a slider grip that he has modified to a 77-79 mph slurve. His firm mid-80s changeup features plus life when he stays on top of it. A long arm action complicates the matter of control. Portillo made big strides in 2012, though he needs to be more stingy with free passes and improve his changeup to guarantee a future in the rotation. He has a fallback option as a late-game reliever if those things don't happen. He'll open 2013 in San Antonio's rotation.

BA GRADE
50
HIGH

Year	Club (League)	Class	W	L	ERA	G	GS	CG	SV	IP	H	HR	BB	SO	K/9	WHIP	AVG
2009	Padres (AZL)	R	1	9	5.13	13	12	0	0	53	67	2	28	44	7.5	1.80	.321
2010	Eugene (NWL)	SS	2	6	4.79	14	14	0	0	62	55	2	40	62	9.0	1.53	.241
	Fort Wayne (MWL)	LoA	0	0	4.50	1	0	0	0	2	2	1	1	1	4.5	1.50	.286
2011	Fort Wayne (MWL)	LoA	3	11	7.11	23	20	0	0	82	89	10	55	97	10.6	1.75	.278
2012	Fort Wayne (MWL)	LoA	6	6	1.87	18	18	0	0	92	54	3	45	81	8.0	1.08	.169
	San Antonio (TL)	AA	2	5	7.20	8	8	0	0	35	34	4	25	26	6.7	1.69	.250
Minor League Totals			14	37	4.86	77	72	0	0	326	301	22	194	311	8.6	1.52	.247

10 ROBBIE ERLIN, LHP

Born: Oct. 8, 1990. **B-T:** L-L. **Ht.:** 5-11. **Wt.:** 190. **Drafted:** HS—Scotts Valley, Calif., 2009 (3rd round). **Signed by:** Butch Metzger (Rangers).

Just like fellow Top 10 Prospects Casey Kelly and Joe Wieland, Erlin missed a significant chunk of 2012 with an elbow injury. In his case, he lost three months to elbow tendinitis. If healthy, all three pitchers would have spent the majority of the season in the San Diego rotation. He joined the organization in July 2011 along with Wieland in the trade that sent Mike Adams to the Rangers. Erlin is almost a smaller, lefthanded version of Wieland. Erlin similarly emphasizes feel over raw stuff. He sits at 88-90 mph, tops out at 92 and commands his fastball to both sides of the plate. That sets up a quality curveball and a fading changeup that averages more than 10 mph of separation from his heater. Erlin fully trusts his low-70s downer curve, throwing it in any count and buckling knees when batters aren't expecting it. Since reaching Double-A, he has begun mixing in a low-80s cutter/slider and a two-seamer to give righties something else to worry about. Just like Kelly and Wieland, he's almost around the zone too much, leaving him susceptible to homers. Erlin got back on track in the Arizona Fall League, recording a 2.28 ERA in seven starts and finishing second with 31 strikeouts in 24 innings. Like any Padres pitching prospect, he stands to benefit from pitching half his games in Petco Park, though he'd profile as a No. 4 starter ready to contribute in 2013 in any organization.

BA GRADE
50
HIGH

Year	Club (League)	Class	W	L	ERA	G	GS	CG	SV	IP	H	HR	BB	SO	K/9	WHIP	AVG
2009	Rangers (AZL)	R	0	0	2.25	3	0	0	0	4	5	0	1	9	20.3	1.50	.294
2010	Hickory (SAL)	LoA	6	3	2.12	28	17	0	1	115	89	6	17	125	9.8	0.92	.213
2011	Myrtle Beach (CAR)	HiA	3	2	2.14	9	9	0	0	55	25	7	5	62	10.2	0.55	.132
	Frisco (TL)	AA	5	2	4.32	11	10	0	0	67	73	9	7	61	8.2	1.20	.282
	San Antonio (TL)	AA	1	0	1.38	6	6	0	0	26	26	2	4	31	10.7	1.15	.265
2012	Padres (AZL)	R	0	2	2.16	3	3	0	0	8	7	0	2	8	8.6	1.08	.206
	San Antonio (TL)	AA	3	1	2.92	11	11	0	0	52	53	6	14	72	12.4	1.28	.255
Minor League Totals			18	10	2.64	71	56	0	1	327	278	33	50	368	10.1	1.00	.227

11 JACE PETERSON, SS

BA GRADE
50
HIGH

Born: May 9, 1990. **B-T:** L-R. **Ht.:** 6-0. **Wt.:** 200. **Drafted:** McNeese State, 2011 (1st round supplemental). **Signed by:** Kevin Ellis.

Peterson starred as a cornerback on the McNeese State football team when he wasn't putting his plus athleticism to use on the diamond. He hit .335 as a junior and set a school record with 78 career stolen bases, indicating that his future was in baseball. Despite his two-sport background, Peterson's baseball skills are refined. No one tool elevates him above the field, though he has no glaring weakness either. A lefthanded hitter, Peterson makes steady line-drive contact (particularly versus righties) and has led his two minor league teams in walks, brandishing a career walk-to-whiff ratio of nearly 1-to-1. He won't hit many homers, but that's not his game. Though he's only a tick above-average runner by the stopwatch, Peterson's base-stealing savvy and ability to get good jumps enabled him to swipe 51 bases (in 64 tries) to finish second in the Midwest League last year. His range and first-step quickness are average, but he positions himself well and rarely botches routine plays. He has fringy arm strength now, but the Padres believe he will improve his accuracy and carry by keeping his elbow up and by continuing his long-toss program. San Diego has used Rule 5 pick Everth Cabrera, utilityman Jerry Hairston Jr. and veteran Jason Bartlett as regular shortstops since Khalil Greene left town after the 2008 season, but Peterson could one day add stability to the position.

Year	Club (League)	Class	AVG	G	AB	R	H	2B	3B	HR	RBI	BB	SO	SB	CS	OBP	SLG
2011	Eugene (NWL)	SS	.243	73	276	48	67	9	5	2	27	50	53	39	10	.360	.333
2012	Fort Wayne (MWL)	LoA	.286	117	444	78	127	23	9	2	48	62	63	51	13	.378	.392
Minor League Totals			.269	190	720	126	194	32	14	4	75	112	116	90	23	.371	.369

12 WALKER WEICKEL, RHP

BA GRADE
50
HIGH

Born: Nov. 14, 1993. **B-T:** R-R. **Ht.:** 6-6. **Wt.:** 195. **Drafted:** HS—Orlando, 2012 (1st round supplemental). **Signed by:** Willie Bosque.

Weickel grew nearly two inches to 6-foot-6 between his junior and senior years of high school, evoking body comparisons with a young Adam Wainwright with his tall, lean, broad-shouldered build. His velocity backed up in the spring leading up to the draft, throwing some teams off his scent, but the Padres were excited to land him with the 55th overall pick, signing him for $2 million. San Diego believes Weickel's downturn in stuff can be attributed to a lack of body control as he learned to pitch with additional height. They love his arm action, delivery and heavy sinking fastball that ranges from 90-93 mph and bumps 95. He can spin a breaking ball, but he'll need to add power to his low-70s curveball, and throw his changeup more often to improve his feel for the pitch. Scouts who like Weickel project his fastball, curve and changeup to be average or better, with his feel for pitching serving as separators that could make him a mid-rotation starter.

Year	Club (League)	Class	W	L	ERA	G	GS	CG	SV	IP	H	HR	BB	SO	K/9	WHIP	AVG
2012	Padres (AZL)	R	1	3	4.50	9	6	0	0	14	16	0	6	12	7.7	1.57	.262
Minor League Totals			1	3	4.50	9	6	0	0	14	16	0	6	12	7.7	1.57	.262

13 KEYVIUS SAMPSON, RHP

BA GRADE
50
HIGH

Born: Jan. 6, 1991. **B-T:** R-R. **Ht.:** 6-0. **Wt.:** 185. **Drafted:** HS—Ocala, Fla., 2009 (4th round). **Signed by:** Rob Sidwell.

Sampson's early-career elbow and shoulder trouble seem like a thing of the past after he made at least 24 starts and averaged 120 innings over the past two seasons. He stifled low Class A Midwest League competition in 2011, finishing second in the league with a .192 opponent average and third with 143 strikeouts, and jumped to Double-A to open the 2012 season. He continued to miss bats in the Texas League, leading the loop with 122 strikeouts but also ranking fourth with 57 walks. Sampson throws a pair of present major league average pitches that could develop into consistent plusses down the line. He throws his fastball at 90-93 mph and tops out near 95 with late running action. His changeup arrives from the same arm slot and speed as the fastball, inducing opponents to swing over the top of it or beat it into the ground. His low-70s curveball continues to lack the consistent break or precise location that would make him a frontline starter. In fact, he struck out nearly twice as many lefthanders (29 percent) as righties (18 percent) last year, relying on his deceptive changeup. A lack of consistent fastball command also holds him back, and while he has a big league arm, Sampson may fit best at the back of the rotation or in the bullpen.

Year	Club (League)	Class	W	L	ERA	G	GS	CG	SV	IP	H	HR	BB	SO	K/9	WHIP	AVG
2009	Padres (AZL)	R	0	0	3.00	2	1	0	0	3	1	0	0	3	9.0	0.33	.111
	Eugene (NWL)	SS	0	0	3.60	2	1	0	0	5	3	0	3	5	9.0	1.20	.176
2010	Eugene (NWL)	SS	3	3	3.56	10	10	0	0	43	35	4	17	58	12.1	1.21	.226
2011	Fort Wayne (MWL)	LoA	12	3	2.90	24	24	0	0	118	81	8	49	143	10.9	1.10	.192
2012	San Antonio (TL)	AA	8	11	5.00	26	25	0	0	122	108	11	57	122	9.0	1.35	.233
Minor League Totals			23	17	3.89	64	61	0	0	291	228	23	126	331	10.2	1.22	.214

14 JOE ROSS, RHP

BA GRADE
55
EXTREME

Born: May 21, 1993. **B-T:** R-R. **Ht.:** 6-3. **Wt.:** 185. **Drafted:** HS—Oakland, 2011 (1st round). **Signed by:** Noah Jackson.

Both Ross and catcher Austin Hedges, a pair of 2011 high school draft picks with minimal pro experience, made the Fort Wayne roster out of spring training. Ross, who signed for $2.75 million as the 25th overall pick, came down with shoulder tendinitis in early May that the Padres treated with extreme caution, holding him out of action until July 25, when he debuted with short-season

Eugene. His older brother Tyson spent parts of three seasons in the big leagues with the Athletics from 2010-12, then got traded to San Diego in November. The Padres have procured a rotation's worth of tall, projectable high school righties in the past two drafts—Ross, Matt Wisler, Walker Weickel, Zach Eflin and Mike Kelly—but Ross might have more arm strength than any of them. He pitches at 92-93 mph and bumps his heater up to 96 with riding life when he needs it, though he's still learning his delivery and tends to scatter the zone. Likewise, his slider features good tilt at times, and though his command wavers, he'll throw it in any count. Ross throws a decent changeup in bullpen sessions, but it has too much velocity in games, about 85 mph. The Padres appreciate Ross' easygoing nature because he doesn't get too high or too low, but they'd like to see him on the mound more often in 2013, when he'll take another crack at low Class A.

Year	Club (League)	Class	W	L	ERA	G	GS	CG	SV	IP	H	HR	BB	SO	K/9	WHIP	AVG
2011	Padres (AZL)	R	0	0	0.00	1	0	0	0	1	2	0	0	0	0.0	2.00	.400
2012	Fort Wayne (MWL)	LoA	0	2	6.26	6	6	0	0	27	33	2	11	27	8.9	1.61	.297
	Padres (AZL)	R	0	0	13.50	1	1	0	0	1	2	0	2	1	13.5	6.00	.500
	Eugene (NWL)	SS	0	2	2.03	8	8	0	0	27	16	1	9	28	9.5	0.94	.178
Minor League Totals			0	4	4.20	16	15	0	0	56	53	3	22	56	9.1	1.35	.252

15 BRAD BOXBERGER, RHP

BA GRADE
45
LOW

Born: May 27, 1988. **B-T:** R-R. **Ht.:** 6-2. **Wt.:** 200. **Drafted:** Southern California, 2009 (1st round supplemental). **Signed by:** Rex de la Nuez (Reds).

The third prospect acquired by the Padres from the Reds—along with Yonder Alonso and Yasmani Grandal—in the trade that sent Mat Latos to Cincinnati before the 2012 season, Boxberger served three tours of duty in San Diego in 2012, each one more successful than the last. During his September callup, he fanned 13 in 12 innings, while allowing five walks and a .150 opponent average. As a Reds farmhand, Boxberger learned the virtue of not overthrowing and maintaining a consistent arm slot, but the lesson seemed to take only after initial struggles at a new level of competition. San Diego hopes history repeats for Boxberger, who struck out 10.7 batters per nine innings but also walked 5.9 per nine as a major league rookie. He uses a 91-93 mph fastball that features sharp cutting action and tops out near 95, and he favors a changeup almost to the exclusion of an average slider. The change of pace generates the highest percentage of swings and misses, but the Padres would like to see Boxberger incorporate his slider more frequently and continue to pitch as aggressively as he did in September, when he went right after batters with his fastball. If he can keep the baserunners in check, he can be an important part of San Diego's bullpen because he has strikeout stuff.

Year	Club (League)	Class	W	L	ERA	G	GS	CG	SV	IP	H	HR	BB	SO	K/9	WHIP	AVG
2010	Lynchburg (CAR)	HiA	4	6	3.19	14	13	0	0	62	57	3	20	70	10.2	1.24	.249
	Carolina (SL)	AA	1	4	8.49	22	0	0	0	30	35	4	22	40	12.1	1.92	.289
2011	Carolina (SL)	AA	1	2	1.31	30	0	0	4	34	16	2	13	57	14.9	0.84	.139
	Louisville (IL)	AAA	1	2	2.93	25	0	0	7	28	16	2	15	36	11.7	1.12	.167
2012	Tucson (PCL)	AAA	2	2	2.70	37	0	0	5	43	37	0	19	62	12.9	1.29	.233
	San Diego (NL)	MAJ	0	0	2.60	24	0	0	0	28	22	3	18	33	10.7	1.45	.222
Major League Totals			0	0	2.60	24	0	0	0	28	22	3	18	33	10.7	1.45	.222
Minor League Totals			9	16	3.52	128	13	0	16	197	161	11	89	265	12.1	1.27	.224

16 ZACH EFLIN, RHP

BA GRADE
50
HIGH

Born: April 8, 1994. **B-T:** R-R. **Ht.:** 6-4. **Wt.:** 200. **Drafted:** HS—Oviedo, Fla., 2012 (1st round supplemental). **Signed by:** Willie Bosque.

Eflin did not pitch last April due to triceps tendinitis, and if not for the injury he might have been a first-round pick. Still, he went 33rd overall to the Padres as the second pick in the sandwich round and came to terms for $1.2 million, eschewing a Central Florida commitment. He made four appearances in the Rookie-level Arizona League, going through the lineup roughly once, but he didn't pitch after July 14 after contracting mononucleosis. A strapping 6-foot-4 righty, Eflin bumped 96 mph as an amateur and showed consistent solid velocity after signing. He throws strikes while pitching at 92, though San Diego loves his arm action and repeatable delivery, believing he could sit a tick higher once he adjusts to a pro routine. He had one of the best changeups in last year's prep ranks, sitting at 80-82 mph with late, biting action that causes the pitch to bottom out as it reaches the plate. He doesn't throw a breaking ball with the same consistency, and his slurvy curveball has average shape. Some scouts project the curve to be average to a tick above. An MRI on Eflin's elbow last spring revealed no damage, so he could represent a significant draft bargain if he regains the form he showed in late 2011 and early 2012. The Padres see a mid-rotation workhorse based on his big frame and potential for at least solid stuff across the board.

Year	Club (League)	Class	W	L	ERA	G	GS	CG	SV	IP	H	HR	BB	SO	K/9	WHIP	AVG
2012	Padres (AZL)	R	0	1	7.71	4	3	0	0	7	9	0	3	4	5.1	1.71	.300
Minor League Totals			0	1	7.71	4	3	0	0	7	9	0	3	4	5.1	1.71	.300

17 FERNANDO PEREZ, 3B

BA GRADE
50
HIGH

Born: Sept. 13, 1993. **B-T:** L-R. **Ht.:** 6-2. **Wt.:** 190. **Drafted:** Central Arizona JC, 2012 (3rd round). **Signed by:** Dave Lottsfeldt.

Born in Mexico, Perez moved to the United States in 2010 to live with his uncle and play for Otay Ranch High in Chula Vista, Calif. He had enough credits to graduate a year early, so he moved on to Central Arizona JC in 2012, batting a loud .338/.399/.571 with wood bats as the equivalent of a high school senior. The Padres were thrilled to land Perez with a third-round pick last June and sign him for $400,000, citing the advanced timing and balance of his lefthanded swing as reasons for their excitement. He drives the ball to all fields, slugging five extra-base hits in 14 games in the Arizona League, despite playing through a wrist injury that required surgery and knocked him out of instructional league. Perez could grow to be an above-average hitter with solid power output. His defensive home is a bigger question than his bat because his thick lower half and below-average speed probably mean he'll lack the agility to play second base. His arm is strong and his hands soft, so third base could be his long-term home. Some in the organization believe Perez has the best pure hitting stroke in the system, which ought to allow him to produce in low Class A in 2013.

Year	Club (League)	Class	AVG	G	AB	R	H	2B	3B	HR	RBI	BB	SO	SB	CS	OBP	SLG
2012	Padres (AZL)	R	.273	14	55	6	15	2	1	2	16	2	17	1	0	.298	.455
Minor League Totals			.273	14	55	6	15	2	1	2	16	2	17	1	0	.298	.455

18 JAMES DARNELL, 3B/OF

BA GRADE
45
MEDIUM

Born: Jan. 19, 1987. **B-T:** R-R. **Ht.:** 6-2. **Wt.:** 195. **Drafted:** South Carolina, 2008 (2nd round). **Signed by:** Anthony Byrd.

While 2008 draft picks such as second baseman Logan Forsythe (sandwich round), righthander Anthony Bass (fifth) and relievers Nick Vincent (18th) and Brad Brach (42nd) carved out playing time in San Diego, Darnell (second) spent the final four months of 2012 on the big league disabled list. He parlayed a huge half-season in Double-A in 2011 into a September callup that year, then returned to San Diego last May, only to leave his seventh game after injuring his shoulder while diving for a ball in left field. Darnell has had two surgeries in two years on his left shoulder, an arthroscopic procedure to stabilize a strain in 2011 and then another surgery last August to repair a partial dislocation. Despite his lost year, other clubs continue to ask about him because he offers righthanded power and enough athleticism to handle third base or the corner outfield. His strong, sometimes erratic arm probably plays best in the outfield. With strong hands, ample loft in his swing and a good hitting approach, Darnell's above-average power plays in games, though righties with good breaking stuff can give him trouble. It's a different story versus southpaws, against whom he has batted .367/.451/.590 with 14 homers and just 36 strikeouts in 359 plate appearances in the high minors. While he'll be 26 this season, Darnell still has time to carve out a role for a club looking for righty power.

Year	Club (League)	Class	AVG	G	AB	R	H	2B	3B	HR	RBI	BB	SO	SB	CS	OBP	SLG
2008	Eugene (NWL)	SS	.373	16	67	9	25	6	1	2	15	11	12	1	1	.462	.582
2009	Fort Wayne (MWL)	LoA	.329	66	222	40	73	17	2	7	38	57	51	5	5	.468	.518
	Lake Elsinore (CAL)	HiA	.294	60	235	40	69	18	2	13	43	30	38	3	1	.377	.553
2010	Fort Wayne (MWL)	LoA	.360	7	25	5	9	4	0	1	8	5	4	0	0	.500	.640
	San Antonio (TL)	AA	.265	101	373	46	99	21	1	10	50	44	64	2	0	.348	.408
2011	San Antonio (TL)	AA	.333	76	288	62	96	25	1	17	62	52	48	2	1	.434	.604
	Tucson (PCL)	AAA	.261	35	134	20	35	4	0	6	17	16	30	0	0	.344	.425
	San Diego (NL)	MAJ	.222	18	45	2	10	2	0	1	7	5	7	1	0	.294	.333
2012	Tucson (PCL)	AAA	.267	31	116	22	31	6	0	7	21	16	25	1	1	.365	.500
	San Diego (NL)	MAJ	.235	7	17	1	4	1	0	1	1	2	2	0	0	.316	.471
Major League Totals			.226	25	62	3	14	3	0	2	8	7	9	1	0	.300	.371
Minor League Totals			.299	392	1460	244	437	101	7	63	254	231	272	14	9	.398	.508

19 DONN ROACH, RHP

BA GRADE
45
MEDIUM

Born: Dec. 14, 1989. **B-T:** R-R. **Ht.:** 6-1. **Wt.:** 200. **Drafted:** JC of Southern Nevada, 2010 (3rd round supplemental). **Signed by:** Jeff Scholzen (Angels).

A teammate of Bryce Harper's at JC of Southern Nevada in 2010, Roach was the second Coyote drafted that year, going in the supplemental third round to the Angels. Los Angeles helped Roach soften his landing and improve his direction to the plate, and he turned in a fine relief season at low Class A in 2011, fanning 68 in 70 innings and notching a 3.6 groundout/airout ratio. He continued to keep the ball on the ground while shifting to the rotation in 2012, both before and after the Angels traded him (along with Alexi Amarista) to the Padres for Ernesto Frieri in May. He generated 3.5 groundball outs for every one in the air in 2012 to rank first among minor league pitchers with at least 100 innings. Roach lacks premium stuff, but he buys into the sinkerballer mentality, pounding the zone with a steady diet of 89-92 mph two-seamers with sinking action, seeking to induce groundball contact in the first two or three pitches. He'll throw a tumbling splitter for swings and misses when he gets two strikes, while incorporating a slurve for a different look the second time through the order. He completes the package by fielding his position and holding baserunners (he allowed 13 steal attempts all year). San Diego shut down Roach in mid-July due to his jump in innings, but he profiles as a back-of-the-rotation starter or groundball-oriented reliever.

Year	Club (League)	Class	W	L	ERA	G	GS	CG	SV	IP	H	HR	BB	SO	K/9	WHIP	AVG
2010	Orem (PIO)	R	4	1	6.04	16	10	0	0	54	64	6	16	59	9.9	1.49	.294
2011	Cedar Rapids (MWL)	LoA	5	5	3.45	45	0	0	2	70	73	1	20	68	8.7	1.32	.266
2012	Inland Empire (CAL)	HiA	5	0	2.16	6	6	0	0	42	36	1	3	29	6.3	0.94	.228
	Lake Elsinore (CAL)	HiA	5	1	1.74	8	7	0	0	47	41	1	11	44	8.5	1.11	.233
	San Antonio (TL)	AA	1	1	1.59	4	3	0	0	17	9	0	8	5	2.6	1.00	.155
Minor League Totals			20	8	3.34	79	26	0	2	229	223	9	58	205	8.0	1.23	.252

20 MATT ANDRIESE, RHP

BA GRADE
50
HIGH

Born: Aug. 28, 1989. **B-T:** R-R. **Ht.:** 6-3. **Wt.:** 210. **Drafted:** UC Riverside, 2011 (3rd round). **Signed by:** Josh Emmerick.

Andriese declined to sign with the Rangers as a 37th-round pick out of high school in 2008, but he came to terms with the Padres three years later, following an up-and-down career at UC Riverside, for $270,000 out of the third round. A physical righty with a chance for three solid pitches, he survived the jump from short-season ball in 2011 to high Class A in style, winning the California League ERA title (3.58) and ranking third in WHIP (1.22). His fastball sits at 91-92 mph, tops out at 95 and plays up thanks to sinking and tailing action that batters struggle to lift. Cal League righthanders managed to hit just .223/.259/.302 against him. Andriese throws slightly across his body, which along with a long arm action adds deception but also affects his command, particularly to his arm side. His control is fine, though, and he finds the zone with a hard downer curveball with plus potential as well as a tumbling splitter. He began throwing a mid-80s cutter in pro ball, but he uses it sparingly. If Andriese keeps lefties at bay, then he has mid-rotation potential. If not, he has the type of arm that will play in the bullpen. He's ready for Double-A.

Year	Club (League)	Class	W	L	ERA	G	GS	CG	SV	IP	H	HR	BB	SO	K/9	WHIP	AVG
2011	Eugene (NWL)	SS	5	1	1.51	12	8	0	0	42	29	0	10	42	9.1	0.94	.197
2012	Lake Elsinore (CAL)	HiA	10	8	3.58	27	26	0	0	146	140	9	38	131	8.1	1.22	.252
Minor League Totals			15	9	3.12	39	34	0	0	188	169	9	48	173	8.3	1.16	.241

21 TRAVIS JANKOWSKI, OF

BA GRADE
50
HIGH

Born: June 15, 1991. **B-T:** L-R. **Ht.:** 6-2. **Wt.:** 190. **Drafted:** Stony Brook, 2012 (1st round supplemental). **Signed by:** Jim Bretz.

Jankowski hit .414 and led NCAA Division I with 79 runs, 110 hits and 11 triples as a Stony Brook junior last spring, serving as the lynchpin for the club's improbable run to the College World Series. The Padres signed him for $975,000 as the 44th overall pick in the draft. He appeared worn down after essentially heading straight from campus to low Class A, then rallied to hit .333 (47-for-141) from July 27 on. Including the Midwest League playoffs, Jankowski collected a hit in his final 23 games, though his season ended prematurely when he broke a rib when hit by a pitch. Plus speed and range in center field are his carrying tools, and he makes steady line-drive contact with a handsy, lefthanded swing. Though he has a knack for barreling the ball, he's slightly built and projects to hit for little over-the-fence power. He stole 17 bases in 24 tries with Fort Wayne, and he'll need to improve both his proficiency and efficiency to get the most out of his speed. He doesn't throw well enough to profile in right field, but defense shouldn't be an issue. Expect Jankowski to tread the same path as 2011 first-rounder Cory Spangenberg and head to high Class A for his first full year out.

Year	Club (League)	Class	AVG	G	AB	R	H	2B	3B	HR	RBI	BB	SO	SB	CS	OBP	SLG
2012	Padres (AZL)	R	.250	2	8	1	2	0	0	0	4	0	1	0	0	.222	.250
	Fort Wayne (MWL)	LoA	.282	59	238	32	67	10	4	1	23	13	44	17	7	.318	.370
Minor League Totals			.280	61	246	33	69	10	4	1	27	13	45	17	7	.314	.366

22 BURCH SMITH, RHP

BA GRADE
50
HIGH

Born: April 12, 1990. **B-T:** R-R. **Ht.:** 6-4. **Wt.:** 215. **Drafted:** Oklahoma, 2011 (14th round). **Signed by:** Lane Decker.

The Indians tried twice to sign Smith, drafting him out of Howard (Texas) JC in both 2009 (49th round) and 2010 (20th), but they didn't get him either time. The Padres had more luck, signing him for $250,000 as a 14th-round selection out of Oklahoma in 2011. Like Matt Andriese, Smith had no trouble jumping to high Class A his first year out, and the two teamed with Donn Roach to front a Lake Elsinore pitching staff that led the California League with a 4.31 ERA and 1.33 WHIP. Smith throws the hardest of the three, giving him a higher ceiling, but he doesn't have a go-to second pitch like Andriese's curve or Roach's splitter. He tops out near 97 mph and generates fierce cutting action on his fastball, which usually ranges from 90-95 mph. San Diego projects his changeup to be solid, assuming he develops more consistent arm speed, but he hasn't refined or settled on a consistent breaking ball yet. His curveball needs more power and his slider more tilt. Smith has no trouble throwing strikes—his 5.1 K-BB ratio topped the Cal League—but he'll need one of his secondary pitches to step forward to continue thriving as a starter at Double-A in 2013.

Year	Club (League)	Class	W	L	ERA	G	GS	CG	SV	IP	H	HR	BB	SO	K/9	WHIP	AVG
2011	Padres (AZL)	R	0	0	4.50	2	0	0	1	2	3	0	1	4	18.0	2.00	.300
2012	Lake Elsinore (CAL)	HiA	9	6	3.85	26	26	0	0	129	127	11	27	137	9.6	1.20	.256
Minor League Totals			9	6	3.86	28	26	0	1	131	130	11	28	141	9.7	1.21	.257

23 JAFF DECKER, OF

BA GRADE
45
MEDIUM

Born: Feb. 23, 1990. **B-T:** L-L. **Ht.:** 5-10. **Wt.:** 190. **Drafted:** HS—Peoria, Ariz., 2008 (1st round supplemental). **Signed by:** Dave Lottsfeldt.

The Padres placed Decker on the 40-man roster in November, but it was potential more than performance that got him there. The talk of 2012 spring training camp, Decker hit .295 with eight extra-base hits in 23 games, but that momentum vanished when he returned to Double-A for a second straight year. He hit just .184/.365/.293 through May, then spent the final three months sidelined with plantar fasciitis in his right foot. Short with a thick lower half, Decker is more athletic than he looks, and in the words of one club official, he looks "hitterish" thanks to a short lefty stroke and great eye at the plate. He sports a .371 on-base percentage at the Double-A level despite hitting just .224, taking a walk-first, hit-second approach that scouts agree needs to be evened out. San Diego would like to see him let the bat fly more often because he has solid power from left-center to right field and home run juice to his pull side. Decker plays all three outfield spots but fits best on the corners, with fringy speed and average range and arm strength. He has a shot at assuming a platoon role or perhaps serving as an offensive-minded reserve.

Year	Club (League)	Class	AVG	G	AB	R	H	2B	3B	HR	RBI	BB	SO	SB	CS	OBP	SLG
2008	Padres (AZL)	R	.352	49	159	51	56	11	2	5	34	55	36	9	1	.523	.541
	Eugene (NWL)	SS	.200	3	10	2	2	0	0	0	0	2	5	0	0	.333	.200
2009	Fort Wayne (MWL)	LoA	.299	104	358	78	107	25	2	16	64	85	92	10	6	.442	.514
2010	Lake Elsinore (CAL)	HiA	.262	79	290	53	76	14	2	17	58	47	80	5	4	.374	.500
2011	San Antonio (TL)	AA	.236	133	496	90	117	29	2	19	92	103	145	15	5	.373	.417
2012	San Antonio (TL)	AA	.184	47	147	30	27	3	2	3	9	40	37	6	2	.365	.293
	Padres (AZL)	R	.296	9	27	5	8	1	2	1	7	4	3	0	0	.394	.593
Minor League Totals			.264	424	1487	309	393	83	12	61	264	336	398	45	18	.406	.459

24 YEISON ASENCIO, OF

BA GRADE
50
HIGH

Born: Nov. 14, 1989. **B-T:** R-R. **Ht.:** 6-1. **Wt.:** 175. **Signed:** Dominican Republic, 2009. **Signed by:** Randy Smith/Felix Feliz/Martin Jose.

Asencio represented himself as a 16-year-old named Yoan Alcantara when San Diego signed him for $135,000 on July 2, 2009. In reality, he is Yeison Asencio and three years older than advertised, his identity having been vetted by a crooked contract investigator working for MLB. Playing as Alcantara, he pulled down the No. 1 ranking on the 2011 Arizona League prospect list. He didn't receive his visa to re-enter the United States until May 2012, but it didn't take him long to shake off the rust in low Class A. He hit .361 from July 13 onward to win the Midwest League batting title. Asencio swings at nearly every pitch he sees and barrels up most of those he can reach. A pronounced bat wag often foils his timing, but he has bat speed to spare and at least fringy power potential. Though he's a below-average runner and not the most agile defender, he makes the routine plays in right field and has a terrific arm thanks to a quick release and uncanny accuracy. He led MWL outfielders with 21 assists. Asencio's age change—he's now 23—cost the Padres an evaluation year, so they added him to the 40-man roster in November.

Year	Club (League)	Class	AVG	G	AB	R	H	2B	3B	HR	RBI	BB	SO	SB	CS	OBP	SLG
2010	Padres (DSL)	R	.241	66	228	43	55	14	3	5	37	27	40	12	5	.332	.395
2011	Padres (AZL)	R	.348	50	210	50	73	13	8	7	46	4	25	8	2	.367	.586
2012	Fort Wayne (MWL)	LoA	.323	92	350	47	113	21	4	8	61	16	38	7	6	.353	.474
Minor League Totals			.306	208	788	140	241	48	15	20	144	47	103	27	13	.350	.481

25 MILES MIKOLAS, RHP

BA GRADE
45
MEDIUM

Born: Aug. 23, 1988. **B-T:** R-R. **Ht.:** 6-5. **Wt.:** 220. **Drafted:** Nova Southeastern, 2009 (7th round). **Signed by:** Rob Sidwell.

The most predictable feature of the Padres' Top 30 Prospects list is the presence on the back end of at least one quality relief prospect with a modest ceiling who is on the cusp of a regular gig in the major leagues. In recent years, that description has fit Brad Brach (2012), George Kontos (2011), Ryan Webb (2010) and Ernesto Frieri (2009), big leaguers all. This year, Mikolas is the best bet to join that group, and he served his apprenticeship in San Diego last season, working low-leverage relief innings.

Despite throwing a firm 92-95 mph fastball that tops out at 98, he favors his above-average curveball because his heater lacks life and can be turned around when it catches too much of the plate. His curve, on the other hand, features firm mid-70s velocity and true 12-to-6 break. He throws it for both called and swinging strikes. According to Pitch f/x data, Mikolas threw his curveball 35 percent of the time in 2012, a frequency greater than any righthanded reliever with at least 30 innings, save for veteran Jose Veras. While Mikolas might top out as a middle reliever or maybe a set-up man, he has a high probability of reaching his ceiling.

Year	Club (League)	Class	W	L	ERA	G	GS	CG	SV	IP	H	HR	BB	SO	K/9	WHIP	AVG
2009	Eugene (NWL)	SS	1	8	5.94	15	11	0	0	53	77	1	9	39	6.6	1.62	.332
2010	Fort Wayne (MWL)	LoA	6	3	2.20	60	0	0	13	82	76	3	15	78	8.6	1.11	.240
2011	Lake Elsinore (CAL)	HiA	3	0	1.13	34	0	0	12	40	31	1	9	42	9.5	1.01	.214
	San Antonio (TL)	AA	1	0	1.67	28	0	0	9	32	29	0	6	27	7.5	1.08	.240
2012	San Antonio (TL)	AA	1	1	2.92	12	0	0	4	12	16	0	3	11	8.0	1.54	.320
	Tucson (PCL)	AAA	2	1	3.20	17	0	0	0	20	20	1	8	17	7.8	1.42	.260
	San Diego (NL)	MAJ	2	1	3.62	25	0	0	0	32	32	4	15	23	6.4	1.45	.256
Major League Totals			2	1	3.62	25	0	0	0	32	32	4	15	23	6.4	1.45	.256
Minor League Totals			14	13	2.90	166	11	0	38	239	249	6	50	214	8.1	1.25	.264

26 JUAN ORAMAS, LHP

BA GRADE
50
HIGH

Born: May 11, 1990. **B-T:** L-L. **Ht.:** 5-10. **Wt.:** 215. **Signed:** Mexico, 2006. **Signed by:** Robert Rowley.

Signed out of Mexico at age 16, Oramas made slow progress early in his career before vaulting into the big league picture with a strong 2011 season at Double-A, prompting San Diego to add the 21-year-old to its 40-man roster following the season. That status proved to be short-lived, however. He showed up at 2012 spring training worn down from a winter spent pitching in the Mexican Pacific League, where he had logged nine starts for Hermosillo. His balky elbow required Tommy John surgery in mid-June after he ran up a 6.37 ERA through eight Double-A starts. Though his stuff played down a half-grade in 2012, Oramas when healthy has three pitches that grade as average to a tick above. He sits 89-92 mph and bumps 94, working both sides of the plate and occasionally dropping down versus lefties. The Padres like his aggressive, fearless pitching style, which coupled with strong command, helps his curve and changeup play up. To make room on the 40-man for other players, San Diego nontendered Oramas in November, subsequently re-signing him to a minor league deal a month later. He racked up 157 innings (counting the playoffs) in the MPL from 2009-11, so his injury rehab at least gives him a respite from pitching year-round.

Year	Club (League)	Class	W	L	ERA	G	GS	CG	SV	IP	H	HR	BB	SO	K/9	WHIP	AVG
2007	Padres (DSL)	R	2	3	3.81	16	5	0	0	54	39	1	20	63	10.4	1.09	.196
2008	Padres (DSL)	R	3	2	1.02	19	5	0	3	53	23	0	24	70	11.9	0.89	.125
2009	Mexico City (MEX)	AAA	9	1	2.31	25	14	0	0	90	72	4	44	89	8.9	1.29	--
2010	Fort Wayne (MWL)	LoA	0	1	1.20	5	0	0	0	15	9	0	3	25	15.0	0.80	.176
	Lake Elsinore (CAL)	HiA	7	3	3.00	24	21	0	0	84	64	10	26	90	9.6	1.07	.209
2011	Tucson (PCL)	AAA	0	1	14.73	1	1	0	0	4	7	3	1	4	9.8	2.18	.389
	San Antonio (TL)	AA	10	5	3.10	19	18	0	0	105	99	10	28	102	8.8	1.21	.249
2012	San Antonio (TL)	AA	3	4	6.37	8	8	0	0	35	39	5	16	33	8.4	1.56	.267
Minor League Totals			34	20	3.05	117	72	0	3	440	352	33	162	476	9.7	1.17	.215

27 MATT STITES, RHP

BA GRADE
45
MEDIUM

Born: May 28, 1990. **B-T:** R-R. **Ht.:** 5-11. **Wt.:** 170. **Drafted:** Missouri, 2011 (17th round). **Signed by:** Jeff Stewart.

The Cubs overlooked Stites' short stature when they took the Jefferson (Mo.) CC ace in the 33rd round of the 2010 draft, but the two sides couldn't agree to terms after he fanned a batter per inning in the Cape Cod League. He headed to Missouri, where he served as the Tigers' No. 1 starter, and went to the Padres in the 17th round in 2011. Stites signed quickly and shifted to the bullpen, a role for which he seems well suited given his quick-twitch athleticism, two plus pitches and feel for the strike zone. He opened 2012 as the closer for Fort Wayne, a role that mitigates concerns about his stamina (he made two trips to the disabled list) and a lack of plane on his fastball. He incorporates his lower half into his delivery, throwing 92-96 mph heat without a lot of effort. His slider shows sharp tilting action and plus potential, and he owns a fringe changeup and curveball from his starter days. Stites' fearless approach leads scouts to confidently project him as a big league reliever, and some like him as a late-rotation starter given his control. He struck out 60 and walked three as closer for the TinCaps. San Diego sent him to the Arizona Fall League, a rare step for a second-year player in low Class A, which suggests that he could move quickly to Double-A in 2013.

Year	Club (League)	Class	W	L	ERA	G	GS	CG	SV	IP	H	HR	BB	SO	K/9	WHIP	AVG
2011	Padres (AZL)	R	0	0	0.00	2	0	0	0	2	0	0	0	3	13.5	0.00	.000
	Eugene (NWL)	SS	4	0	1.93	24	0	0	5	33	14	1	8	36	9.9	0.67	.125
2012	Fort Wayne (MWL)	LoA	2	0	0.74	42	0	0	13	49	25	4	3	60	11.1	0.58	.148
Minor League Totals			6	0	1.19	68	0	0	18	83	39	5	11	99	10.7	0.60	.136

28 MALLEX SMITH, OF

BA GRADE
50
HIGH

Born: May 6, 1993. **B-T:** L-R. **Ht.:** 5-9. **Wt.:** 155. **Drafted:** Santa Fe (Fla.) JC, 2012 (5th round). **Signed by:** Willie Bosque.

Coming out of high school in Tallahassee, Fla., Smith turned down the Brewers as a 13th-round selection in 2011. He improved his stock considerably after spending a year in junior college, going to the Padres in the fifth round of the 2012 draft and signing for an above-slot $375,000. Smith's entire game revolves around 80 speed on the 20-to-80 scouting scale. He flies down the first-base line, placing extreme pressure on defenders on the left side of the infield, stretches singles into doubles and makes use of his wheels to outrun his mistakes in center field. Despite his athleticism and speed, he remains a raw defender and below-average thrower. He stole 31 bases in 37 attempts in junior college and went 17-for-21 as a pro, but he has only scratched the surface of his potential for base thievery. A short, slender lefty hitter, Smith understands the importance of bunting and putting the ball in play, though he has quick hands and feel to hit, suggesting he won't get the bat knocked out of his hands. San Diego believes his competitiveness and worth ethic will enable him to improve his defensive play, making him a potential regular center fielder and leadoff man if everything breaks right.

Year	Club (League)	Class	AVG	G	AB	R	H	2B	3B	HR	RBI	BB	SO	SB	CS	OBP	SLG
2012	Padres (AZL)	R	.344	25	96	23	33	2	1	1	10	5	19	13	3	.379	.417
	Eugene (NWL)	SS	.188	10	32	6	6	0	0	1	5	6	8	4	1	.333	.281
Minor League Totals			.305	35	128	29	39	2	1	2	15	11	27	17	4	.366	.383

29 KEVIN QUACKENBUSH, RHP

BA GRADE
45
MEDIUM

Born: Nov. 28, 1988. **B-T:** R-R. **Ht.:** 6-3. **Wt.:** 207. **Drafted:** South Florida, 2011 (8th round). **Signed by:** Willie Bosque.

Quackenbush's control improved dramatically as a South Florida senior, once he teamed up with former big league pitching coach Chuck Hernandez. He hasn't stopped throwing strikes after turning pro for $5,000 as an eighth-round pick in 2011, and he spent his first full season as closer for Lake Elsinore. Quackenbush befuddles batters with a single-minded plan of attack—throwing fastballs nine out of every 10 pitches—but the strategy has worked up through high Class A because opponents just don't pick up the ball out of his hand. The angle he creates, coupled with a short arm action, make him difficult to square up even when batters do make contact with his 89-91 mph heat. He'll throw a fringy slider on occasion, and a changeup even less frequently, but to this point he simply hasn't needed them. Quackenbush navigated the perilous conditions of the Arizona Fall League in 2012, not allowing a hit over his first nine innings and finishing with six saves and a 2.45 ERA. Double-A will be a big test in 2013, after which the Padres will have a better idea whether he's big league material or a one-pitch oddity.

Year	Club (League)	Class	W	L	ERA	G	GS	CG	SV	IP	H	HR	BB	SO	K/9	WHIP	AVG
2011	Eugene (NWL)	SS	1	0	0.44	17	0	0	9	21	13	0	6	33	14.4	0.92	.188
	Fort Wayne (MWL)	LoA	1	1	0.84	18	0	0	9	21	12	0	6	38	16.0	0.84	.158
2012	Lake Elsinore (CAL)	HiA	3	2	0.94	52	0	0	27	58	42	1	22	70	10.9	1.11	.205
Minor League Totals			5	3	0.81	87	0	0	45	100	67	1	34	141	12.7	1.01	.191

30 JOHNNY BARBATO, RHP

BA GRADE
45
HIGH

Born: July 11, 1992. **B-T:** R-R. **Ht.:** 6-2. **Wt.:** 185. **Drafted:** HS—Miami, 2010 (6th round). **Signed by:** Rob Sidwell/Bob Filotei.

Barbato signed for $1.4 million at the 2010 deadline, the beneficiary of surplus money that materialized when the Padres failed to sign first-rounder Karsten Whitson. That outlay more than doubled the amount received by any other San Diego draft pick that year. After starting games for Eugene in 2011, Barbato moved into a set-up role for closer Matt Stites last season on a prospect-laden Fort Wayne club that advanced to the Midwest League finals. He unleashes 91-94 mph heat and bumps 96 with a quick arm, mixing in a sharp, 12-to-6 knuckle-curve. MWL righties had almost no chance, batting .139/.233/.188 in 165 plate appearances. Barbato has some feel for a changeup he used as a starter, but it's below average and not often front-and-center when he pitches out of the bullpen. Some in the organization believe he could return to a starting role, but his mentality and mechanics—he struggles to say online to the plate with an unathletic delivery—seem better suited to a relief role. Regardless of Barbato's role, the Padres would like to see him attack batters with his fastball and not rely so much on his curve. Barring huge strides in his development, he is probably in the bullpen to stay.

Year	Club (League)	Class	W	L	ERA	G	GS	CG	SV	IP	H	HR	BB	SO	K/9	WHIP	AVG
2011	Eugene (NWL)	SS	1	4	4.89	15	13	0	0	57	52	4	31	50	7.9	1.46	.248
2012	Fort Wayne (MWL)	LoA	6	1	1.84	48	0	0	3	73	52	4	31	84	10.3	1.13	.195
Minor League Totals			7	5	3.18	63	13	0	3	130	104	8	62	134	9.3	1.27	.218

San Francisco Giants

BY ANDREW BAGGARLY

The Giants strived for more than a half-century to win their first World Series title in San Francisco. They didn't make their faithful wait nearly as long for the next parade down Market Street.

The road was far more treacherous than in 2010. This time, it included six elimination games in the first two rounds against the Reds and Cardinals, and those fiery hoops only forged stronger steel. Upon reaching the Fall Classic, the Giants overwhelmed the Tigers to claim a four-game sweep and win second championship in three seasons—the closest the National League has come to a dynasty since the Big Red Machine repeated in 1975-76.

Those Reds had Johnny Bench. These Giants have Buster Posey, who won the Bench Award as college baseball's top catcher at Florida State in 2008, along with the Golden Spikes and Baseball America's College Player of the Year awards. Four years later, he racked up a whole new set of hardware after leading the majors with a .336 average, a Silver Slugger award, National League comeback player of the year honors and a landslide selection as the NL MVP.

Prior to Posey, San Francisco hadn't drafted and developed an all-star position player since Matt Williams. Instead, the organization's strength remains its ability to churn out pitchers.

Though Tim Lincecum took a severe step backward from his two Cy Young Award-winning seasons, a rotation of Matt Cain, Madison Bumgarner, Ryan Vogelsong and Barry Zito was firm enough when it mattered most. Cain, who received a five-year, $112.5 million extension in April, further etched his legacy on June 13 when he threw the 22nd perfect game in major league history and the first by a Giant in the franchise's 128-year existence.

Though the pitching staff was largely the same on both World Series winners, Posey was the only everyday position player held over from the team that took down the Rangers in 2010. But if San Francisco's first World Series title since 1954 was something of a happy accident won by a band of misfits and castoffs, its second championship featured the kind of lineup that longtime general manager Brian Sabean had coveted.

Sabean assembled a younger, more athletic and defensively skilled team that sought to use AT&T Park's ample dimensions as an advantage instead of an excuse. The Giants became the first team since the 1985 Cardinals to reach the playoffs despite hitting

In his two healthy seasons, Buster Posey has led the Giants to two World Series crowns

BILL NICHOLS

the fewest homers in the majors, including just 31 longballs in 81 home games.

Sabean utilized prospects such as catcher Tommy Joseph, second baseman Charlie Culberson and right-hander Seth Rosin in July deals for Marco Scutaro (the NLCS MVP) and Hunter Pence (who became San Francisco's inspirational leader).

The farm system lacks depth as a result of trades, such as the 2011 rental of Carlos Beltran that cost current Mets No. 1 prospect Zack Wheeler, but the Giants still have their share of quality pitchers, starting with Kyle Crick, Chris Stratton and Mike Kickham. Pitching guru Dick Tidrow must matriculate some of those arms to the big leagues soon, because Lincecum and Zito could be spending their last season in a San Francisco uniform.

It's going to get tougher for the Giants now that the Dodgers have deep-pocketed ownership and are threatening to become the Yankees of the West. Though the Giants aren't run on a shoestring budget, they probably won't turn themselves into the Red Sox in order to compete.

Expect Sabean and his staff to adhere to their blend of scouting, pragmatic assessment and turning over rocks to find athletic, two-way players. That strategy couldn't be working any better.

THIS YEAR'S TOP 30

Player, Pos.	Grade
1. Kyle Crick, rhp	60/High
2. Joe Panik, ss	50/Medium
3. Chris Stratton, rhp	55/High
4. Gary Brown, of	55/High
5. Mike Kickham, lhp	50/Medium
6. Clayton Blackburn, rhp	50/High
7. Heath Hembree, rhp	50/High
8. Francisco Peguero, of	50/High
9. Roger Kieschnick, of	45/Medium
10. Adalberto Mejia, lhp	50/High
11. Adam Duvall, 3b	45/Medium
12. Gustavo Cabrera, of	55/Extreme
13. Andrew Susac, c	50/High
14. Edwin Escobar, lhp	50/High
15. Martin Agosta, rhp	50/High
16. Mac Williamson, of	50/High
17. Chris Heston, rhp	45/Medium
18. Steven Okert, lhp	50/High
19. Chris Marlowe, rhp	50/High
20. Josh Osich, lhp	50/Extreme
21. Stephen Johnson, rhp	50/Extreme
22. Juan Perez, of	45/Medium
23. Nick Noonan, ss/3b	45/Medium
24. Ehire Adrianza, ss	45/Medium
25. Eric Surkamp, lhp	45/High
26. Cody Hall, rhp	45/High
27. Ricky Oropesa, 1b	45/High
28. Jacob Dunnington, rhp	45/High
29. Shawn Payne, of	45/High
30. Brett Bochy, rhp	40/Medium

LAST YEAR'S TOP 30

Player, Pos.	Status
1. Gary Brown, of	No. 4
2. Tommy Joseph, c/1b	(Phillies)
3. Heath Hembree, rhp	No. 7
4. Joe Panik, ss	No. 2
5. Francisco Peguero, of	No. 8
6. Andrew Susac, c	No. 13
7. Eric Surkamp, lhp	No. 25
8. Kyle Crick, rhp	No. 1
9. Ehire Adrianza, ss	No. 24
10. Hector Sanchez, c	Majors
11. Charlie Culberson, 2b	(Rockies)
12. Brett Pill, 1b/2b	Majors
13. Conor Gillaspie, 3b	Dropped out
14. Hector Correa, rhp	(Dodgers)
15. Jarrett Parker, of	Dropped out
16. Chris Dominguez, 3b	Dropped out
17. Ricky Oropesa, 1b	No. 27
18. Chuckie Jones, of	Dropped out
19. Chris Marlowe, rhp	No. 19
20. Mike Kickham, lhp	No. 5
21. Clayton Blackburn, rhp	No. 6
22. Jesus Galindo, of	Dropped out
23. Josh Osich, lhp	No. 20
24. Ray Black, rhp	Dropped out
25. Stephen Harrold, rhp	Dropped out
26. Adalberto Mejia, lhp	No. 10
27. Roger Kieschnick, of	No. 9
28. Adam Duvall, 3b	No. 11
29. Leonardo Fuentes, of	Dropped out
30. Rafael Rodriguez, of	Dropped out

BEST TOOLS

Best Hitter for Average	Joe Panik
Best Power Hitter	Adam Duvall
Best Strike-Zone Discipline	Joe Panik
Fastest Baserunner	Gary Brown
Best Athlete	Gary Brown
Best Fastball	Kyle Crick
Best Curveball	Chris Marlowe
Best Slider	Mike Kickham
Best Changeup	Chris Heston
Best Control	Clayton Blackburn
Best Defensive Catcher	Jeff Arnold
Best Defensive Infielder	Ehire Adrianza
Best Infield Arm	Chris Dominguez
Best Defensive Outfielder	Gary Brown
Best Outfield Arm	Francisco Peguero

PROJECTED 2016 LINEUP

Catcher	Buster Posey
First Base	Brandon Belt
Second Base	Joe Panik
Third Base	Pablo Sandoval
Shortstop	Brandon Crawford
Left Field	Angel Pagan
Center Field	Gary Brown
Right Field	Hunter Pence
No. 1 Starter	Matt Cain
No. 2 Starter	Madison Bumgarner
No. 3 Starter	Kyle Crick
No. 4 Starter	Tim Lincecum
No. 5 Starter	Chris Stratton
Closer	Heath Hembree

TOP PROSPECTS OF THE DECADE

Year	Player, Pos.	2012 Org.
2003	Jesse Foppert, rhp	Out of baseball
2004	Merkin Valdez, rhp	Athletics
2005	Matt Cain, rhp	Giants
2006	Matt Cain, rhp	Giants
2007	Tim Lincecum, rhp	Giants
2008	Angel Villalona, 3b/1b	Giants
2009	Madison Bumgarner, lhp	Giants
2010	Buster Posey, c	Giants
2011	Brandon Belt, 1b	Giants
2012	Gary Brown, of	Giants

TOP DRAFT PICKS OF THE DECADE

Year	Player, Pos.	2012 Org.
2003	David Aardsma, rhp	Yankees
2004	Eddy Martinez-Esteve, of (2nd rd)	(Atlantic Lge)
2005	Ben Copeland, of (4th round)	Indians
2006	Tim Lincecum, rhp	Giants
2007	Madison Bumgarner, lhp	Giants
2008	Buster Posey, c	Giants
2009	Zack Wheeler, rhp	Mets
2010	Gary Brown, of	Giants
2011	Joe Panik, ss	Giants
2012	Chris Stratton, rhp	Giants

LARGEST BONUSES IN CLUB HISTORY

Buster Posey, 2008	$6,200,000
Zack Wheeler, 2009	$3,300,000
Rafael Rodriguez, 2008	$2,550,000
Angel Villalona, 2006	$2,100,000
Tim Lincecum, 2006	$2,025,000

SAN FRANCISCO GIANTS

TOP 2013 ROOKIE: Roger Kieschnick, of. He was close to breaking through when he injured his shoulder crashing into a wall last May.

BREAKOUT PROSPECT: Stephen Johnson, rhp. He can overpower hitters with his fastball and curve, and the Giants hope he'll throw enough strikes to develop as a starter.

SLEEPER: Shilo McCall, of. The New Mexico prepster is the best hitter San Francisco signed in the 2012 draft.

SOURCE OF TOP 30 TALENT			
Homegrown	29	Acquired	1
College	20	Trades	1
Junior college	1	Rule 5 draft	0
High school	3	Independent leagues	0
Nondrafted free agents	1	Free agents/waivers	0
International	4		

LF	CF	RF
Shawn Payne (29)	Gary Brown (4)	Francisco Peguero (8)
Leonardo Fuentes	Gustavo Cabrera (12)	Roger Kieschnick (9)
Rafael Rodriguez	Juan Perez (22)	Mac Williamson (16)
Randy Ortiz	Jesus Galindo	Jarrett Parker
Nick Liles	Shilo McCall	
Brett Krill	Tyler Hollick	

3B	SS	2B	1B
Adam Duvall (11)	Joe Panik (2)	Nick Noonan (23)	Ricky Oropesa (27)
Chris Dominguez	Ehire Adrianza (24)	Brock Bond	Angel Villalona
Conor Gillaspie	Carter Jurica	Ryan Cavan	
Natanael Javier	Kelby Tomlinson		
Mitch Delfino			

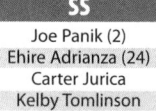

C
Andrew Susac (13)
Trevor Brown
Jackson Williams
Jeff Arnold
Johnny Monell

LHP		RHP	
LHSP	**LHRP**	**RHSP**	**RHRP**
Mike Kickham (5)	Steven Okert (18)	Kyle Crick (1)	Heath Hembree (7)
Adalberto Mejia (10)	Josh Osich (20)	Chris Stratton (3)	Chris Marlowe (19)
Edwin Escobar (14)	Bryce Bandilla	Clayton Blackburn (6)	Cody Hall (26)
Eric Surkamp (25)	Mason McVay	Martin Agosta (15)	Jacob Dunnington (28)
Ty Blach	Joe Kurrasch	Chris Heston (17)	Brett Bochy (30)
Ryan Bradley		Stephen Johnson (21)	Jake Dunning
		Shawn Sanford	Dan Otero
		Justin Fitzgerald	Jean Machi
		Joan Gregorio	E.J. Encinosa
			Matthew Graham
			Jose Valdez
			Ray Black
			Stephen Harrold
			Armando Paniagua

2012

BEST PURE HITTER: OF Shilo McCall (9), the only prep position player the Giants drafted in the first 36 rounds. He combines a good setup and short stroke with natural strength and decent speed.

BEST POWER HITTER: OF Mac Williamson's (3) 6-foot-4, 240-pound frame is loaded with plus-plus raw power. He led the Atlantic Coast Conference with 11 homers in the spring and went deep nine times in his pro debut. 1B Joey Rapp (28) has similar pop and homered 11 times at short-season Salem-Keizer.

FASTEST RUNNER: OF Tyler Hollick (14) has plus speed out of the batter's box and is quicker once under way. He stole 21 bases in 23 tries in 32 pro games.

BEST DEFENSIVE PLAYER: Hollick plays a fine center field. SS Matt Duffy (18) has good hands and the versatility to play anywhere in the infield.

BEST FASTBALL: RHP Stephen Johnson (6) worked at 94-98 mph in his pro debut and reportedly hit 101 as an amateur. He was the draft's best college prospect outside Division I, starring for St. Edward's (Texas). LHP Steven Okert (4) and RHP Ian Gardeck (16) can reach 97, while RHP Martin Agosta (2) touches 96. RHPs Chris Stratton (1) and E.J. Encinosa (7) don't throw quite as hard, but their 91-95 mph heaters have good life. Stratton's fastball has tailing action, while Encinosa's features heavy sink that led to a 3.2 groundout/airout ratio in his pro debut.

BEST SECONDARY PITCH: Stratton manipulates his slider well, throwing it for strikes and getting hitters to chase it out of the zone. Okert's slider helped him limit lefties to a .158 average in pro ball.

BEST PRO DEBUT: Williamson batted .321/.375/.588, mostly at Salem-Keizer. LHP Mason McVay (26) had a 1.19 ERA and 43 strikeouts in 30 innings for the same club, with his deceptive delivery helping his low-90s fastball play up.

BEST ATHLETE: Williamson has the best combination of strength and speed. He's a solid runner with a strong arm and fits the right-field profile well. Stratton is athletic for a pitcher, giving him strong command of his lively stuff.

MOST INTRIGUING BACKGROUND: Unsigned SS Drew Jackson's (37) brother Brett made his big league debut with the Cubs last summer.

CLOSEST TO THE MAJORS: Stratton, whose progress was slowed when he was hit in the head by a batting-practice liner in mid-August. As a lefty reliever with power stuff, Okert could jump on the fast track.

BEST LATE-ROUND PICK: Hollick offers speed, defense and a patient approach that bodes well for his ability to hit for average. Gardeck lacks consistency but has a power arm and good stuff when he's on.

THE ONE WHO GOT AWAY: Jackson is a quality runner and defender who's now at Stanford. RHP Tyler Ferguson (40) took his 88-94 mph fastball to Vanderbilt.

ASSESSMENT: For the second straight year, the Giants stocked up on pitching, taking arms with seven of their first eight picks. That wasn't necessarily the plan, but they were pleased to land Stratton and Co.

2011

San Francisco's top two prospects, RHP Kyle Crick (1s) and SS Joe Panik (1) came from this crop. C Andrew Susac (2) and RHPs Chris Marlowe (5) and Clayton Blackburn (16) offer promise as well.

GRADE: B+

2010

OF Gary Brown (1) is the Giants' center fielder of the future, and RHP Heath Hembree (5) could be their closer. LHP Mike Kickham (6) and 3B Adam Duvall (11) are intriguing in their own right. RHP Seth Rosin (4) was part of the Hunter Pence trade last summer.

GRADE: C+

2009

RHP Zack Wheeler (1) looks like he'll be the next stud pitcher to come out of the San Francisco system—but he's now with the Mets after getting traded for Carlos Beltran in 2011. 1B Brandon Belt (5) still may develop into a star for the Giants. They used C/1B Tommy Joseph (2) as another piece in the Pence deal.

GRADE: B+

2008

There's no more valuable player in baseball than C Buster Posey (1), who has two World Series rings to show for his two healthy big league seasons. SS Brandon Crawford (4) was a key part of the 2012 championship team as well. Other big leaguers include 3B Conor Gillaspie (1s), LHP Eric Surkamp (6) and since-traded LHPs Scott Barnes (8) and Ryan Verdugo (9).

GRADE: A

Draft analysis by Jim Callis. Numbers in parentheses indicate draft rounds.

1 KYLE CRICK, RHP

Born: Nov. 30, 1992. **B-T:** L-R. **Ht.:** 6-4. **Wt.:** 225.
Drafted: HS—Sherman, Texas, 2011 (1st round supplemental). **Signed by:** Todd Thomas.

BA GRADE
60
HIGH

TOM PRIDDY

The Giants weren't shy about throwing out Matt Cain comparisons when they spent the 49th overall pick in the 2011 draft on Crick. Over the course of his first full pro, he convinced most coaches, managers and roving intsructors that his fastball was firmer and had more movement than Cain's did at the same stage a decade ago. If that wasn't impressive enough, Crick remains relatively new to the mound. He mostly played first base in high school and didn't concentrate on pitching until he hit 94 mph on the showcase circuit before his senior season. San Francisco loved his size, arm speed and the life on his pitches, and wasn't concerned that his mechanics needed to be cleaned up. A $900,000 bonus bought out a commitment to Texas Christian and delivered a perfect project for vice president of player personnel Dick Tidrow and pitching coordinator Bert Bradley. They turned Crick from a short-arming, max-effort thrower into a pitcher who could stay within a smoother delivery. By the end of 2012, he got better at correcting himself mid-inning when he got off track. Competing as a 19-year-old in low Class A, Crick recorded a 4.05 ERA in his first nine starts, when his pitch counts soared before he could get deep into games. Then he didn't allow an earned run in June and finished with a 1.91 ERA over the final three months before hitting his innings limit.

Crick maintains a 93-95 mph into the late innings and can reach 99 mph. He combines strength, stamina and athleticism, creating plenty of leverage as he drives down the mound with his long, powerful legs. He drops his arms as he starts from the windup and separates his hands late, which isn't a problem because of his arm speed. His delivery gives him a bit of deception to go along with power stuff that seemingly explodes out of his hand. Crick threw a slider in high school but now operates with a hard curveball. Managers voted it the best breaking ball in the South Atlantic League last summer, even though he basically used it as a show-me offering while learning to throw it for strikes. His changeup became his most dependable offspeed pitch by the end of the year and will be a key to his success as a starter. Crick benefited from pitching in the same Augusta rotation as Clayton Blackburn, a fellow 2011 high school draftee who had an advanced feel for four pitches. "That was the best thing to happen to him, to sit in the stands and chart Blackburn," Bradley said. Crick doesn't have anywhere near Blackburn's command, though. He walked 5.4 batters per nine innings and tended to labor and overanalyze when he had trouble locating his pitches. He also overthrows when things don't go is way, something he'll address as he matures. He's extremely competitive, which leads to occasional battles with coaches when he wants to stay in games. He's intelligent and inquisitive, always trying to soak up knowledge.

After giving up Zack Wheeler in a short-sighted trade with the Mets for Carlos Beltran in 2011, the Giants now have another frontline starter in the making. Crick will be part of one of the minors' most talented rotations at high Class A San Jose in 2013, and San Francisco won't be far off if he improves his control and consistency. Cain made his debut before his 21st birthday, after all.

SCOUTING GRADES

Fastball: 70.	**Control:** 55.
Curveball: 60.	**Command:** 50.
Changeup: 50.	

Based on 20-80 scouting scale, where 50 represents major league average, and future projection rather than present tools.

Year	Club (League)	Class	W	L	ERA	G	GS	CG	SV	IP	H	HR	BB	SO	K/9	WHIP	AVG
2011	Giants (AZL)	R	1	0	6.43	7	0	0	0	7	9	0	8	8	10.3	2.43	.321
2012	Augusta (SAL)	LoA	7	6	2.51	23	22	0	0	111	75	1	67	128	10.3	1.28	.193
Minor League Totals			8	6	2.74	30	22	0	0	118	84	1	75	136	10.3	1.34	.202

2 JOE PANIK, SS

BARRY COLLA

Born: Oct. 30, 1990. **B-T:** L-R. **Ht.:** 6-1. **Wt.:** 195. **Drafted:** St. John's, 2011 (1st round). **Signed by:** John DiCarlo.

Somewhat of a surprise selection as the 29th overall pick in the 2011 draft, Panik signed for $1.116 million and had a terrific pro debut, winning the short-season Northwest League MVP award and batting title (.341). He had a tougher time making the jump to high Class A in 2012, but he still drew more walks than strikeouts and hit .337 in the second half. Panik's bat remains his only plus tool, but no position player in the system is a better bet to become an everyday big leaguer. He works counts, makes consistent line-drive contact on all types of pitching and flashes some gap power. He has uncanny situational-hitting acumen and a terrific two-strike approach. Panik is an opportunistic baserunner despite average speed. Managers rated him the best defensive shortstop in the California League last year, though he's more reliable than flashy. He has average range and arm strength, and he gets rid of the ball quickly and makes accurate throws. Panik continues to establish himself as a smart, contact-oriented No. 2 hitter in the mold of Marco Scutaro or Freddy Sanchez—the kind of hitter who has even more value to the Giants, a team that must move runners in their spacious ballpark. It's probably a matter of time before Panik moves to second base, where he could form a smooth tandem with Brandon Crawford in another year or two. He'll open 2013 at Double-A Richmond.

BA GRADE
50
MEDIUM

Year	Club (League)	Class	AVG	G	AB	R	H	2B	3B	HR	RBI	BB	SO	SB	CS	OBP	SLG
2011	Salem-Keizer (NWL)	SS	.341	69	270	49	92	10	3	6	54	28	25	13	5	.401	.467
2012	San Jose (CAL)	HiA	.297	130	535	93	159	27	4	7	76	58	54	10	4	.368	.402
Minor League Totals			.312	199	805	142	251	37	7	13	130	86	79	23	9	.379	.424

3 CHRIS STRATTON, RHP

Born: Aug. 22, 1990. **B-T:** R-R. **Ht.:** 6-3. **Wt.:** 186. **Drafted:** Mississippi State, 2012 (1st round). **Signed by:** Hugh Walker.

The first Mississippi State player taken by the Giants in the first round since 1985, Stratton went 20th overall in June and signed for $1.85 million. He probably won't make the same franchise-altering impact that Will Clark did, but Stratton has solid No. 2 starter potential. Undrafted out of high school, he went from bullpen arm to legitimate ace with the Bulldogs, winning Southeastern Conference pitcher of the year honors in 2012. San Francisco scouting director John Barr was on hand when Stratton struck out 17 against Louisiana State, showing size, athleticism and feel for four pitches. He pitches to both sides of the plate with a 91-93 mph fastball that touches 95 and has easy, late carry. He has a short slider that he can throw for strikes or use as a chase pitch. Stratton worked more on his changeup after signing and was told he could throw it to righthanders. His body, delivery, stuff and savvy remind longtime Giants coaches of 1999 first-round pick Kurt Ainsworth. Stratton sustained a concussion and was hospitalized overnight after he was struck by a batting-practice line drive in mid-August, ending his pro debut and knocking him out of instructional league. He's expected to make a complete recovery before spring training. There's a good chance he'll skip a level and open his first full pro season in high Class A.

BA GRADE
55
HIGH

Year	Club (League)	Class	W	L	ERA	G	GS	CG	SV	IP	H	HR	BB	SO	K/9	WHIP	AVG
2012	Salem-Keizer (NWL)	SS	0	1	2.76	8	5	0	0	16	14	1	10	16	8.8	1.47	.237
Minor League Totals			0	1	2.76	8	5	0	0	16	14	1	10	16	8.8	1.47	.237

4 GARY BROWN, OF

Born: Sept. 28, 1988. **B-T:** R-R. **Ht.:** 6-0. **Wt.:** 185. **Drafted:** Cal State Fullerton, 2010 (1st round). **Signed by:** Brad Cameron.

The 24th overall pick in 2010, Brown signed for $1.45 million and put together an outstanding first full pro season, batting .336 with 53 steals and a San Jose-record 188 hits. He couldn't duplicate that performance in Double-A last year, and he's no longer considered a lock to be a big league leadoff hitter. The tools are still there, however. Brown stands out most with his top-of-the-scale speed, but he brings a lot more to the table. He has a quick bat, fine center-field skills and solid arm strength. His ability to make adjustments will determine how much he gets out of his tools. Brown has an unorthodox setup and swing, choking up on the bat and pinning his hands behind his chest before beginning his load. He has modest power to begin with, and none when he opens up too much in his swing. He bears some similarity to a righthanded Randy Winn and destroys

BA GRADE
55
HIGH

lefthanders, but he has trouble when righties pound him inside. For all his speed, Brown still has a lot to learn as a basestealer after getting caught 18 times in 51 tries last year. Brown has a lot on his to-do list for Triple-A Fresno this year, but his primary goals are to get on base more often and wreak more havoc when he does. He remained upbeat and tenacious throughout his struggles, and the livelier ballparks in the Pacific Coast League could help get him back on track.

Year	Club (League)	Class	AVG	G	AB	R	H	2B	3B	HR	RBI	BB	SO	SB	CS	OBP	SLG
2010	Giants (AZL)	R	.182	6	22	6	4	1	0	0	0	4	5	2	0	.333	.227
	Salem-Keizer (NWL)	SS	.136	6	22	2	3	0	1	0	2	2	7	0	1	.259	.227
2011	San Jose (CAL)	HiA	.336	131	559	115	188	34	13	14	80	46	77	53	19	.407	.519
2012	Richmond (EL)	AA	.279	134	538	73	150	32	2	7	42	40	87	33	18	.347	.385
Minor League Totals			.302	277	1141	196	345	67	16	21	124	92	176	88	38	.374	.444

5 MIKE KICKHAM, LHP

Born: Dec. 12, 1988. **B-T:** L-L. **Ht.:** 6-4. **Wt.:** 210. **Drafted:** Missouri State, 2010 (6th round). **Signed by:** Hugh Walker.

A recurring blister issue contributed to an underwhelming 2011 full-season debut, but Kickham re-established himself as one of the most talented arms in the system following an aggressive assignment to Double-A. The recipient of an above-slot $410,000 bonus as a draft-eligible sophomore, he had stretches when he dominated Eastern League hitters and ranked second in the circuit in strikeouts (137) and opponent average (.219). Kickham's raw stuff easily is the best among lefthanders in the system. He works off a two-seam fastball that he throws in the low 90s with sinking and tailing action. His slider and changeup both arrive in the low 80s and are solid offerings. He'll also mix in a curveball that has its moments. His ability to vary his breaking ball reminds Giants coaches of Jeremy Affeldt and has them convinced Kickham could move quickly. The key for him is throwing strikes. He can be effectively wild but will need to be more efficient as he progresses. He has trouble hiding his displeasure when he doesn't get calls behind the plate, but he pitched with more maturity as the season went on. Kickham is expected to receive an invite to major league camp this spring and could establish himself as a viable major league option, though he's expected to begin the season in Triple-A. If he puts everything together, he could be a No. 3 starter.

BA GRADE
50
MEDIUM

Year	Club (League)	Class	W	L	ERA	G	GS	CG	SV	IP	H	HR	BB	SO	K/9	WHIP	AVG
2010	Giants (AZL)	R	0	0	11.57	3	0	0	0	2	4	0	2	3	11.6	2.57	.400
2011	Augusta (SAL)	LoA	5	10	4.11	21	21	0	0	112	112	9	37	103	8.3	1.33	.261
2012	Richmond (EL)	AA	11	10	3.05	28	27	1	0	151	119	8	75	137	8.2	1.29	.219
Minor League Totals			16	20	3.57	52	48	1	0	265	235	17	114	243	8.3	1.32	.239

6 CLAYTON BLACKBURN, RHP

Born: Jan. 6, 1993. **B-T:** L-R. **Ht.:** 6-3. **Wt.:** 220. **Drafted:** HS—Edmond, Okla., 2011 (16th round). **Signed by:** Daniel Murray.

Blackburn was ready to start his pro career and the Giants knew it, so they positioned themselves to get one of the biggest steals out of the 2011 draft. His commitment to Oklahoma dropped him to the 16th round, where San Francisco signed him for $150,000. After he posted a 1.08 ERA in the Rookie-level Arizona League during his pro debut, the Giants had no hesitation sending him to low Class A in 2012. At age 19, he led the South Atlantic League in strikeouts (143), K-BB ratio (7.9) and WHIP (1.02). Blackburn has a stocky build reminiscent of Brad Penny, but with less steam on his fastball. Blackburn tops out at 92 mph but pitches at 87-89. He has advanced feel for a curveball and slider that he can shape to fit any situation. He also has an inconsistent changeup. Blackburn will make his curve a little harder when he needs a strikeout, but he's more interested in pitching to contract. His mound presence, command and ability to set up hitters are uncanny for a pitcher his age. His body doesn't have much projection remaining and he'll have to work harder to stay in good shape. He doesn't have enough pure stuff to project as a staff ace, but Blackburn can be a solid mid-rotation option. He'll open 2013 in San Jose, where he won a California League playoff opener with seven strong innings last September.

BA GRADE
50
HIGH

RODGER WOOD

Year	Club (League)	Class	W	L	ERA	G	GS	CG	SV	IP	H	HR	BB	SO	K/9	WHIP	AVG
2011	Giants (AZL)	R	3	1	1.08	12	6	0	0	33	16	2	3	30	8.1	0.57	.140
2012	Augusta (SAL)	LoA	8	4	2.54	22	22	0	0	131	116	3	18	143	9.8	1.02	.232
Minor League Totals			11	5	2.24	34	28	0	0	165	132	5	21	173	9.5	0.93	.215

7 HEATH HEMBREE, RHP

Born: Jan. 13, 1989. **B-T:** R-R. **Ht.:** 6-4. **Wt.:** 205. **Drafted:** College of Charleston, 2010 (5th round). **Signed by:** Jeremy Cleveland.

Hembree lasted five rounds in the 2010 draft because he was a seldom-used college closer who didn't pitch as a high school senior while rehabbing a knee injury sustained in a football game. He breezed through his first three stops in pro ball before hitting a speed bump at Triple-A Fresno in 2012. A strained flexor tendon cost him five weeks, though he rebounded with a solid Arizona Fall League. With a fastball that approaches triple digits and the makings of a power slider, Hembree has closer stuff. He works at 93-96 mph with quality life when fully healthy, and he got back up to 95 in the AFL. He's doing a better job of maintaining his arm slot, which has helped the consistency of his 82-85 mph slider. His changeup probably won't become anything more than a show-me pitch, but he has made some progress with it. If anything, Hembree's injury and diminished velocity showed him the importance of having dependable offspeed stuff. While he can be overpowering, he also has bouts of wildness and gets into trouble with walks. The Giants could use Hembree sooner rather than later in their bullpen, which is light on hard throwers from the right side. He'll probably begin 2013 in Triple-A, but a solid spring would put him in line for a callup the first time San Francisco finds itself short an arm.

BA GRADE: 50 HIGH

Year	Club (League)	Class	W	L	ERA	G	GS	CG	SV	IP	H	HR	BB	SO	K/9	WHIP	AVG
2010	Giants (AZL)	R	0	0	0.82	12	0	0	3	11	9	0	0	22	18.0	0.82	.220
2011	San Jose (CAL)	HiA	0	0	0.73	26	0	0	21	25	16	1	12	44	16.1	1.14	.182
	Richmond (EL)	AA	1	1	2.83	28	0	0	17	29	20	1	13	34	10.7	1.15	.194
2012	San Jose (CAL)	HiA	0	0	0.00	5	0	0	0	5	0	0	1	7	12.6	0.20	.000
	Fresno (PCL)	AAA	1	1	4.74	39	0	0	15	38	29	2	20	36	8.5	1.29	.207
Minor League Totals			2	2	2.68	110	0	0	56	107	74	4	46	143	12.0	1.12	.191

8 FRANCISCO PEGUERO, OF

Born: June 1, 1988. **B-T:** R-R. **Ht.:** 5-11. **Wt.:** 186. **Signed:** Dominican Republic, 2006. **Signed by:** Pablo Peguero.

Peguero's career was slowed when he had arthroscopic surgery on his left knee just before the start of the 2011 season and again during the offseason. He had the worst season of his seven-year pro career in 2012, though he put together a 22-game hitting streak in Triple-A that ended one day before he received his first big league callup. The Giants used him in pinch-running situations and took him along in the postseason even though he wasn't on the active playoff roster. Peguero still has the most exciting combination of speed and power in the system, along with perhaps the best bat speed. He is a high-energy, hyper-aggressive hitter reminiscent of Pablo Sandoval, even if their body types are nothing alike. Peguero is an exceptional athlete with the plus speed needed for center field and a cannon arm that fits in right. He hits the ball a long way in batting practice but is still learning to implement his power at game speed. He hurts himself by being too aggressive at the plate, and he'll need to develop a better gameplan and adjust when pitchers challenge him on the inner half. San Francisco is anxious to see how Peguero will perform against Triple-A pitching when he's fully healthy in 2013. He has the tools to profile as a regular, but he'll need better strike-zone awareness to be able to stick in a major league lineup.

BA GRADE: 50 HIGH

Year	Club (League)	Class	AVG	G	AB	R	H	2B	3B	HR	RBI	BB	SO	SB	CS	OBP	SLG
2006	Giants (DSL)	R	.275	56	182	24	50	10	3	4	16	6	37	3	2	.307	.429
2007	Giants (DSL)	R	.294	69	235	51	69	12	2	1	17	15	39	25	5	.341	.374
2008	Augusta (SAL)	LoA	.261	50	180	23	47	2	4	2	15	12	43	15	1	.309	.350
	Salem-Keizer (NWL)	SS	.307	50	202	33	62	11	4	2	28	9	43	10	3	.349	.431
2009	Salem-Keizer (NWL)	SS	.394	17	71	14	28	3	1	0	12	3	9	7	0	.421	.465
	Augusta (SAL)	LoA	.340	58	238	28	81	12	4	1	34	5	39	15	5	.359	.437
2010	San Jose (CAL)	HiA	.329	122	510	78	168	19	16	10	77	18	88	40	22	.358	.488
2011	San Jose (CAL)	HiA	.324	16	68	12	22	2	0	2	9	7	8	4	0	.387	.441
	Richmond (EL)	AA	.309	71	285	34	88	12	6	5	37	5	45	8	1	.318	.446
2012	Fresno (PCL)	AAA	.272	105	449	46	122	20	10	5	68	15	82	1	0	.297	.394
	San Francisco (NL)	MAJ	.188	17	16	6	3	0	0	0	0	0	7	3	0	.188	.188
Major League Totals			.188	17	16	6	3	0	0	0	0	0	7	3	0	.188	.188
Minor League Totals			.305	614	2420	343	737	103	50	32	313	95	433	128	39	.335	.428

9 ROGER KIESCHNICK, OF

Born: Jan. 21, 1987. **B-T:** L-R. **Ht.:** 6-3. **Wt.:** 229. **Drafted:** Texas Tech, 2008 (3rd round). **Signed by:** Todd Thomas.

After back problems plagued him the previous two seasons, Kieschnick was on the cusp of putting it all together in Triple-A in 2012. Then he ran into an outfield wall on May 29, sustaining a stress fracture in his left shoulder that knocked him out for three months. The Giants have loved Kieschnick's size, strength and athleticism ever since taking him in the same 2008 draft that netted Buster Posey and Brandon Crawford. Before he got hurt, Kieschnick was showing vastly improved patience and pitch recognition that enabled him to punish mistakes in the strike zone. He has worked to shorten up his stroke and take a more direct path to the ball, though he still likes to take an aggressive cut when ahead in the count. He still has trouble covering the outer half of the plate at times, but he isn't chasing as many pitches as he did earlier in his pro career. He runs well for his size and has a plus arm that plays well in right field. Kieschnick showed he was healthy while spending a month in the Dominican League. His two-month run at Fresno caught San Francisco's attention, and he's a good bet to contribute at the big league level in 2013—if he can finally stay healthy.

BA GRADE

45

MEDIUM

Year	Club (League)	Class	AVG	G	AB	R	H	2B	3B	HR	RBI	BB	SO	SB	CS	OBP	SLG
2009	San Jose (CAL)	HiA	.296	131	517	86	153	37	8	23	110	36	130	9	1	.345	.532
2010	Richmond (EL)	AA	.251	60	223	21	56	8	3	4	23	18	55	2	3	.305	.368
2011	Richmond (EL)	AA	.255	126	459	71	117	22	5	16	65	34	121	13	7	.307	.429
2012	Giants (AZL)	R	.083	3	12	0	1	1	0	0	4	0	5	0	0	.077	.167
	Fresno (PCL)	AAA	.306	55	222	49	68	13	4	15	40	24	68	0	2	.376	.604
Minor League Totals			.276	375	1433	227	395	81	20	58	242	112	379	24	13	.329	.482

10 ADALBERTO MEJIA, LHP

Born: June 20, 1993. **B-T:** L-L. **Ht.:** 6-3. **Wt.:** 205. **Signed:** Dominican Republic, 2011. **Signed by:** Pablo Peguero.

Mejia signed for $350,000 and dominated the Rookie-level Dominican Summer League in 2011, then showed in instructional league that he could throw strikes and change speeds. So the Giants decided to get aggressive and assign him to low Class A as an 18-year-old. Mejia gave up 11 runs over five innings in his first two starts, leading to a two-month stay in the bullpen, but he bounced back to go 4-1, 1.58 in his final six starts. With his size, loose arm and potential for three solid or better pitches, Mejia could fit in the middle of a big league rotaton. He's a flyball pitcher who works off an 89-91 mph fastball that touches 93 and should gain steam as he continues to mature. He can get outs with both of his secondary offerings, a slider that flashes good tilt and depth, and a changeup, more advanced than the slider, that he sells effectively. Mejia's ability to throw consistent strikes and keep the ball down in the zone is unusual for such a young pitcher. San Francisco doesn't need to rush him, but Mejia has earned the right to open 2013 in high Class A at age 19. He'll be part of a prospect-laden San Jose rotation that should also include Kyle Crick, Chris Stratton and Clayton Blackburn.

BA GRADE

50

HIGH

Year	Club (League)	Class	W	L	ERA	G	GS	CG	SV	IP	H	HR	BB	SO	K/9	WHIP	AVG
2011	Giants (DSL)	R	5	2	1.42	13	13	0	0	76	58	0	8	71	8.4	0.87	.209
2012	Augusta (SAL)	LoA	10	7	3.97	30	14	1	0	107	122	4	21	79	6.7	1.34	.284
Minor League Totals			15	9	2.91	43	27	1	0	183	180	4	29	150	7.4	1.14	.255

11 ADAM DUVALL, 3B

BA GRADE

45

MEDIUM

Born: Sept. 4, 1988. **B-T:** R-R. **Ht.:** 6-1. **Wt.:** 205. **Drafted:** Louisville, 2010 (11th round). **Signed by:** Kevin Christman.

Duvall couldn't figure out why he felt so weak toward the end of spring training last year. A medical exam revealed that he had diabetes, and though he began the season 15 pounds under his normal weight while getting used to an insulin pump, he soon had his strength and stamina back. Though he was old for high Class A at age 23, he led the entire level with 30 homers and 100 RBIs. Signed for a mere $2,500 as an 11th-rounder in 2010, Duvall might be the most successful Giants farmhand at getting the barrel to fastballs. His tremendous top hand allows him to hit all pitches hard to all fields, and he has the most functional power in the system. It wasn't just a California League phenomenon, as he slugged .527 at hitter-unfriendly Augusta the previous year. He strikes out and may not hit for high averages, though he does draw walks. Almost all of Duvall's value comes from his power. He's a well below-average runner and a subpar defender at third base. He has average arm strength but lacks accuracy on this throws, so San Francisco is working to change him to a three-quarters arm slot. He lacks consistent footwork and his 29 errors easily led Cal League third basemen last year. The Giants once had visions of turning him into a second baseman along the lines of Jeff Kent, but that's unrealistic. If Duvall can continue his power production at Double-A this year, he could become part of San Francisco's future plans.

Year	Club (League)	Class	AVG	G	AB	R	H	2B	3B	HR	RBI	BB	SO	SB	CS	OBP	SLG
2010	Salem-Keizer (NWL)	SS	.245	54	192	30	47	10	1	4	18	14	45	2	3	.318	.370
2011	Augusta (SAL)	LoA	.285	116	431	69	123	30	4	22	87	59	98	4	4	.385	.527
2012	San Jose (CAL)	HiA	.258	134	534	101	138	24	4	30	100	47	116	8	2	.327	.487
Minor League Totals			.266	304	1157	200	308	64	9	56	205	120	259	14	9	.348	.482

12 GUSTAVO CABRERA, OF

BA GRADE
55
EXTREME

Born: Jan. 23, 1996. **B-T:** R-R. **Ht.:** 6-0. **Wt.:** 190. **Signed:** Dominican Republic, 2012. **Signed by:** Pablo Peguero/Felix Peguero.

The Giants signed Cabrera for $1.3 million, and he might have received three times as much if not for MLB's new rules that cap international spending. In terms of raw tools and athleticism, Cabrera was the most coveted July 2 signee in Latin America. He is a plus-plus runner who profiles well in right field, which excites club officials. "He's ideal for us because in our ballpark, we almost need three center fielders," scouting director John Barr said. Cabrera went 2-for-3 with a walk and a steal and earned MVP honors while leading the Dominican team to the junior division Reviving Baseball in Inner Cities World Series at Minnesota's Target Field in 2011. At the plate, Cabrera has a long swing and struggles with balance issues but has plus power and bat speed to spare. If he plays in the United States at all in 2013, it'd be in the Arizona League. More likely, San Francisco will give Cabrera time to work on developing a functional swing and fundamental approach before he faces pro pitching.

Year	Club (League)	Class	AVG	G	AB	R	H	2B	3B	HR	RBI	BB	SO	SB	CS	OBP	SLG
2012	Did Not Play—Signed 2013 Contract																

13 ANDREW SUSAC, C

BA GRADE
50
HIGH

Born: March 22, 1990. **B-T:** R-R. **Ht.:** 6-1. **Wt.:** 200. **Drafted:** Oregon State, 2011 (2nd round). **Signed by:** Matt Woodward.

The Giants expected more from Susac in his 2012 pro debut, and he might be asked to repeat high Class A as a result. But all the tools are still there for the Sacramento native, who might have been a first-round pick if not for a hamate fracture that ended his college career a month before the draft. Susac has quick feet, and he's an athletic receiver with good flexibility, through his hips and arm are slightly above average. But his focus wavered behind the plate (as evidenced by his California League-high 14 errors), and he has a lot to learn about calling a game. He is still refining his technique, which is apparent when his throws are off target. Still, he managed to throw out Reds speedster Billy Hamilton twice in one game, and his 32 percent caught-stealing rate was second-best among Cal League regulars. Susac had a tough year at the plate, striking out in 28 percent of his at-bats, and had to smooth out a high leg kick that kept him from staying back on breaking pitches. His adjustments helped him hit .333 in August and he showed flashes of the plus power that earned him an over-slot $1.1 million bonus as a second-round pick in 2011. Even with his struggles, San Francisco still felt confident enough about Susac that it was willing to sacrifice catching prospect Tommy Joseph to get Hunter Pence from the Phillies. Susac now ranks as the best catcher in the system.

Year	Club (League)	Class	AVG	G	AB	R	H	2B	3B	HR	RBI	BB	SO	SB	CS	OBP	SLG
2012	San Jose (CAL)	HiA	.244	102	361	58	88	16	3	9	52	55	100	1	1	.351	.380
Minor League Totals			.244	102	361	58	88	16	3	9	52	55	100	1	1	.351	.380

14 EDWIN ESCOBAR, LHP

BA GRADE
50
HIGH

Born: April 22, 1992. **B-T:** L-L. **Ht.:** 6-1. **Wt.:** 195. **Signed:** Venezuela, 2008. **Signed by:** Wilmer Becerra/Rafic Saab (Rangers).

The Giants loved "Esky" Escobar's size and arm action as a teenager in Venezuela, and they didn't toss their scouting reports after he signed with the Rangers. In the spring of 2010, Texas couldn't keep Rule 5 pick Ben Snyder on its big league roster, so rather than take Snyder back, San Francisco suggested a trade for Escobar, whom they were ecstatic to bring into the system. The solidly-built lefthander got hit hard at lower levels for Texas but Giants officials noted that he hadn't allowed many homers, he still struck out better than a batter per inning, and his strikeout-to-walk ratio remained excellent. Although it took a year and a half, Escobar made the leap forward that San Francisco envisioned in low Class A last season, using cleaner mechanics and better conditioning to throw 92-93 mph—a jump from the 88 mph he threw in short-season ball the previous summer—and develop a viable changeup. That K-BB ratio (122-32) looked better than ever, and he ranked third in the South Atlantic League in ERA (2.96) and WHIP (1.17). Escobar's curve is more of a slurve and it'll have to get better as he advances. That'll be a project for pitching coach Steve Kline at San Jose.

Year	Club (League)	Class	W	L	ERA	G	GS	CG	SV	IP	H	HR	BB	SO	K/9	WHIP	AVG
2009	Rangers (AZL)	R	2	5	5.00	13	12	0	0	45	53	1	16	48	9.6	1.53	.279
2010	Salem-Keizer (NWL)	SS	2	4	4.86	14	14	0	0	63	64	6	40	69	9.9	1.65	.270
2011	Augusta (SAL)	LoA	1	3	18.00	4	2	0	0	6	15	0	5	5	7.5	3.33	.455
	Giants (AZL)	R	2	4	5.09	15	12	0	0	46	51	2	17	42	8.2	1.48	.293
2012	Augusta (SAL)	LoA	7	8	2.96	22	22	0	0	131	121	7	32	122	8.4	1.17	.241
Minor League Totals			14	24	4.33	68	62	0	0	291	304	16	110	286	8.9	1.42	.267

15 MARTIN AGOSTA, RHP

BA GRADE
50
HIGH

Born: April 7, 1991. **B-T:** R-R. **Ht.:** 6-1. **Wt.:** 180. **Drafted:** St. Mary's, 2012 (2nd round). **Signed by:** Keith Snider.

Agosta's size scared off some scouts, so it's no surprise that he lists Tim Lincecum as his favorite pitcher. San Francisco liked Agosta's feel for pitching and his competitiveness, going back to their reports on him at Jesuit High in Sacramento—where his catcher for a time was current Giants minor leaguer Andrew Susac. Signed for $612,500 as a second-round pick in 2012, Agosta throws a 91-93 mph fastball that tops out at 96, although he makes more location mistakes when he tries to reach back. He's better off letting his sinking, running fastball do its own thing. It gets on hitters because he has some deception and hides the ball well in his delivery. Agosta throws an average slider and uses a cutter that serves as a change of pace and was a plus pitch at times while he became the first nine-game winner for the Gaels since 1991. His lack of a true changeup might limit him to relief, but the Giants plan to try him as a starter. There's a good chance he and Susac will unite again as batterymates, perhaps as soon as 2013 in the California League if Susac repeats high Class A.

Year	Club (League)	Class	W	L	ERA	G	GS	CG	SV	IP	H	HR	BB	SO	K/9	WHIP	AVG
2012	Giants (AZL)	R	0	0	4.22	5	5	0	0	11	8	0	9	19	16.0	1.59	.205
Minor League Totals			0	0	4.22	5	5	0	0	11	8	0	9	19	16.0	1.59	.205

16 MAC WILLIAMSON, OF

BA GRADE
50
HIGH

Born: July 15, 1990. **B-T:** R-R. **Ht.:** 6-4. **Wt.:** 240. **Drafted:** Wake Forest, 2012 (3rd round). **Signed by:** Jeremy Cleveland.

It's hard to get power to play at AT&T Park. So the Giants have taken their draft shots at plus-plus power-hitting college juniors with questionable contact skills, hoping they can file off the raw edges in the minor leagues. Their latest gamble is on Williamson (full name: Johnathan Mackensey Williamson), and the early returns are encouraging. Widely seen as a third-round overdraft who signed for $390,000 ($22,300 under the assigned value for his pick), Williamson had a monster August for short-season Salem Keizer that included six homers, almost certainly buying him an express pass past Augusta to San Jose for 2013. Williamson has power to all fields and is a max-effort player who impressed coaches with his work ethic and desire. He played center field at Wake Forest but profiles best in right, where he shows plus arm strength if not accuracy. He is not an instinctive outfielder but was determined to improve in instructional league. Williamson is a solid runner who had less than a 50 percent success rate on stolen bases in each of his three seasons at Wake Forest. For a power hitter, Williamson doesn't have a long swing. He usually gets in trouble when he hits off his back leg and spins out on pitches. He's shown the ability to take walks, stay on breaking balls and hit mistakes a long way.

Year	Club (League)	Class	AVG	G	AB	R	H	2B	3B	HR	RBI	BB	SO	SB	CS	OBP	SLG
2012	Giants (AZL)	R	.176	4	17	4	3	0	0	2	7	2	5	0	0	.263	.529
	Salem-Keizer (NWL)	SS	.342	29	114	22	39	8	0	7	25	6	19	0	0	.392	.596
Minor League Totals			.321	33	131	26	42	8	0	9	32	8	24	0	0	.375	.588

17 CHRIS HESTON, RHP

BA GRADE
45
MEDIUM

Born: April 10, 1988. **B-T:** R-R. **Ht.:** 6-4. **Wt.:** 185. **Drafted:** East Carolina, 2009 (12th round). **Signed by:** Pat Portugal.

Heston improved on a terrific 2011 season in high Class A and established himself as a legitimate prospect with a banner year in which he led the Double-A Eastern League in ERA (2.24) and WHIP (1.10) and finished fourth in strikeouts (135). Heston has been older for his league and his 87-89 mph fastball won't make scouts salivate, but he's a durable performer who just knows how to pitch. Heston has great pace on the mound and shows such a knack for setting up hitters that his teammates call him "Hesto Presto." Pitching coordinator Bert Bradley was so impressed with Heston's presence and smarts that he would screen video of him when he visited other affiliates. Heston's curveball is his best offspeed pitch, and he likes to save it for strikeout situations. He has a solid changeup that ranks as the best in the system and a decent slider but likes to pitch off his two-seam fastball, which he throws down and to both sides of the plate. Heston is a groundball machine, especially with runners on base. The Giants added Heston to the 40-man roster to shield him from the Rule 5 draft and will send him to Triple-A in 2013.

Year	Club (League)	Class	W	L	ERA	G	GS	CG	SV	IP	H	HR	BB	SO	K/9	WHIP	AVG
2009	Giants (AZL)	R	1	5	4.11	11	6	0	0	35	30	0	10	34	8.7	1.14	.233
2010	Augusta (SAL)	LoA	5	13	3.75	26	26	1	0	149	161	6	33	124	7.5	1.30	.272
2011	San Jose (CAL)	HiA	12	4	3.16	24	24	1	0	151	144	10	40	131	7.8	1.22	.259
2012	Richmond (EL)	AA	9	8	2.24	25	25	1	0	149	124	2	40	135	8.2	1.10	.230
Minor League Totals			27	30	3.13	86	81	3	0	483	459	18	123	424	7.9	1.20	.253

18 STEVEN OKERT, LHP

BA GRADE
50
HIGH

Born: July 9, 1991. **B-T:** L-L. **Ht.:** 6-2. **Wt.:** 210. **Drafted:** Oklahoma, 2012 (4th round). **Signed by:** Daniel Murray.

Okert has all the equipment to become a difference-making bullpen arm in the late innings. Drafted twice previously by the Brewers out of Grayson County (Texas) CC, Okert added velocity at Oklahoma and continued to refine a hard slider that makes him especially effective against lefthanders. He topped out at 97 mph in college to climb up the Giants' 2012 draft board and showed the same heat in instructional league after signing for $270,000 as a fourth-round pick. Health and conditioning will be keys for Okert, who toned up quite a bit over the last year. He steps over his front leg in his delivery and cross-fires but has a good feel for repeating his mechanics and throws hard without obvious effort. He is competitive and likes a relief role, where he doesn't have to hold back. San Francisco expects to develop him along the lines of a Dan Runzler, a lefthander who can throw multiple innings. Okert will need to further refine a changeup to have more success against righthanders. He's headed to a Class A affiliate for his first full pro season.

Year	Club (League)	Class	W	L	ERA	G	GS	CG	SV	IP	H	HR	BB	SO	K/9	WHIP	AVG
2012	Giants (AZL)	R	0	0	0.00	2	0	0	0	2	2	0	1	6	27.0	1.50	.250
	Salem-Keizer (NWL)	SS	2	0	2.36	15	0	0	0	27	26	0	11	22	7.4	1.39	.255
Minor League Totals			2	0	2.20	17	0	0	0	29	28	0	12	28	8.8	1.40	.255

19 CHRIS MARLOWE, RHP

BA GRADE
50
HIGH

Born: Oct. 26, 1989. **B-T:** R-R. **Ht.:** 6-1. **Wt.:** 175. **Drafted:** Oklahoma State, 2011 (5th round). **Signed by:** Daniel Murray.

Marlowe's calling card is a 12-to-6 curveball that gets some 80 grades on the 20-80 scouting scale. "It's hard and late and he can make hitters look really bad with it," pitching coordinator Bert Bradley said. The key in his first full pro season was developing fastball command to get into counts to use his curve as a finishing pitch. Marlowe, who signed for $145,000, made some progress on that front, moving to a three-quarters arm angle that he could repeat better while adding velocity. He was up to 93-94 mph by the end of the season but command is another matter, attested by his 16 wild pitches and 6.4 walks per nine innings last year. Marlowe throws a slider as well that he used to overpower Big 12 hitters at Oklahoma State. The Giants used Marlowe both as a starter and in relief in low Class A, sliding him to the bullpen after July 4 in part to manage his workload. He's a good, wiry athlete whose frame, stuff and delivery draw some comparisons to Tim Lincecum. Marlowe might be the best-fielding pitcher in system. He'll have to fill up the strike zone this spring to earn a promotion to high Class A.

Year	Club (League)	Class	W	L	ERA	G	GS	CG	SV	IP	H	HR	BB	SO	K/9	WHIP	AVG
2011	Giants (AZL)	R	1	0	0.00	3	0	0	0	3	3	0	1	5	15.0	1.33	.231
2012	Augusta (SAL)	LoA	1	9	4.20	30	14	0	2	84	66	5	59	86	9.3	1.49	.216
Minor League Totals			2	9	4.05	33	14	0	2	87	69	5	60	91	9.5	1.49	.216

20 JOSH OSICH, LHP

BA GRADE
50
EXTREME

Born: Sept. 3, 1988. **B-T:** L-L. **Ht.:** 6-3. **Wt.:** 230. **Drafted:** Oregon State, 2011 (6th round). **Signed by:** Matt Woodward.

The Giants knew they'd have to use kid gloves with Osich, who signed for second-round money ($450,000) despite a Tommy John surgery in his recent past and more health concerns in the weeks leading up to the 2011 draft. He didn't pitch on back-to-back days and ended up logging just 32 innings over 27 appearances in high Class A, including two starts. When more arm soreness presented itself, Osich began to work with coaches to lower his arm angle. He felt encouraged by the new delivery but skipped instructional league as a precaution. If healthy, Osich is a big league arm with a mentality to match. He throws consistently in the upper 90s and can touch 98 with a solid slider and changeup while keeping everything around the zone. His fastball has movement in addition to heat, with a lot of late life. Osich has all the tools to develop as a starter. As an amateur, he threw a no-hitter to beat Trevor Bauer and UCLA, the first no-no by an Oregon State pitcher since 1947. More likely, San Francisco will monitor his innings as a reliever while keeping all options open down the road.

Year	Club (League)	Class	W	L	ERA	G	GS	CG	SV	IP	H	HR	BB	SO	K/9	WHIP	AVG
2012	San Jose (CAL)	HiA	0	2	3.62	27	2	0	1	32	34	1	11	34	9.5	1.39	.272
Minor League Totals			0	2	3.62	27	2	0	1	32	34	1	11	34	9.5	1.39	.272

21 STEPHEN JOHNSON, RHP

BA GRADE
50
EXTREME

Born: Feb. 21, 1991. **B-T:** R-R. **Ht.:** 6-4. **Wt.:** 205. **Drafted:** St. Edward's (Texas), 2012 (6th round). **Signed by:** Todd Thomas.

Widely regarded as last year's best small-college draft prospect, Johnson is a late bloomer who didn't make his Colorado high school varsity team until his senior year. He came back from a partially torn elbow ligament to post triple-digit heat as a closer while striking out 63 in 36 innings and holding opponents to a .131 average at NCAA Division II St. Edward's (Texas). He signed for $180,000 in the sixth round. In terms of pure arm strength and velocity, Johnson has few peers. He throws 94-98 mph with a fastball that tops out at 101, and he also has a hard breaking ball in the mid-80s. His mechanics are far from textbook and he stabs the ball behind his back like Rick Sutcliffe as he loads in his delivery. Consistency is his major issue, along with throwing offspeed pitches for strikes. Giants manager Bruce Bochy loves to assemble a bullpen with different looks, and some club officials see Johnson as a funky reliever with overpowering stuff who would fit in well. Others don't want to rule out trying him as a starter, even though he didn't arrive on the prospect map until he turned to relief. He's likely to begin 2013 doing a little of both, as Marlowe did, in low Class A.

Year	Club (League)	Class	W	L	ERA	G	GS	CG	SV	IP	H	HR	BB	SO	K/9	WHIP	AVG
2012	Giants (AZL)	R	0	0	4.50	2	0	0	0	2	1	0	2	2	9.0	1.50	.167
	Salem-Keizer (NWL)	SS	0	2	4.66	17	0	0	2	19	19	2	12	19	8.8	1.60	.257
Minor League Totals			0	2	4.64	19	0	0	2	21	20	2	14	21	8.9	1.59	.250

22 JUAN PEREZ, OF

BA GRADE
45
MEDIUM

Born: Nov. 13, 1986. **B-T:** R-R. **Ht.:** 5-11. **Wt.:** 185. **Drafted:** Western Oklahoma State JC, 2008 (13th round). **Signed by:** Todd Thomas.

You have to dream a little bit on Perez, who is old for a prospect and stayed in the game between high school and junior college by playing night ball for El Caribe—the Bronx's well known amateur men's league—while working as a plumbing apprentice for his father. Now entering his fifth season in the Giants organization, Perez just continues to compete well wherever they send him. He played alongside Gary Brown at Richmond and was every bit as good a defensive outfielder while outhitting Brown in a pitcher's park in a pitcher's league. The Flying Squirrels even played Perez in center and Brown in left a few times. Perez has above-average arm strength. He's an aggressive hitter with an upright stance who resembles Ian Kinsler in the way he arches backward at times. He doesn't have a flat path through the zone and often swings for the fences, which won't work once he arrives at AT&T Park. He'll have to do a better job controlling ball flight and thinking line drive, allowing him to better employ his plus speed. Perez gets out of the box as fast as anyone in the system. He's not a good baserunner, stealing just 18 bases while getting caught 15 times. Perez should be a candidate to make the big league club as a fifth outfielder this spring. San Francisco added him to its 40-man roster in November.

Year	Club (League)	Class	AVG	G	AB	R	H	2B	3B	HR	RBI	BB	SO	SB	CS	OBP	SLG
2009	Augusta (SAL)	LoA	.244	123	447	56	109	29	3	9	54	23	101	18	4	.283	.383
2010	San Jose (CAL)	HiA	.298	131	551	83	164	37	10	13	63	31	116	17	15	.337	.472
2011	Richmond (EL)	AA	.256	131	457	58	117	25	10	4	40	28	95	22	6	.303	.381
2012	Richmond (EL)	AA	.302	126	483	65	146	26	4	11	53	22	85	18	15	.341	.441
Minor League Totals			.277	511	1938	262	536	117	27	37	210	104	397	75	40	.317	.422

23 NICK NOONAN, SS/3B

BA GRADE
45
MEDIUM

Born: May 4, 1989. **B-T:** L-R. **Ht.:** 6-1. **Wt.:** 180. **Drafted:** HS—San Diego, 2007 (1st round supplemental). **Signed by:** Ray Krawczyk.

A former top-10 prospect, Noonan dropped off the map for a couple years because of one simple reason: He stopped hitting the fastball. The 32nd overall selection in 2007 and recipient of a $915,750 bonus, he hit the a wall at Double-A in 2010 when he hit .237, then followed up by batting just .229 over three levels the following year. But something clicked in Triple-A and he hit .296 while getting back to the line-drive approach that once made him one of the system's most promising hitting prospects. Noonan might not profile as a future all-star, but he has a bit more than gap power and added to his value by playing adequately at three infield positions at Fresno while making a major improvement on backhand plays at shortstop. He marries a quick transfer with much-improved throwing accuracy, and his solid arm strength allows him to play on the left side of the infield. He's an average runner but smart on the bases. The Giants got several trade hits on Noonan around the July 31 deadline, so clearly they aren't the only ones who see him contributing as an extra infielder. He was added to the 40-man roster to protect him from the Rule 5 draft.

Year	Club (League)	Class	AVG	G	AB	R	H	2B	3B	HR	RBI	BB	SO	SB	CS	OBP	SLG
2007	Giants (AZL)	R	.316	52	206	33	65	11	4	3	40	12	20	18	3	.357	.451
2008	Augusta (SAL)	LoA	.279	119	499	79	139	27	7	9	68	23	98	29	4	.315	.415
2009	San Jose (CAL)	HiA	.259	124	459	82	119	26	8	7	64	48	97	9	5	.330	.397
2010	Richmond (EL)	AA	.237	101	372	43	88	12	2	3	26	22	74	7	3	.280	.304
2011	Richmond (EL)	AA	.212	71	260	28	55	11	0	3	25	33	60	2	2	.303	.288
	Fresno (PCL)	AAA	.297	13	37	6	11	0	0	1	4	4	2	1	0	.366	.378
	San Jose (CAL)	HiA	.246	28	122	14	30	6	1	1	16	12	18	1	2	.311	.336
2012	Fresno (PCL)	AAA	.296	129	490	65	145	26	3	9	62	40	84	7	3	.347	.416
Minor League Totals			.267	637	2445	350	652	119	25	36	305	194	453	74	22	.322	.380

24 EHIRE ADRIANZA, SS

BA GRADE
45
MEDIUM

Born: Aug. 21, 1989. **B-T:** B-R. **Ht.:** 6-0. **Wt.:** 168. **Signed:** Venezuela, 2006. **Signed by:** Ciro Villalobos.

Adrianza is one of those players who inspires coaches to rub their chins and say, "If only we could make him a .250 hitter . . ." The switch-hitter did better than that in 2011 while finishing with a .300 average in high Class A, but he couldn't compete against more advanced pitching in Double-A. Adrianza remains the Giants' most gifted defensive infielder, with soft hands, plus range and terrific playmaking ability—all-star level tools. He hasn't developed physically as hoped and has trouble keeping on weight or adding strength. He's a better hitter from his natural right side, where he has better barrel accuracy and can turn on a fastball. But from the left side, he doesn't have the bat speed to trust his hands and let the ball get deep, allowing him to use the whole field. A lot of at-bats ended with ground outs to first base. Adrianza has good instincts on the bases and is a plus runner, if not a burner. He hit better in winter ball in his native Venezuela He's a candidate to repeat Double-A for sure, but perhaps San Francisco will send him to the livelier Pacific Coast League in an effort to get him rolling at the plate.

Year	Club (League)	Class	AVG	G	AB	R	H	2B	3B	HR	RBI	BB	SO	SB	CS	OBP	SLG
2006	Giants (DSL)	R	.156	44	122	17	19	2	1	0	7	24	31	3	2	.311	.189
2007	Giants (DSL)	R	.241	66	249	44	60	17	2	0	30	41	31	23	6	.351	.325
2008	Fresno (PCL)	AAA	.500	2	6	2	3	1	0	0	0	2	1	0	0	.625	.667
	Giants (AZL)	R	.255	15	55	13	14	4	0	1	6	7	4	0	1	.349	.382
	Salem-Keizer (NWL)	SS	.400	1	5	3	2	0	0	0	0	0	1	0	0	.400	.400
2009	Augusta (SAL)	LoA	.258	117	388	54	100	15	3	2	46	42	66	7	1	.333	.327
2010	San Jose (CAL)	HiA	.256	124	445	70	114	22	5	3	35	47	87	33	15	.333	.348
2011	Augusta (SAL)	LoA	.231	38	143	18	33	10	1	3	17	18	32	3	2	.315	.378
	San Jose (CAL)	HiA	.300	56	230	34	69	24	3	3	27	23	46	5	1	.375	.470
2012	Richmond (EL)	AA	.220	127	451	52	99	22	5	3	32	41	90	16	4	.289	.310
Minor League Totals			.245	590	2094	307	513	117	20	15	200	245	389	90	32	.330	.341

25 ERIC SURKAMP, LHP

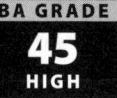

BA GRADE
45
HIGH

Born: July 16, 1987. **B-T:** L-L. **Ht.:** 6-5. **Wt.:** 220. **Drafted:** North Carolina State, 2008 (6th round). **Signed by:** Pat Portugal.

Surkamp entered last spring as an outside candidate to make the Giants rotation after a strong 2011 season in which he led the Eastern League in the pitching triple crown categories before receiving his first big league callup. But Surkamp's elbow had other plans. He was shut down after one exhibition game with a strained forearm, tried to rehab for two months without success and ultimately had Tommy John surgery in July. His rehab has gone well, but he won't be ready to return until midseason. When healthy, Surkamp profiles as a good back-of-the-rotation starter. He features a dynamic curveball and isn't afraid to throw inside even though his best fastball is a two-seamer that just brushes 90 mph. Surkamp has a solid changeup and has been successful at getting ground-ball outs. He has flashed a cutter, too. Surkamp probably won't get much late life back on his fastball until 2014, but his one premium pitch and his presence on the mound make him a name to keep in mind.

Year	Club (League)	Class	W	L	ERA	G	GS	CG	SV	IP	H	HR	BB	SO	K/9	WHIP	AVG
2008	Giants (AZL)	R	0	0	2.70	2	0	0	0	3	3	0	0	7	18.9	0.90	.231
	Salem-Keizer (NWL)	SS	0	2	6.43	5	4	0	0	14	20	1	5	16	10.3	1.79	.351
2009	Augusta (SAL)	LoA	11	5	3.30	23	23	2	0	131	129	6	39	169	11.6	1.28	.257
2010	San Jose (CAL)	HiA	4	2	3.11	17	17	1	0	101	79	5	22	108	9.6	1.00	.218
2011	Richmond (EL)	AA	10	4	2.02	23	22	1	0	142	110	5	44	165	10.4	1.08	.213
	San Jose (CAL)	HiA	1	0	0.00	1	1	0	0	6	4	0	1	5	7.5	0.83	.190
	San Francisco (NL)	MAJ	2	2	5.74	6	6	0	0	27	32	1	17	13	4.4	1.84	.311
2012	Did Not Play—Injured																
Major League Totals			2	2	5.74	6	6	0	0	27	32	1	17	13	4.4	1.84	.311
Minor League Totals			26	13	2.85	71	67	4	0	398	345	17	111	470	10.6	1.15	.234

26 CODY HALL, RHP

Born: Jan. 6, 1988. **B-T:** R-R. **Ht.:** 6-4. **Wt.:** 220. **Drafted:** Southern, 2011 (19th round). **Signed by:** Hugh Walker.

BA GRADE
45
HIGH

Hall was among several power arms the Giants took in the middle to late rounds of the 2011 draft, and while he had less pedigree than some of the others, coaches knew early on that they'd give him first chance to close at Augusta. Hall is a physically imposing reliever who doesn't have any trouble maintaining a mid-90s fastball that hits 97 mph on occasion. He had a tremendous year in low Class A, earning a promotion for the stretch run and California League playoffs. He is a prototypical closer, with exaggerated body language on the mound and hyper-competitiveness that sometimes gets the best of him. He would rate higher if he had a dependable breaking ball. His slider is a raw pitch and he'd rather power his way through lineups with his four-seamer. He made more progress with his changeup, which probably rates as his second best pitch for now. Hall had barely any formal pitching instruction before arriving at Southern, where ex-big leaguers Dave Stewart and Lee Smith regularly provide preseason coaching assistance, so he has everything to learn. He is set to return to high Class A, likely as the closer.

Year	Club (League)	Class	W	L	ERA	G	GS	CG	SV	IP	H	HR	BB	SO	K/9	WHIP	AVG
2011	Salem-Keizer (NWL)	SS	3	1	2.63	23	0	0	4	27	21	1	19	42	13.8	1.46	.210
2012	Augusta (SAL)	LoA	3	0	1.60	36	0	0	20	39	36	0	12	54	12.4	1.22	.247
	San Jose (CAL)	HiA	1	1	3.24	9	0	0	1	8	12	0	4	10	10.8	1.92	.333
Minor League Totals			7	2	2.16	68	0	0	25	75	69	1	35	106	12.7	1.39	.245

27 RICKY OROPESA, 1B

Born: Dec. 15, 1989. **B-T:** L-R. **Ht.:** 6-3. **Wt.:** 225. **Drafted:** Southern California, 2011 (3rd round). **Signed by:** Michael Kendall.

BA GRADE
45
HIGH

Oropesa was one of the best collegiate power hitters in the 2011 draft. He led the Cape Cod League with seven homers in 2010, and as a sophomore, he became the first player to top Southern California in all three triple crown categories (.353-20-67) since Jeff Clement in 2005. He showed a knack for driving in runs in high Class A, but his first pro season was a bit underwhelming considering the hitter-friendly California League and his 150 strikeouts. Oropesa doesn't have a lot of rhythm in his swing and he didn't make an adjustment when Cal League pitchers—especially lefthanders—fed him offspeed pitches off the plate. His barrel accuracy must improve as well as his approach when behind in the count to profile as something more than a platoon player. Oropesa is a station-to-station runner and probably doesn't have the hands or range to play anywhere besides first base. He has plenty of arm, though, and could pile up plenty of outfield assists if the Giants stuck him in left field to give him another avenue to the big leagues. He'll move up the ladder to Double-A in 2013.

Year	Club (League)	Class	AVG	G	AB	R	H	2B	3B	HR	RBI	BB	SO	SB	CS	OBP	SLG
2012	San Jose (CAL)	HiA	.263	134	518	70	136	30	3	16	98	59	150	1	1	.338	.425
Minor League Totals			.263	134	518	70	136	30	3	16	98	59	150	1	1	.338	.425

28 JACOB DUNNINGTON, RHP

Born: Feb. 2, 1991. **B-T:** L-R. **Ht.:** 6-2. **Wt.:** 160. **Signed:** HS—Redmond, Wash., NDFA 2009. **Signed by:** Matt Woodward.

BA GRADE
45
HIGH

Dunnington might have weighed 140 pounds when he graduated from high school and didn't start hitting 90 mph until after the draft, but he didn't give up his dream of becoming a pro pitcher. Giants scout Matt Woodward offered him a contract after seeing the Seattle-area righthander throw at a workout. Then he was nearly untouchable in the low minors. Although Dunnington has put on 20 pounds over the past two years, he's still rail thin. Coaches sometimes hold up a fungo bat to indicate that they want him to start warming up in the bullpen. He's got more room to fill out and his stuff keeps missing bats, while his funky delivery bears some resemblance to former Angels all-star set-up man Scot Shields. In 119 pro innings, he has allowed just three homers. Dunnington throws downhill while mixing a lively 92-94 mph fastball with a plus curveball and solid slider. He's had a tender arm at times over the last two years. San Francisco jumped him to Double-A to finish last season and then sent him to the Arizona Fall League. He'll have to prove his durability in 2013, and a starting role isn't out of the question if he does. He'll likely begin at Double-A.

Year	Club (League)	Class	W	L	ERA	G	GS	CG	SV	IP	H	HR	BB	SO	K/9	WHIP	AVG
2010	Giants (AZL)	R	3	0	0.63	17	0	0	3	29	10	0	15	45	14.1	0.87	.109
2011	Augusta (SAL)	LoA	3	0	3.77	32	0	0	1	43	29	1	32	53	11.1	1.42	.193
	San Jose (CAL)	HiA	2	1	2.82	16	0	0	1	22	13	1	10	31	12.5	1.03	.167
2012	Augusta (SAL)	LoA	1	0	4.50	11	0	0	0	10	8	1	5	14	12.6	1.30	.216
	Richmond (EL)	AA	0	0	1.76	13	0	0	0	15	12	0	8	18	10.6	1.30	.222
Minor League Totals			9	4	2.64	89	0	0	5	119	72	3	70	161	12.1	1.19	.175

29 SHAWN PAYNE, OF

BA GRADE
45
HIGH

Born: July 13, 1989. **B-T:** R-R. **Ht.:** 6-1. **Wt.:** 190. **Drafted:** Georgia Southern, 2011 (35th round). **Signed by:** Ron Merrill.

A lightly regarded college senior, Payne was old for the South Atlantic League last season but his terrific leadoff skills should translate as he moves up the line. An upbeat and positive player, Payne is a plus runner and a premium basestealer who was successful on 53 of 56 attempts at Augusta. In his first full pro season, he ranked second in the SAL in steals, fourth in on-base percentage (.413) and sixth in hitting (.309). Payne has a quiet stance, a short stride and shows good hand strength and bat speed. He's a line-drive hitter who reminds some of Andres Torres with his ability to surprise by popping one over the fence. Payne is a below-average defender, and a below-average arm likely will limit him to left field as he advances, but his bat and speed will carry him. He has a decent knowledge of the strike zone and worked on his bunting and two-strike approach in instructional league. Payne's road to the big leagues is as an extra outfielder, but the Giants don't have many promising leadoff men in the system behind Gary Brown. So he'll receive every opportunity to advance.

Year	Club (League)	Class	AVG	G	AB	R	H	2B	3B	HR	RBI	BB	SO	SB	CS	OBP	SLG
2011	Salem-Keizer (NWL)	SS	.306	57	160	37	49	8	3	0	19	29	32	21	6	.431	.394
2012	Augusta (SAL)	LoA	.309	116	405	66	125	19	6	6	57	61	71	53	3	.413	.430
	San Jose (CAL)	HiA	.333	2	9	1	3	1	0	0	2	0	2	0	0	.333	.444
Minor League Totals			.308	175	574	104	177	28	9	6	78	90	105	74	9	.417	.420

30 BRETT BOCHY, RHP

BA GRADE
40
MEDIUM

Born: Aug. 27, 1987. **B-T:** R-R. **Ht.:** 6-2. **Wt.:** 192. **Drafted:** Kansas, 2010 (20th round). **Signed by:** Hugh Walker.

It took all spring, but Giants manager Bruce Bochy finally worked his son into a Cactus League exhibition just before San Francisco broke camp. The former Jayhawks closer responded by casually recording three outs—including a strikeout of Brewers catcher Jonathan Lucroy—on a handful of pitches. It brought great satisfaction to the manager, who hasn't been present for most of his son's baseball career. Like his dad, Bochy is the laconic sort who carries himself with confidence and knows what pitch is called for in a given situation. There's no nepotism in a pitcher who conquered Double-A in his second pro season just two years removed from April 2010 Tommy John surgery. Bochy has a disappearing 88-90 mph fastball that he throws from a deceptive arm angle. He has plus command of a tight slider that he can make bigger when needed, and he can sink or cut his fastball when he wants a ground ball. He's a bit of an arm swinger, throwing across his body, so durability remains the biggest question. Bochy was shut down late in the season because of shoulder fatigue, precluding him from possibly pitching for France in the World Baseball Classic qualifier. His medicals checked out and he's done plenty to deserve a promotion to Triple-A.

Year	Club (League)	Class	W	L	ERA	G	GS	CG	SV	IP	H	HR	BB	SO	K/9	WHIP	AVG
2011	Augusta (SAL)	LoA	1	0	1.38	35	0	0	10	39	22	1	8	53	12.2	0.77	.161
2012	Richmond (EL)	AA	7	3	2.53	41	0	0	14	53	29	3	18	69	11.6	0.88	.161
Minor League Totals			8	3	2.05	76	0	0	24	92	51	4	26	122	11.9	0.83	.161

Seattle Mariners

BY CONOR GLASSEY

Though the Mariners finished last in the American League West for the third straight season, they continue to make marginal improvements under general manager Jack Zduriencik and rebuild patiently after former GM Bill Bavasi left the team with bad contracts and a gutted farm system.

While the past few years have been bleak, Seattle's future appears brighter. It has a young core at the big league level, starting with Felix Hernandez, who threw the first perfect game in franchise history on Aug. 15 and continues to rank among the best pitchers in the game. Kyle Seager broke out and led the team with 20  home runs. Rookie Jesus Montero, acquired from the Yankees along with Hector Noesi for Michael Pineda and righthander Jose Campos in the offseason, became the youngest player (age 22) to hit 15 homers for the Mariners since Alex Rodriguez in 1998.

Despite the positives, the Mariners expected more from the likes of Dustin Ackley and Justin Smoak. Drafted No. 2 overall behind Stephen Strasburg in 2009, Ackley batted just .226/.294/.328. Smoak, the key player in the Cliff Lee trade with the Rangers in 2010, was just as bad for most of the season but provided some hope by hitting .338 with five homers in September.

After finishing last in the AL in scoring for the fourth straight year, Seattle announced it would move the fences in at Safeco Field for 2013.

Hope is on the horizon, as the Mariners have one of the best farm systems in baseball. Seattle has top-tier talent, most notably an outstanding group of pitching prospects, along with depth and balance, even after graduating closer Tom Wilhelmsen (who recorded 29 saves in 2012 after taking over as the team's closer in June) and starter Erasmo Ramirez, who strung together five quality starts (out of eight).

Scouting director Tom McNamara and his staff have restocked the system in a short time, identifying quality players with their top picks—Ackley, righthander Taijuan Walker, lefty Danny Hultzen and catcher Mike Zunino—and finding value in the later rounds.

The Double-A Jackson Generals led the Southern League with a 3.37 ERA with a staff that featured all of the organization's top pitching prospects at some point. Carter Capps and Stephen Pryor contributed to the big league bullpen by the end of the season, while starters Walker, Hultzen, James Paxton and Brandon Maurer could arrive in 2013 after some Triple-A time.

Third baseman Kyle Seager led the Mariners with 35 doubles and 20 home runs

The Mariners also have a few hitters on the way. Zunino had a stellar pro debut and reached Double-A after signing for $4 million as the No. 3 overall pick in the 2012 draft. Seattle has a number of middle-infield options in the upper minors as well, highlighted by Nick Franklin, Stefen Romero and Brad Miller.

After the season ended, the Mariners significantly revamped their international scouting department. They fired Latin America coordinator Patrick Guerrero, a move that prompted international scouting director Bob Engle to announce he wouldn't return when his contract expired. Both Engle and Guerrero joined the Dodgers.

Engle, who had been with Seattle since January 2000, oversaw the signings of Hernandez, Pineda, Shin-Soo Choo, Asdrubal Cabrera and several other big leaguers. He previously had been the scouting director for the Blue Jays, with whom he was involved in drafting Cy Young Award winners Chris Carpenter, Roy Halladay and Pat Hentgen.

To replace Engle, the Mariners hired Cubs crosschecker Tim Kissner, who grew up in Alaska and played at Oregon State. They also tabbed Red Sox crosschecker Tom Allison, a former Diamondbacks scouting director, as their pro scouting director, a position that had been vacant since September 2010.

THIS YEAR'S TOP 30

Player, Pos.		Grade
1.	Mike Zunino, c	60/Low
2.	Taijuan Walker, rhp	70/High
3.	Danny Hultzen, lhp	65/Medium
4.	James Paxton, lhp	55/Medium
5.	Nick Franklin, ss/2b	55/Medium
6.	Brandon Maurer, rhp	55/Medium
7.	Carter Capps, rhp	55/Medium
8.	Stefen Romero, 2b	50/Medium
9.	Brad Miller, ss	50/Medium
10.	Victor Sanchez, rhp	55/High
11.	Stephen Pryor, rhp	45/Low
12.	Luiz Gohara, lhp	60/Extreme
13.	Joe DeCarlo, 3b	50/High
14.	Tyler Pike, lhp	50/High
15.	Gabriel Guerrero, of	55/Extreme
16.	Carson Smith, rhp	45/Medium
17.	Leon Landry, of	50/High
18.	Patrick Kivlehan, 3b	50/High
19.	Edwin Diaz, rhp	50/High
20.	Jack Marder, 2b/c/of	45/Medium
21.	John Hicks, c	45/Medium
22.	Francisco Martinez, 3b/of	50/High
23.	Julio Morban, of	50/High
24.	Jabari Blash, of	50/High
25.	Timmy Lopes, 2b	50/High
26.	Vinnie Catricala, 3b/of	45/Medium
27.	Chance Ruffin, rhp	45/Medium
28.	Chris Taylor, ss	45/Medium
29.	Ramon Morla, 3b	50/High
30.	Anthony Fernandez, lhp	45/Medium

LAST YEAR'S TOP 30

Player, Pos.		Status
1.	Taijuan Walker, rhp	No. 2
2.	Danny Hultzen, lhp	No. 3
3.	James Paxton, lhp	No. 4
4.	Nick Franklin, ss/2b	No. 5
5.	Jose Campos, rhp	(Yankees)
6.	Francisco Martinez, 3b	No. 22
7.	Chance Ruffin, rhp	No. 27
8.	Tom Wilhelmsen, rhp	Majors
9.	Vinnie Catricala, 3b/1b/of	No. 26
10.	Phillips Castillo, of	Dropped out
11.	Brad Miller, ss	No. 9
12.	Guillermo Pimentel, of	Dropped out
13.	Erasmo Ramirez, rhp	Majors
14.	Alex Liddi, 3b/ss	Majors
15.	Stephen Pryor, rhp	No. 11
16.	Carter Capps, rhp	No. 7
17.	Victor Sanchez, rhp	No. 10
18.	Tyler Marlette, c	Dropped out
19.	Forrest Snow, rhp	Dropped out
20.	Jabari Blash, of	No. 24
21.	Brandon Maurer, rhp	No. 6
22.	John Hicks, c	No. 21
23.	Marcus Littlewood, c/ss/2b	Dropped out
24.	Chih-Hsien Chiang, of	(Free Agent)
25.	Carlos Triunfel, ss	Dropped out
26.	Mauricio Robles, lhp	Dropped out
27.	Steven Proscia, 3b/1b	Dropped out
28.	Johermyn Chavez, of	(Cubs)
29.	Rich Poythress, 1b	Dropped out
30.	Cavan Cohoes, ss	Dropped out

BEST TOOLS

Best Hitter for Average	Stefen Romero
Best Power Hitter	Mike Zunino
Best Strike-Zone Discipline	Brad Miller
Fastest Baserunner	Mike Faulkner
Best Athlete	Patrick Kivlehan
Best Fastball	Carter Capps
Best Curveball	James Paxton
Best Slider	Carson Smith
Best Changeup	Danny Hultzen
Best Control	Anthony Fernandez
Best Defensive Catcher	Mike Zunino
Best Defensive Infielder	Gabriel Noriega
Best Infield Arm	Carlos Triunfel
Best Defensive Outfielder	Denny Almonte
Best Outfield Arm	James Jones

PROJECTED 2016 LINEUP

Catcher	Mike Zunino
First Base	Justin Smoak
Second Base	Nick Franklin
Third Base	Kyle Seager
Shortstop	Brad Miller
Left Field	Dustin Ackley
Center Field	Michael Saunders
Right Field	Stefen Romero
Designated Hitter	Jesus Montero
No. 1 Starter	Felix Hernandez
No. 2 Starter	Taijuan Walker
No. 3 Starter	Danny Hultzen
No. 4 Starter	James Paxton
No. 5 Starter	Brandon Maurer
Closer	Carter Capps

TOP PROSPECTS OF THE DECADE

Year	Player, Pos.	2012 Org.
2003	Rafael Soriano, rhp	Yankees
2004	Felix Hernandez, rhp	Mariners
2005	Felix Hernandez, rhp	Mariners
2006	Jeff Clement, c	Pirates
2007	Adam Jones, of	Orioles
2008	Jeff Clement, c	Pirates
2009	Greg Halman, of	Deceased
2010	Dustin Ackley, of/1b	Mariners
2011	Dustin Ackley, 2b	Mariners
2012	Taijuan Walker	Mariners

TOP DRAFT PICKS OF THE DECADE

Year	Player, Pos.	2012 Org.
2003	Adam Jones, ss (1st round supp.)	Orioles
2004	Matt Tuiasosopo, ss (3rd round)	Mets
2005	Jeff Clement, c	Pirates
2006	Brandon Morrow, rhp	Blue Jays
2007	Phillippe Aumont, rhp	Phillies
2008	Josh Fields, rhp	Red Sox
2009	Dustin Ackley, of	Mariners
2010	Taijuan Walker, rhp (1st round supp.)	Mariners
2011	Danny Hultzen, lhp	Mariners
2012	Mike Zunino, c	Mariners

LARGEST BONUSES IN CLUB HISTORY

Danny Hultzen, 2011	$6,350,000
Dustin Ackley, 2009	$6,000,000
Ichiro Suzuki, 2000	$5,000,000
Mike Zunino, 2012	$4,000,000
Jeff Clement, 2005	$3,400,000

SEATTLE MARINERS

TOP 2013 ROOKIE: Mike Zunino, c. The No. 3 overall pick in the 2012 draft showed he could handle a full season's worth of catching.

BREAKOUT PROSPECT: Luiz Gohara, lhp. The 16-year-old Brazilian lefthander draws comparisons to a young C.C. Sabathia for his size, athleticism and plus fastball.

SLEEPER: Yoervis Medina, rhp. A move to the bullpen got the big righty with a mid-90s fastball back on track.

SOURCE OF TOP 30 TALENT			
Homegrown	27	Acquired	3
College	12	Trades	3
Junior college	1	Rule 5 draft	0
High school	7	Independent leagues	0
Independent/drafted	1	Free agents/waivers	0
International	6		

LF
Vinnie Catricala (26)
Guillermo Pimentel
Phillips Castillo
Mike McGee
Dario Pizzano
Isaiah Yates
Joe Dunigan

CF
Leon Landry (17)
Denny Almonte
Jamal Austin
James Zamarripa
Jamodrick McGruder
Mike Faulkner
Jabari Henry

RF
Gabriel Guerrero (15)
Julio Morban (23)
Jabari Blash (24)
James Jones

3B
Stefen Romero (8)
Joe DeCarlo (13)
Patrick Kivlehan (18)
Francisco Martinez (22)
Ramon Morla (29)
Steven Proscia
Mario Martinez

SS
Brad Miller (9)
Chris Taylor (28)
Carlos Triunfel
Ketel Marte
Gabe Franca
Cavan Cohoes
Gabriel Noriega

2B
Nick Franklin (5)
Jack Marder (20)
Timmy Lopes (25)
Eric Farris
Dan Paolini

1B
Rich Poythress
Taylor Ard
Mickey Wiswall
Ji-Man Choi
Dennis Raben
Kristian Brito

C
Mike Zunino (1)
John Hicks (21)
Marcus Littlewood
Tyler Marlette
Steve Baron
Michael Dowd

LHP

LHSP	LHRP
Danny Hultzen (3)	Bobby LaFromboise
James Paxton (4)	Mauricio Robles
Luiz Gohara (12)	Brian Moran
Tyler Pike (14)	
Anthony Fernandez (30)	
Jordan Shipers	
Jimmy Gillheeney	
Roenis Elias	
Steven Ewing	

RHP

RHSP	RHRP
Taijuan Walker (2)	Carter Capps (7)
Brandon Maurer (6)	Stephen Pryor (11)
Victor Sanchez (10)	Carson Smith (16)
Edwin Diaz (19)	Chance Ruffin (27)
D.J. Mitchell	Yoervis Medina
Seon Gi Kim	Jochi Ogando
Andrew Carraway	Danny Farquhar
Bobby Shore	Matt Brazis
Steve Landazuri	Tyler Burgoon
Matt Anderson	George Mieses
Trevor Miller	Dominic Leone
Neritzon Osorio	Forrest Snow
	Stephen Kohlscheen
	Blake Hauser
	Matt Vedo
	Levi Dean
	Mayckol Guaipe
	Brett Shankin

2012   BONUSES: $9.3 MILLION

BEST PURE HITTER: C Mike Zunino (1) has the ability to backspin balls and use the whole field. A smart hitter, he has an advanced approach at the plate and puts together consistent at-bats.

BEST POWER HITTER: Zunino's plus power is his best tool. He's the rare catcher who profiles to hit in the middle of a batting order. 3Bs Joe DeCarlo (2), who signed for $1.3 million, and Patrick Kivlehan (4) also have promising power, as does 1B Taylor Ard (7).

FASTEST RUNNER: OF/2B Jamodrick McGruder (9) and OF Mike Faulkner (12) are both plus-plus runners who clock in at 6.5 seconds in the 60-yard dash. Faulkner is a more explosive runner than McGruder.

BEST DEFENSIVE PLAYER: SS Chris Taylor (5) is a pure shortstop with good fundamental skills. He has smooth hands and feet, takes direct routes to balls and has solid arm strength. Zunino projects as a solid defender behind the plate.

BEST FASTBALL: On the radar gun, RHP Edwin Diaz (3) wins with a heater that tops out at 97 mph, with the potential for even more velocity when he adds weight to his skinny frame. LHP Tyler Pike (3s) pitches at 89-91 mph, but his fastball sneaks up on hitters because of its late life and deception. He also can reach back for 94 mph when he needs it.

BEST SECONDARY PITCH: Pike's curveball is a tight 11-to-5 downer that he throws at 72-76 mph.

BEST PRO DEBUT: Zunino hit .360/.447/.689 with 14 doubles and 13 homers between short-season Everett and Double-A Jackson. Kivlehan won short-season Northwest League MVP honors after batting .301/.373/.511, topping the circuit in homers (12) and slugging. RHP Matt Brazis (28) reached low Class A while posting a 0.65 ERA, seven saves, a 51-5 K-BB ratio and a .117 opponent average in 28 innings.

BEST ATHLETE: Kivlehan played defensive back for Rutgers' football team for four years.

MOST INTRIGUING BACKGROUND: Unsigned OF Mike Yastrzemski's (30) grandfather Carl is a Hall of Famer. Kivlehan took three years off from baseball, then returned this spring and won player of the year honors in the Big East Conference and NWL. Zunino's father Greg scouts for the Reds. 2B Timmy Lopes' (6) brother Christian plays in the Blue Jays system.

CLOSEST TO THE MAJORS: Zunino has the tools and intangibles to get to the big leagues in 2013 and stay there for a long time.

BEST LATE-ROUND PICK: Brazis has a fastball that gets up to 96 mph and the chance for a plus slider. OF Dario Pizzano (15) has a pure lefthanded swing with some strength.

THE ONE WHO GOT AWAY: The Mariners liked 1B Nick Halamandaris' (8) strong lefthanded bat and makeup, but they weren't able to pry him away from his commitment to California. RHP James Kaprielian (40) might have gone in the first three rounds had he been signable away from UCLA.

ASSESSMENT: The Mariners solved their future catching needs by taking Zunino with the third overall pick. After that, Seattle got a mix of hitters and pitchers with upside.

2011   BONUSES: $11.3 MILLION

LHP Danny Hultzen (1), the No. 2 overall pick, surprisingly struggled with his control in his pro debut but still looks like a frontline starter. SS Brad Miller (2) has hit .341/.414/.513 as a pro while getting to Double-A, and RHP Carter Capps (3s) already is a key part of Seattle's bullpen.

GRADE: B+

2010   BONUSES: $4.9 MILLION

Even without a first-round pick, the Mariners had a bountiful draft. RHP Taijuan Walker (1s) has ace potential, and LHP James Paxton (4) isn't far behind. RHP Stephen Pryor already has reached the majors. 2B Stefen Romero (12) is the system's best pure hitter. Unsigned RHP Ryne Stanek (3) and 3B D.J. Peterson (33) could be first-rounders in 2013.

GRADE: B+

2009   BONUSES: $10.9 MILLION

Another No. 2 overall choice, 2B Dustin Ackley (1), is much better than he showed in Seattle last year. 3B Kyle Seager (3) gives the Mariners another infield regular, and SS/2B Nick Franklin (1) could join them soon. LHP Anthony Vasquez (18) has pitched in the majors.

GRADE: B+

2008   BONUSES: $4.3 MILLION

RHP Brandon Maurer (23) had a breakthrough 2012, giving this draft class one hope. RHPs Josh Fields (1), Aaron Pribanic (3) and Brett Lorin (5) were used in trades that haven't helped anyone.

GRADE: C

Draft analysis by Conor Glassey (2012) and Jim Callis (2008-11). Numbers in parentheses indicate draft rounds.

1 MIKE ZUNINO, C

Born: March 25, 1991. **B-T:** R-R. **Ht.:** 6-2. **Wt.:** 220.
Drafted: Florida, 2012 (1st round). **Signed by:** Rob Mummau.

BA GRADE
60
LOW

BILL MITCHELL

Zunino has grown up around the game. His father Greg has been a scout for more than 25 years and currently works with the Reds. Coming out of Mariner High (Cape Coral, Fla.) in 2009, Zunino was regarded as a fifth-round talent but fell to the Athletics in the 29th round because of his strong commitment to Florida. He hit 47 homers in three seasons with the Gators, improving each season and leading them to three College World Series. He won the Baseball America College Player of the Year and Golden Spikes awards in 2012, when he batted .322/.394/.669 while ranking third in NCAA Division I with 28 doubles, fourth with 19 homers and fifth with 150 total bases. The first college player selected and the third overall pick in the 2012 draft, he signed for $4 million. His year continued to get better, as he batted .360/.447/.689 with 13 homers while reaching Double-A Jackson, then married his high school sweetheart before heading to the Arizona Fall League.

From a pure tools standpoint, Zunino doesn't have a single attribute that really wows evaluators. Power is his best tool and it's his only one that scouts grade as plus. He shows an excellent ability to backspin balls, generating above-average pop to all fields. With his strong hands and forearms, he stays through the ball well and shows an advanced ability to drive pitches to the opposite field. He never gives away at-bats and has a patient, balanced approach. Zunino has below-average speed, but he has keen instincts and is a sound baserunner. Even with his muscular frame, he's agile behind the plate. He has a take-charge attitude and pitchers love throwing to him. Though Zunino handled plenty of talented pitchers at Florida, he'll need to continue to make subtle adjustments to handling a pro staff. He has strong hands but can box balls at times, and he allowed nine passed balls in 44 pro games. His arm strength is average to a tick above, and he gets the most out of it with smooth footwork and a quick transfer. He threw out 43 percent of basestealers during his first pro season. Overall, Zunino's sum is greater than his parts and his tools play up

SCOUTING GRADES

Batting: 55.   **Defense:** 55.
Power: 60.   **Arm:** 50.
Speed: 30.

Based on 20-80 scouting scale, where 50 represents major league average, and future projection rather than present tools.

because of his makeup. He has a strong work ethic and is a natural leader on and off the field. He has the requisite toughness for his position and an excellent baseball IQ.

The last time the Mariners spent the No. 3 overall pick on a catcher, they passed up Troy Tulowitzki to take Jeff Clement in 2005. Taking Zunino should work out better, and he's on a fast track to the big leagues. He'll presumably attend big league spring training, though it's doubtful he'll be with the Mariners on Opening Day. More likely, he'll start the season with Triple-A Tacoma. Zunino has all-star potential as a middle-of-the-order hitter at an up-the-middle position, drawing comparisons to Jason Varitek. There's no need to rush Zunino, but he could force the team's hand and he renders moot any questions about Jesus Montero's ability to stay behind the plate.

Year	Club (League)	Class	AVG	G	AB	R	H	2B	3B	HR	RBI	BB	SO	SB	CS	OBP	SLG
2012	Everett (NWL)	SS	.373	29	110	29	41	10	0	10	35	18	26	1	0	.474	.736
	Jackson (SL)	AA	.333	15	51	6	17	4	0	3	8	5	7	0	0	.386	.588
Minor League Totals			.360	44	161	35	58	14	0	13	43	23	33	1	0	.447	.689

2 TAIJUAN WALKER, RHP

Born: Aug. 13, 1992. **B-T:** R-R. **Ht.:** 6-4. **Wt.:** 210. **Drafted:** HS—Yucaipa, Calif., 2010 (1st round supplemental). **Signed by:** John Ramey.

A late convert to the mound after playing more shortstop and basketball early in his high school career, Walker signed for $800,000 as the 43rd overall pick in 2010. The Mariners' 2011 minor league pitcher of the year, he skipped a level to Double-A in 2012. He was the youngest pitcher in the Southern League by nearly a full year and part of the most prospect-laden pitching staff in the minors. Walker is a premium athlete with an ideal pitcher's frame. He sits 93-95 mph with his fastball, tops out at 97 and holds that velocity deep into games and over an entire season. His heater can flatten out at times, but he did a better job of commanding it in 2012. He short-arms his curveball at times, but when he stays loose and gets extension, it shows the potential to be a plus offering. Walker is getting more comfortable using his changeup, which has similar upside. He's also working on adding a cutter to his repertoire. He has electric stuff at times but still needs to command it better. His 2012 stats may not show it, but Walker is one of the best pitching prospects in the game and a potential ace. He could return to Jackson to start 2013, though the Mariners may decide to keep their top pitching prospects together in Triple-A.

BA GRADE 70 HIGH

Year	Club (League)	Class	W	L	ERA	G	GS	CG	SV	IP	H	HR	BB	SO	K/9	WHIP	AVG
2010	Mariners (AZL)	R	1	1	1.29	4	0	0	0	7	2	0	3	9	11.6	0.71	.087
2011	Clinton (MWL)	LoA	6	5	2.89	18	18	1	0	97	69	4	39	113	10.5	1.12	.202
2012	Jackson (SL)	AA	7	10	4.69	25	25	0	0	127	124	12	50	118	8.4	1.37	.258
Minor League Totals			14	16	3.83	47	43	1	0	230	195	16	92	240	9.4	1.25	.231

3 DANNY HULTZEN, LHP

Born: Nov. 28, 1989. **B-T:** L-L. **Ht.:** 6-3. **Wt.:** 200. **Drafted:** Virginia, 2011 (1st round). **Signed by:** Mike Moriarty.

Hultzen set Virginia records for career wins (32) and strikeouts (395) while leading the Cavaliers to their first two College World Series appearances. The No. 2 overall pick in the 2011 draft, he signed an $8.5 million big league contract that included a club-record $6.35 million bonus. He dominated Double-A in his pro debut, but his control disappeared following a promotion to Triple-A in June. Despite his reputation as a polished strike-thrower, Hultzen walked as many batters in his first pro season (75) as he totaled in three years at Virginia. When he got into jams, he tended to overthrow instead of backing off a little or pitching smarter. While his numbers aren't pretty, his stuff was consistent. Hultzen works at 90-92 mph, can touch 95 and gets good movement on his fastball. His changeup is an above-average offering, though he sometimes throws it too hard. He's getting more consistent with his 80-84 mph slider, staying on top of the pitch more often. He uses an extreme knee bend and throws across his body, which helps create deception. The Mariners love his maturity. Hultzen's control issues aren't a long-term concern. He still has the upside of a No. 2 starter. He'll return to Tacoma but should join Seattle's rotation during the season.

BA GRADE 65 MEDIUM

Year	Club (League)	Class	W	L	ERA	G	GS	CG	SV	IP	H	HR	BB	SO	K/9	WHIP	AVG
2012	Jackson (SL)	AA	8	3	1.19	13	13	0	0	75	38	2	32	79	9.4	0.93	.151
	Tacoma (PCL)	AAA	1	4	5.92	12	12	0	0	49	49	2	43	57	10.5	1.89	.258
Minor League Totals			9	7	3.05	25	25	0	0	124	87	4	75	136	9.9	1.31	.197

4 JAMES PAXTON, LHP

Born: Nov. 6, 1988. **B-T:** L-L. **Ht.:** 6-4. **Wt.:** 220. **Drafted:** Grand Prairie (American Association), 2010 (4th round). **Signed by:** Brian Williams/Jesse Kapellusch.

The Blue Jays picked Paxton, a native Canadian, 37th overall out of Kentucky in 2009 but didn't sign him. Team president Paul Beeston told a Toronto newspaper he had negotiated with Paxton's agent Scott Boras, effectively ending Paxton's NCAA eligibility. He spent a spring in the independent American Association, went in the fourth round of the 2010 draft and signed for $942,500 in March 2011. He has carved up minor league hitters, slowed only by patellar tendinitis in his right knee that sidelined him for six weeks early in the 2012 season. Paxton is an imposing presence on the mound with his strong, workhorse build and two above-average pitches. His fastball sits at 92-95 mph and gets as high as 98. He has the best curveball in the system, a 76-79 mph hammer with 12-to-6 break. He's developing better feel for a changeup that he throws with a circle grip. Paxton

BA GRADE 55 MEDIUM

has a long arm action and comes right over the top, creating deception and allowing him to pitch with good downward plane. However, the length in his delivery can hamper his command. Paxton will get his first taste of Triple-A to start the 2013 season. The development of his changeup will determine if he can be a No. 2 starter. His fastball/curveball combination also could make him a closer.

Year	Club (League)	Class	W	L	ERA	G	GS	CG	SV	IP	H	HR	BB	SO	K/9	WHIP	AVG
2010	Grand Prairie (A-A)	IND	1	2	4.24	4	4	0	0	17	15	1	7	18	9.5	1.29	—
2011	Clinton (MWL)	LoA	3	3	2.73	10	10	0	0	56	45	1	30	80	12.9	1.34	.225
	Jackson (SL)	AA	3	0	1.85	7	7	0	0	39	28	2	13	51	11.8	1.05	.201
2012	Jackson (SL)	AA	9	4	3.05	21	21	0	0	106	96	5	54	110	9.3	1.41	.244
Minor League Totals			15	7	2.73	38	38	0	0	201	169	8	97	241	10.8	1.32	.231

5 NICK FRANKLIN, SS/2B

Born: March 2, 1991. **B-T:** B-R. **Ht.:** 6-1. **Wt.:** 180. **Drafted:** HS—Altamonte Springs, Fla., 2009 (1st round). **Signed by:** Chuck Carlson.

BA GRADE
55
MEDIUM

Franklin signed for $1.28 million as the 27th overall pick in 2009 and led the Midwest League with 23 homers in his first full season. He found 2011 rockier while battling a concussion, mononucleosis and food poisoning, but got back on track in 2012 and reached Triple-A at age 21, making him the youngest position player in the Pacific Coast League. Franklin has a tightly wound build with quick-twitch athleticism and surprising strength. Those factors lead to sneaky power from his short, compact stroke. He projects to hit 15 homers a year in the big leagues while adding plenty of doubles. Though he's a switch-hitter, he has had little success from the right side because his stride gets too long. He might be more productive batting solely lefthanded. He's an adequate defender at shortstop, but he may fit better at second base because his range, hands and arm are all average. He's a solid runner with good instincts on the bases. He plays with a lot of confidence and can take his game up a notch when necessary. Expected to return to Triple-A, Franklin should reach Seattle by the second half of the season. He profiles as a solid regular who could play in a few All-Star Games.

Year	Club (League)	Class	AVG	G	AB	R	H	2B	3B	HR	RBI	BB	SO	SB	CS	OBP	SLG
2009	Mariners (AZL)	R	.302	10	43	6	13	2	0	1	4	1	6	0	0	.318	.419
	Everett (NWL)	SS	.400	6	20	4	8	2	1	0	2	1	2	1	0	.429	.600
2010	Clinton (MWL)	LoA	.281	129	513	89	144	22	7	23	65	50	123	25	10	.351	.485
	West Tenn (SL)	AA	.667	1	3	3	2	0	0	0	0	1	0	0	0	.750	.667
2011	High Desert (CAL)	HiA	.275	64	258	50	71	10	5	5	20	31	56	13	1	.356	.411
	Mariners (AZL)	R	.091	3	11	1	1	0	0	0	0	0	6	0	0	.091	.091
	Jackson (SL)	AA	.325	21	83	13	27	3	2	2	6	6	18	5	3	.371	.482
2012	Jackson (SL)	AA	.322	57	205	25	66	17	4	4	26	24	38	9	2	.394	.502
	Tacoma (PCL)	AAA	.243	64	267	39	65	15	5	7	29	24	68	3	2	.310	.416
Minor League Totals			.283	355	1403	230	397	71	24	42	152	138	318	56	18	.351	.458

6 BRANDON MAURER, RHP

Born: July 3, 1990. **B-T:** R-R. **Ht.:** 6-5. **Wt.:** 200. **Drafted:** HS—Orange, Calif., 2008 (23rd round). **Signed by:** Tim Reynolds.

BA GRADE
55
MEDIUM

Maurer missed the Area Code Games before his senior high school season because of strep throat, but he got plenty of looks that spring pitching in the rotation at Orange (Calif.) Lutheran High with Gerrit Cole. Signed for $150,000, Maurer had elbow problems in 2010 and shoulder woes in 2011, though he avoided surgery. Healthy in 2012, he nearly doubled his career high with 138 innings and the Mariners named him their most improved minor leaguer. Maurer, who was added to the team's 40-man roster this winter, has an athletic frame and shows the potential for four solid pitches. His two best weapons are his 93-95 mph fastball (which tops out at 97) and a swing-and-miss slider. He sharpened his curveball and improved his ability to throw it for strikes in 2012. He also developed better feel for his changeup and the confidence to throw it 12-15 times a game. He shows above-average control but still needs to learn when to expand the strike zone and entice hitters to chase. The key to his health was his commitment to conditioning in the offseason, as he moved to Arizona for the winter to work out at the Mariners' training complex. Maurer's emergence gives Seattle yet another pitching prospect with frontline potential and he'll open 2013 in Triple-A.

Year	Club (League)	Class	W	L	ERA	G	GS	CG	SV	IP	H	HR	BB	SO	K/9	WHIP	AVG
2008	Mariners (AZL)	R	1	2	3.09	8	5	0	0	23	20	1	8	25	9.6	1.20	.247
2009	Pulaski (APP)	R	3	4	3.61	13	12	1	0	67	67	4	18	51	6.8	1.26	.266
2010	Mariners (AZL)	R	0	1	1.64	4	4	0	0	11	8	0	2	14	11.5	0.91	.205
	Clinton (MWL)	LoA	0	1	2.08	2	0	0	0	4	5	1	0	6	12.5	1.15	.294
2011	Clinton (MWL)	LoA	1	3	3.41	7	6	0	0	37	28	2	14	44	10.7	1.14	.211

	High Desert (CAL)	HiA	2	4	6.38	9	7	0	0	42	47	8	11	37	7.9	1.37	.275
2012	Jackson (SL)	AA	9	2	3.20	24	24	1	0	138	133	4	48	117	7.6	1.31	.260
Minor League Totals			16	17	3.65	67	58	2	0	323	308	20	101	294	8.2	1.27	.256

7 CARTER CAPPS, RHP

Born: Aug. 7, 1990. **B-T:** R-R. **Ht.:** 6-5. **Wt.:** 220. **Drafted:** Mount Olive (N.C.), 2011 (3rd round supplemental). **Signed by:** Garrett Ball.

A catcher in high school, Capps redshirted in his first year at NCAA Division II Mount Olive (N.C.) before converting to pitcher in 2010. After going 24-1 in two seasons, he signed for $500,000 in 2011. Capps did not allow an earned run in May or June and became the third player from the 2011 draft to reach the majors. Capps' fastball is easily an 80 pitch on the 20-80 scouting scale. He sits at 97-99 mph and had the second-highest average fastball velocity (98.3) in the majors in 2012, behind only the Royals' Kelvin Herrera. Capps also misses bats with a plus breaking ball. It has slider velocity and movement at 83-86 mph, but he calls it a curveball and uses a curveball grip. His third pitch is an average changeup. Capps hides the ball well, and his drop-and-drive, crossfire delivery makes it seem as though he's starting pitches behind the backs of righthanders. His to-do list includes sharpening his command and getting quicker to the plate with runners on base. Capps already has earned a late-inning role for the Mariners in 2013. He has the potential to develop into a dominant closer.

BA GRADE

55

MEDIUM

Year	Club (League)	Class	W	L	ERA	G	GS	CG	SV	IP	H	HR	BB	SO	K/9	WHIP	AVG
2011	Clinton (MWL)	LoA	1	1	6.00	4	4	0	0	18	19	1	10	21	10.5	1.61	.284
2012	Jackson (SL)	AA	2	3	1.26	38	0	0	19	50	40	2	12	72	13.0	1.04	.212
	Tacoma (PCL)	AAA	0	0	0.00	1	0	0	0	1	0	0	0	3	20.3	0.00	.000
	Seattle (AL)	MAJ	0	0	3.96	18	0	0	0	25	25	0	11	28	10.1	1.44	.260
Major League Totals			0	0	3.96	18	0	0	0	25	25	0	11	28	10.1	1.44	.260
Minor League Totals			3	4	2.47	43	4	0	19	69	59	3	22	96	12.5	1.17	.227

8 STEFEN ROMERO, 2B

Born: Oct. 17, 1988. **B-T:** R-R. **Ht.:** 6-2. **Wt.:** 205. **Drafted:** Oregon State, 2010 (12th round). **Signed by:** Joe Ross.

Romero hit 13 home runs as an Oregon State junior in 2010, but he still lasted 12 rounds in the draft, in part because he broke his elbow late in the season. After signing for $100,000 he focused on improving his conditioning and agility, which gave him a better chance to stick at second base. He won Mariners minor league player of the year honors in 2012, leading the system in hitting (.352) and slugging (.599). The Mariners view Romero as the best pure hitter in the system. His swing has balance and rhythm, and he shows good bat control along with strong wrists and forearms. He doesn't draw a lot of walks, but he also doesn't strike out much for a player with solid power. He has a grinder mentality and the ability to make in-game adjustments. Romero is an outlier with his size at second base, where he's adequately defensively. He has below-average speed and range, though he does possess solid arm strength. He played third base in college and profiles better there or on an outfield corner. Romero profiles as an above-average hitter with the potential for 20 homers a season. If he can do that, Seattle will find a spot in its lineup for him, perhaps at some point during the 2013 season.

BA GRADE

50

MEDIUM

Year	Club (League)	Class	AVG	G	AB	R	H	2B	3B	HR	RBI	BB	SO	SB	CS	OBP	SLG
2011	Clinton (MWL)	LoA	.280	116	429	62	120	22	4	16	65	32	69	16	9	.342	.462
2012	High Desert (CAL)	HiA	.357	60	258	47	92	19	3	11	51	13	35	6	2	.391	.581
	Jackson (SL)	AA	.347	56	216	38	75	15	4	12	50	14	37	6	3	.392	.620
Minor League Totals			.318	232	903	147	287	56	11	39	166	59	141	28	14	.368	.534

9 BRAD MILLER, SS

Born: Oct. 18, 1989. **B-T:** L-R. **Ht.:** 6-2. **Wt.:** 185. **Drafted:** Clemson, 2011 (2nd round). **Signed by:** Garrett Ball.

The 2011 Atlantic Coast Conference player of the year, Miller went in the second round that June and signed for $750,000. He hasn't batted lower than .320 at any of his three pro stops, reaching Double-A and ranking second in the minors with 186 hits in his first full pro season. Miller long has drawn comparisons to Craig Counsell, mostly because of his similar stance at the plate. Miller does start with his hands high, but isn't as unorthodox as Counsell and has a simple load and quick swing. He uses a contact-oriented approach, letting his hands work and shooting balls from gap to gap. He hits towering home runs in batting practice and could have close to average power. Miller always has been an erratic defender, and his 36 miscues ranked 10th in the minors in 2012. He has smooth actions and good footwork at shortstop, but his inconsistent arm slots result in errant throws. He has average range and arm strength that may be a better fit at second base. He has solid speed and runs the bases well. Miller's feel for hitting, leadership and desire can make him an everyday player in the majors. He's similar to Kyle Seager but offers more defensive versatility. Miller likely will return to Double-A with the chance for another midseason promotion.

BA GRADE

50

MEDIUM

Year	Club (League)	Class	AVG	G	AB	R	H	2B	3B	HR	RBI	BB	SO	SB	CS	OBP	SLG
2011	Clinton (MWL)	LoA	.415	14	53	9	22	4	1	0	7	4	9	1	0	.458	.528
2012	High Desert (CAL)	HiA	.339	97	410	89	139	33	5	11	56	52	79	19	6	.412	.524
	Jackson (SL)	AA	.320	40	147	21	47	7	2	4	12	22	26	4	1	.406	.476
Minor League Totals			.341	151	610	119	208	44	8	15	75	78	114	24	7	.414	.513

10 VICTOR SANCHEZ, RHP

Born: Jan. 30, 1995. **B-T:** R-R. **Ht.:** 6-0. **Wt.:** 255. **Signed:** Venezuela, 2011. **Signed by:** Luis Martinez/Emilio Carrasquel/Bob Engle.

The best pitcher on the international market in 2011, Sanchez signed for $2.5 million, the most the Mariners ever have spent on a foreign amateur. Assigned to the short-season Northwest League for his pro debut, at 17 he was the youngest player in a circuit where the average pitcher was 21. He finished second in the NWL in innings (85) and strikeouts (69). Everett teammates called him "Ray Lewis" after the Baltimore Ravens linebacker because Sanchez is a tough competitor with broad shoulders, a powerful lower half and long arms with huge hands. He pitches at 90-94 mph with his fastball and can spot it on both sides of the plate. He loves to throw his above-average changeup, which has nice fade. Sanchez throws both a curveball and slider, but the pitches tend to blend together. Seattle wants him to focus on the slider for now. He also needs to work on repeating his delivery and some of the finer aspects of pitching. He shows poise beyond his years when it comes to adding and subtracting from his pitches to keep hitters off balance. Sanchez's physicality, stuff and feel will allow him to handle a full-season assignment to low Class A Clinton in 2013. While he doesn't have a lot of projection remaining in his chiseled frame, he profiles as a solid No. 3 starter.

BA GRADE

55

HIGH

Year	Club (League)	Class	W	L	ERA	G	GS	CG	SV	IP	H	HR	BB	SO	K/9	WHIP	AVG
2012	Everett (NWL)	SS	6	2	3.18	15	15	0	0	85	69	5	27	69	7.3	1.13	.223
Minor League Totals			6	2	3.18	15	15	0	0	85	69	5	27	69	7.3	1.13	.223

11 STEPHEN PRYOR, RHP

BA GRADE

45

LOW

Born: July 23, 1989. **B-T:** R-R. **Ht.:** 6-4. **Wt.:** 245. **Drafted:** Tennessee Tech, 2010 (5th round). **Signed by:** Alvin Rittman.

After signing for $153,000 as a fifth-round pick in the 2010 draft, Pryor zipped through the system and made his major league debut on June 2 against the White Sox, striking out all-star Paul Konerko as the first batter he faced. Pryor has a big, strong frame and his stuff is just as intimidating as his appearance. He loads up on his back leg and fires his fastball between 94-97 mph, topping out at 99. The pitch sometimes can get straight, but he makes up for it with premium velocity, and he keeps hitters off balance with his nasty 91-93 mph cutter. He can take a little off the cutter and make it an 87-90 mph slider with more downward break. Scouts don't love his arm action, but Pryor has cleaned up his delivery considerably every year since leaving Tennessee Tech. His control is below-average and he doesn't really have a pitch to combat lefthanders, which makes him profile better as a set-up man than a closer.

Year	Club (League)	Class	W	L	ERA	G	GS	CG	SV	IP	H	HR	BB	SO	K/9	WHIP	AVG
2010	Everett (NWL)	SS	0	0	0.49	11	0	0	4	18	7	0	7	26	12.8	0.76	.119

Club (League)	Class	W	L	ERA	G	GS	CG	SV	IP	H	HR	BB	SO	K/9	WHIP	AVG
Clinton (MWL)	LoA	0	2	3.71	12	0	0	1	17	17	0	6	29	15.4	1.35	.250
2011 High Desert (CAL)	HiA	1	0	7.67	22	0	0	4	27	28	2	26	34	11.3	2.00	.264
Jackson (SL)	AA	2	1	1.19	17	0	0	6	23	9	0	7	27	10.7	0.71	.123
2012 Jackson (SL)	AA	1	0	1.13	11	0	0	7	16	7	0	5	24	13.5	0.75	.125
High Desert (CAL)	HiA	0	0	6.75	2	1	0	0	3	0	0	3	3	10.1	1.13	.000
Tacoma (PCL)	AAA	0	0	0.00	16	0	0	3	20	11	0	11	20	9.0	1.10	.159
Seattle (AL)	MAJ	3	1	3.91	26	0	0	0	23	22	5	13	27	10.6	1.52	.253
Major League Totals		3	1	3.91	26	0	0	0	23	22	5	13	27	10.6	1.52	—
Minor League Totals		4	3	2.77	91	1	0	25	124	79	2	65	163	11.9	1.16	.199

12 LUIZ GOHARA, LHP

BA GRADE
60
EXTREME

Born: July 31, 1996. **B-T:** L-L. **Ht.:** 6-3. **Wt.:** 220. **Signed:** Brazil, 2012. **Signed by:** Emilio Carrasquel/Hide Sueyoshi.

No player born and raised in Brazil has made it to the big leagues yet (Yan Gomes was born in Brazil but moved to the United States as a child), and the Mariners hope Gohara will be the first after making him the centerpiece of their 2012 international signing crop with an $880,000 bonus. He'll open the 2013 season at 16 and already has a burly frame with broad, square shoulders and long arms. He started playing in Brazilian amateur national tournaments when he was 10, and some scouts regarded him as the best pitcher available on this year's international market. Gohara's fastball sits at 88-91 mph and has been clocked as high as 94. His curveball shows the potential to be a plus pitch down the road, but he needs to be more consistent with it, and he will have to learn a changeup. He is surprisingly agile for his size and fared well in athletic tests during instructional league. He repeats his delivery well, shows rhythmic, balanced mechanics and a fast, clean arm action. The fact that the Mariners brought Gohara to instructs as a 16-year-old is encouraging, and coaches were impressed with his work ethic and aptitude. He spent part of the winter in the Mariners' Venezuelan academy to learn the organization's conditioning program. There's no need to rush him, so Gohara will stay in Arizona during extended spring training to continue to get adjusted to changes in culture, learn English and pitch in a low-stress environment. There's no higher risk than a 16-year-old pitcher, but his combination of size, stuff, athleticism and makeup give him the makings of a frontline starter and draw comparisons to C.C. Sabathia.

Year	Club (League)	Class	W	L	ERA	G	GS	CG	SV	IP	H	HR	BB	SO	K/9	WHIP	AVG
Did Not Play—Signed 2013 Contract																	

13 JOE DeCARLO, 3B

BA GRADE
50
HIGH

Born: Sept. 13, 1993. **B-T:** R-R. **Ht.:** 5-10. **Wt.:** 205. **Drafted:** HS—Glen Mills, Pa., 2012 (2nd round). **Signed by:** Mike Moriarty.

DeCarlo comes from an athletic family. His father played football at Delaware, his two older brothers played Division I baseball and his older sister played lacrosse at Virginia. A second-round pick in June, he received a $1.3 million bonus to pass on a commitment to Georgia. DeCarlo has a solid, muscular build and is already maxed out physically. His best asset is his bat. He has a short swing with above-average bat speed and a high finish, and he projects as an average hitter with the potential for plus power. He tracks pitches well, letting them get deep, and puts together professional at-bats. DeCarlo played shortstop in high school, but with his build and below-average speed, a move to third base was necessary as a pro. He shows good hands and above-average arm strength. Like many players from the Northeast, he plays with an edge. His hard-nosed mentality, physique and swing path remind some of Brett Lawrie, though he doesn't run as well or have Lawrie's bat speed. Coming from the Northeast also puts DeCarlo behind the developmental curve because he hasn't played as much as players from warmer climates. He'll likely begin 2013 in extended spring training before heading to Everett.

Year	Club (League)	Class	AVG	G	AB	R	H	2B	3B	HR	RBI	BB	SO	SB	CS	OBP	SLG
2012	Mariners (AZL)	R	.236	53	182	29	43	12	3	4	31	31	47	0	2	.368	.401
Minor League Totals			.236	53	182	29	43	12	3	4	31	31	47	0	2	.368	.401

14 TYLER PIKE, LHP

BA GRADE
50
HIGH

Born: Jan. 26, 1994. **B-T:** L-L. **Ht.:** 6-0. **Wt.:** 180. **Drafted:** HS—Winter Haven, Fla., 2012 (3rd round supplemental). **Signed by:** Rob Mummau.

Pike had a couple of worthy mentors growing up. His father Mark is a former Indians minor league outfielder, and his high school assistant coach was Pat Borders, who spent parts of 17 years in the big leagues and was MVP of the 1992 World Series. With a 2012 supplemental third-round pick received for not signing Kevin Cron the year before, the Mariners took Pike and lured him away from a Florida State commitment with $850,000. He's a quality athlete who would have been a two-way player for the Seminoles. His athleticism helps him repeat a fluid, simple delivery which in turn leads to above-average control and good fastball command. Pike's fastball sits at 89-91 mph and occasionally touches 94 with natural tailing action. His fastball is sneaky fast and appears quicker to hitters because of his deception and smooth delivery. Pike showed flashes of a plus curveball in high school, and Seattle worked with him on getting better feel for varying speeds with it. At its best, the pitch ranges from 72-76 mph with tight 11-to-5 break. He didn't use a changeup much in high school, so the biggest things he needs to work on are developing that pitch and getting stronger. He profiles as a back-of-the-rotation starter and has enough polish and poise to earn a full-season assignment to low Class A in 2013.

Year	Club (League)	Class	W	L	ERA	G	GS	CG	SV	IP	H	HR	BB	SO	K/9	WHIP	AVG
2012	Mariners (AZL)	R	2	1	1.78	11	11	0	0	51	34	1	21	57	10.1	1.09	.193
Minor League Totals			2	1	1.78	11	11	0	0	51	34	1	21	57	10.1	1.09	.193

15 GABRIEL GUERRERO, OF

BA GRADE
55
EXTREME

Born: Dec. 11, 1993. **B-T:** R-R. **Ht.:** 6-3. **Wt.:** 190. **Signed:** Dominican Republic, 2011. **Signed by:** Patrick Guerrero/Bob Engle/Franklin Taveras Jr..

The Mariners signed Vladimir Guerrero's nephew as a 17-year-old for $400,000, in part because his build and hitting mechanics draw comparisons to his uncle. Gabriel is a free swinger who has the bat control and hand-eye coordination to hit just about any pitch near the plate. He shows good pitch recognition for his age and has budding strength that will improve as he continues to add muscle to his thin, projectable frame. He has explosive bat speed and strength in his wrists. Guerrero led the Rookie-level Dominican Summer League with 11 homers before being promoted to the Rookie-level Arizona League to finish the season. He has a slight uppercut at the plate and shows power to all fields, but the Mariners are working to shorten his swing a bit. His bat is ahead of his glove, as Guerrero is still raw defensively and needs to improve his routes and angles in right field. He's a below-average runner with a strong arm, and he lacks accuracy on his throws. There's no need to rush Guerrero, so he could start 2013 in extended spring training and report to Everett in June. His bat is advanced enough that an aggressive assignment to Clinton isn't out of the question.

Year	Club (League)	Class	AVG	G	AB	R	H	2B	3B	HR	RBI	BB	SO	SB	CS	OBP	SLG
2011	Mariners (DSL)	R	.236	57	191	24	45	9	0	1	14	14	29	4	3	.288	.298
2012	Mariners (DSL)	R	.355	50	200	38	71	9	4	11	54	21	28	4	6	.409	.605
	Mariners (AZL)	R	.333	18	75	17	25	5	0	4	18	3	13	0	0	.350	.560
Minor League Totals			.303	125	466	79	141	23	4	16	86	38	70	8	9	.351	.472

16 CARSON SMITH, RHP

BA GRADE
45
MEDIUM

Born: Oct. 19, 1989. **B-T:** R-R. **Ht.:** 6-6. **Wt.:** 205. **Drafted:** Texas State, 2011 (8th round). **Signed by:** Kyle Van Hook.

In Carter Capps and Stephen Pryor, the Mariners have already gotten two pitchers from recent drafts to the big leagues, and Smith is another hard-throwing reliever who shouldn't be far behind. A 2011 eighth-rounder who signed for $215,000, he didn't pitch in his first pro summer while recovering from shoulder issues that he pitched through at Texas State. His shoulder didn't prevent him from winning consecutive Southland Conference pitcher of the year awards, and he performed well in his pro debut to finish second in the system behind Capps with 15 saves. Smith has a big, physical frame and throws from a low three-quarters arm slot that gives him a lot of movement on his fastball. He typically works at 92-95 mph and gets as high as 97. With his fastball's heavy sink and late life, he gets plenty of groundballs. His hard slider pairs nicely with his heater and serves as an out pitch. Smith worked last season to add a changeup to his repertoire, in order to give hitters something extra to think about and to combat lefthanders. He has some violence in his delivery, including spinning off the rubber and a head whack, which leads to below-average control. Still, he has the potential to be a solid set-up man and another quality arm in Seattle's young, homegrown bullpen.

Year	Club (League)	Class	W	L	ERA	G	GS	CG	SV	IP	H	HR	BB	SO	K/9	WHIP	AVG
2012	High Desert (CAL)	HiA	5	1	2.90	49	0	0	15	62	54	2	28	77	11.2	1.32	.234
Minor League Totals			5	1	2.90	49	0	0	15	62	54	2	28	77	11.2	1.32	.234

17 LEON LANDRY, OF

BA GRADE
50
HIGH

Born: Sept. 20, 1989. **B-T:** L-R. **Ht.:** 5-11. **Wt.:** 190. **Drafted:** Louisiana State, 2010 (3rd round). **Signed by:** Matt Paul (Dodgers).

The Mariners acquired Landry along with righthander Logan Bawcom from the Dodgers for Brandon League at the 2012 trading deadline. Landry put together an excellent season, winning the high Class A California League batting title (.341). leading the minors in triples (18) and ranking second in the league in doubles (34) and slugging (.584). He had a similarly strong pro debut in 2010 before regressing in his first full pro season. Landry holds his bat low and has a quick, handsy swing. He gets his foot down early and utilizes mostly a flat bat path, which is why most of his power goes to the gaps. He profiles as a solid hitter with below-average power, but he'll make up for his lack of homers with plenty of doubles. A solid runner, he's a threat to bunt for a hit. He is still learning to read pitchers so he can become a better basestealer. He's even quicker once he gets going, which allows him to cover the gaps in center field. He's a fearless defender who will lay out for balls and go up against a wall. He has a below-average arm. Landry will face a major test as a hitter in 2013 when he heads to Double-A for the first time.

Year	Club (League)	Class	AVG	G	AB	R	H	2B	3B	HR	RBI	BB	SO	SB	CS	OBP	SLG
2010	Ogden (PIO)	R	.349	57	249	46	87	20	4	4	38	20	36	13	9	.399	.510
2011	Great Lakes (MWL)	LoA	.250	125	500	59	125	21	11	4	41	37	67	28	12	.307	.360
2012	R. Cucamonga (CAL)	HiA	.328	80	345	63	113	26	15	8	51	14	52	20	9	.358	.559
	High Desert (CAL)	HiA	.385	24	104	25	40	8	3	5	25	5	14	7	2	.414	.663
Minor League Totals			.305	286	1198	193	365	75	33	21	155	76	169	68	32	.350	.475

18 PATRICK KIVLEHAN, 3B

BA GRADE
50
HIGH

Born: Dec. 22, 1989. **B-T:** R-R. **Ht.:** 6-2. **Wt.:** 210. **Drafted:** Rutgers, 2012 (4th round). **Signed by:** Mike Moriarty.

Kivlehan's success was one of the best stories in the 2012 draft. After playing defensive back on Rutgers' football team for four years, he got the itch to play baseball again last spring for the first time since high school. He became the first Scarlet Knight honored as Big East Conference player of the year since Todd Frazier in 2007, then signed with the Mariners for $300,000 as a fourth-round pick. The Mariners sent him to the Northwest League, an aggressive assignment considering his relative inexperience, and he responded by leading the circuit in homers (12) and slugging (.511) en route to winning MVP honors. While Kivlehan has plenty of strength and above-average raw power, he needs to improve his pitch recognition and adapt to how pitchers are attacking him. He topped the NWL with 93 strikeouts. Kivlehan has length and stiffness to his rotational, upper-half swing, but scouts believe he'll be able to make adjustments because of his athleticism. When he makes contact, he squares the ball up with authority. Seattle is working with him to drive breaking balls to the opposite field. A solid runner, Kivlehan is adequate defensively at third base. His arm is fringy for the position and he may wind up moving to left field. He plays hard and shows natural leadership on and off the field. Kivlehan will play his first full pro season at age 23, so the Mariners may push him to high Class A High Desert.

Year	Club (League)	Class	AVG	G	AB	R	H	2B	3B	HR	RBI	BB	SO	SB	CS	OBP	SLG
2012	Everett (NWL)	SS	.301	72	282	46	85	17	3	12	52	19	93	14	1	.373	.511
Minor League Totals			.301	72	282	46	85	17	3	12	52	19	93	14	1	.373	.511

19 EDWIN DIAZ, RHP

BA GRADE
50
HIGH

Born: March 22, 1994. **B-T:** R-R. **Ht.:** 6-2. **Wt.:** 165. **Drafted:** HS—Caguas, P.R., 2012 (3rd round). **Signed by:** Noel Sevilla.

Diaz is relatively new to pitching, not taking the mound until he was 15 years old. But he has a mentor in his cousin Jose Melendez, who pitched in the big leagues for parts of five seasons in the early 1990s, and Diaz learned his lessons well. He went in the third round of the 2012 draft, signing for a discounted $300,000 after a postdraft physical raised some minor issues, but he hasn't had any health concerns so far. Thin with long arms and legs, Diaz's arm action is loose, whippy and explosive, and his fastball sits at 92-94 mph and tops out at 97. His curveball shows flashes of being an average pitch, but it's inconsistent because he tends to get under it. He didn't throw a changeup much as an amateur, so he will have to learn one as a pro. Like many tall, gangly pitchers, Diaz sometimes has trouble with controlling his body and his pitches. He walked nearly a batter an inning in his brief pro debut. The Mariners will give him plenty of time to develop as a starter, realizing that he needs to fill out and improve his secondary pitches and control. Diaz will start 2013 in extended spring training as he seeks to add weight to his frame, improve his English and work on repeating his delivery.

Year	Club (League)	Class	W	L	ERA	G	GS	CG	SV	IP	H	HR	BB	SO	K/9	WHIP	AVG
2012	Mariners (AZL)	R	2	1	5.21	9	1	0	0	19	12	2	17	20	9.5	1.53	.176
Minor League Totals			2	1	5.21	9	1	0	0	19	12	2	17	20	9.5	1.53	.176

20 JACK MARDER, 2B/C/OF

BA GRADE
45
MEDIUM

Born: Feb. 21, 1990. **B-T:** R-R. **Ht.:** 5-11. **Wt.:** 185. **Drafted:** Oregon, 2011 (16th round). **Signed by:** Joe Ross.

A shortstop in high school and a right fielder/first baseman as an Oregon freshman, Marder moved behind the plate as a sophomore in 2011. He hit just .209/.360/.295 but was draft-eligible as a 21-year-old and commanded a $200,000 bonus as a 16th-round pick. The Mariners sent him to high Class A, and he has batted .352/.416/.564 the past two years. Marder's hands work well in his swing, and he has natural rhythm and surprising strength for his size. He has a gap-to-gap approach and consistently squares the ball up. He caught 15 games in 2012, but Seattle decided to move him from behind the plate after two concussions sidelined him for six weeks. For the second half of the season, he played second base and left field. He fits best in the outfield, where he's an average defender with average arm strength, because he doesn't quite have the quickness for second base. He has fringy speed but always runs hard and is a smart baserunner. Coaches, teammates and scouts love Marder for his hustle, heart and leadership. His competitive drive helps his tools play up and will get him to the big leagues in some capacity, most likely as a utility player.

Year	Club (League)	Class	AVG	G	AB	R	H	2B	3B	HR	RBI	BB	SO	SB	CS	OBP	SLG
2011	High Desert (CAL)	HiA	.324	18	71	11	23	6	0	2	12	2	12	3	1	.380	.493
2012	High Desert (CAL)	HiA	.360	65	278	68	100	24	4	10	56	21	44	16	6	.425	.583
Minor League Totals			.352	83	349	79	123	30	4	12	68	23	56	19	7	.416	.564

21 JOHN HICKS, C

BA GRADE
45
MEDIUM

Born: Aug. 31, 1989. **B-T:** R-R. **Ht.:** 6-2. **Wt.:** 205. **Drafted:** Virginia, 2011 (4th round). **Signed by:** Mike Moriarty.

Twelve players have been drafted out of Virginia the past two years, with the Mariners responsible for one-third of them: Danny Hultzen, Hicks and Steven Proscia in 2011, and Chris Taylor in 2012. Hicks, who comes from the same Goochland (Va.) High program that produced Justin Verlander, signed as a fourth-rounder for $240,000. Hicks shows good hand-eye coordination and bat control. He mostly produces doubles power with his line-drive stroke, but does have the strength to hit balls out of the park on occasion. He has a chance to be an average hitter with fringy power, enough offense for him to be a solid option behind the plate. Hicks started catching full-time in 2011. While his exchange and arm strength grade out as average, he led all minor league catchers last year by throwing out 54 percent of basestealers. He handles a pitching staff well and calls a good game, but he needs to improve his receiving and blocking. Hicks is an average runner with enough athleticism to try other positions. He's a natural leader and a smart player who shows the ability to learn and adjust quickly. He profiles as a solid backup catcher and should spend most of 2013 in Double-A.

Year	Club (League)	Class	AVG	G	AB	R	H	2B	3B	HR	RBI	BB	SO	SB	CS	OBP	SLG
2011	Clinton (MWL)	LoA	.309	38	139	21	43	9	2	2	26	5	17	2	3	.331	.446
2012	High Desert (CAL)	HiA	.312	121	506	87	158	32	2	15	79	28	73	22	8	.351	.472
Minor League Totals			.312	159	645	108	201	41	4	17	105	33	90	24	11	.347	.467

22 FRANCISCO MARTINEZ, 3B/OF

BA GRADE
50
HIGH

Born: Sept. 1, 1990. **B-T:** R-R. **Ht.:** 6-2. **Wt.:** 210. **Signed:** Venezuela, 2007. **Signed by:** Alejandro Rodriguez/Pedro Chavez (Tigers).

In the July 2011 trade that sent Doug Fister and David Pauley to the Tigers, Martinez came to the Mariners along with Charlie Furbush, Chance Ruffin and Casper Wells. He ranked among each team's Top 10 Prospects the previous two years, but his first full season in the Seattle system was one to forget. He missed a month with a left hamstring strain and was anemic at the plate, posting the second-lowest slugging percentage (.295) in the Southern League among batting qualifiers. Martinez has a quick bat and projects to be an average hitter, but he needs to tone down his swing and be more consistent. He doesn't have profile home run power for a corner spot, though he has the stroke and speed to hit plenty of doubles and triples. His plus speed is actually his best tool, and he ranked third in the system with 28 steals in 2012. Because of his speed, the Mariners tried Martinez in center field for 15 games last year. He should be at least an average defender wherever he winds up, with arm strength to match. He was one of the youngest players in the Southern League last year, so repeating Double-A was a no-brainer.

Year	Club (League)	Class	AVG	G	AB	R	H	2B	3B	HR	RBI	BB	SO	SB	CS	OBP	SLG
2008	Tigers (VSL)	R	.321	68	249	32	80	4	0	1	23	28	28	20	10	.394	.349
2009	Tigers (GCL)	R	.222	43	153	21	34	9	0	2	23	5	38	11	1	.256	.320
	Lakeland (FSL)	HiA	.167	6	18	1	3	0	0	0	2	0	3	1	0	.167	.167
2010	Lakeland (FSL)	HiA	.271	89	340	47	92	17	1	3	29	28	71	12	5	.330	.353
2011	Erie (EL)	AA	.282	91	348	63	98	14	4	7	46	19	80	7	8	.319	.405
	Jackson (SL)	AA	.310	33	129	20	40	7	3	3	23	4	24	3	2	.326	.481
2012	Jackson (SL)	AA	.227	95	352	55	80	16	1	2	23	43	85	27	7	.315	.295
	Mariners (AZL)	R	.286	8	28	7	8	2	2	0	7	1	6	1	0	.323	.500
Minor League Totals			.269	433	1617	246	435	69	11	18	176	128	335	82	33	.325	.359

23 JULIO MORBAN, OF

BA GRADE
50
HIGH

Born: Feb. 13, 1992. **B-T:** L-L. **Ht.:** 6-1. **Wt.:** 203. **Signed:** Dominican Republic, 2008. **Signed by:** Patrick Guerrero/Bob Engle.

Nagging injuries have limited Morban to an average of 55 games during the past four seasons after he signed out of the Dominican Republic for $1.1 million. Even so, the Mariners added him to their

40-man roster this winter because of his above-average hitting ability. He uses a balanced setup and a compact swing to hit to all fields with ease. He frequently squares the ball up and mostly has a line-drive stroke, but shows the efficiency and bat speed for at least average power potential from left-center to the right-field line. Morban is a good athlete and a solid runner who saw time at all three outfield spots last season, getting his most action in center field. He profiles better on a corner, however, and has the plus arm strength for right field. Hamstring problems have plagued Morban repeatedly, leading to a pair of disabled-list stints in 2012, and he hurt his wrist last year when he ran into a wall. Because he's 21 and has just 810 pro at-bats, starting him back in high Class A this year is a logical move.

Year	Club (League)	Class	AVG	G	AB	R	H	2B	3B	HR	RBI	BB	SO	SB	CS	OBP	SLG
2009	Pulaski (APP)	R	.333	4	9	3	3	1	0	0	0	0	3	0	0	.400	.444
	Mariners (AZL)	R	.266	42	154	28	41	9	7	5	23	7	49	8	3	.303	.513
2010	Pulaski (APP)	R	.100	4	10	1	1	0	0	0	0	4	3	0	0	.357	.100
	Mariners (AZL)	R	.400	3	5	0	2	0	0	0	1	0	1	0	0	.400	.400
	High Desert (CAL)	HiA	.333	2	6	0	2	0	0	0	1	0	2	0	0	.333	.333
	Everett (NWL)	SS	.250	1	4	0	1	0	0	0	0	0	2	0	0	.250	.250
2011	Clinton (MWL)	LoA	.256	80	301	44	77	12	7	4	28	26	99	10	5	.315	.382
2012	High Desert (CAL)	HiA	.313	76	300	56	94	16	2	17	52	21	67	5	1	.361	.550
	Mariners (AZL)	R	.238	6	21	2	5	0	0	0	3	0	3	0	0	.227	.238
Minor League Totals			.279	218	810	134	226	38	16	26	108	58	229	23	9	.330	.462

24 JABARI BLASH, OF

Born: July 4, 1989. **B-T:** R-R. **Ht.:** 6-5. **Wt.:** 224. **Drafted:** Miami Dade JC, 2010 (8th round). **Signed by:** Mike Tosar.

BA GRADE: 50 HIGH

A native of the Virgin Islands, Blash didn't sign out of high school as a 29th-round pick of the White Sox in 2007, instead choosing to attend Alcorn State. Ruled academically ineligible in 2008, he transferred to Miami Dade JC the following season and was drafted in the ninth round by the Rangers, but again turned down pro ball. He returned to the Sharks but was kicked off the team in April 2010 before signing that July for $140,000 as an eighth-rounder. There's nothing subtle about Blash's game. His chiseled physique would stand out in a big league clubhouse and his tools can be just as loud. He is still raw and streaky, however. On some nights he'll look like a future all-star, and on others he'll look like he won't make it to Triple-A. The biggest question is how much he'll hit. Blash has excess movement in his set-up and questionable pitch recognition. He struck out in 34 percent of his at-bats last year while repeating low Class A, though he did show more patience than he had in the past. When Blash does make contact, the ball goes a long way. He shows plus-plus raw power in batting practice. His defense and speed both improved in 2012, when he saw action in center field. Right field is his natural position, however, because he's an average runner with a plus arm. He'll spend 2013 in high Class A.

Year	Club (League)	Class	AVG	G	AB	R	H	2B	3B	HR	RBI	BB	SO	SB	CS	OBP	SLG
2010	Pulaski (APP)	R	.266	32	109	21	29	6	1	5	20	13	44	1	1	.362	.477
2011	Clinton (MWL)	LoA	.218	42	124	13	27	5	1	3	13	38	43	5	2	.401	.347
	Everett (NWL)	SS	.292	57	195	26	57	16	3	11	43	28	65	10	3	.393	.574
2012	Clinton (MWL)	LoA	.245	113	400	71	98	20	5	15	50	60	134	13	7	.355	.433
Minor League Totals			.255	244	828	131	211	47	10	34	126	139	286	29	13	.372	.459

25 TIMMY LOPES, 2B

Born: June 24, 1994. **B-T:** R-R. **Ht.:** 5-11. **Wt.:** 180. **Drafted:** HS—Huntington Beach, Calif., 2012 (6th round). **Signed by:** John Ramey.

BA GRADE: 50 HIGH

Growing up, Lopes was overshadowed by his older brother Christian, who ranked as the nation's top 13-year-old prospect in 2006 and signed for $800,000 as a Blue Jays seventh-rounder in 2011. Timmy was more of a late bloomer who came into his own as a high school senior. Many scouts now believe Timmy will be a better player than his brother, and the Mariners paid $550,000 to buy him away from a UC Irvine commitment last summer. Lopes' best tool is his advanced hitting ability. He has a short, fluid swing built for line drives and a knack for centering the ball. He'll never be a home run threat but will wear out the gaps with plenty of doubles and triples. He has a good eye at the plate, puts together professional at-bats and performs well under pressure. Lopes has a thick lower half but is a solid runner. His speed plays up a little because of his instincts for the game and ability to read pitchers. Like his brother, Lopes played shortstop in high school and can fill in there in a pinch, but he fits better at second base because of his below-average arm strength. He's a steady defender with smooth actions and an advanced baseball IQ. He was promoted to high Class A for the final four games of his pro debut, but he'll likely begin 2013 in low Class A.

Year	Club (League)	Class	AVG	G	AB	R	H	2B	3B	HR	RBI	BB	SO	SB	CS	OBP	SLG
2012	Mariners (AZL)	R	.316	53	215	42	68	11	12	0	32	24	29	7	3	.381	.479
	High Desert (CAL)	HiA	.250	4	12	2	3	0	1	0	1	0	1	0	0	.250	.417
Minor League Totals			.313	57	227	44	71	11	13	0	33	24	30	7	3	.375	.476

26 VINNIE CATRICALA, 3B/OF

Born: Oct. 31, 1988. **B-T:** R-R. **Ht.:** 6-3. **Wt.:** 220. **Drafted:** Hawaii, 2009 (10th round). **Signed by:** Tim Reynolds.

BA GRADE
45
MEDIUM

The Mariners signed Catricala for $90,000 as a 10th-round pick in 2009, a deal that looked like a steal two years later. He was the organization's minor league player of the year in 2011, when he ranked second in the minors in extra-base hits (77) and total bases (313), third in hits (182), fourth in batting (.349) and sixth in OPS (1.022). So his downfall last season was just as surprising as his breakout. He was a shell of himself in Triple-A, posting the second-lowest OPS (.640) among Pacific Coast League qualifiers. Catricala has the potential to be a solid hitter with average power. Some said his struggles were partly mental and that just as things snowballed for him in a positive way in 2011, the effect happened in reverse in 2012. Catricala does have mechanical issues with his swing, however. After batting .322 and showing a consistently compact stroke in his first three pro seasons, he got longer with his swing last year. His hips sometimes leaked open early and he started leaning out over the plate, throwing his swing off balance. He'll have to bounce back with the bat to be a useful player. He has average arm strength, but he's an erratic fielder at the hot corner and fits better in left field or first base. He has fringy speed. After batting .279/.329/.412 in the Arizona Fall League, he'll take a second crack at Triple-A in 2013. Seattle still thinks highly enough of him to have protected him on its 40-man roster in November.

Year	Club (League)	Class	AVG	G	AB	R	H	2B	3B	HR	RBI	BB	SO	SB	CS	OBP	SLG
2009	Pulaski (APP)	R	.301	59	219	33	66	14	2	8	40	18	34	6	1	.363	.493
2010	Clinton (MWL)	LoA	.302	135	496	90	150	41	0	17	79	56	112	7	3	.386	.488
2011	High Desert (CAL)	HiA	.351	71	282	56	99	19	1	14	61	33	45	8	3	.421	.574
	Jackson (SL)	AA	.347	62	239	45	83	29	3	11	45	24	47	9	1	.420	.632
2012	Tacoma (PCL)	AAA	.229	122	463	58	106	23	1	10	60	37	88	4	2	.292	.348
Minor League Totals			.297	449	1699	282	504	126	7	60	285	168	326	34	10	.369	.485

27 CHANCE RUFFIN, RHP

Born: Sept. 8, 1988. **B-T:** R-R. **Ht.:** 6-1. **Wt.:** 195. **Drafted:** Texas, 2010 (1st round supplemental). **Signed by:** Tim Grieve (Tigers).

BA GRADE
45
MEDIUM

Ruffin followed in his father Bruce's footsteps, starring at Texas, going in the first 50 picks in the draft and getting to the big leagues in his first full pro season. Signed for $1.15 million by the Tigers in 2010, he reached Detroit the following July. Five days later, the Tigers included him in a trade package for Doug Fister. Ruffin pitched well in Seattle after the deal, but he spent all of 2012 in Triple-A and the results weren't pretty. His control and command haven't been as polished as they were in college, though his stuff is still solid. His fastball sits in the 90-93 mph range and reaches 95. He has a quick arm, and the ball jumps out of his hand from his low three-quarters arm slot. He has an out pitch in his plus slider with late break. His curveball and changeup are both below-average but give hitters something else to think about. In the past, Ruffin just reared back and threw, but the Mariners are working to make his delivery quicker and more efficient. He lands on a stiff front leg and throws across his body, hurting his ability to locate his pitches where he wants. His long arm swing in the back and lower release point make it easy for lefthanders to pick up his pitches, and they hit .294/.348/.516 against him last year. Ruffin has the upside of a set-up man if he can cut down on his walks, and he'll break in as a middle reliever in Seattle because the team has better options ahead of him. He'll likely head back to Tacoma to start 2013.

Year	Club (League)	Class	W	L	ERA	G	GS	CG	SV	IP	H	HR	BB	SO	K/9	WHIP	AVG
2011	Erie (EL)	AA	3	3	2.12	31	0	0	10	34	23	2	16	43	11.4	1.15	.190
	Detroit (AL)	MAJ	0	0	4.91	2	0	0	0	4	5	2	0	3	7.4	1.36	.313
	Toledo (IL)	AAA	0	0	1.84	13	0	0	9	15	14	1	6	17	10.4	1.36	.241
	Seattle (AL)	MAJ	1	0	3.86	13	0	0	0	14	13	2	9	15	9.6	1.57	.245
2012	Tacoma (PCL)	AAA	0	5	5.99	50	0	0	1	71	75	8	35	54	6.9	1.56	.268
Major League Totals			1	0	4.08	15	0	0	0	18	18	4	9	18	9.2	1.53	.261
Minor League Totals			3	8	4.37	94	0	0	20	119	112	11	57	114	8.6	1.42	.207

28 CHRIS TAYLOR, SS

Born: Aug. 29, 1990. **B-T:** R-R. **Ht.:** 6-0. **Wt.:** 170. **Drafted:** Virginia, 2012 (5th round). **Signed by:** Mike Moriarty.

BA GRADE
45
MEDIUM

The Mariners signed Taylor for $500,000—the biggest bonus in the fifth round of the 2012 draft—because of his athleticism, polish and hitting ability. He has a quick, loose swing and the ability to turn around any fastball. He puts together quality at-bats with a compact, line-drive stroke, though his power rates only a 30 on the 20-80 scouting scale. At shortstop, Taylor shows excellent hands, takes proper angles to balls and makes smooth transfers. Range will be a question, though. Some scouts got below-average running times from Taylor last summer, but the Mariners say he's above-average in that regard. He could have just been tired. He played every game at Virginia during his sophomore and junior years and was shut down as a pro with a dead arm. He's fundamentally sound with a good knowledge of the game and a businesslike approach. Taylor draws divergent opinions about his upside. Some scouts see him as an everyday big league shortstop, while others think he'll be more of a utilityman. Everyone agrees, however, that he's a baseball rat who plays the game with confidence and on an even keel. He'll start his first full pro season at one of Seattle's Class A affiliates.

Year	Club (League)	Class	AVG	G	AB	R	H	2B	3B	HR	RBI	BB	SO	SB	CS	OBP	SLG
2012	Everett (NWL)	SS	.328	37	137	26	45	12	1	2	18	21	18	13	5	.430	.474
	Clinton (MWL)	LoA	.304	12	46	5	14	0	0	0	4	2	4	4	1	.373	.304
Minor League Totals			.322	49	183	31	59	12	1	2	22	23	22	17	6	.417	.432

29 RAMON MORLA, 3B

BA GRADE
50
HIGH

Born: Nov. 20, 1989. **B-T:** R-R. **Ht.:** 6-1. **Wt.:** 203. **Signed:** Dominican Republic, 2006. **Signed by:** Patrick Guerrero.

Signed out of the Dominican Republic in 2006, Morla has moved slowly and wasn't able to handle full-season pitching until 2012, his sixth pro season. His best tool is his plus-plus raw power. He has a short, balanced swing with strong wrists and forearms. The ball screams off his bat, and while he'll likely be a below-average hitter, he should make enough contact to hit at least 15 homers a year. Pitch recognition will determine how much Morla will produce at the plate. He's an aggressive hitter who strikes out a lot and doesn't draw many walks. His speed and defense are both fringy. He doesn't have good footwork at third base and made 34 errors last season, the fourth-most in the Midwest League. He does have well above-average arm strength, which would still be an asset if he has to move to an outfield corner. He'll spend 2013 in high Class A at age 23. Because Morla has been slow to develop, the Mariners haven't protected him on their 40-man roster even though he became eligible for the Rule 5 draft after the 2010 season.

Year	Club (League)	Class	AVG	G	AB	R	H	2B	3B	HR	RBI	BB	SO	SB	CS	OBP	SLG
2007	Mariners (DSL)	R	.233	34	116	23	27	7	0	2	13	18	35	4	7	.364	.345
2008	Mariners (DSL)	R	.256	55	164	34	42	7	1	2	17	28	38	7	4	.399	.348
2009	Mariners (AZL)	R	.294	28	102	20	30	2	1	2	12	6	29	4	2	.345	.392
2010	Pulaski (APP)	R	.323	62	251	60	81	17	2	17	49	15	65	13	4	.364	.610
2011	Clinton (MWL)	LoA	.170	28	106	7	18	3	3	0	7	4	28	5	2	.196	.255
	Mariners (AZL)	R	.250	3	12	1	3	1	0	0	1	0	2	1	1	.250	.333
	Everett (NWL)	SS	.263	48	179	24	47	5	2	4	21	18	44	10	5	.332	.380
2012	Clinton (MWL)	LoA	.278	102	410	63	114	27	7	13	68	17	102	7	1	.312	.473
Minor League Totals			.270	360	1340	232	362	69	16	40	188	106	343	51	26	.334	.435

30 ANTHONY FERNANDEZ, LHP

BA GRADE
45
MEDIUM

Born: June 8, 1990. **B-T:** L-L. **Ht.:** 6-4. **Wt.:** 207. **Signed:** Dominican Republic, 2006. **Signed by:** Franklin Taveras/Patrick Guerrero.

Fernandez flies under the radar because he wasn't a high-profile signing and gets overshadowed by the system's pitching depth. He has quietly pitched his way to Double-A and ranked third among Mariners farmhands with 134 strikeouts while topping them with 164 innings in 2012. Protected on the 40-man roster in November, Fernandez has a durable build and a solid repertoire. His fastball operates at 88-91 mph and plays up because it has good movement. He's a smart pitcher and can reach back for a little extra when he gets in trouble. His changeup is his lone plus pitch, featuring nice fade and deception. He throws two breaking balls, a solid slider and an average curveball. Fernandez is efficient with his pitches and pairs above-average control with average command. He's a competitor who does the little things well, like holding runners and fielding his position. He'll probably return to Jackson to start 2013, with a midseason promotion to Triple-A a possibility.

Year	Club (League)	Class	W	L	ERA	G	GS	CG	SV	IP	H	HR	BB	SO	K/9	WHIP	AVG
2007	Mariners (DSL)	R	1	2	3.80	18	0	0	2	24	13	3	24	22	8.4	1.56	.163
2008	Mariners (DSL)	R	4	4	3.93	16	6	0	0	50	42	0	27	41	7.3	1.37	.227
2009	Mariners (AZL)	R	5	3	3.40	13	2	0	0	53	56	0	13	53	9.0	1.30	.268
2010	Everett (NWL)	SS	8	3	2.59	15	15	0	0	83	75	1	18	69	7.5	1.12	.245
2011	High Desert (CAL)	HiA	1	1	7.39	7	7	0	0	28	48	4	13	26	8.4	2.18	.384
	Clinton (MWL)	LoA	7	4	2.80	21	19	0	0	125	109	6	42	107	7.7	1.20	.238
2012	High Desert (CAL)	HiA	2	5	3.68	14	14	1	0	88	89	6	14	79	8.1	1.17	.263
	Jackson (SL)	AA	4	3	3.32	13	13	2	0	76	74	6	24	55	6.5	1.29	.259
Minor League Totals			32	25	3.45	117	76	3	2	528	506	26	175	452	7.7	1.29	.252

Tampa Bay Rays

BY BILL BALLEW

The Rays fell three games short of making their fourth playoff appearance in five years in 2012, but they continued to serve as the template for small-revenue team success.

Tampa Bay won 90 games despite baseball's sixth-lowest Opening Day payroll ($64.2 million) and a string of injuries. Perennial MVP candidate Evan Longoria and incumbent closer Kyle Farnsworth each missed half the season, and Jeff Niemann made just eight starts. The Rays had as many as 10 players on the disabled list at one time.

The offense wasn't a juggernaut to begin with and sputtered to an 11th-place finish in the American League in scoring (4.30 runs per game) with Longoria sidelined for so long. But the Rays are used to doing more with less, and they compensated with pitching and defense.

Tampa Bay led the AL in ERA (3.19) and opponent average (.229) and set an AL record for strikeouts (1,383). David Price topped the league with 20 wins and a 2.56 ERA en route to winning the AL Cy Young Award, while Fernando Rodney took over as closer and converted 48 of 50 save opportunities while establishing a major league relief record with a 0.60 ERA.

Though the Rays continued to rank near the bottom of the major leagues in payroll, their Opening Day figure did represent a 56 percent increase from 2011, and the club made a huge commitment to Longoria after the season, extended his contract through 2022 (with a club option for 2023). The club's efforts still have not been reciprocated by the fan base, however. Tampa Bay ranked last in the majors in attendance at 1.6 million—an average of 19,255 per game—which commissioner Bud Selig called inexcusable.

Tropicana Field is outdated, but no progress is being made toward a new stadium, and political sparring between the cities of St. Petersburg (site of the current stadium) and Tampa hasn't helped matters. As a result, the Rays are unlikely to keep boosting their payroll. They couldn't dream of retaining B.J. Upton when the Braves offered him a free-agent deal worth $75 million over five years.

Tampa Bay's financial limitations mean that it will have to continue growing its own talent, but it now faces a lull in farm system production. The Rays are the only club that hasn't graduated a single pick from the last five drafts to the majors.

David Price led the American League in wins and ERA and won the AL Cy Young Award

After grabbing Price with the No. 1 overall pick and stealing Matt Moore in the eighth round of the 2007 draft, Tampa Bay chose infielder Tim Beckham over Buster Posey with the top overall selection in 2008. Beckham has hit just .264/.330/.379 in five minor league seasons and served a 50-game drug suspension in 2012. The Rays undermined their 2009 draft by failing to sign their top two choices, LeVon Washington and Kenny Diekroeger.

Tampa Bay's more recent drafts show some promise, especially a 2011 crop that included a record 12 picks in the first two rounds. But with most of their best prospects currently in the lower levels of the minors, the Rays opted to inject some young talent into their system with a December trade that sent righthanders James Shields and Wade Davis to the Royals.

In return, Tampa Bay received outfielder Wil Myers, righthander Jake Odorizzi, lefty Mike Montgomery and third baseman Patrick Leonard. Baseball America's 2012 Minor League Player of the Year, Myers is the system's top hitting prospect since Longoria graduated to the majors in 2008 while Odorizzi is a polished starting pitcher who has already made a pair of starts in the big leagues as a Royals' September callup.

THIS YEAR'S TOP 30

Player, Pos.		Grade
1.	Wil Myers, of/3b	70/Low
2.	Chris Archer, rhp	60/Medium
3.	Taylor Guerrieri, rhp	60/High
4.	Hak-Ju Lee, ss	55/Medium
5.	Jake Odorizzi, rhp	55/Medium
6.	Alex Colome, rhp	55/Medium
7.	Richie Shaffer, 3b	55/High
8.	Enny Romero, lhp	55/High
9.	Blake Snell, lhp	55/High
10.	Tim Beckham, ss/2b	50/Medium
11.	Drew Vettleson, of	55/High
12.	Mikie Mahtook, of	50/Medium
13.	Jeff Ames, rhp	55/High
14.	Jesse Hahn, rhp	55/High
15.	Mike Montgomery, lhp	50/High
16.	Tyler Goeddel, 3b	50/High
17.	Brandon Martin, ss	50/High
18.	Jake Hager, ss	50/High
19.	Andrew Toles, of	55/Extreme
20.	Felipe Rivero, lhp	50/High
21.	Todd Glaesmann, of	50/High
22.	Ryan Brett, 2b	50/High
23.	Jose Mujica, rhp	55/Extreme
24.	Josh Sale, of	50/High
25.	Parker Markel, rhp	50/High
26.	Patrick Leonard, 3b	50/High
27.	Bralin Jackson, of	50/High
28.	Ty Morrison, of	45/Medium
29.	Spencer Edwards, ss	50/High
30.	Nick Sawyer, rhp	50/Extreme

LAST YEAR'S TOP 30

Player, Pos.		Status
1.	Matt Moore, lhp	Majors
2.	Hak-Ju Lee, ss	No. 4
3.	Chris Archer, rhp	No. 2
4.	Taylor Guerrieri, rhp	No. 3
5.	Alex Colome, rhp	No. 6
6.	Alex Torres, lhp	Dropped out
7.	Tim Beckham, ss	No. 10
8.	Enny Romero, lhp	No. 8
9.	Drew Vettleson, of	No. 11
10.	Mikie Mahtook, of	No. 12
11.	Brandon Guyer, of	Dropped out
12.	Jake Hager, ss	No. 18
13.	Derek Dietrich, ss	(Marlins)
14.	Ryan Brett, 2b	No. 22
15.	Luke Bailey, c	Dropped out
16.	Parker Markel, rhp	No. 25
17.	Albert Suarez, rhp	Dropped out
18.	Tyler Goeddel, 3b	No. 16
19.	Matt Bush, rhp	(Released)
20.	Blake Snell, lhp	No. 9
21.	Braulio Lara, lhp	(Marlins)
22.	Stephen Vogt, c/of/1b	Dropped out
23.	Wilking Rodriguez, rhp	Dropped out
24.	Lenny Linksy, rhp	Dropped out
25.	Brandon Martin, ss	No. 17
26.	Kes Carter, of	Dropped out
27.	Justin O'Conner, c	Dropped out
28.	Felipe Rivero, lhp	No. 20
29.	Tyler Bortnick, 2b	(Diamondbacks)
30.	Jake Thompson, rhp	Dropped out

BEST TOOLS

Best Hitter for Average	Wil Myers
Best Power Hitter	Wil Myers
Best Strike-Zone Discipline	Richie Shaffer
Fastest Baserunner	Andrew Toles
Best Athlete	Andrew Toles
Best Fastball	Jesse Hahn
Best Curveball	Taylor Guerrieri
Best Slider	Chris Archer
Best Changeup	Mike Montgomery
Best Control	Taylor Guerrieri
Best Defensive Catcher	Mark Thomas
Best Defensive Infielder	Brandon Martin
Best Infield Arm	Tim Beckham
Best Defensive Outfielder	Ty Morrison
Best Outfield Arm	Drew Vettleson

PROJECTED 2016 LINEUP

Catcher	Mark Thomas
First Base	Richie Shaffer
Second Base	Tim Beckham
Third Base	Evan Longoria
Shortstop	Hak-Ju Lee
Left Field	Ben Zobrist
Center Field	Desmond Jennings
Right Field	Wil Myers
Designated Hitter	Matt Joyce
No. 1 Starter	David Price
No. 2 Starter	Matt Moore
No. 3 Starter	Chris Archer
No. 4 Starter	Jeremy Hellickson
No. 5 Starter	Jake Odorizzi
Closer	Taylor Guerrieri

TOP PROSPECTS OF THE DECADE

Year	Player, Pos.	2012 Org.
2003	Rocco Baldelli, of	Out of baseball
2004	B.J. Upton, ss	Rays
2005	Delmon Young, of	Tigers
2006	Delmon Young, of	Tigers
2007	Delmon Young, of	Tigers
2008	Evan Longoria, 3b	Rays
2009	David Price, lhp	Rays
2010	Desmond Jennings, of	Rays
2011	Matt Moore, lhp	Rays
2012	Matt Moore, lhp	Rays

TOP DRAFT PICKS OF THE DECADE

Year	Player, Pos.	2012 Org.
2003	Delmon Young, of	Tigers
2004	Jeff Niemann, rhp	Rays
2005	Wade Townsend, rhp	Out of baseball
2006	Evan Longoria, 3b	Rays
2007	David Price, lhp	Rays
2008	Tim Beckham, ss	Rays
2009	*LeVon Washington, of	Indians
2010	Josh Sale, of	Rays
2011	Taylor Guerrieri, rhp	Rays
2012	Richie Shaffer, 3b	Rays

LARGEST BONUSES IN CLUB HISTORY

Matt White, 1996	$10,200,000
Rolando Arrojo, 1997	$7,000,000
Tim Beckham, 2008	$6,150,000
David Price, 2007	$5,600,000
B.J. Upton, 2002	$4,600,000

TAMPA BAY RAYS

TOP 2013 ROOKIE: Wil Myers, of/3b. The James Shields' trade brought back a much-needed middle-of-the-order bat who is big league ready.

BREAKOUT PROSPECT: Brandon Martin, ss. He could emerge as a premier prospect if his pitch recognition catches up with his defensive skills.

SLEEPER: Cameron Seitzer, 1b. A professional hitter with a sweet swing and a great approach, he has the skills to add more power.

SOURCE OF TOP 30 TALENT

Homegrown	24	Acquired	6
College	3	Trades	6
Junior college	4	Rule 5 draft	0
High school	13	Independent leagues	0
Draft-and-follow	0	Free agents/waivers	0
Nondrafted free agents	0		
International	4		

LF
Josh Sale (24)
Granden Goetzman
Johnny Eierman

CF
Andrew Toles (19)
Bralin Jackson (27)
Ty Morrison (28)
Kevin Kiermaier
Kes Carter
Joey Rickard
Clayton Henning

RF
Wil Myers (1)
Drew Vettleson (11)
Mikie Mahtook (12)
Todd Glaesmann (21)
Brandon Guyer
Raul Mondesi Jr.

3B
Richie Shaffer (7)
Tyler Goeddel (16)
Patrick Leonard (26)
Cole Figueroa

SS
Hak-Ju Lee (4)
Brandon Martin (17)
Jake Hager (18)
Spencer Edwards (29)

2B
Tim Beckham (10)
Ryan Brett (22)
Tommy Coyle

1B
Cameron Seitzer
Jeff Malm

C
Mark Thomas
Luke Bailey
Justin O'Conner
Oscar Hernandez
Taylor Hawkins
Luke Maile
Stephen Vogt
Robinson Chirinos
David Rodriguez

LHP

LHSP	LHRP
Enny Romero (8)	Frank de los Santos
Blake Snell (9)	Chris Rearick
Mike Montgomery (15)	Jacob Partridge
Felipe Rivero (20)	C.J. Riefenhauser
Alex Torres	
Jose Castillo	
Benjamin Molina	
Ryan Carpenter	
Grayson Garvin	
Chris Kirsch	

RHP

RHSP	RHRP
Chris Archer (2)	Nick Sawyer (30)
Taylor Guerrieri (3)	Dane de la Rosa
Jake Odorizzi (5)	Josh Lueke
Alex Colome (6)	Lenny Linsky
Jeff Ames (13)	Kirby Yates
Jesse Hahn (14)	Andrew Bellatti
Jose Mujica (23)	Jason McEachern
Parker Markel (25)	Zach Quate
Roberto Gomez	Willie Gabay
Damion Carroll	
Jorman Durate	
Jake Thompson	
Wilking Rodriguez	
Albert Suarez	
German Marquez	
Nolan Gannon	

2012

BEST PURE HITTER: OF Andrew Toles (3) has the bat speed and foot speed to hit for high averages. Multiple scouting directors thought 3B Richie Shaffer (1) was the best all-around college hitter available in the entire draft.

BEST POWER HITTER: Shaffer not only has power to all fields, but he also has a patient approach that allows him to tap into it regularly. He's more refined than OF Bralin Jackson (5) and C Taylor Hawkins (12), high school picks with similar raw strength. Hawkins hit 74 homers in his prep career, one shy of Jeff Clement's national record.

FASTEST RUNNER: Toles and SS Spencer Edwards (2) have plus-plus speed, and OF Clayton Henning (11) is close behind them. Toles draws comparisons to Michael Bourn but needs to learn how to make the most of his quickness, as he didn't have a single bunt hit in his pro debut.

BEST DEFENSIVE PLAYER: OF Joey Rickard's (9) outstanding instincts in center field helped his teams win championships at the College World Series and in the short-season New York-Penn League. Toles' wheels give him more pure range in center, and he has a solid arm as well.

BEST FASTBALL: RHP Nick Sawyer (40) is just 5-foot-11 but generates consistent 94-96 mph fastballs that get on hitters quick. RHP Damion Carroll (6) maxes out at 95 mph but has a lot more projection remaining in his athletic 6-foot-4 frame.

BEST SECONDARY PITCH: Sawyer also owns a power 81-83 mph curveball with short, sharp break.

BEST PRO DEBUT: Sawyer was unhittable at three stops, making it to low Class A while posting a 0.28 ERA, 59 strikeouts in 32 innings and a .097 opponent average. Shaffer produced as expected, batting .308/.406/.487 in the NY-P. 3B Ben Kline (32) made the Rookie-level Gulf Coast League all-star team by hitting .347 with 10 steals.

BEST ATHLETE: Toles edges Edwards and Henning because he knows how to use his considerable tools better at this point.

MOST INTRIGUING BACKGROUND: OF Marty Gantt (7) has an underdeveloped right hand that lacks fingertips, but he overcame that to win the Southern Conference 2012 player of the year award. Toles' father Alvin was an NFL first-round pick in 1985 as a linebacker. Position players who bat righthanded and throw lefty are rare, but the Rays signed three of them in Jackson, Gantt and Rickard.

CLOSEST TO THE MAJORS: Shaffer is the biggest impact bat drafted by the Rays since Evan Longoria in 2006.

BEST LATE-ROUND PICK: Sawyer. The Rays also are bullish on Henning, Hawkins, crafty RHP Dylan Floro (13) and Coyle.

THE ONE WHO GOT AWAY: Tampa Bay signed all but three of its selections. It pursued defensive-minded C Taylor Ward (31) but ran out of money, so he headed to Fresno State.

ASSESSMENT: The Rays were pleasantly surprised to find Shaffer available with the 25th overall pick. He set the tone for a Tampa Bay draft class that should be most notable for its position players.

2011

With a record 12 picks in the top two rounds, the Rays added depth to their system but not necessarily a lot of star power. RHP Taylor Guerrieri (1) has a huge ceiling. OF Mikie Mahtook (1), SSs Jake Hager (1) and Brandon Martin (1s), 3B Tyler Goeddel (1s), RHP Jeff Ames (1s) and Blake Snell (1s) could be solid contributors.

GRADE: B

2010

OF Josh Sale (1) and C Justin O'Conner (1) haven't produced at the plate as hoped, but OF Drew Vettleson (1s) and SS/2B Derek Dietrich (2) have picked up the slack. RHP Jesse Hahn (6) could be a steal as he bounces back from Tommy John surgery.

GRADE: C+

2009

In a disastrous draft, Tampa Bay failed to sign its first two choices, OF LeVon Washington (1) and INF Kenny Diekroeger (2), as well as a pair of future first-rounders in RHP Pierce Johnson (15) and LHP Andrew Heaney (24). It gave over-slot bonuses to several players to try to compensate, but only OF Todd Glasemann (3) has shown signs of panning out.

GRADE: D

2008

The Rays famously passed up Buster Posey to take SS/2B Tim Beckham (1) with the No. 1 overall pick. Beckham has yet to live up to his $6.15 million bonus, and LHP Kyle Lobstein (2) has been slow to pay dividends on his $1.5 million.

GRADE: C

Draft analysis by Jim Callis. Numbers in parentheses indicate draft rounds.

1 WIL MYERS, OF/3B

Born: Dec. 10, 1990. **B-T:** R-R. **Ht.:** 6-3. **Wt.:** 205.
Drafted: HS—High Point, N.C., 2009 (3rd round).
Signed by: Steve Connelly (Royals).

BA GRADE
70
LOW

ANDREW WOOLLEY

As a junior at Wesleyan Christian Academy in High Point, N.C., Myers had more success as a pitcher than a hitter, and he would have been a two-way player had he followed through on his commitment to South Carolina. But after his $2 million asking price dropped him to the third round of the 2009 draft, the Royals met his price. He began his pro career as a catcher, but after splitting time with Salvador Perez at high Class A Wilmington in 2010, Myers agreed to move to the outfield to expedite getting his bat to the majors. In 2012, he made the decision to tweak his stance, setting up more upright and working on backspinning the ball for more carry. It paid off to the tune of 37 homers, the second-most in the minors and 23 more than he had ever hit in a pro season. In the last 50 years, only one 21-year-old has hit more homers in a minor league season (Arlo Engel, with 41 in 1963). Myers joined Tom Gordon as the only Royals to win Baseball America's Minor League Player of the Year award, then became the first recipient to get traded before playing in the majors for his original organization. Kansas City sent Myers and three other prospects (righthander Jake Odorizzi, lefty Mike Montgomery, third baseman Patrick Leonard) to the Rays in December for James Shields, Wade Davis and a player to be named.

Myers combines outstanding raw power with an advanced approach at the plate and excellent hand-eye coordination. When he uses the opposite field and doesn't worry about hitting homers, he can post high batting averages and on-base percentages. His decision to try to hit for more power last year meant that he took more aggressive swings in two-strike counts, resulting in a career-high 140 strikeouts. After struggling with chasing balls that were too far in on his hands to hit fair in 2011, he made adjustments to lay off those pitches while showing he could pull fastballs on the inner half for extra bases. Myers has fringy speed but is a heady baserun-

SCOUTING GRADES

Batting: 60. **Defense:** 55.
Power: 70. **Arm:** 60.
Speed: 45.

Based on 20-80 scouting scale, where 50 epresents major league average, and future projection rather than present tools

ner. He fits best in right field, where he should become a solid defender. He responded well to the challenge of center field, but his lack of quickness limits him there. The Royals thought he had a chance to become an average center fielder, but scouts on other teams grade him as well below-average there.

Though the Rays have an outfield vacancy after losing free agent B.J. Upton to the Braves, it's unclear whether Myers will get the opportunity to fill it immediately. It wouldn't be a surprise to see him start 2013 at Triple-A Durham, which would allow him to work on cutting down his strikeouts while also delaying his arbitration and free-agent eligibility. Regardless, he'll be in the major leagues before long and eventually should bat fourth behind Longoria.

Year	Club (League)	Class	AVG	G	AB	R	H	2B	3B	HR	RBI	BB	SO	SB	CS	OBP	SLG
2009	Burlington (APP)	R	.125	4	16	1	2	0	1	1	4	0	3	0	0	.125	.438
	Idaho Falls (PIO)	R	.426	18	68	18	29	7	1	4	14	9	15	2	0	.488	.735
2010	Burlington (MWL)	LoA	.289	68	242	42	70	19	1	10	45	48	55	10	3	.408	.500
	Wilmington (CAR)	HiA	.346	58	205	28	71	18	2	4	38	37	39	2	3	.453	.512
2011	NW Arkansas (TL)	AA	.254	99	354	50	90	23	1	8	49	52	87	9	2	.353	.393
2012	NW Arkansas (TL)	AA	.343	35	134	32	46	11	1	13	30	16	42	4	1	.414	.731
	Omaha (PCL)	AAA	.304	99	388	66	118	15	5	24	79	45	98	2	2	.378	.554
Minor League Totals			.303	381	1407	237	426	93	12	64	259	207	339	29	11	.395	.522

2 CHRIS ARCHER, RHP

Born: Sept. 26, 1988. **B-T:** R-R. **Ht.:** 6-3. **Wt.:** 200. **Drafted:** HS—Clayton, N.C., 2006 (5th round). **Signed by:** Bob Mayer (Indians).

After signing with the Indians for $161,000 as a fifth-round pick in 2006, Archer struggled in his first three pro seasons and never advanced beyond low Class A. He began to blossom after the Cubs acquired him in a trade for veteran infielder Mark DeRosa in 2008, then was traded again, this time to the Rays in an eight-player deal for Matt Garza in January 2011. Inconsistent in his first year in the Tampa Bay system, Archer led Rays farmhands and the Triple-A International League in strikeouts (139) and strikeouts per nine innings (9.8) in 2012. He also made his major league debut in June when Jeremy Hellickson went on the disabled list. During a September callup, he fanned 11 and yielded just two runs on four hits in seven innings against the Rangers and beat the Red Sox for his first big league win. Archer throws two well above-average pitches with his quick arm and easy delivery. His fastball sits at 92-96 mph, has been clocked as high as 98 and features good run and sink. His success in the second half of the season coincided with his willingness to pitch aggressively off his fastball, which allowed him to get ahead in the count more often. In turn, that helped him do a better job of setting up his slider, his most consistent and best all-around pitch. His slider operates in the mid-90s with hard, cutting tilt and impressive depth. He has improved his changeup over the past two seasons, but it's average at best and he just uses it as a show-me pitch to keep hitters off balance. Archer's mechanics are fine, which leaves most observers to believe his command issues result from his inconsistent focus and mental approach. He moves well off the mound but is prone to making errors and must do a better job of controlling the running game. His inability to throw consistent strikes leads some scouts to suggest that Archer could wind up in the bullpen, perhaps even as a closer. But the progress he made after the all-star break showed that he has the ability to be a No. 2 or 3 starter, particularly if he can trust his changeup more against major league hitters. He's a good bet to earn a spot on Tampa Bay's 25-man roster in 2013.

BA GRADE
60
MEDIUM

Year	Club (League)	Class	W	L	ERA	G	GS	CG	SV	IP	H	HR	BB	SO	K/9	WHIP	AVG
2006	Indians (GCL)	R	0	3	7.45	7	6	0	0	19	17	1	17	21	9.8	1.76	.224
	Burlington (APP)	R	0	0	10.80	1	0	0	0	2	1	1	1	1	5.4	1.80	.333
2007	Indians (GCL)	R	1	7	5.64	12	11	0	0	53	56	4	21	48	8.2	1.46	.271
	Lake County (SAL)	LoA	0	0	9.00	1	0	0	0	4	5	0	3	5	11.3	2.00	.333
2008	Lake County (SAL)	LoA	4	8	4.29	27	27	0	0	115	92	8	84	106	8.3	1.53	.220
2009	Peoria (MWL)	LoA	6	4	2.81	27	26	0	0	109	78	0	66	119	9.8	1.32	.202
2010	Daytona (FSL)	HiA	7	1	2.86	15	14	0	0	72	54	4	26	82	10.2	1.11	.202
	Tennessee (SL)	AA	8	2	1.80	13	13	0	0	70	48	2	39	67	8.6	1.24	.198
2011	Montgomery (SL)	AA	8	7	4.42	25	25	0	0	134	136	11	80	118	7.9	1.61	.266
	Durham (IL)	AAA	1	0	0.69	2	2	0	0	13	11	0	6	12	8.3	1.31	.224
2012	Durham (IL)	AAA	7	9	3.66	25	25	0	0	128	99	6	62	139	9.8	1.26	.216
	Tampa Bay (AL)	MAJ	1	3	4.60	6	4	0	0	29	23	3	13	36	11.0	1.23	.215
Major League Totals			1	3	4.60	6	4	0	0	29	23	3	13	36	11.0	1.23	.215
Minor League Totals			42	41	3.75	155	149	0	0	720	598	37	405	718	9.0	1.39	.227

3 TAYLOR GUERRIERI, RHP

Born: Dec. 1, 1992. **B-T:** R-R. **Ht.:** 6-3. **Wt.:** 195. **Drafted:** HS—Columbia, S.C., 2011 (1st round). **Signed by:** Brad Matthews.

Though he had one of the most electric arms in the 2011 draft, Guerrieri lasted 24 picks because of questions about his maturity. The Rays believed those concerns were exaggerated and were thrilled to land him for $1.6 million. He rewarded them with an impressive pro debut in 2012, ranking as the top prospect in the short-season New York-Penn League. Clocked as high as 98 mph in high school, Guerrieri pitched at 90-95 with his fastball in his first pro summer. His two-seamer has hard, late sink and armside run, and he does an excellent job of spotting it on both sides of the plate and down in the strike zone. His sharp 77-81 mph curveball has good depth and is a swing-and-miss offering at times. His changeup has a chance to give him a third plus pitch as he incorporates it more into his repertoire. Guerrieri has a solid delivery and ideal pitcher's body, and he walked just five batters in his 12 starts. He displays a strong competitive drive and there were no issues with his makeup in 2012. A potential frontline starter, Guerrieri should open 2013 at low Class A Bowling Green. The Rays usually develop their high school pitchers slowly, but he could force their hand if he repeats his New-York Penn League performance when he opens next year in a full-season league.

BA GRADE
60
HIGH

Year	Club (League)	Class	W	L	ERA	G	GS	CG	SV	IP	H	HR	BB	SO	K/9	WHIP	AVG
2012	Hudson Valley (NYP)	SS	1	2	1.04	12	12	0	0	52	35	0	5	45	7.8	0.77	.186
Minor League Totals			1	2	1.04	12	12	0	0	52	35	0	5	45	7.8	0.77	.186

4 HAK-JU LEE, SS

Born: Nov. 4, 1990. **B-T:** L-R. **Ht.:** 6-2. **Wt.:** 170. **Signed:** South Korea, 2008. **Signed by:** Steve Wilson (Cubs).

Two of the Rays' three best prospects are products of the Matt Garza trade with the Cubs in January 2011. Signed by Chicago for $725,000 out of South Korea, Lee hit well in the lower minors but has leveled off in Double-A the last two years, batting .249/.325/.351 at Montgomery. He did post a 21-game hitting streak and a 46-game on-base streak this season before an oblique injury sidelined him in mid-August. Lee's calling card is his defensive acumen. He has quick-twitch actions, plus speed and a sixth sense about where to position himself. His hands are soft and he bolsters his above-average arm strength with good accuracy and a quick release. At the plate, Lee tends to slap at pitches and uses the opposite field more often than not. While his power is modest, he can drive the ball to the gaps. He needs to do a better job of working counts and getting on base so he can take advantage of his plus speed. He knows how to steal bases and swiped 37 in 46 tries in 2012, an improvement on his 33-for-49 total from the 2011 season. The Rays continue to see Lee as their long-term answer at shortstop, but they want him to improve his strength and make a few more adjustments at the plate and improve his strength. Added to the 40-man roster, he should spend most of 2013 in Triple-A.

BA GRADE

55

MEDIUM

Year	Club (League)	Class	AVG	G	AB	R	H	2B	3B	HR	RBI	BB	SO	SB	CS	OBP	SLG
2009	Boise (NWL)	SS	.330	68	264	56	87	14	2	2	33	31	50	25	8	.399	.420
2010	Peoria (MWL)	LoA	.282	122	485	85	137	22	4	4	40	49	86	32	7	.354	.351
2011	Charlotte (FSL)	HiA	.318	97	400	82	127	16	11	4	23	42	72	28	14	.389	.443
	Montgomery (SL)	AA	.190	24	100	16	19	1	4	1	7	11	22	5	2	.272	.310
2012	Montgomery (SL)	AA	.261	116	475	68	124	15	10	4	37	51	102	37	9	.336	.360
Minor League Totals			.287	427	1724	307	494	68	31	12	140	184	332	127	40	.359	.383

5 JAKE ODORIZZI, RHP

Born: March 27, 1990. **B-T:** R-R. **Ht.:** 6-2. **Wt.:** 175. **Drafted:** HS—Highland, Ill., 2008 (1st round supplemental). **Signed by:** Harvey Kuenn Jr. (Brewers).

Since signing for $1.06 million as the 32nd overall pick in the 2008 draft, Odorizzi has been involved in two major trades. The Brewers included him with Lorenzo Cain, Alcides Escobar and Jeremy Jeffress to get Zack Greinke from the Royals in December 2010, and Kansas City used him to acquire James Shields and Wade Davis from the Rays two years later. Odorizzi doesn't really have an out pitch, but his ability to throw four offerings for strikes makes him hard to hit. He works both sides of the plate with a fastball that sits at 89-92 mph, touches 94 and features nice sink. His curveball and slider are both average pitches, and his changeup has similar potential. Odorizzi will need more consistent control and command if he's going to thrive in the big leagues with average stuff. A star shortstop and wide receiver in high school, he's a good athlete who repeats his delivery well. Odorizzi is a longshot to make Tampa Bay's rotation in spring training, and he'll probably get some more time in Triple-A. He has a relatively low floor but his lack of plus stuff limits him to a ceiling as a No. 3 or 4 starter.

BA GRADE

55

MEDIUM

Year	Club (League)	Class	W	L	ERA	G	GS	CG	SV	IP	H	HR	BB	SO	K/9	WHIP	AVG
2008	Brewers (AZL)	R	1	2	3.48	11	4	0	0	21	18	2	9	19	8.3	1.31	.220
2009	Helena (PIO)	R	1	4	4.40	12	10	0	0	47	55	3	9	43	8.2	1.36	.296
2010	Wisconsin (MWL)	LoA	7	3	3.43	23	20	0	1	121	99	7	40	135	10.1	1.15	.220
2011	Wilmington (CAR)	HiA	5	4	2.87	15	15	0	0	78	68	4	22	103	11.8	1.15	.235
	NW Arkansas (TL)	AA	5	3	4.72	12	12	0	0	69	66	13	22	54	7.1	1.28	.254
2012	NW Arkansas (TL)	AA	4	2	3.32	7	7	0	0	38	27	2	10	47	11.1	0.97	.191
	Omaha (PCL)	AAA	11	3	2.93	19	18	0	0	107	105	12	40	88	7.4	1.35	.254
	Kansas City (AL)	MAJ	0	1	4.91	2	2	0	0	7	8	1	4	4	4.9	1.64	.267
Major League Totals			0	1	4.91	2	2	0	0	7	8	1	4	4	4.9	1.64	.267
Minor League Totals			34	21	3.50	99	86	0	1	481	438	43	152	489	9.2	1.23	.241

6 ALEX COLOME, RHP

Born: Dec. 31, 1988. **B-T:** L-R. **Ht.:** 6-2. **Wt.:** 185. **Signed:** Dominican Republic, 2007. **Signed by:** Eddy Toledo.

Colome pitched well in 2012 but had a hard time staying on the mound. He missed a month and a half when he hurt his left oblique while fielding a bunt in his second start, and his season came to a premature end with a lat strain in mid-August. His uncle Jesus pitched 10 seasons in the majors, including six with the Rays. Colome has a special arm that generates impressive velocity and good movement. His fastball sits at 93-95 mph with excellent sink and some armside run. He also throws two breaking balls, a sharp curveball with tight spin and an upper-80s slider that's less consistent. He has added fade to his changeup, but he lacks the confidence to throw it when behind in the count. Colome made the transition from a thrower to a pitcher in 2012 after trying to strike out every batter earlier in his career. He struggled at the beginning of his starts early in the campaign before he improved his pitch selection and command. If his feel for pitching continues to get better, Colome has what it takes to be a solid mid-rotation starter in the big leagues. At worst, he should be a late-inning reliever. He'll open 2013 in the Durham rotation, with a big league promotion a strong possibility later in the season.

BA GRADE 55 MEDIUM

Year	Club (League)	Class	W	L	ERA	G	GS	CG	SV	IP	H	HR	BB	SO	K/9	WHIP	AVG
2007	Devil Rays (DSL)	R	1	6	2.97	14	11	0	0	39	30	1	31	50	11.4	1.55	.208
2008	Princeton (APP)	R	0	5	6.80	12	11	0	0	46	50	5	26	52	10.1	1.64	.272
2009	Hudson Valley (NYP)	SS	7	4	1.66	15	15	2	0	76	46	0	32	94	11.1	1.03	.174
2010	Bowling Green (MWL)	LoA	6	6	3.95	22	22	1	0	114	98	14	45	118	9.3	1.25	—
	Charlotte (FSL)	HiA	0	0	2.25	1	1	0	0	4	5	0	0	8	18.0	1.25	.333
2011	Charlotte (FSL)	HiA	9	5	3.66	19	19	1	0	106	78	8	44	92	7.8	1.15	.214
	Montgomery (SL)	AA	3	4	4.15	9	9	1	0	52	41	5	28	31	5.4	1.33	.219
2012	Montgomery (SL)	AA	8	3	3.48	14	14	1	0	75	69	2	34	75	9.0	1.37	.252
	Durham (IL)	AAA	0	1	3.24	3	3	0	0	17	12	1	9	15	8.1	1.26	.207
Minor League Totals			34	34	3.66	109	105	6	0	529	429	36	249	535	9.1	1.28	.224

7 RICHIE SHAFFER, 3B

Born: March 15, 1991. **B-T:** R-R. **Ht.:** 6-3. **Wt.:** 210. **Drafted:** Clemson, 2012 (1st round). **Signed by:** Brian Hickman.

The Rays considered Shaffer the best all-around hitter in the 2012 draft, so they were surprised when he fell to them with the 25th overall pick. He signed for $1.71 million and had no problem handling pro pitching. He hit a game-deciding three-run homer in the second game of the New York-Penn League finals, helping Hudson Valley to its first league title in 12 years. Shaffer is the most polished hitter and biggest impact bat in the system. He employs a patient approach with good discipline, uses his hands well and has power to all fields. His swing generates leverage and impressive bat speed that creates loud contact. He'll chase out of the strike zone at times but has the ability to recognize pitches. Just the second third baseman ever drafted in the first round by the Rays, he's blocked by the first, Evan Longoria. Capable of playing first base and right field, Shaffer will remain at the hot corner for now. He has solid athleticism and ability to make throws from a variety of angles. He possesses average speed, plus arm strength and good instincts. He's a hard worker who loves to play. Given his tools and savvy, Shaffer could move quickly. He could start his first full professional season at high Class A Charlotte and crack Tampa Bay's lineup at some point in 2014.

BA GRADE 55 HIGH

Year	Club (League)	Class	AVG	G	AB	R	H	2B	3B	HR	RBI	BB	SO	SB	CS	OBP	SLG
2012	Hudson Valley (NYP)	SS	.308	33	117	25	36	5	2	4	26	16	31	0	0	.406	.487
Minor League Totals			.308	33	117	25	36	5	2	4	26	16	31	0	0	.406	.487

8 ENNY ROMERO, LHP

Born: Jan. 24, 1991. **B-T:** L-L. **Ht.:** 6-3. **Wt.:** 165. **Signed:** Dominican Republic, 2008. **Signed by:** Eddy Toledo.

In three years in the United States, Romero has led the Rookie-level Appalachian League with a 1.95 ERA (2010), the low Class A Midwest League with 11.1 strikeouts per nine innings (2011) and the high Class A Florida State League with a .201 opponent average (2012). He pitched in the Futures Game last July before falling into a second-half slump, posting a 5.09 ERA and 39 walks in his final 53 innings. Romero can dominate with his plus fastball when he's in rhythm and pounding the strike zone. He was unhittable at times in the FSL, but struggled at others because of self-inflicted mistakes. His 92-97 mph fastball has great movement and armside run. He throws a hard curveball in the low 80s but battles to command it from his three-quarters release point. His changeup is a work in progress but shows promise when he maintains his arm slot. Romero's greatest need is to repeat his delivery with more consistency so he can throw more strikes. The Rays believe he'll continue to improve as his projectable frame develops and adds strength. Romero could move quickly if he harnesses his command and control. His ability to do so will determine whether he becomes a No. 3 starter or late-inning reliever. Added to the 40-man roster in the offseason to protect him from the Rule 5 draft, he'll make the jump to Double-A in 2013.

BA GRADE 55 HIGH

Year	Club (League)	Class	W	L	ERA	G	GS	CG	SV	IP	H	HR	BB	SO	K/9	WHIP	AVG
2008	Rays (DSL)	R	1	0	2.76	10	0	0	0	16	11	0	8	20	11.0	1.16	.175
2009	Rays (GCL)	R	2	4	4.81	11	4	0	0	39	38	2	21	33	7.6	1.50	.255
2010	Princeton (APP)	R	4	1	1.95	13	13	0	0	69	51	2	14	72	9.3	0.94	.204
	Hudson Valley (NYP)	SS	1	0	1.80	1	1	0	0	5	1	0	5	4	7.2	1.20	.071
2011	Bowling Green (MWL)	LoA	5	5	4.26	26	26	0	0	114	104	9	68	140	11.1	1.51	.245
2012	Charlotte (FSL)	HiA	5	7	3.93	25	23	1	0	126	89	5	76	107	7.6	1.31	.201
Minor League Totals			18	17	3.67	86	67	1	0	370	294	18	192	376	9.1	1.31	.219

9 BLAKE SNELL, LHP

Born: Dec. 4, 1992. **B-T:** L-L. **Ht.:** 6-4. **Wt.:** 180. **Drafted:** HS—Shoreline, Wash., 2011 (1st round supplemental). **Signed by:** Paul Kirsch.

The Rays' sixth pick (52nd overall) in the 2011 draft, Snell has surged past all the players they took ahead of him except for Taylor Guerrieri. He has compiled a 2.44 ERA while being kept on tight pitch counts in two years of pro ball. He would have led the Appalachian League with a 2.09 ERA in 2012 if he hadn't fallen seven innings short of qualifying because Tampa Bay shut him down with fatigue in mid-August. Snell's fastball sits in the low 90s and touches 94 mph with good sinking action that results in a lot of groundouts. His low-80s slider is tough on lefthanders when he throws it for strikes. His curveball and changeup lag behind his other two pitches and require plenty of work, but his biggest need is to add strength to his lanky frame in order to handle the wear and tear of a full season. Snell still is learning that strikeouts aren't everything, and that he can reduce his pitch counts if he's more efficient. Though he's slow to the plate, he gave up just one steal in four attempts over 11 starts in 2012. Scouts like Snell's arm and projectable body, and they see a potential No. 3 starter on the verge of a breakthrough. The Rays will be conservative with his development, so his next stop could be Hudson Valley.

BA GRADE 55 HIGH

Year	Club (League)	Class	W	L	ERA	G	GS	CG	SV	IP	H	HR	BB	SO	K/9	WHIP	AVG
2011	Rays (GCL)	R	1	2	3.08	11	8	0	0	26	30	0	11	26	8.9	1.56	.291
2012	Princeton (APP)	R	5	1	2.09	11	11	1	0	47	34	4	17	53	10.1	1.08	.202
Minor League Totals			6	3	2.44	22	19	1	0	74	64	4	28	79	9.7	1.25	.236

10 TIM BECKHAM, SS/2B

Born: Jan. 27, 1990. **B-T:** R-R. **Ht.:** 6-0. **Wt.:** 190. **Drafted:** HS—Griffin, Ga., 2008 (1st round). **Signed by:** Milt Hill.

As the first overall selection in the 2008 draft, Beckham always will be compared to Buster Posey, who went four picks later to the Giants. Since signing for $6.15 million, Beckham has made a rocky ascent through the minor leagues. He has hit just .256/.314/.389 in Triple-A during the last two seasons and was suspended for 50 games in 2012 after testing positive a second time for a drug of abuse. Beckham continues to maintain plus bat speed that generates raw power to all fields. His lack of consistency at the plate comes from his below-average pitch recognition and refusal at times to shorten his swing. The Rays are encouraged by adjustments he has made, including lowering his hands and reducing his pre-swing movement. Questions have centered on Beckham's ability to remain at shortstop since he signed, and he saw action at second base for the first time in 2012. He has a plus arm, but his average speed and decent range and hands are

BA GRADE

50

MEDIUM

better suited for second. Beckham is knocking on the door to the big leagues, something further evidenced by his addition to the 40-man roster during the offseason. His ticket appears to be developing into an offensive-minded second baseman, though the Rays have a greater need at shortstop.

Year	Club (League)	Class	AVG	G	AB	R	H	2B	3B	HR	RBI	BB	SO	SB	CS	OBP	SLG
2008	Princeton (APP)	R	.243	46	177	30	43	12	0	2	14	13	43	5	1	.297	.345
	Hudson Valley (NYP)	SS	.333	2	6	5	2	1	0	0	0	2	1	1	0	.556	.500
2009	Bowling Green (SAL)	LoA	.275	125	491	58	135	33	4	5	63	34	116	13	10	.328	.389
2010	Charlotte (FSL)	HiA	.256	123	465	68	119	23	5	5	57	62	119	22	14	.346	.359
2011	Montgomery (SL)	AA	.275	107	418	82	115	25	2	7	57	39	91	15	4	.339	.395
	Durham (IL)	AAA	.255	24	106	12	27	3	2	5	13	3	29	2	1	.282	.462
2012	Durham (IL)	AAA	.256	72	285	40	73	10	1	6	28	29	71	6	0	.325	.361
Minor League Totals			.264	499	1948	295	514	107	14	30	232	182	470	64	30	.330	.379

11 DREW VETTLESON, OF

BA GRADE

55

HIGH

Born: July 19, 1991. **B-T:** L-R. **Ht.:** 6-1. **Wt.:** 185. **Drafted:** HS—Silverdale, Wash., 2010 (1st round supplemental). **Signed by:** Paul Kirsch.

Vettleson first captured attention as a switch-pitcher when he was in high school, but he went 42nd overall in the 2010 draft because of his hitting ability. Vettleson set a Bowling Green franchise record with 139 hits and ranked second in the low Class A Midwest League with 218 total bases. Vettleson has all the tools to be a solid right fielder. He has a short swing and is capable of driving the ball to all fields. He does a good job of getting around on premium fastballs and makes consistent contact, even when he's behind in the count. He should have solid power once his body fills out. He sells out for home runs at times, adding length to his swing. Vettleson has average speed and good instincts on the basepaths and in the outfield. He's working on refining his basestealing jumps and defensive routes. Managers rated his arm as the best among Midwest League outfielders, and he finished second in the league with 20 assists. If Vettleson makes the necessary adjustments, he could have solid tools across the board. He's expected to spend the majority of 2013 in high Class A.

Year	Club (League)	Class	AVG	G	AB	R	H	2B	3B	HR	RBI	BB	SO	SB	CS	OBP	SLG
2011	Princeton (APP)	R	.282	61	234	33	66	13	4	7	40	27	53	20	6	.357	.462
2012	Bowling Green (MWL)	LoA	.275	132	505	80	139	24	5	15	69	51	117	20	11	.340	.432
Minor League Totals			.277	193	739	113	205	37	9	22	109	78	170	40	17	.345	.441

12 MIKIE MAHTOOK, OF

BA GRADE

50

MEDIUM

Born: Nov. 30, 1989. **B-T:** R-R. **Ht.:** 6-1. **Wt.:** 200. **Drafted:** Louisiana State, 2011 (1st round). **Signed by:** Rickey Drexler.

Mahtook was part of a 2009 national championship at Louisiana State and led the Southeastern Conference in batting (.383) and steals (29) as an All-American two years later, then went 31st overall in the 2011 draft. After signing for $1.15 million, he got a taste of pro ball in the Arizona Fall League and headed to high Class A for his official pro debut last spring. He made quick adjustments at Charlotte and did well initially after a late-July promotion to Double-A Montgomery before the length of his first full season seemed to take its toll. Mahtook doesn't have a dominating tool but he does a lot of things well and has a hard-nosed approach. Employing a deep crouch at the plate, he drives the ball to all fields and generates excellent backspin and distance with his short stroke. He should hit for a solid average with 12-15 home runs annually as he continues to improve his plate discipline. With slightly above-average speed, Mahtook runs the bases aggressively and covers ground in the outfield with his ability to take proper angles on flyballs. He played both center and right field last year, though he's likely destined for a corner. He has average arm strength with good accuracy.

Mahtook is moving rapidly through the system and could fill a role in Tampa Bay at some point during the 2014 season. He may be more of a quality extra outfielder than a regular, unless he can stick in center or develop more power. He'll open 2013 back at Montgomery, with a promotion to Triple-A a possibility during the summer.

Year	Club (League)	Class	AVG	G	AB	R	H	2B	3B	HR	RBI	BB	SO	SB	CS	OBP	SLG
2012	Charlotte (FSL)	HiA	.290	92	341	44	99	15	7	5	37	29	71	19	6	.358	.419
	Montgomery (SL)	AA	.248	39	153	17	38	10	1	4	25	11	31	4	3	.308	.405
Minor League Totals			.277	131	494	61	137	25	8	9	62	40	102	23	9	.342	.415

13 JEFF AMES, RHP

BA GRADE
55
HIGH

Born: Jan. 31, 1991. **B-T:** R-R. **Ht.:** 6-4. **Wt.:** 225. **Drafted:** Lower Columbia (Wash.) CC, 2011 (1st round supplemental). **Signed by:** Paul Kirsch.

The 42nd overall pick in the 2011 draft, Ames signed for a below-slot $650,000 before posting a 7.12 ERA at Rookie-level Princeton in his pro debut. He did an impressive job of harnessing his raw stuff in his second year in the system, employing better command and keeping his delivery tight and over his front leg more consistently. He recorded the third-lowest ERA (1.96) in the New York-Penn League while ranking fourth in opponent average (.195) and strikeouts (70). Ames uses his 6-foot-4 frame to throw on an excellent downhill angle. His four-seam fastball sits at 93-95 mph, but it can become straight when he overthrows it. He added a sinking two-seamer during the 2012 season, and it complements his four-seamer well. The two-seamer also does a better job of setting up his plus slider, which resides at 83-88 mph but flattens when he fails to stay on top of it. His changeup is coming along yet still lacks consistent fade and depth. Ames is a work in progress who could have a nice four-pitch mix and become a middle-of-the-rotation starter. He'll open 2013 in low Class A.

Year	Club (League)	Class	W	L	ERA	G	GS	CG	SV	IP	H	HR	BB	SO	K/9	WHIP	AVG
2011	Princeton (APP)	R	4	2	7.12	11	5	0	1	30	40	4	7	39	11.6	1.55	.317
2012	Hudson Valley (NYP)	SS	6	1	1.96	14	13	0	0	64	44	1	20	70	9.8	0.99	.195
Minor League Totals			10	3	3.61	25	18	0	1	95	84	5	27	109	10.4	1.17	.239

14 JESSE HAHN, RHP

BA GRADE
55
HIGH

Born: July 30, 1989. **B-T:** R-R. **Ht.:** 6-5. **Wt.:** 185. **Drafted:** Virginia Tech, 2010 (6th round). **Signed by:** Lou Wieben.

Hahn looked like he had pitched himself into the first round of the 2010 draft before he came down with a sore elbow. The injury dropped him to the sixth round (where he signed for $525,000) and resulted in Tommy John surgery that delayed his pro debut until 2012. A broken foot last March dragged out his debut further, but he finally took the mound in June and showed the same arm strength and feel for pitching that had attracted scouts. Hahn's four-seam fastball sits at 94-96 mph and touches 99, and his heavy two-seamer resides at 91-96 mph with excellent sink. His secondary pitches also have promise, including an overhand curveball with a sharp drop and a changeup that flashes good depth. He started to use his hard slider again as the season progressed, though it lacked its previous sharp break. Hahn employs a good downhill delivery, but his release point is inconsistent. He tends to muscle the ball to the plate, though the Rays believe his delivery is better now than before his elbow reconstruction. If he can stay healthy, Hahn could reach his ceiling of a No. 2 starter. His next stop will be low Class A, and he could start to move quickly.

Year	Club (League)	Class	W	L	ERA	G	GS	CG	SV	IP	H	HR	BB	SO	K/9	WHIP	AVG
2010	Did Not Play—Injured																
2011	Did Not Play—Injured																
2012	Hudson Valley (NYP)	SS	2	2	2.77	14	14	0	0	52	38	0	15	55	9.5	1.02	.199
Minor League Totals			2	2	2.77	14	14	0	0	52	38	0	15	55	9.5	1.02	.199

15 MIKE MONTGOMERY, LHP

BA GRADE
50
HIGH

Born: July 1, 1989. **B-T:** L-L. **Ht.:** 6-4. **Wt.:** 185. **Drafted:** HS—Newhall, Calif., 2008 (1st round supplemental). **Signed by:** Dan Ontiveros (Royals).

Signed for $988,000 as the 36th overall pick in 2008, Montgomery projected as the Royals' future ace for years. But after he struggled for two straight seasons in Triple-A and was even worse after a demotion to Double-A in mid-2012, Kansas City decided it couldn't wait any longer. The Royals included him in the four-prospect package that pried James Shields and Wade Davis from the Rays in December. At his best, Montgomery still shows a 92-93 fastball that touches 95 mph, along with a plus changeup. But as he tried to implement a lower arm slot last season, his fastball often dipped to 88-90 mph. Montgomery never has gotten comfortable with his erratic curveball, and he'll try to work on a slider and a cutter as he looks for something to reverse his surprising lack of a platoon advantage. Lefties were way too comfortable against him in 2012, posting a .993 OPS. Montgomery will return to Triple-A and try to regain the confidence and swagger.

Year	Club (League)	Class	W	L	ERA	G	GS	CG	SV	IP	H	HR	BB	SO	K/9	WHIP	AVG
2008	Royals (AZL)	R	2	1	1.69	12	9	0	0	43	31	2	12	34	7.2	1.01	.211
2009	Burlington (MWL)	LoA	2	3	2.17	12	12	0	0	58	42	1	24	52	8.1	1.14	.206
	Wilmington (CAR)	HiA	4	1	2.25	9	9	0	0	52	38	0	12	46	8.0	0.96	.196
2010	Wilmington (CAR)	HiA	2	0	1.09	4	4	0	0	25	14	0	4	33	12.0	0.73	.165
	Royals (AZL)	R	0	1	1.04	3	3	0	0	9	6	0	1	7	7.3	0.81	.207
	NW Arkansas (TL)	AA	5	4	3.47	13	13	0	0	60	56	4	26	48	7.2	1.37	.255
2011	Omaha (PCL)	AAA	5	11	5.32	28	27	0	0	151	157	15	69	129	7.7	1.50	.271
2012	Omaha (PCL)	AAA	3	6	5.69	17	17	1	0	92	110	12	43	67	6.6	1.67	.298
	NW Arkansas (TL)	AA	2	6	6.67	10	10	0	0	58	69	12	21	44	6.8	1.55	.299
Minor League Totals			25	33	4.15	108	104	1	0	546	523	46	212	460	7.6	1.35	.254

16 TYLER GOEDDEL, 3B

BA GRADE
50
HIGH

Born: Oct. 20, 1992. **B-T:** R-R. **Ht.:** 6-4. **Wt.:** 180. **Drafted:** HS—Mountain View, Calif., 2011 (1st round supplemental). **Signed by:** Brian Morrison.

The Rays had seven supplemental first-round picks in 2011, and all but one signed at or below Major League Baseball's slot recommendations. The exception was Goeddel, who went 41st overall and landed a $1.5 million bonus to pass up his UCLA commitment. The younger brother of Mets farmhand Erik Goeddel, Tyler made his pro debut in 2012 in low Class A—an almost unheard of assignment for a Tampa Bay high school draftee. He earned a spot in the Midwest League all-star game and held his own as one of the youngest players in the league. Goeddel has an athletic, projectable frame but needs to get stronger to produce at the plate. He generates good bat speed but tends to get a little long with his approach to the ball because of his lanky body. He could develop into a solid hitter with plus power once he matures physically and shortens his swing. Goeddel runs the bases with above-average speed and instincts, as evidenced by his 30 steals in 35 attempts last season. He also has a strong arm and good hands, with the Rays believing he could play any one of several positions should a need arise. He made 29 errors in 93 games at third base in 2012, but he profiles well there and has the tools to play the hot corner, so he'll stay there for now. Goedel will be one of the younger players in the Florida State League in 2013.

Year	Club (League)	Class	AVG	G	AB	R	H	2B	3B	HR	RBI	BB	SO	SB	CS	OBP	SLG
2012	Bowling Green (MWL)	LoA	.246	103	329	52	81	19	2	6	46	38	94	30	5	.335	.371
Minor League Totals			.246	103	329	52	81	19	2	6	46	38	94	30	5	.335	.371

17 BRANDON MARTIN, SS

BA GRADE
50
HIGH

Born: Aug. 24, 1993. **B-T:** R-R. **Ht.:** 5-11. **Wt.:** 185. **Drafted:** HS—Corona, Calif., 2011 (1st round supplemental). **Signed by:** Jake Wilson.

Another supplemental first-rounder from the Rays' 2011 draft class, Martin stood out for his defensive ability and earned an $860,000 bonus as the 38th overall pick. He lived up to his reputation with the leather in 2012, leading Appalachian League shortstops in putouts (78), assists (194), total chances (286) and double plays (37). Scouts rave about his intelligence and decision-making as well as his overall feel for the position. Martin has soft hands and a quick exchange with a strong, accurate arm. An average runner, he has a quick first step and impressive anticipation, traits that should allow him to remain at the position for the long haul. At the plate, Martin struggles to make consistent contact because he chases breaking balls outside the strike zone and struggles with pitch recognition. He hit just .194/.249/.358 against righthanders. He does have solid pop when he connects. Martin has the tools and talent to make adjustments at higher levels and hit enough to develop into a big league shortstop. He'll make the jump to low Class A in 2013.

Year	Club (League)	Class	AVG	G	AB	R	H	2B	3B	HR	RBI	BB	SO	SB	CS	OBP	SLG
2011	Rays (GCL)	R	.255	19	47	10	12	1	0	1	3	7	12	5	3	.386	.340
2012	Princeton (APP)	R	.209	63	254	46	53	11	4	10	32	21	73	8	1	.272	.402
Minor League Totals			.216	82	301	56	65	12	4	11	35	28	85	13	4	.292	.392

18 JAKE HAGER, SS

BA GRADE
50
HIGH

Born: March 4, 1993. **B-T:** R-R. **Ht.:** 6-1. **Wt.:** 170. **Drafted:** HS—Las Vegas, 2011 (1st round). **Signed by:** Jayson Durocher.

Few players in the Rays system are more focused than Hager. A mature player who has an impressive even-keel approach, he doesn't have standout tools but the sum is greater than the individual parts. Drafted 32nd overall in 2011 and signed for $963,000, Hager uses his hands well at the plate. He has excellent pitch recognition and does a good job of waiting on the ball and employing the entire field. He can drive the ball on occasion and could hit a dozen or more homers annually as his body continues to get stronger. With his average speed and keen baserunning instincts, he should reach double digits in steals as well. Hager isn't as gifted defensively as Brandon Martin, who was selected six picks after him, but he has soft hands and solid range and arm strength. He should be able to play shortstop at higher levels, though he'd probably shift to second base if he were on the same team as Martin. That won't happen in 2013, when Hager will be one of the younger players in the Florida State League.

Year	Club (League)	Class	AVG	G	AB	R	H	2B	3B	HR	RBI	BB	SO	SB	CS	OBP	SLG
2011	Princeton (APP)	R	.269	47	193	29	52	11	1	4	17	9	26	5	7	.305	.399
2012	Bowling Green (MWL)	LoA	.281	114	442	63	124	22	3	10	72	40	60	17	11	.345	.412
Minor League Totals			.277	161	635	92	176	33	4	14	89	49	86	22	18	.334	.408

19 ANDREW TOLES, OF

Born: May 24, 1992. **B-T:** L-R. **Ht.:** 5-10. **Wt.:** 185. **Drafted:** Chipola (Fla.) JC, 2012 (3rd round). **Signed by:** Milt Hill.

The Marlins drafted Toles in the fourth round in 2010 out of a Georgia high school, but he opted to attend Tennessee instead. He batted .270 with 21 stolen bases as a freshman in 2011, but after a new coaching staff came in he was dismissed from the program in the fall of 2011, even though talent like his was in short supply. He transferred to Chipola (Fla.) JC but was benched and suspended last spring. The Rays believe his talent will allow him to blossom as a pro after he signed for $394,200 as a third-round pick in June. The son of former NFL first-round pick Alvin Toles, Andrew was one of the fastest players available in the entire 2012 draft. He has plus-plus speed, runs the bases well and covers a lot of ground in center field. He also shows solid arm strength and makes accurate throws. Toles has offensive upside as well, with a quick bat and above-average raw power. His swing can get long at times, and he needs to improve his plate discipline and bunting ability so he can get on base and maximize the value of his speed. Team officials said he has impact tools and the ability to climb quickly through its system. They do not see his makeup as a long-term concern. He'll open his first full pro season in low Class A.

Year	Club (League)	Class	AVG	G	AB	R	H	2B	3B	HR	RBI	BB	SO	SB	CS	OBP	SLG
2012	Princeton (APP)	R	.281	51	199	31	56	13	3	7	33	12	36	14	5	.327	.482
Minor League Totals			.281	51	199	31	56	13	3	7	33	12	36	14	5	.327	.482

20 FELIPE RIVERO, LHP

Born: July 5, 1991. **B-T:** L-L. **Ht.:** 6-0. **Wt.:** 151. **Signed:** Venezuela, 2008. **Signed by:** Ronnie Blanco.

Rivero received significant attention for the first time in his career last year when he was selected to the Futures Game. He earned the spot with a strong start at Bowling Green, where he didn't allow an earned run while striking out 20 batters in his first 22 innings. Tampa Bay took note of his overall progress and added him to its 40-man roster in November. Rivero's fastball sat around 90 mph when he broke into pro ball in 2009, but it now resides at 92-93 and tops out at 95 with good run and decent sink. His quick arm also generates a three-quarters breaking ball that can be a swing-and-miss pitch at times. He's not afraid to throw his changeup, which can become an average offering, and he does a nice job of mixing his pitches. One scout said Rivero is reminiscent of Enny Romero with less command. Rivero has no problem throwing strikes but gets in trouble when he leaves his pitches up in the zone, which happens too regularly. A projected No. 3 or 4 starter who could become a reliever if organization needs dictate it, he'll advance to high Class A this year.

Year	Club (League)	Class	W	L	ERA	G	GS	CG	SV	IP	H	HR	BB	SO	K/9	WHIP	AVG
2009	Rays (VSL)	R	6	4	3.74	16	0	0	1	34	38	0	12	25	6.7	1.49	.286
2010	Rays (VSL)	R	3	3	2.09	14	9	0	2	52	46	1	10	44	7.7	1.08	.243
2011	Princeton (APP)	R	3	3	4.62	14	12	0	0	60	64	7	13	57	8.5	1.28	.264
2012	Bowling Green (MWL)	LoA	8	8	3.41	27	21	0	0	113	115	5	29	98	7.8	1.27	.266
Minor League Totals			20	18	3.47	71	42	0	3	259	263	13	64	224	7.8	1.26	.264

21 TODD GLAESMANN, OF

Born: Oct. 24, 1990. **B-T:** R-R. **Ht.:** 6-4. **Wt.:** 220. **Drafted:** HS—Midway, Texas, 2009 (3rd round). **Signed by:** Pat Murphy.

The light came on for Glaesmann in 2012, when he was named Rays minor league player of the year after leading the system with 21 home runs. Tampa Bay's top signee from the 2009 draft, when he went in the third round and landed $930,000, he entered the season having gone deep just 11 times in his first three pro seasons combined. Fully healthy for his first extended period as a pro, he learned to relax, improved his pitch recognition and started taking advantage of pitchers' mistakes. With his short stroke and willingness to use all fields, Glasemann should hit for average. More patience also would allow him to tap into his solid power potential on a more regular basis. He runs well for his size and has one of the strongest outfield arms in the system, a combination that led managers to rate him as the best defensive outfielder in the Midwest

League last year. He played mostly center field at Bowling Green, then saw most of his Charlotte action in right field. If Glaesmann can repeat the progress he made last year in Double-A this season, he'll be knocking on the door to the big leagues.

Year	Club (League)	Class	AVG	G	AB	R	H	2B	3B	HR	RBI	BB	SO	SB	CS	OBP	SLG
2009	Rays (GCL)	R	.278	5	18	1	5	1	0	0	2	0	3	1	0	.278	.333
2010	Princeton (APP)	R	.233	62	236	41	55	17	5	4	24	13	70	13	6	.297	.398
2011	Rays (GCL)	R	.216	11	37	7	8	1	0	0	0	5	10	6	1	.341	.243
	Bowling Green (MWL) LoA	.229	63	210	28	48	8	2	4	21	14	85	6	0	.286	.343
2012	Bowling Green (MWL) LoA	.281	91	352	57	99	17	5	13	53	22	89	8	3	.338	.469
	Charlotte (FSL)	HiA	.295	36	139	20	41	8	2	8	22	8	35	0	0	.333	.554
Minor League Totals			.258	268	992	154	256	52	14	29	122	62	292	34	10	.316	.426

22 RYAN BRETT, 2B

Born: Oct. 9, 1991. **B-T:** R-R. **Ht.:** 5-9. **Wt.:** 180. **Drafted:** HS—Burien, Wash., 2010 (3rd round). **Signed by:** Paul Kirsch.

BA GRADE
50
HIGH

Brett was putting together a solid all-around season at Bowling Green when he failed a drug test in late August, drawing a 50-game suspension that will carry over into the 2013 season. One of four Hot Rods to test positive for methamphetamine and an amphetamine in 2012, he said through his agent that the positive test was the result of taking an energy pill that contained Adderall. That was the first blemish on his pro career, as Brett has produced consistently at each of his three pro stops. Employing a blue-collar approach at the top of the lineup, he makes consistent contact, controls the strike zone and can drive the ball in the gaps with a compact swing. A switch-hitter in high school who has batted from the right side as a pro, he hits righties well but has struggled against southpaws, including a .188/.266/.217 performance last year. Brett has above-average speed and baserunning instincts to match, and he stole 48 bases in just 56 attempts last year. His quick first step and plus range help compensate for average arm strength and less-than-smooth hands at second base. When he's eligible to play in 2013, he'll make the climb to high Class A.

Year	Club (League)	Class	AVG	G	AB	R	H	2B	3B	HR	RBI	BB	SO	SB	CS	OBP	SLG
2010	Rays (GCL)	R	.303	27	89	8	27	5	2	0	9	8	17	12	3	.364	.404
2011	Princeton (APP)	R	.300	61	240	42	72	22	5	3	24	26	24	21	3	.370	.471
2012	Bowling Green (MWL) LoA	.285	100	410	77	117	20	3	6	35	37	73	48	8	.348	.393
Minor League Totals			.292	188	739	127	216	47	10	9	68	71	114	81	14	.357	.419

23 JOSE MUJICA, RHP

Born: June 29, 1996. **B-T:** R-R. **Ht.:** 6-2. **Wt.:** 180. **Signed:** Venezuela, 2012. **Signed by:** Ronnie Blanco.

BA GRADE
55
EXTREME

The Rays gave seven-figure bonuses to two Venezuelan pitchers last summer. Though Mujica ($1 million) signed for less than lefthander Jose Castillo ($1.55 million), Latin American scouts considered him the better prospect. A product of former all-star Carlos Guillen's academy in Venezuela, Mujica impressed scouts at a Major League Baseball showcase in the Dominican Republic in February and continued to show advanced skills prior to the July 2 signing date. Despite turning 16 just three days prior to signing, he has a fluid delivery and clean arm action. Mujica throws a heavy fastball with late life that has reached 93 mph. He does a good job of working both sides of the plate with his heater, and Tampa Bay believes he should sit in the mid-90s once his lean body gets stronger. He throws his changeup with excellent deception and consistent sink, giving it a chance to become a plus pitch. His breaking ball needs the most work, but the Rays believe it will develop because of his feel for pitching and work ethic. He'll probably make his pro debut in the Rookie-level Dominican Summer League and won't come to the United States until 2014.

Year	Club (League)	Class	W	L	ERA	G	GS	CG	SV	IP	H	HR	BB	SO	K/9	WHIP	AVG
Did Not Play—Signed 2013 Contract																	

24 JOSH SALE, OF

Born: July 5, 1991. **B-T:** L-R. **Ht.:** 6-0. **Wt.:** 215. **Drafted:** HS—Seattle, 2010 (1st round). **Signed by:** Paul Kirsch.

BA GRADE
50
HIGH

The 17th overall pick in the 2010 draft, Sale earned an above-slot $1.62 million bonus based on his bat, but he looked like a bust during his 2011 pro debut and appeared to panic at the plate at times. After the season he worked with his some of his amateur coaches in the Seattle area to rework his hitting mechanics while rededicating himself to the game. Tampa Bay had him spend a month in extended spring training before turning him loose at Bowling Green in May. Sale responded by hitting .370 with seven homers in his first 19 games. He couldn't keep that encouraging start going, however, as he batted just .232 with three homers in the next 55 games and then became one of four Hot Rods to test positive for methamphetamine and an amphetamine, resulting in a 50-game suspension. Though Sale slipped into bad habits, such as becoming too pull-conscious, the Rays said he looked more like the player they thought they were getting in 2010. He demonstrated a stronger mental approach and did a better job of using the entire field and incorporating his hands in his swing. Sale has a good feel for the strike zone, drawing more than his share of walks, though he also strikes out a lot because he works deep counts. His power stands out more than his hitting ability at this point. Sale has solid speed but needs to improve his feel for running the bases. He provides below-average defense and arm strength in left field, so his bat will have to carry him. Tampa Bay will get a better idea if it can after he serves out his suspension and moves to high Class A in 2013.

Year	Club (League)	Class	AVG	G	AB	R	H	2B	3B	HR	RBI	BB	SO	SB	CS	OBP	SLG
2011	Princeton (APP)	R	.210	60	214	24	45	11	3	4	15	23	41	4	3	.289	.346
2012	Bowling Green (MWL)	LoA	.264	74	239	35	63	10	4	10	44	51	62	7	6	.391	.464
Minor League Totals			.238	134	453	59	108	21	7	14	59	74	103	11	9	.345	.408

25 PARKER MARKEL, RHP

BA GRADE

50

HIGH

Born: Sept. 15, 1990. **B-T:** R-R. **Ht.:** 6-4. **Wt.:** 220. **Drafted:** Yavapai (Ariz.) JC, 2010 (39th round). **Signed by:** Jayson Durocher.

It was a tale of two seasons for Markel in 2012. He went 1-4, 6.17 in his first nine starts in low Class A, before his nasty changeup keyed a 10-1, 2.44 run in his final 15 outings. He continues to impress with his fastball, which ranges from 91-97 mph with sink and armside run. He maintains his arm speed on his deceptive changeup, which resides in the low 80s and has solid fade. He also throws a slider that's inconsistent but shows flashes of becoming a solid pitch. Maintaining his release point with his low three-quarters delivery has been Markel's biggest problem, and his short stride contributes to his inconsistency. He's an average athlete with a big frame, and the Rays moved him to the rotation in hopes of getting his mechanics ironed out with more innings. The scouting report on Markel as an amateur was that he had arm strength but lacked a clean arm action and profiled as a reliever, and he still may be better suited for the bullpen at the major league level unless he can improve his slider and command. Markel will remain in the rotation for now and head to high Class A.

Year	Club (League)	Class	W	L	ERA	G	GS	CG	SV	IP	H	HR	BB	SO	K/9	WHIP	AVG
2010	Rays (GCL)	R	2	0	1.74	7	0	0	0	10	8	0	3	13	11.3	1.06	.222
2011	Hudson Valley (NYP)	SS	3	4	3.14	13	13	0	0	57	42	3	23	44	6.9	1.13	.207
2012	Bowling Green (MWL)	LoA	11	5	3.53	24	24	0	0	120	117	6	34	96	7.2	1.26	.249
Minor League Totals			16	9	3.31	44	37	0	0	188	167	9	60	153	7.3	1.21	.236

26 PATRICK LEONARD, 3B

BA GRADE

50

HIGH

Born: Oct. 20, 1992. **B-T:** R-R. **Ht.:** 6-3. **Wt.:** 224. **Drafted:** HS—Houston, 2011 (5th round). **Signed by:** Brian Rhees (Royals).

The least known and least advanced of the four prospects acquired from the Royals in the James Shields/Wade Davis trade in December, Leonard signed for a well above-slot $600,000 as a fifth-round pick in 2011. In his final game as an amateur, his three-run homer led Houston's St. Thomas High to the Texas state 5-A private school state title. Some scouts questioned how well Leonard would handle stronger competition, viewing him as a raw hitter who would struggle with premium velocity. But since turning pro, he has cleaned up his swing and shown he can make enough contact to tap into his plus raw power. A shortstop in high school, Leonard also has made a smooth transition to third base. He led Appalachian League third basemen in fielding percentage (.929) and total chances (196) during his 2012 pro debut. He's a below-average runner with enough first-step quickness to remain at the hot corner. Leonard is ready to make the jump to low Class A.

Year	Club (League)	Class	AVG	G	AB	R	H	2B	3B	HR	RBI	BB	SO	SB	CS	OBP	SLG
2012	Burlington (APP)	R	.251	62	235	37	59	9	3	14	46	30	55	6	2	.340	.494
Minor League Totals			.251	62	235	37	59	9	3	14	46	30	55	6	2	.340	.494

27 BRALIN JACKSON, OF

BA GRADE

55

EXTREME

Born: Dec. 12, 1993. **B-T:** R-L. **Ht.:** 6-1. **Wt.:** 185. **Drafted:** HS—Raytown, Mo., 2012 (5th round). **Signed by:** J.D. Elliby.

The Rays love athletes, which led them to draft Jackson in the fifth round last June and sign him away from a Missouri commitment for $322,500. He stands out most with his bat speed, which Tampa Bay believes will generate above-average power as he develops and his body matures. He'll need to make more consistent contact and become more disciplined at the plate. Jackson has solid speed and arm strength, traits that give him a chance to stay in center field. To do so, he must improve his routes to balls in the gaps and do a better job going back on balls hit over his head. His baseball instincts aren't overwhelming, but his athleticism should allow him to overcome some of his mistakes. Raw in all phases of the game and not ready for full-season ball, Jackson will move up to one of the Rays' more advanced short-season stops, Princeton or Hudson Valley, in 2013. He may need a year at each level, but the wait could be worth it.

Year	Club (League)	Class	AVG	G	AB	R	H	2B	3B	HR	RBI	BB	SO	SB	CS	OBP	SLG
2012	Rays (GCL)	R	.253	39	146	16	37	5	4	0	11	6	39	5	3	.286	.342
Minor League Totals			.253	39	146	16	37	5	4	0	11	6	39	5	3	.286	.342

28 TY MORRISON, OF

BA GRADE

45

MEDIUM

Born: July 22, 1990. **B-T:** L-R. **Ht.:** 6-2. **Wt.:** 170. **Drafted:** HS—Tigard, Ore., 2008 (4th round). **Signed by:** Paul Kirsch.

Morrison has been one of the best all-around athletes in the system since signing as a fourth-round pick in 2008. His overall development has been slow, but Rays officials say he's making steady progress and can develop into a major league regular. He has demonstrated his above-average speed by ranking among the leaders in stolen bases and triples in multiple leagues while doing a good job in center field. Morrison's biggest flaw is his high strikeout totals for a speed-oriented player. He has closed up some of the holes in his swing but still needs to make more consistent contact. He has added strength to his tall, broad-shouldered frame, but power never will be a big part of his game. An above-average defender who takes good routes to the ball, he makes accurate throws but has below-average arm strength. After a solid showing following a promotion to Double-A last season, he should make the jump to Triple-A in 2013.

Year	Club (League)	Class	AVG	G	AB	R	H	2B	3B	HR	RBI	BB	SO	SB	CS	OBP	SLG
2008	Princeton (APP)	R	.265	10	34	2	9	0	0	0	1	2	12	3	1	.297	.265
2009	Princeton (APP)	R	.271	59	225	34	61	9	2	3	18	27	61	20	5	.365	.369
2010	Bowling Green (MWL)	LoA	.250	131	452	65	113	21	13	6	56	43	133	58	10	.324	.394
2011	Charlotte (FSL)	HiA	.264	67	265	36	70	8	2	0	18	11	67	19	7	.306	.309
2012	Charlotte (FSL)	HiA	.281	32	135	15	38	8	2	0	14	9	29	11	2	.340	.370
	Montgomery (SL)	AA	.269	102	405	56	109	17	8	3	35	35	88	20	8	.341	.373
Minor League Totals			.264	401	1516	208	400	63	27	12	142	127	390	131	33	.333	.365

29 SPENCER EDWARDS, SS

BA GRADE

50

HIGH

Born: April 7, 1993. **B-T:** R-R. **Ht.:** 6-0. **Wt.:** 170. **Drafted:** HS—Rockwall, Texas, 2012 (2nd round). **Signed by:** Pat Murphy.

A second-team BA High School All-American after batting .440 with 17 steals in 2012, Edwards went in the second round of the draft and gave up a commitment to Texas to sign for $554,400. He struggled in his pro debut, striking out 42 times and committing 12 errors in 33 games in the Rookie-level Gulf Coast League, but he still showed the tools and all-around ability that got him picked 88th overall. Edwards has a live body and well above-average speed that he employs to his advantage on defense and on the basepaths. He has a quick bat as well, and he should be able to drive the ball in the gaps as he gains strength. Some scouts were concerned about a hitch in his swing in high school, but Tampa Bay worked with him to smooth out his stroke. While he has plus arm strength and good range at shortstop, he doesn't have soft hands and many evaluators project Edwards as a center fielder. The Rays plan on keeping him at shortstop for the immediate future, however, and they'll see how he develops over the course of the 2013 campaign, which he'll most likely spend in Princeton.

Year	Club (League)	Class	AVG	G	AB	R	H	2B	3B	HR	RBI	BB	SO	SB	CS	OBP	SLG
2012	Rays (GCL)	R	.188	33	128	14	24	5	2	1	7	9	42	8	4	.250	.281
Minor League Totals			.188	33	128	14	24	5	2	1	7	9	42	8	4	.250	.281

30 NICK SAWYER, RHP

BA GRADE

50

EXTREME

Born: Sept. 23, 1991. **B-T:** R-R. **Ht.:** 5-11. **Wt.:** 175. **Drafted:** Howard (Texas) JC, 2012 (40th round). **Signed by:** Pat Murphy.

The Rays' final pick in June appeared headed to Oregon before signing for $50,000. He wound up having a spectacular pro debut, recording a 0.28 ERA and 59 strikeouts in 32 innings, holding opponents to a .097 average and reaching low Class A. Sawyer got overlooked because he didn't pitch much on a talented Howard (Texas) JC staff and combines a small frame with a maximum-effort delivery. But he has a pair of plus pitches in his 94-96 mph fastball and a power 81-83 mph curveball with short, sharp break. He creates a lot of deception with his short arm action, and his pitches appear to jump on hitters. He'll likely open his first full pro season back in Bowling Green but may not stay there for long.

Year	Club (League)	Class	W	L	ERA	G	GS	CG	SV	IP	H	HR	BB	SO	K/9	WHIP	AVG
2012	Rays (GCL)	R	1	0	0.00	3	0	0	0	5	3	0	2	6	11.6	1.07	.231
	Princeton (APP)	R	2	1	0.37	15	0	0	5	24	6	0	10	50	18.5	0.66	.074
	Bowling Green (MWL)	LoA	1	0	0.00	2	0	0	0	3	1	0	2	3	9.0	1.00	.111
Minor League Totals			4	1	0.28	20	0	0	5	32	10	0	14	59	16.6	0.75	.097

Texas Rangers

BY MATT EDDY

Rookie Yu Darvish ranked second in the majors with 10.4 strikeouts per nine innings

With nine games to go in the regular season, the Rangers had the best record in the American League and looked poised to make a run to their third straight American League pennant. But when Texas lost seven of its final nine contests, including five to the hard-charging Athletics, it ceded the AL West crown to Oakland.

The A's defeated the Rangers 12-5 in the final game of the season, relegating Texas to the AL Wild Card Game, which it lost at home to the Orioles by a score of 5-1.

Much like his team, Josh Hamilton faded down  the stretch. He seemed destined for his second AL MVP award in three seasons when he batted .368/.420/.764 with 21 homers in the first two months, but he did little in June or July and didn't homer in his final 52 at-bats of the season.

Rangers fans booed Hamilton lustily after he struck out twice and grounded out weakly, seeing just eight pitches, in the wild-card game defeat. No doubt they remembered that he dropped a routine flyball in center field the day before to key an A's rally.

The boos were a sign of how much expectations for him—and the team—have changed during the last three seasons.

Hamilton will test free-agent waters this offseason, coming off a career-high 43 homers, with a cloud of uncertainty hovering over his potential return. If he departs Texas—as premier free agents Cliff Lee and C.J. Wilson did following the 2010 and 2011 seasons—then the Rangers have the talent to replenish from within.

The roster retooling actually began in 2012, when the Rangers spent $111.7 million ($51.7 million posting fee, $60 million contract) to import Yu Darvish from Japan. The 26-year-old went 16-9, 3.90 in 29 starts and struck out 10.4 batters per nine innings, the second-best rate in the majors. Darvish stayed strong in the Texas heat, going 5-1, 2.35 in his final eight starts with 67 strikeouts in 57 innings.

Elsewhere, rookie relievers Robbie Ross and Tanner Scheppers carved out significant bullpen roles, while second-year lefty Michael Kirkman held opponents to a .182 average.

Texas also gave a preview of coming attractions by promoting shortstop Jurickson Profar and third baseman Mike Olt from Double-A before the end of the season. Two of the game's top prospects, neither played much but could carve out regular big league roles in 2013 despite being blocked by all-stars Elvis Andrus and Adrian Beltre at their best positions.

For the third year in a row, the Rangers sacrificed minor league talent during the season to strengthen the big league team. The most significant losses came when they surrendered third baseman Christian Villanueva and righthander Kyle Hendricks to acquire Ryan Dempster from the Cubs at the July deadline.

In recent years, trades for Mike Adams, Cliff Lee and Koji Uehara cost the Rangers young players like Blake Beavan, Chris Davis, Robbie Erlin, Tommy Hunter, Justin Smoak and Joe Wieland. That the system continues to thrive even after the defections testifies to the job Texas does scouting at all levels, domestic, international and professional.

The Rangers continue to be as active in Latin America as any club. One year after committing $13.4 million in bonuses to sign Cuban outfielder Leonys Martin and Dominican outfielders Ronald Guzman and Nomar Mazara, Texas agreed to terms in February with Dominican outfielder Jairo Beras for $4.5 million.

MLB later suspended Beras for one year—though his contract was approved, and he can be reinstated July 1—when it learned that the outfielder originally had understated his age.

THIS YEAR'S TOP 30

Player, Pos.	Grade
1. Jurickson Profar, ss/2b	75/Low
2. Mike Olt, 3b/1b	65/Medium
3. Martin Perez, lhp	55/Medium
4. Leonys Martin, of	50/Medium
5. Justin Grimm, rhp	50/Medium
6. Luke Jackson, rhp	55/High
7. Luis Sardinas, ss/2b	60/Extreme
8. Cody Buckel, rhp	50/Medium
9. Jorge Alfaro, c/1b	60/Extreme
10. Joey Gallo, 3b	60/Extreme
11. Rougned Odor, 2b/ss	50/Medium
12. Lewis Brinson, of	55/Extreme
13. Roman Mendez, rhp	50/High
14. C.J. Edwards, rhp	50/High
15. Hanser Alberto, ss/3b	50/High
16. Nomar Mazara, of	55/Extreme
17. Ronald Guzman, 1b	55/Extreme
18. Jairo Beras, of	55/Extreme
19. Nick Tepesch, rhp	50/High
20. Leury Garcia, 2b/ss	50/High
21. Drew Robinson, 3b/2b	50/High
22. Wilmer Font, rhp	50/High
23. Neil Ramirez, rhp	45/Medium
24. Zach Cone, of	50/High
25. Nick Williams, of	55/Extreme
26. Keone Kela, rhp	50/High
27. Nick Martinez, rhp	50/High
28. Matt West, rhp	50/Extreme
29. Randy Henry, rhp	45/High
30. Joe Ortiz, lhp	40/Low

LAST YEAR'S TOP 30

Player, Pos.	Status
1. Jurickson Profar, ss	No. 1
2. Martin Perez, lhp	No. 3
3. Mike Olt, 3b	No. 2
4. Leonys Martin, of	No. 4
5. Neil Ramirez, rhp	No. 23
6. Cody Buckel, rhp	No. 8
7. Jorge Alfaro, c	No. 9
8. Christian Villanueva, 3b	(Cubs)
9. Rougned Odor, 2b	No. 11
10. Matt West, rhp	No. 28
11. Leury Garcia, ss	No. 20
12. Jordan Akins, of	Dropped out
13. Ronald Guzman, 1b/of	No. 17
14. Robbie Ross, lhp	Majors
15. Justin Grimm, rhp	No. 5
16. Tanner Scheppers, rhp	Majors
17. Luis Sardinas, ss	No. 7
18. Luke Jackson, rhp	No. 6
19. Roman Mendez, rhp	No. 13
20. Barret Loux, rhp	(Cubs)
21. Will Lamb, lhp	Dropped out
22. Kevin Matthews, lhp	Dropped out
23. Kellin Deglan, c	Dropped out
24. Jake Skole, of	Dropped out
25. Tomas Telis, c	Dropped out
26. David Perez, rhp	Dropped out
27. Odubel Herrera, 2b	Dropped out
28. Michael Kirkman, lhp	Majors
29. Miguel de los Santos, lhp	(Brewers)
30. Nomar Mazara, of	No. 16

BEST TOOLS

Best Hitter for Average	Jurickson Profar
Best Power Hitter	Joey Gallo
Best Strike-Zone Discipline	Jurickson Profar
Fastest Baserunner	Leury Garcia
Best Athlete	Lewis Brinson
Best Fastball	Wilmer Font
Best Curveball	Justin Grimm
Best Slider	Nick Tepesch
Best Changeup	Martin Perez
Best Control	Nick Tepesch
Best Defensive Catcher	Jorge Alfaro
Best Defensive Infielder	Luis Sardinas
Best Infield Arm	Leury Garcia
Best Defensive Outfielder	Engel Beltre
Best Outfield Arm	Preston Beck

PROJECTED 2016 LINEUP

Catcher	Jorge Alfaro
First Base	Mike Olt
Second Base	Jurickson Profar
Third Base	Adrian Beltre
Shortstop	Elvis Andrus
Left Field	Ian Kinsler
Center Field	Lewis Brinson
Right Field	Leonys Martin
Designated Hitter	Joey Gallo
No. 1 Starter	Yu Darvish
No. 2 Starter	Matt Harrison
No. 3 Starter	Derek Holland
No. 4 Starter	Martin Perez
No. 5 Starter	Justin Grimm
Closer	Neftali Feliz

TOP PROSPECTS OF THE DECADE

Year	Player, Pos.	2012 Org.
2003	Mark Teixeira, 3b	Yankees
2004	Adrian Gonzalez, 1b	Dodgers
2005	Thomas Diamond, rhp	Out of baseball
2006	Edinson Volquez, rhp	Padres
2007	John Danks, lhp	White Sox
2008	Elvis Andrus, ss	Rangers
2009	Neftali Feliz, rhp	Rangers
2010	Neftali Feliz, rhp	Rangers
2011	Martin Perez, lhp	Rangers
2012	Jurickson Profar, ss	Rangers

TOP DRAFT PICKS OF THE DECADE

Year	Player, Pos.	2012 Org.
2003	John Danks, lhp	White Sox
2004	Thomas Diamond, rhp	Twins
2005	John Mayberry Jr., of	Phillies
2006	Kasey Kiker, lhp	Rockford (Frontier)
2007	Blake Beavan, rhp	Mariners
2008	Justin Smoak, 1b	Mariners
2009	*Matt Purke, lhp	Nationals
2010	Jake Skole, of	Rangers
2011	Kevin Matthews, lhp	Rangers
2012	Lewis Brinson, of	Rangers

*Did not sign.

LARGEST BONUSES IN CLUB HISTORY

Leonys Martin, 2011	$5,000,000
Nomar Mazara, 2011	$4,950,000
Mark Teixeira, 2001	$4,500,000
Jairo Beras, 2012	$4,500,000
Justin Smoak, 2008	$3,500,000

TEXAS RANGERS

TOP 2013 ROOKIE: Jurickson Profar, ss. Baseball's top position-player prospect has tools and skills that ought to translate to rapid big league success.

BREAKOUT PROSPECT: C.J. Edwards, rhp. He pairs incredible velocity and cutting action on his fastball with solid secondary stuff.

SLEEPER: Victor Payano, lhp. He ran out of gas in the second half of 2012, but he tops out at 94 mph, throws a downer curveball and shows feel for a changeup.

SOURCE OF TOP 30 TALENT			
Homegrown	28	Acquired	2
College	5	Trades	2
Junior college	1	Rule 5 draft	0
High school	9	Independent leagues	0
Nondrafted free agent	0	Free agents/waivers	0
International	13		

LF
Nick Williams (25)
Jared Hoying
Ryan Strausborger
Alejandro Selen

CF
Leonys Martin (4)
Lewis Brinson (12)
Engel Beltre
Chris Grayson
Jordan Akins
Jake Skole
Jamie Jarmon
Chris Garia

RF
Nomar Mazara (16)
Jairo Beras (18)
Zach Cone (24)
Joey Butler
Preston Beck
Eduard Pinto

3B
Mike Olt (2)
Joey Gallo (10)
Drew Robinson (21)

SS
Jurickson Profar (1)
Luis Sardinas (7)
Hanser Alberto (15)
Leury Garcia (20)
Luis Marte
Greg Miclat

2B
Rougned Odor (11)
Odubel Herrera
Yangervis Solarte
Alberto Triunfel
Janluis Castro

1B
Ronald Guzman (17)
Brandon Snyder
Mike Bianucci

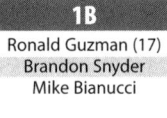

C
Jorge Alfaro (9)
Luis Martinez
Tomas Telis
Kellin Deglan
Konrad Schmidt
Zach Zaneski
Pat Cantwell

LHP

LHSP	LHRP
Martin Perez (3)	Joe Ortiz (30)
Victor Payano	Tommy Hottovy
Andrew Faulkner	Jimmy Reyes
Will Lamb	
Kevin Matthews	
Chad Bell	
Yohander Mendez	
Sam Stafford	

RHP

RHSP	RHRP
Justin Grimm (5)	Roman Mendez (13)
Luke Jackson (6)	Wilmer Font (22)
Cody Buckel (8)	Keone Kela (26)
C.J. Edwards (14)	Matt West (28)
Nick Tepesch (19)	Randy Henry (29)
Neil Ramirez (23)	Coty Woods
Nick Martinez (27)	Lisalverto Bonilla
Collin Wiles	Justin Miller
Jake Brigham	Cory Burns
Alec Asher	Carlos Pimentel
Eric Brooks	Jose Valdespina
David Perez	Connor Sadzeck
Kyle Castro	Tyler Tufts
Jerad Eickoff	Johan Yan
Tyler Smith	Phil Klein
	Ryan Bores
	Jose Mavare
	Jose Leclerc

2012
BONUSES: $7.4 MILLION

BEST PURE HITTER: OF Nick Williams (2) baffled scouts with an inconsistent spring, then hit .313 in his pro debut. He has excellent bat speed, a knack for barreling balls and good hitting instincts.

BEST POWER HITTER: 3B Joey Gallo (1s) had the best raw power in the entire draft and can make a claim to having the most in the minor leagues. He hit 22 homers and slugged .660 in his pro debut. OF Lewis Brinson (1) won the home run derby at the 2011 Under Armour All-America Game.

FASTEST RUNNER: Brinson is a well above-average runner with long, gliding strides. He runs the 60-yard dash in 6.5 seconds.

BEST DEFENSIVE PLAYER: Stony Brook made a shocking run to the College World Series, thanks in part to C/1B Pat Cantwell (3), whose blue-collar work ethic prompts Pat Borders comparisons. Cantwell has good hands and feet to go with solid arm strength, and his toughness and intelligence help his tools play up behind the dish. Brinson covers a lot of ground in center field.

BEST FASTBALL: RHP Keone Kela (12) threw 89-91 mph when the Mariners drafted him in the 29th round out of high school in 2011, worked at 91-95 mph last spring at Everett (Wash.) CC and was up to 96-100 mph during instructional league. He has good athleticism and cleaned up his delivery after signing, which also improved his control. RHP Alec Asher (4) consistently hits the mid-90s.

BEST SECONDARY PITCH: RHP Collin Wiles (1s) has good feel for his 72-74 mph curveball. The pitch shows tight rotation and should continue to firm up as he gets stronger.

BEST PRO DEBUT: Gallo broke the Rookie-level Arizona League home run record with 18 in just 43 games on his way to winning the league MVP award. His 22 homers ranked fourth among Rangers minor leaguers in just a half season.

BEST ATHLETE: Brinson draws Cameron Maybin comparisons and shows five-tool ability. OF Jamie Jarmon (2) and Williams also have a wide array of tools.

MOST INTRIGUING BACKGROUND: Unsigned OF Jameis Winston (15) was one of college football's top quarterback recruits and one of the baseball draft's best pure athletes. He headed to Florida State. OF Royce Bolinger's (6) uncle Russ played nine seasons in the NFL as an offensive lineman.

CLOSEST TO THE MAJORS: There's no obvious candidate because Texas signed so many toolsy but raw players. OF Preston Beck (5) is the only college draftee who received a six-figure bonus.

BEST LATE-ROUND PICK: Kela. The Rangers will see if he can transition to a starter in 2013.

THE ONE WHO GOT AWAY: Texas took several high-profile high school players later in the draft but ran out of money to sign them. In addition to Winston, LHP Alex Young (32, Texas Christian) and RHP Ryan Burr (33, Arizona State) had early-round talent.

ASSESSMENT: The Rangers loaded up on high school position players with big tools—Brinson, Gallo, Jarmon and Williams. That group cost a combined $5 million and combines upside with risk.

2011
BONUSES: $4.2 MILLION

The Rangers like their top two picks, LHP Kevin Matthews (1) and OF Zach Cone (1s), but their best prospect is hard-throwing RHP C.J. Edwards (48), who came 47 rounds later. RHP Kyle Hendricks (8) was used in the Ryan Dempster trade with the Cubs.
GRADE: C

2010
BONUSES: $8.5 MILLION

3B Mike Olt (1s) is a future all-star who just needs an opportunity. He and RHP Justin Grimm (5) already have reached the majors, and RHPs Luke Jackson (1s) and Cody Buckel (2) have the talent to join them. That group makes up for the slow starts by OF Jake Skole (1) and C Kellin Deglan (1).
GRADE: B+

2009
BONUSES: $4.7 MILLION

MLB killed a $6 million deal for LHP Matt Purke (1), who has had problems staying healthy since. Both he and unsigned RHP Eddie Butler (35) landed seven-figure deals in later drafts. The best pros who did sign with Texas are big league RHP Tanner Scheppers (1s) and LHP Robbie Erlin (3), part of the Mike Adams deal with the Padres in mid-2010.
GRADE: C

2008
BONUSES: $7.4 MILLION

1B Justin Smoak (1) hasn't lived up to his billing as the No. 11 pick, but he was the key piece in the 2010 trade for Cliff Lee that sparked the franchise's first World Series appearance. RHP Joe Wieland (4) got to the majors after going to San Diego in the Adams deal. LHP Robbie Ross (2) and since-waived RHP Cody Eppley (43) are big league relievers, as is unsigned RHP Stephen Pryor (42).
GRADE: B

Draft analysis by Conor Glassey (2012) and Jim Callis (2008-11). Numbers in parentheses indicate draft rounds.

1 JURICKSON PROFAR, SS/2B

Born: Feb. 20, 1993. **B-T:** B-R. **Ht.:** 6-0. **Wt.:** 165.
Signed: Curacao, 2009. **Signed by:** Mike Daly/Chu Halabi/Jose Felomina.

BA GRADE
75
LOW

BILL MITCHELL

Profar served as the bellwether for the Rangers' renewed emphasis and success in Latin America. As an amateur in Curacao, he garnered attention more as a pitcher with low-90s heat and feel for a breaking ball, but Texas acquiesced to his desire to play shortstop after signing him for $1.55 million in 2009. Neither party has any regrets. No prospect this side of Mike Trout has a better minor league résumé than Profar. He ranked as the top prospect in the short-season Northwest League in his 2010 pro debut, then for an encore won MVP honors in the low Class A South Atlantic League in 2011. He earned a promotion to Double-A Frisco for 2012, skipping over high Class A entirely, and ranked as not only the Texas League's youngest player (19) but also its No. 1 prospect. Profar's body of work in the Futures Game includes a triple against the Twins' Kyle Gibson in 2011 and a solo homer off the Royals' Jake Odorizzi in 2012.

To paraphrase one Rangers instructor, Profar may not have the most power, the most speed or the strongest arm on the field, but typically he's the best player out there. A natural righthanded hitter, he learned to switch-hit after signing and now shows uncommon bat speed from both sides of the plate, lending him more power than his lean 6-foot frame suggests. Profar surprises some opponents with his pop—which is above-average for a middle infielder—but he may have to tone down his swing to maximize his overall production. He takes a disciplined approach to hitting, with strong knowledge of the strike zone that ought to make him a consistent .300 hitter in his prime. An above-average defender at shortstop, Profar has instincts that outstrip his plus range. His hands and arm are above-average as well. Some of his throws to first base tend to sail when he gets on the side of the ball, but that's just a matter of adjustment. He has solid speed and knows how to use it on the bases, stealing 16 bases in 20 tries in 2012. Observers rave about Profar's mental toughness, leadership skills and grace under pressure.

When he signed, Profar told the Rangers he would reach the big leagues by the time he was 20. He actually completed his journey five months ahead of schedule last September. He played sporadically down the stretch but made the Rangers' playoff roster for their Wild Card Game against the Orioles. Even if he begins the 2013 season in Triple-A, Profar's talent probably will win out and result in a promotion to Texas during the season. He likely will move to second base in deference to Elvis Andrus, pushing Ian Kinsler to the outfield. Few prospects represent a safer bet to develop into a first-division regular and all-star than Profar.

SCOUTING GRADES

Batting: 70.   **Defense:** 65.
Power: 60.   **Arm:** 60.
Speed: 55.

Based on 20-80 scouting scale, where 50 represents major league average, and future projection rather than present tools.

Year	Club (League)	Class	AVG	G	AB	R	H	2B	3B	HR	RBI	BB	SO	SB	CS	OBP	SLG
2010	Spokane (NWL)	SS	.250	63	252	42	63	19	0	4	23	28	46	8	3	.323	.373
2011	Hickory (SAL)	LoA	.286	115	430	86	123	37	8	12	65	65	63	23	9	.390	.493
2012	Frisco (TL)	AA	.281	126	480	76	135	26	7	14	62	66	79	16	4	.368	.452
	Texas (AL)	MAJ	.176	9	17	2	3	2	0	1	2	0	4	0	0	.176	.471
Major League Totals			.176	9	17	2	3	2	0	1	2	0	4	0	0	.176	.471
Minor League Totals			.276	304	1162	204	321	82	15	30	150	159	188	47	16	.367	.450

2 MIKE OLT, 3B/1B

Born: Aug. 27, 1988. **B-T:** R-R. **Ht.:** 6-2. **Wt.:** 210. **Drafted:** Connecticut, 2010 (1st round supplemental). **Signed by:** Jay Heafner.

The 49th overall pick in the 2010 draft, Olt raced to Texas in little more than two years despite missing half of the 2011 season after breaking his collarbone in a home-plate collision. He led the Double-A Texas League with 28 homers and a .579 slugging percentage in 2012 before being called up in August. Plantar fasciitis in his left foot kept him out of the lineup for most of September. With plus raw power and a strong hitting approach, Olt is a threat to go deep anytime he steps to the plate. He works deep counts and piles up both walks and strikeouts, so his average will settle in the .260-.270 range. Pitchers have had success exploiting the length in his swing by attacking him with high fastballs, and he continues to work to identify and stay back on breaking balls. Scouts say Olt is a joy to watch defensively, owing to his agility and ability to make throws from any angle. He's a well below-average runner. Like Profar, Olt has advanced rapidly thanks to his tools, work ethic and mental toughness. He's blocked in Texas by Adrian Beltre, so a shift to first base or an outfield corner could be in the works. A potential all-star, he could open 2013 in the big league lineup or get a couple of months in Triple-A.

BA GRADE
65
MEDIUM

Year	Club (League)	Class	AVG	G	AB	R	H	2B	3B	HR	RBI	BB	SO	SB	CS	OBP	SLG
2010	Spokane (NWL)	SS	.293	69	263	57	77	16	1	9	43	40	77	6	0	.390	.464
2011	Rangers (AZL)	R	.214	4	14	2	3	0	0	1	4	1	5	0	0	.267	.429
	Myrtle Beach (CAR)	HiA	.267	69	240	39	64	15	0	14	42	48	70	0	1	.387	.504
2012	Frisco (TL)	AA	.288	95	354	65	102	17	1	28	82	61	101	4	0	.398	.579
	Texas (AL)	MAJ	.152	16	33	2	5	1	0	0	5	5	13	1	1	.250	.182
Major League Totals			.152	16	33	2	5	1	0	0	5	5	13	1	1	.250	.182
Minor League Totals			.282	237	871	163	246	48	2	52	171	150	253	10	1	.391	.521

3 MARTIN PEREZ, LHP

Born: April 4, 1991. **B-T:** L-L. **Ht.:** 6-0. **Wt.:** 180. **Signed:** Venezuela, 2007. **Signed by:** Rafic Saab/Manny Batista/Don Welke.

Signed for $580,000, Perez sped to Double-A as an 18-year-old. His progress stalled in Triple-A the last two seasons, when he posted a 4.86 ERA over 176 innings with pedestrian strikeout (5.4) and walk (3.9) rates per nine innings. Called to Texas in late June as an injury fill-in, he struggled to locate his pitches and got hit hard. Despite Perez's lackluster results, scouts continue to give him positive evaluations for his above-average stuff, compact and repeatable delivery, clean arm action and youth. His fastball sits at 91-92 mph and tops out near 95, and his low-80s changeup gives him a second plus pitch at times. His curveball ranges from the low to high 70s and often features depth. Perez gets hit when he falls behind, so the Rangers introduced a two-seam fastball and slider to his repertoire. That gave him two weapons with horizontal action and a chance to induce groundouts early in counts. While expectations for Perez have downshifted from future ace to solid mid-rotation starter, he's a reasonable bet to get there. He seemed to respond to a consultation with Rangers special assistant Greg Maddux during the season, where the two reviewed pitch sequencing and game planning. Perez could be ready for an expanded role in Texas in 2013.

BA GRADE
55
MEDIUM

Year	Club (League)	Class	W	L	ERA	G	GS	CG	SV	IP	H	HR	BB	SO	K/9	WHIP	AVG
2008	Spokane (NWL)	SS	1	2	3.65	15	15	0	0	62	66	3	28	53	7.7	1.52	.274
2009	Hickory (SAL)	LoA	5	5	2.31	22	14	0	1	94	82	3	33	105	10.1	1.23	.236
	Frisco (TL)	AA	1	3	5.57	5	5	0	0	21	29	2	5	14	6.0	1.62	.326
2010	Frisco (TL)	AA	5	8	5.96	24	23	0	0	100	117	12	50	101	9.1	1.68	.290
2011	Frisco (TL)	AA	4	2	3.16	17	16	1	0	88	80	6	36	83	8.5	1.31	.245
	Round Rock (PCL)	AAA	4	4	6.43	10	10	0	0	49	72	4	20	37	6.8	1.88	.343
2012	Round Rock (PCL)	AAA	7	6	4.25	22	21	2	0	127	122	10	56	69	4.9	1.40	.258
	Texas (AL)	MAJ	1	4	5.45	12	6	0	0	38	47	3	15	25	5.9	1.63	.297
Major League Totals			1	4	5.45	12	6	0	0	38	47	3	15	25	5.9	1.63	.297
Minor League Totals			27	30	4.23	115	104	3	1	540	568	40	228	462	7.7	1.47	.272

4 LEONYS MARTIN, OF

Born: March 6, 1988. **B-T:** L-R. **Ht.:** 6-2. **Wt.:** 190. **Signed:** Cuba, 2011. **Signed by:** Chu Halabi/Jose Fernandez/Don Welke.

BA GRADE

50
MEDIUM

A backup to Yoenis Cespedes on Cuba's 2009 World Baseball Classic squad, Martin defected the following year and signed a five-year, $15.6 million major league deal in May 2011. Among Triple-A Pacific Coast League players with at least 250 plate appearances, he ranked second in hitting (.359) and third in on-base percentage (.422) and slugging (.610) in 2012. He missed five weeks after tearing a ligament in his left thumb in May. The Rangers say Martin has more power than he gets credit for, and he hits home runs with ease during batting practice. They would like him to tone down his swing and focus more on lining balls to the gaps, however, in order to take advantage of his plus speed. That attribute also boosts his average via bunts and infield hits as well as providing him with solid range in center field. Martin knows the strike zone and has the bat path to hit for average, so he profiles as a top-of-the-order threat capable of providing 20 steals and strong defense. He also has an above-average arm. Despite hitting .324/.390/.502 in the high minors, Martin has struggled during brief stints with the Rangers. His injury and inactivity in the big leagues cut into his development time in 2012, but at worst he figures to be a platoon option for Texas in 2013.

Year	Club (League)	Class	AVG	G	AB	R	H	2B	3B	HR	RBI	BB	SO	SB	CS	OBP	SLG
2011	Rangers (AZL)	R	.267	4	15	2	4	0	2	0	1	1	6	0	1	.313	.533
	Frisco (TL)	AA	.348	29	112	24	39	9	2	4	24	15	8	10	8	.435	.571
	Round Rock (PCL)	AAA	.263	40	175	27	46	7	1	0	17	11	24	9	2	.316	.314
	Texas (AL)	MAJ	.375	8	8	2	3	1	0	0	0	0	1	0	0	.375	.500
2012	Round Rock (PCL)	AAA	.359	55	231	48	83	18	2	12	42	24	39	10	9	.422	.610
	Texas (AL)	MAJ	.174	24	46	6	8	5	2	0	6	4	12	3	0	.235	.370
Major League Totals			.204	32	54	8	11	6	2	0	6	4	13	3	0	.254	.389
Minor League Totals			.323	128	533	101	172	34	7	16	84	51	77	29	20	.388	.503

5 JUSTIN GRIMM, RHP

Born: Aug. 16, 1988. **B-T:** R-R. **Ht.:** 6-3. **Wt.:** 195. **Drafted:** Georgia, 2010 (5th round). **Signed by:** Ryan Coe.

BA GRADE

50
MEDIUM

Grimm adapted quickly to the routine of pro ball following a wildly erratic college career at Georgia, where he ran up a 5.80 ERA in three seasons. He beat the Astros in his June 16 debut, little more than a year and a half after making his pro debut in low Class A. Grimm decimated Double-A competition with a strong three-pitch mix and plus control. He found the going tougher in Triple-A and the big leagues when batters tended not to chase his 12-to-6 curveball. He pitches at 91-94 mph while commanding his fastball to both sides of the plate. That helps him work ahead of batters and set up his curve, changeup and slider/cutter hybrid. His changeup has come the farthest since turning pro, helping him hold minor league lefties to a .231 average while sporting a 4-1 K-BB ratio against them in 2012. Adding the slider gives Grimm the ability to change the speed and shape on his breaking ball, while also helping him stay in the zone more frequently. Texas bypassed Martin Perez, who already was on the 40-man roster, when it called on Grimm in June. Both could earn larger roles with the Rangers in 2013, whether starting or relieving. Most scouts see Grimm as a potential mid-rotation starter.

Year	Club (League)	Class	W	L	ERA	G	GS	CG	SV	IP	H	HR	BB	SO	K/9	WHIP	AVG
2011	Hickory (SAL)	LoA	2	1	3.40	9	9	0	0	50	45	5	18	54	9.7	1.25	.247
	Myrtle Beach (CAR)	HiA	5	2	3.39	16	16	0	0	90	84	2	30	73	7.3	1.26	.247
2012	Round Rock (PCL)	AAA	2	3	4.59	9	8	0	0	51	53	2	16	30	5.3	1.35	.273
	Frisco (TL)	AA	9	3	1.72	16	14	0	0	84	70	3	14	73	7.9	1.00	.227
	Texas (AL)	MAJ	1	1	9.00	5	2	0	0	14	22	1	3	13	8.4	1.79	.367
Major League Totals			1	1	9.00	5	2	0	0	14	22	1	3	13	8.4	1.79	.367
Minor League Totals			18	9	3.11	50	47	0	0	275	252	12	78	230	7.5	1.20	.246

6 LUKE JACKSON, RHP

Born: Aug. 24, 1991. **B-T:** R-R. **Ht.:** 6-2. **Wt.:** 185. **Drafted:** HS—Fort Lauderdale, 2010 (1st round supplemental). **Signed by:** Juan Alvarez.

Jackson offered perhaps the best combination of present velocity and future projection among Florida high school arms in the 2010 draft when the Rangers snagged him with the 45th pick and paid him $1.545 million. His stuff has been more impressive than his results in pro ball, though Texas says none of its pitching prospects made more progress in 2012. Jackson can touch 97 mph and works steadily at 93-94 with his fastball, holding that velocity deep into starts and delivering the ball on a steep downhill plane. His curveball frequently features tight rotation and power, grading as a potential well above-average pitch if he learns to locate it. The changeup is a relatively new addition to his arsenal and needs further refinement. A lengthy arm action and busy delivery affect Jackson's fastball command and contribute to his curve squirting out of his hand when he holds the ball too long in an effort to generate spin. He leans backward at his balance point and often fails to transfer his weight up front, blocking off the extension in his delivery. Jackson could grow into a No. 2 starter or shutdown reliever, and he ought to get his first taste of Double-A at some point in 2013.

BA GRADE
55
HIGH

Year	Club (League)	Class	W	L	ERA	G	GS	CG	SV	IP	H	HR	BB	SO	K/9	WHIP	AVG
2011	Hickory (SAL)	LoA	5	6	5.64	19	19	0	0	75	83	9	48	78	9.4	1.75	.276
2012	Hickory (SAL)	LoA	5	5	4.92	13	13	1	0	64	63	4	33	72	10.1	1.50	.259
	Myrtle Beach (CAR)	HiA	5	2	4.39	13	13	0	0	66	67	2	32	74	10.1	1.51	.273
Minor League Totals			15	13	5.01	45	45	1	0	205	213	15	113	224	9.9	1.59	.270

7 LUIS SARDINAS, SS/2B

Born: May 16, 1993. **B-T:** B-R. **Ht.:** 6-1. **Wt.:** 150. **Signed:** Venezuela, 2009. **Signed by:** Mike Daly/Rafic Saab/Pedro Avila.

Sardinas and Jurickson Profar both signed seven-figure deals with the Rangers as 16-year-old shortstops on July 2, 2009. While Profar has rocketed to the big leagues, Sardinas has made slower progress while contending with injures since signing for $1.2 million. A broken finger delayed his 2010 pro debut, and a dislocated shoulder that required surgery limited him to 14 games the following year. He was mostly healthy in 2012, missing time here and there with shoulder soreness. Sardinas has some of the most intriguing tools in the system. His speed, arm strength and defensive potential all grade as double-plus. He has a knack for hitting and shows looseness from both sides of the plate. Because he's skinny, he likes to use an exaggerated load, but Texas has stressed that proper hitting position and a balanced, direct swing will translate to some natural power. Sardinas is an effective basestealer who succeeded on 32 of 41 tries in 2012. With quick feet and plenty of agility, he can make all the plays at shortstop. Sardinas hit .326/.366/.436 in 181 second-half at-bats and gained further experience in the Arizona Fall League, readying him for the jump to high Class A in 2013.

BA GRADE
60
EXTREME

Year	Club (League)	Class	AVG	G	AB	R	H	2B	3B	HR	RBI	BB	SO	SB	CS	OBP	SLG
2010	Rangers (AZL)	R	.311	26	103	22	32	4	0	0	8	7	15	8	2	.363	.350
2011	Rangers (AZL)	R	.308	14	52	11	16	2	1	0	7	4	10	2	1	.367	.385
2012	Hickory (SAL)	LoA	.291	96	374	65	109	14	2	2	30	29	52	32	9	.346	.356
Minor League Totals			.297	136	529	98	157	20	3	2	45	40	77	42	12	.352	.357

8 CODY BUCKEL, RHP

Born: June 18, 1992. **B-T:** R-R. **Ht.:** 6-1. **Wt.:** 170. **Drafted:** HS—Simi Valley, Calif., 2010 (2nd round). **Signed by:** Todd Guggiana.

Like sub-6-foot Rangers prospects Robbie Erlin and Robbie Ross before him, Buckel combines short stature, swing-and-miss stuff and results. An offseason workout routine with Diamondbacks prospect Trevor Bauer prior to the 2012 season provided Buckel with ammunition for his long-toss regimen, mechanics and repertoire. Buckel claims tweaks to his delivery—which scouts compare to Tim Lincecum's—allowed him to maintain his velocity deeper into starts as he climbed to Double-A at age 20 in late June. He sits at 90-91 mph and touches 94 with running life, though his fastball plane tends to be flat. As a result, he leans on a repertoire of secondary pitches that grade as average or better. Buckel likes to pitch up in the strike zone with his fastball, then change eye levels with a plus curveball. He'll work to his glove side with a tight slider or slow bats with a solid changeup. He got in trouble at Frisco when he pitched backward, but improved as his fastball location got better. Buckel's repertoire and polish could be attractive in a back-of-the-rotation role to the

BA GRADE
50
MEDIUM

Rangers or a club that trades for him. He could be ready for a big league audition in late 2013 or early 2014.

Year	Club (League)	Class	W	L	ERA	G	GS	CG	SV	IP	H	HR	BB	SO	K/9	WHIP	AVG
2010	Rangers (AZL)	R	0	0	0.00	4	0	0	0	5	2	0	1	9	16.2	0.60	.125
2011	Hickory (SAL)	LoA	8	3	2.61	23	17	0	0	97	83	7	27	120	11.2	1.14	.229
2012	Myrtle Beach (CAR)	HiA	5	3	1.31	13	13	0	0	76	49	2	25	91	10.8	0.98	.186
	Frisco (TL)	AA	5	5	3.78	13	10	0	0	69	56	7	23	68	8.9	1.14	.228
Minor League Totals			18	11	2.48	53	40	0	0	246	190	16	76	288	10.5	1.08	.214

9 JORGE ALFARO, C/1B

Born: June 11, 1993. **B-T:** R-R. **Ht.:** 6-2. **Wt.:** 185. **Signed:** Colombia, 2010. **Signed by:** Rodolfo Rosario/Don Welke.

Going unsigned during the 2009 international signing period prompted Alfaro to shift from third base to catcher and move his home base from Colombia to the Dominican Republic, broadening his appeal. He signed for $1.3 million in January 2010, establishing a record for a Colombian amateur. He wowed observers with his raw tools while making his full-season debut in 2012, but he caught just 29 games as he dealt with a hamstring injury and shoulder inflammation. Alfaro's mature frame and wicked bat speed produce plus raw power, but he'll need to tone down his aggressiveness to tap into it. Texas widened his hitting base to cut down on his lunging, and in order to enhance his discipline they encouraged him to trust his hands and not go outside his preferred hitting zone. With plus-plus arm strength and a live body, Alfaro engenders confidence that he can develop into an asset on defense. At this stage, however, his blocking and receiving skills are raw and his arm a bit scattershot. He threw out just 15 percent of basestealers in 2012. Exceptionally athletic for a catcher, he has close to average speed. Alfaro headed to the Puerto Rican League to continue to work with Rangers catching instructor Hector Ortiz, who manages at Ponce. If he can learn to slow the game down, Alfaro could be an all-star.

BA GRADE: 60 EXTREME

Year	Club (League)	Class	AVG	G	AB	R	H	2B	3B	HR	RBI	BB	SO	SB	CS	OBP	SLG
2010	Rangers (DSL)	R	.221	48	172	18	38	5	2	1	23	5	48	1	4	.278	.291
2011	Spokane (NWL)	SS	.300	45	160	18	48	9	1	6	23	4	54	1	0	.345	.481
2012	Hickory (SAL)	LoA	.261	74	272	40	71	21	5	5	34	16	84	7	3	.320	.430
Minor League Totals			.260	167	604	76	157	35	8	12	80	25	186	9	7	.315	.404

10 JOEY GALLO, 3B

Born: Nov. 19, 1993. **B-T:** L-R. **Ht.:** 6-5. **Wt.:** 205. **Drafted:** HS—Las Vegas, 2012 (1st round supplemental). **Signed by:** Todd Guggiana.

Gallo established a pair of home run records in 2012, a year in which he signed for a well above-slot $2.25 million as the draft's 39th overall selection. He set a Nevada high school record with 65 career homers, then blasted 18 in the Rookie-level Arizona League to establish its single-season standard and win the circuit's MVP award. Top-of-the-scale raw power is Gallo's calling card, as he uses his quick hands to drive the ball to all fields. The question is how much he can tap into it because he swings and misses a lot. He expanded his strike zone in pro ball and piled up strikeouts after oppponents began pitching him backward. He works deep counts and takes his walks, and the Rangers think he can reduce his strikeouts and streakiness if he continues to shorten his path to the ball. Gallo has sure hands but subpar range at third base, so Texas has put him through agility drills to improve his first-step quickness. He sat in the mid-90s as a pitcher in high school and has a plus arm, but he made 17 errors in 56 pro games because he has trouble setting his feet on throws. If Gallo can improve his feel for hitting and prove himself at third base, he could make a relatively quick climb.

BA GRADE: 60 EXTREME

GREGG FORWERCK

Year	Club (League)	Class	AVG	G	AB	R	H	2B	3B	HR	RBI	BB	SO	SB	CS	OBP	SLG
2012	Rangers (AZL)	R	.293	43	150	44	44	10	1	18	43	37	52	6	0	.435	.733
	Spokane (NWL)	SS	.214	16	56	9	12	2	0	4	9	11	26	0	0	.343	.464
Minor League Totals			.272	59	206	53	56	12	1	22	52	48	78	6	0	.412	.660

11 ROUGNED ODOR, 2B/SS

BA GRADE: 50 MEDIUM

Born: Feb. 3, 1994. **B-T:** L-R. **Ht.:** 5-11. **Wt.:** 170. **Signed:** Venezuela, 2011. **Signed by:** Rafic Saab/Mike Daly.

The nephew of Indians Double-A hitting coach Rouglas Odor, Rougned signed out of Venezuela for $425,000 in January 2011 and has been the youngest player in the Northwest and South Atlantic leagues in successive seasons. He teamed with catcher Jorge Alfaro and shortstop Luis Sardinas with Hickory last year to form one of the most prospect-centric middle configurations in the minors. Like them, he also spent time on the disabled list, in his case with a separated shoulder. Odor batted .293/.357/.482 in 49 first-half games but tired badly down the stretch and hit just .232/.277/.336 after the all-star break. One of the toughest players in the system and lauded for having plus instincts, he has the classic lefty swing and hand-eye coordination to hit .280 or better in the big leagues. He has the strength to drive the ball despite a smaller frame, and scouts who like him peg him for 12-15 homers annually. The Rangers believe Odor can improve his hitting consistency by toning down a leg kick that can throw off his timing and by implementing the mental discipline to lay off pitches outside his preferred hitting zones. Signed as a shortstop, Odor is a fringy runner who has all the requisites to play a big league second base, including strong range and arm strength, a quick exchange and the fortitude to hang in on double plays. While Jose Altuve is the only Latin second-base regular in the big leagues today who spent his entire minor league career at the keystone, the Rangers believe Odor is another player who breaks the mold.

Year	Club (League)	Class	AVG	G	AB	R	H	2B	3B	HR	RBI	BB	SO	SB	CS	OBP	SLG
2011	Spokane (NWL)	SS	.262	58	233	33	61	9	3	2	29	13	37	10	4	.323	.352
2012	Hickory (SAL)	LoA	.259	109	432	60	112	23	4	10	47	25	65	19	10	.313	.400
Minor League Totals			.260	167	665	93	173	32	7	12	76	38	102	29	14	.317	.383

12 LEWIS BRINSON, OF

BA GRADE

55

EXTREME

Born: May 8, 1994. **B-T:** R-R. **Ht.:** 6-3. **Wt.:** 170. **Drafted:** HS—Coral Springs, Fla., 2012 (1st round). **Signed by:** Frankie Thon.

Brinson cemented his prospect status as an amateur by winning the Under Armour All-America Game home run derby at Wrigley Field in 2011 and by performing well at the World Wood Bat Association tournament that fall. Though he had a disappointing high school senior year, the Rangers stayed on him, took him with the 29th pick in June and signed him for $1.625 million. He topped the Arizona League in runs (54), doubles (22), extra-base hits (36) and strikeouts (74) in his pro debut. Brinson draws comparisons to Cameron Maybin and Dexter Fowler for his tall, lean, long-limbed physique and outstanding bat speed. The ball carries off Brinson's bat, and with a more consistent approach he could hit 15-20 homers. Getting to that power could be a challenge if he doesn't refine his swing mechanics to cut down on strikeouts. Texas is working with him to reduce his stride and keep his hands back on breaking pitches in order to take some of the loop out of his swing path. Scouts expect Brinson to develop into a plus defender in center field, with above-average arm strength and speed. If he improves his lower-half strength and explosiveness he could become a basestealing threat. Texas may have him take the minors one level at a time, but the ultimate payout could be a five-tool center fielder.

Year	Club (League)	Class	AVG	G	AB	R	H	2B	3B	HR	RBI	BB	SO	SB	CS	OBP	SLG
2012	Rangers (AZL)	R	.283	54	237	54	67	22	7	7	42	21	74	14	2	.345	.523
Minor League Totals			.283	54	237	54	67	22	7	7	42	21	74	14	2	.345	.523

13 ROMAN MENDEZ, RHP

BA GRADE

50

HIGH

Born: July 25, 1990. **B-T:** R-R. **Ht.:** 6-2. **Wt.:** 190. **Signed:** Dominican Republic, 2007. **Signed by:** Luciano del Rosario (Red Sox).

Mendez joined the Rangers in the July 2010 trade that sent Jarrod Saltalamacchia to the Red Sox and also yielded first baseman Chris McGuiness. Mendez hadn't thrown a pitch above the low Class A level when Texas added him to its 40-man roster in November 2011. Despite his obvious arm strength and quickness, he struggles to locate his pitches because of an inconsistent arm slot brought on in part by a hooking arm action. So after Mendez missed time in June with arm tightness, the Rangers converted him to the bullpen in high Class A and he proceeded to experience his first run of sustained success. In 11 relief appearances there and in Double-A, he struck out 24, walked six and allowed just 13 hits in 24 innings. Mendez pitches at 94-96 mph and approaches triple digits with his fastball as a reliever. He deceives batters with the torque and upper-half rotation in his pitching motion. His average mid-80s slider runs away from righthanders, who hit a mere .227 against him in 211 at-bats last season. Mendez's fair splitter/changeup leads some to believe he can return to starting at some point, though he'd have to improve his command drastically to find success. He could get a refresher with Frisco to begin 2013, then surface in the Texas bullpen at some point during the season. He has closer upside.

Year	Club (League)	Class	W	L	ERA	G	GS	CG	SV	IP	H	HR	BB	SO	K/9	WHIP	AVG
2008	Red Sox (DSL)	R	3	1	2.65	11	11	0	0	51	43	1	16	46	8.1	1.16	.222
2009	Red Sox (GCL)	R	2	3	1.99	12	10	0	0	50	33	1	8	47	8.5	0.83	.184
2010	Greenville (SAL)	LoA	0	2	11.40	6	6	0	0	15	29	5	10	18	10.8	2.60	.392
	Lowell (NYP)	SS	2	3	4.36	8	8	0	0	33	31	5	19	35	9.5	1.52	.240
	Spokane (NWL)	SS	1	1	2.31	3	3	0	0	12	19	2	3	13	10.0	1.89	.373
2011	Hickory (SAL)	LoA	9	1	3.31	26	20	0	1	117	117	7	45	130	10.0	1.38	.259
2012	Myrtle Beach (CAR)	HiA	4	6	5.14	18	12	0	1	70	69	7	25	71	9.1	1.34	.260
	Rangers (AZL)	R	0	1	3.00	3	3	0	0	9	7	1	1	7	7.0	0.89	.219
	Frisco (TL)	AA	2	0	1.46	5	0	0	1	12	8	2	4	9	6.6	0.97	.174
Minor League Totals			23	18	3.71	92	73	0	3	369	356	31	131	376	9.2	1.32	.250

14 C.J. EDWARDS, RHP

BA GRADE
50
HIGH

Born: Sept. 3, 1991. **B-T:** R-R. **Ht.:** 6-2. **Wt.:** 155. **Drafted:** HS—Prosperity, S.C., 2011 (48th round). **Signed by:** Chris Kemp.

The story of Edwards' signing will sound like an apocryphal tale if he one day makes the big leagues. Lightly scouted in high school because he didn't play in high-profile showcases, he fell to the 48th round of the 2011 draft. The Rangers selected him based on the recommendation of area scout Chris Kemp, who had recruited him to play for Spartanburg Methodist (S.C.) JC while he served as an assistant coach there. Edwards elected to turn pro for $50,000 at the Aug. 15 signing deadline despite a lack of instruction or feel for pitching. Texas remedied those issues during instructional league and in extended spring training the following year, teaching him to long-toss and to repeat his delivery. The lanky righthander then promptly breezed through the Arizona League in his 2012 pro debut, allowing just six hits and no runs in 20 innings on his way to a promotion to short-season Spokane. In the span of one year, the quick-armed Edwards increased his velocity from the mid-80s to 90-94 mph with a high of 98. He also has developed feel for two secondary pitches. He imparts natural cutting action on the ball because his fingers are offset slightly to the right. Edwards can spin a mid-70s breaking ball and throw an effective changeup with fading action, but he needs to stay on top of all his pitches to get the most out of them. The Rangers rave about his makeup and projection—he could add 25 pounds easily, they say—and they intend to give him every opportunity to win a spot in the Hickory rotation.

Year	Club (League)	Class	W	L	ERA	G	GS	CG	SV	IP	H	HR	BB	SO	K/9	WHIP	AVG
2012	Rangers (AZL)	R	3	0	0.00	4	3	0	0	20	6	0	6	25	11.3	0.60	.094
	Spokane (NWL)	SS	2	3	2.11	10	10	0	0	47	26	0	19	60	11.5	0.96	.160
Minor League Totals			5	3	1.48	14	13	0	0	67	32	0	25	85	11.4	0.85	.141

15 HANSER ALBERTO, SS/3B

BA GRADE
50
HIGH

Born: Oct. 17, 1992. **B-T:** R-R. **Ht.:** 5-11. **Wt.:** 175. **Signed:** Dominican Republic, 2009. **Signed by:** Rodolfo Rosario/Willy Espinal/Mike Daly.

Alberto hit .358 to win the Rookie-level Dominican Summer League batting title during his 2010 pro debut, but he didn't gain prospect helium until he reached full-season ball two years later. He made the South Atlantic League all-star team during the first half of 2012, then moved on to high Class A and served as the Carolina League's second-youngest regular. Alberto doesn't have standout tools, but he does have quick hands and a knack for squaring up the ball, which should enable him to hit for a solid average. He doesn't swing and miss much but he doesn't walk much either, and he offers just gap power potential. Alberto runs well underway, but he grades more as solid in that regard and isn't as explosive on the bases or in the field as Leury Garcia or Luis Sardinas, the shortstops one level ahead of and one level behind him. Alberto plays to his strengths better than they do, however, giving him a higher floor. He flashes a plus arm and has steady range, hands and actions at shortstop. A stint in the Arizona Fall League could prepare Alberto for an assignment to Double-A, which would keep the organization's shortstops in the same lock-step pattern as 2012.

Year	Club (League)	Class	AVG	G	AB	R	H	2B	3B	HR	RBI	BB	SO	SB	CS	OBP	SLG
2010	Rangers (DSL)	R	.358	50	179	25	64	15	2	0	24	6	9	16	3	.377	.464
2011	Spokane (NWL)	SS	.267	53	187	21	50	8	1	0	16	9	15	7	1	.308	.321
2012	Hickory (SAL)	LoA	.337	62	246	37	83	17	1	4	38	18	22	15	4	.385	.463
	Myrtle Beach (CAR)	HiA	.265	66	279	36	74	11	2	4	34	2	27	9	3	.273	.362
Minor League Totals			.304	231	891	119	271	51	6	8	112	35	73	47	11	.333	.402

16 NOMAR MAZARA, OF

BA GRADE
55
EXTREME

Born: April 26, 1995. **B-T:** L-L. **Ht.:** 6-4. **Wt.:** 200. **Signed:** Dominican Republic, 2011. **Signed by:** Rodolfo Rosario/Mike Daly.

The Rangers committed a combined $8.4 million to sign lefty-hitting Dominican outfielders Mazara and Ronald Guzman during the 2011 international signing period. Mazara's international-record $4.95 million bonus may never be surpassed with the spending limits established in the new Collective Bargaining Agreement. Both Dominicans made their pro debuts as 17-year-olds in the Arizona League last summer and ranked among the circuit's brightest prospects. Rangers officials rave about not only Mazara's tools but also his makeup, maturity and ability to take things in stride. He has taken to a number of routines—weightlifting, long-tossing, power-shagging—that made him one of the system's most improved players. Despite his youth and easy plus raw power, Mazara already shows plate discipline and ranked second in the AZL with 37 walks. The ball jumps off his bat, though he'll need to make more contact to hit for average. Reducing his leg kick would help, as would a more-refined two-strike approach and ability to spoil quality pitches. Mazara has prototype right-field tools with solid range and plus arm strength. While he has fringy speed, he's a solid baserunner. Mazara could patrol right field in Arlington one day, but he may need at least four years to develop his feel for hitting.

Year	Club (League)	Class	AVG	G	AB	R	H	2B	3B	HR	RBI	BB	SO	SB	CS	OBP	SLG
2012	Rangers (AZL)	R	.264	54	201	40	53	13	3	6	39	37	70	5	2	.383	.448
Minor League Totals			.264	54	201	40	53	13	3	6	39	37	70	5	2	.383	.448

17 RONALD GUZMAN, 1B

Born: Oct. 20, 1994. **B-T:** L-L. **Ht.:** 6-4. **Wt.:** 205. **Signed:** Dominican Republic, 2011. **Signed by:** Willy Espinal/Mike Daly.

BA GRADE
55
EXTREME

Guzman signed for $3.45 million on the same day that fellow Dominican outfielder Nomar Mazara got $4.95 million, and they were Arizona League teammates for their pro debuts in 2012. Many international scouts favored Guzman to Mazara because he showed a more advanced feel to hit and had a track record in the United States, having participated in a Reviving Baseball in Inner Cities tournament and the Under Armour All-America Game in 2010. Guzman has leverage in his swing and can juice the ball in batting practice. He focuses on driving the ball from line to line in games, and it shows—he batted .321 and led the AZL with 68 hits. As his body matures, he could produce gaudier home run totals because his ball ought to carry. Signed as an outfielder, Guzman has below-average speed and played first base almost exclusively last summer. His arm strength and instincts are lacking, so he'll require a lot of work to become even average defensively. He figures to advance with Mazara to low Class A in 2013, and their bats will determine how far they climb.

Year	Club (League)	Class	AVG	G	AB	R	H	2B	3B	HR	RBI	BB	SO	SB	CS	OBP	SLG
2012	Rangers (AZL)	R	.321	52	212	29	68	15	3	1	33	19	42	7	1	.374	.434
Minor League Totals			.321	52	212	29	68	15	3	1	33	19	42	7	1	.374	.434

18 JAIRO BERAS, OF

Born: Dec. 25, 1994. **B-T:** R-R. **Ht.:** 6-6. **Wt.:** 190. **Signed:** Dominican Republic, 2012. **Signed by:** Danilo Troncoso/Roberto Aquino/Paul Kruger/Mike Daly.

BA GRADE
55
EXTREME

The Rangers have signed many of the organization's top prospects as international amateurs, yet as of March 2011 the most they had committed to any one of them was $1.55 million to Jurickson Profar in 2009. Anticipating changes to the signing protocol, Texas drastically altered its operating procedure in 2011, doling out three of the four largest bonuses ever for international amateurs in the span of eight months. They spent a combined $8.4 million to sign Nomar Mazara and Ronald Guzman in July 2011, and $4.5 million (a sum eclipsed only by Mazara) in February 2012 to sign Beras. Following an investigation, Major League Baseball determined that he had presented two different birthdates to clubs and suspended him for one year. By claiming to be 17 instead of 16, he effectively circumvented the new budgetary restrictions that kicked in when the international signing period started on July 2. MLB approved his contract, however, and allowed him to participate in instructional league and extended spring training. Like Mazara and Guzman, Beras is both immense and immensely talented. He's a 6-foot-6 right fielder who projects to hit for prototype corner power and possibly for average. Texas hasn't done much at this stage to alter his hitting mechanics. He doesn't project to offer much in the way of speed or project as much more than an average defender, though he does have a strong arm. Beras probably will follow Mazara and Guzman's path and make his U.S. debut in the Arizona League once he's reinstated on July 1.

Year	Club (League)	Class	AVG	G	AB	R	H	2B	3B	HR	RBI	BB	SO	SB	CS	OBP	SLG
Did Not Play—Signed 2013 Contract																	

19 NICK TEPESCH, RHP

Born: Oct. 12, 1988. **B-T:** R-R. **Ht.:** 6-4. **Wt.:** 225. **Drafted:** Missouri, 2010 (14th round). **Signed by:** Dustin Smith.

BA GRADE
50
HIGH

Tepesch floated a seven-figure bonus demand coming out of high school in 2007, which pushed him to the 28th round of the draft. He declined to sign with the Red Sox and instead attended Missouri, where he was supposed to be the next in line following Tigers first-round pitchers Max Scherzer, Aaron Crow and Kyle Gibson. Tepesch didn't live up to that standard, though he did get an over-slot $400,000 bonus after sliding to the 14th round of the 2010 draft. His solid performance in Double-A during the second half of 2012 leads some club officials to believe that he could make an impact on the big league pitching staff in 2013. Because he doesn't throw 95 mph, however, he flies under the radar. Tepesch's strengths include durability and a knack for throwing four pitches for strikes, reading swings and locating the ball down in the zone consistently. He sits at 91-92 mph and muscles up to 94 on occasion, though he typically allows the late sinking action on his fastball to do the heavy lifting. Tepesch's high-70s curveball and high-80s cutter continue to improve each season—they're borderline plus pitches—and have come a long way in his two pro seasons. His diving changeup and two-plane slider are average pitches more often than not. Tepesch has mid-rotation upside and could be next in line to get a look in the Rangers rotation.

Year	Club (League)	Class	W	L	ERA	G	GS	CG	SV	IP	H	HR	BB	SO	K/9	WHIP	AVG
2011	Hickory (SAL)	LoA	7	5	4.03	29	23	2	0	138	147	14	33	118	7.7	1.30	.279
2012	Myrtle Beach (CAR)	HiA	5	3	2.89	12	12	1	0	72	68	3	18	59	7.4	1.20	.253
	Frisco (TL)	AA	6	3	4.28	16	14	0	0	90	97	10	26	68	6.8	1.36	.280
Minor League Totals			18	11	3.84	57	49	3	0	300	312	27	77	245	7.3	1.30	.273

20 LEURY GARCIA, 2B/SS

Born: March 18, 1991. **B-T:** B-R. **Ht.:** 5-7. **Wt.:** 153. **Signed:** Dominican Republic, 2007. **Signed by:** Jesus Ovalle.

BA GRADE
50
HIGH

Garcia continues to attract attention in a system overflowing with talented young middle infielders. He's the fastest runner—a borderline 80 on the 20-to-80 scouting scale—and has the best infield arm among Rangers farmhands. He's also a flashy defender at shortstop who ranges well to both sides and makes plays in the hole with ease because of his elite arm strength. Garcia spent most of his time at second base with Double-A Frisco in 2012, however, in deference to shortstop Jurickson Profar, though he did return to short later in the season and also gained brief exposure to center field. Wiry strong and 5-foot-7, Garcia has the power to drive the ball into the gaps but his swing tends to get too big. As one Rangers instructor put it, the hitter Garcia should be is not the hitter he wants to be. Texas would like to see him focus more on bunting, hitting the ball on the ground and working walks to take maximum advantage of his terrific speed. He's a switch-hitter whose swing is a bit long from the left side, and he batted a modest .282/.330/.370 against righthanders in 2012. Garcia continues to make careless mistakes in the field and on the bases, but he still has time on his side. The Rangers added him to their 40-man roster in November. He ultimately fits best in their plans as a super-utility player who can play short, second and center.

Year	Club (League)	Class	AVG	G	AB	R	H	2B	3B	HR	RBI	BB	SO	SB	CS	OBP	SLG
2008	Rangers (AZL)	R	.209	41	129	17	27	3	3	0	14	8	40	12	3	.250	.279
2009	Hickory (SAL)	LoA	.232	83	276	28	64	6	3	1	18	18	64	19	6	.288	.286
2010	Hickory (SAL)	LoA	.262	89	359	57	94	5	4	3	22	23	57	47	9	.307	.323
	Rangers (AZL)	R	.500	6	18	5	9	2	0	0	2	4	4	4	2	.591	.611
2011	Myrtle Beach (CAR)	HiA	.256	109	442	65	113	19	5	3	38	28	100	30	12	.306	.342
2012	Frisco (TL)	AA	.292	100	377	55	110	12	11	2	30	22	79	31	7	.337	.398
Minor League Totals			.260	428	1601	227	417	47	26	9	124	103	344	143	39	.309	.339

21 DREW ROBINSON, 3B/2B

Born: April 20, 1992. **B-T:** L-R. **Ht.:** 6-1. **Wt.:** 185. **Drafted:** HS—Las Vegas, 2010 (4th round). **Signed by:** Todd Guggiana.

BA GRADE
50
HIGH

Excluding Bryce Harper, scouts liked Robinson more than any hitter in the Four Corners area leading up to the 2010 draft. He did little to justify that faith by face-planting in the Northwest League the following year, when he hit .163/.266/.265 in 45 games. Playing on a talent-laden Hickory team in 2012 reduced the pressure on Robinson and he recovered his feel to hit, ranking third in the South Atlantic League in walks (86) and fifth in on-base percentage (.409). He also racked up 123 strikeouts, the product of working deep counts, pulling off the ball and timing issues when his hips drifted too far forward. With a sweet lefty swing, Robinson hits for average first and power second, and he continues to show the same gap-to-gap approach he did as an amateur. A below-average runner, he played shortstop in high school but hasn't settled into a defensive home in pro ball. He landed at third base with Hickory and also spent 15 games at second, but his feet and hands are just OK, so he might make his way to an outfield corner before all is said and done. He has a tick above-average arm. Robinson will graduate to high Class A in 2013.

Year	Club (League)	Class	AVG	G	AB	R	H	2B	3B	HR	RBI	BB	SO	SB	CS	OBP	SLG
2010	Rangers (AZL)	R	.286	44	140	26	40	6	2	0	11	26	41	6	3	.406	.357
2011	Rangers (AZL)	R	.500	6	18	9	9	2	0	1	5	6	4	4	1	.640	.778
	Spokane (NWL)	SS	.163	45	147	18	24	6	0	3	25	22	46	3	1	.266	.265
2012	Hickory (SAL)	LoA	.273	123	410	72	112	23	4	13	67	86	123	10	7	.409	.444
Minor League Totals			.259	218	715	125	185	37	6	17	108	140	214	23	12	.387	.399

22 WILMER FONT, RHP

Born: May 24, 1990. **B-T:** R-R. **Ht.:** 6-4. **Wt.:** 210. **Signed:** Venezuela, 2006. **Signed by:** Manny Batista/Andres Espinosa.

BA GRADE
50
HIGH

Font flashed a 98-mph fastball as a 17-year-old during his 2007 pro debut, but he missed almost all of the next season with injuries. He worked his way to high Class A in 2010, only to experience elbow soreness that eventually required Tommy John surgery, which erased his entire 2011 season. Texas added him to its 40-man roster in November 2010 even knowing he wouldn't get back on a mound for more than a year. When Font returned to action in 2012, the Rangers assigned him to high Class A with the goal of getting him 100 or so innings, and he actually finished the year with a three-game trial in the big leagues. Font shows the same wicked arm strength he showed pre-surgery, sitting at 94 mph and touching 99, but also the same lengthy arm action that inhibits his feel for a slider. His high-70s changeup has its moments, but without more precise fastball command he won't find himself in many counts where he can use the changeup as a chase pitch. Font's heater alone might be enough for a low-leverage relief role, but he has the potential for more because he's hard to hit when he's around the plate. Look for him to spend time in Triple-A and the majors in 2013.

Year	Club (League)	Class	W	L	ERA	G	GS	CG	SV	IP	H	HR	BB	SO	K/9	WHIP	AVG
2007	Rangers (AZL)	R	2	3	4.53	14	10	0	0	46	41	2	24	61	12.0	1.42	.238
2008	Rangers (AZL)	R	1	0	10.38	3	0	0	0	4	1	1	1	6	12.5	0.46	.071
2009	Hickory (SAL)	LoA	8	3	3.49	29	24	0	0	108	93	4	59	105	8.7	1.40	.231
2010	Hickory (SAL)	LoA	4	1	5.16	7	7	0	0	30	35	3	13	33	10.0	1.62	.294
	Bakersfield (CAL)	HiA	1	2	3.86	9	9	0	0	49	38	5	32	52	9.6	1.43	.217
2011	Did Not Play—Injured																
2012	Myrtle Beach (CAR)	HiA	2	5	4.21	23	19	0	0	83	58	10	37	109	11.8	1.14	.198
	Frisco (TL)	AA	2	0	3.00	10	0	0	1	15	9	1	7	29	17.4	1.07	.170
	Texas (AL)	MAJ	0	0	9.00	3	0	0	0	2	0	0	4	1	4.5	2.00	.000
Major League Totals			0	0	9.00	3	0	0	0	2	0	0	4	1	4.5	2.00	.000
Minor League Totals			20	14	4.08	95	69	0	1	335	275	26	173	395	10.6	1.34	.224

23 NEIL RAMIREZ, RHP

BA GRADE
45
MEDIUM

Born: May 25, 1989. **B-T:** R-R. **Ht.:** 6-4. **Wt.:** 210. **Drafted:** HS—Virginia Beach, 2007 (1st round supp). **Signed by:** Russ Ardolina.

Ramirez has made halting progress after signing for $1 million as the 2007 draft's 44th pick. He took two cracks at low Class A before rocketing up the minor league ladder and this list (all the way to No. 5) following a 2011 season that he finished in the Round Rock rotation. His success vanished as quickly as it had arrived during a rocky 2012 campaign, during which he dealt with shoulder fatigue and earned a late-June demotion to Double-A. He made his final appearance of the season out of the bullpen and showed a consistent 95-97 mph fastball after settling in at 90-94 as a starter. The Rangers believe relieving better suits his personality because Ramirez tends to overthink things as a starter. He has cleaned up his arm circle in recent years, reducing the severity of a high-elbow backswing, but an inconsistent release point still affects the quality of his secondary pitches when he doesn't stay on top of them. He sells a high-80s changeup with natural deception, and it's a plus pitch at times. He started throwing a slider in 2012, and it flashes promising tilt. He hangs his curveball too much for it to be viable at higher levels. If he stays in the bullpen, Ramirez could vie with fellow 40-man roster members Wilmer Font and Roman Mendez for relief innings in Arlington this year.

Year	Club (League)	Class	W	L	ERA	G	GS	CG	SV	IP	H	HR	BB	SO	K/9	WHIP	AVG
2008	Spokane (NWL)	SS	1	2	2.66	13	13	0	0	44	25	5	29	52	10.6	1.23	.166
2009	Hickory (SAL)	LoA	3	6	4.75	18	14	0	0	66	58	8	41	56	7.6	1.49	.235
2010	Hickory (SAL)	LoA	10	8	4.43	28	26	1	0	140	150	14	37	142	9.1	1.33	.281
2011	Myrtle Beach (CAR)	HiA	0	0	0.00	1	1	0	0	5	1	0	1	9	17.4	0.43	.063
	Frisco (TL)	AA	1	0	1.89	6	6	0	0	19	13	1	8	24	11.4	1.11	.194
	Round Rock (PCL)	AAA	4	3	3.63	18	18	0	0	74	63	6	35	86	10.4	1.32	.229
2012	Round Rock (PCL)	AAA	6	8	7.66	15	15	0	0	74	78	12	31	63	7.7	1.47	.271
	Frisco (TL)	AA	2	5	4.20	13	12	0	0	49	47	6	16	45	8.2	1.28	.258
Minor League Totals			27	32	4.52	112	105	1	0	472	435	52	198	477	9.1	1.34	.247

24 ZACH CONE, OF

BA GRADE
50
HIGH

Born: Dec. 14, 1989. **B-T:** R-R. **Ht.:** 6-2. **Wt.:** 205. **Drafted:** Georgia, 2011 (1st round supplemental). **Signed by:** Ryan Coe.

One of the top high school athletes available in the 2008 draft, Cone couldn't agree to terms with the Angels as a supplemental third-round pick. He hit .363 as a sophomore at Georgia but regressed badly as a junior in 2011—the year the NCAA instituted less-potent bats—but the Rangers still loved his athleticism, work ethic and physicality, and they signed him for $873,000 as a sandwich pick in 2011. While questions remain as to whether Cone will hit for average, his other tools are stout. He has above-average power, speed and range. He led a loaded Hickory squad with 17 homers and a .461 slugging percentage last season. Texas thinks Cone developed too many bad habits as an amateur. He's so strong that he relied on upper-body strength and neglected his lower half. The Rangers have worked to get Cone to stop overstriding to his front side, and to keep his head centered and his hands back and in position to hit offspeed pitches. He's a solid defender at any outfield position thanks to his range and average arm strength.

Year	Club (League)	Class	AVG	G	AB	R	H	2B	3B	HR	RBI	BB	SO	SB	CS	OBP	SLG
2011	Spokane (NWL)	SS	.201	62	224	37	45	15	2	4	29	16	57	11	2	.278	.339
2012	Hickory (SAL)	LoA	.262	112	432	66	113	27	4	17	64	39	110	10	0	.326	.461
Minor League Totals			.241	174	656	103	158	42	6	21	93	55	167	21	2	.309	.419

25 NICK WILLIAMS, OF

Born: Sept. 8, 1993. **B-T:** L-L. **Ht.:** 6-3. **Wt.:** 195. **Drafted:** HS—Galveston, Texas, 2012 (2nd round). **Signed by:** Jay Heafner.

Area scouts zeroed in on Williams and Courtney Hawkins, a pair of Texas Gulf Coast area high school outfielders, as potential 2012 first-round picks when they were sophomores. While Hawkins went No. 13 overall to the White Sox in June, Williams had an uneven senior year and slipped to Texas in the second round. After signing for $500,000, he hit .313 in his pro debut while showcasing excellent bat speed, hitting instincts and a knack for barreling the ball. The Rangers said he had the quickest hands in their instructional league camp. By contrast, amateur scouts thought he was too spread out at the plate and had trouble picking up spin on breaking balls. Williams has been clocked at 6.5 seconds in the 60-yard dash, but he turns in fringy running times during games. He lacks the instincts to handle center field on an everyday basis, and his substandard arm mandates that he spend most of his time in left, particularly if paired with 2012 first-rounder Lewis Brinson.

Year	Club (League)	Class	AVG	G	AB	R	H	2B	3B	HR	RBI	BB	SO	SB	CS	OBP	SLG
2012	Rangers (AZL)	R	.313	48	201	34	63	9	6	2	27	16	50	15	2	.375	.448
Minor League Totals			.313	48	201	34	63	9	6	2	27	16	50	15	2	.375	.448

26 KEONE KELA, RHP

Born: April 16, 1993. **B-T:** R-R. **Ht.:** 6-1. **Wt.:** 195. **Drafted:** Everett (Wash.) CC, 2012 (12th round). **Signed by:** Gary McGraw.

The Mariners made Kela a 29th-round pick in 2011 but failed to sign him out of a Seattle high school, so he headed to Everett (Wash.) CC. The Rangers had better luck getting him under contract as a 12th-rounder in 2012, signing him for $100,000. Kela's velocity has increased exponentially in two years, jumping from 89-91 mph in high school to 96-98 with a peak of 100 in short stints. His athleticism allowed him to clean up his delivery after signing and get more extension out front, which did wonders for his overall control. Texas believes his mid-80s slider has above-average potential. He's only now working on a changeup that he'll need as he attempts to transition from reliever to starter in 2013. Kela's fastball features plenty of late life, so he'll profile as a relief prospect if starting doesn't work out. He could open his first full pro season in low Class A.

Year	Club (League)	Class	W	L	ERA	G	GS	CG	SV	IP	H	HR	BB	SO	K/9	WHIP	AVG
2012	Rangers (AZL)	R	0	1	1.59	9	0	0	0	11	4	0	4	15	11.9	0.71	.105
Minor League Totals			0	1	1.59	9	0	0	0	11	4	0	4	15	11.9	0.71	.105

27 NICK MARTINEZ, RHP

BA GRADE
50
HIGH

Born: Aug. 5, 1990. **B-T:** L-R. **Ht.:** 6-1. **Wt.:** 175. **Drafted:** Fordham, 2011 (18th round). **Signed by:** Jay Heafner.

Martinez had pitched all of 26 relief innings in three years at Fordham when the Rangers made him an 18th-round pick in 2011. He spent most of his time as the Rams' shortstop and No. 3 hitter, but Texas scouts correctly gauged that Martinez had the type of pitchability that would enable him to start in pro ball. He impressed club officials by precisely locating his 90-94 mph fastball in his pro debut, and he worked his way into the Hickory rotation during his first full pro season in 2012. Martinez's quick-twitch athleticism, fast arm and clean, repeatable pitching motion serve him well. He sits steadily at 92-93 mph and shows an average curveball at times. His breaking ball has made the most progress of any of his pitches since he signed, and he's still gaining confidence in his fringy changeup. Martinez's secondary pitches play up because he sets them up well by commanding his fastball to both sides of the plate. Other young Rangers pitching prospects may have higher ceilings, but Martinez won't have to improve much to profile as a safe No. 4 starter.

Year	Club (League)	Class	W	L	ERA	G	GS	CG	SV	IP	H	HR	BB	SO	K/9	WHIP	AVG
2011	Rangers (AZL)	R	2	1	1.83	6	4	0	0	20	21	0	2	19	8.7	1.17	.256
	Spokane (NWL)	SS	1	2	2.54	9	7	0	0	39	37	0	16	37	8.5	1.36	.252
2012	Hickory (SAL)	LoA	8	6	4.83	31	20	0	1	117	121	8	37	109	8.4	1.35	.265
Minor League Totals			11	9	3.99	46	31	0	1	176	179	8	55	165	8.4	1.33	.262

28 MATT WEST, RHP

BA GRADE
50
EXTREME

Born: Nov. 21, 1988. **B-T:** R-R. **Ht.:** 6-1. **Wt.:** 200. **Drafted:** HS—Houston, 2007 (2nd round). **Signed by:** Randy Taylor.

West built serious prospect momentum in 2011 by notching a 35-1 K-BB ratio in his first year on the mound after spending four seasons as a light-hitting third baseman. After pitching his way onto the 40-man roster, he probably couldn't have imagined a worse encore season than the one he endured. West sprained the ulnar collateral ligament in his elbow during spring training but recovered in time to take the mound in high Class A in mid-June. He struggled through 17 appearances before having Tommy John surgery in late August. Before he got hurt, he drew comparisons to Jason Motte as a converted position player with a squat build and true power stuff. A healthy West showcased a 94-96 mph fastball and an 82-84 mph slider with serious two-plane tilt. If he makes a full recovery, he could ride a fast track to big leagues when he returns in 2014.

Year	Club (League)	Class	AVG	G	AB	R	H	2B	3B	HR	RBI	BB	SO	SB	CS	OBP	SLG
2007	Rangers (AZL)	R	.301	29	103	21	31	1	4	0	17	9	21	1	3	.397	.388
2008	Spokane (NWL)	SS	.258	67	240	48	62	12	0	4	30	26	68	1	0	.367	.358
2009	Hickory (SAL)	LoA	.234	135	471	61	110	29	2	5	55	54	136	12	4	.336	.335
2010	Hickory (SAL)	LoA	.223	115	391	52	87	25	2	13	48	38	125	7	2	.326	.396
Minor League Totals			.241	346	1205	182	290	67	8	22	150	127	350	21	9	.344	.364

Year	Club (League)	Class	W	L	ERA	G	GS	CG	SV	IP	H	HR	BB	SO	K/9	WHIP	AVG
2011	Spokane (NWL)	SS	1	2	3.12	23	0	0	9	26	23	3	1	35	12.1	0.92	.242
	Myrtle Beach (CAR)	HiA	0	0	0.00	1	0	0	0	1	1	0	0	0	0.0	1.00	.250
2012	Myrtle Beach (CAR)	HiA	0	3	6.64	17	0	0	0	20	18	1	16	14	6.2	1.67	.240
Minor League Totals			1	5	4.56	41	0	0	9	47	42	4	17	49	9.3	1.25	.241

29 RANDY HENRY, RHP

BA GRADE 45 HIGH

Born: May 10, 1990. **B-T:** R-R. **Ht.:** 6-3. **Wt.:** 190. **Drafted:** South Mountain (Ariz.) CC, 2009 (4th round). **Signed by:** John Gillette (Orioles).

The Rangers and Orioles consummated three trades in 2011. Baltimore acquired Chris Davis, Tommy Hunter, Pedro Strop and Taylor Teagarden, all of whom contributed to their stunning wild-card run in 2012. Texas acquired big league relievers Mike Gonzalez and Koji Uehara, minor league infielder Greg Miclat and Henry. A fourth-round pick in 2009, Henry pitched sparingly at South Mountain (Ariz.) CC as he recovered from Tommy John surgery. Now that he's healthy, he may be coming into his own. He pitched so well out of the Myrtle Beach bullpen last season (0.98 ERA, 25-9 K-BB ratio) that the Rangers moved him to the rotation for the second half. He went just 1-7, 4.53 in 11 starts, so his future probably lies in the bullpen. That's OK because Henry has firm stuff. He works fast, throws strikes and sits at 91-93 mph with natural cutting action on his fastball. His tight mid-80s slider and solid changeup also generate swings and misses. He could be a solid middle-relief option—and maybe more—for Texas in the near future. His next step will be Double-A.

Year	Club (League)	Class	W	L	ERA	G	GS	CG	SV	IP	H	HR	BB	SO	K/9	WHIP	AVG
2010	Delmarva (SAL)	LoA	1	1	5.64	10	0	0	0	22	28	1	5	30	12.1	1.48	.289
	Aberdeen (NYP)	SS	0	1	13.50	1	0	0	0	1	2	0	1	0	4.50	.667
2011	Delmarva (SAL)	LoA	4	0	1.67	20	0	0	1	38	31	3	6	29	6.9	0.98	.223
	Frederick (CAR)	HiA	0	3	3.60	9	0	0	1	15	17	1	2	11	6.6	1.27	.298
2012	Myrtle Beach (CAR)	HiA	5	9	3.35	29	11	0	7	83	88	7	33	65	7.0	1.45	.272
Minor League Totals			10	14	3.34	69	11	0	9	159	166	12	47	135	7.6	1.34	.268

30 JOE ORTIZ, LHP

BA GRADE 40 LOW

Born: Aug. 13, 1990. **B-T:** L-L. **Ht.:** 5-7. **Wt.:** 175. **Signed:** Venezuela, 2006. **Signed by:** Edgar Suarez.

The Rangers left Ortiz unprotected in both the 2010 and 2011 Rule 5 drafts, but they elected not to risk exposing him a third time, so they added him to their 40-man roster in November. The diminutive reliever turned a corner in 2012, so much so that Texas contemplated calling him up when it needed an extra bullpen lefty. The Rangers love Ortiz's aggressive approach and willingness to throw his plus slider in any count. His low-80s breaking ball makes him a prime candidate for a matchup reliever role in the big leagues. He struck out 25 and walked only one of the 100 lefthanders he faced in 2012, holding them to a .214/.222/.398 line. Thanks to a quick arm, Ortiz throws a 91-92 mph fastball with armside run, keeping hitters from sitting on his slider. However, the list of successful pitchers standing 5-foot-8 and shorter is, well, short. In the past decade, Tim Collins and Danny Ray Herrera are the only two hurlers that short who have worked 100 innings in the majors. Ortiz will try to buck those odds and should get his first callup some point in 2013.

Year	Club (League)	Class	W	L	ERA	G	GS	CG	SV	IP	H	HR	BB	SO	K/9	WHIP	AVG
2007	Rangers (DSL)	R	1	2	2.70	18	0	0	7	27	21	0	8	38	12.8	1.09	.212
2008	Rangers (AZL)	R	0	0	0.00	1	0	0	1	1	1	0	0	1	9.0	1.00	.333
	Clinton (MWL)	LoA	2	0	1.97	23	0	0	4	32	23	1	16	25	7.0	1.22	.204
2009	Hickory (SAL)	LoA	0	1	6.00	4	0	0	0	6	11	1	4	6	2.50	.344
	Spokane (NWL)	SS	2	0	2.95	18	0	0	0	37	32	4	5	38	9.3	1.01	.237
2010	Bakersfield (CAL)	HiA	0	0	3.86	2	0	0	0	2	3	0	1	4	15.4	1.71	.333
	Hickory (SAL)	LoA	4	1	1.50	26	0	0	5	42	30	2	5	59	12.6	0.83	.190
2011	Myrtle Beach (CAR)	HiA	5	5	2.15	40	0	0	5	67	54	4	14	55	7.4	1.01	.216
2012	Frisco (TL)	AA	1	2	2.35	27	0	0	4	31	26	2	6	29	8.5	1.04	.226
	Round Rock (PCL)	AAA	1	1	1.97	24	0	0	2	32	31	6	3	23	6.5	1.06	.254
Minor League Totals			16	12	2.28	183	0	0	28	276	232	20	62	278	9.1	1.06	.224

Toronto Blue Jays

BY NATHAN RODE

The Yankees and Red Sox long have dominated the American League East, while the Rays have bucked the financial odds and consistently contended for the last five seasons. With the Orioles' surprise run to the playoffs in 2012, the Blue Jays are the only team in the division that hasn't made the postseason in the last four years. Toronto hasn't visited the playoffs since 1993, when it won the second of consecutive World Series championships.

After spending his first two seasons on the job mostly trading veterans for prospects, GM Alex Anthopoulos has moved aggressively to end that drought in the last two offseasons. He took that to new levels in November, when he worked a 12-player megadeal with the Marlins, highlighted by the additions of shortstop Jose Reyes, lefthander Mark Buehrle and righthander Josh Johnson to the roster. It cost Toronto seven players, including three of its top eight prospects, but positions the team as one of the favorites in the AL East heading into 2013.

The Blue Jays had planned on contending in 2012, but injuries piled up and contributed to a 9-26 run from late July to early September. Jose Bautista, Kyle Drabek, promising rookies David Cooper and Drew Hutchison and trade acquisitions J.A. Happ and Sergio Santos ended the season on the disabled list. Toronto finished 73-89 for its fifth straight fourth-place finish and worst record since 2004.

Going into 2012, Anthopoulos had sent righthander Nestor Molina to the White Sox for Santos. With the Jays still trying to contend in July, they parted with four prospects (righthanders Kevin Comer, Joe Musgrove and Asher Wojciechowski, plus catcher Carlos Perez) to get Happ, David Carpenter and Brandon Lyon from the Astros. Toronto also gave up on two outfielders, shipping Travis Snider to the Pirates for Brad Lincoln, and Eric Thames to the Mariners for Steve Delabar.

While those deals have cost the organization a lot of its prospect depth, Toronto has continued to aggressively bring in talent through the draft and the international market. Toronto was as aggressive as any team under the new draft rules that went into effect in 2012, taking high-upside, high-dollar players with its seven picks in the first three rounds and then cheap college seniors in rounds four through 10.

The biggest bonus went to supplemental first-rounder Matt Smoral, a big lefty who signed for $2

John Farrell will head to Boston after the Blue Jays' disappointing 2012 season

million. Toronto also gave seven-figure bonuses to power righthander Marcus Stroman ($1.8 million), athletic outfielder D.J. Davis ($1.75 million) and power-hitting third baseman Mitch Nay ($1 million). They got the best athlete in the draft, outfielder Anthony Alford in the third round for $750,000, but with no guarantee he'll give up football.

On the international market, the Jays signed Venezuelan shortstop Franklin Barreto for $1.45 million and Dominican shortstop Richard Urena for $725,000. Baseball America rated Barreto as the top international prospect available in the 2012 class. Toronto landed another Venezuelan shortstop, Luis Castro, for $800,000 but voided the deal when he failed his physical.

After the draft, Toronto promoted scouting director Andrew Tinnish to assistant GM and called on professional crosschecker Brian Parker to replace Tinnish.

They made another significant personnel change in mid-October, trading manager John Farrell to the Red Sox for Mike Aviles. Boston showed interest in Farrell, its former pitching coach, a year earlier, but those talks broke down when Toronto asked for Clay Buchholz in return. The relationship between Anthopoulos and Farrell reportedly chilled in 2012, and the manager was entering the final season of his three-year contract.

THIS YEAR'S TOP 30

Player, Pos.		Grade
1.	Travis d'Arnaud, c	60/Medium
2.	Noah Syndergaard, rhp	60/High
3.	Aaron Sanchez, rhp	60/High
4.	Roberto Osuna, rhp	55/High
5.	Marcus Stroman, rhp	55/High
6.	D.J. Davis, of	60/Extreme
7.	John Stilson, rhp	50/Medium
8.	Daniel Norris, lhp	60/Extreme
9.	Matt Smoral, lhp	60/Extreme
10.	Anthony Alford, of	60/Extreme
11.	A.J. Jimenez, c	50/High
12.	Tyler Gonzales, rhp	50/High
13.	Franklin Barreto, ss/of	55/Extreme
14.	Santiago Nessy, c	50/High
15.	Alberto Tirado, rhp	50/High
16.	Dwight Smith Jr., of	50/High
17.	Matt Dean, 3b	50/High
18.	Chad Jenkins, rhp	45/Medium
19.	Sean Nolin, lhp	45/Medium
20.	Deck McGuire, rhp	45/Medium
21.	Kevin Pillar, of	45/Medium
22.	Chase DeJong, rhp	50/High
23.	Christian Lopes, 2b/ss	50/High
24.	Mitch Nay, 3b	50/High
25.	Wuilmer Becerra, of	50/Extreme
26.	Dawel Lugo, ss	50/Extreme
27.	Dickie Joe Thon, ss	50/Extreme
28.	Jairo Labourt, lhp	50/Extreme
29.	Yeyfry del Rosario, rhp	45/High
30.	Chris Hawkins, of	45/High

LAST YEAR'S TOP 30

Player, Pos.		Status
1.	Travis d'Arnaud, c	No. 1
2.	Anthony Gose, of	Majors
3.	Jake Marisnick, of	(Marlins)
4.	Daniel Norris, lhp	No. 8
5.	Justin Nicolino, lhp	(Marlins)
6.	Aaron Sanchez, rhp	No. 3
7.	Noah Syndergaard, rhp	No. 2
8.	Deck McGuire, rhp	No. 20
9.	Drew Hutchison, rhp	Majors
10.	Asher Wojciechowski, rhp	(Astros)
11.	Matt Dean, 3b	No. 17
12.	A.J. Jimenez, c	No. 11
13.	Adeiny Hechavarria, ss	(Marlins)
14.	Carlos Perez, c	(Astros)
15.	Moises Sierra, of	Majors
16.	Dwight Smith Jr., of	No. 16
17.	Kevin Comer, rhp	(Astros)
18.	Adonys Cardona, rhp	Dropped out
19.	Kellen Sweeney, 3b	Dropped out
20.	Joe Musgrove, rhp	(Astros)
21.	Jake Anderson, of	Dropped out
22.	David Cooper, 1b	Majors
23.	Michael Crouse, of	Dropped out
24.	Marcus Knecht, of	Dropped out
25.	Chris Hawkins, of	No. 30
26.	John Stilson, rhp	No. 7
27.	Dickie Joe Thon, ss	No. 27
28.	Chad Jenkins, rhp	No. 18
29.	Christian Lopes, ss	No. 23
30.	Roberto Osuna, rhp	No. 4

BEST TOOLS

Best Hitter for Average	Travis d'Arnaud
Best Power Hitter	Travis d'Arnaud
Best Strike-Zone Discipline	Kellen Sweeney
Fastest Baserunner	D.J. Davis
Best Athlete	Anthony Alford
Best Fastball	Aaron Sanchez
Best Curveball	Aaron Sanchez
Best Slider	Marcus Stroman
Best Changeup	John Stilson
Best Control	Sean Nolin
Best Defensive Catcher	A.J. Jimenez
Best Defensive Infielder	Jorge Flores
Best Infield Arm	Dickie Joe Thon
Best Defensive Outfielder	D.J. Davis
Best Outfield Arm	Anthony Alford

PROJECTED 2016 LINEUP

Catcher	Travis d'Arnaud
First Base	Edwin Encarnacion
Second Base	Emilio Bonifacio
Third Base	Brett Lawrie
Shortstop	Jose Reyes
Left Field	Melky Cabrera
Center Field	Anthony Gose
Right Field	Colby Rasmus
Designated Hitter	Jose Bautista
No. 1 Starter	Josh Johnson
No. 2 Starter	Noah Syndergaard
No. 3 Starter	Aaron Sanchez
No. 4 Starter	Brandon Morrow
No. 5 Starter	Mark Buehrle
Closer	Marcus Stroman

TOP PROSPECTS OF THE DECADE

Year	Player, Pos.	2012 Org.
2003	Dustin McGowan, rhp	Blue Jays
2004	Alex Rios, of	White Sox
2005	Brandon League, rhp	Dodgers
2006	Dustin McGowan, rhp	Blue Jays
2007	Adam Lind, of	Blue Jays
2008	Travis Snider, of	Pirates
2009	Travis Snider, of	Pirates
2010	Zach Stewart, rhp	Red Sox
2011	Kyle Drabek, rhp	Blue Jays
2012	Travis d'Arnaud, c	Blue Jays

TOP DRAFT PICKS OF THE DECADE

Year	Player, Pos.	2012 Org.
2003	Aaron Hill, ss	Diamondbacks
2004	David Purcey, lhp	Phillies
2005	Ricky Romero, lhp	Blue Jays
2006	Travis Snider, of	Pirates
2007	Kevin Ahrens, 3b	Blue Jays
2008	David Cooper, 1b	Blue Jays
2009	Chad Jenkins, rhp	Blue Jays
2010	Deck McGuire	Blue Jays
2011	*Tyler Beede, rhp	Vanderbilt
2012	D.J. Davis, of	Blue Jays

*Did not sign.

LARGEST BONUSES IN CLUB HISTORY

Adeinys Hechavarria, 2010	$4,000,000
Adonys Cardona, 2010	$2,800,000
Ricky Romero, 2005	$2,400,000
Felipe Lopez, 1998	$2,000,000
Deck McGuire, 2010	$2,000,000
Daniel Norris, 2011	$2,000,000
Matt Smoral, 2012	$2,000,000

TORONTO BLUE JAYS

TOP 2013 ROOKIE: Travis d'Arnaud, c. If he can just stay healthy, he could take over behind the plate in Toronto by the all-star break.

BREAKOUT PROSPECT: Dwight Smith Jr., of. The son of the ex-big leaguer with the same name, he's figuring out his timing at the plate.

SLEEPER: Tyler Ybarra, lhp. A 43rd-round pick in 2008, he has a fastball that can reach 95 mph and a slider that's a plus pitch at times.

SOURCE OF TOP 30 TALENT			
Homegrown	29	Acquired	1
College	5	Trades	1
Junior college	1	Rule 5 draft	0
High school	15	Independent leagues	0
Draft-and-follow	0	Free agents/waivers	0
Nondrafted free agents	0		
International	8		

LF	CF	RF
Dwight Smith Jr. (16)	D.J. Davis (6)	Jake Anderson
Wuilmer Becerra (25)	Anthony Alford (10)	Sawyer Carroll
Chris Hawkins (30)	Kevin Pillar (21)	Michael Crouse
Marcus Knecht	Dalton Pompey	Jesus Gonzalez
Eric Arce	Will Dupont	
John Tolisano	Dennis Jones	
Josh Almonte		
Nathan DeSouza		

3B	SS	2B	1B
Matt Dean (17)	Franklin Barreto (13)	Christian Lopes (23)	K.C. Hobson
Mitch Nay (24)	Dickie Joe Thon (27)	Ryan Goins	Art Charles
Dawel Lugo (26)	Andy Burns	Ryan Schimpf	
Kellen Sweeney	Richard Urena	Ronniel Demorizi	
Gustavo Pierre	Jorge Flores	Justin Atkinson	
	Kevin Nolan		

C
Travis d'Arnaud (1)
A.J. Jimenez (11)
Santiago Nessy (14)
Sean Ochinko
John Silviano

LHP		RHP	
LHSP	**LHRP**	**RHSP**	**RHRP**
Daniel Norris (8)	Tyler Ybarra	Noah Syndergaard (2)	Marcus Stroman (5)
Matt Smoral (9)	Evan Crawford	Aaron Sanchez (3)	John Stilson (7)
Sean Nolin (19)	Mitchell Taylor	Roberto Osuna (4)	Sam Dyson
Jairo Labourt (28)		Tyler Gonzales (12)	Ronald Uviedo
Griffin Murphy		Alberto Tirado (15)	Danny Barnes
Ryan Borucki		Chad Jenkins (18)	Chuck Ghysels
Zak Wasilewski		Deck McGuire (20)	
Alonzo Gonzalez		Chase DeJong (22)	
Colton Turner		Yeyfry del Rosario (29)	
		Adonys Cardona	
		Jesus Tinoco	
		Taylor Cole	
		Jeremy Gabryszwski	
		Tom Robson	
		Javier Avendano	

2012   BONUSES: $10.5 MILLION

BEST PURE HITTER: OF D.J. Davis (1) draws attention because of his supreme athleticism, and he has the tools to hit as well. He has strong hands, a fast bat and a sound lefthanded swing.

BEST POWER HITTER: 3B Mitch Nay (1s), whose pro debut was curtailed by a broken foot, generates easy power to all fields.

FASTEST RUNNER: Davis was the fastest player in the entire draft, running 6.4-second 60-yard dashes and consistently getting from home to first in less than four seconds. His speed is in the same class as that of minor league stolen base king Billy Hamilton, a fellow Mississippi high school prospect.

BEST DEFENSIVE PLAYER: SS Jorge Flores (19) made the short-season Northwest League all-star team in large part because of his glove. Just 5-foot-5, he has plus range and hands along with solid arm strength.

BEST FASTBALL: LHP Matt Smoral (1s) has the best fastball package as a lefthander with 92-96 mph heat from a difficult angle. The Blue Jays, who gave him $2 million, eased him back into action after he broke a bone in his right foot in March.

BEST SECONDARY PITCH: Stroman had the best slider in the entire draft, a nasty mid-80s pitch with nice depth. Toronto's draftees have a number of quality secondary offerings, including Smoral's slider, Tyler Gonzales' (12) slider, and RHP Chase DeJong's (2) curveball and changeup.

BEST PRO DEBUT: Stroman struck out 23 in 19 innings and reached Double-A before getting a 50-game ban for testing positive for a stimulant.

BEST ATHLETE: Alford gets the nod over Davis because of his superior strength. Alford informed teams in April that he wanted to play quarterback at Southern Mississippi rather than professional baseball, but the Blue Jays signed him for $750,000 while letting him play football as well.

MOST INTRIGUING BACKGROUND: Unsigned SS Nick Lovullo's (38) father Torey played in the majors and is the Red Sox's bench coach. Nay's grandfather Lou Klimchock also played in the big leagues. Gonzales' uncle Jimmy crosschecks for the Nationals.

CLOSEST TO THE MAJORS: Though his suspension will carry over into May, Stroman could pitch for the Blue Jays in the second half of 2013. They still haven't ruled out developing him as a starter.

BEST LATE-ROUND PICK: Borucki's $426,000 bonus was the largest after the 10th round in the entire draft. He slid after injuring his elbow in the spring, but avoided surgery and threw 90-94 mph during instructional league.

THE ONE WHO GOT AWAY: OF Grant Heyman (11), who went to Miami, has intriguing strength and speed.

ASSESSMENT: With five picks before the second round and an aggressive approach, the Blue Jays had an extremely productive draft. There's risk with many of the picks, but no team acquired more upside.

2011   BONUSES: $11.0 MILLION

Even without signing RHP Tyler Beede (1), the Blue Jays still spent $11 million. Most of the players are off to slow starts, leaving RHP John Stilson (3) as the crop's best prospect to this point. RHPs Joe Musgrove (1s), Kevin Comer (1s) and LHP David Rollins (24) were part of a 10-player deal that brought J.A. Happ and Brandon Lyon from the Astros in July. RHP Anthony DeSclafani (6) was a piece in the 12-player November trade with the Marlins.

GRADE: B

2010   BONUSES: $11.6 MILLION

Toronto loaded up on pitching, with RHPs Aaron Sanchez (1s) and Noah Syndergaard (1s) looking like its aces of the future. RHP Deck McGuire (1) regressed last year, while RHP Asher Wojciechowski (1s) was part of the Houston trade and LHP Justin Nicolino (2) departed in the Miami deal. RHP Sam Dyson (4) has pitched briefly in the majors.

GRADE: B+

2009   BONUSES: $4.9 MILLION

Though the Jays failed to sign three of its top four picks, including LHP James Paxton (1s), they did find talent in OF Jake Marisnick (3) and RHP Drew Hutchison (15). They lost Marisnick in the Marlins deal, however, and Hutchison had Tommy John surgery last year. RHP Chad Jenkins (1), LHP Aaron Loup (9) and since-traded C/1B/3B Yan Gomes (10) have seen big league action.

GRADE: B

2008   BONUSES: $4.4 MILLION

Toronto found five big leaguers in 1B David Cooper (1), SS Tyler Pastornicky (5), OF Eric Thames (7), LHP Evan Crawford (8) and RHP Danny Farquhar (10). But none may be a regular, Pastornicky and Thames have been traded and Farquhar was waiver. C A.J. Jimenez (9) may be the best.

GRADE: C+

Draft analysis by Jim Callis. Numbers in parentheses indicate draft rounds.

1 TRAVIS D'ARNAUD, C

Born: Feb. 10, 1989. **B-T:** R-R. **Ht.:** 6-2. **Wt.:** 195.
Drafted: HS—Lakewood, Calif., 2007 (1st round supplemental). **Signed by:** Tim Kissner (Phillies).

The Phillies made d'Arnaud the 37th overall pick and signed him for $837,500 in 2007, one year before the Pirates took his older brother Chase in the fourth round out of Pepperdine. While Chase made it to the majors first, debuting in 2011, Travis has a much brighter future. Had Philadelphia gone a different route, the Blue Jays would have chosen d'Arnaud with the 38th selection in 2007, but they managed to acquire him two years later. He came to Toronto in a package with Kyle Drabek and Michael Taylor for Roy Halladay in December 2009. Slowed by back problems in his first year with Toronto, d'Arnaud broke out in 2011 by overcoming an April concussion to hit .311/.371/.542 with 21 homers at Double-A New Hampshire. After winning the Eastern League MVP award and helping the Fisher Cats to a championship, he joined Team USA for the World Cup in Panama but tore a ligament in his left thumb. D'Arnaud came out swinging again in 2012, batting .333/.380/.595 with 16 homers in 67 games at Triple-A Las Vegas. On track to get his first call to the majors, he tore the posterior cruciate ligament in his left knee while trying to break up a double play in late June. He didn't require surgery but did miss the rest of the season.

D'Arnaud has the tools to become an all-star if he can stay healthy. He's a rare catcher with the potential to be an above-average hitter with plus power. He doesn't walk much but makes consistent hard contact, getting hits even when his timing is off or he gets off balance. He has the bat speed and strength to hit plenty of homers and lets his power come naturally, employing a short stroke and all-fields approach. Though he has played in extremely hitter-friendly home ballparks the last two years, his pop is legitimate, as 18 of his 37 homers have come on the road. D'Arnaud made good strides with his defense in 2011 by working with then-New Hampshire manager Sal Butera, who caught in the majors for nine seasons. Those improvements carried over to 2012, when d'Arnaud threw out a career-high 30 percent of basestealers. He has average to plus arm strength and has refined his footwork and throwing accuracy. He's a solid receiver who moves well behind the plate, and he's a good leader who works well with his pitching staffs. Like most catchers, he's a below-average runner but isn't a liability on the bases.

The Blue Jays control J.P. Arencibia through 2016, so they don't need to rush d'Arnaud, but he is a better overall hitter and defender. D'Arnaud likely will return to Triple-A for some refinement at the beginning of 2013, but he's clearly Toronto's backstop of the future and arguably the best catching prospect in the minor leagues. He's on the 40-man roster, and if he avoids another injury, he may be ready for his major league debut by midseason.

SCOUTING GRADES

Batting: 60. **Defense:** 55.
Power: 60. **Arm:** 55.
Speed: 30.

Based on 20-80 scouting scale, where 50 represents major league average, and future projection rather than present tools.

Year	Club (League)	Class	AVG	G	AB	R	H	2B	3B	HR	RBI	BB	SO	SB	CS	OBP	SLG
2007	Phillies (GCL)	R	.241	41	141	18	34	3	0	4	20	4	23	4	2	.278	.348
2008	Williamsport (NYP)	SS	.309	48	175	21	54	13	1	4	25	18	29	1	0	.371	.463
	Lakewood (SAL)	LoA	.297	16	64	12	19	5	0	2	5	5	10	0	0	.357	.469
2009	Lakewood (SAL)	LoA	.255	126	482	71	123	38	1	13	71	41	75	8	4	.319	.419
2010	Dunedin (FSL)	HiA	.259	71	263	36	68	20	1	6	38	20	63	3	1	.315	.411
2011	New Hampshire (EL)	AA	.311	114	424	72	132	33	1	21	78	33	100	4	2	.371	.542
2012	Las Vegas (PCL)	AAA	.333	67	279	45	93	21	2	16	52	19	59	1	1	.380	.595
Minor League Totals			.286	483	1828	275	523	133	6	66	289	140	359	21	12	.343	.474

2 NOAH SYNDERGAARD, RHP

BA GRADE

60

HIGH

Born: Aug. 29, 1992. **B-T:** R-R. **Ht.:** 6-5. **Wt.:** 200. **Drafted:** HS—Mansfield, Texas, 2010 (1st round supplemental). **Signed by:** Steve Miller.

The Blue Jays promoted area scout Steve Miller to crosschecker after he diligently followed Syndergaard in 2010. Syndergaard went from throwing 87-90 mph at the start of the spring to 92-94 mph just before the draft, and Miller persuaded Toronto to draft him 38th overall. Signed for a below-slot $600,000, he has posted a 2.35 ERA and averaged 10 strikeouts per nine innings as a pro. Syndergaard's big frame gives him an imposing presence on the mound, and his fastball only adds to it. His heater ranges from 92-98 mph with excellent downward angle and armside run. His curveball has gained velocity since he signed and now sits in the mid-70s with downward action. It's inconsistent and eventually may develop into a slider, but it gets outs and features good spin. He maintains his arm speed well on his changeup. He has good body control for his size, which leads to quality command and control. Syndergaard and fellow 2010 sandwich pick Aaron Sanchez have risen through the minors together and will team again in 2013 at high Class A Dunedin. Both have the ceiling of a frontline starter, with Syndergaard not quite matching Sanchez in stuff but outshining him in terms of polish.

Year	Club (League)	Class	W	L	ERA	G	GS	CG	SV	IP	H	HR	BB	SO	K/9	WHIP	AVG
2010	Blue Jays (GCL)	R	0	1	2.70	5	5	0	0	13	11	0	4	6	4.1	1.13	.229
2011	Bluefield (APP)	R	4	0	1.41	7	5	0	0	32	23	1	11	37	10.4	1.06	.198
	Vancouver (NWL)	SS	1	2	2.00	4	4	0	0	18	15	0	5	22	11.0	1.11	.221
	Lansing (MWL)	LoA	0	0	3.00	2	2	0	0	9	8	0	2	9	9.0	1.11	.235
2012	Lansing (MWL)	LoA	8	5	2.60	27	19	0	1	104	81	3	31	122	10.6	1.08	.212
Minor League Totals			13	8	2.35	45	35	0	1	176	138	4	53	196	10.0	1.09	.213

3 AARON SANCHEZ, RHP

BA GRADE

60

HIGH

Born: July 1, 1992. **B-T:** R-R. **Ht.:** 6-4. **Wt.:** 180. **Drafted:** HS—Barstow, Calif., 2010 (1st round supplemental). **Signed by:** Blake Crosby.

With his lanky frame and long limbs, Sanchez drew comparisons to Orel Hershiser on the high school showcase circuit in 2009. The Blue Jays were excited to get him with the 34th overall pick the following June and signed him for a below-slot $775,000. Toronto generally handles its young arms with caution, and has limited Sanchez to 170 innings in three pro seasons. He has the best stuff in the system and some of the best in the entire minors. His quick arm generates fastballs that range from 94-98 mph with little effort. His curveball has tight spin and gives him a second plus pitch, and even his changeup features effective late movement. There's still projection remaining in his body as well. The knock against Sanchez is his command. He has averaged five walks per nine innings as a pro, and he has gotten many of his strikeouts when lower-level hitters have chased pitches out of the zone. Even if he doesn't add any strength, Sanchez has enough stuff to succeed at higher levels. More advanced hitters will force him to throw more strikes, but he won't need pinpoint command to pitch in the front half of a big league rotation. He'll advance to high Class A in 2013.

Year	Club (League)	Class	W	L	ERA	G	GS	CG	SV	IP	H	HR	BB	SO	K/9	WHIP	AVG
2010	Blue Jays (GCL)	R	0	2	1.42	8	8	0	0	19	19	1	12	28	13.3	1.63	.271
	Auburn (NYP)	SS	0	1	4.50	2	2	0	0	6	4	0	5	9	13.5	1.50	.182
2011	Bluefield (APP)	R	3	2	5.48	11	6	0	1	43	45	4	18	43	9.1	1.48	.269
	Vancouver (NWL)	SS	0	1	4.63	3	3	0	0	12	8	0	8	13	10.0	1.37	.195
2012	Lansing (MWL)	LoA	8	5	2.49	25	18	0	0	90	64	3	51	97	9.7	1.27	.204
Minor League Totals			11	11	3.34	49	37	0	1	170	140	8	94	190	10.1	1.38	.228

4 ROBERTO OSUNA, RHP

Born: Feb. 7, 1995. **B-T:** R-R. **Ht.:** 6-2. **Wt.:** 230. **Signed:** Mexico, 2011. **Signed by:** Marco Paddy.

The nephew of Antonio Osuna, a major league reliever for 11 seasons, Roberto attracted attention by popping 94 mph with his fastball as a 15-year-old at an international tournament in 2010. He made his pro debut at age 16 in the Mexican League with the Mexico City Red Devils, who sold his rights to Toronto in August 2011 for $1.5 million. Osuna turned in a strong U.S. debut as a 17-year-old, fanning 49 in 44 innings and holding his own against much older hitters in the short-season Northwest League. Osuna doesn't have the same projection as fellow Mexican righthander Luis Heredia, whom the Pirates signed in 2010 for $2.6 million, but scouts say their stuff is similar. Osuna has a plus fastball that ranges from 91-96 mph, with the ability to add and subtract from it as needed. His changeup is a plus pitch, and he's still seeking a consistent grip and release point for his slurvy slider. Some scouts had concerns about Osuna's thick frame, but he has done a good job of keeping his conditioning in check. He has a clean delivery and enough athleticism to maintain at least average command. With his moxie and feel for pitching, Osuna may advance more quickly than expected. The Blue Jays have no reason to rush the potential No. 3 starter, however, and he'll spend 2013 in low Class A Lansing.

BA GRADE
55
HIGH

Year	Club (League)	Class	W	L	ERA	G	GS	CG	SV	IP	H	HR	BB	SO	K/9	WHIP	AVG
2011	Mexico City (MEX)	AAA	0	1	5.49	13	2	0	0	20	25	3	11	12	5.5	1.83	—
2012	Bluefield (APP)	R	1	0	1.50	7	4	0	0	24	18	1	6	24	9.0	1.00	.209
	Vancouver (NWL)	SS	1	0	3.20	5	5	0	0	20	14	1	9	25	11.4	1.17	.192
Minor League Totals			2	1	3.27	25	11	0	0	63	57	5	26	61	8.7	1.31	.201

5 MARCUS STROMAN, RHP

Born: May 1, 1991. **B-T:** R-R. **Ht.:** 5-9. **Wt.:** 185. **Drafted:** Duke, 2012 (1st round). **Signed by:** John Hendricks.

After starring in college, with Team USA and in the Cape Cod League during the summer, Stroman became Duke's first-ever first-round pick. The Blue Jays drafted him 22nd overall in June with the pick they received for failing to sign 2011 first-rounder Tyler Beede. Stroman signed for $1.8 million and quickly reached Double-A before testing positive for a stimulant and drawing a 50-game suspension. Don't be fooled by Stroman's diminutive frame. He has quick-twitch athleticism and the ball explodes out of his hand. His fastball sits at 92-94 mph when he starts and can reach 98 when he relieves. He has two variations of a breaking ball: a mid-80s slider with big break and a harder, shorter cutter at 88-90 mph. He also mixes in a good changeup. He maintains his velocity well into starts but will need better command to remain a starter. The Blue Jays aren't ruling out developing Stroman as a starter despite his size. He relieved in his pro debut to keep his workload light, and if he stays in that role he could surface in Toronto before the end of 2013. He has the upside of a frontline starter or a closer. When his suspension ends in May, he'll probably return to Double-A.

BA GRADE
55
HIGH

Year	Club (League)	Class	W	L	ERA	G	GS	CG	SV	IP	H	HR	BB	SO	K/9	WHIP	AVG
2012	Vancouver (NWL)	SS	1	0	3.18	7	0	0	0	11	8	0	3	15	11.9	0.97	.190
	New Hampshire (EL)	AA	2	0	3.38	8	0	0	0	8	8	1	6	8	9.0	1.75	.258
Minor League Totals			3	0	3.26	15	0	0	0	19	16	1	9	23	10.7	1.29	.219

6 D.J. DAVIS, OF

Born: July 25, 1994. **B-T:** R-R. **Ht.:** 5-11. **Wt.:** 170. **Drafted:** HS—Wiggins, Miss., 2012 (1st round). **Signed by:** Brian Johnston.

With their first of five picks before the second round of the 2012 draft, the Blue Jays selected Davis 17th overall. He signed quickly for $1.75 million, allowing him to play 60 pro games and reach short-season Vancouver before the end of the summer. The track record of Mississippi high school prospects is downright poor, but Davis is more athletic and polished than most of them. Some scouts believe his pure speed rivals that of fellow Mississippi burner Billy Hamilton, who destroyed the minor league stolen base record in 2012. Davis repeatedly gets from the right side of the plate to first base in less than four seconds, creates havoc on the basepaths and has excellent range in center field. He can use his quickness to get on base too, though he's more than a slap hitter. He has a short, whippy swing and keeps the bat in the hitting zone for a long time. He has strong hands

BA GRADE
60
EXTREME

and can pull the ball with authority, giving him the potential for double-digit home run totals. His weakest tool is his arm, which is fringy but playable. Davis may be advanced enough at the plate to handle an assignment to low Class A at the start of 2013. More likely, he'll hang back in extended spring training before returning to Vancouver in June.

Year	Club (League)	Class	AVG	G	AB	R	H	2B	3B	HR	RBI	BB	SO	SB	CS	OBP	SLG
2012	Blue Jays (GCL)	R	.233	43	163	30	38	7	2	4	12	18	54	18	7	.339	.374
	Bluefield (APP)	R	.340	12	47	9	16	3	1	1	6	4	10	6	2	.415	.511
	Vancouver (NWL)	SS	.167	5	18	3	3	0	0	0	0	5	6	1	1	.348	.167
Minor League Totals			.250	60	228	42	57	10	3	5	18	27	70	25	10	.355	.386

7 JOHN STILSON, RHP

Born: July 28, 1990. **B-T:** R-R. **Ht.:** 6-3. **Wt.:** 200. **Drafted:** Texas A&M, 2011 (3rd round). **Signed by:** C.J. Ebarb.

BA GRADE
50
MEDIUM

Stilson led NCAA Division I with a 0.80 ERA in 2010 and was pitching himself into the first round of the 2011 draft before hurting his shoulder that May. The injury turned out to be a torn labrum, and the initial diagnosis called for shoulder surgery. Stilson got a second opinion from Dr. James Andrews, however, who said the tear was not as bad as originally believed and that rest, rehabilitation and a throwing program would suffice. The Blue Jays gambled a third-round pick and $500,000 on Stilson, who reached Double-A in his 2012 pro debut. Stilson has two plus pitches in a fastball that usually ranges from 93-96 mph and a wipeout changeup with tremendous sink. He also has a hard breaking ball that he can manipulate to resemble either a curveball or a slider. He throws with a lot of effort and across his body, which adds deception but also puts stress on his shoulder and hampers his command, so he probably fits best in the bullpen. Stilson has the stuff and competitive demeanor to be a set-up man or closer. He spent a short stint on the disabled list at midseason with shoulder tightness, which Toronto deemed minor, but the organization shifted him to the bullpen in August to limit his innings. Staying there might be the best way to keep him healthy and could get him to the big leagues in 2013. He got knocked around at New Hampshire, so he may return there to start the season.

Year	Club (League)	Class	W	L	ERA	G	GS	CG	SV	IP	H	HR	BB	SO	K/9	WHIP	AVG
2012	Dunedin (FSL)	HiA	3	0	2.82	13	13	0	0	54	56	2	19	47	7.8	1.38	.265
	New Hampshire (EL)	AA	2	4	5.04	17	9	0	1	50	54	6	23	44	7.9	1.54	.277
Minor League Totals			5	4	3.88	30	22	0	1	104	110	8	42	91	7.8	1.46	.271

8 DANIEL NORRIS, LHP

Born: April 25, 1993. **B-T:** L-L. **Ht.:** 6-2. **Wt.:** 180. **Drafted:** HS—Johnson City, Tenn., 2011 (2nd round). **Signed by:** Nate Murrie.

BA GRADE
60
EXTREME

The top high school lefthander in the 2011 draft class, Norris was projected as a mid-first-round pick, but teams were wary of his commitment to Clemson. Taking advantage of extra picks, the Blue Jays selected him in the second round—their sixth choice at No. 74 overall—and handed him a $2 million bonus at the signing deadline. His signing took some of the sting out of failing to land first-round pick Tyler Beede, who headed to Vanderbilt, but Norris' 2012 pro debut couldn't have gone much worse. He posted an 8.44 ERA as lower-level hitters batted .320 against him. Toronto attributed his struggles to adapting to changes in his delivery and approach. His mechanics were out of sync much of the season, and he couldn't find a consistent balance point, causing his arm to drag and costing him extension out front. That detracted from his fastball command, leading him to pitch behind in the count and up in the zone. Norris is very athletic—he was a quarterback until his senior year and showed easy power as a hitter—so he should be able to adapt to the adjustments over time. When he's on, Norris has a low-90s fastball that touches 96 mph, flashes the ability to spin a plus curveball and shows feel for a changeup. For all his struggles, he still struck out more than a batter per inning. Norris has front-of-the-rotation stuff but clearly needs better command to maximize his potential. His performance in spring training will determine his 2013 assignment, and he could begin the season in low Class A.

Year	Club (League)	Class	W	L	ERA	G	GS	CG	SV	IP	H	HR	BB	SO	K/9	WHIP	AVG
2012	Bluefield (APP)	R	2	3	7.97	11	10	0	0	35	44	4	13	38	9.8	1.63	.301
	Vancouver (NWL)	SS	0	1	10.57	2	2	0	0	8	14	0	5	5	5.9	2.48	.400
Minor League Totals			2	4	8.44	13	12	0	0	43	58	4	18	43	9.1	1.78	.320

9 MATT SMORAL, LHP

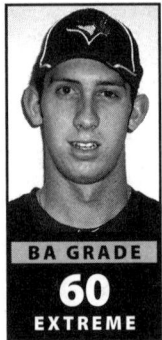

Born: March 18, 1994. **B-T:** L-L. **Ht.:** 6-8. **Wt.:** 220. **Drafted:** HS—Solon, Ohio, 2012 (1st round supplemental). **Signed by:** Couslon Barbiche.

Entering his high school senior season in 2012, Smoral was in the running to be the top prep lefthander in the draft. He carried over a strong performance on the high school showcase circuit into his first scrimmage of the spring, when he dominated in front of 50 scouts. In his first regular-season start, however, he struggled to throw strikes and left the game early with blisters. It would be his last time on the mound for Solon High, as doctors found he had a broken bone in his right foot. He had surgery in early April and wasn't able to pitch before the signing deadline, but the Blue Jays still took him 50th overall and signed him away from a North Carolina commitment for $2 million. When healthy, Smoral fires a 92-96 mph fastball from a low three-quarters arm slot that creates a tough angle for hitters. His slider is a plus pitch that sits in the low 80s. Like most high school pitchers, he needs to develop a changeup. He's tall and lanky, so he's still growing into his body and learning to repeat his pitches, but he has the athleticism to figure it out. A potential frontline starter, Smoral returned to the mound in instructional league. He'll head to extended spring training and make his professional debut at one of the Jays' short-season stops in June.

BA GRADE

60

EXTREME

Year	Club (League)	Class	W	L	ERA	G	GS	CG	SV	IP	H	HR	BB	SO	K/9	WHIP	AVG
Did Not Play—Injured																	

10 ANTHONY ALFORD, OF

Born: July 20, 1994. **B-T:** R-R. **Ht.:** 6-1. **Wt.:** 195. **Drafted:** HS—Petal, Miss., 2012 (3rd round). **Signed by:** Brian Johnston.

The best athlete in the 2012 draft class, Alford likely would have been a first-round pick if not for his standout two-sport prowess. He had a scholarship to play quarterback at Southern Mississippi and told teams that he intended to play both baseball and football in college, which also raised questions about his signability. Alford was the first player to win Mississippi's football player of the year award as both a junior and senior, and he led Petal High's baseball team to 6-A baseball championships as a sophomore and junior. The Blue Jays drafted him in the third round and signed him for $750,000, with the provision that they would allow him to play college football. Alford was arguably Southern Miss' best player as a freshman, starting five games and appearing in four more with a team-high 993 yards of total offense. But he also dealt with knee and ankle injuries that kept him out of three games and limited him in several others, and the Golden Eagles suffered through the worst season in school history at 0-12. Alford was then arrested in November after an on-campus fight in which another student reportedly brandished a gun. After hiring a new coach, Southern Miss released Alford from his scholarship. Alford has more polish in baseball than most two-sport stars. He has a short, quick swing and power to all fields. He has the tools to be an excellent defender in center field because he's a plus-plus runner with solid arm strength. The Blue Jays believed Alford's athleticism made him worth the gamble, but it's a considerable one, and it's not clear how recent events could affect his football future. He could transfer to another school for football, or turn his focus completely to baseball. Though he may not be ready for a full-season assignment, Toronto may send him to low Class A in the spring to maximize his at-bats.

BA GRADE

60

EXTREME

Year	Club (League)	Class	AVG	G	AB	R	H	2B	3B	HR	RBI	BB	SO	SB	CS	OBP	SLG
2012	Blue Jays (GCL)	R	.167	5	18	1	3	0	0	1	1	2	4	4	0	.250	.333
Minor League Totals			.167	5	18	1	3	0	0	1	1	2	4	4	0	.250	.333

11 A.J. JIMENEZ, C

BA GRADE

50

HIGH

Born: May 1, 1990. **B-T:** R-R. **Ht.:** 5-11. **Wt.:** 200. **Drafted:** HS—Bayamon, P.R., 2008 (9th round). **Signed by:** Jorge Rivera.

Some clubs considered Jimenez a third-round talent in 2008, but questions about his elbow dropped him to the ninth round, where he signed for $150,000. He stayed healthy in his first four pro seasons, emerging as the system's best defensive catcher, but his elbow issues resurfaced in 2012. He appeared in just 27 games before requiring Tommy John surgery. The track record with elbow reconstruction is encouraging, so Jimenez should regain the above-average, accurate arm that has helped him throw out 43 percent of pro basestealers. He also blocks and receives well, and he shows aptitude for handling a pitching staff. Jimenez's offense has started to catch up to his defense. He has good bat speed and has improved his pitch recognition. He lacks power, but he can drive the ball to the opposite field and should be able to handle the bat well enough to be an everyday big leaguer. He's a below-average runner, but not bad for a catcher. Once he's back to full strength,

Jimenez will return to Double-A. The Blue Jays protected him on their 40-man roster in November.

Year	Club (League)	Class	AVG	G	AB	R	H	2B	3B	HR	RBI	BB	SO	SB	CS	OBP	SLG
2008	Blue Jays (GCL)	R	.191	19	47	5	9	2	0	0	5	3	16	5	2	.255	.234
2009	Lansing (MWL)	LoA	.263	80	278	30	73	15	1	3	31	7	72	5	2	.280	.356
2010	Lansing (MWL)	LoA	.305	70	262	35	80	22	0	4	54	18	56	17	4	.347	.435
	Dunedin (FSL)	HiA	.111	2	9	1	1	0	0	1	1	0	5	0	0	.111	.444
2011	Dunedin (FSL)	HiA	.303	102	379	49	115	29	1	4	52	28	60	11	2	.353	.417
2012	New Hampshire (EL)	AA	.257	27	105	14	27	4	1	2	10	5	14	2	3	.295	.371
Minor League Totals			.282	300	1080	134	305	72	3	14	153	61	223	40	13	.322	.394

12 TYLER GONZALES, RHP

BA GRADE

50

HIGH

Born: Jan. 22, 1993. **B-T:** R-R. **Ht.:** 6-2. **Wt.:** 170. **Drafted:** HS—San Antonio, 2012 (1st round supplemental). **Signed by:** Mike Burns.

A two-way player in high school, Gonzales showed modest stuff the summer before his senior year but took a big step forward in 2012. His fastball velocity jumped at least a grade and his slider also blossomed, and the nephew of Nationals crosschecker Jimmy Gonzales pitched his way into the supplemental first round of the draft. Signed for $750,000, he wasn't quite as sharp in his pro debut. After sitting at 88-92 mph with his fastball in his first spring outing, Gonzales jumped to 93-95 and touched 98 several times. He maintains his velocity deep into games. He also possesses an overpowering slider that operates in the mid-80s and has hit 90 mph. Gonzales will need a changeup and improved command to stay a starter, but his fastball and slider give him a ceiling of a closer if he shifts to the bullpen. The effort in his delivery also might dictate a future in relief. Old for his draft class, Gonzales will pitch at age 20 in 2013. Given the limited innings in his debut, he may start the season in extended spring training.

Year	Club (League)	Class	W	L	ERA	G	GS	CG	SV	IP	H	HR	BB	SO	K/9	WHIP	AVG
2012	Blue Jays (GCL)	R	1	1	8.40	9	3	0	0	15	20	1	4	7	4.2	1.60	.328
Minor League Totals			1	1	8.40	9	3	0	0	15	20	1	4	7	4.2	1.60	.328

13 FRANKLIN BARRETO, SS/OF

BA GRADE

55

EXTREME

Born: Feb. 27, 1996. **B-T:** R-R. **Ht.:** 5-9. **Wt.:** 175. **Signed:** Venezuela, 2012. **Signed by:** Ismael Cruz/Luis Marquez.

Rated the top prospect in the 2012 international amateur class, Barreto began playing for Venezuela in international tournaments at age 10. He was the MVP at the 12-and-under Pan American Championship in 2008 and at the 14-and-under Pan Am Championship in 2010. Signed for $1.45 million, he has advanced skills that could lead him to bypass the Rookie-level Dominican Summer League and debut in the Rookie-level Gulf Coast League in 2013. Barreto's best tools are his bat and speed. More mature at the plate than most international prospects, he has quick hands and a short swing. He recognizes pitches well and projects as an above-average hitter. He has a small frame and doesn't offer a lot of physical projection, but he's already strong and could hit for average power. Barreto is a plus-plus runner with solid arm strength, though there isn't much support for him staying at shortstop in the long term. The Blue Jays will have him play there to open his career, but he lacks classic footwork and actions for the position. His speed would fit well in center field if shortstop doesn't work out.

Year	Club (League)	Class	AVG	G	AB	R	H	2B	3B	HR	RBI	BB	SO	SB	CS	OBP	SLG
Did Not Play—Signed 2013 Contract																	

14 SANTIAGO NESSY, C

BA GRADE

50

HIGH

Born: Dec. 8, 1992. **B-T:** R-R. **Ht.:** 6-2. **Wt.:** 220. **Signed:** Venezuela, 2009. **Signed by:** Rafael Moncada.

Since signing with Toronto for $750,000 as a 16-year-old in 2009, Nessy has moved through the system step by step. He has yet to play in a full-season league, though he did finish last season in Vancouver at age 19. Nessy stands out most for his above-average raw power. He combines strength and a quick bat to drive balls a long way. However, he's still raw at the plate because he takes an overly aggressive swing and is too pull-conscious. Nessy weighed 190 pounds when he signed but now checks in at 220, leading to skepticism about his chances to stick behind the plate. He earned high marks for his defense in the Rookie-level Appalachian League, where he threw out 33 percent of basestealers. He has an above-average, accurate arm, though he can rush his throws at times. He blocks balls well, and his bilingual skills help him manage a pitching staff. Nessy should get his first crack at full-season ball in 2013.

Year	Club (League)	Class	AVG	G	AB	R	H	2B	3B	HR	RBI	BB	SO	SB	CS	OBP	SLG
2010	Blue Jays (DSL)	R	.248	44	141	15	35	12	0	2	17	14	44	4	0	.327	.376

Year	Club (League)		AVG	G	AB	R	H	2B	3B	HR	RBI	BB	SO	SB	CS	OBP	SLG
2011	Blue Jays (GCL)	R	.306	35	134	12	41	7	0	3	19	8	29	0	2	.347	.425
2012	Bluefield (APP)	R	.256	45	160	26	41	8	0	8	23	13	47	0	0	.320	.456
	Vancouver (NWL)	SS	.091	6	22	4	2	1	0	1	3	3	7	0	0	.200	.273
Minor League Totals			.260	130	457	57	119	28	0	14	62	38	127	4	2	.324	.414

15 ALBERTO TIRADO, RHP

BA GRADE
50
HIGH

Born: Dec. 10, 1994. **B-T:** R-R. **Ht.:** 6-1. **Wt.:** 175. **Signed:** Dominican Republic, 2011. **Signed by:** Marco Paddy/Domingo Toribio.

The Blue Jays have emphasized amateur talent acquisition under general manager Alex Anthopoulos, spending heavily on the draft as well as the international market. They gave 12 international amateurs six-figure bonuses in 2011, including a $300,000 deal for Tirado. He came straight to the United States for his 2012 pro debut, pitching well in two Rookie leagues at age 17. Tirado isn't imposing on the mound, but he has long, skinny arms and plenty of projection. Toronto expected him to add velocity to a fastball that topped out at 91 mph as an amateur, and he's already working at 91-94 mph and touching 96. He commands his fastball in the lower half of the strike zone, leading to plenty of groundouts. He also does a good job of locating his solid changeup. His slider lags behind his other two pitches, and he has abandoned a curveball he threw as an amateur. Tirado is far away from the big leagues, but has the fastball, command and athleticism to be a mid-rotation starter if his secondary stuff develops. There's no need to rush him, so he probably won't make his full-season debut until 2014.

Year	Club (League)		Class	W	L	ERA	G	GS	CG	SV	IP	H	HR	BB	SO	K/9	WHIP	AVG
2012	Blue Jays (GCL)		R	1	2	2.68	11	11	0	0	37	28	0	12	34	8.3	1.08	.217
	Bluefield (APP)		R	2	0	2.45	3	3	0	0	11	4	0	5	5	4.1	0.82	.121
Minor League Totals				3	2	2.63	14	14	0	0	48	32	0	17	39	7.3	1.02	.198

16 DWIGHT SMITH JR., OF

BA GRADE
50
HIGH

Born: Oct. 26, 1992. **B-T:** L-R. **Ht.:** 5-11. **Wt.:** 180. **Drafted:** HS—McIntosh, Ga., 2011 (1st round supplemental). **Signed by:** Eric McQueen.

Scouts lauded the son of the former big leaguer as one of the best high school bats in the 2011 draft. The Blue Jays swayed him from a commitment to Georgia Tech by taking him 53rd overall and paying him $800,000. He signed too late to debut in 2011, and his performance last summer didn't live up to his scouting reports. While his .212/.279/.315 batting line raised concerns, the Blue Jays note that Smith was just 19 and that he didn't struggle to make contact. He has a simple swing that allows him to consistently make hard contact. He has the bat speed to generate solid power, and he could take off once he tones down a high leg kick that can hinder his timing. Smith saw time in both center and left field in 2012, but his solid speed and below-average arm make him a better fit in left. That would put more demands on his bat, and he'll show more about how well he can meet them when he gets to low Class A this year. Toronto gave him a look at second base in instructional league and could revisit that in the future.

Year	Club (League)		Class	AVG	G	AB	R	H	2B	3B	HR	RBI	BB	SO	SB	CS	OBP	SLG
2012	Bluefield (APP)		R	.226	41	159	20	36	6	0	4	21	11	22	1	1	.289	.340
	Vancouver (NWL)		SS	.175	18	63	5	11	3	1	0	8	6	11	0	0	.254	.254
Minor League Totals				.212	59	222	25	47	9	1	4	29	17	33	1	1	.279	.315

17 MATT DEAN, 3B

BA GRADE
50
HIGH

Born: Dec. 22, 1992. **B-T:** R-R. **Ht.:** 6-3. **Wt.:** 190. **Drafted:** HS—The Colony, Texas, 2011 (13th round). **Signed by:** Michael Wagner.

As an amateur, Dean grabbed scouts' attention with his physical frame and projection. He didn't wow them on the showcase circuit, but a strong senior season made him the top third-base prospect in the 2011 draft class. His strong commitment to Texas scared teams off and dropped him to the 13th round, but the Blue Jays were able to sign him for $737,500. Like many high-priced Toronto draft picks, Dean had a modest pro debut at Bluefield in 2012. He has a lot of work to do with his hitting. He tends to jump at the ball rather than letting it travel deep, and he has too much head movement. He has been able to get his upper and lower half in sync better, after he used to be an upper-body pull hitter. He has plus power to all fields but won't tap into it unless he makes adjustments and more contact. A shortstop in high school, Dean should develop into a good defender at third with a plus arm, though he made 24 errors in 47 games last season. He's an average runner who may lose a half-step as he matures physically. Dean's progress in the spring will determine his 2013 assignment, and he may need time at Vancouver before he's ready for full-season ball.

Year	Club (League)		Class	AVG	G	AB	R	H	2B	3B	HR	RBI	BB	SO	SB	CS	OBP	SLG
2012	Bluefield (APP)		R	.222	49	167	22	37	8	4	2	24	12	60	3	2	.282	.353
Minor League Totals				.222	49	167	22	37	8	4	2	24	12	60	3	2	.282	.353

18 CHAD JENKINS, RHP

Born: Dec. 22, 1987. **B-T:** R-R. **Ht.:** 6-4. **Wt.:** 235. **Drafted:** Kennesaw State, 2009 (1st round). **Signed by:** Matt Briggs.

BA GRADE
45
MEDIUM

When scouts traveled to Kennesaw State to see righthander Kyle Heckathorn in 2009, they came away more enamored with his teammate. Jenkins went 20th overall—27 picks ahead of Heckathorn—and signed for $1,359,000. He hasn't dominated as a pro, but he made steady progress until he repeated Double-A last season. His strikeout rate dropped to a career-low 4.5 per nine innings as opponents hit .310 against him. A slew of injuries at the big league level left the Blue Jays looking for arms, however, so they called Jenkins up for the final two months and he posted similar numbers as a swingman. Jenkins doesn't blow hitters away, relying instead on getting quick outs with his sinker/slider combination. His fastball sits at 87-91 mph with heavy sink and his slider is a solid pitch in the low 80s. He also shows a splitter/changeup that can be effective. Jenkins has a durable frame and projects as an innings-eater at the back of a big league rotation. He has yet to pitch in Triple-A, so he'll probably begin 2013 there.

Year	Club (League)	Class	W	L	ERA	G	GS	CG	SV	IP	H	HR	BB	SO	K/9	WHIP	AVG
2010	Lansing (MWL)	LoA	5	4	3.63	13	13	1	0	79	87	5	13	64	7.3	1.26	.277
	Dunedin (FSL)	HiA	2	6	4.33	13	13	1	0	62	73	6	18	42	6.1	1.46	.281
2011	Dunedin (FSL)	HiA	4	5	3.07	11	11	0	0	67	71	3	14	44	5.9	1.26	.267
	New Hampshire (EL)	AA	5	7	4.13	16	16	1	0	100	93	8	27	74	6.6	1.20	.247
2012	New Hampshire (EL)	AA	5	9	4.96	20	20	0	0	114	145	17	31	57	4.5	1.54	.310
	Toronto (AL)	MAJ	1	3	4.50	13	3	0	0	32	32	5	11	16	4.5	1.34	.260
Major League Totals			1	3	4.50	13	3	0	0	32	32	5	11	16	4.5	1.34	.260
Minor League Totals			21	31	4.12	73	73	3	0	424	469	39	103	281	6.0	1.35	.279

19 SEAN NOLIN, LHP

Born: Dec. 26, 1989. **B-T:** L-L. **Ht.:** 6-5. **Wt.:** 235. **Drafted:** San Jacinto (Texas) JC, 2010 (6th round). **Signed by:** Aaron Jersild.

BA GRADE
45
MEDIUM

Nolin wasn't a premium prospect coming out of the 2010 draft, but he has had a lot of success since the Blue Jays took him. He went 10-0, 2.07 that spring at San Jacinto (Texas) JC, and has gone 14-6, 3.04 and reached Double-A since signing for $175,000 as a sixth-round pick. Compared to a lefthanded version of former Baylor and Rockies pitcher Jason Jennings, Nolin has a burly frame and thrives on his feel for pitching. He has an average fastball that ranges from 88-94 mph and regularly sits at 90-91. He also mixes in a two-seamer that sits in the high 80s and features nice sink. His best secondary offering is a solid changeup, and he throws a curveball and slider. He has a longer history with the curve and has added power to it, while his slider needs shorter and quicker break. Projected as a back-of-the-rotation starter, Nolin will return to New Hampshire to begin 2013 but could advance to Triple-A quickly.

Year	Club (League)	Class	W	L	ERA	G	GS	CG	SV	IP	H	HR	BB	SO	K/9	WHIP	AVG
2010	Blue Jays (GCL)	R	0	0	0.00	1	1	0	0	2	1	0	1	4	18.0	1.00	.167
	Auburn (NYP)	SS	0	2	6.05	6	6	0	0	19	25	0	9	22	10.2	1.76	.313
2011	Lansing (MWL)	LoA	4	4	3.49	25	21	0	1	108	102	9	31	113	9.4	1.23	.253
2012	Dunedin (FSL)	HiA	9	0	2.19	17	15	0	0	86	72	7	21	90	9.4	1.08	.226
	New Hampshire (EL)	AA	1	0	1.20	3	3	0	0	15	9	0	6	18	10.8	1.00	.170
Minor League Totals			14	6	3.04	52	46	0	1	231	209	16	68	247	9.6	1.20	.243

20 DECK McGUIRE, RHP

Born: June 23, 1989. **B-T:** R-R. **Ht.:** 6-6. **Wt.:** 220. **Drafted:** Georgia Tech, 2010 (1st round). **Signed by:** Eric McQueen.

BA GRADE
45
MEDIUM

The Blue Jays made McGuire the 11th overall pick in the 2010 draft and signed him for $2 million, but he has seldom shown his college form as a pro. The book on him was that his command and polish would help his solid stuff play up and get him to Toronto quickly, but he got crushed in Double-A last season. He led the Eastern League in losses (15), home runs allowed (22), runs (103) and earned runs (94) while posting the second-worst ERA (5.88) among qualifiers. McGuire's fastball still sits at 88-92 mph and touches 94 with average sink. His slider is his best secondary offering and has a chance to become a plus pitch. He also has a mediocre curveball he can throw for strikes and a fringy changeup that he still is gaining confidence in using regularly. The problem is that McGuire doesn't have a pitch that can consistently miss bats, and his control and command haven't been as good as advertised. He has a sound delivery, so he should be able to throw more strikes and work down in the zone more often. He'll try to get back on track in 2013, when he might have to return for a third stint in New Hampshire. He looked like a No. 4 or 5 starter at best last year, and a long way from reaching that point.

Year	Club (League)	Class	W	L	ERA	G	GS	CG	SV	IP	H	HR	BB	SO	K/9	WHIP	AVG
2011	Dunedin (FSL)	HiA	7	4	2.75	19	18	0	0	105	89	9	38	102	8.8	1.21	.228
	New Hampshire (EL)	AA	2	1	4.35	4	3	1	0	21	20	4	7	22	9.6	1.31	.253
2012	New Hampshire (EL)	AA	5	15	5.88	28	28	0	0	144	162	22	62	97	6.1	1.56	.286
Minor League Totals			14	20	4.54	51	49	1	0	269	271	35	107	221	7.4	1.40	.261

21 KEVIN PILLAR, OF

BA GRADE 45 MEDIUM

Born: Jan. 4, 1989. **B-T:** R-R. **Ht.:** 6-0. **Wt.:** 200. **Drafted:** Cal State Dominguez Hills, 2011 (32nd round). **Signed by:** Kevin Fox.

Pillar set an NCAA Division II record with a 54-game hitting streak as a junior in 2010 and a Cal State Dominguez Hills mark with a .367 career average. After four seasons with the Toros, he signed for $1,000 and kept hitting as a pro. He batted .347 in his pro debut and a system-best .323 last season, when he won the Midwest League MVP award. Pillar easily makes contact at the plate, thanks to a short swing and quiet approach with few moving parts. He has good feel for the barrel and provides gap power. Pillar used solid speed and keen instincts to steal 51 bases in 60 tries in 2012. His quickness and savvy also serve him well in the outfield, where he can play all three positions. He has average arm strength and accuracy. Pillar already is 24 and will have to keep proving himself, but he looks like he can serve as at least a fourth outfielder in the big leagues. He's ready for Double-A and could get to Toronto by season's end if he continues to produce.

Year	Club (League)	Class	AVG	G	AB	R	H	2B	3B	HR	RBI	BB	SO	SB	CS	OBP	SLG
2011	Bluefield (APP)	R	.347	60	236	44	82	17	3	7	37	10	36	8	4	.377	.534
2012	Lansing (MWL)	LoA	.322	86	335	49	108	20	4	5	57	35	53	35	6	.390	.451
	Dunedin (FSL)	HiA	.323	42	164	16	53	8	2	1	34	5	17	16	3	.339	.415
Minor League Totals			.331	188	735	109	243	45	9	13	128	50	106	59	13	.375	.469

22 CHASE DeJONG, RHP

BA GRADE 50 HIGH

Born: Dec. 29, 1993. **B-T:** L-R. **Ht.:** 6-4. **Wt.:** 195. **Drafted:** HS—Long Beach, 2012 (2nd round). **Signed by:** Joe Aversa.

DeJong is a product of Long Beach's Wilson High, which has sent 13 players to the big leagues, including Hall of Famer Bob Lemon, six-time all-star Bobby Grich and former American League MVP Jeff Burroughs. DeJong helped his 2012 draft cause with a pair of stellar outings against Lakewood (Calif.) High and righthander Shane Watson, who went on to become a Phillies supplemental first-rounder. DeJong struck out 12 while taking a tough 1-0 loss in the first matchup, then threw 8 2/3 shutout innings to secure a 3-0 win in the rematch. The Blue Jays selected him 81st overall and lured him away from a commitment to Southern California with an $860,000 bonus. DeJong has the projectable frame that scouts look for in high school righthanders, but he's highly regarded more for his feel for pitching than his pure stuff. His fastball sits at 87-91 mph and peaks at 93. He has a sharp downer curveball that shows the potential to be a plus pitch, and his changeup has similar upside. His delivery still needs cleaning up, but he's doing a better job of throwing less across his body and landing softer on his front leg. DeJong has the ceiling of a mid-rotation starter if everything comes together. Toronto is conservative with its young arms, so he'll likely open 2013 at one of the organization's more advanced short-season stops.

Year	Club (League)	Class	W	L	ERA	G	GS	CG	SV	IP	H	HR	BB	SO	K/9	WHIP	AVG
2012	Blue Jays (GCL)	R	1	0	1.50	6	0	0	0	12	7	0	1	15	11.3	0.67	.171
Minor League Totals			1	0	1.50	6	0	0	0	12	7	0	1	15	11.3	0.67	.171

23 CHRISTIAN LOPES, 2B/SS

BA GRADE 50 HIGH

Born: Oct. 1, 1992. **B-T:** R-R. **Ht.:** 6-0. **Wt.:** 185. **Drafted:** HS—Huntington Beach, Calif., 2011 (7th round). **Signed by:** Joe Aversa.

Lopes drew acclaim early in his amateur career, ranking as the top 13-year-old in the nation in 2006 and projecting as a future first-round pick as a high school freshman. But his physical skills didn't develop as expected, and he seemed to wilt under the pressure. He failed to hit .300 as a junior and started tinkering with his swing, eventually falling to the seventh round of the 2011 draft. The Blue Jays still believed in his bat and signed him away from a Southern California scholarship for $800,000. He outperformed his fellow 2011 draftees at Bluefield last summer, earning team MVP honors. Despite his prolonged slumps as an amateur, Lopes has shown an ability to handle the bat. He has a sound approach and a quick swing that he's not afraid to turn loose. As a pro, he's doing a better job of not thinking too much or panicking at the plate. He should have more pop than most middle infielders, with a chance for average power as he matures. Lopes' below-average speed has prompted a move from shortstop to second base, but he has soft hands and a solid arm to go with good instincts, so he should be fine defensively. He could open 2013 in low Class A.

Year	Club (League)	Class	AVG	G	AB	R	H	2B	3B	HR	RBI	BB	SO	SB	CS	OBP	SLG
2012	Bluefield (APP)	R	.280	49	186	33	52	16	5	4	29	15	34	6	1	.343	.484
	Vancouver (NWL)	SS	.270	10	37	4	10	1	1	0	4	2	6	0	0	.317	.351
Minor League Totals			.278	59	223	37	62	17	6	4	33	17	40	6	1	.339	.462

24 MITCH NAY, 3B

BA GRADE
50
HIGH

Born: Sept. 20, 1993. **B-T:** R-R. **Ht.:** 6-3. **Wt.:** 195. **Drafted:** HS—Chandler, Ariz., 2012 (1st round supplemental). **Signed by:** Blake Crosby.

After missing time on the high school showcase circuit in 2011 because of a back injury, Nay started slowly as a high school senior last spring. He relaxed and started heating up as the draft neared, however, and moved up draft boards dramatically. The Blue Jays took him 58th overall and signed him away from an Arizona State commitment for $1 million. He broke his foot during agility workouts during his first week with the organization, preventing him from making his debut. Nay has a projectable frame with broad shoulders, making it easy to predict that he'll have plus power to all fields. There are questions about whether he'll make consistent contact and hit for average, however. He did adjust nicely to the steady diet of offspeed stuff that pitchers fed him last spring. Nay has an above-average arm that will play at third base, but he'll have to put in the work to stay there. He has below-average speed and quickness, though he moves well enough laterally. If he has to change positions, his power and arm should profile in right field. He'll start 2013 in extended spring training before reporting to Bluefield or Vancouver.

Year	Club (League)	Class	AVG	G	AB	R	H	2B	3B	HR	RBI	BB	SO	SB	CS	OBP	SLG
Did Not Play—Injured																	

25 WUILMER BECERRA, OF

BA GRADE
50
EXTREME

Born: Oct. 1, 1994. **B-T:** R-R. **Ht.:** 6-4. **Wt.:** 190. **Signed:** Venezuela, 2011. **Signed by:** Marco Paddy/Rafael Moncada.

Another big signing from the 2011 international class, Becerra brought home $1.3 million that July. Like Alberto Tirado, he also came to the United States for his debut, but his first foray into pro ball was short-lived. He had 32 at-bats before taking a pitch off the face and breaking his jaw on July 3. His jaw was wired shut and he missed the rest of the regular season, but he reported to instructional league and eased back into baseball activities. Becerra has strength and above-average raw power, but his bat draws mixed reviews. His swing can get long and has an uppercut, which may detract from his ability to hit for average. Becerra is a plus runner who fits best in the outfield despite playing shortstop as an amateur. He doesn't have the hands or arm for shortstop and figured to get too big for the position anyway. He fits in center field now and may have to shift to left if he loses speed when he fills out. Becerra essentially lost a season of development, so he may be destined to return to the GCL in 2013.

Year	Club (League)	Class	AVG	G	AB	R	H	2B	3B	HR	RBI	BB	SO	SB	CS	OBP	SLG
2012	Blue Jays (GCL)	R	.250	11	32	5	8	4	0	0	4	4	7	0	1	.359	.375
Minor League Totals			.250	11	32	5	8	4	0	0	4	4	7	0	1	.359	.375

26 DAWEL LUGO, SS

BA GRADE
50
EXTREME

Born: Dec. 13, 1994. **B-T:** R-R. **Ht.:** 6-0. **Wt.:** 190. **Signed:** Dominican Republic, 2011. **Signed by:** Marco Paddy/Hilario Soriano.

One of the top hitters in the 2011 international class, Lugo matched Wuilmer Becerra's $1.3 million bonus and joined him in the Gulf Coast League for his pro debut last year. Lugo batted just .224/.275/.329, but he also was one of the youngest players in the league at age 17. He routinely makes contact but must learn to let some pitches go if he can't drive them with authority. He has a quick bat and projects to hit for plus power, though he can try to pull the ball too much. He's an average runner. He plays a sound shortstop and could be a Jhonny Peralta type, but most scouts think Lugo will have to shift to third base. He has the arm and athleticism to make the transition. He'll probably spend 2013 in Bluefield and not get his first taste of full-season ball until the following year.

Year	Club (League)	Class	AVG	G	AB	R	H	2B	3B	HR	RBI	BB	SO	SB	CS	OBP	SLG
2012	Blue Jays (GCL)	R	.224	47	170	20	38	2	5	2	20	7	25	5	1	.275	.329
Minor League Totals			.224	47	170	20	38	2	5	2	20	7	25	5	1	.275	.329

27 DICKIE JOE THON, SS

Born: Nov. 16, 1991. **B-T:** R-R. **Ht.:** 6-2. **Wt.:** 190. **Drafted:** HS—San Juan, P.R., 2010 (5th round). **Signed by:** Jorge Rivera.

BA GRADE
50
EXTREME

While Thon was the Blue Jays 11th pick (fifth round) in 2010, he received the second-highest bonus in their draft class at $1.5 million because of his all-around skills and athleticism as well as the leverage of a scholarship to Rice. His father Dickie was an all-star shortstop and played 15 big league seasons. The younger Thon has yet to show much in pro ball, batting .222/.349/.315 in two years of Rookie ball and spending 2011 battling an unspecified blood disorder. He moved up to Rookie-level Bluefield for 2012 and continued to struggle at the plate, hitting .221/.331/.309 in 149 at-bats. Thon has a good swing and can drive the ball to all fields, but he needs to settle down at the plate. He gets too anxious and gives at-bats away, striking out in 29 percent of his at-bats in pro ball. Thon has plus speed, range and arm strength, so he has a shot to stick at shortstop. If he has to move, he figures to stay up the middle at second base or center field. At age 21, Thon faces a crucial season in 2013, when he should get his first full-season assignment.

Year	Club (League)	Class	AVG	G	AB	R	H	2B	3B	HR	RBI	BB	SO	SB	CS	OBP	SLG
2011	Blue Jays (GCL)	R	.223	45	121	23	27	3	0	3	15	23	44	6	2	.369	.322
2012	Bluefield (APP)	R	.221	48	149	18	33	5	1	2	14	19	34	7	3	.331	.309
Minor League Totals			.222	93	270	41	60	8	1	5	29	42	78	13	5	.349	.315

28 JAIRO LABOURT, LHP

Born: March 7, 1994. **B-T:** L-L. **Ht.:** 6-4. **Wt.:** 205. **Signed:** Dominican Republic, 2011. **Signed by:** Marco Paddy/Hilario Soriano.

BA GRADE
50
EXTREME

Another product of Toronto's aggressive international spending in 2011, Labourt signed for $350,000 on his 17th birthday. A skinny 185-pounder when he signed, he already has added 20 pounds and has more room to add strength on his broad-shouldered frame. His fastball velocity has increased as well, sitting at 88-92 mph last summer and in the low 90s during instructional league, topping out at 94. He pitches mostly with his fastball at this point, though he shows feel for a curveball when needed. His changeup is a work in progress. Labourt still has a long way to go in refining the consistency of his pitches and learning to command them. He needs to do a better job of repeating his delivery and holding runners. He has the upside of a mid-rotation starter but won't be ready for full-season ball until 2014.

Year	Club (League)	Class	W	L	ERA	G	GS	CG	SV	IP	H	HR	BB	SO	K/9	WHIP	AVG
2011	Blue Jays (DSL)	R	0	4	2.23	12	12	0	0	36	29	0	14	29	7.2	1.18	.220
2012	Blue Jays (GCL)	R	0	3	3.79	12	12	0	0	38	38	2	23	39	9.2	1.61	.253
Minor League Totals			0	7	3.03	24	24	0	0	74	67	2	37	68	8.2	1.40	.238

29 YEYFRY DEL ROSARIO, RHP

Born: April 27, 1994. **B-T:** R-R. **Ht.:** 6-2. **Wt.:** 180. **Signed:** Dominican Republic, 2011. **Signed by:** Marco Paddy/Domingo Toribio.

BA GRADE
45
HIGH

The Blue Jays signed both Jairo Labourt and del Rosario out of the Dominican Republic on March 7, 2011. Del Rosario fetched only $70,000—one-fifth of Labourt's bonus—because his fastball resided in the mid-80s at the time. Toronto believed there was more there because he could spin a curveball in the mid-70s, and he since has boosted his fastball to 88-90 mph with a high of 92. A throwing program has helped him add arm strength, and there might be a little more to come. He doesn't have as much velocity as Labourt, but del Rosario shows better feel for pitching and ate up inexperienced Gulf Coast League hitters in his U.S. debut. His best secondary pitch is a changeup that he commands well, while his curve has room for improvement. Del Rosario currently projects to fit in the back of a big league rotation, but he could find a higher ceiling if he adds velocity and develops plus command. He'll advance to Bluefield or Vancouver this season.

Year	Club (League)	Class	W	L	ERA	G	GS	CG	SV	IP	H	HR	BB	SO	K/9	WHIP	AVG
2011	Blue Jays (DSL)	R	1	8	2.78	14	13	0	0	45	33	2	10	31	6.2	0.95	.195
2012	Blue Jays (GCL)	R	1	5	3.63	13	12	0	0	45	37	1	12	52	10.5	1.10	.222
Minor League Totals			2	13	3.20	27	25	0	0	90	70	3	22	83	8.3	1.02	.208

30 CHRIS HAWKINS, OF

Born: Aug. 17, 1991. **B-T:** L-R. **Ht.:** 6-2. **Wt.:** 195. **Drafted:** HS—Suwanee, Ga.,
2010 (3rd round). **Signed by:** Eric McQueen.

BA GRADE

45

HIGH

A third-round pick in 2010, Hawkins signed for $350,000 and passed up a scholarship
to Tennessee. A shortstop in high school, he initially moved to the hot corner in pro ball before landing in left
field. The position shifts have increased the offensive demands on him, and he took a step back with a lackluster
performance in low Class A in 2012. Hawkins can look stiff and awkward, but his quick hands and strong wrists
help him get around an arm bar in his swing. He makes consistent contact, almost to a fault, routinely putting
pitches in play that he can't drive. He walks at a decent clip and could develop into a solid hitter with average
power if he refines his plate discipline. He's still learning his swing. A fringy runner who's quicker once he gets
going, Hawkins went 11-for-11 stealing bases last season. Despite his 14 assists in 2012, his arm is below-average
and not particularly accurate. After getting through the pitcher-friendly Midwest League, he'll face another difficult hitting environment when he moves up to the Florida State League in 2013.

Year	Club (League)	Class	AVG	G	AB	R	H	2B	3B	HR	RBI	BB	SO	SB	CS	OBP	SLG
2010	Blue Jays (GCL)	R	.255	46	157	29	40	9	3	0	15	15	37	8	3	.324	.350
2011	Dunedin (FSL)	HiA	.000	2	4	0	0	0	0	0	0	0	2	0	0	.000	.000
	Bluefield (APP)	R	.318	68	242	49	77	15	6	5	52	22	46	14	4	.375	.492
2012	Lansing (MWL)	LoA	.269	123	491	67	132	17	4	2	43	46	78	11	0	.331	.332
Minor League Totals			.279	239	894	145	249	41	13	7	110	83	163	33	7	.340	.377

Washington Nationals

BY AARON FITT

After years spent building a rock-solid foundation, the Nationals were rewarded for their planning and opportunistic drafting with a resoundingly successful 2012 campaign.

They posted their first winning season since moving to Washington in 2005, leading the majors with 98 wins, cruising to the National League East title and snapping the franchise's 31-year postseason drought. The city embraced a team that spent all but a handful of days atop the division, capped by the first playoff appearance by a Washington baseball club since 1933.

But the dream season had a nightmarish finale.

After splitting the first four games of an NL Division Series against the Cardinals, the Nationals blew a 6-0 advantage in the decisive fifth game. Drew Storen failed to hold a two-run lead with two out in the ninth, and St. Louis rallied for four runs to complete a stunning comeback.

Still, Washington could take solace in the knowledge that it has perhaps the best young core in baseball and looks poised to contend for championships for years to come.

The Nationals led the National League with a 3.33 ERA in 2012, as homegrown arms meshed with offseason acquisitions to form a deep, talented staff. They traded four of their best prospects (Brad Peacock, A.J. Cole, Derek Norris and Tommy Milone) to get ace lefthander Gio Gonzalez from the Athletics in December, and he rewarded them by topping the NL with 21 wins and 9.3 strikeouts per nine innings. In his first full season back from Tommy John surgery, Stephen Strasburg was dominant at times and would have outranked Gonzalez with 11.1 strikeouts per nine innings—if Washington hadn't made the controversial decision to shut him down after 159 innings.

The organization took the same approach a year earlier with righty Jordan Zimmermann, ending his 2011 season after 161 innings to ease him back after the same surgery. He responded with his best season in 2012, going 12-8, 2.94 in 195 innings. Another homegrown pitcher, lefty Ross Detwiler, also took a major step forward. Free-agent signee Edwin Jackson rounded out a rotation in which all five starters won at least 10 games.

Storen and Tyler Clippard—two more pitchers who were developed ably by the Washington minor league staff—anchored a rock-solid bullpen.

The lineup featured more player-development success stories. Bryce Harper's rookie season was one

Washington made the controversial decision to sit Stephen Strasburg down in September

of the most anticipated in baseball history, and the 19-year-old phenom didn't disappoint. Called up in late April, he earned a trip to the All-Star Game and hit .270 with 22 homers—the second-most ever for a big league teenager.

Beyond Harper, Ian Desmond blossomed into one of baseball's best shortstops as a 26-year-old, validating the work of minor league instructors who spent five long years easing him along and major league coaches who didn't give up on him after a trying 2011 campaign. Desmond and Danny Espinosa give Washington a pair of dynamic homegrown middle infielders to go with cornerstone third baseman Ryan Zimmerman.

The future is bright for Washington largely because ownership, general manager Mike Rizzo and scouting director Kris Kline have shown they aren't afraid to take chances and spend money in the draft. After hitting the jackpot with Strasburg and Harper as back-to-back No. 1 overall picks in 2009-10, the Nationals pounced on elite prospects who slipped because of health questions with their next two top choices. Third baseman Anthony Rendon (2011) and righthander Lucas Giolito (2012) now rank as the top prospects in a system that has been thinned by graduations and trades.

THIS YEAR'S TOP 30

Player, Pos.		Grade
1.	Anthony Rendon, 3b	65/High
2.	Lucas Giolito, rhp	70/Extreme
3.	Brian Goodwin, of	60/High
4.	Matt Skole, 3b	50/Medium
5.	Nate Karns, rhp	50/Medium
6.	Christian Garcia, rhp	45/Low
7.	Eury Perez, of	50/Medium
8.	Sammy Solis, lhp	50/High
9.	Matt Purke, rhp	55/Extreme
10.	Zach Walters, ss	45/Medium
11.	Michael Taylor, of	55/Extreme
12.	Tony Renda, 2b	50/High
13.	Taylor Jordan, rhp	50/High
14.	Jason Martinson, ss/3b	50/High
15.	Sandy Leon, c	45/Medium
16.	Rick Hague, ss/2b	50/High
17.	Destin Hood, of	50/High
18.	Robbie Ray, lhp	50/High
19.	Brett Mooneyham, lhp	50/High
20.	Corey Brown, of	45/Medium
21.	Estarlin Martinez, of	50/High
22.	Brandon Miller, of	50/High
23.	Chris Marrero, 1b	45/Medium
24.	Carlos Rivero, 3b/ss/1b	45/Medium
25.	Steven Souza, of	50/Extreme
26.	Billy Burns, of	45/High
27.	Ivan Pineyro, rhp	50/Extreme
28.	Paul Demny, rhp	45/High
29.	Wirkin Estevez, rhp	50/Extreme
30.	Jhonatan Solano, c	40/Low

LAST YEAR'S TOP 30

Player, Pos.		Status
1.	Bryce Harper, of	Majors
2.	Anthony Rendon, 3b	No. 1
3.	Brad Peacock, rhp	(Athletics)
4.	A.J. Cole, rhp	(Athletics)
5.	Brian Goodwin, of	No. 3
6.	Alex Meyer, rhp	(Twins)
7.	Matt Purke, lhp	No. 9
8.	Sammy Solis, lhp	No. 8
9.	Derek Norris, c	(Athletics)
10.	Steve Lombardozzi, 2b/ss	Majors
11.	Destin Hood, of	No. 17
12.	Chris Marrero, 1b	No. 23
13.	Tom Milone, lhp	(Athletics)
14.	Michael Taylor, of	No. 11
15.	Rick Hague, ss	No. 16
16.	Tyler Moore, 1b	Majors
17.	Robbie Ray, lhp	No. 18
18.	Kylin Turnbull, lhp	Dropped out
19.	Zach Walters, inf	No. 10
20.	Jeff Kobernus, 2b	(Tigers)
21.	Matt Skole, 3b	No. 4
22.	Eury Perez, of	No. 7
23.	Daniel Rosenbaum, lhp	(Rockies)
24.	Sandy Leon, c	No. 15
25.	Jason Martinson, ss	No. 14
26.	Cole Kimball, rhp	Dropped out
27.	David Freitas, c	(Athletics)
28.	Adrian Sanchez, 2b	Dropped out
29.	Paul Demny, rhp	No. 28
30.	Kevin Keyes, of	Dropped out

BEST TOOLS

Best Hitter for Average	Anthony Rendon
Best Power Hitter	Matt Skole
Best Strike-Zone Discipline	Anthony Rendon
Fastest Baserunner	Billy Burns
Best Athlete	Brian Goodwin
Best Fastball	Lucas Giolito
Best Curveball	Lucas Giolito
Best Slider	Aaron Barrett
Best Changeup	Christian Garcia
Best Control	Taylor Hill
Best Defensive Catcher	Sandy Leon
Best Defensive Infielder	Anthony Rendon
Best Infield Arm	Zach Walters
Best Defensive Outfielder	Michael Taylor
Best Outfield Arm	Michael Taylor

PROJECTED 2016 LINEUP

Catcher	Wilson Ramos
First Base	Ryan Zimmerman
Second Base	Danny Espinosa
Third Base	Anthony Rendon
Shortstop	Ian Desmond
Left Field	Brian Goodwin
Center Field	Denard Span
Right Field	Bryce Harper
No. 1 Starter	Stephen Strasburg
No. 2 Starter	Lucas Giolito
No. 3 Starter	Gio Gonzalez
No. 4 Starter	Jordan Zimmermann
No. 5 Starter	Ross Detwiler
Closer	Drew Storen

TOP PROSPECTS OF THE DECADE

Year	Player, Pos.	2012 Org.
2003	Clint Everts, rhp	Blue Jays
2004	Clint Everts, rhp	Blue Jays
2005	Mike Hinckley, lhp	Out of baseball
2006	Ryan Zimmerman, 3b	Nationals
2007	Collin Balester, rhp	Tigers
2008	Chris Marrero, 1b	Nationals
2009	Jordan Zimmermann, rhp	Nationals
2010	Stephen Strasburg, rhp	Nationals
2011	Bryce Harper, of	Nationals
2012	Bryce Harper, of	Nationals

TOP DRAFT PICKS OF THE DECADE

Year	Player, Pos.	2012 Org.
2003	Chad Cordero, rhp	Out of baseball
2004	Bill Bray, lhp	Reds
2005	Ryan Zimmerman, 3b	Nationals
2006	Chris Marrero, of	Nationals
2007	Ross Detwiler, lhp	Nationals
2008	*Aaron Crow, rhp	Royals
2009	Stephen Strasburg, rhp	Nationals
2010	Bryce Harper, of	Nationals
2011	Anthony Rendon, 3b	Nationals
2012	Lucas Giolito, rhp	Nationals

*Did not sign.

LARGEST BONUSES IN CLUB HISTORY

Stephen Strasburg, 2009	$7,500,000
Bryce Harper, 2010	$6,250,000
Anthony Rendon, 2011	$6,000,000
Brian Goodwin, 2011	$3,000,000
Ryan Zimmerman, 2006	$2,975,000

WASHINGTON NATIONALS

TOP 2013 ROOKIE: Christian Garcia, rhp. After a 2.13 ERA in 13 appearances for Washington in 2012, he's ready to assume a full-time role as a power reliever in the majors.

BREAKOUT PROSPECT: Taylor Jordan, rhp. He returned from Tommy John surgery stronger than ever, touching 96 mph in the late summer and fall.

SLEEPER: Shawn Pleffner, 1b. After a sports hernia sidelined him in 2011, he showed advanced feel for hitting and emerging lefthanded pop last year.

SOURCE OF TOP 30 TALENT			
Homegrown	26	Acquired	4
College	11	Trades	2
Junior college	3	Rule 5 draft	0
High school	6	Independent leagues	0
Nondrafted free agents	0	Free agents/waivers	2
International	6		

LF
Destin Hood (17)
Estarlin Martinez (21)
Erik Komatsu
Kevin Keyes
Caleb Ramsey
Matt Foat

CF
Brian Goodwin (3)
Eury Perez (7)
Michael Taylor (11)
Corey Brown (20)
Billy Burns (26)
Narciso Mesa
Hayden Jennings

RF
Brandon Miller (22)
Steven Souza (25)
Randy Novas
Wander Ramos
Randolph Oduber

3B
Anthony Rendon (1)
Matt Skole (4)
Carlos Rivero (24)

SS
Zach Walters (10)
Jason Martinson (14)
Stephen Perez
Wilmer Difo
Bryce Ortega

2B
Tony Renda (12)
Rick Hague (16)
Adrian Sanchez
Cutter Dykstra
Mike McQuillan

1B
Chris Marrero (23)
Shawn Pleffner
Justin Bloxom

C
Sandy Leon (15)
Jhonatan Solano (30)
Raudy Read
Pedro Severino
Adrian Nieto
Spencer Kieboom
Craig Manuel

LHP

LHSP	LHRP
Sammy Solis (8)	Joel Barrientes
Matt Purke (9)	Elliott Waterman
Robbie Ray (18)	Nick Lee
Brett Mooneyham (19)	Patrick McCoy
Kylin Turnbull	Christian Meza
Matt Grace	R.C. Orlan

RHP

RHSP	RHRP
Lucas Giolito (2)	Christian Garcia (7)
Nate Karns (5)	Paul Demny (28)
Taylor Jordan (13)	Cole Kimball
Ivan Pineyro (27)	Erik Davis
Wirkin Estevez (29)	Aaron Barrett
Tanner Roark	Derek Self
Taylor Hill	Robert Benincasa
Brian Rauh	Rob Wort
Blake Schwartz	Neil Holland
Pedro Encarnacion	Pat Lehman
	Ronald Pena
	Austin Dicharry
	Travis Henke

DRAFT ANALYSIS

2012 BONUSES: $4.9 MILLION

BEST PURE HITTER: 2B Tony Renda (2) is undersized, but he's a gritty performer with excellent bat control.

BEST POWER HITTER: OF Brandon Miller (4) led NCAA Division I with 23 homers at Samford in the spring. His raw power grades as a 70 on the 20-80 scouting scale.

FASTEST RUNNER: OF Hayden Jennings (6) has plus speed and doubled as a wide receiver in high school. SS Stephen Perez (8) is also an above-average runner.

BEST DEFENSIVE PLAYER: Perez plays with flair at shortstop. He has quick, flashy hands and can make difficult plays, though he needs to improve his consistency. Cs Spencer Kieboom (5) and Craig Manuel (10) are sound defenders behind the plate. Kieboom threw out 43 percent of basestealers at short-season Auburn, while Manuel erased 41 percent.

BEST FASTBALL: RHP Lucas Giolito (1) pitched from 92-100 mph in the spring before spraining the ulnar collateral ligament in his elbow. The injury took him out of the running to be the No. 1 overall pick and eventually required Tommy John surgery in August after he pitched two innings as a pro. RHP Derek Self (9) boosted his fastball from 87-91 mph in 2011 to 92-95 in 2012. LHP Brett Mooneyham (3) once touched 97 mph but ranges from 91-94 these days.

BEST SECONDARY PITCH: Giolito also has two quality secondary pitches in his hard curveball and changeup.

BEST PRO DEBUT: Self's 14 saves tied for the short-season New York-Penn League lead. Miller hit .292/.354/.549 with 18 extra-base hits in 29 games at Auburn.

BEST ATHLETE: Perez has the potential for average or better tools across the board, though he frustrated scouts by underachieving during his college career at Miami.

MOST INTRIGUING BACKGROUND: Giolito's parents, Rick Giolito and Lindsay Frost, are actors who have appeared on several television shows. Giolito and Max Fried (Padres) are the seventh pair of prep teammates taken in the first round of the same draft. Mooneyham's father Bill played in the majors, as did unsigned 2B Jake Jefferies' (34) dad Gregg, a two-time all-star. Unsigned SS Ricky Gutierrez (40) is a wide receiver at Connecticut and another son of a big leaguer (Ricky).

CLOSEST TO THE MAJORS: Self and RHP Robert Benincasa (7) could be fast-tracked as relievers. Giolito should move quickly once he returns to health.

BEST LATE-ROUND PICK: LHP R.C. Orlan (30) had Tommy John surgery in June, but the Nationals are excited about his potential. When healthy, he has an 88-93 mph fastball, a hard curveball and a bulldog mentality.

THE ONE WHO GOT AWAY: RHP Freddy Avis (25) could have gone in the top two rounds if he hadn't been so strongly committed to Stanford.

ASSESSMENT: The Nationals used two-thirds of their bonus pool to sign Giolito for $2,925,000. They knew the injury risk, and the success of their draft will hinge on his ability to recover his pre-injury form.

2011 BONUSES: $15.0 MILLION

Washington invested a combined $16.35 million in 3B Anthony Rendon (1), RHP Alex Meyer (1), OF Brian Goodwin (1s) and LHP Matt Purke (3). Meyer brought back Denard Span in a trade this offseason. 3B Matt Skole (5) was the low Class A South Atlantic League MVP in his first full pro season.

GRADE: A

2010 BONUSES: $11.9 MILLION

OF Bryce Harper's (1) legend continues to grow after an outstanding rookie season. RHP A.J. Cole (4) signed for $2 million and became a key part of the Gio Gonzalez trade.

GRADE: A

2009 BONUSES: $11.5 MILLION

The first team ever to have two top-10 picks in the same draft, the Nationals used them on an ace (RHP Stephen Strasburg, 1) and closer (RHP Drew Storen, 1) who rocketed to the majors. RHP Nate Karns (12) bounced back from injuries to have a spectacular full-season debut in 2012.

GRADE: A

2008 BONUSES: $4.8 MILLION

Washington drafted seven big leaguers—but only signed four of them: 2B Danny Espinosa (3), LHP Tom Milone (10, part of the Gonzalez deal), OF/1B Tyler Moore (16) and 2B/OF/3B Steve Lombardozzi (19). RHP Aaron Crow (1) got away—though he did yield the compensation pick that produced Storen—as did RHP Louis Coleman (14) and C Rob Brantly (46).

GRADE: B+

Draft analysis by Conor Glassey (2012) and Jim Callis (2008-11). Numbers in parentheses indicate draft rounds.

BaseballAmerica.com   Baseball America 2013 Prospect Handbook • **481**

1 ANTHONY RENDON, 3B

Born: June 6, 1990. **B-T:** R-R. **Ht.:** 6-0. **Wt.:** 195.
Drafted: Rice, 2011 (1st round). **Signed by:** Tyler Wilt.

BA GRADE
65
HIGH

ED WOLFSTEIN

Rendon is one of the most accomplished college players of the last decade, and his rise to elite prospect status has been slowed only by a succession of injuries. A 27th-round pick by the Braves out of Houston's Lamar High in 2008, Rendon burst onto the national scene at Rice the following spring, hitting .388/.461/.702 with 20 homers to win Baseball America's Freshman of the Year award. He tore ligaments in his right ankle after stepping on a sprinkler head during NCAA super regionals that June, but he rebounded to hit .394/.530/.801 with 26 homers in 2010 to win BA College Player of the Year honors. Once again his summer was lost to injury, as he broke the same ankle while running the bases in his second game with the U.S. collegiate national team. A strained throwing shoulder largely limited him to DH duties as a junior, and he got few pitches to hit, leading NCAA Division I with 80 walks while producing just six homers. Rendon still ranked as the 2011 draft's top prospect, but uncertainty about his shoulder caused him to drop to the Nationals as the sixth overall pick. He signed a $7.2 million big league contract that including a $6 million bonus at the Aug. 15 deadline. After a stellar spring training, Rendon once more succumbed to the injury bug on April 7, slightly fracturing his left ankle while running the bases in his second pro game. He returned to action on July 19 and quickly reached Double-A Harrisburg, but he didn't truly find his stride until the Arizona Fall League, where he batted .338/.436/.494.

Rendon stands out most for his strong, lightning-quick hands, which Rice coach Wayne Graham has often compared to those of Hank Aaron. Rendon's tension-free swing allows him to stay back and then whip his bat through the zone, generating hard line drives from foul pole to foul pole. He has excellent balance, advanced pitch recognition and a patient approach (as evidenced by his 176-78 BB-K ratio at Rice), though his timing and pitch selection were off somewhat in his injury-shortened 2012 pro debut. Though he isn't overly physical, he has enough leverage in his swing to hit 20 or more homers annually while contending for batting titles. Rendon compiled an impressive defensive highlight reel in college, and the Nationals have been impressed with his body control, hands, footwork and instincts. He had a plus arm at Rice, but it now rates as more of a solid tool. He also has lost a step or two after his three ankle injuries, making him a slightly below-average runner.

If he can stay healthy, Rendon can an all-star third baseman with a middle-of-the-order bat and quality defensive skills. But with Ryan Zimmerman in his prime and locked into Washington's third-base job for the foreseeable future, Rendon figures to wind up elsewhere—perhaps second base, where he has played on occasion in college and in spring training. His solid athleticism and baseball savvy should allow him to adapt to a number of defensive positions, and his bat should make him an impact big leaguer. He figures to return to Double-A to start 2013, and he could get his first taste of the majors later in the year because his skills are advanced.

SCOUTING GRADES

Batting: 65.   **Defense:** 60.
Power: 55.   **Arm:** 55.
Speed: 45.

Based on 20-80 scouting scale, where 50 represents major league average, and future projection rather than present tools.

Year	Club (League)	Class	AVG	G	AB	R	H	2B	3B	HR	RBI	BB	SO	SB	CS	OBP	SLG
2012	Nationals (GCL)	R	.364	5	11	2	4	1	0	2	6	3	3	0	0	.500	1.000
	Auburn (NYP)	SS	.259	8	27	7	7	2	0	1	3	4	6	0	0	.375	.444
	Potomac (CAR)	HiA	.333	9	27	5	9	2	3	0	0	5	4	0	0	.438	.630
	Harrisburg (EL)	AA	.162	21	68	14	11	3	1	3	3	11	16	0	0	.305	.368
Minor League Totals			.233	43	133	28	31	8	4	6	12	23	29	0	0	.363	.489

2 LUCAS GIOLITO, RHP

Born: July 14, 1994. **B-T:** R-R. **Ht.:** 6-6. **Wt.:** 225. **Drafted:** HS—Studio City, Calif., 2012 (1st round). **Signed by:** Mark Baca.

Giolito's combination of elite stuff, size and polish gave him a chance to be the first high school righthander ever drafted No. 1 overall. But he sprained his ulnar collateral ligament in early March, ending his season and clouding his draft stock. The son of Hollywood actors Lindsay Frost and Rick Giolito, he made it clear a hefty bonus would be required to lure him away from a UCLA commitment. After drafting him 16th overall, the Nationals exceeded his assigned pick value by $800,000 and signed him for $2,925,000. He appeared in one game before having Tommy John surgery on Aug. 31. When healthy, Giolito works from 92-100 mph with his fastball, sitting comfortably at 94-96. He complements it with a plus-plus 82-86 mph curveball with depth and bite. He even flashes an above-average 82-84 mph changeup, giving him a third swing-and-miss pitch. He has an easy delivery, an advanced feel for pitching, a tenacious mound presence and a tireless work ethic. Giolito has true No. 1 starter upside, and his makeup and command give him a solid chance to reach that ceiling. The Nationals successfully nursed Stephen Strasburg and Jordan Zimmermann back from Tommy John surgery, and should be able to do the same with Giolito, though he might not pitch in 2013.

BA GRADE

70

EXTREME

Year	Club (League)	Class	W	L	ERA	G	GS	CG	SV	IP	H	HR	BB	SO	K/9	WHIP	AVG
2012	Nationals (GCL)	R	0	0	4.50	1	1	0	0	2	2	0	0	1	4.5	1.00	.286
Minor League Totals			0	0	4.50	1	1	0	0	2	2	0	0	1	4.5	1.00	.286

3 BRIAN GOODWIN, OF

Born: Nov. 2, 1990. **B-T:** L-L. **Ht.:** 6-1. **Wt.:** 195. **Drafted:** Miami Dade JC, 2011 (1st round supplemental). **Signed by:** Alex Morales.

Signed for $3 million as a 2011 sandwich pick, Goodwin made progress refining his impressive raw tools in his first full pro season. He showed speed, power and plate discipline while starring at low Class A Hagerstown, then continued to dazzle with his physical ability despite having less success in Double-A and the Arizona Fall League. Goodwin has worked hard to put his hands into better hitting position, free up his swing and make it less rotational. When he's going well, he stays short to the ball, waits on offspeed stuff and drives pitches from left-center to right field. When he struggled at Harrisburg, he got pull-happy and chased pitches up and away. Goodwin must improve against southpaws, who held him to a .246 average last season. But his quick hands and feel for the strike zone give him a chance to be a tablesetter, and he generates enough leverage to add solid power. He's also an above-average runner, though he's still learning to use his speed on the basepaths and in center field. He has a chance to be a plus defender with a solid arm. He could be a dynamic player in the mold of Curtis Granderson with less power and better on-base skills. Goodwin figures to start 2013 back in Double-A, and Washington's center-field job could be his in 2014.

BA GRADE

60

HIGH

Year	Club (League)	Class	AVG	G	AB	R	H	2B	3B	HR	RBI	BB	SO	SB	CS	OBP	SLG
2012	Hagerstown (SAL)	LoA	.324	58	216	47	70	18	1	9	38	43	39	15	4	.438	.542
	Harrisburg (EL)	AA	.223	42	166	17	37	8	1	5	14	18	50	3	3	.306	.373
Minor League Totals			.280	100	382	64	107	26	2	14	52	61	89	18	7	.384	.469

4 MATT SKOLE, 3B

Born: July 30, 1989. **B-T:** L-L. **Ht.:** 6-4. **Wt.:** 230. **Drafted:** Georgia Tech, 2011 (5th round). **Signed by:** Eric Robinson.

After hitting 47 homers in three years at Georgia Tech, Skole led the short-season New York-Penn League with 23 doubles and 48 RBIs in his 2011 pro debut. He was even better in 2012, winning low Class A South Atlantic League MVP honors and topping the circuit in homers (27), walks (94), on-base percentage (.438) and slugging (.574). His prospect stock has climbed higher than that of his younger brother Jake, a Rangers first-round pick in 2010. The Nationals have helped Skole get more out of his big, physical frame by minimizing his leg kick, solidifying his base and improving his balance. As he has implemented a more consistent load and better posture, he has hooked fewer balls and started driving back-door breaking pitches to the opposite field. Most of his plus power comes to the pull side. His improving ability to use all fields, good pitch recognition and patient approach suggest he can be an average hitter. Skole will never be a rangy defender at third base, but he has improved his footwork and body control. His hands are sure enough to play at either corner and his arm is solid. Blocked at third by Ryan Zimmerman and Anthony Rendon, Skole has more of a

BA GRADE

50

MEDIUM

future with Washington as a slugging first baseman. He should reach Double-A in 2013.

Year	Club (League)	Class	AVG	G	AB	R	H	2B	3B	HR	RBI	BB	SO	SB	CS	OBP	SLG
2011	Auburn (NYP)	SS	.290	72	272	43	79	23	1	5	48	42	52	2	1	.382	.438
2012	Hagerstown (SAL)	LoA	.286	101	343	73	98	18	0	27	92	94	116	10	0	.438	.574
	Potomac (CAR)	HiA	.314	18	70	11	22	10	1	0	12	5	17	1	0	.355	.486
Minor League Totals			.291	191	685	127	199	51	2	32	152	141	185	13	1	.410	.511

5 NATE KARNS, RHP

Born: Nov. 25, 1987. **B-T:** R-R. **Ht.:** 6-5. **Wt.:** 230. **Drafted:** Texas Tech, 2009 (12th round). **Signed by:** Jimmy Gonzales.

Karns has flashed power stuff since his high school days in Texas, but his command held him back in college at North Carolina State and Texas Tech. He appeared to turn the corner in 2009 in the Texas Collegiate League, where he ranked as the top prospect before signing for $225,000 as a 12th-round pick, but he tore the labrum in his shoulder shortly afterward and didn't pitch again until 2011. He came out of nowhere to lead the minors in opponent average (.174) in his 2012 full-season debut. Karns throws a heavy fastball at 92-94 mph, topping out at 96. He always has been able to get hitters to chase his downer curveball, a low-80s hammer with depth and finish, and he improved his ability to throw it for strikes last season. His curve should become a true plus pitch as he continues to learn to repeat it, and his changeup has a chance to be average. He has smoothed out his delivery somewhat, and his command has improved so much that he has a chance to stick as a starter. Added to the 40-man roster in November, Karns will advance to Double-A in 2013 and could reach Washington in the second half. He could be a mid-rotation workhorse or a late-inning reliever, depending on how his changeup and feel for pitching progress.

BA GRADE

50 MEDIUM

Year	Club (League)	Class	W	L	ERA	G	GS	CG	SV	IP	H	HR	BB	SO	K/9	WHIP	AVG
2010	Did not play—Injured																
2011	Nationals (GCL)	R	0	0	0.00	5	5	0	0	19	2	0	6	26	12.5	0.43	.035
	Auburn (NYP)	SS	3	2	3.44	8	8	0	0	37	27	1	27	33	8.1	1.47	.211
2012	Hagerstown (SAL)	LoA	3	0	2.03	11	5	1	2	44	23	1	21	61	12.4	0.99	.148
	Potomac (CAR)	HiA	8	4	2.26	13	13	1	0	72	47	1	26	87	10.9	1.02	.190
Minor League Totals			14	6	2.21	37	31	2	2	171	99	3	80	207	10.9	1.04	.168

6 CHRISTIAN GARCIA, RHP

Born: Aug. 24, 1985. **B-T:** R-R. **Ht.:** 6-5. **Wt.:** 215. **Drafted:** HS—Miami, 2004 (3rd round). **Signed by:** Dan Radison (Yankees).

After converting from catcher to pitcher as a prep senior, Garcia rocketed into the third round of the 2004 draft and signed with the Yankees for $390,000. But his career was derailed by two Tommy John surgeries, costing him all of 2007 and most of 2010. He signed with Washington as a minor league free agent in July 2011 and thrived in his first full season as a reliever in 2012, earning a September callup and a spot on the playoff roster. Garcia's stuff is electric. His fastball sits at 93-96 mph and regularly bumps 97 with good life and angle. His plus changeup has late sink, and he trusts it against both lefties and righties. The shape of his hard-biting curveball can vary, making it look more like a slider at times, but it has tight spin and good power in the low 80s. He's still learning how to command its break consistently, though it shows flashes of becoming a plus pitch. Garcia's command is a tick below average, but his stuff is good enough that he doesn't need pinpoint accuracy to succeed. Garcia has a smooth delivery without much effort, but his medical history will keep him in the bullpen. He'll open 2013 as a set-up man for the Nationals.

BA GRADE

45 LOW

Year	Club (League)	Class	W	L	ERA	G	GS	CG	SV	IP	H	HR	BB	SO	K/9	WHIP	AVG
2004	Yankees (GCL)	R	3	4	2.84	13	6	0	0	38	26	1	17	47	11.1	1.13	.188
2005	Yankees (GCL)	R	0	0	4.50	2	1	0	0	6	4	0	5	7	10.5	1.50	.200
	Charleston, SC (SAL)	LoA	5	6	3.91	21	20	0	0	106	102	3	53	103	8.7	1.46	.249
2006	Yankees (GCL)	R	0	1	9.53	5	3	0	0	11	15	1	4	15	11.9	1.68	.313
	Charleston, SC (SAL)	LoA	2	3	3.46	7	7	0	0	42	37	2	12	45	9.7	1.18	.243
2007	Did not play—Injured																
2008	Yankees (GCL)	R	0	2	14.73	3	3	0	0	7	19	3	2	9	11.0	2.86	.487
	Tampa (FSL)	HiA	4	2	2.90	10	10	0	0	50	45	2	17	60	10.9	1.25	.241
	Trenton (EL)	AA	0	0	3.38	1	0	0	0	5	4	0	6	5	8.4	1.88	.211
2009	Trenton (EL)	AA	2	0	0.71	5	5	0	0	25	15	1	17	24	8.5	1.24	.172
2010	Trenton (EL)	AA	1	0	0.00	1	1	0	0	6	2	0	1	3	4.8	0.53	.111
2011	Auburn (NYP)	SS	3	1	2.95	10	0	0	1	18	17	1	2	28	13.7	1.04	.239
	Syracuse (IL)	AAA	0	0	0.00	1	0	0	0	2	0	0	1	2	9.0	0.50	.000
2012	Harrisburg (EL)	AA	1	0	1.35	18	0	0	7	20	13	0	6	28	12.6	0.95	.181

	Class	W	L	ERA	G	GS	CG	SV	IP	H	HR	BB	SO	K/9	WHIP	AVG
Syracuse (IL)	AAA	1	1	0.56	27	0	0	14	32	18	0	11	38	10.6	0.90	.157
Washington (NL)	MAJ	0	0	2.13	13	0	0	0	13	8	2	2	15	10.7	0.79	.186
Major League Totals		0	0	2.13	13	0	0	0	13	8	2	2	15	10.7	0.79	.186
Minor League Totals		22	20	3.22	124	56	0	22	369	317	14	154	414	10.1	1.28	.229

7 EURY PEREZ, OF

Born: May 30, 1990. **B-T:** R-R. **Ht.:** 6-0. **Wt.:** 180. **Signed:** Dominican Republic, 2007. **Signed by:** Dana Brown/Moises de la Mota.

BA GRADE
50
MEDIUM

Perez hit .303 in his first five pro seasons and made great strides with his mental approach in his sixth, helping him advance three levels and earn a September callup in 2012. He improved his English and became a better communicator, implemented a plan for practice as well as games and did a better job staying within himself at the plate. Perez's carrying tool is his speed, which rates an 80 on the 20-80 scale. He's learning to make better use of it by maintaining a slashing approach at the plate, after trying to muscle up and pull pitches in the past—something that makes little sense with his well below-average power. He cut down his high leg kick and focused on hitting balls up the middle. He has good feel for the barrel and makes consistent contact, though he still needs to become more patient in order to realize his potential as a tablesetter. Perez has dramatically improved his pre-pitch positioning and reads, translating to well above-average range at times. He still gets late jumps and takes bad routes a times, however. His arm is solid. Washington's November trade for Denard Span leaves Perez looking at a reserve job in Washington. A little more time in Triple-A Syracuse could be good for him.

Year	Club (League)	Class	AVG	G	AB	R	H	2B	3B	HR	RBI	BB	SO	SB	CS	OBP	SLG
2007	Nationals1 (DSL)	R	.253	51	158	41	40	5	1	0	14	32	39	15	5	.399	.297
2008	Nationals 1 (DSL)	R	.324	60	213	51	69	9	2	4	44	32	36	28	6	.428	.441
2009	Nationals (GCL)	R	.381	47	181	38	69	3	5	3	24	15	20	16	8	.443	.503
2010	Hagerstown (SAL)	LoA	.299	131	438	88	131	17	5	3	42	23	74	64	13	.345	.381
2011	Potomac (CAR)	HiA	.283	119	424	54	120	9	2	1	41	22	63	45	15	.319	.321
2012	Nationals (GCL)	R	.409	5	22	4	9	1	0	0	2	1	0	5	0	.435	.455
	Harrisburg (EL)	AA	.299	82	351	34	105	11	2	0	30	7	53	26	10	.325	.342
	Syracuse (IL)	AAA	.333	40	159	21	53	7	1	0	10	8	26	20	5	.373	.390
	Washington (NL)	MAJ	.200	13	5	3	1	0	0	0	0	0	0	3	0	.200	.200
Major League Totals			.200	13	5	3	1	0	0	0	0	0	0	3	0	.200	.200
Minor League Totals			.306	535	1946	331	596	62	18	11	207	140	311	219	62	.363	.374

8 SAMMY SOLIS, LHP

Born: Aug. 10, 1988. **B-T:** R-L. **Ht.:** 6-5. **Wt.:** 230. **Drafted:** San Diego, 2010 (2nd round). **Signed by:** Tim Reynolds.

RODGER WOOD

BA GRADE
50
HIGH

By visiting the AIDS orphanage his family owns in Africa, the laid-back Solis gained an uncommon sense of perspective, which has been an asset during his injury-plagued career. He missed almost all of 2009 at San Diego with a herniated disc in his back. Signed for $1 million as a 2010 second-rounder, he saw his first full pro season in 2011 delayed by a quadriceps injury. He returned to post a strong season in Class A, but after impressing in the Arizona Fall League, he felt some discomfort in his elbow, which eventually required Tommy John surgery last spring. Solis has quality stuff when healthy, starting with a 90-94 mph fastball that peaks at 96 and has late, tailing life. The depth, speed and shape of his spike curveball varies, looking like a plus downer curve at times and more like a slider at others. He has good feel for his changeup, which projects as a solid or better pitch. He throws strikes but gets in trouble when he leaves balls up in the zone. Solis was progressing well in his rehabilitation and throwing again by the fall. The Nationals expect him to begin 2013 in extended spring training, but he could see game action at high Class A Potomac or Harrisburg by June 1. He projects as a mid-rotation starter, though he must prove he can stay healthy.

Year	Club (League)	Class	W	L	ERA	G	GS	CG	SV	IP	H	HR	BB	SO	K/9	WHIP	AVG
2010	Hagerstown (SAL)	LoA	0	0	0.00	2	2	0	0	4	2	0	0	3	6.8	0.50	.143
2011	Hagerstown (SAL)	LoA	2	1	4.02	7	7	0	0	40	39	3	12	40	8.9	1.26	.253
	Potomac (CAR)	HiA	6	2	2.72	10	10	0	0	56	61	5	11	53	8.5	1.28	.279
2012	Did Not Play—Injured																
Minor League Totals			8	3	3.13	19	19	0	0	101	102	8	23	96	8.6	1.24	.264

9 MATT PURKE, LHP

Born: July 17, 1990. **B-T:** L-L. **Ht.:** 6-4. **Wt.:** 205. **Drafted:** Texas Christian, 2011 (3rd round). **Signed by:** Ed Gustafson.

The 14th overall pick in the 2009 draft, Purke agreed to a $6 million bonus with the Rangers, but MLB controlled the club's finances and refused to approve the deal. He went 16-0 to lead Texas Christian to its first College World Series and win Baseball America's Freshman of the Year award in 2010, but shoulder bursitis hampered him as a draft-eligible sophomore in 2011. The Nationals took him in the third round and signed him to a big league deal with a $2.75 million bonus and $4.15 million total guarantee. He pitched just 15 innings in his 2012 pro debut before having surgery in August to relieve the bursitis and clean out scar tissue in his shoulder. When he's at his best, Purke can pound the strike zone with a 91-94 mph fastball that reaches 96. He backs it up with a plus 78-82 mph slider and shows good feel for a changeup. He was never healthy in 2012 and his stuff was down in the three starts he did make. He has a slingy, low three-quarters delivery, and Washington has worked to raise his arm angle in order to prevent his pitches from flattening out. Purke's history of shoulder problems clouds his prospect status, but he has shown No. 2 starter upside in the past. He's expected to be ready for spring training and to open 2013 in low Class A.

BA GRADE

55

EXTREME

Year	Club (League)	Class	W	L	ERA	G	GS	CG	SV	IP	H	HR	BB	SO	K/9	WHIP	AVG
2012	Hagerstown (SAL)	LoA	0	2	5.87	3	3	0	0	15	15	1	12	14	8.2	1.76	.263
Minor League Totals			0	2	5.87	3	3	0	0	15	15	1	12	14	8.2	1.76	.263

10 ZACH WALTERS, SS

Born: Sept. 5, 1989. **B-T:** B-R. **Ht.:** 6-2. **Wt.:** 195. **Drafted:** San Diego, 2010 (9th round). **Signed by:** Jeffrey Mousser (Diamondbacks).

Acquired from the Diamondbacks for Jason Marquis in July 2011, Walters broke the hamate bone in his right hand during his first spring training with the Nationals. The injury limited him to eight games in April but he played his way to Triple-A by August. He had a solid winter in Puerto Rico as well. Walters stands out for his smooth, fluid swing from both sides of the plate, though he fared markedly better from the left side than the right in 2012. His swing has excellent extension and leverage, giving him a chance to be an average hitter with fringy power if he can improve his plate discipline. He needs to stick with a plan at the plate and avoid chasing pitches early in counts. Walters' other notable tool is his plus arm, which is accurate and gives him a chance to play shortstop in the big leagues. His hands work in the infield, but he must improve his pre-pitch positioning and routes. He's a fringy runner. Washington believes Walters has the athleticism and aptitude to play six different positions, suggesting he could be a valuable utilityman with a quality bat if he can't force his way into an everyday role. He'll head back to Syracuse in 2013.

BA GRADE

45

MEDIUM

Year	Club (League)	Class	AVG	G	AB	R	H	2B	3B	HR	RBI	BB	SO	SB	CS	OBP	SLG
2010	Yakima (NWL)	SS	.302	69	275	44	83	18	4	4	43	16	59	14	4	.338	.440
2011	South Bend (MWL)	LoA	.302	97	361	69	109	27	6	9	56	42	96	12	10	.377	.485
	Potomac (CAR)	HiA	.293	30	116	15	34	7	1	0	11	8	33	7	1	.336	.371
2012	Potomac (CAR)	HiA	.269	54	193	24	52	8	1	5	24	10	43	6	3	.304	.399
	Harrisburg (EL)	AA	.293	43	164	23	48	11	4	6	19	8	38	1	0	.326	.518
	Syracuse (IL)	AAA	.214	29	98	9	21	4	0	1	6	6	28	0	0	.260	.286
Minor League Totals			.287	322	1207	184	347	75	16	25	159	90	297	40	18	.337	.438

11 MICHAEL TAYLOR, OF

BA GRADE

55

EXTREME

Born: March 26, 1991. **B-T:** R-R. **Ht.:** 6-2. **Wt.:** 190. **Drafted:** HS—Fort Lauderdale, Fla., 2009 (6th round). **Signed by:** Tony Arango.

Drafted as a shortstop, Taylor adapted quickly when the Nationals converted him to center field in instructional league after his rough 2010 debut. He complemented his sometimes-dazzling defense with improved offense in 2011, but he failed to build upon that last year in high Class A. He missed time in August after spraining his foot when it got caught under a pad in the outfield fence. Taylor earns comparisons to Mike Cameron and B.J. Upton for his rangy athleticism, his gracefulness in center field, his raw power—and his tendency to swing and miss. The length in Taylor's stroke causes scouts to wonder if he'll ever hit enough to reach the big leagues The Nationals want him to learn to trust his hands, and they think that will come as he continues to get stronger. Taylor hit all three of his home runs last season in July when he simplified his load, stayed more upright and maintained a better direction in his stride. He could grow into average power down the line. For now, defense is Taylor's calling card. He has plus speed underway and outstanding instincts in center field, translating to excellent range. His above-average arm generates low, accurate throws with good carry. Washington would like the mild-mannered Taylor to play with more urgency in 2013, when he will likely repeat high Class A.

Year	Club (League)	Class	AVG	G	AB	R	H	2B	3B	HR	RBI	BB	SO	SB	CS	OBP	SLG
2010	Nationals (GCL)	R	.195	38	128	14	25	4	3	1	12	14	31	1	2	.270	.297
	Hagerstown (SAL)	LoA	.231	5	13	0	3	1	0	0	1	1	2	0	0	.333	.308
2011	Hagerstown (SAL)	LoA	.253	126	442	64	112	26	7	13	68	32	120	23	12	.310	.432
2012	Potomac (CAR)	HiA	.242	109	384	51	93	33	2	3	37	40	113	19	9	.318	.362
Minor League Totals			.241	278	967	129	233	64	12	17	118	87	266	43	23	.308	.385

12 TONY RENDA, 2B

BA GRADE
50
HIGH

Born: Jan. 24, 1991. **B-T:** R-R. **Ht.:** 5-10. **Wt.:** 170. **Drafted:** California, 2012 (2nd round). **Signed by:** Fred Costello.

Renda's makeup turned him into a favorite of Pacific-12 Conference coaches and scouts alike during his standout career at California, which included a conference player of the year award and a trip to the College World Series in 2011. Drafted in the second round last June, he signed quickly for $500,000 and went to short-season Auburn, where he got off to a slow start but came on strong down the stretch. Nationals minor league hitting coordinator Rick Schu worked with Renda to eliminate a wrap in his load, getting his hands into better hitting position. He doesn't stride in his swing, relying on his strong, quick wrists and his hand-eye coordination. He's an aggressive hitter, but aggressive in the strike zone and doesn't chase many bad pitches. He has a knack for squaring up the ball and producing hard line drives from gap to gap, giving him a chance to be an above-average hitter. Renda's power is below average at best, and none of his other tools stand out. He's an average runner with average range and arm strength at second base. He needs to improve his reads, angles, footwork and double-play turns, but he projects as a steady defender. No one will outwork Renda, who has the aptitude to move quickly. Though he's undersized, he has the baseball savvy and bat to be an everyday second baseman.

Year	Club (League)	Class	AVG	G	AB	R	H	2B	3B	HR	RBI	BB	SO	SB	CS	OBP	SLG
2012	Auburn (NYP)	SS	.264	71	295	47	78	9	0	0	32	31	33	15	3	.341	.295
Minor League Totals			.264	71	295	47	78	9	0	0	32	31	33	15	3	.341	.295

13 TAYLOR JORDAN, RHP

BA GRADE
50
HIGH

Born: Jan. 17, 1989. **B-T:** R-R. **Ht.:** 6-3. **Wt.:** 190. **Drafted:** Brevard (Fla.) CC, 2009 (9th round). **Signed by:** Tony Arango.

Jordan was an 18th-round pick by the Reds out of high school in 2007, but it took him a few years to mature off the mound. The Nationals signed him for $99,500 as a ninth-rounder out of Brevard (Fla.) CC, his second junior college. He generated buzz with a strong first half in 2011 but had Tommy John surgery at the end of the summer. He returned to game action last June, and he was showing the best velocity of his career at the end of last season, bumping 96 mph with sink. Jordan's fastball has natural, hard sink and armside run, and it sits at 89-94 mph. He also has the makings of a solid slider with good depth and has a chance for an average changeup. His command hasn't come all the way back yet, but it figures to improve as he gets further away from surgery. He never has had trouble throwing strikes, and Washington believes he has the repertoire, frame and feel to be a starter. The Nationals didn't protect him on the 40-man roster after the season, gambling correctly that he was too far away from the majors to get taken in the Rule 5 draft. He should advance to high Class A in 2013, with a chance to reach Double-A by the second half.

Year	Club (League)	Class	W	L	ERA	G	GS	CG	SV	IP	H	HR	BB	SO	K/9	WHIP	AVG
2009	Nationals (GCL)	R	2	0	3.63	10	6	0	0	35	25	4	9	33	8.6	0.98	.194
2010	Hagerstown (SAL)	LoA	0	1	13.50	1	0	0	0	3	4	0		5	13.5	2.10	.308
	Vermont (NYP)	SS	2	3	4.94	13	13	0	0	62	73	6	17	54	7.8	1.45	.296
2011	Hagerstown (SAL)	LoA	9	4	2.48	18	17	1	0	94	90	1	23	63	6.0	1.20	.247
2012	Auburn (NYP)	SS	0	3	8.16	6	6	0	0	14	19	0	2	17	10.7	1.47	.302
	Hagerstown (SAL)	LoA	3	4	4.05	9	9	0	0	40	52	2	9	28	6.3	1.53	.319
Minor League Totals			16	15	3.98	57	51	1	0	249	263	13	63	200	7.2	1.31	.269

14 JASON MARTINSON, SS/3B

BA GRADE
50
HIGH

Born: Oct. 15, 1988. **B-T:** R-R. **Ht.:** 6-1. **Wt.:** 190. **Drafted:** Texas State, 2010 (5th round). **Signed by:** Tyler Wilt.

Martinson arrived at Texas State on a football scholarship, but he tore his hamstring on his first catch as a wide receiver and decided to focus on baseball. He has made plenty of progress on the diamond at Texas State and in pro ball, but he remains a long-term project with impressive raw tools. After he struck out 144 times in 2011, the Nationals sent him back to low Class A last year to work on his approach, and they promoted him after he made strides in that department. Martinson has plenty of bat speed and leverage in his swing, translating to solid power potential. He can backspin balls out of the park from right-center to left field, but he'll get into funks where he pulls off balls on the outer half, chases sliders out of the zone and passively lets fastballs go by. An above-average runner, Martinson is an accomplished basestealer. His quickness also plays at shortstop, where he has good range and actions. He has a slightly above-average arm, but he needs to do a better job attacking grounders rather than letting the ball play him. He also has seen action at third base. Already 24, Martinson still has plenty of rough edges to smooth out, but he has the tools to be an everyday shortstop. He faces a crucial year in 2013, when he'll likely head back to high Class A after struggling there last season.

Year	Club (League)	Class	AVG	G	AB	R	H	2B	3B	HR	RBI	BB	SO	SB	CS	OBP	SLG
2010	Vermont (NYP)	SS	.241	70	253	38	61	8	6	2	36	38	74	4	2	.346	.344
2011	Hagerstown (SAL)	LoA	.252	129	433	64	109	22	3	19	64	66	144	26	6	.360	.448
2012	Hagerstown (SAL)	LoA	.272	69	265	68	72	11	3	10	63	47	88	23	3	.391	.449
	Potomac (CAR)	HiA	.215	66	237	36	51	2	4	12	43	21	79	7	2	.279	.409
Minor League Totals			.247	334	1188	206	293	43	16	43	206	172	385	60	13	.349	.418

15 SANDY LEON, C

BA GRADE
45
MEDIUM

Born: March 13, 1989. **B-T:** B-R. **Ht.:** 5-11. **Wt.:** 220. **Signed:** Venezuela, 2007. **Signed by:** Mike Rizzo/Dana Brown.

When he was still assistant GM, Mike Rizzo and former scouting director Dana Brown signed Leon on a trip to Venezuela in 2007. He gradually worked his way through the system as a defense-first catcher, and his bat developed enough to help him earn a big league callup when injuries struck the Nationals last May. He sprained his right ankle in a home-plate collision with Chase Headley during his big league debut, but he returned to the majors for stints in July, August and September. Leon has made himself competitive at the plate by tweaking his set-up, getting his hands into better hitting position and improving his balance. He has learned to use all fields and put the ball in play from both sides of the plate. He won't ever hit for power, but he should be a serviceable hitter with outstanding catch-and-throw skills. Leon is a plus receiver with good footwork and agility, making him adept at blocking balls in the dirt. His above-average arm is efficient and accurate, routinely producing pop times in the 1.9-second range and helping him shut down the running game. He threw out 38 percent of basestealers between the majors and minors in 2012. He's still refining his game-calling, but pitchers love throwing to him. He's a well below-average runner, but that's true of most backstops. Leon profiles as a strong backup catcher with a chance to be a defense-first regular, and he's big league-ready.

Year	Club (League)	Class	AVG	G	AB	R	H	2B	3B	HR	RBI	BB	SO	SB	CS	OBP	SLG
2007	Nationals (GCL)	R	.202	31	94	10	19	0	0	0	11	17	15	0	0	.324	.202
2008	Nationals (GCL)	R	.189	26	74	12	14	1	1	0	11	9	18	1	2	.294	.230
2009	Hagerstown (SAL)	LoA	.218	23	78	7	17	3	0	0	6	5	21	0	0	.265	.256
	Vermont (NYP)	SS	.247	50	166	16	41	10	1	2	18	24	29	1	1	.345	.355
2010	Hagerstown (SAL)	LoA	.249	98	325	48	81	10	6	2	36	50	79	3	5	.345	.335
2011	Potomac (CAR)	HiA	.251	109	370	36	93	21	1	6	43	33	69	1	3	.312	.362
2012	Harrisburg (EL)	AA	.311	40	135	15	42	12	0	1	19	9	16	1	0	.358	.422
	Washington (NL)	MAJ	.267	12	30	2	8	2	0	0	2	4	11	0	0	.389	.333
	Auburn (NYP)	SS	.333	5	15	3	5	2	0	0	3	3	2	0	0	.444	.467
	Syracuse (IL)	AAA	.346	19	52	8	18	5	0	2	4	12	12	0	0	.469	.558
Major League Totals			.267	12	30	2	8	2	0	0	2	4	11	0	0	.389	.333
Minor League Totals			.252	401	1309	155	330	64	9	13	151	162	261	7	11	.335	.345

16 RICK HAGUE, SS/2B

BA GRADE
50
HIGH

Born: Sept. 18, 1988. **B-T:** R-R. **Ht.:** 6-2. **Wt.:** 190. **Drafted:** Rice, 2010 (3rd round). **Signed by:** Tyler Wilt.

A three-year standout at Rice, Hague showed plenty of offensive potential in his 2010 pro debut, but he dislocated his throwing shoulder after just four games in 2011, halting his progress. The Nationals eased him back into action last year, holding him back in extended spring training until assigning him to high Class A on April 30. Washington's primary goal for Hague in 2012 was for him to stay healthy for a full season, and he accomplished that, though his numbers were modest. He figures to grow into some power as he matures. He started to hit balls with authority in the second half last year as he learned to make better use of his lower half. He has a chance to be a line-drive, gap-to-gap hitter with average pop, in the mold of Michael Young. A shortstop in college, Hague split time between short and second base last season. His range fits better at second, where his shoulder isn't taxed as heavily. He gradually regained arm strength over the course of the season, and the Nationals expect it to be at least fringy in 2013. He had a slightly above-average arm before his injury. He's a below-average runner but can steal an occasional base. Hague should get a crack at Double-A this year.

Year	Club (League)	Class	AVG	G	AB	R	H	2B	3B	HR	RBI	BB	SO	SB	CS	OBP	SLG
2010	Nationals (GCL)	R	.275	10	40	7	11	1	0	0	6	8	9	3	0	.380	.300
	Hagerstown (SAL)	LoA	.327	39	159	26	52	12	5	3	27	14	34	3	2	.386	.522
2011	Potomac (CAR)	HiA	.357	4	14	4	5	2	0	1	4	2	1	1	0	.438	.714
2012	Potomac (CAR)	HiA	.258	105	395	58	102	20	3	6	48	28	93	20	5	.312	.370
Minor League Totals			.280	158	608	95	170	35	8	10	85	52	137	27	7	.339	.413

17 DESTIN HOOD, OF

Born: April 3, 1990. **B-T:** R-R. **Ht.:** 6-1. **Wt.:** 225. **Drafted:** HS—Mobile, Ala.,
2008 (2nd round). **Signed by:** Eric Robinson.

BA GRADE
50
HIGH

Hood has progressed slowly since eschewing an Alabama football scholarship to sign
for $1.1 million in 2008. It looked like he turned a corner in 2011 at high Class A, but a bout with the flu
followed by a wrist injury plagued his 2012 campaign, during which his power numbers regressed. Physical and
athletic, Hood looks the part of a power hitter, and the ball explodes off his barrel in batting practice. He has
worked hard to make his swing short to the ball, an adjustment that has cost him pop. The Nationals are working with him to maximize his leverage and get himself into better hitters' counts, with a goal of turning some
of his doubles into homers. His ability to hit hard line drives to right field suggests he has a chance to hit for
average. He also rolls over a lot of balls, so some scouts question his feel for hitting. One positive for Hood in
2012 was his development in right field, where his routes and his throwing continued to improve. His arm now
rates as average, though he still profiles best in left field. He's an average runner. Hood will repeat Double-A as
a 23-year-old, and he needs to start translating his potential into production.

Year	Club (League)	Class	AVG	G	AB	R	H	2B	3B	HR	RBI	BB	SO	SB	CS	OBP	SLG
2008	Nationals (GCL)	R	.256	25	86	18	22	6	1	0	14	8	19	5	2	.333	.349
2009	Nationals (GCL)	R	.330	25	88	18	29	10	3	3	24	8	19	3	0	.388	.614
	Vermont (NYP)	SS	.246	38	138	12	34	4	1	2	24	11	45	2	1	.302	.333
2010	Hagerstown (SAL)	LoA	.285	129	492	56	140	30	3	5	65	33	119	5	7	.333	.388
2011	Potomac (CAR)	HiA	.276	128	463	61	128	29	5	13	83	58	96	21	6	.364	.445
2012	Harrisburg (EL)	AA	.245	94	355	45	87	20	3	3	45	24	89	6	1	.301	.344
	Auburn (NYP)	SS	.176	5	17	3	3	1	0	0	0	2	7	0	0	.300	.235
Minor League Totals			.270	444	1639	213	443	100	16	26	255	144	394	42	17	.335	.398

18 ROBBIE RAY, LHP

Born: Oct. 1, 1991. **B-T:** L-L. **Ht.:** 6-2. **Wt.:** 170. **Drafted:** HS—Brentwood,
Tenn., 2010 (12th round). **Signed by:** Paul Faulk.

BA GRADE
50
HIGH

Ray first generated scouting buzz in 2009, when he flashed mid-90s heat on the high
school showcase circuit, but he hasn't shown that kind of stuff since. After signing for $799,000 in 2010, he put
together a solid first full season before struggling mightily against older competition as a 20-year-old in high
Class A last year. Ray has average fastball velocity for a lefthander, sitting at 87-91 mph and bumping 92-93 on
occasion. The Nationals had him commit to a four-seam fastball with some tail, and they think his numbers
took a hit as he got used to pitching without a sinker. He also made a change to his below-average slider, throwing more of a power slurve with better power and depth in the second half of the season. His changeup made
considerable progress in 2012, and it projects as a solid pitch. A short strider, Ray has worked to make better use
of his legs in his delivery and prevent his arm from dragging behind. The Nats made progress giving his delivery
more turn and deception in instructional league. Ray's command is still a work in progress, but he does have feel
for pitching, giving him a chance to be a big league starter. He'll likely repeat high Class A in 2013.

Year	Club (League)	Class	W	L	ERA	G	GS	CG	SV	IP	H	HR	BB	SO	K/9	WHIP	AVG
2010	Vermont (NYP)	SS	0	0	0.00	1	0	0	0	1	0	0	0	2	18.0	0.00	.000
2011	Hagerstown (SAL)	LoA	2	3	3.13	20	20	0	0	89	71	3	38	95	9.6	1.22	.221
2012	Potomac (CAR)	HiA	4	12	6.56	22	21	0	0	106	122	14	49	86	7.3	1.62	.292
Minor League Totals			6	15	4.97	43	41	0	0	196	193	17	87	183	8.4	1.43	.260

19 BRETT MOONEYHAM, LHP

Born: Jan. 24, 1990. **B-T:** L-L. **Ht.:** 6-5. **Wt.:** 235. **Drafted:** Stanford, 2012 (3rd
round). **Signed by:** Fred Costello.

BA GRADE
50
HIGH

Mooneyham's father Bill was a first-round pick in the secondary phase of the June 1980
draft and reached the big leagues with the Athletics in 1986. Erratic control kept Brett from living up to expectations at Stanford, and he missed all of 2011 after having surgery to repair a cut on his left middle finger. He had
a solid pro debut after signing for $428,500. At his best, Mooneyham works with a 92-93 mph fastball, a solid
slider and an average changeup. At other times, his fastball sits at 90-91 and his secondary stuff is below-average.
Mooneyham needs to smooth out his delivery in order to improve what one area scout described as "shotgun
command." He leans back too much when he starts his motion, causing alignment problems and making him
miss to his arm side. When he stays on line and downhill, he's better able to pitch inside against righthanders and
his stuff is crisper. He's an excellent athlete with a durable frame, giving him a chance to be a mid-rotation starter
if he can harness his mechanics and command. Mooneyham could jump to high Class A Potomac in 2013.

Year	Club (League)	Class	W	L	ERA	G	GS	CG	SV	IP	H	HR	BB	SO	K/9	WHIP	AVG
2012	Auburn (NYP)	SS	2	2	2.55	10	9	0	0	42	36	2	16	29	6.2	1.23	.225
Minor League Totals			2	2	2.55	10	9	0	0	42	36	2	16	29	6.2	1.23	.225

20 COREY BROWN, OF

BA GRADE
45
MEDIUM

Born: Nov. 26, 1985. **B-T:** L-L. **Ht.:** 6-1. **Wt.:** 210. **Drafted:** Oklahoma State, 2007 (1st round supplemental). **Signed by:** Blake Davis (Athletics).

Physical and athletic, Brown drew interest from college football programs as a wide receiver coming out of high school, but he opted to play baseball at Oklahoma State and signed with the Athletics for $544,500 as a 2007 sandwich pick. Acquired in the December 2010 deal for Josh Willingham, Brown struggled to make consistent contact at Triple-A in 2011. He got back on track last year, smacking 25 homers at Syracuse and earning a September callup to Washington, where his first career hit was a pinch-hit homer. Brown made better use of his lower half in 2012, staying more balanced in the box and improving his leverage and bat path. He has above-average power to all fields, but he still strikes out a lot and scouts doubt he'll hit enough to be a big league regular. He's an average runner who needs to be more aggressive on the basepaths. Brown has average range and a fringy arm in center field, making him a better fit in left. He profiles better as a power bat off the bench than an everyday player and could win a big league reserve job in spring training.

Year	Club (League)	Class	AVG	G	AB	R	H	2B	3B	HR	RBI	BB	SO	SB	CS	OBP	SLG
2007	Vancouver (NWL)	SS	.268	59	213	31	57	18	4	11	48	37	77	5	3	.379	.545
2008	Kane County (MWL)	LoA	.270	85	300	44	81	18	2	14	49	41	96	12	0	.359	.483
	Stockton (CAL)	HiA	.260	49	196	34	51	9	0	16	34	17	72	4	1	.322	.551
2009	Midland (TL)	AA	.268	66	250	46	67	20	4	9	43	27	69	5	2	.349	.488
2010	Midland (TL)	AA	.320	90	331	63	106	14	8	10	49	52	93	19	1	.415	.502
	Sacramento (PCL)	AAA	.193	41	135	21	26	4	3	5	20	11	36	3	1	.253	.378
2011	Syracuse (IL)	AAA	.235	124	396	50	93	18	3	14	39	47	134	4	7	.326	.402
	Washington (NL)	MAJ	.000	3	3	0	0	0	0	0	0	0	2	0	0	.000	.000
2012	Syracuse (IL)	AAA	.285	126	484	83	138	22	9	25	71	59	139	18	7	.365	.523
	Washington (NL)	MAJ	.200	19	25	4	5	2	0	1	3	1	9	0	0	.231	.400
Major League Totals			.179	22	28	4	5	2	0	1	3	1	11	0	0	.207	.357
Minor League Totals			.269	640	2305	372	619	123	33	104	353	291	716	70	22	.355	.486

21 ESTARLIN MARTINEZ, OF

BA GRADE
50
HIGH

Born: March 8, 1992. **B-T:** R-R. **Ht.:** 6-1. **Wt.:** 185. **Signed:** Dominican Republic, 2009. **Signed by:** Dana Brown/Kris Kline.

After treading water for three years in Rookie ball as a third baseman, Martinez found a home in left field last year at Auburn and took a major step forward offensively, earning all-star honors in the New York-Penn League. He's a quick-twitch athlete with strength in his righthanded swing. He has worked hard to calm down his approach, which had been far too active in the past. His mechanics still break down when he gets pull-happy and tries to muscle up on balls, but he's learning to use the middle of the field. He has cut down his exaggerated leg kick and does a better job swinging at strikes. Martinez is strong enough to drive the ball out of the park to all fields, and he's an average runner. He's working on his reads and routes in left field. While he doesn't have a great feel for throwing distances yet, he has above-average raw arm strength. Martinez needs plenty of refinement but his tools are intriguing. He'll advance to low Class A in 2013.

Year	Club (League)	Class	AVG	G	AB	R	H	2B	3B	HR	RBI	BB	SO	SB	CS	OBP	SLG
2009	Nationals (DSL)	R	.240	60	233	42	56	6	3	3	34	32	28	11	6	.335	.330
2010	Nationals (GCL)	R	.239	32	92	13	22	8	1	0	14	10	22	1	1	.321	.348
2011	Nationals (GCL)	R	.289	50	187	36	54	8	4	6	28	29	36	11	2	.379	.471
2012	Auburn (NYP)	SS	.319	66	257	43	82	16	2	5	44	26	43	13	4	.385	.455
Minor League Totals			.278	208	769	134	214	38	10	14	120	97	129	36	13	.360	.408

22 BRANDON MILLER, OF

BA GRADE
50
HIGH

Born: Oct. 8, 1989. **B-T:** R-R. **Ht.:** 6-2. **Wt.:** 215. **Drafted:** Samford, 2012 (4th round). **Signed by:** Eric Robinson.

Miller was a highly regarded catching prospect who began his college career at Georgia Tech before transferring to Northwest Florida State JC and then to Samford. Moving to the outfield helped his bat blossom, and he topped Division I with 23 homers as a senior in 2012. He homered in his first two pro games before a hip strain sidelined him for six weeks. He posted solid numbers in the season's final month. One club official called Miller "hyper in the box," and another said he "hits with his hair on fire." He has a pull-happy approach and is prone to chasing breaking balls out of the zone, but he has plus-plus raw power. Miller's other premium tool is his arm, though he's still learning to lengthen his arm action rather than throwing from behind his ear like a catcher. A below-average runner, he needs to improve his jumps and angles in order to become an adequate right fielder. The Nats figure to push the 23-year-old if he proves he can handle low Class A next year.

Year	Club (League)	Class	AVG	G	AB	R	H	2B	3B	HR	RBI	BB	SO	SB	CS	OBP	SLG
2012	Auburn (NYP)	SS	.292	29	113	20	33	11	3	4	21	10	36	0	0	.354	.549
Minor League Totals			.292	29	113	20	33	11	3	4	21	10	36	0	0	.354	.549

23 CHRIS MARRERO, 1B

Born: July 2, 1988. **B-T:** R-R. **Ht.:** 6-3. **Wt.:** 220. **Drafted:** HS—Opa Locka, Fla., 2006 (1st round). **Signed by:** Tony Arango.

The 15th overall pick in the 2006 draft, Marrero ranked as the system's top prospect after his first full pro season. He had his best pro season in 2011 at Triple-A but tore his left hamstring playing in the Dominican Republic that November. A setback with his right shoulder in May kept him sidelined until June, and he missed close to another month when he felt discomfort in his surgically repaired hamstring. When he was on the field, Marrero was not himself, as he hit just three homers in 180 at-bats between five levels. He struggled to get in sync, repeatedly pulling off pitches and pressing at the plate. The Nationals are writing off last year and hope Marrero can regain his 2011 form, which would make him an average hitter with slightly above-average game power. He has plus raw pop and is still learning to fully tap into it. Marrero has improved his footwork at first base and his ability to pick balls out of the dirt, making him a fringy defender with an adequate arm. He was already a well below-average runner before the hamstring injury slowed him down further. Marrero no longer looks like a star, but if healthy he could be a solid bat off the bench or the righthanded half of a platoon.

Year	Club (League)	Class	AVG	G	AB	R	H	2B	3B	HR	RBI	BB	SO	SB	CS	OBP	SLG
2006	Nationals (GCL)	R	.309	22	81	10	25	9	0	0	16	8	19	0	0	.374	.420
2007	Hagerstown (SAL)	LoA	.293	57	222	31	65	14	0	14	53	14	39	0	4	.337	.545
	Potomac (CAR)	HiA	.259	68	255	40	66	11	3	9	35	32	63	0	0	.338	.431
2008	Potomac (CAR)	HiA	.250	70	256	40	64	15	2	11	38	25	55	0	0	.325	.453
2009	Potomac (CAR)	HiA	.287	112	414	58	119	21	2	16	65	42	97	2	3	.360	.464
	Harrisburg (EL)	AA	.267	23	75	9	20	6	0	1	11	8	18	0	1	.345	.387
2010	Harrisburg (EL)	AA	.294	141	524	73	154	28	0	18	82	43	102	1	3	.350	.450
2011	Syracuse (IL)	AAA	.300	127	483	59	145	30	0	14	69	58	97	3	2	.375	.449
	Washington (NL)	MAJ	.248	31	109	6	27	5	0	0	10	4	27	0	0	.274	.294
2012	Syracuse (IL)	AAA	.244	37	127	13	31	6	1	0	12	16	28	0	0	.333	.307
	Hagerstown (SAL)	LoA	.250	2	4	1	1	1	0	0	0	1	2	0	0	.500	.500
	Potomac (CAR)	HiA	.462	4	13	1	6	1	0	1	4	0	2	0	0	.462	.769
	Harrisburg (EL)	AA	.273	5	22	2	6	2	0	1	3	0	3	0	0	.304	.500
	Auburn (NYP)	SS	.357	5	14	4	5	1	0	1	3	2	6	0	0	.438	.643
Major League Totals			.248	31	109	6	27	5	0	0	10	4	27	0	0	.274	.294
Minor League Totals			.284	673	2490	341	707	145	8	86	391	249	531	6	13	.353	.452

24 CARLOS RIVERO, 3B/SS/1B

Born: May 20, 1988. **B-T:** R-R. **Ht.:** 6-3. **Wt.:** 215. **Signed:** Venezuela, 2005. **Signed by:** Stewart Ruiz (Indians).

Rivero failed to tap into his potential with the Indians, and the Phillies claimed him off waivers in the winter of 2010 and moved him from shortstop to third base. The Nationals got him on a waiver claim in November 2011 and he had his best pro season last year in Triple-A, resuscitating his faded prospect status. Rivero stands out for his above-average defense at the hot corner, where he has sure hands and a plus arm. He's still capable of filling in at shortstop, though he lacks the range to play the position every day. Rivero shortened up his swing in 2012 and had success peppering line drives from gap to gap. He has quick, strong hands and above-average raw power, though it doesn't play in games. He still chases too many breaking balls and likely lacks the plate discipline to be a full-time big leaguer. His defense, versatility and bat speed could make him a solid utility player. He could get his first taste of the big leagues if injuries create a need in 2013.

Year	Club (League)	Class	AVG	G	AB	R	H	2B	3B	HR	RBI	BB	SO	SB	CS	OBP	SLG
2005	Indians1 (DSL)	R	.257	66	237	21	61	6	0	0	31	12	26	7	5	.295	.283
2006	Indians (GCL)	R	.284	37	134	17	38	6	0	2	22	10	20	0	0	.338	.373
	Burlington (APP)	R	.212	16	66	3	14	3	0	1	7	5	11	0	1	.264	.303
2007	Lake County (SAL)	LoA	.261	115	436	59	114	26	0	7	62	47	84	1	2	.332	.369
2008	Kinston (CAR)	HiA	.282	108	411	46	116	27	1	8	64	36	84	1	2	.342	.411
2009	Akron (EL)	AA	.242	132	480	50	116	24	2	7	58	50	73	1	0	.309	.344
2010	Akron (EL)	AA	.232	110	406	39	94	16	2	6	43	28	81	0	3	.278	.325
2011	Reading (EL)	AA	.275	129	491	70	135	36	0	15	66	38	106	5	3	.331	.440
	Lehigh Valley (IL)	AAA	.185	7	27	1	5	2	1	1	5	1	6	0	0	.233	.444
2012	Syracuse (IL)	AAA	.303	126	455	57	138	28	1	10	64	33	87	6	5	.347	.435
Minor League Totals			.264	846	3143	363	831	174	7	57	422	260	578	21	21	.320	.379

25 STEVEN SOUZA, OF

Born: April 24, 1989. **B-T:** R-R. **Ht.:** 6-3. **Wt.:** 220. **Drafted:** HS—Everett, Wash., 2007 (3rd round). **Signed by:** Doug McMillan.

The Nationals have raved about Souza's raw tools since they signed him for $346,000 in 2007, but scouts have questioned his maturity for years. He hit a low point in 2010, when he broke his thumb and served a 50-game suspension after testing positive for a performance-enhancing drug. He struggled to make consistent contact in 2011 and had to repeat low Class A as a 23-year-old last year, but he turned a corner and earned a promotion to high Class A. Physical and athletic, Souza has three above-average tools in his raw power, speed and arm strength. He used to be a tall, erect hitter who got off his back side quickly, but he did a much better job incorporating his legs and using the whole field while slashing his strikeout rate last year. Scouts still worry about his pitch recognition and holes in his swing, doubting he'll have the aptitude to hit in the majors. Souza responded well to a move to the outfield in 2012 after playing third base and first base earlier in his career, but he has a lot to learn in order to become an average defender there. He has the raw ability to be an everyday big league right fielder, but he's 24 and must prove himself above the Class A level first.

Year	Club (League)	Class	AVG	G	AB	R	H	2B	3B	HR	RBI	BB	SO	SB	CS	OBP	SLG
2007	Nationals (GCL)	R	.194	44	144	17	28	9	0	4	19	18	46	4	1	.299	.340
2008	Hagerstown (SAL)	LoA	.266	23	79	14	21	4	0	2	10	8	26	8	2	.348	.392
	Vermont (NYP)	SS	.189	48	175	27	33	7	0	5	25	24	54	14	7	.296	.314
2009	Hagerstown (SAL)	LoA	.237	126	447	52	106	18	3	4	47	54	116	25	10	.325	.318
2010	Hagerstown (SAL)	LoA	.231	81	303	49	70	16	6	11	56	27	85	18	4	.306	.432
2011	Potomac (CAR)	HiA	.228	122	390	58	89	17	2	11	56	75	131	25	9	.360	.367
2012	Hagerstown (SAL)	LoA	.290	70	262	48	76	20	2	17	72	22	49	7	7	.346	.576
	Potomac (CAR)	HiA	.319	27	91	16	29	2	1	6	13	13	25	7	1	.421	.560
Minor League Totals			.239	541	1891	281	452	93	14	60	298	241	532	108	41	.333	.398

26 BILLY BURNS, OF

BA GRADE
45
HIGH

Born: Aug. 30, 1989. **B-T:** B-L. **Ht.:** 5-9. **Wt.:** 180. **Drafted:** Mercer, 2011 (32nd round). **Signed by:** Eric Robinson.

Burns' father Bob played running back for Joe Namath's New York Jets in 1974. Billy hit .353 with 70 steals in 79 tries during a three-year career at Mercer. A switch-hitter in high school, Burns hit solely from the right side in college before the Nationals turned him back into a switch-hitter in instructional league in 2011. He has an opposite-field, slap approach from the left side, and more strength and natural hitting ability from the right, though he has no power either way. He batted .320 against righthanders and .324 versus lefties last year. The undersized Burns knows his game and excels at making use of his game-changing speed, which scouts rate at 80 on the 20-80 scale. He works counts and puts the ball in play, often on the ground. His speed makes him a formidable basestealer, though he's still learning to get better jumps. Burns has excellent range in center, but his arm is fringy. He has limited offensive upside, but his speed and tablesetting skills give him a chance to be an extra outfielder in the majors. He'll move to high Class A Potomac this year.

Year	Club (League)	Class	AVG	G	AB	R	H	2B	3B	HR	RBI	BB	SO	SB	CS	OBP	SLG
2011	Auburn (NYP)	SS	.262	32	107	21	28	3	2	1	18	12	22	13	1	.367	.355
2012	Hagerstown (SAL)	LoA	.322	113	398	83	128	14	5	0	41	65	68	38	9	.432	.382
Minor League Totals			.309	145	505	104	156	17	7	1	59	77	90	51	10	.418	.376

27 IVAN PINEYRO, RHP

BA GRADE
50
EXTREME

Born: Sept. 29, 1991. **B-T:** R-R **Ht.:** 6-1. **Wt.:** 198. **Signed:** Dominican Republic, 2010. **Signed by:** Johnny DiPuglia.

After carving up the Rookie-level Dominican Summer League in his 2011 pro debut, Pineyro took a line drive to the face during extended spring training in 2012. He missed six weeks of action with a broken jaw, though he continued his-long toss program with his jaw wired shut to keep his arm in shape. When he returned, he dominated in five starts in the Rookie-level Gulf Coast League to earn a promotion to Auburn. He encountered adversity as a 20-year-old facing older competition there, but he held his own. The Nationals rave about Pineyro's maturity and professionalism, and his quick arm is intriguing. His fastball velocity jumped to 90-94 mph last year. He also has good feel for a changeup that projects as an average to plus pitch. His curveball isn't as advanced, however, and its development will be a key going forward. He also needs to refine his command, but his aptitude is encouraging. Pineyro should get a crack at low Class A in 2013.

Year	Club (League)	Class	W	L	ERA	G	GS	CG	SV	IP	H	HR	BB	SO	K/9	WHIP	AVG
2011	Nationals (DSL)	R	4	6	2.20	14	14	1	0	70	63	2	20	73	9.4	1.19	.237
2012	Nationals (GCL)	R	0	0	2.38	5	5	0	0	23	13	2	7	23	9.1	0.88	.163
	Auburn (NYP)	SS	3	2	5.50	8	8	0	0	34	49	2	8	27	7.1	1.66	.345
Minor League Totals			7	8	3.13	27	27	1	0	127	125	6	35	123	8.7	1.26	.256

28 PAUL DEMNY, RHP

BA GRADE
45
HIGH

Born: Aug. 3, 1989. **B-T:** R-R. **Ht.:** 6-2. **Wt.:** 200. **Drafted:** Blinn (Texas) JC, 2008 (6th round). **Signed by:** Tyler Wilt.

After spending two full seasons in low Class A working to harness his mechanics and his emotions, Demny took a step forward in 2011 and moved to Double-A in 2012. His fastball command

and performance remained inconsistent, however, so the Nationals moved him to the bullpen in the Arizona Fall League. He figures to be better suited for relief. Demny's fastball ranges from 90-95 mph in a starting role and could play up in shorter stints. His two-seamer has some sink, but his four-seamer is straight and he must improve his ability to locate it. He has the makings of an average 83-86 mph slider, a below-average curveball and a fringy changeup that he uses sparingly. It isn't dominating secondary stuff, but he has some feel for how to use it. His delivery has a lot of effort and a stiff front leg, contributing to his hit-or-miss command. He has a durable, physical build and enough arm strength to carve out a role as a big league middle reliever. He'll likely head back to Harrisburg to start 2013 and has a chance to reach Triple-A by the second half.

Year	Club (League)	Class	W	L	ERA	G	GS	CG	SV	IP	H	HR	BB	SO	K/9	WHIP	AVG
2008	Nationals (GCL)	R	4	0	2.50	11	6	0	0	36	29	1	14	40	10.0	1.19	.221
2009	Hagerstown (SAL)	LoA	3	11	5.14	23	23	0	0	105	101	8	42	110	9.4	1.36	.250
2010	Hagerstown (SAL)	LoA	6	10	4.23	27	27	1	0	130	128	10	47	106	7.4	1.35	.253
2011	Potomac (CAR)	HiA	10	10	4.32	26	26	0	0	144	144	18	54	108	6.8	1.38	.261
2012	Harrisburg (EL)	AA	6	8	5.46	28	23	0	0	124	138	13	61	97	7.1	1.61	.285
Minor League Totals			29	39	4.60	115	105	1	0	538	540	50	218	461	7.7	1.41	.260

29 WIRKIN ESTEVEZ, RHP

BA GRADE
50
EXTREME

Born: March 15, 1992. **B-T:** R-R. **Ht.:** 6-1. **Wt.:** 170. **Signed:** Dominican Republic, 2010. **Signed by:** Johnny DiPuglia.

Estevez made noise in his 2010 pro debut, leading the Rookie-level Dominican Summer League with 95 strikeouts. He held his own a year later in the New York-Penn League with an 88-90 mph fastball and an advanced feel for a changeup. His velocity jumped in 2012 in low Class A, though it remained inconsistent, and he had Tommy John surgery at the end of the season. At his best, Estevez flashes 92-96 mph heat with sink or cutting action, though he works at 88-93 at other times. His changeup has a chance to be a plus pitch as he matures. Estevez's breaking ball remains a work in progress, sometimes showing biting downer break and other times flattening out. He has a loose arm action and a decent delivery with a three-quarters slot, but he needs to become more consistent. Estevez figures to miss all of 2013 and will need to prove himself in low Class A as a 22-year-old in 2014. He has big league starter upside, with plenty of risk.

Year	Club (League)	Class	W	L	ERA	G	GS	CG	SV	IP	H	HR	BB	SO	K/9	WHIP	AVG
2010	Nationals (DSL)	R	6	7	2.61	15	14	3	0	83	74	1	12	95	10.3	1.04	.233
2011	Auburn (NYP)	SS	6	3	4.01	14	13	0	0	67	72	2	22	55	7.4	1.40	.278
2012	Hagerstown (SAL)	LoA	5	2	5.76	12	12	0	0	59	57	6	25	49	7.4	1.38	.254
	Nationals (GCL)	R	0	0	0.00	3	3	0	0	9	3	0	2	10	10.0	0.56	.103
Minor League Totals			17	12	3.79	44	42	3	0	218	206	9	61	209	8.6	1.22	.248

30 JHONATAN SOLANO, C

BA GRADE
40
LOW

Born: Aug. 12, 1985. **B-T:** R-R. **Ht.:** 5-9. **Wt.:** 205. **Signed:** Colombia, 2005. **Signed by:** Ismael Cruz.

In 2005, Solano hitched a ride from his native Colombia to a baseball tryout in Venezuela in a van full of people and produce—a story that earned him the nickname "Onion" from teammates. The Nationals signed him out of that tryout, and they have valued his defense and leadership behind the plate for years. As his bat has become serviceable over the last two years, he has forced his way into the major league picture. When injuries struck Jesus Flores and Wilson Ramos, Washington called up Solano. He played in his first big league game May 29 at Miami, with his younger brother Donovan (who had debuted eight days earlier) in the opposite dugout. A heady player, Solano handles pitching staffs well. He is an outstanding blocker with solid catch-and-throw skills. When he stays under control in the batter's box, Solano can barrel line drives to the gaps, but he offers little power and won't hit enough to be an everyday player. The Nationals are loaded with big league catching options, so he figures to head back to Triple-A, just a call away from Washington should the need arise.

Year	Club (League)	Class	AVG	G	AB	R	H	2B	3B	HR	RBI	BB	SO	SB	CS	OBP	SLG
2006	Nationals (GCL)	R	.256	37	129	16	33	3	0	0	11	6	15	3	1	.300	.279
2007	Hagerstown (SAL)	LoA	.248	83	298	39	74	15	0	3	38	42	53	0	3	.348	.329
2008	Hagerstown (SAL)	LoA	.218	16	55	6	12	2	0	1	5	6	6	1	1	.302	.309
	Potomac (CAR)	HiA	.258	68	225	35	58	11	0	4	24	16	30	2	1	.315	.360
2009	Harrisburg (EL)	AA	.280	26	93	7	26	7	0	1	11	2	16	0	0	.295	.387
	Syracuse (IL)	AAA	.202	63	183	17	37	11	0	1	9	24	2	1	.239	.279
2010	Harrisburg (EL)	AA	.252	90	317	28	80	15	0	6	42	21	28	1	1	.302	.356
2011	Syracuse (IL)	AAA	.275	78	255	27	70	14	0	5	33	19	36	1	1	.325	.388
2012	Syracuse (IL)	AAA	.250	13	52	8	13	2	0	0	2	3	6	0	0	.298	.288
	Washington (NL)	MAJ	.314	12	35	6	11	3	0	2	6	2	5	1	0	.351	.571
	Nationals (GCL)	R	.333	2	3	1	1	1	0	0	1	0	0	0	0	.250	.667
	Harrisburg (EL)	AA	.195	11	41	4	8	1	0	1	7	0	12	0	0	.209	.293
Major League Totals			.314	12	35	6	11	3	0	2	6	2	5	1	0	.351	.571
Minor League Totals			.250	487	1651	188	412	82	0	22	191	124	226	10	9	.306	.339

2012 DRAFT SPENDING BY TEAM

Major league teams spent $207.9 million on draft bonuses in 2012, the second-highest total ever. The record was set in 2011, when the clubs combined to spend $228 million on bonuses and another $8.1 million on guaranteed salaries as part of major league contracts.

With new draft rules allocating specific bonus pools and prescribing harsh draft-pick penalties to teams that exceeded them by more than 5 percent, several clubs changed their shopping patterns. The Pirates and Nationals were the two biggest draft spenders under the old Collective Bargaining Agreement, which covered the 2007-11 seasons. Pittsburgh plummeted from a record $17 million in 2011 to $3.8 million in 2012, while Washington dropped from $15 million (and another $2.6 million in salary guarantees) to $4.9 million.

On the other side of the spectrum, both the Twins and Astros had ranked in the bottom third in bonus spending under the old CBA. With the top two draft slots and bonus pools this year, Minnesota and Houston led all clubs by paying $12.6 million and $12.1 million in bonuses, respectively.

Team	2012	2011	2007-11 Average
Twins	$12,602,400	$5,902,300	$4,720,740
Astros	$12,074,200	$5,545,800	$5,032,526
Padres	$10,993,000	$11,020,600	$7,153,620
Blue Jays	$10,486,000	$10,996,500	$7,685,920
Cardinals	$9,909,490	$4,554,000	$5,363,640
Mariners	$9,325,200	$11,330,500	$7,211,180
Cubs	$9,164,700	$11,994,550	$6,481,420
Athletics	$8,300,600	$3,067,300	$5,042,100
Red Sox	$7,908,000	$10,978,700	$8,819,450
Royals	$7,573,000	$14,066,000	$9,040,980
Reds	$7,450,400	$6,378,900	$5,533,770
Orioles	$7,433,200	$8,432,100	$8,243,940
Rangers	$7,394,400	$4,193,000	$6,276,860
Brewers	$7,200,100	$7,509,300	$5,870,300
Mets	$7,007,400	$6,782,500	$4,983,860
Rockies	$6,978,700	$3,967,900	$4,900,780
White Sox	$6,450,100	$2,786,300	$3,665,490
Dodgers	$6,277,300	$3,509,300	$4,721,610
Marlins	$5,755,700	$4,135,000	$4,342,210
Indians	$5,330,000	$8,225,000	$6,635,860
Yankees	$4,898,400	$6,324,500	$6,739,800
Nationals	$4,880,500	$15,002,100	$10,216,920
Phillies	$4,787,800	$4,689,800	$4,560,540
Braves	$4,758,000	$3,735,700	$4,402,210
Giants	$4,630,500	$6,266,000	$6,632,480
Diamondbacks	$4,594,800	$11,930,000	$7,052,200
Rays	$4,427,300	$11,482,900	$8,116,440
Pirates	$3,830,700	$17,005,700	$10,411,480
Tigers	$3,172,300	$2,878,700	$6,253,840
Angels	$2,289,800	$3,318,100	$4,538,880
Total	**$207,883,990**	**$228,009,050**	**$190,651,046**
Average	**$6,929,466**	**$7,600,302**	**$6,355,035**

2012 DRAFT SPENDING VS. BUDGETS

Most teams spent very close to their allocated bonus pools in the 2012 draft, which cover the first 10 rounds and any bonus money over $100,000 paid to players in subsequent rounds. The Pct. column below reflects the percentage of pool money spent by a club, while the Plus/Minus column shows how much more or less a team spent in relation to its pool once the money for unsigned players in the top 10 rounds was removed. (The assigned pick value for an unsigned player is removed from a team's signing budget.)

The Yankees ($406,300) and Twins ($298,500) saved the most money versus their bonus pools, though that wasn't necessarily their intention. New York renegotiated its bonus with first-rounder Ty Hensley (from $1.6 million to $1.2 million) and Minnesota did the same with sixth-rounder Andre Martinez ($260,000 to $80,000) after physical examinations prompted questions about their shoulders.

No club exceeded its bonus pool by more than 5 percent, which would have resulted in the loss of a 2013 first-round pick. The Blue Jays came within $341 of doing so and are one of 10 teams that must pay a 75 percent tax on their pool overage.

The tax bill for those teams comes to $1,588,193. The tax money will be divided up among 12 revenue-sharing recipients who didn't exceed their bonus pools: the Athletics, Brewers, Diamondbacks, Indians, Marlins, Orioles, Padres, Pirates, Rays, Reds, Rockies and Tigers. The Cardinals and Royals also would have qualified for tax proceeds if they hadn't surpassed their pools

Team	Pool Spending	Bonus Pool	Pct.	Plus/Minus	Tax
Blue Jays	$9,272,000	$8,830,800	105.0%	-$441,200	$330,900
Cubs	$8,307,700	$7,933,900	104.7%	-$373,800	$280,350
Red Sox	$7,167,000	$6,884,800	104.1%	-$282,200	$211,650
Dodgers	$5,401,300	$5,202,800	103.8%	-$198,500	$148,875
Cardinals	$9,443,990	$9,131,100	103.4%	-$312,890	$234,668
Nationals	$4,548,500	$4,436,200	102.5%	-$112,300	$84,225
Royals	$6,250,000	$6,101,500	102.4%	-$148,500	$111,375
Astros	$11,335,200	$11,177,700	101.4%	-$157,500	$118,125
Giants	$4,130,500	$4,076,400	101.3%	-$54,100	$40,575
White Sox	$5,915,100	$5,915,100	100.0%	$0	
Tigers	$2,099,300	$2,099,300	100.0%	$0	
Brewers	$6,759,100	$6,764,700	99.9%	$5,600	
Braves	$4,007,000	$4,030,800	99.4%	$23,800	
Padres	$9,813,000	$9,903,100	99.1%	$90,100	
Mariners	$8,120,200	$8,223,400	98.7%	-$36,600	$27,450
Rays	$3,821,800	$3,871,000	98.7%	$49,200	
Rangers	$6,484,400	$6,568,200	98.7%	$83,800	
Reds	$6,561,400	$6,653,800	98.6%	$92,400	
Marlins	$4,860,700	$4,935,100	98.5%	$74,400	
Angels	$1,598,800	$1,645,700	97.2%	$46,900	
Diamondbacks	$3,704,800	$3,818,300	97.0%	$113,500	
Rockies	$6,406,700	$6,628,300	96.7%	$221,600	
Twins	$11,938,900	$12,368,200	96.5%	$298,500	
Orioles	$6,564,700	$6,826,900	96.2%	$200	
Indians	$4,387,500	$4,582,900	95.7%	$195,400	
Athletics	$7,875,600	$8,469,500	93.0%	$144,200	
Yankees	$3,785,900	$4,192,200	90.3%	$406,300	
Mets	$6,285,400	$7,151,400	87.9%	$185,600	
Phillies	$4,198,800	$4,916,900	85.4%	$218,100	
Pirates	$3,234,200	$6,563,500	49.3%	$92,600	
Total	**$184,279,490**	**$189,903,500**	**97.0%**		**$1,588,193**

2012 DRAFT

FIRST FIVE ROUNDS

These are the bonuses and assigned pick values for the first five rounds of the 2012 draft. New draft rules that went into effect in 2012 establish assigned values for every pick in the first 10 rounds. The aggregate of all of a team's pick values constitute its draft signing budget. Teams are not required to adhere to the assigned value of any particular pick, but if they exceed their aggregate budget they face penalties that range from fines to lost draft picks. Major league contracts are no longer allowed for draft signees. Crosses signify a two-sport contract, which allows the club to spread the bonus over as many as five years.

FIRST ROUND

Pick. Team: Player, Pos.	Pick Value	Bonus
1. Hou: Carlos Correa, ss	$7,200,000	$4,800,000
2. Min: Byron Buxton, of	$6,200,000	$6,000,000
3. Sea: Mike Zunino, c	$5,200,000	$4,000,000
4. Bal: Kevin Gausman, rhp	$4,200,000	$4,320,000
5. KC: Kyle Zimmer, rhp	$3,500,000	$3,000,000
6. ChC: Albert Almora, of	$3,250,000	$3,900,000
7. SD: Max Fried, lhp	$3,000,000	$3,000,000
8. Pit: Mark Appel, rhp	$2,900,000	Did Not Sign
9. Mia: Andrew Heaney, lhp	$2,800,000	$2,600,000
10. Col: David Dahl, of	$2,700,000	$2,600,000
11. Oak: Addison Russell, ss	$2,625,000	$2,625,000
12. NYM: Gavin Cecchini, ss	$2,550,000	$2,300,000
13. CWS: Courtney Hawkins, of	$2,475,000	$2,475,000
14. Cin: Nick Travieso, rhp	$2,375,000	$2,000,000
15. Cle: Tyler Naquin, of	$2,250,000	$1,750,000
16. Was: Lucas Giolito, rhp	$2,125,000	$2,925,000
17. Tor: D.J. Davis, of	$2,000,000	$1,750,000
18. LAD: Corey Seager, 3b	$1,950,000	$2,350,000
19. StL: Michael Wacha, rhp	$1,900,000	$1,900,000
20. SF: Chris Stratton, rhp	$1,850,000	$1,850,000
21. Atl: Lucas Sims, rhp	$1,825,000	$1,650,000
22. Tor: Marcus Stroman, rhp	$1,800,000	$1,800,000
23. StL: James Ramsey, of	$1,775,000	$1,600,000
24. Bos: Deven Marrero, ss	$1,750,000	$2,050,000
25. TB: Richie Shaffer, 3b	$1,725,000	$1,710,000
26. Ari: Stryker Trahan, c/of	$1,700,000	$1,700,000
27. Mil: Clint Coulter, c	$1,675,000	$1,675,000
28. Mil: Victor Roache, of	$1,650,000	$1,525,000
29. Tex: Lewis Brinson, of	$1,625,000	$1,625,000
30. NYY: Ty Hensley, rhp	$1,600,000	$1,200,000
31. Bos: Brian Johnson, lhp	$1,575,000	$1,575,000

SUPPLEMENTAL FIRST ROUND

Pick. Team: Player, Pos.	Pick Value	Bonus
32. Min: J.O. Berrios, rhp	$1,550,000	$1,550,000
33. SD: Zach Eflin, rhp	$1,525,000	$1,200,000
34. Oak: Daniel Robertson, 3b	$1,500,000	$1,500,000
35. NYM: Kevin Plawecki, c	$1,467,400	$1,400,000
36. StL: Stephen Piscotty, of/3b	$1,430,400	$1,430,400
37. Bos: Pat Light, rhp	$1,394,300	$1,000,000
38. Mil: Mitch Haniger, of	$1,359,100	$1,200,000
39. Tex: Joey Gallo, 3b/rhp	$1,324,800	$2,250,000
40. Phi: Shane Watson, rhp	$1,291,300	$1,291,300
41. Hou: Lance McCullers, rhp	$1,258,700	$2,500,000
42. Min: Luke Bard, rhp	$1,227,000	$1,227,000
43. ChC: Pierce Johnson, rhp	$1,196,000	$1,196,000
44. SD: Travis Jankowski, of	$1,165,800	$975,000
45. Pit: Barrett Barnes, of	$1,136,400	$1,000,000
46. Col: Eddie Butler, rhp	$1,107,700	$1,000,000
47. Oak: Matt Olson, 1b	$1,079,700	$1,079,700
48. CWS: Keon Barnum, 1b	$1,052,500	$950,000
49. Cin: Jesse Winker, of	$1,025,900	$1,000,000
50. Tor: Matt Smoral, lhp	$1,000,000	$2,000,000
51. LAD: Jesmuel Valentin, 2b	$984,700	$984,700
52. StL: Patrick Wisdom, 3b	$969,700	$678,790
53. Tex: Collin Wiles, rhp	$954,800	$975,000
54. Phi: Mitch Gueller, rhp	$940,200	$940,200
55. SD: Walker Weickel, rhp	$925,900	$2,000,000
56. ChC: Paul Blackburn, rhp	$911,700	$911,700
57. Cin: Jeff Gelalich, of	$897,800	$825,000
58. Tor: Mitch Nay, 3b	$884,100	$1,000,000
59. StL: Steve Bean, c	$870,600	$700,000
60. Tor: Tyler Gonzales, rhp	$857,200	$750,000

SECOND ROUND

Pick. Team: Player, Pos.	Pick Value	Bonus
61. Hou: Nolan Fontana, ss	$844,100	$875,000
62. Oak: Bruce Maxwell, c/1b	$831,200	$700,000
63. Min: Mason Melotakis, lhp	$818,500	$750,000
64. Sea: Joe DeCarlo, 3b	$806,000	$1,300,000
65. Bal: Branden Kline, rhp	$793,700	$793,700
66. KC: Sam Selman, lhp	$781,600	$750,000
67. ChC: Duane Underwood, rhp	$769,600	$1,050,000
68. SD: Jeremy Baltz, of	$757,900	$625,000
69. Pit: Wyatt Mathisen, c	$746,300	$746,300
70. SD: Dane Phillips, c/1b	$734,900	$450,000
71. NYM: Matt Reynolds, 3b	$723,600	$525,000
72. Min: J.T. Chargois, rhp	$712,600	$712,600
73. Col: Max White, of	$701,700	$1,000,000
74. Oak: Nolan Sanburn, rhp	$691,000	$710,000
75. NYM: Teddy Stankiewicz, rhp	$680,400	Did Not Sign
76. CWS: Chris Beck, rhp	$670,000	$600,000
77. Phi: Dylan Cozens, of	$659,800	$659,800
78. Cin: Tanner Rahier, ss	$649,700	$649,700
79. Cle: Mitch Brown, rhp	$639,700	$800,000
80. Was: Tony Renda, 2b	$630,000	$500,000
81. Tor: Chase DeJong, rhp	$620,300	$860,000
82. LAD: Paco Rodriguez, lhp	$610,800	$610,800
83. Tex: Jamie Jarmon, of	$601,500	$601,500
84. SF: Martin Agosta, rhp	$592,300	$612,500
85. Atl: Alex Wood, lhp	$583,300	$700,000
86. StL: Carson Kelly, 3b/rhp	$574,300	$1,600,000
87. Bos: Jamie Callahan, rhp	$565,600	$600,000
88. TB: Spencer Edwards, of	$556,900	$554,400
89. NYY: Austin Aune, of	$548,400	$1,000,000
90. Ari: Joe Munoz, 3b	$540,000	$520,500
91. Det: Jake Thompson, rhp	$531,800	$531,800
92. Mil: Tyrone Taylor, of	$523,600	$750,000
93. Tex: Nick Williams, of	$515,600	$500,000
94. NYY: Peter O'Brien, c	$507,800	$460,000
95. Phi: Alec Rash, rhp	$500,000	Did Not Sign

THIRD ROUND

Pick. Team: Player, Pos.	Pick Value	Bonus
96. Hou: Brady Rodgers, rhp	$495,200	$495,200
97. Min: Adam Brett Walker, 1b	$490,400	$490,400
98. Sea: Edwin Diaz, rhp	$485,700	$300,000
99. Bal: Adrian Marin, ss	$481,100	$481,100
100. KC: Colin Rodgers, lhp	$476,500	$700,000
101. ChC: Ryan McNeil, rhp	$471,900	$425,000

Pick. Team: Player, Pos.	Pick Value	Bonus
102. SD: Fernando Perez, 3b	$467,400	$400,000
103. Pit: Jon Sandfort, rhp	$462,900	$462,900
104. Mia: Avery Romero, 3b	$458,400	$700,000
105. Col: Tom Murphy, c	$454,000	$454,000
106. Oak: Kyle Twomey, lhp	$449,700	Did Not Sign
107. NYM: Matt Koch, rhp	$445,400	$425,000
108. CWS: Joey DeMichele, 2b	$441,100	$400,000
109. Cin: Dan Langfield, rhp	$436,800	$436,800
110. Cle: Kieran Lovegrove, rhp	$432,700	$400,000
111. Was: Brett Mooneyham, lhp	$428,500	$428,500
112. Tor: Anthony Alford, of	$424,400	$750,000
113. LAD: Onelki Garcia, lhp	$420,300	$382,000
114. LAA: R.J. Alvarez, rhp	$416,300	$416,300
115. SF: Mac Williamson, of	$412,300	$390,000
116. Atl: Bryan de la Rosa, c	$408,300	$408,300
117. StL: Tim Cooney, lhp	$404,400	$404,400
118. Bos: Austin Maddox, rhp	$400,500	$350,000
119. TB: Andrew Toles, of	$396,700	$394,200
120. Ari: Jake Barrett, rhp	$392,900	$392,900
121. Det: Austin Schotts, ss	$389,100	$389,100
122. Mil: Zachary Quintana, rhp	$385,400	$325,000
123. Tex: Pat Cantwell, c	$381,700	$50,000
124. NYY: Nathan Mikolas, 1b	$378,000	$400,000
125. Phi: Zach Green, 3b	$374,400	$420,000

SUPPLEMENTAL THIRD ROUND

Pick. Team: Player, Pos.	Pick Value	Bonus
126. Sea: Tyler Pike, lhp	$370,800	$850,000
127. Mia: Kolby Copeland, of	$367,200	$367,200
128. Col: Ryan Warner, rhp	$363,700	$363,700

FOURTH ROUND

Pick. Team: Player, Pos.	Pick Value	Bonus
129. Hou: Rio Ruiz, 3b	$360,200	$1,850,000
130. Min: Zack Jones, rhp	$356,700	$356,700
131. Sea: Patrick Kivlehan, 3b	$353,300	$300,000
132. Bal: Christian Walker, 1b	$349,900	$349,900
133. KC: Kenny Diekroeger, 2b	$346,600	$500,000
134. ChC: Josh Conway, rhp	$343,200	$280,000
135. SD: Walker Lockett, rhp	$340,000	$393,000
136. Pit: Brandon Thomas, of	$336,700	Did Not Sign
137. Mia: Austin Dean, 2b	$333,500	$367,200
138. Col: Seth Willoughby, rhp	$330,300	$330,300
139. Oak: B.J. Boyd, of	$327,100	$300,000
140. NYM: Branden Kaupe, ss	$323,900	$225,000
141. CWS: Brandon Brennan, rhp	$320,800	$320,800
142. Cin: Jon Moscot, rhp	$317,800	$317,800
143. Cle: D'vone McClure, of	$314,700	$765,000

Pick. Team: Player, Pos.	Pick Value	Bonus
144. Was: Brandon Miller, of	$311,700	$100,000
145. Tor: Tucker Donahue, rhp	$308,700	$5,000
146. LAD: Justin Chigbogu, 1b	$305,700	$250,000
147. LAA: Alex Yarbrough, 2b	$302,800	$302,800
148. SF: Steven Okert, lhp	$299,900	$270,000
149. Atl: Justin Black, of	$297,000	$300,000
150. StL: Alex Mejia, ss	$294,200	$250,000
151. Bos: Ty Buttrey, rhp	$291,300	$1,300,000
152. TB: Nolan Gannon, rhp	$288,500	$202,500
153. Ari: Chuck Taylor, of	$285,800	$250,000
154. Det: Drew VerHagen, rhp	$283,000	$392,500
155. Mil: Tyler Wagner, rhp	$280,300	$250,000
156. Tex: Alec Asher, rhp	$277,600	$150,000
157. NYY: Corey Black, rhp	$275,000	$215,000
158. Phi: Chris Serritella, 1b	$272,300	$200,000

FIFTH ROUND

Pick. Team: Player, Pos.	Pick Value	Bonus
159. Hou: Andrew Aplin, of	$269,700	$220,000
160. Min: Tyler Duffey, rhp	$267,100	$267,100
161. Sea: Chris Taylor, ss	$264,500	$500,000
162. Bal: Colin Poche, lhp	$262,000	Did Not Sign
163. KC: Chad Johnson, c	$259,500	$340,000
164. ChC: Anthony Prieto, lhp	$257,000	$200,000
165. SD: Mallex Smith, of	$254,500	$375,000
166. Pit: Adrian Sampson, rhp	$252,100	$250,000
167. Mia: Austin Nola, ss	$249,700	$75,000
168. Col: Matt Wessinger, ss	$247,300	$75,000
169. Oak: Max Muncy, 1b	$244,900	$240,000
170. NYM: Brandon Welch, rhp	$242,600	$200,000
171. CWS: Nick Basto, ss	$240,200	$250,000
172. Cin: Mason Felt, lhp	$237,900	$317,800
173. Cle: Dylan Baker, rhp	$235,600	$200,000
174. Was: Spencer Kieboom, c	$233,400	$200,000
175. Tor: Brad Delatte, lhp	$231,100	$5,000
176. LAD: Ross Stripling, rhp	$228,900	$130,000
177. LAA: Mark Sappington, rhp	$226,700	$218,000
178. SF: Ty Blach, lhp	$224,500	$224,500
179. Atl: Blake Brown, of	$222,400	$222,000
180. StL: Cory Jones, rhp	$220,300	$220,300
181. Bos: Mike Augliera, rhp	$218,100	$25,000
182. TB: Bralin Jackson, of	$216,000	$322,500
183. Ari: Ronnie Freeman, c	$214,000	$200,000
184. Det: Joe Rogers, lhp	$211,900	$211,900
185. Mil: Damien Magnifico, rhp	$209,900	$285,000
186. Tex: Preston Beck, of	$207,900	$207,900
187. NYY: Robert Refsnyder, 2b	$205,900	$205,900
188. Phi: Andrew Pullin, of	$203,900	$203,900

2011 DRAFT

Bonuses and estimated slot recommendations by Major League Baseball for the first 100 selections of the 2011 draft. Asterisks indicate bonuses that were part of a major league contract, and crosses signify a two-sport contract, which allows the club to spread the bonus over as many as five years.

FIRST ROUND

Pick. Team: Player, Pos.	'11 Bonus	'11 Slot
1. Pit: Gerrit Cole, rhp	$8,000,000	$4,000,000
2. Sea: Danny Hultzen, lhp	*$6,350,000	$3,250,000
3. Ari: Trevor Bauer, rhp	*$3,400,000	$3,000,000
4. Bal: Dylan Bundy, rhp	*$4,000,000	$2,750,000
5. KC: Bubba Starling, of	+$7,500,000	$2,520,000
6. Was: Anthony Rendon, 3b	*$6,000,000	$2,340,000
7. Ari: Archie Bradley, rhp	+$5,000,000	$2,178,000
8. Cle: Francisco Lindor, ss	$2,900,000	$2,043,000
9. ChC: Javier Baez, ss	$2,625,000	$1,962,000
10. SD: Cory Spangenberg, 2b	$1,863,000	$1,863,000
11. Hou: George Springer, of	$2,525,000	$1,791,000
12. Mil: Taylor Jungmann, rhp	$2,525,000	$1,719,000
13. NYM: Brandon Nimmo, of	$2,100,000	$1,656,000
14. Fla: Jose Fernandez, rhp	$2,000,000	$1,602,000
15. Mil: Jed Bradley, lhp	$2,000,000	$1,557,000
16. LAD: Chris Reed, lhp	$1,589,000	$1,512,000
17. LAA: C.J. Cron, 1b	$1,467,000	$1,467,000
18. Oak: Sonny Gray, rhp	$1,540,000	$1,422,000
19. Bos: Matt Barnes, rhp	$1,500,000	$1,386,000
20. Col: Tyler Anderson, lhp	$1,400,000	$1,359,000
21. Tor: Tyler Beede, rhp	Did Not Sign	$1,332,000
22. StL: Kolten Wong, 2b	$1,300,000	$1,287,000
23. Was: Alex Meyer, rhp	$2,000,000	$1,260,000
24. TB: Taylor Guerrieri, rhp	$1,600,000	$1,242,000
25. SD: Joe Ross, rhp	$2,750,000	$1,215,000
26. Bos: Blake Swihart, c	$2,500,000	$1,197,000
27. Cin: Robert Stephenson, rhp	$2,000,000	$1,161,000
28. Atl: Sean Gilmartin, lhp	$1,134,000	$1,134,000
29. SF: Joe Panik, ss	$1,116,000	$1,116,000
30. Min: Levi Michael, ss	$1,175,000	$1,089,000
31. TB: Mikie Mahtook, of	$1,150,000	$972,000
32. TB: Jake Hager, ss	$963,000	$954,000
33. Tex: Kevin Matthews, lhp	$936,000	$936,000

SUPPLEMENTAL FIRST ROUND

Pick. Team: Player, Pos.	'11 Bonus	'11 Slot
34. Was: Brian Goodwin, of	$3,000,000	$918,000
35. Tor: Jacob Anderson, of	$990,000	$900,000
36. Bos: Henry Owens, lhp	$1,550,000	$889,200
37. Tex: Zach Cone, of	$873,000	$873,000
38. TB: Brandon Martin, ss	$860,000	$858,600
39. Phi: Larry Greene, of	$1,000,000	$844,200
40. Bos: Jackie Bradley, of	$1,100,000	$829,800
41. TB: Tyler Goeddel, 3b	$1,500,000	$815,400
42. TB: Jeff Ames, rhp	$650,000	$802,800
43. Ari: Andrew Chafin, lhp	$875,000	$789,300
44. NYM: Michael Fulmer, rhp	$937,500	$776,700
45. Col: Trevor Story, ss	$915,000	$764,100
46. Tor: Joe Musgrove, rhp	$500,000	$751,500

TOP 100 PICKS

47. CWS: Keenyn Walker, of	$795,000	$739,800
48. SD: Michael Kelly, rhp	$718,000	$728,100
49. SF: Kyle Crick, rhp	$900,000	$717,300
50. Min: Travis Harrison, 3b	$1,050,000	$705,600
51. NYY: Dante Bichette Jr., 3b	$750,000	$694,800
52. TB: Blake Snell, lhp	$684,000	$684,000
53. Tor: Dwight Smith Jr., of	$800,000	$674,100
54. SD: Brett Austin, c	Did Not Sign	$663,300
55. Min: Hudson Boyd, rhp	$1,000,000	$653,400
56. TB: Kes Carter, of	$625,000	$643,500
57. Tor: Kevin Comer, rhp	$1,650,000	$634,500
58. SD: Jace Peterson, ss	$624,600	$624,600
59. TB: Grayson Garvin, lhp	$370,000	$614,700
60. TB: James Harris, of	$490,000	$605,700

SECOND ROUND

Pick. Team: Player, Pos.	'11 Bonus	'11 Slot
61. Pit: Josh Bell, of	$5,000,000	$596,700
62. Sea: Brad Miller, ss	$750,000	$587,700
63. Ari: Anthony Meo, rhp	$625,000	$579,600
64. Bal: Jason Esposito, 3b	$600,000	$570,600
65. KC: Cam Gallahager, c	$750,000	$562,500
66. Phi: Roman Quinn, ss	$775,000	$555,000
67. Cle: Dillon Howard, rhp	$1,850,000	$545,400
68. ChC: Dan Vogelbach, 1b	$1,600,000	$537,300
69. Hou: Adrian Houser, rhp	$530,100	$530,100
70. Mil: Jorge Lopez, rhp	$690,000	$522,000
71. NYM: Cory Mazzoni, rhp	$437,500	$514,800
72. Fla: Adam Conley, lhp	$625,000	$506,700
73. LAD: Alex Santana, 3b	$499,500	$499,500
74. Tor: Daniel Norris, lhp	$2,000,000	$492,300
75. TB: Granden Goetzman, of	$490,000	$485,100
76. Det: James McCann, c	$577,900	$477,900
77. Col: Carl Thomore, of	$480,000	$470,700
78. Tor: J. Gabryszwski, rhp	$575,000	$463,500
79. StL: Charlie Tilson, of	$1,275,000	$457,200
80. CWS: Erik Johnson, rhp	$450,000	$450,000
81. Bos: Williams Jerez, of	$443,700	$443,700
82. SD: Austin Hedges, c	$3,000,000	$436,500
83. Tex: Will Lamb, lhp	$430,200	$430,200
84. Cin: Gabriel Rosa, of	$500,000	$423,900
85. Atl: Nick Ahmed, ss	$417,600	$417,600
86. SF: Andrew Susac, c	$1,100,000	$411,300
87. Min: Madison Boer, rhp	$405,000	$405,000
88. NYY: Sam Stafford, lhp	Did Not Sign	$398,700
89. TB: Leonard Linsky, rhp	$392,400	$392,400
90. Phi: Harold Martinez, 3b	$387,000	$387,000

THIRD ROUND

Pick. Team: Player, Pos.	'11 Bonus	'11 Slot
91. Pit: Alex Dickerson, 1b	$380,700	$380,700
92. Sea: Kevin Cron, 1b	Did Not Sign	$375,300
93. Ari: Justin Bianco, of	$369,000	$369,000
94. Bal: Mike Wright, rhp	$363,600	$363,600
95. KC: Bryan Brickhouse, rhp	$1,500,000	$358,200
96. Was: Matt Purke, lhp	*$2,750,000	$351,900
97. Cle: Jake Sisco, rhp	$325,000	$346,500
98. ChC: Zeke DeVoss, of	$500,000	$341,100
99. Hou: Jack Armstrong Jr., rhp	$750,000	$335,700
100. Mil: Drew Gagnon, rhp	$340,000	$330,300

2010 DRAFT

Bonuses and estimated slot recommendations by Major League Baseball for the top 100 picks of the 2010 draft. Asterisks indicate bonuses that were part of a major league contract, and crosses signify a two-sport contract, which allows the club to spread the bonus over as many as five years.

FIRST ROUND

Pick. Team: Player, Pos.	'10 Bonus	'10 Slot
1. Was: Bryce Harper, of	*$6,250,000	$4,000,000
2. Pit: Jameson Taillon, rhp	$6,500,000	$3,250,000
3. Bal: Manny Machado, ss	$5,250,000	$3,000,000
4. KC: Christian Colon, ss	$2,750,000	$2,750,000
5. Cle: Drew Pomeranz, lhp	$2,650,000	$2,520,000
6. Ari: Barret Loux, rhp	Did Not Sign	$2,340,000
7. NYM: Matt Harvey, rhp	$2,525,000	$2,178,000
8. Hou: Delino DeShields Jr., 2b	$2,150,000	$2,043,000
9. SD: Karsten Whitson, rhp	Did Not Sign	$1,962,000
10. Oak: Michael Choice, of	$2,000,000	$1,863,000
11. Tor: Deck McGuire, rhp	$2,000,000	$1,791,000
12. Cin: Yasmani Grandal, c	*$2,000,000	$1,719,000
13. CWS: Chris Sale, lhp	$1,656,000	$1,656,000
14. Mil: Dylan Covey, rhp	Did Not Sign	$1,602,000
15. Tex: Jake Skole, of	+$1,557,000	$1,557,000
16. ChC: Hayden Simpson, rhp	$1,060,000	$1,512,000
17. TB: Josh Sale, of	$1,620,000	$1,467,000
18. LAA: Kaleb Cowart, 3b/rhp	$2,300,000	$1,422,000
19. Hou: Mike Foltynewicz, rhp	$1,305,000	$1,386,000
20. Bos: Kolbrin Vitek, 2b/of	$1,359,000	$1,359,000
21. Min: Alex Wimmers, rhp	$1,332,000	$1,332,000
22. Tex: Kellin Deglan, c	$1,000,000	$1,287,000
23. Fla: Christian Yelich, of	$1,700,000	$1,260,000
24. SF: Gary Brown, of	$1,450,000	$1,242,000
25. StL: Zack Cox, 3b	*$2,000,000	$1,215,000
26. Col: Kyle Parker, of	+$1,400,000	$1,197,000
27. Phi: Jesse Biddle, lhp	$1,160,000	$1,161,000
28. LAD: Zach Lee, rhp	+$5,250,000	$1,134,000
29. LAA: Cam Bedrosian, rhp	$1,116,000	$1,116,000
30. LAA: Chevez Clarke, of	$1,089,000	$1,089,000
31. TB: Justin O'Conner, c	$1,025,000	$972,000
32. NYY: Cito Culver, ss	$954,000	$954,000

SUPPLEMENTAL FIRST ROUND

Pick. Team: Player, Pos.	'10 Bonus	'10 Slot
33. Hou: Mike Kvasnicka, 3b/c	$936,000	$936,000
34. Tor: Aaron Sanchez, rhp	$775,000	$918,000
35. Atl: Matt Lipka, ss	$800,000	$900,000
36. Bos: Bryce Brentz, of	$889,200	$889,200
37. LAA: Taylor Lindsey, ss	$873,000	$873,000
38. Tor: Noah Syndergaard, rhp	$600,000	$858,600
39. Bos: Anthony Ranaudo, rhp	$2,550,000	$844,200
40. LAA: Ryan Bolden, of	$829,800	$829,800
41. Tor: Asher Wojciechowski, rhp	$815,400	$815,400
42. TB: Drew Vettleson, of	$845,000	$802,800
43. Sea: Taijuan Walker, rhp	$800,000	$789,300
44. Det: Nick Castellanos, 3b	$3,450,000	$776,700
45. Tex: Luke Jackson, rhp	$1,545,000	$764,100
46. StL: Seth Blair, rhp	$751,500	$751,500
47. Col: Peter Tago, rhp	$982,500	$739,800
48. Det: Chance Ruffin, rhp	$1,150,000	$728,100
49. Tex: Mike Olt, 3b	$717,300	$717,300
50. StL: Tyrell Jenkins, rhp	+$1,300,000	$705,600

SECOND ROUND

Pick. Team: Player, Pos.	'10 Bonus	'10 Slot
51. Was: Sammy Solis, lhp	$1,000,000	$694,800
52. Pit: Stetson Allie, rhp	$2,250,000	$684,000
53. Atl: Todd Cunningham, of	$674,100	$674,100
54. KC: Brett Eibner, of/rhp	$1,250,000	$663,300
55. Cle: LeVon Washington, of	$1,200,000	$653,400
56. Ari: J.R. Bradley, rhp	$643,500	$643,500
57. Bos: Brandon Workman, rhp	$800,000	$634,500
58. Hou: Vincent Velasquez, rhp	$655,830	$624,600
59. SD: Jedd Gyorko, 2b	$614,700	$614,700
60. Oak: Yordy Cabrera, 3b	$1,250,000	$605,700
61. Tor: Griffin Murphy, lhp	$800,000	$596,700
62. Cin: Ryan LaMarre, of	$587,700	$587,700
63. CWS: Jacob Petricka, rhp	$540,000	$579,600
64. Mil: Jimmy Nelson, rhp	$570,600	$570,600
65. ChC: Reggie Golden, of	$720,000	$562,500
66. TB: Jake Thompson, rhp	$555,000	$555,000
67. Sea: Marcus Littlewood, ss	$900,000	$545,400
68. Det: Drew Smyly, lhp	$1,100,000	$537,300
69. Tor: Kellen Sweeney, 3b	$600,000	$530,100
70. Atl: Andrelton Simmons, rhp	$522,000	$522,000
71. Min: Niko Goodrum, ss	$514,800	$514,800
72. Tex: Cody Buckel, rhp	$590,000	$506,700
73. Fla: Rob Rasmussen, lhp	$499,500	$499,500
74. SF: Jarrett Parker, of	$700,000	$492,300
75. StL: Jordan Swaggerty, rhp	$625,000	$485,100
76. Col: Chad Bettis, rhp	$477,000	$477,900
77. Phi: Perci Garner, rhp	$470,700	$470,700
78. LAD: Ralston Cash, rhp	$463,500	$463,500
79. TB: Derek Dietrich, 3b	$457,200	$457,200
80. Tor: Justin Nicolino, rhp	$615,000	$450,000
81. LAA: Daniel Tillman, rhp	$443,700	$443,700
82. NYY: Angelo Gumbs, of	$750,000	$436,500

THIRD ROUND

Pick. Team: Player, Pos.	'10 Bonus	'10 Slot
83. Was: Rick Hague, ss	$430,200	$430,200
84. Pit: Mel Rojas Jr., of	$423,900	$423,900
85. Bal: Dan Klein, rhp	$499,900	$417,600
86. KC: Mike Antonio, ss	$411,000	$411,300
87. Cle: Tony Wolters, ss	$1,350,000	$405,000
88. Ari: Robby Rowland, rhp	$395,000	$398,700
89. NYM: Blake Forsythe, c	$392,400	$392,700
90. Hou: Austin Wates, 2b	$550,000	$387,000
91. SD: Zach Cates, rhp	$765,000	$380,700
92. Oak: Aaron Shipman, of	$500,000	$375,300
93. Tor: Christopher Hawkins, 3b	$350,000	$369,000
94. Cin: Devin Lohman, ss	$363,600	$363,600
95. CWS: Addison Reed, rhp	$358,200	$358,200
96. Mil: Tyler Thornburg, rhp	$351,900	$351,900
97. ChC: Micah Gibbs, c	$350,000	$346,500
98. TB: Ryan Brett, 2b	$341,100	$341,100
99. Sea: Ryne Stanek, rhp	Did Not Sign	$335,700
100. Det: Rob Brantly, c	$330,300	$330,300

COLLEGE TOP 100

Rank	Player	Pos.	B/T	Ht.	Wt.	College	Last Drafted
1.	Mark Appel	RHP	R/R	6-4	215	Stanford	Pirates '12 (1)
2.	Sean Manaea	LHP	L/L	6-5	215	Indiana State	Never
3.	Ryne Stanek	RHP	R/R	6-4	190	Arkansas	Mariners '10 (3)
4.	Colin Moran	3B	L/R	6-3	209	North Carolina	Never
5.	Jonathon Crawford	RHP	R/R	6-1	205	Florida	Marlins '10 (42)
6.	Kris Bryant	OF/3B/1B	R/R	6-5	215	San Diego	Blue Jays '10 (18)
7.	Bobby Wahl	RHP	R/R	6-3	200	Mississippi	Indians '10 (39)
8.	Phillip Ervin	OF	R/R	5-11	190	Samford	Never
9.	Austin Wilson	OF	R/R	6-5	245	Stanford	Cardinals '10 (12)
10.	D.J. Peterson	3B/1B	R/R	6-1	190	New Mexico	Mariners '10 (33)
11.	Marco Gonzales	LHP	L/L	6-1	185	Gonzaga	Rockies '10 (29)
12.	Ryan Eades	RHP	B/R	6-3	198	Louisiana State	Rockies '10 (19)
13.	Aaron Judge	OF	R/R	6-7	230	Fresno State	Athletics '10 (31)
14.	Dillon Overton	LHP	L/L	6-2	160	Oklahoma	Red Sox '10 (26)
15.	JaCoby Jones	2B/OF	R/R	6-3	205	Louisiana State	Astros '10 (19)
16.	Colby Suggs	RHP	R/R	6-0	225	Arkansas	Never
17.	A.J. Vanegas	RHP	L/R	6-1	205	Stanford	Padres '10 (7)
18.	Karsten Whitson	RHP	R/R	6-4	225	Florida	Padres '10 (1)
19.	Tom Windle	LHP	L/L	6-4	210	Minnesota	White Sox '10 (28)
20.	Eric Jagielo	3B	L/R	6-3	215	Notre Dame	Cubs '10 (50)
21.	Kent Emanuel	LHP	L/L	6-4	209	North Carolina	Pirates '10 (19)
22.	Trey Masek	RHP	R/R	6-1	195	Texas Tech	Never
23.	Alex Balog	RHP	R/R	6-6	225	San Francisco	Never
24.	Scott Frazier	RHP	R/R	6-6	215	Pepperdine	Phillies '10 (5)
25.	Brian Ragira	1B	R/R	6-2	200	Stanford	Rangers '10 (30)
26.	Dan Slania	RHP	R/R	6-5	275	Notre Dame	Red Sox '10 (42)
27.	Michael Lorenzen	OF/RHP	R/R	6-3	200	Cal State Fullerton	Rays '10 (7)
28.	Kevin Ziomek	LHP	R/L	6-3	200	Vanderbilt	Diamondbacks '10 (13)
29.	Trevor Williams	RHP	R/R	6-3	228	Arizona State	Never
30.	Chad Pinder	3B	R/R	6-2	192	Virginia Tech	Never
31.	Braden Shipley	RHP	R/R	6-2	170	Nevada	Never
32.	Chase Johnson	RHP	R/R	6-3	190	Cal Poly	Rangers '10 (26)
33.	Mike Mayers	RHP	R/R	6-3	195	Mississippi	Never
34.	Dylan Covey	RHP	R/R	6-2	200	San Diego	Brewers '10 (1)
35.	Konner Wade	RHP	L/R	6-3	182	Arizona	Diamondbacks '10 (35)
36.	Jonathan Gray	RHP	R/R	6-4	239	Oklahoma	Yankees '11 (10)
37.	Jason Hursh	RHP	R/R	6-1	197	Oklahoma State	Pirates '10 (6)
38.	Aaron Blair	RHP	R/R	6-5	220	Marshall	Astros '10 (21)
39.	Corey Littrell	LHP	L/L	6-3	190	Kentucky	Nationals '10 (43)
40.	Stephen Tarpley	LHP	R/L	6-1	185	Scottsdale (Ariz.) CC	Indians '11 (8)
41.	Conrad Gregor	1B	L/R	6-3	215	Vanderbilt	White Sox '10 (40)
42.	Hunter Renfroe	OF	R/R	6-2	211	Mississippi State	Red Sox '10 (31)
43.	Aaron Brown	LHP/OF	L/L	6-1	200	Pepperdine	Pirates '11 (17)
44.	Daniel Palka	OF/1B	L/L	6-2	228	Georgia Tech	Phillies '10 (10)
45.	Jared King	OF	B/L	5-11	220	Kansas State	Never
46.	Jason Monda	OF	L/L	6-4	201	Washington State	Rockies '10 (32)
47.	Tyler Horan	OF	L/R	6-2	232	Virginia Tech	Never
48.	John Simms	RHP	R/R	6-3	210	Rice	Nationals '10 (39)
49.	Michael Wagner	RHP	R/R	6-4	185	San Diego	Never
50.	Ben Wetzler	LHP	L/L	6-1	200	Oregon State	Indians '10 (15)

Rank	Player	Pos.	B/T	Ht.	Wt.	College	Last Drafted
51.	Daniel Gibson	LHP	L/L	6-3	220	Florida	Brewers '10 (26)
52.	Kyle Finnegan	RHP	R/R	6-1	165	Texas State	Never
53.	David Garner	RHP	R/R	5-11	175	Michigan State	Reds '10 (33)
54.	Brandon Trinkwon	SS	L/R	6-1	160	UC Santa Barbara	Never
55.	Tyler Linehan	LHP	L/L	6-0	220	Fresno State	Mariners '10 (14)
56.	Matt Boyd	LHP	L/L	6-3	215	Oregon State	Reds '12 (13)
57.	Brandon Thomas	OF	B/R	6-3	205	Georgia Tech	Pirates '12 (4)
58.	Michael O'Neill	OF	R/R	6-1	195	Michigan	Cardinals '10 (31)
59.	Drew Dosch	3B	L/R	6-2	190	Youngstown State	Never
60.	Ryon Healy	1B	R/R	6-5	215	Oregon	Never
61.	Buck Farmer	RHP	L/R	6-3	228	Georgia Tech	Brewers '12 (15)
62.	Andrew Mitchell	RHP	R/R	6-3	220	Texas Christian	Never
63.	Jimmie Sherfy	RHP	R/R	6-0	175	Oregon	Never
64.	Corey Knebel	RHP	R/R	6-3	195	Texas	Never
65.	Barrett Astin	RHP	R/R	6-1	200	Arkansas	Never
66.	Teddy Stankiewicz	RHP	R/R	6-4	215	Seminole State (Okla.) JC	Mets '12 (2)
67.	Dan Child	RHP	R/R	6-5	225	Oregon State	Padres '10 (48)
68.	Keenan Kish	RHP	L/R	6-3	205	Florida	Yankees '10 (34)
69.	Randy LeBlanc	RHP	R/R	6-4	195	Tulane	Marlins '10 (16)
70.	Josh Dezse	RHP	R/R	6-5	225	Ohio State	Yankees '10 (28)
71.	Austin Kubitza	RHP	L/R	6-5	202	Rice	Pirates '10 (7)
72.	Adam Plutko	RHP	R/R	6-3	192	UCLA	Astros '10 (6)
73.	T.J. Pecoraro	RHP	R/R	6-0	170	Vanderbilt	Astros '10 (48)
74.	Dominic Ficociello	1B	B/R	6-4	185	Arkansas	Tigers '10 (23)
75.	Alex Haines	LHP	L/L	6-4	215	Seton Hill (Pa.)	Never
76.	Trey Williams	3B	R/R	6-2	210	JC of the Canyons (Calif.)	Cardinals '12 (11)
77.	Shane Carle	RHP	R/R	6-4	185	Long Beach State	Never
78.	Chad Green	RHP	R/R	6-4	215	Louisville	Blue Jays '10 (37)
79.	Johnny Magliozzi	RHP	R/R	5-10	195	Florida	Rays '11 (35)
80.	Billy Waltrip	LHP	L/L	6-2	215	Oklahoma	Orioles '12 (12)
81.	Justin Topa	RHP	R/R	6-4	190	Long Island	Reds '12 (33)
82.	Jacob May	OF	B/R	5-10	175	Coastal Carolina	Reds '10 (39)
83.	Ben Lively	RHP	R/R	6-4	205	Central Florida	Indians '10 (26)
84.	Hunter Dozier	SS	R/R	6-4	210	Stephen F. Austin State	Never
85.	Dale Carey	OF	R/R	6-2	184	Miami	Pirates '10 (21)
86.	L.J. Mazzilli	2B	R/R	6-1	190	Connecticut	Twins '12 (9)
87.	Ryan Tella	OF	L/L	6-0	175	Auburn	Giants '12 (11)
88.	Adam Nelubowich	3B	L/R	6-2	184	Washington State	Mariners '09 (14)
89.	David Whitehead	RHP	R/R	6-5	247	Elon	Blue Jays '10 (36)
90.	Andrew Knapp	C	B/R	6-1	192	California	Athletics '10 (41)
91.	Austin Voth	RHP	R/R	6-1	209	Washington	Never
92.	Jon Keller	RHP	R/R	6-5	215	Tampa	Mariners '10 (11)
93.	Nick Vander Tuig	RHP	R/R	6-3	195	UCLA	Blue Jays '10 (39)
94.	Matt Reida	SS	L/R	5-11	178	Kentucky	White Sox '10 (47)
95.	Lonnie Kauppila	SS	R/R	6-0	175	Stanford	Athletics '10 (44)
96.	Adam Engel	OF	R/R	6-1	213	Louisville	Never
97.	Adam Frazier	SS/2B	L/R	5-10	172	Mississippi State	Never
98.	C.K. Irby	RHP	R/R	6-2	190	Samford	Never
99.	Sam Moll	LHP	L/L	5-11	187	Memphis	Never
100.	Dace Kime	RHP	R/R	6-5	215	Louisville	Pirates '10 (8)

HIGH SCHOOL TOP 100

Rank	Player	Pos.	B/T	Ht.	Wt.	School	Commitment
1.	Austin Meadows	OF	L/L	6-3	200	Grayson HS, Loganville, Ga.	Clemson
2.	Clint Frazier	OF	R/R	6-1	190	Loganville (Ga.) HS	Georgia
3.	Trey Ball	OF/LHP	L/L	6-6	180	New Castle (Ind.) HS	Texas
4.	Reese McGuire	C	L/R	6-1	190	Kentwood HS, Covington, Wash.	San Diego
5.	J.P. Crawford	SS	L/R	6-2	180	Lakewood (Calif.) HS	Southern California
6.	Dominic Smith	1B/OF	L/L	6-1	200	Serra HS, Gardena, Calif.	Southern California
7.	Jordan Sheffield	RHP	R/R	6-1	175	Tullahoma (Tenn.) HS	Vanderbilt
8.	Ryan Boldt	OF	L/R	6-1	190	Red Wing (Minn.) HS	Nebraska
9.	Kohl Stewart	RHP	R/R	6-3	195	St. Pius X HS, Houston	Texas A&M
10.	Jonathan Denney	C	R/R	6-2	205	Yukon (Okla.) HS	Arkansas
11.	Oscar Mercado	SS	R/R	6-2	175	Gaither HS, Tampa	Florida State
12.	Rob Kaminsky	LHP	B/L	6-0	190	St. Joseph Regional HS, Montvale, N.J.	North Carolina
13.	Stephen Gonsalves	LHP	L/L	6-5	205	Cathedral Catholic HS, San Diego	San Diego
14.	Ian Clarkin	LHP	L/L	6-2	190	Madison HS, San Diego	San Diego
15.	Garrett Williams	LHP	L/L	6-2	195	Calvary Baptist HS, Shreveport, La.	Oklahoma State
16.	Rowdy Tellez	1B	L/L	6-5	250	Elk Grove (Calif.) HS	Southern California
17.	Travis Demeritte	3B	R/R	6-1	185	Winder-Barrow HS, Winder, Ga.	South Carolina
18.	A.J. Puk	LHP/1B	L/L	6-6	205	Washington HS, Cedar Rapids, Iowa	Florida
19.	Nick Ciuffo	C	L/R	6-1	205	Lexington (S.C.) HS	South Carolina
20.	Justin Williams	OF	L/R	6-3	215	Terrebonne HS, Houma, La.	Louisiana State
21.	Brett Morales	RHP	R/R	6-2	190	King HS, Tampa	Florida
22.	Dustin Driver	RHP	R/R	6-2	200	Wenatchee (Wash.) HS	UCLA
23.	Matt McPhearson	OF	L/L	5-10	170	Riverdale Baptist HS, Upper Marlboro, Md.	Miami
24.	Andy McGuire	SS	R/R	6-1	185	Madison HS, Vienna, Va.	Texas
25.	Cavan Biggio	3B	L/R	6-1	185	St. Thomas HS, Houston	Notre Dame
26.	Chris Okey	C	R/R	6-0	175	Eustis (Fla.) HS	Clemson
27.	Casey Shane	RHP	R/R	6-4	200	Centennial HS, Burleson, Texas	Texas A&M
28.	Terry McClure	OF	R/R	6-2	185	Riverwood Int'l HS, Sandy Springs, Ga.	Georgia Tech
29.	Ivan Wilson	OF	R/R	6-3	220	Ruston (La.) HS	Uncommitted
30.	J.B. Woodman	OF	L/R	6-2	190	Edgewater HS, Orlando	Mississippi
31.	Jeremy Martinez	C	R/R	5-11	195	Mater Dei HS, Santa Ana, Calif.	Southern California
32.	Hunter Green	LHP	L/L	6-3	160	Warren East HS, Bowling Green, Ky.	Kentucky
33.	Cord Sandberg	OF	L/L	6-3	215	Manatee HS, Bradenton, Fla.	Mississippi State
34.	Jan Hernandez	SS	R/R	6-3	195	Beltran Baseball Acadmey, Florida, P.R.	Uncommitted
35.	Hunter Harvey	RHP	R/R	6-3	175	Bandys HS, Catawba, N.C.	Uncommitted
36.	Connor Jones	RHP	R/R	6-3	190	Great Bridge HS, Chesapeake, Va.	Virginia
37.	Ryder Jones	3B/RHP	L/R	6-3	190	Watauga HS, Boone, N.C.	Stanford
38.	Billy McKinney	OF	L/L	6-1	195	Plano (Texas) West HS	Texas Christian
39.	Devin Williams	RHP	R/R	6-3	165	Hazelwood (Mo.) West HS	Missouri
40.	Tucker Neuhaus	3B	L/R	6-3	190	Wharton HS, Tampa	Louisville
41.	Chris Kohler	LHP	L/L	6-3	200	Los Osos HS, Rancho Cucamonga, Calif.	Oklahoma
42.	Zack Collins	C/1B	L/R	6-3	210	American Heritage HS, Plantation, Fla.	Miami
43.	Keegan Thompson	RHP	R/R	6-2	175	Cullman (Ala.) HS	Auburn
44.	Josh Hart	OF	L/L	6-0	180	Parkview HS, Lilburn, Ga.	Georgia Tech
45.	Thomas Milone	OF	L/L	6-0	185	Masuk HS, Monroe, Conn.	Connecticut
46.	Mark Armstrong	RHP	R/R	6-3	200	Clarence (N.Y.) HS	Pittsburgh
47.	Cal Quantrill	RHP	L/R	6-3	165	Trinity College School, Port Hope, Ont.	Stanford
48.	Tyler Alamo	C	R/R	6-4	205	Cypress (Calif.) HS	Cal State Fullerton
49.	Marcus Doi	OF	R/R	6-0	185	Mid-Pacific Institute, Honolulu	Hawaii
50.	Jordan Paroubeck	OF	S/R	6-2	190	Serra HS, San Mateo, Calif.	Fresno State

Rank	Player	Pos.	B/T	Ht.	Wt.	School	Commitment
51.	Mason Smith	OF	R/R	6-2	195	Rocky Mountain HS, Meridian, Idaho	Utah
52.	Brian Navarreto	C	R/R	6-3	225	Arlington Country Day HS, Jacksonville	Uncommitted
53.	Stephen Wrenn	OF	R/R	6-2	175	Walton HS, Marietta, Ga.	Georgia
54.	Dom Nunez	C/SS	L/R	6-1	175	Elk Grove (Calif.) HS	UCLA
55.	John Sternagel	3B	R/R	6-2	195	Rockledge (Fla.) HS	Florida
56.	Brandon Gilson	LHP	L/L	6-5	225	Prosper (Texas) HS	Texas Christian
57.	Billy Roth	3B/RHP	R/R	6-3	190	Vista (Calif.) HS	Arizona
58.	Derik Beauprez	RHP	L/R	6-5	220	Cherry Creek HS, Greenwood Village, Colo.	Miami
59.	Corey Simpson	C/1B	R/R	6-3	220	Sweeny (Texas) HS	Houston
60.	Clinton Hollon	RHP	R/R	6-1	195	Woodford County HS, Versailles, Ky.	Kentucky
61.	Jonah Wesely	LHP	L/L	6-2	215	Tracy (Calif.) HS	UCLA
62.	Chris Oakley	RHP	R/R	6-8	220	St. Augustine Prep. HS, Richland, N.J.	North Carolina
63.	Josh Adams	OF	L/L	6-2	195	Pleasant Grove HS, Elk Grove, Calif.	UC Santa Barbara
64.	Jake Brentz	LHP/OF	L/L	6-1	180	Parkway South HS, Manchester, Mo.	Jefferson (Mo.) JC
65.	Carlos Salazar	RHP	R/R	6-2	205	Kerman (Calif.) HS	Fresno State
66.	Ryan McMahon	3B	L/R	6-3	180	Mater Dei HS, Santa Ana, Calif.	Uncommitted
67.	Tyler Alexander	LHP	L/L	6-2	175	Carroll HS, Southlake, Texas	Texas Christian
68.	Trevor Clifton	RHP	R/R	6-4	180	Knoxville HS	Kentucky
69.	Nick Longhi	OF	R/L	6-2	210	Venice (Fla.) HS	Louisiana State
70.	Chris Rivera	SS/C/RHP	R/R	6-0	180	El Dorado HS, Placentia, Calif.	Uncommitted
71.	Alec Hansen	RHP	R/R	6-7	210	Loveland (Colo.) HS	Oklahoma
72.	Dustin Peterson	SS	R/R	6-2	180	Gilbert (Ariz.) HS	Arizona State
73.	Dane McFarland	OF	R/R	6-4	210	JSerra HS, San Juan Capistrano, Calif.	Oregon
74.	Terrian Arbet	SS	R/R	6-0	180	Great Oak HS, Temecula, Calif.	San Diego
75.	Willie Abreu	OF	L/L	6-3	195	Mater Academy, Hialeah Gardens, Fla.	Miami
76.	Eugene Vazquez	OF	L/L	6-2	190	Timbercreek HS, Orlando	Central Florida
77.	Kevin Franklin	3B	R/R	6-2	220	Gahr HS, Cerritos, Calif.	Arizona State
78.	Connor Heady	SS	R/R	6-0	165	North Oldham HS, Goshen, Ky.	Kentucky
79.	Akeem Bostick	RHP	R/R	6-5	185	West Florence (S.C.) HS	Georgia Southern
80.	Kacy Clemens	RHP	L/R	6-2	195	Memorial HS, Houston	Texas
81.	K.J. Woods	OF	L/R	6-4	210	Fort Mill (S.C.) HS	South Carolina
82.	T.J. McDonald	RHP	L/R	6-3	185	Village Christian Acad., Fayetteville, N.C.	East Carolina
83.	Wesley Jones	SS	R/R	6-2	180	Redan HS, Stone Mountain, Ga.	Georgia
84.	Cody Thomas	OF	L/R	6-5	215	Heritage HS, Colleyville, Texas	Oklahoma (FB)
85.	Tyler O'Neill	C	R/R	6-0	200	Garibaldi SS, Maple Ridge, B.C.	Oregon State
86.	Joey Martarano	3B	R/R	6-3	230	Fruitland (Idaho) HS	Boise State (FB)
87.	Ian McKinney	LHP	L/L	5-11	185	Boone HS, Orlando	Central Florida
88.	Anfernee Grier	OF	R/R	6-0	175	Russell County HS, Seale, Ala.	Auburn
89.	Casey Meisner	RHP	R/R	6-7	185	Cypress (Texas) Woods HS	Texas Tech
90.	Andrew Church	RHP	R/R	6-1	185	Palo Verde HS, Las Vegas	San Diego
91.	Dakota Hudson	RHP	R/R	6-5	190	Sequatchie County HS, Dunlap, Tenn.	Mississippi State
92.	Errol Robinson	SS	R/R	5-10	170	St. John's College HS, Washington, D.C.	Mississippi
93.	Cory Thompson	SS/RHP	R/R	6-0	185	Mauldin (S.C.) HS	South Carolina
94.	A.J. Bogucki	RHP	R/R	6-3	200	Boyertown (Pa.) HS	North Carolina
95.	Thomas Hatch	RHP	R/R	6-2	205	Jenks (Okla.) HS	Oklahoma State
96.	Josh Greene	OF	L/L	5-10	155	Forest HS, Ocala, Fla.	Uncommitted
97.	Iolana Akau	C	R/R	5-11	170	St. Louis School, Honolulu	Hawaii
98.	Robert Tyler	RHP	L/R	6-3	185	Crisp County HS, Cordele, Ga.	Georgia
99.	Chandler Eden	RHP	R/R	6-1	165	Yuba City (Calif.) HS	Oregon State
100.	Edwin Diaz	SS	R/R	6-2	175	Vega Alta (P.R.) HS	Uncommitted

FROM EVERY MINOR LEAGUE

As a complement to the organization prospect rankings, Baseball America also ranks prospects in all the minor leagues at the end of their seasons. Like the organization lists, they place more weight on potential than performance and should not be regarded as all-star teams. Unlike the organization lists, which are from more of a scouting perspective, the minor league lists reflect the views of minor league managers, who give more weight to what a player does on the field now. We think both perspectives are useful, so we give you both, even though they don't always match up. For a player to qualify for a league prospect list, he must have spent at least one-third of the season in a league. Also unlike the organization lists, players can make the league lists even if they exhausted their rookie eligibility during the 2012 season.

TRIPLE-A

INTERNATIONAL LEAGUE
1. Matt Harvey, rhp, Buffalo Bisons (Mets)
2. Starling Marte, of, Indianapolis Indians (Pirates)
3. Chris Archer, rhp, Durham Bulls (Rays)
4. Julio Teheran, rhp, Gwinnett Braves
5. Chris Parmelee, 1b, Rochester Red Wings (Twins)
6. Ryan Lavarnway, c, Pawtucket Red Sox
7. Didi Gregorius, ss, Louisville Bats (Reds)
8. Jacob Turner, rhp, Toledo Mud Hens (Tigers)
9. Jeff Locke, lhp, Indianapolis Indians (Pirates)
10. Tim Beckham, ss, Durham Bulls (Rays)
11. Jose Iglesias, ss, Pawtucket Red Sox
12. Cory Kluber, rhp, Columbus Clippers (Indians)
13. Cody Allen, rhp, Columbus Clippers (Indians)
14. Jeurys Familia, rhp, Buffalo Bisons (Mets)
15. L.J. Hoes, of, Norfolk Tides (Orioles)
16. Zach McAllister, rhp, Columbus Clippers (Indians)
17. Jenrry Mejia, rhp, Buffalo Bisons (Mets)
18. Casey Crosby, lhp, Toledo Mud Hens (Tigers)
19. Tyler Cloyd, rhp, Lehigh Valley IronPigs (Phillies)
20. Christian Garcia, rhp, Syracuse Chiefs (Nationals)

PACIFIC COAST LEAGUE
1. Wil Myers, of/3b, Omaha Storm Chasers (Royals)
2. Travis d'Arnaud, c, Las Vegas 51s (Blue Jays)
3. Trevor Bauer, rhp, Reno Aces (Diamondbacks)
4. Tyler Skaggs, lhp, Reno Aces (Diamondbacks)
5. Anthony Rizzo, 1b, Iowa Cubs
6. Shelby Miller, rhp, Memphis Redbirds (Cardinals)
7. Danny Hultzen, lhp, Tacoma Rainiers (Mariners)
8. Anthony Gose, of, Las Vegas 51s (Blue Jays)
9. Yasmani Grandal, c, Tucson Padres
10. Jedd Gyorko, 3b/2b, Tucson Padres
11. Jake Odorizzi, rhp, Omaha Storm Chasers (Royals)
12. Adam Eaton, of, Reno Aces (Diamondbacks)
13. Dan Straily, rhp, Sacramento River Cats (Athletics)
14. Adeiny Hechavarria, ss, Las Vegas 51s (Blue Jays)
15. Brett Jackson, of, Iowa Cubs
16. Nick Franklin, 2b/ss, Tacoma Rainiers (Mariners)
17. Leonys Martin, of, Round Rock Express (Rangers)
18. Derek Norris, c, Sacramento River Cats (Athletics)

19. Matt Adams, 1b, Memphis Redbirds (Cardinals)
20. Patrick Corbin, lhp, Reno Aces (Diamondbacks)

DOUBLE-A

EASTERN LEAGUE
1. Manny Machado, ss, Bowie Baysox (Orioles)
2. Zack Wheeler, rhp, Binghamton Mets
3. Gerrit Cole, rhp, Altoona Curve (Pirates)
4. Nick Castellanos, 3b/of, Erie Seawolves (Tigers)
5. Jackie Bradley, of, Portland Sea Dogs (Red Sox)
6. Oswaldo Arcia, of, New Britain Rock Cats (Twins)
7. Brian Goodwin, of, Harrisburg Senators (Nationals)
8. Aaron Hicks, of, New Britain Rock Cats (Twins)
9. Jake Marisnick, of, New Hampshire Fisher Cats (Blue Jays)
10. Tommy Joseph, c, Richmond (Giants)/Reading Phillies
11. Avisail Garcia, of, Erie Seawolves (Tigers)
12. Bruce Rondon, rhp, Erie Seawolves (Tigers)
13. Mike Kickham, lhp, Richmond Flying Squirrels (Giants)
14. Jonathan Schoop, 2b/ss, Bowie Baysox (Orioles)
15. Rob Brantly, c, Erie Seawolves (Tigers)
16. Gary Brown, of, Richmond Flying Squirrels (Giants)
17. Cody Asche, 3b, Reading Phillies
18. Wilmer Flores, 3b/2b, Binghamton Mets
19. Jon Pettibone, rhp, Reading Phillies
20. Drake Britton, lhp, Portland Sea Dogs (Red Sox)

SOUTHERN LEAGUE
1. Trevor Bauer, rhp, Mobile (Diamondbacks)
2. Taijuan Walker, rhp, Jackson (Mariners)
3. Tyler Skaggs, lhp, Mobile (Diamondbacks)
4. Danny Hultzen, lhp, Jackson (Mariners)
5. Billy Hamilton, ss, Pensacola (Reds)
6. Andrelton Simmons, ss, Mississippi (Braves)
7. Nick Franklin, ss/2b, Jackson (Mariners)
8. Hak-Ju Lee, ss, Montgomery (Rays)
9. Allen Webster, rhp, Chattanooga (Dodgers)
10. James Paxton, lhp, Jackson (Mariners)
11. Tony Cingrani, lhp, Pensacola (Reds)
12. Matt Davidson, 3b, Mobile (Diamondbacks)
13. Zach Lee, rhp, Chattanooga (Dodgers)
14. Brad Miller, ss, Jackson (Mariners)
15. Didi Gregorius, ss, Pensacola (Reds)
16. Tyler Thornburg, rhp, Huntsville (Brewers)
17. Daniel Corcino, rhp, Pensacola (Reds)
18. Christian Bethancourt, c, Mississippi (Braves)
19. Carter Capps, rhp, Jackson (Mariners)
20. Sean Gilmartin, lhp, Mississippi (Braves)

TEXAS LEAGUE
1. Jurickson Profar, ss, Frisco Roughriders (Rangers)
2. Oscar Taveras, of, Springfield Cardinals
3. Wil Myers, of, Northwest Arkansas Naturals (Royals)
4. Mike Olt, 3b, Frisco Roughriders (Rangers)
5. Jonathan Singleton, 1b/of, Corpus Christi Hooks (Astros)
6. Carlos Martinez, rhp, Springfield Cardinals
7. Dan Straily, rhp, Midland Rockhounds (Athletics)
8. Nolan Arenado, 3b, Tulsa Drillers (Rockies)
9. Trevor Rosenthal, rhp, Springfield Cardinals
10. Rymer Liriano, of, San Antonio Missions (Padres)
11. Jedd Gyorko, 3b/2b, San Antonio Missions (Padres)
12. Jean Segura, ss, Arkansas Travelers (Angels)
13. Josh Rutledge, ss/2b, Tulsa Drillers (Rockies)
14. Cody Buckel, rhp, Frisco Roughriders (Rangers)

15. Johnny Hellweg, rhp, Arkansas Travelers (Angels)
16. Kolten Wong, 2b, Springfield Cardinals
17. Sonny Gray, rhp, Midland Rockhounds (Athletics)
18. Edwar Cabrera, lhp, Tulsa Drillers (Rockies)
19. Jarred Cosart, rhp, Corpus Christi Hooks (Astros)
20. Keyvius Sampson, rhp, San Antonio Missions (Padres)

HIGH CLASS A

CALIFORNIA LEAGUE
1. Billy Hamilton, ss, Bakersfield Blaze (Reds)
2. George Springer, of, Lancaster JetHawks (Astros)
3. Joc Pederson, of, Rancho Cucamonga Quakes (Dodgers)
4. Kaleb Cowart, 3b, Inland Empire 66ers (Angels)
5. Zach Lee, rhp, Rancho Cucamonga Quakes (Dodgers)
6. Rymer Liriano, of, Lake Elsinore Storm (Padres)
7. Miles Head, 3b, Stockton Ports (Athletics)
8. Kyle Parker, of, Modesto Quakes (Rockies)
9. C.J. Cron, 1b, Inland Empire 66ers (Angels)
10. Andrew Chafin, lhp, Visalia Rawhide (Diamondbacks)
11. Tony Cingrani, lhp, Bakersfield Blaze (Reds)
12. Chris Owings, ss, Visalia Rawhide (Diamondbacks)
13. David Holmberg, lhp, Visalia Rawhide
(Diamondbacks)
14. Domingo Santana, of, Lancaster JetHawks (Astros)
15. Leon Landry, of, Rancho Cucamonga (Dodgers)/High
Desert (Mariners)
16. Nick Maronde, lhp, Inland Empire 66ers (Angels)
17. Donn Roach, rhp, Inland Empire (Angels)/Lake
Elsinore (Padres)
18. Brad Miller, ss, High Desert Mavericks (Mariners)
19. Cory Spangenberg, 2b, Lake Elsinore Storm (Padres)
20. Joe Panik, ss, San Jose Giants

CAROLINA LEAGUE
1. Dylan Bundy, rhp, Frederick Keys (Orioles)
2. Xander Bogaerts, ss, Salem Red Sox
3. Matt Barnes, rhp, Salem Red Sox
4. Jackie Bradley, of, Salem Red Sox
5. Cody Buckel, Myrtle Beach Pelicans (Rangers)
6. Carlos Sanchez, ss/2b, Winston-Salem Dash (White Sox)
7. J.R. Graham, rhp, Lynchburg Hillcats (Braves)
8. Yordano Ventura, rhp, Wilmington Blue Rocks (Royals)
9. Christian Villanueva, 3b, Myrtle Beach Pelicans
(Rangers)
10. Orlando Calixte, ss, Wilmington Blue Rocks (Royals)
11. Erik Johnson, rhp, Winston-Salem Dash (White Sox)
12. Hanser Alberto, ss, Myrtle Beach Pelicans (Rangers)
13. Nick Ahmed, ss, Lynchburg Hillcats (Braves)
14. Edward Salcedo, 3b, Lynchburg Hillcats (Braves)
15. Nathan Karns, rhp, Potomac Nationals
16. Luke Jackson, rhp, Myrtle Beach Pelicans (Rangers)
17. Christian Vazquez, c, Salem Red Sox
18. Trayce Thompson, of, Winston-Salem Dash (White
Sox)
19. Ronny Rodriguez, ss/2b, Carolina Mudcats (Indians)
20. Cheslor Cuthbert, 3b, Wilmington Blue Rocks (Royals)

FLORIDA STATE LEAGUE
1. Jose Fernandez, rhp, Jupiter Hammerheads (Marlins)
2. Gerrit Cole, rhp, Bradenton Marauders (Pirates)
3. Jameson Tallon, rhp, Bradenton Marauders (Pirates)
4. Christian Yelich, of, Jupiter Hammerheads (Marlins)
5. Nick Castellanos, 3b, Lakeland Flying Tigers (Tigers)
6. Enny Romero, lhp, Charlotte Stone Crabs (Rays)
7. Oswlado Arcia, of, Fort Myers Miracle (Twins)
8. Tyler Austin, of, Tampa Yankees

9. Gary Sanchez, c, Tampa Yankees
10. Jesse Biddle, lhp, Clearwater Threshers (Phillies)
11. Jake Marisnick, of, Dunedin Blue Jays
12. Adam Morgan, lhp, Clearwater Threshers (Phillies)
13. Avisail Garcia, of, Lakeland Flying Tigers (Tigers)
14. Bruce Rondon, rhp, Lakeland Flying Tigers (Tigers)
15. Marcell Ozuna, of, Jupiter Hammerheads (Marlins)
16. Jimmy Nelson, rhp, Brevard County Manatees
(Brewers)
17. Slade Heathcott, of, Tampa Yankees
18. Nik Turley, lhp, Tampa Yankees
19. Wilmer Flores, 3b, St. Lucie Mets
20. Gift Ngoepe, ss, Bradenton Marauders (Pirates)

LOW CLASS A

MIDWEST LEAGUE
1. Javier Baez, ss, Peoria Chiefs (Cubs)
2. Miguel Sano, 3b, Beloit Snappers (Twins)
3. Francisco Lindor, ss, Lake County Captains (Indians)
4. Archie Bradley, rhp, South Bend Silver Hawks (Dbacks)
5. Noah Syndergaard, rhp, Lansing Lugnuts (Blue Jays)
6. Aaron Sanchez, rhp, Lansing Lugnuts (Blue Jays)
7. Austin Hedges, c, Fort Wayne TinCaps (Padres)
8. Kaleb Cowart, 3b, Cedar Rapids Kernels (Angels)
9. Matt Wisler, rhp, Fort Wayne TinCaps (Padres)
10. A.J. Cole, rhp, Burlington Bees (Athletics)
11. Justin Nicolino, lhp, Lansing Lugnuts (Blue Jays)
12. Eddie Rosario, 2b/of, Beloit Snappers (Twins)
13. Jorge Bonifacio, of, Kane County Cougars (Royals)
14. Tyrell Jenkins, rhp, Quad Cities River Bandits (Cardinals)
15. Drew Vettleson, of, Bowling Green Hot Rods (Rays)
16. Kyle Smith, rhp, Kane County Cougars (Royals)
17. Travis Jankowski, of, Fort Wayne TinCaps (Padres)
18. Adys Portillo, rhp, Fort Wayne TinCaps (Padres)
19. Jace Peterson, ss, Fort Wayne TinCaps (Padres)
20. Stephen Piscotty, 3b, Quad Cities River Bandits
(Cardinals)

SOUTH ATLANTIC LEAGUE
1. Jose Fernandez, rhp, Greensboro Grasshoppers
(Marlins)
2. Trevor Story, ss/3b, Asheville Tourists (Rockies)
3. Gregory Polanco, of, West Virginia Power (Pirates)
4. Tyler Austin, of, Charleston Riverdogs (Yankees)
5. Gary Sanchez, c, Charleston Riverdogs (Yankees)
6. Alen Hanson, ss, West Virginia Power (Pirates)
7. Kyle Crick, rhp, Augusta Greenjackets (Giants)
8. Brian Goodwin, of, Hagerstown Suns (Nationals)
9. Mason Williams, of, Charleston Riverdogs (Yankees)
10. Alex Meyer, rhp, Hagerstown Suns (Nationals)
11. Michael Foltynewicz, rhp, Lexington Legends (Astros)
12. Delino DeShields Jr., 2b, Lexington Legends (Astros)
13. Michael Fulmer, rhp, Savannah Sand Gnats (Mets)
14. Adam Conley, lhp, Greensboro Grasshoppers (Marlins)
15. Garin Cecchini, 3b, Greenville Drive (Red Sox)
16. Maikel Franco, 3b, Lakewood BlueClaws (Phillies)
17. Blake Swihart, c, Greenville Drive (Red Sox)
18. Domingo Tapia, rhp, Savannah Sand Gnats (Mets)
19. Matt Skole, 3b, Hagerstown Suns (Nationals)
20. Rougned Odor, 2b/ss, Hickory Crawdads (Rangers)

SHORT-SEASON

NEW YORK-PENN LEAGUE
1. Taylor Guerrieri, rhp, Hudson Valley Renegades (Rays)
2. Luis Heredia, rhp, State College Spikes (Pirates)

3. Roman Quinn, ss, Williamsport Crosscutters (Phillies)
4. Richie Shaffer, 3b, Hudson Valley Renegades (Rays)
5. Luis Mateo, rhp, Brooklyn Cyclones (Mets)
6. Patrick Wisdom, 3b, Batavia Muckdogs (Cardinals)
7. Deven Marrero, ss, Lowell Spinners (Red Sox)
8. Jeff Ames, rhp, Hudson Valley Renegades (Rays)
9. Danry Vasquez, of, Connecticut Tigers
10. Barrett Barnes, of, State College Spikes (Pirates)
11. Brandon Nimmo, of, Brooklyn Cyclones (Mets)
12. Hansel Robles, rhp, Brooklyn Cyclones (Mets)
13. Jesse Hahn, rhp, Hudson Valley Renegades (Rays)
14. Vincent Velasquez, rhp, Tri-City ValleyCats (Astros)
15. Clay Holmes, rhp, State College Spikes (Pirates)
16. Tyler Naquin, of, Mahoning Valley Scrappers (Indians)
17. Pat Light, rhp, Lowell Spinners (Red Sox)
18. Phillip Evans, ss, Brooklyn Cyclones (Mets)
19. Tim Cooney, lhp, Batavia Muckdogs (Cardinals)
20. Breyvic Valera, 2b/ss, Batavia Muckdogs (Cardinals)

NORTHWEST LEAGUE
1. Mike Zunino, c, Everett AquaSox (Mariners)
2. Dan Vogelbach, 1b, Boise Hawks (Cubs)
3. Victor Sanchez, rhp, Everett AquaSox (Mariners)
4. Joe Ross, rhp, Eugene Emeralds (Padres)
5. Tom Murphy, c, Tri-City Dust Devils (Rockies)
6. Marco Hernandez, ss, Boise Hawks (Cubs)
7. Jeimer Candelario, 3b, Boise Hawks (Cubs)
8. C.J. Edwards, rhp, Spokane Indians (Rangers)
9. Gioskar Amaya, 2b, Boise Hawks (Cubs)
10. Patrick Kievlehan, 3b, Everett AquaSox (Mariners)
11. Mac Williamson, of, Salem-Keizer Volcanoes (Giants)
12. Rosell Herrera, ss/3b, Tri-City Dust Devils (Rockies)
13. Jose Valdespina, rhp, Spokane Indians (Rangers)
14. Dane Phillips, c, Eugene Emeralds (Padres)
15. Stephen Bruno, inf, Boise Hawks (Cubs)
16. Trey Martin, of, Boise Hawks (Cubs)
17. Tayler Scott, rhp, Boise Hawks (Cubs)
18. Jeremy Baltz, of, Eugene Emeralds (Padres)
19. Ketel Marte, ss/2b, Everett Aqua Sox (Mariners)
20. Taylor Cole, rhp, Vancouver Canadians (Blue Jays)

ROOKIE

APPALACHIAN LEAGUE
1. Byron Buxton, of, Elizabethton Twins
2. Courtney Hawkins, of, Bristol White Sox
3. Bubba Starling, of, Burlington Royals
4. Blake Snell, lhp, Princeton Rays
5. Mauricio Cabrera, rhp, Danville Braves
6. Luke Sims, rhp, Danville Braves
7. Max Kepler, of, Elizabethton Twins
8. Roberto Osuna, rhp, Bluefield Blue Jays
9. Victor DeLeon, rhp, Johnson City Cardinals
10. Santiago Nessy, c, Bluefield Blue Jays
11. Brandon Martin, ss, Princeton Rays
12. Gavin Cecchini, ss, Kingsport Mets
13. Carson Kelly, 3b, Johnson City Cardinals
14. Daniel Norris, lhp, Bluefield Blue Jays
15. Andrew Toles, of, Princeton Rays
16. Patrick Leonard, 3b, Burlington Royals
17. Adrian Houser, rhp, Greeneville Astros
18. Jose Peraza, ss, Danville Braves
19. Jochi Ogando, rhp, Pulaski Mariners
20. Cameron Gallagher, c, Burlington Royals

ARIZONA LEAGUE
1. Addison Russell, ss, Athletics

2. Albert Almora, of, Cubs
3. Joey Gallo, 3b, Rangers
4. Jorge Soler, of, Cubs
5. Dorssys Paulino, ss, Indians
6. Lewis Brinson, of, Rangers
7. Stryker Trahan, c, Diamondbacks
8. C.J. Edwards, rhp, Rangers
9. Daniel Robertson, ss/3b, Athletics
10. Clint Coulter, c, Brewers
11. Nomar Mazara, of, Rangers
12. Ronald Guzman, 1b, Rangers
13. Renato Nunez, 3b, Athletics
14. Dan Vogelbach, 1b, Cubs
15. Mitch Brown, rhp, Indians
16. Nick Travieso, rhp, Reds
17. Gabriel Guerrero, of, Mariners
18. Tyler Pike, lhp, Mariners
19. Zach Bird, rhp, Dodgers
20. Matt Olson, 1b, Athletics

GULF COAST LEAGUE
1. Byron Buxton, of, Twins
2. Carlos Correa, ss, Astros
3. D.J. Davis, of, Blue Jays
4. Rio Ruiz, 3b, Astros
5. Wyatt Mathisen, c, Pirates
6. Carlos Tocci, of, Phillies
7. Dilson Herrera, 2b, Pirates
8. Tzu-Wei Lin, ss, Red Sox
9. Tyler Glasnow, rhp, Pirates
10. Jose Peraza, ss, Braves
11. Steve Bean, c, Cardinals
12. Alberto Tirado, rhp, Blue Jays
13. Luis Merejo, lhp, Braves
14. Jake Thompson, rhp, Tigers
15. Austin Schotts, of, Tigers
16. Kolby Copeland, of, Marlins
17. Avery Romero, 3b/2b, Marlins
18. Harold Castro, 2b, Tigers
19. Jin-De Jhang, c, Pirates
20. Francellis Montas, rhp, Red Sox

PIONEER LEAGUE
1. David Dahl, of, Grand Junction Rockies
2. Robert Stephenson, rhp, Billings (Reds)
3. Adalberto Mondesi, ss, Idaho Falls Chukars (Royals)
4. Corey Seager, ss, Odgen Raptors (Dodgers)
5. Jesse Winker, of, Billings Mustangs (Reds)
6. Eddie Butler, Grand Junction Rockies
7. Michael Perez, c, Missoula Osprey (Diamondbacks)
8. Sam Selman, lhp, Idaho Falls Chukars (Royals)
9. Mark Sappington, rhp, Orem Owlz (Angels)
10. Dan Langfield, rhp, Billings Mustangs (Reds)
11. Jeff Gelalich, of, Billings Mustangs (Reds)
12. Chris Beck, rhp, Great Falls Voyagers (White Sox)
13. Wilfredo Rodriguez, rhp, Grand Junction Rockies
14. Julian Yan, of, Grand Junction Rockies
15. Ross Stripling, rhp, Ogden Raptors (Dodgers)
16. Brandon Brennan, rhp, Great Falls Voyagers (White Sox)
17. Jayson Aquino, lhp, Grand Junction Rockies
18. Seth Mejias-Brean, 3b, Billings Mustangs (Reds)
19. Wendell Soto, ss, Orem Owlz (Angels)
20. Ismael Guillon, lhp, Billings Mustangs (Reds)

Dahl, David (Rockies) 147
Darnell, James (Padres) 393
Davidson, Matt (Diamondbacks) 20
Davies, Zach (Orioles) 57
Davis, D.J. (Blue Jays) 468
Davis, Glynn (Orioles) 55
Davis, Kentrail (Brewers) 268
Davis, Khris (Brewers) 264
Dayton, Grant (Marlins) 251
de la Cruz, Keury (Red Sox) 75
de la Rosa, Bryan (Braves) 43
de la Rosa, Edgar (Tigers) 173
Dean, Austin (Marlins) 249
Dean, Matt (Blue Jays) 472
DeCarlo, Joe (Mariners) 423
Decker, Jaff (Padres) 395
DeFratus, Justin (Phillies) 345
DeGrom, Jake (Mets) 294
DeJong, Chase (Blue Jays) 474
del Rosario, Yeyfry (Blue Jays) 476
DeLeon, Victor (Cardinals) 376
Delmonico, Nick (Orioles) 52
DeMichele, Joey (White Sox) 106
Demny, Paul (Nationals) 492
Den Dekker, Matt (Mets) 296
DePaula, Rafael (Yankees) 310
DeShields Jr., Delino (Astros) 180
Diaz, Edwin (Mariners) 425
Diaz, Pedro (Reds) 121
Dickerson, Alex (Pirates) 358
Dickerson, Corey (Rockies) 151
Dietrich, Derek (Marlins) 247
Drake, Oliver (Orioles) 60
Drury, Brandon (Braves) 44
Dunnington, Jacob (Giants) 412
Duvall, Adam (Giants) 406
Dwyer, Chris (Royals) 202

E

Eaton, Adam (Diamondbacks) 20
Eckels, Ben (Diamondbacks) 26
Edwards, C.J. (Rangers) 456
Edwards, Spencer (Rays) 445
Eflin, Zach (Padres) 392
Eibner, Brett (Royals) 204
Elander, Josh (Braves) 41
Encinas, Gabe (Yankees) 317
Erlin, Robbie (Padres) 390
Esch, Jake (Marlins) 251
Escobar, Edwin (Giants) 407
Estevez, Wirkin (Nationals) 493
Evans, Phillip (Mets) 296

F

Familia, Jeurys (Mets) 293
Federowicz, Tim (Dodgers) 231
Fedroff, Tim (Indians) 137
Fernandez, Anthony (Mariners) 429
Fernandez, Arjenis (Angels) 218
Fernandez, Jose (Marlins) 242
Fields, Daniel (Tigers) 173
Fields, Josh (Astros) 187
Figueroa, Pedro (Athletics) 327
Fletcher, Brian (Royals) 205
Flores, Ramon (Yankees) 311
Flores, Wilmer (Mets) 292
Flynn, Brian (Marlins) 251
Foltynewicz, Mike (Astros) 180
Font, Wilmer (Rangers) 458
Fontana, Nolan (Astros) 182
Ford, Fred (Royals) 202
Fornataro, Eric (Cardinals) 378

Franco, Carlos (Braves) 42
Franco, Maikel (Phillies) 341
Franklin, Nick (Mariners) 420
Frazier, Parker (Rockies) 157
Freeman, Sam (Cardinals) 378
Fried, Max (Padres) 387
Fujikawa, Kyuji (Cubs) 86
Fulmer, Michael (Mets) 293

G

Gagnon, Drew (Brewers) 265
Gallagher, Cameron (Royals) 200
Gallo, Joey (Rangers) 454
Garcia, Avisail (Tigers) 163
Garcia, Christian (Nationals) 484
Garcia, Leury (Rangers) 458
Garcia, Onelki (Dodgers) 229
Garcia, Willy (Pirates) 361
Garrett, Amir (Reds) 120
Gast, John (Cardinals) 380
Gattis, Evan (Braves) 37
Gausman, Kevin (Orioles) 51
Gelalich, Jeff (Reds) 120
Geltz, Steven (Angels) 220
Gennett, Scooter (Brewers) 261
Gibson, Kyle (Twins) 276
Giles, Kenny (Phillies) 345
Gillies, Tyson (Phillies) 348
Gilmartin, Sean (Braves) 36
Gindl, Caleb (Brewers) 268
Giolito, Lucas (Nationals) 483
Glaesmann, Todd (Rays) 442
Glasnow, Tyler (Pirates) 361
Goeddel, Tyler (Rays) 441
Goforth, David (Brewers) 265
Gohara, Luiz (Mariners) 423
Gomes, Yan (Indians) 140
Gonzales, Tyler (Blue Jays) 471
Goodrum, Niko (Twins) 283
Goodwin, Brian (Nationals) 483
Gould, Garrett (Dodgers) 233
Graham, J.R. (Braves) 35
Gray, Sonny (Athletics) 324
Green, Grant (Athletics) 325
Green, Tyler (Diamondbacks) 28
Greene, Larry (Phillies) 342
Gregorius, Didi (Reds) 116
Grichuk, Randal (Angels) 212
Griffin, Jon (Diamondbacks) 25
Griggs, Scott (Dodgers) 233
Grimm, Justin (Rangers) 452
Grossman, Robbie (Astros) 185
Gueller, Mitch (Phillies) 344
Guerrero, Gabriel (Mariners) 424
Guerrieri, Taylor (Rays) 435
Guillon, Ismael (Reds) 118
Gumbs, Angelo (Yankees) 309
Guzman, Ronald (Rangers) 457
Gyorko, Jedd (Padres) 387

H

Hader, Josh (Orioles) 57
Hager, Jake (Rays) 441
Hague, Rick (Nationals) 488
Hahn, Jesse (Rays) 440
Hale, David (Braves) 40
Haley, Trey (Indians) 135
Hall, Cody (Giants) 412
Hamilton, Billy (Reds) 114
Haniger, Mitch (Brewers) 262
Hanson, Alen (Pirates) 356
Harrison, Travis (Twins) 280

Hatcher, Chris (Marlins) 250
Hatley, Marcus (Cubs) 93
Hawkins, Chris (Blue Jays) 477
Hawkins, Courtney (White Sox) 98
Head, Miles (Athletics) 325
Heaney, Andrew (Marlins) 243
Heathcott, Slade (Yankees) 307
Hechavarria, Adeiny (Marlins) 245
Heckathorn, Kyle (Brewers) 269
Hedges, Austin (Padres) 387
Hefflinger, Robby (Braves) 45
Heineman, Tyler (Astros) 189
Hellweg, Johnny (Brewers) 260
Hembree, Heath (Giants) 405
Henry, Randy (Rangers) 461
Hensley, Ty (Yankees) 310
Heredia, Luis (Pirates) 355
Hermsen, B.J. (Twins) 281
Hernandez, Cesar (Phillies) 344
Hernandez, Elier (Royals) 200
Hernandez, Marco (Cubs) 90
Herrera, Dilson (Pirates) 362
Herrmann, Chris (Twins) 280
Heston, Chris (Giants) 408
Hicks, Aaron (Twins) 276
Hicks, John (Mariners) 426
Hoes, L.J. (Orioles) 52
Holaday, Bryan (Tigers) 171
Holmberg, David (Diamondbacks) 21
Holmes, Clay (Pirates) 358
Holt, Brock (Pirates) 362
Hood, Destin (Nationals) 489
Hoover, J.J. (Reds) 117
Houser, Adrian (Astros) 184
Howard, Dillon (Indians) 139
Hudson, Kyrell (Phillies) 349
Hultzen, Danny (Mariners) 419
Hyatt, Nathan (Braves) 44

I

Iglesias, Jose (Red Sox) 69

J

Jackson, Bralin (Rays) 444
Jackson, Brett (Cubs) 84
Jackson, Luke (Rangers) 453
Jackson, Ryan (Cardinals) 376
Jacobs, Brandon (Red Sox) 71
Jaime, Juan (Braves) 42
James, Chad (Marlins) 252
Jankowski, Travis (Padres) 394
Jenkins, Chad (Blue Jays) 473
Jenkins, Tyrell (Cardinals) 373
Jhang, Jin-De (Pirates) 364
Jimenez, A.J. (Blue Jays) 470
Jimenez, Luis (Angels) 216
Johnson, Brian (Red Sox) 72
Johnson, Erik (White Sox) 100
Johnson, Kevin (Angels) 221
Johnson, Micah (White Sox) 107
Johnson, Pierce (Cubs) 84
Johnson, Stephen (Giants) 410
Johnson, Steve (Orioles) 56
Jones, Devin (Orioles) 58
Jones, Tyler (Twins) 282
Jordan, Taylor (Nationals) 487
Jorge, Felix (Twins) 283
Joseph, Corban (Yankees) 316
Joseph, Donnie (Royals) 199
Joseph, Tommy (Phillies) 339
Jungmann, Taylor (Brewers) 259
Junis, Jake (Royals) 204

K

Kahnle, Tommy (Yankees)	317
Karns, Nate (Nationals)	484
Kela, Keone (Rangers)	460
Kelly, Carson (Cardinals)	373
Kelly, Casey (Padres)	386
Kelly, Ty (Orioles)	61
Kepler, Max (Twins)	278
Keys, Brent (Marlins)	253
Kickham, Mike (Giants)	404
Kieschnick, Roger (Giants)	406
Kingham, Nick (Pirates)	361
Kivlehan, Patrick (Mariners)	425
Kline, Branden (Orioles)	54
Kobernus, Jeff (Tigers)	170
Kozma, Pete (Cardinals)	375
Kubitza, Kyle (Braves)	43
Kukuk, Cody (Red Sox)	76

L

Labourt, Jairo (Blue Jays)	476
Lake, Junior (Cubs)	88
LaMarre, Ryan (Reds)	122
Lamb, Jake (Diamondbacks)	24
Lamb, John (Royals)	198
Landry, Leon (Mariners)	424
Langfield, Dan (Reds)	118
Lazo, Raudel (Marlins)	250
Leathersich, Jack (Mets)	298
Lee, Chen (Indians)	134
Lee, Hak-Ju (Rays)	436
Lee, Zach (Dodgers)	228
Leesman, Charlie (White Sox)	102
Leon, Arnold (Athletics)	333
Leon, Sandy (Nationals)	488
Leonard, Patrick (Rays)	444
Light, Pat (Red Sox)	74
Lin, Tzu-Wei (Red Sox)	72
Lindor, Francisco (Indians)	130
Lindsey, Taylor (Angels)	213
Lipka, Matt (Braves)	39
Liriano, Rymer (Padres)	388
Lo, Chia-Jen (Astros)	186
Lobstein, Kyle (Tigers)	169
Lohman, Devin (Reds)	123
Loosen, Matt (Cubs)	92
Lopes, Christian (Blue Jays)	474
Lopes, Timmy (Mariners)	427
Lopez, Eduar (Angels)	219
Lopez, Jack (Royals)	201
Lopez, Jorge (Brewers)	267
Lorenzo, Greg (Orioles)	61
Lotzkar, Kyle (Reds)	119
Lough, David (Royals)	203
Loux, Barret (Cubs)	92
Lovegrove, Kieran (Indians)	138
Lugo, Dawel (Blue Jays)	475
Lugo, Luis (Indians)	135
Lutz, Donald (Reds)	121

M

Machado, Dixon (Tigers)	172
Magill, Matt (Dodgers)	229
Mahtook, Mikie (Rays)	439
Maness, Seth (Cardinals)	379
Manzanillo, Santo (Brewers)	268
Maples, Dillon (Cubs)	89
Marder, Jack (Mariners)	425
Margot, Manuel (Red Sox)	74
Marin, Adrian (Orioles)	54
Marinez, Jhan (White Sox)	103

Marisnick, Jake (Marlins)	243
Markel, Parker (Rays)	444
Marlowe, Chris (Giants)	409
Maron, Cam (Mets)	301
Maronde, Nick (Angels)	211
Marrero, Chris (Nationals)	491
Marrero, Deven (Red Sox)	70
Marshall, Brett (Yankees)	308
Marshall, Evan (Diamondbacks)	24
Marte, Alfredo (Diamondbacks)	25
Martin, Brandon (Rays)	441
Martin, Cody (Braves)	39
Martin, Ethan (Phillies)	340
Martin, Leonys (Rangers)	452
Martin, Trey (Cubs)	93
Martinez, Carlos (Cardinals)	371
Martinez, Estarlin (Nationals)	490
Martinez, Francisco (Mariners)	426
Martinez, Jose (Diamondbacks)	27
Martinez, Nick (Rangers)	460
Martinson, Jason (Nationals)	487
Marzilli, Evan (Diamondbacks)	29
Mata, Angel (Twins)	282
Mateo, Luis (Mets)	291
Mathisen, Wyatt (Pirates)	360
Matthes, Kent (Rockies)	152
Matz, Steve (Mets)	301
Matzek, Tyler (Rockies)	149
Maurer, Brandon (Mariners)	420
Maxwell, Bruce (Athletics)	330
May, Trevor (Twins)	277
Mazara, Nomar (Rangers)	456
Mazzoni, Cory (Mets)	294
McCann, James (Tigers)	166
McClure, D'Vone (Indians)	136
McCullers Jr., Lance (Astros)	179
McElroy, C.J. (Cardinals)	376
McFarland, T.J. (Orioles)	58
McGuiness, Chris (Indians)	137
McGuire, Deck (Blue Jays)	473
McHugh, Collin (Mets)	299
McNutt, Trey (Cubs)	91
McPherson, Kyle (Pirates)	357
Mejia, Adalberto (Giants)	406
Mejias-Brean, Seth (Reds)	121
Melotakis, Mason (Twins)	279
Mendez, Roman (Rangers)	455
Meo, Anthony (Diamondbacks)	23
Mercedes, Melvin (Tigers)	167
Mercedes, Simon (Red Sox)	76
Merejo, Luis (Braves)	42
Mesa, Melky (Yankees)	313
Meyer, Alex (Twins)	275
Michael, Levi (Twins)	280
Mikolas, Miles (Padres)	395
Miller, Aaron (Dodgers)	236
Miller, Brad (Mariners)	422
Miller, Brandon (Nationals)	490
Miller, Shelby (Cardinals)	371
Mitchell, Bryan (Yankees)	311
Mitchell, Jared (White Sox)	102
Molina, Nestor (White Sox)	108
Mondesi, Adalberto (Royals)	196
Montas, Frank (Red Sox)	74
Montero, Rafael (Mets)	292
Montgomery, Mark (Yankees)	310
Montgomery, Mike (Rays)	440
Mooneyham, Brett (Nationals)	489
Moore, Navery (Braves)	40
Morban, Julio (Mariners)	426
Morgan, Adam (Phillies)	340
Morla, Ramon (Mariners)	429
Morris, Bryan (Pirates)	359
Morris, Hunter (Brewers)	259

Morrison, Ty (Rays)	445
Moya, Steven (Tigers)	168
Mujica, Jose (Rays)	443
Muncy, Max (Athletics)	328
Munoz, Joe (Diamondbacks)	26
Munson, Kevin (Diamondbacks)	28
Murphy, J.R. (Yankees)	312
Murphy, Tom (Rockies)	151
Myers, Wil (Rays)	434

N

Naquin, Tyler (Indians)	131
Nay, Mitch (Blue Jays)	475
Neal, Thomas (Indians)	140
Nelson, Jimmy (Brewers)	260
Nessy, Santiago (Blue Jays)	471
Ngoepe, Gift (Pirates)	365
Nicolino, Justin (Marlins)	244
Nimmo, Brandon (Mets)	291
Nolin, Sean (Blue Jays)	473
Noonan, Nick (Giants)	410
Norris, Daniel (Blue Jays)	469
Northcraft, Aaron (Braves)	45
Nunez, Renato (Athletics)	327

O

O'Neill, Mike (Cardinals)	380
Oberholtzer, Brett (Astros)	186
Odor, Rougned (Rangers)	454
Odorizzi, Jake (Rays)	436
Okert, Steven (Giants)	409
Olacio, Jefferson (White Sox)	109
Oliver, Andy (Pirates)	359
Olson, Matt (Athletics)	326
Olt, Mike (Rangers)	451
Omogrosso, Brian (White Sox)	107
Oramas, Juan (Padres)	396
Oropesa, Ricky (Giants)	412
Ortega, Jose (Tigers)	168
Ortega, Rafael (Rockies)	151
Ortiz, Joe (Rangers)	461
Osich, Josh (Giants)	409
Osuna, Jose (Pirates)	363
Osuna, Roberto (Blue Jays)	468
Owens, Henry (Red Sox)	68
Owings, Chris (Diamondbacks)	21
Ozuna, Marcell (Marlins)	244

P

Paniagua, Juan Carlos (Cubs)	86
Panik, Joe (Giants)	403
Parker, Kyle (Rockies)	147
Parker, Stephen (Athletics)	332
Partch, Curtis (Reds)	124
Paulino, Brenny (Tigers)	170
Paulino, Dorssys (Indians)	131
Paxton, James (Mariners)	419
Payne, Shawn (Giants)	413
Peacock, Brad (Athletics)	323
Pederson, Joc (Dodgers)	227
Peguero, Francisco (Giants)	405
Pena, Ariel (Brewers)	266
Pena, Miguel (Red Sox)	77
Peralta, Starling (Diamondbacks)	28
Peralta, Wily (Brewers)	258
Peraza, Jose (Braves)	38
Perez, Carlos (Astros)	189
Perez, Carlos (Braves)	44
Perez, Eury (Nationals)	485
Perez, Felipe (Diamondbacks)	26
Perez, Fernando (Padres)	393

Perez, Hernan (Tigers)	172
Perez, Juan (Giants)	410
Perez, Martin (Rangers)	451
Perez, Michael (Diamondbacks)	23
Peterson, Jace (Padres)	390
Petricka, Jake (White Sox)	104
Pettibone, Jonathan (Phillies)	339
Phegley, Josh (White Sox)	105
Phillips, Brett (Astros)	185
Pike, Tyler (Mariners)	423
Pill, Tyler (Mets)	299
Pillar, Kevin (Blue Jays)	474
Pimentel, Stolmy (Red Sox)	77
Pineyro, Ivan (Nationals)	492
Piscotty, Stephen (Cardinals)	374
Plawecki, Kevin (Mets)	298
Polanco, Gregory (Pirates)	355
Polanco, Jorge (Twins)	279
Pollock, A.J. (Diamondbacks)	22
Portillo, Adys (Padres)	390
Prince, Josh (Brewers)	269
Profar, Jurickson (Rangers)	450
Pryor, Stephen (Mariners)	422
Puello, Cesar (Mets)	297
Puig, Yasiel (Dodgers)	227
Pullin, Andrew (Phillies)	348
Purke, Matt (Nationals)	486
Putkonen, Luke (Tigers)	171

Q

Quackenbush, Kevin (Padres)	397
Quinn, Roman (Phillies)	339

R

Rahier, Tanner (Reds)	122
Ramirez, Harold (Pirates)	364
Ramirez, Jose (Indians)	139
Ramirez, Jose (Yankees)	312
Ramirez, Neil (Rangers)	459
Ramos, A.J. (Marlins)	248
Ramsey, James (Cardinals)	374
Ranaudo, Anthony (Red Sox)	71
Rasmussen, Rob (Astros)	185
Rathjen, Jeremy (Dodgers)	237
Ray, Robbie (Nationals)	489
Realmuto, J.T. (Marlins)	246
Reed, Chris (Dodgers)	228
Renda, Tony (Nationals)	487
Rendon, Anthony (Nationals)	482
Reynolds, Matt (Mets)	299
Reynoso, Jonathan (Reds)	118
Rienzo, Andre (White Sox)	101
Riggins, Harold (Rockies)	155
Rivera, Yadiel (Brewers)	267
Rivero, Carlos (Nationals)	491
Rivero, Felipe (Rays)	442
Roach, Donn (Padres)	393
Roache, Victor (Brewers)	261
Robertson, Daniel (Athletics)	326
Robertson, Montreal (Tigers)	169
Robinson, Clint (Pirates)	365
Robinson, Drew (Rangers)	458
Robles, Hansel (Mets)	295
Rodgers, Brady (Astros)	187
Rodgers, Colin (Royals)	203
Rodriguez, Aderlin (Mets)	297
Rodriguez, Eduardo (Orioles)	52
Rodriguez, Henry (Reds)	123
Rodriguez, Luigi (Indians)	133
Rodriguez, Paco (Dodgers)	229
Rodriguez, Ronny (Indians)	133
Rodriguez, Santos (White Sox)	107
Rodriguez, Wilfredo (Rockies)	156
Rodriguez, Yorman (Reds)	120
Rogers, Chad (Reds)	125
Rogers, Mark (Brewers)	262
Romano, Sal (Reds)	125
Romero, Avery (Marlins)	249
Romero, Enny (Rays)	438
Romero, Stefen (Mariners)	421
Romine, Andrew (Angels)	218
Romine, Austin (Yankees)	313
Rondon, Bruce (Tigers)	163
Rondon, Jorge (Cardinals)	379
Rondon, Jose (Angels)	217
Rosa, Gabriel (Reds)	125
Rosario, Amed (Mets)	300
Rosario, Eddie (Twins)	277
Rosenbaum, Danny (Rockies)	154
Rosenthal, Trevor (Cardinals)	371
Ross, Joe (Padres)	391
Roth, Michael (Angels)	221
Ruf, Darin (Phillies)	341
Ruffin, Chance (Mariners)	428
Ruiz, Rio (Astros)	181
Rupp, Cameron (Phillies)	346
Russell, Addison (Athletics)	322
Rutledge, Lex (Orioles)	59
Ryu, Hyun-Jin (Dodgers)	226

S

Saladino, Tyler (White Sox)	108
Salazar, Danny (Indians)	132
Salcedo, Adrian (Twins)	284
Salcedo, Edward (Braves)	41
Sale, Josh (Rays)	443
Sampson, Adrian (Pirates)	362
Sampson, Keyvius (Padres)	391
Sanburn, Nolan (Athletics)	326
Sanchez, Aaron (Blue Jays)	467
Sanchez, Angel (Dodgers)	235
Sanchez, Carlos (White Sox)	99
Sanchez, Gary (Yankees)	307
Sanchez, Jesus (Brewers)	266
Sanchez, Tony (Pirates)	359
Sanchez, Victor (Mariners)	422
Sano, Miguel (Twins)	274
Santana, Alex (Dodgers)	235
Santana, Daniel (Twins)	278
Santana, Domingo (Astros)	182
Santander, Anthony (Indians)	135
Sappington, Mark (Angels)	214
Sardinas, Luis (Rangers)	453
Sawyer, Nick (Rays)	445
Scahill, Rob (Rockies)	150
Scarpetta, Cody (Brewers)	267
Schafer, Logan (Brewers)	263
Schoop, Jonathan (Orioles)	51
Schotts, Austin (Tigers)	164
Schrader, Clay (Orioles)	56
Schugel, A.J. (Angels)	215
Scoggins, Reid (Angels)	216
Seager, Corey (Dodgers)	227
Seaton, Ross (Astros)	186
Selman, Sam (Royals)	196
Semien, Marcus (White Sox)	104
Shaffer, Richie (Rays)	437
Shaw, Travis (Red Sox)	74
Shipman, Aaron (Athletics)	331
Siegrist, Kevin (Cardinals)	375
Silverio, Alfredo (Marlins)	247
Simon, Kyle (Phillies)	349
Sims, Lucas (Braves)	36
Singleton, Jonathan (Astros)	179
Skaggs, Tyler (Diamondbacks)	18
Skole, Matt (Nationals)	483
Smith Jr., Dwight (Blue Jays)	472
Smith, Blake (Dodgers)	237
Smith, Burch (Padres)	394
Smith, Carson (Mariners)	424
Smith, Jordan (Indians)	141
Smith, Kevan (White Sox)	108
Smith, Kyle (Royals)	199
Smith, Mallex (Padres)	397
Smoral, Matt (Blue Jays)	470
Snell, Blake (Rays)	438
Snodgress, Scott (White Sox)	100
Solano, Jhonatan (Nationals)	493
Soler, Jorge (Cubs)	83
Solis, Sammy (Nationals)	485
Solorzano, Jesus (Marlins)	250
Soptic, Jeff (White Sox)	109
Soto, Neftali (Reds)	124
Souza, Steven (Nationals)	491
Spangenberg, Cory (Padres)	389
Springer, George (Astros)	179
Spruill, Zeke (Braves)	38
Stamets, Eric (Angels)	215
Starling, Bubba (Royals)	195
Stassi, Max (Athletics)	327
Stephenson, Robert (Reds)	115
Stilson, John (Blue Jays)	469
Stites, Matt (Padres)	396
Story, Trevor (Rockies)	147
Straily, Dan (Athletics)	324
Stratton, Chris (Giants)	403
Streich, Seth (Athletics)	330
Stripling, Ross (Dodgers)	230
Stroman, Marcus (Blue Jays)	468
Suarez, Eugenio (Tigers)	166
Sullivan, Josh (Rockies)	153
Summers, Matt (Twins)	285
Surkamp, Eric (Giants)	411
Susac, Andrew (Giants)	407
Swagerty, Jordan (Cardinals)	377
Swanner, Will (Rockies)	154
Swihart, Blake (Red Sox)	68
Syndergaard, Noah (Blue Jays)	467
Szczur, Matt (Cubs)	88

T

Tago, Peter (Rockies)	157
Taillon, Jameson (Pirates)	355
Tapia, Domingo (Mets)	293
Taveras, Oscar (Cardinals)	370
Taylor, Beau (Athletics)	329
Taylor, Chris (Mariners)	428
Taylor, Drew (Angels)	220
Taylor, Michael (Athletics)	328
Taylor, Michael (Nationals)	486
Taylor, Tyrone (Brewers)	264
Teheran, Julio (Braves)	34
Tekotte, Blate (White Sox)	104
Tepesch, Nick (Rangers)	457
Terdoslavich, Joey (Braves)	41
Thompson, Jake (Tigers)	164
Thompson, Trayce (White Sox)	99
Thon, Dickie Joe (Blue Jays)	476
Thornburg, Tyler (Brewers)	259
Tillman, Daniel (Angels)	218
Tilson, Charlie (Cardinals)	377
Tirado, Alberto (Blue Jays)	472
Tocci, Carlos (Phillies)	342
Toles, Andrew (Rays)	442
Tonkin, Michael (Twins)	284
Torres, Ramon (Royals)	202
Tovar, Wilfredo (Mets)	295
Tracy, Matt (Yankees)	316

Trahan, Stryker (Diamondbacks) 22
Travieso, Nick (Reds) 116
Tropeano, Nick (Astros) 182
Turley, Nik (Yankees) 311

U

Underwood, Duane (Cubs) 89
Urena, Jose (Marlins) 245
Urrutia, Henry (Orioles) 55
Urshela, Giovanny (Indians) 138

V

Valentin, Jesmuel (Dodgers) 231
Valle, Sebastian (Phillies) 343
Van Slyke, Scott (Dodgers) 232
Vance, Kevin (White Sox) 105
Vargas, Kennys (Twins) 285
Vasquez, Danry (Tigers) 164
Vaughn, Cory (Mets) 295
Vazquez, Christian (Red Sox) 73
Velasquez, Vincent (Astros) 183
Velazquez, Andrew (Diamondbacks) 27
Ventura, Yordano (Royals) 195
VerHagen, Drew (Tigers) 167
Verrett, Logan (Mets) 300
Vettleson, Drew (Rays) 439
Villanueva, Christian (Cubs) 87
Villar, Jonathan (Astros) 183
Vinicio, Jose (Red Sox) 72
Vitters, Josh (Cubs) 92
Vizcaino, Arodys (Cubs) 83
Vogelbach, Dan (Cubs) 85
Vollmuth, B.A. (Athletics) 328

W

Wacha, Michael (Cardinals) 372
Wada, Tsuyoshi (Orioles) 58
Walding, Mitchell (Phillies) 344
Waldrop, Kyle (Reds) 122
Walker, Christian (Orioles) 55
Walker, Keenyn (White Sox) 100
Walker, Taijuan (Mariners) 419
Wall, Josh (Dodgers) 234
Walters, Zach (Nationals) 486
Warner, Ryan (Rockies) 156
Warren, Adam (Yankees) 315
Wates, Austin (Astros) 188
Watkins, Logan (Cubs) 89
Watson, Shane (Phillies) 342
Webb, Brenden (Orioles) 60
Webster, Allen (Red Sox) 67
Weickel, Walker (Padres) 391
Welker, Duke (Pirates) 364
West, Aaron (Astros) 189
West, Matt (Rangers) 460
Wheeler, Jason (Twins) 283
Wheeler, Ryan (Rockies) 150
Wheeler, Tim (Rockies) 150
Wheeler, Zack (Mets) 290
White, Max (Rockies) 155
Whitenack, Robert (Cubs) 91
Wieland, Joe (Padres) 389
Wilk, Adam (Tigers) 166
Wilkins, Andy (White Sox) 103
Williams, Mason (Yankees) 306
Williams, Nick (Rangers) 460
Williamson, Mac (Giants) 408
Willoughby, Seth (Rockies) 155

Wilson, Alex (Red Sox) 73
Wilson, Justin (Pirates) 357
Wilson, Tyler (Orioles) 60
Winker, Jesse (Reds) 117
Winkler, Kyle (Diamondbacks) 27
Wisdom, Patrick (Cardinals) 374
Wisler, Matt (Padres) 388
Witherspoon, Travis (Angels) 219
Withrow, Chris (Dodgers) 230
Wojciechowski, Asher (Astros) 183
Wolters, Tony (Indians) 136
Wong, Kolten (Cardinals) 372
Wood, Alex (Braves) 37
Wood, Austin (Angels) 212
Workman, Brandon (Red Sox) 71
Wright, Austin (Phillies) 345
Wright, Mike (Orioles) 53

Y

Yambati, Robinson (Royals) 204
Yan, Julian (Rockies) 153
Yarbrough, Alex (Angels) 214
Yelich, Christian (Marlins) 243
Ynoa, Gabriel (Mets) 298
Ynoa, Michael (Athletics) 329

Z

Zimmer, Kyle (Royals) 194
Zunino, Mike (Mariners) 418
Zych, Tony (Cubs) 90